AN IMPOSTER OF
NO ORDINARY RANK

AN IMPOSTER OF NO ORDINARY RANK

The True Story of
Loreta Janeta Velazquez, alias Confederate Lt. Harry T. Buford,
and her Civil War Memoir, *The Woman in Battle*

William L. Post Jr.

Copyright ©2023 by William L. Post Jr.
All rights reserved. No reproduction in any form without prior written permission of the copyright holder. Contact- animposterofnoordinaryrank@gmail.com

First Edition

Library of Congress Control Number: 2023902547
ISBN-13: 979-8-9875827-1-8

Publisher's Cataloging-in-Publication data

Names: Post, William L., Jr., author.
Title: An imposter of no ordinary rank: the true story of Loreta Janeta Velazquez, alias Confederate Lt. Harry T. Buford, and her Civil War memoir, The Woman in Battle / William L. Post Jr.
Description: Includes bibliographical references and index. | Pensacola, FL: William L. Post Jr., 2023.
Identifiers: LCCN: 2023902547 | ISBN: 979-8-9875827-1-8 (hardcover) | 979-8-9875827-0-1 (paperback)
Subjects: LCSH Velazquez, Loreta Janeta, 1842-1923. | Women soldiers--Confederate States of America--Biography. | Cubans--Confederate States of America--Biography. | United States--History--Civil War, 1861-1865--Participation, Female. | BISAC HISTORY / United States / Civil War Period (1850-1877) | BIOGRAPHY & AUTOBIOGRAPHY / Women | BIOGRAPHY & AUTOBIOGRAPHY / Military | BIOGRAPHY & AUTOBIOGRAPHY / Historical
Classification: LCC E628.P67 2023 | DDC 973.7/13092--dc23

Dedicated to:

Catti, my wife, a chemical engineer by profession, who lovingly and wonderfully never lets an illogical supposition or conclusion go unchallenged;

Eric and Sara, my children, who give love and encouragement;

Shirley Laurent Post, my mother, who was a school teacher, an avid reader and lover of books (especially mysteries) and awaited, but never saw the completion of this mystery of Velazquez;

William L. Post, my father, who was a chemical engineer, and upon retirement was a farmer for many years- he skillfully distinguished the bull from the bull droppings whether dealing with livestock or people.

Table of Contents

Introduction xiii
    Part 1: Events in the Time Frame of *The Woman in Battle* 1

Chapter 1 1
Synopsis of *The Woman in Battle (TWIB)* 1
Meeting Men of Influence 10
1861, Arrested in Lynchburg, Taken to Richmond 12
April 1862, First Arrest in New Orleans 19
Shiloh and Velazquez 21
A Love Letter- Oh, Really? 24
The Union Navy's Arrival/Arrest of William B. Mumford 26
Running the Lines of the Union Army at New Orleans 32

Chapter 2 35
October 1862, Second Arrest in New Orleans 35
The 7th Louisiana, First Battle of the Manassas (Bull Run) 42
The 11th Louisiana, Battle of Shiloh 44
Nelly Bremer's House of Prostitution 45
Escaped and Captured 47
The Charity Hospital Record 47
1863, Departed New Orleans as a "Registered Enemy" 48
Arrived in Jackson, Mississippi 51
The Battle of Leesburg (or the Battle of Ball's Bluff) 58
A Spy Trip to Washington in Female Attire 64

Chapter 3 69
The Battle of Shiloh and Velazquez's Wounds 69
The Battle of Shiloh and Lieutenant Philip Hastings 70
Three Noteworthy Items in the June 6, 1863 *Mississippian* 72
A Rare Bird 73
Lieutenant Colonel Fremantle saw a Female Soldier 74
1863, at the Battle House (Hotel) in Mobile, Alabama 76
Applied for a Commission, Yes She Did! 78
Arrested in Mobile, Taken to Richmond 83
Married Thomas C. DeCaulp 98

Chapter 4 109
In Indianapolis 109
Was Velazquez in Two Places at the Same Time? 110
Looking for Thomas 111
Love Letters between Thomas and Nettie 116

The Yankee Spy within Her 123
Departed Milwaukee and St. Paul Areas for New York City 125
1864, Arrested in Nashville 129
1864, Revisited Richmond in December? 141

Chapter 5 145
1865, Where was Velazquez? 145
Famed Secret Courier for the St. Alban's Raiders? 148
Another Velazquez Sighting? 152
Grand Reappearance in Memphis and St. Louis 152
1866, the Explosion of Steamboat *Miami* 158
Gallant, Fearless, Good-looking, Perfect Lady, Angel of Mercy 164
Defended her Honor and her Husband's too 165
Get Your Books Right Here 168

Chapter 6 185
In New Orleans Again 185
The Venezuela Emigration Company 192
1867, Married John Wasson 197
Who was John Wasson? 200
The Sailing of the *Elizabeth* and its Arrival in Venezuela 201
A Letter to U.S. President Andrew Johnson 206
A Letter to the Governor 208
Unhappy in Venezuela 210
Departed Venezuela, Visited the Caribbean 215

Chapter 7 219
A Sea Tale 219
Visited Cuba… and was Welcomed by General Manzano?! 224
Returned to America 227
Across the Western Plains and "The Delights of Julesburg" 236
At Cheyenne 241
The Road to Nevada 243

Chapter 8 251
1868, a New Husband 251
Moved to Utah 259
Silver City, One Stays and One Goes 267
That Stagecoach Driver 273

Illustrations 277

Part 2: Events After the Time Frame of *The Woman in Battle* 301

Chapter 9 301
1874, Mobile (Alabama) Interview 301

1874, Atlanta (Georgia) Interview 307
Who wasn't Thomas C. DeCaulp? 320
DeCaulp's Military record 320
Arrived in Louisville 326
Encounter with Her Old Friend, Philip Arnold the Swindler 329

Chapter 10 335
Philip Arnold and The Great Diamond Hoax of 1872 335
The Mark Twain Dispute and the Salt Lake City Letter 337
A Letter to Jefferson Davis, Ex-Confederate President 342
A Letter to A. H. Stephens, Ex-Confederate Vice-President 344
1875, Returned to Atlanta and Defended Her Name 345
Velazquez the Reporter 357
A Letter to President Ulysses S. Grant 358
The Southern Publishing Company Fails Velazquez 360
A Woman in a Street Fight 362
Uncle Remus Knows 364

Chapter 11 367
The Woman in Battle is Born 367
Southern Historical Society's Criticism 371
The Publisher's Circular 376
Dr. Hammond, I Presume, or Not 385
Hammond's Firsthand Account 388
Conclusion of Publisher's Testimonials 388
1876, Other Book Reviews 389
Another Letter to Alexander H. Stephens 390
1877, Married McLeod 392
Who was Doctor McLeod? 395

Chapter 12 397
Going, Going, Gone from Wilmington 397
A Good Book Review 398
1878, Promoting Her Book, Herself and Cuba's Freedom 399
1878, Defending Her Book from General Jubal Early 404
General Jubal Early's Objections 408
Who Was General Jubal Early? 418
Departed Washington 419
She was a Former Arkadelphian 422
Velazquez's Son Died in New Orleans 423
An Opportunity in the Theatre 425
1878 and 1879, All Business in St. Louis 425
Departed St. Louis 428

Chapter 13 431
  1879, the Ridiculous Story and Investigator Glover 431
  A Firsthand Account from One Who Believed 436
  1881, *North and South American* in New York............................ 440
  1884, the Cigar Makers and President Grover Cleveland............ 443
  1885, the People's Party and Another Letter to Cleveland 446
  1886, Cohabited with Edward Goddard in New York 449
  1887, Married William Beard 453
  Who was William Beard? 455
  William Beard is Swindled 457
  1888, Ex-Confederate General Longstreet's Letter 458
  Another Respected Man Who Just Didn't Know 462
  1889, William Beard's Interest in Railroads 463
  1891, Still in New York, as Businesslike as a Man 464

Chapter 14 469
  1891, Saving George Washington's Mother 469
  1890 to 1893, Awarded $4,000 474
  1893, the Southern Immigration Scheme 475
  1894, Second Try, New Company 480
  1893, Ménie Muriel Dowie's *Women Adventurers* 485
  H. W. Hageman and Richard Worthington 486
  Was C. J. Worthington the Editor of *The Woman in Battle?* 488
  1895, 1896, 1897 Norfolk, Philadelphia and Wilmington 496
  1896, Myth Building 500

Chapter 15 503
  1898, the Death of William Beard 503
  1899, Fans of the Legend 516
  1900, Railroad Promoter 519
  About Albert Owen 524
  1900, the Promotion of the Railroad Continued 525
  About Alexander K. Coney and Mr. Alphonso B. Smith 526
  Another Try with a New Railroad Company 528
  1900, Mrs. Velazquez Beard Departed Phoenix 531
  1900, Traveled to New Orleans, Then to Atlanta 535
  1901, Tampa Could Not be Persuaded 537
  1901, Last Chance in Philadelphia 538

Chapter 16 543
  Mrs. Velazquez Beard's Train Wreck 543
  1901, Author Marian West was Skeptical 548
  1903, Some Heroic Women 550
  1905, Returned to New York 551

1905 to 1908, the Myth Revived 552
1908, a Heroine in Need of Rescuing 556
Relocated to Washington, D.C. 559
1914, Swan Song 565
1912, Petition, a Matter of Insanity 566
1913 to 1922, Out of Sight, but Not Out of Mind 568
1923, a Death Hardly Noticed 569
Was Velazquez Cuban? 571
A Father by Any Other Name 573
Making the Case that She was a Cuban 575
Making the Case that She was a Mississippian 580
Other Claimed Places of Residence 582

Chapter 17 585
Parade of Books, Newspapers, Magazines and Films 585
Sustained Myth Concluded 681

A Parable 685
Acknowledgements 689
Appendix 693
Abbreviations 705
About the Author 706
Index 707

Introduction

When Abraham Lincoln was elected as the 16th President of the United States of America, in November 1860, the southerly located states of the country reacted against his presidency with hostility. Lincoln was burned in effigy in Pensacola, Florida, "near the Navy Yard." The newspaper wrote, "The wildest extravagances are reported and measurably accredited." Lincoln's effigy also was reported hung and/or burned in other places such as Charleston, South Carolina and Aiken, Georgia.[1]

Southern states understood Lincoln and his new Republican Party were vehemently opposed to slavery's extension into new U.S. territories, and moreover, the Southern states believed Lincoln and his party were not supporters of the continuation of legal slavery anywhere in the country; after all, Lincoln had clearly said that slavery was a "moral, social and political evil."[2] But Lincoln also had loudly and clearly stated, "I have no purpose, directly or indirectly, to interfere with the institution of slavery in the States where it exists. I believe I have no lawful right to do so, and I have no inclination to do so."[3]

The South relied on slave labor for the cultivation of cotton which provided wealth for that section of the country. The North benefited from the slave grown cotton which supplied their textile producing mills. Southern states, believing that they were going to lose their slave labor, refused to submit to Lincoln's leadership and called for state conventions to decide by vote whether their states would withdraw from the United States of America. Shouts for secession had been heard for years before Lincoln's election, but now it was happening.

Florida's state secession convention was called to order on January 3, 1861. Rumors circulated that Governor Perry intended to seize Federal properties, that is, forts and arsenals in Florida. Pensacola, located in northwest Florida and the largest city in the state at the time, was the home of a significant Federal Navy shipyard and three Federal forts (four counting the Advanced Redoubt, protecting the rear of Fort Barrancas), which protected the entrance to Pensacola harbor.

Lieutenant Adam J. Slemmer, who was in command of the army troops while the regular commander was on leave, understood his small company of 46 men were too few to defend the Federal properties on the mainland and retreated to the more defensible Fort Pickens on Santa Rosa Island, across the mouth of Pensacola Bay. At the time Fort Pickens was an inactive

---

1. *Commercial Advertiser* (New York), Nov 10, 1869; *Alexandria Gazette* (Virginia), Nov 12, 1860; *Charleston Courier* (South Carolina), Nov 13, 1860.
2. Lincoln-Douglas fifth debate in Galesburg, Illinois, Oct 7, 1858.
3. Lincoln's first inaugural speech.

property which was occupied only by a hired watchman. Thirty sailors joined Lieutenant Slemmer's force making a total of 76 men and two officers. All worked furiously to make the Fort ready for an assault and the men were in place by January 10, the same day the Florida convention passed its ordinance of secession by a vote of sixty-two to seven.

As predicted by Lieutenant Slemmer, opposition came in the shape of two Florida militias (the Confederate army was not yet organized) and Alabama volunteers.[4] They marched on the Navy Yard and demanded of its commander, James Armstrong, its surrender. Slemmer's command of the army and Armstrong's command of the Navy Yard were separate. Unlike Slemmer, Armstrong had failed to understand the serious threat, and besides, he had not received orders to destroy and abandon Navy property, so had not. He had received orders to "protect the public property," and to cooperate with Slemmer and the army. Likewise, Slemmer had received orders to prevent seizure and to cooperate with the Commander of the Navy Yard. Slemmer had tried, but had not convinced Armstrong of the impending danger. Slemmer, to the best of his ability, disabled the equipment left behind at Forts Barrancas and McRee, but the supplies at the Navy Yard, which were the responsibility of Commander Armstrong, were seized by the Rebels.

Warrington, which lies five miles to the southwest of Pensacola, now hummed with activity with the arrival of Rebels preparing for a fight. Ultimately 8,000 Rebels dug in at Fort Barrancas, Fort McRee, the Navy Yard and all along the mainland opposite Fort Pickens. The Federals reinforced Fort Pickens by naval ships, unloading troops and supplies. The naval vessels themselves stood alert with their cannons in support of Fort Pickens. All was ready for the eruption of the Civil War. However, the war did not begin at Fort Pickens as most people at the time thought likely, but instead it erupted at Fort Sumter, in Charleston Harbor, South Carolina.

Historic Fort Pickens is about 10 miles from my home. I visit it regularly and have studied its history. It came to my attention that one Madame Loreta Janeta Velazquez wrote a memoir, published in 1876, in which she claimed she delivered a "battalion" of 236 Arkansas men, called the "Arkansas Grays," to Pensacola to oppose Fort Pickens in the opening days of the war. Curiously, she claimed she disguised herself in the uniform of a military officer, called herself Lieutenant Harry T. Buford, and solely through her own effort enlisted the Arkansas men, trained them, paid for all the necessary military supplies to sustain them, then delivered them to her husband who had earlier arrived in Pensacola. Her husband, "William," did not recognize his wife in disguise, until she "took him aside where [she] could speak to him in private, and disclosed [her] identity," whereupon he

---

4. Pensacola is near the Alabama state line and was an easy destination for Alabama troops.

was "intensely astonished and greatly grieved" at her revelation. I was no doubt as equally "astonished" upon reading her claim and wished someone could tell me whether it was true.

Luckily, George F. Pierce, retired history professor and author of *Pensacola in the Civil War* (2000), lived a mere three-minute walk down the block. On a pleasant day in May 2009, I paid him a visit with that question in mind. Mr. Pierce, in spite of being an expert on Pensacola's Civil War history, answered that he knew nothing of the "Arkansas Grays" or of Velazquez. Yet, if Velazquez's claim was true, she certainly deserves proper recognition by historians!

With my curiosity peaked, I commenced reading *The Woman in Battle* (*TWIB*), Velazquez's 606-page memoir, the central theme of which is her role as a combatant in the American Civil War while disguised as a male Confederate lieutenant. Both the author's and editor's Prefatory Notices emphatically stated the memoir is told "with simplicity and truth"; is a story of "plain, straightforward, and unpretending a style"; is "a true story in every particular"; and is "the only authentic account of the career of a Confederate heroine that has issued from the press."

Velazquez wrote (*TWIB*, p37), "[readers] will find in these pages an unaffected and unpretending, but truthful, and I hope interesting narrative...." The editor asserted (p10) that "there are thousands of officers and soldiers who fought in the Confederate armies who can bear testimony, not only to the valor she displayed in battle, and under many circumstances of difficulty and danger, but to her integrity, her energy, her ability, and her unblemished reputation." Velazquez echoed (p38) the same, "...some of the most distinguished officers of the Confederate army and many equally distinguished civilians, can and will testify to the truthfulness of the story I am about to relate, and to the unblemished character I bore while in the Confederate service." Far into her memoir (p275), Velazquez reminded readers, "I aim at giving in plain language an unadorned narrative of the personal experiences of a single adherent of the Confederacy...." and (p347) "In writing this narrative, it has seemed to me that the only proper method is to represent events as they actually occurred...." and (p390) "I have no hesitation whatever in giving to the world a plain, unadorned statement of the enterprises in which I was engaged...."

Contrary to these assertions, it became clear to me while reading *The Woman in Battle* that it contained much exaggeration and many deliberate lies. Exaggeration, grafted onto the truth is not an unknown habit of storytellers, and might be acceptable to some. However, deliberate lies are disturbingly not acceptable and ought not to be present in a memoir which emphatically purports to be "truthful." Surely, most readers would agree.

Velazquez seemingly challenged her reading public to ferret out the truth of her claims when she wrote (p5), "… the best I can hope to do is to relate my story with simplicity and truth, and then let it find its fate, whether it be praise or condemnation." The challenge, whether real or imagined, in any case, was accepted. The process of separating the truth from the lies commenced and it became rather like searching for clues in a mystery, a fun challenge, but also at times frustrating because of dead ends. The result of the investigation is *An Imposter of No Ordinary Rank*.

The real reward was the discovery of the fascinating life of a unique and highly energetic woman, who marched to the beat of her own drum, and who was perhaps the most traveled and most often married woman of that era. Besides the unexpected discoveries about Velazquez, the most surprising find is the existence of a vast number of Velazquez adherents, past and present, who have embraced or embrace Velazquez's embellishments because they claim the embellishments facilitate the excitement of her narrative. Many adherents, through the years and now, refuse to understand that the memoir is full of lies- or worse still, they know of the lies and willfully perpetuate the lies to mask the true Velazquez. By the conclusion of this book, readers will know the difference between embellishments, unwittingly accepted lies, and purposely perpetuated lies.

The true Loreta Janeta Velazquez was captivatingly loquacious, intelligent and perfectly capable of looking out for herself. More significantly, she was a con-artist, a forger, an exaggerator and a liar much of the time, particularly on points of importance. She flogged her mostly fabricated story to the newspapers and it was believed by much of the public, even though there were those who denounced her and her memoir as untruthful.

Even before the publication of her memoir, Mark Twain, in a letter to one Owen S. McKinney, said "the woman is a fraud" and McKinney replied that Velazquez was "an imposter of no ordinary rank." McKinney further wrote, "She is one of the most intelligent as well as one of the 'cheekiest' women I ever saw." Velazquez had asked Twain to write her memoir and when he declined, she represented anyway that he was to write it and forged Twain's signature in a ruse. McKinney, in a letter, brought Twain's attention to this fact. Twain's involvement will be addressed in detail.

To her credit, Velazquez's enchanting memoir is still working its deceitful magic and it has come into print once again. It continues to dupe readers, even Civil War scholars. Reprints are in libraries, bookstores and free at www.google.com/books/edition/The_Woman_in_Battle.

In light of the newly popular reprints and in consideration of their many unwary readers, I offer *An Imposter of No Ordinary Rank*. Hopefully, its ultimate effect will be the un-duping of the duped.

Part 1: Events in the Time Frame of *The Woman in Battle*

Chapter 1

Synopsis of *The Woman in Battle* (*TWIB*)

"The woman in battle is an infrequent figure on the pages of history," yet what a bad thing it would be if their history was "obliterated" because when they have "rushed to the battle-field they have invariably distinguished themselves," wrote Velazquez in her memoir's first chapter. She noted Deborah of the Hebrews, who led her warriors to victory; Tomyris, the Scythian queen who took away command of her army from her son after it suffered a defeat under his leadership and led it to victory against Persian king Cyrus; Boadicea, who led a British uprising against Roman occupation; and Bona Lombardi, who "fought in male attire by the side of her noble husband."

Velazquez was particularly fond of Catalina de Erauso, the Spanish nun-lieutenant. Catalina ran away as a teenager from the convent she had entered, cut her hair, disguised herself in young men's clothing and went to the New World and in Peru joined the army. She was promoted to the rank of lieutenant, was quick with a sword and dagger and never shied from a fight which resulted in her injuring or killing her opponents. She was arrested, confessed her true sex, rid herself of her legal troubles and returned to Spain. Her story became known and she became a celebrity.

Velazquez cited another heroine, but "nearer our own time," Apolonia Jagiello, who fought for Poland's independence. At the age of 21, during the Kraków Insurrection of 1846, Apolonia assumed male attire and joined the fight. Later she fought as a soldier in the Hungarian Revolution and attained the rank of lieutenant. She traveled to America in December 1849, married Major Gaspard Tochman of Washington, D.C. and was a social success. When the American Civil War erupted her husband went South, but she stayed loyal to the Union, even though she was briefly arrested on suspicion of Southern sympathies.[1]

Velazquez's imagination was most fired by Joan of Arc whose "glorious deeds" Velazquez wished to "emulate." Velazquez admired her courage and leadership which "rallied the defeated and demoralized [French] army" against the British army. Velazquez called her a great patriot who dared and dared to do greatly. Velazquez readily admitted that her circumstances were different from Joan's; in particular, Velazquez was happy she had avoided a

---

1. Mary W. Schaller and Martin N. Schaller, ed., *Soldiering for Glory: The Civil War Letters of Colonel Frank Schaller Twenty-second Mississippi Infantry* (Columbia, SC: Univ. of South Carolina Press, 2007), 162; H. G. Adams, ed., *A Cyclopædia of Female Biography Consisting of Sketches of all Women who have been distinguished by Great Talents, Strength of Character, Piety, Benevolence, or Moral Virtue of any Kind* (London: Groombridge and Sons, 1857), 409; *National Era* (Washington, DC) Oct 3, 1850, Sep 30, 1851, Jun 3, 1852; *Alexandria Gazette* (Virginia), Aug 14, 1851.

similar fate as Joan's. Velazquez's friends assured her that the adventures that befell Velazquez "while playing the part of a warrior" were worth telling.

Velazquez viewed the outbreak of the American Civil War, as an opportunity offered her to emulate her martial heroines; she wrote (*TWIB*, p51) she wished to make "[her] name famous above that of any of the great heroines of history" and that her "heart was fixed on achieving fame (p62)."

She said that fellow soldiers would be surprised to read her story and learn, for the first time, that Lieutenant Harry Buford was a woman. They should "blush with shame" when they realize the "profanity and ribaldry" they used in the presence of a woman, especially "a modest woman at that." Throughout her book she made clear she was neither an admirer of cursing nor drinking of alcohol. No matter how disagreeable the language of camp life was, she claimed that she never wavered from her determined goal of serving the Confederacy. She asserted she maintained "unblemished character" while "in the Confederate service" and "labored with efficiency, courage, and energy to secure the independence of the Confederacy, but with [her] womanly reputation unblemished by even a suspicion of impropriety...."

Velazquez was proud of her name and "of the ancestry from whom [she] inherited it." She said the Velazquez family name was that of Castilian nobles whose impressive deeds fill Spanish history and that she never discredited "the noble name." She counted as her kin, Don Diego Rodriguez Velazquez, the famous painter, and Don Diego Velazquez, the conqueror and first governor of Cuba. She figured she inherited some of the "adventuresome blood of old Governor Don Diego" which "fired [her] brain and steeled [her] nerves" to seek for herself "a warrior's fame."

Velazquez explained that her father was a native of "Carthagena [*sic*]," Spain and was educated "at the universities of Madrid and Paris" where he was a scholar of Latin, French and German. "He went to Paris as an attaché of the Spanish embassy." While living there he met and married the daughter of a French naval officer and an American woman. Señor Velazquez left Paris to return to Madrid where Loreta's three brothers and two sisters were born. Her father was then "appointed to an official position in Cuba" and moved the family there. Two years later, on the 26th of June, 1842, Loreta was born in a house on "Calle Velaggas [*sic*]" in Havana. She was christened Loreta Janeta.

Her father left his job in Cuba, when he inherited "a large estate in Texas, which was then a part of the republic of Mexico," and moved the family to San Luis Potosí. When the Mexican-American War erupted her father joined the Mexican forces as an officer and sent his family away to the Caribbean island of St. Lucia where her mother's brother lived. Velazquez wrote that with the conclusion of the war, her father abandoned his estate because it was part of the territory ceded to the United States and he refused to live under its rule. He was terribly embittered by his loss, but in any case, he fell "heir to another valuable estate at Puerto de Palmas" in Cuba. The plantation thrived and the family was wealthy.

While in Cuba, Velazquez received a proper education by a hired English governess until 1849 at which time her parents sent her to live in New Orleans with an aunt, "[her] mother's only surviving sister," who tutored her for two years. Velazquez then attended the Sisters of Charity School.

While residing with her aunt she dressed herself in the clothes of her male cousin and practiced a man's gait when no one was likely to discover her. She aspired to be another Joan of Arc, or wished she was a man who could discover new worlds as Columbus and Captain Cook had done. When she wrote to her father in Cuba, her letters were filled with such notions and Velazquez said that her father reprimanded her and she was lucky he did not "remove her from influences."

Velazquez related particulars of her childhood in Cuba and girlhood in New Orleans. She told how in New Orleans she stole for herself Nellie V's boyfriend, "William," a "young American army officer." Velazquez claimed that Nellie V. was her best friend and classmate, but curiously, as will be seen, Velazquez seemingly memorialized Nellie B. or Nellie Bremer, the owner of a New Orleans whorehouse at which Velazquez briefly resided.

"William" and Velazquez were "clandestinely married" and upon its later revelation, the news horrified her aunt and parents, who disinherited her (*TWIB*, p49). Since Velazquez gave the date of this marriage and the date of her birth, one can determine that she would have been aged 13 years, 9 months and 10 days. Velazquez narrated that her army officer husband William was ordered to accompany the expedition to Utah against the Mormons in 1857. She, however, stayed in St. Louis. After the expedition he was assigned to Fort Leavenworth (Kansas) and she too went. Her husband then was sent to Fort Arbuckle (Oklahoma), at which time she returned to St. Louis. Velazquez claimed that they had three children by the end of 1860, but all died of fever in St. Louis. Then with the rumblings of war and her "husband's state determined to secede," she persuaded him to resign his United States army commission.

When war erupted and after William departed to fight for the South, Velazquez disguised herself in her husband's clothes, sought out a German tailor in Memphis, who measured her and from whom she ordered two uniform suits.[2] She clothed herself as a male Confederate soldier, applied a

---

2. There indeed were German-born tailors in Memphis; one was Frederick G. Bauer at 332 Main Street and another was Peter Marmann at 265 Main Street. Source is Tanner, Halpin & Co., *Memphis City Directory for 1859* (Memphis: Hatton and Clark Publishers, 1859), 47, 122 and U.S. Census, 1860.

false mustache and named herself Lieutenant Harry T. Buford. Then posing as Lieutenant Buford she traveled to "Hurlburt [*sic* Hulbert] Station" (Arkansas) where she raised in four days a "battalion" of 236 Arkansas men. She claimed she provided the money necessary to outfit the men and had "eighty-eight thousand dollars with which to see [herself] through." These dollars from 1861 would be equivalent to more than 3.3 million dollars in 2023.

She marched the men to the Mississippi River, loaded them on a steamboat and took them to New Orleans. From there she took them to Mobile (Alabama) where its citizens gave them a rousing welcome. She continued eastward to Pensacola (Florida) with her "battalion" and delivered it to her husband, William, who was stationed there. Her husband did not recognize that Lieutenant Buford was his wife and was astonished when she revealed herself to him. She turned over the command of the men to William.

Please see the images taken from *TWIB* of Velazquez in male military attire and female attire in Illustrations, Figure 1.

Lieutenant Harry T. Buford immediately departed Pensacola and was on a supply run in New Orleans when news of the death of her husband at Pensacola reached her. "Terribly shocked, and nearly wild with grief," she returned to Pensacola and learned he was killed by the accidental explosion of a carbine; she mentioned nothing about a funeral or burial. As will be seen, the story of this husband and his death was untrue. Lieutenant Buford left her "battalion" under the command of Lieutenant Thomas C. DeCaulp and departed for Virginia on June 16, 1861. DeCaulp will become integral in this story.

Velazquez claimed that as Lieutenant Harry Buford, she made a stop in Montgomery (Alabama) and met Confederate Secretary of War Leroy P. Walker at the Exchange Hotel who expressed "the prospects of the contest with the North." In the course of this book, it will be shown that Secretary Walker, by June 16, had already departed Montgomery and was in the newly designated Confederate capital of Richmond. Secretary Walker was the first of many, many, many dignitaries who Velazquez claimed to meet- even U.S. President Lincoln and Confederate President Davis.

Upon her arrival in Virginia, Velazquez claimed she fought at the First Battle of Bull Run (First Battle of Manassas) and then at the Battle of Ball's Bluff. Later in Tennessee she fought at the Battle of Shiloh (April 1862), so she said.

Three days before and leading up to the First Battle of Bull Run, there occurred a skirmish at Blackburn's Ford. Here Velazquez claimed that as the enemy "broke and ran" she "fired a last shot at them with a dead man's musket." She said she was "placed temporarily in command of a company, the senior officer of which had been killed," and she hoped the "big fight" (Bull Run) would come off soon so she could retain command of this company, yet she failed to say another word about it. It was the evening after the skirmish at Blackburn's Ford that she unbelievably claimed she went to sleep on the battlefield and woke-up some 50 miles to the northwest and then marched back to the battlefield at Bull Run; the claim will be challenged.

The second battle in which she proclaimed her bravery was at the Battle of Ball's Bluff (Virginia), where she again said she "took charge of a company which had lost all its officers." She said that after the fighting was over, the company's first lieutenant reappeared and she thought he had slinked away to the safety of the rear in a "cowardly trick."

At the Battle of Shiloh (Tennessee) she claimed she concealed herself along the banks of the Tennessee River during the evening and by chance saw General Ulysses S. Grant with another officer go past in a small boat. She wrote (p213):

My heart began to beat violently when I saw Grant, and my hand instinctively grasped my revolver. Both he and the officer with him, were completely at my mercy, for they were within easy pistol shot, and my first impulse was to kill them, and run the risk of all possible consequences to myself. I even went so far as to take good aim, and in a second more, had I been a little firmer-nerved, the great Federal general, and future President of the United States, would have finished his career. It was too much like murder, however, and I could not bring myself to do the deed, although it would have been as justifiable as any killing that takes place in warfare.

Prior to this Grant episode, Velazquez tells of her arrival at the impending battlefield when she "spied the Arkansas boys whom [she] had enlisted at Hurlburt [*sic* Hulbert] Station nearly a year before." Velazquez wrote (p204):

Dismounting from my horse, I forced my way through the ranks until I reached Captain De Caulp, who shook me heartily by the hand, and was evidently delighted to see me, as we had not met since I parted from him in Pensacola the previous June, when starting for Richmond. My pleasure at the interview, especially at meeting him again under such circumstances as those I am describing, was of a very different and much more intense kind than his, for reasons that will appear hereafter.

Her intense pleasure "for reasons that will appear hereafter" is that DeCaulp is the object of her affections and she his, only he does not yet know that Lieutenant Harry T. Buford is one and the same as the lady he loves. It will be seen that DeCaulp and Velazquez meet again and express their love for one another. However, it is provably false that DeCaulp and his company were at the Battle of Shiloh.

Her claimed deeds in these three battles will be discussed in detail. There were other battles as well; she said she fought at the Battle of Woodsonville (Rowlett's Station) in Kentucky and two months later she participated in the siege of Fort Donelson, Tennessee.

Velazquez claimed (p309) she "managed to severely hurt the foot which had been wounded shortly after the battle of Fort Donelson," and that she, posing as Lieutenant Buford, was sent to Atlanta, Georgia for treatment. In Atlanta, she expected to see Captain Thomas DeCaulp because she knew he was there, sick. She (as herself) and DeCaulp had already expressed their mutual affection in letters and became engaged and now she had determined to go to him, nurse him back to health and marry him. First, she knew she must reveal that the lady with whom he had been communicating was one and the same as his comrade-in-arms Lieutenant Harry T. Buford, who DeCaulp knew in Pensacola and at the Battle of Shiloh, but failed to realize was his fiancée. Velazquez explained, "Captain DeCaulp and I were under an engagement of marriage, having been in correspondence with each other since my departure from Pensacola."

In Atlanta, her condition worsened because, in addition to being lame, she now had fever. She, as Lieutenant Harry Buford, was admitted into the hospital where she learned that DeCaulp also was a patient. Once she recovered, she went to his bedside, posing as comrade Lt. Harry Buford and expressed her happiness to see him once more. Buford asked if DeCaulp had yet married the woman to whom he was engaged. DeCaulp replied no, and that he had not heard from her in several months and then handed a picture of female Velazquez to Lieutenant Buford and said, "That is the woman I love; what do you think of her?" Velazquez narrated (p327):

This was almost too much for me; and all trembling with emotion, I handed it back to him, saying, "She is a fine-looking woman;" and wondering he did not observe the resemblance between the portrait and the original before him.

"Yes," said he, "and she is just as good as she is good-looking. I think the world of her, and want to see her again- O, so bad!"

"Have you known her long, captain?" I asked, with a trembling voice, and scarcely daring to trust myself to speak, for these words, and the tender tone in which they were spoken, made my heart leap with joy, and brought tears to my eyes. I was afraid that he would notice my agitation, and in some way surmise the cause of it; and I did not want him to do this, for I was not yet ready to reveal myself, but desired further to hear what he would say about me before I told him my secret. So I turned away, and pretended to be attracted by some object in another part of the room while I wiped the tears from my eyes, and attempted to recover my composure.

"Yes," he went on, "I have known her for a long time. She is a widow, and her husband was an excellent friend of mine." Then, apparently suddenly recollecting the circumstances under which he first made my acquaintance in the character of a

Confederate officer, he said, glancing quickly and eagerly at me, "Why, you ought to know her; her husband was the first captain of our company; you recollect him, surely."

"O," said I, as if rather surprised at this revelation, "she is his widow, is she?"

"Yes," said Captain De Caulp; "you have met her, have you not?"

I could scarcely help smiling at the turn this conversation was taking; and still wondering whether my lover would be shrewd enough to detect the likeness between the picture he was holding in his hand, and fondly gazing at, and the original of it who was sitting by his bedside, I said, "Yes, I have had a slight acquaintance with her, but you, probably, have known her longer than I have. When did you see her last?"

"I have not seen her for three years," he replied.

"Have you been engaged to her that long?"

"O, no; I did not become engaged to her until about six months after the death of her husband. He was killed, as you know, at Pensacola, just after the war commenced, by the bursting of a carbine."

"Well, if you have not seen her all that time, how have you managed to do your courting?"

"O, that was easy enough. After her husband's death, we had some correspondence about the settlement of his affairs, and we kept on writing to each other after these were arranged. I always had a great liking for her, as I thought that she was a first-rate woman, of the kind that you don't meet every day; and, consequently, after about six months, I asked her to marry me. She was a sound, sensible, patriotic woman, who admired me for going to the front more than she would have done had I remained at home to court her, and she accepted me without hesitation."

Please see the "In the Hospital" drawing from *TWIB* in Illustrations, Figure 2.

After DeCaulp proclaimed that he "would almost give [his] existence in heaven" if he could go to her, Velazquez became all choked-up and made a "hasty excuse" and an abrupt departure.

The next morning, Velazquez, as herself, sent DeCaulp a note saying she was coming to visit. She waited until DeCaulp had time to read the note and to predictably become overjoyed, then she entered his room posing again as comrade Lt. Harry Buford. DeCaulp announced the happy news of the arrival of his fiancée to Buford who congratulated him on his fortune. DeCaulp requested a private room of the doctors, who complied, and he received a shave and a cleaning-up in anticipation of the arrival of his fiancée.

Now Buford, although very nervous to finally reveal her secret, said (p332):

"Well, captain, don't you think that the picture of your lady-love looks the least bit like your friend Harry Buford?"

A light seemed to suddenly break upon him; he gasped for breath, and sank back overcome on his pillow, the great drops of perspiration standing out all over his forehead. Then, raising himself, he looked me hard in the face, and, grasping my hand tightly, exclaimed, "Can it be possible that you are she?"

"Yes," said I, clasping his hand still tighter, "I am, indeed, your own Loreta. It was your sweetheart who fought by your side at the great battle of Shiloh; and not only on that occasion, but ever since the outbreak of the war she has been doing a soldier's work for the cause of the Confederacy. Can you love her a little for that as well as for herself? or will you despise her because she was not willing to stay at home like other women, but undertook to appear on the battle-field in the guise of a man for the purpose of doing a man's duty?"

"I love you ten times more than ever for this, Loreta!" he said, with a vehemence that brought tears of joy to my eyes.

For the moment, Harry Buford could not pursue the marriage as she had to go to Montgomery to attend to some unspecified business. When she returned to Atlanta, she went to the hospital; she found DeCaulp's health had improved and he was on his feet. They made arrangements for the wedding to take place at the Thompson Hotel and took into their confidence Drs. Benton and Hammond, who were astonished since they were only then told that Lt. Harry Buford was a female. They agreed to be present the next day.

Velazquez, in Harry Buford disguise, purchased suitable female apparel at several stores, telling the clerks the clothes were for someone out of town or presents for "the girls at the hotel- in fact, making up whatever story [she] thought would answer [her] purpose (p335)." In this gathered wardrobe, she and DeCaulp were married in the parlor of the hotel by "Rev. Mr. Pinkington," the post chaplain.

After the wedding, Velazquez yielded to her husband's wish for her not to reassume her military uniform or return to the front. After a week's honeymoon DeCaulp returned to the war, over Velazquez's protests, but "before reaching his command, Captain DeCaulp was taken sick again; and before [she] obtained any information of his condition, he had died in a Federal hospital in Chattanooga." She lamented, "Within three short weeks, I was a widow again!" She continued, "This was a terrible blow to me, for I tenderly loved my husband, and was greatly beloved by him." She eulogized him for three paragraphs.

At this point in her memoir, she expressed weariness of her male soldier impersonation, resumed female attire and determined she could be of more benefit to the South by performing spy activities against the North. She claimed she traveled to Washington, D.C. where she said she met Abraham Lincoln, whom she was induced to believe was "not a bad man, but that he was an honest and well-meaning one, who thought that he was only doing his duty in attempting to conquer the South," and also Secretary of War Cameron who failed to impress her favorably.

As a spy, she claimed she was given the duty to inform the Confederate prisoners at Johnson's Island prison camp (Ohio) of a planned prison break which was to be forced from the outside. The scheme failed. She said it would have succeeded "had everybody been as enthusiastic and as determined as [her]self and had there been no traitors with [them]."

Also, while working as a spy, she claimed to have participated in a successful scheme in which she received stolen printing plates from the U.S. Treasury capable of turning out "one hundred dollars' compound interest notes" and later "obtained another one for printing fractional currency."

She then traveled to Europe to sell some Confederate bonds, and had just returned to New York when she heard of General Lee's surrender. The war ended soon after.

Seemingly every page of her fast-paced book contains a new and scarcely believable war adventure. Not only did Velazquez tell of her war adventures and pre-war childhood, she also told of her post-war adventures.

After the war, she went to New Orleans where she met "Major Wasson" who also had just arrived in the city. She "saw a great deal of Major Wasson, and a strong attachment sprang up between [them]" and they married. Research shows they knew one another for less than 12 days, the details of which will be discussed in due course. Wasson was a member of a party of ex-Confederates preparing to exile themselves to Venezuela (South America) because they could not "remain in their old homes under the domination of their heartless victors."[3] The new Mrs. Wasson along with the party endured a rough sea voyage to Venezuela and had not been there long trying to establish their colony when John Wasson died of fever. Velazquez then left the country.

Her route took her by ship through the Caribbean and once again to the United States, arriving in New York. From there she headed west by train and stagecoach, finally stopping in the silver mining boomtown of Austin, Nevada. After residing in Austin approximately 60 days she married a miner, whose name she never mentioned in her memoir, but research reveals he was Edward Hardy Bonner.

Velazquez wrote that her husband briefly quit mining when they moved to California, but then he wished to resume mining so they went to Utah. In Salt Lake City Velazquez had a son whom she also did not name in her book, but research has revealed his name. She and her son departed the Salt Lake area, headed eastward through Colorado, then south through New Mexico. Facts show that her husband had already left Utah to mine in Silver City, New Mexico and that was the reason for their journey there, however,

---

3. *Evening Post* (New York, New York), Sept 18, 1886.

Velazquez purposely avoided saying so. She simply wrote that upon her arrival there, the place did not suit her and she departed eastward traveling through Texas. She did not explain whether her intention at that time was to leave her husband permanently, but research shows she married again within weeks and never saw Bonner again.

Her narrative ends with her and her child crossing Texas, in 1874 (though she didn't say the date), when she would have been about 34 years old (if her given birth year was truthful) and it was two years later in 1876 that she published her book.

Of the claims found in her memoir, many are true. She did wear a Confederate uniform. She was arrested. She did visit the towns and cities and stayed in the hotels she claimed. After the War, Velazquez did marry Wasson and sailed to Venezuela, and upon her return to the United States she indeed traveled to Nevada and married a miner. During the War, Velazquez did marry Confederate soldier Thomas DeCaulp in Atlanta. However, Velazquez also wrote that only a week after they were married, her husband returned to the front and died in Chattanooga, but it was a lie. The truth is that DeCaulp deserted the Confederacy, went North, joined the Yankee army and she went North to join him. He received a medical discharge from the Union army and died in Philadelphia- after the War had ended. If Velazquez would tell a lie of this magnitude about her beloved husband, wouldn't she lie about almost anything? To answer the question, the task of analyzing her many claims now commences.

Meeting Men of Influence

Throughout her book Velazquez made many claims of meeting important political and military men, both Union and Confederate. Most of the meetings were brief and all business, but sometimes her meetings were conversational. These alleged meetings "stretched her credibility by claiming too much," according to writer Sylvia D. Hoffert in her 1978 *Civil War Times Illustrated* article "Heroine or Hoaxer" which probed Velazquez.[4] Hoffert pointed out that in a mere four years, and during a tumultuous war no less, it was "incredible" that Velazquez could have met so many people, especially in light of the difficulty of travel during the war (because of military restrictions). Obviously, Hoffert intuitively felt something was amiss.

But Velazquez did travel and did so extensively. Facts uncovered make it clear she was probably the most traveled female of her generation. Also, facts make clear Velazquez was not timid and if any of the claimed meetings were possible, she would have not shied away. It will be seen later, in her railroad scheme of the 1900's, that she relished meeting men of influence. Her approach was always bold, disregarding any imposition. Still,

---

4. Reprinted in *Civil War Times*, Aug 1999.

documented behaviors of travel and of meeting some people does not make it true that she met all the people she claimed, as will be seen.

She claimed she met: U.S. President Abraham Lincoln, and Secretary of War Simon Cameron; Confederate President Jefferson Davis and Secretary of War Leroy P. Walker; Governors Brough of Ohio and Morton of Indiana; Confederate Generals Milledge Bonham, James Longstreet, Stonewall Jackson, John Winder, William Hardee and Earl Van Dorn; Union Generals Benjamin Butler and William Rosecrans. This list includes only some of the governors and generals, there were more of each. She also claimed many colonels, majors and captains who became distinguished during the war.

The first meeting claimed was with the Confederate Secretary of War, Leroy P. Walker in Montgomery, Alabama. Velazquez wrote (p88) that from Pensacola, Florida she started for Virginia "on the 16th of June [1861]." It should be pointed out that she could not possibly have mistaken the date of her Pensacola departure. It was right after the death of her husband, "William," from a carbine rifle explosion, which left her "terribly shocked and nearly wild with grief," a memorable day to be sure. En route she stopped at Montgomery's Exchange Hotel where she met Secretary Walker "with whom [she] had a very pleasant conversation about the prospects of the contest with the North, the political situation, and other matters of interest."

Montgomery was chosen as the first capital of the Confederate States of America and here Jefferson Davis was chosen the new country's president on February 18, 1861.[5] The Exchange Hotel was built in 1848 on the northwest corner of Commerce and Montgomery Streets and was the hub of Montgomery activity for years.

On May 16, 1861, Confederate clerk and diarist John B. Jones wrote, "Here there is an incessant influx of strangers coming from all directions on business with the new government."[6] However, by June 16, 1861, when Velazquez claimed she was there, the excited crowds had dispersed because the Confederate Government had relocated its capital to Richmond, Virginia. President Jefferson Davis had gone there and this included the Executive Cabinet, which meant that Secretary of War Leroy P. Walker had gone to Richmond!

The evidence which places Walker in Richmond, instead of Montgomery, on June 16 is indisputable and provided by Secretary Walker's correspondence clerk, John B. Jones. Baltimore-born Jones had been the editor of a Philadelphia newspaper "devoted to Southern interests." When he became convinced that the nation would erupt in war, and fearing for his

---

5. M.P. Beale & S.H. Phelan, *City Directory and History of Montgomery, Alabama* (Montgomery, AL: T.C. Bingham), 1878.
6. John B. Jones, *A Rebel War Clerk's Diary* (Philadelphia, PA: J.B. Lippincott, 1866), 36.

safety in the North, he abandoned his paper and went South. After his departure he wrote, "It was said ten thousand had visited my office, displaying a rope with which to hang me. Finding their victim had escaped, they vented their fury in sacking the place." He said he had no idea if the building was destroyed, but it was owned by a Unionist, in any case.

The fifty-one-year-old Jones went to Montgomery to offer his services to the newly formed Confederate government and was hired by Leroy P. Walker as his correspondence secretary on May 19, 1861. Jones departed Montgomery on May 28, arrived in Richmond on May 31 and on June 1 prepared "five offices" for the impending arrival of Secretary Walker. John Jones reported, "June 3d.- The Secretary arrived today, sick" and "June 4th.- The Secretary is still sick." Skipping ahead to the date in question, June 16, Jones wrote, "The Secretary got me to send a telegraphic dispatch to his family to repair hither without delay...." On June 17, Jones wrote a "short editorial for one of the newspapers" and Jones explained, "This I carried to the Secretary at his lodgings, and he was so well pleased with it he wanted me to accompany him to the lodgings of the President... and show it to him." On June 23 Jones wrote, "Everyday... the Secretary... invites me to ride with him in quest of a house," but they had yet to locate a suitable one.[7]

Secretary of War Walker was in Richmond by June 3 and no longer in Montgomery on June 16. Clearly Velazquez invented her June 16, 1861 Montgomery meeting with him.

Further evidence is Secretary of War Walker's telegram register book which documents his departure for Richmond and contains telegrams sent by him from Richmond during the time in question.[8] Walker's letters written from Richmond to generals and governors, reproduced in *War of the Rebellion... Official Records* (OR), as well as the newspapers of the time, place Walker in Richmond.[9]

1861, Arrested in Lynchburg, Taken to Richmond

Velazquez's first found appearance as Lieutenant Buford is recorded in the *Lynchburg* (Virginia) *Republican* newspaper of Thursday morning, September 26, 1861:

ARRIVAL EXTRAORDINARY.- On the [railroad] cars of the Tennessee Company, which arrived here on Tuesday evening [September 24], among many other officers was one whose gay and dashing appearance attracted universal

---

7. Ibid, 19, 2-54.
8. U.S. National Archives and Records Administration (NARA), Record Group (RG)109, Microfilm (M)524, Telegrams Sent by the Confederate Secretary of War.
9. OR, Ser 1 Vol 2, Chap IX, p906; OR, Ser 1Vol 52, pt 2, p111; OR, Ser 1 Vol 3, Chap X, p597; William C. Harris, "Leroy Pope Walker: Confederate Secretary of War," *Confederate Centennial Studies*, No. #20 (1962), 102; *Edgefield Advertiser* (SC), Jun 12, 1861; *Daily Dispatch* (Richmond, VA), Jun 11, 1861; *Keowee Courier* (SC), Jun 15, 1861.

attention, and led to the firm belief on the part of all that he was one of the chief dignitaries of the military world. Decked out in all the "pomp and pride, and circumstance of glorious war," and with an air that seemed to say, "I am the master of the great Wellington and Bonaparte," he trod the streets the observed of all observers, when, in an evil hour, it became noised [rumored] about that the gallant officer was sailing under false colors- in other words, that he who had become the envy of all the men, and the admiration of all the women, was herself a woman dressed up in the habilaments [*sic*] of the sterner sex. Our police, ever on the alert for suspicious characters, and knowing of no good reason why the gay one should have donned the "pants" instead of the gown, quickly arrested her, and carried her before Alderman Saunders, who, after a tedious examination, being unable to find out much either favorable or unfavorable to the suspected party, determined to send her to Richmond for the Secretary of War to examine. She gave her name as Mrs. Mary Ann Keith, of Memphis, Tennessee, but registered at the Piedmont House as Lieut. Buford. Said she had been married twice, her first husband having been a member of Sherman's famous Battery; her second was in the Southern army, but she stated that she was separated from him for some reason she did not make known. She declared she was alright on the Southern question, and scouted the idea of being a spy. She said her reason for dressing in soldier clothes was, that she had determined to fight the battles of her country, and thought such a disguise more likely to enable her to accomplish her object. She may be all sound as far as we know to the contrary, but a proper regard for our safety requires that all such characters should be strictly examined wherever they are found in the South. The prisoner was sent to Richmond yesterday morning.

The story drew much attention and many newspapers, local and distant, repeated the story, some full length and some paraphrased. One newspaper, the *Memphis Daily Appeal* repeated the story, but surprisingly failed to add information about "Mrs. Mary Ann Keith of Memphis." It would seem that a hometown newspaper would have discovered who she was, but it did not, and neither did any other newspaper.

In one detail, the *Republican's* description of Velazquez is at odds with Velazquez's self-description. The newspaper failed to mention the mustache which Velazquez claimed (p68) she wore: "then my friend carefully fastened the mustache to my upper lip with glue." Recall in the illustration of Lieutenant Harry T. Buford, in *TWIB* between pages 61 and 62, she sports a mustache and a goatee which adds more hair to the mystery. And Velazquez never explained the adoption of her goatee. She just popped-up with the claim (p186) that she sported an "imperial" (or goatee) along with her mustache.

The portrait of Velazquez wearing a mustache and goatee is reproduced in Illustrations, Figure 1.

It is curious that no newspapers which reported her various arrests ever mentioned a facial hair disguise. If the reporters had witnessed a facial hair disguise, it can be sure they would have stated so and likely made the most of it with puns and jokes. A case in point is one Alice Flynn who, when in Baltimore, assumed a male disguise and was arrested "while walking in the street, dressed in a suit of black cloth, and with huge whiskers *a la* Burnside." Union General Ambrose Burnside wore admirable side whiskers from which the word "sideburns" originates. Alice had run away from her Washington, D.C. home, was just married in Baltimore, now intended to go South with her husband and "he had suggested that she would get along much better so disguised."[10]

As will be seen, the lack of comment about Velazquez's alleged hairy disguise at the time of each of her several arrests, leads one to believe she wasn't wearing one on those occasions. It was only well after the timeline of her <u>narrated</u> arrests in Lynchburg and other arrests to come, in New Orleans and Richmond, that Velazquez wrote that she was no longer wearing her mustache. More significant is the fact that this admitted lack of a mustache was after the <u>true</u> timeline of her <u>true</u> arrests in Lynchburg, Richmond, New Orleans and Mobile. These arrests will be presented later.

In her memoir (p308), the first occasion she claimed she was not wearing her mustache was when she returned from the North on a spy mission, as her female self. She relocated her hidden uniform, put it on and crossed the military lines near Chattanooga. She approached a Confederate picket and asked to see "the officer of the guard." Velazquez wrote, "I was much afraid lest he should suspect something, for I had no mustache, and having become somewhat bleached [She had previously tanned her skin with a solution.], was not by any means so masculine in appearance as I had been at one time." She was allowed to proceed into the South. She soon found out that the object of her affections, Captain DeCaulp, was sick in Atlanta. She went there and her narrative continued with the story of her marriage to DeCaulp.

One can see in her memoir, in the illustration titled "In the Hospital," that she is shown without a mustache; see Illustrations, Figure 2.

Even in Velazquez's many interviews she never mentioned she sported a mustache and goatee. However, there was one instance in 1874 (September 4) when an *Atlanta Constitution* reporter wrote about Velazquez: "She was frequently seen upon the streets, and at the depot in her full lieutenant's uniform, and a lovely imperial." This reporter's recollection was 10 years after he saw her in Atlanta. The reporter's memory certainly could have been accurate, but it by no means allows the conclusion that Velazquez always wore a facial hair disguise. The lack of comment by reporters on other occasions supports the conclusion that she mostly did not wear facial hair. It would seem her claim, to have mostly worn a mustache and goatee disguise, originated at the time of the book's creation, after the War, for the benefit of the readership.

---

10. *Plain Dealer* (Cleveland, OH), Apr 27, 1863.

Velazquez, herself, was not consistent when she explained how she got her mustache. She first wrote (p53) that when her husband took her out on the town, with her wearing a male disguise, she braided her hair, "put on a man's wig, and a false mustache." Then fifteen pages later, in seeming contradiction, she explained (p68) that once her husband left for the war, she determined to disguise herself in a uniform and an unnamed male friend, thinking he could improve her disguise, to give her a "more manly air... obtained a false mustache... [and] carefully fastened the mustache on [her] upper lip with glue." Clearly, Velazquez had forgotten that she had already introduced the adoption of a mustache and proceeded to spin a new and contradictory version. This fuzzy mustache contradiction is enough to set one's nose a-twitching and for good reason. It gets worse. Velazquez then narrated that she looked in the mirror and noted the mustache "was a very great improvement... and laughed at the thought of what [her] husband would say when he saw [her] in this disguise." What?! Her husband had already seen her in her mustache! He had taken her out in Memphis when she was wearing "a man's wig and a false mustache." It can be sure there is a lie hidden somewhere, likely in the bushy mustache!

With or without facial hair, the question arises as to how successful Velazquez was at her disguise, or even if she diligently tried to stay in disguise. As will be seen on the occasion of her 1863 arrest (about which much will be written later), she characterized it (*TWIB*, p288), "my recent unpleasantness with Richmond and Lynchburg authorities with regard to my right to wear male attire." Clearly, the authorities arrested her "on the charge of being a woman in disguise" and at that time it was illegal for a woman to dress as a man, much less impersonate a soldier and officer. Velazquez said little about the soldier and officer part, but commented that she had the right to wear male attire. Then in a passage on page 341 of *TWIB*, Velazquez seems to have unwittingly admitted that she was routinely discovered:

> For having dared to assume a man's garb, for the purpose of doing a man's work, I had been treated with contumely, on more than one occasion, by those who ought at least to have given me credit for my intentions, and although my comrades of the camp and the battle-field--or at least all of them whose good opinion was worth having--esteemed me for what I had done, and for what I tried to do, bestowing ample praise upon me for my valor and efficiency as a soldier, I was getting out of the notion of subjecting myself to the liability of being locked up by every local magistrate within whose jurisdiction I happened to find myself, simply because I did not elect to dress according to his notions of propriety.

If she was routinely discovered while in disguise, was she ever successful at performing the deeds she claimed she performed while in disguise? And still more questionable is the fact that she wrote to the Confederate government signing both her then married name and Lt. Harry T. Buford (which will be addressed).

The *Republican's* September 26 account of alias "Lieut. Buford" has a not so obvious problem. The article lacked any claim by her to have been at the First Battle of Manassas (Bull Run) which had just occurred in July, only two months prior to the article. It is inconceivable that Velazquez would have failed to tell the newspaper of her participation, if true. At this date, she simply had not yet thought to include it in her developing story. It was only much later when she first claimed to have fought there and thereafter claimed it at every opportunity to newspapers and in her memoir. However, in every retelling of her participation in the battle, she made claims which are easily proven falsehoods. These claims are addressed further along.

In the *Republican* article Velazquez claimed, in effect, that her "first husband" fought at the First Battle of Manassas, as a Federal soldier, when she asserted that he was "a member of Sherman's famous Battery." This assertion is in total contradiction to her memoir's version of her first husband, "William," which indicates at least one of the versions was a lie and as will be seen, both versions were lies.

"Sherman's famous Battery" was the Federal artillery battery commanded by Captain Thomas W. Sherman, which saw much action in the Mexican-American War and became renowned. After the Mexican War, the battery did duty at Fort Ridgely and Fort Snelling in Minnesota, dealing with Indian uprisings and at Fort Leavenworth dealing with violence in Kansas.[11] When the Civil War erupted, the battery was quick to aid in securing Washington, D.C., then found itself at the First Battle of Manassas as Battery E. Third U.S. Artillery, under Captain Romeyn B. [Beck] Ayers, but still known as Sherman's Battery.[12]

If Velazquez had thought at this early date of the *Republican* article to claim she had fought at Manassas, then she could have claimed she fought against her "first husband"! It would have been a wonderfully sensational claim had she thought of it.

Velazquez never again claimed to the newspapers or asserted in her memoir that her first husband was with "Sherman's famous battery," thereby wisely avoiding getting caught in a provable lie. But it is a curiosity that Velazquez claimed in her memoir to have been at Fort Leavenworth prior to the War, as the Sherman's Battery had been, and later facts surface

---

11. Solon J. Buck, ed., *Minnesota History Bulletin*, Vol 3 (1919), 426.
12. *The United States Army and Navy Journal and Gazette of the Regular and Volunteer Forces*, 1870-1871, Vol VIII, No. #43 (New York: Publication Office, 1871), 683; Steve Soper, *The "Glorious Old Third" A History of the Third Michigan Infantry 1855 to 1927* (Old Third Publishing, 2007), 13.

in newspaper articles which seem to indicate that she was in Minnesota prior to the War, just like Sherman's Battery.

The *Lynchburg Republican,* two days later, again reported on Lieutenant Buford:[13]

TURNED UP AGAIN.- Mrs. Mary Ann Keith, alias Lieut. Buford, whose arrival we noticed in our Wednesday's issue, turned up again quite unexpectedly yesterday evening. As we stated before, she was dressed in uniform, and attempted to pass herself here as an officer in the Confederate army, and after examination was sent to Richmond to the Secretary of War. About the time of the arrival of the South Side cars, yesterday, a telegram was received from General Winder directing the police of the city to look out for her, and detain her until further orders. The arrest was effected, and the prisoner taken to the Mayor's office to await the requisition of the military authorities at Richmond. In conversation with the Mayor, Mrs. K stated that upon getting to Richmond she went before the Secretary of War in the costume she first appeared in here, and requested a pass to Memphis under her *nomme de plume* of Lieut. Buford, which was given, and after donning her female attire again called upon the Secretary for a pass to the same place under the name of Mrs. Martha Keith, which was also given. We know nothing about Mrs. K. but we are inclined to the opinion that there is something suspicious about her movements, or she is a very erratic person. The examination which she will undergo when she again visits Richmond- which we suppose will be today- will probably develop her true character. She was committed to jail by Mayor Branch for safe keeping until Gen. Winder could be heard from.

The Richmond *Daily Dispatch* of October 21, 1861 wrote:

The *Lynchburg Virginian* says: In answer to the numerous inquiries which have been made of us concerning the disposal of Mrs. Keith, we will state that after remaining in jail several days, she was discharged by an order from Gen. Winder, at whose insistence she was arrested a second time. Upon her discharge she appeared in the apparel of her sex, and we suppose will not again soon undertake to play the "bowld soger [bold soldier] boy." She immediately left here for Memphis which she claimed as her home.

Several observations are in order about these two articles.

First, this is the first found hint that Velazquez was interested in writing about events surrounding her, evident by her claim that her alias was a *nomme de plume.*

Second, Velazquez, in her memoir, did not mention this Lynchburg arrest, being taken to Richmond, her release or her rearrest in Lynchburg. Instead, she told (p89) of her (as Buford) accompanying a "jovial party" during her train ride to Lynchburg, where she was compelled to stay overnight. The next day upon boarding the Richmond-bound train, an

---

13. *Lynchburg Republican*, Sep 28. The article was repeated by the *Nashville Union and American* on Oct 4, 1861, from which it was taken.

elderly gentleman asked Lt. Harry T. Buford if he wouldn't be so kind as to escort "five ladies and two children," which Velazquez said she did. In Richmond, she took a room at the Ballard House. All the while she claimed she had her slave boy Bob with her. Clearly, the newspapers did not mention her slave and it will be seen that her claim of even the existence of Bob fails on all questions.

In her memoir, she claimed she stayed briefly in Richmond, then left to join "the forces of the Confederacy in the face of the enemy," which precipitated into the First Battle of Bull Run (Manassas). She wrote (p95-106) in great detail about her participation in the Battle; the problem is, this battle had already occurred before her documented arrival in Lynchburg and Richmond, and not after, as she claimed!

It will be seen that in July 1863 Velazquez was arrested in Mobile and escorted to Richmond and put in Castle Thunder Prison. The newspapers of the time reported this arrest and Velazquez told (p278) of it, but not truthfully. It was at the time of her Castle Thunder imprisonment that she claimed to have been arrested and upon her release then rearrested, which the newspapers clearly don't corroborate. Velazquez blended her 1861 arrest and rearrest, and her 1863 arrest into one event. More about the 1863 arrest will be detailed later.

It is unclear where Velazquez went upon her departure from Richmond, but she may have been back in town on November 20, 1861. It was on this date that John B. Jones encountered someone who might have been Velazquez. On page 94 of his diary, *A Rebel War Clerk's Diary*, Jones wrote:

November 20th.- I had a protracted and interesting interview to-day with a gaudily dressed and rather diminutive lieutenant, who applied for a passport to the Mississippi River, *via* Chattanooga, and insisted upon my giving him transportation also. This demand led to interrogatories, and it appeared that he was not going under special orders of the adjutant-general. It was unusual for officers, on leave, to apply for transportation, and my curiosity was excited. I asked to see his furlough. This was refused; but he told me to what company he belonged, and I knew there was such a company in Bishop or Gen. Polk's command. Finally he escaped further interrogatories by snatching up the passport I had signed and departing hastily. But instead of the usual military salute at parting, he *courtesied* [*sic*]. This, when I reflected on the fineness of his speech, the fullness of his breast, his attitudes and his short steps, led me to believe the person was a woman instead of a lieutenant. Gen. Winder coming in shortly after, upon hearing my description of the stranger, said he would ascertain all about the sex.

November 21st.- My mysterious lieutenant was arrested this morning, on the western route, and proved, as I suspected, to be a woman. But Gen. Winder was ordered by the Secretary to have her released.

Velazquez does not mention this occasion and no further corroborating evidence has been located which might identify the woman. This episode could not have been the same arrest and rearrest described by the October 4 and October 21 newspapers since those arrests were the month prior.

April 1862, First Arrest in New Orleans

Velazquez narrated (p177-181) her return to New Orleans where she also was arrested. She stated that upon her arrival in New Orleans she was "thunderstruck" by her arrest "on the charge of being a spy, and taken before the provost marshal." She said the officer asked her "a very few questions," determined there was "no justification for holding" her and let her go. She then said that she was again arrested the next evening, "this time on suspicion of being a woman."

She wrote that she was taken before Mayor Monroe, and interrogated "in a style that [she] did not at all admire." It was decided to remand her "to the calaboose, until it should be settled to his satisfaction who [she] was, and whether [she] was a man or woman." Velazquez determined her best course of action was "to confess frankly to the mayor that [she] was really a woman." She "told him who [she] was, and gave him what [she] hoped would be satisfactory reasons for assuming the garb [she] wore." The mayor apparently did not feel sympathetic and fined her ten dollars, not a small amount at the time, and sentenced her to ten days in jail. It should be noted that at that date it was unlawful for a woman to dress in male attire and the newspapers occasionally reported that some woman donned male attire and was arrested and fined.

The New Orleans *Daily True Delta* newspaper article of April 24, 1862 contradicts Velazquez's claim that she was hauled in. The article stated that she "surrendered herself" because of her "fear of detection, and consequent trouble." In light of the recent trouble she had with her arrest in Lynchburg and Richmond, it seems reasonable that Velazquez revealed herself in order to avoid similar problems in New Orleans. The reporter's account sounds like the true version of events. It will become clear further along that Arnold of this article, titled "Female Soldier," was Velazquez:

> Yesterday a female, dressed in soldier's clothes, surrendered herself to the mayor, and was sent before the provost-marshal. She gave Arnold as her name.
>
> We had not the pleasure of an introduction to this female patriot, but learn from those who were more fortunate, that she appears to be a woman of intelligence and gentle breeding. She gave the name of respectable houses here in the city who knew her in her proper sphere, when she resided in Arkansas, where she says she owns a plantation. Her story is quite a romantic one.
>
> She asserts that she was arrested in Richmond on suspicion of being unfriendly to the South, but was treated very civilly while being held prisoner. She claims to have been in the battles of Manassas [July 21, 1861] and Belmont [Nov. 7, 1861], and to have been with the army in Kentucky.
>
> She says she left here in response to the call of Gen. Beauregard for ninety days' volunteers, and that she was in the battles of the 6th and 7th [This was the Battle of

Shiloh.], in which she was wounded in the foot and hand. She came back to the city with the wounded.

Her reason for making known her sex at this time was the fear of detection, and consequent trouble. She was before the provost-marshal yesterday, and is to have another interview with that functionary to-day.

Her reason for the course she has adopted is, that she is collecting material for a history of the war, and that she adopted male attire as the plan best calculated to enable her to carry out her design.

She has no desire to abandon her project if permitted to prosecute it in her own way. There are others engaged with her, but their names she deems proper to withhold. That she is an extraordinary woman there is no question, and our curiosity is excited to know more of her history and her adventures in male attire.

Note, her claim at this time was that her male attire was to enable her to collect a history of the war, not to fight in it.

For the first time Velazquez claimed that she had been at the First Battle of Manassas (also known as Bull Run). Her claimed participation, of which she wrote much (p96-106) will be eviscerated later.

Also interesting in this article is her claim to have been in the Battle of Belmont, Missouri. The problem is she never claimed in her memoir to have been at Belmont and it is inconceivable that she would have failed to include a firsthand account, if it was true. This much reported-on battle was Union Brigadier General Ulysses S. Grant's first test which would be followed by victories and public acclaim. Also, in no later newspaper accounts does she make this claim. She seemly forgot this one-time claim and moved on with a different storyline.

There is equally a problem with the fact that she did not claim to the *Daily True Delta* that she participated in the October 21, 1861 Battle of Ball's Bluff (or Battle of Leesburg). The battle was only six months in the past, yet she failed to mention it, but then she claimed it 20 months after the battle in a newspaper article dated, June 6, 1863. She also claimed it 15 years later in her memoir, devoting pages 116-125 to a recitation of her deeds and what she witnessed, which she said left an impact on her emotional state which was hard to shake off. Did Velazquez drop the Battle of Belmont from her storyline and add the Battle of Ball's Bluff?

She stated to the newspaper that she was at the Battle of Shiloh. She also claimed in her memoir her presence at Shiloh and she wrote (p213) about her failure there to assassinate General Grant when the opportunity arose. This implausible claim, which is presented later, casts doubt on other claimed activity at Shiloh. It is conceivable that she could have been there or nearby and may even have been in harm's way, but she did not do what she claimed she did. Also troubling is that there exists a problem in her timeline.

In her memoir (p179) she placed this first arrest in New Orleans several weeks <u>before</u> the Battle of Shiloh, April 6 & 7, when in fact the newspapers make clear her reported April 24 arrest was <u>after</u> the Battle of Shiloh. Considering that both her arrest and the battle would have been memorable events in her life, and considering her intellectual capacity, memory was not to blame. Worse still, Velazquez explained (p202) that her motivation for seeking out the impending battle was to redeem herself from the indignity of her arrest in New Orleans:

... my mortification at the indignities I had endured at the hands of Mayor Monroe and his satellites in New Orleans, was overcome by the thought that, notwithstanding the fact that I was a woman, I was as good a soldier as any man around me, and as willing to fight valiantly and to the bitter end before yielding. The fighting blood of my ancestor, old Governor Don Diego, was making itself felt in my veins as I prepared to follow Hardee's corps to the scene of action with all possible expedition [advancing on Shiloh Church].

It is clear that her error in the timeline was not a mistake of memory, but was a purposeful disregard for the truth to facilitate a fabricated storyline.

Shiloh and Velazquez

Velazquez claimed (*TWIB*, p201-204) that she had been in Corinth, Mississippi and decided to go to where "a surprise was to be attempted," at Shiloh, Tennessee, a distance of 23 miles. (It was true that this Rebel offensive caught the Federals by surprise.) She wrote that on April 5 she traveled about halfway to Shiloh, stopped in the village of Monterey and camped the night. A torrential rain forced her into a vacant house in the village. In the morning she reached her destination. She narrated:

I found the general stationed near Shiloh Church, and rode up and saluted him just as he was mounting his horse. Showing him my pass, I said I wanted to have a hand in this affair. [General William J.] Hardee looked at the pass, and replied, "All right; fall in, and we'll see what can be done for you."

She said the fighting had already commenced between the armies' skirmishing lines, "In obedience to Hardee's command, I fell in with his men, and we advanced briskly upon the enemy's camp." The Rebels routed the "only half dressed" Federals, who left their breakfast un-eaten, which she said she ate and "enjoyed it immensely." She continued:

I had scarcely finished eating when I came across General Hardee again. He was in a high good humor at the course events had taken thus far, and said to me, in a jocular sort of way; "Well, lieutenant, what can I do for you?"

I replied that I was anxious to do my share of the fighting, and wanted to be stationed where there was plenty of work to be done.

The general laughed a little at my enthusiasm, but just then his attention was called away for a moment, and I, glancing down the line, spied the Arkansas boys whom I had enlisted at Hurlburt [*sic* Hulbert] Station[14] nearly a year before. I was immediately seized with a desire to go into the fight with them; so I said, "Ah, there is my old company, general; with your permission, I will see the captain. Perhaps he can give me a chance."

"Hardee nodded an assent, and giving him a salute," Harry Buford said she went to the Arkansas boys. However, at this point in her narrative a fabrication seems evident. She wrote, "Dismounting from my horse, I forced my way through the ranks until I reached Captain DeCaulp [of the Arkansas boys], who shook me heartily by the hand." The problem is this. She claimed she arrived on horseback at the Arkansas company when she had not explained prior that she had been mounted in the battle line when she had participated in taking the Yankee camp and eating their breakfast only shortly before. It is not believable that she was mounted while in the advancing battle line of Rebel infantry because the Yankees poured furious musket fire into their ranks. If she had been mounted in the battle line, she would have been an easy target and the first to go down. A good reading of any history about the Battle of Shiloh makes it clear that she was not going around on horseback where the fighting was taking place. This horse fabrication may not be much to get excited about, but it is worth getting excited about the claim that Captain DeCaulp and his regiment were at Shiloh. Military records make clear, they were not.

From this point, Velazquez narrated (p204) a rousing account of events at Shiloh. Captain DeCaulp's company advanced into battle, "the second lieutenant of the company fell" and she "immediately stepped into his place, and assumed the command of his men." Since DeCaulp's company in truth was not at Shiloh, it follows that her subsequent narration of the death of its corporal, who was by her side and who was shot through the heart with a "Minie ball,"[15] was false. Velazquez wrote, "He fell heavily against me, and all my clothing was reddened by his blood."

She incautiously and falsely claimed (p210), "During the afternoon, I succeeded in gaining a good deal of very important information from several prisoners, and particularly from a sergeant belonging to the twenty-seventh Illinois regiment." This regiment also was not at the Battle of Shiloh, but was some 105 miles away! Seemingly every Illinois regiment under the sun was there, but not this one. Velazquez expressed confidently of which she spoke, singling out the sergeant and regiment with the qualifier, "particularly," so why the error?

After the first day's battle, that evening, she was placed "with the advanced picket line." She left her post and sneaked through the Federal

---

14. Today part of West Memphis, AR, west of the Mississippi River and about 8 miles west of Memphis, TN.
15. Minié ball named after Claude-Étienne Minié, inventor of the French Minié rifle.

picket line to spy. With difficulty she succeeded and discovered Federal reinforcements arriving. It was at this time she claimed she had a chance to assassinate General Grant, but "could not bring herself to do the deed" because "it was too much like murder." She then claimed she returned to her own side.

A visit to the Shiloh National Military Park reveals that the terrain which Velazquez claimed to have traversed would have included the impossibly steep Dill Branch Ravine and a penetration of the concentrated Federal lines located on the north rim of the ravine. It is simply not believable that she crossed the precipitous ravine, sneaked through the thick Federal line and then out again, recrossing the ravine. Also, she would have had to cross her own line twice without getting shot.

Velazquez thought the Confederate general needed to know of her discovery of Yankee troop reinforcements so she told Captain DeCaulp who expressed that "attempting to instruct the general of an army was a risky business" and that the general was probably already "well informed." Since it is simply false that Captain DeCaulp was at Shiloh, it follows that his refusal to take her to the general was also false. In any case, continuing, she said "for [her] own sake," she thought she had "better hold her tongue." She wrote (p215):

I finally came to the conclusion that the responsibilities were [the general's], and not mine, and I had no fancy for being put under arrest, and of ruining all my future prospects by going through with my New Orleans experiences again, under circumstances that would almost inevitably expose me to indignities worse even than those I had suffered at the hands of his honor Mayor Monroe.

Whoa, now historians know! The reason for the Confederate defeat at Shiloh is because Velazquez refused to report the Federal troop reinforcements to the Confederate general because she did not want to get into trouble because of her male disguise, and ruin "all [her] future prospects." This claim is ludicrous! If Velazquez had reported to the general, her future prospects would have been unlimited. She would have found fame as the female soldier who saved an army and saved a new nation, the Confederate States of America. This was the exact fame she sought! The entire theme of Velazquez's memoir was that she endeavored to imitate Joan of Arc, seeking a similar fame and here was an opportunity for fame maybe even surpassing Joan of Arc. Yet Velazquez failed to report her discovery because she did not want to get in trouble for dressing like a man!

Having decided against reporting her findings, she wrote (p215), "I accordingly concluded to wait and see what the result of the next day's battle would be, declaring energetically to Captain DeCaulp that if we were defeated, I would never raise my sword in the army of Tennessee again." Well, first and once again, DeCaulp wasn't at Shiloh. Second, neither was "the army of Tennessee." The Army of Tennessee was not created until seven months later, on November 20, 1862. It was General Johnston's Army of Mississippi which was at Shiloh. Then, in her memoir, some thirteen pages later (but only several days after Shiloh), she again asserted her "desire to get as far away from the army of Tennessee as possible, before the fact that Lieutenant Harry T. Buford was a woman became generally known...." The good news is that she saved her male disguise, even if she had to destroy an army in doing so!

Much of what Velazquez narrated about Shiloh is clearly embellishment or lies, such as everything she wrote about DeCaulp. However, she convincingly gave details (all of which were found in the newspapers of the times) of bad weather, the ground, leaders and troop movements, but she made mistakes and at least one of these was probably a lie in the making which failed in the attempt. Velazquez, about the second day's battle, wrote (p217), "On our side, Terril's battery did excellent service, and succeeded in holding the enemy at bay, giving the infantry a breathing spell that they sorely needed." No, no, no! Captain William R. Terrill's Battery H was a Yankee battery which slaughtered Rebels! It was placed near the Hamburg-Savannah Road in support of Union Brigadier General William Nelson's 4th Division. "Its fire was terrific. It was handled superbly. Wherever Captain Terrill turned his battery silence followed on the part of the enemy."[16]

Velazquez claimed that she stayed with Captain DeCaulp and his men, but after the second day when she saw the defeat at hand, she "determined to leave the field." She said (*TWIB*, p218) the road was blocked by the retreating Rebels and she "remained in the woods all night," and was caught by a "furious storm of rain and hail." After the worst of the storm, she said she found a "tolerably dry place, where, completely used up by the fatigues [she] had undergone, [she] fell into a sound sleep." At daybreak she mounted her horse and started back to Corinth (Mississippi). Then confusingly, five paragraphs later, she wrote, "On arriving at camp I found a mail waiting for me." She had already said that she spent the night in the woods, without the benefit of a camp and then was headed to Corinth. But here in contradiction, she arrived at camp. And just how and where she found camp while the army was in full retreat to Corinth is a mystery.

A Love Letter- Oh, Really?

In camp, Velazquez claimed there were letters waiting for her, among them was "a love letter." A discerning person should question how her mail could have possibly found her considering she explained that she had just arrived at Shiloh, was not officially attached to a company and only by chance had found her Arkansas companions and joined them. It is an

---

16. *OR*, Ser 1, Vol 10, pt 1, Chap XXII, 325.

impossibility that the mail carrier could have found her and besides the letter writers could not have known in which company to address her. The "love letter" was sent from "Memphis, Tennessee, April 2, 1862" and Velazquez said it was received the second day of the battle which was April 7. Delivery in this time frame was possible if one knew where to find the addressee, Lieutenant Harry T. Buford, but another problem looms.

Velazquez reproduced the love letter (p221-223) and about it said:

> I give this as a favorable specimen of the love-letters I was in the habit of receiving during my military career, and I have the less hesitation in doing so as it is one that no woman need be ashamed of having written.

The letter was indeed "a favorable specimen," and was very long, 695 words, as if the writer wished to linger in the presence of the intended recipient. In part it reads:

> My dear, I am afraid that this will appear unintelligible, being wet with tears from beginning to end… dear Harry, my fidelity to you shall remain… Your loving intended till death, [signed] M—.

The letter was beautifully written, passionate, and sensitive; it was a textbook perfect letter in every sense... because it was, in fact, plagiarized straight out of a textbook! The letter came out of *The Universal Letter-Writer; or, New Art of Polite Correspondence; Containing a Course of Interesting Original Letters on the Most Important, Instructive, and Entertaining Subjects, Which May Serve as "Copies" for Inditing Letters on the Various Occurrences in Life.* The book was written by the Rev. Thomas Cook, A. B. and published in London in 1812. The book was popular enough that it was reprinted in 1827 by G. Davidson, Charlestown. The letter is found in both editions and is titled, "The Lady's Answer."

It is clear that Velazquez used the 1812 edition because in one sentence she reproduced the word "Alas," exactly as in that edition. The 1827 edition dropped the word "Alas" probably because by that date it sounded out of fashion. Velazquez very nimbly inserted appropriate words to personalize the letter. For example: The textbook letter stated "and although unmarried, will remain a widow till death." Velazquez wrote, "and although unmarried, I will ever remain the widow Buford until death." Velazquez also substituted "Harry," where appropriate, replacing the original letter's addressee, Charles. Another example: in the original letter, the writer stated that her father was reading the newspaper, but Velazquez changed it to the writer's grandpa was reading the *"Appeal"* which was/is the local Memphis newspaper, Memphis being the residence of the young writer. Looking for the differences in the two letters is good entertainment, rather like the cartoons which challenge the reader to find ten differences between two pictures which only appear to be the same. Without taking on the tedious task of actually counting the minor changes Velazquez made to the original text, it can be guessed she copied more than 98% of the original, which would warrant an A+ in plagiarism.

Or was Velazquez the unwitting recipient of a plagiarized letter? Maybe Miss M was a heartbroken girl, struggling for words of her own and in desperation plagiarized from a forty-year-old text book. But please consider that there is no good reason to disparage Miss M and call her a plagiarist, when there are good reasons to disparage Velazquez as a prevaricator. And now a plagiarist.

The Union Navy's Arrival/Arrest of William B. Mumford

The New Orleans *Daily True Delta* of April 26, 1862 presented a follow-up article about "Mrs. Arnold" titled "That Female Soldier":

> The female soldier, of whom we made brief mention a day or two since, was sent to the Parish Prison to await an examination before the [Confederate] provost-marshals. She gave her name as Mrs. M. M. Arnold, but she has flourished under several aliases, such as Gibbons and Lieut. Buford. Change of circumstances will probably prevent us from learning more of her history than we have already given. She is certainly a very extraordinary woman, and her history must have been an eventful one.

There was indeed "a change of circumstance." The Union navy had fought its way past the Confederate forts at the mouth of the Mississippi River and was expected to arrive shortly at now indefensible New Orleans. Admiral Farragut's Navy was met by a hostile mob of residents gathered on the Mississippi River levee, "all animated by a common hatred of the detested Yankees."[17] The retreating Confederate troops, by orders of General Lovell, set fire to 15,000 bales of cotton, cotton ships, steamboats, stockpiles of coal and wood for steamboats, the dry docks, barrels of turpentine and tar, and anything else which might benefit the conquerors. "The heavens were black with smoke."[18] Events in the city moved quickly and the news reporters now had work enough, so reported no more on "that female soldier," even if she was "a very extraordinary woman."

It can be believed that Velazquez was out of custody in time to witness the Union fleet's arrival about which she gave (*TWIB*, p232-237) a firsthand account. She wrote she "found [herself] in the anxious and angry crowd on the levee" and saw the arrival of "these splendid vessels." Velazquez accurately enough narrated how Mayor Monroe declined to surrender the city.

---

17. Admiral David Dixon Porter, *The Naval History of the Civil War* (NY: Sherman Publishing Co., 1886), 247.
18. James Parton, *General Butler in New Orleans* (NY: Mason Brothers, 1864), 265.

James Parton, Union General Butler's biographer, wrote how Captain Theodorus Bailey's party was rowed ashore at the river levee to demand, on Admiral Farragut's orders, the surrender of the city. Captain Bailey was conducted to City Hall by several respectable persons of courage as they were followed by "a yelling and infuriated multitude." At City Hall Captain Bailey met with the mayor and demanded of him the surrender of the city and the raising of the Union flag, which the mayor refused. "Captain Bailey requested protection during their return to the levee, the crowd being evidently in no mood to allow their peaceful departure."[19] Protective escorts were provided.

Velazquez, in her never-ending claims of meeting important people, claimed (p237) she met Captain Bailey. Velazquez, now as a woman, was determined to act as a spy, an "active *attaché* of the [Rebel] detective corps," by gathering information on the Yankees. First, she figured she had better ingratiate herself with the Yankees. She wrote:

> desirous of being in favor with the captors, I sought an opportunity to speak to Captain Bailey, and to welcome him to the city. He shook hands with me, and said that he would see me again; but he had no time for conversation just then, and as my object was accomplished by introducing myself to his notice as a pretended friend of his cause, I did not make any endeavor to further attract his attention.

The problem with her claim is that New Orleanians were extremely hostile to Captain Bailey's presence and it is barely believable that she chanced bringing the wrath of the mob upon herself by extending a friendly welcome to the Yankee captain. Such Yankee lovers, if lucky, were only pummeled. However, as will become clear, Velazquez had audacity to do what she wanted.

In a published letter to the City Council, Mayor John T. Monroe explained that he was only a municipal officer, not a military man, and he had no authority to surrender anything. He refused to hoist the Union flag at the Customhouse, Post Office or (coin) Mint, or haul down the Louisiana flag from City Hall. In effect, he said that the city was conquered, and he could not prevent the conquerors from raising any flag they wished.[20] The Mayor explained that Confederate General Lovell refused to surrender and had departed with his army, leaving the civil authorities to manage the best that they could.

Union Admiral Farragut, on Saturday, April 26, sent Captain Morris of USS *Pensacola*, the ship anchored off the Mint, ashore to hoist the flag of the

---

19. Ibid, 269-271.
20. *Daily True Delta* (New Orleans, LA), Apr 27, 1862.

United States on that building. When it was done, it "excited the inhabitants of the neighborhood."[21] The captain then

> warned the by-standers that the guns of the *Pensacola* would certainly open fire upon the building if anyone should be seen molesting the flag. Without leaving a guard to protect the flag, he returned to his ship, and the howitzers [cannons] in the maintop of the *Pensacola*, loaded with grape [shot of multiple projectiles instead of a single cannon ball], were aimed at the flagstaff, and the guard was ordered to fire the moment anyone should attempt to haul down the flag.[22]

The warning was not heeded and at about eleven o'clock four rebellious citizens dashed out onto the roof "in spite of a volley of grape"[23] and cut down the flag, one William Bruce Mumford doing the cutting. The two cannon shots fired by *Pensacola* did not stop the men, but only damaged a few neighboring roofs.

Mumford, along with his co-gallants, Lieutenant N. Holmes, Sergeant Burns and James Reed were identified and praised by the *Picayune* as deserving "great credit for their patriotic act." A fifth participant was identified as Vincent Heffernan by the New Orleans *Crescent*.[24]

James Parton wrote:

> The four men having secured their prize, trailed it in the mud of the streets amid the yells of the mob; mounted with it upon a furniture car and paraded it about the city with fife and drum; tore it, at last, into shreds, and distributed the pieces among the crowd.

An eye-witness and a staunch Southerner, Mrs. Eugenia Levy Phillips, saw this act under her window and wrote, "the infuriated mob tore this flag into tatters, each one struggling for a piece, dancing, yelling, howling over the mad act, which was too soon to be fatally expiated."[25] The mob, which consisted of "thousands," had followed behind "Mumford and his two friends" from the Mint to City Hall, where next door lived Mrs. Phillips. It is not clear why Mrs. Phillips failed to count the fourth or fifth man. They simply may have not been standing near Mumford when Mrs. Phillips took note of the scene or they may have dropped out of the mob parade by then.

At the time of this affair, the city had not technically surrendered, and a permanent presence of the Union army had not yet been established. It was during these several days that "each hour witnessed some fearful lawlessness." Mrs. Phillips witnessed several people cut to death when they

---

21. *Commercial Bulletin* (New Orleans, LA), Apr 28, 1862.
22. Parton, 274.
23. *Commercial Bulletin* (New Orleans, LA), Apr 28, 1862.
24. Apr 28, 1862.
25. Eugenia Levy Phillips, *Journal of Mrs. Eugenia Levy Phillips, 1861-1862*, Library of Congress.

shouted "Hurrah for Lincoln!" and a drunken woman hanged- for what, Phillips did not specify, but implied because of the woman's Northern sympathy.

The "horrors of mob rule" finally ended when General Butler arrived on May 1 with his 5000 troops. To be sure, the troops were not welcomed and it took months of military presence to subdue the residents' exhibited hatred for the Northern occupiers. In the meantime, Mumford was still free in the city bragging of his exploits and inciting unrest. James Parton wrote:

> Mumford still appeared in the streets, bold, reckless and defiant, one of the heroes of the populace. He was seen even in front of the St. Charles hotel, [where Union headquarters had been set up] relating his exploit to a circle of admirers, boasting of it, daring the union authorities to molest him.[26]

Admiral Farragut, who had been "indignant and embarrassed" by the affair at the Mint, had not forgotten it. Mumford was arrested on May 12 and tried by Military Commission on May 14.[27] A witness testified he heard Mumford say that "[he] was the first man who put a hand to the flag to tear it down." The Recorder and Legal Advisor for the Commission wrote, "[Mumford had] no reputation for veracity, and did not seem to be either intoxicated or inebriated at the time he admitted the fact. He is a sporting man, and has been much accustomed to drinking."[28] The Commission "condemned him to death, and General Butler approved the sentence, and ordered its execution."[29]

Velazquez claimed (p237) that she met Mumford after his arrest, while he was in prison:

> The United States flag which was raised upon the mint was pulled down again by Mumford, who paid the penalty of his life for the act after Butler took command of the city. The execution of this young man was an outrage on civilization, and a crime on the part of the man who ordered it which entitles his memory to execration. Mumford told me himself that he perpetrated the act through a mistaken idea that the flag had been displayed by some traitor, and that he was not aware at the time that the Federals had assumed control of the city.

This claim that Mumford "himself" told Velazquez that he "perpetrated the act through a mistaken idea" is not believable.

First, all New Orleanians, including Mumford, were painfully aware of the arrival of the Union navy and that it was the Union marines who had raised the Stars and Stripes at the Mint.

---

26. Parton, 346
27. Parton, 276; *New Orleans Delta*, May 13, 1862.
28. Jessie Ames Marshall, *Private and Official Correspondence of Gen. Benjamin F. Butler* Vol 1 (Massachusetts: Plimpton Press, 1917), 483.
29. Parton, 346.

Second, after his arrest, Mumford had a chance to speak in his own behalf and never claimed he acted on "a mistaken idea." The Union cannon fire was surely unmistakable!

Third, among the prominent citizens appealing on Mumford's behalf, was "the venerable Dr. Mercer," and even he never said that Mumford's action was based on "a mistaken idea."

Fourth, various newspaper accounts of the time never wrote that Mumford's actions were based on "a mistaken idea."

Fifth, Mumford was a bold and tough character and never minimized his hand in the affair. Even when permitted to address the crowd which had gathered to witness his hanging, he did not claim he had taken action based on "a mistaken idea." The *New Orleans Delta* reported that Mumford did say that 'the offense for which he was condemned was committed under excitement, and he did not consider he was suffering justly." The *Delta* wrote further:

He conjured all who heard him to act justly to all men, to rear their children properly, and that when they met death, they would meet it firmly. He was prepared to die; and as he had never wronged any one, he hoped to receive mercy.[30]

It must be concluded that Mumford never said that he had acted under "a mistaken idea" and particularly never told Velazquez such a thing.

Mumford's gallows was built out of the second story window of the Mint facing Esplanade Street, directly under the flag staff where he cut down the Union flag. On June 7, Mumford, described as "five feet eight inches high, stoutly built... black hair and dark complexion, and deeply pitted with the smallpox [he wore a beard to cover the scars]" met his death with "composure."[31] The forty-seven-year-old North Carolina-born Mumford had a "wife and three or four children" who had appealed to General Butler for Mumford's pardon, to no avail.[32]

Mumford was hung alone; the other identified men in the flag affair were never apprehended.

Velazquez wrote (p237), "The execution of this young man was an outrage on civilization, and a crime on the part of the man [Butler] who ordered it which entitles his memory to execration." Butler's memory did not have to wait. Confederate President Jefferson Davis issued a proclamation stating that Mumford's execution was "deliberate murder" and declared Butler "to be a felon, deserving of capital punishment... an outlaw and [a] common enemy of mankind" and if captured, would be

---

30. Parton, 352; *New Orleans Delta* (New Orleans, LA) Jun 8, 1862.
31. Parton, 351; *Daily Delta* (New Orleans, LA) Jun 6, 1862.
32. The 1860 U.S. Census shows four children.

"immediately executed by hanging."[33] Richard Yeadon, editor of the South Carolina *Courier*, offered a $10,000 reward to anyone delivering Butler, "dead or alive, to any proper Confederate authority."[34]

Velazquez's condemnation of Butler was in agreement with that of Confederate patriots of the time. However, Butler's biographer, James Parton, explained that Butler could not have issued a pardon as it would have been construed as "weakness and cowardice" and perpetuated the "continued turbulence of the mob of the city" which could have only been "quelled by final grape and canister [cannon fire]."

Eighty-year-old Dr. William N. Mercer, "one of the best gentlemen in the city," president of the Bank of Louisiana and a secessionist with whom Butler had formed "the most friendly relations," asked Butler to sign a pardon for Mumford's life. Dr Mercer, with "tears running down his cheeks," pleaded, "It is but a scratch of your pen." Biographer Parton wrote of the General's answer, "True, replied the general. But a scratch of my pen could burn New Orleans. I could as soon do the one act as the other. I think one would be as wrong as the other."[35] Butler in his autobiography wrote that he replied to the doctor's plea thus, "'No, Doctor,' I said, 'it is your life, and my life, and the life of every good man in this city which I must save. The question is now to be settled whether law and order or mob shall govern.'"[36]

To her credit, Velazquez correctly predicted that General Butler's memory would be "execrated." Those who today still rail loudly against Butler's historical record in New Orleans, willingly or unwittingly, fail to acknowledge facts which shed positive light on Butler's administration of the city. He abated crime, cleaned the diseased and filthy streets, and fed the poor. His entire adult life, he was a champion of the poor and downtrodden. When he was elected governor of Massachusetts, he sought improvements for the state's insane asylums and prisons, even meeting with prisoners to hear their complaints.

In the analysis of General Butler's capacity for compassion, it must be noted that one day prior to the execution order of Mumford, Butler gave six Confederates a reprieve from the gallows. Butler considered the men mere ignorant pawns of greater powers over them and refused to hang them.

One last proof of Butler's compassion should be mentioned. After the war, when Mumford's widow was in dire financial straits, she sought Butler's help and he located a job for her at the Internal Revenue Department. When

---

33. OR, Ser I, Vol XV, 906- 908.
34. *Life and Public Services of Major-General Butler, The Hero of New Orleans* (Philadelphia: T. B. Peterson & Brothers, 1864), 100.
35. Benj. F. Butler, *Butler's Book* (Boston: A.M. Thayer & Co., 1892), 443; Parton, 351.
36. Butler, 443.

that job was cut, he found her a job with the postal service. One Boston newspaper[37] wrote:

> General Butler has cared for Mumford's widow as though she was a relative... took [Mumford's] family under his care, cleared off a mortgage upon the widow's home.... The widow and her children feel that no harm will come to them as long as General Butler lives.

General Butler lived until 1893, thirty-one years after the flag affair at the Mint.

Running the Lines of the Union Army at New Orleans

Velazquez claimed (*TWIB*, p242-263) she daringly ran through the Union military lines during the summer of 1862. At this time the Union had taken control of New Orleans, but the surrounding countryside remained in Rebel hands. A daring person stood to profit handsomely by secreting medicine out of New Orleans and selling it to the needy Rebels or anyone with the ability to pay. Trade in Confederate currency was also a big moneymaker. Since Confederate currency had been declared illegal by Union authorities and therefore worthless, it could be obtained for a pittance and used or traded in Rebel territory where it was still legal tender. Smuggling letters from New Orleans citizens to the outside or dispatches to the Rebels were other possible sources of income. Smuggling military dispatches might have been done strictly for patriotic reasons and not for pay. Velazquez claimed to have participated in all these activities.

Velazquez claimed that by befriending Union authorities and representing herself as friendly to the Union, and mistreated by the Confederacy, she obtained passes which enabled her to visit Mandeville, across Lake Pontchartrain from New Orleans, and even Mobile, Alabama. She also claimed that she did some line crossing without a permit.

She told of two adventures during her smuggling career while in New Orleans. The first was a trip to Havana, Cuba to deliver a dispatch intended for Confederate shipping raider *Alabama*. She did not claim to have seen the ship, only to have delivered the message to the person to whom she was directed to deliver it. The narration of her "pleasant cruise" is believable enough, but she failed to explain how she succeeded in departing the Gulf Coast aboard any Havana-bound ship. This omission reduces the believability of her story.

At this date, after the conquest of New Orleans, the Union navy's blockade of the Gulf Coast, by her own words, "was now fully established," so it can be surmised that her departure was not on a Rebel blockade runner and besides she did not narrate any adventurous running of the blockade.

---

37. *Boston Evening Transcript* (Boston, MA) Sep 23 1881, taken from the *New York Sun*.

She implied she left New Orleans aboard a Union vessel because she said (p243) she had "the despatch secreted" on her person, meaning hiding it from Yankee enemies. If she had taken passage on a Union vessel, she would have needed a military permit to facilitate an open departure. How did she get one? She only implied, without giving details, that she procured one. Obtaining such a permit, surely through a clever pretext, should have warranted mentioning, especially considering the permit would have been from the infamous and wily General Butler, her nemesis, as will be seen.

This claimed successful mission warranted details that a curious reader might wish to know, yet she provided none. She did not even express a modicum of tension or fearful exhilaration in describing her departure or return. She characterized her trip as "agreeable" and "delightful." She made clear that her return was not clandestine, but in the open, and that when she "set foot on the levee at New Orleans," she "felt in better condition than [she] had been in for a long time...." Something's fishy, or is that just the waterfront?

The second instance of a smuggling adventure was her trip to deliver a dispatch to Rebel forces outside of Union controlled New Orleans. She explained (p255):

Not a great while after my return from Havana, I undertook to go to Robertson's Plantation, for the purpose of sending some despatches [sic], as well as some verbal information, to the Confederate forces stationed at Franklin. It was necessary to walk the entire distance of seventeen miles; and that such a tramp could scarcely be a particularly pleasant exercise, those who are acquainted with the country around New Orleans need not be reminded.

She then told an exciting story of avoiding Union sentries and of her "terribly lonesome walk," during which she heard alligators bellowing and of their plunging into the stream when alarmed by her approach. The mosquitoes "attacked [her] with the greatest fury and [her] face and hands were terribly bitten." She reached her destination "foot-sore and completely tired out, but satisfied with having accomplished [her] errand." However, her story does not check out.

The Robertson Plantation can only be presumed to be that which was located some 80 miles west of New Orleans and about 30 miles east of Franklin, Louisiana. It was located on Lake Palourde and Bayou Boeuf near today's Amelia, Louisiana.[38] She said she walked "the entire distance of seventeen miles," but, in fact, the distance is 80 miles. The mighty Mississippi River was directly in her path, but she failed to mention this obstacle or how she crossed the River. She said that after walking all night she reached her destination at daybreak, and "found some Confederate

---

38. *Louisiana Planter and Sugar Manufacturer*, Vol XIX, No. #10 (Sep 4, 1897): 153.

soldiers preparing to cross the lake...." This was presumably the eastern shore of Lake Palourde, some 30 miles east from Franklin. She gave the soldiers verbal messages and the dispatches she carried, to be delivered to headquarters in Franklin. Her duty done, she sought food and shelter from hospitable locals. She wrote:

> I was in a most dilapidated condition... My clothing was heavy with the night dews, and my skirts were bedraggled with dirt; my shoes were nearly worn through, and were covered with mud; and taking me altogether, I was as forlorn a looking creature as could be imagined.

The locals understood her situation and would "not permit [her] to make any excuses or apologies" for her appearance, but rejuvenated her with food, fresh clothes and much needed sleep. The locals then led her back to New Orleans on horseback, as far as was safe, then bid her farewell expressing their obligation to "a brave woman, who was willing to venture, as [she] had done, for the purpose of advancing the welfare of a cause which was a common one with [them] all." From that point she claimed she "made [her] way into the city on foot," once again "eluding the pickets," and also failing to tell her readership how she recrossed the Mississippi River.

Her failure with the fact of the true distance renders unbelievable her version of the smuggling trip. Velazquez said that Robertson's Plantation was within one day's walk, 17 miles, and lying in "the country around New Orleans," which it was not. She encountered "the lake," implying it was in line with the road to Franklin, making the only possibility Lake Palourde. She did not identify "the lake," but somewhat implied it was Lake Ponchartrain which it could not have been and she might not have known better. Velazquez's omission in naming "the lake" or stating the road and direction traveled seems purposeful, designed to keep the truth out of the reader's grasp.[39]

However, it is believable that Velazquez had some role in smuggling and maybe was involved in some portion of the Robertson's Plantation trip and simply took full credit for it. The news of the day confirmed her participation in smuggling. The *Daily Delta*[40] said, "The police accuse her of having been engaged frequently to run the blockade with letters by parties in the city- and say that she is a very dangerous character." (This news report is presented further along.) In addition, simple logic adds credence that she smuggled, since smuggling paid money and she needed money, evident by the fact that she was arrested for stealing.

---

39. A. Persac, *Norman's Chart of the Lower Mississippi River*, 1858.
40. Nov 2, 1862.

Chapter 2

October 1862, Second Arrest in New Orleans
The *Daily Delta* of October 31, 1862 wrote:

A HEROINE IN A FIX.- Our readers will recollect the female soldier, about whom there was some excitement in the city just after the battle of Shiloh. She had arrived in the city just after that event, clad in a full suit of "soger close" [soldier clothes], and claimed, truthfully, too, we believe, to have been in that terrible battle, and showed a wound in the wrist which was received there. This of course made her quite a lioness, when it became known, which it soon did, from the fact that she was arrested by the police for appearing in male apparel. Yesterday we found her appearing on the police reports in a very unheroic attitude, under the name of Anne Williams. She is charged by Mr. Chester, whose house she has had the freedom of for some days, which having returned his hospitality by stealing a gold watch and chain and gold thimble...

Within two days the local newspapers had gathered important details about the heroine and on November 2 the *Picayune* provided some:

There was one case up, which attracted considerable attention. The prisoner was a woman who, for some years past, appears to have led a checkered existence. She appeared under the name of Ann Williams, but until recently she had been known as Mrs. Arnold. Ann can talk glibly, and her story is quite a romantic one. She had been with the Santa Fé expedition, and could describe all its officers; she had also journeyed over the mountains and plains of the West, with the Utah expedition. After the existing war broke out she followed the fortunes of the Confederacy, and was present with a Louisiana regiment at the first battle of Manassas. After that she returned to this city, and was for a while an inmate of a house, the reputation of which is not exceedingly high.

Eventually she returned to the army and took part in soldier's clothes in the battle of Shiloh, where she was wounded in the wrist. About two months ago she got back to the city and was arrested for being in Confederate uniform. She then assumed female apparel, and figured as the wife of a soldier named Williams, at Camp Lewis, and one night induced him to join her in an attempt to get beyond the lines. They failed, and returned to camp. Afterwards she tried to get away by a route through a bayou to the lake, but failed. She then went to a respectable house here, told a touching tale of how she, as a Union lady, had fallen into the hands of the guerillas and suffered fearfully. A number of Union people, whom she sent for, gave her money to enable her to get to New York. She then went to the house of another lady whom she had known at St. Paul, Minnesota, and when the lady was out one morning she absconded, taking with her a watch and other articles. The case was given to Officer O'Conner [*sic*], who found the prisoner at Camp Lewis, drawing the rations as a soldier's wife. She managed the case very skillfully...

Velazquez's arrest is recorded in a register book titled *Proceedings of the Provost Court, New Orleans, La.,* which is archived at the National Archives in

Washington, D.C.[1] She was brought before Judge Kinsman on Thursday October 30 for arraignment, then sent to the Parish Prison to "await trial." Two days later, on Saturday November 1, she was again in court before Judge Kinsman. The register book states the verdict and sentence, "stealing watch & chain six months P. P. [Parish Prison]." No more information is revealed by this register about her case. This (and New Orleans newspapers) make clear Judge Lieut. Col. Kinsman heard her case and sentenced her, but Velazquez claimed in her memoir General Butler sentenced her.

Another local newspaper, the *Daily True Delta* added details worth knowing:

... Annie is quite a character, and has passed through adventures enough to fill a portly volume with exciting yellow-covered literature interest. She had been attached to the Utah expedition, in the course of which she became the wife of a Lieutenant Arnold. She had been in the Confederate army, and was at Manassas, Shiloh and other battles, and got wounded in the wrist. Finally, she claims to be the wife of a man named Williams, of Company E, Thirteenth Connecticut Volunteers, now stationed at Camp Lewis. She is known also to have been an inmate of Nelly Bremer's, where she was picked up by a well-to-do man named Bachman, from Arkansas, but who sent her back on becoming acquainted with her character. In short, she has been everywhere. Lately she had endeavored to make her way out of the lines, and induce others to do so, but they were detected. She was detected by a picture taken of her dressed in soldier's clothes. She is understood to have been very free fingered; and numerous reports are given of her doings in this line. Some of the jewelry, for stealing which she was sentenced yesterday, was found pawned at Jacobs', corner of St. Charles and Poydras streets, in the name of Mrs. Williams. She has been suspected of being a spy...

And the *Daily Delta* on November 2, for the second time, reported similarly, now explaining "The Fate of a Heroine":[2]

... It appears that she resided in this city several years ago, in a house of questionable character, but managed by some deceptive arts, which are best known to women, to win the affections of an Arkansas planter, who carried her with him to "Rackensack" [nickname for Arkansas] and married her. She soon tired of married life, however, left him, and next turned up with our army in Utah, where she became acquainted with many under the name of Mrs. Arnold. The rebellion broke out, and Mrs. Arnold, alias Mrs. Williams, was next found doing the duty of a private soldier in the battle of Manassas, as a member of the 7th Louisiana Regiment. She was brought into public notice again last spring, just after the battle of Shiloh, having been wounded in that engagement, as a member of the 11th Louisiana. On that occasion she visited the city, and was arrested for appearing in

---

1. NARA, RG393, Register of Persons Brought Before the Provost Court, 10/1862-09/1865.
2. Distant newspapers such as the Peoria, Illinois *Morning Mail* of Dec 17, 1862 titled the article, "The Adventures of a Rebel Female."

male attire, but on account of what was then called her patriotic conduct, she was dismissed with honor... She is a little *passé*, but still quite a handsome woman, with a very masculine nature. She spoke right sharply in her own defense before the Court- said that although she had been to Richmond, and in the rebel army, and participated in several battles, she had never descended to play the spy. She declared that she was now strongly for the Union, and was raising her children up to revere the old flag. The police accuse her of having been engaged frequently to run the blockade with letters by parties in the city- and say that she is a very dangerous character. The Judge, after hearing the evidence in regard to the robbery of which she stood accused, concluded that she was guilty of the crime charged, and accordingly sent her to the Parish Prison for six months. This is a rather unromantic termination to a most romantic career. In our opinion, women should continue to be women, and whenever they unsex themselves should be treated, as they desire to be considered, like men under similar circumstances.

It is curious that Velazquez claimed that she "was raising her children up to revere the old flag" since at this date, according to her memoir, she had no children, her three having died of fever some two years earlier. In addition, the Richmond newspapers, when she was there, and New Orleans papers made no mention of children with her. If she had any, she must have left them in the care of someone else, but it is more likely she was trying to elicit sympathy to try to keep a mother out of jail.

The newspapers recalled that "Annie Williams" had been previously called Arnold, probably remembering when she presented herself to the mayor which was reported on April 24. At that time the newspapers called her "Mrs. M. M. Arnold." The April newspaper also noted that she had "flourished under several *aliases*, such as Gibbons and Lieut. Buford." So, what of the names Arnold, Gibbons and Bachman, this last from Arkansas?

Velazquez claimed that she was with the Utah Expedition, "[She] next turned up with our army in Utah, where she became acquainted with many under the name of Mrs. Arnold." The Utah Expedition, also known as the Mormon Rebellion, was a confrontation between the members of the Church of the Latter-day Saints or Mormons, who controlled the Utah Territorial government and the Federal government whose authority the Mormons ostensibly rejected, with the Mormons' polygamy as a central issue. The date of the Expedition is generally stated as from May 1857 to July 1858. The oldest that Velazquez could have been at that time was sixteen years old, if she was truthful about her birth date of June 26, 1842. However, in a huge contradiction, Velazquez wrote in her memoir (p49) she did not actually go to Utah with the troops, instead she claimed she "was compelled to submit to remaining behind" in St. Louis because she was pregnant. And when she tells (*TWIB*, p581) of a later trip in 1867 to Utah she makes it clear it was her first time there.

It is impossible that she participated in the Santa Fe Expedition, as she claimed to the newspaper, since that was in 1841 and she claimed she was born in 1842!

When the April newspaper first noted Mrs. Arnold, it failed to state that her husband was a soldier, but now the newspaper wrote, "She had been attached to the Utah expedition, in the course of which she became the wife of a Lieutenant Arnold." With Arnold now identified as an officer, verifying whether he was on the Utah Expedition becomes rather easy.

Prior to the Civil War, the United States army consisted of approximately 15,000 soldiers and officers. Officers were people of note and recorded in history. The 2500 officers and soldiers of the Utah Expedition are identified by author Roger B. Nielson in his book, *Roll Call at Old Camp Floyd, Utah Territory* (2006). A search was conducted for "Lieutenant Arnold" using Nielson's valuable reference book and there was none. Moreover, there was no soldier by the name of Arnold.

Expanding the Arnold search, is it possible that he was later a Confederate officer? No Confederate officer by the name of Lieutenant M. M. Arnold is found in the records. However, there is one soldier with the rank of private, M. (Madison) M. Arnold of 2nd Battalion Mississippi Infantry, Company B, and he is weakly suspected simply because of fact that he was from Mississippi. Further along it will be clear that Velazquez had a connection to Mississippi. It is possible, of course, that the "M. M." initials were not those of her husband, but were her initials or initials she invented.

A search for Velazquez's connection to the name Gibbons yielded no results. Gibbons was even searched for among the soldiers of the Utah Expedition, but no candidates are obvious.

The name Bachman from "Rackensack" is another mystery which might be impossible to solve. Since the gentleman was said to have taken her back to Arkansas and married her, a search was initiated for him and the marriage, but nothing of value was revealed. Maybe a future researcher will discover this connection.

The next gentleman in line to examine is Williams. The newspapers wrote that "she claims to be the wife of a man named Williams, of Company E, Thirteenth Connecticut Volunteers, now stationed at Camp Lewis," and that "[she] was at Camp Lewis, drawing the rations as a soldier's wife" when she was arrested.

Who was Williams of the 13th Connecticut, Company E? And was Velazquez married to him?

Military records show that the 13th Connecticut was formed in New Haven in November 1861 and shipped out on March 17, 1862 aboard *City of New York*. "After a rough voyage, with two severe gales and a narrow escape from shipwreck on the Florida coast, the regiment disembarked at

Ship Island," off the coast of Mississippi, on April 13. After three weeks of drilling on the stark island, the regiment struck their tents and shipped out for New Orleans, arriving on May 12. The regiment took temporary quarters near the New Orleans levee, but then on May 15 marched to the U.S. Custom House, now the military center for the Union occupation.

The 13th Connecticut Regiment was stationed at the Custom House for more than four months; during the summer Company E was detached from the regiment and assigned Provost Guard.[3] It was during this time that William B. Mumford was arrested, tried and hung. The men of the Company served as Mumford's prison guards. Recall Velazquez claimed she spoke to Mumford while he was imprisoned and it might have been possible through Williams of Company E.

The regiment departed the Custom House on September 30, at which time they went to Camp Lewis (newly christened Camp Kearney) and spent twenty-four days there.[4] Then on October 24 it departed Camp Lewis and went to Donaldsonville, 90 miles upriver.[5] It is clear that Velazquez was in New Orleans on April 24, 1862 when she first surrendered to the mayor and was still (or again) in New Orleans on November 2 when she was arrested for stealing. It is clear that the 13th Connecticut was in New Orleans from May 15 until October 24, 1862 when it departed. Company E ostensibly did not depart on October 24 with the rest of the regiment, since it was serving as Provost Guard in New Orleans. Company E was still at Camp Lewis when policeman O'Connell found Velazquez there, and that date, at the latest, was October 29. Recall she first made the court appearance on October 30.

In order to add one more piece to the puzzle, it is necessary to jump ahead to when she departed New Orleans and traveled to Jackson, Mississippi where the *Mississippian* newspaper of June 6, 1863 reported she claimed her husband was a lieutenant in the 13th Connecticut regiment and on duty as provost guard.

So now Williams was a lieutenant (not just a "soldier," as claimed before), which was clearly not true because there is no record of Lieutenant Williams in the very complete archived records of Company E of the 13th Connecticut. However, Velazquez truthfully told the *Mississippian* that

---

3. Homer B. Sprague, *History of the 13th Connecticut Infantry Volunteers during the Great Rebellion* (Hartford, Conn: Case, Lockwood & Co., 1867), 68.
4. Ibid, 74.
5. NARA, RG94, M594, Records of the Adjutant General's Office, 1780's-1917, Compiled Records Showing Service of Military Units in Volunteer Union organizations, Reel 7, Twelfth Infantry through Seventeenth Infantry; *Record of Service of Connecticut Men in the Army and Navy of the United States during the War of the Rebellion* compiled by authority of the General Assembly, 1889, 523; Sprague.

Williams had served as provost guard; it is factual that Company E pulled provost guard duty in New Orleans at the time.[6]

There were three Williams in the 13th Connecticut Infantry, Company E, but none were lieutenants. They were: John, Charles E., and Henry. All three men went in as privates and mustered-out as privates.

The first soldier, Private John Williams, must be eliminated because records show that it was only later in 1865 that John was in Company E. He was in Company C from May to December 1862 when an association with Velazquez was possible and besides that company did not do provost guard duty.[7]

The second soldier, Private Charles E. Williams, cannot be eliminated. The 22-year-old mustered-in on January 28, 1862 in Connecticut and arrived at Ship Island, Mississippi, with the 13th Connecticut Infantry. When the troops struck their tents on May 4 and departed the island, Charles was apparently missing. He was recorded as "deserted May 6, 1862 at Ship Island." It is difficult to accept that Charles succeeded in escaping the island since it is 10 miles to the mainland and the island was crawling with Yankee troops who would have easily witnessed any desertion attempt. At best, Charles may have concealed himself in the island's brush. In any case, the guards found him because he was still in the army when he was again documented in the military record as "deserted at New Orleans, La. July 1862." However, this was still not the end of Charles; he ostensibly continued to serve with Company E until he mustered-out at New Haven, Connecticut in January 1865.[8]

Charles E. Williams might have been Velazquez's man. Recall that the *Picayune* of November 2 said that Velazquez had "one night induced him [Williams] to join her in an attempt to get beyond the lines. They failed, and returned to camp." This was likely the aforementioned July desertion. Charles had the propensity to desert, evident by this and May's desertion. And on August 14 the *New Orleans Bee* wrote, "Charles Williams, was arrested on Rampart Street, last night, as a dangerous and suspicious character, and was endeavoring to obtain a pass under false pretenses." It is impossible to know if this Charles Williams was from the 13th Connecticut and the newspaper didn't say so and the name Charles Williams was too common to be certain it was the same man.

The third soldier, Private Henry Williams, cannot be eliminated, either. Henry had "black eyes, black hair, dark complexion" and stood five feet and

---

6. Sprague, 23.
7. NARA, Compiled Military Service Records (CMSR) for John Williams.
8. NARA, CMSR for Charles Williams.

eight inches. At age 28 Henry mustered-in the 13th Connecticut, Company E in Colebrook, Connecticut in December 1861.[9]

Henry appears to have been an earnest soldier during 1862 when it would have been possible to associate with Velazquez. His military record shows him "present" with his company from July to December 1862. For the months of May and June his presence or absence was recorded as "not stated," but it is easily assumed Henry was "present" as the regiment and company were newly arrived and busy settling in at their new post assignment in New Orleans.

It might be instructive to follow Henry's army career to its completion to understand his nature and to see if he was the type of man with whom Velazquez might have associated. Long after any possible association with Velazquez, in May of 1863, Henry was taken prisoner by the Confederates, paroled and returned to his company on June 12, 1863. From July to October, he was recorded as "under arrest in jail"; the reason was not stated. By November and December, he was again recorded on the roll as "present."

Henry mustered-out in February 1864 and re-enlisted at Thibodaux, Louisiana as a "veteran" and received a $300 "local bounty." His reenlistment document states that his occupation was "teamster" and clearly, he was not schooled enough to sign his own name to the document, marking only an "X" next to his name.

The regiment then went to Baltimore where it was to be shipped out to join General Sherman's army. Along with some other men, Henry "left the wharf without permission" and went into the city and got "intoxicated." In the morning Henry found his regiment had left. Henry stated, "he went about the city until arrested by a detective about January 16, 1865 who took [him] to the Provost Marshal who sent him to Fort McHenry, thence to Prince Street Military Prison in Alexandria, Virginia." This Federal prison held its own deserters. This imprisonment resulted in Henry being listed from January to March 1865 as "absent without leave."

When Henry was released, he was sent South where on May 22, 1865 at Sister's Ferry, Georgia, he died of smallpox. At this date the war was generally accepted to be over; General Lee had long since surrendered on April 9.

It is impossible to eliminate Henry Williams as the possible "husband," so he must remain alongside Charles E. Williams, the other possibility.

Since the newspaper stated that Velazquez was "living as the wife" of Williams at Camp Lewis, an effort was made to locate this possible marriage. Camp Lewis was located in Jefferson Parish so a search there was

---

9. NARA, CMSR for Henry Williams.

conducted, but failed to show results. On the other hand, it is possible the couple married in New Orleans, prior to the regiment moving to Camp Lewis, so marriage records for Orleans Parish were also searched. There was no 1862 marriage in Jefferson or Orleans Parish for a Henry or Charles Williams. No other man in the records named Williams appears to be the man. No bride in the records appears to be Velazquez.[10]

In her memoir (p301-303), in the correct time frame, Velazquez said that she "gave [her] name as Mrs. Williams," telling the readers that she invented the name to fool Yankee picket guards and Union General Rosecrans:

> I represented that I was a widow woman, who was endeavoring to escape from the Confederacy, and who desired to go to her friends in the North; and judging from appearances, I quite won upon the sympathies of the Federal commander... I could not help smiling at the ease with which I deceived General Rosecrans....

This was the only time in her memoir she claimed "Mrs. Williams."

She most certainly did not tell her readers that her husband, Williams, was a Yankee soldier because this would have flown in the face of her never-ending claim to have been a loyal Southerner! It may be true that Velazquez was married to Williams, or at least, she considered herself married to him, bothering to recall this married name ten years afterwards in her memoir, but she wasn't a widow woman as she told Rosecrans. By this small lie, she wished her readership to know she was cleverly deceitful by claiming it. The big lie was she claimed that she crossed the lines at this time to go on a self-directed spy mission just to see what she could learn which might benefit the Southern cause. It is a ridiculous claim and the facts of her true movements refute the claim. Even if she had gone North, all she would have had to do was tell authorities she had married a Yankee soldier and wished to go North and not all the drama she claimed to her readers about it, all the while purporting to be a loyal Southerner.

In conclusion, either Charles E. Williams or Henry Williams could have been the man identified as Velazquez's "husband" soldier in Company E of the 13th Connecticut Infantry. However, it is possible that the couple was not married by civil authorities and was instead cohabitating; some undiscovered document may yet give the answer.

The 7th Louisiana, First Battle of the Manassas (Bull Run)

The *Daily Delta* article of November 2, 1862 accredited Velazquez for having been "a member of the 7th Louisiana Regiment" at the First Battle of Manassas. The reporter's information no doubt came from Velazquez herself. It is a fact that the 7th Louisiana Regiment was at this battle, but was

---

10. Jefferson Parish Clerk of Court, Jefferson Parish Marriage License Index; New Orleans Public Library, City Archives & Special Collections, Index to the Justice of the Peace Marriage Records, 1846-1880.

Velazquez "a member of the 7th Louisiana Regiment"? Does Velazquez's memoir substantiate the claim? Trying to corroborate the newspaper report with her memoir's version of her activity at Manassas is tricky because in her book she failed to name the company or regiment in which she claimed to have been a soldier during the battle.

She described (p96) her arrival at the soon-to-be battlefield. She wrote she introduced herself to Confederate Brigadier General Bonham (commanding the First Brigade), who told her that if she stayed around, she would "be able to find plenty of work." She said, "I took this as a hint that I might make myself at home…." General Bonham was defending against a Union army crossing at Mitchell's Ford on Bull Run (Creek). Velazquez gave no more details of her or Confederate activity at Mitchell's Ford, but suddenly jumped with her narrative a mile away to the east, along the creek to Blackburn's Ford, which was being defended by General Longstreet's Fourth Brigade. When the Union army attacked at Blackburn's Ford, General Longstreet asked for re-enforcements from General Jubal Early's Sixth Brigade which had been held in reserve about a mile in the rear for the purpose of reinforcing either Longstreet or Bonham, depending on where the Union army's attack came. The 7th Louisiana was one of the regiments of Jubal Early's Sixth Brigade. It was at this time that the 7th Louisiana was brought into the engagement. If we are to believe that Velazquez was a member of the 7th Louisiana, she makes it difficult to do so. Velazquez failed to explain how or why she left Bonham's First Brigade. Upon leaving the First Brigade she would have had to travel one mile to the southeast to join Early's Sixth Brigade, which had been held in reserve, and then together with the Sixth Brigade march due north one mile to join in the fight with Longstreet's Fourth Brigade at Blackburn's Ford. Or she would have had to join the Sixth Brigade, of which the 7th Louisiana was part, after it reached Blackburn's Ford. She only wrote that she jumped from Mitchell's Ford to Blackburn Ford, a mile apart, with no explanation.

The skirmish at Blackburn's Ford was a prelude to the First Battle of Manassas (or Bull Run). Of the skirmish she had just participated in, Velazquez wrote:

> I was the more anxious for a big fight soon, as I had been placed temporarily in command of a company, the senior officer of which had been killed, and I was afraid that if a fight was long delayed I should be superseded, and should be compelled to lose my best chance of distinguishing myself.

Oddly, in her narrative, she just dropped any more discussion of her good fortune at having obtained command of a company. She did not explain how, when, where or if she lost her command position of this company. She said she was afraid she might be "superseded," yet she did not state if she was. Considering the major theme of her book was her quest for the honorable position of an officer, it is puzzling that she failed to give every detail of her unique on-the-battlefield promotion. She simply wandered off in another direction with a narrative about her crossing Ashby's Gap (a mountain pass), which turns out to be a gaping lie and will be shown why later.

Was Velazquez "placed temporarily in command of a company"? The simple answer is no. A full company consisted of 100 men under the command of a captain. If the captain was killed, the next in command was the 1st lieutenant, then the 2nd lieutenant, followed by sergeants and corporals. Besides, the men would not have followed the leadership of an unknown walk-on.

Did a company in the 7th Louisiana Regiment have its captain, "the senior officer," killed at Blackburn's Ford and was Velazquez given command of the company? The 7th Louisiana consisted of ten companies, Companies A through K, totaling about 850 men. (A full regiment would have been 1000 men.) Of these, nine were killed at Blackburn's Ford and none was a captain, or "the senior officer." Velazquez's claim could not have been true.

The 11th Louisiana, Battle of Shiloh

The *Daily Delta* article of November 2, 1862 also accredited Velazquez for having been "a member of the 11th Louisiana" at the Battle of Shiloh and wounded. Again, the reporter's information surely came from Velazquez herself. The information does not corroborate Velazquez's book version of events. In fact, it contradicts her book.

Of the 11th Louisiana, Velazquez wrote (*TWIB*, p205) that she glanced "over the field" and "saw the eleventh Louisiana regiment, with a friend of [hers], and a brave officer, Colonel Sam Marks, at its head…." She did not claim to be a member of the regiment. Instead, she explained that she took "part in [the] great battle along with [her] own company that [she] raised over in the Arkansas swamp…." Velazquez wrote:

We had not been long engaged before the second lieutenant of the company fell. I immediately stepped into his place, and assumed the command of his men.

In this passage she also explained she fought beside Captain DeCaulp of this Arkansas company. This claim creates a huge problem because Captain DeCaulp was with the 3rd Arkansas Cavalry and the 3rd Arkansas Cavalry was not at Shiloh! It logically follows that Velazquez did not assume the command of any second lieutenant's men since the company was not at Shiloh.

Clearly, in the *Daily Delta* article, Velazquez was playing to the New Orleans audience by falsely claiming to have been "a member of the 11th Louisiana" since it is a fact that this regiment was at Shiloh. However, she was not a member of it and she didn't glance over the field to see the 11th Louisiana regiment from her position with DeCaulp's Arkansas company since the company was not there.

Nelly Bremer's House of Prostitution

In the various newspaper accounts of Velazquez in New Orleans it is clear that the reporters had some knowledge of her earlier years, stating that she had been an "inmate" at Nelly Bremer's house, "the reputation of which is not exceedingly high" and also "a house of questionable character." Nelly Bremer operated "a house of ill fame" or prostitution. The 1860 Census listed "Mrs. Bremer" as a white 24-year-old, "furnished rooms keeper" from Ohio with a "Value of Personal Estate" of $1000. There were seven other women with ages ranging from 20 to 28 living in the same house. One of the women had a 2-year-old son. There also was a 45-year-old female servant living there. No men are listed as residents.

Among the names of the women listed in the 1860 Census living at Nelly Bremer's is one name which is confusing and at the same time curious because it might have been Velazquez. Two different census databases interpret the written name differently, one as Mina Ahah and the other as Mina Aliah. The rest of the census information for this individual is clear and not in doubt- Mina was 22 years old and born in Kentucky. A problem arises because no surname, either Ahah or Aliah, existed in Kentucky, much less in the United States in the 1860 Census or any prior census. The interpretation of the surname as Aliah is not convincing and that leaves only the name Ahah seemingly the correct interpretation. Did Mina give the census taker a made-up surname, maybe with a joke intended, such as- ahah, I pulled a fast one on you? A records search for anything related to one Mina Ahah yielded no results, and further searching probably never will.

One of the occupants of the whorehouse was Lilly Chester from Ohio, age 25, and is of some interest because, recall, Velazquez stole from the Chesters and was arrested. These Chesters were identified as from Minnesota, so maybe it was just a surname coincidence, but there lingers suspicion of a connection.

A year prior to when the press reported that Velazquez had been an "inmate" of Nelly Bremer's "house of ill fame," the place burned down. The four-a.m. fire totally destroyed the building, valued at $2,000, and Nelly's furniture, paintings and other decorations, worth ten to fifteen thousand dollars. All was insured. The fire was thought to be a case of arson, "the result of jealousy."[11] "The inmates were only to save themselves from the

---

11. *Daily True Delta*, Nov 1, 1861, the building was on Customhouse Street, between Villeré and Robertson Streets; *Daily Delta*, Nov 3, 1861.

flames."[12] One report added, "If we mistake not, this is the second time Miss Nelly Bremer sees her furniture destroyed by fire, in the course of a few months."[13]

It is unclear if Velazquez worked as a prostitute or if she just resided in a house that would have her. She could have earned her keep as a drink pusher and a clever swindler of loose change from drunken customers. If she did prostitute herself, it must be supposed it was for only a brief time in her young years. Her history, after New Orleans, does not indicate she had anything to do with prostitution and no evidence found in the many cities she frequented indicates any involvement in prostitution. In her memoir she made plain she held a low opinion of immoral conduct, including drinking.

It appears that Velazquez memorialized Nelly Bremer as her dear "schoolmate, Nellie V" on page 45 of *The Woman in Battle:*

> Nellie was a beautiful girl, of about sixteen years of age, and a very warm regard subsisted between us up to the time of her discovery that I was endeavoring to capture her lover. Her affection for me did not last long after that, and she said a great many disagreeable things about me, for which I have long since forgiven her, as I doubt not she has me for running away with her handsome young officer.

Velazquez said she stole Nellie V's boyfriend whom Velazquez soon clandestinely married. This man, only identified as "William" in her memoir, was the first of Velazquez's claimed husbands. The asserted date of this alleged marriage would have made Velazquez a bride at the age of 13 years, 9 months and 10 days, calculating from the date of her birth given in the memoir. In later newspaper articles she identified this husband as William Burnet, which will be addressed.

"Nellie V" was never a "schoolmate" of Velazquez's because Velazquez did not attend the school she claimed to have attended. Velazquez claimed that while living with her aunt in New Orleans, she attended "the school conducted by the Sisters of Charity, to learn the ornamental branches." The only school run by the Sisters of Charity in New Orleans was St. Elizabeth's Industrial School at 1314 Napoleon Avenue, founded in 1845 for the "care and training of needy girls."[14] Velazquez could not have qualified to attend the school; she said that her father in Cuba, who had sent her to New Orleans to study, had "acquired great wealth, and was able to surround his family with every luxury." Such a wealthy family did not send their child to the Sisters of Charity School, nor could they have qualified to send their child there. Either Velazquez lied about attending the school or she lied

---

12. *Commercial Bulletin*, Nov 1, 1861.
13. *Times Picayune*, Nov 1, 1861.
14. *Benevolent Institutions 1904* (Washington, DC: Government Printing Office, 1905), 76.

about coming from such a wealthy family.[15] If one believes both, then one might just as well believe that her wealthy family paid her room and board at Nelly B's whorehouse.

Escaped and Captured

Recall Velazquez had just been convicted of theft and sent to the Parish Prison? Well, she escaped. Several New Orleans newspapers[16] reported her capture under various titles: The Female Warrior; Anne Williams Again; The Heroine Again.

Pure chance would have it that on November 14 Officer J. D. O'Connell was walking along Poydras Street, when he saw a female pass whom he recognized. "Quickening his pace, he soon came along side... She turned around, and he found that it was Anne Williams, the heroine of Shiloh and many other moving scenes, incidents and adventures by flood and field."

O'Connell was surprised since he had arrested her two weeks ago and she had been sent to the Parish Prison for six months. He questioned her as to how she got out and she "equivocated," said that Butler gave her a pardon. O'Connell did not believe her and demanded they visit Butler and then the Police Station. "She declined both invitations, but he insisted." O'Connell took her to see Police Lieutenant Boyd Robinson.

Anne explained she had been sick and was sent to Charity Hospital and that the Hospital Surgeon had given her a pass to go out that morning. "On inquiry this was found to be true. On entering the hospital, she had given the name of Loretta Williams Clark, native of Nassau, N. P. [New Providence]." Officer O'Connell said it was "all only a ruse to escape justice." One newspaper said she had not been very sick and concluded, "She is a wily heroine."

The Charity Hospital Record

A valuable record of Velazquez's visit to the hospital survives in the form of the *Charity Hospital Admission Book*.[17] The entered date of her admission, November 16, is in conflict with the newspaper's date of November 15 which announced her escape and arrest, "yesterday." It should be noted that the book is not sequentially dated, indicating that the names and dates might have been transferred from another record or the admitting clerk may have made a simple error. In any case, she was admitted into Ward 35 under the name "Lauretta Williams born Clark." The entry for "Occupation" was left blank. The entry for "Place of Birth" was noted as "Nassau, N. [New]

---

15. According to the Office of Archives for the Archdiocese of New Orleans, enrollment records exist for 1872 and after, so Velazquez's claimed enrollment, circa 1851-1856, is impossible to confirm.
16. The *Picayune*, the *Bee*, the *Daily True Delta* and the *Daily Delta*, all from Nov 15, 1862.
17. *Volume 31, Years 1862-1865* archived at the New Orleans Public Library.

Providence, West Indies." Her age was written as a "1" superimposed on a "2," followed by an "8." It is not clear if the "1" was intended to correct the "2" or just the opposite. She claimed either 18 years or 28 years. According to her memoir's claimed birthdate, she should have been 21 years old. The other entries are: "Last Place From - Arkansas; Residence in N. Orleans - 7 mths [months]; Single or Married- M; Long Sick- 10 days; Malady- Prolapsus of womb."

"Prolapsus of womb" must have been a clerical entry and not a doctor's diagnosis. That medical condition varies in severity, but almost always requires surgical repair of the supporting muscles or removal of the uterus. The condition does not remedy itself and a patient does not go "on her way rejoicing" or "sailing along Poydras street." If she, in truth, had this medical condition it was the mildest of cases; ostensibly nothing was done medically and she was sent back to jail. Her reproductive system was in good working order in about 1869 when she had a child and in 1886 when she had another, and in 1888 when she had another. It can only be concluded that she told the admitting clerk what she thought her malady was or she simply "adopted the ruse of getting in the Hospital in order the more easily to effect her escape from confinement" as the newspaper reported. In any case, the newspaper reported "she had not been very sick."

It is noteworthy that Velazquez's answer for "Residence in N. Orleans" was seven months, which corroborates the newspaper report of her arrival in the city on about April 24. And her stated "Last Place From" was "Arkansas" which seems to corroborate the newspapers' assertion she went there with the intention of marrying Bachman. Recall at her 1861 Lynchburg arrest she confessed she was Mary Ann Keith from Memphis; Arkansas lies only across the Mississippi River from Memphis.

In the hospital register is the first found usage of "Lauretta," that is "Lauretta Williams born Clark." Velazquez will use "Lauretta" in the future, but she will vary its spelling. Also in the register, she claimed she was married- if true, that could have been to Williams of the 13th Connecticut.

Nowhere in her memoir does Velazquez reveal the story of her arrest for stealing, her sentencing, her admission to the hospital, her escape from the hospital and subsequent rearrest. Only in a January 5, 1867 interview by the *Daily Picayune* did she vaguely reference the theft, the newspaper wrote, "For some indiscretion, she was arrested by Gen. Butler, but being subsequently released, managed to make her way through the lines to Richmond."

1863, Departed New Orleans as a "Registered Enemy"

Velazquez surely served her full six months in prison since nothing was heard of her during that time and only after more than six months, did she reappear. At the time of her release, the Federal authorities were requiring citizens of New Orleans to take an "Oath of Allegiance to the Union," or to register as an enemy. Those signed-up as "registered enemy" were permitted to cross the military lines to be with their fellow secessionists. Velazquez ostensibly exiled herself as a "registered enemy."

The process of winnowing the registered enemy from the loyal citizen was initiated on September 24, 1862 by command of Major-General Butler. Any citizen over 18 years of age had to declare, by October 1, their loyalty to the Union, or otherwise. Each person was required to list their "property and property rights, both real, personal, and mixed" and each head of a household was to submit a list of people under their roof. Failure to register was punishable by a fine. The local policeman was responsible to see the order enforced on his beat.

Conditions were made harsher on December 5, when another order was issued that all registered enemies "desiring to go within the rebel lines, and not return, because they prefer to live there" report themselves on, or before, the 10th to the Provost-Marshal for transportation. Each adult was "allowed to take personal clothing only, not exceeding $50 in value."

The *Daily Delta*[18] assured the "People of the North" that the Rebels, once across the lines, would not raise arms against the Union. The reporter said "the registered enemy is not a character intensely martial," that is, with military ambition. Among people going were those who "shine in bar-rooms and on street corners," and who were clearly unhappy since General Butler's crackdown on the shady side of the city. The newspaper said, "Some women have taken pains to enroll themselves as enemies. Some of them are simply silly. Some of them are malignant." To date, "only some two hundred applications" had been made for "the privilege of going beyond the lines not to return again."

Just how many registered enemies were on the books was being asked and it was reported the number was 2127, mostly men. The number was revised to "1103, of which about 300 were women and 100 children." The men were said to be of all ages and mostly in no condition to serve the Rebel Army. In any case, the departure was postponed 10 days.[19]

One Northern newspaper pointed out the "insanity" of these registered enemies for leaving personal safety, even though at the loss of some civil liberties if they stayed, and abandoning their houses and other property to go live among the starving, rag-wearing Rebels. Anyone feeling sorry for the soon-to-be exiles for leaving their homes need to save their sympathy. The haughty residents "brought it on their own heads" when "they deliberately rejected the clemency shown them."[20]

---

18. Dec 10, 1862.
19. *Daily Delta*, Dec 16, 18, 1862.
20. *New York Times*, Dec 19, 20, 1862.

A final offer on January 12 "invited those who have registered themselves as enemies to take the oath of allegiance, and withdraw their previous registration."[21] It should be noted that the "registered enemies" were not compelled to leave, they were permitted to leave. Even so, there were those who left.

On January 21, the first group boarded the small steamboat, *S. B. Brown*, on the south shore of Lake Pontchartrain. The boat carried them across to Madisonville, Louisiana on the north shore.[22] There were subsequent trips and Velazquez was on one of those.

Velazquez must not have taken the Oath of Allegiance and it would have made no sense to stay in a city where her reputation was tarnished; she must have been anxious to get away. Upon her release from the Parish Prison, she likely took the 5-mile-long Pontchartrain Railroad which ran from the City neighborhood of Marigny, down Elysian Fields to its terminus on the south shore of the lake at the town of Milneburg, now the location of University of New Orleans. Milneburg at the time was waterfront and the embarkation point for the steamboat *S. B. Brown*. The steamer was scheduled to depart at 12 o'clock on May 17 and the officers were instructed to be on board by 8 a.m. to receive baggage.[23]

By the date of Velazquez's May 17 departure, the authorities had become more lenient, allowing the exiles to take "a sufficient quantity of food for ten days' subsistence, a reasonable amount of clothing, and the beds and bedding necessary for their own use."[24] On an earlier trip when the authorities searched for contraband items, it was reported that the search among the females incited "no little indignation in the feminine bosom. 'They searched them even to taking off the stockings,' said one lovely rebel...." When some smuggled letters were found they were read and returned to their custodians, with one exception. Also discovered were six bottles of cognac in the trunk of a matron who explained "that she was an invalid and that the cognac was intended to 'rub her with.'" She was allowed to pass.[25]

It can be surmised that the *S. B. Brown* carried Velazquez across the lake, and after about 5 hours docked at the town of Madisonville, Louisiana. She was now beyond the Federal lines and free once again to roam.

---

21. *Daily Picayune*, Jan 15, 1863.
22. Ibid, Jan 25, 1863.
23. Ibid, May 17, 1863.
24. Ibid, May 12, 1863.
25. Ibid, Mar 8, 1863.

Arrived in Jackson, Mississippi

Velazquez next appeared in Jackson; her presence noted by the *Mississippian* on June 6, 1863:[26]

ADVENTURES OF A YOUNG LADY IN THE ARMY.

Among the registered enemies of the United States government who have been recently sent across the lines from New Orleans, there is now in this city [Jackson, Mississippi], a lady whose adventures place her in the ranks of the Mollie Pitchers [Revolutionary War heroine] of the present revolution.

At the breaking out of the war Mrs. Laura J. Williams was a resident of Arkansas. Like most of the women of the South, her whole soul was enlisted in the struggle for independence. Her husband was a Northern man by birth and education, and a strong Union man. After Arkansas seceded from the Union he went to Connecticut, he said, to see his relations and settle up some business.—Mrs. Williams suspected his purpose and finally she received information that he had joined the Yankee army. Possessing little of the characteristic weakness of her sex, either in body or mind, Mrs. W. vowed to offer her life upon the altar of her country. Disguising herself in a Confederate uniform, and adopting the name of "Henry Benford," she proceeded to Texas, where she raised and equipped an independent company, and went to Virginia with it as first Lieutenant. She was in the battle of Leesburg and several skirmishes; but finally, her sex having been discovered by the surgeon of the regiment—the 5th Texas Volunteers, to which the company had been attached—she returned to her home in Arkansas. After remaining there a short time she proceeded to Corinth, and was in the battle of Shiloh, where she displayed great coolness and courage. She saw her father on the field, but, of course, he did not recognize her and she did not make herself known to him. In the second day's fighting she was wounded in the head, and was ordered to the rear. She wrote to her father, and then came on down to Grenada, where she waited for some time, but never saw or heard from him.

She then visited New Orleans, was taken sick, and while sick the city was captured. On recovery she retired to the coast, where she employed herself in carrying communications, assisting parties to run the blockade with drugs and cloths for uniforms. She was informed on by a negro and arrested and brought before Gen. Butler. She made her appearance before Gen. B. in a Southern homespun dress. She refused to take the oath, told him she gloried in being a rebel—had fought side by side with Southern *men* for Southern rights, and if she ever lived to see "Dixie" she would do it again. Butler denounced her as the most incorrigible she rebel he had ever met with. By order of the Beast she was placed in confinement, where she remained three months. Some time after her release she was arrested for carrying on "contraband correspondence," and kept in a dungeon fourteen days on bread and water. At the expiration of which time she was placed in the State Prison as a dangerous enemy. Her husband, it so happened, was a Lieutenant in the 13th Conn. regiment, and on duty as provost guard in the city. He accidentally found her out and asked if she wanted to see him. She sent him word

---

26. Repeated by the Richmond *Daily Whig*, Jun 19, where taken by author.

she never wanted to see him so long as he wore the Yankee uniform. But he forced himself upon her, tried to persuade her to take the oath, get a release, when he said he would resign and take her to his relations in Connecticut. She indignantly spurned his proposition, and he left her to her fate. When Gen. Banks assumed command he released a great many prisoners, but kept her in confinement until the 17th of May last, when she was sent across the lines to Meadesville [*sic* Madisonville] with the registered enemies.

An article was recently published in the New York World[27] in relation to the part Mrs. Williams has played in the war, but the above is, we are assured, a true account of her remarkable career. We understand she has attached herself to the medical staff of a brigade now in this city, and will render all the assistance in her power to the wounded in the approaching struggle for possession of the great Valley of the Mississippi.

Velazquez's account of her arrest and life as she told the *Mississippian* contained lies more numerous than boll weevils plaguing a Mississippi cotton field.

First, Velazquez claimed, "She saw her father on the field, but, of course, he did not recognize her and she did not make herself known to him." It is not believable that her father was at the Battle of Shiloh and she never claimed it in her book. Instead, she claimed that he was wealthy at this time with a plantation in Cuba. Any genuine Cuban plantation owner of Spanish birth, who had "received a very thorough education" and was "a careful and accurate business man," as she claimed (*TWIB*, p39-40), would have been too busy smartly making war money in Cuba rather than marching about the South, participating in the dirty aspects of a war in which he could have scarcely had a desire to fight. In any case, everything she ever said about her father was a lie and her many preposterous claims will be shown false, and the claims get much worse.

Second, it was untrue that she raised and equipped an independent Texas company "and went to Virginia with it as first Lieutenant." Much more will be said about this later and also her alleged participation in the battle of Leesburg (Ball's Bluff) will be addressed.

Third, in her memoir, she never claimed that before the War she was married to a Northerner (implying from Connecticut), who later turned out to be Yankee soldier Williams of the 13th Connecticut Regiment in New Orleans. Her memoir weaves a different story.

Fourth, she was not arrested for running the "blockade with drugs and cloths for uniforms." She was arrested only on the charge of stealing a watch and other articles; the New Orleans newspapers reported it. She never mentioned this arrest in her memoir. However, it can be believed that she

---

27. A search for this article failed to find it; if it exists, it was probably a repeat of a Southern newspaper story about her arrest in New Orleans.

participated in running the blockade with various items, since she had to earn a living by some means, but that was not the reported reason for her arrest. Recall, the police said that she was known to frequently engage in running the "blockade with letters by parties in the city- and that she is a very dangerous character."

Fifth, she claimed to have been confined to prison for three months, released, then rearrested and "kept in a dungeon for 14 days on bread and water." This account contradicts the New Orleans newspapers which reported she received a six-month sentence. And there is no evidence that she failed to serve her full sentence. She was sentenced on November 2, 1862 and re-emerged in the public on May 17, 1863, six months and 2 weeks later. Her claimed three-month arrest, release and fourteen-day rearrest could have been her twisted version of her April arrest and release and then her rearrest in October; or it could have been her October arrest and her escape from the hospital then her rearrest. In any case, it was not true as she told the *Mississippian*.

Sixth, she claimed to the *Mississippian* that, "By order of the Beast [General Butler] she was placed in confinement, where she remained three months," but the New Orleans newspapers and military record contradict this, reporting Judge Kinsman sentenced her, not General Butler. She would never have been brought before General Butler because he did not preside over cases concerning fights, drunks, and thefts; those crimes were the purview of the court. Interestingly in her memoir (p 263) she wrote that she was released the same day as she was arrested through the efforts of the British Consul. This of course contradicts the *Mississippian*- that she was jailed for three months. Neither the *Mississippian* version nor her book tells the true story.

It is neither likely nor believable that Velazquez crossed swords with General Butler, as she claimed she did. She told the *Mississippian* that:

> She made her appearance before Gen. B. in a Southern homespun dress. She refused to take the oath—told him she gloried in being a rebel—had fought side by side with Southern *men* for Southern rights, and if she ever lived to see "Dixie" she would do it again. Butler denounced her as the most incorrigible she-rebel he had ever met with.

Velazquez was apparently feeling much haughtiness due to her now safe distance from the General. In any case, there is no evidence that she was ever "before" Butler, instead it is conclusive that she was before Judge Kinsman in the New Orleans court, and then she wasn't so defiant. The *Daily Delta* reported, "She declared that she was now strongly for the Union, and was raising her children up to revere the old flag."[28] However, the paper

---

28. Nov 2, 1862.

also said she was known to have previously supported the Southern cause in various ways.

Please see the "Before Butler" drawing in Illustrations, Figure 3.

Clearly, Velazquez intended to impress her Jackson, Mississippi audience with her claim of Southern loyalty and her defiance before General Butler. It was fortunate for her that her encounter was only invented, because Southerners who crossed swords with Butler came away the loser. He did not suffer fools gladly and made sure that he prevailed in his efforts to secure law and order of New Orleans. Butler was a demanding no-nonsense administrator of Union-occupied New Orleans and because of his heavy handedness earned himself the nickname, the Beast. Actually, a Union officer first called him by this epithet, but Southerners approvingly adopted the slur. Behind this epithet was a 44-year-old highly educated, intelligent individual. He had studied law and maintained a successful law practice before the war. *Harper's Weekly* said of him, "His forte is in the trial of cases. It is said that he has tried more jury cases for the last ten years than any other lawyer in the United States."[29] Butler was admitted to practice before the United States Supreme Court at the age of 27 and was "one of the youngest lawyers to attain that privilege."[30] Butler's courtroom antics and wit along with his "brutal" cross-examination skills were legendary. After the war, during the President Johnson impeachment case at which Butler was prosecutor, Butler caused the imposing witness General Lorenzo Thomas to crumble and "confess that his testimony was wrong."[31]

Velazquez wrote (p259-263) of her "contest of wits" with General Butler:

Butler was not the handsomest man I ever saw in my life, and he certainly looked the tyrant that he was. It was a favorite amusement with him to browbeat people who were brought before him, and he was remarkably skillful in terrifying those who were weak enough to submit to being bullied by him into making just the admission he wanted them to make.

She invented a clever and perfectly believable dialog in which Butler could not get the upper hand and she would not admit that she was the author and carrier of an illegal dispatch. Butler angered and "roared out, 'Well, madam, if you won't confess without compulsion, I'll see whether I can't compel you.'" The General then "gave an order that [she] should be locked up in a cell in the Custom House until [her] case was investigated further." Velazquez said she "left the presence of the general, feeling tolerably well satisfied with having gotten the best of him thus far...."

---

29. Jun 1, 1861.
30. David Detzer, *Dissonance, The Turbulent Days Between Fort Sumter and Bull Run* (NY: Harcourt, 2006), 81.
31. Richard S. West Jr., *Lincoln' Scapegoat General, A Life of Benjamin F. Butler, 1818-1893* (Boston: Houghton Mifflin, 1965), 326.

So how easy was it to out-wit or get the best of General Butler? The answer is- it was impossible, especially judging from the case of Mrs. Phillips. Mrs. Eugenia Levy Phillips was the wife of Alabama Congressman Philip Phillips, both of whom had left Washington, D.C. because of Mrs. Phillips' ardent support of the South, though Mr. Phillips was far from a rabid secessionist. They had taken up residence in New Orleans where she was ordered arrested by Butler and later wrote of her ordeal.[32]

A Union soldier came to her house and arrested her to her puzzlement and disbelief, for she could not imagine the reason for her arrest. The soldier took her to "The Hall of Justice... held in the Customhouse" to appear before Butler. Mrs. Phillips wrote:

> As I advanced, Butler's loud and vulgar voice greeted me, while an arm was thrust into my face. The greeting ran thus, while the face from which the bellowing came was distorted with passion, fury, and loyalty. He screamed, "You are seen laughing and mocking at the remains of a Federal officer. I do not call you a common woman of the town, but an uncommonly vulgar one, and I sentence you to Ship Island for the War."

She had not shown proper respect and laughed out loud as the funeral procession of Union Lieutenant DeKay passed by Mrs. Phillips who was on her balcony. In the sentence order Butler wrote she was "laughing and mocking at [Dekay's] remains."[33]

Mr. Phillips, who had accompanied his arrested wife, protested against Butler's insult, but "the general bawled: 'Arrest this man, gag him, take him away.'" Mrs. Phillips turned to her husband and said, "Mr. P., go out and leave this man to me." (Mr. Phillips was not imprisoned.) She then responded to Butler saying, "I was in good spirits the day of the funeral." She said that "all restraint seemed to have deserted" General Butler and with his "face inflamed," proceeded to write out her sentence. She said:

> I noted that he took a mighty long time to write my sentence, and I suspected that he hoped by delay I would throw myself on his mercy, or beg his pardon, or promise never to do so again. Nothing of this kind ever crossed my brain, and, full of holy indignation and determination to meet with silent contempt this outrageous insult, I quietly folded my arms and looked on him while he wrote. Not a word of appeal or explanation broke the ominous silence.

She was "condemned to imprisonment as a bad and dangerous woman, stirring up strife and inciting riot."[34]

Because of Phillips' haughty attitude and unwillingness to yield her Southern loyalty, she suffered months of imprisonment on Ship Island,

---

32. *Journal of Mrs. Eugenia Levy Phillips, 1861-1862*, Library of Congress.
33. Parton, 441; *Commercial Bulletin* (New Orleans), Jul 2, 1862.
34. *Commercial Bulletin*, Jul 2, 1862.

indeed an inhospitable barrier island. A summer visit to Ship Island, off the coast of Mississippi, about 60 miles from New Orleans, will confirm its discomfort. It is a mere large sandbar devoid of shade trees and hot in the summer. It is exposed to the elements and voracious insects, mostly the biting kind: chiggers, mosquitoes, dog flies, and yellow flies. Phillips' sentence ran the worst months to be on Ship Island, from June 30, 1862 until her early release on September 14. Fort Massachusetts, on the western end, was a staging area for the Union navy's assault on New Orleans' defenses and it was here that she was imprisoned. Mrs. Phillips was assigned living quarters in "one of the houses for hospital purposes," she was supplied with daily "soldier's ration" or allowed to cook the same (in addition her husband was allowed to send her some food) and was allowed to bring one female servant.[35] Phillips claimed to have scarcely survived the two and a half months imprisonment.

The question must be asked, If General Butler was infuriated at Mrs. Phillips' provocative laughter during a passing funeral and her unrepentant behavior, then how can one believe that Butler was not equally infuriated with Velazquez's alleged carrying of illegal dispatches and her unrepentant behavior? Mrs. Phillips did not even offer any back talk, yet Butler sentenced her severely, whereas Velazquez was all back talk, and received a lesser sentence. Velazquez should have counted herself lucky that, in truth, she did not come before General Butler on charges for it can be sure Butler would have dealt with her severely. In any case, the facts of her arrest and trial were clearly reported by the newspapers; she was arrested for stealing and was sentenced by Judge Kinsman.

Velazquez's memoir's treatment of this arrest contradicts both the New Orleans and the Mississippi newspapers' accounts on every point. In her memoir (p262), Velazquez warned General Butler that she "was a British subject, and that she claimed the protection of the British flag." Velazquez stated that with the help of friends, she procured pen and paper and wrote to British Consul Mr. Coppell, asking for his assistance. When he came to her, she gave Mr. Coppell her hotel room number and the key to her trunk which contained forged papers, "proofs of British citizenship." Earlier in her memoir (p239), Velazquez explained that she had obtained these papers from "an English lady with whom [she] had become slightly acquainted." Velazquez heard that the lady was leaving America, tired of the turmoil of war and returning to "Old England." Velazquez wrote:

> I went to her, and expressed a desire to purchase her passport and other foreign papers, confident that, armed with such documents as these, I would be able to make a fair start against the Federal authorities, and gain some immediate

---

35. West Jr., 154-155.

advantages that would probably be otherwise out of the question. The lady readily consented to part with the papers for a fair price....

This claim is not believable simply because the English lady would have been left without "her passport and other foreign papers" which she would need to safeguard her own travel.

Velazquez said that she did not know what transpired between Consul Coppell and the General, but that she was subsequently escorted out of her cell by Mr. Coppell, implying within one day. Greatly relieved, she then determined to get away from New Orleans and applied for a pass which was refused her. What? She claimed her false British citizenship got her out of jail, but yet it could not secure her a travel pass to leave New Orleans!

Velazquez wrote she then clandestinely hired a fishing boat to sail her across Lake Ponchartrain and away from New Orleans. She prepared herself, wearing a double layer of clothes, as she did not wish to carry luggage. She "secreted about [her] person all the Confederate money [she] had purchased, about nine thousand dollars in greenbacks, and [her] jewelry." In truth, Velazquez had no money or jewelry; that's the reason she robbed the Chesters which got her thrown in the Parish prison. Velazquez explained she had "a reasonable amount of confidence in the fidelity of the boatman," but just in case she "had provided [herself] with a six-shooter, and had taken pains to see that it was loaded, and all in condition for instant use." She went to the lake shoreline, checked that the coast was clear before approaching the boat and rendezvoused with the boatman. Velazquez wrote, "On taking my seat in the boat I placed my hand on this weapon, and was resolved to put it to the head of the man if he showed the slightest inclination of a desire to betray me." She said she would have used it to avoid being sent to prison on Ship Island. She concluded, "I was not sorry to get away, and considered myself fortunate in being able to make my escape with as much ease as I did."

Of course, her memoir's rendition of her trip across the lake is false and the *Mississippian's* account of her coming across on the "registered enemies" boat, *S. B. Brown*, is clearly the truth. The only truthful thing that Velazquez wrote (p265) about her departure from New Orleans was that she was headed to Jackson, Mississippi.

Velazquez's telling (*TWIB*, p262-263) of how British Consul (George C.) Coppell helped secure her release has a ring of truth and the fact that she pulled in this detail is impressive. But there are points which muffle the ring. The newspapers at the time made no mention of George Coppell assisting her and Velazquez ostensibly made no mention of his help to the *Mississippian* newspaper, and so shortly after the alleged help. Besides, Coppell would not have likely been of any real assistance to a British citizen who had been convicted of stealing a watch and other articles. She was not released in one day, but was incarcerated for six months!

The reason that Velazquez was able to pull Mr. Coppell into her storyline was because she knew his name well, as it had been made very public in the news all year due to his conflict with General Butler, which came close to inflaming an international crisis. Mr. Coppell had assumed the position of British Consul when the regular and credentialed Consul had left New Orleans returning to England because of ill health. However, Mr. Coppell was unable to present the proper documents from the British Government validating his official status so General Butler would not recognize his authority. General Butler claimed that certain behaviors and actions of Coppell's British subjects were pro-Confederate and undermining Butler's control of the city, and Butler was determined to thwart them and him.

Velazquez noted (p254) General Butler's "favorite punishment… was a sojourn on Ship Island, a desolate strip of sand on Mississippi Sound…." She wrote, "[I] only escaped such a fate through my address and courage, and the thoroughness of the preparations I had made to meet such an emergency."

Is it possible that Velazquez had ready at her convenience fake proof of British citizenship? Did she cleverly anticipate that these papers would be handy to get her out of her scrape?

But here's another question. What was Velazquez doing running around claiming British citizenship when in her book she claimed she was the daughter of a Spanish father and half-French mother and that she was born in Spanish-owned Cuba, all of which would have clearly given her Spanish citizenship and maybe even French citizenship? She could have forgone the trouble of buying British papers and simply and truthfully claimed her Spanish citizenship, *si*? *¡Ay Dios mio! Mon ami* there seems to be a blooming lie somewhere in the pudding.

The Battle of Leesburg (or the Battle of Ball's Bluff)

The *Mississippian* newspaper (June 6, 1863) is the first found of a published claim that Velazquez fought at the Battle of Leesburg (Ball's Bluff) which occurred on October 21, 1861. The article stated, "She was in the battle of Leesburg and several skirmishes, but finally, her sex having been discovered by the surgeon of the regiment—the 5th Texas Volunteers, to which the company had been attached…." If one is to understand this sentence to mean she was with the 5th Texas Volunteers at that battle, it just is not true, since that regiment was not there. Disregarding this troubling fact, is it true that she was there anyway? It is known that she was in Richmond only 125 miles away, 25 days before, on September 27, so it is conceivable that she found her way to the Ball's Bluff vicinity. However, even if she was near or on the battlefield, it is certain she did not do what she claimed she did during the battle for the following reasons.

Velazquez, in her memoir, called the Battle of Leesburg by its Union name, the Battle of Ball's Bluff, and gave a rousing narration (p116-125) of the battle. She explained (p110) how she came to finding her way to that locale; she met some boys from Leesburg "who persuaded [her] to go there with them, as there was every prospect of another fight coming off soon." She said she arrived at Leesburg on October 10, went to the headquarters of General Evans and "asked to be employed." He sent her to Colonel Burt who said he had "no vacancy in his command." She said she was disappointed, but figured to wait around so that she could have "a hand in the expected battle, whenever it came off." And then for the third time in her narration, she stated that a battle was expected; she said the night prior to the battle, she told her slave boy, Bob, "to cook plenty of provisions, as we expected something to happen." Well, actually Velazquez made the claim four times. Earlier, Lieutenant Buford told young Miss E in Leesburg, with whom Buford was flirting, that Miss E might see Buford again if he was "not killed, but a battle was expected shortly."

It was impossible that Buford or the Confederate forces could have anticipated the Battle of Ball's Bluff. The Union had sent across the Potomac River a reconnaissance force, which also had the assignment to capture what they believed was a small Rebel encampment. The encampment turned out not to be an encampment, but just trees, the physical features of the landscape misjudged in the dark of the night. The Union force was discovered and the Rebels brought up their men to repel it. "Thus, the opening round of the battle pitted some forty Confederates against about sixty Yanks."[36] It was a chance encounter and not predictable by Velazquez or anyone else. The skirmish grew into a battle as the combatants threw more men into the conflict.

Velazquez's recitation of the events of the battle is not 100% accurate, but there is some accuracy. Most notable is her purposeful avoidance of details which might be used as points of investigation.

In a trivial mix-up, she mistakenly said Colonel Burt was in command of "the eight Virginia regiment." Then shortly afterwards she correctly wrote that Colonel Eppa Hunton commanded the 8th Virginia. In another error, she said Colonel Burt was in charge of the 13th Mississippi Regiment and Colonel Barksdale was in charge of the 18th Mississippi Regiment. A few paragraphs later she also corrected that mistake stating that Colonel Burt was in charge of the 18th Mississippi Regiment. These brief mix-ups are not the real problem.

---

36. James A. Morgan III, *A Little Short of Boats: The Civil War Battles of Ball's Bluff & Edwards Ferry, October 21-22, 1861* (New York and California: Savas Beatie), 47.

The real problem comes from her self-proclaimed deeds. She wrote, "Shortly after the fight commenced, I took charge of a company <u>which lost all its officers</u>, and I do not think that either my men or myself failed to do our full duty." She continued with her story:

After the battle was over, the first lieutenant of the company which I was commanding came in and relieved me, stating that he had been taken prisoner, but had succeeded in making his escape in the confusion incident to the Federal defeat. I did not say anything, but I had my very serious doubts as to the story which he told being the exact truth. He had a very sheepish look, as if he was ashamed of himself for playing a sneaking cowardly trick; and I shall always believe that when the firing commenced, he found an opportunity to slink away to the rear for the purpose of getting out of the reach of danger.

The historical truth is that there was no Confederate company at Ball's Bluff which lost all of its officers! No company even came close to losing all of its officers. Recall, a company was led by a captain, then first lieutenant and second lieutenant. In addition, there was a first sergeant, plus 4 more sergeants, plus 6 corporals. The *Official Records*[37] show 3 killed officers and 12 wounded officers out of the entire force of the Confederates at Ball's Bluff which was stated at 1709 men!

Velazquez did not say which company she led, and clearly, she did not wish the reader to know; by making known the company, her claim could have been checked. It will be explained in the course of this book how Velazquez unfailingly told her readers the correct names of inn keepers, insignificant acquaintances, yet refused to name military companies upon which her important leadership claims hinged and thereby the claims might be tested.

To whittle it down more- Although Velazquez evaded naming the company she commanded, she weakly implied she was with the 13th Mississippi Regiment by stating the names of other regiments and their positions, though in error she wrote Colonel Burt and the 18th Mississippi was "on the left of our line." Colonel Burt was on the right. If Velazquez meant to imply she was with the 13th Mississippi Regiment, then it can be noted the 13th regiment supplied only Company D at Ball's Bluff and it had all of its officers available. If any first lieutenant from the company went missing during the battle, it can be certain that there was a full complement of officers ready to assume command and the company did not avail itself of Velazquez's walk-on leadership. Only one man from Company D was killed and he was not an officer.

The bottom line is that she fabricated the story of her participation. It is galling that she wasn't content to elevate her own importance, but in the

---

37. Ser 1, Vol 5, p353.

process, she disparaged a comrade-in-arms, calling him cowardly and accusing him of skirting his duty.

Velazquez shot off another fib (p125), "I fired my revolver at another officer--a major, I believe... I saw him... fall... An officer near me exclaimed, 'Lieutenant, your ball took him.'" Records show no Union major was killed, as she implied, at Ball's Bluff. Of course, she left herself an out; she said she believed he was a major.

The Rebels pushed the Federals back into the Potomac River, which the Federals had just crossed in the night. Some Union soldiers threw their weapons into the river and tried to escape death or capture by swimming the river. Many drowned or were shot dead by the Rebels high on the banks of the river. There were not enough boats to transport all the retreating Union soldiers or evacuate all the wounded, and the men in the few boats were shot. One scow capsized midway across the river and all drowned, but one.[38]

Velazquez evoked Ball's Bluff because this Union defeat was shocking at that time, though today is overshadowed historically by big battles like Gettysburg. The nation was shocked by the death of Colonel Edward D. Baker, a sitting U.S. Senator and a dear friend of Lincoln's, who had named his son after Baker. Ball's Bluff was characterized as a calamity and a Congressional Joint Committee on the Conduct of the War was formed to find who was responsible. The stunned nation wanted answers.

Other of Velazquez's claims cast doubt that she was at Ball's Bluff.

First, Velazquez stated that the Confederates had "six pieces of artillery" in the battle. In contradiction, the *Confederate Military History* states, "The Confederates had no artillery in the fight, while the Federals had three light guns."[39] Agreeing with this fact is James A. Morgan III, Ball's Bluff historian, battlefield tour guide and author of *A Little Short of Boats: The Civil War Battles of Ball's Bluff & Edwards Ferry*.

Second, Velazquez said, "At that point where I stood the Potomac River was very wide...." The River is not "very wide" at this location since Harrison's Island sits in its middle. The west channel (Virginia side) which Velazquez would have seen is approximately 280 feet wide and the east channel (Maryland side) which was out of her sight is about 670 feet wide.[40] Above and below the Island, the Potomac is generally 1000 feet wide, but Velazquez would not have been able to see that portion of the River.

---

38. Charles Lawrence Peirson, *Ball's Bluff: An Episode and its Consequences to Some of Us* (Salem, MA: The Salem Press Co., 1913), 12.
39. Ed. Gen. Clement Evans, Vol 3 Chap XI (Atlanta, GA: Confederate Publishing Co., 1899), 191.
40. *Frank Leslie's Illustrated Newspaper* of Nov 16, 1861 said the Virginia channel was "about 100 yards wide" and the Maryland channel "a distance of 200 yards."

Velazquez failed to note, just off the bluff, the dominate land feature, Harrison's Island, which played a major role in the Union retreat. It would have been impossible for Velazquez not to have seen the island and to have mistaken the river as "very wide" at that location. In fact, the battle is known by a third name, the Battle of Harrison's Island, which Velazquez should have learned by the time she wrote her memoir.[41]

Please see the map of the Battle of Ball's Bluff in Illustrations, Figure 4.

Third, Velazquez related (p124) the story of the "escape of Colonel Devens" of the 15th Massachusetts Regiment:

Directly, one of the prisoners whom I was guarding, shouted, "There goes my colonel!"

"What is his name?" I inquired.

"Colonel Devens, of the fifteenth Massachusetts regiment," he replied, as he pointed to a figure striking out in an attempt to swim across the river.

I said, "I hope the poor fellow will get safely to land, for he has fought bravely, and deserves a better fate than a watery grave."

Colonel Devens, it appears, in the confusion got separated from his men, and seeing no chance of rallying them, or of doing anything to turn the tide of defeat, had, when all hope of ever effecting an orderly retreat was gone, sought to save himself in the desperate manner I have indicated. He was, apparently, a powerful swimmer, for he was soon out of musket-shot, and I believe he managed to gain the other shore.

Velazquez's rendition of Colonel Devens' escape drowns in the facts.

Colonel Charles Devens' escape was told by Lieutenant Charles H. Eager[42] who said that after his company was ordered to retreat, his men went to the river where Colonel Devens ordered them to throw their weapons into the river and to "take care of [themselves] as best as [they] could."

Lieutenant Eager and his men found on the riverbank a limb and a floor joist board, both about ten feet long, which they were pushing off the bank when "Colonel Devens came to the water's edge and stripped of his equipment and clothing. Asked if he could swim, he replied that he could not and one man replied, 'Hop on to our craft and we will take you across, too. After satisfying himself that we were all swimmers but me [Eager], he waded in.'"

Separately, another officer, Lieutenant Derby, who had succeeded in crossing the river, was an eye-witness to Devens' crossing, "Colonel Devens, swimming across on a log, landed where I lay."

---

41. In 1861 the Island was 300-400 yards wide & two miles long. Source- Morgan III, xxii.
42. Andrew E. Ford, *The Story of the Fifteenth Regiment Massachusetts Volunteer Infantry in the Civil War 1861-1864* (Clinton, MA: The Press of W. J. Coulter, Courant Office, 1898), 90-92.

It is conclusive that Colonel Devens was not a "powerful swimmer," but instead, was a non-swimmer and that he did not strike out across the river alone, but went in a group.

Worse still is the fact that darkness had already fallen at the time of Devens' swim which would have prevented the prisoner from even seeing Devens. Colonel Devens testified to the Joint Committee on the Conduct of the War, which investigated the defeat of the Federals, that when he was going among his men and instructing them to save themselves "by the river, or in any other way," it was dark: "When I got to the rear of the regiment [meaning the men along the riverbank farthest upriver] it had become quite dark." After giving his men "[his] leave," Devens prepared to save himself; he explained how he crossed the river on "a bit of log floating" with the help of the other men and said, "It was entirely dark before I got over."

Records from the U.S. Naval Observatory for Leesburg for this day indicate that sunset was at 5:23 p.m., the end of twilight at 5:50 p.m. and moonrise was an hour afterwards, at 6:50 p.m. It appears that it was during this interval Devens crossed. However, the Rebels might have been able to see retreating dark figures enough to take potshots, this based on Devens continued narration, "At that time the enemy were pouring down a terrific fire on the island and on the water, in which every man who could swim was making an attempt to swim across...."[43]

Velazquez held the prisoner atop the bluff which is some 110 feet above the river. At this time during the battle, no Rebel, including Velazquez, descended to the riverbank; the Rebels went down only after dark. In addition, the bluff is set back about 150 feet from the water's edge with the river's flood plain in-between, so line of sight from the top of the bluff to the water's edge was some 186 feet, according to Pythagoras of Samos, Greece, who wasn't actually at the battle. At even a greater distance than 186 feet and in the darkness, it would have been impossible for the prisoner to identify a swimming Devens. At best, Velazquez and her alleged prisoner might have seen a dark figure swimming.

It is impossible to ascertain what purpose Velazquez had in telling her story and attributing it to the captured soldier. Did she hope to disparage the Colonel by stating that he "sought to save himself in the desperate manner I have indicated"? In any case, her version of Colonel Devens' escape is not believable. Colonel Devens survived the war and he will reappear in Velazquez's life five years hence.

A final note about Velazquez's narration of the events surrounding Ball's Bluff is in order. At headquarters in Leesburg prior to the battle, Velazquez

---

43. *Report of the Joint Committee on the Conduct of the War* (Washington, DC: GPO, 1863), 411-412.

met "Colonel Featherstone [*sic*], of the seventeenth Mississippi regiment," who was indeed there. She narrated (*TWIB*, p117):

> This fine officer I had known when I was quite a small child, and I was decidedly amused at the idea of renewing my acquaintance with him under existing circumstances. He had not the shadow of an idea that the dashing little lieutenant who stood before him was a woman whom he had known as a child.

The question arises as to when and how Featherston could have known Velazquez "as a child" when she claimed she did not leave Cuba before the age of seven. She wrote that at that age she moved to New Orleans where she spent the next seven years attending to her education. First, she spent two years under the tutelage of her aunt and then from about 1851 until 1856 was in a "school conducted by the Sisters of Charity." She wrote she got married on April 6, 1856, as a fourteen-year-old bride. This all took place in New Orleans, where Featherston never resided.

So where did Featherston and Velazquez earlier cross paths? Winfield Featherston was born in Tennessee in 1820.[44] He studied in Tennessee and Georgia and became a lawyer in Houston, Mississippi, in 1840, where he rose to prominence. He was elected to serve as a U.S. Congressman from 1847 to 1851 and moved to Holly Springs, Mississippi in 1857.[45] Holly Springs, in Marshall County, is some 76 miles northwest of Houston, in Chickasaw County.

It would appear that if Velazquez (who claimed to have been born in 1842) was a child when she first knew Featherston, it had to have been in Mississippi. She may have lived in any of the Mississippi counties in which Featherston campaigned for Congress and saw him then. If a childhood in Mississippi is the truth, then it contradicts Velazquez's story of her youth in Cuba and New Orleans. A Mississippi childhood has a ring of truth compared to the provable falsehoods she proffered about her birth in Cuba or of her father's governmental office in Cuba or of his inherited ranch in Texas or of his inherited plantation in Cuba or of his immense wealth. And what she wrote about her time in New Orleans is questionable; for example, recall the impossibility that Velazquez attended the Sisters of Charity School as a child from a wealthy family. Other possible clues of Mississippi origins are presented elsewhere.

A Spy Trip to Washington in Female Attire

In her memoir, Velazquez explained (p127-129) that after the Battle of Ball's Bluff she was "disillusioned" because she "discovered that actual

---

44. Ed. Clement A. Evan, *Confederate Military History Vol 7* (Atlanta, GA: Confederate Publishing Co., 1899), 251.
45. University of Mississippi Libraries, Featherston Collection, 1824-1952, Special Collections, MUM00181.

warfare was far different from what [she] had supposed it to be." But worse were the "trivial devices adopted to kill time" in camp life and general soldiering, to the point that these became "most oppressive." She "chafed under the ennui of the camp, and felt irresistibly impelled to be moving about and doing something." She recognized that

> a woman like [herself], who had a talent for assuming disguises, and who like [her], was possessed of courage, resolution, and energy, backed up by a ready wit, a plausible address, and attractive manners, had it in her power to perform many services of the most vital importance, which it would be impossible for a man to even attempt.

She acknowledged that "to be a second Joan of Arc was a mere girlish fancy" which was now "dissipated forever." Understanding she could not be someone else, she resolved she "must be simply [herself]." She determined to resume female attire and to cross into enemy territory to gather information for her commander and "to see and to hear for [herself]."

Velazquez wrote (p132) she procured women's clothing with the help of "an old negro woman, who washed for [her] and who had shown considerable fondness for [her]," and hired "an old negro who had a boat" to take her across the Potomac River to the Maryland shore. She said the river crossing was "during a chilly night in the latter part of October." This would have been in 1861, since she said the trip was immediately after the Battle of Ball's Bluff which was on October 21, 1861. However, recall that she was arrested in Lynchburg and Richmond on September 26, while using the name "Mrs. Mary Ann Keith." Then on October 21, 1861 the Richmond *Daily Dispatch* wrote:

> The *Lynchburg Virginian* says: In answer to the numerous inquiries which have been made of us concerning the disposal of Mrs. Keith, we will state that after remaining in jail several days, she was discharged by an order from Gen. Winder, at whose insistence she was arrested a second time. Upon her discharge she appeared in the apparel of her sex, and we suppose will not again soon undertake to play the "bowld soger boy." She immediately left here for Memphis which she claimed as her home.

If Velazquez was in "jail several days" after her September 26 arrest and she did not, in fact, "immediately [leave] for Memphis," but instead went to Leesburg, then one might believe she was in the vicinity of the Battle of Ball's Bluff. Admittedly, she could have by chance gone to Leesburg or, as now claimed, crossed to Maryland. Since the newspapers lost track of her, we shall follow her narration as to her whereabouts. Be attentive to her claims, because after they are accumulated, they will be analyzed.

She wrote that upon her successful crossing of the Potomac, she arrived in Washington, D.C. and took a room at Brown's Hotel.[46] She contacted "an officer of the regular Federal army" who had been a friend of her husband from their old military days and he showed her great kindness. He spoke freely of the military situation, which Velazquez noted he shouldn't have done had he known her true mission. He also "greatly lamented the defeat which the Federals had met with at Ball's Bluff… little thinking that he was conversing with one who had played a most active part in the very thickest of the battle."

Since Velazquez had never visited the city, her friend volunteered to show her the sights. He took her to the Patent Office, the Treasury Department, and the War Department. At the War Department she coaxed her friend into introducing her to Secretary of War Simon Cameron, whom she thought was courteous enough, but had "a crafty look in his eyes and a peculiar expression about his mouth, that [she] thought indicated a treacherous disposition."

She then met "General Wessells, the Commissary General of Prisoners," with whom she was more favorably impressed. She took the opportunity to tell (p141) the General her brother was a Rebel prisoner and asked if it was possible to visit him. He replied yes and she said that she would "shortly avail [herself] of his kindness." Velazquez assured her readers that she took in all she "saw and heard" in the War Department to be used for the benefit of the Rebels.

She next went to the White House, "where [her] friend said he would introduce [her] to the President." Velazquez narrated:

Mr. Lincoln, however, was an agreeable disappointment to me, as I have no doubt he was to many others. He was certainly a very homely man, but he was not what I should call an ugly man, for he had a pleasant, kindly face, and a pleasant familiar manner, that put one at ease with him immediately.

I did not have an opportunity to exchange a great many words with Mr. Lincoln, but my interview, brief, as it was, induced me to believe, not only that he was not a bad man, but that he was an honest and well-meaning one, who thought that he was only doing his duty in attempting to conquer the South.

Velazquez said that when she bid Lincoln good-bye, she left "if not with a genuine liking for him, at least with many of [her] prejudices dispelled, and different feelings towards him than [she] had when [she] entered."

She next visited the Capitol where she "listened to the debates in Congress for a while."

She then went to the Post Office where her friend transacted some business. There she heard many conversations which revealed "really

---

46. Located between 6th and 7th Streets on Pennsylvania Avenue.

important information" which she thought behooved the speakers to mind their "loud talking" among strangers. She wrote (p142):

> I was really annoyed at some of the conversation I heard between government officials while at the Post Office, and wondered how the Federal authorities ever expected to prevent the Confederates from finding out their plans if this kind of thing was going on all the time.

Instead of annoyed, one would have expected her to have been elated by the government officials' laxity, considering Velazquez unfailingly trumpeted a most pure Southern loyalty! Velazquez's questionable annoyance will be overshadowed momentarily by undoubtable facts.

She said she recrossed the military lines to the Confederacy, her round trip having taken her 13 days. She once again assumed the Lieutenant Harry T. Buford disguise.

Is this spy trip believable?

First, in the time frame Velazquez set, she could not have seen Congress in session, since it was not! Velazquez said her departure was the "latter part of October" and lasted 13 days. The earliest she could have left was October 22, 1861, the day after the Battle of Ball's Bluff. The latest departure would have been October 31. Her latest return would have been November 12. Congress was not in session in October and November.[47]

Second, Velazquez could not have met General Wessells since he was nowhere near Washington, D.C. or at the military post or rank which Velazquez claimed. He did not become Commissary of Prisoners until November 11, 1864. On the date Velazquez claimed, Wessell was posted "on the Northwest frontier." During the winter of 1861-'2 he organized the 8th regiment of Kansas volunteers and was made its colonel.[48] In addition, Velazquez evoked her captured brother to Wessells, when this brother, as subsequent evidence makes clear, most surely did not exist, at least not in any form ever told by her.

Third, it would have been very possible for Velazquez to meet Lincoln since he made himself accessible to the public at every opportunity. He dutifully and rather fondly met the public as routine. The only problem is, she said the introduction to Lincoln was made by a friend of her dead husband "William" and subsequent evidence shows that "William" was fabricated by Velazquez. Since this husband never existed, then his friend did not exist either. The same logic applies to the alleged introduction to

---

47. 37th Congress, Special session was Mar 4-28, 1861; 1st session was Jul 4, 1861- Aug 6, 1861; 2nd session was Dec 2, 1861- Jul 17, 1862; 3rd session was Dec 1, 1862- Mar 4, 1863.
48. Ed. William A. Ellis, *Norwich University, Her History, Her Graduates, Her Roll of Honor* (Concord, NH: Rumford Press, 1898), 199; ed. George Ripley and Charles A. Dana, *New American Cyclopædia*, Vol XVL (NY: Appleton & Co., 1872), 847.

Secretary Cameron (who may have been more or less accessible than Lincoln).

If in truth Velazquez crossed military lines and went spying in Washington, she destroyed any possible chance to have it believed due to these falsehoods. Velazquez made clear (p139) her trip was her own undertaking "without authority from anybody," in other words, she was not an official Confederate spy on this occasion.

Chapter 3

The Battle of Shiloh and Velazquez's Wounds

The *Mississippian* (June 6, 1863) reported that Velazquez had been at the Battle of Shiloh (April 6 and 7, 1862) and that "in the <u>second</u> day's fighting she was wounded in the <u>head</u>, and was ordered to the rear...." She had apparently forgotten her previous claim printed a mere 17 days after the battle, when she was in New Orleans and "dressed in soldier's clothes, surrendered herself to the mayor." The local *Daily True Delta* of April 24, 1862, reported she was "wounded in the <u>foot</u> and <u>hand</u>." And then on November 2, still in New Orleans and arrested for stealing, the *Daily True Delta* wrote, "[She] was at Manassas, Shiloh and other battles and got wounded in the <u>wrist</u>."

As will be seen, in the coming years, Velazquez was even more confused as to the body locations of her wounds, and she varied the day the wounds were inflicted.

The St. Louis *Republican* of March 7, 1866 wrote, "At the battle of Shiloh... while gallantly leading her company in a charge, she was <u>twice</u> wounded and carried from the field."

The *Memphis Daily Avalanche* of March 21, 1866 wrote, "... this chivalric woman, whose <u>three</u> wounds, and experience of a score of battles, adds so much luster to the name of woman."

The New Orleans *Daily True Delta* of March 29, 1866 wrote, "Lieut. Buford was wounded <u>four</u> times during her military career."

The Augusta, Georgia *Daily Constitutionalist* of May 22, 1866 reported, "she was <u>twice</u> wounded, going into action on one occasion with the scar of her first hurt yet uncicatrized [unhealed]... receiving one hurt at Stillwater and the other in a cavalry skirmish a <u>few</u> <u>days</u> <u>after</u> Shiloh."

The *Pulaski Citizen* (Tennessee) of June 22, 1866 wrote she "was <u>twice</u> wounded at the battle of Shiloh."

The *Mobile Daily Register* of August 25, 1874 stated she was at "Shiloh, where she was badly wounded in the <u>right</u> <u>shoulder</u> on the <u>first</u> day of the battle, April 7th, 1862." To clarify, April 6 was the first day of the battle and was a Sunday.

Only ten days after the *Mobile Daily Register*'s report, the *Atlanta Constitution* of September 4, 1874 interviewed her and reported, "She was in the battle of Shiloh, and on Monday evening after the fight, was wounded badly in the <u>right</u> <u>shoulder</u> and <u>hand</u> by the bursting of a shell." Monday would have been the <u>second</u> day.

A reporter for the *Georgia Weekly Telegraph and Georgia Journal & Messenger* of February 1, 1876 wrote that he yesterday met "Mde. Velazquez... [who] was wounded <u>three</u> times- in her <u>foot</u>, <u>neck</u>, and <u>breast</u>."

Turning to Velazquez's book to settle the question of when and what wounds she received seems reasonable since in great detail Velazquez addressed (p200-227) her role at the Battle of Shiloh. She does not tell of wounds in the foot, neck, breast, or head, instead, she claimed she was wounded "severely in the <u>arm</u> and <u>shoulder</u>" while burying some dead. She said, "My <u>shoulder</u> was found to be out of place, my <u>arm</u> cut, and my <u>little finger</u> lacerated- a disagreeable and exceedingly painful, but not necessarily a very dangerous wound." This wound, she claimed, occurred on the <u>third</u> day, after the full battle of the 6th and 7th, and that day would have been a Tuesday, the 8th.

Nearly forgotten was her claim (p309), "I managed to severely hurt the <u>foot</u> which had been <u>wounded</u> shortly <u>after</u> the battle of Fort Donelson...." The Battle of Fort Donelson was February 11-16, 1862 and clearly before the Battle of Shiloh on April 6-7, 1862, so Velazquez was wounded in her foot in addition and previous to her wounds at the Battle of Shiloh.

In summary, Velazquez was wounded on the <u>first</u>, <u>second</u> and <u>third</u> day of the Battle of Shiloh, while burying some dead or "in a cavalry skirmish a <u>few</u> <u>days</u> <u>after</u> Shiloh," or "while gallantly leading her company in a charge," in the <u>head</u>, <u>foot</u>, <u>wrist</u>, <u>hand</u>, <u>shoulder</u>, <u>neck</u>, <u>breast</u>, <u>arm</u> and <u>little</u> <u>finger</u> and she was wounded <u>twice</u> at Shiloh. During her entire service she was wounded <u>one</u>, <u>two</u>, <u>three</u> or <u>four</u> times.

Please see the "Making a Charge" drawing in Illustrations, Figure 5.

There is a grave problem with Velazquez's wounding at Shiloh. She claimed (p225) in her memoir, it was the third day of battle while she was burying some "dead men belonging to the tenth Tennessee regiment" that she was wounded by a bursting shell. The 10th Tennessee regiment was not at the Battle of Shiloh! They had all been captured some 51 days prior, on February 16, 1862, at the Battle of Fort Donelson and "the field and staff officers were taken to Fort Warren, the line officers to Johnson's Island, and the non-commissioned officers and men to Camp Douglas, at Chicago."[1] After the men were released in a prisoner exchanged, they returned South and reorganized on October 2, 1862 in Clinton, Mississippi. It is certain that Velazquez did not bury anyone from the 10th Tennessee Regiment.

Please see the "Wounded by a Shell" drawing in Illustrations, Figure 6.

The Battle of Shiloh and Lieutenant Philip Hastings

Velazquez narrated (p186) an event two weeks prior to the Battle of Shiloh which requires scrutiny. Lieutenant Harry T. Buford was in Memphis and "came across a friend whom [Lt. Buford] was very glad to meet. This was Lieutenant Philip Hastings, a whole-souled fellow, for whom [Buford] had an especial liking, and whom [Buford] accordingly greeted with great cordiality. Hastings returned [Buford's] greeting in an equally cordial

---

1. Ed. John Berrien Lindsley, *The Military Annals of Tennessee. Confederate. First Series: Embracing a Review of Military Operations, with Regimental Histories and Memorial Rolls, Compiled from Original and Official* (Nashville, TN: J. M. Lindsley & Co., 1886), 284.

manner." After a brief conversation of where they had been and their thoughts for the future, Velazquez claimed their conversation turned to the subject of a young Memphis woman, Miss M, for whom Hastings had marital desires. Hastings explained that the lady had a "deucedly pretty sister, about fifteen years of age" who would suit Buford and suggested that Buford go with him to visit the ladies. Buford agreed to go, but before they went, Hastings, who had already been imbibing, insisted on having some drinks. Hastings took a "brandy smash" and Buford drank only cider. (Velazquez always claimed as Buford that she never drank alcohol.) Afterwards, "lighting [their] cigars, [they] strolled down the street...."

The hour became late, too late for a proper visit to the ladies, and Buford convinced Hastings that they shouldn't go. Hastings then figured to spend the rest of the night out on the town. Harry Buford made her excuse to return to her room wishing to avoid any trouble which a night on the town may bring. Buford worried for Hastings' safety considering his condition, but could not convince him to retire for the night. Finally, Buford talked Hastings into letting her hold his money, leaving him only small change.

The next morning when Hastings came around to collect his money, he expressed remorse for his drinking and expressed his doubts that he would succeed in wooing "his love-lady." Buford suspected that his lady was aware of his behavior and the lady was put-off. In any case, Buford offered to "aid him in any way" to gain the affection of the lady.

Velazquez went on entertainingly for pages (p191-199) about how she (as Buford) tried to assist Phil in his conquest of Miss M with carriage rides and theater visits only to have Miss M fall in love with Harry T. Buford. This Miss M is the same young lady who Velazquez claimed later sent Harry Buford a "love letter" which Buford received just after Shiloh. Velazquez wrote that she felt "really sorry for the writer, and reproached [herself] for having permitted [Miss M's] flirtation with her to go to the length it did." Of course, this is the "love letter" shown to be a plagiarism.

Velazquez lamented:

Alas poor Phil! his affections were bestowed in the wrong direction, but he lived in hope that things would finally shape themselves according to his wishes, and he confidently expected that in time he would be able to soften the lady's heart towards him, that she would accept his hand. His dreams of happiness, however, were cut short in an untimely manner, for I saw him fall, while fighting bravely, about two weeks subsequently, at the head of his company, at the battle of Shiloh.

Velazquez further grieved:

There was no braver soldier belonging to the Confederate army engaged in that bloody battle than Phil Hastings, and his death was doubly a source of regret to me, as by it I lost a warm-hearted and sincere friend, and also an opportunity to undo the wrong I had unwittingly done him through capturing the affections of the girl he loved, by endeavoring to make matters right between him and her.

Oh, dear. So, who was the courageous and unintentionally wronged best comrade Phil Hastings?

It is rare that Velazquez provided enough detail about a comrade to enable a researcher to conduct a search of the historical record. In the case of Hastings, Velazquez provided his first and last name, his rank and his death. A search of the Consolidated Military Service Records of Confederate soldiers which is archived at the National Archives reveals no Lieutenant Philip Hastings. Officers' records are generally complete enough to find the target of a search, yet Lieutenant Philip Hastings is not found.

Did Velazquez embellish Hastings' rank and, in truth, he was an enlisted (a private) instead? No enlisted soldier by that name is found in the record, either. There are some Hastings soldiers with an initial of "P" in their first or middle name, but they are not likely candidates for Velazquez's Hastings.

Was there a Lieutenant Philip Hastings killed at Shiloh? Although there is, to date, no single comprehensive list of all Confederate dead at Shiloh, there exist multiple lists and it should be noted these are especially attentive to listing dead officers. The *Memphis Daily Appeal*, from April 8 and into May, almost daily, presented impressive casualty lists, naming brigades, regiments, companies, ranks and names. No Lieutenant Philip Hastings was found in the search.

During and after the Civil War, regimental and company pride was evident in every soldier and they identified themselves by it. Velazquez chose not to identify Hastings' regiment or company and it can only be thought that she purposefully failed to because Hastings was a lie she wished to go undetected. Recall, she said she saw Hastings fall in battle? It will be seen in 1866 she told a newspaper, "At the battle of Shiloh Captain Phillips fell mortally wounded, and the command then devolved upon her." In this case Captain Phillips was a real person, but it is false that Captain Bruce L. Phillips died at Shiloh. Instead, he surrendered at the end of the War (more on Phillips later). And in 1874, Velazquez told a newspaper that she was "near Drew [Colonel Dreux] when he was killed" at the First Battle of Manassas. In truth, the Colonel had died days earlier and miles away. This is addressed later. If Velazquez lied about Captain Phillips and Colonel Dreux, real people, why wouldn't she invent someone with no discoverable history about whom she might feel even freer to lie?

Three Noteworthy Items in the June 6, 1863 *Mississippian*

1) Stated: "At the breaking out of the war Mrs. Laura J. Williams was a resident of Arkansas." The first public reference to her residency in Arkansas comes from the New Orleans *Daily Delta* of April 24, 1862 which wrote, "She gave the name of respectable houses here in the city who knew

her in her proper sphere, when she resided in Arkansas, where she says she owns a plantation." Recall that she claimed in her November 1862 hospital admission in New Orleans, that she came from Arkansas seven months prior which would have been April. The *Daily Delta* of November 2, 1862 wrote she "managed by some deceptive arts, which are best known to women, to win the affections of an Arkansas planter, who carried her with him to Rackensack." In her memoir she never mentioned living or marrying in Arkansas.

2) Stated: "She disguised herself in a Confederate uniform, and adopting the name of 'Henry Benford,' she proceeded to Texas, where she raised and equipped an independent company and went to Virginia with it as 1st Lieutenant." Why did she use a different name other than Harry T. Buford? Did the newspaper type setter misread the reporter's handwriting? It seems so, because it will be seen another report out of Jackson by a correspondent called her Buford, and shortly, she will write to the Confederate government using Buford. She never called herself Benford in any letters. Or maybe Velazquez used Henry Benford for some reason she deemed good. She might have been trying it on for size, so to speak. She had a clear pattern of varying her female names, even her first name. She was Ann Williams and Laura Williams and soon will be Alice Williams. It will later be seen she was Jeruth DeCaulp, Lauretta DeCaulp and Mary DeCaulp. In many cases it appears that she is trying to separate herself from a history that she feared would be remembered by citizens in the area she was re-transiting.

3) Stated:

He [her husband] accidentally found her out and asked if she wanted to see him. She sent him word she never wanted to see him so long as he wore the Yankee uniform. But he forced himself upon her, tried to persuade her to take the oath, and get a release, when he said he would resign and take her to his relations in Connecticut. She indignantly spurned his proposition, and he left her to her fate.

This contradicts the facts, which are, that her husband, Williams of the 13th Connecticut Regiment, did not "accidently find her out." Instead, the New Orleans newspapers from November 1862 make it clear they were living together in the military camp where and when the policeman arrested Velazquez!

A Rare Bird

Velazquez's presence in Jackson, Mississippi was noted by another newspaper. A correspondent for the *Memphis Daily Appeal* wrote from Jackson, June 24th, 1863 (in part):[2]

---

2. Atlanta, Georgia- this was the Atlanta edition of Jun 29, 1863 which printed a "Letter from Jackson," indicating the letter was "Special Correspondence of *Memphis Daily Appeal*."

There is this morning on the streets a *rara avis*, a well made, but not pretty, Confederate lieutenant, of the *genus famina*, with a very perceptible strut, and a trifle of a swagger. Madame rummer [*sic* rumor] gives *him* (?) two names, i. e. Mrs. Buford and Miss Williams, and says she (the lieutenant) is an officer in a Texas company. Her husband is in the Yankee service, for which baseness, on his part, she (the said lieutenant) donned the apparel of a "bold soldier boy." We admire angels in calico, but we never could see the charm of dressing up "the last and best gift of heaven" in pantaloons, though the trowsers [*sic* trousers] were of nice Confederate gray, with brass buttons thrown in. It may be a splendid opportunity for showing a well-turned ankle, but "While it makes the unthinking laugh, It cannot but make the judicious grieve." And we being of the latter class, have been in tears ever since.

It should be noted that Velazquez did not succeed in staying undetected in her male lieutenant or Harry T. Buford disguise, as she regularly claimed she did in her memoir.

Lieutenant Colonel Fremantle saw a Female Soldier

Velazquez wrote (p269) that upon leaving New Orleans she went to Jackson, Mississippi "with what haste [she] could, and arrived just in time to witness... the burning of the Bowman House." This assertion should be believed true to a slight degree; maybe she saw the ashes. However, she also claimed she was staying at the hotel when the fire broke-out and "barely succeeded in escaping from the building with [her] life." This assertion should not be believed to any degree.

Velazquez claimed (p270) that she had "taken rooms, and was proceeding to make [herself] comfortable, when all of a sudden, [she] found it was in flames, and that it would be as much as [she] could do to get out unscathed." The problem is, the newspaper reported the fire was discovered at about 2 o'clock in the morning (another said 3:20 a.m.) and it was necessary to arouse the hotel guests.[3] So did Velazquez seek a room that late at night and did the front desk clerk rent her a room that late? And had she just gotten comfortable at 2 or 3 a. m.? Once the reader has read the upcoming 1866 newspaper reports of her claimed escape from steamboat *Miami's* explosion and burning, revisit this question and give an answer.

Velazquez explained that Southern forces burned the hotel because they became infuriated when they thought that the hotel proprietor had charged the Yankees one-third less for services when the Yankees had come through town. Velazquez sympathized with the owner and said that he had no choice but to host the Yankee occupiers or he would have been burned out, just as the Southerners did to him anyway. It was a fact that the Bowman House

---

3. *Times-Picayune*, Jun 21, 1863, from the *Advertiser's* Jackson correspondence of Jun 10; *Montgomery Daily Mail*, Jun 17, 1863, taken from the *Jackson Mississippian*.

was the only hotel left by the Yankees and newspapers reported it burned on June 10 by Southerners, just as Velazquez related.[4]

Recall that the *Mississippian* article of June 6 reported her presence in Jackson. Most likely the interview was done and the article prepared, at the least, the day before the article appeared. Using this reference date and that of the hotel burning, it may be thought Velazquez was in Jackson at least from June 5 to June 10, which is important for making the next point.

A seemingly firsthand sighting of Velazquez survives in history which must be examined. The famous English military officer, Lieutenant Colonel Arthur Lyon Fremantle of the Coldstream Guards, who made a trip through the South during the War to satisfy his military curiosity, was witness to a female soldier who ninety-one years later was suspected by editor Walter Lord of being Velazquez. In the published diary[5] of his travels Fremantle wrote:

5th June [1863] (Friday)... I left Chattanooga for Atlanta at 4:30 P.M. The train was much crowded with wounded and sick soldiers returning on leave to their homes. A goodish-looking woman was pointed out to me in the cars as having served as a private soldier in the battles of Perryville and Murfreesboro. Several men in my car had served with her in a Louisiana regiment, and they said she had been turned out a short time since for her bad and immoral conduct. They told me that her sex was notorious to all the regiment, but no notice had been taken of it so long as she conducted herself properly. They also said that she was not the only representative of the female sex in the ranks. When I saw her, she wore a soldier's hat and coat, but had resumed her petticoats.

Fremantle's diary was first published in 1863. It was later, in 1954, reprinted and edited, with abundant commentary by Walter Lord, and he titled the work *The Fremantle Diary*. About this diary passage, Walter Lord wrote (p282):

Fremantle's discovery may have been Madame Loreta Janeta Velasquez [*sic*], who posed as Lieutenant Harry T. Buford and served in a Louisiana regiment under Bragg about this time. Certainly, the time and place seem about right, and there couldn't have been too many girls fighting beside the Louisiana boys.

However, the time and place were not right since it has been shown that she was in Jackson and could not have been on the Chattanooga train *en route* to Atlanta at the date said. This was not Velazquez. It was another female seen by Fremantle. Besides, Velazquez never claimed to have been at the battles of Perryville or Murfreesboro, as this woman soldier was

---

4. *New York Times*, Jun 24 1863, date line Jackson, Wed, Jun 10.
5. Lieut.-Col. Fremantle, *Three Months in the Southern States: April-June 1863* (Edinburg and London: William Blackwood and Sons, 1863), 172-173; Ed. Walter Lord, *The Fremantle Diary*.... (Boston: Little, Brown and Co., 1954).

represented to have been. And besides, again, Velazquez asserted that she never exhibited "bad and immoral conduct."

1863, at the Battle House (Hotel) in Mobile, Alabama

After Velazquez left Jackson, Mississippi she traveled to Mobile, Alabama, 190 miles to the southeast. She wrote (*TWIB*, p346), "On arriving at Mobile, I took up my quarters at the Battle House, with the intention of taking a good rest, for I was weary with much travel...."

The Battle House was a fine hotel, and expensive, which raises the question of where Velazquez got money enough to stay there. She seemed not to have had any money while in New Orleans; at least, she acted as though she needed money when she stole from the Chesters for which she was jailed. And while in prison, it is unlikely that she got any significant money. Even if she possessed some items of value, she would have been commanded by military order, as a "registered enemy," to leave them behind in New Orleans.

So where did she get the money to stay at the Battle House? She probably elicited the sympathy of the citizens of Jackson, who would have understood her sacrifice of leaving behind all of her property, and they most likely gave her money to enable her to depart Jackson. A pattern of receiving money from sympathetic citizens is seen later in her life. For example, she wrote (p554) that a ship's officer, in 1867, passed the hat for her benefit. In another, she implied (p577) that in 1867, when she was traveling West, the people in Julesburg gave her money to enable her to continue her journey. In still another, in 1900 the newspaper reported that she was "aided by money furnished by sympathetic citizens" of Phoenix, Arizona which enabled her to leave that city.[6] Finally, it should be noted that she wasn't above running out on a hotel bill, either. In 1901 she sneaked away owing "three weeks of board" at the Palmetto Hotel in Tampa, Florida.[7] And there is a possibility that she failed to pay her bill at the Battle House, because (as will be seen) she was likely a guest there at the moment when Mobile's Provost Marshal arrested her and sent her to Richmond.

The Battle House "was a five-story brick building... with 240 sleeping and living rooms, gas fittings, baths, hot and cold water...." The furniture was shipped in from Boston and was "the best that money could buy." It opened to the public in November 1852 and well received. A traveler in 1853 said it was an "excellent hotel; but with higher charge than [he] had ever paid before." After the commencement of the war and with luxuries diminishing, a traveler reported (in 1862) "the absence of wine at the hotel

---

6. *Weekly Republican*, May 24, 1900.
7. *Morning Tribune* (Tampa), Feb 24, 1901.

tables."[8] One month prior to Velazquez's arrival, the aforementioned Sir Author James Lyon Fremantle arrived there and wrote in his diary that he paid eight dollars for a room.[9] Keeping in mind the elegance and expense of the hotel, it is commendable that Velazquez went from a prison cell to such a luxury hotel in the period of one month!

Many Confederate luminaries stayed at the Battle House, such as, President Jefferson Davis; Admiral Raphael Semmes; L. H. Hunley, inventor of submarine Hunley; and now alias Lieutenant Harry T. Buford.

On Friday, June 26, 1863 Velazquez registered at the Battle House, her name appearing clearly in the wonderfully and miraculously preserved *Hotel Register* as, "Lieut. H. Buford." In the space for "Occupation" was written "C.S.A." She was given room number 60. By Monday, a different guest is shown occupying that room.[10]

Unfortunately, her name in the *Register* appears not to be written by her own hand. It is not a good handwriting match with the "Harry T. Buford, C. S. A." signature presented in her memoir, as an autograph below her portrait on the illustration page between pages 60 and 61 or with the handwriting style found in her many known letters.

In the *Register*, the two names above her name, her name and the name below her name are all in the same handwriting. This leads one to conclude that either a clerk wrote their names or that one of the four registrants wrote all of their names when they checked-in. If all of the names were written by one of the registrants, which one was it?

Velazquez, because of the signature mismatch, has been dismissed as the writer in the *Register*. The two men above her signature were H. W. Virden from Canton, Mississippi and A. S. Coleman from Oakland, Mississippi and were likely together as they both were given room #117. Their military records show that they were privates. The name listed below that of "Lieut. H. Buford" was "Capt. —" from "Ponchatoula, Ala." and he was given room #81. This guest's entry presents several problems. First, Ponchatoula is not in Alabama, but is in Louisiana. Second, the man refused to write his surname. Refusal to enter a surname was not unprecedented; another guest, noticed elsewhere in the register, also did not supply a surname. Still, it is clear that "Capt. —" was acting mysteriously, not using his name and failing in a lie about from where he came. It is probable that "Capt. —" wrote the names of all four of the registrants since it would not have been fitting of the stations of privates to enter a captain and lieutenant in the register, even

---

8. James Frederick Sulzby Jr., *Historic Alabama Hotels & Resorts* (Tuscaloosa and London: Univ. of Alabama Press, 1960).
9. Fremantle, May 24, 1863, 7:15 p.m.
10. *The Battle House Guest Register 1863*, A. S. Williams III Americana Collection, Amelia Gayle Gorgas Library, University of Alabama, Tuscaloosa.

if the lieutenant was not a real lieutenant and maybe the captain wasn't a real captain, either.

Please see the Battle House guest register in Illustrations, Figure 7.

The "Lieut. H. Buford" of the hotel guest register was most surely Velazquez, using her alias and falsely claiming attachment to the C.S.A. because there was no possible true "Lieut. H. Buford" in the Confederate army. The well-regarded reference, *The Roster of Confederate Soldiers, 1861-1865*, Vol 3, by Janet B. Hewett, Broadfoot Publishing Co., reveals no possible "Lieut. H. Buford." The National Park Service's "Search for Soldiers" database identifies no Confederate Harry Buford, although some H. Bufords are found, none are possible matches. Also, the more complete form of her alias name, "Harry T. Buford," is not found in any index or list of soldiers. It should be remembered that on a previous occasion, in September 1861, Velazquez registered at another the hotel, in Lynchburg, Virginia, as "Lieut. Buford."

Applied for a Commission, Yes She Did!

While in Mobile, Velazquez applied for a military commission! Velazquez, in her memoir, never said she did this, but instead she substituted a claimed in-person request for a commission to Jefferson Davis. Velazquez took a commendable truth and debased it into a lie. In any case, Velazquez was most certainly ahead of her time in even thinking of requesting a commission and can be recognized for it.

The National Archives in Washington, D.C. preserves the following record:

> Williams, Mrs. Lauretta Tennett, June 25/[18]63 alias H. T. Buford Lt. C. S. A. Mobile, Ala., June 16/[18]63 Applies for a commission in Confederate Army.

The record book noted that her application letter was presented, "Presd," on July 10 and returned, "Retd," to her on August 4. It is almost beyond explanation that Velazquez applied for the commission using her female name, Mrs. Lauretta Tennett Williams, and included her alias, H. T. Buford Lt. C. S. A., but apparently this was the case! Since the record is an index book, it is not possible to see what the application said. Anyway, the Confederate authorities denied a commission to both personas, Mrs. Williams, and "H. T. Buford Lt. C. S. A."[11] Further along it will be seen that she wrote another letter to the Confederate Government and again stated boldly that she was a female using the "alias Lieut. H. T. Buford." Of course, these two examples fly in the face of her claimed secret disguise with which

---

11. NARA, War Department Collection of Confederate Records, ARC 6925795, Chapter 1, Vol 56, Register of Letters Received, Adjutant and Inspector General's Office, Apr-Jul 1863, M-Z, 04/1863-07/1863, entry #1145.

she fooled people time and again. It is clear she was not at all times trying to keep her male disguise a secret. Perhaps she never really tried ever.

An explanation for why Velazquez applied for the commission using her female name and included her male soldier alias, is that she was extremely optimistic, at best, or delusional, at worst.

First, notice that she applied for a commission using the rank of "Lt.," that is, lieutenant. She explained in her memoir that she did not earn this rank, but self-designated the rank. The issue of her rank is addressed in detail elsewhere.

Second, she seriously thought that the military was going to officially accept a female into its ranks- one sporting a self-appointed rank and male alias! It can only be surmised that Velazquez thought the Confederate military would be equally impressed with her as she was impressed with herself. She thought that her (alleged) loyalty to and sacrifice for the Confederate effort would be rewarded. She said as much on page 345 of *TWIB*. Before checking what she said on that page, it is necessary to review where she had been for the past year in order to make a point.

It is known that Velazquez was in New Orleans on April 23, 1862. The newspaper reported that she turned herself in at the mayor's office. After the Federal Army conquered the city, it was then that she claimed she ran in and out of the military lines at New Orleans. She was arrested in October and sentenced on November 1 to six months in the Parish Prison. Once released from prison she left New Orleans on May 17, 1863, went to Jackson, Mississippi and her presence reported there on June 6. She then turned up at Mobile's Battle House on June 26, 1863. In summary, she was in New Orleans for the period of a year and when she went outside of New Orleans, please note, that she was nowhere near Richmond.

Now back to page 345 of *TWIB*, Velazquez stated she went to Richmond right before she went to Mobile where she stayed at the Battle House. As just explained, the facts of the time do not support her claim to have gone to Richmond. If she did not go to Richmond, then what she wrote she did while there must be considered untrue. However, what she claimed she did is instructive and is the point which is in the making. She asserted she interviewed with Confederate States President Jefferson Davis:

> I represented to President Davis that I had been working hard for the Confederacy, both as a soldier and a spy, and that I had braved death on more than one desperately fought battle-field while acting as an independent, and that now I thought I was deserving of some official recognition. Moreover, I had lost my husband through his devotion to the cause, and, both for his sake and for my own, I desired that the government would give me such a position in the secret service corps or elsewhere as would enable me to carry on with the best effect the work that he and I had begun.

Mr. Davis was opposed to permitting me to serve in the army as an officer, attired in male costume, while he had no duties to which he could properly assign me as a woman. I left his presence, not ungratified by the kindness of his manner towards me, and the sympathy which he expressed for my bereavement, but none the less much disappointed at the non-success of my interview with him.

If it was true that Velazquez met President Davis in order to ask for a commission, just prior to going to Mobile, then why did she apply for a commission once she arrived in Mobile? The simple answer is that she invented the interview which probably represented her feelings at the time she applied for a commission. She probably believed the things about herself she pretended to tell President Davis. Velazquez was simply endowed with an unrestrained imagination and a huge self-confidence to do as she pleased, and if reality did not match her imagination or deeds, she just invented it.

It might be noted that, if in truth the conversation occurred, which it did not, she would have been lying to President Davis' face when she said "I had lost my husband through his devotion to the cause." This false claim even succeeded in getting "sympathy" for her "bereavement" from Davis. The husband to whom she referred she made clear was Captain Thomas C. DeCaulp. In truth, he did not die for the Southern cause as she claimed in her memoir, but instead deserted the Confederate army and then joined the Yankee army. Even more disjointed is the fact that she did not, in truth, marry DeCaulp until three months after her visit to the Battle House in Mobile, and therefore, also after the alleged meeting with President Davis.

There was more lying going on than just to President Davis. Velazquez hid her arrest for stealing, and subsequent prison time, from her readers by claiming that she, instead, made the trip to Richmond. Since the trip would not have covered all the time of her prison sentence, she filled in the time by claiming she went "On Another Grand Tour" of the South on her way to Mobile in order to collect information which might be useful in her spy endeavors. This claimed "grand tour of the entire Southern Confederacy" is just not believable, especially since she glosses over the trip, not even bothering to recount one incident which might have been of interest. In summary, she did not go to Richmond, she did not meet President Davis and she did not make a grand tour of anything- she was in jail.

Another Confederate register[12] also recorded Velazquez's same application for a commission. Entered is the request of "Buford, H. T." for a commission on Monday, July 27, 1863. The adjacent column was left blank and fails to show the disposition of the request letter.

From both the Confederate registers it can be understood that the date of Velazquez's application letter was June 16, 1863, sent from Mobile,

---

12. NARA, Confederate Records, Chapter 9, Vol 90, Applications in Military Service, Confederate States.

Alabama. The letter was received by officials on June 25. The request was presented or considered on July 15 and recorded in the Applications index on July 27. The application was denied and her request letter returned to her on August 4. It is clear that Velazquez was in Mobile on June 26, when she registered at the Battle House as "Lieut. H. Buford," but can Velazquez be placed in Mobile on June 16 when she sent her application letter?

The Battle House guest register for Monday, June 16, contains the signature of one "Mrs. Capt. Williams." She was given room #20. No companions are indicated in the register. The registrant's handwriting cannot be determined to be that of Velazquez, but this might have been Velazquez. Recall that she had assumed her husband's surname, Williams of the 13th Connecticut Regiment, in New Orleans. She used the name "Mrs. Laura J. Williams" in Jackson, Mississippi on June 6 and had by then been using the Williams surname for eight months. In her June 16 letter for an "Application for a Commission," she applied under the name of Mrs. Lauretta Tennett Williams. If she called herself in the guest register at this time "Mrs. Capt. Williams," it certainly would have matched her propensity (as will be seen) to attach a rank to her name, whether she considered the rank her own or that of her husband, even if she had to inflate his rank.

If "Mrs. Capt. Williams" of the guest register, who was in Mobile on June 16, was Velazquez, and it was on this date that the "Confederate Records" placed Velazquez there, what should be thought of the aforementioned and seemingly contradictory newspaper article by "Special Correspondence of *Memphis Appeal*" which by letter dated "Jackson, June 24th, 1863," placed Velazquez in Jackson "this morning" on the 24th? Recall, "There is this morning on the streets a *rara avis*, a well made, but not pretty, Confederate lieutenant, of the *genus famina*, with a very perceptible strut...."

The answer is that it is an error to infer that she had been in Jackson continuously since June 6 when she was first written-up and only appeared in Mobile on June 26 at the Battle House as "Lieut. H. Buford." She explained in her memoir that she did not stay in Jackson continuously and it should probably be believed somewhat.

Velazquez narrated (*TWIB*, p271) that after arriving in Jackson, she left for Hazlehurst, Mississippi (about 30 miles south), once again figuring as Lieutenant Harry T. Buford. She said, there she was given a message to be taken to Port Hudson, Louisiana (about 115 miles southwest), but was met in Clinton, Louisiana, (about 24 miles shy of Port Hudson) by a special courier and turned back to Jackson.

Then once again in Jackson, Lieutenant Harry T. Buford learned that her lost slave boy Bob was in Grenada (about 114 miles north) so she proceeded there and returned with him. She then decided to speed her way to Richmond. Of course, it is clear that she did not go to Richmond then, as she narrated- but she did go there, instead, under arrest from Mobile (addressed shortly). Also, any claimed trip which involved her slave boy Bob, must be doubted. Common sense does not allow one to believe she ever owned a slave boy named Bob simply because of the unbelievable claimed events surrounding him. For example, she explained that he by accident took the wrong road and "had gone plump into a Federal camp... but not liking the company he found there, had slipped away at the earliest opportunity, and had wandered about in a rather aimless manner for some time, seeking [her] out." It is just not believable that Bob obtained his freedom through the Yankee lines, but then willingly returned to slavery, and no less looking for her, when at this time countless runaway slaves eagerly sought the Yankee lines and freedom. Near the end of the book in hand, facts and logic will show that Velazquez's slave Bob was surely a fabrication.

In any case, Velazquez's narrative is instructive because she claimed that she was not continuously in Jackson during the time in question, coming and going, so it is possible that she might have gone to Mobile twice in June.

If one accepts that "Mrs. Capt. Williams" of the guest register was Velazquez, then one might speculate that she first came to Mobile as "Mrs. Capt. Williams." As a result of her incarceration in New Orleans, her exile from there, and then her travel to Jackson and Mobile, she no longer had presentable male attire, so wore female attire. She needed time to reorganize her male attire. Upon her arrival at the Mobile hotel, she wrote on June 16 her request for a military commission and sent it to Richmond. She stayed in the room less than a week, maybe trying to organize her attire and left that room on June 22 or earlier. At least, on that date, the guest register shows room #20 occupied by a new party. Velazquez went back to Jackson where she was noted on June 24 as the *"rara avis...* Confederate lieutenant, of the *genus famina."* When she returned to Mobile, she was ready to register at the hotel on June 26 as "Lieut. H. Buford, C. S. A.," which she did. Maybe future research will validate or invalidate this speculation.

There can be no doubt that Velazquez applied for a commission in the Confederate army, military records make this clear. Interestingly, this record contains a bit of information which may prove of value in determining her true identity, the middle name, "Tennett." It may be suspected that "Tennett" is associated with the "T" of her alias, Harry T. Buford. To date "Tennett" has not led to a useful next step, but further research on it could be revealing. It should be noted that researchers/authors of a 2002 book[13] read the name as "Fennett." The name can be clearly determined not "Fennett," when one studies the entire page of the document for writing

---

13. DeAnne Blanton and Lauren M. Cook, *They Fought Like Demons*, (Baton Rouge: Louisiana State University Press, 2002), 69.

similarity. There are both capital "Ts" and "Fs" found in the document and they are plainly distinguishable. The name written is "Tennett."

Arrested in Mobile, Taken to Richmond

Velazquez's visit to Mobile was cut short when she was arrested by the city's Provost Marshal. It is unclear if she was in male disguise and was discovered, or if she simply assumed the garb of a soldier without worrying about whether anyone understood she was a woman. It seems that she wasn't particular about keeping her alias Lieutenant H. Buford, or her sex, a secret, evident by her application for a commission in which she clearly identified herself both as Mrs. Williams and Lieutenant Buford.

She was taken to Richmond and it will be seen, that along the way, she visited Selma, Montgomery and Atlanta and got noticed. She arrived in Richmond about July 1 and was imprisoned in Castle Thunder. The *Daily Richmond Examiner* of July 2, 1863 reported:

A FEMALE LIEUTENANT. - Recently a glowing account of a female, in Confederate uniform, went the rounds of the Southern press. She was a second Joan of Arc, and had done, and was to do more remarkable things. Yesterday the hero or heroine, whichever you please, was received in this city from the Provost Marshal of Mobile, and lodged in Castle Thunder. She bears her assumed name, Lieutenant Benford, and persists in wearing the uniform of an officer of that rank. We did not understand that any charge, except that of unsexing herself, is alleged against her.

This report contradicts Velazquez's memoir- what she claimed she did and where she claimed she traveled.

Recall, Velazquez claimed that she went to Richmond to seek a commission from President Davis and that he would not give her one and she had to be satisfied with a "letter of recommendation" from General Winder. It has been shown that this claimed meeting was pure fantasy and that at the time she was in a New Orleans jail for stealing. She claimed it was after her meeting with President Davis that she went to Mobile. However, the truth is that it was after her release from the New Orleans jail that she traveled to Jackson, then to Mobile.

In her memoir Velazquez narrated (p348) how shortly after her arrival in Mobile she received a mysterious note asking for a secret meeting. She was at first reluctant, but not fearful, to meet the stranger and thought it might be a request for her to "undertake some such enterprise as [she] for a long time had been ardently desirous of engaging in," noting that she was "traveling under credentials from General Winder, and was in a manner an attaché of the Secret Service Department." It is impressive that after ten paragraphs, Velazquez elevated her "letter of recommendation" to having attained the position of "in a manner an attaché." In any case, it has been shown that she was not in Richmond at the time she claimed she received the "letter of recommendation." As it will be seen shortly, she did meet General Winder upon this Castle Thunder incarceration.

According to her narrative, upon arriving at the secret meeting spot in a Mobile square, the mysterious correspondent revealed himself to be "Lieutenant Shorter of Arkansas," working in the secret service. In order to make a point momentarily, it is noted now, that no Confederate army records are found for "Lieutenant Shorter of Arkansas." He asked her to carry a dispatch through the military lines. She agreed to try and they set another rendezvous in Meridian, Mississippi. The next day she traveled to Meridian where Lieutenant Shorter met her at the train depot and escorted her to "the hotel kept by a Mr. Jones, and was received with great cordiality from him and by his wife." Mr. Jones was, no doubt, "W. H. Jones, Inn Keeper," and his wife was Mary A., as noted in the 1860 Census for Meridian.[14] It can be sure that Velazquez was familiar with Mr. Jones and Meridian, Mississippi. Most of the time when Velazquez narrated about lodging she took, and incidental people, she was accurate, indicating her correct knowledge because she was there- though maybe not at the time or under the circumstances which she asserted, but she was there at some time.

The point of contention in the making is that whenever she narrated about people that mattered, in particular comrade-in-arms who might have supported her claims of military deeds, or better yet, battlefield deeds, she provided names which fail to be verified by military records or she gave incomplete names by which she never intended that a reader would know of whom she wrote. Velazquez named the significant Lieutenant Shorter who fails to be found in historical records and then two pages later she named insignificant Mr. Jones, the innkeeper, who is easily found in historical records. In the same vein, please recall the aforementioned Lieutenant Philip Hastings about whom Velazquez provided much, but surely false information, and who is not found in military records. And it will be seen that Velazquez wrote (p378) that while in Memphis she asked a "Lieutenant B. of Arkansas" for news of her brother, "Captain——." What purpose would it serve to shield her own brother's name or the officer who gave her news of him except to elude verification? Both men were significant and might have added credence to her narrative, yet she refused to provide their correct names. She does this repeatedly; watch for the Confederate "General F" incident to be addressed shortly.

Lieutenant Shorter asked her to carry a fake report of Confederate movements to Union General Washburn and a real dispatch for Confederate General Forrest, to be given to his "Confederate secret agent in Memphis." Lieutenant Shorter then gave her $136 in Union money for travel. She next took the train to Okolona, Mississippi where she met

---

14. U.S. Census 1860, Mississippi, Lauderdale County, Beat No. 3, p98.

Confederate General Ferguson and received additional instructions and a pistol, but he advised her not to take the pistol into the Federal lines as the Yankees would construe her to be a spy. He gave her an additional $90. She was provided an escort to "conduct [her] to a point somewhere to the northeast of Holly Springs, from whence [she] would have to make [her] way alone, getting into the Federal lines as best [she] could."

She and the escort rode "all that night and nearly all the next day through lonesome woods, past desolate clearings, - all occupied, if at all, by poor negroes, or even poorer whites." They finally rested at a "negro's cabin" where they paid for "coarse quality food" and a "miserable bed." The next morning her Confederate escort left to return to his company and the "old negro" led the way to the Federal military lines. Upon seeing a country church and knowing they were near the lines, Velazquez paid her guide and warned him to skedaddle or Yankee soldiers would catch him and "give [him] to the abolitionists." Velazquez narrated:

> I said this in a very severe way, and it evidently made an impression on the darkey, who probably thought the abolitionists were cannibals, who would proceed to use him as a substitute for beef. He opened his eyes as big as saucers, and his teeth chattered so that he could scarcely say, 'Good-by, miss,' as he darted off, clutching the ten-dollar Confederate bill that I had handed him in payment for his services.

In rebuttal, records show that, at this date, any slave who could find his way to the Federal lines did so and runaway slaves came in droves. The Federal Army provided food and employment for the runaways and it is not believable that the "old negro" scurried back to the safety of an existence of hunger and bondage. In addition, it is highly unlikely that the "old negro" did not know what an abolitionist was, since the country had been killing one another for the past two years over that word. Solomon Northup, the free New York black man, who was kidnapped into slavery in 1841 and who subsequently told of his ordeal in his 1853 autobiography, *Twelve Years a Slave*, wrote (p158), "... ninety-nine out of every hundred [slaves] are intelligent enough to understand their situation and to cherish in their bosoms the love of freedom...."

After the old man had left her, Velazquez entered the country church and "raised a plank in the flooring" and concealed her pistol. She then contemplated the appropriateness of using the "settled plan" Lieutenant Shorter had advised her to use to conceal her true self. She wrote (p355):

> Experience had taught me, however, that no settled plan, in a matter of this kind, amounts to much, so far as the details are concerned, and that it is necessary to be governed by circumstance. I resolved, therefore, to regulate my conduct and conversation according to the character and behavior of those I chanced to meet....

In cryptic fashion Velazquez revealed a *modus operandi* which will be evident as her life's story is revealed; tell your listener what you think they might believe. Similarly, when Velazquez later went to Washington, D.C., she claimed (p 394) she met a general (unnamed) to whom she "had a plausible story ready to tell him, in which fact and fiction were mingled with some degree of skill...." Of course, Velazquez intended her readers to understand how clever she was at making up her life's story to fool the Yankees, but ultimately it will be clear she was fooling her readers as well.

Mounted on horseback, Velazquez departed the church and proceeded about two miles where she encountered a Federal sentry. She informed the soldier that she wanted to go to Memphis to give "some papers" to General Washburn. He asked, "Where are you from, Madam?" and she replied, "I am from Holly Springs."

Velazquez's claim to be from Holly Springs, Mississippi was meant to be understood by her reader that she was telling a lie to the sentry. The reader had already been told in detail how she was born in Havana and raised in New Orleans. However, as it will be seen, she made statements of personal connections with people from Holly Springs and Mississippi in general, more often than any from Havana or New Orleans where she claimed she was a school girl. She told the Richmond *Examiner* of July 11, 1863 that her father was "Major J. B. Roche of Mississippi." This newspaper article follows shortly. Recall, Velazquez offhandedly claimed (*TWIB*, p117) she knew General Featherston when she was a "small child." Indeed, Winfield S. Featherston was a prominent citizen of Holly Springs during the years when she would have been a child. This connection to Holly Springs will be addressed some more.

Velazquez narrated that she was then escorted by a soldier to Moscow, Tennessee where a Union colonel tried to trip her up on her cover story, but she kept her composure and insisted on seeing General Washburn in Memphis in order to give him the dispatch and "to tell him alone certain things." She was then taken to Memphis by a young naive lieutenant who spoke too freely of Yankee army movements, providing useful information for her spying activity.

It is clear from her narrative that Velazquez, at some time in her life, had traversed the ground, from Mobile to Meridian to Okolona to Holly Springs to Moscow to Memphis because she knew it well. She also wrote, "It is scarcely necessary to say that I was well acquainted with Memphis...." She no doubt intended that the reader recall that she was acquainted with the city because she had previously told of her adventures in its saloons while wearing male attire, under the watchful eyes of her accompanying husband. However, the odds are that she knew Memphis well because it was the nearest large city to Holly Springs, Mississippi where she likely had lived. It is clear that she had firsthand knowledge of the Memphis area, evident by the fact that she used the small community of Hulbert Station, Arkansas, a mere eight miles away from Memphis and across the Mississippi River, as the location where she claimed she raised a battalion of Rebel soldiers. And she had claimed Memphis as her home at the time of her 1861 Richmond arrest when she identified herself as Mrs. Mary Ann Keith.

Upon her arrival in Memphis, Velazquez immediately insisted on being taken to Union General Washburn's headquarters and the young lieutenant, whose confidence Velazquez had gained through her flirtation during their travel, happily complied. At headquarters Velazquez was not allowed to see General Washburn as he was indisposed. The Provost Marshal insisted that she hand the message to him and he would see that General Washburn received it or come back later when the General could see her. After some reflection, Velazquez said she wrote a note to accompany the bogus intelligence message and left both with the Provost Marshal and then departed. She, still escorted by the young lieutenant, went to the Hardwick House (hotel) and registered as Mrs. Fowler. Of course, Velazquez, with great correctness, named another hotel in another city which indicates her firsthand knowledge.[15]

After dark, she, being "well acquainted with Memphis," sought out and met secretly with the Confederate agent and delivered the authentic dispatch intended for General Nathan Bedford Forrest. The agent said he believed a Federal troop movement was imminent and asked Velazquez to learn more; he could wait no more than two days for her to find out before departing to find Forrest. Velazquez claimed within the two days she learned from Federal officers, and others who called on her, that the Union army was strengthening their force at Collierville (30 miles east of Memphis), news which she passed to the Confederate agent and he "started for Forrest's headquarters without more delay." Velazquez wrote (p374):

The concentration of the Federal force at Colliersville [sic Collierville], I had every reason to believe, was induced by the dispatch I delivered to General Washburn. At any rate, it had the effect of leaving a gap in the Federal line beyond Grand Junction for Forrest to step through; and, when in a day or two, intelligence was received that he was on a grand raid through Western Tennessee, I knew that the plot in which I had been engaged had succeeded in the best manner.

I made a great to-do when the news of Forrest's raid was received, and pretended to be frightened lest an attack should be made on Memphis, and the rebels should capture me. The fact is, that Forrest, before he got through, did come very near the city, and some of my new acquaintances were just as much frightened in reality as I pretended to be. He, however, did not make any demonstration in the

---

15. The hotel was operated at #65 Adams Street from April 1863 to 1868 when it changed its name to Central House.

city, but after a brilliant campaign of several weeks slipped by the Federals again, carrying back with him into Mississippi sufficient cattle and other booty to amply repay him for his trouble.

I thought that I had reason to congratulate myself upon the success of the enterprise in which I had been engaged. Taking it altogether, it was as well planned and as well executed a performance as any I ever attempted during the whole of my career in the Confederate service.

There arises a serious conflict between the truth of the calendar and Velazquez's narrative of Forrest's activities. Recall that Velazquez was in Mobile on June 26. When she was arrested in Mobile, she was taken to Richmond appearing there on July 1. She was committed to Castle Thunder Prison under suspicion of being a "Yankee spy" and was subsequently released no later than July 10, as will be momentarily made clear. Velazquez's claim that she left Mobile, went to Holly Springs and then crossed military lines and went to Memphis was not true. She instead was arrested in Mobile and taken to Richmond under guard!

In addition, at the end of June 1863, the time frame when Velazquez places herself in Memphis, General Forrest was nowhere near Grand Junction, Tennessee, but instead was some 200 miles east fighting (all the while retreating) against Union General Rosecrans' forces near Shelbyville and Tullahoma, Tennessee.[16] Forrest's infamous raid into West Tennessee, to which Velazquez must have been referring, did not happen until December 1, 1863 and the expedition took the entire month.

Is it possible that Velazquez altered events in her life causing them to not match the known calendar of events, and therefore making her appear to be lying about her contribution to General Forrest's successful raid? Research shows that after she was released from Castle Thunder she went to Atlanta where she was married about the first week of September. She then returned to Richmond where she was noticed by the newspaper on September 16. But was she indeed in Memphis just prior to General Forrest's raid? Some evidence suggests that she was there in October 1863, after her September visit to Richmond. This information comes from a letter she wrote, much later, on July 27, 1864 in Nashville, where she wrote asking to be released from yet another jail. In that letter she claimed that she had arrived in "Memphis last October."

Even if she was in Memphis in October, that was too early of a date for any provided military information to be used by General Forrest on his December 1 raid, as military intelligence turns stale quickly. Recall, Velazquez claimed that within "a day or two" after she delivered the

---

16. John Allen Wyeth, *Life of Lieutenant-General Nathan Bedford Forrest* (NY and London: Harper & Brothers, 1908), 233; Jack Hurst, *Nathan Bedford Forrest, A Biography* (NY: Vintage Books, 1994), 130.

intelligence to General Forrest, General Forrest acted. Other evidence shows that Velazquez was nowhere near Memphis at the time of General Forrest's raid. By November 15, 1863, Mrs. Alice Williams (Velazquez?) was in Baltimore, according to Federal military records, and had signed on as a Union spy. Still more certain is Velazquez is documented on the payroll of the Indianapolis Indiana Arsenal in November 1863. If Velazquez was (maybe) in Baltimore on November 15 and was positively in Indianapolis in November, then she would have been in no position to supply intelligence related to West Tennessee to General Forrest. No matter how one slices Velazquez's claim- to have carried dispatches to Forrest which directly resulted in his successful raid- no truth can be found in it.

In her memoir, Velazquez wrote (p375) that while in (Federal controlled) Memphis she spotted a Confederate officer, "Lieutenant B. of Arkansas," out of uniform "who belonged to [her] brother's command." Exactly how she would have known anyone in her brother's military unit is unclear, especially if the reader is to construe that the unit was from Arkansas. Why would Velazquez's Spanish/Cuban brother be in an Arkansas military unit? Velazquez failed to make herself any more believable when she wrote (p379), "I had not seen him [her brother] for a number of years, and, as the reader will remember, had only learned of his being in the Confederate army some little time before my second marriage." It is clear that she had not been in touch with her brother, so how could she know his associations?

In any case, then Velazquez cleverly and secretly made arrangements to meet Lieutenant B who told her that her brother, "Captain—," was in Camp Chase Federal prison in Columbus, Ohio. Why did Velazquez again hide the identity of another soldier, Lieutenant B., when if she had stated his name in full, it would have been a proper and deserving thank you for his unselfish help in locating her poor brother, "Captain—," whose identity was also kept hidden and who would have probably appreciated some thanks for his service and sacrifice to the Cause? Hmm?

It seems as early as page 141 in her memoir she had already told her readers her brother was a prisoner unless she was just testing "General Wessells, the Commissary General of Prisoners," with invented information. She wrote, "On the impulse of the moment, and just for the sake of feeling my ground with him, I said, in a careless sort of way, during our conversation, that I had a brother who was a prisoner, and whom I would like to see, if it could be permitted, notwithstanding that he was on the wrong side." Of course, it has been shown that it was a blatant lie that General Wessells was at this time Commissary General of Prisoners or that he was then in Washington, D.C.

This news about her brother in Camp Chase Prison, she claimed, changed her plans to return to Mobile. Now she desired to go North to her brother and gain his release. With the assistance of the Federal lieutenant who was still infatuated with her, she procured "a pass and transportation from General Washburn." She departed Memphis and "pushed forward as rapidly as [she] could, and made no stoppage of any moment until [she] reached Louisville, Kentucky, where [she] took a room at the Galt House...." Once again, she identified another of her many hotel stays, correctly naming the Galt House this time.[17]

Velazquez departed Louisville and traveled to Columbus, Ohio, and upon her arrival booked a room at the Neil House. Yes, the Neil House also existed, in its second version, the original hotel having burned down in November 1860.

Even though Velazquez convincingly narrated her northern progress, it is not true that at this claimed time she went North, instead she went later. The following reports show her still in the South and arrested in Mobile and taken to Richmond.

The *Richmond Enquirer* of July 2, 1863 noted Velazquez's arrival in Richmond:

A SUPPOSED FEMALE SPY IN MALE ATTIRE. On yesterday morning, a young gentleman, in appearance, rigged out in a new Confederate uniform, was brought before General Winder. He had just arrived from Mobile, and was known on the hotel register as Lieutenant Bensford, C. S. A. An investigation into the suspicious character of the young man, revealed the little circumstance that he was sailing under false colors- the rank, title and habiliments of a man- where, in fact, "he" was a woman. The secret being thus being discovered, the she Lieutenant, who, by the way, was not quite as pretty as the romance of her case might admit, informed the General that her name was Mrs. Alice Williams, that she had a husband in the Federal army, but was herself true to the South. Upon being informed that she would have to be imprisoned, she said, with an independent air, if that was tried she would "claim foreign protection, being a British subject, and bound by no laws to be arrested as a prisoner by the Confederate authorities." It was quite evident that there was something wrong about her and she was sent to prison, where she will find ample time to cogitate upon her new idea of international law, and the folly of trying to wear breeches in a sphere where even Bellona [Roman goddess of war] wears petticoats.

This dashing Lieutenant passes for the same valiant Joan, who, under the name of Lieutenant Bensford, is represented to have fought so heroically in several battles in the Southwest, an account of which appeared in the papers some time ago.[18] The

---

17. The hotel, located at First and Main Streets, burned in 1865; today the luxury hotel exists in its fourth version, located a block from its original location. - www.galthouse.com.
18. The Southwest at that date was basically along the southern portion of the Mississippi River, for example, West Tennessee, and not the Southwest of today, that is New Mexico, Arizona, etc. The Western battle theater was the area between the Mississippi River and Appalachian Mountains which included Tennessee, Kentucky and most of the three states

identity is by no means improbable, the lady being evidently a "whole team," and not of the build to be frightened greatly by either gun or goblin.

Velazquez was noted to be "rigged out in a new Confederate uniform" which must have been one she acquired either in Jackson or Mobile or someplace in-between. She most certainly did not have it with her in the New Orleans jail and then carried it across the military lines with her. Her noted new uniform seems to support the speculation that Velazquez first appeared in Mobile as "Mrs. Capt. Williams" without the benefit of a uniform which she had not yet acquired. Once she located a new uniform, she was again Lieutenant Buford.

Recall that Velazquez wrote she used a claim of British citizenship to get out of the New Orleans jail and she explained how she used a false British passport to achieve the deception. She also claimed that her New Orleans incarceration was brief because the British Consul got her out; the truth was, she was jailed for six months for stealing and received no help related to any claim of British citizenship. However, it cannot be denied that Velazquez was bold when she challenged the Richmond Confederate authorities with a defense of "being a British subject." In her memoir, she narrated nothing about her "British citizenship" getting her out of Castle Thunder Prison.

In any case, her claim to British citizenship had nothing to do with her release from Castle Thunder. On July 11 the Richmond *Enquirer* told of the "DISCHARGE OF THE FAIR LIEUTENANT":

We are pleased to learn that Lieut. Buford (otherwise Mrs. Alice Williams,) who has performed such valuable service to the South, in the character, both of nurse and soldier, has been discharged from custody and will proceed as early as possible to the field again. This young woman was arrested because she appeared in officer's attire, and was incarcerated in Castle Thunder until her identity with the distinguished female Lieutenant could be established. It is now fully confirmed, and it is but just to her to say that she appears to be all her published history represents her to be- a woman of heroic character, fearing no danger, dreading no trial, shunning no duty that her self-chosen fortune may send her. May she live long to enjoy her fame.

The article is revealing in several of ways.

First, Velazquez now used the name "Mrs. Alice Williams" although "Alice" might have been the newspaper's mistake for Ann or Anne. In New Orleans she called herself "Anne Williams... wife of a soldier named Williams," and in Jackson, she called herself "Mrs. Laura J. Williams."

Second, Velazquez informed the newspapers that her *nom de guerre* was Lieutenant Buford. Recall, that prior to her registration as "Lieut. H.

---

of Alabama, Mississippi and Louisiana. The referenced account about her in the Southwest probably came from the *Mississippian's* report.

Buford" at the Battle House hotel, Velazquez provided a version of her life to the Jackson, Mississippi newspaper (June 6), which called her "Henry Benford." The Benford name was likely a typesetter's error reading the reporters handwriting. In any case, now the Richmond newspapers of July 1863 wrote that Velazquez was on the "hotel register as Lieutenant Bensford," and also "Benford." The hotel register referred to was not a Richmond hotel register, but was the register of the Battle House in Mobile. Since it is certain that the Richmond newspaper reporters did not see firsthand the name Buford under which she had registered in Mobile, it might be assumed the newspaper was following the *Mississippian's* lead. Or Velazquez herself told the newspapers her Benford/Bensford *nom de guerre*. Maybe during this period Velazquez was simply undecided which *nom de guerre* she liked best. After her Castle Thunder imprisonment, she was always Buford.

Third, the newspaper claimed that she did the duty of a nurse, which Velazquez never claimed in her memoir and only claimed once much later in 1908 to a newspaper, as will been seen.

Fourth, just what did the reporter do to confirm her "identity" or her "published history" or her claimed deeds? There would not have been much that the Richmond newspaper could have discovered about her. It can be certain that Velazquez herself presented a copy of the flattering June 6, 1863 *Mississippian* article to the Richmond newspaper and to the local authorities as her identification. In addition, Velazquez surely spoke persuasively in her own behalf and the *Enquirer* reporter was charmed and convinced, and reported accordingly.

The Richmond *Examiner* of July 11, 1863 was clearly more dedicated to gathering facts about Buford and presented the article, "THE FEMALE LIEUTENANT." Of course, the reporter could not have known more than what Velazquez told him:

"Lieutenant Buford," the female Lieutenant from the South, arrested in this city, and sent to Castle Thunder, has been released by General Winder. The charge of being a Yankee spy was never alleged against her, and she is indignant that such a thing was ever intimated. She persists in sporting her military costume, and it was this that got her into trouble with the Richmond authorities.- Her real name is Mrs. S. T. Williams, and her husband is a 1st Lieutenant in company E, 13th Connecticut regiment, under Banks in Louisiana. Her father is Major J. B. Roche, of Mississippi, but she was born in the West Indies. Her people were wealthy, and her annual income before the war was $20,000, most of which she spent in getting medicines for the Confederate Government. Her penchant was to follow the army in a private ambulance with medicines, bandages and servant, and apply herself to the relief of the wounded, though she has been known to lend a helping hand with the musket at several battles in which she participated.

It is most curious that Velazquez, for the moment, minimized her soldier/battle claims and offered an alternate and impressive version of herself as a nurse. In her memoir, she never claimed to do the duty of a nurse; she also never claimed to have spent $20,000 ($765,000 in year 2023) of her money for medicines for the Confederate Government. Instead, she wrote that she had eighty-eight thousand dollars (more than $3.3 million in year 2023) of her own money which she intended to use to raise a battalion of men at Hulbert Station, Arkansas. By the end of this book, it will be clear she did not spend her own money to raise a battalion, because she did not raise a battalion, and she did not spend $20,000 of her own money to buy medicines for the Confederate Government. These claims were false.

Velazquez had already called herself Alice Williams upon her arrival in Richmond and now called herself Mrs. S. T. Williams. One might assume that "S. T." referred to the first and middle names of her "husband," Williams of Company E, 13th Connecticut regiment. However, a Williams with those initials did not exist in Company E, 13th Connecticut. Recall, that either Charles E. Williams or Henry Williams has been identified as the most likely candidate for her husband. It is possible that "S. T." initials were her first name, "S" and her maiden name, "T." Recall she called herself "Tennett" when she applied for a commission as "Williams, Mrs. Lauretta Tennett." The "T" of her alias, Harry T. Buford, might have the same connection.

On July 15 the Richmond *Enquirer* wrote:

LIEUT. BUFORD.- The female Lieutenant who has created such a sensation lately, has received an appointment as clerk at Castle Thunder. She longs for the wars, however, and will not be content to hold it long.

Mrs. Alice Williams was released from Castle Thunder and the Richmond *Sentinel* (July 16, 1863) reported:

Lieut. Buford, otherwise known as Mrs. Alice Williams, who was committed to Castle Thunder some weeks ago, for dressing in male apparel, is to be sent South this morning, to Atlanta, Ga.- The history of this female lieutenant is full of romantic interest. Report says that she participated in the battles of Kentucky and Mississippi, and at Shiloh received a dangerous wound. Her husband, it is said, is in the federal army, but she, with true Southern feelings, sympathizes with our cause, and illustrates her sympathy in a practical way. She is brave, but eccentric, and certainly has an ambition to distinguish herself in the sphere allotted to man. If she is allowed the opportunity, she will doubtless take a hand in the fight at Jackson, Miss.

At least, Velazquez was back to making battle claims, but she forgot to claim battles in Virginia- recall, the Battle of Bull Run and the Battle of Ball's Bluff?

Velazquez's persistent claim to be married to a soldier in the federal army, this being Williams of the 13th Connecticut, lends credence that she may have indeed married Williams in New Orleans, even though research failed to confirm this marriage. Maybe she felt a fond enough attachment to persist in her claim or maybe she felt it safer to represent herself as married.

The *Daily Richmond Examiner*[19] shed some light on her treatment while in prison, "[she] quite took the Castle before she left. She got acquainted with everybody, ordered everybody about, and by her bustling manner and busy ways threw the commandant quite in the shade." Velazquez wrote (*TWIB*, p278) of her kind treatment by the prison's commander and his wife and declared her arrest was the best thing that could have happened to her.

Another local newspaper[20] noted Velazquez's release from Castle Thunder and speculated, "It is hardly probable that this brave but eccentric woman will be kept out of the fights in Mississippi." A Selma, Alabama newspaper[21] remembered "Mrs. Alice Williams" when it saw the Richmond newspapers and noted:

> This far-famed female soldier who passed through this place *en route* to Richmond a few weeks ago, under arrest for appearing in officer's attire, has been released from Castle Thunder, and will again proceed to active service in the field. She has already been in the service a great while, and is represented to be a woman of heroic character, fearing no danger and shrinking from no undertaking. She was first commissioned as a Lieutenant, and served several months before her sex was suspected. When arrested and brought to trial she only had to prove her identity to secure her release.

The Augusta, Georgia *Daily Constitutionalist* of July 18, 1863 also noted that she had "passed through Atlanta en route to Richmond a few weeks ago." It seems that Velazquez, upon arrest in Mobile and escort to Richmond, transited Selma, then Montgomery and then Atlanta on the way to Richmond which is still further confirmation that she did not go to Meridian, then Holly Springs and then Memphis, as a secret courier, in the time frame she claimed.

Velazquez addressed her arrest in Richmond and confinement in Confederate Castle Thunder in Chapter 23 of her book in which she told she "was arrested on the charge of being a woman in disguise, and supposedly a Federal spy" and held "until [she] could give a satisfactory account of [herself]." Velazquez explained "it compelled [her] to reveal [her]self" to the "commander of Castle Thunder, Major G. W. Alexander," and "his lovely wife" who became sympathetic to her and took an interest in her. Velazquez said, "they treated me with such kindness and

---

19. Jul 16, 1863.
20. *Daily Dispatch* (Richmond), Jul 16, 1863.
21. *Morning Reporter,* Jul 18, 1863.

consideration" that now she was "proud to number [them] among [her] best and most highly-esteemed friends."

Some twelve years later G. W. Alexander wrote a testimonial on Velazquez's behalf in a "publisher's circular" which promoted *The Woman in Battle*. His testimonial will be later introduced and analyzed. It is a curiosity that considering Velazquez counted Alexander among her best friends and that he later provided a testimonial for her, she, either in error or on purpose, failed to get G. W. Alexander's rank correct. She called him a major, but he was a captain at the time of her Castle Thunder stay; records have him as "Captain" in July and August, 1863, and also all throughout 1864. Did Velazquez, who claimed extensive military knowledge and held rank in the highest regard, make an error or exaggerate?[22]

Please see the images of Castle Thunder and G. W. Alexander in Illustrations, Figure 8.

There are contradictions between her book's version of events surrounding the time of her incarceration in Richmond and newspaper reports.

First, in her book, she claimed that after her confinement in Castle Thunder in Richmond and her release, she was rearrested in Lynchburg, Virginia. She tells an amusing and possibly fabricated story of a nosy old woman who visited her during her Lynchburg confinement to discover her true sex. However, in reality this arrest in Lynchburg had already occurred 22 months earlier, on September 4, 1861 and she was sent to Richmond for further questioning. She was released, but returned to Lynchburg, where she was rearrested by telegraphic orders from Richmond. After the authorities determined she was benign, she was sent on her way. She characterized (*TWIB*, p288) this episode as a "little unpleasantness with the Richmond and Lynchburg authorities with regard to [her] right to wear male attire." Velazquez blended the 1861 Lynchburg-Richmond-Lynchburg arrest with the 1863 Mobile-Richmond Castle Thunder arrest.

Second and most troubling was Velazquez's claim (p282) that after her release from Castle Thunder, Confederate General Winder sent her on a test assignment as a "secret service" courier. She narrated that upon her imprisonment, she confessed all to Castle Thunder's "Major Alexander" (he was a captain) and "his lovely wife"; she told them "what [her] purposes were in assuming male garb, what adventures [she] had passed through, and what [her] aspirations were for the future." The couple urged her to abandon

---

22. NARA, CMSR for G. W. Alexander; *OR*, Ser 2, Vol 5- Alexander's rank is evident in many other volumes of *OR*; *Sun* (Baltimore), Feb 22, 1895, Obituary- The obit said he was promoted to "colonel in the Army of Northern Virginia," but his CMSR does not confirm this assertion. As well, the *Richmond Times-Dispatch*, Mar 3, 1895, Obituary called him a colonel.

her disguise, but she refused, so the kind Alexander let her have her way. Velazquez then claimed that Alexander released her and represented her case to General Winder and "induced him to give [Buford] a trial in his corps." She implied that Alexander kept her secret and did not tell General Winder of her disguise. If this is what she meant, then the assertion is just not believable. Captain Alexander would never have tried such foolishness on General Winder. But this disbelief and speculation will be seen unnecessary in just a moment.

Velazquez told how the General Winder played a trick on her when he gave her a job to deliver some military dispatches to General Earl Van Dorn. Actually, she narrated two tricks. She wrote she traveled by train to Charlotte, North Carolina where "a gawky member of the North Carolina home-guard" attempted to arrest her. Velazquez figured that the local provost marshal had been telegraphed by General Winder to do so, the first trick to test her. The soldier was "not the brightest-witted specimen ever created" and showed "some degree of trepidation" in arresting Lieutenant Buford. She wrote, "He blinked his eyes at a terrible rate, and great drops of sweat oozed from his forehead, which he wiped off with the sleeve of his jacket, as he tried to argue the matter with me." She was able to present defensive replies to all his arrest attempts.

Finally, by much trouble she arrived at General Van Dorn's headquarters with the dispatch. When Van Dorn read a letter accompanying the blank dispatch, which explained that the courier was being tested, "he burst into a laugh." Velazquez wrote, "I did not particularly admire having been sent all this distance on such a fool's errand, and was very much disposed to resent it."

It is an amusing story to be sure, but it cannot be true, that is, if Velazquez did not alter the true time frame of this anecdote. The story can be determined untrue because Velazquez was released from Castle Thunder on July 10 or 11, 1863 as announced by the newspaper. At that date General Van Dorn had already been dead 65 days. On May 7 he was shot by jealous Doctor James Peters, who claimed that Van Dorn was having an affair with Peters' wife. Velazquez did not deliver a message to the already dead General.

Upon her release from Castle Thunder, Velazquez headed south and a newspaper noted her passing through Columbia, South Carolina on Saturday, July 18, 1863, "Mrs. Alice Williams, the far-famed female soldier, who we never heard of before passed through Columbia on the same day [as Vice President Stephens- meaning the aforementioned date]." Stephens had addressed a greeting crowd on that date. The Alice Williams article followed the Vice President Stephens article and the newspaper facetiously interjected, "whether [Mrs. Alice Williams was an] aide to Mr. Stephens, (who is a bachelor, we believe) is not stated."[23]

Velazquez is next placed in Atlanta based on a July 20, 1863 letter she wrote to the Confederate Government, "relative to idle men who ought to be in service."[24] Her letter[25] is presented verbatim:

> July 20, 1863
> Provost Marshal Office, Atlanta, ga
> Col Cooper Adjutant General-
>
> Dear Sir:
> I have just arrived here last Evening from your city [Richmond] of A visit and now avail myself of giving you my oppinion [*sic* opinion] of the war and the idle men on the Railroads and in the different commisary [*sic* commissary] & quartermasters departments who are able bodied young men that at the present crises of times ought to be in the army as their [*sic* there] are plenty of Old men & criples [*sic* cripples] that can fill those positions, and I hope And trust to god that the president will look into this mater [*sic* matter] and isue [*sic* issue] and [*sic* an] Order to send them to the feild [*sic* field] as Speedy as posible [*sic* possible] Or Else we will be lost. their [*sic* there] can be mustered into the service to my calculation 110000 hundred & ten thousand which can and are able to go do good service-. I take this Liberty of addressing you and hope you will not think me bold by so doing for boldness in woman I deprecate[,] the want of it in man at the present crisis of times I deplore. this is from your sincere friend the female Lieutenant whoes [*sic* whose] whole soul is Enlisted in her countrys [*sic* country's] cause. I must come to A close pleas [*sic* please] answer in care of Colnel [*sic* Colonel] S. W. Lee- commanding.
>
> Yours most Obedient Servant
> Mrs. Lauretta J. Williams
> Alias Lieut H. T. Buford

Most curious, and already pointed out when she applied for a commission, is the fact that Velazquez willingly revealed her alias. This behavior is in violent contradiction to the claims in her memoir that she earnestly endeavored to maintain her disguise as Lieutenant H. T. Buford! Also curious, is she signed neither "Alice" nor "S. T." Williams, the names she went by in Richmond.

---

23. The *Yorkville Enquirer*, Jul 22, 1863 and the *Abbeville Press*, Jul 24, 1863, both South Carolina newspapers repeated information from the *Daily South Carolinian* (Columbia, S. C.). Archived *Carolinian* newspapers contain a date gap; thus, the original report of Mrs. Alice Williams' presence was not found.
24. NARA, RG109, War Department Collection of Confederate Records, ARC 6925795, Chapter 1, Vol 56, Register of Letters Received, Adjutant and Inspector General's Office, Apr-Jul 1863, M-Z, 04/1863-07/1863, entry #1310.
25. NARA, RG109, Letters Received by the Confederate Adjutant General and Inspector General Office, 1861-1879, Jul-Oct 1863. Microfilm 474, Letter W (1255-1879), Roll 88, entry #1310.

To clarify the confusing letterhead- Velazquez addressed Adjutant and Inspector General Samuel Cooper, her friend in Richmond, apparently boldly writing from the office of Atlanta's Provost Marshal, S. W. Lee and requesting an answer there. At this point her Richmond fame was likely a calling card of sorts for entry into the presence of Atlanta's Provost Marshal or the Provost Marshal did his job and took her in for questioning.

Married Thomas C. DeCaulp

Except for Velazquez's July 20 Atlanta letter to the Adjutant Cooper, nothing is known of her activity in Atlanta from July 19 to September, other than activity about which she narrated.

Velazquez wrote (p312) that upon her arrival in Atlanta (as Lieutenant Harry T. Buford) and registration at a hotel, she was "surrounded by a number of officers, who were eager to learn what was going on at the front." She continued:

Among them was General F.,- I do not give his name in full for his own sake,- an individual who thought more of whiskey than he did of his future existence, and who was employing his time in getting drunk at Atlanta, instead of doing his duty at the front leading his men.

She then provided an animated account of the General bullying Buford, he taking Buford for "a little fellow" easily accosted with "offensive and insulting remarks" and "insolent questions." Buford went to the washroom and "the general evidently considered this a retreat due to his prowess,- prowess which he was careful not to make any great display of within the smell of gunpowder, - and he followed [Buford], apparently determined to provoke [Buford] to the utmost." The two exchanged insults and fighting words. Buford- "let me be, or it will be worse for you." He- "What'll be worse for me? What do you mean? I'll lick you out of your boots. I can lick you, or any dozen like you." Buford- "You are too drunk, sir, to be responsible. I intend, however, when you are sober, that you shall apologize to me for this, or else make you settle it in a way that will, perhaps, not be agreeable to you."

General F dismissed Buford, stating to his accompanying colonel, "Come, colonel, let's take another drink; he won't fight" and they "walked off towards the bar-room together." These last words of insult enraged her. Then after supper and once "again at the bar" the dispute continued. She wrote:

I was on the point of going up and slapping his face, when Major Bacon and Lieutenant Chamberlain, thinking that it was not worthwhile for me to get into trouble about such a fellow, induced me to go to my room.

The dispute was compellingly narrated and all, but the incident is certainly a fabrication. Once again when significant officers are named by which Velazquez might solidify some truth in her memoir, she fails. No Confederate Major Bacon or Lieutenant Chamberlain fit the bill as her named comrades, just like the previously addressed phony Lieutenants Hastings and Shorter.

Worse still, there was no Confederate "General F" who fits her characterization of such a person. There were fourteen Confederate generals whose surname began with "F" and none ran from the smell of gunpowder, none was notorious for drinking and none would have wasted their time in a silly fuss with Lieutenant Harry T. Buford. And Lieutenant Buford was going to slap General F? The fuss sounds like it was between a woman and a man. Was she at this time not hiding her sex, but was wearing the uniform? No, she said she was a successfully disguised male lieutenant intent on striking a general. Oh, come on now!

Taking each general by name and studying his history, medical history too, none fits Velazquez's characterization.[26] A detailed biography for each of the fourteen generals could be presented in order to prove that none was the general described by Velazquez, but will not. Rest assured by noting, of the fourteen generals at least ten were wounded in battle and, at least, five of the generals were wounded multiple times. Their presence at the front is clearly contrary to Velazquez's assertion. One was a non-drinker and another expressed a disdain for spirits. One was a Federal prisoner of war during the period in question. One was not yet a general. One had gone to Canada, without leave, to reunite with his displaced Southern family and never returned to the military. One, whose bravery might be questioned, had already lost his commission and died before the date of Velazquez's fuss. Significantly, none of the generals have been placed in Atlanta at the time Velazquez claimed.

Velazquez herself removed two of the generals as the likely abuser. She wrote (p352) that General Ferguson received her near Okolona, Mississippi with "the greatest politeness, and invited [her, as a woman] into his quarters…." Likewise, she wrote (p117) that she, disguised as Lt. Harry T. Buford, met Colonel Featherston just prior to the Battle of Ball's Bluff and he "took a very polite interest" in her. Colonel Featherston made general in March 1862; clearly, he would have been a general at the time of the General F incident which Velazquez indicated happened in 1863. So, the fourteen generals are reduced to twelve possible candidates and still none of them was her abuser either.

In conclusion, no "General F" of Velazquez's allegation existed! If any doubt lingers, feel free to take the Find the General F Challenge; a prize awaits the General's discoverer.

---

26. Jack D. Welsh, *Medical Histories of Confederate Generals* (Kent, OH and London: Kent State Univ. Press, 1995.

Possibly Velazquez experienced similar abuse by someone, even someone in uniform. If so, maybe she felt the need to elevate the abuser to the rank of a general to make the incident more engagingly important. As will be understood by the conclusion of this book, Velazquez never hesitated to exaggerate rank whenever she felt like it. However, the "General F" incident in Atlanta, as narrated, did not happen.

What really happened in Atlanta is that Velazquez married Thomas DeCaulp, probably the first week in September. However, before the wedding, Velazquez narrated (p334) that she had "to go to Montgomery, where [she] had some business to attend to." The next day she returned to Atlanta. This trip seems corroborated by the *Montgomery Mail* newspaper, "We have seen the gallant Lieutenant on the streets of Montgomery for several days." The rest of the *Mail* article basically repeated the *Examiner's* story of July 11, 1863, that her real name was Mrs. S. T. Williams and so on.[27]

About a week after her Atlanta marriage to Thomas, Velazquez returned to Richmond. On September 14, Monday, New Orleans-born Henri Garidel met her in the parlor of Richmond's Ballard Hotel. Garidel had exiled himself for two years from his home in Yankee-occupied New Orleans and during that time kept a remarkable daily journal and wrote of meeting Velazquez.[28]

Major Juan Miangolara of New Orleans made the introduction to "First Lieutenant Henry Buford," who "turned out to be a fine-looking woman." Garidel said that they spoke a long time with her and noted that she "expressed herself well, with a slight lisp." He also saw "she was missing some of her front teeth." This is the sole observation of her missing front teeth in the many notices of her; she must have worn partial dentures, but for some reason she did not have them at the moment. He noted she wore "a black muslin skirt with white flowers on it and a white blouse."

Garidel said that she told him she was first lieutenant in a company of which her husband had been captain, but that he had been killed early in the war. "Her first name was Alice Williams and her second Mrs. Deschamps." Of course, this second name would seem to have been meant to be DeCaulp's name, her current husband. "She told us that she had just remarried," wrote Garidel. Curiously, it will be seen that in August 1887 she gave her mother's maiden name as DeChaump. Garidel, the precise diarist that he was, would seemingly have gotten correct what Velasquez told him, in particular, her Alice name. But Garidel also explained that he "had heard

---

27. The Chattanooga *Daily Rebel* of Aug 4, 1863 reprinted a *Montgomery Mail* story. A search for the original *Montgomery Mail* yielded no results.
28. Ed. Michael Bedout Chesson and Leslie Jean Roberts, *Exile in Richmond, The Confederate Journal of Henri Garidel* (Charlottesville: Univ. Press of Virginia, 2001), 69-71.

a lot about her and had wanted to meet her," so he may have just picked up her first name from the press, never having addressed her in an ungentlemanly way by her first name. And what about the name Henry by which Garidel called her? Did she herself say that name or did Garidel pick it up from an earlier newspaper article?

Garidel wrote that Velazquez showed him "all her papers and her commission," and all her collected pay she intended to give to "the poverty stricken who had been taken ill in Atlanta." This might have been the truth in a distorted way for she said to Garidel that her husband was ill in Atlanta; maybe her husband qualified for her fake charity from her fake pay from her fake commission. Note that she did not say her husband was wounded, but she did claim she had been wounded three times.

Garidel concluded, "After having a good talk, we wished her good night. She invited us warmly to come and visit her."

During his conversation with her, Garidel learned that she had been "exchanged and left New Orleans" on May 17 aboard *Brown*, the lake steamer. That confirms her date and method of departure from New Orleans, as has been previously learned, but it was surely false that she was exchanged. Unfortunately, Garidel did not mention a New Orleans hometown connection with her which might have shed some light on her history.

The *Daily Richmond Examiner* on September 16, 1863 reported her return to Richmond and of her recent marriage in Atlanta:[29]

THE FEMALE LIEUTENANT.- The public will remember the numerous paragraphs published concerning one "Lieutenant Harry Buford," *nee* Mrs. Williams, with a history romantic in war as that of Joan of Arc. Last summer the Lieutenant got into Castle Thunder, her sex not corresponding with the dashing uniform she wore. She was released, and went from Richmond to Chattanooga, where she joined General Bragg's army, got upon the staff of General A. P. Stewart, and for a time was employed in the secret service, and doing some very daring things.

The other day she visited Richmond again, not as the gay Lieutenant, but in the garments more becoming her sex, and bearing the name of Mrs. Jeruth DeCaulp, she having, in the interval, married an officer of the Confederate States Provisional army of that name, first obtaining a divorce from her first husband, Williams, who is in the army of General Grant.

In consideration of her services, the Confederate Government has commissioned Mrs. DeCaulp with the rank of Captain, and since her arrival in Richmond, she has drawn $1,600 back pay. She is now at the Ballard House, en route for Georgia, and the home of her new husband.

---

29. Many newspapers repeated the story or published abridged versions: *Staunton Spectator* (Virginia), Sep 22; *Republican* (Savannah, GA), Sep 25; *Weekly Columbus Enquirer* (Georgia), Oct 6, 1863.

The heroine of this sketch is a native of Mississippi, and a devoted Southern woman.

Mr. Henri Garidel said he cut out this "article about the famous female lieutenant." With Velazquez placed in Richmond on September 14, it is instructive to compare where Velazquez said she was at this date. On page 343 of *TWIB* Velazquez wrote, "While I was in the hospital [in Atlanta], Bragg gained his great victory at Chickamauga...." This battle was fought on September 19-20, 1863 so it is clear that Velazquez was not in the hospital in Atlanta. She had already departed Atlanta and had been seen in Richmond. The battle was indeed a great event and one would think that Velazquez could have remembered where she was at the time. If the false claim was intentional, it is not clear what purpose it served, but it is not unusual to find falsehoods in Velazquez's narrative and/or newspaper interviews which seem to serve no purpose other than getting pleasure out of putting one over on the public.

When the newspaper noted Velazquez's presence at the Ballard House it said she was "en route for Georgia." She departed Richmond, headed for Georgia, and was spotted by Fitzgerald Ross, Captain of Hussars in the Imperial Austrian Service, who was riding the train from Augusta, Georgia to Atlanta between about September 17-18. This gentleman published a book in 1865 titled *A Visit to the Cities and Camps of the Confederate States,* in which he wrote he encountered a woman who claimed to have been a Confederate soldier:

... Colonel Geary, one of our party, discovered a Confederate captain in one of the ladies. Her husband was a major in the Confederate army, and she had taken an active part herself in the war, and fairly earned her epaulettes. She was no longer in uniform, having lately retired from the service, was young, good-looking, and lady-like, and told her adventures in a pleasant quiet way.

The date of Ross' sighting can be established based on information provided in Ross' narrative and it fits Velazquez's likely return trip to Georgia. Her train route to Atlanta would have necessitated that Velazquez travel through Augusta. Adding to the circumstantial evidence is the fact that Velazquez, while in Richmond only days before, had called herself a "captain," the same as the lady on the train. And it will be seen that in 1866, Velazquez did not hesitate to call husband Thomas DeCaulp a "major."

Even though this sighting was certainly Velazquez, it unfortunately did nothing to confirm her claimed deeds of fighting in battles or spying. The sighting only confirmed her existence and her willingness to lie about her rank and that of her husband.

The biggest news contained in the September 16 Richmond article was that Velazquez got married. The Richmond newspaper could not have known first-hand of the Atlanta marriage; it only knew of it because Velazquez said it was so. But it was true.

Velazquez told the paper that her new name was Mrs. Jeruth DeCaulp. Recall that immediately before she left Richmond for Atlanta, before she got married, she called herself Mrs. Alice Williams. Now with this marriage and her return to Richmond, not only had she changed her surname, but she changed her first name, from Alice to Jeruth, or she changed Thomas' name. It is not clear what purpose it served to claim a new first name. In any case, neither Jeruth nor Alice was likely her real name. Recall before Alice, she was Annie or Ann and before that she was Laura J. and Mary Ann.

There were other inconsistencies, as well. She said that Georgia was the home of her new husband, which it wasn't, and once again, a falsehood which served no clear purpose. She claimed that she collected back pay as a captain. She never was a captain and besides she never claimed in her book that she was one. Thus, if she was not a captain, it follows that she did not collect the back pay of one.

Velazquez devoted the entirety of Chapter 28 to compellingly telling of the events surrounding her new husband, how she located her husband-to-be sick at the Empire Hospital in Atlanta and how she revealed her disguise to him. It might be helpful for the next point of contention to review the dialog (*TWIB*, p326 or in Synopsis of *The Woman in Battle*) with her husband-to-be DeCaulp, who is not yet aware that his comrade Lieutenant Harry T. Buford and "William's" widow are one and the same person. DeCaulp is trying to explain to Lieutenant Harry T. Buford the identity of the woman who is the object of his love. Velazquez wrote (p328):

"Yes," [DeCaulp] went on, "I have known her for a long time. She is a widow, and her husband was an excellent friend of mine." Then, apparently suddenly recollecting the circumstances under which he first made my acquaintance in the character of a Confederate officer, he said, glancing quickly and eagerly at me, "Why, you ought to know her; her husband was the first captain of our company; you recollect him, surely."

"O," said I, as if rather surprised at this revelation, "she is his widow, is she?"

"Yes," said Captain De Caulp; "you have met her, have you not?"

At first glance the passage seems just fine, but with a whit of wit it becomes clear it was written for blockheads. Of course Captain DeCaulp knew that Lieutenant Harry T. Buford knew "the first captain ["William"] of our company"! Buford determinedly delivered the 236-man "battalion" to William in Pensacola (p86). After William "took command of the men... Thomas C. DeCaulp was appointed first lieutenant (p86)." When William was tragically killed, Buford "turned over the command of [her] battalion to Lieutenant DeCaulp (p87)." How on earth did DeCaulp not know of Lieutenant Buford's contribution or suspect Buford didn't know William?

The dialog was a simpleminded fabrication and the lie is made clear by other facts, as well, for example: Velazquez did not raise a battalion; DeCaulp wasn't in Pensacola; Velazquez's first husband was not the "William" of her description. These facts will be shown to be solid.

Velazquez wrote, "Captain DeCaulp and I were married in the parlor of the hotel by Rev. Mr. Pinkington [*sic*], the post chaplain, in as quiet and unpretentious way as either of us could desire." She was, in fact, referring to Reverend Samuel J. Pinkerton who was appointed to "Hospt, Atlanta, Ga." as post chaplain by the Secretary of War on February 12, 1863.[30] One Confederate army document shows Chaplain S. J. Pinkerton in Atlanta from October 1 to December 31, 1863.[31] No document was discovered placing Pinkerton in Atlanta the first part of September, the likely time frame of Velazquez's marriage, but it can anyway be believed that he was there.

The location of the marriage, Velazquez claimed, was the Thompson Hotel also called the Atlanta Hotel and it was in downtown Atlanta, Fulton County. A search of Fulton County (and adjacent counties) marriage records was made. The Reverend is found as the signer of marriage certificates in August and December of 1863. No marriage certificates at all for September were found with Pinkerton as the signer, thus no marriage certificate for DeCaulp was discovered either. It seems that because of the distractions of the war, the marriage never got registered in the civil records. Some future researcher could possibly still find it.

Velazquez wrote that after their marriage, her new husband Thomas C. DeCaulp went back to his command and she never saw him again. She said that she learned he "was taken sick again" and died in a "Federal hospital in Chattanooga." She wrote, "within three short weeks of my marriage, I was a widow again!" She did not explain how she learned he ended up in a Federal hospital. She grieved, "This was a terrible blow to me, for I tenderly loved my husband, and was greatly beloved by him."

The only problem with the tale of Thomas' death was, it was a lie. Discovered correspondence dating from the following year, 1864, in which they address one another as "My Dear Husband," "Your Affectionate Wife" and "Dear Wife" clearly show that her husband did not die "within three short weeks." In addition, military records show DeCaulp deserted the Confederate army, went North and joined the Yankee army.

Velazquez wrote (p337) that at the time of his alleged death, Captain Thomas C. DeCaulp was "about twenty-nine years of age." According to his

---

30. Clement Anselm Evans et al., *Confederate Military History: Georgia* (Wilmington, NC: Broadfoot, reprint 1987), 918-920; Joseph Blount Cheshire, *The Church in the Confederate States, A History of the Protestant Episcopal Church in the Confederate States* (NY: Longmans, Green & Co., 1912), 105.
31. NARA, CMSR for S. J. Pinkerton.

Confederate records he was 25 years old at the time of his enlistment on July 29, 1861 at Pocahontas, Arkansas. In September 1863, when he allegedly died, he would have been 27 or 28. Curiously, on the date thought to have been his true death, in December 1865, he would have indeed been about 29 years old. More will be revealed about DeCaulp.

Recall for a moment Velazquez's release from Castle Thunder. One "Harvey Birch" wrote a letter, dated October 17, 1863, to the editor of the *New York Herald* in which he told of "Mrs. Alice Williams." Harvey Birch was one of many pseudonyms used during the War by the infamous liar and forger, Charles A. Dunham. He wrote letters and articles, crafted with just enough facts mixed with fiction to make them believable. He seemingly lied just for the pleasure of deception and a pay check. For pay, he supplied to the newspapers stirring articles, complete with invented facts, in which he criticized both the North and South in their handling of the war.

Later Dunham, using the alias Sandford Conover, became embroiled in the aftermath of the Lincoln assassination plot. He fooled Federal investigators into sending him substantial amounts of money in order for him to produce witnesses who he claimed could testify that Confederate President Jefferson Davis had ordered the assassination. At this time Conover remembered "Mrs. Alice Williams" from the war years and said she had participated in a different plot to kill Lincoln with poison. This and Dunham will be addressed in detail.

According to Dunham, he was a prisoner in Castle Thunder at the same time as was Mrs. Alice Williams. Indeed, the record is clear that he was in Castle Thunder on May 7, 1863. On that day he wrote a letter to Confederate General John H. Winder in which he presented a smart argument that he was unjustly arrested. Dunham had already been "brought before" the General on May 2, so his arrest was probably a few days prior.[32]

It was after his release from Castle Thunder[33], and again back North, that Harvey Birch wrote to the *New York Herald* editor warning that this "spy," Mrs. Alice Williams, who had already been released from prison, was probably now among the good people of the North gathering information for the benefit of the Rebels' war effort. The *New York Herald* published "Harvey Birch's" letter and it, in part, stated:[34]

In July last the celebrated she-Lieutenant Buford was sent north to act as a spy, and is now probably cutting a figure with some of the officers in our army, and serving the rebels with such information as she can acquire. [Here he inserted an

---

32. Confederate Military Manuscripts in microfilm, Ser A, Reel 8, the Virginia Historical Society.
33. About Aug 1, this was after Velazquez's release. Source- NARA, Turner Files, #1561, letter from C. A. Dunham to Col. L. C. Baker.
34. Oct 19.

article from the *Richmond Enquirer* which gave news of her arrest and release from Castle Thunder] After her release this valiant Joan remained several days in the castle, boarding, drinking, gambling and carousing with Capt. Alexander and other officers. Corporal Herbert, of the prison, told me that she was going to leave the service, and was going North on the truce boat from City Point. I remarked that she would pass herself off for one of the women captured at Winchester. When the corporal told me this, he believed me to be a hater of the Yankees. The day before the fair lieutenant left, she said in a jocular way to me that she hoped I would soon be released, and that she should see me in Baltimore. Three weeks later Capt. Alexander confidentially told a person, whose name it would not be fair in me to mention, that he had received under truce a letter from her, from Washington. I have not a particle of doubt as to the accuracy of my information on this subject, and I know from my own observation there would have been no difficulty in passing this woman over to Major Mumford, agent for exchange, as a Yankee female captured at Winchester, or elsewhere, and as soon as the boat reaches Annapolis civilian prisoners are permitted to go where they please. This is wrong. They should be turned over to the Provost Marshal or some officer, to inquire and ascertain who they are before setting them at liberty. Unless this is done many he and she wolves in sheep's clothing will be loose upon us.

Dunham was wrong that Velazquez went North on the truce boat upon her release from Castle Thunder, even though he claimed as proof a letter supposedly written by Mrs. Williams in Washington, D.C. to Captain Alexander.

Upon Mrs. Alice Williams' release on July 11 she traveled to Atlanta, arriving on the 19th, where she wrote the "idle men" letter dated July 20. Also in Atlanta, she married Captain Thomas C. DeCaulp about the first week in September 1863. She then returned to Richmond and was noticed by the newspapers on September 16, 1863.

It was while Velazquez was once again in Richmond that her new husband, Thomas DeCaulp, deserted the Confederacy at Chattanooga on about September 14. Records show that on October 23 he took the Oath of Allegiance to the Union and was freed by Federal officials.

It is unclear if his desertion was pre-planned. DeCaulp likely sent his wife a letter telling of his fate, though such a letter might have had trouble crossing the military lines and finding her. Just when the newly married Mrs. L. J. DeCaulp received word is unknown. It seems unlikely that it was while in Richmond, but instead when she returned to Atlanta. She then started her efforts to reunite with her husband in the North. She first went to Memphis, Tennessee. She explained in a letter, dated July 27, 1864 that she was in Memphis in October of 1863. (This letter will be addressed.) There is no record which reveals precisely where she crossed the Federal military lines in order to go North, but based on this letter it can be assumed to have been near Union controlled Memphis. In her book, she claimed exactly that. On pages 346 to 381 she tells of her (surely exaggerated) odyssey. Recall this is when Velazquez's claimed she met a "Lieutenant Shorter of Arkansas" who asked her to carry a "bogus account of the movement of our troops to [Union] General Washburn" in Memphis and to deliver a secret Rebel dispatch.

In Memphis she told Union officers that she had been badly treated by the Rebels and only wished to travel to Ohio where she had friends. She explained (*TWIB*, p378) that while in Memphis she approached a "Lieutenant B. of Arkansas" to ask if he knew anything of her brother "Captain—" and he replied that her brother had been captured four months before. She now wished to go to him. She invented for her readers the story of her trip to find her prisoner of war brother held at Federal prison Camp Chase, Columbus, Ohio, but the truth was, she was going to meet her husband who had deserted to the North.

If she ever had a brother, all she told about him was false.

First, she refused to state her brother's surname, instead called him "Captain—." This goes beyond odd since she would or should have known that any reader would understand his surname was the same as her maiden name and the same as her father's surname. However, no Captain Velazquez is found in Confederate military records. And no Captain Velazquez is found in prisoner of war records or Camp Chase records. A captain in the Confederate army, especially one with doctor training as Velazquez implied, was someone important and is not lost in the dust of history. He would survive in the records. However, there is a caveat which needs consideration. In Spanish culture, children take the surname of their mother as their last name. In 1887, Velazquez supplied on a Return of Marriage document her mother's name, DeChaump. It was most certainly an invented name, but for the moment assume it was truthful in order to complete the search path. Her brother would have been Captain DeChaump. There existed no Confederate soldier by that name at Camp Chase or anywhere else in the Confederacy.

Second, Velazquez supplied (p42) readers with her Spanish brother's first name, but she seemingly did not even know how to spell it. She called him "Josea" which is not a Spanish name at all. She surely was trying to spell José. One would think that she could spell her own brother's name, especially when it is not difficult. Velazquez wrote, "I wished that I could only change places with my brother Josea. If I could have done so I would never have been a doctor...." Velazquez again mentioned her brother on page 49, and forever desirous of casting the big lie, she let one fly. She wrote that her brother "had graduated with distinction from the College de France," presumably in medicine, as she implied. The problem with this statement is the fact that the College de France "does not set examinations nor does it award diplomas." In other words, one never graduates from the college, as it is just one big lecture series! The college exists today and maintains its policy. At the time of the brother's alleged graduation, the institution was called Collège Impérial. Its name changed in 1870, so Velazquez used its new name, not the name of the institution at the time her brother "graduated," when she wrote about it in 1876.[35]

Third, she did not have a Spanish-born brother (*TWIB*, p40) in the Confederate army. She wrote (p290) she was first aware in the summer of 1863 that he had enlisted when she received a letter from him. Velazquez never explained that her brother had moved away from Cuba and the family; she only mentioned that he once visited her in St. Louis, well before the war. This brother had seemingly been staying in Cuba. The question arises: Why wasn't this Spanish-born/Cuba-residing brother helping their Spanish-born/Cuba-residing father attend to the Cuban plantation at Puerto de Palmas which dealt in "sugar, tobacco and coffee" which allowed her father to "speedily acquire great wealth… [which enabled him] to surround his family with every luxury"? Why would her Spanish-born/Cuba-residing brother leave a profitable Cuban plantation and career, no doubt enhanced by the war, to fight, but mostly suffer, for a neophyte foreign government, not his own, which by 1863 most people could see was losing the war? Velazquez's assertion of this brother defies common sense and is not believable. She might have had a brother somewhere, only it was not the one she portrayed!

---

35. www.college-de-france.fr.

Chapter 4

In Indianapolis

The exact travel path Velazquez took from the South to the North is not clear, but it is clear that she was in Indianapolis in November 1863. Her presence is documented as an employee at the Indiana Arsenal in Indianapolis by the November payroll records of the Arsenal.[1] That month's paycheck is consistent with an entire month's pay, so it might be concluded she started the job on the first of the month. She also was on the payroll in December.

At this time DeCaulp was ostensibly with her. In early December, Velazquez wrote a letter to the Governor of Indiana requesting that he grant her husband a Union army recruiting job in Indianapolis. After not getting the job, it seems that DeCaulp left for Baltimore or was already there waiting for positive news.

Velazquez's short letter to the Governor contains valuable information:[2]

December 7, 1863
Indianapolis Arsenal Indiana

Mr. O. P Morton
Dear Sir
I now avail myself of the present opportunity to State to you that my husband is desireous [sic] of Joining the army at this post he requested me to say to you if you would give him A recruiting commission and grant him the privileges of going in to Camp Morton, he will esure [sic assure] you one hundred or more men who were Like himself in the South was forced to take up arms. he has just received A letter from Maj. General W. D. Rosecrans- in regards to his Loyalty he is A northern man borned [sic born] in Philadelphia. you will pleas give this matter A thought and answer by Mr. Milock. Am very much Oblige yours
Mrs. Lauretta J. Decaulp

First, Velazquez stated to Governor Morton that her husband was a "northern man borned [sic] in Philadelphia." This assertion is revealing and will be addressed later.

Second, Velazquez was working at the arsenal on December 7, 1863. (The arsenal is her location, not that of Governor Morton.) The Indiana State Archives which preserves this letter has wrongly dated it 1865.[3] Payroll records for the arsenal show her employed for December and November, 1863.

---

1. Indiana State Archives, Civil War Miscellany AG Civil War Drawer 107, Folder 43, 1937002, 002613, 7/12, 47-1-5.
2. Ibid, Governor Oliver P. Morton Papers, Collection 401-A-3, microfilm, Roll 10.
3. An enlarged view of the letter's date makes clear the date is 1863. Velazquez, with her pen, swept in from the right with a long line and then made a very small upper curve of the number three and then the larger curve of the lower part of the three. The long sweep at the top of the three has been mistaken for the top of the number five. It is not.

Third, Velazquez tried to get her husband a recruiting job in Indianapolis, so he could be near her. This requested commission to recruit captured and surrendered Southern soldiers for the Union army is startling and contradictory since she vociferously claimed in her memoir (and in upcoming newspaper reports) that she and her husband were ardent Southern loyalists.

Velazquez's request failed and DeCaulp enlisted anyway in the Union army on December 17, 1863 in Baltimore, records show. He possibly knew he would be sent to Milwaukee (as will be seen) and maybe even knew he would go to Minnesota, as many "Galvanized Yankees" were sent here. Minnesota had recently, in August and September 1862, suffered a great conflict between Sioux Indians and settlers which resulted in the death of an estimated 500 to 800 civilians, 77 soldiers and 150 Sioux warriors.

In any case, this may have been the section of country in which Velazquez and DeCaulp decided to take-up residence, evident by their appearance in Indianapolis; it was distant from the war.

Fourth, it was surely true that her husband had some paper signed by Major General Rosecrans stating that DeCaulp had taken the Oath of Allegiance to the Union and that Rosecrans ordered DeCaulp released. Military documents confirm the Oath and Rosecrans' release of DeCaulp. When Velazquez identified "Maj. General W. D. Rosecrans," she used the wrong initials; the General's correct initials were W. S., for William Starke. Admittedly, using the wrong initials of a person is not a serious mistake and barely worth mentioning. However, for Velazquez, it was another example of the plentiful and curious habit she had of writing the wrong initials for prominent men. This habit will be evident time and again in her book and in her letters; for example, she wrote a letter to Samuel Clemens and addressed him as Mr. S. P. Clemens, instead of Mr. S. L. Clemens. And she forged a letter she signing M. D. Hascall and not the correct M. S. Hascall (Milo Smith Hascall), which helps confirm the forgery, the facts of which will be detailed later. More will be said of this habit as it relates to Samuel Clemens and other prominent men.

Was Velazquez in Two Places at the Same Time?

The following document places one "Mrs. Alice Williams" in Baltimore on November 15, 1863 when she was appointed "U.S. Special Agent." It has been asserted by authors/researchers that this "Mrs. Alice Williams" was one and the same as Velazquez because the newspapers made clear she used this name. Recall, prior to her marriage to DeCaulp, she claimed she married "Williams," the Union soldier from the 13th Connecticut Regiment, Company E, stationed in New Orleans. While in New Orleans she called herself Anne Williams, but by the time she was arrested in Mobile, sent to Richmond, and imprisoned in Castle Thunder, the newspapers reported she called herself Mrs. Alice Williams. Once she was released from Castle Thunder, she went to Atlanta where she married DeCaulp about the first week of September 1863. From then onwards, she was Mrs. DeCaulp.

The handwritten appointment letter of Mrs. Alice Williams follows:

Headquarters, Middle Department, 8th Army Corps,
Office Provost Marshal
Baltimore, Md. Nov. 15, 1863

This certifies that the bearer Mrs. Alice Williams has this day been appointed as U. S. Special Agent to act in Middle Depart until further orders. She will report only to me and will endeavor scrupulously to avoid notoriety or permitting any person to learn that she is acting in such capacity unless absolutely necessary. Compensation for service will be reckoned at $2.00 per day. By Command Maj. Gnl Robert C. Schenck [written by] Wm. S. Fish Col & P. Marshal[4]

The obvious question is; how can this Mrs. Alice Williams be the same as Velazquez when it is clear that Velazquez was working at the Arsenal during the month of November? It seems impossible that she went to Baltimore in the middle of the month when she ostensibly was on the Arsenal's payroll for the entire month. Also, by this time she had, for more than a month, been using DeCaulp's surname and not Williams' surname. Adding more doubt is the fact that Velazquez claimed (*TWIB*, p407) that she was hired by United States Secret Service Chief Lafayette Baker and said nothing of General Schenck. So, if indeed this Mrs. Alice Williams was Velazquez, then she was hired by Schenck which would make Velazquez's claim to have been hired by Baker a lie. At this juncture, it is simply not believable this Mrs. Alice Williams was one and the same as Velazquez.

Although General Schenck's document fails to establish that Velazquez was in the secret service for the Union, a different document, Captain Ewald Over's (6th West Virginia Infantry) travel order "No. 330," adds credence and it is presented momentarily.

Looking for Thomas

Mrs. DeCaulp left Indianapolis and was in Washington, D.C. by early January 1864. At least that is what she explained in a letter dated July 30, 1864, written during her Nashville detention, which will be addressed. Velazquez went to the Washington area to find her husband. Recall her husband enlisted on December 17, 1863 in Baltimore, but also recall that a conflicting document stated his place of enlistment as Washington, D.C. In any case, the cities are near enough to one another and she clearly was trying

---

4. NARA, RG110, Provost Marshal General's Bureau, entry 36, Williams, Alice; Major General Schenck was in command of the Middle Department from Oct 10 to Dec 5, 1863. His promotion to major general was on Sep 18, 1862, retroactive to Aug 30, 1862. He resigned his commission on Dec 3, 1863.

to reunite with him in that region. If she succeeded, their time together was limited because he was shipped out to Milwaukee by February 8.

Mrs. DeCaulp left Washington to follow Thomas to his new post, and was in Wheeling, West Virginia. There she received the help of Union Captain Ewald Over who gave her transportation to Columbus, Ohio. Travel order, "No. 330," identifies her working "in secret service:"

H Qrs Military Commander
Wheeling WV, January 26/64,
Capt. F. Moor, A. Q. M. Wheeling, Will furnish transportation for Mrs. Lauretta Decaulp, in secret service, from Wheeling to Columbus Ohio. [signed] Ew.Over [Ewald Over] Capt 6th W. V. Infantry Military Commander

This handwritten document was taken from Velazquez upon her July 1864 arrest in Nashville (to be addressed). To date, the nature of her secret service assignment is undiscovered.

She failed to find Thomas in Columbus and now sought the help of the military district commander, Major General Samuel P. Heintzelman,[5] who wrote of their meeting:

Columbus, Ohio Wed., Jan. 27, 1864
After tea the clerk in the office of the Hotel told me that Mrs. Major DeCaulp wished to see me on some very private business. In a little while I went with him to the parlor. She was not in. We then went to her room & he introduced & left me. She commenced & told a queer tale. She expected to join her husband on his way out to the Department of the Northwest & missed him. She has a letter from Dr. [Boner/Bonu/Bonee?] Actg. hosp. [Genl.?] to the Medical Director to give her a situation in the hospital- matron. She has been a detective & know numbers of officers in Washington & out West some of our Generals. I let her run on & she passed from one thing to another for an hour & a half at the least.

She has been all through the rebel lines & armies & has been twice in the Richmond prisons. She then met Gen. Ricketts & Gen. Corcoran. The accounts she gave of her adventures were really quite interesting.

She wanted my advice what to do. She is off the road her husband takes & don't know when, where or how to find him. From her statement I advised her to telegraph or write to Major Pelouse [*sic* Pelouze][6] & learn from him what she had better do. From one moment she was ready to burst into tears & the next she was in the midst of her adventures & you suppose that she had nothing to trouble her.

From the name of places & people & events there is no doubt of the facts. She is middle sized tolerably full 25 or 30 years of age & apparently quite intelligent. She is dressed in black.

---

5. Samuel Peter Heintzelman, Journal, ID. No.: MSS25676, Library of Congress.
6. Major L. H. Pelouze who had examined Thomas in Washington, D.C.

The next day[7] Heintzelman recorded they again met and "had another long talk... She has passed through some very interesting scenes." On January 30, Heintzelman reported:

> Mrs. DeCaulp sent for me in distress & wished for me to aid her in getting as far as Chicago. I advanced her $20. I think I will get it back as I think there is little doubt of the truth of her story.

Velazquez's story telling and powers of persuasion had hooked the General for twenty dollars! But by February 5, he "[felt] a little doubtful about her" and wrote to Major Pelouze about her. Heintzelman, upon a reply from Major Pelouze, now "fear[ed] she is a scamp."[8]

She had told a twisted version of the truth.

First, Velazquez had an exceptional memory for places, people and events and used them both truthfully and untruthfully, as the situation demanded.

Second, she did not truthfully explain the nature of her two imprisonments in Richmond. Recall, the first was in 1861 when she was arrested in Lynchburg, dressed in Confederate male attire, taken to Richmond on September 25 and discovered to be Mrs. Mary Ann Keith. The second was in July 1863 when she was arrested in Mobile wearing a Confederate male uniform, taken to Castle Thunder prison in Richmond and identified as Mrs. Alice Williams. To Heintzelman she implied she was pro-Union at these times, and claimed to have met Generals Ricketts and Corcoran, two prominent Union officer prisoners, implying in 1861 since that is when they were prisoners in Richmond. But she positively did not meet Corcoran then and it is not credible that she met Ricketts.

The officers had been wounded at the First Battle of Bull Run, captured and taken to Richmond. Colonel Michael Corcoran (later General) was no longer in Richmond, having been sent by September 11 to Castle Pinckney, Charleston Harbor.[9] And Captain James B. Ricketts (later General) was in a Richmond hospital, not in the regular prison population.[10] So, if she met him, she would have had to visit him in the hospital, which is not likely, since she was busy making a public show of herself in her soldier clothes.

Third, her recommendation as a hospital matron did not get her the job; she moved on to other pastures. The document could have been a forgery.

---

7. Jan 28, 1864.
8. Feb 13, 1864.
9. *Examiner* (Richmond), Sep 11, 1861 repeated by *The Manitowoc Pilot*, Sep 20, 1861; Michael Corcoran, *The Captivity of Michael Corcoran* (Philadelphia: Barclay & Co., 1864), 39.
10. NARA, RG94, Letters Received by the Adjutant General (Main Series), 1861-1870, File Unit: 1861-Ricketts, James B. -File No. R775.

Fourth, Heintzelman stated that she claimed "she has been a detective" (implying past tense). One can guess at this time she showed her "in secret service" travel orders from Capt. Ewald Over.

Fifth, Heintzelman guessed her age at between 25 and 30; she would have been 22 and a half, according the date of birth in her memoirs.

Velazquez continued her search for Thomas, who upon his enlistment had been assigned on February 1 to the 30th Wisconsin Regiment and joined his company on the 8th. The company was for a while at Camp Reno, Milwaukee and then subsequently, no later than May, sent to St. Paul, Minnesota.[11] Thomas DeCaulp enlisted using the alias William Irwin to avoid trouble from knowledge of his antecedents as a Rebel, as will be seen.

By February 3 Velazquez reached her destination of Milwaukee, Wisconsin, maybe even ahead of DeCaulp's arrival. The *Milwaukee Sentinel* of February 5 took notice of her, though at first misnamed her:

A modern Bellona [Roman goddess of war] has been among us for a day or two, in the person of "Mrs. Gage, Major U.S.A." This officer arrived by the Chicago train on Wednesday [February 3], and has been seen several times since promenading the streets, wearing a closely fitting basque [jacket] ornamented with a neat pair of Major's shoulder straps. Her mission here is a source of much speculation among those not "thoroughly acquainted with military matters," like the man who makes predictions for the press, at Washington- some conjecturing that she is John Morgan in disguise, others asserting that she has been sent to raise a battalion of nine month's women to bring this rebellion to a speedy termination, and still others maintaining other equally improbable things. The charming Major has evidently learned to stand fire, as every one that she passed on the street stopped and *shot* a glance at her.

The Detroit papers of this week mention her having been at that city, and states that she has a commission from the Secretary of War and an appointment on Gen. Thomas's staff.- We are consuming to know what may be her whence, wherefore, whereby, whereupon, and how-come-you-so. *Nous verrons*.

The next day the *Milwaukee Sentinel* obligingly corrected Velazquez's identity:

The Major Again.- We have received a note from Mrs. Lauretta de Caulp, the lady referred to yesterday as 'Mrs. Gage,' in which she denies being John Morgan 'or any other man.' We didn't believe it at all. We will do more tomorrow towards making the 'speedy correction' which the Major de Caulp requests.

The *Milwaukee Sentinel* had initially identified "Mrs. Lauretta de Caulp" as "Mrs. Gage" because, just days before, the *Detroit Free Press* of February 2 (Tuesday) had reported in Detroit a "Mrs. Gage, Major, U.S.A.,

---

11. "Thirtieth Regiment Wisconsin Infantry Vols. mustered into the Service of the United States at Madison, Wisconsin, October 21st 1862 Major R. S. Smith mustering officer." Source- NARA regimental records.

Washington" who, last Friday, had registered (January 29) at the Michigan Exchange hotel. Then on Saturday (January 30), she "distinguished the colored regiment with her presence" and "took dinner with Captain Tuttle, tea with the Quartermaster." She possessed "several documents of a public character... a commission bearing the autograph signature of the immortal Stanton; an appointment on General Thomas' staff; blank transportation from General Orr...." The newspaper speculated who she was and what her business might be, but did not know.[12]

A "Mrs. Major Gates [*sic*]" next showed up in Cleveland, where she married "a private in the 49th New York Regiment- a mere boy."[13] At a local photographic studio (on February 1), Mrs. Gates tried to get their photo taken for free, she showing "several badges, & c., and made known her name and position." The operator refused, but adjusted the price.[14]

The "Mrs. Gage" and "Mrs. Gates" antics seem like Velazquez's behaviors, but the dates do not fit. She was with Heintzelman in Columbus on January 30; this woman registered at the hotel in Detroit on January 29 and visited local troops on January 30. Not convincing either is the line of travel, from Detroit, eastwards to Cleveland. Velazquez was not "Mrs. Gage" or "Mrs. Gates." Whoever she was, she appeared to have been borrowing the surname of renowned Frances Dana Baker Gage (at this date 56 years-old) who was then on the lecture circuit, speaking on the condition of Freedmen in South Carolina.[15] The real Mrs. Gage was known nationwide for her anti-slavery, women's voting-rights and temperance stances.

Naturally, Velazquez denied she was "Mrs. Gage." But more convincing is that the *Detroit Free Press* said that "Mrs. Gage" had "red hair, ditto complexion and nose," a description unlike Velazquez's. Velazquez could have worn a red wig, but it is not clear how the red complexion and red nose fit.

It is curious that in Milwaukee Velazquez paraded herself dressed in a stylish military uniform... ostensibly a Yankee uniform, no less! If the spy "Mrs. Alice Williams" was in fact Velazquez, then she clearly was not following General Schenck's instructions given less than four months prior, to "endeavor scrupulously to avoid notoriety." There was nothing secret about public promenading in a military uniform.

The fact that Velazquez attired herself in a uniform in Yankeeland is inexplicable, since the entire premise of her book was that she disguised

---

12. *Detroit Free* Press, Feb 2, 1864.
13. This marriage was likely not true. A search of marriage records for Cleveland, Cuyahoga County for January 29-31 and February 1, 1864 yielded no groom whose name matched a name on the roster of soldiers from the 49th NY Infantry Regiment. No Mrs. Gates or other likely female, either.
14. *Cleveland Daily Plain Dealer*, Feb 2, 1864.
15. Ibid, Feb 8, 1864.

herself in a Confederate uniform solely to enable her to fight for the noble cause of the South; her editor wrote (*TWIB*, p11) that "the Confederate cause had no more enthusiastic or zealous supporter." Her propensity to wear male military uniforms was seemingly greater than her loyalty to any cause, as she clearly was not particular about which side's uniform she wore! Also, it appears that her desire for the uniform and for public attention was greater than any desire to follow orders, specifically, "avoid notoriety," if she was General Schenck's hired U.S. Secret Service agent.

Velazquez wore her jacket "ornamented with a neat pair of Major's shoulder straps," implying she was commissioned the rank of major in the Yankee army and all the while making it clear she positively was not a man. Of course, it was not true that she held that rank in the Yankee army (or Confederate army) and she certainly was not foolish enough to claim it in her book. Her walking around in public exhibiting a false martial appearance to onlookers who probably understood (or at least should have) that she was not a woman soldier, and could not have been one since at this date there were no female soldiers, is reminiscent of a kindergartener who wears cowboy boots and spurs to school pretending to have a pony, or more likely wishing for one. The child does it for their own fantasy pleasure or to impress or fool classmates. The fun of fantasies is very cute for a child, but rather eccentric for an adult.

Love Letters between Thomas and Nettie

A letter survives which Velazquez wrote from Milwaukee to her husband who had been assigned to military duty at Fort Snelling, St. Paul, Minnesota.[16] Ostensibly, Velazquez took possession of the letter when she reunited with her husband and it was later taken from her when she was arrested in Nashville in July 1864, which will be addressed.

The letter is handwritten and is presented here, retaining Velazquez's original punctuation, spelling, and sentence construction. Her sentences were shorter due to the width of the paper she used, but reproduced here are allowed to run the width of the page. It should be pointed out that Velazquez consistently used a period where a comma should have been used. There can be no doubt that the marks are periods and not commas. It is possible that a period was her comma, though in other places she uses obvious commas. Seen also, is she seldom capitalized the first word of a sentence and randomly capitalized others. Her writing habits may provide clues to her claimed Hispanic origin:

---

16. NARA, Union Provost Marshal Files of Papers Relating to Individual Citizens, DeCaulp.

May 12, 1864
Milwaukee Wisconsin-

My Dear husband,
I have just returned from the post Office and not getting a letter from you since thursday [*sic*] weak [*sic* week]. I feel somewhat worried to disappointment. I wept bitterly to think you would treat me so unkind. after my being so kind to you when you were not able to help yourself. this is the fourth letter I have written to you. I received no answers to them. I received two from you. Signed T. C. Decaulp- One signed Benjamine F. Carter- which you thought I would not no [*sic* know] your hand write. this I Look Over for the present and Leave it for us to discus [*sic*] to One another when we meet if we should ever meet again. but sometimes things Looks very dark and gloomy to me. the way you are acting I do not feel satisfied. for you no [*sic* know] I Love you dearly and have suffered a great deal for you and am suffering Everything all most woman could suffer for man. if you are sick Let me know it. and Let me know what you intend to do. I am some times tempted to go to the front and try and win my glory back. but my present condition will not permit me for the present but by August or Sept- I will be able. What comfort is this world to me. separated [*sic*] from all I love. you promised to write to me every two days. the Ministers wife has assisted me in getting some clothes. this Leaves me well as could be Expected. Mrs [Swed ?] & Mr. send their Love
[page 2]
to you allso [*sic*] Mr. & Mrs. Greenwood. I directed my other Letter to your own name Thomas C. Decaulp. I direct this to your assumed name. Write or come home soon. Your Affectionate wife a kiss+ Mrs. Lauretta J. Decaulp

There are several observations made and conclusions drawn by studying the letter's contents.

Velazquez directed her letter to DeCaulp's "assumed name," William Irwin. More about Irwin is in store.

Velazquez was still in Milwaukee on May 12, 1864. She did not have much money, as she was depending on the help of the Minister's wife to get clothes. If she had no money, then it may be assumed that she was not receiving money, even if she was serving as a Union spy at some $2.00 per day.

The Greenwoods were probably Thomas, a grocer of some wealth and his wife Fannie.[17] Velazquez was likely getting help with her food.

She intimated that she was pregnant and due before or in August/September. She does not sound pleased to have entered into domestic life and was "tempted" to resume her activity at the "front."

Her English positively does not sound like that of a native speaker, in particular, her use of the phrase, "this I Look Over for the present...." In 1878, when Ex-Confederate General Jubal Early met her, he thought she

---

17. U.S. Census, 1860.

did not use English of a Southerner, or of a non-native English speaker, but that of a Northerner! General Early might have been wrong on this point and this will be addressed elsewhere.

Lauretta questioned DeCaulp as to what he was doing sending her a letter signed Benjamin F. Carter. She raised a good question; she said she knew the letter was from him because she recognized his "hand write." It will be seen that his response was that he was perplexed and that someone in his company must have written the letter to her. But was he telling the truth? Was the name Benjamin F. Carter a previous alias or even his real name? It is easier to imagine that Thomas DeCaulp unthinkingly signed this letter out of habit, using a name he had used in prior years, than to believe that someone in his company would waste the time, effort and the cost of an envelope, paper and stamp to send some foolish letter to someone. These soldiers did not have money to waste and, as DeCaulp explained (in his response letter), his company had not been paid in a while. It is easier to believe that DeCaulp was sick, which he was, or exhausted, and unthinkingly signed a previous alias or his true name.

There was one more thing about DeCaulp's past which Velazquez maybe did not know and maybe would have wanted to know. He was already married. Only ten months before Velazquez married DeCaulp, one 27-year-old "Thomas R. Decalp" had married 32-year-old Mrs. Sarah Haralson,[18] on December 9, 1862, in Little Rock, Arkansas at the residence of the bride.[19] DeCaulp returned to duty in the Confederate Army and it appears that he wrote Sarah a letter which was awaiting her pick-up at the Post Office on December 31.[20]

This Thomas R. DeCalp was surely Thomas C. DeCaulp; his noted age matches other mentions of age. Before this date the DeCaulp surname, or its variant, Decalp, did not exist in Arkansas and it can only be thought that he invented the name with his arrival there. While Velazquez was busy marrying DeCaulp in Atlanta, the first week of September 1863, back in Arkansas his other wife, Sarah, was busy giving birth to her child Thomas Edwin DeCaulp, born on September 5, 1863. From that date foreward the DeCaulp surname became common in Arkansas.

DeCaulp's response letter is presented verbatim and there are particulars which are immediately noticeable.

---

18. Sarah's maiden name was Hollinshead and she had been previously married (March 23, 1843) to much older Herndon Haralson (b. 1796) at the Church of Christ in Little Rock. Source- www.familysearch.com, Marriage Record 1838-1901, Pulaski County, film #007578561, Book "B," p65.
19. www.familysearch.com, Arkansas Marriages 1838-1901, film #007578561, Pulaski County, Book B2, p66.
20. *True Democrat* (Little Rock, Arkansas), Jan 7, 1863.

First, DeCaulp was not "very highly educated," as Velazquez claimed (p337); he had "studied in England and France with the intention of becoming a physician." As can be seen, his spelling, punctuation, syntax and capitalizations, or lack of, are atrocious. If indeed he studied as she claimed, maybe he failed spelling and composition.

Second, he was not born in Edinburgh, Scotland and did not come to America in 1857, as Velazquez claimed (p337). Is a discerning reader to believe his Scottish English syntax and vocabulary just disappeared? Recall his stated age was 25 at his July 1861 enlistment in the 3rd Arkansas Cavalry, so he would have been 21 years old when he came to America in 1857. It is not believable that he came to America as a 21-year-old adult, and by the time of this letter, seven years later, he had lost all of his Scottish English. His handwriting was pretty and neat, and considering that Velazquez, in her book, had already killed him off by the end of September 1863, it might be facetiously noted that his writing hand should have been very stiff eight months later. Velazquez, in newspaper interviews, killed him off at varying places and times and all were lies. For the moment he was alive:

[page] 1
Fort Snelling
Minn., May the 12, 1864

Dear, Wife
having don [*sic* done] no duty scince [*sic* since] I arived [*sic*] here gives me ampel [*sic* ample] time to write to you which gives me more pleasure then [*sic* than] any other way my leasure [*sic*] time can be ocupied [*sic*] scince [*sic*] we ar [sic] designed to be seperated [*sic*] by unavoidable circumstances which grives [*sic* grieves] me much when I reflect over the past scenes of falisity [*sic* felicity] that we have enjoyed to gather [*sic* together] mitigating that blited [*sic* blighted] love that like the early flowers of spring which ar [*sic* are] kissed by the late frosts of winter and left withered in cilence [*sic* silence] untill [*sic*] aroused by the genial sunshine of affection into its original state by womans [*sic*] love the only consoling friend of man when trials and adversities of this cheerless world gather around him, my health has much improved from the pure air and salubrious
[page] 2
climate generaly [*sic*] although I have suffered somwhat [*sic*] from my rheumatism which is caused by the debilitated state of my system, I however hope it will leave me as the warm weather aproches [*sic*], I have suffered much solicitude of minde [*sic*] about your situation fearing that you would grieve yourself by beeing [*sic*] seperated [*sic*] from me I hope however to be soon able to over com [*sic* overcome] this difficulty for if I live to get out of the infernal serves [*sic* service] I will work to subort [*sic* support] and be with you if I should be compelled to preform [*sic*] my daily labors bent double but we cannot help this at present oing [*sic* owing] to the pecular [*sic*] situation under which we ar [*sic*] placed we therefore can only over com [*sic*] the present by hoping for better in the future and bare our present calamities

by trusting in <u>God</u> who bore and suffered that we should enjoy everlasting life we much less than he must be patient if we would enjoy the blessings prommist [*sic* promised] by him to those who keepe [*sic*] his commandents [*sic* commandments]

[page] 3

Dear. Nettie I commenced writing this letter a day or two cince [*sic* since] inwhich [*sic*] I intended saying much of the past present and future whellfare [*sic* welfare] of our weded [*sic* wedded] life, but alass,, [*sic*] I am compelled to abridge it on receipt of a very abstruce [*sic* abstruse] complicated lette [*sic*] I recieved [*sic*] this morning which I am totaly [*sic*] at a loss to understand or fathom it couses [*sic* accuses] me of many groos [*sic* gross] and unhusbant [*sic*] like things togather [*sic*] with demands to know why I wrote such a letter, I know of but three letters that I have writen [*sic*] to you scince [*sic*] I left Milwaukee inwhich I remember of writing nothing unbecoming or ufaithfull [*sic*], my last I will admit was hastey [*sic* hastily] writen [*sic*] but I know of it containing nothing but advice and afection [*sic*] such as is beccomming [*sic*] for a devoted Husbant [*sic*] to impart to the nearest and dearest to him on Earth who holdes [*sic*] the cord of future happines [*sic*] or misery to the grave, it spoke of knowing no such a name in Atlanta I neather [*sic* neither]

[page] 4

know of mentioning that plase [*sic* place] or any person therein I am also shure [*sic* sure] signing my one name if I signed any other I must have been delerious [*sic*] at the time, I know [*sic* now] wish to ask you a few questions in proofe [*sic*] of my devotion towards you which from I hope you will take no exception for <u>god</u> forbid that I should bare the sin of planting a thorn in that devoted relenting [*sic* unrelenting] heart that watched over me with cuch [*sic* such] care and anxiety during the long days and restless nights of my sickness who shared alike my joys and sorrows forsaked all for riches and dear friends to follow the object of her heart in the sight of <u>Almighty God</u> when I seace [*sic* cease] to love you it will be when the toung [*sic* tongue ?] seases [*sic* ceases] to keep the heart to beat and the mind unconcious [*sic*] of all wourldly [*sic*] things have I ever by word or action shown the slightest cause for you to doupt [*sic* doubt] my love towards you and have I

[page] 5

not always when I maid [*sic* made] the slightest breach on your feelings which was always in amusment [*sic*] taken every pains to amend it even on my bended kees [*sic* knees], did I not labor cheerfully and untiring, smiling at my affliction keeping from you nothing that was in my power to aid your comfort cocealing [*sic* concealing] my feelings and pain fearing that it would worry you it was on that account that I enlisted in the army, and get you away from Indianapolas [*sic*] knowing that your health would not last if you continued at at the arsnel [*sic* arsenal] from the long walk, and further my minde [*sic*] was never easy during the day knowing the daingerous [*sic*] situation under which you were placed it was always a pleasure on returning at night to finde you safe at home your Thomas is a man of few words always concealing his feelings especlaly [*sic* especially]

[page] 6

when they ar [*sic*] such as to give sorrow and if you knew the long days spent in silent thought in regards to your whelfare [*sic* welfare], the fervent prayers and apeals [*sic*] to the <u>almighty</u> for your whelfare [*sic*], during the restless and silent midnight hours you would not have writen [*sic*] a letter acusing [*sic*] me of such groos [*sic* gross] crimes as being tirde [*sic* tired] of you and not wishing to support you a thing that has never entered my mind it has rather been utmost in my mind how I could best promote your comfort and when I saw you best situated it was then my heart knew most joy, it is true scince [*sic* since] I have been in the army I have not been able to give you any money on acunt [*sic* account] of not being paid which has given me much trouble and partly the cause of my sickness which the men of company (C) told you they could see me pining for sum [*sic* some] time before I was taken sick although they did not know the caus [*sic* cause] nor

[page] 7

did I let you know it untill [*sic*] now but yet it is nothing now the <u>almighty</u> has seene [*sic*] fit to spare me with your presence and attension [*sic*] during my loest [*sic* lowest] hours, the most severe blow of all that went deepe [*sic*] into my heart which caused me to shed tears was the acusation [*sic*] of being unwilling to support my Infant the next dearest to me on earth and when I refuse to provide for you or it may the <u>almighty</u> God punnish [*sic*] me with the punishment he has promest [*sic* promised] thos [*sic* those] who shall offend them which is, <u>Hellfire</u> when you recive [*sic*] this letter write amediatly [*sic* immediately] and let me know the particulars of this letter you have recived [*sic*] and if there is a man here who dare to write you a letter good bad or indifferent he shall fight me for life or death the minet [*sic* minute] I finde [*sic*] him I have sufferd [*sic*] much in minde [*sic*] from the little trouble at camp Reano [*sic* Camp Reno in Milwaukee] and woe be unto them if i [*sic* I] have the pleasure of meeting them on the plains this summer

[page] 8

I have all ready born [*sic* borne] to [*sic* too] much from men and woe woe [*sic* same word twice] be unto all that has or will cross my path for I would rather suffer death than know you sufferd [*sic*] insult from any, the men have been scatterd [*sic*] in different parties 41 lefte [*sic* left] for the plains yesterday, on last sunday [*sic*] a company of ex rebel cavalry arived [*sic*] from the front they where [*sic* were] in the 1st coneticut [*sic*] regiment [*sic*] 13 of us have been asigned [*sic*] to them it is thought they will remain here we ar [*sic*] daily expecting pay as soon as I get it I shall forward it to you I would have retained this letter untill [*sic*] I sent it had I not received this morning a letter which has inflicted a wound of much sorrow and pain, give my pious regards to Mr. Mrs. [Sweede ?] write soone [*sic*] and amende [*sic* amend] the unjust breach you have made on your loving devoted and sanguine husbant [*sic*] untill [*sic*] death non [*sic* none] but thee and non [*sic* none] without thee [signed] T. C. DeCaulp kiss [And next to the word is a small drawing of lips.]

Thomas DeCaulp's letter is noteworthy.

First, he called his wife by a pet name, Nettie, presumably for Janeta, the middle name she used in the authorship of her book. Her middle initial "J" has been used before.

Second, Thomas refers to his "infant," but seems to imply that the child was not yet born and Velazquez herself seems to verify this because she only referred to her "present condition." No birth record (July-September, 1864, the likely time frame) for this child was found. The child may never have been born or died young. However, there is an additional hint of the existence of a child.

Velazquez submitted, in December 1864, a forged and bogus letter to the newspapers purporting to announce the death of her father and the disposition of his estate. It stated, "Her son, is to be educated at the expense of the estate, at the military school at London, and at the age of 21 years, shall receive $30,000 with interest." The entire letter was a fantastic lie, but it is significant that she thought to address the needs of her son which might be indicative that she actually had a son at the time. The details of this inheritance letter are presented later.

Third, Thomas confirmed that Velazquez worked at the federal arsenal in Indianapolis. Velazquez claimed (p446-448) to have visited Indiana Governor Morton to ask him for a job, representing herself as a widow in need. She also told her readership that she was a widow, which she was not. That makes two lies for the price of one! Velazquez said that Governor Morton suggested the arsenal and she asked for a letter of introduction. She got the job, claimed she was unhappy and quit after "two weeks."

But the truth is different. She worked there at least two months. The Indiana State Archives contain the payroll records for the arsenal for that time period. "Mrs. Lauretta DeCaulp" signed the salary receipt book for November 1863 for ten dollars. Curiously her pay was much higher than the other 50 females listed on that page; the average salary was $5.31 for the month. For the month of December 1863 "Lauretta DeCaulp" received six dollars; the average for the 50 females on that page of the payroll book[21] was $12.51.

Velazquez said (p447) she quit the Arsenal because she wanted to remove herself from the temptation of blowing-up the place for the Southern cause. She said the likely civilian casualties were not justifiable, so she "shrank from doing this." She reflected that even though she was in the Confederate service, "there was a wide difference between killing people in a fair fight and slaughtering them in this fashion." She said that she was forever pleased she didn't, just as she also was pleased, she did not assassinate General Grant when the opportunity had presented itself.

Her reason is just not believable. Neither her hatred of the North nor her loyalty to the South ran deep enough to consider blowing-up the arsenal. After all, she married DeCaulp probably knowing of his intention to desert the Rebel army and surely knowing that he was a Northerner born in Pennsylvania. Even if she did not know of his desertion plans, once he went North, she gladly followed him there. When she arrived in Milwaukee, she

---

21. Indiana State Archives, Civil War Miscellany AG Civil War Drawer 107, Folder 43, 1937002, 002613, 7/12, 47-1-5.

was wearing a Yankee uniform. In Indianapolis she tried to land her husband a job recruiting Rebel prisoners of war for the Union army! When he failed to get the job and he joined the Yankee army, she did not denounce him. Somehow bits of this information must have gotten back to the citizens of the Southern cities in which she had stayed and when she once again visited those cities (it will be seen) she had to vigorously defend DeCaulp's Southern loyalty and her own as well.

And before her marriage to DeCaulp, she claimed (to newspapers) to have been married to Yankee soldier Williams of the 13th Connecticut Regiment, part of the Union army's occupation of New Orleans. Apparently, her attraction to Yankee soldiers was stronger than her attraction to Southern loyalty. The bottom line is that Velazquez was not particularly worried about any noble Southern cause. She worried about her welfare and cash flow, justifiably. It can be seen that she took a 40% pay cut from November to December and that was likely her reason for quitting. Maybe she was demoted to a less desirable job and corresponding pay, or maybe she missed too much work due to her "present condition" and her pay was docked which she resented and quit. In any case, it was not true that she worked at the arsenal for only "two weeks," like she wrote, and her stated reasons for not blowing-up the place are ludicrous in light of the facts.

Fourth, Thomas DeCaulp, in his letter, confirmed the financial need which Velazquez claimed in her book as the motivating factor of her seeking the job. He worried about her health because of the "long walk" to the arsenal. If she was compelled to walk and was unable to afford public transportation, then their financial situation was indeed stressed. In her memoir she claimed (p448) that she was "anxious to leave Indianapolis," but was unable to because she had a "lack of orders, and also a lack of cash."

Finally, note that neither at this point in her book, nor anywhere else, does she mention that she, in fact, lived with her alive, deserter husband in Indianapolis, who she killed off long ago.

The Yankee Spy within Her

Velazquez now narrated (p449) a story of a spying trip. She received, in Indianapolis, a package containing cash, and then received telegraphic orders to proceed to Cairo, Illinois. From there she was instructed to go to St. Louis, Missouri "for the purpose of seeing if [she] could not find out something about projected federal movements from the officers who were making their headquarters [there]." She befriended a chambermaid at the Planters' House (Hotel), stole her pass key and looked for dispatches in the hotel rooms of Yankee officers. Once again and to her credit, Velazquez correctly evoked the name of a real hotel with which she was familiar. This second version of the hotel was located on Fourth Street between Chestnut and Pine Streets.

Velazquez excitingly narrated how she was nearly caught by the bellboy while conducting her search. Returning to her own lodgings, she made out a report of her findings and sent it to an agent, who in reply sent her a telegraphic order to proceed to Hannibal where she picked up a package containing a dispatch for "Major T., of the Confederate army" to whom she gave it. At this point (p452) Velazquez makes a very confusing statement, "The delivery of this dispatch to Major T. was the last transaction of the western trip which I made under the auspices of Colonel Baker."

What? Clearly from the beginning, the alleged mission was under the auspices of the Confederate government, but by the conclusion, the sponsorship is claimed to have come from Federal Colonel Baker. Why would Baker wish for Velazquez to relay dispatches to a Confederate officer? It would seem that Velazquez messed up her own story in the telling. Did Velazquez stumble on her own lie or did she simply fail to make clear her narrative? In any case, Velazquez claimed that it was after this job that she wrote to Colonel Baker and resigned as an agent.

Her claim that she worked for Union Secret Service boss Colonel Baker is thought to be false. No record of Williams' or DeCaulp's association with Baker has been found. However, the record does show that Major-General Robert C. Schenck hired one Mrs. Alice Williams "as U.S. Special Agent" and that she was to report "only" to him. Velazquez appears to have invented her business with Baker instead of simply stating that she was hired and worked for Schenck, that is, if this Mrs. Alice Williams was Velazquez. Another military record dated two months later shows that "Mrs. Decaulp" was "in secret service" and received a travel pass to Columbus, Ohio.

However, there are no found documents which confirm whether she traveled to Cairo, then St. Louis, and then Hannibal as an agent for the North or South. For argument's sake, let's accept that Velazquez was hired by Union Major General Schenck, on November 15, 1863- then it must be asked if she even did any work. Judging by her lack of money in Milwaukee in May 1864, she seems not to have collected any large sums for her service. Most likely, if she had produced, she would have gotten paid and not been in financial straits. As will be seen, the record shows "Mrs. Alice Williams" resigned on July 15, 1864.

Rather than departing Indianapolis and going on a spying trip to Cairo, Illinois, then to St. Louis, Missouri and then to Hannibal as she claimed, there is evidence (her Milwaukee letter) that after Velazquez left Indianapolis, she traveled to Milwaukee where her husband was posted. Then circumstantial evidence indicates she went to Fort Snelling, St. Paul, Minnesota, where her husband was newly posted. At Fort Snelling she probably stayed at Mrs. Adams' boarding house. At least, Velazquez was in possession, upon her arrest in Nashville, of a slip of paper containing "Mrs.

Adams boarding house, Fort Snelling, Minn." Mrs. Adams pioneered the area and ran a well-known boarding house for many years. And at that time there were limited rooming opportunities, so if Velazquez went to Fort Snelling, she likely stayed at Mrs. Adam's.

Departed Milwaukee and St. Paul Areas for New York City

Velazquez claimed that by June 14, 1864 she had departed Milwaukee, Wisconsin and St. Paul, Minnesota. This is the date she claimed in a letter she wrote on July 30, 1864. In this same letter, she stated she went to New York with the intention of visiting friends, and the friends suggested that she seek a job with the National Union Life & Limb Insurance Co. in New York. Velazquez explained, "The President [Mr. Orvis P. Blunt] made out a commision [sic] for the Department of Tennessee...." This was a job as an insurance sales agent.

Velazquez pursued her new sales job and evidence found in a Baltimore military document, dated June 26, 1864, shows she sought an audience with General Grant. It can be supposed that she was trying to obtain permission to sell insurance policies to Federal officers and soldiers. It should be noted that this document has a letterhead with the year 1863 pre-printed and the month and day to be filled-out. It is clear that the author of the document failed to cross out the "3" of 1863 and replace it with a "4." The contents and supporting documents make it clear that the correct date was 1864. Simply explained, Velazquez had not yet married Captain Thomas DeCaulp in June of 1863, but instead married him in September 1863, so she could not have used his name if the document was correctly dated as June 26, 1863. The letter follows:

> Head-Quarters, Middle Department, 8th Army Corps,
> Baltimore, Md. June 26th 1863 [sic 1864]
>
> Acting Provost Marshal
> 8th Army Corps-
Maj_
The bearer Mrs DeCaulp claims to be en rout for Gen Grants HD Qrs [headquarters] on important business, of which I have no Knowledge, but on her producing Satisfactory evidence of the fact, and that she goes by proper authority, you are authorized to give her a pass to procede to Ft. Monroe [Hampton, Virginia] on Govt AC [government account].
E. B. Tyler, Brig Gen, Comdg HQ [Erastus Bernard Tyler, who at the time commanded Baltimore defenses.]

Velazquez likely did not succeed in meeting General Grant. She did not mention any such meeting in her memoir and neither did the newspapers. She seems not have gone to Fort Monroe in Virginia because she returns too soon to New York. She next appeared requesting permission to solicit money from soldiers at Fort Columbus in New York harbor. Curiously, she claimed that she was raising money for the children of disabled Federal soldiers. In light of her vociferous claims in her book and to the newspapers, to embrace only Southern loyalty, it is interesting that she sought to raise money for Northerners. She certainly made no public admission for Southern consumption of such fundraising. Her request was granted:

> Fort Columbus N. Y. H. [New York Harbor]
> July 4, 1864
> Mrs. L. J. DeCaulp is permitted to visit the officers & soldiers of this garrison, to obtain aid for the Volunteers Institute for disabled soldiers' children, NY, NY
> [signed] G. Loomis [Gustavus Loomis, Superintendent of Recruitment]

The NY State Volunteers Institute was a legitimate organization founded by Colonel William H. Young. After Colonel Young resigned[22] from the Union army, he in 1863 founded "an asylum for soldier's orphan boys." By March 1865 he had under his care 160 boys.[23] It will be seen further along that in a July 30, 1864 letter by Velazquez she claimed she visited her "friends" Colonel Young and his wife in Suspension Bridge, New York. It appears Colonel Young gave his approval of Velazquez's fundraising, but it cannot be certain. Suspicion is raised because Velazquez seemingly in error told Loomis that the aid was for "disabled soldiers' children" when more correctly it was for soldiers' orphaned children.

If Velazquez succeeded in collecting money, one must be doubtful that she delivered all of it to the children, unless Colonel Young provided her a salary and money for expenses. If not, then she probably pocketed some cash, as she was in need of it; her need is understood from the letter to her husband, Thomas DeCaulp, and his reply letter, which referenced their lack of money. In addition, she herself admitted she did not handle money in the manner in which she pretended, so it is difficult not to be skeptical. It will be seen in an August 25, 1874 interview with the *Mobile Daily Register* she claimed she diverted $780 in funds donated by the sailors of the Union navy which she "sent to Southern hospitals, although the money was supposed to have been given for the benefit of Federal soldiers." This claim was false (which will be detailed later), but the claim hints at an attitude.

Velazquez presented herself impressively enough and the gentlemanly 75-year-old Commander Loomis of the Fort Columbus did not deny the lady's request. Besides a gentleman, Loomis had served as a professional soldier with an admirable career ever since his 1811 graduation from the U.S. Military Academy. Maybe he was charmed by Velazquez telling of her

---

22. Aug 14, 1862; Ryan A. Conklin, *The 18th NY Infantry in the Civil War: A History and Roster* (Jefferson, NC: McFarland & Co., 2016).
23. *Brooklynn Daily Eagle*, Mar 21, 1865; Ed. J. G. Wilson and John Fiske, *Appleton's Cyclopædia of American Biography*, Vol VI (NY: D. Appleton & Co., 1889), 651.

recent trip to Fort Snelling; he had been commander of Fort Snelling, as a captain, some ten years before the war and would have been most attentive to news of the place.[24]

There exists the possibility that Velazquez earnestly solicited money from soldiers at Fort Columbus for Yankee children and at the same time used the occasion to try to sell life insurance to the soldiers. In that case, she could easily be credited with an honest day's work on both accounts. In her memoir, Velazquez did not mention a pass to visit Fort Columbus to collect money for Yankee children.

At this point in her memoir (p405-413) Velazquez weaved a contradictory story which was nothing but a whopper. She claimed she "was asked [as a Confederate agent] to attempt a trip to Richmond… to consult with, and receive final instructions from Richmond authorities, with regard to the proposed raid on the lake shores…." This raid was the planned prison break to free Confederate prisoners of war from the Johnson's Island Federal prison on Lake Erie. She now approached Lafayette Baker, head of the Federal Secret Service, whom she had already befriended, and convinced him that she should go to Richmond to seek out the name of a particular Confederate spy and other information which might be helpful to the Union. Baker hired her. So, now she claimed she was a double spy.

With a Federal pass provided by Baker, she easily crossed the Federal lines and upon arriving at the Confederate lines, she "declared [her] real errand" and was allowed to continue to Richmond where she completed her business. She narrated (p409) she was given important dispatches to carry back North and was compelled to take a longer, but safer, route through Parkersburg, West Virginia. There, she obtained a travel pass from General Kelley and proceeded to Baltimore where she took a room at Barnum's Hotel. She wrote (p411), "General E. B. Tyler, who was very affable and courteous, and who, learning that I was anxious to travel northward, and was short of money, kindly procured for me a travel pass to New York."

No evidence has been located that General Tyler gave her a pass to travel to New York. She claimed she made a brief stop in Philadelphia, staying at the Continental Hotel. Velazquez then wrote (p412) that upon arriving in New York she was "met at the Desbrosses Street ferry, by an associate in that city, who conducted [her] to Taylor's Hotel, where he had engaged a room for [her]." He told her a detective was on her trail, but he had steered the detective away by providing him a photo of some "very different looking woman."

In her memoir, Velazquez recalled almost 100% correctly the names of hotels and their cities. Here, she accurately identified three hotels in their

---

24. Edward D. Neill, "Fort Snelling Echoes," *Magazine of Western History* Vol 11 (Nov 1889): 22-28.

cities which indicates her knowledge of them. In addition, she accurately mentioned that in New York she took the Desbrosses Street Ferry and then went to Taylor's Hotel. This Jersey City hotel was located at Exchange Place, on the Hudson River front at the Jersey City Ferry Slips.[25] Clearly, she had to take a ferry across the Hudson River, and this was the ferry to use. Velazquez's recall of these locations points to the fact that she was a remarkable traveler and hotel guest, but be aware that many times the claimed circumstances of her visits to these hotels and places were not true, as momentarily will be shown.

Velazquez was anxious to depart New York (p413):

Having cashed my drafts, and gotten everything ready, I started for Canada, carrying, in addition to valuable letters, orders, and packages, the large sum of eighty-two thousand dollars [more than 3.3 million U.S. dollars in 2023 money] in my satchel.

Recall Velazquez claimed (p68) she had eighty-eight thousand dollars she used to raise her battalion? That eighty thousand range must have been a favorite, cha-ching!

Velazquez narrated that she was being seen off to Canada, at the train station, by her fellow spy when he pointed out a man and told her that he was the detective who had been looking for her, so for her to beware. Once the train left the station Velazquez discovered that the detective too had boarded the train and with the picture of the alleged female spy in hand, checked the passengers and asked around if anyone had seen the woman. Velazquez wrote (p414):

I concluded that I would try and strike up an acquaintance with this gentleman, in order to find out what he had to say for himself, and because I thought that perhaps I could say or do something to make him even more bewildered than he was already.

She did, and a clever conversation ensued.

Velazquez put on "a touch of Irish brogue" and claimed she lived in England and was only a visitor to America. The detective showed her the fake photo of the female which Velazquez's associate had given him some days prior and asked, "Did you ever see anybody resembling this? I am after the lady, and would like very much to find her." Velazquez replied, "She is very handsome, is she your wife?" Velazquez "look[ed] him straight in the eyes as [she] said this." The witty dialog continued until they reached the end of the line and the detective, in gentlemanly fashion and unbeknownst to him, helped her carry to the waiting passenger boat her satchel with the eighty-two thousand dollars plus the secret dispatches. When Velazquez

---

25. *1887, Quarter-Century's Progress of New Jersey's Leading Manufacturing Centres, Dover* (NY, NY: International Publishing Co., 1887) 134; *Hudson County Map*, 1873.

arrived at Canadian customs, she winked and "whispered the password [she] had been instructed to use" and zipped right through with her satchel undisturbed- Oh, sure! And when she was at Niagara Falls, it started flowing uphill. Hey, what's one more lie? A wink and a whispered password to Canadian customs- for cryin' out loud!

"On reaching the Canada shore," she was met by Mr. L., to whom Velazquez pointed out the still snooping detective "anxiously surveying the crowd." She "related [her] adventure with the detective… and [Mr. L.] thought it a capital good joke" and said it seemed as though Velazquez was "tolerably well able to take care of [her]self."

In Canada, Velazquez busied herself with "a good many matters… which demanded [her] immediate consideration," implying she stayed a long time before returning to New York. She explained (p417) that she "mailed packages for the commanders of the cruisers *Shenandoah* and *Florida*, which [she] had received with especial injunctions to be particularly careful of…." She identified the date of the mailing of the packages to the Confederate commerce raiders well before the attempted prison break at Johnson's Island which was September 19, 1864, but the *Shenandoah* was not even purchased until September 1864 and commissioned on October 19, making the assertion seemingly false. It isn't clear how she could have sent a message to the commander of *Shenandoah* when it did not yet exist in the Confederate service. Maybe the message was sent to the anticipated commander of the impending *Shenandoah*.

In conclusion, it is false that Velazquez was the spy who carried the "final instructions from Richmond authorities, with regard to the proposed raid on the lake shores." In truth, Velazquez, in order to be near her husband, was in the Milwaukee and St. Paul areas, about which she wrote nothing in her memoir, and in its place claimed the spy trip to Richmond. She was not returning from Richmond when she obtained a travel pass from General Tyler to go New York, but instead, got a pass from him to go south, to Fort Monroe on the Virginia Peninsula, about which she wrote nothing. When she did go to New York she, in truth, got a respectable job selling insurance, about which she wrote nothing. While in New York she did not meet with some unnamed spy associate who helped her evade a Federal detective. And it is not true that she proceeded to Canada upon her departure from New York. She went to Nashville, about which she wrote nothing, but it will be told now.

1864, Arrested in Nashville

Upon her arrival in Nashville in July 1864 Velazquez set herself up as an agent of the National Union Life and Limb Insurance Company. The Federal authorities occupying the city arrested her shortly after she set up her sales office, probably wishing to verify the truth of her agency.

Velazquez asserted (*TWIB*, p452), "I wrote a letter to Colonel Baker, resigning from the secret service, under the plea that I had obtained other employment of a more remunerative and more congenial character." She pretended to her readers that she next went into the blockade-running business, but she was surely selling insurance. She explained in convincing detail of buying Yankee goods and shipping them to the West Indies, to then be shipped into the South by blockade-running ships.

Velazquez disparaged Yankee merchants who professed their Union loyalty because they knew, or suspected, the merchandise she purchased was being sent South and supplied it anyway. Once she had her chartered schooner loaded, it set sail from Pier No. 4, North River. She jumped aboard a steamer and hastened to Havana to meet other pending orders. From Havana she claimed she went to Bridgetown, Barbados, through St. Thomas and upon her return to St. Thomas she saw Confederate cruiser *Florida*, which was taking on coal. It is a huge and provable falsehood that she saw this ship, while she was conducting her claimed blockade-running business. Cruiser *Florida* will be addressed in detail later.

In conclusion, it is most certainly not true she conducted blockade-running (in the manner she narrated) upon her resignation from the Federal secret service, but instead she went into the insurance business, the narration of which now continues.

Upon her arrest in Nashville, many personal papers in her possession were confiscated and today are found preserved at the National Archives and Records Administration. Among the papers is the (already presented) letter to her husband, Thomas C. DeCaulp, and his (already presented) reply. Also preserved are her letters to Federal authorities in which she declared her innocence, requesting her release.[26]

Was Velazquez a bona fide agent for National Union Life and Limb Insurance Company? Since that distance time, the company has undergone two name changes and today is the well-known Metropolitan Life, adopting that name in March 1868. The author contacted the Company Archivist[27] and he stated that there was no record of DeCaulp, but also stated that records for that date "are few." The archivist wrote:

> MetLife's first female agent began work with the company in 1881. If Mrs. DeCaulp was indeed an agent for National Union in 1864, she must have been a real trailblazer.

There are only two possible answers as to whether Velazquez, in 1864, was an agent for the National Union Life and Limb Insurance Company,

---

26. NARA, Union Provost Marshal Files of Papers Relating to Individual Citizens, microcopy 345, roll 70.
27. Jan 13, 2011.

yes or no. If no, then she was selling fake insurance policies and pocketing all the money. This would have been a bold scam, even for Velazquez, considering that she was openly selling to Federal officers and soldiers. The poster which she used, and was confiscated, stated:

National
Life and Limb
Insurance Company
of Nashville, Tenn.,
Office on North Summer St., No. 52
~~~~~~~~~~~~~~~~~~~

Soldiers, Insure your Limbs for your own benefit. Insure your Lives for the benefit of your Families.
FRIENDS AT HOME
Can Insure the "*absent ones*" who are fighting for the "*Loved ones at Home*," and their country's honor.
Parents can Insure their absent Sons.
Brothers, Sisters and Friends
Can Insure the Soldier in the field, as though he were personally present.
Every Patriot at Home
Should Insure at least one Soldier, so that in case he should lose a Limb, he would be comparatively independent.
~~~~~~~~~~~~~~~~~~~
Come one, Come all, for this may be the last opportunity you will have to insure your Limbs and Lives.
Mrs. Maj. L. J. DeCAULP, Agt
Office hours from 8 A. M., to 6 P. M.

(The original font of the poster is approximated; the text is verbatim.)

One clear problem with this advertisement is that Velazquez represented herself as "Mrs. Major." Considering her propensity for exaggeration and/or lying, it comes as no surprise that she represented herself as being married to a major, which Captain Thomas C. DeCaulp was not. And his captaincy was in the Rebel army, not the Union army, which no doubt she was implying her major was in. Or maybe she was implying that she herself was a major, which also, she was not. With the exception of this obvious falsehood, all the other circumstantial evidence supports that she did indeed represent the insurance company as its agent.

The National Union Life and Limb Insurance Company had only recently started to operate. Velazquez was one of the first of the Company's agents hired, male or female, so she could indeed be called a "trailblazer." Life insurance companies of the time, as a general rule, did not actively seek customers in the ranks of soldiers. And life insurance companies, by law, could not sell disability insurance. The war now created a need which was not being satisfied.

The New York Legislature endeavored to fill the need and Governor Horatio Seymour, on April 25, 1863, signed the Legislature's bill which allowed the company to sell "insurance on the lives and limbs and health" of soldiers. The company "intended to write military business only and to solicit it actively," and so Velazquez was hired to seek out business. By the time Velazquez arrived in Nashville, in July 1864, the Company had elected officers, sold the required $100,000 worth of stock, purchased $3680.66 worth of furniture and occupied "two and a half second floor rooms at 243 Broadway, opposite City Hall."[28]

Back to Velazquez's resignation from the Secret Service- A surviving historical record may be evidence of Velazquez's resignation, at least the date is good. Military records of July 15, 1864, state, "Detective commission surrendered by Mrs. Alice Williams."[29] The document does not state to whom the resignation was sent, Colonel Baker or anyone else. But by this date Major General Schenck, who had hired "Mrs. Alice Williams" and had said to only communicate with him, had resigned his commission, December 3, 1863.

If it is believed that the resignation of "Mrs. Alice Williams" was Velazquez, then it might be concluded that the hiring of "Mrs. Alice Williams" by Major General Schenck also was Velazquez. However, Velazquez claimed she was hired by Baker. The bigger problem which has already been presented is that evidence shows Velazquez was working at the Arsenal in Indianapolis which makes it unclear how she could have been hired in Baltimore by Schenck at the same time. It should be noted that at the time of Mrs. Alice Williams' employment and resignation, Velazquez's surname was DeCaulp, having already married DeCaulp in September 1863. It was earlier, between October 1862 and September 1863, that Velazquez used the surname Williams, and particularly Mrs. Alice Williams in July 1863, because of her claimed marriage to Williams of the 13th Connecticut

---

28. Marquis James, *The Metropolitan Life, a Study in Business Growth* (NY: Viking Press, 1947), 24.
29. NARA, RG110, Provost Marshal Records on Spies, Scouts, Guides, and Detectives/ Correspondence, Reports, Appointments, and Other Records Relating to Individual Scouts, Guides, Spies, and Detectives, 1861-1867, Reel 9, Frame Number 0537.

Infantry, Company E in New Orleans, reported by the newspapers in New Orleans, Jackson and Richmond.

Still, there's another problem. "Mrs. Alice Williams'" hiring and resignation dates would have made her service last eight months. If Mrs. Alice Williams is believed to have been Velazquez or, in fact, was Velazquez, then a lie becomes evident in her memoir. Velazquez wrote (p396) she was employed "for nearly a year and a half." Alternatively, if Velazquez was hired and resigned under some other name, such as DeCaulp, and her records lost to history, then her claimed "nearly a year and a half" employment remains unconfirmed.

It can be assumed that Velazquez had little luck selling insurance policies. Author Marquis James wrote, "On December 31, 1864, seventeen life and fifty-six accident policies had been written for premiums aggregating $3,687.76." An optimist might point out that at least the Company paid for its furniture and had seven dollars and ten cents remaining. The Company's total "receipts from all sources" for the year were $10,407.76 against $11,824.41 in expenditures. In this business environment, there can be little doubt that her employment was short lived. In defense of Velazquez's ability as a salesman, it must be noted that Marquis James said the war ended "before the company's soldier insurance scheme was properly launched...." And as history shows, the company soon thrived.

Other items confiscated from her included: a door poster which stated, "**NO ADMITTANCE** EXCEPT ON BUSINESS"; a slip of paper on which was handwritten the name of a presumed employee of the insurance company, "Captain S. O. Post, National Life & Limb Insurance Co., 243 Broadway, N. Y."; and a blank insurance policy.

In addition to the Baltimore pass and the Fort Columbus pass there was a Nashville military pass request which shows Velazquez's propensity and ability to travel. It should be noted that after her book was published, Ex-Confederate General Jubal Early in 1878, raised the question of how was it possible for her to travel to all the places she claimed without military passes. This evidence makes it clear that she had her ways of getting passes. General Early was partially correct in that she lied on many occasions about where she traveled... but she did travel! It can easily be supposed that there was no greater woman traveler during the War years.

The first of the three papers which make-up the Nashville pass was a request by W. W. Tuttle to Captain S. B. Brown to ostensibly supply railroad transportation for Velazquez. The second paper was from Captain Brown in which he forwarded the request to Captain Crane. The third paper was the final compliance with the request. The three requests follow:

[Letter 1]
US Military Railroads/Div. of the Mississippi/Office of General Agent

Nashville, Tenn., July 12th 1864
Capt S B Brown, AQM [Assistant Quartermaster, May 1864 to January 1, 1866]

Capt
This will introduce to you Mrs. Maj L J Decaulp who is the Agt of the National Life & Limb Ins Co of New York_ She will make her wishes known
Very Truly Yours
W. W. Tuttle [He was the general freight agent at Nashville]

[Letter 2]
AQM Office/RR [Railroad] Transportation
Nashville July 12, 1864

Respectfully referred to Capt J. C. Crane AM [Assistant Quartermaster] with the request that he aid the bearer if practicable. I can not furnish her the aid she desires.
S. B. Brown, Capt & AQM

[Letter 3]
Assistant Quartermaster's Office
Nashville, July 18, 1864

Madam,
I will endeavor to comply with your request
Very Respy
[? unclear word] [? unclear word] [? D. T. Mousanat]

Taken from her was a brief letter which is likely evidence of Velazquez trying to sell insurance policies in Nashville. Colonel Donaldson does not seem to be a target for a transportation pass, so maybe she had another reason to ask for a meeting, such as selling him a policy. Union officers, not enlisted men, would have been the most likely able to purchase insurance. Velazquez wrote:

July 23, 1864
No. (blank space) Front st., Nashville, Tenn.

Col Donaldson
Respective Sir
Would be pleased to see you at 6 Oclock if it is convenient. I should have called to have seen you [in] your office, but having mislaid the Letters of Introduction to you from Brig Gen Judah & Col [? Aldby]

Velazquez had not worked very long at her new job before she found herself under suspicion and detained by Union military authorities. She wrote a flurry of five letters in which she proclaimed her innocence. She fussed about her place of detention and wrote, "[it is a] miserable place. it is not fit for any Lady. thrown among all kind of low people. it is not any place for a man wife [*sic*]." There can be no doubt that she inflicted more torture on the syntax and grammar of her letters than she herself had to endure from her captors. These five letters, like her previous letters, are presented as written (with two small obvious edits in the second letter) and follow in chronological order:

[Letter 1]
July 26, 1864
St. Cloud Hotel Nashville Tenn

Captain Stockdale
Respective Sir
Will you have the kindness to investigate my case as soon as posible [*sic*] as I am under Expense. I feel sure that the charge professed against me is an unjust one. it is without foundation. it has been through malicious persons. One of the parties I spoke of. he is in Chatanooga [*sic*]- A Mr. Hubbards- I am willing to meet with any person or persons before and [*sic* a] court of jury in the U S. and after a thorough Examination Either by act or word done anything that has any tendency to Injure the government I am perfectly satisfied to suffer any punishment here Orthorities [*sic*] may deem just. I thus call your immediate attention to my case
    Yours Very Respectfuly [*sic*]
    Mrs. Lauretta J. DeCaulp

[Letter 2]
July 27, 1864
No. 49 St. Cloud Hotel Nashville Tenn

Captain Stockdale
Respective Sir
Will call your immediate attention to Statements in regards to my arrival at Memphis Last October. I received my passes & permit from his provost marhial [*sic* marshal] for to carry two pistols & A Rebbel belt I captured from A Rebbel[.] gen Furgusons Courier [note- removed a period] he will Leave this Eavening [*sic*] and says if you wish to get those statements can do so by calling Or sending to his room. he is sick. You will pleas [*sic*] attend to this matter as soon as posible [*sic*]
    Yours truly,
    Mrs. L. J. DeCaulp

[Letter 3]
July 29, 1864
No. 49 St. Cloud Hotel Nashville Tenn

Captain Stockdale
Respective Sir
Will you have the kindness to call and see me, or call me for trial. it is very unjust to keep me under guard without I was guilty. Of course you have to do your duty,

but if you can not give me a trial parole me until you can give and [*sic* an] honorable trial. I do not wish to leave the city of Nashville if it was in my power. there are many of the Officers here seem to think it a shame to arrest me upon Suposition [*sic*]. Captain I am here without my baggage or any apparel and no one to attend to it. you will pleas [*sic*] take these matters into consideration and let me know as soon as posible [*sic*]. You will Learn a Little more of me when you see me. pleas [*sic*] answer this by the bearer.

Yours Mrs. L. J. DeCaulp

[Letter 4]
Office of Military Prison
Nashville, Tenn., July 30th 1864

Brig Gen Webster
Respective Sir
Will you have the kindness to have my case attended to as soon as posible [*sic*] as I feel sure that I am here under a false supposition by Order of Maj Gen Sherman- who I have been informed by Several staff Officers knows nothing about me I beseech the Orthorities [*sic*] to give me a hearing. I am able to answer any charge professed against me. here And if necessary am willing to go to Washington- Where I was last December & January- and since then have been in Milwaukee Wis-. and Fort Snelling Minn. until the 14th of June last is where my husband is Stationed at Headquarters or detached duty under Brig Gen Sibbley- whose Hd Qrs is at St paul in the International Hotel. my husband is captain of comp [C ?] [2nd ?] Connetticut [*sic*] Cav Rebbel [*sic*] deseters, sent from the army of the Potomac, by order of secretary of war. he was elected by the camp- his health was so much impaired the Ds [*sic* doctors] did not think him fit to join the Expedition against the Indians, having friends in New York I left and went to New York on a visit, visiting

[page 2]
my friends from Suspension bridge Col Young & lady and Mr Chamberlyn. the vice council [*sic*] to [mexico ?] who was interested in the National Life & Limb Insurance Co 243 Broadway NY he offered me an Agency which I Excepted [*sic* accepted]. The President (Mr. Orvis P Blunt) made out commision [*sic*] for the Department of Tennessee- with the instructions to stop at Chatanooga [*sic*]- and Establish an Office- and there communicate with Maj Gen W. T. Sherman to know if he would permit me to go to the front. Gen Thomas Ajt Gen US- allso [*sic*] advised me to do the same as there was no accommodations in the front for a lady. Gen I should not excepted [*sic* accepted] this position but my husband has not received any pay for Over Eight months and it was the general Oppinion [*sic*] they would not be paid before August or September- and I wished to be doing something to for [*sic*] a livelyhood and to assist my husband as I think it is Every Ladies duty to help her husband in this hour of trouble. Gen Sir I have not been in the Rebbel [*sic*] Lines since Last September. I was then sent through after my husband who was sick at Atlanta Ga. I had no intention to Leave Nashville until I received a letter from my husband & and Gen Sherman. I will thus close soliciting your immediate attention to this matter.

Yours Very Respectfuly [*sic*]
Mrs. Lauretta J. DeCaulp

[Letter 5]
Office of Military Prison
Nashville, Tenn., <u>August 1st</u> 1864

Captain S. A. Stockdale
Dear Sir
You will pleas [*sic*] to give me a hearing to day as I am desireous [*sic*] of knowing what they have me hear [*sic* here] for, keeping from my business and withall- my bagage [*sic*]. and keeping me in this miserable place. it is not fit for any Lady. thrown among all kind of low people, it is not any place for a man wife. if they have any respect for a lady I hope they will attend to this at an Early period. you promised my [*sic* me] you would attend to this matter the next day. I shall go home as soon as my trial come [off ?] to my husband at Fort Snelling Minn who wrote me a few day ago do they think that this is the way to make Soldiers Or Officers do their duty to arrest their wives. upon innocent charges. I will thus close and Leave you to judge for yourself just placing you in the same position
Your truly
Mrs L. J. DeCaulp

Please see the image of St. Cloud Hotel in Illustrations, Figure 9.

Velazquez finally succeeded in getting herself released. "Civil War Prisoner of War Records, 1861-1865" documents her release: "Mrs. Major DeCaulp, Rlease [*sic* Release] Aug 1, 1864 By one capt Stockdale." She was probably relieved to be able to now concentrate on other matters, particularly her husband's situation in Minnesota. As she stated in her August 1 letter to Captain Stockdale, she had just received a letter from her husband "a few days ago." No doubt she had been apprised of her husband's situation at Fort Snelling, Minnesota and felt compelled to help him.

Velazquez now made a bold move. She, using an altered handwriting, posed as Union "Colonel M. D. Hascall," and forged a letter asking Union Brigadier General (Henry Hastings) Sibley, who commanded the military department which included Minnesota, to extend "any favor" in his power to "a soldier by name William Irwin."[30] This was DeCaulp, under his "assumed name."

One might reasonably think that great care would have been taken in the execution of a forged letter, if it was to be convincing, but this plainly was not the case. The letter was another example of Velazquez's ability to butcher every aspect of grammatical norms. The forged letter contains the same sort of errors seen in her other letters. When Velazquez wrote in haste, or excitement, her letters were horribly done. However, if her letters were

---

30. NARA, CMSR for William Irwin.

written with care, they showed some improvement. The question arises as to how she could have produced such an error burdened letter when she should have been at the top of her spy game, that is, if she ever had a spy game. Was she still a little rattled three days after her week-long arrest? The letter, unedited, follows:

August 4, 1864
Louisville ky
Brig Gen Sibley

Dear Sir
allow me to inquire of you if there, is in your command. now at Fort Snelling Minn, a soldier by name (William Irwin) a Rebbel [sic] deserter he deserted the Rebbels at Chickamagau [sic Chickamauga] in October 1863, where he held the Commission of Capt. in the 3rd Reg Arks. Vol Cav. under Forrest.) he was a union man forced to take up arms against his county or hang. and Escaped as soon as opportunity admitted. his name is (DeCaulp) but by friends. advised to change it for his own safety. any favor that Mr. DeCaulp. alias, William Irwin, ask of you I have every confidence you will to the Extent of your power grant. at the same time will call to your notice he has family the daughter of Rear Admiral Rosche Eng [English] Navy is his wife. who deserves great credit from the patriot in the feild [sic field]. Please feel for her situation which she will Explain to your Entire satisfaction. any kindness shown them will be highly appreciated by
Yours Truly
M. D. Hascall
Col q m 2nd Div 23 ac

ps pleas [sic] see for refference [sic] Letter of mine to Capt Wilson, Mineopolis [sic] of this date

How can it be certain that this letter is not genuine, but instead, is a forgery by Velazquez?

First, there existed no Union military man named "M. D. Hascall" whose signature is found on the letter.[31] The officer must have been meant to be M. S. Hascall (Milo Smith Hascall). The signature is clear and a misreading of it is not possible. It is impossible that M. S. Hascall incorrectly wrote his own name. Recall, in a December 1863 letter, she addressed Union General W. S. Rosecrans incorrectly as General W. D. Rosecrans and in 1874 she wrote to Mark Twain, incorrectly calling him Mr. S. P. Clemens, instead of Mr. S. L. Clemens. Even in her memoir (page 189), Velazquez exhibited the same shortcoming when she incorrectly called General Lucius E. Polk, by the name of "General Lucius M. Polk." The General's full name was Lucius Eugene Polk and he was a nephew to the more famous General Leonidas

---

31. A thorough check of databases and books of Union soldiers and officers reveals no one by this name and/or rank.

Polk. At the time of her supposed chance meeting with Lucius in a Memphis dining room, two weeks prior to the April 6, 1862 Battle of Shiloh, Lucius E. Polk was not a general, but a second lieutenant. Maybe Velazquez, who described Polk as "my old friend," called Polk a general in an effort to add a greater air of importance to their acquaintance. Or maybe it was just too much trouble for her to say she ran into a second lieutenant who later became a general of some renown. Or maybe she just lied. It was only after Shiloh that Lucius Polk was promoted to colonel and then later to brigadier general on December 13, 1862. The point is, Velazquez routinely erroneously used peoples' initials.

Second, Hascall was highly educated. He could not have written such a poor letter, devoid of logic and syntax, even if a Navy Colt Model 1861 cap & ball six-shot revolver had been held to his head. Nor could Hascall have written the words, "Chickamagau," "Rebbel," feild," "pleas," "refference," and "Mineopolis" even if a "Rebbel" had forced Hascall's hand with the point of a Confederate Bowie knife. Please recall Velazquez's use of the word "Rebbel" in her letter to Brig. Gen. Webster just three days prior. (It is arguable whether "rebbel" was a misspelling since it was used by others at the time, but the majority of the populace wrote "rebel.") In addition, recall the same words, "Rebbel" and "pleas," in her Nashville letters written to Captain S. A. Stockdale. Years after the war, in a June 27, 1875 letter to Jefferson Davis, Velazquez again used the word "refferences."

A short illustrative history of Hascall's education is in order to make the point. Hascall, at the age of sixteen, taught school. The local congressman understood young Hascall's potential and appointed him to a Cadetship at the U.S. Military Academy at West Point. Hascall graduated from the Academy in 1852, with a class ranking of 14th out of a class of 43 members. After a brief military duty, he resigned, became a railroad contractor, and then a lawyer. He was elected Prosecuting Attorney for the Court of Common Pleas; then in the fall of 1859, he was elected Clerk of Elkhart Circuit Court, working there until the outbreak of the war.[32] In summary, Hascall overflowed with education and was incapable of violating the rules of grammar such as found in the forged letter.

Third, Velazquez's other known letters are a collection of violated rules of syntax and grammar of exactly the same nature. In this and other letters, she habitually did not start a new sentence with a capitalized word. She used periods in the middle of sentences, which might have been meant to be commas, but regardless, it is a repeated habit found in all of her letters. The awkward construction of the Hascall letter is identical to that of her letters.

---

32. *Thirty-Sixth Annual Reunion of the Association Graduates of the United States Military Academy, at West Point, New York, June 13th 1905* (Saginaw, MI: Seeman & Peters, 1905), 317.

140

Fourth, Hascall would never have written such a mundane letter to a general. He would never have been so impressed that William Irwin's wife was "the daughter of rear Admiral Rosche Eng Navy" to have warranted even mentioning it. The only person impressed with this made-up story of the "daughter of rear Admiral Rosche Eng Navy" was Velazquez herself, and it was for this reason Velazquez was compelled to include this irrelevant fact in her forged letter. (Some researchers have asserted that alias William Irwin stated that "he was married to the daughter of a [*sic*] English rear admiral residing in Philadelphia," but he did not say it.)

Fifth, the date and the location on the forged letter fit a logical time and location for Velazquez; the date was August 4, 1864. This makes sense if one supposes that Velazquez, upon her August 1 release from her Nashville detention, went to Louisville, Kentucky, where the letterhead indicates the letter was written. She was presumably on her way back North to be with her husband. In the letter, she stated as much. She said that Irwin's wife (herself) would be happy to explain all to General Sibley's satisfaction, so it is clear that she was on her way North and was trying to set the stage for a meeting with General Sibley. The letter has annotations that it was received "in the Dist. of Minn." on August 9 and replied to by General Sibley on August 11.

General Sibley was an educated, no-nonsense man, wise to the ways of the world. He was born to a Detroit attorney who insisted that his son study Greek, Latin and law. But Sibley wanted adventure, went to the Northwest wilderness, became a fur trader with the Indians, became fluent in the Dakota language and attained wealth. At the age of thirty-eight he ran for the U.S. Congress and won. Upon leaving Washington, he won a seat in the Minnesota Legislature and later became Minnesota's first governor. When the Sioux Uprising of 1862 began, the first person Governor Ramsey sought out to quell the unrest was Sibley. Indians by the hundreds were arrested for attacking Indian agency personnel and settlers. Some 303 Indians were sentenced to death; all but 38 got a reprieve and those were hung in December 1862, the largest mass execution in U.S. history.[33] Now in 1864, Sibley was still commanding the troops which maintained the peace and these were the troops in which William Irwin was serving.

Did General Sibley recognize the letter as a forgery? His reply[34] indicates no:

Colonel,

---

33. Duane Schultz, *Over the Earth I Came, The Great Sioux Uprising of 1862* (NY: St. Martin's Press, 1992).
34. NARA, RG 393, Letters and Telegrams Sent, Nov 1862- Jun 1873, Sibley to Hascall, Aug 11, 1864, part 3, entry 343, p384.

In reply to your dispatch of 4th instant relative to William Irwin a rebel deserter. You are respectfully informed that he is now at Fort Snelling with his wife in comfortable quarters. Mrs. Irwin (or DeCaulp) came to see me in person shortly after her husband had been assigned to duty in this Military District and her representations of the facts agrees with your own.

I have not seen your letter to Captain Wilson of Minneapolis to which you refer.

Sixth, a perfect handwriting match is found on an envelope which was taken from Velazquez upon her arrest in Nashville. The envelope has a pre-printed return address for the National Life and Limb Insurance Co. and upon it is handwritten, "Official Business." The envelope is addressed to "Lieut. Gen. U.S. Grant USA, Head Quarters, City Point." The handwriting is a bold, heavy, dark, back slanted, very distinctive, and not at all characteristic of Velazquez's normal handwriting. The handwriting of the forged letter is a perfect match to this addressed envelope in every regard. The faked writing of both was clearly meant to be perceived as the heavy style of writing more typical of a man.

Seventh, preserved documents show that Milo Smith Hascall's forward slanting, medium pressure handwriting is not remotely similar to that of the handwriting of the forged letter. His true signature does not match the signature of the forged letter, even vaguely.

Eight, the alleged signer, "M. D. Hascall," identifies his rank as "Col Q M 2nd Div. 23 AC." This should be interpreted as: Colonel, Quartermaster, 2nd Division, 23rd Army Corps. The 2nd Division, 23rd Army Corps was in Knoxville at this date. M. S. Hascall, who had been a colonel in 1861, was promoted to Brigadier-General in April 1862. In August 1864 (date of the letter) he was not a colonel or a quartermaster. A document from April 24, 1864 makes clear he was, on that date, Brigadier-General of the 2nd Brigade, 2nd Div., 23rd Army Corps.[35]

Please see the images of the "M. D. Hascall" letter and evidence in Illustrations, Figure 10.

1864, Revisited Richmond in December?

From the time of her detention release in Nashville, August 1, 1864, until March 1866, Velazquez's whereabouts is undiscovered. Circumstantial evidence places her in Richmond in December 1864, but that would have meant she crossed the military lines back into a Confederate controlled city. The Augusta, Georgia *Daily Constitutionalist* of December 31, 1864 re-printed from the "Personal" section of the *Richmond Enquirer*, a letter which was allegedly written to Velazquez, announcing the death of her father and of her inheritance. This paid-to-place *Richmond Enquirer* "Personal" could have only been supplied by Velazquez and must be judged a contrivance,

---

35. *OR*, Ser 1, Vol 52, part 1, p549.

probably designed to ease the fears of Richmond citizens from whom she had borrowed money or sought to borrow. The Augusta article[36] was titled "In Luck":

> We clip the subjoined Personal from the *Richmond Enquirer*.
> Madame Laure De Caulp, formerly of St. James' Parish, La.- The following is an extract from a letter from Don Augustus V. Steinhosse, of Havana:
> "Died on the 20th of November, at the residence of his sister, Mrs. Horatio Flagg, at Hayti, W. I., Commodore J. B. Roach, of the British Navy, aged 72 years and 4 months.- In distribution of his estate, his daughter, residing in the Confederate States of America, is to receive, at the expiration of five years, the sum of $10,00, with interest. [*sic* The number is clear, but the typographical error makes the amount unclear; it can be supposed to be $10,000, judging from further content.] Her son is to be educated at the expense of the estate, at the military school at London, and at the age of 21 years, shall receive $30,000 with interest."
> The plate, valued at twenty thousand dollars ($20,000,) [*sic*] was also left you, and your jewelry and manuscripts are on deposit in the Bank of England for you. The estate was valued at $1,810,000 and after deducting your own and your son's portion, it is to be equally divided between the remaining eight children. Your father expressed in his will a dissatisfaction with your late marriage, and acted accordingly. The only member of the family present at your father's death was your brother Harry, who is acting British Consul at Hayti. The remains were sent to Glasgow, Scotland, for interment.

The falsehoods are quickly revealed! The letter stated that Velazquez had eight siblings. In contradiction, she claimed (p40) in her book, that she was the "sixth and last child" in the family. And it will be seen that she wrote (p517) that she and her brother, in April 1865, were the "sole remnants of our family," so apparently all eight siblings or five siblings, take your pick, dropped dead in less than a four-month period. That's a lot of droppings!

Recall, Velazquez, in the forged letter to General Sibley, claimed that her father was "Rear-Admiral Rosche of the English Navy." In a mere five months the poor gentleman was demoted from a rear-admiral to a commodore and underwent a name change too, from Rosche to Roach and Velazquez had provided both spellings. No wonder the man died; the shock was too much! At the least, it should have made him feel ill. The poor gentleman's suffering was not yet over, because twelve years later, Velazquez, in her memoir, caused her dear father to have a tricky medical gene rearrangement when she wrote that her father was Velazquez of Spain and was of noble heritage as a bonus.

---

36. *Charleston Courier* (South Carolina) Dec 29, 1864 had reported the same news two days prior. It reproduced only the first paragraph and it stated a different sum, $5,000, to be received by the daughter. It noted that the paragraph was, "Copied from a letter received by a brother-in-law, in Havana, Cuba. DON AUGUSTINE V. STAINHOSS."

The inheritance letter claimed to be from one Don Augustus V. Steinhosse in Havana informing Velazquez of her father's death at Roach's sister's house (Mrs. Horatio Flagg) in Haiti. It further claimed that her "brother Harry, who is acting British Consul at Hayti," was the only family member present at his death. Oh, wasn't the commodore's sister a family member? In any case, it should be noted that none of the presumably important people named in the letter are found in any archival records; no Steinhosse, no Flagg, no Roach as a Commodore, and no son of a Roach as a British Consul.

The letter was plainly bogus, designed to impress the newspaper's readers of Velazquez's pending inheritance or maybe just of her important lineage.

It gets worse. Recall the *Mississippian* article of June 6, 1863 in which Velazquez claimed she saw her father on the battlefield of Shiloh, but that he did not recognize her in her disguise? By all measures it is remarkable that a commodore in the British Navy, who would have been 69 years and 9 months on the date of Shiloh (April 6-7, 1862), devoted his sweat and blood for the glory of the South. Indeed, it must have been terribly inconvenient to carry a cane plus a musket. And shore leave from the British Navy must have been a little tricky… Oh, the Commodore could have written his own shore leave pass! And it was fortuitous the old chap had time enough to scurry to Haiti, write his will making Velazquez a beneficiary, before he died. Recall, about a year and a half prior to the inheritance article Velazquez told the Richmond *Examiner* (July 11, 1863) that her father was "Major J. B. Roche, of Mississippi." These must have been troubling times for the old man, not knowing his own rank or whether he was in the navy or army or even which country he served. Of course, in her memoir Velazquez made no claim of a father named "Commodore J. B. Roach" or of his will. Or of a father "Major J. B. Roche of Mississippi." Or that her father fought at Shiloh and that he did not recognize her when they were near to one another on that battlefield.

One point in the article is a curiosity- the "manuscripts are on deposit in the Bank of England for you." It is clear that at this date, 1864, Velazquez considered herself an author and she was glad to let the public know it. As early as 1862, she had stated her intentions to write a history of the war; the New Orleans *Daily True Delta* (April 24, 1862) reported, "Her reason for the course she has adopted is, that she is collecting material for a history of the war, and that she adopted male attire as the plan best calculated to enable her to carry out her design."

Chapter 5

1865, Where was Velazquez?

For a year and two months, Velazquez seems to have gone into hiding. Uncharacteristically, she does not make herself known to the newspapers and they take no notice of her from January 1865 to March 1866. There exist several hints where she might have been.

According to her book (p505), Velazquez places herself in New York sometime between February 1 and March 7, 1865 (or later). She wrote she visited her associate in New York who feared the collapse of Confederate bonds because General Sherman was marching through the Carolinas. The dates of Sherman's march are clear; he crossed into South Carolina about February 1, 1865 and by March 7, he began crossing into North Carolina. At her associate's urging she undertook a quick trip to Europe- London, Paris and Liverpool. She arrived back in New York the day after General Lee's surrender, which was on April 9, 1865.

Then on page 519 Velazquez claimed a second European trip, this time with her brother and his family. Velazquez makes clear their departure for Europe was after April 30 since she claimed (p511) that she was in Columbus, Ohio, staying at the Neil House, when Lincoln's body was lying in state in Columbus and that date was April 29, 1865 (assassinated April 14). The telling of the trip regaled readers with the wonders of Paris, Rheims, Frankfurt, Kraków and London and it has all the markings of truthfulness because of the wonderful detail. One observation Velazquez offered was: "I have every reason to believe that wines, as fine in flavor as any of the European brands, can be, and in time will be, made in America." Velazquez should be credited with visionary/sommelier powers.

Her claimed second European trip is full of inconsistencies and there are at least six problems.

First, Velazquez claimed she made this trip with a brother, whose very existence should be doubted. At this point in her memoir, Velazquez claimed (p517) she and her brother "were the sole remnants of [their] family." Velazquez explained that her brother, along "with his wife and child," were going to Europe and proposed Velazquez join them. But then two pages later (p519) Velazquez lost count of her brother's children and wrote that her brother and "his wife [and] two children... one of whom was a name-sake of [her] own" made the trip. Oops!

Recall that Velazquez said that this brother was awarded a degree in medicine from the College de France, which he was not because it doesn't confer degrees. During the narration of this trip, Velazquez again made the claim (p523), "The College de France, where my brother had been educated, and the Medical School in which he had studied, interested him greatly, but I was satisfied with looking at them from the outside."

Adding to the doubt is that she refused to identify her brother, instead she called him "Captain –" when clearly his surname would have been the same as her maiden name. No Captain Velazquez existed, and if by chance he called himself in the Spanish manner which uses the mother's name, there existed no captain by the name which some years later Velazquez provided for her mother. More on this elsewhere. Recall, she claimed her brother's name was "Josea," which is a completely nonsensical name if it was meant to be Spanish. It will be seen that in November 1868, Velazquez called her brother by the name of "Colonel R. D. Clapp" (a provable falsehood) which in no way hints at the first name of "Josea."

Second, Velazquez claimed that her prime motivation for going on the second trip was to escape the onerous task of "finding herself" which was pushed on her by U.S. Secret Service Chief Lafayette Baker. Velazquez narrated (p516) Baker's demand:

> I want you to find this woman who is travelling and figuring as a Confederate agent... she is a slippery customer... I knew it was myself Baker meant....

It is not believable that Baker would obsess, at this late date, (after April 30) over the capture of some nebulous woman who was an alleged Confederate agent. General Robert E. Lee had already surrendered on April 9, followed by General Joe Johnston's surrender on April 26; the collapse of the Confederacy was clear to everyone. Baker would have had nothing to do with her decision to go to Europe, if she even went.

In fact, archived records show that if she worked "as U.S. Special Agent," it was for General Robert C. Schenck and not Baker, and any association between her and Baker has, to date, not been discovered.[1] Still more telling is the fact that "Mrs. Alice Williams," who is thought by some researchers to have been Velazquez, had resigned as an agent in the Federal secret service on July 15, 1864, which would have been some nine months prior to when she claimed this European trip occurred. She would have had no reason to avoid Baker since she had resigned long before, so her stated motive for the trip was false!

Third, on June 16, 1866 the *Daily Union and American* reported her presence in Nashville and wrote:

> She was in the City of New York at the time of the Confederate surrender, on the eve of her departure 'for Europe;' but upon that event, changed her destination, and sometimes afterwards presented herself to the nearest Commander as a Confederate soldier, and asked and obtained the parole usual in such cases, which she still retains.

Fourth, the Atlanta *Daily Intelligencer* (May 9, 1866) said that she had been held in a Yankee prison and implied this was after the death of her husband

---

1. In 1894 Baker published his own book, *Spies. Traitors and Conspirators of the Late Civil War*, relating the Secret Service's activities and his own activity and made no mention of anyone who was Velazquez.

(which research suggests was in December 1865). The paper wrote, "Mrs. Lorreta J. DeCaulp… informs us that she surrendered herself a prisoner in Washington City, to the authorities there and was treated with great kindness." No evidence of this arrest has been located. However, remember her arrest in Nashville? Why did she fail to mention that arrest to the newspapers? Was it a lie of omission? Did she choose not to tell of the Nashville arrest, and instead, swapped arrest stories, claiming she was arrested in Washington in an effort to gain prestige? Or did she get arrested in Washington, too? A search of the prisoner register for Washington's Old Capitol Prison[2] for the years 1863 to 1865 did not uncover anyone named DeCaulp or DeCamp, the names she used at that time. This same article claimed, "She had been a great traveler- having visited Europe twice…."

Fifth, the St. Louis *Republican* (March 7, 1866) after an interview with her, wrote that she was up north at the close of the war:

After the final collapse of the Confederacy [April- June 1865], Mrs. De Camp remained in the North until January [1866], when she returned to her home in Louisiana; but remaining there only a few days, she proceeded to Memphis….

Sixth, Velazquez wrote:

In Paris we [she and her brother] met Mr. Dayton, the minister from the United States, and were quite cordially received by him. I had carefully avoided going near this gentleman on my former visit, because I was aware that he knew me, and thought that, perhaps, he might bear me some ill will.

The described meeting seems genuine, but take a closer look.

Recall Velazquez claimed this trip was sometime after President Lincoln's death, April 15, 1865, and even after General Joe Johnston's April 26, 1865 surrender. William Lewis Dayton, Minister to France, had already died on December 1, 1864, at least 3 months and 26 days prior to Velazquez's earliest possible departure for Europe and even longer before her claimed visit to him! Clearly, this claim falls in the category of "Meeting Men of Influence"; remember some of the other prominent people she claimed to have met. In this case the claim is a provable lie. It might be considered that this second European trip was earlier than she claimed and she really did see Mr. Dayton. The problem with that line of thought is, then her claim to have witnessed the arrival of Lincoln's funeral train in Columbus, Ohio could not have been the truth.

In summary, Velazquez did not go to Europe with her brother and she most certainly did not visit an alive Mr. Dayton, and she did not visit a dead one either, as his body had been taken to and buried in New Jersey. (Dayton,

---

2. NARA, United States Records of Confederate Prisoners of War, 1861-1865, M598, list prisoners and visitors.

New Jersey is named in his honor.) There is a very slim chance that Velazquez did go to Europe, but lied about aspects of her trip.

It is more believable that Velazquez remained "in the North" after the death of Thomas C. DeCaulp, (alias William Irwin) which might have been in December 1865 in Philadelphia. She probably stayed in Philadelphia awhile and then went to New York which was consistently her favorite city. Velazquez told contradictory versions of her location and activity for the time frame in question and it is certain that all the versions cannot be the truth.

Famed Secret Courier for the St. Alban's Raiders?

In 1864 Confederate operations commenced against the United States in the North, behind the lines. It remains in question just how closely these operations were directed by the Confederate Government in Richmond. In any case, sanctioned or not, the Rebels who were involved in the various schemes were mostly like-minded and they worked to damage United States property and personal property of its citizens, as the Rebels felt the Federals were doing to their own government and families. The operations also were an effort to open another war front which would demand manpower and resources of the United States to defend. The new war front was to be made-up of freed Rebel prisoners of war, some 30,000, held in several large Federal prison camps.

The Rebel scheme, which raises questions about Velazquez, became known as the St. Albans Raid. Twenty-one Confederate soldiers staying in Canada, under the leadership of Lieutenant Bennett H. Young, crossed the nearby U.S. border and robbed St. Albans' (Vermont) three banks.

The raiders killed one citizen and wounded another and fled back to Canada. The perpetrators were caught and brought to trial by the Canadians. American officials wanted the men extradited as common thieves and murderers. The raiders claimed they had conducted a legitimate act of war against the United States which was at war with their own country, the Confederate States of America. A Canadian judge was willing to listen to that argument, but demanded proof of their enlistment in the Confederate army.

The Confederates asked the Federal Government for safe passage for a courier to go to Richmond to get documentation, but were refused. So, four Confederate messengers were sent out in secret from Montreal to Richmond to obtain the proof. Federal officials learned of the messengers, determined to thwart them, and they succeeded in capturing one, Samuel Davis. Another messenger, Wilson, drowned in the Potomac River. Confederate army Chaplain Reverend Stephen F. Cameron almost drowned along with Wilson, but he succeeded in reaching the shore, then completed his mission to Richmond and returned to Montreal, where the trial had been granted a 30-

day delay. He arrived in time to deliver the documents and testified to the facts surrounding his obtaining them. The Judge accepted the documents and the raiders were set free. The fourth messenger arrived in Montreal the same day as Cameron (alternatively reported as the day after Cameron's arrival).

This fourth messenger, a female, is our person of interest because it has been suspected she was Velazquez.

In 1906 one of the Confederate operatives, John W. Headley, wrote about his participation in several of these northern Confederate activities. In his book, *Confederate Operations in Canada and New York*, he specifically addressed (p376) the female Confederate messenger:

Mrs. -----,* a widow only 24 years old, employed by the Confederate Government for secret service in the Northern States, had come to Montreal and called on the prisoners at the jail. She volunteered for the journey to Richmond. After leaving the railroad in Maryland she walked much of the way through the country occupied by the enemy in Virginia. She departed from Richmond with the necessary papers, well concealed, one day before Rev. Mr. Cameron arrived there. These two messengers, traveling by different routes, reached Montreal on the same day. She declined to accept from Col. Jacob Thompson any compensation whatever for her services or expenses. This devotee of the South was a Kentucky lady. About 1867 she visited Frankfort when the legislature was in session. During a recess of fifteen minutes taken in her honor she was the recipient of an ovation, being presented by Hon. Thomas T. Coger [*sic* Cogar], of Jessamine County, the home of Lieut. Bennett H. Young.

* The prisoners never met this lady before or after her visits to the jail at Montreal. One of the survivors secured her photograph at the jail, but after forty years her name is forgotten.

In memory of her heroic interest when the lives of the Confederate prisoners were hanging by a thread all the tribute that can be paid on their behalf is cheerfully recorded.---Author [John W. Headley]

The photo of a young dark-haired woman was reproduced in Headley's book and it rather resembles the drawings depicting Velazquez produced in her own book. The photo might easily be thought to be Velazquez especially considering that Velazquez claimed she was a Confederate spy in the North, with trips to Canada.

Please see the photo of the mystery woman in Illustrations, Figure 11.

One earlier researcher of women in the Civil War, Richard H. Hall (d. 2009), thought there was a "striking resemblance" between the woman in the photo and the illustration of Velazquez from her book. He compared them side-by-side in his book, *Patriots in Disguise, Women Warriors of the Civil War* (1993). Hall was intrigued and wrote that he "intend[ed] to continue this research."

Mr. Hall pursued Velazquez in a second book, titled *Women on the Civil War Battlefront* (2006), "Much more has been learned about Velazquez after ten years additional years of research...." Mr. Hall again addressed the alleged photograph of Velazquez, "My previous research on Velazquez was reported in detail in *Patriots in Disguise*, including the discovery of an apparent photograph of her during a trip to Canada in which she was helping Confederate soldiers who were prisoners there."

So, is the photograph of Velazquez? To answer the question an examination of the facts and evidence is in order.

First, Velazquez at no time claimed an association with the St. Albans raiders. If she had indeed taken the trip on behalf of the raiders, from Montreal to Richmond and return, it would have been a deed worth telling and Velazquez would not have failed to tell it. Of the four messengers sent for documents, one was captured, one drowned and two succeeded, one was a reverend and the other was a woman. The importance, intrigue, difficulty and success of the mission were remarkable in every way, much more so than a courier's petty mission to Robertson's Plantation in Louisiana about which she happily wrote (p255), dedicating three pages to it. She explained that she walked all night covering 17 miles, suffering from hunger, fatigue and fear of capture. She was clearly pleased and impressed with herself. Simply stated, if a 34-mile round trip to Robertson's Plantation was worth telling, then wouldn't a 1400-mile trip from Montreal to Richmond and back, all the while avoiding Federals looking for her be even more noteworthy? If Velazquez had made the trip, logic dictates she would have told of it.

Second, Velazquez wrote (p418) of her first trip to Canada:

> As this was my first visit to Canada, there was much for me to do, and much to learn. I therefore became acquainted with as many people as I could, and found out all I could about the methods of transacting commercial and financial business, who the proper parties to deal with were, and everything else worth knowing that I could think of.

On her return from Canada, she said she went to New York. She placed this trip well before Lincoln's re-election, November 8, 1864. The captured raiders first appeared in court in November, so this trip had nothing to do with the Raiders.

She claimed (p499) she "made a number of trips to Canada," but of these, she said she would not make the effort to give the details, as it would "but increase the bulk of this volume without adding to its interest, and would weary, rather than entertain the reader." Nothing to see here people, please move along.

The last time Velazquez deemed it important enough to mention a trip to Canada, she wrote nothing of the St. Albans raiders' imprisonment,

November 1864 through February 1865, and only said the trip was extremely brief. She wrote (page 504), "Proceeding as rapidly as I could to Canada, I had a conference with the agent there, and then hastened to New York."

Third, the mystery woman was stated to be a young widow. At the date of the St. Albans raiders' imprisonment Velazquez was not a widow. She was still married to DeCaulp, who had just received a discharge from the Yankee army on January 14, 1865 and claimed he was going to live in Holmesburg, Philadelphia County, Pennsylvania.

Fourth, recall that John W. Headley wrote:

This devotee of the South was a Kentucky lady. About 1867 she visited Frankfort when the legislature was in session. During a recess of fifteen minutes taken in her honor she was the recipient of an ovation, being presented by Hon. Thomas T. Coger [*sic* Cogar], of Jessamine County, the home of Lieut. Bennett H. Young.

The referenced Legislative session was from December 2, 1867 to March 9, 1868 in which Representative Cogar was in attendance.[3] In order to determine if the mystery woman who appeared at this session was Velazquez, a simple question needs to be answered: Is there any evidence which places her there or elsewhere?

Not yet discussed, but will be shortly, is the fact that on November 11, 1867 Velazquez (documented as Laura Wasson, 28 years old) arrived in New York aboard the 424-ton American bark *Elba* from Cuba. This was her return trip from her misadventure to Venezuela. Velazquez wrote (p571) that in New York she bought a train ticket to Omaha and went there by way of the "Niagara (New York), Fort Wayne (Indiana) and Chicago (Illinois) route." In other words, she went nowhere near Frankfort, Kentucky during the period in question; she was out West well before the Legislative session began. If she had gone to Kentucky and was honored by the Legislature, even if in recess, one can be sure she would have included that fact in her memoir, which is not scarce of self-accolades. The conclusion, based on the date of the Legislative session and of Velazquez's movements, must be that the mystery woman was not Velazquez. And Velazquez never at any time claimed any connection to Kentucky.

If the claimed origin of the mystery woman's photograph is correct, then the lady in the photograph was not Velazquez. The author of the book in hand, for one, wished for the opposite conclusion, but facts and logic prohibit it. However, if the photograph's source was incorrectly identified and it came from elsewhere, in that case, and also considering the photo's

---

3. *Frankfort Commonwealth*, Dec 7, 1867.

startling likeness to Velazquez's portrait in her memoir, then the woman could be Velazquez, but in no case was she the messenger!

Another Velazquez Sighting?

In his second book, *Women on the Civil War Battlefront* (2006), Richard Hall suspected he had identified a sighting of Velazquez in an archived letter, dated March 15, 1864.[4] One H. Winslow was answering orders and updating Confederate Major J. C. Denis, the Provost Marshal General of Mobile, Alabama:

> I have also placed within the lines a person who will within the next few weeks traverse a large part of the West and North, gathering all the general movements of the enemy, their strength, and future plans as far as an individual can. This person is a highly intelligent and observant lady, and one who from her connections has access to influential and popular leaders of different political parties. She proposes to be in Richmond during the month of April.

Hall noted, "The date and circumstances described fit exactly with the account in her memoirs of her spying activities at this time." Is Hall correct this was Velazquez?

Like the mentioned lady, Velazquez was highly intelligent and observant, but unlike the mentioned lady, Velazquez did not have high connections.

By the date of Winslow's letter, March 15, 1864, Velazquez had long ago gone North. The *Milwaukee Sentinel* placed her in Milwaukee as early as February 6, 1864 and earlier still, on January 26, 1864, "Mrs. Lauretta DeCaulp" was documented in Wheeling, West Virginia receiving a travel pass to proceed to Columbus, Ohio. Is it to be believed that H. Winslow, who was anxious to acknowledge that he had complied with orders, told Major Denis, delaying two months after the fact, that he had placed a spy across the lines?

In conclusion, the date and circumstances do not "fit exactly."

Grand Reappearance in Memphis and St. Louis

The Civil War, in effect, ended with the surrender of General Lee, though it officially ended by declaration on May 9, 1865; there were still sporadic shots fired afterwards. Velazquez now emerged from her yearlong obscurity arriving in Memphis, noted by the *Memphis Daily Avalanche* of March 1, 1866:

> Mrs. L. D. Camp [*sic*].- This lady, whose romantic career as a Lieutenant in the late C. S. A., under the name of H. T. Buford, attracted so much attention during the war, is now in our city, and is stopping at the Commercial Hotel. In male attire, full Confederate uniform, she went into a number of battles with a heroism equal to that of Joan of Arc. She was twice wounded during the war, but nothing daunted, fought to the end. Mrs. Camp [*sic*] is on her way to St. Louis, to purchase a stock

---

4. *OR*, Ser 1, Vol 32, part 3, p633.

of dry goods and plantation supplies, with a view of opening a business house at Mulberry Grove, Jefferson County, Ark.

Velazquez indeed proceeded to St. Louis as she said, and on arrival she contacted the *Republican* newspaper[5] which reported, March 7, 1866:

Romance of the War-Thrilling Adventures of a Young and Beautiful Woman.- Among the many thrilling events of the late war none can exceed the adventures of Mrs. Loretta De Camp [*sic*], the subject of this sketch. Mrs. De Camp, whose maiden name was Roach, was born in the West Indies, in 1838, and is now about 28 years of age. At an early period her parents moved to the United States and settled in the parish of St. James, Louisiana. The current of her life ran smoothly on, until the outbreak of the war for Southern Independence, when, fired by enthusiasm in, as she thought, the cause of liberty, she donned the male attire, and was among the first to rush to arms. Raising a company of cavalry, and equipping it at her own expense, she proceeded to Virginia, and there served eight months on the Peninsula, under the command of the celebrated Colonel Dreux, before her sex was discovered. When this occurred she was at once mustered out and ordered home. Instead of obeying the order she proceeded to Columbus, Ky., and was serving with General Polk at the evacuation of that place. She proceeded to Island No. 10, but not being satisfied with the manner in which affairs were conducted there, she left and went to Fort Pillow, where she was elected First Lieutenant in Captain Phillips' Company of Independent Tennessee Cavalry. With her company she proceeded to Corinth, and reported to General A. S. Johnston. At the battle of Shiloh Captain Phillips fell mortally wounded, and the command then devolved upon her. While gallantly leading her company in a charge, she was twice wounded and carried from the field. After the retreat from Corinth she was taken to New Orleans for surgical treatment, and when the city fell into the Federal hands she was among those taken prisoner. After a confinement of several months she was paroled, and soon after exchanged.

Proceeding at once to Richmond, the disguised female soldier was commissioned 1st Lieutenant in the Adjutant General's department, and ordered to report to General Marcus J. Wright, commanding the district of Atlanta. Upon reporting, she was assigned to duty with the Provost Marshal, as chief of detectives and military conductor. Serving for several months in this capacity, she met Maj. De Camp, of the 3d Arkansas cavalry, to whom she was engaged to be married previous to the war. The ceremony was then performed at Atlanta, and from the dashing Lieutenant Roach she was transformed to the sober Mrs. Major De Camp. From this time her services ceased as an officer in the field and she was engaged in secret service- sometimes in the Confederacy, again in England, and then in Canada. In 1864 she spent several months traveling in the United States, and even went as far as Sioux country in Minnesota. Her husband, who was taken prisoner in the fall of 1863, while serving with his regiment in Georgia, was carried to New York. After a long and arduous siege she at length succeeded in getting him paroled in January, 1865, but he lived only eight days after his release from prison.

---

5. Many newspapers nationwide repeated the article.

Subsequent to the death of her husband (in January, 1865,) she proceeded to Columbus, Ohio, to watch over the interests of the Confederate prisoners confined at Camp Chase.

After the final collapse of the Confederacy, Mrs. De Camp remained in the North until January, when she returned to her home in Louisiana; but remaining there only a few days, she proceeded to Memphis and purchased a stock of goods, which were shipped on the ill-fated steamer Miami, which was blown up on the Arkansas in February. She was one of the two ladies who were saved, but with the sacrifice of all her baggage and goods. By an unfortunate oversight on the part of her merchants, her goods were not insured, and, consequently, she lost her all.

Mrs. De Camp is now in this city, and sojourning at the Southern Hotel. Many who served in the Confederate army will remember the dashing Lieut. Roach, of whom so much was said in Mobile and Selma in 1863. Our space will not permit a full recital of her adventures.

It was a good thing that the newspaper's space did not "permit a full recital" because the abundance and boldness of the lies, and the contradictions to her book's story line, are almost beyond endurance. Understand that surely the reporter wrote what was told him and mustn't be blamed if the facts fail.

First, she claimed her maiden name was Roach. She went through a phase when she liked to use that name. In contradiction, in her book she narrated the extensive family history of her noble father, surname Velazquez. One name is most certainly a lie.

Second, she claimed she was born in 1838. In her book, she named June 26, 1842 as her birthday. The true date is unknown. She used various dates and ages.

Third, she claimed that her family came to St. James' Parish, Louisiana when she was young. In her book, she said her family remained in Cuba and sent her to live with an aunt in New Orleans. She never wrote that her family resided in Louisiana.

Fourth, she said she was fired by enthusiasm, donned male attire, rushed to arms, raised a <u>company</u> of <u>cavalry</u> at her own expense and proceeded to Virginia. In contradiction, in her book she wrote that her first husband "William" played a role, in that, she proved herself to him by her raising an <u>infantry</u> <u>battalion</u>, not cavalry and not company, and delivered the battalion to him in Pensacola, Florida, not Virginia.

Fifth, it is untrue that she "served eight months on the Peninsula [Virginia], under the command of the celebrated Colonel Dreux." The good Colonel lived only long enough to serve 86 days. That's just short of three months, not eight months. He joined the army on April 11 as captain of the company known as the Orleans Cadets and died on July 5, 1861, as the colonel of the 1st Battalion of Louisiana Infantry. Nothing she ever said about Dreux was true. In her book, she never claimed she served under Colonel Dreux and it was wise of her.

Sixth, she claimed that "she proceeded to Columbus, Ky., and [served] with General Polk at the evacuation of that place." In her book (p145) she claimed she went to Columbus, Tennessee (of course, she meant Kentucky) where "General Polk, who had been a bishop before the war broke out" gave her a job as a military railroad conductor. To clarify, this General Polk, the ex-bishop, and in command at Columbus, was General Leonidas Polk.

According to her book, Velazquez's "duty was to run on the trains and examine passes, furloughs, and leaves of absence" and arrest anyone without proper papers. She was the victim of a complaint against her from "a malicious scoundrel" who she had refused travel since he had no pass, so "General Lucius M. Polk... undertook to look into the matter himself." Velazquez told how "General Polk" rode the train and as a trick, pretended not to have papers and how she threatened to arrest him. In significant confusion for the reader, the trickster General was unexpectedly identified, not as General Leonidas Polk, the ex-bishop who had given her the conductor job, but instead as "General Lucius M. Polk." Worse still, she mistakenly called the man, "General Lucius M. Polk," who, in reality, was Lucius E. Polk, the nephew of Leonidas. For verifying this railroad conductor story, Velazquez conveniently created a time frame by placing it after the Battle of Ball's Bluff, October 21, 1861 and before the Battle of Woodsonville, December 17, 1861. The problem is at this time Lucius E. Polk was not a general! He was a 1st lieutenant in the 15th Arkansas Regiment, Yell Rifles Company (F). He was not promoted to general until December 20, 1862.[6]

It is clear that, if the railroad pass trick was even factual, she did not stand her ground against "General Lucius Polk" because he was not then a general. Later, she mentioned (p189) that she again met her "old friend" and again misnamed the old friend, calling him General Lucius M. Polk.

Seventh, she claimed that "she proceeded [from Columbus, KY] to Island No. 10, and not being satisfied with the manner in which affairs were conducted there, she left and went to Fort Pillow...." In contradiction, in her book (p226-232), she wrote that she left Shiloh, went to Corinth, MS; then Grand Junction, TN; then Grenada, MS; then Jackson, MS; then Osyka, MS and finally to New Orleans. She wrote, "I heard the news that Island No. 10 had been captured, after reaching New Orleans...." In her detailed narration of that travel, she never claimed she went to Island No. 10 and she never did.

---

6. NARA, CMSR; Ed. William Robertson Garrett, *American Historical Magazine*, Vol 3 (1898), 50.

Eighth, she claimed that at Fort Pillow "she was elected First Lieutenant in Captain Phillips' Company of Independent Tennessee Cavalry." She never claimed in her book to have been elected to the rank of an officer. Worse still, on page 181, she claimed she enlisted in Captain Moses' Company of 21st Louisiana Regiment and "the next day we started for Fort Pillow, to join the balance of the regiment." So, while she was at Fort Pillow, was she enlisted in the 21st Louisiana Regiment or the Independent Tennessee Cavalry? The answer is neither.

While on the question of rank- the newspaper asserted she claimed, "Proceeding at once to Richmond, the disguised female soldier was commissioned 1st Lieutenant in the Adjutant General's department...." In her book, she contradicted this and stated that she never received a real commission and that she gave rank to herself as part of her alias, Lieutenant Harry T. Buford.

Ninth, she claimed, "At the battle of Shiloh Captain Phillips fell mortally wounded, and the command then devolved upon her." Captain Bruce L. Phillips did not die at Shiloh, April 6-7, 1862, but surrendered and was paroled at Fort Donelson on May 6, 1865, at the conclusion of hostilities.[7] The command did not "devolve upon her" and she wisely never made this claim in her book, which presents a totally different storyline.

Tenth, she claimed, "While gallantly leading her company in a charge, she was twice wounded and carried from the field." In her book she never claimed this, but instead claimed that it was the third day of the conflict, when burying the dead, that she was wounded by an exploding shell. Through the years she made many contradictory claims as to the how, when, and where of her wounds. Much more is said about this elsewhere.

Eleventh, she claimed "...when [New Orleans] fell into the Federal hands she was among those taken prisoner. After a confinement of several months she was paroled, and soon after exchanged." This was untrue and contradictory to her book in which she claimed that she was detained only several days, after which, she hired a fisherman who clandestinely took her across the lake to her freedom (p265), but that was untrue, as well. It is clear from the New Orleans newspapers that she was not "taken prisoner," but arrested for stealing and sentenced to six months in prison. She was not "paroled" and "exchanged," but was sent out of Federal New Orleans as a "registered enemy" aboard a lake steamer.

Twelfth, she claimed that she was "assigned to duty with the Provost Marshal as chief of detectives and military conductor" in the Atlanta district which was under the command of General Marcus J. Wright. It is true that General Wright commanded Atlanta in 1863-64. In her book, Velazquez makes no mention of serving under the General's command or even

---

7. NARA, CMSR.

mentions him. She does not write anything about being given the job of "chief of detectives and military conductor" in the Atlanta district.

Thirteenth, she claimed while doing duty in Atlanta she met "Maj. De Camp, of the 3d Arkansas Cavalry, to whom she was engaged to be married previous to the war." Confederate military records show that "Maj. De Camp" was never a major, but was a captain, Captain Thomas C. DeCaulp. In contradiction, in her book Velazquez narrated that prior to the war, in 1856, she married a "William." When the war broke out William joined the Confederacy, went to Pensacola, where she followed and delivered to him a "battalion" of soldiers she had raised at her own expense, and all the while in male military disguise. In short order William was killed while explaining "the use of the carbine to one of the sergeants" Velazquez then wrote that DeCaulp, who she claimed was at Pensacola, took command of the company. Military records show that DeCaulp was never at Pensacola and history makes clear that William did not exist. And please answer a question: If Velazquez was engaged to DeCaulp prior to the War, did she have her husband William's approval of the engagement?

Fourteenth, she claimed that she was in Minnesota in 1864. That was the truth. She traveled there to be with her deserter husband, DeCaulp, who had joined the Union army. And she may have been there prior to the war.

Fifteenth, she claimed her husband was "taken prisoner in the fall of 1863" and was "carried to New York in 1865." False. Records indicate that he deserted in 1863 and went North the same year. Velazquez claimed in the article that "after a long and arduous siege" she succeeded in getting him released only to have him die eight days later. She did nothing of the kind and he did nothing of the kind, and the claim of "eight days" is not true. After his desertion, he took the "Oath of Allegiance" and went North where he joined the Union army. He was discharged because of poor health in middle of January 1865 and died, it appears, in December 1865. Since the war had ended on May 9, 1865 (by declaration), she seems to have killed him off in January, so that she could depict him to be a loyal Southerner who was a military prisoner casualty. Her book contradicts the truth and this false New York claim.

Sixteenth, she claimed that "she proceeded to Columbus, Ohio, to watch over the interests of the Confederate prisoners confined at Camp Chase." In contradiction, in her book (p381-382) she said that when she went to Camp Chase it was to secure the release of her brother and she did not claim to perform humanitarian services for any prisoners.

Seventeenth, the newspaper asserted she claimed that "after the final collapse of the Confederacy, Mrs. De Camp remained in the North until January." This might be true. It is likely that she was there with her husband until his death. In her book she said she had just returned from Europe and was in New York harbor, still shipboard, when she learned of General Lee's surrender from the boarding pilot. Note that in this *St. Louis Republican* article she made no claim to have been in Europe at that time.

Eighteenth, she claimed, now while in St. Louis (March 7, 1866) that she had gone "to Memphis and purchased a stock of goods, which were shipped on the ill-fated steamer *Miami*, which was blown up on the Arkansas [River] in February." The falsehood becomes obvious when one compares what she told the *Memphis Daily Avalanche* (March 1, 1866) only six days prior while in Memphis, which was that she was "on her way to St. Louis, to purchase a stock of dry goods and plantation supplies." It is notable that while in Memphis, she did not mention the steamboat *Miami*, but now in St. Louis, six days later, she was ready to tell the tale of her losing all her possessions and investment of "dry goods." She did not dare make the claim of her loss to the people of Memphis because they were too close to the disaster and knew the true details. A skeptic might suppose that she was using a ploy of a great financial loss to elicit money from sympathetic and uninformed citizens to help her get back on her feet. Her life's history will make clear she used similar ploys when necessary.

Nineteenth, she claimed, "She was one of the two ladies who were saved" in the explosion of the steamboat *Miami*. This will be shown to be false, now.

1866, the Explosion of Steamboat *Miami*

The Cincinnati-built three-year-old sternwheeler *Miami* advertised itself as "commodious and elegant… fast gaining favor with the… traveling public, and with urbane and attentive officers."[8] It ran a route from Memphis, Tennessee to Pine Bluff and Little Rock, Arkansas and intermediate points. The vessel's outbound leg took it down the Mississippi River, then it turned northwest up the Arkansas River to Little Rock.[9]

The *Miami* departed the Memphis dock at 9 p.m. Saturday, January 27, 1866, fully loaded with cargo and passengers. One passenger, Major J. E. Rankin "estimated three hundred souls aboard including 40-50 cabin passengers; ninety-five men of company E, Third [United States] Regulars; one hundred deck passengers, including many negroes, being carried up the Arkansas river for farm hands; and a crew, say fifty."[10]

The boat was about seven miles up the Arkansas River by 7 p.m. Sunday the 28th. After dinner, the passengers had congregated in the hall deck for conversation and to get warm by the stove. Aboard was Ashley's Band, a

---

8. *New York Times*, Feb 6, 1866.
9. *Memphis Daily Appeal*, Jan 27, 1866.
10. *Memphis Daily Appeal*, Jan 31, 1866- Two of cabin crew stated the number of cabin passengers at 50-60.

black musical band from Little Rock, playing for the passengers.[11] Lieutenant Hildeburne's company of soldiers had gone forward on the hurricane roof in a response to a call "for their ration of whiskey." Two soldiers had been tied, as reprimand for "disorderly and unruly conduct," to the guide chains which supported the smokestacks on the hurricane roof.[12]

Without any warning, hell came to earth when one of the boat's boilers exploded "tearing up the forward cabin and hurricane roof, and immediately took fire." Some of the soldiers on the hurricane roof were sent, headless and limbless, into the air. Others were "hurled into the air for an instant, and fell back into the hull of the boat among the wreck of iron and timbers, never more to be heard of."[13] Most of the socializing passengers gathered by the stove were obliterated. Those who survived the blast fell into the chasm of fire and were burned or scalded by steam.

Those who did not fall into the chasm were forced away from the burning mid-section, towards the vessel's bow and stern, and many began to throw themselves overboard into the freezing and turbulent water of the Arkansas. Initially the boat was close to the south bank and some passengers who jumped into the river reached that shore. Others used bales of hay or wooden debris from the vessel for flotation. "Young Tallaferro… floated down the river on a cabin door, nearly a mile and a half before he was rescued."[14] The steamboat then drifted across the river to the north bank.

The two soldiers who were tied up survived the explosion, but were unable to free themselves and no one responded to their screams for help. The fire undermined the portion of the roof where they were tied and in the end their cries, and they, were consumed by the flames. Two other men, reportedly one a corporal and the other a citizen, "deliberately [blew] their brains out with revolvers to escape the more terrible death of burning."[15]

Captain E. A. Levy, who was in his cabin, survived the explosion and the collapse of his cabin to a lower deck. Miraculously he extricated himself and commenced heroic efforts to save passengers. Seeing that the boat was being pushed near the north bank, he tried to get a plank ashore to enable crew to fasten a line to the bank. The panicked passengers rushed upon the plank and "swamped it, nearly all of them falling into the angry stream." A second effort ended with the same outcome, but on the third attempt Captain Levy succeeded in securing the bow of the boat to the bank of the river which enabled the passengers huddling on the bow to get off. The stern of the boat was well away from the shore, out in the river's deep water, which prevented

---

11. Ibid, Feb 1, 1866.
12. *New York Times*, Feb 6, 1866.
13. *Memphis Daily Avalanche*, Jan 31, 1866.
14. Ibid, Feb 1, 1866.
15. *Memphis Daily Appeal*, Jan 31, 1866; *Daily Southern Star* (New Orleans), Feb 1, 1866.

those survivors from getting ashore. All the while the fire was consuming the boat, and the passengers on the stern had to increase the distance between themselves and the flames by climbing onto the stern paddle. The ship's carpenter, now safely ashore, waded "into the water as far as he could and with the aid of a pole, rescued nearly all of them."[16]

Survivors, on the north shore, built bonfires to warm themselves. Someone located, in the now mangled hull, some whiskey which was passed around and "the chilliest were revived." A supply of shoes was discovered and distributed among the survivors, many of whom had lost their shoes. Survivor Major J. E. Rankin stated:

Some deeds of noble heroism and charity were seen whilst the suffering and dying were being administered to, by giving water, and plastering blisters with mud, that had an effect none can credit who have never experienced or seen its happy relief. Negro women disrobed themselves of their garments and made bandages, and negro men cleared their coats, whilst many a fortunate man either gave his pants or drawers to those without any.[17]

It was now one o'clock in the morning, seven hours after the explosion, and to the great joy of those with any life remaining, they heard the whistle of an approaching steamboat. The *Henry Ames* was bound from New Orleans to St. Louis when it heard of the disaster. Captain Tom Crawford hastened his vessel up the Arkansas River to help the victims. Captain Tom was highly praised for his humanity and the fact that he took a great personal financial risk, knowing that he voided his insurance policy which only permitted operation on the Mississippi. The steamboat *Mary E. Forsythe* also came to the rescue.

The precise death toll can never be known. Many victims were blown to bits, reduced to ashes or lost to the river. About 50 were buried on the river bank.[18] Many who initially survived, died later because of burns and scalded lungs. Compounding the difficulty of an accurate count was that "the cabin register was lost." In any case, the register would not have enumerated black deck passengers. Captain Levy guessed the death toll at about 125, but not more than 150.[19] Crew member, James Wolfe thought at least 150 lives were lost. Other estimates were as high as 200 dead.[20]

---

16. *Memphis Daily Appeal*, Feb 1, 1866.
17. Ibid, Jan 31, 1866.
18. *Daily Southern Star* (New Orleans), Feb 5, 1866.
19. *Memphis Daily Appeal*, Feb 1, 1866.
20. Ibid, Jan 31, 1866; Company E "suffered thirteen Troopers killed, nine injured, and twelve missing."- www.hood.army.mil, *The History, Customs, and Traditions of the 3d Cavalry Regiment BLOOD AND STEEL*, Published by 3d Cavalry Public Affairs in collaboration with the Third Cavalry Museum, Fort Hood, Texas, 2013 edition.

An accurate count of survivors was not possible. Survivors were on both river banks and rescue vessels took them to different points, such as Napoleon and Memphis. Adding to the uncertainty, some passengers and crew who were first reported dead were later found alive and some of the wounded but alive, soon died. Even the reported number of band members composing the Ashley Band varied from five to ten, and those who survived were reported at none to three.[21]

The number of (white) female passengers was generally stated as three.[22] Survivor S. Page, who claimed to be the only Eastern man onboard as far as he knew and "one of the victims of *incompetency* and *gross carelessness*" wrote, "There were about fifty cabin passengers, three of them ladies, one of them the wife of the clerk, with an infant.... One lady swam ashore and the other two were lost."[23]

The ship's clerk was Mr. John P. Lusk and it was his wife of less than fifteen months, Mrs. Lusk, and child who perished. The mother and child drowned when they tried to escape on a floating door. Mr. Lusk, who was seated at the stove in the hall deck, was killed instantly. Miss M. Jennie Bacon, who was accompanying Mrs. Lusk, drowned too.[24]

One lady, Mrs. S. Jacobs of Chicago, was identified as saved and the newspapers said she was "a German just from her native land."[25] "The woman was saved by the timely aid of Major Rankin, who caught her in the water and swam ashore with her." She had been scalded in the blast.[26]

There was another woman who was not included in the commonly reported count of three female passengers. She was listed as "Barrett Brasius and wife" in the *Memphis Daily Avalanche* of February 2 and she and her husband survived.[27] It is clear from the various newspaper accounts that two women were killed; two survived, Mrs. Jacobs and Mrs. Brasius.

---

21. The Ashley Band "was aboard the boat at the invitation of its captain, Emanuel Levy. He had taken them to a music festival in Memphis." Four of the seven original band members died; three brothers and a brother-in-law. In July of 1866, two surviving original members renewed the band with the addition of five members to the delight of Little Rock.- Sources: *Memphis Daily Appeal*, Feb 1, 1866; *Daily Arkansas Gazette*, Jul 24, 1866; *Arkansas Historical Quarterly*, Vol. 15, No. 1 (Spring, 1956), p53-61 and www.oldstatehouse.com, displaying "*The Arkansas News*, A Newspaper of History Published by The Old State House an Agency of The Department of Arkansas Heritage, Fall (November) 1995," containing the article titled "Ashley Band Restored to Play Again after Steamboat Disaster."
22. The *Daily Southern Star* (New Orleans) of Feb 5, 1866 stated the number at two.
23. *Boston Journal*, Feb 13, 1866.
24. *Memphis Daily Appeal*, Feb 1, 1866.
25. *Memphis Daily Avalanche*, Feb 1, 1866; *Richmond Whig*, Feb 6, 1866; *Arkansas Weekly Gazette*, Feb 10, 1866.
26. *Memphis Daily Avalanche*, Jan 31, 1866; *Arkansas Weekly Gazette*, Feb 10, 1866.
27. Listed as "Barnett Brasius and wife" in the *Arkansas Weekly Gazette* of Feb 10, 1866.

Was Velazquez a passenger and survivor, as she claimed? Only 31 days after the explosion Velazquez traveled to Memphis and the *Memphis Daily Avalanche* of March 1, 1866 reported, "Mrs. Camp [*sic*] is on her way to St. Louis, to purchase a stock of dry goods and plantation supplies, with a view of opening a business house at Mulberry Grove, Jefferson County, Ark." Please note, Velazquez had not yet purchased the merchandise and the explosion occurred 31 days prior to the intended purchase! This was the merchandise (which she never bought anyway) she later claimed was lost in the tragedy. And she did not mention that she was a survivor of the *Miami!* The reason she did not claim it was that she did not dare lie to the Memphis citizens who had an intimate knowledge of the disaster. It was only later, when she was some 285 miles further away in St. Louis, that she floated the lie. Velazquez told the *St. Louis Republican* of March 7 that she was "one of the two ladies who were saved."

The explosion of the *Miami*, which one newspaper called "one of the most heartrending accidents that it has ever been our misfortune to chronicle,"[28] was a human tragedy of the first magnitude, surely not easily forgotten. Yet Velazquez, in her memoir, never mentioned she was a survivor; in fact, she never wrote a word about the *Miami*.

Did Velazquez use this human tragedy to call attention to herself? Was Velazquez making a veiled appeal for financial contributions using the alleged loss of her uninsured possessions as a pretext? Collections were taken for victims, for example:

Mr. Wm. Lynch, one of the sufferers of the ill-fated Miami, is very low, at the Commercial Hotel. The river men have generously subscribed a purse of $400 for his benefit. Steamboatmen are noted for their generosity.[29]

Or did Velazquez simply derive pleasure in casting a lie and embellishing her life's story? Maybe Velazquez was pleased if people believed her story and even more pleased if they gave her money. Later she will ask for contributions to ameliorate this alleged loss. No evidence was found showing she received any money, but the evidence does show that Velazquez was not on the *Miami* when it exploded.

Velazquez departed St. Louis and backtracked to Memphis. There, she again wisely avoided telling the newspaper that she was a survivor of the *Miami*. She could not risk the lie being discovered as everyone in Memphis knew the true story of the *Miami* and its survivors, many of whom were taken there. And the Memphis newspapers especially knew the details; after all, they had reported them. The *Memphis Daily Avalanche* of March 21, 1866 reported:

---

28. *Memphis Daily Appeal,* Jan 31, 1866.
29. *Memphis Daily Avalanche,* Feb 8, 1866.

We copied a few days since from the St. Louis *Republican*, a very handsome notice of one of our gallant comrades in the late war, in which her name was spelt wrong. It should have been Mrs. Lauretta J. DeCamp [*sic*]- or Lieutenant Harry S.[*sic*] Buford, of the C. S. A. We make the correction in justice to this chivalrie woman, whose three wounds, and experience of a score of battles, adds so much luster to the name of woman. The circumstances that forced this lady to wear the garb of a soldier are of a romantic and stirring characteristic, but once a soldier, none were braver or more zealous. Now that she has resumed her wonted costume, no one can be more womanly than the subject of this notice. Many of her old comrades have called on her at her hotel- the Commercial- where she will be happy to see any of her friends.

Particular notice should be taken that the Memphis newspaper credited her with "experience of a score of battles." That would be 20 battles and Velazquez never claimed such a thing in her memoir. And inexplicably the Memphis newspaper, in its repetition of the St. Louis paper, said she received "three wounds," instead of the "twice wounded" of the St. Louis paper. The Memphis paper had reprinted on March 17 in its entirety the St. Louis *Republican* article of March 7 so why the Memphis paper did not see the falsehood Velazquez told to the St. Louis *Republican* paper is a mystery, recall, "She was one of the two ladies who were saved, but with the sacrifice of all her baggage and goods." It can only be thought the Memphis reporter did not read the original St. Louis claims which his own newspaper had reprinted; after all, the article was very long.

Velazquez departed Memphis and traveled to New Orleans where she made her arrival known to the *Daily True Delta* (March 29, 1866):

DISTINGUISHED VISITOR
We were honored by a call this morning from Mrs. Major T. C. De Camp, better known throughout the South as Lieut. H. T. Buford, of the late Confederate States Army, under which name she achieved such deeds of daring during the late war. Of course this gallant soldier-ess [*sic*] has dropped the garb *militare*, in which she once did such excellent service in the cause of the South; and now appears attired as the accomplished lady, which she most unquestionably is. Lieut. Buford was wounded four times during her military career, and has also been blown up on a steamboat (being the only lady passenger saved), but she now appears to be enjoying excellent health. Few women have had such an eventful life.
This distinguished lady is now stopping at the St. James Hotel. We sincerely hope her visit to the Crescent City will be a pleasant one.

Notice the similarity of this *Daily True Delta* article to the previous two articles in the Memphis *Daily Avalanche*. Velazquez likely presented copies of those Memphis articles to the New Orleans newspaper to help excite its interest. What the New Orleans paper might have added was that Velazquez was already familiar with the city's police, court, parish prison and Nelly

Bremer's whorehouse, but clearly the newspaper's memory did not go back that far.

"Mrs. L. J. De Camp," from "Miss [Mississippi]," registered at the St. James Hotel and was noted by the *Daily Picayune* of March 29, 1866, in section "Arrivals at the Principal Hotels." The fact that Velazquez registered that she was from Mississippi raises the question of why. According to her memoir she should have claimed Cuba or the West Indies or even New Orleans, but never Mississippi. Was she a Mississippian? The question will be raised several more times.

Now in New Orleans and once again far away from Memphis and the people who knew the details of the explosion of the *Miami*, Velazquez resumed her lie of survivorship. With the passage of only 22 days, she changed her story from being "one of the two ladies who were saved" (*St. Louis Republican*, March 7) to being "the only lady passenger saved." Maybe she forgot her first version or maybe claiming that she was one of two women survivors wasn't dramatic enough for her and she decided to distinguish herself by stating that she was the only woman survivor. One wonders why the New Orleans newspaper did not see the discrepancy. Maybe it did and Velazquez extricated herself by explaining that the other woman died of injuries.

It should be noted that this report stated that she was wounded four times during the War which is the highest number claimed in any of the many reports. The number has been also reported as one, two and three times, and has been addressed.

Gallant, Fearless, Good-looking, Perfect Lady, Angel of Mercy

The country's newspapers continued to shine the light of heroism on Velazquez without knowing, and maybe just not caring to know, the real person. For example, the *Dallas Weekly Herald* (Texas) of April 14, 1866 picked up an article from the *Houston Star* (Texas) which had seen the *Daily True Delta's* (New Orleans) report of her in town:

> We see from the New Orleans papers that Mrs. Major T. C. De Camp, better known throughout the South as Lieut. H. T. Buford, is in that city.
> We knew her well during Confederate times. She was a gallant soldier-ess; was wounded three times during the war, and was noted for her fearless daring. Good-looking and in speech and manner a perfect lady, in the hour of battle she was ever among the foremost; but when the carnage was over, she would drop the garb *militare* and become an angel of mercy to the wounded and dying.- *Houston Star*

How did the Houston *Star* know Lieutenant H. T. Buford well during Confederate times? The editor of the *Star* was Mississippian Robert H. Purdom who had been the editor of the *Jackson* (Mississippi) *Eagle* before the War.³⁰ With the threat of war, his state militia company was ordered to Pensacola on April 8, 1861.³¹ At Pensacola the company was joined into the Confederate army on April 20.³² Purdom's enlistment was for one year, as was the entire company's; all were mustered out, it is believed, in April 1862.³³ Recall that Velazquez claimed to have been in Pensacola as well, but since everything she wrote about her activity there is false, she surely was not there.

Robert Purdom had already left the military in April 1862 and had probably returned to Jackson when the *Mississippian's* huge article of June 6, 1863 reported Lieutenant H. T. Buford in Jackson. Purdom's presence there cannot be confirmed, but if he wasn't there, he likely read the widely repeated article. Even if he met her then, he would have learned nothing firsthand of her service, only what she told him. And undoubtedly, he read other circulating articles about her.

The article credits Velazquez with being "an angel of mercy to the wounded and dying," but only once and briefly did Velazquez claim in her memoir that she made "the wounded men as comfortable as possible, until [she] saw that, if [she] intended to escape (from Fort Donelson), [she] must go at once." (p172) In the thousands of Civil War soldier narratives and diaries, never yet has Velazquez been identified as nursing soldiers, except by Captain Thomas C. DeCaulp, who gratefully acknowledged, in a letter to Velazquez, her help when he was sick in Atlanta. Does this acknowledged aid confer to her the status of "angel of mercy" since she was trying to get DeCaulp well in order to mercifully marry him?

It might be noted that she went from being wounded four times, claimed on March 29 by the New Orleans paper, back to being wounded three times here on April 14, just a space of 16 days. Prior, on March 21, the Memphis paper had stated she was wounded three times.

Defended her Honor and her Husband's too

Velazquez departed New Orleans and headed to Atlanta. Her travel took her through Mobile, Alabama where she made a stopover. Neither the date of Velazquez's arrival nor length of stay is clear, but it can be roughly calculated to have been between the first week of April and the first week of May, 1866. She did not find a cordial reception there as she had in New Orleans, instead she came under criticism. She was compelled to write a

---

30. 1860 U.S. Census; *Louisville Daily Courier*, Jan 20, 1859.
31. *Weekly Whig* (Vicksburg), Feb 13, 1861, taken from the *Mississippian* of the 8th; *OR*, Ser I, Vol LII, part II, p40.
32. Roland, 875.
33. NARA, CMSR for R. H. Purdom.

"card" in her defense and had it printed in the advertising section of the *Mobile Tribune*:[34]

> To the Public.- The undersigned has been pained by the circulation of slanders concerning her loyalty to the late confederacy. She takes this means of pronouncing them all false, and without a shadow of foundation. Those who desire a refutation of them can see her at the Battle House, and those who persist in circulating them will do so at their peril. MRS. LORRETA J. DECAULP, formerly Lieutenant T. Buford, C.S.A.

Several newspapers took notice of the "card," such as the Philadelphia *Evening Telegraph* which said it came from one "noted as a skillful officer and for indomitable perseverance and pluck."[35]

The "card" makes clear her presence at Mobile's Battle House hotel, her old favorite hotel from her June 1863 stay. The local newspaper had recently reported the hotel was "thoroughly repainted and partly refurnished and is daily improving its accommodations so as to be unsurpassed by any Hotel in the South. The bath rooms have also been refitted in splendid style, where Hot, Cold and Shower Baths can be obtained at all times."[36] It might be supposed that the comforts of the hotel's luxury assuaged the discomforts of the criticism she received.

Surely, Velazquez thought she was leaving behind the criticism in Mobile when she headed to Atlanta, but upon her arrival she found, no doubt to her chagrin, she had not escaped it after all. Some Atlantans remembered her husband, Captain DeCaulp, and understood that he had deserted the Southern army and went North. Velazquez vigorously refuted those who called the Captain a deserter. So besides defending herself, she now had to defend her husband's good "name" and "memory" from the "base slander." Of course, the "base slander" was true, but nevertheless, she refuted all critics and threatened them with physical harm.

Velazquez was obviously willing to chance criticism because she did not stop seeking publicity which generated it. The following article by Atlanta's *Daily Intelligencer* of May 9, 1866 contains her refutation. The newspaper was apparently too busy praising Velazquez to bother looking into whether her critics were correct. The same *Daily Intelligencer* had, only 54 days prior, on March 16, reprinted the huge article taken from the St. Louis *Republican* of March 7 which detailed her claimed history. The paper clearly did not seek to compare the *Republican's* facts to its own gathered facts, because the

---

34. The original *Mobile Tribune* article is not found, as few editions of this newspaper have survived, but it can be surmised to have been the first week of May because the *Daily Mississippi Clarion* of May 8 repeated the article in brief.
35. May 12, 1866.
36. *Mobile Daily Advertiser and Register*, Apr 21, 1866.

falsehoods were there for easy picking. Instead, the *Daily Intelligencer* was simply pleased to be contacted by Velazquez and to write her story:

> Mrs. DeCaulp
>
> It was in 1863, we first met in this city, this second "Joan of Arc." She was then attired in the garb of an officer and was introduced to us as Lieutenant Buford, in the Confederate service. There are many now in this city who will remember this heroine, and her marriage with her late husband Mr. DeCaulp, a soldier also in the same service, since deceased. We had lost sight of, and knowledge of the whereabouts of this daring and romantic girl, until a few days ago, when we saw in one of our Southern exchanges a complimentary notice of her, and of her return to the South.- Of this fact, we had occular [*sic*] demonstration on yesterday, for while we were engaged, scissors in hand, clipping from our exchanges, there entered into our sanctum, an elegantly dressed lady, still in the bloom of youth, and beautiful to behold, whom we soon recognized as the veritable Lieutenant Buford, now a widow, her husband having died shortly after her alliance with him. Mrs. Lorreta J. DeCaulp- for that is the lady's name in full- informs us that she surrendered herself a prisoner in Washington City, to the authorities there and was treated with great kindness. She had been a great traveler- having visited Europe twice, Canada also and on each occasion in Confederate service. She is now engaged in writing her history, in which will be embraced, of course, the dangers through which she passed in the tented and on the battle field, on the high seas and amid the crowded cities of Europe, at Nassau and in running the blockade and for the publication of which, she solicits subscribers and contributions. She tells us that an old military friend has kindly consented to receive either the one or the other, during her absence from the city, and all who may be disposed to aid her in her design can do so by calling upon him at the Agency of the Georgia Railroad, and making their deposits. Mrs. DeCaulp, desires us also to say, that the report circulated against her husband, that he had deserted the Confederate cause, and gone over to the other side, is a base slander; that she is here now in the South to defend his name; and will meet any one who dares or has dared to asperse his memory; that she has already received two wounds upon the battle field, and will defy death itself in vindication of her departed husband's honor. We do not envy the man who will accept this challenge, for though gentle in peace, "in arms" this lady is sure to conquer.

One must marvel at Velazquez's audacity to refute the facts of her husband's desertion to his detractors when they obviously knew something about it.

The reporter wrote that her husband "died shortly after her alliance with him," an obvious contradiction compared to the March 16 article, which stated in part:

> Her husband, who was taken prisoner in the fall of 1863, while serving with his regiment in Georgia, was carried to New York. After a long and arduous siege, she at length succeeded in getting him paroled in January, 1865, but he lived only eight days after his release from prison.

From "the fall of 1863," when they were married and when her husband was "captured," to the time of his death, January 1865, is not a period of time which can be characterized as "shortly," instead it was about a year and four months' time. In any case, everything she said about her husband DeCaulp's capture, imprisonment, release and death was a lie, as has been explained.

It is noteworthy that it is in this May 9, 1866 *Intelligencer* article we find out that Velazquez is "now engaged in writing her history" and she is "solicit[ing] subscribers and contributions" to sustain the effort. It will be seen that the endeavor will take ten years, surely a credit to her tenacity.

And she is back down to being wounded twice.

Get Your Books Right Here

Velazquez now departed Atlanta, traveled to Augusta, Georgia and was noticed by the local paper:[37]

Mrs. DeCaulp- C. S. [Confederate Service] Lt. Buford: This lady, who was a celebrity during the late war, is now in our city, *en route* to Savannah. She is now engaged in writing a "History of the late war," which will comprise not only all the public documents of both sides, but also a large collection of military orders not heretofore published: and a narrative of events which will embrace her own romantic, personal adventures, both by land and by sea- in the strife of battle and in the craft of diplomacy.

To enable her to publish her Book, she solicits subscribers and contributions. She bears with her very high testimonials. We subjoin the following notice from the Atlanta Intelligencer:

Mrs. DeCaulp.- It was in 1863, we first met.... [What followed was the complete previously presented May 9 *Intelligencer* article.]

Velazquez spent no more than a couple of days in Augusta and proceeded to Savannah, as she told the newspaper she would, and arrived there on Friday May 11 where she registered at the Pulaski House. The Savannah newspaper,[38] under "Arrivals at Hotels," took note of her- "Mrs. DeCaulp, Ala." The state of Alabama presumably was identified in the guest register in response to the question, "where from?" Velazquez had indeed just traveled from Alabama to Georgia. The register was apparently not asking for the place of birth.

On Monday morning, May 14, the Savannah paper had much more to say about Velazquez:

A FEMALE LIEUTENANT FOUR YEARS IN THE CONFEDERATE SERVICE.- Mrs. Loretta J. DeCaulp, well-known as Lieutenant T. Buford, of the Confederate States Army, is now temporarily in this city, and residing at the Pulaski

---

37. *Augusta Chronicle*, May 12, 1866.
38. *Daily News and Herald*, May 12, 1866.

House, but will soon leave for Charleston. Her object here is to collect subscriptions for three forthcoming works which she is preparing, entitled "The Cruise of the Shenandoah, or the last of the Confederacy;" "The History of the Southern Confederacy, including Personal Adventures of the Authoress;" and "Buford's Poems."

At the commencement of the War she devoted her property and her personal exertions to the Confederate cause, and in male disguise raised a company in Texas, which she commanded at Manassas. She was afterwards connected with a cavalry company at the west. She was three years in active service, and was three times wounded and once taken prisoner. She was also for about a year in the C. S. Government service North and in Europe. Her adventures were of a remarkable character, and her material for interesting works relating to the war, historical, reminiscental [sic] and documentary are unrivalled.

She desires to publish the works as soon as she can obtain the requisite means, and that those friendly to the object will send contributions or subscriptions to her in care of this office, the Pulaski House, or her agent, Mr. A. B. Watt, Exchange Hotel, Montgomery, Ala. The following is from the Atlanta Intelligencer:

Mrs. DeCaulp.- It was in 1863, we first met in this city, this second "Joan of Arc." She was.... [Again, the complete previously presented May 9 *Intelligencer* article followed.]

Newspapers nationwide repeated the story; the distant *Boston Journal* of May 25, 1866 used the title "A WOMAN'S ADVENTURES IN THE REBEL ARMY."

Velazquez claimed she raised a company in Texas which she commanded at Manassas, but it is a fact that no company from Texas fought at this battle. However, the Independent Squad Texas Rangers, which consisted of three men, was present at Manassas. They volunteered as aides to (Fourth Brigade) Confederate Brigadier-General James Longstreet's staff.[39] It can be sure Velazquez had nothing to do with them. Ten years later, in her memoir, she contradicted the Texas company claim when she wrote that she raised "a battalion" in Arkansas and took them to Pensacola. Also in her memoir, she did not claim to take any company to Manassas, instead, she claimed she traveled there alone and then joined the battle. Both versions of her participation at Manassas are provably false and the truth of her participation at Manassas is covered in detail later.

In the Savannah *Daily News and Herald* article, she boldly claimed she was "three years in active service," which ten years later she contradicted in a letter (October 1876) she wrote to Reverend Jones defending her book, stating, "I only was 5 months in the Army regular [sic]." In her memoir, she wrote (p181) that she enlisted in a regiment only a "short time" and that was

---

39. The Texas Historical Association referencing *Hood's Texas Brigade: Lee's Grenadier Guard* (1970) by Harold B. Simpson.

so she could slip away from New Orleans unnoticed. Credibility about this enlistment suffers greatly and is addressed later.

It should be noticed that in the period of two days, between her Augusta newspaper article and her Savannah newspaper article, she improved her claim about book writing by the addition of two books- *Buford's Poems* and *The Cruise of the Shenandoah, or the last of the Confederacy*. These books apparently were never published and maybe she never meant to write them, but instead, only wished to impress the locals enough to sell them subscriptions. The evidence that she never intended to write *The Cruise of the Shenandoah* is simply the fact that she did not know the first thing about commerce raider CSS *Shenandoah*. This vessel was never remotely near places where she ever was. Velazquez knew no more about *Shenandoah* than what the newspapers knew and they knew very little of the vessel's activity in the distant Pacific Ocean.

It is clear that Velazquez was capitalizing on the much reported-on surrender of *Shenandoah* only six months prior, in November 1865, in England. It was of great interest what was to become of the vessel's crew, considered pirates by the Federal Government. Worse yet, the vessel's crew had continued to fight for six months after the War was over, they not believing it was over, even after an American vessel had shown the Rebel sailors a Northern newspaper with news of the surrender of the Confederacy. The officers of *Shenandoah* suspected the newspaper might be propaganda. Finally, a British ship which they stopped convinced them of the South's surrender.

In any case, by claiming to write a book about CSS *Shenandoah* and a poetry book, in addition to a history of the War, Velazquez was casting a wide net to catch more subscriptions from a larger section of the population. It is curious that she was compelled to raise money in order to publish her books, considering her prior newspaper claim that she was soon to get a substantial inheritance resulting from her father's 1864 death. Recall the forged inheritance letter from "Don Augustus V. Steinhosse, of Havana" announcing the death of "Commodore J. B. Roach, of the British Navy"? There was a "five years" waiting period which had not yet passed, so the inheritance would not yet have come through, however, with such a large and legal inheritance pending, might she have used it as collateral to secure the cash she needed for her publications? The simple answer is no, because the inheritance was a lie and the letter a forgery. Her father was a lie. His death was a lie. She, at present, had no money or she would not have been soliciting "subscriptions" against future delivery of books not yet written. She even asked for "contributions" towards her efforts. If she received any, it can be certain that she was exponentially pleased since she would not have been obliged to repay a "contribution" by the delivery of a book, as in the case of a "subscription."

Well shoot! Velazquez didn't think to ask her other father for the money; remember the father of her autobiography, the wealthy Señor Velazquez who owned vast plantations in Cuba and "surround[ed] his family with every luxury." Even though Velazquez claimed he disowned her because of her marriage to William, she could have at least begged for forgiveness and asked for the money. Bet she'll remember to ask him next time!

Her money raising scheme was probably not very successful. If she collected any, she slipped it into her pocket and as will be seen, she abandoned the immediate publication of her book, putting it on hold for the next ten years. By then subscribers probably had given up hope of receiving their book, even forgetting about it. When the book was finally published, the subscribers surely did not recognize author "Velazquez" as one and the same as Mrs. DeCaulp who sold them the subscription. If Velazquez, after ten years, sought out her subscribers and delivered their pre-paid book, she would warrant commendation.

Criticism of Mrs. DeCaulp seems to have become less frequent or at least she quit adding fuel to the fire by responding publicly in the newspapers. Soon the newspapers reverted to presenting, with admiration, Velazquez's life story. The *Pulaski Citizen* (Tennessee) of May 18, 1866 parroted information gathered from other papers:

> The last 'lioness' in Atlanta is Mrs. Loretat [sic] J. DeCaulp, who was well known in the Confederate army as Lieutenant Buford. Mrs. DeCaulp- entered the army early in the war, and fought bravely in many engagements, and was once wounded. In 1864 she was married to Lieutenant D. [sic] Caulp, at the Atlanta Hotel.

From Savannah, Velazquez took a short trip up the coast to Charleston, South Carolina, probably by coastal steamer; at least four steamers, the *Fannie*, *Emile*, *Kate* and *Dictator*, made that run.[40] She continued soliciting money to ostensibly enable her to publish her book or books. A Charleston correspondent for the *Cincinnati Daily Gazette* of June 2, 1866 reported her salient presence:

> A Rebel Bloomer. A Charleston correspondent writes: The latest sensation here is the presence of a Mrs. De Camp [sic], alias Lieut. Buford (C. S.) She was the cynosure of all eyes as she rode out this afternoon, accompanied by a very awkward escort. She was attired in a plain riding skirt and Confederate gray basque [closely fitted bodice or jacket], trimmed *a la militare*, and with the insignia of a 1st Lieutenant on the collar; a Derby set jauntily on the side of her head, completed her costume. The object of her visit is to obtain subscriptions for a true and correct (?) history of the war which she designs publishing.

The reporter doubted whether Velazquez's book was going to be a "correct (?) history of the war" by his insertion of a question mark.

---

40. *Daily News and Herald* (Savannah), May 26, 1866.

A second newspaper, in witty ridicule, noted her presence:[41]

The sober, staid citizens of this burg, were considerably excited-by observing a fair equestrienne, on the streets this morning dressed a la militaire, with the insignia of a First Lieutenant in the Confederate States army. Speculation was rife as to who she was and where she came from, and if the United States knew she was around. It was discovered at length that she was the celebrated Mrs. DeCamp alias Lieut. Buford, (whose arrival was mentioned in a former letter). Her novel dress attracted considerable attention and gladdened the eyes of many of the "unharmonized."

It appears that she paid her devoirs to the powers that be, and the lion and lamb sat down peaceably together. Confederate buttons which were hid away have been brought from darkness to light. The fair lieutenant has flashed upon us like a dream that is past, and if the most of us were not thoroughly reconstructed, there is no telling what disastrous effects might accrue from this visitation.

The newspaper and public were "gladdened" by Velazquez's show of the Confederate uniform because just now this sort of display wasn't acceptable to occupying Federal military authorities who routinely suppressed public Southern patriotism. To be sure, her display illustrates her bravado and individualism.

Velazquez attired herself in a stylish, but clearly non-military issued, female soldier's uniform, or her idea of one. She had dressed similarly, in 1864, when she followed her husband to Milwaukee; that city's newspaper said, "[She] has been seen several times... promenading the streets, wearing a closely fitted basque ornamented with a neat pair of Major's shoulder straps." Velazquez had preferred to call herself "Major DeCaulp" while in Yankee territory, and presumably wore a Federal blue basque, instead of a "Confederate gray basque." However, in Charleston she demoted herself to first lieutenant. In any case, she succeeded in gaining the attention to help her sell subscriptions and no doubt enjoyed the notoriety. At the same time, she probably did not enjoy her lack of cash, the reason she was compelled to try sell a book which she had not yet written.

Velazquez addressed this Charleston horseback ride in *The Woman in Battle* (p533-534) and gave a lively, but exaggerated version, if one accepts the correspondent's version. She explained that on a social occasion in Charleston, she met a Federal officer to whom she showed only "considerable coolness." She was then surprised when he asked her out for a horseback ride. At first she said no, but her friends "suggested that [she] should accept the invitation, and give him a genuine specimen of [her] abilities as a horsewoman." Velazquez narrated:

I accordingly went to every livery stable in the city, until I at length found a very swift horse, that I thought would suit my purpose. This being secured, I wrote a

---

41. *Newberry Herald* (SC), May 30, 1866 repeating the *Charleston Cor.[respondent] Col.[umbia] Carolinian*, no date given.

challenge for him to ride a race with me. We were to ride down the main street. He, without being aware of what was on foot, accepted; and the next afternoon, therefore, we mounted our steeds and started. When we arrived at the appointed place, I said, "Let us show these people what good equestrians we are."

He gave his horse a lash, but I reined mine in, telling him that I would give him twenty feet. When he had this distance, I gave my steed a cut with the whip, and flew past my cavalier like the wind, saying, loud enough for everyone to hear me, "This is the way we caught you at Blackburn's Ford and Bull Run."

This was enough for him; and turning his horse, he rode back to the hotel, to find that a large party there were [*sic*] interested in the race, and that there were some heavy bets on the result, the odds being all against him. This gentleman, apparently, did not desire to continue his acquaintance with me, for I saw no more of him.

There can be no doubt that the Charleston correspondent encountered Velazquez and collected first-hand the details of her horseback ride. Is it possible that the correspondent missed, in broad daylight, the big horse race right "down the main street"? Suppose that he only heard of the race after-the-fact, wouldn't he have reported on the excited crowd and the betting? His failure to mention the race surely indicates that it did not take place, with the exception of in Velazquez's own mind.

Velazquez pressed on with her book promotional efforts, even offering for sale photographs of herself to her admirers. This is the first found public sale of photographs of her. She placed an advertisement in the *Charleston Daily Courier* of May 17, 1866:

MRS. L. J. DeCAMP,
KNOWN IN THE WESTERN DEPARTMENT OF THE late C. S. Army as Lieut. H. D. [*sic*] Buford, being now in this city, announces to the citizens of Charleston and the vicinity, that she is here with the view of securing subscriptions for a CORRECT and TRUTHFUL HISTORY OF THE LATE WAR. The works are to be entitled, the CRUISE OF THE SHANADOAH, or the LOST WAR, BUFORD'S POEMS, etc. Mrs. DeCamp has contributed largely, pecuniarily, to the late war, and was twice wounded. Contributions to these publications will be received at the OFFICE OF THE CHARLESTON HOTEL, or will be acknowledged if forwarded to A. P. WATT, Exchange Hotel, Montgomery, Ala. Photographs of herself are now for sale at QUIMBY & CO'S Gallery, King street.

N. B.- To Major-General DEVENS and A. A. General O. H. HART, Mrs. Decamp returns her thanks for attentions received.

The next day the newspaper corrected the spelling of her name, "MRS. L. J. DeCAULP," in the advertisement.

The N. B., *nota bene*, should indeed be noted well, as it contains a curious thank you from Velazquez to Brevet Major General Charles Devens and Assistant Adjutant General O. H. Hart (Brevet Brigadier General). These gentlemen were Federal Army officers in the Yankee occupation army of which Southerners were none too fond. In fact, Major General Devens was in command of the Military District of Charleston, and both gentlemen had just, on April 21, concluded a more than two-month Military Commission Court (Devens, the President of the Commission) which tried four Southern men for the October 8, 1865 murder of three Federal soldiers. Three of the accused men were South Carolinians and were therefore of great interest to other South Carolinians.

Because of the supposed weakness of the evidence, the community expected an acquittal for all the men charged and was shocked when "the court found all of the accused guilty, and sentenced them to execution." The verdict caused a "great sensation" because the accused were of "unblameable [sic] character," one of them an "intimate friend" from childhood of South Carolina Governor Orr, who appeared on his behalf.

The sentence was commuted to life in prison for two of the men. The other two men (one a Georgian) were ordered to be hanged on April 27. The correspondent wrote:

[The verdict], of itself, is unfortunate enough, but when I add that the condemned are *ordered to be executed five days after their conviction, and before, by any possibility, they can have an opportunity of taking leave of their families*, your readers will join me in the honest mortification which is felt by our people at this extra-judicial proceeding.[42]

In order not to leave the reader hanging, so to speak, let it be noted that the U.S. President intervened and "suspended" the execution order, to the "great rejoicing" of the Charlestonians. In the meantime, the citizens had circulated a petition in the city which had "received thousands of signatures, and [was] to be forwarded to the President, beseeching him to give the accused a trial before a jury of the countrymen."[43] The prisoners were not tried before a jury, but instead, by Presidential order, were sent to Fort Jefferson military prison on Dry Tortugas (Florida) for life sentences.[44]

At this time the citizens of Charleston were not feeling friendly towards General Devens and General Hart and their "extra-judicial proceeding," so by Velazquez evoking the Generals' names in the advertisement, she could not have hoped to gain herself favor in the eyes of the Charlestonians to whom she hoped to sell books. So why did she publicly thank Generals Devens and Hart for "attentions received"?

One can speculate she was taken before the military officials to determine the nature of her business in Charleston. After all, she was dressed in a "Confederate gray basque, trimmed *a la militare*, and with the insignia of a

---

42. *Edgefield Advertiser* (SC), May 2, 1866, reprinting a Charleston correspondent's article in the *Constitutionalist*, April 22.
43. *Anderson Intelligencer* (SC), May 3, 1866.
44. *Charleston Daily News*, Aug 3, 1866.

1st Lieutenant on the collar" which was plenty enough to get her in trouble with the Federal military. Routinely, ex-soldiers still wearing their Confederate uniforms were in trouble with authorities, and if not the authorities, then Unionist men would trouble them with a beating or even killing them. Her wearing of the uniform surely caused a trip to the authorities.

Velazquez likely explained to the officials that she was not trying to cause trouble or show militarism, but was simply trying to promote book subscriptions by drawing attention to herself. To the Generals, she would have displayed her exceptional charm and easily reassured them. They would have shown her gentlemanly courtesy, according to their education and station in life, if not outright friendliness. In kindness, they might have even invited her to dinner, who knows? Indeed, "It appears that she paid her devoirs to the powers that be, and the lion and lamb sat down peaceably together." The gravest interpretation for her professed "thanks for attentions received" can be thought to be a thank you for not immediately tossing her in jail.

Remember Velazquez wrote (p124) a vivid account of Colonel Charles Devens' swim across the Potomac River to escape from overwhelming Rebels? That Colonel Devens was the now Major General Charles Devens. Her account of Devens' swim, with Rebels high on the bluff taking rifle shots at him, left her wondering if Colonel Devens succeeded in crossing the river. It would have been the opportune moment and logical thing for Velazquez to bring the story of Devens' swim and fate to a satisfactory conclusion by telling her readers that she was delighted to meet the gentleman and learn that he had indeed found safety, but she didn't. It's as though she herself didn't realize he was the same person. In any case, if she saw anyone swimming across the Potomac it was positively not Colonel Devens, as already explained, and she surely fabricated her version of the swim.

Velazquez did not linger in Charleston, but returned to Augusta, likely by the 7 a.m. train, May 21. The Augusta, Georgia, *Daily Constitutionalist* of May 22, 1866 presented some fresh information, rather, fresh falsehoods, which surely came directly from Velazquez. Velazquez claimed some success at gathering contributions in Charleston, no doubt with an eye to enticing the citizens of Augusta to likewise contribute:

JOAN OF ARC.- We were favored yesterday by a visit from Madame Lauretta DeCaulp, widow of Major DeCaulp, of Arkansas, slain in the military service of the late CONFEDERATE STATES, now canvassing the South for means wherewith to publish what will undoubtedly be a very valuable compilation of Federal documents relative to the causes and conduct of the war. Madame DeCaulp was, during that struggle, known as Lieutenant Buford, and, from the testimonials shown us, did good service, both as a cavalier in the field- where she was twice wounded, going into action on one occasion with the scar of her first hurt yet uncicatrized- and by ministrations, more peculiar to her sex, at the bedside of many a wounded Confederate soldier. Serving equally in the East and West, Lieut. B. has fought under both Forrest and that *preux chevalier*, Jeb Stuart, receiving one hurt at Stillwater and the other in a cavalry skirmish a few days after Shiloh.- Mr. Trenholm, of Charleston, as well as other prominent men in Carolina have, we learn, contributed largely to Madame DeC.'s subscription list, and in our own city a liberal response has been made.

Her claim, to have fought under the commands of Nathan B. Forrest and "Jeb" Stuart, in their cavalries, defies credibility on every level. She never fought under the command of one of these men, much less both. If the claim was true, it should have been a claim that she was forever proud of, in fact, so very proud of, that she did not even bother to mention it in the book she wrote ten years later. "Jeb" Stuart's name does not even appear in her book. That of Nathan B. Forrest only appears when she explained (p351) that she delivered a secret dispatch to a Confederate agent who was then to deliver it to Forrest. If the claims were true, they would have warranted their own book.

To beat a dead horse, so to speak, Forrest rode his horses and men so hard that often both were left broken down in his trail. Only the most ironed-willed and physically capable men rode with Forrest. With no intent to disparage women of exceptional physical abilities, who might have indeed ridden with Forrest if given the chance, it must be pointed out, that Velazquez was not one of these women.

The article pointed out that she was wounded "in a cavalry skirmish a few days after Shiloh," but this claim contradicts her book, in which she claimed (p225), she was injured by a bursting shell while burying the dead the day after Shiloh. The claimed wounds varied in number and body location in the many newspaper articles over the years. These discrepancies are covered in detail elsewhere. In this article she pointed out that the other wound of the two was received at Stillwater. She never claimed in her book to have been wounded at Stillwater, though she did claim to be wounded at other places, but never at Stillwater. And it is unclear where Velazquez's Stillwater occurred, even after a search of *An Alphabetical List of the Battles of the War of the Rebellion* by J. W. Wells and N. A. Strait, 1875, revised 1883; and *4000 Civil War Battles from Official Records* compiled by J. W. Carnahan, 1899; and *Civil War Monographs*, Vol 6 Number 7 October 1964, "Checklist of Battles, Skirmishes and Encounters of the Civil War, Arranged Alphabetically."

Please note the triple lie contained in a single sentence- that Velazquez was the "widow of Major DeCaulp, of Arkansas, slain in the military service of the late CONFEDERATE STATES." The truth is, DeCaulp was never a major and he deserted the Confederate army, joined the Union army, was given a medical discharge and died as a civilian.

From Augusta, Georgia, Velazquez would have likely proceeded to Atlanta, then to Montgomery, Alabama to see if any contributions had been mailed there as she had asked of the Charleston citizens. To date, no record of her transiting these cities has been located. From Montgomery she proceeded to Meridian, Mississippi, at least her next public notice was there.

The *New Orleans Times* of June 5, 1866, under "Southern Items," repeating the *Meridian Messenger* (Mississippi) of June 2, wrote:

LIEUT. H. T. BUFORD.- This distinguished personage, who served three years in the field in the Confederate service, and bears upon her person honorable scars as a testimony of her bravery and devotion to the cause of her adopted country, was in our city yesterday at the Jones House. Her history is well known. She is Mrs. L. J. DeCaulp, who, as a Lieutenant in an Arkansas company, signalized her bravery on several hotly contested fields. She donned the apparel of the sterner sex, and for a long time kept her secret well, and was accounted one of the bravest of the youths who rushed to arms in defence [*sic*] of the Southern cause.

Mrs. DeC. has now prepared for the press three books. "The Cruise of the Shenandoah, or the Last of the Confederacy," "History of the Southern Confederacy, with personal adventures of the Authoress," and "Buford's Poems." Having lost all her means by the deplorable disaster of the steamer Miami last winter, she will ask the Southern public to assist her with the means to get her books out- *Meredian* [*sic*] *Messenger*, 2.

The article, with typical mindless flattery, bestowed Velazquez with heroine status. However, the article is not totally useless since it contains significant information. First, it must be clarified she was in Meridian, Mississippi, staying "at the Jones House," which starting in 1863 was operated by one Josiah Jones and, unlike many structures, survived the war.[45]

In the article she claimed that she was "a Lieutenant in an Arkansas company." However, in her book (p70-85) she pushed this claim farther, that she raised an Arkansas "battalion" while in male disguise, solely through her own effort and paid for all the company's military accouterments by herself. Recall, only 12 days prior, the *Boston Journal* (May 25, 1866) reported that she claimed she raised a company in Texas. In any case, all accounts of her raising a company, and of her being an officer in it, are not true.

For the first time, in any found public statement, she claimed she was not American born. The article stated that her devotion was to the cause of "her adopted country." It should be recalled in November 1862 she registered at Charity Hospital in New Orleans, claiming she was born in "Nassau, N. [New] Providence, West Indies." This might have been false since she could

---

45. Fred W. Edmiston, *Lauderdale, Mississippi's Empire County, The Early Years, 1830-1865* (Meridian, MS, 2005).

have been deceiving hospital authorities. At other times she claimed she was from Mississippi, Arkansas, Tennessee and Louisiana. The location of her birth is addressed in detail elsewhere.

The last sentence of the article, "Having lost all her means by the deplorable disaster of the steamer Miami last winter, she will ask the Southern public to assist her with the means to get her books out," confirms the earlier suspicion that Velazquez was claiming she was a victim of the explosion of *Miami* in order to elicit charitable contributions from the public. Velazquez understood the inherent generosity of people. She had adopted the steamboat explosion ploy as early as March 7 and must have realized some success using it because she was still using it three months later. Her claim to have "lost all her means" in the explosion has been shown false. Recall, when she first claimed she lost all of her means it meant the loss of merchandise which was intended to start a dry goods store, but now the loss prevented the publishing of her three books.

From Meridian she traveled to Nashville, Tennessee, arriving June 15. She was still asking for subscribers for her planned books and she managed to get help from at least two newspapers. The *Nashville Daily Union* (June 16) wrote:

Mrs. Lauretta DeCaulp, who served several years in the Southern Army, and attained distinction for gallantry and heroic courage as Lt. Buford, arrived in this city yesterday. She is making a tour of the Southern States soliciting subscriptions for a couple of volumes which she proposes to publish relative to the late war, and incidents growing out of it. We have no doubt they will be more than usually entertaining, coming from a lady who participated in the bloody struggle, and who wields a ready and racy pen.

A second newspaper, the *Daily Union and American* (June 16) reported:

MRS. L. J. DECAULP is on a brief visit to this city, which she proposes to canvass for subscribers to one or more works which she proposes shortly to publish, in relation to the late war and her connection with it. Of the extent and scope of these publications we are not precisely informed, but if nothing more than her own romantic experience is given in the simple language of truth, they will possess unusual interest.

During and since the war the papers have so fully stated the leading points in her career, that it is scarcely necessary to repeat them here. She entered the war as a soldier, was severely wounded in her first battle, at Shiloh- and was afterwards in the service as an officer in various of its branches. She was a widow at the time of entering the army, and was afterwards married to Maj. De Caulp who died in a Federal prison. During the latter part of the war she spent a good portion of the time in the United States, sometimes in prison, at other times as a Federal detective and spy, and again as a clerk in the War office at Washington, under appointment from Secretary Stanton. She was in the City of New York at the time of the Confederate surrender, on the eve of her departure "for Europe;" but upon that event, changed her destination, and sometime afterwards presented herself to the nearest Commander as a Confederate soldier, and asked and obtained the parole in such cases, which she still retains.

She has now cast aside the male attire, retaining only the regular Confederate button as decoration to her dress.

These incidents are sufficient to show the eccentricities of a strongly marked character, extreme shrewdness and readiness of address, combined with great energy and self-possession.

Although the article is brief, it provides important information which greatly contradicts her memoir. Here, she claimed that her first battle was Shiloh, but in her book, she claimed her first battle was Manassas (Bull Run). And it will be seen momentarily in a newspaper article only six days later she claimed she was at Manassas.

She said she was already a widow at the time she entered the army, which contradicts her memoir in which she claimed she raised troops and delivered them to her very much alive husband.

She claimed husband DeCaulp died in a Federal prison, but in her book, she said it was in a Federal hospital. Of course, it has been shown that both these claims are false.

She asserted she was on the verge of departing for Europe at the time of the Confederate surrender, but in her book, she said she had just returned from Europe at this time. One claim is surely a lie and likely both are.

Amazing is her claim that she worked "as a clerk in the War office at Washington, under appointment from Secretary Stanton." Never in her book did she claim or admit that she worked in the Federal War Department. In fact, both in her book and in her many newspaper interviews she vehemently declared she was the most loyal Confederate possible, which would rule out working for the Yankees. It is strange that she or maybe the newspaper failed to explain that she had operated as a Southern spy while at the Federal War Department, if that had been the case. The simple conclusion is, if she in truth worked there, she did not operate as a Southern spy, but instead was probably happy just to have a job. This claim to have worked in the Federal War Department may have been a lie to replace the truth that she worked in the Federal Arsenal in Indianapolis.

Velazquez may have indeed been working in Washington, D.C. in 1865, the year when her whereabouts is undetermined. A National Archives search of clerks employed by the War Department produced a seemingly complete list of employees and a DeCaulp or Williams or Velazquez was not discovered.

In the same vein is the fact that in this article she claimed she was "a Federal detective and spy." Again, she or the newspaper made no effort to explain whether she was a spy for the South. Research shows she indeed worked for the Federal secret service, but it has not been discovered, to date, that she was at the same time a Southern agent.

Velazquez continued her self-promotion and again offered for sale photographs of herself through an advertisement in a Nashville newspaper:[46]

PHOTOGRAPHS OF LT. BUFORD
MRS. L. J. DECAULP, (Lt. Buford, late of the Confederate army) has for sale several hundred beautifully executed Photographs of herself, which can be procured of Mr. Saltzman, at his gallery, on Union street, or from Mrs. DeCaulp, at the St. Cloud Hotel. The old companions in arms of Mrs. DeCaulp will find her at the St. Cloud, between the hours of 5 and 8 P.M.

These photos were probably a new pose, not the photos taken in Charleston. Unfortunately, neither of these photographs has been located. It is likely one will yet be discovered, so Civil War enthusiasts please keep a lookout. Remember there was an earlier photograph of Buford circulating in New Orleans in October 1862 which was used to identify and arrest her, "She was detected by a picture taken of her dressed in soldier's clothes." Watch for this one too.

It may be recalled that Velazquez wrote (p174) that after the fall of Fort Donelson and her departure from there, she sought refuge at the St. Cloud Hotel (calling it "a good hotel") to recover from exhaustion.[47] Whether, in truth, she was at Fort Donelson and then went to the St. Cloud Hotel to recover is unclear. However, it is clear that in 1864 she was held in the St. Cloud Hotel while under arrest, an arrest she avoided mentioning in her memoir. At that time, she wrote letters of protest to her captors, calling the hotel a "miserable place… not fit for any Lady." Now she had returned to the familiar hotel. To be sure, Velazquez was an inveterate hotel resident, her life's history shows.

From Nashville she took a southward side trip and next made an appearance at Pulaski, Tennessee and made herself known to the newspaper:[48]

Lieutenant Buford,
We had the pleasure yesterday of meeting the world-renowned heroine and Confederate officer, Lieut. Buford, whose exploits during the war are familiar to our readers. She entered the army in disguise, was at the first battle of Manassas, was twice wounded at the battle of Shiloh,- promoted to a Lieutenantcy [sic] for gallantry in that position throughout the war. She is now the widow of Maj. De Caulp, of an Arkansas regiment, and is soliciting subscribers to a volume of poetry

---

46. *Daily Union and American*, Jun 20, 1866.
47. Located on the NW corner of 5th and Church Street, at 500 Church Street.
48. *Pulaski Citizen*, Jun 22, 1866.

and a historical work which she has just completed. She is stopping at the Tennessee House.

The article claimed more than Velazquez claimed in her book. She never claimed to have been wounded "twice" at Shiloh, only once. She never claimed in her book that she was "promoted to a Lieutenancy for gallantry in that position throughout the war," but only that her rank was self-designated. She never in her book claimed husband DeCaulp was a major.

Why did this newspaper tell a different story than Velazquez would tell ten years later? Did the newspaper erroneously report what Velazquez correctly told it? For that matter, what about the many other papers which printed assertions about Velazquez which are provably false? Did they too erroneously report what Velazquez told them? The simple answer is that when the newspapers interviewed her, they repeated accurately enough what she told them. However, at times, newspapers grabbed an original story off the telegraph wires and reprinted it incorrectly. Their errors do not make Velazquez a truthful person; it just makes it more difficult for a researcher to understand when Velazquez told the paper a lie and when the newspaper made an inadvertent error.

And was it true that she had "just completed" a volume of poetry and a historical work? Only 20 days earlier, June 2, it was reported that she had "now prepared for the press three books." She obviously un-prepared one of the three books which trimmed down the book count to two. The truth was that none of the books were prepared and it took her ten years from this date to "complete" her one book, *The Woman in Battle*.

After Velazquez's departure from Pulaski, she traveled west and her next public notice was in Memphis, Tennessee. A "GRAND BALL" was announced:[49]

> A ball is to be given tomorrow evening at the Charleston Hotel, for the benefit of Mrs. Lauretta J. DeCaulp, better known as Lieut. Buford, of the Confederate army. This lady acquired a brilliant reputation as an officer in the field, until wounded and her sex revealed, after which she went North and to Europe on a secret service mission, rendering invaluable aid to the "lost cause." Her many friends in this city have tendered her this benefit, as an appreciation of her merits, and we hope their efforts will be crowned with success.

In the course of five days, Velazquez seemingly dropped her plea for subscriptions and took a different course. It might be supposed that her financial needs were dire enough that she permitted a charity benefit for herself.

One wonders the identity of the friends who gave the benefit ball and a disparager might question if her friends were receiving a cut of the funds

---

49. *Public Ledger*, Jun 27, 1866.

raised. In her book, Velazquez mentioned one particular friend in Memphis who helped her with her disguise, but mentioned no others. Just how she came to having a significant number of friends in Memphis where she never claimed she spent her youth, is not clear. It would be natural to expect that she had many friends in New Orleans where she claimed she was raised as an older child and teenager, but why "many friends" in Memphis?

The "grand ball" was seemingly neither the event of the year nor the failure of the year, either of which would have probably caused a follow-up newspaper report and there appears to have been no additional news of the event.

The article stated that she went to Europe "on a secret service mission, rendering invaluable aid to the 'lost cause'" and in her memoir she did write that she went to Europe to sell some Confederate bonds. The problem is that in her memoir she explained or implied that she was profiteering and not conducting transactions for the benefit of the Confederacy or "lost cause." She wrote, "I accordingly proceeded to London... was soon plunged into business... Confederate bonds were not selling very well just at that time, but as ours cost us very little, we could afford to dispose of them at very moderate figures and still make a handsome profit."

The benefit ball likely provided some money; from this date forward, it seems that Velazquez ceased subscription peddling. In any case, with the money raised she resumed her journey and headed east to Richmond. Which route she took and where she lingered are unknown. A local newspaper[50] noted her arrival:

IN THE CITY.- We were distinguished by a call yesterday from Mrs. Lauretta J. De Caulp, who, was known during the war as "Lieutenant Buford, Confederate States Army." Mrs. De Caulp retains a warm interest in her old companions-in-arms, and requests us to say that she will gladly see any of them at the Spotswood Hotel where she is at present staying. We learn that she expects to visit Europe during the coming fall. Her home is in Dallas county, Arkansas.

Considering that she had no money and had been in need of a benefit ball, it is admirable that she set her sights on a trip to Europe in the fall. As will be seen, she did not go. It is curious that she claimed her home was in Dallas County, Arkansas. This claim is addressed elsewhere.

After Velazquez left Richmond, she traveled to Washington, D.C., arriving no later than August 13, 1866. Now instead of selling book subscriptions, she took up a new goal- the building of an asylum for the disabled. The Washington *Evening Star* (August 13) wrote of her arrival in the city and her purpose:

---

50. *Richmond Whig*, Aug 10, 1866.

Mrs. Lauretta J. De Caulp, who was known during the war as 'Lieutenant Buford, Confederate States Army,' is at the Kirkwood House, and is seeking an interview with the President regarding the building of an asylum for the disabled and destitute of the South.

Many newspapers repeated the asylum story because they had prior knowledge of her and that appears to be the case with the *Pulaski Citizen* which carried it on August 31, surely recalling her June 22 visit to Pulaski. Later, on September 28, the *Pulaski Citizen* repeated the old article from the March 7 *St. Louis Republican* and told its readers, "It will be remembered that the subject of this sketch honored our town with a visit some three months since," of course, referring to the June 22 visit. It might be speculated Velazquez left the *Citizen* a copy of the old *Republican* article and now the *Citizen* was sufficiently stirred to reprint it.

Did Velazquez meet with the President Johnson? Although no record to date has been found of a meeting, it can be believed the case. She was certainly bold enough to seek a meeting. In a letter Velazquez wrote to the President on March 23, 1867, she referenced a meeting with him in August of 1866. In addition, her sincere intentions cannot be discounted. She narrated (p535) that "[her] journey through the South had disclosed a pitiable state of things" and she searched "whether there was anything [she] could do to advance the interest of the people among whom [her] lot had been cast for so many years...." Although it seems true that she was affected and it is true she sought to bring attention to the plight of the South, this effort in Washington was short-lived, as was her stay there. She abandoned her efforts to build an asylum; she now had a new mission in mind.

Velazquez went to New York and was probably there by September 18, 1866, when she likely read in the *Evening Post* about a venture of "Southern Emigration to Venezuela." The article explained that Dr. Henry Price's "Venezuela Emigration Company" offered relief to such persons "as cannot remain in their old homes under the domination of their heartless victors, and more especially for the poor Confederate soldiers and their widows and orphans." The newspaper said that Dr. Price had "issued a circular setting forth the advantages of emigration from the southern states to Venezuela." Velazquez likely came into possession of the circular.

Possibly this was not the first time she heard about the Venezuela Emigration Company, as the project had received publicity earlier in 1866. Newspapers in many of the southern cities through which Velazquez had traveled, had run articles about it. Velazquez probably learned of the scheme early in the year and then continuously heard about it for the rest of the year. By the end of 1866, she had determined to explore any opportunity with the Venezuela Emigration Company.

Velazquez wrote (p536):

I was much interested in these emigration schemes when I first heard of them, and was extremely anxious to investigate them, for my own sake as well as for that of my suffering fellow-country people of the South. Venezuela was one of the countries which it was proposed to colonize, and representations were made, to the effect that the Venezuelan government would extend a cordial welcome to emigrants, and would aid them in establishing themselves.

Velazquez further explained, "I longed to quit the scene of so much misery...." Her travels through the war-tattered South revealed the "general prostration of business and impoverishment of all classes" which she claimed was caused by "ambitious and unscrupulous politicians" taking advantage of "the forlorn condition of the South for the furtherance of their own bad ends."

Chapter 6

In New Orleans Again

Four months after Velazquez abandoned her asylum building efforts, she boarded a ship in New York, bound for New Orleans to look into the Venezuela emigration scheme. Velazquez departed on December 22, 1866 aboard the Black Star Line's steamship *Montgomery*, advertised as "one of our best and safest steamships," as well as, a "fast" and a "favorite steamship" by the New Orleans agent at 162 Common Street. The company claimed the vessel was "provided with everything to make passengers comfortable," and it had "elegant accommodations." It is unknown what accommodations Velazquez booked, but her choices were: "First Cabin Passage $60, Second Cabin $40 and Steerage $30." The *Montgomery* arrived safely, as promised, in New Orleans on Tuesday, January 1, 1867 and likely docked at the wharf at Ursulines Street.[1]

Once ashore Velazquez booked a room at the City Hotel and in her typical fashion made her presence known to the *Daily Picayune* newspaper:[2]

> Mrs. Mary De Caulp
>
> This is the name of the person who arrived in our city a few days since, upon the steamship Montgomery, from New York, and who claims to be the agent for the Southern States for a Venezuela Emigration Company, the president of which is Mr. John Walker, of St. Louis, Mo. Mrs. De Caulp has taken rooms at the City Hotel, and intends to open an office, in a few days, in some central locality, for the purpose of transacting business connected with her mission.
>
> Mrs. De Caulp's life, according to her account, and what is generally known, has been quite an adventurous one, and would furnish data for a half dozen such books as "Belle Boyd in Prison," and other sensational biographies of that class.
>
> At the opening of the late war, having donned male attire, she vaulted in the saddle of a 1st lieutenancy of a Texas cavalry company, and saw service in the first battle of Manassas. Subsequently she was transferred to the Western army, and was wounded in the battle of Shiloh, in which memorable engagement she claims to have performed splendid service.
>
> While recovering from her wound, she visited New Orleans, and took quarters with a regiment stationed out upon the Delachaise Grounds, where her sex being discovered, she was arrested and brought before Mayor Monroe, upon violating the city's ordinance in figuring in male attire. The writer of this paragraph remembers to have seen her at the time, dressed in a rough gray jacket and pants, the suit rather the worse for wear, with her hair cut short, and supporting a bandaged foot with a crutch of the most primitive pattern.
>
> Finding there was no objection to her appearing in male attire in this latitude, Mrs. De Caulp (or Lieut. Bufort [sic], as she was then known,) paid a visit to one of our fashionable dress makers, and arranged for a wardrobe more in keeping with her sex, decked in which she bade adieu to the Crescent City and went up the river

---

1. *Times-Picayune*, Apr 20, 1866; *Times-Picayune*, Dec 7, 1866; *Commercial Bulletin*, Jan 3, 1867; *Times-Picayune*, Mar 8, 1867; *Times-Picayune*, Apr 16, 1867.
2. Jan 5, 1867.

to some point above. Before the city fell, however, she had returned, and on the day the Federal fleet came up, she was recognized in her male attire while dashing about the streets upon horseback.

For some indiscretion, she was arrested by Gen. Butler, but being subsequently released, managed to make her way through the lines to Richmond.

From Richmond she was ordered out to the Western army, where she was detailed as passport agent on the line of the railroad between Chattanooga and Atlanta, in which service she remained for some six months or more. About the time of the battle of Chickamauga she was married to Capt. De Caulp, who belonged to an Arkansas regiment, and she was afterwards upon duty in the passport office at Tyler Station.

Mrs. De Caulp claims to have been sent during the last year of the war as a special agent to Europe by the Confederate Government for the purchase of clothing and other necessaries. Her description of campaign life, both in Virginia and Tennessee, would impress one with the idea that she certainly saw a good deal of active service.

Mrs. De Caulp, the Southern agent, as she claims to be, of the Venezuelan Emigration Company, is a very different looking person from the "bould soger boy" who came to New Orleans during the war; and it was very difficult for us to recognize as the rather graceful and elegantly attired lady in black, who called upon the Mayor yesterday, the rather shabby looking Lieut. Bufort of Confederate times.

About the emigration scheme in which Mrs. De Caulp is engaged, we can say but little, as her ideas about the matter appear to be yet quite crude and vague.

She states that she will, in the course of a few days, receive certain documents and circulars which will fully explain the purposes of the enterprise in which she is enlisted.

She is quite enthusiastic about the inducements offered to parties wishing to try the volcanic lands of Venezuela, but only in general terms, and is apparently not sufficiently versed to enter into those minor details which emigrants would like to converse about a little before setting sail with their families for the new Eldorado.

Mrs. De Caulp has not had the pleasure of meeting any of the Kentucky Venezuelan Emigration company at present in our city.

Velazquez, in her memoir, named the hotel in which she stayed and it is seen here confirmed by news of the day, she wrote (p537), "It having been announced that I intended to go to Venezuela, I was called upon at the City Hotel, where I had my quarters, by Captain Fred. A. Johnston [*sic* Johnson], who was fitting out an expedition." It is questionable if Captain Johnson came to her in the manner she described, to persuade her into going, but instead, it is more likely he came to see her in confused reaction to what she had told the newspapers- that she was an agent for the emigration company.

This *Daily Picayune* article was a substantial bit of reporting and contains plenty of points which can and will be disputed. It is suggested the reader go back and read the 1862 New Orleans newspaper reports about Velazquez. The contradictions between those 1862 articles and this one are only too clear. Obviously, the reporter didn't look in his own newspaper's archives or he would have been forced to produce a different report.

First, why did Velazquez use the name of "Mary"? Did she wish not to be recognized by the locals? But that wouldn't make much sense since she readily admitted her history there, though she told it falsely. Recall she was "Annie Williams" at her 1862 New Orleans arrest. Earlier at her 1861 Lynchburg arrest, she was "Mrs. Mary Ann Keith" and later at her 1863 Mobile/Richmond/Castle Thunder arrest, she was "Mrs. Alice Williams." Afterwards she went to Atlanta, married Thomas C. DeCaulp, returned to Richmond and called herself "Jeruth DeCaulp." So why now Mary? The likely three-part answer is, she was a congenital liar, she was hiding a past history and she was a paranoid person. Her propensity to lie has already been made clear, some of her history was worth hiding and a paranoia will become evident in her later history.

Second, the article stated that "At the opening of the late war, having donned male attire, she vaulted in the saddle of a 1st lieutenancy of a Texas cavalry company, and saw service in the first battle of Manassas." No, no, and no. In 1862, in an effort to endear herself to the same New Orleans audience, she claimed that she was at Manassas with the 7th Louisiana Regiment. Now, at this later date in 1866, she did not dare make the same claim to New Orleanians who might have been veterans of the 7th Louisiana and could have caught her in her lie. In her 1876 memoir, she claimed that at a prelude to the big battle she was in General Bonham's First Brigade, then somehow joined-up with Longstreet's Fourth Brigade. And on the actual day of the battle, she said she was with General Bee's command, the Third Brigade. This claim would have required her to switched armies within the Confederate army, going from the Army of the Potomac on the first day to the Army of the Shenandoah on the second day. The remainder of her lies of her participation in the First Battle of Manassas are exposed elsewhere.

Third, if the reader will review the news articles of her wartime visits to New Orleans, it can be understood that almost nothing she said at this date, about that earlier time, is true. She was not arrested while "with a regiment" at Delachaise Grounds and "brought before Mayor Monroe, upon violating the city's ordinance in figuring in male attire." Velazquez blended her two scrapes with the law into one event. Recall, the first time she "surrendered herself to the mayor" in order to avoid any problems similar to those she had encountered at Lynchburg and Richmond in 1861. She had arrived in New Orleans in April 1862 wearing her male attire and wanted to stay out of trouble.

When she was arrested in October 1862, it was for stealing from the Chesters. At the time of this arrest, she was "with a regiment," but not as a soldier. Instead, she was living as the wife of a Yankee soldier who was with his regiment at the "Delachaise Grounds." She most certainly did not tell the newspaper that she was living with a Yankee soldier in a Yankee camp! The reporter probably correctly remembered having "seen her at the time, dressed in a rough gray jacket and pants, the suit rather the worse for wear, with her hair cut short, and supporting a bandaged foot with a crutch of the most primitive pattern." The reporter implied that he understood her, at the time, to be a woman in male attire.

It is certainly possible that "on the day the Federal fleet came up, she was recognized in her male attire while dashing about the streets upon horseback." Again, the reporter seemed to know that she was a woman in male attire. At that moment she was still free, not in jail. It was after the fleet's arrival, that she was arrested for stealing from the Chesters. Clearly, at the time, she had no money and was forced to steal, so it can be assumed that the horse upon which she rode was borrowed. Still, it is remarkable that Velazquez conducted herself as she did, outside typical behavior norms of the times for women; no other women were dashing about the street on horseback in male attire!

Notice that the reporter said after Velazquez's first New Orleans arrest, she "arranged for a wardrobe more in keeping with her sex, decked in which she bade adieu to the Crescent City and went up the river to some point above. Before the city fell, however, she had returned...." In great contradiction, in her memoir, Velazquez made no mention of going "up the river to some point above," but instead said she went on the mission to Havana and then on the mission to Robertson's Plantation.

Velazquez claimed and the newspaper reported, "For some indiscretion, she was arrested by Gen. Butler, but being subsequently released, managed to make her way through the lines to Richmond." The 1862 New Orleans newspapers make clear that the "indiscretion" which Velazquez obviously wished to avoid mentioning was theft. She was not brought before Butler and he had nothing to do with her trial. A judge sentenced her to the parish prison for common criminals. Once released, she was sent out of Union occupied New Orleans and across the military lines along with other "registered enemies." Details of this are given elsewhere.

Upon her departure from New Orleans, she did go to Richmond. However, it was no problem "to make her way through the lines to Richmond," as she had already passed the military lines when she left New Orleans. The article stated, "From Richmond she was ordered out to the Western army, where she was detailed as passport agent on the line of the railroad between Chattanooga and Atlanta, in which service she remained for some six months or more." It is possible that she was hired for this position. The article did not say she assumed a male disguise for the job, but in her memoir, she claimed (p148-153) she disguised herself as a man. Whether it is true that she served in this position, either as a woman or man, is still inconclusive. However, it is clear that she lied in this article or in her memoir about the time she held the position. In her memoir she said she quit after three weeks!

It is almost true that "about the time of the battle of Chickamauga she was married to Capt. De Caulp, who belonged to an Arkansas regiment." They actually married prior to that battle and it was during that campaign the Captain deserted.

According to the article, Velazquez then "afterwards" had "duty in the passport office at Tyler Station." The reporter surely meant Tyner's Station, which was slightly east of Chattannoga, and is today within the city limits of Chattanooga. To date no military record found supports the claim, but it is possibly true, but not likely. It will be seen later that Lieutenant General Bromfield Ridley wrote in his 1906 book, that Velazquez showed up there asking for a job as a scout, but was found out to be a woman and was turned away. Ridley must be believed that Velazquez showed up at Tyner's Station, but he also made clear she was turned away as a scout, the job she came to request. Is it possible she then was placed in the passport office at Tyner's Station? If so, it is clear that she would have done the job as a woman because she had been discovered; Ridley said she was discovered. However, it is unclear when she might have found the time for the job since it was very shortly after her marriage to DeCaulp and his desertion to the North, that she followed him North.

Two soldier diaries corroborate Velazquez's Tyner's Station or Chattanooga presence, but at a date prior to her DeCaulp marriage (first-week of September), in Atlanta. This earlier date possibly supports Velazquez's memoir's claim to have quit after three weeks. Private (later 2nd Lieutenant) Robert Hodges Jr.[3] wrote from Turners [*sic*-Tyner's] Station on August 7-8, 1863:

> Pa, among the curiousities [*sic*] I have seen since I left home, one I must mention, a female first lieutenant! I had heard of her deeds of bravery in several battles and a few evenings I was [at a point] to [near] the station about a quarter of a mile distant from camp. I discovered quite a crowd. Approaching, I enquired what was up. One of the soldiers directed my attention to a youth apparently about seventeen years of age well dressed with a lieutennat's [*sic*] badge on his collar. I remarked that I saw nothing strange. He told me that the young man was not a man but a female. It is said she volunteered with her husband as a private, fought through the Battles of Shiloh where her husband was killed. She performed the rites of burial with her own hands. She then continued with Braggs army in Ky,

---

3. Darst, Maury (1971) "Robert Hodges, Jr.: Confederate Soldier," *East Texas Historical Journal*: V 9; Iss 1, Art 6.

fighting in the ranks as a commissioned soldier, until she was twice wounded in the ankle and then in the breast. When she fell prisoner into the hands of the Yankees her sex was discovered by the Federals and she was regularly paroled as a prisoner of war, but they did not permit her to return until she had donned female apparrell [sic]. She has since her return, I suppose, being promoted to the office of Lt.

Robert Hodges' sighting was real; she was at the train station, a quarter-mile from camp. Hodges did not name Velazquez, but surely this was her. Clearly, he did not confirm her military claims and could only write of the rumors he heard. Velazquez never claimed to have served as a private nor that she had a husband killed at Shiloh, who she buried with her own hands, nor that she was "promoted" to lieutenant.

The second soldier did use her name. Private (later Corporal) Van Buren Oldham[4] wrote in his diary, August 5, 1863:

> Sometime since a Mrs. P. Williams was arrested and found in [an] army uniform and passing herself as Lieut[enant] Buford. She was sent to [the] castle. No charges being preferred against her. She was released and is now in Chattanooga with her uniform and still persists in being known as Lieut[enant] Buford.

Obviously, Mr. Oldham knew nothing of Velazquez, except what he had just read in the *Chattanooga Daily Rebel* newspaper the day prior, August 4th. The newspaper had repeated a story from the *Montgomery Mail* which had clearly taken their information from a Richmond newspaper reporting her release from Castle Thunder. What is interesting is the Montgomery newspaper wrote, "We have seen the gallant Lieutenant on the streets of Montgomery for several days." This means that Velazquez boarded the train prior to Montgomery's report, and traveled to Chattanooga (transiting Atlanta), arriving by August 5th.

Back to the *Daily Picayune* newspaper, the article stated, "Mrs. De Caulp claims to have been sent during the last year of the war as a special agent to Europe by the Confederate Government for the purchase of clothing and other necessaries." Doubt that she ever went to Europe has already been expressed and now here her claim adds to the doubt because she said she went to purchase "clothing and other necessaries" which hugely contradicts her memoir in which she wrote (p505) the purpose of the European trip was to sell Confederate bonds for personal profit.

It is interesting to note that in one year, 1866, Velazquez went from an entrepreneur seeking "to purchase a stock of dry goods and plantation supplies, with a view of opening a business house at Mulberry Grove, Jefferson County, Ark.," to an impending authoress of three books, selling

---

4. Civil War Diaries of Van Buren Oldham, Dieter C. Ullrich, ed. Originals at Sp. Coll./Univ.Archives, Univ. of Tennessee at Martin, utm.edu/departments/special-collections/E579%20Oldham/text/vboldham-1863.php.

book subscriptions throughout the South, to a champion asking the U.S. President to build an asylum for the disabled. Now Velazquez claimed she was an agent for the Venezuela Emigration Company. Nowhere in her book did she claim to have been an agent using the name of Mrs. Mary DeCaulp or any other name.

Fourth, was Velazquez an agent for the Venezuela Emigration Company or did she just think that she was an agent, or did she have the intention to commit fraud? Well, she falsely claimed that John Walker was the President which points to her deliberate will to lie. Could she have made an innocent mistake? Not likely; it would have been abundantly clear to her, from all the newspaper reports, that Dr. Henry Price was the President. On the other hand, if she intended to commit fraud, it is indeterminable how her plan might have worked.

Maybe she had a less sinister intention and only figured to push her way into a job. She might have intended to collect money from passengers and then assert her prowess to the company, and thus gain an agency. But such boldness is barely imaginable.

Had she received a vague and unsecured promise of an agency in some roundabout way from John Walker? Did "Mr. John Walker, of St. Louis" misrepresent himself as President of the company to her? This was Ex-Confederate Major General John G. Walker, native of Missouri and it is a fact that in "November-December, 1866 Walker was at the Southern Hotel, St. Louis"[5] and Velazquez may have met him sometime in 1866, when she was traveling through the South.

Or did Velazquez lie simply because she couldn't help herself? In any case, she was denounced, as quickly as the mail permitted, by one of the company's principals, John A. Doll. He wrote a letter to the *Times-Picayune* which published it on February 9, 1867:

Mrs. De Caulp and the Venezuela Company.
The following explains the non-connection between these two. Mrs. De C. must be connected with some other company:
SCOTTSVILLE, Albemarle county, Va.,
January 28, 1867

Editors of the Picayune:
Dear Sirs- A gentleman in New Orleans has sent me a slip from the Picayune, giving an account of the arrival in your city, of a Mrs. De Caulp, who claims to be an agent of the "Venezuela Emigration Company," and that she has her authority from Gen. John Walker, who she says, is "President of said company." Now I know of but one Venezuela Company, at present, in existence. Dr. Henry M. Price,

---

5. Alfred Jackson Hanna and Kathryn Abbey Hanna, *Confederate Exiles in Venezuela* (Tuscaloosa, AL: Confederate Publishing Co., 1960), 23.

of Scottsville, Va., is the President and Grantee, and Col. R. H. Musser, of St. Louis, Vice President. Gen. John G. Walker, No. 1 Alderman's Walk, London, is a Director, and also one of the agents for England. I cannot believe that Gen. Walker would assume the authority to appoint any one as agent to act anywhere, without the knowledge and direction of the President. My opinion is, that Mrs. De Caulp is a self-constituted agent, and does not know even the title of our company. The name of our company is simply "The Venezuela Company," and we have but one authorized agent in New Orleans, Benjamin P. Vancourt, Esq., No. 13 New Levee street. As I am a Director and Treasurer of the "Venezuela Company," and have almost daily interviews with the President and grantee, Dr. H. M. Price, I claim to know who are the authorized agents. Yours respectfully, John A. Doll

It can be certain that well before this letter was mailed, the true agent in New Orleans, Benjamin P. Vancourt[6] had corrected Velazquez in the error of her ways. She was probably forced off her claim within a day and well before John A. Doll's letter was even composed, much less mailed. In any case, Doll's letter was too late to matter. By then, some 25 days prior, Velazquez had departed New Orleans. She no longer posed as an agent of the company, but had joined the party of emigrants then en route, across the Gulf of Mexico and Caribbean Sea, to Venezuela.

The Venezuela Emigration Company

At the conclusion of the Civil War, some ex-Confederate soldiers and government officials refused to accept "the new political, social and economic life being forced upon them" by the victorious North.[7] These Southerners concluded that there was no financial opportunity in the war-devastated South or they believed that their Southern traditions were lost forever, or they simply did not want to take the "Oath of Allegiance" to the United States.

In addition, the defeated Rebels understandably feared prosecution by the Federal Government which had called the Southerners traitors. Traitors could be hung. To satisfy the dissatisfied, there came into existence several emigration schemes which promoted a new life by starting colonies in foreign lands, Mexico, Brazil and Venezuela being the best known. Other destinations of fleeing ex-Confederates were Canada, Cuba, British Honduras (now Belize), Jamaica, Japan, Egypt and Europe.[8] It is estimated that about 10,000 people became expatriates, making this diaspora the largest to that date in U.S. history, if you don't consider most of them eventually returned.

---

6. Vancourt later went to Venezuela and died at LaGuaira on May 8, 1868.
7. Hanna and Hanna, 14.
8. Andrew R. Rolle, *The Lost Cause, the Confederate Exodus to Mexico* (Norman, OK: Univ. of Oklahoma Press, 1965), 9.

Many ex-Confederates fled to Mexico. They went by any conveyance available, some by ship, but mostly by horse and mule. They loaded wagons with provisions and trekked through the desert with an eye out for bandits. At that time Mexico was ruled by Emperor Maximilian who had been placed on the throne by Napoleon III of France through military force which deposed Mexican President Benito Juárez. Napoleon III determined to set up a profitable little empire in the New World and used as his excuse the money which Mexico owed France. Maximilian supported the ex-Confederates immigration, but he was captured and shot by firing squad by Benito Juárez's army and the estimated 3,000 ex-Confederates were killed or driven back to where they came.

The Brazilian colony was the most successful of the schemes, but not very. To this day, the remnants of the colony are found in family names, place names, and customs. Of the approximately 4,000 emigrants, less than half remained five years later, the others returned to the U.S.

The scheme of the Venezuela Emigration Company was the vision of Dr. Henry Manore Price. Price petitioned the Venezuelan government to provide a large tract of land and it responded favorably, undoubtedly already with a tract of land in mind. Ever since its independence from Spain, Venezuela sought to develop the endless land of the state of Guyana, surrounding the Orinoco River. The land had potential, especially for cotton production, but it was lacking farmers because continuous Venezuelan civil wars had decimated the region's population. Now with the American Civil War ended, a new labor force in the form of expatriated Confederates was available to develop the region. Both parties to the agreement were poised to profit; Henry Price wanted the land concession and the government wanted the settlers to develop the unoccupied land and add to the prosperity of the region and country.

Dr. Price's efforts resulted in the September 13, 1865 drafting of conditions of agreement by the Venezuelan Ministry of the Interior in Caracas. The document granted the new arrivals exemption from all taxes for five years. Within one year the colonist could be citizens. They would be guaranteed freedom of religion, press and speech and could have representation in congress.

The land given was a huge area, roughly 240,000 square miles, four times the area of the state of Georgia. The document defined the region in typical verbose survey style; the Emigration Company simply said "all vacant lands in the State of Guyana and the District of Amazonas." In addition, "All mineral and vegetable wealth products to be found in the lands they occupy" were conceded to the settlers. Dr. Price wrote[9] of the attractions, "Its gold mines are richer than those of California, every pound of quartz yielding an

---

9. *Charleston Courier*, Mar 10, 1866.

ounce of gold." It is startling to think that readers would believe such an impossibility. Gold quartz deposits with such yields cannot be found in nature. A mine which yields an ounce per ton would be wildly rich! Maybe the readership missed this basic truth because they were dazzled by the overflowing description of the land.

The most urgent issue facing the Emigration Company was a numbers and time constraint defined by the grant document. It stipulated that the first colonization party must consist of a minimum of fifty people and must begin within eighteen months of the date of the agreement, February 5, 1866, or the grant was void.

The Venezuela Emigration Company was now in a hurry. It met on March 25, 26 and 27 in Richmond, to write a charter, appoint officers and write the by-laws.[10] The charter officially designated the company as the "Venezuela Company." Two months prior, Dr. Price had used the name "Venezuelan Land Company," and newspapers said that according to the circulars sent out by the company, it was called the "Venezuela Emigration Company."[11]

The Venezuela Company's charter provided for a president and sixteen directors, establishing a "Court of Directory." Of the 80,000 planned stock shares, 10,000 "reserved" shares stayed in possession of the grantee, Dr. Price, for his discretionary use. Forty-thousand "authorized" shares were designated to be sold at $1,000 per share. Profit from these sales was to be used for construction of infrastructure. The remaining 30,000 "gratuitous" shares were to go to "late Confederate soldiers and other Southern citizens." Dr. Price explained[12] the 30,000 shares were "granted to *poor* Confederate soldiers- the preference being given to men of family, simply upon the payment to us of *Office Fees* necessary to expenses, etc., $4." He also wrote that there was a $60 ship passage fee.

"A large company of emigrants is organized in St. Louis for Venezuela," reported the newspaper.[13] This first emigrant party, not surprisingly, came from St. Louis where Missouri native Gen. John Walker had been promoting the emigration scheme. More promotion there followed in mid-December by a "Mr. Anaslyne, a native of Venezuela," who presented to prospective emigrants the land grant document and "examined... interpreted, [and] pronounced [it] correct." He showed samples of Venezuelan corn and cotton and explained that three crops a year could be grown.[14] The cotton

---

10. *Richmond Whig*, May 1, 1866.
11. *Evening Post* (New York), Sep 18, 1866.
12. *The Charleston Courier*, Mar 10, 1866.
13. *New Orleans Times*, Dec 16, 1866.
14. *Times-Picayune*, Dec 20, 1866.

was "compared favorably with the finest Sea Island cotton," then raised in coastal South Carolina and Georgia and highly prized.

The group departed St. Louis on December 20 and one newspaper wrote that "Several of those who had agreed to emigrate, backed out when the hour of departure arrived."[15] One correspondent[16] thought that the forty departing emigrants were "a sorry looking crowd of forlorn fellows indeed... down the back streets they marched, more like a pack of half-starved emigrants just from Dublin than like American citizens going to start a new colony." He noted that prior to their departure, a benefit held for the emigrants at De Bar's Opera House "yielded nothing" and some emigrants did not have money enough to pay their passage fee and barely had clothes on their backs.

Upon the emigrants' arrival in New Orleans, a newspaper[17] treated them more tenderly:

There are in our city at the present time fifty stalwart, whole-souled sons of Kentucky bound to Venezuela, where they are promised 1400 acres of land and $200 apiece upon their settlement. They are mostly from Georgetown [Kentucky] and the neighborhood, and we are glad to see that, during the fitting out of their vessel, they are enjoying themselves among their many friends here.

The newspaper reported they were leaving on Saturday, but thought they were making a mistake leaving, that no "better homes or truer friends" could be found than in the "old blue grass country." The newspaper wished them Godspeed, stating that without a doubt:

They will soon rise to the dignity of generals and governors in that country of earthquakes, volcanic eruptions and political revolutions. We warn them, however, to beware of the black-eyed señoritas.

The emigrants' layover in New Orleans was supposed to be a short one. The departure for Venezuela was set for January 5 aboard "the staunch vessel" *United States*.[18] In the meantime, Agent B. P. Vancourt promoted, "We now have about sixty emigrants and can take a few more" and the settlers would find "a new and better home," be a citizen in one year, be exempt from military duty for ten years and be free from taxes for five years. All the tobacco, cotton, sugar, coffee, etc., produced would be free from export duty for five years. "Each emigrant will receive... 1280 acres of land, one town lot of one acre, an interest in the General Stock Company, and

---

15. *Times-Picayune*, Dec 20, 1866; *New Orleans Times*, Dec 22, 1866; Mar 13, 1867 letter from "Derby" in the *Daily Picayune*, May 20, 1867.
16. *Boston Herald*, Jan 2, 1867, the correspondent's report was dated Dec 24.
17. *Daily Picayune*, Jan 3, 1867.
18. *Crescent* (New Orleans), Jan 1, 1867.

one steerage passage, upon the payment of $55." In other words, the emigrant had to pay for their passage.

In charge of the expedition was thirty-year-old Captain Frederick A. Johnson, a native of St. Louis. After the War, Johnson became interested in the emigration scheme when he read the circular sent out by Dr. Price and was convinced of the opportunities of immigrating to Venezuela.[19] Johnson had accompanied the colonist aboard the *Columbian* during their trip from St. Louis, down the Mississippi River to New Orleans where Captain Johnson sent a letter to the editors of the *Crescent* newspaper[20] "in order to correct some misapprehensions." He listed the same attributes of the grant, previously made public. He concluded with what sounded like his farewell address:

> Political wrongs at home, whether actual or imaginary, have always had the effect of causing new colonies and countries to spring up like magic. God Almighty has decreed it, if we are to judge from histories of the past. The majority of the parties leaving are from Missouri, which we leave to the negroes and the Dutch [as Germans were routinely called] and we go from home, like our ancestors, to found a new home, and to endeavor to improve upon the management of our own country. [Signed] F. A. J.

But still there was no departure. One reason given was the *United States* was in dry dock, but another reason given was that the vessel had too many outstanding claims against it.[21] Even if the vessel had been available, the hired agent for the emigration company, Mr. Williams of the agency Williams and Long, was unable to offer enough money to secure a charter because the poor emigrants had not put up enough money. Mr. Williams was ineffectual in the eyes of the colonists and was criticized.

Wishing to minimize the delay, Captain Johnson sought to charter another vessel and Mr. Williams ostensibly hired schooner *Elizabeth*. The settlers moved aboard with their baggage on January 12 and the crew assisted them in building additional bunks.[22] The vessel was moved from Algiers, across the River from New Orleans, to the wharf next to Jackson Square in New Orleans and made ready for departure.[23] On January 14, the *New Orleans Times* advertised that "the fast-sailing clipper schooner" would "sail positively" for Venezuela on Tuesday the 15th. Again, there was no departure.

The Emigration Company had only paid a retainer for the vessel and the owner wanted to be paid in full prior to the vessel's departure. Johnson

---

19. Hanna and Hanna, 49.
20. Jan 5, 1867.
21. *Daily Picayune*, May 20, 1867, letter from "Derby" letter dated Mar 13, 1867.
22. *New Orleans Commercial Bulletin*, Jan 24, 1867.
23. Hanna and Hanna, 49.

rounded up cash and notes, and even added $950 in notes of his own to make a total of some $3184. The boat's owner, one George P. Deshon (Albert also was given as his first name), refused the money because he now wished to take a more profitable cargo of sugar to Northern markets and he wanted the colonist off the boat.[24] When Johnson and the colonist refused to get off, Deshon had them arrested for trespass. "F. A. Johnson and about fifty others" were arraigned before Recorder Gastinel, on January 23.[25] Deshon testified that the first time he saw the colonist was when he went to his vessel on the 13th and found them living onboard. Mr. Williams, the agent, testified that he had hired the *Elizabeth* through Kane & C., who "represented themselves to be the owner." Mr. Williams testified that it was Kane & Co. who ordered Johnson and the settlers aboard. Mr. Williams was again criticized by the colonists for this mess up.

"It was proven that the defendants... had paid their passage money $45 each to parties representing themselves as owners of the Elizabeth."[26] The judge ruled the vessel's ownership needed to be resolved by a civil court, not his criminal court. The case was dismissed and the colonists were ordered returned to the vessel from which they were taken when arrested.

Velazquez truthfully, though only briefly, narrated (p540) the arrest:

> A small schooner was finally procured.... Just as we were on the point of sailing, however, the owners of the vessel, who had not received their money for her attempted to regain possession. We were all arrested, therefore, but after a long investigation of the case, were released, and the schooner delivered into our hands.

The colonist had the sympathy of the press[27] which renewed its best wishes:

> We regret to learn the party... from St. Louis and Kentucky... en route to Venezuela have, through no fault of their own, had trouble with their vessel. It gives us pleasure, however, to learn that they are all right now, and will be able to sail Saturday next. If they must go, we wish them joy and good fortune, leaving each for himself to make his way with the pretty senoritas of Hispaniola after they arrive... and leave a black-eyed, dark-haired progeny behind them.

1867, Married John Wasson

In the middle of the chaos of the emigrants acquiring a boat and their arrest, Velazquez married a young man in the emigrants' party.

Upon "Mrs. Mary De Caulp's" arrival in New Orleans, she stated to the newspaper that she had "not had the pleasure of meeting any of the

---

24. Ibid, 50.
25. *Times-Picayune*, Jan 24, 1867.
26. *New Orleans Commercial Bulletin*, Jan 24, 1867.
27. *Daily Picayune*, Jan 24, 1867.

Kentucky Venezuelan Emigration company at present in [the] city."[28] In her memoir, Velazquez explained that she made it known to Johnson that she was interested in emigrating and Johnson called on her at her hotel. She wrote, that after they became acquainted, he "was apparently beginning to consider [her] a valuable ally, came and invited [her] to go over to Algiers... for the purpose of meeting the others who were going." She crossed the Mississippi River to meet the emigrants, she wrote, "A meeting was called for the purpose of consultation with regard to chartering a vessel and arranging for supplies, and Johnson greatly desired me to deliver an address. This I declined to do...." The question arises why would she, as an undecided emigrant, be asked to address the committed emigrants? Those daring souls had already invested their time and money traveling from Missouri, down the Mississippi River, and Velazquez was going to do... what? Encourage them? Share her wisdom? Can any reason be thought of why Johnson would ask her? In any case, it was at this time that she met her future husband (p539):

> Among the emigrants who had enlisted in Johnston's [*sic* Johnson] band was a young Confederate officer, Major Wasson. He was a remarkably fine-looking man, with long, wavy, flaxen hair, which he wore brushed off his forehead, blue eyes, and fair complexion. The day before going over to Algiers with Johnston I had seen him on one of the street cars, and was very much struck with him. At Algiers I had some conversation with him, and invited him to call on me at the hotel. This he did; and I discovered that he was a stranger to all the rest of the band of emigrants, that he was anxious to get out of the country, and that, attracted by Johnston's representations, he had resolved to go to Venezuela with his expedition.
>
> After that I saw a great deal of Major Wasson, and a strong attachment sprang up between us. A few days before we were to sail, he asked me to accept his hand, and I did so willingly; for not only did I admire him greatly, but I felt that it would be better in every way that I should accompany the expedition as a married woman.
>
> We were accordingly married, and for some days kept the matter secret, it being our original intention not to say anything about it until after we were out at sea. As I was, however, pursued by the attentions of several other gentlemen, we finally concluded that the fact of our being husband and wife had best be announced.

Shortly after their meeting in Algiers, John Wasson married Lauretta DeCaulp on January 17, 1867, before the Third Justice of the Peace, Paul W. Collins, in the Parish of Orleans- City of New Orleans, the marriage certificate shows. The witnesses who stood for them were Daniel Clary and John Whitman, both members of the emigrants' group.

From the time of her arrival in New Orleans until her marriage, 17 days later, Velazquez changed her name from Mary DeCaulp back to her previous and regularly used name, Lauretta DeCaulp. One wonders how that was

---

28. Ibid, Jan 5, 1867.

explained to Wasson or the other emigrants, that is, if they had even been aware that she had arrived in New Orleans as Mary DeCaulp.

Please see the Wasson and Velazquez marriage certificate in Illustrations, Figure 12.

The marriage license (a separate document from the certificate) was obtained the same day and witnessed by the same two men, who swore they "were well acquainted with" the betrothed and that the couple was over the age of twenty-one. A fee or bond was paid by John Wasson, and Daniel Clary signed as "Surety," however, the amount of money written on the license cannot be clearly read. (Due to the poor quality of the license, no attempt was made to reproduce it in the illustrations section.)

Velazquez truthfully wrote that she did not know Wasson many days before marrying him and the number of days can be calculated within a range. It is known that Velazquez arrived in New Orleans on January 1 and in the January 5th published interview she said she had "not had the pleasure of meeting" the Kentucky emigrants. This statement could not have been made prior to the 2nd of January, which makes 15 days the maximum number of days before the wedding. But the time was less, based on Velazquez's own narrative. She said it was when she went to Algiers, to visit the emigrants who were waiting on a vessel, that she met Wasson. Their originally scheduled vessel, *United States*, was still thought to be departing on January 5 and only sometime after that date was it positive it was not able to go. The newspaper account of the court hearing indicated that the group boarded the second vessel chosen, the *Elizabeth*, on the 12th. Extrapolating the information given by Velazquez, it was between the 5th and the 13th that she met Wasson. The previous liberal estimation of fifteen days can now be recalculated to be a minimum of four days and a maximum of twelve days. In any case, she said that during this short period she, "saw a great deal of Major Wasson, and a strong attachment sprang up between [them]."

There exists a falsehood in her assertion about her marriage, "We were accordingly married, and for some days kept the matter secret, it being our original intention not to say anything about it until after we were out at sea...." But Daniel Clary and John Whitman, the witnesses, were members of the emigrants' party! It is clear that Velazquez did not keep the marriage a secret from those fellow emigrants.

There exists another not-so-obvious falsehood, that of the rank of "Major Wasson." Circumstantial evidence and common logic dictate that Wasson was not a major.

First, recall that Velazquez lied when she called herself "Mrs. Major DeCaulp," in effect, attributing the higher rank of major to Captain DeCaulp.

Second, the rank of major was accomplished (educated) and esteemed. High ranking officers were publicly known and their names can be easily found in Civil War records. Major Wasson does not exist in the records.

Third, fellow emigrants wrote several letters to newspapers in which the colony's progress was told and the letters made no mention of "Major Wasson." The party would have been proud to have such an estimable, high-ranking major in their group, surely worth mentioning, since he would have been an endorsement of the scheme and he probably would have ascended to a natural leadership in the expedition.

Fourth, a colonist wrote a letter to a friend in St. Louis who then gave it to a newspaper for the letter to be made public. The letter gave news of fellow colonists and it named eight newly married colonist men and their wives. These marriages had taken place after the group's departure from St. Louis. The newspaper[29] reported:

> Probably the following extract from the letter will be information to the most of their friends in this State: Mr. John Wasson has been united in wedlock with Madame Lauretta J. DeCaulp, a widow lady, young, gay and fascinating, who is the daughter of an English Admiral; Daniel Clary is married to Senorita Auguara, a young Spanish lady, who speaks English and is young, beautiful and wealthy....

If Wasson had been a major, and a known public figure, the letter writer would have, in typical manner, used the rank with Wasson's name, but instead called him only "Mr." At least, Wasson rated a "Mr." as a title; poor Daniel Clary, who stood as a witness in the Wasson/DeCaulp wedding, did not even get a "Mr."!

Another point about this letter: it sounds like Velazquez wrote it. Did anyone among the emigrants except herself care if she was "the daughter of an English Admiral"? The simple answer is no. However, if by chance, a fellow emigrant wrote the letter, then Velazquez herself must have shown one of the articles written previously about herself, which mentioned her "English Admiral" father. If it is accepted that Velazquez wrote the letter, then it should be noted that she did not address Wasson as "Major," but only "Mr." And it will be seen that in a September 1874 interview with the Atlanta *Constitution* that Velazquez claimed she was married to "Mr. John W. Wasson of Kentucky."

It is a certainty that "young Confederate officer, Major Wasson" did not exist in the Civil War and Velazquez falsely credited Wasson with the rank.

Who was John Wasson?

Velazquez stated that Wasson was unacquainted with the emigrant party when he joined the group. This party consisted mostly of Missourians. She,

---

29. *Daily Missouri Republican* (St. Louis, MO), May 24, 1867.

in September 1874, stated to the *Atlanta Constitution* that "John W. Wasson" was from Kentucky.

The only likely "John Wasson" or "John W. Wasson," was one John W. Wasson, born in Oldham County Kentucky in 1845. He is found in the 1850 U.S. Census.[30] His father was Robert Wasson Jr., 28 years old, and his mother was Sarah, 29. John was 5 years old; his sister Sarah was three and his sister Elizabeth was one. The family's value of "real estate owned" was $2500, which was substantial for the times.

The 1860 U.S. Census records "Wasson" and shows that the Robert Jr. was absent, most likely dead, but Robert Jr.'s father, Robert (age 65), was living in La Grange, (Oldham County). Under his roof was Robert Jr.'s wife, Sarah (40), and daughters Sarah C. (12) and Elizabeth (11). John W. Wasson was not present and it is assumed he was living independent of his family. He would have been 15 years old in 1860. When the Civil War broke-out he was of prime age for the ranks, and surely served, though the military records show no conclusive matches for John W. Wasson of any rank; there are some nebulous possibilities with the rank of private.

When Wasson and Velazquez married, he was 21 or 22 years old.

The Sailing of the *Elizabeth* and its Arrival in Venezuela

Captain Frederick Johnson, the expedition leader, successfully negotiated an agreement with the owner of the *Elizabeth*. (It should be noted that Johnson was not captain of the vessel, Captain Frith was.) Now the colonists were free to depart New Orleans, which they did on January 29.[31] After descending the Mississippi River, the vessel set sail February 4.[32] The colonists were finally on their way. Of the fifty-one colonists, all were men, except five children and four women- Mrs. Austin, Mrs. Whitman, Mrs. Beasley and Mrs. Wasson, who was, of course, the newly married Velazquez. Velazquez narrated (p540) correctly enough that "the expedition consisted of forty-nine persons, including children."

The *Elizabeth* was a slow vessel, but sturdy. Colonist F. A. Derbyshire, "Derby," wrote that rough seas caused by "a heavy gale, lasting several days," impeded her progress. Johnson was the first to "cave" with seasickness. After a rough 30-day passage, on about March 5, the ship dropped anchor at the mouth of the Orinoco River. The vessel took aboard

---

30. In error, the recorded name was "Warson."
31. *Daily Picayune*, May 20, 1867, a letter from "Derby" dated Mar 13, 1867.
32. *Times* (New Orleans), Feb 1, 1867, Feb 5, 1867; Mar 13, 1867, Derby letter in the *Daily Picayune*, May 20, 1867.

a pilot, proceeded up the Orinoco and arrived at Ciudad Bolívar on March 14.[33] In general agreement with Derby's account, Velazquez wrote:

> It was a terrible voyage; and, although I had passed through some rather rough experiences in my life, and was accustomed to hardships, it will always live in my memory as one of my most painful experiences. My sufferings, however, were nothing in comparison with those of some of the poor women and children who were with us, and I was indignant, beyond expression, at the idea of their being victimized in the manner they were.

Derby wrote that while Captain Frith was trying to determine his bearings and how to safely navigate up the river, the outbound British schooner *Isabel*, whose homeport was Demerara (British Guyana), pulled-up alongside the *Elizabeth*. The *Isabel* transferred the river pilot to the *Elizabeth* and with his guidance she safely ascended the river. Derby wrote, "The pilot gave us good accounts of our new home, confirming all the previous accounts we had of the richness, etc., of the country."

Velazquez's account (p542) of the vessel's arrival and the way it took on a pilot is in conflict with Derby's account:

> We had not been in the neighborhood of the mouth of the river long before a small, light canoe put out towards us, and its occupant, hailing us in Spanish, asked whether we did not want a pilot.
>
> I was the only person on board who understood him, and as he came alongside the captain refused to let him come on board. Some of the men, thinking that he had hostile intentions, produced their pistols, and for a time there was a prospect of trouble.
>
> I accordingly went to Johnston [sic], and said, "Now, Captain Johnston, you are in a nice fix. This man is a pilot, and you cannot go up the river without his assistance. If you attempt anything of the kind you will be considered a pirate."
>
> This frightened Johnston, and I laughed in my sleeve to see the perplexity he was in. After leaving him to his reflections for a few moments, I said, in a whisper, "This man is a government pilot, and your vessel and crew are in imminent danger. It won't do to trifle with these Spaniards, I can tell you, for if you do, they will make short work of the whole party."
>
> Johnston saw the point, and telling the captain of the schooner who the man was, he was permitted to come on board. The arrival of the pilot created quite a commotion, and no little surprise was expressed at the fact of his being a negro. The man, however, understood his business, and managed the vessel very skilfully [sic]. Without his assistance we would never have been able to have ascended the beautiful Orinoco, or have steered the schooner among the numerous islands.

---

33. Hanna and Hanna, 51; *Daily Picayune*, May 19, 1867; *Daily Picayune*, May 20, 1867, "Derby" letter dated Mar 13, 1867; *Daily Missouri Republican*, Jun 16, 1867, Letter from unnamed colonist dated Apr 11, 1867.

Derby's account must be considered true because he had no reason to lie, whereas, Velazquez's account of anything must always be suspect, since time and again she is caught lying and this is one of them. Instead of simply telling of how the outbound *Isabel* transferred the river pilot to them, she chose to invent an account which she probably thought would elevate in the readers' eyes her status in the expedition. She might have figured it was a good place to demonstrate her prowess at understanding Spanish though she earlier in her memoir claimed (p365, 501, 521) "to speak Spanish." But here, there would have been no need of her alleged Spanish because the pilot spoke English. Remember, Derby wrote that the pilot gave a good accounting of the colonists' destination. The pilot presumably spoke English, because Derby did not say there was a language problem and he did not say that there was a need for Velazquez or anyone else to translate.

A different source tells that the Orinoco pilot spoke English. The pilot boarded, on May 3, 1867, the second ship of the emigration company, the schooner *United States* and he spoke English to those onboard. That same day, in a letter home to his wife, Dr. Henry Price, grantee of the colony and leader of the second wave of emigrants, wrote:

> The pilot seemed glad of immigration- enquired "when more *como*- heap? heap?" He informed us that the *Elizabeth*, with emigrants from New Orleans, reached the mouth of the Caroni about a month ago, and went out about twenty days ago, all safe and well.

It is clear that Dr. Price communicated in English with the pilot and understood the communication. It is easily believed that it was the same pilot since he knew all about the first batch of settlers.[34]

The most obvious evidence that her account was contrived is the fact that the pilot did not come from the shore in a canoe, but was passed to the *Elizabeth* from the outbound *Isabel*. However, pilots did indeed come away from the shore in a canoe, but not in this case. The Orinoco River pilot lived in "a long, thatched cottage" located on Cangrejo (Crab) Island; this was the Orinoco's pilot station. When a ship came abreast of the station, the pilot put out in a canoe, boarded the vessel and provided pilot service. The canoe was either loaded aboard the vessel or towed behind if a small vessel.[35] In the case of transferring the pilot from the *Isabel* to the *Elizabeth*, the crew of the *Isabel* would have put the pilot's canoe in the water if carried on board, or not, if it was towed. The pilot then would have rowed the short distance over to the *Elizabeth*, climbed aboard, and his canoe taken on board or towed.

---

34. James Frederick Pattison, *The Emigrant's Vade-Mecum or Guide for the Price Grant in Venezuelan Guayana*, (London: Messrs. Truber and Co., 1868), 101, Price letter, May 3, 1867.
35. Ibid., 99.

Did Velazquez speak Spanish as she claimed? One might suppose that a valuable Spanish-speaking member of the party would have been praised in some letters by Derby or other colonist, but no mention of her is found. In fact, opposite evidence is found. Recall, the St. Louis *Daily Missouri Republican* reported, "Madame Lauretta J. De Caulp, a widow lady, young, gay and fascinating, who is the daughter of an English Admiral...."[36] Why did Velazquez claim to the colonists that her father was an English Admiral, then later, in her book, claim a Spanish father who was a civil servant with the blood of "Castilian nobles" and that she could speak Spanish?

Whether Velazquez spoke Spanish might be questioned, but it is conclusive that she could not spell in Spanish. She misspelled almost all the place names she visited: "Coraeppa," correct is Curiapo; "Baranco," correct is Barrancas; "Los Tablos," correct is Las Tablas; and "Caraccas," correct is Caracas. It might be argued that others before her had misspelled Caracas. It is true that some sixty years before Velazquez's visit, the famous Prussian explorer and geographer Alexander von Humboldt visited and misspelled "Caraccas," but during Velazquez's visit, Caracas was Caracas.

Her Spanish spelling errors are so wrong that it's incomprehensible. One of the odd errors is that she used "p" as a double consonant, which does not exist in Spanish! Spanish uses double "r" and "l," sometimes "c" and "n," but no others. How could she make such a basic mistake that any 1st grader likely would not? Remember that in her book she claimed that she was educated in Cuba until 1849 or the age of seven, so she should have known these simple Spanish grammar rules. In addition, on page 319, she claimed that while in Cuba she "had read when a girl" the "Spanish *novela*" about the heroine, Estela. This 1637 Spanish story was written for adults and not easily read by a child, so in effect, she was claiming considerable mastery of Spanish.

Captain Frederick A. Johnson landed on March 14, 1867 at Ciudad Bolívar with the minimum of 50 colonists as the conditions of the land grant required. He also beat the deadline which would have voided the land grant. An unidentified emigrant wrote to the *Daily Picayune* that Ciudad Bolívar was "a handsome, clean little town of about 5000 people" and that they were "very cordially received by the people, the officials vying with each other in showing us attention."[37]

Velazquez did not mention the colonists' cordial reception by the officials, but instead, wrote of the party's "dissatisfaction" when "the order was given that nobody should go ashore." By whom the order was given, she did not say. Exasperated, Velazquez then "resolved to land and look out" for herself. She wrote:

---

36. May 24, 1867.
37. *Daily Picayune* (New Orleans), May 19, 1867.

My husband, however, refused to go, and said that he would stick by the expedition to the last. I suggested that they would be far from sticking to him in case he was left destitute, and, thoroughly disgusted with the whole business, I left the schooner and went to the hotel.

Besides Velazquez taking offense, it seems Dixie, one of the colonist's "noble old bull dog," was offended when it was unceremoniously gobbled-up by a crocodile. Dixie had traveled from the U.S. with the colonists, who had grown fond of him because they were entertained by his shipboard antics. When the colonists arrived in Ciudad Bolívar, they purchased a sloop to take the group farther up the river to inspect the land they thought to settle. When Dixie attempted to swim back to the sloop, the crocodile struck.

Poor Dixie, his master fairly shed tears, as hearing the dog howl, he saw him bit in two and swallowed at one mouthful by the monster, and many have been the attempts since to revenge ourselves by taking his life. He is bullet proof, however, and is careful to balk us now by showing his nose only.[38]

Velazquez made no claim that the separation from her husband was permanent, but clearly the couple was not of one mind in happy domesticity.

Velazquez claimed that she busied herself ashore collecting information about the true advantages and disadvantages of emigration which she had promised to send back to parties in America. Earlier in her narrative, she claimed she "would go and see for [herself] and would bring back such an account as could be relied on." Meanwhile, her husband "stuck to the schooner." She wrote (p545):

Finally, however, he too became so much disgusted that he concluded to take my advice, and abandon Johnston and his whole enterprise. In a day or two he left, and started for the gold mines, to find that the black fever was raging there to such an extent that it was dangerous for him to remain. He therefore returned, and went to Caraccas [sic], where, shortly after his arrival, he was taken ill with the black vomit and died.[39]

It can be accepted as true Wasson went to the mines. A letter written by an unidentified writer, on March 23, 1867 in Ciudad Bolívar stated, "part of [the] company, composed of the bone and sinew of the expedition… proceeded this day to the mines…."[40] John Whitman, an emigrant and witness to the Wasson wedding, and maybe the writer of the aforementioned letter, wrote in a letter that "ten or fifteen" of the company were going with

---

38. *Daily Picayune,* Jun 9, 1867, Apr 23, 1867 letter from Derby to the *Picayune.*
39. Yellow fever was so named because black matter is vomited in the final stage. The patient has high fever and their skin and eyes become yellow, thus the name yellow fever.
40. *Commercial Advertiser* (New York), May 17, 1867, correspondence of the *New Orleans Picayune.*

Captain Johnson to select a town site, but the remainder of the company were going to the mines. The mines were stated to be 125 miles from the confluence of the Caroni and Orinoco Rivers.[41] More will be said about Wasson momentarily.

A Letter to U.S. President Andrew Johnson

On March 23 Velazquez wrote a letter[42] to the "President of US of NA." Presented now, all spelling and punctuation remain faithful to the original. One must read most of the "periods" as "commas," as Velazquez seldom made the pen stroke required to produce a comma, but merely made a period. She wrote:

> Ciudad Bolivar, State of Guayana, Venezuela
> South Amarica [sic], March 23. A. D. 1867
>
> To His Excellency
> Andrew Johnson
> President US of NA [sic North America]
> Hon. Sir
> I had the Pleasure of an interview with your Excellency last August, in regard to Erecting a home at Atlanta, Georgia for the benefit of the Suffering Widows & Orphants [sic] of Southern Soldiers. I proceeded to New York not meeting with Sucess [sic] visited Europe, London and Parris [sic]. I can cheerfuly [sic] say widow & Orphant [sic] Ought to be thankful for the aid bestowed upon them by their foreign friends but at the same time there is no government like the United States. (She has bin [sic] the Land of adoption for 17 years though my interest temperaly [sic] is here. but I still claim her as my home. She has my prayers for her prosperity May the god of natives smile upon his people.)
>
> I beg leave to say to you that having bin [sic] one of the Suffers [sic] of the late Rebbelion [sic] lost all I possessed. I Excepted [sic accepted] a deed of gift from this government under grant given to Dr. Henry M. Price of (Virginia) by an act of congress at Caracus [sic Caracas]. 17 of September, 1865. Second year of the Seventh Confederation also one acre lot in the city of Orinoca, situated 20 miles above this point on the Orinoco River, founded by fifty Emigrants. under the Direction of Capt. Frederick. S. Johnson. Representative of Dr. Price. at the same time I hold my allegiance to the US,A- having every facility of traveling through the interior with my Protective Papers Endorsed by the President of the Venezuelean [sic] US. [sic United States] which guarantees my assistance in the State of Guayana under Dela Costa. Govnor [sic]. I beg ask at the Sugestion [sic] of Senor Dalton – our consul, the authority to be appointed as Special Correspondent for the US at this point. as my associations with the American Colony and Dr. Price is such as gives me the opportunity of furnishing the government, with correct history

---

41. Pattison, 122, letter from John Whitman, Mar 23, 1867, Ciudad Bolívar.
42. NARA, RG59, General Records of the Department of State, Letters of Application and Recommendation During the Administrations of Abraham Lincoln and Andrew Johnson, 1861-1869, M650, Reel 14.

of the Proceedings of the young Colonists and of the mining district. Some of the finest Specimines [sic]. of gold & silver. for reference I refer you to Senor Dela Costa. & Dr. H. M. Price & Capt. Johnson. Orinoco City.

Should this meet your favorable consideration a reply will reach me through the Consul or Govnor [sic].

Hon Sir, with my prayers for your prosperity Allow me to Subscribe myself your
Sincere friend
Madam Lauretta J. De Caulp

Several comments are in order before continuing with the narration of the events in Venezuela.

First, even though Velazquez had recently married Wasson, she signed her former married name, DeCaulp, probably with the hope that President Johnson would remember her by that name from her asylum building effort.

Second, Velazquez clearly did not consider herself an unrepentant Rebel who was escaping from a tyrannical Yankee government. It is evident that her Southern loyalty ran only so deep, "I hold my allegiance to the US,A [sic]." She wisely did not mention that her party consisted of self-exiled Rebels, but instead only said they were "suffers."

Third, Velazquez's whereabouts between August and December 22, 1866 is unclear. She could have had time to go to Europe, as claimed, but if so, while there, she clearly did not learn how to spell "Parris." And besides did she really have the money for such a trip? She had spent the first half of 1866 trying to raise money by evoking the pity of people because of her alleged loss on the *Miami*, then by preselling book subscriptions, then by a charity ball for herself. It's difficult to believe that she raised enough money to make a European trip. This would have been her third claimed trip to Europe; she claimed two others in her book.

Fourth, Velazquez took another stab at spelling Caracas, this time writing "Caracus."

Fifth, Velazquez clearly stated that the United States was her "Land of adoption for 17 years," but unfortunately, she did not clarify her native land. This is one of the earliest references to her not being American born. In *TWIB* she claimed (p41) she arrived in New Orleans in 1849, which corroborates close enough her claim of 17 years in the United States.

Sixth, at this date, she was not yet disgusted with Dr. H. M. Price and Capt. Johnson, and used them as references. She seemed still content with her existence in Venezuela, "South Amarica [sic]." Maybe she was optimistic that her husband's efforts in the mines would secure wealth.

A Letter to the Governor

Twenty-seven days after her letter to U.S. President Johnson, Velazquez wrote a letter[43] to the Governor of Guayana:

Ciudad Bolivar
April 19, 1867
To His Excellency Senor John Dala Costa

Honored Sir

I take the liberty of addressing you hoping the following details of my history & appeal will meet your favorable consideration. I arrived here on the 14th of March. Per Schooner Elizabeth. from New Orleans, a member of Dr. Henry M. Price's Venezuelan Emigration Company numbering 50 persons under the supervision of Captain F. A. Johnson, I joined the comp the 15th of January at NO. Previous to my arrival, I was appointed agent for the State of Louisiana. with instructions to proceed forthwith by Brig Gen John Walker of London. I left New York the 8 of December arrived the 29 NO. On my arrival Captain Johnson noticing my arrival and my mission through the press, he called upon me, and presented me one of his comps circulars. and held out every inducement for me to join him he called a special meeting and left it to the voice of the company whether, I should become a member, which was unanimous with a guarantee, that I should have any assistance I needed and on my arrival if I wished to return I should be furnished with the necessary means, which they have not done. Now I appeal to your generosity as a lady and one. who has served her country under the most trying of circumstances from the feild of Battle to the hospital attending to the wants of our suffering, [?] I had the honor to unsheathe the first sword

[page 2]
(or among the first) for my adopted countrys cause. in January 1861 I raised and equipped at my own expense a company for the Services No. 136 officers & men. in the State of Texas. which I kept in readiness for service when for defense my state Arkansas. waiting for her to Seceed after the act of secession was passed by the legislature, I proceeded to the scene of Battle. serving through three severe battles, and some twenty skirmishes, in a charge I was wounded and after my recovery I was commissioned 1 Lieutenant by the government in the Regular Army. by the Secretary of War. Hon James. A. Sedon. C'S. and approved by the President and his cabbinet, I was ordered to join the north western army under Major Gen Braxton Bragg. commander in cheif, was Placed on special duty as Passport conductor on the Rail Road from the Army to Atlanta, and in the retreat of our forces I was placed on duty in the Provost Martials Office, from thence I was detailed on Major Gen Joseph. E. Johnsons., staff Ajutant until October 1863. I was removed by an order from the War dpt. and commissioned to Europe to bear dispatches & make purchases. of supplies for the Army. I served in this capacity until the surrender, on receiving the sad inteligence of Lees surrender. I proceeded to Washington, and surrendered to the Orthorities. was treated very kindly by the

---

43. La Casa del Congreso de Angostura, Ciudad Bolívar, Venezuela.

President and the Hon E. M. Stanton & Gen Thomas the agt gen of the US. received my parole of honor and Proceeded to Richmond. to consult with Mr Sedon & Gen. Lee. what would be best for me to do. they advised me to proceed to Mescico. and join Gen Price & his colony. I after a period of four months visited Europe and returned

[page 3]

to the states, hoping to find peace restored and to find our members admitted as of [?gove] to congress. but to my sad disappointment found my adopted country under a Military despot. I was received with open arms by my many comrads & friends. who showed their appreciation by giving me balls and diners calling on me to adress them Politicaly. which I had the honor to do so at the several Respective Places Mobile, Ala-Montgomery, Atlanta Ga. Charleston SC Columbia. Rauliegh NC Petersburg & Richmond Va, my last address was at Charleston. was on the rights of secession. the presidents veto of the civil rights Bill, the right of Taxation without representation to Congress. Freedmans Bureau Bill. the right to enact laws. without the voice of congress (by Mr Lincoln) Sir for the facts of this statements I will send you some of my testimonials and the notices of my arrivals in the diferent Papers. also my Photograph. in uniform now I have complied with the terms set forth in the grant to the American Emigration. I consider I am a citizen of the state of Guyana, and appeal to your excellency for some Position in which I can be of service to my new country and at the same time support myself, as my present position is not compatable to my former having lost a large Estate infact. I am almost dependent upon my own exertion for a support I will commit my case to your consideration if you desire you can speak with Captain Johnson & Major Garner who know me reputably, you will pleas to examine my testimonials and return them by the bearer and if request meet yours favorable approbation pleas

[page 4]

State when and where I can have an interview with your excellency if at my house. Mr [?Rodrigues] will inform you where I am I will close hoping to hear soon allow me to subscribe myself

Yours most obedient
Mrs Lauretta. J. DeCaulp
or Lieutenant H. T. Buford of the Confederate States Army of NA

Note she signed her DeCaulp name. It was supposed that she used DeCaulp in her letter to President Johnson to remind him of her, before she married John Wasson. However, "Dala Costa" had no prior knowledge of her by that name. Señor Juan Bautista Dalla Costa would have met her as Mrs. Wasson upon her arrival, so why did she use a previous married name? Had she cast off John Wasson? Wasson likely had not died by this date, but if so, one would think that she would have respectfully and advantageously called herself Wasson's widow and not by a former husband's name.

The letter contains other problems as well. It is false she "raised and equipped at [her] own expense a company 136 officers & men in the State of Texas" which she then kept in readiness in Arkansas, a truly novel and illogical claim. In her memoir she claimed it was 236 men from Arkansas. It is false she was "commissioned 1 Lieutenant by the government in the Regular Army by the Secretary of War Hon James A. Sedon and approved by the President and his cabbinet [*sic*]." In her memoir she asserted she never received a commission, though she claimed contradictory versions over the years to the newspapers.

She claimed she "was detailed on Major Gen Joseph E. Johnsons staff Ajutant [*sic*] until October 1863." And that she "was removed by an order from the War dpt and commissioned to Europe to bear dispatches & make purchases of supplies for the Army [she] served in this capacity until the surrender." She did not go to Europe until the surrender. Instead, she followed deserter husband DeCaulp north and was in Indianapolis, in Milwaukee and in New York. Then in July 1864 she was under arrest in Nashville.

It was simply false that she "was appointed agent for the State of Louisiana" for the Venezuelan Emigration Company. Recall Treasurer and co-Director John A. Doll's letter of refutation? Benjamin P. Vancourt was the agent in New Orleans. And it is nonsensical that Captain Johnson upon learning of her arrival in New Orleans "presented [her] one of his companys [*sic*] circulars and held out every inducement for [her] to join him...." Questions: She was an official agent, yet did not have her own supply of circulars which she had studied in detail? And only when Johnson showed her one, she was induced to join the group?

Velazquez was broke and wisely appealed to the highest local authority, the Governor of Guayana, "His Excellency Senor John Dala Costa." Surprisingly she failed to spell Señor (Mr.) with "ñ" which any person educated as a youth in Cuba, as she claimed she was, would have done. And she had been exposed daily to Spanish since her arrival in Venezuela.

Unhappy in Venezuela

A letter by Henry M. Price dated July 6, 1867[44] all but confirmed Wasson's death, "Out of the party who went to the mines, all were sick, and four died." "Derby" in a July 8, 1867 letter to Governor Dalla Costa named two dead and two others dying and asserted "many are sick."[45] John Wasson, not named, must have been among the sick. A contradiction is evident in Velazquez's assertion that Wasson went to Caracas, where he died. She had already explained that Wasson said that "he would stick by the expedition to the last" and was not willing to separate himself from his fellow emigrants. It is not believable that Wasson left the group and went to Caracas. Besides, Wasson surely did not have the money or good enough health to manage the sea voyage around the coast to Caracas (no land route existed). No

---

44. *Charleston Mercury*, Sep 17, 1867.
45. La Casa del Congreso de Angostura, Ciudad Bolívar, Venezuela.

emigrants wrote, in their letters, telling of any members of the party going to Caracas. Two sources said the miners were sick at the mines and died there. Velazquez's claim is implausible in light of the evidence.

After the death of John Wasson, Velazquez claimed she stayed in Ciudad Bolívar "for several months, making occasional excursions into the country in the neighborhood." She said her object was to "find out all [she] could about the natural resources and climate of Venezuela, for the purpose of advising [her] friends in New Orleans." It must be asked, who were these friends in New Orleans? Judging from the newspaper account of her 1867 arrival as "Mrs. Mary De Caulp," she had no friends there. Friends would not have let her stay at the City Hotel, instead would have invited her into their home as a guest. And why not have her friends as witnesses to her marriage instead of strangers Mr. Clary and Mr. Whitman of the colonists?

She claimed that while staying in Ciudad Bolívar, she wrote a letter containing all the facts gathered and "had it countersigned by the governor, his brother, the consul, and a number of Americans who were in the city." Velazquez narrated (p546):

I accordingly wrote a letter advising those who thought of emigrating to Venezuela, to let it alone, and denouncing Johnston and Price for holding out inducements to poor and ignorant people which they had no assurance whatever would be realized. I said that it would be useless for any persons from the States to come to Venezuela without plenty of capital to carry on any such operations as they might engage in, and that if they did come they would have to submit to the laws of the country, and take their chances with its citizens. One great objection to any emigration schemes, however, was the instability of the government, and the fact that Venezuela had no national credit. The Governor of Bolivar said that Venezuela would be glad to have industrious people come to it from the United States, or any other country, and that facilities would be afforded for them to take up lands at low rates, but he had no supplies to give half-starved men and women who might be landed within his jurisdiction, and was anxious that no one should come under any misapprehensions as to what reception they would be likely to have on their arrival.

It is unknown if she actually wrote this letter. In any case, she correctly stated the facts, and whether she knew it or not, she foreshadowed the colony's ultimate failure.

Earlier in her memoir, she wrote that she had "no difficulty in reading Captain Johnston's [*sic*] character," and he was "more bombast than true enterprise." He was a "good talker... it was no wonder a number were deceived by him." In contradiction to this denunciation, the historical record does not show Captain Johnson was deceitful or that he was an irresponsible expedition leader. It might be remembered that Johnson put up $950 of his own to secure the *Elizabeth* and that he fought in court to secure the vessel.

Authors, Alfred and Kathryn Hanna, in their book *Confederate Exiles in Venezuela* wrote:

> As leader of the first contingent of settlers on the Price Grant, Johnson had acquitted himself well under difficult circumstances... He had exhausted his own pocket in behalf of his party, at one time his assets having been reduced to 65 cents. Nor had he spared himself physically; during one period he slept only eight hours in ninety-one... He was given a testimonial by a 'committee' of the colonists ... who expressed appreciation for his devotion to the settlement....

In addition, Velazquez's characterization of Johnson does not corroborate in the least with what his friends said of him in 1887, at the time of his death, age 52. Reverend Dr. A. J. Witherspoon, who was chaplain of the New Orleans Seamen's Bethel said:

> Captain Johnson was noted for taking more interest in others than in himself, while he was the most unselfish of mortals. He had not much money, although liberal with what he had, but his encouragement and counsel to young people were better than silver or gold. He presided for years over the temperance association of the Upper Bethel and in less than fourteen months enrolled over 1400 names, besides being instrumental in the reform of many young men.[46]
>
> He was a true and loyal man to the bethel cause, which he espoused some ten years ago, and he would rise at midnight to serve it... [he] taxed himself beyond his strength in working for the patriotic and public and benevolent associations of the country, and especially of the city of New Orleans. I knew of no man who devoted himself more to the public welfare of the Crescent city, and whose services were more a kind of free-will offering.[47]

Velazquez's denunciation of Johnson and Price was no doubt the results of her personal experience, but according to the historical evidence, Johnson, as the expedition's leader, seems not to deserve the condemnation. Personal dislikes are subjective and Velazquez had her reasons for her low opinion. She cannot be accused of falsely claiming dissatisfaction, since eighteen other colonists, by their leaving, also indicated dissatisfaction, though more likely of their new home and not Johnson.

On April 21, Johnson sailed for the United States aboard the steamship *Pioneer*. It is believed that he never returned to Venezuela. On his outbound voyage Johnson must have passed Dr. Henry Price leading the second group of colonists, fifteen in number, on the inbound *United States*. Price wrote in a letter to his wife that the *United States* arrived at the mouth of the Orinoco on April 30 and went up the river, arriving at Ciudad Bolívar on May 9.[48]

Velazquez wrote that she was in Ciudad Bolívar when Price arrived there. She said that it was "after the arrival of Price's expedition" that she

---

46. *Times-Picayune* (New Orleans), Nov 22, 1887 and Sep 29, 1887- Obituary.
47. Ibid, Oct 12, 1887.
48. Hanna and Hanna, 58-59; Pattison, 99, 108, Price's letter to his wife.

composed the letter of denunciation. About this same time, on May 11, Price wrote to his wife from Ciudad Bolívar, stating, "I find all our emigrants are satisfied."

Maybe he wasn't aware of their dissatisfaction or maybe they had not yet become dissatisfied. By July 6, Dr. Price wrote a letter to an associate telling of dissatisfaction and at the same time he tried to make excuses for it:

> We now have three settlements; but nineteen persons, including women and children have become dissatisfied, and all these Yankees, except two, who smuggled themselves among us. Every Confederate who went to farming and trading has done well. Out of the party who went to the mines, all were sick and four died. They have left the mines and gone to farming, and are healthy.[49]

It is true that during the War, the states of Missouri and Kentucky from which the colonists came were viciously divided between Rebel and Yankee sentiments, but to call the disenchanted colonists Yankees seems a slur of the worst kind. Indeed, it is not even logical that any Yankee would choose to leave their country, which was once again tranquil, especially after their side was victorious. Price's extreme attitude might be indicative of what triggered Velazquez's denunciation of Price and his scheme.

Of the sixty-five colonists (50 people from the first expedition plus 15 people from the second), nineteen departed Venezuela and among them were three women, Velazquez being one of them.

Velazquez remarked that she wanted to "visit other portions of the country, and accordingly made a trip around by sea to La Guyra, and thence to Caraccas." She persisted in misspelling "Caraccas" and added another Spanish misspelling, "La Guyra" to her growing list; however, three pages further along she did spell La Guayra correctly, for the times. Today the place is called La Guaira. She stated that a suitor from Ciudad Bolívar followed her to Caracas, but that she gave him very "little encouragement." She said she might "have done well to have been more gracious to him" because he came from a wealthy family.

She gave no details of her claimed Caracas trip, as a tourist might, and as she habitually did of her travels. This omission is an indication that she did not actually make this trip. Travelers of this era seldom failed to remark on the journey from La Guaira, on the coast, to Caracas, inland. There was no pier or wharf at La Guaira, so ships' passengers had to climb down the ship's ladder into row boats which then took them to the beach, sometimes through frightening surf since La Guaira was not a protected harbor, but open to the weather.

Next the traveler had to mount one of the mules of the mule train which trudged the 25 miles of switchback trails just to cover the seven-mile straight

---

49. *Charleston Mercury*, Sep 17, 1867.

line distance to Caracas. The "old Spanish muletrack" went past the forts of El Vigía and San Carlos which protectively overlooked La Guaira. The trail, which offered panoramic views, was uphill all the way to the 3,000-foot elevation of Caracas.[50] Velazquez tells nothing of landing on the beach or ascending, by muleback, a remarkable trail about which other travelers routinely commented. Other convincing evidence that Velazquez did not go to La Guaira and Caracas is the fact that she did not tell her readers in which hotels she stayed; she unfailingly named the hotels at which she stopped.

Velazquez narrated that when she departed Venezuela, it was from La Guaira aboard the *Isabel*, with "a rather unsavory cargo in the shape of cattle," bound for Demerara (which at that time was a region in the colony of British Guiana) and that the *Isabel* arrived at Georgetown. From there she claimed she departed to the U.S. This claimed departure scenario is just not believable for the following reasons.

She claimed that "there were two lady passengers, besides [herself], whose companionship [she] found very agreeable." One must suspect that these two ladies were fellow colonists. They and all the rest of the nineteen dissatisfied colonists probably left at the same time. These colonists did not have money and would have had to negotiate their best deal and most direct route. It is most probable that Velazquez, and the rest, left Venezuela from Ciudad Bolívar directly to Georgetown, British Guiana and from there northward to America. It makes no sense that Velazquez went from Ciudad Bolívar to La Guaira, some 870 miles distance by water and well to the northwest, then back-tracked some 865 miles to Georgetown, which lies some 220 miles southeast of the Orinoco River and then departed from there to the United States via St. Thomas and Cuba, which she claimed. Check a map for clarity and convincing.

If Velazquez had sailed from La Guaira to Georgetown, it would have been on a better coastal trader and not a cattle boat as she claimed it was. It would make little sense that the *Isabel* hauled cattle from the distant (865 miles) La Guaira region to Georgetown when Georgetown merchants could have purchased cattle, surely cheaper, in the much closer (about 515 miles) Ciudad Bolívar region. And it is known that *Isabel* freighted cattle from the vast *llanos* of the Orinoco River to the populated center of Georgetown.

There existed steamer service between La Guaira and St. Thomas- she would have used it, instead of back-tracking to Georgetown.[51]

---

50. T. R. Ybarra, *Young Man of Caracas* (NY: Ives Washburn, Inc., 1941), 5.
51. NARA, RG59, General Records of the Department of State, Despatches from U.S. Ministers to Venezuela, 1835-1906, M79, Roll 17, Telegram to Secretary of State Seward dated Nov 20, 1867 which explains that a regular steamer is believed lost in a storm. This suspected loss was well after Velazquez's departure. The steamer was probably *Columbian II*, owned by West India and Pacific Steamship Company, driven ashore at St. Thomas by hurricane number 9, Oct 29, 1867. Source- www.theshipslist.com, www.nhc.noaa.gov and

One more point remains to be made. One would think that Velazquez would have mentioned that she visited the Caracas gravesite of husband John Wasson, yet she wrote nothing. Remember she said he went to Caracas where he died. The reason she didn't visit his grave there is because he did not go to Caracas- and neither did she.[52]

It can be guessed that Velazquez left Ciudad Bolívar between May 11 and the first week of June 1867.

Departed Venezuela, Visited the Caribbean

Velazquez stated she left Venezuela with "personal gratification which the trip afforded [her]" and thought Venezuela "a portion of the world that was well worth looking at." She said she did a praiseworthy duty for her Southern brethren by warning them not to emigrate and that she "was the means of preventing a great number of persons in the Southern states from being swindled by speculators...." In any case, Dr. Price's venture was destined to fail with or without her purported warning.

At this point in her narrative, she told (p554) of a pleasant visit in Georgetown. Velazquez is back to describing in great detail the hotel in which she stayed, called the Prince of Wales, and the woman hotel keeper- her beauty, intelligence and housekeeping. Velazquez mentioned the woman's dead husband, her daughters, even one daughter's husband, Mr. Waite. The abundance of description is convincing that Velazquez was there. Recall the lack of detail about Velazquez's stay in Caracas? She wasn't there.

Velazquez tells (p553-555) of several interesting events while in Georgetown, but one is notable because it confirms her presence there and also shows a pattern which has been seen and will be seen a few more times. At Georgetown, "an officer belonging to a United States man-of-war which

---

Notes on the Tropical Cyclones of Puerto Rico, 1508-1970 by José Colón, edited by Orland Pérez.

52. Later some unidentified colonists did pass through La Guaira on their return to the United States, but they seem not to have been the much earlier-departing Velazquez and her companions. Charles Loehr, U.S. Consul at La Guaira, wrote in his monthly report ending Sep 30, 1867: "Hundreds of people of our Southern States imigrated [sic] from New Orleans to Ciudad Bolivar last year, allured by false reports to the mines of Guayana. All appear to have been sadly disappointed and while a great number of them have already returned to their old homes, the remainder arrive at this port in a most deplorable condition. I do not wonder about this failure, similar results have been and will yet be seen in this country." It would appear that Consul Loehr had received bad information because "hundreds" had not immigrated and besides the earliest arrivals landed in Ciudad Bolívar on March 14, not last year. Even if somehow Velazquez went through La Guaira, it seems that she did not go to Caracas because of the aforementioned reasons. Source- NARA, RG59, General Records of the Department of State, Despatches from U.S. Consuls in La Guaira, Venezuela, 1810-1906, M84, Roll 10, Letter #38, Oct 4, 1867 from Consul Charles H. Loehr to Frederick W. Seward, Assistant Secretary of State.

was lying in the harbor," upon meeting Velazquez, understood her to be "in destitute circumstances" and raised among his sailors "a considerable sum of money" which he gave her.

Research shows this man-of-war was USS *Penobscot*, Lieutenant Commander Charles E. Fleming commanding, which arrived on May 22 from Barbados and was on its way to Rio de Janeiro; *Penobscot* departed Georgetown on June 9, 1867.[53] There can be little doubt Velazquez was in Georgetown sometime between May 22 and June 9, 1867.

Recall Velazquez wrote she saw Dr. Price arrive in Ciudad Bolívar on May 9. On May 11 Dr. Price wrote all the emigrants were satisfied, and said nothing of departures. That leaves 11 to 20 days available for Velazquez's claimed departure and travel from Ciudad Bolívar to La Guaira, and to Caracas, then back to La Guaira and to Georgetown. This short time adds to the doubts of this claimed trip.

Now, it is no crime for a person in need to accept financial help, things happen and life can be hard. But recall, Velazquez claimed that she came from an immensely wealthy family in Cuba and she and her brother, by this date, were the only surviving members of the family. Her Spanish father still had his vast estate in Cuba; she never said he didn't. And she was wonderfully close to her dear brother, who would have happily given her some money if he had been the sole heir. But she too, in 1864, was set to inherit lots of money from a different deceased father, "Commodore J. B. Roach, of the British Navy." This different deceased father didn't disinherit her like the one in her book (p49). Well, fathers and inheritances can be tricky, don't cha know?

As was seen in her 1864 letter to her husband DeCaulp, she had no money- she accepted charity from the preacher's wife. In June 1866, she had no money- she accepted the proceeds from a charity ball held for her in Memphis, Tennessee. It will be seen upon her return to America in 1867 and traveling West, she implied the hat was passed for her at Julesburg, Colorado and still much later, in 1900, she accepted money from the "sympathetic citizens" of Phoenix to enable her to leave town, she had no money. The fact is, she lied about her rich family.

From Georgetown it was by ship to Trinidad and then to Barbados. It is impossible to separate fact from the fiction in this part of her memoir, such as her claim that in Barbados she got reacquainted with friends from her war time blockade-running days. She spiced-up her story by telling (p558) how a "Captain F., of Liverpool, came with a handsome carriage" and took her

---

53. NARA, RG59, General Records of the State Department, Despatches from U.S. Consuls in Georgetown, Demerara, British Guiana, 1827-1906, Microfilm T336, Roll 8. Letter #77, Jun 11, 1867 from the U.S. Consul Philip Figyelmesy at Demerara to Honorable William H. Seward, Secretary of State, Washington, D.C.

on an outing and later how her "whole party" was invited to "dine with a wealthy American gentleman, who had just arrived by the steamer, and who was on a visit to a number of West India Islands." Captain F. regretted that he would be unable to see more of her, as his ship was to depart the next day, and in any case, she had explained to him that she was soon departing for Saint Lucia.

She said that she then traveled by steamer to Saint Lucia, "for the purpose of visiting the home of my early childhood [and] my mother's birth-place." Upon her arrival there, the ship's steward delivered a basket of fruit from Captain F., who was obliged to stop there to make repairs to his ship. She sent a note to Captain F. asking him to call on her "at the residence of [her] cousin, the old family homestead." This he did and was introduced to the family. Velazquez explained that his visit was a short one, they said their goodbyes and she never saw him again. This part of the narrative may have been true or maybe it was only for romantic effect. She always claimed to have had suitors, and there is no reason to doubt it. However, there is information she reveals about her visit to St. Lucia which must be considered whether it can be part of her true history.

Velazquez claimed she had lived "in the old-fashioned stone house… with her father and mother, and brothers and sisters, when a little girl." She remembered a "happy family," of which "most of its members were dead." She said she went to "the family burying-ground in search of the weather-stained vault… which contained the earthly remains… of a sister and brother, whose faces [she] never beheld after [she] left Cuba to go to New Orleans to attend school."

In *The Woman in Battle* Velazquez explained (p40) that she had three brothers and two sisters, all born in Madrid and all before 1840. She claimed to have been born in Cuba in 1842, "the last" child. However, recall, in 1864 she had claimed,[54] in the phony inheritance letter, that her father's money, after deducting her own, was to be "equally divided between the remaining eight children." So that would have made her one of nine children, all still alive in 1864. It is inexplicable how she went from claiming she was one of nine siblings in 1864 to being the last of six siblings in 1876. Might one of these claims be a lie?

The question arises as to when and how the brother and sister could have been buried in St. Lucia. Velazquez, in the preceding quote, stated they were alive in Cuba at the time she left for New Orleans in 1849. Did they die in Cuba and were buried in St. Lucia, some 1550 miles away? Velazquez doesn't provide enough clues about her siblings to investigate the truthfulness of her claim. The only sister relationship Velazquez referenced was when she wrote (*TWIB*, p290) that a sister living in Matanzas (Cuba) sent her a letter

---

54. *Daily Constitutionalist* (Augusta, Georgia), Dec 31, 1864.

in the year 1863. Velazquez mentioned Matanzas once again (p569) when she claimed to have made "a brief stoppage" there during her visit of Cuba, but it is notable that then she did not claim any relatives there. If this was the same sister buried in St. Lucia, Velazquez does not help the reader understand it.

Also casting the shadow of doubt on these buried siblings is the fact that Velazquez lied about her brother, "Josea," who supposedly studied medicine and graduated from the College de France and whose name she misspelled if she meant the Spanish name José. In any case, Velazquez left the buried siblings where she found them and she wrote that she "was reluctant to leave" St. Lucia, her "visit to it having been the happiest episode of [her] journey." She next traveled to St. Thomas.

In St. Thomas, "one of her friends of the war time," to whom she had written a letter telling of her intended visit, met her. As a bonus, another old friend, the Italian consul, met her, as well. He asked her what she "had been doing since the blockade-running business had come to a stand-still." Both men walked her to her hotel. Once settled-in the large room, which had been booked for her, "the visitors came pouring in… first the proprietor and his wife, then the Danish commandant's wife, then half a dozen others…." She said that she had never been welcomed anywhere with such a "hearty and sincere courtesy, or with more evident disposition to make a heroine of [her]."

Chapter 7

A Sea Tale

Velazquez refreshed the reader's memory that on her previous visit to St. Thomas, during the War, she "had the satisfaction of seeing the Confederate cruiser *Florida* come in, and coal, and get away in safety, through a clever trick played upon the Federals." She wrote (p564):

> The Florida took in her coal and supplies at the King's wharf, and when she was ready for sea, one of the sailors, pretending to be an Englishman, went to the consul, Mr. Smith, and told him, that as they were coming in they saw the Florida off to the westward of the island. Mr. Smith, accordingly, gave orders to the Federal man-of-war to go out and look for her, and so soon as the Federal cruiser was out of the harbor, and heading westward, Captain Maffitt, having steam up, put on all speed and went out after her. Before the Federal commander discovered that he had been duped, the Florida was out of sight and out of danger.

The tale is simply illogical and foolish. Everyone in port, including "Mr. Smith," would have known which vessels were at the wharf. For some strange Englishman to seek out Mr. Smith to tell him he saw the *Florida* in the distance and for Mr. Smith to not question the man as to how he would even know what it looked like and then to issue orders to a Federal man-of-war to give chase- it did not happen! Can a U.S. Consul even give orders to a Federal man-of-war?

Curiously, one-hundred pages earlier in her book (p463) Velazquez had already told of this event. She said the Federal vessel "was deluded into giving chase to a mail steamer," and then *Florida* slipped out of port. Her conflicting versions cast doubt that Velazquez was present on the occasion, making it necessary to consider the facts more closely.

Velazquez placed the date of her visit to St. Thomas, when she saw *Florida* escape, after September 19, 1864. She made the date clear because she said that it was after the attempted prison break at Johnson's Island, Ohio, which occurred on that date. She claimed she had participated in the escape plot, as a Southern agent and the failure of the plot irked her because she had "labor[ed] so hard to promote [it]." She now wanted nothing more to do with the secret agent business because of the risks involved and sought opportunities in blockade-running. She traveled to St. Thomas to carry-out her new business and it was at this time she witnessed *Florida's* escape.

It is necessary to bracket the dates on which it was possible for Velazquez to have witnessed *Florida's* escape. The earliest possible date was identified as September 19, 1864. The latest possible date was October 7, 1864 because on that day *Florida's* career as a Confederate commerce raider came to a halt at Bahia, Brazil when she was captured by USS *Wachusett*. *Florida* had anchored in Bahia on the October 4, three days before its capture, so the only period for Velazquez to have seen the vessel was from September 19 to October 4, 1864, sixteen days.

Velazquez explained that "a day or two" after September 19, she was in Hannibal, Missouri when she found out about the failure of the Johnson's Island prison escape. From Hannibal, she said she went to Philadelphia where she commenced her career as a blockade-runner with a "few transactions with Philadelphia houses." She then went to New York, where she "labored for a number of weeks, with all possible zeal, being resolved to make the venture a profitable one...." But remember, she only had a 16-day window. She did not have "a number of weeks" in which to labor, as she claimed.

It gets worse. She then wrote that she traveled from New York to Havana, to St. Thomas and to Barbados. It was on the return trip, when she stopped at St. Thomas and was "compelled to wait some days for the steamer" that she witnessed *Florida's* escape. It was impossible that in 16 days she traveled from Hannibal to Philadelphia, to New York, to Havana, to St. Thomas, to Barbados and back to St. Thomas. Even if she, by some amazing travel feat, succeeded in being present in St. Thomas, the *Florida* was not present!

The *Florida* was not present in St. Thomas because she was at sea and had been for sixty-one days prior to her arrival at Bahia, Brazil. Her purpose for going to Bahia was to take on coal. *Florida's* Commander D. Manigault Morris wrote these facts in his report of the surrender of the vessel. He wrote the vessel arrived in Bahia on October 4 at 9 p.m., "to procure coal and provisions, and also to get some slight repairs, after a cruise of sixty-one days."[1] The obvious question is: Why would *Florida* put in at Bahia for coal if it had taken on coal some 16 days prior in St. Thomas, as Velazquez claimed? The easy answer is that *Florida* did not put in at St. Thomas.

In the second telling of her tale about *Florida's* escape, Velazquez's wrote, "Captain Maffitt, having steam up, put on all speed and went out...." Once again Velazquez's story wilts under the facts. Captain Maffitt was not at any time during 1864 the commander of *Florida* nor was he aboard or anywhere near the vessel. He had resigned his position in September 1863.

Maffitt, in early September 1863, requested to be detached from the *Florida* because he was debilitated by the effects of yellow fever.[2] He received orders on September 17, 1863 from Commander M. F. Maury who wrote, "consider yourself detached from her...."[3] Maffitt never returned to CSS *Florida*, even after his health was restored. Instead, upon returning to duty, he was assigned to other Confederate vessels.

---

1. The Navy Department Library, Capture of CSS *Florida* by USS *Wachusetts*, 7 Oct 1864, www.history.navy.mil/docs/civilwar/64-10-7a.htm.
2. Emma Martin Maffitt, *The Life and Service of John Newland Maffitt* (New York: Neale Publishing Company, 1906), 327.
3. Ibid, 322.

The reason Velazquez determined to evoke Captain Maffitt's name was that he was a celebrity in his own time, especially during his Confederate career and admired by many. Commander Raphael Semmes was highly complimentary of Maffitt's perfect social manners with both ladies and gentlemen, "but this was the mere outside glitter of the metal," in other words of Maffitt's internal steel![4]

Maffitt first went to sea in 1832 as a thirteen-year-old midshipman. He served three years aboard the famous USS *Constitution* on duty in the Mediterranean Sea. When the vessel arrived (August 19, 1836) in Athens, Greece, numerous dignitaries, including the King and Queen, were invited for an onboard visit. The Marine Band played the Greek national anthem and later when the Band played a spirited waltz, Queen Amalia, only seventeen years old, begged with her eyes for a dance. Commander Elliott introduced his young aid, Midshipman Maffitt, to lead her in the dance. "In less than thirty minutes at least twenty couples, including the King were whirling upon the deck to their hearts' content." The party lasted until two in the morning.[5]

As a pre-Civil War U.S. Navy officer, Maffitt earned an unblemished record. Among his achievements, he captured three illegal slave trading vessels with their human cargo. He spent fifteen years doing the "Coast Survey" and he intimately knew the coastline of the Carolinas and Georgia. Maffitt's Channel, an alternative to the main channel to Charleston, was named after him. His knowledge of hydrography of the East Coast was unsurpassed. It was said that if Maffitt had stayed with the Union he would have had Union Admiral Farragut's position.[6]

Maffitt resigned from the U.S. Navy,[7] joined the Confederacy and was made commander of the newly designated blockade runner *Cecile* which performed astonishing feats, all the while avoiding capture or destruction by the Union navy. Maffitt's coastline knowledge triumphed.

On May 2, 1862 Maffitt traveled to Nassau where he was given command of the *Oreto*. This steamer had been built in a British shipyard under the cover that it was ordered by an Italian customer, when in fact, the true customer was the Confederacy. She fell under suspicion from the very beginning. After its construction, *Oreto* departed England and was delivered to Nassau. She had no weapons mounted, still her presence caused great suspicions and accusations by Federal officials in the Bahamas, and she was seized and placed in Admiralty Court. The court convened and "It was

---

4. Royce Shingleton, *High Seas Confederate, The Life and Times of John Newland Maffitt* (Columbia, SC: Univ of South Carolina Press, 1994), 44.
5. Maffitt; Shingleton, 16; Note, both authors said Amalia was fifteen.
6. Maffitt, 378.
7. Ibid, 219.

clearly proven that she left England unarmed and unequipped, and had continued so during her stay at Nassau... Judge Lee gave his decision and she was released from bondage."[8]

The now free *Oreto* slipped away at night and traveled ninety miles south of Nassau to "a desolate, uninhabited islet." There, a rendezvousing vessel came along side with war matériel. With an undermanned force, Maffitt hoisted on board eight cannons, powder, shot, shell, general equipment and stores. It was an arduous task in the August tropics; the men stripped to the waist and toiled in the broiling sun. One man fell sick and died in 8 hours, surely from heat stroke. After more than a week, the job was done, but the accessories necessary to make the cannons operational had been forgotten by the supply ship. They had no rammers, sponges, sights, locks, beds, and quoins (wedges to raise the level of a gun). These items would have to be found somewhere if the vessel was to do her duty as a commerce raider.

The outfitting was completed as much as possible and *Oreto* sailed away as the newly christened *Florida*. Maffitt wrote, "...with loyal cheers for the *Florida* we flung the Confederate banner to the breeze." However, the crew's cheer soon vanished. Yellow fever ran through the vessel and *Florida* was compelled to seek anchorage at Cardenas, Cuba on August 19. Captain Maffitt personally nursed his sick crew and sent for medical help ashore. Then Maffitt was stricken with fever. He suffered horribly and the physicians forecast his death, but he survived.

Once recovered, Maffitt buried his dead sailors ashore, settled his bills with the Cuban authorities and determined to depart the harbor on August 31, 1862. However, a Federal squadron of men-of-war had gotten word that *Florida* was in the harbor, therefore, was waiting outside for *Florida's* departure. Maffitt wrote:

'Twas whispered about that we were leaving and the American consul dispatched a swift craft to inform the Federal squadron. At 8 p.m. the Spanish mail boat for Havana left, and when outside was chased by the Federals... They mistook her for the *Florida*, consequently at 9:30 we sailed, and ran the coast along unmolested.[9]

Recall that Velazquez narrated (p463-564) this exact escape of *Florida* only she relocated it to St. Thomas and injected herself into the story. She created a falsehood with a custom fit. Velazquez must have heard of the event or read a news account; in any case, Velazquez's version was invented.

After *Florida* left Cuba, the vessel proceeded to Mobile, Alabama in order to obtain the forgotten hardware, in addition to enlisting sailors to replace those felled by yellow fever. In broad daylight *Florida* approached the

---

8. Ibid, 245.
9. Ibid, 251.

blockaded entrance to Mobile Bay after running up the British flag as a ruse, hoping to buy some minutes of unimpeded progress. After a couple of warning shots, the Federal fleet opened up with the cannons of three of the ships. The ships pursued *Florida* "for nearly two hours at a distance of only eighty yards."[10] Maffitt wrote, "In truth, so terrible became the bombardment, every hope of escape fled from my mind." One large shell came through *Florida*, but it failed to explode. Even so, it caused nine men to be wounded and took the head off of James Duncan, who was "captain of the top main and one of [their] best men." Of course, Florida could not return fire since it lacked the cannon accessories for which she was going to Mobile. A sailor was ordered to haul down the English flag and raise the Confederate flag and succeeded in doing so, but "lost his forefinger with shrapnel shot" in the process. One cannon shot entered 3 inches above the water line and would have sunk *Florida* had the seas not been completely calm. Maffitt wrote to his daughter, "It was awful- the little craft is riddled, riddled. Such a run!"[11]

Maffitt's unbelievable feat was praised by those who witnessed it from Confederate Fort Morgan and Fort Gaines at the mouth of Mobile Bay. The newspapers and well-wishers heaped "extreme adulation" on Maffitt.[12] Letters of praise, from Admiral Buchanan and Secretary of the Navy, S. R. Mallory, arrived.

It took three months to repair the ship; she now had a newly painted gray hull and fresh crew. She was ready to depart Mobile Bay, but had to wait for the right conditions for running the blockade. Maffitt counted thirteen ships waiting on him. On January 16, 1863 the night was windy, rainy and bitterly cold, but then the stars came out and there was a mist upon the sea. *Florida* slipped pass two vessels undetected, but a third raised the alarm. The chase was on with half a dozen Federal ships in pursuit. The outcome of the chase was uncertain until Maffitt ordered to "shortened sail" and to put the "engines at rest." This action made the ship's sails difficult to see in the night. *Florida* also was aided by its newly painted gray hull and the Federals lost sight of her, passing her at a distance thinking they were still pursuing her.

Captain Maffitt opened his "sea orders" and *Florida* began her career as a commerce raider. Maffitt wasted no time; three days later he made his first capture. Under Maffitt's command, *Florida* destroyed an estimated 15 million dollars ($573 million in 2023) of goods and Yankee vessels, capturing

---

10. Ibid, 262.
11. Ibid, 261.
12. Ibid.

some 23 vessels. After Maffitt resigned his command of *Florida*, she continued to capture vessels until she herself was captured in Brazil.[13]

Visited Cuba… and was Welcomed by General Manzano?!

Velazquez wrote she departed St. Thomas aboard the steamer "*Pelyo*" bound for Cuba. In forever consistent form, Velazquez misspelled another Spanish name; the vessel was named *Pelayo*. Earlier in her narration (p462), at the time she claimed she saw Confederate raider *Florida's* escape, she also claimed she had traveled on the "*Pelyo*" from Havana to St. Thomas. It was while in Havana she claimed she saw "Moro Castle," misspelling still another Spanish name (Morro) and a major error for someone claiming, as she did, to have received an education in Cuba until the age of seven. Pointing this out may appear petty, but it is a piece of the puzzle when considering whether Velazquez was of Cuban birth and/or heritage, and it sets the stage for pointing out a major error. In any case, the vessel was real and it was the mail steamer which served the Havana to St. Thomas route.[14]

Velazquez's first port of call in Cuba was Santiago de Cuba. She narrated a pleasant stay, being "waited upon by many distinguished people." She then continued to Havana. She narrated she was once more on familiar ground, visiting family and friends. She visited her brother and niece, but not her sister-in-law with whom she had "differences." Velazquez then narrated a curious story:

> In addition to my relatives, I had many acquaintances in Havana who were glad to extend the hospitalities of the place to me. Among others, General Juaquin Mansana, and other officers of his staff, were all warm friends of mine, and they seemed never to tire of paying me attention.

This assertion will not stand!

She misnamed the general who she claimed was one of her "warm friends"! She bungled his first name which was not "Juaquin," and she bungled his last name which was not "Mansana." Velazquez came closer to calling the General an apple than by his real name. Apple in Spanish is *manzana*. The General's name was Joaquín del Manzano y Manzano.

And he was no ordinary general, but was Capitán General de Cuba, in effect, Cuba's highest official or the Governor of Cuba, appointed by Spain. It is strange that she neither mentioned that he was the highest-ranking official in Cuba nor explained his supreme importance, but instead, stated simply that he was "a good man" and "he deserved and enjoyed a great popularity."

---

13. Ibid, 343.
14. The Spanish West Indies Mail Steam Packet Company received a contract on Aug 29, 1866 to run the mail. Source- *Accounts and Papers of the House of Commons*, Vol 41.

Worse still, Velazquez's claimed interactions with Manzano are beyond belief. She narrated that Manzano suggested Velazquez participate in a "grand religious festival" parade by appearing in military uniform, posing as a male. The General supplied her with a "handsome Spanish military suit" and she was asked to keep her identity a secret. She rode in the parade, right behind the General's carriage, in a carriage with Colonel Montero, who was in on the ruse. Throughout the day she "several times passed quite close to Mr. Savage, the United States consul[15] and the members of his staff" and they did not have the "slightest suspicion as to who [she] was." She, as well, succeeded in fooling all the "members of the [General's] staff." Velazquez wrote:

[I was] introduced to a number of ladies as a young Spanish officer, who had been educated in England. This plea was put in on my behalf, because my Spanish accent was none the best, my long non-use of the language having caused me to lose the faculty of speaking it in such a manner as to do entire credit to my ancestry.

It might be believed her Spanish accent was not perfect, but her fluency should have been good. After all, she had just spent months in Venezuela where she interacted in abundance with the Venezuelans. Her knowledge of the language should have been good enough not to mistake the General's name and nearly calling him an apple.

Velazquez claimed that after the procession, General Manzano and his group, including her, went to the theatre. "General Mansana said that he was hungry, and retired." The rest of the group stayed until the end of the performance, and then went to supper. Afterwards she went to her room and changed to female attire:

As I was coming out, Colonel Montero met me in the hall, and said that the general had been taken quite sick. I asked if I could see him; and on a messenger being sent, word was conveyed to the colonel that the general wished to speak with him. He soon returned, and invited me to go into the sick chamber. The general was in bed, and the doctor was in attendance on him. He complained of severe cramps, but did not think that anything serious was the matter, and invited me to call on him the next morning, when he expected to be better.

After breakfast, the next morning, I went to the general's quarters; but the guard had orders not to admit any one. I sent in my card, however, and in a few moments the chief of staff came down and asked me to walk up to the reception-room. The surgeon in attendance made his appearance, and said that the general was worse instead of better; but that I could see him if I would promise not to speak. I accordingly went into the sick-room, and found the general looking very bad indeed. He smiled at me, and seemed to be glad that I had called. I then retired, as I found that I could be of no assistance, and went to see....

---

15. At that date, Thomas Savage was Vice-Consul and acting Consul-General of Cuba.

On Sunday morning I learned, to my infinite sorrow, that General Mansana was dead! The funeral took place the next day, and the body, having been embalmed, was carried through the streets, followed by his carriage, dressed in crape, and his favorite horse. The funeral was an imposing but sorrowful spectacle, for the general was a good man; and although, like other public men, he had his enemies, he deserved and enjoyed a great popularity.

The first evident flaw in her story is that she claimed that General Manzano died on Sunday morning. In truth, he died at 4 a.m. on Tuesday morning, September 24, 1867. In addition, the funeral was not the following day, but was two days later, on September 26, this all reported by Thomas Savage, U.S. Consul at Havana.[16]

Velazquez's credibility suffers further because she only described the funeral as "imposing but sorrowful," a great understatement. The funeral procession, in fact, took 45 minutes to pass any single point and it was composed of almost every Cuban governmental agency and military department in existence. There were multiple cannonades of military salute and single cannon fire on the half-hour. It is inconceivable how Velazquez understated the event, even though it is likely that she was in Cuba about that time. It can only be supposed that she was in Matanzas and not Havana, and misunderstood just who this "public [man]" was.

Her described personal association with the General is not believable. She might have helped her own credibility if she had narrated how she had made the General's prior acquaintance. One would think that the story of how one became "warm friends" with the supreme leader of Cuba was worth telling, especially when considering how prideful she was of her alleged birth there, her ancestor Don Diego Velazquez who was Cuba's first governor, and how she held in such high esteem military officers. She failed to explain anything.

The real problem is that Velazquez simply fabricated her own version of Manzano's death. The lie becomes clear when compared to the *New York Times*' correspondent's report, dateline Wednesday September 25, 1867:[17]

[Manzano], it seems, attended, on the 16th, a banquet given by the Marquis Almendares, and on the following evening was at a ball at the Puentes. While at the *fête* he complained of indisposition, and on his way home a choking sensation came over him, causing him to loosen his cravat and collar. Having reached his dwelling, Capt. Manzano took a warm bath. On the morrow he was unable to leave his bed, a high fever having set in. Two days later he was unable to speak. He subsequently

---

16. NARA, RG59, General Records of the State Department, Despatches from U.S. Consuls in Havana, Cuba, 1783-1906, M899, Roll 49. Letter dated Oct 1, 1867 from Thomas Savage to William H. Seward, Secretary of State.
17. *New York Times*, Oct 2, 1867.

rallied a little, but sank again, and after lingering six days he died in the arms of his bosom friend, Señor M. A. Herrera.

In summary, Manzano took to his sick bed on the 16th and never left it. It is clear that he lingered the last six days of his life in bed, so it is impossible that he participated in a parade or went to the theatre or socialized with Velazquez the last two days before his death, as Velazquez claimed. Besides the reporter said he first got sick at a "ball at the Puentes."

Considering that Velazquez boldly lied about facts surrounding Manzano's death, facts which she must have known could have been easily checked through the newspapers, it raises questions: What other Cuba related assertions did she fearlessly lie about, claims which could never have been in the purview of the newspapers, therefore unverifiable? Did she in truth visit relatives or her brother in Cuba? Can anything she said about her Cuban family, her Cuban brother or Cuba be true?

One last question is in order. Did she dress-up as a male in a military uniform in Cuba? The answer is no. Recall she claimed the uniform was supplied by Manzano, which was impossible because he was, at that time, on his death bed.

Returned to America

Velazquez claimed she left Havana, making "one brief stoppage at Matanzas," aboard a steamer which took her to New York. Evidence shows her arrival in New York was on November 11, 1867. The passenger list for the 424-ton American bark *Elba*, commanded by John Peterson, and dated November 12, shows that taken aboard at Matanzas was "Laura Wasson," a 28-year-old female whose occupation was listed as "Lady." The document stated that she occupied a "cabin," and that the "US" was "The country to which they [she] severally belong," meaning her residence, and also as "The country of which they [she] intend to become inhabitants," meaning her destination.[18] Three points in the document are of interest: she stated her age at 28 which would have made her born in 1839, instead of 1842, the date given in her memoir; she was the only passenger onboard; and she came aboard at Matanzas, which contradicts her claim to have boarded at Havana and then the vessel made a brief stop at Matanzas.

In the year 1867, Bark *Elba* routinely made the Cuba-New York run carrying sugar and molasses. It loaded at Matanzas or Cardenas. The coming and goings of the vessel were noted in the "Marine Intelligence" section of the *New York Times*. The particular trip of which Velazquez availed herself was noted as "Arrived" on "Monday, Nov. 11." and *Elba* had loaded at

---

18. NARA, RG36, Records of the U.S. Customs Service, Passenger Lists of Vessels Arriving at New York, New York, 1820-1897, M237, Roll 288.

Matanzas 11 days prior. No other passengers are mentioned; *Elba* was not routinely a passenger vessel.[19]

Back in America, Velazquez said that she wanted to settle in the South, but thought the "financial and political situations" there were "more deplorable than ever." Velazquez wrote (p570):

> The people were oppressed and harried without mercy and without hope of redress by the black and white adventurers whom the fortunes of war had given the control over their affairs, and it was very apparent that there could be no revival of business worth speaking of while such a state of affairs existed.

She said her "own fortunes were at a low ebb" and she "saw very plainly" that she would have to "go elsewhere." "After mature consideration" and some inquiries she determined to try her "luck in the mining regions of the Pacific slope." She said her decision was not solely based on her desire for "pecuniary profit," but she had a desire to explore the territory about which she had heard so much. Also, right before she left New Orleans bound for Venezuela she was told by "an old gentleman who had been a good deal in California" that "there was not a country in the world equal to California" and it would be "vastly better" to go there than to South America. So now she headed West, purchasing a ticket to Omaha, Nebraska, traveling by train through Niagara, Fort Wayne and Chicago. By rail it was two days to Chicago and four more days to Omaha.[20]

On arrival at Omaha, she found snow on the ground and cold weather, and said that she was not properly attired, having just come from the tropics. She dreaded the upcoming stagecoach ride with inadequate clothing and tried to buy some woolen underclothing at a dry goods store, but found none. She then by chance met a woman, also staying at the International Hotel (another hotel which she correctly identified), who was willing to sell her own woolen undergarments to Velazquez.

Velazquez's luck continued (p571):

> At the International I had the good fortune to meet an old friend whom I had not seen for a number of years, and with whom it was a pleasure of the most genuine kind to renew my acquaintance. This was the veteran soldier, General W. S. Harney. He was, apparently, as glad to see me as I was to see him, and insisted on escorting me in to dinner, rather, I think, to the astonishment of some of the guests. The general had a special table for himself and friends, and as we took our seats the eyes of everyone in the room were fixed on us.

About the dinner conversation, Velazquez wrote (p572):

> [Harney] said that he was a true Southerner in his sympathies, and that his extreme age alone had prevented him from offering his services to the

---

19. *New York Times*, Nov 12, 1867.
20. *Reese River Reveille* (Austin, Nevada), Dec 18, 1867.

Confederacy. He, however, had helped the cause as much as he could with his means and influence, and his only regret was that he had not been able to take an active part in the great conflict.

Did this former Yankee officer, in truth, make such a statement of regret, and worse still, as Velazquez said, he helped the Confederacy with his means and influence? Did Velazquez in reality meet Yankee General William Selby Harney in Omaha, Nebraska? An examination of evidence is called for.

There is no doubt that Harney and Velazquez were in Omaha at the same time, she traveling West to seek her fortune and he as part of a Congressional appointed Indian Commission sent West to seek a treaty with the Indians. The Commission had passed through Omaha outbound in August, but Velazquez was still in the Caribbean at that time. It was only possible for Harney and Velazquez to have crossed paths when the Commission was in Omaha on its return, about the middle of November. Recall that Velazquez arrived in New York on November 11 and seemingly left immediately on her westward journey.

The Indian Commission's meeting with the Indians was big news which attracted nationwide attention; nine newspaper correspondents covered it. The Commissioners were escorted by 500 horse-mounted soldiers wearing their dress uniforms.[21] Some sixty army wagons extended for two miles in route to Medicine Lodge Creek, the meeting grounds.[22] The Indians arrived even more impressively to the meeting. A teamster named Billy Dixon wrote:

> I shall never forget the morning... For a moment I was dumbfounded at sight of what was rising over that crest and flowing with vivid commotion toward us. It was a glittering, fluttering, gaily colored mass of barbarism, the flower and perfection of the war strength of the Plains Indian tribes. The resplendent warriors, armed with all their equipment and adorned with all the regalia of battle, seemed to be rising out of the earth. Their number was estimated at 15,000, but I cannot vouch for its accuracy.

The young Billy Dixon was in awe, a more correct estimate was 4,000.[23]

The Indian Commission hauled in the sixty wagons "a large supply of Indian goods" to entice the Indians to the treaty table. General William Tecumseh Sherman, who was one of the several luminaries composing the Commission, stated he had no confidence that the Indians wouldn't just "accept all the presents they [had] to give," and would then just continue with their war path proclivities in the spring.[24]

---

21. S. C. Gwynne, *Empire of the Summer Moon* (New York: Scribner, 2010), 225.
22. Billy Dixon, *Life and Adventures of "Billy" Dixon of Adobe Walls, Texas Panhandle* (1914), 57.
23. Gwynne, 225.
24. *Daily National Intelligencer* (Washington, D.C.), Aug 23, 1867.

Velazquez wrote, "[Harney] then gave me a revolver, saying that I might have need of it, and also a buffalo robe and a pair of blankets, which he was certain I would find useful." It is easily imagined that the blankets gifted by Harney came from the "Indian goods" in the government supply. The buffalo robe had probably been given to Harney by the Indians and it was generous of him to give it to her. A revolver might have in truth been gifted or Velazquez might have created it for dramatic literary effect. Curiously, Velazquez never mentioned the nature of Harney's business in Omaha, or the source of the "goods," maybe figuring these facts irrelevant.

One curious detail she claimed was that Harney was "an old friend whom [she] had not seen for a number of years." There exist two possibilities where their paths may have previously crossed. The first was when General Harney served as the Commander of the Utah Expedition in May of 1857. It was then that an expedition was sent to suppress the Mormon rebellion against the Federal Government's civil law in the Mormon dominated Utah Territory.

On two occasions Velazquez made reference to her firsthand knowledge of the Mormon rebellion and it is credible that she had an association with a soldier or soldiers who participated in the expedition. In the *New Orleans Picayune* of November 2, 1863, she claimed to have "journeyed over the mountains and plains of the West, with the Utah expedition." This newspaper said that at that time she went by the name of "Gibbons" or "Mrs. Arnold." Research did not reveal her association with any soldier by those names.

However, later in her memoir she contradicted the newspaper's assertion by writing (p49) that she did not actually go on the expedition, but at the time was pregnant and "was compelled to submit to remain behind." She claimed that after the expedition was over, she lived with her husband, "William," at Fort Leavenworth. In newspaper articles she further identified "William" as the rather known William Burnet. Her claimed association with him is false for many reasons, which are explained elsewhere. Besides, William Burnet was nowhere near the Mormon Expedition or Fort Leavenworth. In spite of the lie about Burnet being her husband at the time, it is still possible that she was at Fort Leavenworth sometime during 1858 and she made the General's acquaintance. The General arrived at Fort Leavenworth on August 2, 1858 when returning from the Utah expedition.[25]

The second opportune place was in St. Louis with two possible dates, the first, during the Civil War and the second, the year after its end. In 1861 Union Brigadier-General Harney was given command of the Department of the West with his headquarters in St. Louis. However, he was soon relieved

---

25. Ed. Albert Watkins, *Publications of the Nebraska State Historical Society*, Vol 20 (Lincoln, NB: The Society, 1922), 304.

of his command, but stayed in the St. Louis area. In 1865, he bought a house on the SW corner of Locust and 15th Street. (Later, in 1869, he bought a thousand-acre farm, twenty-five miles west of St. Louis.)[26] Velazquez claimed (p449) to have traveled to St. Louis presumably sometime during the first months of 1864. After the war, the St. Louis newspaper wrote a large news story about her March 1866 visit there. Velazquez clearly transited St. Louis at least once and maybe twice and possibly encountered Harney, though no hard evidence exists that they met. She liked St. Louis, made clear by the fact that later, in 1878, she adopted St. Louis as her home for a year.

While Federal General Harney was commanding in St. Louis his allegiance to the Union came into question by Federal authorities. General Harney controlled St. Louis for the Union, and Major-General Sterling Price controlled the rest of the state with his Missouri State Guard. General Price was initially in favor of the Union, but events turned him against the Union. He then decided to support "States rights" and advocated a peaceful transition to this end. He, along with General Harney, wished to avoid more bloodshed, as recently witnessed in Missouri and they signed, on May 21, 1861, a non-aggression agreement which encouraged "peace and good order" of Missourians. (This was all prior to the outbreak of the War.)

Federal authorities were rankled; they believed that General Harney had overstepped his authority to negotiate such a truce. General Harney was replaced on May 30 and thereafter never held a command. For the rest of the War and his career, he only had the "honor of presiding over two or three courts-marshal [sic] and he traveled to Washington, D.C. for those." He was promoted to brevet major general on March 13, 1865. In effect, after the loss of his command in St. Louis, he was taken out of the public's awareness, but with his new appointment to the 1867 Indian Commission he was saved from "painful obscurity." His experience in Indian affairs was extensive before the War and he was highly qualified and well chosen for the new assignment. At the time of this appointment his loyalty to the Union was no longer questioned, instead he was praised in every way.[27]

It is difficult to believe Velazquez's claim, that "[Harney] said that he was a true Southerner in his sympathies, and that his extreme age alone had prevented him from offering his services to the Confederacy." No historical records evince he harbored disloyal feelings toward the Union. General Harney, after being given command in St. Louis, wrote a May 14, 1861 letter "To the people of the State of Missouri" in which he expressed his loyalty

---

26. Adams, 241; United States Department of the Interior, National Park Service, National Register of Historic Places, Inventory- Nomination Form.
27. *Philadelphia Inquirer*, Jul 29, 1867; George Rollie Adams, *General William S. Harney, Prince of Dragoons* (Lincoln, NB: Univ of Nebraska Press, 2001).

to the Union. He wrote that he would "at all times, and all circumstances, endeavor faithfully [to] uphold" the authority of the United States.[28] Biographer Logan Reavis' 1878 book on Harney is a presentation of letter after letter from officials and military officers giving testimonials to Harney's high character and loyalty to the Union!

Another biographer, George Rollie Adams, wrote:

> Harney remained loyal to the Union throughout the war… he never once contemplated aiding secession or joining the Confederacy. Yet the War Department never entrusted another command to him. It ignored both his plea for reassignment to California and a subsequent plea, made in November 1861, to return to the Department of the West.[29]

The fact that Harney was promoted to major general in March 1865, near the end of the War, and well after his actual retirement in August 1863, must have reflected the War Department's regrets over Harney's treatment, and of its ultimate satisfaction and acknowledgement of his loyalty.

Surely, Harney's actions spoke for his true feelings. Even though there was ample opportunity to resign from the U.S. Army and join the Confederate army, the Tennessee-born Harney did not. Other U.S. Army officers resigned and joined the Confederacy and age seems not to have stopped them. Robert E. Lee was only seven years younger than Harney and Lee's age did not prevent his resignation.

The following incident might serve as the final word on the question of the General's true feelings. During the War, General Harney was ordered to Washington, D.C. and during the trip he "was captured by Southern forces but released."[30] If he was Southern in sentiment, why did he not just stay with his captors and ask for a commission in the Confederate army?

Velazquez wrote, "[Harney's] only regret was that he had not been able to take an active part in the great conflict." Harney's biographer, G. Rollie Adams, contradicts this assertion on page 241 of his book, "Harney never indicated any regret about not participating in the war…."

In conclusion, it is easily suspected that Velazquez invented Harney's alleged statements and sentiments, or at least carelessly represented them. Harney's remarkable and impeccable career stands in refutation of Velazquez's claim. It would appear that Velazquez put words in General Harney's mouth, just as she did to William B. Mumford of the New Orleans Mint flag incident.

---

28. Logan Uriah Reavis, *The Life and Military Services of General William Selby Harney* (St. Louis: Bryan, Brand & Co., 1878), 364.
29. Adams, 240.
30. United States Department of the Interior, National Park Service, National Register of Historic Places, Inventory- Nomination Form, page 4 from www.dnr.mo.gov/shpo/nps-nr/85002144.pdf.

When General Harney and Velazquez finished dinner they went to the drawing-room where Velazquez soon was talking to some St. Louis people and the General excused himself and left. Velazquez then claimed that Governor C. introduced himself and asked her to introduce him to General Harney (p572):

> Governor C., a tall, lank, shambling backwoodsman, stalked up to me, and, in an awkward sort of way, introduced himself. He desired to make the acquaintance of General Harney, and wished to know if I would not do the "polite thing" for him, that is, give him an introduction to the general. It struck me that, considering his official position, he might as well have introduced himself; but, as he apparently did not know how to do this gracefully, I told him that if the general was willing, he and the governor should become acquainted after four o'clock, if he would meet me in the drawing-room.

It is curious that Velazquez willingly identified General Harney, but would only identify the Governor by his initial, in some semi-secret manner. In any case, she was referring to the Governor of Kansas, Samuel J. Crawford and he was a country boy, having been raised on a farm in Lawrence County, Indiana, and he was tall and lanky. He described himself as "tall" and "lean."[31] A biographer described a 26-year-old Crawford as six feet one-inch tall, brown hair, hazel eyes, and fair complexion.[32]

Velazquez had made plans to meet the General in his private parlor at four o'clock, so she brought along Governor C. She claimed she made the introduction (p573):

> ...the governor evidently did not know what to say or do, but after a moment's hesitation he extended his hand, and seizing that of the general, shook it as if he were working a pump-handle. The general, who understood what kind of a customer he had to deal with, stood-up and saluted his new friend with a characteristic gesture, and passed a few formal words with him. After a very brief conversation, the governor, impressed by the general's peculiar manner, and appreciating the force of the maxim that "two are company and three a crowd," said that he would give himself the pleasure of calling again, and bowed himself out.

This scenario of the Governor timidly asking for an introduction, Velazquez fabricated. Governor Crawford already knew General Harney! Both Governor Crawford and General Harney had attended the month-long Peace Council at Medicine Lodge Creek in South Central Kansas, starting in early October.[33] There, Governor Crawford read to the Indian Peace Commissioners a lengthy statement (dated October 5) of depredations

---

31. Samuel J. Crawford, *Kansas in the Sixties* (Chicago: A. C. McClurg & Co., 1911), 11.
32. Mark A. Plummer, *Frontier Governor: Samuel J. Crawford of Kansas* (Lawrence, KS: Univ Press of Kansas, 1971), 13.
33. Crawford, 264.

committed by the Indians against settlers and soldiers, and told the Commissioners that "decisive measures should be at once adopted to punish the Indians for what they have done, and secure peace in the future."

It is only barely possible that Velazquez even met Governor Crawford since Velazquez could not have passed through Omaha before November 15 and at that date Governor Crawford by his own statement was back in Kansas, he wrote, "Early in November, 1867, I returned from the Medicine Lodge Council and devoted my time to affairs of State which had necessarily been neglected."[34]

One last point needs making about Governor Crawford. Yes, he was raised on a farm, but he was far from a "backwoodsman" who "did not know what to say or do." The gentleman received his law degree from Cincinnati College and was elected the 3rd Governor of Kansas. It is simply an oxymoron that there ever existed a lawyer-governor who "did not know what to say or do." Moreover, he was a leader of men; at the commencement of the Civil War, he was elected captain of his Union military company and by the War's end he was a brevet brigadier general. The Governor was slightly outranked by Brevet Major General Harney, but Crawford had seen hard battle whereas Harney had been forced to sit out the war. As a brevet brigadier general, a combat veteran and a governor, Samuel J. Crawford would have had full confidence to meet Major General Harney as an equal, if not his superior.

Velazquez, "snugly wrapped up in her blankets and buffalo robe," was now prepared for the long westward stagecoach ride across the plains. General Harney had bid her farewell with his best wishes and the words, "Remember the advice of your best friend. I only wish I was thirty-five years younger; you should not make this journey alone." Velazquez wrote, "This was so flattering that I could not help permitting my wishes to run in the same channel."

It is believable that Harney paid flattering attention to Velazquez; he had no reason not to. His wife, Mary Mullanphy, had left him years before. They had married in 1833 when he was thirty-two and she was thirty. Mary complained of his spending her money and he was seldom present in his children's lives. She and the children went to live in Paris where Mary could get medical help for their son. Their two daughters would grow to womanhood and marry there. Harney traveled to Paris in 1854 to the wedding of daughter Ann, but arrived too late to witness it. While there, Harney received news he was given command of an expedition against the Sioux Indians in Nebraska and he left Paris on Christmas Eve 1854 to return to America.[35] Harney never saw his wife again, she died in 1861.

---

34. Ibid, 281.
35. Adams, 118-119.

In any case, Harney never lacked the companionship of the fairer sex. In 1829 or 1830, when he was based at Fort Winnebago in Wisconsin, he had a daughter, Mary Caroline Harney, with a Winnebago Indian woman named Ke-sho-ko. Harney never formally acknowledged this union and it appears that wife Mary was never told of it.[36] In 1858 Harney had another daughter, Ada Stuart, born by Sarah Ashton Stuart while married to Mary.[37] It is unlikely that Harney's wife knew of this child either and it would have made no difference as the marriage had failed long before.

At the time of his encounter with Velazquez, Harney was a single, handsome gentleman of 67 years. One western newspaper wrote that the six-foot three-inch Harney was "straight as an arrow, and in his younger days used to excel every Indian on the plains, with whom he came in contact in running and jumping and wrestling." During his early military service, before the Civil War, when Harney's company was "encamped at the Mandan village, on the Missouri River," he was challenged by the Indians to run against their chosen fastest runner. The Indians "bet everything they possessed on the result, and the officers of Harney's company also backed their favorite to the fullest extent. The Indians… bet a buffalo robe against a plug of tobacco, or a pony against a few pounds of sugar and coffee."

At the start, the Indian had a fifteen-foot lead which Harney through his "utmost efforts and straining every nerve" managed to close. At the finish line of the 800-yard race, Harney beat the Indian by three feet. "The Indian dropped upon the ground exhausted, and was so chagrined at this defeat that he would, under no circumstances, come near the General again." Harney only kept "trifling things for his winnings, but gave the best back to the Indians." Harney, from that day, was known as "fast runner" and won influence with the Indians through his popularity.[38]

The story is illustrative of Harney's familiarity with the natives and the very good reason he was selected as a member of the Indian Commission. It also illustrates Harney's physical prowess as a youth which still must have been evident for the newspaper reporter to mention the vigor of the 67-year-old Harney. Billy Dixon similarly remembered Harney:

> This fine old warrior made a lasting impression upon me… He was gray-haired, straight, broad-shouldered, and towered to the commanding height of six feet and six inches. General Harney was an experienced Indian fighter, and exerted a powerful influence among the Plains tribes. They knew him and respected him, believing that he had always told them the truth.[39]

---

36. Ibid, 35, 347.
37. Ibid, 347.
38. *Union Vedette* (Salt Lake City), Nov 14, 1867.
39. Dixon, 63.

General Harney told Velazquez that he wished himself 35 years younger, but it might have behooved the General to wish away a few additional years since Velazquez was twenty-five, making their age difference forty-two years.

When Harney did remarry it was in 1884, at the age of 84, and his new wife was 26 years his junior. He lived five more years.

Please see the photo of General Harney in Illustrations, Figure 13.

Across the Western Plains and "The Delights of Julesburg"

Velazquez narrated (p574) her stagecoach ride from Omaha was uncomfortable with "a rather rough set" of characters as fellow passengers. Two men sitting in the front seat, whom she assumed to be "mountaineers," had a bottle whiskey they passed between themselves. In spite of their whiskey consumption, they were not "disagreeable" to her, since they minded their manners. It was a third man, sitting on the same seat as herself, better dressed than the other two, who offended her with his profanity. One of the mountain men, Bill, seeing the disgust on Velazquez's face said, "See here, old chap, just remember there is a female aboard this stage-coach, will you?" The man replied, "I am a captain in the United States army, sir, and I wish you to respect my commission." Bill retorted, "I don't care a d—n who you are, you simmer down mighty quick," and he took hold of the man's "throat and choked him till he was nearly black in his face." Velazquez said that there was no further annoyance for the rest of the trip.

"In course of time" the stage arrived in Julesburg, Colorado, which Velazquez said was "one of the most remarkable products of Western civilization." She was being facetious in this remark and also in claiming there were "delights" in Julesburg. In further description, she said, "Card-playing and whiskey-drinking, embellishment with blasphemy, seemed to be the chief occupations of the Julesburg citizens, while murder was their commonest amusement." She wrote (p576), "The reckless bloodthirstiness of most the men baffles description. Pistols and knives were produced on the slightest provocation." She witnessed the "murder of a young man of about twenty years of age." After the young man was shot and writhing on the ground, the "fiend, in the shape of a human being" stood over him and finished him off with two more shots. The assailant then drew a "huge knife" to cut his victim's throat, but was restrained by the "murderer's comrades." She said the women were worse than the men, she meeting only two "who made the most distant claims to even common decency or self-respect."

A newspaper[40] of the times thought equally of the town and its people:

---

40. *Keowee Courier* (Pickens Court House, SC), Sep 28, 1867, repeating a correspondent of the *Chicago Tribune*.

Along the two long streets running parallel to the rail road, nearly every house is a whisky shop, gambling saloon, or house of prostitution; not unfrequently [*sic*] all of these combined in one great shanty, with here and there a clothing store or a trading establishment, as if thrown in occasionally to prevent the total depravity of the street and preserve to it some slight air of respectability... In short, whiskey-selling, gambling and prostitution in every conceivable and inconceivable shape, occupy about three-fourths of the town. With such a population it may be imagined that murder, robbery and crime of every kind are rife, that life is held cheap, and that punishment seldom follows crime.

Another newspaper[41] reported, "A gentleman recently through from Julesburg reports that during twenty-four hours which he passed in the town no less than eight men were killed by violence. Lively place, Julesburg."

Velazquez wrote that she was "heartily glad" when the stagecoach arrived by which she could leave and that she hoped she would "never be compelled to find [herself] within sight of [Julesburg] again."

Julesburg of that date rightfully earned the title of the "wickedest city in the west," though other boom towns of the West briefly held this dubious title, as well. Ruffians, gamblers, prostitutes and other opportunist were the first to swarm to a location of potential wealth, outpacing the slower arriving law enforcement. Towns which stayed around long enough became reasonably civilized. The Julesburg of Velazquez's visit went from boom to bust, in five months; it never got a chance to become civilized.

The town Velazquez described was the infamous "Hell on Wheels, a foldable city of gambling halls, saloons and brothels that followed the progression of tracks moving west."[42] "Hell on Wheels" arrived on June 25, 1867, the day after the tracks of the Transcontinental Railroad, then under construction, arrived. It invaded the existing little town "of three buildings, all rude frame shanties,"[43] with twelve hundred wood-framed canvas buildings, erected with urgency. Of these, at least nine-hundred served the vice industry. The town's population grew to more than three thousand and the town thrived through a summer and a fall of debauchery. It then folded itself up and followed the track's westward construction towards Cheyenne, leaving a large garbage dump and little more than a ghost town.[44]

A letter dated November 15, 1867 by a newspaper correspondent to the *White Cloud Kansas Chief* stated that the town he saw was "not the Julesburg of 3,000 inhabitants it was a few months ago, but a defunct town, of perhaps

---

41. *Montana Post* (Virginia City, Montana Territory), Sep 21, 1867.
42. Jolie Anderson Gallagher, *A Wild West History of Frontier Colorado* (Charlestown, SC: The History Press, 2011), 103.
43. Alexander Kelly McClure, *Three Thousand Miles Through the Rocky Mountains* (Philadelphia: J. B. Lippincott & Co., 1869), 60, travel journal entry May 11, 1867.
44. Dallas Williams, *Fort Sedgwick: Colorado Territory, Hell Hole on the Platte* (Julesburg, CO: Fort Sedgwick Historical Society, 1996).

300 or 400 people, and nearly all of them preparing to leave immediately."[45] He added that all the stage operations would be conducted out of Cheyenne within ten days, as all equipment was being moved from Julesburg.[46] This dated letter of November 15 is important because it reveals that Velazquez could not have witnessed the lively town of her description. The town at the time of Velazquez's arrival had a population of less than 300 or 400 hundred, and many of those had probably left. She could have only transited the town after November 15, that is based on her documented November 11 New York arrival, plus two days travel to Chicago, then four more days travel to Omaha, plus travel time from Omaha to Julesburg. Bets are, she did not witness the "murder of a young man."

Velazquez's last paragraph about Julesburg (p577) warrants scrutiny because it reveals, in cryptic, her modus vivendi, which was that she received money from kind people when she represented herself as a lady in financial distress. It will be seen that throughout her life she resorted to this scheme. Velazquez unwittingly revealed herself when she explained that the one admirable virtue, among the overwhelming vices, of the Julesburg's "desperadoes" was that "When they have any reason to think that a woman is really respectable, they will protect her, and they are always free with their money, and ready to help anyone who may be in distress." Velazquez knew this to be the case because she was speaking of herself; how else could she have known. She had already said there were no respectable women in town. At this point, she would have been financially depleted having spent what little she had getting away from Venezuela. She probably got her ship's passage free using the lady in distress model. Recall that an officer of a U.S. man-of-war, by passing the hat, "raised a considerable sum of money" for her in Georgetown, Guyana (*TWIB*, p554). If she had any of this money remaining at the time of her arrival in the U.S., she spent it buying train tickets. By the time she arrived in Julesburg, it can be supposed she was out of money.

The narrative of her stagecoach ride from Omaha to Julesburg (about 360 miles) is exciting and all, and it's a shame not to leave it alone as the truth, but her narrative fails a facts test. She wrote falsely that she left Havana bound for New York, a few days after General Manzano's death, which occurred on September 24, 1867. It was shown, in fact, she shipped out of Cuba eleven days prior to her November 11 arrival in New York. If she had walked off the ship and immediately onto the train, it would have taken her about six more days to get to Omaha or until November 17 at the earliest. The Transcontinental Union Pacific railroad had already completed the

---

45. Julesburg did not roll up the streets completely to become a ghost town, but survived, and in the 2010 U.S. Census it claimed a population of 1284.
46. *White Cloud Kansas Chief*, Dec 5, 1867.

tracks to Julesburg by June 24, 1867 and started carrying passengers immediately after. It is not believable that Velazquez chose to travel by stage when the train had been running for almost five months, especially considering her long history of using trains.

Stagecoach travel was dusty and physically punishing to one's body. A British traveler in 1865 wrote, "The severe discomforts of this travelling can hardly be exaggerated."[47] And then there were the dangers of highway robbery and Indian attacks. Julesburg, in 1865, just two years prior to her travel, had been raided by one thousand warriors who killed civilians and soldiers.

During the summer of 1867 Indians were cutting telegraph wires, raiding settlements, stagecoaches and railroad construction parties. Stage travel was disrupted, and also the mail it carried. Settlers sought the protection of the military forts from "the infernal redskins."[48] Soldiers were attacked. In June 1867, Lieutenant Lyman Kidder and ten soldiers departed Fort Sedgwick at Julesburg to deliver a message to Lieutenant Colonel George Custer camped at the Republican River. The party did not find Custer there and thought he had gone to Fort Wallace, so proceeded there, but never arrived; Kidder's party was attacked and all killed. Kidder's "body was mutilated in the most shocking and brutal manner."[49]

Throughout the summer General Harney's Indian Peace Commission worked to remedy the situation. The Commission succeeded in reigning in some tribes with the signing of the Medicine Lodge Treaty on October 29, but in November when Velazquez was traveling, danger still existed. Finally in December, it was reported that the stagecoaches were operational and that "the Indian troubles along the road [had] all been amicably settled, and the savages [had] ceased to molest travel."[50] Not all tribes signed the treaty, because with the onset of winter, they were unable to travel to the meeting and were only able to sign in the spring of 1868. Even after the treaty, there were factions within the tribes who refused to acknowledge them, so there were continuing conflicts with the Indians. For all of 1868 there were Indian raids in abundance which kept settlers and travelers anxious.

Disregard the Indian danger for the moment and consider the greater point- there was no need for Velazquez to take the stagecoach; the train was already running! Why would Velazquez have claimed to have taken such a stagecoach trip, when the Union Pacific Railroad had already completed the

---

47. *An Overland Journey from San Francisco to New York by Way of the Salt Lake City* by Edmund Hope Verney, 1865, published in the *Royal Good Words and Sunday Magazine*, June 1, 1866, Vol 7, p380-383 as presented by genealogytrails.com/main/stagecoachtrip1.html.
48. *Montana Post*, Jun 15, 1867.
49. Board of Commissioners, *Minnesota in the Civil and Indian Wars, 1861-1865*. 2nd ed. (St. Paul, MN: Pioneer Press Co., 1891), 601.
50. *Reese River Reveille* (Austin, NV), Dec 18, 1867.

tracks from Omaha to Julesburg on June 24, 1867 and had been carrying passengers for five months? Only a fool would forgo the safety, the speed and the comfort of the train in order to travel by stagecoach, and Velazquez was no fool, her intelligence evident many times. However, a fabulist might tell such a stagecoach story in order spice-up a narrative and Velazquez was just that, as shown many times. And finally, the stage was no longer running between Omaha and Julesburg.[51] She took the train.

Velazquez was not finished with her narrative of stagecoach misadventures. She continued on her way to her next stop, Cheyenne, Wyoming. She said that her traveling companions were a "rougher and more unpleasant set than the first party." Two men produced a bottle of "fearful smelling whiskey," and they passed it around. Another passenger, a female, took a "good drink every time it was handed to her," and when she spoke "seemed to be unable to open her lips without uttering some blasphemous or obscene expression." After eight or nine drinks she became "stupidly drunk," and lit her "filthy pipe" which produced sickening fumes, but it "at least kept her quiet and soothed her until she fell into a deep and drunken sleep."

Upon their arrival in Cheyenne, the drunken woman had to be helped out of the stagecoach. Velazquez was happy to be finally free of her. Velazquez requested to be shown the washroom before dinner and was shocked to find it filthier than herself. Dinner was "so uninviting in appearance that [she] could eat but little of it." Then she sought out her room at the Cheyenne House and to her "utter astonishment" she found the drunken woman as her roommate, worse yet, even in the same bed, which they would have to share. Velazquez protested to the management, but there was no good option, only sleeping in the hotel parlor with "the roughs congregated there."

The next morning the woman was called to catch the stagecoach; she got up already dressed, never having removed her clothing. She took out from under her pillow a "formidable-looking knife and a six shooter" which she buckled on. The woman asked, "in a rather sarcastic sort of way, 'How did you sleep?'" Velazquez answered, "Not much" and the woman said she would rather "sleep on a board or a rock as on one of these d—d old straw beds!" Velazquez wrote, "Soon, to my infinite relief, this delectable creature was gone, and I was left to myself." Velazquez claimed she remained in Cheyenne for a day or two.

Again, Velazquez's credibility suffers over her claim to have traveled from Omaha to Cheyenne by stagecoach. The track had been completed to

---

51. *Daily Missouri Republican* (St. Louis), Jul 2, 1867, in a "Special dispatch to the *Republican*, Omaha July 2" stated the "Julesburg Station, the present terminus of the Union Pacific… the station opened a week ago.…"

Cheyenne and, by November 12, was already 22 miles west of the city. This date should be noted to be the day after her arrival in New York.[52] A traveler, including Velazquez, would have arrived by train, not by stagecoach.

At Cheyenne

Velazquez claimed she could not secure a seat on the outbound stage and was stuck in town. She was unhappy with the shabby accommodations she found at the Cheyenne House and expressed this to Mr. Stewart, a "road agent."[53] He escorted her to find better lodging in Laporte, Colorado, which is about 39 miles south of Cheyenne and about 6 miles northwest of Fort Collins. There she said that she found herself "under the excellent care of Mrs. Taylor, the station-keeper's wife, and her sister who did all that was in their power to make [her] comfortable." Velazquez correctly named "Mrs. Taylor, the first stationmaster's wife." Mrs. Taylor was known to be a "good cook" and a "gracious hostess" to travelers on the Overland Trail Stage Route.[54]

Besides Velazquez's complaint of having to share a bed at the Cheyenne House with the drunken woman who slept with a knife and six-shooter, she said the Cheyenne House was the "worst apology for a hotel [she] ever met with in the course of [her] rather extensive travels." Velazquez claimed it was this which drove her to seek accommodations in Laporte. The only problem with this claim is that it makes no sense that Velazquez traveled 39 miles out of her way to another hotel when there was a good selection of hotels in Cheyenne. The many and newly constructed hotels leaped into existence as the railroad was nearing completion to Cheyenne and she could have changed to one of these hotels.

There was the Talbot House which advertised "a first-class hotel in every particular" and the Dodge House, which claimed a "new and commodious hotel… [and] no pains [would] be spared for the comfort of guests…." These hotels placed their advertisements prominently in the *Cheyenne Leader* between September 19-28, 1867, well before her arrival there which was sometime after the middle of November.

The Cheyenne House, which was owned by "Holladay and Thompson" placed an advertisement on September 24, "The above popular house is now open for the accommodation of guests. The best in the market shall be found on our table. Terms moderate." The Cheyenne House clearly did not

---

52. *Cheyenne Leader*, Oct 24, 1867; *Deseret News* (Utah), Nov 27, 1867, letter to editor dated Nov 12, 1867, Omaha.
53. This gentleman was Jim Stewart and he was a division agent for the Bitter Creek stretch of the Overland Stage. He "developed into a first-class Indian fighter" due to the continuous Indian attacks experienced in this section. Source- Frank A. Root and William Elsey Connelley, *The Overland Stage to California* (Topeka, KS: Crane & Co., 1901), 103.
54. www.over-land.com/laport.html created and maintained by Elizabeth Larson.

call itself the best, but instead, "popular." It did, however, call its food the best.

The owner, Holladay, was not oblivious to satisfying the public, he had already made a fortune doing so! Benjamin Holladay was the energetic and successful business man who created the famous Overland Stage Line, which, upon the threat of competition from the railroad sold out to Wells Fargo. He sought the patronization of the public, not to mention their money. Holladay and Thompson hurriedly built another hotel down the street from the first hotel and the newspaper of November 9 said it is "one of the finest hotel buildings in the west... and is 26 X 46, two lofty stories in height, and handsomely and substantially put up, and will be fine ornament to that portion of the city."[55]

Velazquez was probably accurate that the original Cheyenne House was none too nice, as indicated by the fact that the proprietors felt compelled to build another; she could have taken a room at the new Holladay and Thompson hotel or any of the others. The lack of quality rooms in Cheyenne was not the true reason she left the hotel and went to Laporte.

The true reason was that she had ridden the railroad to its terminus at Cheyenne and now it was necessary to travel to Laporte's Overland Stage "head" station in order to catch the Overland Stage to continue her journey. By December 18, the stage was connecting directly with the railroad in Cheyenne, but this was <u>after</u> Velazquez went through; she <u>had</u> to make the connection in Laporte, that's why she went there.

Laporte was the headquarters for the Mountain Division of the Overland Stage. "Head" stations furnished sleeping accommodations and meals. They were located 40 or 50 miles apart, and at these, the passengers traveling through were allowed forty minutes in which to eat. Here, fresh drivers relieved weary drivers. The stagecoaches ran 24 hours a day, covering 100 to 125 miles. The passengers were forced to try to sleep in their bouncing seats. About every 10 miles, at "swing stations," there was a quick change of horses and passengers stepped down to stretch their legs, briefly.

Salt Lake City was Velazquez's next city of importance, about a 450-mile stage ride. The route required about 25 coaches, 28 drivers, 400 horses and the support of "station men, hostlers, artisans and others in the service of the company."[56]

Velazquez left a small trail of evidence that she had been through Cheyenne. The *Cheyenne Leader* newspaper posted Velazquez's name,

---

55. *Cheyenne Leader*, Nov 9, 1867.
56. *Reese River Reveille*, Dec 18, 1867. The newspaper explained "The Best Way to go Home" to eastbound travelers, "the most direct, economical, and pleasant route is by Overland stages connecting with the Central Pacific Railroad at Cheyenne."

"Warson [sic], Mrs. L. J.," in a list of unclaimed letters" as of December 13, 1867.[57] Velazquez likely retrieved this letter.

From Laporte, Velazquez traveled by stagecoach to Laramie, and then continued through Wyoming, to Utah. Upon arriving in Utah, she described (*TWIB*, p581) traveling through "Echo Canon [sic cañon or canyon]" where the stage met with an accident.

Velazquez wrote that the horses and stage became stuck in the flooded road caused by rain in the mountains and "the passengers were obligated to swim out on the back of the horses, and escaped with no other damage than wet clothing." This accident was reported by a Salt Lake newspaper,[58] indicating by its dateline, December 26, that it occurred "last night." It reported that while crossing the river at a ford, since the bridge had been washed away by the flood, the stage "was capsized, drowning one of the horses and submerging the coach and several mail bags, in the stream... passengers barely escaping with their lives." The residents of a nearby house gave the passengers shelter; there Velazquez made the "agree[able]" acquaintance with the first Mormons she was to meet.

The stage then traveled through Bear River Valley where she was pleased to see "little cottages or neat log cabins, surrounded by well-cultivated and well-watered farms and orchards." The stagecoach soon arrived in Salt Lake City, Utah and delivered her at the "Kimble House." She claimed that Mr. Stewart, the stagecoach agent, had given her a letter of introduction to the "Mormon proprietor" of the house. More correctly, the name of the house was the Kimball House, the "Mormon proprietor" was Heber C. Kimball.

The Road to Nevada

Velazquez soon departed Salt Lake City by stagecoach westward into Nevada. She mentioned her stop at Ruby Valley, a way station used on its route through the Overland Pass. There she claimed she met a gentleman engaged in mining, who strongly advised her to go to Austin, Nevada located in the "Reese River gold regions." Although she was not terribly impressed with him, he seemed intelligent enough and he confirmed what other people had already advised her. Now on the final push of her arduous journey she had nine more way station stops to make, 113 more miles to Austin.[59]

Her route from Salt Lake City to Austin covered 400 miles[60] and was supported by "twenty-drivers, one hundred and ninety horses and sixty wagons, covering the thirty-six stations."[61] The travel time was 71 hours of

---

57. *Cheyenne Leader*, Dec 14, 1867.
58. *Daily Telegraph*, Dec 28, 1867 and Jan 4, 1868.
59. Root and Connelley, 102.
60. *Reese River Reveille*, Dec 18, 1867.
61. Thomas Wren, *A History of the State of Nevada: Its Resources and People* (NY: Lewis Publishing Co., 1904), 114.

non-stop discomfort, with only brief opportunities to stretch one's legs during the horse changes. At least, it was her final leg. The total trip from New York, where Velazquez began her trip, was said by the newspaper to take "only 15 days."[62]

The stagecoach ticket price from Salt Lake City to Austin in 1868 was $96 or over 25 cents a mile.[63] At the approximate time of Velazquez's Austin arrival, a trip from Omaha to Austin cost $275, "payable in currency, equal to $211.70 in coin."[64] A traveler paid for their own food at $1 to $2 a meal.[65]

To put the price of travel into perspective, the daily wage in Austin for an ordinary laborer was $3.50; skillful miners, $4 to $5; blacksmiths, $6; carpenters, $6 to $7; masons, $7 to $8. "Necessary articles for living" ran as follows: "flour, 11 cents per pound; bacon, 30 cents; hams, 35 cents; sugar, 23 cents; Java coffee, 40 cents; Rio (Brazil) coffee, 35 cents and whiskey, $4 to $5.50 a gallon." "Luxuries" were "limited" and "the few that the market afford[ed] could be had at about the following rates: cocktail at a bar, 25 cents; chicken for the table, $1.50 each; warm bath, $1; hair-cutting, $1; shaving, 50 cents; a seat in church and sermon, 50 cents." Drinking too much and landing before the judge cost $17 and "punching the head of the fellow you do not like" resulted in a fine of $17, as well.[66]

Lodging varied in price from 50 cents to $20 per night. One or two room houses rented for $10-20 a month and houses of several rooms rented for $30 a month. One could eat "at the most excellent restaurants for $10 per week; while one may live upon the fat of the land solitary and alone for the small sum of $5 per week."[67]

The *Reese River Reveille* newspaper diligently reported the names of arriving and departing passengers on the daily stagecoach, both east and west, and Mrs. Wasson or any other person who could have been her is not found. She, in fact, may have arrived on a supply wagon or private wagon of some sort. She could not have arrived prior to December 30, 1867. Recall Velazquez was placed at Echo Canyon on December 25 and she claimed she rested in Salt Lake City "for a day or two" before proceeding on. She still had three and a half days travel from Salt Lake to Austin.

Austin, at the time when Velazquez arrived was a thriving silver mining town, with a population of about eight thousand people. It sprang into existence when in early May 1862 William M. Talcott, an employee at the stagecoach station at Jacob's Springs (later enveloped by Austin) was

---

62. *Reese River Reveille*, Dec 18, 1867.
63. Lucius Beebe and Charles Clegg, *U.S. West, The Saga of Wells Fargo* (NY: E. P. Dutton & Co., 1949), 146.
64. *Reese River Reveille*, Dec 18, 1867.
65. Albert Watkins, *History of Nebraska*, Vol 3 (Lincoln, NB: Western Publishing, 1913), 379.
66. *Reese River Reveille*, Oct 26, 1867.
67. Ibid.

collecting firewood and "discovered a vein of metal-bearing quartz" which "proved to contain silver." A claim was made and named "the 'Pony,' as the discoverer had formerly been a rider of the Pony Express." That same May the Reese River Mining District was formed, covering an "area of 75 miles east and west, and 20 miles north and south."[68]

Both the Overland Stage Company and the Pony Express maintained stations in the Reese River vicinity on the Central Overland Trail. The Trail had been surveyed in 1859 and was adopted as the best transportation route to California. Even though the Pony Express service and its Reese River station existed only eighteen months, April 1860-October 1861, the stage service used the Reese River station and Trail for many years.

The rush was on and miners enough arrived to create the town of Clifton and it was soon followed by the creation the town of Austin, a mile further up the canyon. The towns grew into each other and in early 1864 Clifton was incorporated into Austin.[69] By January 1866 Austin's population was thought to be five thousand[70] and by 1867, Austin could boast of saloons, banks, restaurants, hotels and stores of every kind, as well as professions of every kind- clerks, druggists, saddle makers, doctors, lawyers, bankers, etc. The district's silver production for the year 1867 was valued at $685,172 and for 1868 it increased to $1,493,895.[71] Velazquez's arrival was timed perfectly for rich opportunities.

Austin[72] had already been designated the County Seat in 1863. Its importance was held for years because of its central location to mining activities. However, the Transcontinental Railroad was constructed 89 miles north of town, through Battle Mountain, thus commenced the gradual decline Austin would suffer. The County Seat was moved to Battle Mountain in 1979. Today, Austin is a "living ghost town" sustained by tourism looking for the lore of the West. The 2020 Census noted the population at 167. Some of the original structures of the boom days still exist, including the hotel in which Velazquez stayed, well sort of.

---

68. William P. Blake, *The Production of the Precious Metals* (1869), 129- taking the extract from *Harrington's Directory of the City of Austin for the Year 1866* by Myron Angel and W. P. Harrington.
69. *Nevada Historical Society Quarterly*, Vol XXIV, No. #1 (Spring 1981): 65.
70. J. Ross Browne, "The Reese River Country," *Harper's New Monthly Magazine*, Vol 33 (Jun to Nov 1866): 36.
71. Patrick H. Welsh, *An Historic Overview of the Bureau of Land Management- Shoshone-Eureka Resource Area, Nevada, Technical Report No. 7* (Reno, NV: BLM, 1981), based on Couch and Carpenter (1943) and Ross (1953).
72. Austin is located rather in the middle of Nevada, some 390 road miles west of Salt Lake City, Utah, and 173 miles east of Reno, Nevada, on Highway 50 at its intersection with Highway 305.

Velazquez claimed that she "took lodging at the Exchange Hotel, which was kept by a Slavonian by the name of Mollinely." This hotel was misidentified by Velazquez, which she rarely did, but she correctly named the owner. The hotel was the International and it still exists today as a café and bar, and landmark of interest.

Please see the photos of the International Hotel and Austin, yesteryear and today, in Illustrations, Figures 14 and 15.

The original hotel was moved from Virginia City in pieces, reassembled in Austin and in full operation by May 1863, and maybe before. The 14-room structure had been built in 1860, but by 1863 thriving Virginia City had outgrown it. Now in Austin it was admired even though it was only "37x90 feet in size." (In 1873 it was torn down and a new International Hotel was built at the same location.)[73] At the time of Velazquez's arrival, the proprietors were Molinelli and Crescenzo. After Molinelli took on partner Samuel Crescenzo, in June 1867,[74] they closed the hotel for several days for remodeling and upon its reopening the newspaper wrote, "We imagine that no eyes looked around the beautiful room without admiration." There was a "charming fresco on the wall behind the bar." The newspaper praised, "The hotel would be worthy of notice in any large city in the United States; but in the mountains of Central Nevada the elegance of its style is marvelous."[75]

The hotel advertised in the local newspaper that it offered "Order, Elegance, Pleasure" and enticingly listed as available: ambrosial cocktails, English ale and porter, joyous wines, Havana cigars, billiard tables, a club room and sleeping apartments. About the sleeping apartments, it advertised that they were "unsurpassed for quiet and comfort... 18 rooms neatly furnished, provided with new spring mattresses and fresh bedding...."[76]

Velazquez wrote that her night there was disturbed by the "terrible noise" of "some drunken fellows" in the next room. She voiced her dissatisfaction with her accommodations to some unnamed gentleman and he offered to check on a better place for her. "While he was gone," Velazquez narrated, "the chambermaid brought from the room next to [hers] two pairs of pistols, two large knives, and a razor, and informed [her] that their owner was a noted desperado, called Irish Tom, and that he had killed two men." When Irish Tom returned to claim his weapons and understood that the

---

73. www.hmdb.org, the Historical Marker Database; Thompson and West, *History of the State of Nevada, 1881, with Illustrations, and Biographical Sketches of its Prominent Men and Pioneers* (Berkeley, CA: Howell-North, 1958), 466; Donald R. Abbe, "Austin and the Reese River Mining District: Nevada's Forgotten Frontier," Ph. D. Dissertation in History, Texas Tech University. Abbe citied the *Reese River Reveille*, Aug 14, 1873.
74. *Reese River Reveille*, Jun 24, 1867.
75. Ibid, Sep 27, 1867.
76. Ibid, Nov 11, 1867.

chambermaid had removed them to show Velazquez, he was not vexed in the least, instead was "rather complimented that [Velazquez] should feel an interest in them and him." Of Irish Tom, Velazquez wrote (p584):

> He was a tall, good-looking Irishman, with a very pleasant face, and had as little of the ruffian in his appearance as any man I had met on the frontier. I was informed that he never attempted to hurt well-behaved people, and that he often submitted to the grossest kind of insults from some of his intimates. Men of his acquaintance had been known to slap him in the face, and he would take no notice, but walk away as if nothing had happened. With others, however, he would have no mercy, but would produce a pistol or knife at the slightest provocation. Tom was rather noted for his polite bearing towards the ladies, which I considered as an evidence that he was not as bad, by any means, as he might have been.

Irish Tom was one Thomas A. Carberry and he indeed attained notoriety by killing two men in Austin. The first man killed was Samuel Vance who had entered the Bank Exchange Saloon and on seeing Carberry standing on the outside, Vance asked him to drink with him. It was stated that the two had been friends, but had quarreled. Irish Tom refused the drink. Vance replied, "If you don't drink, I'll take a shot at you," and he fired his derringer pistol, but missed Irish Tom. "Tom instantly drew his revolver and fired at Vance, but the ball missed him and lodged in the jamb of the door." At the moment Tom fired a second shot, Vance was caught by officer Marshall, but it was too late and Vance was hit in the stomach, "a dangerous if not a mortal wound."[77]

Irish Tom was arrested and during an inquiry a witness asserted that Vance took the derringer from his coat pocket, walked towards the door, pointed it at Tom and said that "if he did not take a drink with him he would take a shot at him. Tom asked how big a shot he would take. Vance took a step toward him and fired...." On cross-examination the witness added that the "shooting was done as fast as it could be done" and that the "face of Vance was never away from Tom." With the additional testimony from the two officers present at the shooting the charges against Irish Tom were dropped.[78]

Mortally wounded, but lucid, Vance "sent for Carberry, upon whose arrival [Vance] freely admitted that he was wholly to blame, and asked forgiveness." Samuel Vance died of his wound and the newspaper reported, none too sympathetically, that "Vance had attained a bad notoriety by his turbulent life."[79]

The second man that Irish Tom killed in Austin was named Charles Ridgely. There had existed "some bad feeling" between the two because

---

77. *Reese River Reveille*, Aug 3, 1867.
78. Ibid, Aug 5, 1867.
79. Ibid, Aug 7, 1867.

Ridgely had been Vance's friend. When they encountered one another on a Friday night "high words and vile epithets were exchanged." A while later a police officer walked by and Irish Tom asked him to arrest Ridgely, saying that Ridgely intended to murder Irish Tom. The officer searched Ridgely for weapons, found none, and told both to go home.

The next morning at 11 a.m. Tom was standing near the shoeshine stand opposite Barovich's Saloon when he saw Ridgely and called "him vile names." Tom showed his "cocked six-shooter, and told Ridgley to go and arm himself and fight him there or anywhere else." Ridgely went to the International Hotel and retrieved his pistol left there in the care of the barkeeper.

Tom and Ridgley met in the street in the front of Miller and Wadleigh's store and "fired simultaneously." Both missed and Ridgley advanced towards Tom and they each fired again "within a few feet of each other." Tom hit Ridgley in the chest and Ridgley hit the Lafayette Restaurant. Ridgley continued toward Tom, but finally fell dead in front of the Lick House Saloon. The newspaper said that Irish Tom had "gained for himself a vile and infamous notoriety" and "this makes the second man that this fellow bags near that corner within a year."[80]

This killing occurred exactly a year and three days after the first, making it at least nine months after Velazquez came to town. She might not have remembered that it was after her arrival, when she wrote her book some 7 years afterwards. But if she did remember, then she ignored it and invented the hotel maid's assertion that Irish Tom had killed two men by that date.

In the process of sorting out the facts, it was revealed that Charles Ridgely was really James Archer from Sacramento, about 28-years-old, who had been in prison for highway robbery, escaped and took an alias. He had killed Pat Ford and Johnny Ewing in two separate incidences, and had been shot himself on each of those occasions.[81]

While Irish Tom was locked up and awaiting trial,[82] a Nevada newspaper said it could not see "a demon in one worthless desperado, James Archie, alias Charles Ridgely, and an angel in another, Irish Tom, alias Thomas Carberry."[83] Friends of Irish Tom contested "another falsehood" written in the *Gold Hill News* (Nevada) which asserted that Carberry had killed someone in Idaho in the process of robbing him. The friends would "wager

---

80. Ibid, Sep 5, 1868.
81. *Daily Union* (Sacramento), Sep 9, 1868; *Reese River Reveille*, Sep 8, 1868; *Mariposa Weekly Gazette* (California), Sep 18, 1868, repeating the Virginia City (Nevada) *Daily Trespass*.
82. *Reese River Reveille*, Sep 16, 1868.
83. *Virginia Trespass* (Virginia City) quoted in the *Reese River Reveille*, Sep 21, 1868.

$250 Thomas Carberry never was in Idaho; and in due time legal notice will be taken of these slanders."[84]

Although Tom's friends might have been right that he had never been in Idaho, he was no angel. In 1863 he had been in a gun fight in Aurora, about 175 miles SW of Austin, and was shot in the hip by Tom Lloyd, who was unscathed.[85] A year later in Aurora, he was one of ten "roughs" of the John Daly gang arrested for the murder of William R. Johnson, a well-regarded station-keeper. Samuel Vance was one of this gang. When Vance was en route to an inquiry, a citizen took a revenge shot at Vance hitting him in the groin and still Vance managed three return shots, all missing. A newly formed vigilante committee was determined to stop the lawlessness, arrested the gang, tried them and hung four. Tom escaped the noose by one vote of the committee. Vance also missed the hanging because he was convalescing. By the time Vance recovered, the Nevada governor had stepped in and stopped the vigilante committee. Vance was then tried by jury and found not guilty.

Irish Tom's luck held, and in Austin he was found not guilty of murder in Charles Ridgley's death.[86]

Velazquez's assessment of Irish Tom, based upon their meeting, might be considered about half right and half wrong. She wrote that "he never attempted to hurt well-behaved people," or "intimates," and that "he was not as bad, by any means, as he might have been." Velazquez noted, "but with others, however, he would have no mercy, but would produce a pistol or knife at the slightest provocation." Samuel Vance, dead guy number one, left this life believing he was a friend; at least, he called Tom to his death bed and apologized as a friend might. On the other hand, what kind of friend takes a pot shot at you? Charles Ridgely, dead guy number two, seemingly never was a friend.

In March, after Irish Tom Carberry extracted himself from his legal problems in Austin, he moved 115 miles east to the mining town of Hamilton, White Pine County, today a ghost town with still visible stone and wooden structures. At Hamilton, Irish Tom "acted as a special police officer" and "according to all accounts had studiously avoided getting into trouble, of whatever character, and on all occasions. Indeed, those who knew him most intimately say that he had determined never again participate in difficulties where was at all possible to avoid them."

---

84. *Reese River Reveille*, Sep 21, 1868.
85. *The Grizzly Bear*, Vol X, No. 6 (April 1912), letter to the editor by William Mackey, Mar 6, 1912, Crescent City, California.
86. *Daily Alta California*, Mar 18, 1869, copying the *Reese River Reveille*, Mar 13, 1869.

Irish Tom had little time left on earth and six months later, on September 26, on Sunday morning, he died "after a protracted illness."[87] It is clear from the obituary that Thomas A. Carberry was not completely despised, but was accepted in Hamilton as a "trusted police officer" of sorts.[88]

In the end, Velazquez accurately assessed his character when she wrote (p585) that "he was not as bad, by any means, as he might have been." Velazquez only mentioned meeting Irish Tom the one time and did not state his fate, so it is assumed they had no further association. She made no mention of the infamous September 5, 1868 gunfight with Ridgely which might indicate she was out of town at the time; otherwise, it seems that she would have addressed it. As will be seen, she claimed she didn't remain in Austin for long after her forthcoming marriage.

---

87. *Sacramento Daily Union*, Oct 1, 1869, repeating *Inland Empire* (White Pine), Sep 28, 1869.
88. *Nevada Historical Society Quarterly*, Vol XII, No. #2 (Summer 1969).

Chapter 8

1868, a New Husband

Velazquez stated that thanks to the help of her "friend" who had gone out to search for new quarters, she succeeded in finding a new room. Her "landlady was a Pennsylvanian" who made her comfortable and introduced her to "a number of prominent people of the place." Velazquez was soon on "excellent terms with most of her new acquaintances." A widower of about sixty years of age proposed marriage to her after knowing her for two days. She said he offered to give her an interest in his mines, but she thought that his way of courtship "a rather abrupt style" and declined. He "took [her] refusal good-naturedly enough" and she concluded that he wasn't sufficiently in love with her to let her refusal bother him.

Velazquez wrote (p585):

> Subsequently, I met a gentleman who paid me attention, and to whom I became sincerely attached. We were married in a very quiet manner; for neither of us desired, any more than we could help, to be made the subjects of the gossip of a mining town.

She did not mention this husband's name in her 1876 memoir, some eight and a half years after their marriage. However, in newspaper articles prior to her book she called herself "Mrs. E. H. Bonner" and it is a fact that her husband was Edward Hardy Bonner.

Lander County Courthouse records show that E. H. Bonner applied for a marriage license on January 29, 1868, a Tuesday, and that they were married on the same day. The handwritten license reads:

> State of Nevada
> County of Landers
> E. H. Bonner being duly sworn says that he is a resident of Lander county, that he is over 21 years of age and desires a License to marry L. J. Wasson and that she is over 18 years of age, and he knows of no legal objection to said Marriage.
> Subscribed and sworn to before me this 29th day of Jan'y A. D. 1868 H. D. Spiry Clk [clerk]
> [signed] E. H. Bonner

The marriage of Lauretta J. Wasson and E. H. Bonner was performed by Reverend A. Taylor and witnessed by D. W. Levan and Mrs. D. W. Levan. The minister registered the marriage with the court recorder on January 31 at 10 a.m.:

> E. H. Bonner to Lauretta J. Wasson
> State of Nevada County of Landers
> This is to certify that the undersigned Minister of the Gospel, did, on the 29th of January A. D. 1868 join in lawful wedlock E. H. Bonner and Lauretta J. Wasson with their mutual consent, in the presence of D. W. Levan & Mrs. D. W. Levan, witnesses. A. Taylor Clergyman
> U.S. Int. Rev stp 5d ct [United States Internal Revenue stamp 5 dollars 0 cents]

State Rev. stp 1.00[d] ct [State Revenue stamp 1 dollar 0 cents]
Recorded at request of A. Taylor Jan'y 31st 1868 at 10 O'clock A.M.
D.C. W. Kenney County Recorder

The *Reese River Reveille*[1] wrote:

MARRIED. In this city, Jan. 29th, by Rev. A. Taylor, E. H. Bonner and Lauretta J. Wasson. The REVEILLE is the recipient of substantial compliments from the happy couple, and it drinks bliss and length of days to the hardy prospector and his bride.

The newspaper made the obvious pun using Bonner's name, Hardy. No doubt Velazquez was pleased to receive the kind wishes and was likely even better pleased to have bagged Bonner about 29 days after her arrival in Austin; she indicated (*TWIB*, p585) that she did not meet him right away so she knew Bonner less than 29 days.

D. W. Levan and Mrs. D. W. Levan, the two witnesses, were the operators of a boarding house in Austin. In the first half of September 1867 Mrs. D. W. Levan leased the Graham Lodging House on Union Street, which was the block behind the International Hotel. Mrs. Levan, in a newspaper advertisement, promised the public that the House would "be kept in the neatest and most cleanly manner at all times... [and] Pleasant rooms to let by the night, week or month."[2] It was here that Velazquez took a room.

Velazquez wrote her landlady was Pennsylvanian and indeed both Mr. Daniel W. Levan and his wife Catherine were Pennsylvania-born. Before coming to Austin, Levan was a "hotel keeper" in Placerville, California.[3] It can be certain that the marriage witnesses and Velazquez's Pennsylvanian landlords, the Levans, were one and the same. Velazquez, in a future wedding, will use another landlady as a witness to a marriage.

New husband E. H. Bonner was born in Mississippi. It is unclear when he went West, but he is not found in Mississippi with his family in the 1850 U.S. Census when he would have been 24 years old, as later censuses reveal his age. Bonner seems to have left Mississippi, bound for the California Gold Rush, well before the Civil War; no evidence of military service is found. When he arrived in Austin sometime in 1863 and while the War was in progress, he came as an experienced miner.[4]

He busied himself with the buying and selling mines: On October 19, 1863, he bought interest in the Johnny Grove Ledge; in November he sold

---

1. Jan 30.
2. *Reese River Reveille*, Sep 25, 1867, showing the ad was first taken on Sep 19.
3. U.S. Census, 1860, 1870.
4. Bonner is not in *First Directory of Nevada Territory: the names of residents in the principal towns, etc* compiled by J. Wells Kelly in 1862. He might not have been in any of the towns listed, but instead out prospecting, or maybe even in California working.

interest in the Amador Ledge, the Sierra Ledge and the Sutter Ledge. Also, in November he filed certificates of incorporation in San Francisco for "Bonner Gold and Silver Company. Location, Reese River. Trustees- E. H. Bonner, J. D. Havens, F. T. Potter. Capital, $80,000."[5]

Beginning in December 1863 E. H. Bonner served as "Department Recorder" for the mining district. This entailed visiting claim locations and recording these in the *Reese River Mining Records*. Bonner's handwriting shows good punctuation, spelling and neatness, indicative of an educated person. He held the position until at least January 26, 1864, a short period to be sure, which might mean he was a substitute for the regular Recorder. In any case, it is likely he learned much about the mining district which might have enabled him to make informed mine purchases, such as his partnership in the La Madonna Ledge.[6]

The following year Hardy Bonner, along with three others, went prospecting in and near inhospitable Death Valley, some 200 miles south of Austin. They were in search of the "rich silver lodes discovered by the party that made the disastrous passage of Death Valley in 1852." The only living member of that party was a lady living in Santa Clara County and she had "in her possession some exceedingly rich specimens of ore containing pieces of native silver." Other prospectors had searched for the lady's silver lodes and failed. Bonner's group apparently also failed, but claimed that east of Death Valley they "met with good success... had discovered a rich section of county" and intended to return. This trip had taken the dogged prospectors two months.[7] It is clear that Bonner never pursued this alleged discovered rich section of country.

E. H. Bonner, in Austin, continued with his buying and selling mine shares and in June 1865, together with four others, bought the full claim known as the Mountain Eagle Ledge. During 1865 and 1866 he rented a house on Court Street, between Third and Fourth Streets.[8]

In the early part of 1867 Bonner left Austin and made a 580-mile trip to the vicinity of Prescott, Arizona, likely prospecting[9] and when he returned to Austin, he bought, on September 10, 1867, for $200, a town lot and house. Bonner did not keep this house for long and three months later sold it for $150. This lot was/is two blocks uphill from the International Cafe & Bar on the same side of Main Street. As always, "Hardy Bonner" received

---

5. *Reese River Reveille*, Nov 27, 1863.
6. Jan 25, 1864.
7. *Sacramento Daily Union*, Apr 29, 1865.
8. W. P. Harrington, *Directory of the City of Austin for 1866* (Austin, NV: Harrington, January 1866).
9. *Arizona Miner* (Prescott, AZ), Apr 20, 1867, letter awaiting pick up "Bonner, E. Hardy."

his mail at the Austin Post Office and he had a letter there on October 1, 1867 awaiting pick up.[10]

Velazquez wrote (p586):

> Shortly after my marriage I made a flying trip to New Orleans, for the purpose of seeing my brother, and some of my relatives. Immediately a rumor was started that I had run away; and when I returned I found that all kinds of stories had been set afloat about me. My reappearance, however, set them all at rest; and, as my husband and myself zealously attended to our own business, and let that of other people alone, we were permitted to dwell together in peace.

This claim of a quick trip to New Orleans to visit her "brother and some of [her] relatives" was simply false, as records reveal. On February 4, 1868, which was six days after her marriage, she departed on the westbound stage, alone.[11] This departure, so soon after her wedding, was the cause of the rumors about which she complained. Then on February 19, Mr. Bonner also departed on the westbound stage.[12] It is unclear if he went to join her for pleasure or retrieve her. In any case, both returned to Austin; the records do not reveal if they returned together or singly. Records seem to show that Bonner (and maybe Velazquez, too) had not yet returned to Austin by March 3, at least that was the date the Post Office published a list of unclaimed letters and Bonner had three letters awaiting him.[13] The letters must have arrived after his westward departure and were probably from Velazquez. The couple is next found in the records, again leaving Austin, westbound on February 27.[14] All of her (and his) activity was clearly west of Austin; she did not go east to New Orleans.

One more point about this "flying trip to New Orleans" to visit her "brother and some of my relatives" needs making. When Velazquez, as "Mary De Caulp," went to New Orleans in January 1867 and stayed at the City Hotel, she had no relatives there or she wouldn't have stayed at a hotel, but with relatives. And why weren't her brother and relatives, the worthy recipients of this later Velazquez visit from all the way across the continent, witnesses at her January 17, 1867 wedding to John Wasson? Recall, she left her only living brother in Cuba, when she visited him during her return trip from Venezuela. Velazquez had no brother/relatives in New Orleans!

Velazquez claimed that upon her return from New Orleans the couple "purchased a snug little stone house." A deed search for this purchase failed to confirm it and it remains doubtful. She then "devoted [herself] to advancing [her] husband's interest as much as possible, and to making [their]

---

10. *Reese River Reveille*, Oct 4, 1867.
11. Ibid, Feb 5, 1868, "By Overland Stage, departed west yesterday, Mrs. E. H. Bonner."
12. Ibid, Feb 20, 1868, "By Overland Stage, departed west yesterday, Mr. E. H. Bonner."
13. Ibid, Mar 3, 1868.
14. Ibid, Feb 27, 1868, "By Overland Stage, departed west, E. H. Bonner and wife."

home comfortable and attractive" and Bonner "for a time prospered in his mining operations."

Velazquez wrote that Austin of 1868 was a lively place of about fifteen hundred to two thousand people, with "a dozen stores, one hotel, four or five lodging-houses, half a dozen restaurants, more drinking-saloons than [she] ever undertook to count, Catholic and Methodist churches, a Masonic Hall, and five quartz crushing-mills, only one, however, of which was in operation." The Sacramento *Weekly Rescue* of November 11, 1868 wrote:

> The citizens of Austin (Nev.) drink 100 baskets of champagne per month, besides an incredible amount of other liquors. This is doing very well for a city of 3,500 inhabitants.

The *Weekly Rescue* was the publication of the International Organization of Good Templars, the temperance society.

In September 1868 Bonner's livelihood was good enough that the couple made another trip to the west, probably Sacramento or maybe even San Francisco. Their departure was noted: "By Overland Stage.- Departed West, Hardy Bonner and wife." E. H. Bonner's return to Austin was noted on September 24, and "Mrs. E. H. Bonner" returned ten days afterwards on October 4.[15] Also in 1868 E. H. Bonner is noted in the newspaper as having letters at the Post Office awaiting pick up.[16] One wonders if during this period Bonner was with Velazquez in California or if these letters were sent by Velazquez in California to Bonner who remained in Austin working.

In her memoir Velazquez wrote (p586), "there were envious people who spoke ill of him and me, we succeeded in gaining the esteem of such of our neighbors as were worth knowing, and did not disturb ourselves about what might be said of us by those who were disposed to speak evil." It is likely that Velazquez was not very warmly received by Bonner's longtime friends, and in any case, she didn't think too highly of the citizenry of Austin and characterized them as "queer people."

She claimed to be even more repulsed by the "mining speculation and swindles" about which she learned. It was there that she first learned the meaning of "salting" a mine, explaining that was only one of a variety of "frauds that were practiced every day." Velazquez wrote (p587), "It grieved me greatly that my husband should be compelled to associate, and to transact business with such scoundrels as the men about him." She said that her husband's partner "was as worthless a scamp as there was in the district" and she feared her husband would get the blame for the partner's doings. She encouraged her husband to be rid of these people and seek a "locality that offered greater advantages for living, as descent people ought to live."

---

15. Ibid, Sep 2 & 24, Oct 5, 1868.
16. Ibid, Jun 1, Dec 1& 2, 1868.

Velazquez can easily be believed that mining scams existed in abundance in Austin, as in all mining towns in those days. About Austin, *Harper's* reporter John Ross Browne wrote, "That many swindles have been perpetrated, and many worthless claims palmed off on a credulous public, is beyond dispute…." Browne asserted that this fact did not mean that there were not good mines there to be purchased. He continued, "Mining speculations are much on par with speculations in horse-flesh." His analogy was that just because a buyer was cheated on a horse purchase, did not mean that there were no good horses to be found. He concluded that if a buyer would just inspect the mine or hire an agent "there would be less disappointment in the investment of capital."[17]

Bonner, according to Velazquez, sold out his Austin mining interest and the couple moved to California and "purchased a lovely place" in the Sacramento Valley. Scarce records have been found (to date) relative to this California period and it is doubtful that the couple ever "purchased a lovely place," as their activity will show.

One curious record of Velazquez in California comes from the *Daily Alta California* (San Francisco) dated January 9, 1869. In the column for "DIED" is found:

OBITUARY.
MAZATLAN, November 10, 1868.
The remains of Colonel R. D. Clapp arrived here to-day en route for their resting place, San Luis Potosi. He leaves a wife and four children, and one married sister- Mrs. Lauretta J. Bonner, of Austin- to mourn his sad loss. Died from injuries received at the fall of fort Arequipa, Peru, 13th of August, by the earthquake.
LEOPOLD BEGOCHA
>>> Reese River Reveille, New Orleans and Vicksburg papers copy.

There can be no doubt that this was Velazquez, identified by name and her Austin residence. Note at this date, there is no claimed California residence.

Recall, Velazquez wrote she had recently gone to New Orleans to visit her brother, but now, ten months later, it seems that he is in Peru, thousands of miles away. When she wrote of her brother in New Orleans, she failed to state that he held the prominent position of colonel in the United States Army, a position worth bragging about, especially considering the admiration she held for military personnel of rank. It should be noted that Velazquez claimed by May 1865, she had only one brother living (p517), so he was living in both Cuba and New Orleans and now died in Peru.

---

17. *Harper's New Monthly Magazine*, Vol 33 (Jun to Nov 1866): 38. Reporter Browne visited Austin from May to Oct 1866.

Here, Velazquez identified her brother as R. D. Clapp, but, recall, in her book she gave "Josea" as her brother's first name and clearly that name has no connection to the initials R. D. Remember the 1864 fake inheritance letter which named a brother "Harry, who [was] acting British Consul at Hayti [*sic*]"? It can be certain that if Velazquez had a brother, he was none of these.

This appears to be the first time that Velazquez tested Clapp as her family name. It is necessary to jump ahead to 1874 when Velazquez claimed to the Atlanta *Constitution* that Samuel S. Clapp was her father in order to refute this brother claim. When Velazquez said that Samuel Clapp was her father, she should have first considered his birth date; he was born in August 1828. Velazquez claimed she was born in 1842. This would have made Samuel Clapp a fourteen-year-old father. Recall in her book, Velazquez claimed that she was the youngest of six children. Assume that this brother was the child closest to her in age and assume a two-year spacing in births; Colonel R. D. Clapp would have been born in 1840, making Samuel Clapp a twelve-year-old father. Suppose that brother Colonel R. D. Clapp was two births before Velazquez, father Samuel would have been ten years old. Obviously, it is unnecessary to consider the next three siblings' births. In any case, the records show that Samuel never married and no children are found documented. More about the Clapps will be addressed.

It is a mystery why Velazquez forged such an obituary and it is interesting that she asked the New Orleans and Vicksburg newspapers to copy the announcement. It is known that Velazquez spent time in New Orleans, but nothing is known of a connection to Vicksburg. Of course, her connection to the *Reese River Reveille*, the first paper she wished to copy the notice is understandable.

The death announcement trick was not new to Velazquez. Recall the 1864 forged death announcement of her father "Commodore J. B. Roach" (what happened to Clapp?!) by way of the inheritance letter she advertised in the Virginia newspaper? On that occasion her motive might be supposed that she was trying to impress people with her wealth or maybe to reassure the locals that she could be trusted to pay back borrowed money with the pending inheritance.

The purpose for the death announcement of brother Colonel R. D. Clapp seems to have been that Velazquez was reinforcing some narrative that she had adopted in Austin, such as her father's confiscated Mexican estate. It will be seen that on January 7, 1875, one Adam A. Wilson wrote of her activity in Austin, "She then claimed to have a vast amount of property that had been confiscated...."

There remain a couple of points about Colonel Clapp's death announcement.

First, there exists nowhere in the military records a Colonel R. D. Clapp. Colonels just do not go missing! It can only be assumed that this was the same brother, she claimed in her book, who fought for the Confederacy, achieved rank of captain, was captured and imprisoned at Camp Chase. So, is it believable that the U.S. Government, after the Civil War, enlisted this Rebel captain and gave him a promotion to colonel? The emphatic answer is, no! Ex-Rebels were barred from any position of power by the Federal Government.

Second, indeed there was a hugely destructive earthquake in Peru on August 13 which resulted in 25,000 deaths. There were U.S. Navy vessels at anchor which experienced the earthquake at the coastal town of Arica some 170 miles south of Arequipa which is inland. One ship was beached by a tsunami wave. The officers wrote about the disaster and they did not report the destruction of "fort Arequipa" or the death of any U.S. colonel.

In summary, the earthquake was real, the brother was not. And who was the letter signer, "Leopold Begocha?" She gotcha.

Another curious record of Velazquez's presence in California comes from the San Francisco convention of the Independent Order of Odd Fellows. In attendance were Chapters from nationwide and the Mississippi delegation submitted, on September 27, 1869, a "grateful acknowledgement" for some unspecified kindness to "the ladies of San Francisco, who presented to them, through Mrs. E. H. Bonner, a native Mississippian, a token of respect as tasteful and elegant as the fair donors are generous and lovely."[18]

This "Mrs. E. H. Bonner" seems to have been one and the same as our Mrs. E. H. Bonner. Curiously she was called a native Mississippian. It is known that Mr. E. H. Bonner was a Mississippian, so two questions arise, did Velazquez know him in Mississippi before her Austin trip and was that the reason for her trip? Was their common bond, both were Mississippians? These questions will be addressed later.

Mrs. Bonner's presence in San Francisco about this time is confirmed by letters held in the Post Office to be picked up, noted in the local newspaper in October and December 1869.[19] She then ostensibly left San Francisco and went to Sacramento and started to receive mail there, in December 1869 and January 1870.[20]

---

18. Independent Order of Odd Fellows, *The Journal of Proceeding*, Vol 6 (Baltimore: James L. Ridgely, 1874), 4690.
19. *San Francisco Chronicle*, Oct 12, 1869 and Dec 1, 7, 8, 15, 22, 1869, letters remaining in the Post Office, "Bonner Mrs. L J," "Bonner L C Mrs," "E. H. Bonner," "Bonner L J Miss."
20. *Sacramento Daily Union*, Dec 17, 1869 as "Bannar Mrs E H," Dec 24, 1869 as "Barner Mrs E H," Jan 14, 21, 1870 as "Bonner Mrs E H."

Moved to Utah

Velazquez claimed she and Bonner were settled in California for only a few months when Bonner became restless to be off again to the mines, this time to Utah.

It is clear that while she was in California inventing a fake obituary for her fake brother, making presentations to the Order of Odd Fellows, and receiving mail in San Francisco, that Bonner was still working in Austin and had not yet sold out. His presence there is definite based on three silver ore assays and sales under his name dated September 23, October 4 and October 15, 1869 which pocketed him some good money.[21] Clearly it was sometime after the October 15 assay that Bonner sold out and went to Utah. Mrs. Bonner went too, at some unclear date.

The couple is later found departing Utah, noted on a railway passenger list:

E. H. Bonner and wife (Austin, Nevada)... departed Ogden, Utah on September 25, 1870 on the west-bound Overland Train... arrived at Oakland, California wharf on September 27, 1870.[22]

From Oakland the passengers crossed the Bay to San Francisco by steamer.

It is unexpected that the passenger list indicated the Bonners claimed they were from Austin, Nevada because it can be reasonably ascertained that the Bonners were living, at that date, in the Salt Lake City region, at least Mr. Bonner was. Velazquez related that they rather long ago had left Austin, first moving to California, only to relocate a few months later to Utah. Bonner may have considered himself still from Austin, after such a long residence, and thought his stay in Utah was temporary. The Ogden train station was about 64 miles north of the Alta mining area where Bonner worked and it was the place to catch the Central Pacific Railroad.

Velazquez said, that in Utah, Bonner "passed a year prospecting in Bingham Canon [*sic* cañon], Camp Floyd, Eureka and Tintic, and expended all his money without achieving anything. He then was compelled to accept a foremanship in the Lucine [*sic* Lucin] district, and after he had been working in that capacity for some time, was promoted to superintendent." Velazquez gives the correct names for the mines and towns of the area surrounding Salt Lake City. All her facts relating to the Utah mines and

---

21. Untitled ore assay record book at the Austin Museum, 180 Main Street, Austin, Nevada.
22. *Daily Alta California*, Sep 26, 1870, "Passengers Overland"; Louis J. Rasmussen, *Railway Passenger Lists of Overland Trains to San Francisco and the West*, Vol 1 (Colma, CA: San Francisco Historic Records, 1966), 35, covers Jul 28, 1870 to Nov 13, 1871. Mr. Rasmussen also produced Vol 2 which covers Nov 14, 1871 to Apr 23, 1873; the Bonners are not found in it.

towns are accurate enough, only she mistakenly named (p589) a sub-chapter in her book, "The Gold Regions of Nevada," when she clearly meant Utah.

Evidence of E. H. Bonner's many returns to Salt Lake City, after being out in the mining districts, is the listing of his name in the "Hotel Arrivals" section of the newspaper. He is noted arrived at the Salt Lake House on: February 22, 1871 from East Canyon; March 4 from Ogden; March 9 from Ogden and March 16 from Bingham.[23]

It seems that during this time, Mrs. Bonner was not with Mr. Bonner in Utah, but had stayed in California. Mr. Bonner expected her return soon and came often to town to check. She arrived, registered at the Salt Lake House on March 19 and noted she was from Sacramento.[24]

Velazquez implied she lived in Alta City, the town which supported mining in Little Cottonwood Canyon southeast of Salt Lake City.[25] About this mining district Velazquez said (p589):

> I doubt whether many of the mines in this district will ever be successfully worked. The Emma is one of the best, and I think could be made to pay, if judiciously operated. This mine is situated in the side of the mountain, and is almost perpendicular. On looking at it, it is impossible not to wonder how the owners ever reached it, or are able to work it. I believe that there is an immense lead of silver here which will yet be unearthed.

Please see the photo of Alta City, year 1873, and map of the region in Illustrations, Figure 16.

Velazquez's manner of reference to the Emma mine indicates that she probably wrote about it while in Utah or recently there, and not at a later date and from memory, say between mid-1873 and 1876, the year she published her book. If she wrote about it after mid-1873, then she ignored the public outcry of Emma mine investors and the newspapers which reported, "The Emma Mine Swindle" and "The Emma Mine Fraud."[26]

The story of the Emma mine was big news in its day; the mine owners-speculators-vendors went to England and formed a company called the Emma Silver Mining Company, Limited, with English organizational and financial help[27] to sell the mine to the public based on its past and true reputation of good production. However, the owner-vendors

---

23. *Salt Lake Daily Herald:* Feb 23, 1871; Mar 5, 1871; Mar 10, 1871; Mar 17, 1871.
24. Ibid, Mar 21, 1871, "Hotel Arrivals, Mrs. E. H. Bonner, Sacramento."
25. *Deseret News*, Nov 15, 1871; Edward L. Sloan, *Gazeteer of Utah, and Salt Lake City Directory* (Salt Lake City: Salt Lake Herald Publishing Co., 1874), stated the population of Alta City as 600 and of the mining district as 1300.
26. *Daily Evening Traveller* (Boston) and *New York Herald*, Jun 26, 1873.
27. Lucius Eugene Chittenden, *The Emma Mine: A Statement of the Facts Connected with the Emma Mine* (New York: B. H. Tyrell, 1876), 18. Chittenden was attorney for T. W. Park and H. H. Baxter and prepared the statement for the Chairman Committee of Foreign Affairs, House of Representatives, Mar 9, 1876.

misrepresented the mine's current production and profitability. The company claimed ore stockpiles, which in reality did not exist, neither at the mine nor in transit to the smelter. When the mine failed, the initially eager English investors turned disgruntled stockholders and hollered that they were sold an exhausted, worked-out mine. A resulting lawsuit in the U.S. courts against the owner-vendors found them not guilty of fraud, a surprising verdict to many. It's unclear if the owner-vendors truly understood or believed they were selling a worked-out mine or just a mine not worth the money they asked.

General Robert C. Schenck, who was the U.S. Minister to England,[28] became embroiled in the affair when he was offered shares of stock and accepted a seat on the Board of Directors of the company. Recall, this was the same Major General Schenck who hired one "Mrs. Alice Williams" as a spy during the Civil War.

Schenck was loudly condemned for having seemingly endorsed the company. He had, before the announcement of the mine's failure, resigned his board position, after holding his position for only 28 days, but this did not free him from criticism.[29] Still, he held his diplomatic position until 1876 by which time the U.S. Congress decided to investigate Schenck's involvement. Schenck offered to resign which was accepted and he returned home where he willingly appeared before the investigative committee which concluded that Schenck was not a conspirator to commit fraud, but his relationship to the vendors of the mine as a director and stockholder "cast suspicion on his motives and subject his action to unfavorable criticism." In summary, Schenck's involvement was stated as "ill-advised, unfortunate, and incompatible with the duties of his official position."[30] Schenck maintained through it all that he wasn't part of a conspiracy.

The mine's ownership went back to the American owners to whom the British shareholders owed money.[31] The American Emma Company set to working the mine- not exactly the expected behavior from the American owners if they had knowingly sold a depleted mine to the British.

Then in November 1880, the American Emma Company "consented to hand back the mine and £49,663 [about $248,000 in 1880 money or $7.7 million in 2023 money] in exchange for shares in a reorganized British company, a guarantee that all proceedings against the American defendants… would be discontinued, and mutual releases on both sides."

---

28. The Minister of the U.S. at the Court of St. James.
29. Chittenden, 21.
30. *Reports of Committees of the House of Representatives for the First Session of the Forty-fouth Congress, 1875-76* (Washington, DC: GPO, 1876), XVI. The "Emma Mine Investigation, Report #579" consists of some 879 pages which includes testimony and documents.
31. Clark C. Spence, *British Investments and the American Mining Frontier, 1860-1901* (Moscow, ID: Univ of Idaho Press, 1995), *178*.

This British buy-back is not exactly the behavior one would expect from the British considering they had ranted for years that they were sold an exhausted mine!

By January 1882 the (British) New Emma Silver Mining Company was working the mine. For nearly a quarter of a century, they tried to make the mine profitable and failed. It then took a decade more to let it go back to American owners, who also could never make it pay. Thus was Emma's fate.

Today, Alta's historical marker No. 379 (noting the old town location was a little to the south) states, in part, "To the north is one entrance to famous Emma Mine, first to produce paying ore in this area, located in 1866 by Woodman, Chisholm, Woodhill and Reich."

Velazquez wrote that her husband was the "superintendent of one of the Wellington [silver] mines," which was a neighboring mine to the Emma and was as well located in Little Cottonwood Canyon.[32] Of their time there, Velazquez wrote (p589):

> Alta City, at the foot of the two canons [*sic*],- Big and Little Cottonwood,- is a town of rather more importance [referencing neighboring Tannersville]. When I was there it had three stores, a hotel, a couple of lodging-houses, a livery stable, and a large number of drinking-saloons. The dwelling-houses were mostly very small, and were entirely invisible in winter, being covered by the snow. The snow usually commences to fall about the middle of September, but I have seen it in August. During the winter many parts of the canon are impassable, except by the use of sledges and snow-shoes, and there is constant danger from avalanches, which carry everything before them.
>
> The Wellington mine lost its foreman and a miner through an avalanche while I was there, and many men have lost their lives in this canon, their bodies remaining buried beneath the snow until spring.

Velazquez was in error that Alta is located at the foot of Big and Little Cottonwood Canyons; it is in Little Cottonwood Canyon. This minor error does not detract from the fact that she was there or nearby and her narration of the death of the foreman helps date her presence. A newspaper corroborates the death:[33]

> Salt Lake, April 13th.- The snow avalanches at Little Cottonwood, Thursday and yesterday, are described as the most fearful ever known in that region. A slide at the Wellington mine came from a height of 2,000 feet, carrying away and burying the entire day force of the Wellington workmen. All were finally dug out alive, except H. H. Murray, foreman, who was smothered to death. His body will be

---

32. By 1874 it was stated that 5,000 tons of ore had been extracted from Wellington mines- Source is Edward L. Sloan, *Gazeteer of Utah, and Salt Lake City Directory* (Salt Lake City: Salt Lake Herald Publishing Co., 1874).
33. *Daily Alta California*, Apr 14, 1872 (a San Francisco newspaper not related to Alta City, Utah).

brought here today. Murray was from Rhode Island, thirty-seven years of age and highly esteemed.

Indeed, the snowfall had been great. On the 28th of March, it was reported that the snow was "14 feet deep on the level" and "many houses are entirely covered with snow. The altitude of this city is 8475 feet above sea level."[34]

Already, early that winter, on November 26, 1871, the snow was reported at six feet deep and the residents had to "dig themselves in and out of their dwellings" and there was no relief in sight, "the storm still continues." The newspaper reported that:

> A young man named Jenkins was buried by a snow-slide on Wednesday, near the mouth of the Wellington mine. He was dug out by the miners and buried on Thursday morning. Several of the miners, while at work for the body, were caught in slides and escaped with difficulty.

Jenkins was likely the other man, "a miner," mentioned by Velazquez.

It was no exaggeration by Velazquez that men were lost in the snow and not found until spring. On June 15, men in Alta recovered the "body of Montgomery, who was lost during some of the severe storms last winter... He was standing almost erect when found." However, "The body of Morrison [had] not been found yet."[35]

Alta City was constantly under the threat of snow avalanche and one in January 1875 caused much damage and six deaths. Many residents were unnerved and were reported to have packed and left.[36] News items about snow avalanche victims in Little Cottonwood Canyon from the 1870's until the present are too many to recite. Alta's historical marker No. 379 states its "boothill" cemetery contains 140 people killed by snow slides (and 110 men killed in gunfights).

Ironically, it was not an avalanche which destroyed the town, but fire, and it was some four years after the Bonners had departed the area. The fire started at the Swan Hotel at the west end and the flames swept eastward and "almost totally" destroyed the town, "thirty to forty families" were "rendered homeless," and "the situation of the people [was] deplorable." Only fifteen houses were spared.[37] Adding to the Alta residents' difficulties after the fire, the first snow, measuring four inches, came on September 19.[38]

Mining continued for decades in the canyon, but the town of Alta never regained the energy of a commercial mining center. It thrives today as a

---

34. *Deseret News*, Apr 3, 1872.
35. Ibid, Jun 19, 1872.
36. Ibid, Jan 27, 1875.
37. *Deseret News*, Aug 7, 1878; *St. Louis Post Dispatch*, Aug 3, 1878.
38. *Deseret News*, Sep 25, 1878.

world-class ski resort with snow in abundance. The Little Cottonwood Canyon road which leads to popular ski slopes is well marked with warning signs of potential avalanche. There are gates at intervals on the winding road which can be closed to stop vehicle traffic from entering in times of danger, until avalanche control specialists remove the threat.

It is clear that Mr. Bonner came in from the Bingham mines on March 16, 1871 to meet Velazquez who had returned from Sacramento.[39] Later in the year she accompanied him to the mining districts; her return to Salt Lake House from the Tintic district is noted on September 21, 1871.[40]

In the fall Velazquez accompanied her husband to Silver City, New Mexico, surely to investigate opportunities in mining and living, and returned without him. She was noted in the newspaper's "Hotel Arrivals" returned from there to Salt Lake House on November 2, 1871: "H. K. Tompkins, Mrs. Bonner; Silver City;"[41] No Velazquez connection can be made with one H. K. Tompkins, so whether they traveled and arrived together is unknown.

Velazquez narrated that she and Bonner tired of Alta and moved to Salt Lake City.[42] She said that her husband was interested in going to New Mexico, and, as seen, they had checked out Silver City, but it is likely that Mr. Bonner continued working a little longer in Little Cottonwood Canyon. He would go later. While her husband was away working in the Canyon, Velazquez boarded with a Mormon lady who had "been one of twelve wives and was a strong advocate of polygamy." Velazquez said (p591) that since she was the only boarder, the two women had plenty of time to become personal, and the landlady told her many things in confidence about the history and beliefs of the Mormons. The lady showed Velazquez her "endowment robes, which she wore when she became a member of the Mormon Church."

Velazquez said that the Mormons practiced their religion in everyday life, which was more than she could say about other religions with which she was familiar. She admired their agriculture and said their thrift and industry were superior to that of their neighbors. She said that Mormons had been forced to move west and that they should be left alone. She wrote (p592):

Whether polygamy, however, be right or wrong, there is this to be said in favor of the Mormons. The men marry according to the custom of their church, and they

---

39. *Salt Lake Daily Herald*, Mar 17, 1871.
40. Ibid, Sep 22, 1871.
41. Ibid, Nov 3, 1871.
42. The Bonners are not found in surviving city directories. The *Salt Lake City Directory and Business Guide, for 1869*, compiled and arranged by E. L. Sloan, shows no Bonners. Directories for 1870, 1871, and 1872 were not located. The *Salt Lake City Directory for the Year 1873*, published by Hannaks & Company shows no Bonners.

acknowledge and provide for the women who bear their children- which is a good deal more than a great many people who denounce polygamy and Mormonism do.

She added, "I do not believe in polygamy myself, but if other people think it is right, and choose to practice it, that is their business and not mine."

Velazquez said that she was very interested to learn of the Mormon religion and asked many questions which were kindly answered by her landlady. However, she remained puzzled (p594) on "the status of sealed wives" and "by what theory a Mormon could marry a widow for her lifetime, while all her children born of the second marriage would belong to the first husband in the next world." Velazquez wrote (p595) that during her stay in Utah she learned to regard the Mormons as "hard-working and honest people," but yet, she "could not agree with all of their religious doctrines."

Velazquez became "acquainted with Brigham Young and a number of the bishops" and heard the preaching of the principal bishops and they "never utter[ed] a word that was not good doctrine." Of Young she wrote (p594):

Brigham Young is a light-complexioned man, rather inclined to corpulency, but strong and hearty in spite of his years and the labors he has undergone. He has a large, full head, a keen blue eye, and an easy, affable manner that is very engaging. I found him to be a pleasant, genial gentleman with an excellent fund of humor, and a captivating style of conversation.

It is likely true that Velazquez met the founder of Salt Lake City, Brigham Young, and bishops of the Mormon Church. They were accessible and she had a propensity, throughout her life, to seek out and meet prominent people. However, recall it has been shown she falsely claimed meeting several prominent people.

Velazquez relocated to Sandy Station, which is twelve miles south of Salt Lake City and some fifteen miles west of Alta. The move to Sandy Station is an indication that her husband was still working in Little Cottonwood Canyon. Sandy Station would have been a convenient alternative to living in isolated Alta or distant Salt Lake City.

At Sandy Station she "boarded for several months in the house of Bishop Nilo Andrews." She misnamed the gentleman, but the error is minor considering the uniqueness of his name, Milo Andrus. She liked him well and said, "I never want to receive better hospitality than I did from him," and he was "about sixty years of age and was as hale and hearty as a man of thirty."[43] Of his children Velazquez wrote:

---

43. Milo Andrus was born in 1810 and died in 1893. Source: miloandrus.org.

The bishop was passionately fond of his children, and took the greatest pains to have them educated. His daughters he escorted to all public gatherings and entertainments that it was proper for them to attend, and did all in his power to make life enjoyable for them.

The Andrus Halfway House was built in 1859, on 160 acres, twelve miles south of Salt Lake City and half-way between two other inns (thus its name) on the same road in an area known by several names: Jordan Bottoms, Dry Creek, Crescent, Sandy Station and today, Sandy. The House was simultaneously "a comfortable and convenient two-story pioneer inn... and a residence for 120 years."[44] The Milo Andrus website (miloandrus.org) states, "The inn was built and run by Milos' third wife Lucy Loomis. Wives Adeline Alexander, Mary Webster, Jane Munday, Emma Covert and Francenia Tuttle and their children lived and worked there off and on as well." Velazquez said that she "was on very intimate terms with five of his six wives... they were all smart women." There were actually eleven wives, but the aforementioned wives were associated with the Halfway House. The house's original location[45] is identified by a historical marker provided by the Sons of Utah Pioneers, but the house itself was moved and is preserved at This is The Place Heritage Park in Salt Lake City.

Please see the photos of the Andrus Halfway House in Illustrations, Figures 17 and 18.

In a letter Velazquez later wrote to Mark Twain, she said she lived for 18 months among the Mormons, which probably included her stay in Sandy and all of the Salt Lake City vicinity. The dates which Velazquez moved to Sandy Station and resided there are undiscovered, but it is seen that both she and Bonner had at times mail arriving for them in Salt Lake City. E. H. Bonner had unclaimed mail at the Post Office in April 1872 and she had unclaimed mail in May 1872. Again E. H. Bonner had mail on September 7 and September 22, maybe the same letter.[46]

However, in the spring, Velazquez must have gone to San Francisco, at least for a short visit; her presence there is indicated by the *San Francisco Chronicle's* (May 28, 1872) posting of a list of unclaimed letters at the Post Office and found is "Bonner, L. J. Mrs."

It can be reasonably concluded that at some time while she was settled in Sandy Station, Mr. E. H. Bonner quit the Utah mines and went to New Mexico. At about this time Velazquez was a mother of a newborn, and she and the child would likely have remained behind until they were ready to travel. More will be said about this child.

---

44. Historical marker #26, Sons of Utah Pioneers.
45. Sandy, Utah at 10400 South State Street.
46. *Salt Lake Daily Herald:* Apr 20, 1872; May 18, 1872; Sep 15, 1872; Sep 22, 1872.

Velazquez's name, "Bonner, E. H.," is found in the Salt Lake City newspaper[47] which posted a "Ladies List" of unclaimed letters at the Post Office at Salt Lake City, September 27, 1872. This letter might have been from Mr. Bonner telling her to come to New Mexico now and she did. Five months later, the newspaper[48] again posted her name in a Ladies List of letters, but she likely did not retrieve this letter as she had already left the Salt Lake area, as evidence presented shortly will show.

The *Deseret News* of May 21, 1873, listed a letter to "Bonner, E. H., Fort Barnard [*sic* Bayard, which was just outside of Silver City], New Mexico," which was "Held for Postage." Velazquez might be suspected the writer because of the misspelling of Fort Bayard which is suggestive of other misspellings routinely made by her. However, the date of the newspaper notice is too late to be convincing evidence, since she had left the area much earlier. It seems this letter was from a friend.

Silver City, One Stays and One Goes

In the closing pages of *The Woman in Battle*, Velazquez narrated in good detail her travels through Colorado, New Mexico and Texas. She, with her son in her arms, who she only now revealed- "born during my sojourn in Salt Lake City"- undertook the trip. However, a letter dated January 5, 1875, from a miner named Adam A. Wilson in Salt Lake City, to an Atlanta newspaper stated, "She left here [Salt Lake City] about eighteen months ago with a Jew for San Francisco, intending to marry him," which would have made her departure (if true) for that city about July 1873. Wilson's letter will be presented further along, but his accusation will be examined now.

At this time the San Francisco *Daily Alta California* posted the names of railroad passengers arriving from the east (Salt Lake City). No Mrs. E. H. Bonner or Mrs. L. J. Bonner or name variant is found.[49] Admittedly, if she traveled under her unknown alleged boyfriend's surname, she can't be identified. In addition, hotel arrivals for San Francisco were posted daily in the *Chronicle* and she is not found.

The only near name is "Mrs. J. H. Bonner" and she is found arriving by train on September 7, 1873.[50] This same woman is noted checking into the Cosmopolitan Hotel on September 7 under "Mrs. Bonner, [from]

---

47. *Deseret News*, Oct 2, 1872.
48. Ibid, Mar 26, 1873, letters "remaining in the Post Office at Salt Lake City, March 21, 1873."
49. The "Overland Travel" section of the *Daily Alta California* was carefully examined for dates Apr 1, 1873 to Jan 31, 1874. The search was expanded, covering dates Nov 14, 1871 to Apr 23, 1873, by using the index book, *Railway Passengers List of Overland Trains to San Francisco and the West* by Louis J. Rasmussen, Vol II.
50. *Daily Alta California*, Sep 7, 1873.

Cedarville."[51] Earlier in the year, on May 27, this same "Mrs. J. H. Bonner" had checked into the Cosmopolitan Hotel and was noted from "Sonoma," which also could be construed as the place travelling from, not living.[52] The day before, May 26, "Mr. J. H. Bonner, Cedarville" had checked into the same hotel.[53] Were these two meeting there? Yes. The man was John Heath Bonner, who co-founded the town of Cedarville in Surprise Valley, California in 1867. In 1870, he married Emeline Claflin, now "Mrs. J. H. Bonner."[54] Clearly this wasn't Velazquez.

To date, no convincing evidence shows Velazquez running away with "a Jew to San Francisco." Of course, she and the boyfriend might have fallen out before they left Salt Lake City or during the trip and she just turned around, never arriving in San Francisco. Or she went under a different name. Adam Wilson might have been wrong on this specific, but as will be seen, he was right- Velazquez did run away, in the opposite direction, and in short order married a stagecoach driver in Texas.

Velazquez narrated the progress of her travels to Denver, then Pueblo, then Trinidad and of her visit to the Stockton Ranch, the owner of which she said (p598) was a rough character, "with a fierce black eye," and a bad reputation. In that locale she also correctly identified the Maxwell Ranch of which "Maxwell is the wealthiest American in Southern Colorado" and who married "a Mexican woman, who inherited an extensive Spanish grant." All is true and an interesting history, and a credit to Velazquez's keen talent for gathering facts. Velazquez explained while there, Mr. Stockton had a disagreement with Maxwell's men over some cattle. Velazquez presciently touched on the issue of cattle ownership and as history shows this section of the country later erupted in infamous cattle wars.

From there she went to Dry Cimarron, New Mexico and sixty miles further south to Fort Union, then to Santa Fe. "It was the month of November" that her "little party" of travelers left Santa Fe (*TWIB*, p602). The year was 1872, based on evidence presented next. She said that she went off the normal path to visit Silver City, New Mexico. Velazquez wrote (p604) that she took a look at Silver City and the surroundings with staying in mind. (She never hinted about staying at any other place in this journey.) She gave a favorable enough description of the area and supposed it had a future, but stated, "This country, however, did not hold out any great inducement for me at the time of my visit, and after taking a look at it, I turned back...."

Velazquez did not explain to her readers the true reason for her visit to Silver City, which was, her husband was working in the local mining district.

---

51. *San Francisco Chronicle*, Sep 8, 1873.
52. Ibid, May 28, 1873.
53. Ibid, May 27, 1873.
54. www.findagrave.com.

She made no mention of his existence there. There was more to her Silver City visit than she admitted and she took more than a brief look at Silver City, as she claimed. She and her husband assumed the management of a Silver City hotel, at least by the last week of January 1873. "A fine supper was prepared by Mr. Bonner of the Keystone House" for the "fine ball" at Porter Hall "last week" which was hosted by the mechanics of Silver City.[55] The first advertisement for the Bonner's enterprise appeared in the February 7, 1873 Santa Fe *Daily New Mexican:*

Keystone House, by Mr. & Mrs. E. H. BONNER, SILVER CITY, NEW MEXICO. The above named house is prepared to accommodate travelers and regular boarders with the best the market affords; in the line of a first-class hotel. Charges moderate and the comfort of guest cared for.   11-tf

At the bottom of the advertisement was a printer's note, "11-tf," which meant 11 times "till forbid" or until stopped; the ad ran until March 14. It seems that the Bonners only leased (or managed) the Keystone from Thomas Bull because it was recorded that Thomas Bull sold the Keystone to Enos S. Culver on April 5, 1873.[56] By May 17 Joseph Yankie advertised as the proprietor of the Keystone.[57] Then on August 12 Floyd Higgins advertised as the proprietor and by September 20, 1873 Peter Ott advertised as the proprietor of the Keystone.[58] Considering that no one kept the Keystone very long, it is not surprising the Bonners did not stick with it either.

Velazquez probably stayed in Silver City for seven months, sometime between November 1872 and November 1873. She, at a later date, wrote to Mark Twain and asserted she had resided among the Apache for seven months. The Apache lived in New Mexico, as well as other areas. Upon her departure from Silver City, she went to El Paso and struck out due east, across Texas, where she married again in February 1874, then abandoned him, and was next noted on August 25, 1874 in Mobile, Alabama.

Mr. E. H. Bonner stayed many years in Silver City. He was elected the Justice of the Peace for Precinct No. 1, Lone Mountain area, from at least October 1873 to September 1874. Generally, justices were people who the community held in high regard for their trustworthiness; legal training was not a prerequisite. It can be supposed that Bonner fit into this mold. Recall that in 1863 Bonner was given the job of mining claims recorder in Austin, also a position of trust. In that position his good education was evident and

---

55. *Borderer* (Las Cruces, New Mexico), Feb 1, 1873.
56. Payable in two promissory notes for a total of $1031.59 to be paid on 3 August 1873 and 3 February 1874. Source- Silver City, Clerk of Court, Book 1, p333.
57. *Mining Life* (Silver City, NM), May 17 and 24, 1873.
58. Ibid, Aug 3, 1873; *Tribune* (Silver City, NM), Sep 20, 1873.

this fact is further validated by the quality of his justice of the peace paperwork.

One might speculate that Bonner had an abundance of integrity which was what drove him to seek the office of Justice of the Peace. Could Velazquez's seeming lack of honesty and truthfulness have been a point of contention, damaging the marriage? In any case, she left and he stayed.

Bonner's mining activities were often mentioned in the local newspapers:[59] "The mines of Lone Mountain District are being vigorously worked ... Warren and Bonner are working on the Bismarck lode which has an excellent appearance."

Some thirteen years after Bonner was first noted at Lone Mountain, he was still at it, reported the newspaper:

> E. H. Bonner, on Lone Mountain, has again made a rich strike in his Treasure Mine. Some new development has exposed a four-foot vein of pay quartz, six inches of which will assay about $1,000. As yet the development is not sufficient to judge the extensiveness of the strike. It was from this mine that Bonner and O'Brien took out several thousand dollars of high-grade ore last spring. It looks now as if the old gentleman has encountered a similar pocket.[60]

By 1886, Bonner was indeed an "old gentleman." He was sixty years old, an advanced age for pick and shovel work, but he was obviously still "Hardy."

The newspaper, in a follow-up, reported, "E. H. Bonner came in from Lone Mountain this week. He reports that the body of rich ore upon which he is working still holds out."[61] This surely put some money in his account, but he was not motivated to retire. The newspaper of January 3, 1890 reported the "Bonner and O'Brien" team still working "on the Lone Mountain Mine." Through the years Bonner owned other mines, in part or whole: the Black Diamond Treasure, the Miami and another mine two miles east of Fleming. Besides O'Brien, Bonner also partnered with miners: Campbell, Holson and O'Neill.[62] It was reported that Bonner and Howard were working the Copper Point mine in Lone Mountain and it was turning out 60 ounces of silver per ton and 5 per cent copper.[63]

Bonner was held in good esteem by his fellow citizens. "Mr. Bonner of Lone Mountain" was among three people nominated for the "election of a temporary chairman" at the county Democrat convention.[64] It appears that

---

59. *Tribune* (Silver City), Sep 6, 1873.
60. *Silver City Enterprise*, Nov 26, 1886.
61. Ibid, Dec 17, 1886.
62. Ibid, Apr 11, 1884, Jul 18, 1884, Aug 29, 1884, Jan 3, 1890.
63. *New Mexican* (Santa Fe), May 5, 1897.
64. *Southwest Sentinel*, Oct 11, 1892.

Bonner withdrew his name for consideration and the assembled delegates elected one of the two other selected nominees.

No evidence reconnects Velazquez with Bonner after she left him. She was finished with him in her own mind, evinced by her next marriage to one A. J. Bobo a stagecoach driver in Texas only months after leaving Bonner. Detractor Adam Wilson claimed that Mrs. Bonner divorced E. H. Bonner in Salt Lake City, but no divorce decree, to date, has been found. Publically, Velazquez wasn't finished with Bonner and she claimed to the newspaper on September 7, 1874, and after, and while married to Bobo, that she was married to Bonner and he was mining in New Mexico.

Edward H. Bonner was still in Silver City, New Mexico in 1900 according to the U.S. Census and living in John E. Coleman's household. Bonner was listed as a Mississippi-born 74-year-old miner (born May 1826) and a boarder, and most curiously, he was listed as <u>widowed</u>. However, five years earlier the 1885 Territorial Census listed him as <u>single</u>, living and working as a miner at Lone Mountain. And five years earlier the 1880 U.S. Census listed 52-year-old E. H. Bonner as <u>married</u>. One might conjecture that Bonner still considered himself married in 1880, but by 1885 his wife had not returned and he considered himself single. By 1900, after no longer hearing from her, Bonner believed Velazquez was dead and he therefore called himself widowed. Or did Velazquez forge some kind of death announcement and send it to him? Such a deception would have been in the realm of possible for Velazquez, as has been seen in the case of the false death announcements of her "father" and "brother."

One should interpret Bonner's 1880 Census "married" status to mean that he and Velazquez did not divorce in Salt Lake City, as alleged by Adam A. Wilson. It was not likely that Bonner married another woman by 1880 considering the scarcity of women in the mining towns, not to mention that Bonner was described as a "very quiet, modest miner." No named wife was listed in the Census and no record of him remarrying was found. It is unlikely that Bonner ever divorced Velazquez or vice-versa.

Edward Hardy Bonner ended his days in Silver City. His obituary appeared in the Silver City *Enterprise* of May 4, 1906, a Friday:

> Death of Old Time Residents- E. H. Bonner, one of the old time residents of Silver City, died at the Sisters' Hospital last Sunday [April 29], aged seventy-five years. The funeral was held Monday afternoon with interment in the city cemetery.
>
> Mr. Bonner came to Grant County thirty-three years ago and has lived in this vicinity ever since. For a time he was proprietor of the Tremont House, one of the historic hotels of Silver City and which was destroyed by flood waters a few years ago. Mining and prospecting was his occupation, and for a long time he made his headquarters with John Coleman at the Coleman ranch three miles east of the city. Deceased has been in ill health for a number of years, and death came as a relief to the pain-racked body.

It is clear that John Coleman's ranch is the same location where Bonner was found living during the 1900 Census.

Bonner's proprietorship of the Tremont House probably was stimulated by his earlier interest in the Keystone House. The noted flood (Sunday, July 21, 1895) was caused by a heavy rain which funneled into the valley, occupied by Silver City. The ensuing flash flood carried great boulders and mud, destroyed the railroad tracks and telegraph poles. Buildings were damaged or destroyed and many fine possessions were washed away. "The big safe at the postoffice... which weighed more than a ton... was carried several hundred feet...." The Tremont's first floor was "covered to a depth of more than three feet with water. The people in the hotel thought the "entire building would be washed down" and them with it. There were no deaths.[65]

A brief follow-up newspaper article[66] corrected Bonner's misstated age, "Mr. Bonner would have been 79 years old the 10th of May, had he lived. Two brothers living in Mississippi are known to survive him."

The fact that Bonner had two surviving brothers in Mississippi, facilitate a genealogical tracing of E. H.'s likely parents and siblings. His father was a farmer of considerable wealth in Lawrence County and the two mentioned surviving brothers were Franklin P. and John, who, as well, became farmers in Lawrence County. E. H. Bonner had at least four other brothers and a sister. One brother, five years younger, became a doctor and all the siblings attended school in their teenage years.[67] The propensity of this family to educate its children explains the education evident in E. H. Bonner's positions as mining recorder and justice of the peace.

The question was previously raised whether Bonner and Velazquez knew one another in Mississippi prior to their Nevada marriage? Recall, Velazquez ostensibly had some connection to northern Mississippi counties during her youth, but Lawrence County is located far in the southern part of the State, so the great distance would have been an obstacle to a prior meeting. More significant would have been their age difference. It is clear that Bonner had already left the Mississippi home place by 1850 at about age 24, when Velazquez would have still been a child. They likely never met in Mississippi.

Bonner was buried in Section E of Memory Lane Cemetery on Monday April 30, 1906. No gravestone marks his grave, so its exact location is unknown.[68]

---

65. *Eagle* (Silver City), Jul 24 & 31, 1895.
66. *Enterprise*, May 18, 1906.
67. U.S. Censuses 1840, 1850, 1860, 1870, 1880, 1900.
68. Silver City, City Hall, Utilities Billing Office, 101 W. Broadway, is custodian of cemetery records and has erroneously recorded Bonner's burial as May 29, 1908.

That Stagecoach Driver

Velazquez ended her book with a section titled The Stage Route Across Texas, which is a picturesque progress report of her trip, but there's one detail she failed to tell- she married the stagecoach driver!

The last Texas settlement Velazquez mentioned was Fort Stockton and it was probably in this vicinity she made the acquaintance of Andrew Jackson Bobo, an Alabama-born, ex-Confederate soldier. During the War his duty was teamster (wagon driver) at the rank of private. A newspaper said he fought and received wounds at both Shiloh and Nashville. He was captured in August 1864, near Atlanta, sent to Camp Chase Prison and paroled in March 1865.[69] He was described as "jovial" and was no doubt well regarded as an experienced, responsible driver in the challenging, and many times, dangerous stage operation.[70]

On one occasion, about the first day of June 1870, near Fort Stockton, Bobo's stagecoach was stopped by twenty-five Comanches. On board was Mr. James D. Spears, agent for the El Paso Mail Company, who reacted sharply with his Winchester rifle, felling three Indians immediately. The Indians commenced at full gallop encircling the stage. A "gigantic Indian, bolder than the rest," was killed next by Spears with two shots. "Meanwhile, another dashing brave, riding at full speed upon a superb white horse was shot by Bobo, who fired his carbine with his right hand, while holding the whip and reins in his left." One of the bullets fired by the Indians hit one of the stage mules, frightening the team which broke into a run. Bobo stopped the team on a little elevation where they readied themselves for more fighting. A seven-years-later version said the mules ran back to the station. In any case, the Indians quit the pursuit. The agent and Bobo were reported to have killed nine Indians. The later version said five Indians were killed, four wounded, all removed by their comrades; two of their horses were killed and five crippled. The bleached bones of the killed horses could still be seen on the trail seven years after the 1870 incident and Bobo was still driving stages past the scene.[71] Velazquez possibly passed these bones.

Velazquez and Bobo likely made their acquaintance in December 1873 or January 1874. She proceeded south to Galveston, possibly thinking to take a coastal steamer to New Orleans, and Bobo stayed at his job. It seems that Bobo subsequently wrote her stating his interest. "Wasson L J mrs" had a letter at the Galveston Post Office awaiting pick up for the week ending

---

69. *Galveston Weekly News*, May 28, 1877; NARA, CMSR for Andrew J. Bobo.
70. *Galveston Weekly News*, May 28, 1877.
71. Ibid, May 28, 1877, asserted twenty-six Indians. The New Orleans *Daily Picayune*, June 22, 1870, stated, "A letter from Fort Mason (some 110 miles NW of San Antonio) dated the 8th inst., in the San Antonio *Herald*, says: 'About a week ago, the El Paso stage was attacked... the agent and driver killed nine Indians.'"

January 31, 1874.[72] This letter was surely from Bobo; who else would have written her a letter using her Wasson name? To state the obvious, Velazquez was at this time Mrs. E. H. Bonner. She had abandoned Bonner's name and used Wasson, her previous married name, maybe to evade Bonner's possible pursuit. Of course, Bonner knew her previous married name, so that would seem ineffective. One can only imagine her intention and it's beyond imagination what story she fabricated for Bobo's benefit, but she probably claimed she was Wasson's widow which would have been a truth of sorts.

Mrs. Wasson was not yet in Galveston to pick up the letter, but was probably spending time in Austin or Houston. She arrived in Galveston on February 11 and registered at the Cosmopolitan Hotel as "Mrs. Wasson and son, Jackson, Miss."[73] It is curious that Velazquez claimed she was from Jackson, Mississippi when she never in her memoir claimed to have lived there or been born there. Jackson is just 65 miles north of Lawrence County where Bonner's family resided. Recall, about five years earlier she was called "a native Mississippian" by the Order of Odd Fellows in San Francisco.

Upon retrieving the letter awaiting her, she responded by writing a letter to "A. J. Bobo" at Galveston.[74] She expected he would check at the Post Office for something from her stating her whereabouts. But she worried that Bobo would miss her letter, so on February 19 she placed a newspaper ad to help him find her in Galveston, "Mr. A. J. Bobo will please call at (attorneys) Tucker & Campbell's office, Number 122 Postoffice street, and inquire for Mrs. Wasson."[75] Velazquez bought only one ad, indicated by "1t" at the foot of the ad, which indicates she anticipated Bobo's arrival, no doubt knowledge she gained from his letter.

Bobo must have arrived in Galveston the same day she placed the ad, maybe before it was printed, and found the letter awaiting him. They immediately departed because two days after the ad, February 21, they are found 110 miles away in Hempstead, Texas, northwest of Houston, where they married.

The marriage license/certificate states that Mrs. Loretta J. Wasson was thirty-one years of age which corresponds to the claimed date of birth in her book. It might be remembered that she was "Lauretta" when she married Wasson and she was "Lauretta" when she married Bonner, but now Loretta. Curiously, she said she was "of Galveston" which was slightly correct and as good a place as any from which to be. Bobo said he was thirty and "of

---

72. *Galveston Daily News*, Feb 1, 1874.
73. Ibid, Feb 12, 1874.
74. Ibid, Feb 22, 1874.
75. Ibid, Feb 19, 1874.

Concho." The ceremony was conducted by Justice of the Peace J. H. Adams.[76]

Why they married in Hempstead is undiscovered. They could have been en route to Concho, Texas, Bobo's home, and decided they could not wait or did not want to travel the distance. Two days after the ceremony they ostensibly returned to Galveston, possibly to retrieve luggage she had left there or maybe Velazquez liked Galveston for a honeymoon. They stayed at the Cosmopolitan Hotel and were noted in the local newspaper's "Arrivals" at hotels, as "A. G. Bobo, lady and child, Austin."[77]

Bobo, Velazquez and her child by E. H. Bonner surely set up house, though no records were located saying so, but their domestic bliss was short-lived. Who cried uncle first is unknown, but it can be guessed Velazquez gave it up. She had goals in mind other than being a housewife, living in the boondocks; she had already done that with Bonner. Besides she had probably gotten all she was going to get out of Bobo.

After they separated, A. J. Bobo continued to drive the stage (as noted in 1877) and he later remarried in October 1878 to Lee Anna from Collier County, Texas, seven years his junior and they produced a houseful of kids, three daughters and four sons, all living in 1900. Forever the Southerner, Bobo named his oldest son after Robert E. Lee and his fourth son after Jefferson Davis.

---

76. Marriage records of Waller County, Clerk of the Court, Hempstead, Texas.
77. *Galveston Daily News*, Feb 24, 1874. The "G" must be an error for "J." It is not clear why "Austin" was the place claimed as residence or place traveling from, as was typical of those entries. Austin is 110 miles NW from Hempstead on the road to Fort Concho, Texas, which is 203 miles further still to the NW. Fort Concho's location is in San Angelo.

Illustrations

Figure 1. Velazquez in male military attire and female attire as presented in her memoir.

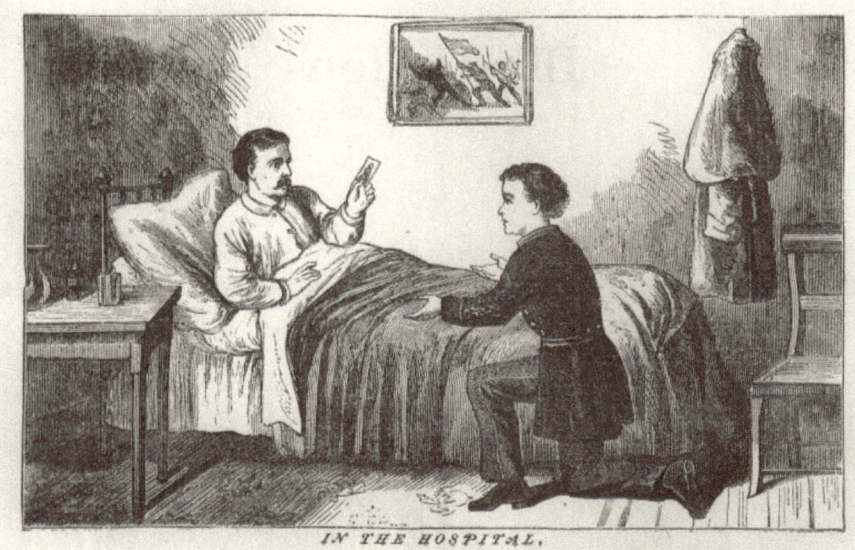

Figure 2. Velazquez narrated in *The Woman in Battle* (pages 327-337) how her husband-to-be, Captain Thomas DeCaulp, did not recognize her in her male military disguise.
What has become of her infamous mustache and goatee?
Illustration from *TWIB*

Figure 3. Velazquez narrated in *The Woman in Battle* (pages 260-263) how she won a "contest of wits" against General Butler.
Illustration from *TWIB*

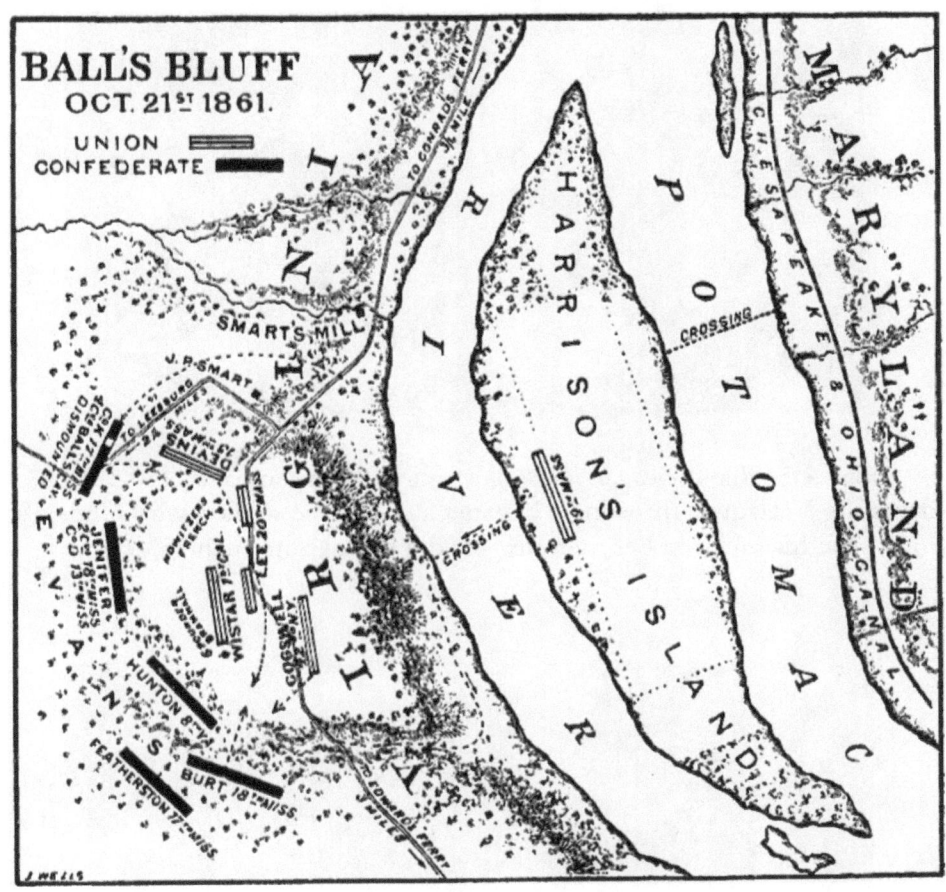

Figure 4. Map of the Battle of Ball's Bluff, October 21, 1861.
West (Virginia) channel is about 280 feet wide,
east (Maryland) channel about 670 feet wide.
Source: *Battles and Leaders of the Civil War, Volume Two*
edited by R. U. Johnson and C. C. Buel, illustration by J. Wells,
published 1884, page 126.

Figure 5. *The Woman in Battle* illustration (between pages 130-131) depicting Velazquez thrusting a bayonet at a Yankee soldier, who fends off with his saber; in her memoir, she did not narrate such an event.

Figure 6. Velazquez narrated in *The Woman in Battle* (pages 225-226) one of her several versions of her battlefield injuries.
Illustration from *TWIB*

281

"Register Battle House," cover of guest register book

First page of guest register, "Battle House, Mobile, Ala[bama], Confederate States of America"

The words "Constantinople" and "Constantinople Circumstances" must have been a clerk's humor referring to the several sieges of Constantinople during the Byzantine Empire. Mobile, in 1863, was under a Federal naval blockade, a siege of a sort.

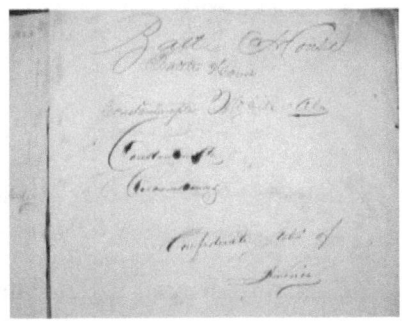

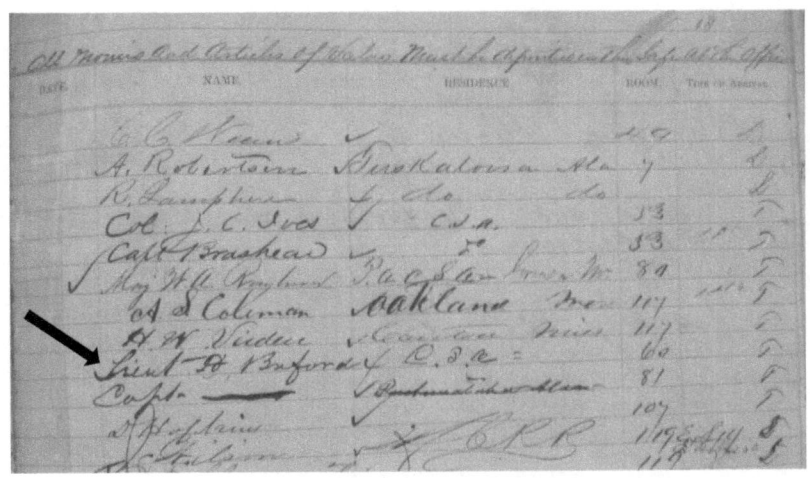

Figure 7. "Lieut. H. Buford CSA" registered at the Battle House, Friday, June 26, 1863. She was given room 60.
Source: A. S. Williams III Americana Collection, Amelia Gayle Gorgas Library,
University of Alabama, Tuscaloosa, Alabama.

Confederate Castle Thunder Prison, Carey Street view, 1865, (Richmond, Virginia), where Velazquez was imprisoned for about ten days in 1863. Source: Courtesy Library of Congress.

Figure 8. Commander of Castle Thunder, G. W. Alexander. Velazquez said he and "his lovely wife" treated her "with such kindness and consideration that [Velazquez] was induced to tell them exactly who [she] was, what [her] purposes were in assuming the male garb, what adventures [she] had passed through, and what [her] aspirations were for the future."

St. Cloud Hotel in Nashville, Tennessee
where Velazquez was held under suspicion in July 1864.
Source: 1860 engraving by M. Bosse, Tennessee State Library and
Archives Dwr 18, Flr 50, Img ID 3532.

Office of Military Prison
Nashville, Tenn., August 1st *1864*

Captain S. A. Stockdale
Dear Sir
You will pleas [sic] to give me a hearing to day as I am desireous [sic] of knowing what they have me hear [sic here] for, keeping from my buisness [sic] and withall my bagage [sic] and keeping me in this miserable place. it is not fit for any Lady. thrown among all kind of low people. it is not any place for a man wife. if they have any respect for a lady...

Figure 9. Velazquez's letter asking for release from her confinement at St. Cloud Hotel, "this miserable place. it is not fit for any Lady."

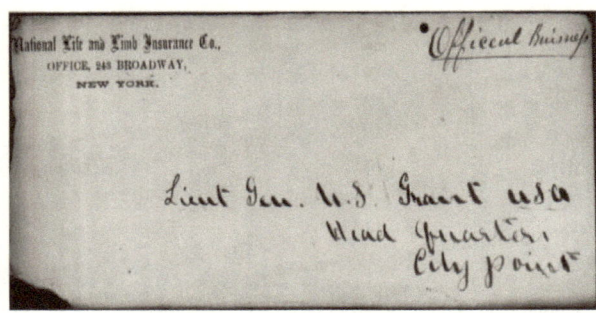

Envelope found in Velazquez's possession.
Compare this handwriting to that in the forged letter.

Figure 10. General Milo S. Hascall and his true signature. Compare this to the forged "M. D. Hascall" signature. Image courtesy of Steve Meadow

The last few sentences of the forged letter by "M. D. Hascall."

...will call to
your notice he has family
the daughter of
Rear Admiral
Rosche Eng [English] Navy
is his wife. who deserves great
credit from the patriot
in the feild [sic field]. Please feel for
her situation which she
will Explain to your Entire
satisfaction. any kindness
shown them will be
highly appreciated by
  Yours Truly
  M. D. Hascall
  Col q m 2nd Div 23 ac

YOUNG CONFEDERATE WIDOW WHO WAS A MESSENGER FOR THE
ST. ALBAN'S RAIDERS IN GETTING THE PROPER PAPERS
FROM THE CONFEDERATE GOVERNMENT

Figure 11. This image has been suspected to be that of Loreta Janeta Velazquez. However, if the alleged circumstances surrounding the acquisition of the photo are true, the photo cannot be Velazquez.

In 1906 ex-Confederate operative, John W. Headley, wrote about his participation in northern Confederate activities. In his book, *Confederate Operations in Canada and New York*, on page 376, he addressed the female messenger who helped the St. Alban's Raiders and included this photo which supposedly had been acquired by one of the raiders. Neither Headley nor the raiders could recall the woman's name.

One researcher on women in the Civil War, Richard H. Hall, thought there was a "striking resemblance" between the woman in the photo and the illustration of Velazquez from her book. He compared them side-by-side in his book, *Patriots in Disguise, Women Warriors of the Civil War* (1993). When Mr. Hall published a second book in 2006, entitled *Women on the Civil War Battlefront*, he again wrote of "the discovery of an apparent photograph of her during a trip to Canada in which she was helping Confederate soldiers who were prisoners there."

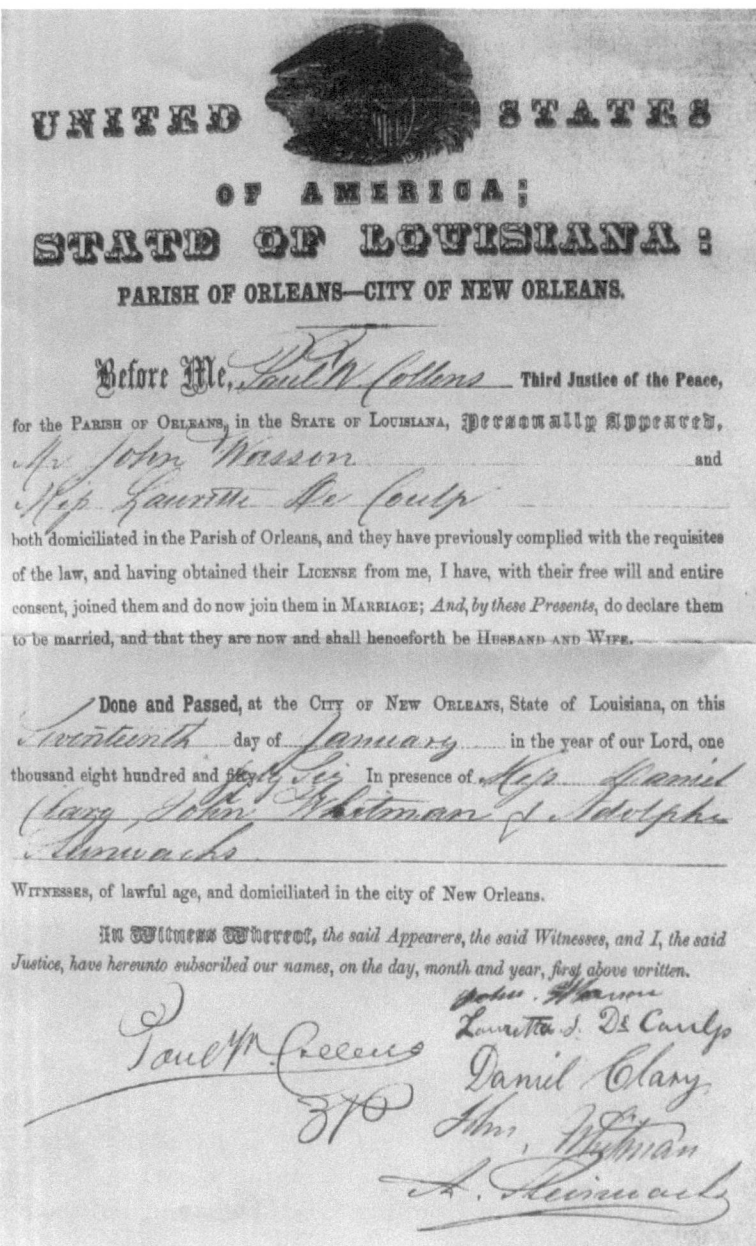

Figure 12. Marriage Certificate, John Wasson and "Miss Laurette (and Lauretta) De Caulp," January 17, 1867.

Figure 13. General William Selby Harney

Velazquez asserted that he said to her, "Remember the advice of your best friend. I only wish I was thirty-five years younger; you should not make this journey alone." Velazquez wrote, "This was so flattering that I could not help permitting my wishes to run in the same channel."
Photo taken by Brady & Company (Washington D.C.) between 1860 and 1870, Repository: LOC Prints and Photographs Division.

International Hotel, circa late 1880's
The original structure, located in Virginia City, was dismantled and moved to Austin, Nevada in 1863.
Courtesy of Austin Museum

Figure 14. International Café and Bar, March 2014
Photo by author

Austin, Nevada, circa 1870
Looking north across the canyon to Lander Hill.
Source: *History of Nevada*, Thompson & West, 1881.

Figure 15. Austin, Nevada, March 2014
Looking north across the canyon to Lander Hill.
Photo by author

Alta, Utah, year 1873
Right side: Drug Store, California Brewery, Grand Hotel, Restaurante.
Left side: Sam Gee Washing & Ironing, Miners Restaurant.
Photo by C. R. Savage, Courtesy of Utah State Historical Society

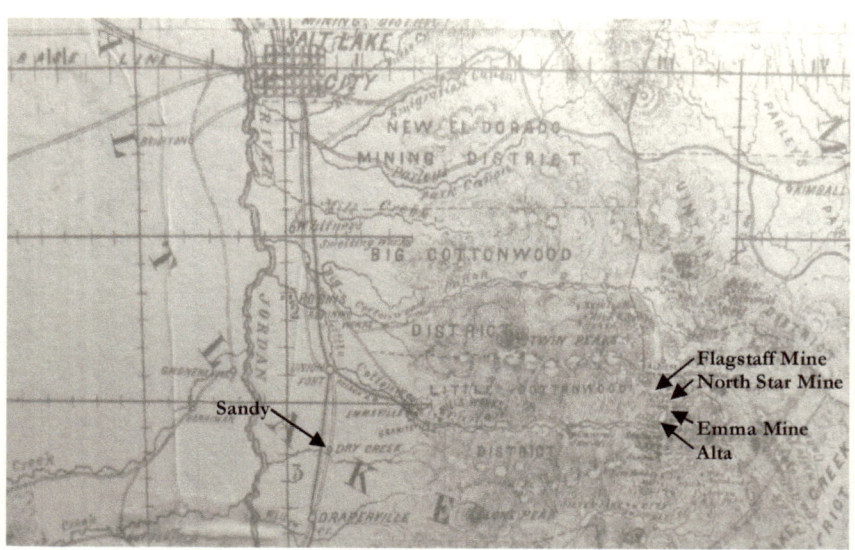

Figure 16. Mining Map of Utah
by R. A. M. Froiseth aided by H. R. Durkee, Salt Lake City, 1871

Andrus Halfway House
The house was originally situated on 160 acres in present day Sandy, Utah, half-way between two other inns on the well-traveled road. A historical marker at the South Towne Center, 10330 South State Street marks the spot. Photo of unknown date from This is The Place Heritage Park.

Figure 17. Andrus Halfway House
Relocated to This is the Place Heritage Park.
Photo by author, March 2014

Andrus Halfway House dining room
where Velazquez dined. Furnishings are not original to the house.
Photos by author, March 2014

Figure 18. Andrus Halfway House bedroom
One of two identical, upstairs, front-facing, two-window bedrooms.
A third upstairs bedroom is smaller and has only one side-facing
window. A front-facing room likely would have been Velazquez's first
choice. The owner's bedroom was downstairs and larger.

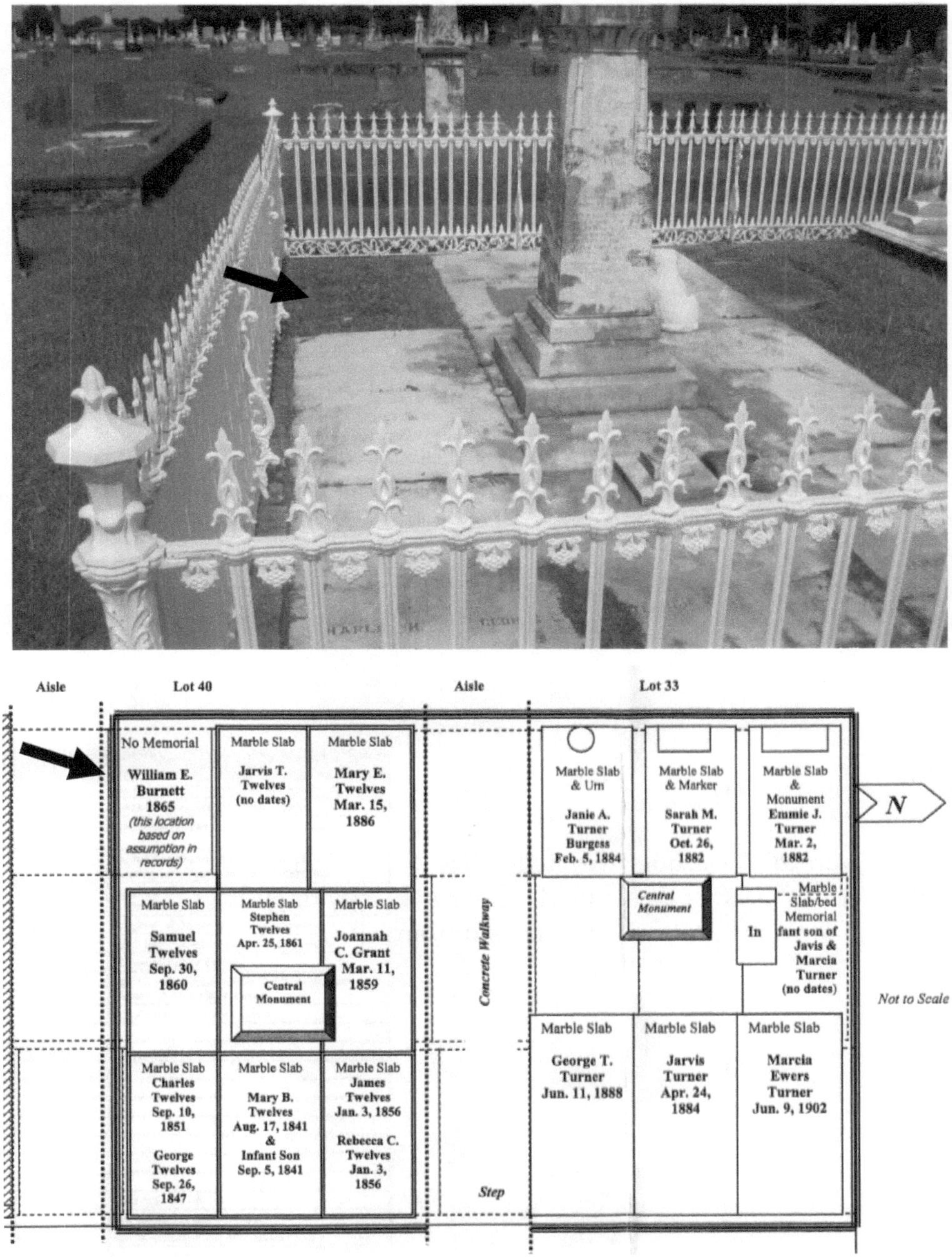

293

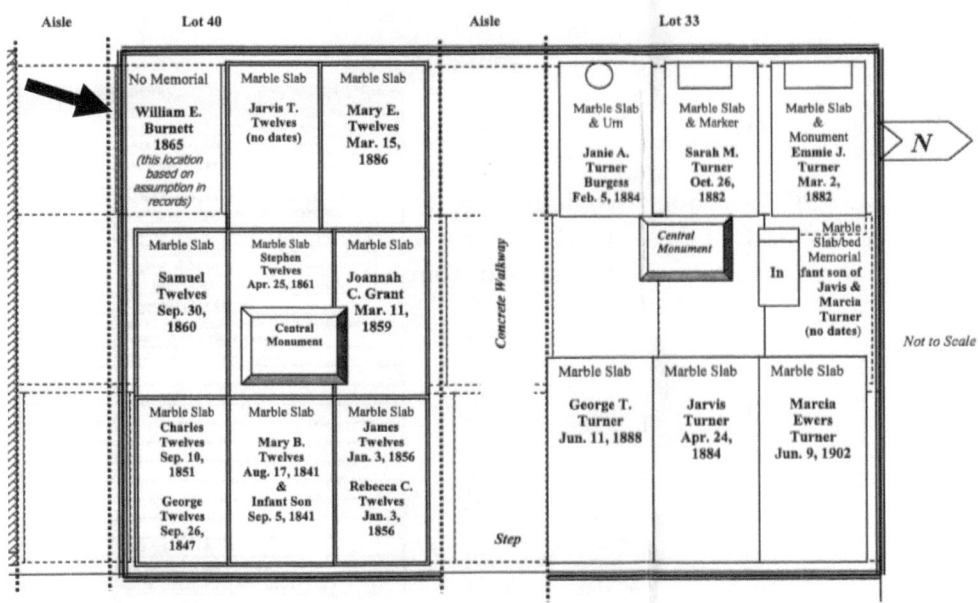

Figure 19. William E. Burnet's grave, Magnolia Cemetery, Mobile, Alabama.

Sources: Photo by author, diagram by H. F. Marston, Sexton of Magnolia Cemetery.

Figure 20. Velazquez narrated in *The Woman in Battle* (pages 56-68) her first day in public in male military disguise.
Illustration from *TWIB*

THE NATIONAL POLICE GAZETTE: NEW YORK.

MRS. GODDARD EXPLAINS

SHE CHASES HER RECREANT HUSBAND INTO A NEW YORK BARBER SHOP AND THERE GIVES HIM A PIECE OF HER MIND

Figure 21. Source: *National Police Gazette*, (New York, N. Y.), May 15, 1886, Xerox University Microfilms, 1973.

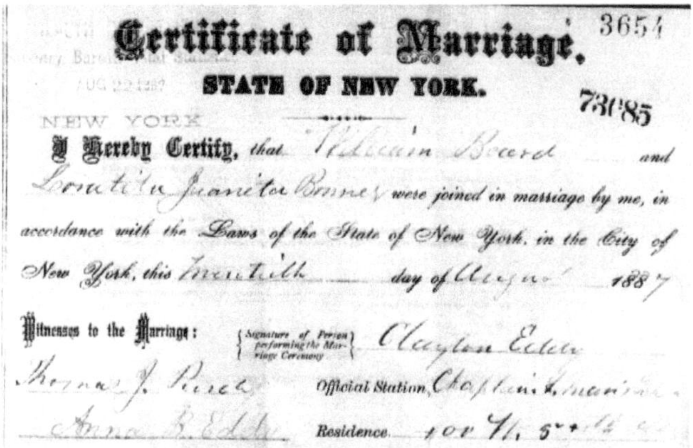

3654

Certificate of Marriage.

STATE OF NEW YORK.

73085

NEW YORK

I Hereby Certify, that William Beard and Loratita Juanita Bonner were joined in marriage by me, in accordance with the Laws of the State of New York, in the City of New York, this Twentieth day of August 1887

Witnesses to the Marriage: {Signature of Person performing the Marriage Ceremony} Clayton Eddy

Thomas J. Pierce Official Station, Chaplain

Anna R. Eddy Residence 100 W. 5

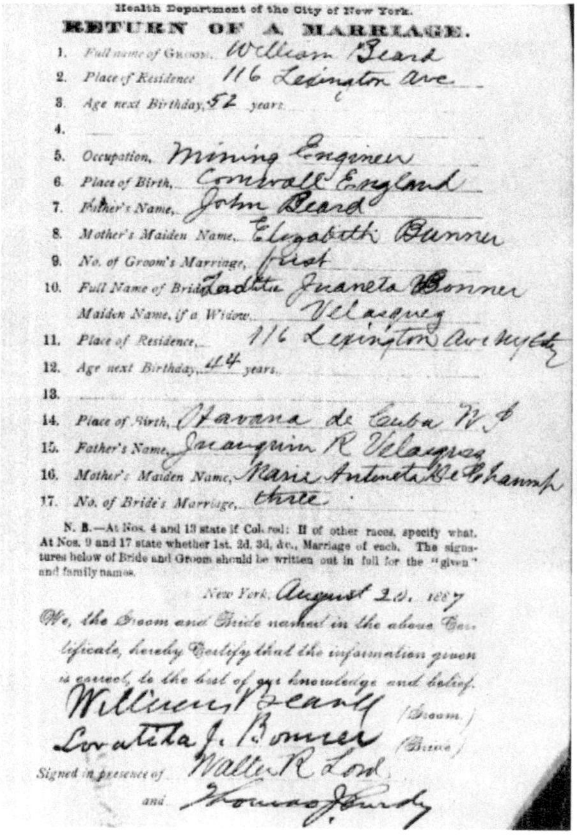

Health Department of the City of New York.

RETURN OF A MARRIAGE.

1. Full name of Groom, William Beard
2. Place of Residence 116 Lexington Ave
3. Age next Birthday, 52 years
4.
5. Occupation, Mining Engineer
6. Place of Birth, Cornwall England
7. Father's Name, John Beard
8. Mother's Maiden Name, Elizabeth Banner
9. No. of Groom's Marriage, first
10. Full Name of Bride Loratita Juaneta Bonner
    Maiden Name, if a Widow, Velasquez
11. Place of Residence, 116 Lexington Ave N.Y. City
12. Age next Birthday, 44 years
13.
14. Place of Birth, Havana de Cuba W.I.
15. Father's Name, Joaquin R Velasquez
16. Mother's Maiden Name, Marie Antonieta De Champ
17. No. of Bride's Marriage, three

N. B.—At Nos. 4 and 13 state if Colored: If of other races, specify what. At Nos. 9 and 17 state whether 1st, 2d, 3d, &c., Marriage of each. The signatures below of Bride and Groom should be written out in full for the "given" and family names.

New York, August 20, 1887

We, the Groom and Bride named in the above Certificate, hereby Certify that the information given is correct, to the best of our knowledge and belief.

William Beard (Groom.)

Loratita J. Bonner (Bride.)

Signed in presence of Walter R Lord

and Thomas J Purdy

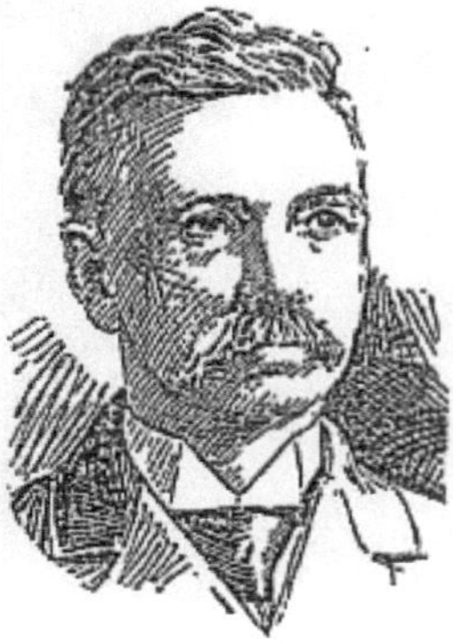

PROFESSOR WILLIAM BEARD.

Figure 22. Certificate of Marriage and Return of a Marriage, William Beard and Loratita Juanita (and Juaneta) Bonner, August 20, 1887. Source: New York City Archives.

Washington, D.C. Police Officer William E. Owens, on or about July 26, 1912, ostensibly arrested Mrs. Beard (Velazquez) which led to her lunatic inquiry. Source: NARA, RG 351, Records of the District of Columbia, Metropolitan Police, Personnel case files, entry 119.

Figure 23. Velazquez was admitted to St. Elizabeth's Hospital for the insane on August 5, 1912 and remained there until her death on January 6, 1923. Source: Center Building at Saint Elizabeth's in Washington, D.C., photo No. 841 by the National Photo Company, taken between 1909 and 1932. LOC, Call Number/Physical Location LOT 12359-10A [P&P], Digital Id cph 3c04691, Library of Congress Control Number 92501098, Reproduction Number LC-USZ62-104691.

ORDER OF THE COURT.

Upon consideration of the foregoing petition...., it is, by the Court, this..22......... day of ..August..................., A. D. 1912..

Ordered, That the rule to show cause why the above-mentioned .Loretta J. Beard.. should not be adjudged to be of unsound mind issue, returnable on the ..29th.. day of ..August............, A. D. 1912., at....10:30..... o'clock, .A.... M.

It is Further Ordered, That the United States Marshal for the District of Columbia summon a jury of twelve good and lawful men of this District, according to the statute in such case made and provided, to appear in this Court at the above-mentioned date and hour to inquire into the mental condition of the aforesaid person.

.........Ashley M Gould...........
Justice.

Figure 24. Order of the Court

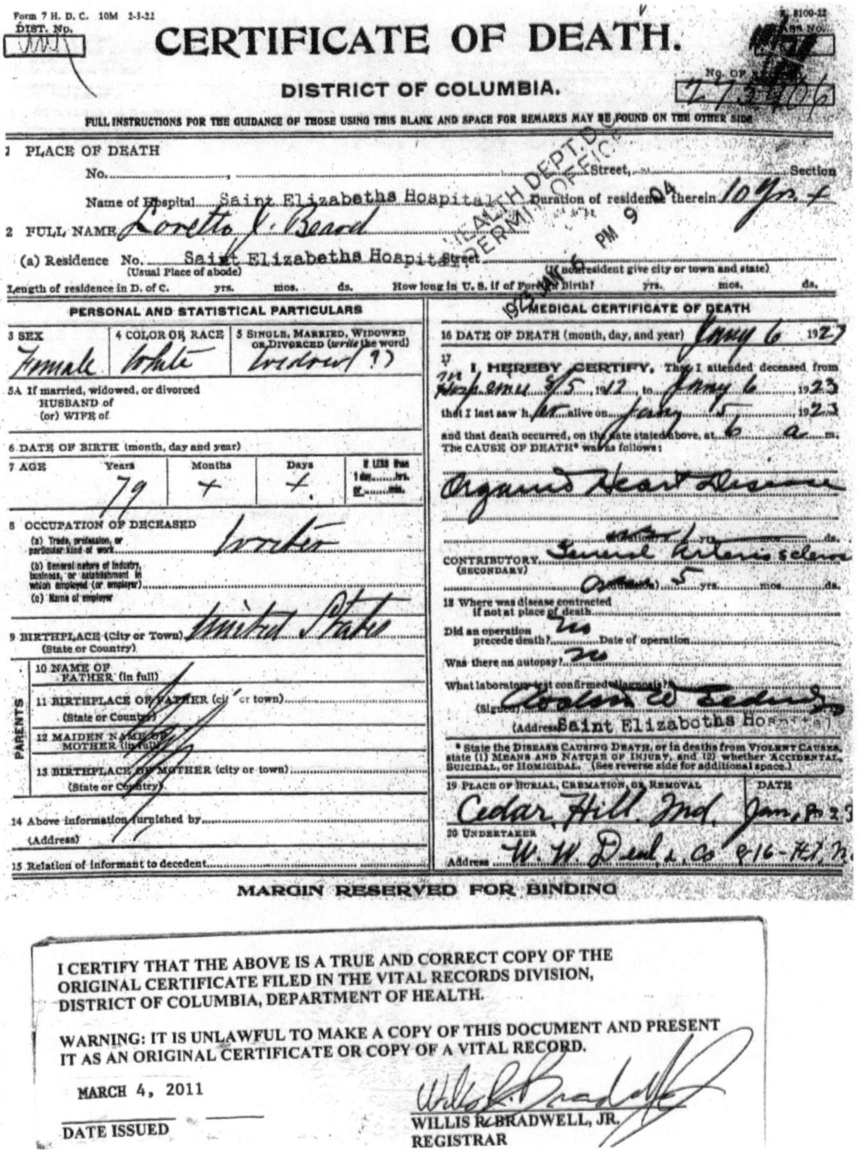

Form 7 H. D. C. 10M 2-1-22
DIST. No.

CERTIFICATE OF DEATH.

DISTRICT OF COLUMBIA.

No. of 273406

FULL INSTRUCTIONS FOR THE GUIDANCE OF THOSE USING THIS BLANK AND SPACE FOR REMARKS MAY BE FOUND ON THE OTHER SIDE

1 PLACE OF DEATH
No. .... Street, ... Section
Name of Hospital Saint Elizabeths Hospital Duration of residence therein 10 yr. +

2 FULL NAME Loretto J. Beard

(a) Residence No. Saint Elizabeths Hospital Street (Usual Place of abode) (If nonresident give city or town and state)
Length of residence in D. of C. yrs. mos. ds. How long in U. S. if of Foreign Birth? yrs. mos. ds.

HEALTH DEPT. D.C. PERMIT OFFICE 1923 JAN 6 PM 9 04

PERSONAL AND STATISTICAL PARTICULARS

3 SEX: Female
4 COLOR OR RACE: White
5 SINGLE, MARRIED, WIDOWED OR DIVORCED (write the word): Widowed (?)
5A If married, widowed, or divorced HUSBAND of (or) WIFE of
6 DATE OF BIRTH (month, day and year)
7 AGE: Years 79 — Months + — Days +.
8 OCCUPATION OF DECEASED: (a) Trade, profession, or particular kind of work: Writer
(b) General nature of industry, business, or establishment in which employed (or employer)
(c) Name of employer
9 BIRTHPLACE (City or Town) (State or Country): United States

PARENTS
10 NAME OF FATHER (in full)
11 BIRTHPLACE OF FATHER (city or town) (State or Country)
12 MAIDEN NAME OF MOTHER (in full)
13 BIRTHPLACE OF MOTHER (city or town) (State or Country)
14 Above information furnished by
(Address)
15 Relation of informant to decedent

MEDICAL CERTIFICATE OF DEATH

16 DATE OF DEATH (month, day, and year) Jany 6 1923
17 I HEREBY CERTIFY, That I attended deceased from Sept. 5 1912 to Jany 6 1923
that I last saw h er alive on Jany 5 1923
and that death occurred, on the date stated above, at 6 a. m.
The CAUSE OF DEATH* was as follows:
Organic Heart Disease
(duration) yrs. mos. ds.
CONTRIBUTORY (SECONDARY) General Arteriosclerosis
(duration) 5 yrs. mos. ds.
18 Where was disease contracted if not at place of death
Did an operation precede death? no Date of operation
Was there an autopsy? no
What laboratory test confirmed diagnosis?
(Signed) [signature]
(Address) Saint Elizabeths Hospital

* State the DISEASE CAUSING DEATH, or in deaths from VIOLENT CAUSES, state (1) MEANS AND NATURE OF INJURY, and (2) whether ACCIDENTAL, SUICIDAL, or HOMICIDAL. (See reverse side for additional space.)

19 PLACE OF BURIAL, CREMATION, OR REMOVAL: Cedar Hill Md. DATE: Jan. 8 23
20 UNDERTAKER
Address W. W. Deal & Co 816-H St. N.

MARGIN RESERVED FOR BINDING

I CERTIFY THAT THE ABOVE IS A TRUE AND CORRECT COPY OF THE ORIGINAL CERTIFICATE FILED IN THE VITAL RECORDS DIVISION, DISTRICT OF COLUMBIA, DEPARTMENT OF HEALTH.

WARNING: IT IS UNLAWFUL TO MAKE A COPY OF THIS DOCUMENT AND PRESENT IT AS AN ORIGINAL CERTIFICATE OR COPY OF A VITAL RECORD.

MARCH 4, 2011
DATE ISSUED

WILLIS R. BRADWELL, JR.
REGISTRAR

Figure 25. Certificate of Death, "Loretto J. Beard," January 6, 1923. Source: Vital Records Div., Dept. of Health, Dist. of Columbia.

Figure 26. Grave of Madame Loreta Janeta Velazquez

Section 10, South D Row, Site 59, Cedar Hill Cemetery, Suitland, Maryland

Loreta's grave is the unmarked plot (X) located to the right (southwest) of the gravestone plaque, that of Bryant Z. McLeroy, seen at the bottom left. There is an unmarked grave to the right of Loreta's, that of surname Almont, followed by the gravestone plaque of Mary A. Satterfield, seen on the extreme right edge of the photo. Photo by author.

Part 2: Events After the Time Frame of *The Woman in Battle*

Chapter 9

1874, Mobile (Alabama) Interview

The first found news item about Velazquez, after she left husbands E. H. Bonner and Andrew J. Bobo and the West, and after the end of the storyline of her memoir, is in the *Mobile Daily Register*, dated August 25, 1874. The article was titled "An Adventurous Lady":

Saturday, Mrs. E. H. Bonner, better known throughout the South as Lieut. Harry T. Buford, arrived in this city from New Orleans, *en route* to New York. This distinguished lady has, perhaps, gone through more hardships and done more for the Confederate States during the "late unpleasantness," than any woman within the borders of the section so designated. Like all Southern women, Mrs. Bonner was filled with that unprecedented love of country and patriotism, so beautifully exemplified by the women of the South during the war, and unwilling to see those whom she held most dear, march to the front, she made preparations, notwithstanding her sex, to participate actively in the strife.

During the month of June, 1861, she left New Orleans, in full uniform of a recruiting officer, and went to Arkansas, where she soon succeeded in raising a company of veterans. As First Lieutenant, under Capt. Weatherford, she left Arkansas with the company and went to Key West. Here she was reluctantly compelled to leave the command which she had organized, and to which she became so much attached, on the ground of incompetency, as alleged by the commander of that post.

Determined to allow no impediment to make her swerve from the line of duty marked by herself, she at once proceeded to Virginia, and joined Drew's [*sic* Dreux] Battalion of New Orleans the day previous to the first battle of Manassas, and participated in that memorable struggle. A short time after this she joined the 8th Louisiana, and for the first time her sex was questioned, and she was arrested and ordered to assume female attire.

Among hundreds of amusing adventures perhaps the best with which she was connected took place during the time of her imprisonment after this arrest. A committee of ladies waited upon her by order of the commander, for the purpose of settling the vexed question, but after seeing the dashing young officer they concluded not to perform their mission. She was taken before the Mayor, released, allowed to retain her uniform, and at once commissioned to perform any service for the Confederacy which she might be called upon to perform. As her sex had been questioned, if not known, she resolved to leave Richmond, and rejoiced when Gen. Winder ordered her to the Western army for the purpose of scouting in the vicinity of Okolona, Mississippi.

The reliability of the daring young recruit was soon recognized and appreciated, and General Quantrell [*sic* Quantrill] sent her with despatches [*sic*] as a spy into Missouri. After rendering inestimable service in this capacity she went to Mississippi, and from there back to New Orleans, where she joined the 21st Louisiana Regiment, then being organized, and reported to Gen. Villipigue [*sic* Villepigue]. Receiving her commission as First Lieutenant, she went to Memphis and from there to Shiloh, where she was badly wounded in the right shoulder on the first day of the battle, April 7th, 1862.

While recovering from the effects of her wound her sex was again discovered, to her mortification, and General Beauregard and others were astonished to find out that the gallant young officer was not of the stronger sex. Unable to dissuade her from participating in active warfare, she was commissioned to go to Atlanta, pass through the lines and act as a spy. Upon reaching Atlanta she was compelled to wait several days for further orders, and instead of staying in that city, she ran up to Dalton and Chattanooga, and participated actively in both fights, returning to Atlanta a day or two before the necessary orders arrived.

From this section of the country she was ordered aboard of blockaders from different Southern ports to the Indies, and often was the bearer of important despatches to foreign ports for the Florida and Shenandoah. She seized every opportunity, whether in the South, in the North, or in a foreign land, to render assistance to the Southern Confederacy. She has a receipt now in her possession for $780, which she collected from the United States soldiers of Commodore Brissol's [sic] fleet, then at Bridgeport, Barbadoes [sic], and sent to Southern hospitals, although the money was supposed to have been given for the benefit of Federal soldiers.

She was now sent to San Diego and Havana for the purpose of buying coffee and sugar for the Confederacy, and from there, after making the necessary purchases she went to South America, in the interest of the Confederate Government, with Price's expedition. From South America she proceeded to the West Indies, charged with some important mission for the country which she loved so well and served so faithfully. The deeds of this noble woman are well known throughout the South, and have been recited on many a hearthstone by well scarred veterans and inmates of Federal dungeons. The starved, inhumanely treated prisoners of camp Chase, have every reason to remember her who nursed them, fed them, and furnished them every cent she could spare, day after day.

She is in possession of genuine documents, given her every step she made, and from all of them it can be seen that she was trusted unhesitatingly, and bore an unblemished character from the beginning to the close of the war. Even after her sexhood had been questioned, throughout the entire war,- be it said to the credit of the men of the South- that not a syllable was ever repeated in her hearing unfit to repeat in the presence of the most reserved lady. Mrs. Bonner removed from New Mexico after her adventurous life, and engaged in mining speculation, and has realized a handsome fortune from her investments. She has been well employed otherwise, and has finished a book giving a truthful account of her adventures during her connection with the Confederacy. She is an intelligent-looking woman, of about thirty-five years of age, and has a particularly refined appearance for one who has experienced the hardships of camp life, and preformed the duties of a man for more than four years.

She is on her way to New York, and has a number of letters of introduction to prominent gentlemen of many Southern and Northern cities, and other evidences of an irreproachable reputation. While here she called upon several of our distinguished citizens, whose connection with the war rendered her desirous of forming their acquaintance, and to many of whom she brought letters of introduction.

Mrs. E. H. Bonner had transited New Orleans. She missed a letter which arrived there for her, unclaimed in the New Orleans Post Office, Sept. 5.[1] This letter would not have been from Bobo, trying to chase her down, as he would have addressed her as Mrs. A. J. Bobo or at worst, Mrs. L. J. Wasson, the names he knew for her. The letter, no doubt, came from Mr. E. H. Bonner, or some other man, trying to chase her down. It will be seen that Velazquez never used her married Bobo name and never mentioned this marriage.

The article was repeated far and wide by many newspapers.[2] Most of the newspapers retitled the article "A Confederate Amazon" and did not express an opinion of the story's veracity, but said only it was found in the Mobile paper.

When the New York *Argus* repeated the story and it drew a reaction from one of its readers who sent a letter to the editor[3] protesting that Mrs. Bonner had diverted the $780 dollars collected for the charity of captured Federal soldiers to Southern hospitals, "an illustration of the demoralizing effects of a civil war." The writer became shriller:

> And the *Register* mentions this without a word of blame… [her act] is contrary to all honorable dealings… is contrary to modern ideas of justice, and to modern rules of warfare. Among civilized nations, as little injury as possible is to be done to non-combatants; and those who have been captured are to be treated with all the kindness consistent with security. To rob them of money contributed by their friends for their use, is as dishonorable as to rob any other helpless persons. And to mention such a deed without blame, in a eulogistic notice, affords another instance of the erroneous views which some of our Southern brethren have of honor and chivalry. [signed X]

Writer "X" was needlessly upset about the incident because it was a fabrication.

First, there was no "Commodore Brissol" in the Union navy as the article asserted. There was no other ranking navy officer by that name, either. Considering the possibility of a misspelled name, a search for variations such as Drissol, Bristol or Dristol was made and still no possible person was found.[4]

---

1. *Times-Picayune*, Sep 6, 1874.
2. *Chicago Daily Tribune*, Oct 10, 1874; *Argus* (Albany, NY), Sep 4, 1874; *Inter Ocean* (Chicago, IL), Sep 8, 1874; *Jackson Citizen Patriot* (Jackson, MI), Sep 12, 1874; *Columbia Weekly Register* (New Haven, CT), Sep 26, 1874; *Frank Leslie's Illustrated Newspaper*, Nov 14, 1874.
3. Sep 8, 1874.
4. Lewis R. Hamersly, *The Records of Living Officers of the U.S. Navy and Marine Corp with a History of Naval Operations During the Rebellion of 1861-5, and a List of the Ships and Officers Participating in the Great Battles* (Philadelphia: J. B. Lippincott, 1870); Ed. Edward W. Callahan, *List of Officers of the Navy of the United States and of the Marine Corps from 1775 to 1900* (NY: L. R. Hamersly & Co., 1901); Ed. Dr. Spencer C. Tucker, Dr. Paul G. Pierpaoli Jr.,

Second, her collecting $780 from the Yankees and giving it to the Rebels never happened. Clearly, no Commodore Brissol means no fleet, which means no men from whom she could collect money. This lie resembles the 1864 true episode when she obtained permission from Commander Loomis at Fort Columbus, New York to solicit money from soldiers for the relief of soldiers' children, money which has been rudely suggested she kept for herself, as she was in need. And recall in Georgetown, Guiana, "an officer belonging to a United States man-of-war" in the harbor collected money for Velazquez who said she was "in destitute circumstances."

Third, the newspaper claimed that she was "in possession of genuine documents" which gave credence to her "unblemished character." This was simply the failure of the newspaper to ask penetrating questions of a lady. The paper would never have suspected Velazquez's audacity to possess forged papers, which she surely did. Recall the 1864 forgery under Colonel Hascall's name, and it will be seen in October 1874, Mark Twain was the victim of her forgery.

Fourth, it is not believable that Velazquez "<u>often</u> was the bearer of important despatches to foreign ports for the *Florida* and *Shenandoah* [commerce raider ships]." In fact, in her memoir she contradicted this claim when she wrote (p417) that she went to Canada where "[she] distributed [her] letters and despatches according to instructions; mailed packages for the commanders of the cruisers *Shenandoah* and *Florida*, which [she] had received with special injunctions to be particularly careful of, as they were very important...." In the article she hand-carried dispatches to the West Indies, but in her memoir, she mailed dispatches from Canada. Remember, she had plenty to write about *Florida*, all of which has been shown to have been lies. However, this was the only time in her memoir Velazquez mentioned any association with *Shenandoah*, the mailing of a package to it. Considering that the *Shenandoah* operated distantly in the Pacific Ocean, so much so, that it did not even know that the War had ended, it is not clear how any dispatch could have been directed to the vessel for Velazquez to "often" carry to it. Exactly to which "foreign port" did Velazquez travel, to "often" deliver her dispatch to *Shenandoah*, maybe Hawaii, on an excursion package with round-trip flight, hotel, meals and surfing lessons included? Recall the 1866 newspapers which reported that Velazquez claimed she had "forth-coming works which she [was] preparing, entitled 'The Cruise of the Shenandoah, or the last of the Confederacy?'" Yes, this was the book about

---

and William E. Whilte III, *Official Records of the Union and Confederate Navies*; Ed. Spencer C. Tucker, Paul G. Pierpaoli Jr., William E. White III, *The Civil War Naval Encyclopedia* (Santa Barbara, CA: ABC-CLIO, 2011); Kenneth E. Thompson, *Civil War Commodores and Admirals, A Biographical Directory of All Eighty-Eight Union and Confederate Navy Officers Who Attained Commissioned Flag Rank During the War* (Portland, ME: Thompson Group, 2001).

the history of *Shenandoah* about which she knew nothing and therefore was never written.

Fifth, it is surely untrue that "General Quantrell [*sic* Quantrill] sent her with despatches [*sic*] as a spy into Missouri." For one thing, William Clarke Quantrill was never a general, instead he was a captain. Briefly he called himself a colonel which might have been the results of his men electing him to that position. No evidence has been found that he was a commissioned colonel.[5]

Nowhere in her memoir does Velazquez claim any activity in Missouri during the War. She twice mentioned Quantrill in her memoir, but she was channeling dispatches to Quantrill, never Quantrill using her as a courier for his dispatches. The first of the Quantrill references (p444) stated that while she was in Indianapolis, she gave a dispatch to some Missourian who "was to report to Quantrell [*sic*], on some business of a secret nature" and that she had no idea what the dispatch was about and didn't ask. This claim cannot be proven or disproven. However, the second occasion is a different matter.

On page 509, Velazquez explained she was in New York when she was asked to deliver a dispatch to Quantrill. She wrote, "My associates suggested that I should proceed immediately to Missouri with despatches for Quantrell...." She accepted the mission and "with scarcely more than a change of clothing in [her] travelling satchel, [she] was soon speeding westward."

Velazquez continued:

> I did not get as far as Quantrell's headquarters, as I was lucky enough to meet with one of his couriers, to whom I delivered the despatches. This man, to whom I was tolerably well known, was very eager to have me go with him to the general, saying that I could be of the greatest possible service in the present juncture by acting as his spy, and as bearer of despatches to the agents in the North. I, however, was compelled to decline....

It is clear that her unbelievable claim in the article, that "General Quantrell ... sent her with despatches as a spy into Missouri" is in perfect contradiction to her memoir's claim. Worse still, the claim in her memoir is provably false. Velazquez conveniently provided a precise date for this mission, stating it was after General Lee's surrender (April 9, 1865) and before General Joe Johnston's surrender (April 26, 1865). The problem is, long before these dates, Quantrill had already left Missouri, never to return, so he did not have a headquarters in Missouri as Velazquez asserted.

---

5. Edward E. Leslie, *The Devil Knows How to Ride: the True Story of William Clarke Quantrill and His Confederate Raiders* (NY: Da Capo Press, 1996), 294.

On the night of January 1, 1865, Quantrill and his men crossed the Mississippi River into Kentucky and he never left. And he had no "headquarters" in Kentucky to which a dispatch could have been sent, either. He and his raiders had disguised themselves as 4th Missouri troopers (Union) and fooled Union garrisons into helping them on their eastward journey. "In a week they traveled some 120 miles as the crow flies, much more than that on horseback."[6] It is claimed that Quantrill and his band were endeavoring to get to Virginia, anticipating the surrender of the Confederacy, where they could find favorable terms, instead of being turned over to a vengeful Missouri population upon which the raiders had dealt murder, and had plundered and burned their houses. The newspapers said that the guerillas were going to Washington, D.C. to seek pardons.[7]

When Quantrill and his followers arrived in central Kentucky, they ostensibly gave up their efforts to get to Virginia and joined some guerrilla bands and made some raids. By now the word was out that Quantrill was in Kentucky; Union garrisons were alerted and forced a skirmish in Bradfordsville, some 65 miles south of Lexington. Although several guerillas were killed, Quantrill escaped and "went into hiding in Spencer County," staying in towns rich in Southern sympathizers. Quantrill did not hide long, but resumed his raids with his followers. On May 10, one Edwin Terrell, a young man of bad reputation, and his men, who had been hired by the military to hunt down Quantrill, caught Quantrill and his men resting in James Wakefield's barn, "five miles south of Taylorsville." In the ensuing gunfight Quantrill was shot and crippled. He was taken to a Louisville military prison infirmary where he died twenty-seven days later.[8]

In conclusion, it is not believable that anyone sent a message to Quantrill in Missouri and asked Velazquez to deliver it, when Quantrill was long gone from there and well into Kentucky. From January until Quantrill's capture in May, the Kentucky newspapers and nationwide newspapers, such as the *New York Tribune*, reported on Quantrill's activity in Kentucky. Recall, Velazquez claimed she got her orders to go to Missouri while in New York City in April, when everyone in New York would have known Quantrill was in Kentucky.

At least Velazquez had the good sense not to falsely claim, in this interview (or her forthcoming book) that she rode with Quantrill, as she had claimed about riding with Nathan B. Forrest and "Jeb" Stuart to the Augusta *Daily Constitution* back in May 1866.

---

6. Ibid, 347.
7. *Daily National Intelligencer* (Washington, D.C.), Dec 1, 1864, dateline "Cairo (Missouri) November 30."
8. Leslie, 369.

There are many other provable lies (since almost everything was a lie) in the Mobile newspaper article and they will be addressed momentarily when they are compared to her forthcoming interview in Atlanta.

1874, Atlanta (Georgia) Interview

The *Atlanta Constitution* of September 4, 1874 noted Mrs. Bonner's arrival in that city only ten days after she was in Mobile. She was passing through Atlanta on her way to New York and once again Mrs. Bonner was interviewed. The discrepancies between the Mobile interview and this Atlanta interview are shocking. Worse still, these interviews conflict with her book's version of events which she published only two years later, in the middle of 1876. The Atlanta newspaper article was titled "Lieut. Harry Bufort [*sic*], The Lady Officer of the Rebel Army- Her Extraordinary Career During and since the War- She is wounded three times on the Battle-field- Her Exploits and Marriage in Atlanta." The reporter wrote:

Wednesday morning a representative of The Constitution had the pleasure of an introduction to Mrs. E. W. [*sic* H.] Bonner, who is at present in our city, and who claims to be the original Lieutenant Harry T. Bufort [*sic*], of the confederate army. Mrs. Bonner has such documentary proof of the truth of her assertion in her possession as to leave scarcely any room for doubt. Her career, taken altogether, is probably the most extraordinary of any woman who ever lived in the southern states, and it is of particular interest to the citizens of Atlanta, from the fact that she was here repeatedly during the war, and was married here to her second husband in 1864. It will be impossible, in the scope of this article, to give more than a brief allusion to the more prominent points in the life of this remarkable lady, for it would take a volume to contain in detail her record and travels since.

Mrs. Bonner's Early History.- Mrs. Bonner is a lady slightly above the average height, thoroughly educated, and very fluent. She is fine looking, and when in conversation her face lights up with interest. She has no hesitancy in talking about the strange events of her life, and answered readily all questions that were asked. Her maiden name was Loretta Jeanett Clapp; she was born in Havana, and is now 31 years of age. One of her uncles, a Mr. Theodore Clapp, flourished for many years in New Orleans as a Universalist minister, and was widely esteemed and known. The family moved from Havana to the United States while Mrs. Bonner was quite young. Her childhood days were spent in Mississippi, but after she grew up to girlhood her family removed to Texas.

The only part of Mrs. Bonner's life is entirely uneventful and about the same as that of any other young lady of the same years. Mrs. Bonner has no brothers or sisters living. Her father, Samuel S. Clapp, died a confederate prisoner in Fort Hamilton, N. Y., in 1863. Her mother died in Texas in 1860. While the family were residing in Texas, Mrs. Bonner made the acquaintance of Mr. William E. Burnett [*sic* Burnet], at the time a student in the military academy at West Point, whose family were her father's neighbors. An attachment sprung up between the young people and they were married in 1857, Mrs. Burnett being at the time under fourteen years of age and her husband a little older. The fact of this marriage was not allowed to become known beyond the families as it would have resulted in the expulsion of young Burnett from the academy at West Point. After his graduation Mr. Burnett was made a lieutenant, and ordered to duty in Pennsylvania, where his young wife followed him.

Transformed Into A Rebel Lieutenant.- The extraordinary part of our heroine's career commences with the war. She followed her husband about previous to that time, from post to post, and became acquainted with a number of the old army officers. In the early part of 1861, at the inauguration of the war, Lieutenant Burnett determined to follow the fortunes of his state. He threw up his commission in the United States army, returned to Texas, raised an independent company, and was ordered to duty in Pensacola, Fla.

This brought about a separation between husband and wife, and now Mrs. Burnett first conceived the idea of entering the army herself. It was arranged between her husband and herself that she should raise a company and join him at Pennsacola [*sic*], thus making him a battalion commander. She accordingly donned the Full Uniform Of A Second Lieutenant [*sic*] in the regular confederate army, and went to Arkansas, where she succeeded in raising a company of one hundred and thirty-six men. She also assumed the name of Lieut. Harry T. Bufort. She speaks even now with much pride of her company. It was composed of splendid material, and not one of the men knew that the gallant young commander was a woman. The lieutenant, with her company, joined her husband in New Orleans, to which place her husband had been ordered, and the two companies were merged in the "Louisiana Greys." In the later part of 1861 her husband was killed, and the lieutenant left a young widow. She went to Fort Pillow with her command, and was promoted to be first lieutenant by General Pillow, then commanding at that place. The lieutenant did not remain long attached to any command. She became what she calls "an independent officer," and so remained until 1864, being employed by the government most of the time in carrying dispatches. It would take a book to hold all of her travels from point to point while on this duty.

Wounded Three Times.- Lieutenant Bufort has seen considerable service in front of the enemy. She was in the first battle of Manassas with Col. Charley Drew's [*sic* Dreux] battalion and was near Drew when he was killed. She went into battle of Malvern Hill, in the 12th Mississippi under Colonel Tailor, and was here wounded in the right foot. She was in the battle of Shiloh, and on Monday evening after the fight, was wounded badly in the right shoulder and hand by the bursting of a shell.

Her Career In Atlanta.- The lieutenant was in Atlanta a number of times, from 1861 to 1864, and was married here in 1864 [*sic* it was 1863] to her second husband, Capt. Byron DeCamp of Van Dorn's cavalry. She knew Captain DeCamp before the war, he being a regular army officer. After the death of her husband he courted her by letter, and the correspondence was kept up for some time. After the battle of Franklin, Tennessee, she met the captain on the battle-field, and was introduced to him. She recognized him and had a bundle of his letters in her pocket, but he did not for an instant suspect that the young officer by his side was his sweetheart. On her trip through this city in 1864 she found the captain sick in the hospital here, when she made herself known to him, and at his earnest solicitation married him.

The ceremony took place at the old Atlanta hotel, and was performed by a resident Methodist minister. After a brief stay here with her second husband they were forced to separate. She had dispatches to carry to a distant place, and he returned to his command in Mississippi. Before she could join him, she received news of his death, and did not reach Corinth, where he died, until after his funeral.

Running The Blockade, Etc.- After the death of her second husband and at her request she was employed by the government on a different kind of service. She made several trips to and from Havanna [sic] to bring supplies. She was also repeatedly in the northern lines and smuggled through supplies as well as much valuable information. She at this time devoted much of her attention to alleviating the sufferings of the southern prisoners.

Travels Since The War.- After the war and in 1866 she was married to Mr. John W. Wasson of Kentucky, and with him went to South America with the expedition organized by Dr. Henry A. Price of Virginia. The emigrants went out under the charge of Mr. Fred Johnson to Venezuela, and found that they had been grossly deceived, as to lands and assistance from the government. Here her husband died. After remaining in South America for a short time, our heroine returned to New York. From this place she went to Austin, Nevada, and there on the 29th of January, 1868, was married to her present husband, Mr. E. H. Bonner. He is in the mining business, and is at present with a mining company in New Mexico.

Mrs. Bonner's Mission Here.- Mrs. Bonner has come east to see about a book she contemplates publishing, containing a history of her life. The book is to be written by Mark Twain, and will sell well. She is now on her way to New York to see this celebrated humorist.

Remembered Here.- This reporter has seen a number of people here who remembered Lieut. Bufort, and several who were at her marriage. She was frequently seen upon the streets, and at the depot in her full lieutenant's uniform, and a lovely imperial. She certainly made a handsome officer, and was as gallant as good looking. Not the least interesting among her collection of papers is a number of love letters from young ladies here and elsewhere whom the lieutenant visited while in the army.

She says her sex was only discovered after she had been wounded, and that she passed for a man here until her marriage. Considerable interest has been taken in Mrs. Bonner by a number of our city officials and citizens. She has been an object of great curiosity during her few days visit here, and her army acquaintance, as Lieut. Bufort, with several ex-confederate officers has been left.

She yesterday renewed for New York, but will return to the October fair. During the fair she has, by invitation, consented to enter the riding contest, and arrangements are on foot to have her deliver several lectures. Mrs. Bonner has one child, a boy five years old- at present in New Orleans, and has lost two.

The article was repeated by newspapers nationwide. Its lies, contradictions and inconsistencies are as large as Stone Mountain, Georgia!

1) The Atlanta article stated that her maiden name was Loretta Jeanett Clapp and that she was born in Havana and was 31 years old. She claimed that "Her father, Samuel S. Clapp, died in a confederate prisoner in Fort

Hamilton, N. Y., in 1863." She also explained that, "One of her uncles, a Mr. Theodore Clapp, flourished for many years in New Orleans as a Universalist minister."

Only two years later, in her book, she claimed her father was Velazquez of a proud and noble Spanish birth and was related to both the first governor of Cuba, Don Diego Velazquez, and the artist, Don Diego Rodríquez Velazquez. It is ironic that she bragged so proudly in her book of her father's heritage, yet in it she didn't even honor him by mentioning him by his first name or telling of his death.

"Samuel S. Clapp" was in reality, Theodore Samuel Clapp, who was the son of Reverend Theodore Clapp, the minister in New Orleans. Velazquez said that Mr. Theodore Clapp was "one of her uncles," but he would have been her grandfather! The Clapp family was well-known and she took the liberty of making them related to her. (Recall, in 1868 she claimed a fake brother, Colonel R. D. Clapp, by his obituary.) The Reverend was a Massachusetts native who was invited to lead the Universalist Church in New Orleans in 1822, until his retirement in 1856. Together with his wife, they had 6 children and Theodore Samuel Clapp was one of the children. Already mentioned, it might have been wise for Velazquez to check when Theodore S. Clapp was born because it was in 1828 and since Velazquez gave (*TWIB*, p40) her own birth date as 1842, this would have made Theodore S. Clapp a 14-year-old father at her birth.

Theodore S. Clapp became a doctor and served as a contract surgeon for the Confederacy and was stationed at Fort Pike near New Orleans. When the Union captured New Orleans, the doctor, after being captured and paroled, sought employment with the Union. Clapp survived the war, and afterwards he was a doctor in New Orleans, later moved to Kentucky, and died there in 1905 at the age of 77. It is a lie that "Samuel S. Clapp" died "a confederate prisoner in Fort Hamilton, N. Y. in 1863" and furthermore it should be noted that Fort Hamilton was never used as a confederate prison!

Recall, as early as 1863, Velazquez claimed that her father was "Major J. B. Roche of Mississippi" (*Richmond Examiner*, July 11, 1863). Then on August 4, 1864 she forged a letter to General Sibley in which she claimed that she was the "daughter of Rear Admiral Rosche Eng. [English] Navy." Velazquez forged another letter, an inheritance letter, four months later, in December 1864 and placed it in the *Richmond Enquirer* which announced the death of her father, "Commodore J. B. Roach, of the British Navy."[9] Remember, this was the old gentleman who died of shock when he was demoted from rear-admiral to commodore?

2) The Atlanta article stated that "The family [the Clapps] moved from Havana to the United States while Mrs. Bonner was quite young. Her

---

9. *Daily Constitution* (Augusta, Georgia), Dec 21, 1864 repeating the *Richmond Enquirer*.

childhood days were spent in Mississippi, but after she grew up to girlhood her family removed to Texas." Well, the Clapps never lived in Cuba or Texas.

In great contradiction, in her book Velazquez explained that her parents (the Velazquezes) remained living in Cuba when she was sent to live with an aunt in New Orleans. She never wrote that her family moved to Texas during her young womanhood. She, in this Atlanta interview, declared her family's move to Texas only so she could support the false claim of meeting her first husband there.

3) The Atlanta article stated that her family, while in Texas was neighbors to the Burnets and that in 1857 fourteen-year-old Velazquez married her little older husband. "The fact of this marriage was not allowed to become known beyond the families as it would have resulted in the expulsion of young Burnett [sic] from the academy at West Point." Upon his graduation he was commissioned a lieutenant and sent to Pennsylvania and his wife followed him there. "In the early part of 1861... he threw up his commission in the United States army, returned to Texas, raised an independent company, and was ordered to duty in Pensacola, Fla."

There was not a single word of truth in the entire paragraph and Velazquez wisely did not inject it into her book, but replaced it- with another lie. She wrote (p48) that in New Orleans she and "William" were "clandestinely married" on the "5th of April 1856," which would have made her 13 years, 9 months and 10 days old. The caveat with this claim is that underage marriages on this date in New Orleans required the appearance of a parent before the Justice of the Peace. There were no underage marriages without a parent's knowledge and consent and her parents were in Cuba anyway. And please recall that on page 48 Velazquez claimed she "present[ed] the certificate of marriage to [her] horror-stricken relative [her aunt]."

The Atlanta article then stated, "It was arranged between her husband and herself that she should raise a company and join him at Pensacola, thus making him a battalion commander." Of course, this version contradicts her book (p84-87) in every way. In her book she claimed she raised a battalion, the "Arkansas Grays," without the knowledge of her husband and delivered it to him in Pensacola to his utter astonishment. But now in this article Velazquez changed her story and claimed she met him in New Orleans with her company and "the two companies were merged in the 'Louisiana Greys.'" Both versions are lies. Other contradictions are clear. In her memoir, Velazquez claimed she got into her disguise in Memphis and from there she crossed the Mississippi River and recruited in Arkansas. However, notice in the Mobile article she said that "she left New Orleans, in full uniform of a recruiting officer, and went to Arkansas, where she soon succeeded in raising a company of veterans."

The Louisiana Greys was a real company, a long-standing state militia company which pre-dated the Civil War and consisted of Louisiana men. With the outbreak of the War, it organized under the command of Captain Edmund Kennedy and was part of the First Brigade.[10] The company consisted of about 100 men, the typical company size. It is absurd that Velazquez claimed that "the two companies were merged in the Louisiana Greys" which means two companies of 100 men were merged to form one company, since a single company consisted of 100 men. But her claim is even more nonsensical because she claimed in the interview that she raised 136 men which then merged with another 100 men to form a company of 100 men. And still, it gets worse! In her memoir Velazquez claimed she raised 236 men, so that would make a merger of her 236 men with another 100 men of her husband's company. Of course, the claim was simply not true and in addition, the historical record shows that at the beginning of the Civil War, companies formed with great pride at their own locale. It is unbelievable that a company of Arkansas men went to New Orleans and intentionally renounced their home turf identity and merged with Louisiana men to <u>form</u> the Louisiana Greys, which in any case already existed! It was only much later in the War that depleted companies might merge with unrelated companies.

Velazquez claimed that her first husband, "William" in her book, was one "William E. Burnet." Nothing Velazquez said about the man was true. Then who was he? William E. Burnet came from a prominent Texas family. His father was New Jersey-born David Gouverneur Burnet, who became the first president of the new Republic of Texas in 1836. Most likely, Velazquez did not know of William's father's prominence because she failed to boast to the newspapers of her connection to this prominent family. On the other hand, if she did know, maybe she did not dare to lie too loudly for fear of discovery. In her book, she purposefully gave nothing about William's history or pedigree, and avoided his surname knowing that someone would see the lie.

William E. (Este- his mother's maiden name) Burnet was David G.'s and wife Hannah's only child of four to reach adulthood. He was born on July 7, 1833 in now Texas, but at that time was Mexico.[11] In the 1850 U.S. Census

---

10. Robert C. Reinders, *End of an Era: New Orleans, 1850- 1860* (Gretna, LA: Pelican Publishing Co., 1964), 81; Ed. Henry Rightor, *Standard History of New Orleans, Louisiana* (Chicago: Lewis Publishing Co., 1900), 160.
11. William E. Burnet letter to S. Cooper, Adjutant General of the United States dated May 12, 1857, acknowledging receipt of his commission as second lieutenant in the 1st Infantry. Source- NARA, RG94, Letters Received by the Office of the Adjutant General Main Series 1822-1860, Records of the Adjutant General's Office.

William E. was recorded as a seventeen-year-old "student at law" under his parents' roof. It is not likely that he completed his law study because he soon sought a military career.

William E. Burnet did <u>not</u> attend or graduate from West Point, as Velazquez claimed. However, he did attend the Kentucky Military Institute where he received A.B. and C.E. degrees in June 1855. He was commissioned second lieutenant in the U.S. Army on February 21, 1857. He later was given an honorary M.A. degree in 1858.[12]

As a U.S. Army officer and prior to the War, William E. Burnet was nowhere near Pennsylvania as claimed by Velazquez in the Atlanta article. He was stationed in Texas and Oklahoma, as the plentiful records show. Velazquez probably thought to claim she and William had gone to Pennsylvania taking her cue from her experience of living in Pennsylvania with Thomas DeCaulp or because of things she learned about Pennsylvania from her Austin, Nevada landlady.

After Burnet resigned his U.S. Army commission and joined the Confederacy, he did not raise a company in Texas. He did not merge his company with her company in New Orleans to form a battalion, the "Louisiana Greys." Burnet did not raise "an independent company" and neither did Velazquez. All these claims in the Atlanta article are pure lies.

On the question of raising a company, it is clear that the Mobile article (August 1874) conflicts with the Atlanta article (September 1874) and with her book (1876). The Mobile article stated:

> During the month of June 1861, she left New Orleans, in the full uniform of a recruiting officer, and went direct to Arkansas, where she soon succeeded in raising a company of veterans. As First Lieutenant, under Capt. Weatherford, she left Arkansas with the company and went to Key West. Here she was reluctantly compelled to leave the command which she had organized....

The historical record is clear- no Rebels got even close to Key West which always remained under Federal control. And there was no Captain Weatherford associated with this claim. Clearly Velazquez understood that she could not say to the Mobile interviewer that she traveled through Mobile with her company, on the way to Pensacola, as she later narrated in her book, "As we passed through Mobile we were heartily cheered, the men waving their hats, and the women their handkerchiefs...." The Mobile newspaper reporter could have seen the lie and the risk was too much for Velazquez to chance. And had she truly marched her men through Mobile, she would have not failed to bring it to the attention of the Mobile reporter in

---

12. Raymond Estep, "Lieutenant Wm. E. Burnet: Notes on Removal of Indians from Texas to Indian Territory, Part 1," *The Chronicles of Oklahoma*, Vol 38 (Autumn 1960): 261.

anticipation of lavish praise. Velazquez did not raise or take a company (or battalion) to Key West or Pensacola or through Mobile.

William E. Burnet achieved an admirable military record in the Confederacy. At the Battle of Corinth (Mississippi), Burnet served as Chief of Artillery for General Dabney H. Maury's Division. Maury wrote:

> Colonel Burnett [*sic*], chief of Artillery of Maury's division, one of the bravest and ablest artillery officers of our army, now saw his opportunity, and rapidly massed all the batteries [cannons] of the division on this eminence [ridge]. About two hundred yards before them lay Davis's bridge, over which Ord's forces must pass to attack us. Burnett charged his guns with double canister, and swept that bridge until near five hundred of the enemy were laid on or about it. Ord was wounded and his army held in check... It is only just to these gallant troops to say that *they* saved Van Dorn's army that day.[13]

General Maury was notified at his Knoxville, Tennessee headquarters that he was given command of the Department of the Gulf, headquarters in Mobile, Alabama,[14] which he assumed on May 19, 1863.[15] It can be understood that Burnet arrived in May with Maury's command in Mobile. Burnet, in a letter from Mobile to his father wrote, "On my return to this place, June 26th, I found your letter dated May 4th...." Burnet does not make clear the nature of his absence, but he probably was away for several days taking care of artillery defense batteries in the Mobile Bay area, since that was his assignment.[16]

It is certain that Velazquez was in Mobile in June 1863, and maybe Velazquez met, or at least, learned of the distinguished officer, Major William E. Burnet, posted there. It also is possible that she met or learned of Burnet somewhere in Mississippi since both spent much time there during the War.

When she passed through Mobile again in August 1874, she likely learned of Burnet's March 1865 death and of his burial in Mobile. She never claimed

---

13. *Ibid*, 303- 304; at this date Burnet's rank was lieutenant or captain. On Apr 4, 1863 he was appointed major, retroactive to Nov 4, 1862. On Jul 7, 1863, Major General Maury requested Burnet's promotion to colonel and the promotion was given on Aug 19, 1863- Source- www.Fold3.com.

14. *OR*, Ser 1, Vol 15, p1056, letter from S. Cooper, Adjutant and Inspector General in Richmond.

15. Arthur W. Bergeron Jr., *Confederate Mobile* (Jackson, MS: University Press of Mississippi, 1991) 28, 206.

16. Letter from William to father dated Jul 13, 1863- Burnet, David Gouverneur Papers, 1788-1870, Galveston and Texas History Center, Rosenberg Library, Galveston, Texas; Burnet may have been able to write to his father as early as Apr 27 to let him know that he was headed to Mobile. His father could have received the letter by May 4 and immediately sent a reply to William in Mobile. If his father was not advised that William was going to Mobile, then the letter was likely forwarded to Mobile from William's last duty post.

the marriage to Burnet any time prior to or during her August 1874 Mobile interview, but waited 10 days later, when she was in Atlanta where no one could see the falsehood. She also needed time to fabricate the marriage details, which probably occupied her mind during the train ride from Mobile to Atlanta. Upon arrival there she was ready for the interview.

4) The Atlanta article stated, "In the later part of 1861 her husband was killed...."

However, in her memoir, Velazquez stated that he was killed prior to June 16, 1861. In reality, the man she claimed was her husband, but was not her husband, was killed on March 31, 1865. Since the basic assertion of marriage to William Burnet was a lie, it is predictable that all assertions about him which followed were lies. In her memoir Velazquez claimed "William" was with her in a Memphis hotel on April 5, 1861 and had previously resigned his commission. The lie is evident because Burnet was nowhere near Memphis on that date; only three days earlier on April 2, 1861, U.S. Army 2nd Lieutenant Burnet wrote a letter placing him at Fort Cobb, Indian Territory (Oklahoma).[17] Worse still, Burnet did not resign his U.S. Army commission as a Second Lieutenant in the First Infantry, Company C, until July 17, 1861, in St. Louis. And afterwards, he could not reach the Confederacy except by first traveling west to Fort Leavenworth, Kansas, then south to Fort Smith, Arkansas. From there he traveled to Richmond. He received a commission in the Confederate army on September 9, 1861, as a first lieutenant. Burnet was nowhere near the Memphis hotel or Pensacola (June 1861) at the times claimed by Velazquez.[18]

5) The Atlanta article stated, "She went to Fort Pillow with her command, and was promoted to be a first lieutenant by General Pillow, then commanding at that place." This claim of her rank, and all others, are false. Only ten days previous, in the Mobile article, she claimed that at the war's commencement she was a "First Lieutenant, under Capt. Weatherford." Further into the same Mobile article she claimed that she went back to New Orleans, "where she joined the Twenty-first Regiment, then being organized, and reported to Gen. Villipigue. Receiving her commission as First Lieutenant, she went to Memphis." It will be seen that on June 24, 1878, after "an *Evening Post* reporter conversed" with her "yesterday," he wrote, "By some means she procured her commission from the Governor of Arkansas, dated May 28, 1861."[19] And recall the *St. Louis Republican* of March 7, 1866 stated that at Fort Pillow she "was elected 1st Lieutenant in Capt. Phillip's Company of Independent Tennessee Cavalry." Moreover, she claimed she tried to buy a commission for $500 (p96). Please take note, no

---

17. Auctioned as lot #312 by Nate D. Sanders, Inc., Los Angeles on Oct 29, 2013.
18. Estep, 261.
19. *St. Louis Evening Post*, Jun 25, 1878.

version of a commissioned rank is true. In her book, she never claimed she was commissioned a rank, instead claimed her rank was self-designated. Velazquez wrote (*TWIB*, p37) she assumed "the *pseudonym* of Lieutenant Harry T. Buford." She must have determined, and correctly, that if she falsely claimed a commissioned rank in her book, she would not get away with it as easily as she could in an interview.

6) The Atlanta article stated, "Lieutenant Bufort [*sic*] has seen considerable service in front of the enemy. She was in the first battle of Manassas, with Col. Charley Drew's [*sic* Dreux's] battalion, and was near Drew when he was killed." The Mobile article echoed the same, that she "joined Drew's Battalion of New Orleans the day previous to the first battle of Manassas."

It is a blatant lie that Colonel Dreux was at the First Battle of Manassas (July 21, 1861) and that she was "near Drew when he was killed." Colonel Dreux was already dead 16 days prior to this date. More on this later.

Nothing Velazquez ever said about her participation at Manassas has any ring of truth. Please see Ex-Confederate General Jubal Early's reasons for rejecting her claim about Manassas, as well as her other claims. It is notable that when she was arrested in Lynchburg, Virginia on September 24, 1861, only two months after the Battle of Manassas, the newspaper stated, "She said her reason for dressing in soldier's clothes was, that she had determined to fight the battles of her country, and thought such a disguise more likely to enable her to accomplish her object." If she had recently fought at Manassas, she would have said so, loudly and proudly. She probably never set foot in Virginia until September 1861, when she was arrested there. The first record found in which she claimed to have fought at Manassas was 9 months after the battle; it probably just then occurred to her to claim it.[20]

In her memoir, Velazquez wisely dropped her Col. Dreux claim, and instead, she weaved another story. She told she took up with "Brigadier General Bonham and his First Brigade who was holding Mitchell's Ford" which was a wagon crossing location on the Bull Run. She then popped up a mile away at Blackburn's Ford, another crossing location, with the Fourth Brigade commanded by Brigadier General James Longstreet. To clarify, at this date the Confederate government had the army divided into two armies, Army of the Potomac and the Army of the Shenandoah. Both of these aforementioned brigades were part of the Army of the Potomac, commanded by General Beauregard. As if her one mile jump from the First Brigade to the Fourth Brigade wasn't impressive enough, she then narrated that she jumped 50 miles away and became part of the Army of the Shenandoah commanded by General Joseph E. Johnston, and specifically part of General Bee's Third Brigade. Velazquez wrote (p98), "General Bee,

---

20. *Daily True Delta* (New Orleans), Apr 24, 1862.

at this place, appointed me special messenger…." She also said (p101), "I attached myself to my favorite officer, Bee, and remained with his command during the entire day."

7) The Atlanta article stated, "She went into the battle of Malvern Hill, in the 12th Mississippi under Colonel Tailor [*sic* Taylor], and was here wounded in the right foot." Velazquez, in her memoir, did not claim to have fought at Malvern Hill with the 12th Mississippi, and it was good thing, too. This regiment did not fight at Malvern Hill. The Battle of Malvern Hill (July 1, 1862) was the final battle of the Seven Days Battle which was a series of six major battles over seven days. The 12th Mississippi did participate in some of the other battles of this week, but not the final day's battle at Malvern Hill. Needless to say, if she was with the 12th Mississippi and the 12th Mississippi was not at Malvern Hill, then she wasn't at Malvern Hill, so neither was her right foot. She did not maintain this claim in her memoir; she probably forgot about it.

In the Atlanta interview, Velazquez claimed that she fought at Shiloh and "on Monday evening [which was April 7] after the fight, was wounded badly in the right shoulder and hand by the bursting of a shell." The Mobile article, written only ten days earlier, gave a different day for the wound, she was "badly wounded in the right shoulder on the first day of the battle [which was April 6]," but then in error, called the first day April 7. Two years later, in her book, she wrote (p225) a bursting shell wounded her "in the arm and shoulder," and that the injury occurred on the third day, after the full battle of the 6th and 7th was over, when she was burying the dead. In her memoir she explained (p226) that once she departed the Shiloh battle area and arrived in Corinth, Mississippi, she sent for a physician she knew who determined that her shoulder was "out of place," her "arm was cut" and her "little finger lacerated." Velazquez claimed the doctor treated her cuts and her "out of place" shoulder by applying a dressing and putting her arm in a sling. What, the doctor treated an out of place shoulder by putting the arm in a sling? Didn't he force the shoulder back into place first? If indeed she sustained this injury, it is more consistent with a fall (from a horse?) than shrapnel from an explosion. In an obvious contradiction twelve years earlier (*Daily True Delta*, April 24, 1862) when she claimed she fought at Shiloh, she said she was "wounded in the foot and hand." She often made conflicting claims about wounds sustained at Shiloh. Once all claims have been accumulated, they will be again addressed.

She had much to say about Shiloh in her book, but the most interesting was her whopper about deciding not to assassinate General U.S. Grant, when opportunity presented itself. This claim (p213-214) of Grant's near premature demise will be exposed further along.

8) The Atlanta article stated that Velazquez had lost two children and had a five-year-old boy. However, two years later, in her 1876 book, she claimed she lost three children, all dying the same year, implying 1860, and had, at present, one boy.

9) The Atlanta article stated that Velazquez's second husband, whom she married in Atlanta in 1864 (It was 1863.), was named "Capt. Byron DeCamp." It is inexplicable how the newspaper got the captain's name 100% wrong. It might be understandable how a name like DeCaulp could be wrongly heard as DeCamp, but how a reporter could mistake her husband's first name, "Thomas C.," and write "Byron" is beyond error. Velazquez purposely misnamed him because she feared that people would have their memories jogged. Recall, DeCaulp's name had been remembered by the Atlanta public in May of 1866 and he was accused of desertion. Velazquez must have feared that his desertion would again be remembered. Maybe the Southern public would even remember his enlistment in the Northern army!

It appears that Velazquez had purposely avoided an association with the name DeCaulp in the first months of 1866, when in March she used the name De Camp or DeCamp. When she visited Memphis on March 1, 1866, the *Memphis Daily Avalanche* mistakenly called her "Mrs. L. D. Camp." Velazquez troubled herself to correct the newspaper's error and it apologized and corrected it to "Mrs. Lauretta J. DeCamp."[21] It is curious that she did not have the paper correct the name to DeCaulp, so it must be assumed she meant to use DeCamp. She appeared in St. Louis on March 7, 1866 (*St. Louis Republican*) as "Mrs. Loretta De Camp" and "Mrs. Maj. De Camp," and in New Orleans on March 29, 1866 (*Daily True Delta*) as "Mrs. Major T. C. De Camp."

By May 1866, Velazquez resumed using her DeCaulp name and it caused her problems. Recall, Velazquez had to fight off accusations in Atlanta that her husband deserted the Confederacy:

> Mrs. DeCaulp, desires us also to say, that the report circulated against her husband, that he deserted the Confederate cause, and gone over to the other side, is a base slander… and will meet any one who dare or has dared to asperse his memory; that she has already received two wounds upon the battle field, and will defy death itself in vindication of her departed husband's honor.[22]

Also remember, Mrs. DeCaulp previously had to defend her own honor in Mobile, Alabama when she took out an advertisement (May 1866) in the *Mobile Tribune* proclaiming false all "slanders concerning her loyalty to the

---

21. *Memphis Daily Avalanche*, March 21, 1866.
22. *Atlanta Daily Intelligencer*, May 9, 1866.

late confederacy" and threatning those who made them. It is unknown who were her detractors.

The 1874 Atlanta article goes on to say that Velazquez knew DeCaulp prior to the war, as he was a friend of her first husband and that DeCaulp had been "a regular army officer." The article claimed, "After the battle of Franklin, Tennessee, she met him on the battle-field," but he did not recognize her in her disguise. Then the article explained his death, "Before she could join him, she received news of his death, and did not reach Corinth, where he died, until after his funeral."

It is true that DeCaulp married Velazquez in 1863. It is not true, as she claimed, that he was an officer in the regular (Federal) army prior to the War. In her memoir, Velazquez claimed (p337) he enlisted prior, but did not say he was an officer. The truth is, after the start of the War, DeCaulp enlisted in the Confederacy and became an officer in the Arkansas 3rd Cavalry Regiment, which fought at Franklin, Tennessee. It is not true, as Velazquez wrote (*TWIB*, p215) that DeCaulp was at the Battle of Shiloh in Tennessee simply because the Arkansas 3rd Cavalry Regiment did not fight at Shiloh. It is not true that DeCaulp died in Corinth as she stated in the Atlanta article, or that he died "in a Federal hospital in Chattanooga… within three short weeks" of her marriage, as she wrote in *TWIB*, page 337. The truth is that he did not die while serving in the Confederate army. Velazquez wrote emotionally of how DeCaulp "fought nobly for the cause which he espoused." Velazquez might have been more precise which "cause" DeCaulp "espoused" because he deserted the Confederate army and joined the Union army and seemingly supported its noble cause too. DeCaulp did not die while serving in the Union army, either. He had already received a medical discharge and died a civilian.

Perhaps the most irksome of Velazquez's many false claims (*TWIB*, p337) is:

> I made an endeavor to procure his body for the purpose of sending it to his relatives in Scotland, in accordance with his last request, but owing to the exigencies of the military situation, -the Federals being in possession of Chattanooga,- I was unable to do so.

The lie was insensitive, at best, and an insult, at worst, to the families who, in reality, were unable to recover the body of their loved one.

By the time Velazquez wrote her book she had apparently forgotten her earlier and equally false claim about DeCaulp's death. Recall, the *St. Louis Republican* of March 7, 1866 announced her presence in that city and wrote:

> Her husband, who was taken prisoner in the fall of 1863, while serving with his regiment in Georgia, was carried to New York. After a long and arduous siege, she at length succeeded in getting him paroled in January, 1865, but he lived only eight days after his release from prison.

Velazquez's many and varying lies about DeCaulp's life and death, dishonors a fellow human being, not to mention a husband, and is inexplicable. A truthful account of the man's life and death is in order.

Who wasn't Thomas C. DeCaulp?

Velazquez claimed (*TWIB*, p337) her husband was a "native" of Edinburg, Scotland and came to the United States in 1857 with his brother; that he joined the regular United States army in 1859; and "He was very highly educated, having studied in England and France with the intention of becoming a physician." None of the claims are believable.

A record search failed to substantiate the DeCaulp surname in Scotland or any brother who came to America with him. A letter written by DeCaulp to Velazquez (May 12, 1864) used language which does not give a single hint of Scottish English. The letter was not that of a "highly educated" person; it abounds in misspellings and sentence construction errors. DeCaulp could have only been unsuccessfully "very highly educated." However, his penmanship is neat, smooth, relaxed and fluid.

The first hint of his true place of birth is found in Confederate army enlistment documents which state that DeCaulp was born in Pennsylvania. It should be noted that other researchers have misread this document, erroneously taking "Penn," for "Tenn," thus believing Tennessee. A comparison of handwriting throughout the document easily reveals the "P" is a "P" and not a "T," making DeCaulp born in Pennsylvania. Other records, presented shortly, confirm Pennsylvania.

DeCaulp's Military record

Prior to the Civil War, the U.S. Regular Army consisted of only about fifteen thousand men. Officers were a select few and their names are well documented in archival records. No DeCaulp was an officer prior to the Civil War, as Velazquez claimed in the 1874 Atlanta interview. In her memoir, two years later, Velazquez dropped her claim that he was an officer prior to the war, but only a soldier, meaning enlisted. No record of DeCaulp serving in the pre-Civil War military, as an enlisted, has been found.

At the outbreak of the Civil War, Thomas C. DeCaulp enlisted, at the age of 25, as a private in the 1st Regiment Arkansas Mounted Volunteers on July 29, 1861 at Pocahontas, Arkansas. If he had prior U.S. Army training and had been an officer, the Confederate army would have given him a rank, not letting him enlist as a private where his experience would be wasted. He was enlisted for the duration of the war by Colonel Solon Borland. DeCaulp was serving as 3rd corporal of Company "D" as early as August 31. He continued as 3rd corporal of Company "D" after the regiment was renamed the 3rd Regiment Arkansas Cavalry on January 15, 1862. But sometime between January 31 and April 30, 1862 he was reduced in rank back to private. He did not remain at that rank long. His leadership qualities must have endeared him to fellow soldiers and by May 26 (A different date of May 15 is given in another document.) he was elected 2nd lieutenant and on July 25 was promoted to 1st lieutenant.

No records found substantiate Velazquez's claim (*TWIB*, p87) that DeCaulp was ever in Pensacola, Florida at the 1861 face-off with the Union army at Fort Pickens. Velazquez claimed (p88) she left Pensacola on June 16, 1861, leaving her "battalion" under the command of DeCaulp, but DeCaulp did not enlist in the Confederacy until a month and a half later, on July 29, 1861, and 530 miles away in Pocahontas, in northern Arkansas.

No records found substantiate Velazquez's claim (*TWIB*, p204) that DeCaulp was at the Battle of Shiloh. The regimental records for DeCaulp's 3rd Arkansas Cavalry are clear; the regiment was not at the Battle of Shiloh or Pensacola.

The 3rd Arkansas Cavalry, which was serving as infantry because they had been dismounted for lack of horses, fought at the Battle of Corinth, Mississippi.[23] The Confederate after-battle report listed DeCaulp as missing; he had been captured on October 2.[24] DeCaulp was paroled and exchanged "at Camp near Helena, [Arkansas] December 2, 1862." He was delivered to the care of Lieutenant R. W. Stevenson "in charge of Flag of Truce, in behalf of Confederate States of America."

Once DeCaulp was exchanged, he was free to rejoin the Rebel army and his Company "D," which he did. The record provides no detail as to his activity or health from January to April 1863, but military records show that he was "Sent to Gen. Hospital May 4, 1863." Velazquez wrote he was in the hospital because of ill health and did not say it was because of a wound. However, an Arkansas newspaper reported "Capt. T. C. Decaulp," commanding Company "D," was wounded at the Battle of Thompson's Station on March 5, 1863.[25] At the time of DeCaulp's hospital admission, his rank was Captain. It can be reasonably assumed that he remained a patient at Empire Hotel Hospital in Atlanta until Velazquez met him. The testimonial of Dr. J. F. Hammond, in the 1876 publisher's advertisement circular (to be addressed), places DeCaulp already a patient there when Velazquez arrived on July 26, 1863. DeCaulp, after considerable time convalescing, regained enough strength to marry Velazquez, about the first week of September.

---

23. Peter Cozzens, *The Darkest Days of the War, The Battles of Iuka & Corinth* (Chapel Hill, NC: University of North Carolina Press, 1997).

24. NARA, RG109, War Department Collection of Confederate Records, Confederate Army Casualty Lists and Narrative Reports, 1861-1865, M836, Roll 2, Confederate Colonel S. G. Earle's "Report of Casualties of 3rd Ark Cavalry in the battle of Corinth" "Killed -10, Wounded-61, Missing-52" and "Lt. T. C. Decaulp" listed as missing.

25. *True Democrat* (Little Rock, Arkansas), May, 27, 1863.

He returned to active duty, but then deserted the Confederate army. All of the military records agree that he deserted, except one Union record which stated that DeCaulp was "captured" on Sept. 14, 1863 at Chattanooga and "appears on a register of Prisoners of War." The record of the "Union Headquarters of the Provost Marshal General in Nashville, Tenn.," noted that the "Des. [Deserter] Rebel has taken oath of allegiance." The Confederate records noted, "Deserted his country Oct. 15, 1863."

Other Union records stated that DeCaulp "Appears on a roll of deserters from the rebel army who have taken the oath of allegiance, and were released at Nashville, Tenn. by Capt. R. M. Goodwin... on Nov. 1, 1863." The Union army document stated that DeCaulp, "Came to our lines at Chattanooga... Sept. 14... was released Oct. 23... [and] Lives in Phila." It should be noted that this place of residence, Philadelphia, is consistent with his Confederate enlistment papers which state he was from Pennsylvania. DeCaulp signed (April 1, 1864) a statement that "he came over in the Federal lines at Chattanooga and reported to [Union] General W. S. Rosecrans on October 13, 1863." In other words, DeCaulp wrote that he deserted. DeCaulp was released by order of Major General Rosecrans on October 23.[26]

Thomas C. DeCaulp then lived in Indianapolis with Velazquez while she worked at the arsenal, but he seems not to have found any employment; Velazquez asked Indiana Governor Morton to give him a Union army commission, without success. DeCaulp then went to Baltimore, Maryland and using the name William Irwin "went as a substitute in the U.S. Service... on the 17th day of December 1863." DeCaulp signed a statement to this fact at Camp Reno, Milwaukee, Wisconsin on April 1, 1864.

Shortly afterwards, at Camp Reno on March 31, 1864, Captain Alen A. Arnold wrote a letter to "certify" the facts of William Irwin. Captain Arnold was the captain of Company "C" of the 30th Regular Wisconsin Volunteers in which Irwin was then serving as a private. The letter, for the Adjutant General's Office, stated that Irwin was assigned to the Company on February 1, 1864 by Brigadier General T. C. H. Smith and had been with the Company since February 8.

Captain Arnold stated that he understood that Irwin was one and the same as Thomas C. DeCaulp, who had been in the "rebel service" and that Irwin "appears to be a gentleman & a good soldier being always ready & willing to do his duty." Captain Arnold asked the addressee to notice Irwin's "request to be commissioned in the U.S. Service" and Irwin's "application & statements containing important information of the so-called Confederate

---

26. NARA, RG109, M598, Roll 8, Descriptive Lists of Confederate Prisoners and Deserters Released on Taking the Oath of Allegiance, vol 10, 1861-64, under "D" Commissioned Officers, entry 2; M598, Roll 39, Department of the Cumberland, Nashville, TN, Register of Prisoners, vol 105, 1864-65, p54, entry 481.

States." In other words, DeCaulp, now Irwin, was telling all he knew of the Rebel army in an effort to secure a Yankee officer's rank. Irwin, on April 1, wrote his own letter to the Assistant Adjutant General[27] requesting the commission he sought, explaining that he had been examined by Acting Assistant Adjutant General Major Louis H. Pelozed [*sic* Pelouze] and provided information on the Confederate States. This fact, of course, is in clear contradiction to Velazquez's many and strident assertions that DeCaulp was a steadfast Southern loyalist.

Captain Arnold wrote that Irwin "was a drafted man and substitute from Mason's [Roosevelt's] Island, District of Columbia." The reason is unclear for the discrepancy between Irwin's assertion that Baltimore was his place of enlistment, and Captain Arnold's statement that the District of Columbia was the location. However, it is clear that DeCaulp had been in Washington because of his claim to have met with Major Pelouze whose office was there. The locations are about 40 miles apart.

Irwin seems to have spent most of 1864 at Fort Snelling, Saint Paul, Minnesota. A letter written by Irwin firmly places him at Fort Snelling on May 12, 1864. He remained with Company "C" except for a brief transfer to Company "B" on April 16, 1864. By the fall of the year, Irwin was back with company "C." The various companies of the 30th Wisconsin did patrol duty to the west. That area was then the frontier, Indian country, and was under the watchful eye of the Irwin's regiment. It appears that he either seldom or never did patrol duty because of chronic poor health. William Irwin, as a Yankee soldier, never fought against the Confederate army. By the end of 1864 William Irwin was on his way to receiving a medical discharge, having served one year. His Certificate of Disability for Discharge states:

Private William Irwin, of Captain Alen A. Arnold Company 'C' of the Thirtieth Wisconsin Regiment of the United States Infantry Volunteers was enlisted by [lined out] Drafted at Baltimore in the 2nd Sub Dist on the Eighteenth day of December, 1863 to serve three years; he was born in Pennsylvania, is Twenty Eight years of age, Five feet Eleven inches high, Fair complexion, Grey eyes, Dark hair, and by occupation when enlisted a Carpenter... has been unfit for duty 60 days.

Once again, a military record asserted DeCaulp was born in Pennsylvania. Recall, his Confederate enlistment was the first. Note there is no mention of Scotland, where Velazquez claimed (*TWIB*, p337) he was born. His stated occupation of carpenter does not very well corroborate Velazquez's claim that he was "very highly educated, having studied in England and France with the intention of becoming a physician." From Irwin's physical

---

27. Edward D. Townsend.

description one might conclude that he was handsome enough to attract Velazquez, which he did.

Next on the certificate was the Acting Assistant Surgeon's statement:

> William Irwin of Captain Arnold's Company... [is] incapable of performing the duties of a soldier because of Chronic Sciatica and Hemorrhage of the Lungs. This soldier has done no duty for four months, Is unfit for Vet Res Corp. Disability two thirds and incurred since being drafted. No subject for bounty.

The Veterans Reserve Corps, previously known as the Invalid Corps, assigned invalid, but capable, soldiers to less strenuous duties, thereby, relieving the healthy soldiers to perform the more strenuous duties.

William Irwin was officially discharged on January 14, 1865 at Fort Snelling, Minnesota. The certificate concluded, "The Soldier desires to be addressed at Town, Holmesbergh [Holmesburg] County, Phila [Philadelphia] State [left blank]." For the fourth time, an official document connects DeCaulp to Pennsylvania and it even connects him to the particular suburb of Philadelphia called Holmesburg.[28]

Reviewing, first, DeCaulp stated in his Confederate army enlistment records his place of birth was Pennsylvania. Second, after his desertion and after he took an oath of allegiance to the Union, he was sent to Philadelphia. Third, his Union army discharge certificate states he was born in Pennsylvania. And finally, when he left the Union army he wished to be addressed at the town of Holmesburg, now part of Philadelphia. The evidence is convincing that DeCaulp was from Pennsylvania when compared to Velazquez's book's unsupported claim that he was born in Scotland. Furthermore, Velazquez contradicted her own book's assertion when she wrote to Governor Morton on December 7, 1863, stating that her husband was a "northern man borned [*sic*] in Philadelphia."

The mystery of DeCaulp's connection to Pennsylvania is not completely solved. The surname DeCaulp (or variant) is not found in any census from Pennsylvania and is not found in the 1850 or 1860 U.S. Census in Arkansas. Circumstantial evidence might lead one to suspect that Thomas C. DeCaulp was not the man's birth name, but a totally invented name. His birth name might have been "Benjamine F. Carter." Speculation about this name was made previously. If accepted that he was born in Philadelphia, then it might be speculated that he went to Arkansas and adopted a new name. Recall, Velazquez wrote that at the "breaking out of the war, he came South and offered his services to the Confederacy." When he went South and enlisted maybe he changed his name to DeCaulp, as he similarly changed his name when he went North and enlisted using the alias, Irwin.

---

28. NARA, CMSR for William Irwin.

William Irwin, after leaving the Union army, probably went to Philadelphia. It is assumed his health did not improve and about one year later, in December 1865, it appears he died. One William Irwin was listed in the "Return of Interments made to the Registrar" for Philadelphia for the "week ending December 16, 1865." The "Return" form contains information spaces for Age, Nativity and Diseases, but all were left blank. The record shows that his body was "removed from Hanover St. Vault" and was buried at the United American Mechanics and United Daughters of America Burial Ground at Islington Lane. The cemetery was subsequently closed and the bodies were removed and reburied at Philadelphia Memorial Park in Frazer, Chester County. A request to Philadelphia's Department of Records for William Irwin's death record received an answer that apparently no record accompanied the transfer of the body and that they were "unable to locate the death record."

Although there is no concrete link that William Irwin of the Philadelphia cemetery was the same William Irwin known as Thomas C. DeCaulp, the circumstantial evidence seems there. Recall, Irwin's discharge papers stated that he wished to be addressed at Holmesburg (part of Philadelphia).

The date of William Irwin's burial, the week of December 16, 1865, does not match any date given by Velazquez. Velazquez said to the *St. Louis Republican* (March 7, 1866) that DeCaulp died in January 1865, eight days after his release from a New York Yankee prison. Clearly this prison assertion is false. If this date too was false, one might speculate she gave it so that his death would have been before the end of the War. If his true death date was after the end the War (April 9, 1865), it would have ruined her story that he died while serving in the army, though it would have been the Yankee army and not the Rebel army as she always claimed.

Velazquez never could decide which story of his death to use. In her book she maintained that he "died in a Federal hospital in Chattanooga," three weeks after her (September) Atlanta marriage to him. The book's implied death date was September 1863, which in truth was when he deserted the Confederacy. And of course, in the 1874 Atlanta interview she claimed DeCaulp died in Corinth, Mississippi in 1864.

Curiously, Velazquez claimed Thomas had a brother who was also a captain in the Confederate army and "he died in Nashville just after the close of the war." This too was a lie, if he didn't use another surname. Military records do not document any "DeCaulp" other than Thomas.

Arrived in Louisville

Velazquez departed Atlanta on her way to New York and made a stop in Kentucky where the *Louisville Courier-Journal* of September 6, 1874 took notice of her in an article[29] titled "An Interesting Visitor":

> Mrs. Bonner, alias Harry Buford, of Mexico, is in the city- a guest of the United States Hotel. In a recent issue of the COURIER-JOURNAL there was published a sketch of her life as a soldier in the Confederate army, taken from a Southern exchange.
>
> Mrs. Bonner arrived in the city Friday [Sept. 4]. Yesterday she visited the Fair Grounds and remained to see a number of the races. She expressed herself pleased with the exhibition of the trotting stock. Mrs. Bonner is on her way to Lexington, Ky. She is about 35 years old, and although not particularly handsome, yet there is something striking about her countenance that renders it rather attractive. There is nothing masculine either in her talk, appearance or carriage. She says that she was the member of a Confederate company for eight months before her sex was ascertained. During that time her husband, who was captain of the company of which she was first lieutenant, was killed by the premature discharge of a gun. She succeeded him in command, but afterwards resigned and engaged as a soldier, free to come and go as she pleased. She says that she was never within hearing of a battle but what she hastened to the scene and entered into the fight. She was wounded three times during the war. After the surrender she married a second time, and her present husband is a miner in Mexico. She is now endeavoring to compose an autobiography, embracing her adventurers as a soldier, and a narrative of her travels in Eastern countries in the interest of the Southern cause. She is also a newspaper correspondent and is constantly writing for the papers.

There are more galloping falsehoods here than there are thoroughbreds in Kentucky.

First, she claimed her current husband, Bonner, was her second husband. Well, Bobo was her current husband. And remember only two days prior, in the Atlanta interview, she said that DeCaulp was her second husband. Later in her published book, she wrote Bonner was her fourth husband.

Second, in the article she made no claim to have raised the men of her company by herself, but in her memoir, she claimed that in the disguise of a lieutenant, she raised a "battalion" by herself. And in prior newspaper interviews she claimed that she raised the company by herself. In any case, it is false that she raised a company or battalion by herself; it is a fact that during the war, lieutenants did not raise companies. Captains raised companies. After a company was formed, the soldiers elected their lieutenants from among themselves.

Third, she claimed her husband was "captain of the company of which she was first lieutenant" and that after her husband was killed, she took

---

29. The article was reprinted in other newspapers.

command, but then resigned. The newspaper contradicts her memoir in which she explained that she, in a lieutenant's disguise, enlisted a "battalion" of 236 soldiers and delivered them to William who had been assigned to Pensacola. He was astonished when she furtively revealed her true identity to him. She wrote that he "took command" of the men and implied that her husband was an officer, a captain, but did not state his rank. If he was a captain of a company already at Pensacola, the question arises as to how he managed an additional 236 men. It was an impossibility that a captain was given a total of some 336 men; the men would have been made into new companies or dispersed into existing companies. In her book, she stated (p87) that upon the men's arrival in Pensacola, "they were mustered in, and stationed in camp, Thomas C. De Caulp was appointed first lieutenant, and Frank Murdock second lieutenant, while [she] was ordered back to New Orleans to purchase more stores and equipment." Well, recall in the article, she just claimed she was the 1st lieutenant. All versions of her leadership of a company or battalion were false.

Velazquez claimed to the newspaper that her husband "was killed by the premature discharge of a gun." However, in her memoir she claimed (p87) that her husband, William, was killed while explaining the use of a carbine, "the weapon exploded in his hands." There is a difference between a discharge and an explosion. In any case, so as to not leave the reader in a pall of sympathy, lingering like the cloud of smoke from the explosion, let the air be cleared with the truth that this accident did not happen. In her memoir she wrote that after her husband was killed, she immediately left Pensacola- so how did she "succeed him in command" then later resign, as she claimed in the article?

What of the exploding carbine? At this time Southern newspaper men were crawling all over the Pensacola Rebel camp looking for stories, almost any story. In one case, the Pensacola *Advertiser* wrote:

> A shark was caught this morning with a pair of red breeches and a whole parcel of Bowie knives in his belly- supposed to be the remains of a Zouave.[30] I didn't see the shark. It will be remembered I reported the drowning of a Zouave the other day.[31]

In another case, on April 1, 1861 the *New-Orleans Commercial Bulletin* reported:

---

30. American Civil War Zouave soldiers dressed in the fashion of the French Army Zouaves which served in North Africa beginning in 1831.
31. *Times-Picayune* (New Orleans), Apr 30, 1861, repeating stories of the Pensacola paper, dateline, "Pensacola, Thursday Evening, April 25."

A man was shot at the Redoubt[32] last night, in attempting to pass the sentry without the countersign. He died soon afterwards. No blame is attached to the sentry, who only performed his duty. The deceased was a member of the Red Eagle Company.

And in still another case, the *Mobile Daily Advertiser* of April 16, 1861 reported:

Killed- Last night, at the quarters of the Chipola Rifles, a member named Joel Brown, a quarrelsome man, and who was intoxicated at the time, insulted another member while sitting around the camp fire, who took up a stick and struck him on the head, making a pretty large gash. Brown was taken to the hospital, where he died this morning. He was perfectly insensible from the moment he was struck.

If this exploding carbine accident had happened, it would have been reported. At this early date in the war, when the public had not yet become accustomed to the death of its soldiers, the newspapers heralded any soldier's death, even if accidental, and especially if the soldier was an officer, and doubly especially if the death was by the explosion of anything. The alleged death of her alleged officer husband "William" wasn't reported by the newspapers because it did not happen. Worse still, this husband she called "William" and who she identified to the Atlanta *Constitution* (September 4, 1874) newspaper as William E. Burnet, was never her husband! And he was not then in Pensacola and did not die there!

About her return to Pensacola from New Orleans, Velazquez wrote (*TWIB*, p87), "Smothering my grief as much as possible, I turned over the command of my battalion to Lieutenant De Caulp." But wait, before she went to New Orleans, she had already turned over command of the men to husband "William" and DeCaulp was "appointed first lieutenant (*TWIB*, p87)." So, upon her return to Pensacola, why was it necessary for her to once again relinquish command of her men to anyone? In any case, as it has been shown, DeCaulp was nowhere near Pensacola, so could not have received command of the men. Besides, DeCaulp did not even join the Confederate army until July 29, 1861 at Pocahontas, Arkansas which was well after June 16, 1861, the date given by Velazquez when DeCaulp assumed 1st lieutenancy of the company.

She then wrote (p88) that, "On the 16th of June I started for Virginia" without her beloved "battalion." Taking note of the date she claimed she put on the uniform and the date she set out for Virginia without her "battalion," she was associated with the "battalion" at maximum from April 12 (*TWIB*, p56, p61) to June 16, which is two months, not eight months, the time which she claimed to the Louisville newspaper. This is the only possible time frame she could have been with this "battalion." But the truth is

---

32. The fort which protects the rear of Fort Barrancas, both west of Pensacola.

simpler; she was not with this or any "Confederate company for eight months" with or without her "husband," even a "husband" who, in truth, did not exist.

In contradiction, the "company" of the Louisville article, she called in her book a "battalion" of 236 recruited men. A battalion consisted of 2 to 8 one-hundred-man companies and was commanded by a major or lieutenant colonel, and not a lieutenant. Besides she could have never assembled a "battalion" or "236 men" without huge publicity. The forming of a 100-man military company was big news and never went unnoticed by the public or press; it was heralded from on high! Did Velazquez recruit a "company," or a "battalion" or both, since she freely claimed both? No, neither.

Encounter with Her Old Friend, Philip Arnold the Swindler

After Velazquez missed her intended train departure from Louisville and she, by chance, learned an old acquaintance was in the local jail, she once again became the topic of a newspaper article. The newspaper[33] of September 7 wrote, "Arnold's Difficulty. He is held Merely as a Witness- 'The Victim of a Swindle and Shameful Outrage.' What Mrs. Bonner Knows About It":

> When a COURIER-JOURNAL reporter conversed with Mrs. Bonner at the United States Hotel Saturday, he was not aware that she was acquainted with Philip Arnold, of Elizabethtown, and of Arizona diamond notoriety, nor did the distinguished lady know that Mr. Arnold was languishing in jail, waiting the pleasure of a California Court. The reporter had another interview with this remarkable person yesterday, and she informed him that she had heard during the morning of Mr. Arnold's incarceration, and rejoicing that she had been accidentally left by the Lexington train Saturday [Sept. 5]. She repaired immediately to see him and she afterwards gave an interesting account of the affair in which Mr. A is so unpleasantly mixed up. She is a woman of remarkable intelligence, having traveled extensively in this country and in Europe, and she has a business manner which will carry her through thick and thin, having already experienced a little of both. She showed evidences of her good name and of her high standing in California and the mining regions, and seems to be entirely truthful in her statements. She says she has no interest whatever in Mr. Arnold's welfare except as an acquaintance, and the statement which she made in writing is made up of facts- "true facts," to use her own expression, which she knew before she met Mr. Arnold at the jail yesterday. The following is her statement, which she wrote herself and which was addressed "To The Public Press:"
>
> In behalf of Mr. Arnold, whom I find here in jail on a requisition from the Governor of California, I wish to make a brief statement. The affair grew out of his connection with the Burra silver mine, located in the southwestern part of New Mexico. Mr. Arnold discovered and located this mine when he was prospecting for G. D. Roberts and Harpending, who were to have an equal interest with him in all

---

33. *Louisville Courier-Journal*, Sep 7, 1874.

the mines located by him. After his discovery of the Burra mine he returned to San Francisco and found from the assays that it was thought by many experienced miners to be very rich: the assays run from $10 to $4,000 a ton. Mr. Arnold then sold his interest for $25,000 to Mr. G. D. Roberts. It appears that Mr. Roberts afterwards sold his interest to a Mr. Treadwell for $30,000. The mine then belonged to Roberts, Harpending, Brown and Treadwell, and these gentlemen appointed Mr. Harpending to go to London to make a sale, giving him entire control of the matter. So Harpending went to London in 1870, organized a stock company and sold 200,000 pounds worth of stock. He came very near being successful, and it was currently rumored in California that Harpending had sold the mine for a million and half of dollars.

But owing to the many failures in mines, about that time, the stockholders became suspicious and drew their money out of the company. They demanded that their money be refunded, and as England's ways are not our ways made him give back the money. Harpending refunded the two hundred thousand which had been paid him by the stockholders and the scheme fell through. At that time there was a quantity of bogus stock dealed upon the market, which I believe Mr. Treadwell, and not Mr. Arnold had caused to be put upon the market for Mr. Arnold owned no interest in the mine.

After this failure of Treadwell and his associates, after a lapse of four years, Mr. Treadwell felt so hurt over the failure of their scheme that he conceived the idea of bringing suit against Roberts and Harpending to recover $30,000, which he paid for his interest in the mine. He still goes farther and has Roberts and Harpending indicted for "salting" the mine. Now in order to force Roberts and Harpending to refund the $30,000 he uses the old diamond indictment against Mr. Arnold, thinking they would refund the money, in order to secure his release from jail.

I have lived, with my husband, in the mining regions of Nevada, California, Colorado, New Mexico (my husband is now on the headwaters of the Gila on a mining expedition) and I have never heard of a miner being arrested for selling a mine to a speculator. We sell a mine for what we have in sight, and the purchaser takes his chances for its being a success. The miner sells for all he can get from the speculators, and it is considered a legitimate transaction. This rule holds good throughout all the mining regions where I have been.

Had Mr. Treadwell and his associates been successful in selling the Burra mine (I do not know how to spell the name of the mine- that is, the Spanish pronunciation of the word, which is donkey in English), by their London scheme, Mr. Arnold would not have been in prison today. I have been witness to so many swindling tricks that I am not surprised at anything they may do. I knew Mr. Arnold to be a very energetic miner, prospector and adventurer; one who has taken more desperate chances to prospect and develop the great mineral sources of the West than any other miner in the West; and he has received but little reward for his labor. He, in company with Messrs. Chisholm and Bowman, discovered the famous Emma mine; but they had to abandon their prospects on account of having no transportation and on account of Mormon difficulties in 1864.

In justice to Mr. Arnold, I must say that I think he is the victim of a swindle and shameful outrage. [signed] Mrs. E. H. Bonner, New Mexico

Velazquez fabricated her information about the Emma mine. J. F. Woodman and Robert B. Chisholm were the discoverers in 1868[34] so they could not have been troubled "Mormon difficulties in 1864" as claimed by Velazquez. Maybe Velazquez mistook Woodman's name and called him Bowman, but it is clear that neither Mr. Treadwell's name nor Philip Arnold's name is found associated with the discovery of the Emma mine.

The Mrs. Bonner and Philip Arnold association is a curiosity. Recall that in her early years, Velazquez called herself Mrs. M. M. Arnold. The alleged Mr. Arnold's first name is not known. It is possible that this husband was related to Philip, but it is clear that Philip was never her husband. Philip was very much married to another (with children together) by any date in which it would have been possible for Velazquez to marry him. If the common thread was not a relative, then, as Mrs. Bonner said, it was their acquaintance in the mining districts of "Nevada, California, Colorado and New Mexico." While married to the miner, E. H. Bonner, she indeed lived in locations where Arnold operated.

Arnold's arrest was based on two suits and both were related to silver mining deals in Grant County, New Mexico. Recall that this was the location where miner E. H. Bonner was working, and Mrs. Bonner stayed briefly, so there is no doubt that she knew, at least, of the existence of the Burro-Burro mine. The first suit involved Mr. Treadwell of California and the Burro-Burro silver mine. The second suit involved a silver mine in which Arnold took an option to purchase, but upon Arnold's inspection and sending an ore sample for assay, he decided against the purchase. Only the first suit is of interest.

Upon Arnold's arrest, his hometown newspaper[35] defended him stating the suits were unjustified and pressure tactics, using the old charges of the diamond swindle, to force Arnold to settle with the plaintiffs. (The story of the diamond swindle will be told shortly.) The newspaper's suspicion was not out of the realm of possible, since Arnold might have been glad to pay what the plaintiffs asked just to avoid extradition to California, where he had cultivated enemies in the diamond swindle. Or the newspaper might have supposed that since the plaintiff, L. L. Treadwell in California, was suing Roberts and Harpending, who were suspected co-conspirators in the diamond swindle, and Treadwell was trying to extradite Arnold, that Roberts and Harpending would apply pressure on Arnold to settle the suit in order

---

34. W. Turrentine Jackson, "The Infamous Emma Mine: A British Interest in the Little Cottonwood District, Utah Territory," Utah Historical Quarterly, Vol. 23, Nos. 1-4 (1955); D. B. Huntley, "Mining Industries of Utah," *Tenth Census, 1880, Vol. 13, Statistics and Technology of the Precious Metals* (Washington, DC: GPO, 1885) 423.; Norman L. Freeman, Reporter, *Reports of Cases at Law and in Chancery Argued and Determined in the Supreme Court of Illinois. Volume 93. Bragg v. Geddes et al.* (1879) (Springfield, 1880), 59.

35. *News* (Elizabethtown, Kentucky), Aug 20, 1874.

to avoid Arnold returning to California, where Arnold could be a potential witness against them.

Arnold was indicted by a San Francisco grand jury on two counts, "conspiracy to cheat" and "obtaining money under false pretense." The Governor of California requisitioned the Governor of Kentucky to arrest Arnold. The grand jury also indicted Asbury Harpending and George D. Roberts "for criminal transactions in the Burro-Burro mine business, in which Arnold was also involved." Harpending was in Europe, so was out of the reach of the law. Roberts paid $1000 bond and awaited trial. He was being sued for $50,000.[36]

The *Sacramento Daily Union* wrote, "Arnold's presence became an imperative necessity." Arnold had been alerted by a friend in California and as long as Arnold remained in his home county, he avoided arrest; his money bought influence with local county authorities. However, Arnold let his guard down by visiting distant Louisville and was arrested, locked in jail, and that was where Mrs. Bonner visited him. Arnold waited to answer the charge of having "swindled L. L. Treadwell out of $75,000 by false pretense."[37]

The California court date was postponed on account of Treadwell's inability to produce witnesses; Asbury Harpending was in Europe and Philip Arnold was still in Kentucky. On the day of the big trial, L. L. Treadwell had not succeeded in producing witnesses, so he did not even show up to pursue the case. The jury found George D. Roberts not guilty.[38] In spite of the verdict, historians agree, in the case of the Burro-Burro Mine, that there was an attempt to defraud investors.

Philip Arnold avoided arrest long enough that the trial proceeded without him. He was never extradited to California; in fact, the trial had already occurred five days before Mrs. Bonner wrote her letter in his defense.

It might be suspected that the Louisville paper paid Mrs. Bonner to write what she knew, since at that time she claimed she wrote for newspapers. Mrs. Bonner was seemingly sincere about Arnold's innocence as she would have had nothing to gain but public scorn for defending the guilty. She simply believed what she believed. To her credit, she wisely made no statement about Arnold's role or guilt as the head swindler in "The Great Diamond Hoax of 1872." Velazquez must have known the story of the diamond swindle, but probably knew there was nothing positive that she could say about it and Arnold, so she said nothing. The backlash came anyway.

---

36. *Sacramento Daily Union*, Aug 25, 1874, Sep 2, 1874.
37. Ibid, Aug 25, 1874.
38. Ibid, Sep 2, 1874.

The *San Francisco Bulletin*,[39] in an article titled "The Diamond Swindle Redivivus [Revived]," was incredulous at her defense of Arnold and wrote she was defending Arnold just like the Kentucky newspapers which try "to show that Arnold is the victim of a swindle and a shameful outrage." It continued:

> The following assertions of Mrs. Bonner will pass current as grim humor among Arnold's victims, and others who know him well: "I know Mr. Arnold to be a very energetic miner, prospector, and adventurer; one who has taken more desperate chances to prospect and develop the great mineral sources of the West than other miner in the West, and he has received but little reward for his labor." Considering the amount of money Arnold disgorged to Lent and Ralston, on account of his bogus-diamond field operations, and the sum expended in beautifying his home in Elizabethtown, to say nothing of the political and other influence secured by his reputation as a man of means, it would appear that Mrs. Bonner is mistaken about that "little reward" matter.

Velazquez was probably never aware of this rebuke. She had already departed Louisville, heading north.

---

39. Sep 14, 1874.

Chapter 10

Philip Arnold and The Great Diamond Hoax of 1872

Philip Arnold was a native of Elizabethtown, Kentucky, born in 1829. As a teenager he was indentured to learn the trade of a hatter, however, the excitement of the outbreak of the Mexican War in 1846 enticed him to enlist. At the War's conclusion, he went to California where he was a successful miner. Also, Arnold was a speculator, buying and selling mining properties.

Often a speculator would find himself with a mine in which he had invested good money, but failed to make it pay and now concluded to dispose of it. A desperate or greedy seller might "salt" the mine; salting in its simplest form was when ore containing gold or silver was dispersed throughout the mine so that it seemed a natural occurrence. If the potential buyer failed to see the trick, they would believe the mine to be rich and buy it.

The Great Diamond Hoax (or more correctly, Swindle or Fraud) of 1872 was a case of a salted mine. In a creative variation, the salters, or swindlers, used diamonds. The swindlers were Philip Arnold, the brains, and his older cousin John B. Slack, the accomplice. Arnold correctly gauged the worldwide excitement of recent South African diamond discoveries and determined that if he invented a diamond mine in the American West, investors would flock to it.[1]

Philip Arnold was associated with a Mister Cooper, the assistant book keeper for a San Francisco diamond drill bit company. From him, Arnold learned all he could about diamonds, and accumulated diamonds enough to mix with garnets, sapphires and rubies which he probably gathered or bought near Fort Defiance, New Mexico Territory (now Arizona). Cooper dropped out of the scheme, but Arnold's cousin, John B. Slack, became the new partner. This bag of "discovered" gems was shown to George D. Roberts who was told to keep the secret. But Roberts was too excited and wrote to his friend and partner Asbury Harpending who was in London, to come home to get in on the deal.

Roberts also told William M. Lent of the discovery and Lent asked to bring in General George S. Dodge for his opinion of the authenticity of the stones. Arnold and Slack played reluctant sellers of any portion of their discovery, but finally agreed to sell a share of their discovery to the eager investors. William C. Ralston of the Bank of California was the most prominent of the initial investors. With this money the miners traveled to London, to the diamond district, and purchased second quality diamonds in

---

1. The best treatment of the subject is *Diamonds in the Salt*, by Bruce A. Woodard, 1967. One of the principal speculators/investors was Asbury Harpending, who some suspected was a conspirator, but he maintained that he "was only a dupe" and wrote his own account of events in *The Great Diamond Hoax and Other Stirring Incidents in the Life of Asbury Harpending*, published by James H. Barry Co., San Francisco, in 1913.

bulk. Arnold returned to the West and used these diamonds to salt the "discovered diamond field."

As word of the discovery, but still secret location, became known to the newspapers, several expressed doubts of its veracity because of the poor reputations of the partnered speculators. William Lent at an earlier date had raffled his house in San Francisco, only to have a friend win, who then gave it back to him. Asbury Harpending had floated stocks in England to a played-out silver mine. It was this stock offering Velazquez addressed in her letter in the Louisville newspaper.

The diamond mine speculators-owners determined to offer public shares of stock for sale, so organized a corporation to do so. But first, the men asked the Mr. Charles Lewis Tiffany of New York to verify the authenticity of the diamonds, which he did. Then the group decided that an expert must evaluate the diamond field and hired Henry Janin, who was taken to the field. Janin reported the diamond field real and diamond fever soared.

The newly discovered diamond field became worldwide news. In London, some diamond dealers announced that they suspected that the large quantity of second quality diamonds which they had sold to some Americans might have been used to create the new field. This revelation should have been explosive, but nothing could subdue the enthusiasm. Even competing diamond prospecting companies were formed to participate in the stampede, that is, once they found out the location, which was still a secret.

Clarence King's U.S. Geological survey party was following the news and doubted the field's authenticity because they had traversed this geography and knew it was not diamond producing. King's party calculated where the field might be and successfully located it by the markings of human activity. It was clear to the geologists that there was salting because some of the diamonds they picked up showed evidence that they had been worked. The European diamond cutters had commenced working them, but then considered them unacceptable and put them in the reject pile. These were among the diamonds purchased in bulk by the swindlers and used in the salting. When King reported the fraud, the corporation failed and the newspapers howled, some with "I told you so."

Luckily for the secondary investors, their money was still sitting in an account in the Bank of California so they were reimbursed. It appears that only the initial speculators lost money. It is certain that Philip Arnold came away with at least $500,000 in 1872 money (about $13.8 million in 2023).

It was not a clean get away for Arnold. Early investor William M. Lent wasn't going to take his loss lying down. He sued Philip Arnold and John B. Slack for $350,000. The case was settled with Arnold paying $150,000,[2]

---

2. *Sacramento Daily Union*, Mar 25, 1873.

probably all from Arnold's portion of the scammed money since Cousin Slack's role was rather small and he had faded away, taking at most $50,000.

Shortly after Velazquez's jail visit to Arnold, he was released and never extradited to California. Arnold settled down comfortably in Elizabethtown with his abundance of cash and established the Arnold & Polk Bank. He fell into a business quarrel with the Longshaw Bank and one of the clerks, Holdsworth, "took an active part in the controversy, and Arnold cowhided him in the street." The two met in a bar and Arnold knocked down the clerk who then "ran to the bank, got a shot-gun, and fired at Arnold as he came from the barroom. Arnold returned the fire with his pistol, shooting five times. None of the shots hit Holdsworth, but one of them struck John Anderson, a farmer, passing entirely through the stomach. The second time Holdsworth fired, the entire load lodged in Arnold's right breast and shoulder...." The shooters were never prosecuted.[3]

The *San Francisco Chronicle*[4] unsympathetically wrote that Holdsworth had artistically planted some buckshot "of fine carat" in Arnold's right shoulder, the diamond pun obvious. Arnold managed not to die then, but he later contracted pneumonia, supposedly not related to his gunshot wound, and died in February 1879.

In conclusion, the only participants who were tagged as swindlers in The Great Diamond Hoax were Arnold and Slack. No evidence has emerged which identify any other conspirators, but there were and are suspicions of others' participation. It might be facetiously stated it was a case of little swindlers out-swindling big swindlers.

Why Velazquez did not address Arnold's diamond hoax is unclear. Either she wisely avoided it, or she missed the biggest scandal in mining of the day.

The Mark Twain Dispute and the Salt Lake City Letter

Mrs. Bonner had been gone from Atlanta about two months when an Atlanta-based correspondent[5] wrote of his skepticism about her:

Mrs. Bonner, the female Confederate Lieutenant, who created somewhat of a sensation here a few weeks since by announcing her intention to have her biography published, has gone North to see Mark Twain. I am informed by a publisher of this city that she had secured Mark Twain's service and that he was now actually engaged upon the task of writing a history of her romantic adventures. Due allowance for exaggeration must however be made weighing this announcement of this Confederate Joan D'Arc.

It will be remembered that it was in the Atlanta *Constitution* of September 4 that she first claimed that her book was "to be written by Mark Twain."

---

3. *Chicago Tribune*, Feb 20, 1879, taken from a Louisville letter to the *New York Sun*.
4. Sep 1, 1878.
5. *Chronicle and Sentinel* (Augusta, Georgia), Nov 1, 1874, dateline Oct 30.

So, this announcement took the claim one step further, that Twain had been "secured" and was "actually engaged upon the task of writing" her story. The "publisher of this city" who "informed" the reporter was surely William A. Ramsay, of whom more will be said when he contracts, in March 1875, to publish her book. Ramsay most likely had preliminary talks with Velazquez concerning her book and was following its progress. It is doubtful that he would have falsely claimed that Mrs. Bonner had procured Twain's services if he did not believe it true and no doubt Mrs. Bonner told him it was true.

Mrs. Bonner arrived in New York City about the second week of September, according to the *Daily Graphic News* of September 9, 1874:

> Mrs. E. H. Bonner, known throughout the South as 'Lieutenant Harry T. Buford,' has arrived in this city. As far as devotion to the Confederate cause was concerned, it seems that Mrs. Bonner was a double concentrated *Belle Lamar*, with the additional advantage of never having indulged in "the wild utterances of despeah [*sic* despair]!"

Belle Lamar was the Southern spy heroine of a Dion Boucicault melodramatic play, by the same name, which had just opened at the Booth's Theatre in New York on August 10, 1874.[6] The plot line is that Belle (nee) Lamar broke her marriage to Union army Colonel Philip Bligh because of her Southern sympathies. When she is captured as a spy, the Colonel must bring her to trial, but is torn because he still loves her. In any case, all ends well, and both Northern and Southern sensibilities are treated gently by the playwright. It can be supposed the heroine character was loosely based on authentic Southern spy Belle Boyd.

It must have been at this time that Velazquez wrote a letter with a New York City letterhead address of "No 155 E 29. St. NY" to "Mr. S. P. [*sic* L.] Clemens" asking him to write her biography. The letterhead contained only the year, 1874, but it can be supposed it was written in September, shortly after her arrival in New York.[7]

Velazquez must not have waited for Twain's reply before she shot off a letter to the "publisher" in Atlanta to say Twain would write her book. After

---

6. *New-York Daily Tribune*, Aug 11, 1874.
7. This letter has been indicated by the Mark Twain Project as having been written June–August 1874, but this seems not possible as she was not in New York at that time. On October 9 Twain wrote a letter to Henry Watterson stating that Mrs. Bonner had written twice "some months ago." However, this statement presents some confusion, as that would seemingly make this letter the third from Mrs. Bonner, but the contents of the letter make it sound like the first letter she would have written. It also will be seen, on October 13 Twain wrote to Owen McKinney that Mrs. Bonner was the "woman who wrote me & *asked* me once to help her write her book."

all, she had been saying for months that Twain would and it might never have occurred to her that Twain would deny her request.

Mrs. Bonner's letter to "Mr. S. P. Clemens" is clearly in her own hand and is typical of her other known letters. Misspellings, random capitalization, and the lack of sentence structure is in great evidence. She even mistook Mr. Clemens' middle initial, writing "P," instead of "L" for Langhorne. Wrong initials and misspellings of people's names were Velazquez's most enduring faults and are seen time and again in her writings. Her letter[8] to "Mr. S. P. Clemens," unedited, follows:

No 155 E 29. St. NY   1874

Mr. S. P. Clemens.
Dear Sir

The university Publishing Co and the author Z O Bond, also Apleton, advise me to correspond with you and to know by writing could you in the spring take hold of my Book, if written up by you it will have a large sale in the South and the West. I will now give you the subject of the Work. My autobiography as a an officer two and 8 months in the Southern Army and 4 years in the mining regions west of the Rocky Mountains 18 months life among the Mormons 7 months among the Apatchee Indians, containing an Exposee of the great Bounty and Banking Frauds here during the War, which came under my observation also the mining swindles, and as you can readily understand how we Californians stand when we say we are almost to the bed Rock. I am struggling along to get ready but am now compelled to have some assistance. I knew you at Virginia City, Karson, and Sanfrancisco. Your Roughing it I know without reading for I have been over the same country, if you should be in NY, call and see me

hoping to see you soon
I remain Yours Rpt-
Mrs. E. H. Bonner

Velazquez was telling tall tales to the premier teller of tall tales, Mark Twain. She asserted that she was "an officer" for "two [years] and eight months in the Southern Army." In her memoir, she never claimed she was a commissioned officer, only that she disguised herself in a rank. Also in her memoir, she claimed to have enlisted in the regular army for a "short time," not two years and eight months. And later, in an 1876 publisher's testimonial, Major John Newman said she served under his command for 3 months. His testimonial will be eviscerated later.

On her way to New York, Mrs. Bonner had passed through Palatine, West Virginia where she made the acquaintance of one Owen S. McKinney. He listened to her story and her claim that Twain was writing her book, but was doubtful and wanted verification.

---

8. Mrs. E. H. Bonner to SLC, June-August 1874, New York, N.Y., (UCLC 32055), Courtesy of the Mark Twain Project, The Bancroft Library, University of California, Berkeley.

McKinney[9] wrote Samuel L. Clemens on October 7, 1874 asking if he knew, during his time in California, a lady named Mrs. E. H. Bonner, alias Harry Buford. He said the Mobile *Register* and the Louisville *Courier-Journal* had given her "prominence" and judging from their articles and his "few brief hours of acquaintance" with her, "she is certainly a very great imposter or a remarkable woman." McKinney said she had documents, "undoubtedly genuine… purporting to be by you," on Clemens' publishing house stationary, which represented that Clemens was jointly with her writing "Harry Buford's Adventures during the War." The fact that she had such "prominent papers" was the reason, McKinney said, for being "taken in." If it was not true, please let him know.

Samuel L. Clemens, from Hartford, Connecticut, answered McKinney's inquiry on October 13, "Mr Dear Sir: The woman is a fraud- her assertions are without any foundation whatever." Clemens went on to say that he wrote to Mr. Watterson of the *Courier-Journal* saying that McKinney had written about Mrs. Bonner and that Clemens was not in a partnership "with any woman in a book." Clemens told McKinney he included a note of denial for Mr. Watterson to print if Watterson had been imposed upon by her. Clemens told McKinney that Mrs. Bonner had written and asked if Clemens could "help her write her book," that he "declined very positively" and Clemens supposed "she has forged my handwriting, now." And Clemens thanked McKinney for writing "about this matter."

"I was not much surprised to learn the woman is a fraud, though her representations were of the most plausible character," wrote Owen S. McKinney in his October 31 letter of reply to Clemens. McKinney explained that she showed letters from prominent people who asked "members of the press" to assist her during her travels. She also had a letter from General Casey, Collector for the Port of New Orleans, to President Grant asking him to help her acquire "some mineral specimens from Smithsonian Institute." She said she was promoting "Southern immigration" to the Gila Valley (Arizona) and was working for the Colonization Society there. The mineral specimens she intended as exhibits when she presented an address, "The Agriculture and Mineral Resources of New Mexico and Arizona as compared with those of the Southern States" at the Atlanta State Fair. McKinney wrote, "The tale she tells is well calculated from its plausibility- and from the documentation she exhibits- to obtain credence."

McKinney said now it was clear to him that Casey's letter was a forgery as well as the "one purporting to come from you" and that "she is one of the most intelligent as well as one of the 'cheekiest' women I ever saw." He explained to Clemens that she exhibited the lengthy articles from the Mobile

---

9. At this time, he was about 25 years of age and probably already a printer. The 1880 U.S. Census lists him as a printer.

Register and the Louisville *Courier-Journal* which seemed to add credibility to all her claims and that "she said she knew you personally in California." McKinney concluded, "She is an imposter of no ordinary rank."

McKinney said he would try to send a copy of the Mobile *Register* article which he had seen in some other newspapers and that perhaps Clemens, because of McKinney's necessarily short letter, would not see how McKinney was "so easily 'taken in,'" but McKinney stressed that "her story is admirably constructed, remarkably well told- being connected and coherent in all its details."[10]

It should be emphasized that McKinney identified two letters in Velazquez's possession as forgeries, the one from Samuel Clemens and one from the Port of New Orleans Collector's Office. Of course, these letters no longer exist to confirm whether they were forgeries. However, the forged letter from "Col. M. D. Hascall" does survive and is solid evidence of her willingness to commit forgery.

Just as Twain told McKinney that he had, Twain mailed a letter to Mr. Watterson, a personal friend and the editor of the *Courier-Journal*. Accompanying this letter was another letter, a public refutation of Mrs. Bonner, which Twain asked to be published in the *Courier-Journal*. The letter to Watterson is dated October 9, 1874, which probably indicates that he sent the letter the same day as he received Owen S. McKinney's letter. Twain wrote "My Dear Mr. Watterson" and explained that the woman had written him "twice, some months ago," asking him to write her story and that he "declined twice," and recommended someone else for the job and then heard nothing more from her. Clemens said he had not seen what Watterson had written about Clemens' association with Mrs. Bonner, but that if Watterson had asserted that Clemens was connected to Mrs. Bonner, it was not true and to print his enclosed "screed" or to write and tell him what to "say in its place." Clemens concluded, "Now I do not want the public defrauded in my name except when I do it myself- & not then, when I know it."

The "screed" that Clemens wished Mr. Watterson to print was printed in the *Courier-Journal*; it explained that Owen S. McKinney had written Clemens stating that Mrs. Bonner "exhibits documents purporting to come from me, & also professes to be joint proprietor" of a book about Harry Buford's adventures. Clemens asserted, "I have not furnished documents of the above sort to anybody. I am not joint proprietor in any book with any woman." Clemens said he wrote his denial because he understood the newspapers had been "imposed upon with the story of the joint book proprietorship" and he wished to make the correction.

---

10. No other letters between McKinney and Twain have been located.

It is unknown if Velazquez immediately saw or heard about Twain's repudiation, but she might have. The Mark Twain Project has in its collection evidence of another letter Velazquez wrote to Twain in the form of an envelope dated October 30, 1875, but with the contents missing; this might have been her letter in reaction to his screed.

Henry Watterson, editor of the *Courier-Journal*, ostensibly had read his own reporter's article, "An Interesting Visitor," the month prior, on September 6, 1874, but one wonders if Watterson had previously read about Lieutenant Harry T. Buford in other newspapers during the War or afterwards.

It seems that Watterson, with all of his peregrinations through the South and as a Southern newspaper man during the War, should have been aware of the multiple reports about and the claims of alias Lieutenant Harry T. Buford. Of particular interest to Watterson might have been her claim to the Augusta *Daily Constitution* of May 22, 1866, that she fought under Nathan B. Forrest. Watterson himself had ridden and fought with Forrest and he surely would have raised an eyebrow. If Watterson did indeed know of Velazquez and her alias, no comment in the known correspondence between him and Mark Twain shows it. In fact, it will be seen that when he replied to Twain, he addressed Velazquez as "this woman" and did not mention her role as alias Lieutenant Harry T. Buford. It is possible that Watterson simply paid no attention to the oddity of a woman in uniform because his all-consuming interest was politics. In particular, at that date, 1874, Henry was doing all he could to see that President Grant did not succeed in running for a third term as President.

Velazquez, when she returned to Atlanta, felt the repercussions of Twain's repudiation and had to defend herself in the newspapers, as will be seen. It also will be seen that she wrote a retort to the "Editors of the Corier [*sic*] Journal."

A Letter to Jefferson Davis, Ex-Confederate President

While still in New York City and from the same address as when she wrote to Mark Twain, Velazquez wrote a letter to Ex-President Jefferson Davis of the defeated Confederate States of America.[11] The letter is presented as Velazquez wrote it, retaining erroneous capitalizations, misspellings and her typical use of periods in place of commas:

Oct 16 1874
No 155 East 29 Street. Bt 3 & Lexington Avenue. New York-

Hon Jefferson Davis

---

11. Mrs. E. H. Bonner to Jefferson Davis, October 16, 1874, Jefferson Davis Papers, Louisiana Historical papers, Louisiana Research Collection, Tulane University.

Dr Sr

I have just been Shown a letter from you containing a photograph of myself in the confederate uniform during my service. in the glorious Confederate States Army, which belongs to your wife. allow me to thank you for your kindness. in Speaking of me. So highly. I have many such. Letters from prominent Officers and men of the South also ladies, but one coming from you has more affect than any of them. I have a very high Recommendation from Judah P. Benjamine, from London- I am now writing my Autobiography.. Lt. Harry T. Buford C'S'A or the woman in battle. by Mrs. E. H. Bonner- if not asking too much of you pleas [sic] give me Some of the most important. Items. in regard to. yourself. as to your capture and treatment together with Other very important. Items

[page 2]

as you may deem worthy of note. pleas [sic] inform me where I can find the Confederate Archives. I shall give you a bright page in the Annals of my work. I assure you. your persecutors will Suffer for there [sic their] Slander. I will give all my proceedings while in the Secret Services. if there is anything you or any of Our dear Old veterans whan [sic when] published you do not wish to be known in I am not afraid for I am going to Expose the US Officials at Washington, during the war I have points from the head quarters proceedings of Mr. Stanton, Johnson, on the assassination of Lincoln, from Cheif [sic] Dect Baker. under whose cloak I served the glorious Southern Cause.. if they refuse to publish my work. there are two English Companies in London & Manchester will take hold of it. there are 3 companies now anxious to take hold of it here. my reviser is afraid he says so far it contains too many plain facts. Let me hear from you at your Earliest Convenience. would be glad

[page 3]

to have a coppy [sic] of the Photograph also yours and Mrs. Davis- tender my Kindest regards to your Excellent wife. my little Son is name [sic] Jefferson for you he is five years old and is a dear little fellow. Should you be in the city. call and see me,

Yours Most Respectfully

Mrs. E. H. Bonner. or Lt. H. T. Buford C'S'A

First, this letter does not make clear that Velazquez had made Davis' acquaintance at a prior date, in particular, the intimate 1863 meeting she claimed (p345) in her memoir.

Second, it is not clear to whom Jefferson Davis' letter was addressed or to whom Mrs. Davis wished to show the photograph of Velazquez. It might be supposed that the photograph of Velazquez was one which Velazquez had sent to Mrs. Davis. The photograph might have been one taken in Charleston at the Quimby & Co. gallery in May 1866 or one taken in Nashville at Mr. Saltzman's gallery in June. To date, none of these photographs have been located, but surely one will surface eventually.

Third, none of the referenced "letters from prominent Officers and men of the South also ladies" or the letter with "a very high Recommendation from Judah P. Benjamine, from London" have been, to date, discovered.

However, her 1876 book's "publisher's circular" did present some endorsements, which will be addressed in detail.

Fourth, at this date Velazquez was content to use Mrs. E. H. Bonner as her authorship name, though she was finished with Bonner. She had since even married stagecoach driver Bobo, leaving him too. As will be seen, she didn't return to either man and decided to use her maiden name in her memoirs, never mentioning Bonner by name or revealing the Bobo marriage.

And lastly, Velazquez gave her son's name, Jefferson, which will shortly be of value in determining his fate.

A Letter to A. H. Stephens, Ex-Confederate Vice-President

Fifteen days after her letter to the Ex-President of the Confederacy, she wrote a similar letter to the Ex-Vice-President of the Confederacy asking for his help or thoughts on the War.

Prior to the War, the Georgian was a prominent politician at the forefront of the Southern issue and had served ten years in the U.S. House of Representatives. He spoke against breaking the Union, though he was adamantly pro-slavery on all points. At the outbreak of the War, he sided with his state and the Confederacy. After the Confederacy's defeat he was captured and imprisoned for five months. Upon his release, Georgians elected him to the U.S. Senate, but he was not permitted by Federal authorities to take office since he was an ex-Confederate. However, in 1873 he was elected to Congress and took his seat. He was re-elected multiple times and was serving as a congressman when he was in communication with Velazquez. The letter[12] is verbatim:

No 155 E 29. Street New York
Oct 31 1874

Hon: Alexander. H. Stephens
Dr Sir

I am first in receipt of a kind letter from Hon Jefferson Davis, who has kindly offered to help me in the way of information relative to our late war. I am writing my autobiography title Lt. Harry T. Buford or the Woman in Battle. together with my travels in Europe, South American. & four years in the mining regions west of the Rocky Mountains. 18 months life among the Mormons. 7 months life among the Toulorosa[13] [*sic* Tularosa] Apatchee [*sic* Apache] Indians. a full and complete discription of all the country South of the Great Salt Lake City to the Pacific also from [?Chihuahua], north to Denver City Col, with my late husband who was a

---

12. LOC, Alexander Hamilton Stephens Papers: General Correspondence, 1784-1886; 1874, Oct. 1-Nov. 25, Image 115 (Box 87, Reel 44).
13. Apaches from the vicinity of Rio Tularosa, Catron County, located immediately north of Grant County where Velazquez was with her husband in Silver City.

minor [*sic*], it will contain the great Bounty & Bank frauds and swindles during the war, which came under my special Observation. I intend to give our Veterans a bright page in my work. Any information you can give me as to the change of currency. Your mind on the causes of our down fall will be thankfully received. There is a gentleman in Richmond. prepairing [*sic*] a synopsis of his military career. hoping to hear from you at your Earliest convenience. I have the honor to escribe Myself.

Yours Most Respectfully
Mrs. E. H. Bonner

Velazquez directed Stephens' attention to a "kind letter" of which she was "in receipt" from Jefferson Davis. This letter appears to be the same letter which Velazquez said she had "been shown."

It is curious that she said her "late husband who was a miner" when he was neither "late" nor ceased being a miner. Maybe it was just a poor language choice. She had recently explained his New Mexico mining in the September 4, 1874 Atlanta interview.

She will again write to Stephens in 1876, gift him a book and name drop him as her advocate.

1875, Returned to Atlanta and Defended Her Name

It can be supposed that Mrs. Bonner spent the last two months of 1874 and the first half of 1875 in the North. An odd report[14] seems to indicate that she was still in New York:

Lieutenant Harry Benford [*sic*], who enlisted in the Confederate service in Memphis, and served with distinction up to the battle of Shiloh, where an ugly bullet wound in the shoulder led to the discovery that the gallant Lieutenant was a woman, is now Madame L. J. Velazquex [*sic*], agent in New York for the Paris house Ch. Fabre & Co., importers of artificial flowers. Upon the discovery of her sex, Lieutenant Benford was honorably discharged and sent to Richmond. She was of decided masculine appearance, and after the civil war attempted to join the Cuban insurgents, but failed, when she resumed petticoats and engaged in the above business.

It is unclear where the newspaper picked up her Benford name which was seen only briefly during the war. The assertion that she enlisted in Memphis is of unknown origin, as is, the assertion that she took a bullet to the shoulder at Shiloh and that she received an honorable discharge. In her book, Velazquez contradicts these three assertions and she never mentioned her Benford/Bensford alias.

The point worth learning is that this is the first public use of a newly chosen surname, "Velazquex," though the reporter certainly applied his own spelling of it. And she was seemingly, at this date, April 15, in New York

---

14. *Daily Memphis Avalanche*, Apr 15, 1875.

where she acquired an agency as an "importer of artificial flowers." If the claim was true, she did not stick with the business and can be placed in Key West on June 27.

Of the eight months which Velazquez spent in the North, she did not spend it all in New York because she would have had to spend time in Philadelphia to collaborate with her editor, "C. J. Worthington." Indeed, in the editor's preface, Worthington wrote he had "a number of interviews with her." Worthington circumstantially placed her both in New York and Philadelphia at that time when he wrote (p13), "In New York [and] Philadelphia… she has a large number of very warm friends…." And in documentation, yet to be presented, it is stated that Philadelphia was the location of her editor. The identity of this editor, to date, is rather a mystery. Further along a case will be made that the editor was none other than Charles A. Dunham, forger and liar extraordinaire. Dunham must have spent many hours, with and without her, turning her manuscript into its finished form, judging from Velazquez's known surviving letters.

While Mrs. Bonner was busy in the North seeking an editor for her book, the Atlanta *Constitution* published several articles which denounced her. Two articles from the January 15, 1875 edition were biting. The first article refreshed readers' minds that Mrs. Bonner, female lieutenant Harry Buford, had appeared in Atlanta some months ago when her history was written up:

> Amongst other things she stated that she had employed Mark Twain to write her life. She also promised to return here during the state fair, and drill the troops contesting for the prize. The woman was adroit, but she had not long left the city before it became known that she was an imposter. We have before us a letter from Mark Twain, denying all knowledge of her history. Now we publish on another page a letter from a correspondent in Salt Lake City, purporting to give some lively developments of her history.

It is worth noting that the newspaper asserted that it had written "her history just as she detailed it." This newspaper, and others, when they wrote their extensive articles after they interviewed Velazquez, wrote what they were told. The great contradictions found in these types of first-person reports were a result of Velazquez telling varying falsehoods of her story. Smaller newspapers sometimes borrowed these stories and occasionally made errors in the repetition. However, in the case of the *Constitution*, it clearly proclaimed its accuracy in reporting.

The second article was a letter to the editor with a letterhead, "Salt Lake City, Utah, January 5, 1875." The article was titled "From Mormondon. The Exploits of Mrs. Bonner. A Salt Lake Correspondent of The Constitution Tells a Strange Story":

> I saw an article of your paper, purporting to be a communication from Mrs. Bonner. I was in Austin, Nevada, when she came there in the winter of 1867-1868.

She then claimed to have a vast amount of property that had been confiscated, and she was taking measures to recover. She immediately COMMENCED A COURTSHIP with E. H. Bonner, who was a very quiet, modest miner. In a short time they were married. He made quite a large amount of money in 1868-1869, and as often as he got enough ore to make a crushing, she would receive a letter from her lawyer that she must come immediately to San Francisco with money to prosecute her suit, sign papers, etc., and by one excuse and another beat Bonner out of a great many thousand dollars. When she got it all, and he had worked out his claim, she applied for A DIVORCE. That was here in Salt Lake. She left here about eighteen months ago with a Jew for San Francisco, intending to marry him. Staid [sic] in San Francisco awhile with him, but he was too smart to be bilked by her.

She is without doubt a low, vulgar, UNPRINCIPLED ADVENTURER. Her ideas of morals are of the loosest kind, and no one in this country would believe her under oath. In a word, she is what the people in this country call an old blister.

I see by your article she is about to engage Mark Twain to write her life and exploits, but she will find Sam will see through her at the first sitting.

You can take the above for what you think it worth. At any rate, she will prove a dead beat, that I am sure.

Yours Truly, ADAM A. WILSON

(Mark Twain denies any knowledge of Mrs. Bonner.-EDS. CONSTITUTION.)

Since Velazquez was not present in Atlanta, she probably wasn't aware of the denunciations. Later, in the second half of 1875, when she returned to Atlanta, the denunciations caused her considerable headaches and she fought back with her words in the newspaper.

However, at this moment she had not yet returned to Atlanta, but was circuitously headed there. Her location is fixed on June 27, 1875 at the St. James Hotel in Key West, Florida[15] where she posted another letter[16] to Jefferson Davis. It would seem that Jefferson Davis had not answered her first letter, as she would have likely thanked him for it or referenced it in the second.

This second letter to "Hon. Jefferson Davis, Dear President," is a curiosity for several reasons. She asked for him to add his name to a list of "Refferences," but whether he did or even answered her letter is unclear. More interesting, perhaps, is that this is the earliest date found in which she wrote that she was born in Cuba and that her name is "Mad. L. J. Velazquez." Her letter is typical of her hurried writings- she readily sacrificed syntax on the scaffold, though she meant herself:

---

15. No Key West newspapers for June-July have been located in any archive (and probably haven't survived) which might provide more information about her visit there.
16. Jefferson Davis Collection, Eleanor S. Brockenbrough Library, Museum of the Confederacy, Richmond, Virginia.

I ask your influence in the Noble Cause of Poor Cuba- will you add to the list of Refferences, I have from many of our worthy Patriots and veterans of our lost cause. the Sunny South. for whom you know woman as I was Risked my life. my all. and would for her noble people again. if it was necessary. on my duty. now I am ready to Sacrifice my life on the Scaffold for. Noble Cuba where I was borned. Why shouldt I. my native Land when I would for the of [sic] my adoption the home of my husband my children. I am not able to Serve her on the Battle feild [sic] as I was disabled in my right shoulder So I can not Carry a Sword or musket. Now I ask you to give me a Letter which will help me at present to help my poor Country. I Only wish I had 2000 of Our Old tried veterans well Armed and Equiped I could drive the destestable Spanish from the Island let me hear from You at your Earliest Convenience. hoping this will find you well. You have my best wishes for your prosperity. pleas when you write direct Ofc Tift & Co
Yours Respectfully
Mad. L. J. Velazquez

Velazquez implied that Davis knew her which he did, at least, from her previous letter. It seems Velazquez was seeking a character reference to enhance anticipated book sales, in a rather indirect and disguised way, by asking for an endorsement for the Cuban freedom fighters and Davis' "influence" with U.S. authorities.

At that time there was a revolution in Cuba against mother country Spain. Cuban exiles and insurgents continually requested Washington officials to apply political pressure on Spain, but the U.S. refused and remained neutral. It is impossible that Jefferson Davis had any influence on U.S. foreign policy, so Velazquez asking for his "influence" seems mindless.

The exiled Cuban community in Key West collected money in support of excursions seeking to overthrow Spanish rule; exiled Cuban communities in New York, New Orleans and elsewhere worked to that end, as well.

Was Velazquez raising funds for the Cuban revolutionaries? She did not say she was, but it is possible, since fundraising for the Cubans was at that time common. If she was, was she dipping into the proceeds? It should be recalled that during the Civil War, in New York, she sought permission to raise money for the children of Yankee soldiers. It is easy to suspect that she pocketed all or some of the children's money because at that time she had none herself. If she was collecting money for Cuba, it might easily be supposed she kept some of the money, as she seemingly had no other income source at that time. However, her concern about Cuba's welfare was sincere as evinced later by the amount of time and energy she expended in addressing Cuba's independence. In about 1877, she tried to direct attention to Cuba in a public paper titled, "Address to the American Congress on Cuba." More on this address later.

Finally, was Velazquez simply seeking a reference from a prominent person, specifically Jefferson Davis, to help her promote her soon to be published book? She spent her entire life collecting character references of all kinds, even if she had to forge them. If Davis replied at all, it can be suspected that she would have found a way to embellish his reply into an endorsement, if necessary. Think Mark Twain.

During her absence from Atlanta, her publisher-designate, William A. Ramsay, was having financial difficulty. The first upset came when "the firm of Ramsey & Brandner" was dissolved.[17] Although the breaking of a partnership is not always a bad thing, it must have left him financially short.

The second upset came when all of Ramsay's Southern Publishing Company's property was placed in the "Fulton Sheriff's Sales for May, 1875." The Fulton Superior Court had issued a lien against the company stemming from a lawsuit against W. A. Ramsay and "all the printing material, types, stands, cases, cabinets, racks, office furniture, presses and fixtures used and now in the printing office" were levied on. Also, a real estate lot owned by Ramsay was levied on "to satisfy his State and county tax for the year 1874."[18]

On June 6, 1875, Ramsay advertised, "Partner wanted… with from $3,500 to $10,000 cash… to extend our facility so as to meet the present and rapidly increasing demands of the public." Ramsay described Southern Publishing Company as "the largest, best and most complete Printing and Publishing House in the South… showing that we can compete with Northern Houses."[19] It appears that Ramsay failed to get his partnership.

It is not known how or when Velazquez and Ramsay sealed the deal on her book. They may have agreed to a contract before she departed for the North, as was implied in a previous news report, or they may have come to an agreement through the mail. A *Constitution* article from March 9, 1876 stated that the contract was entered into "about a year ago" which would have made it sometime around March 1875, when she was not in Atlanta. The earliest found public announcement that "W. A. Ramsey, of Atlanta" was to publish her book was in the *New York Herald* of August 9, 1875, under "Literary Chit-Chat." It is unclear from where the *Herald* gathered the news. This is the first found announcement of the final title of the book.

Velazquez's return to Atlanta was first noted in a *Constitution* news brief on October 2, "Pleasant Pop Calls.- We have been pleased to meet in our sanctum; Madame Velasquez [*sic*] or 'the woman in battle.'" She had arrived on October 1[20] in which case she must have previously supplied, by mail, the (following) catchy summary of her book to Ramsay for advertising.

---

17. *Atlanta Constitution*, Feb 27, 1875.
18. Ibid, May 4, 1875.
19. Ibid, Jun 6, 1875.
20. Ibid, Oct 6, 1875.

On September 11, 1875 the Southern Publishing Company placed a large attractive two-part advertisement in the *Constitution*. The first part touted the Company as the "largest, best and most complete" printing house in the South and stated other admirable capabilities. The second part announced "Agents wanted for the Woman in Battle." The ad then gave a very enticing summary of Velazquez's exploits and of the book's content:

> Madame Velasquez, disguised as a Confederate officer, participated in a number of the hardest fought battles of the late war, and greatly distinguished herself by the extraordinary valor she displayed… and was the heroine of a number of exploits even more interesting than those of the battle-field.

After the summary of the exploits, the ad continued, "The above facts are substantiated by leading men both South and North who participated." The ad included the editor's name, but miswrote it as "J. C. Worthington" instead of "C. J. Worthington." It should be noted that this advertisement establishes September 11, 1875 as the earliest date when Velazquez revealed the name of her editor.

Clearly, Ramsay thought he had a blockbuster of a book and sought agents who were told that they "can make more money by canvassing for this book than any others, as it is the cheapest as well as the best-selling Agents' book ever published." Besides the Atlanta newspaper, at least one other Georgia newspaper carried the same advertisement and it added the headline, "A TRUE SOUTHERN HEROINE."[21] Outside of Georgia, two Tennessee newspapers and a South Carolina newspaper ran the same advertisement and there were others.[22]

The Southern Publishing Company must have appeared at this time to Velazquez as stable and prosperous. The company advertised its upcoming two-dollar city directory to "surpass anything of the kind ever published" and "it is in the hands of undoubted ability."[23] The company claimed itself:

> …the Largest, Best and most Complete Book and Job Printing… Manufacturing ESTABLISHMENT IN THE SOUTH! and the only one that can compete with Northern Houses in price and mechanical execution… satisfaction guaranteed… WM. A. RAMSAY, PRESIDENT[24]

Upon her return to Atlanta, Velazquez became aware of the January 1875 newspaper denunciations of her and she defended herself in the *Constitution*[25]

---

21. *Bainbridge Weekly Democrat*, Dec 16, 23, 1875.
22. *Fayetteville Observer*, Dec 9, 16 and 23; Jonesborough *Herald Tribune*, Dec 2, 9, 16 and 23; The *Newberry Herald* (South Carolina) first ran the advertisement on Dec 1, 1875 and ran it for seven months; *Shepherdstown Register* (W. Virginia), Dec 4, 11, 1875.
23. *Constitution* (Atlanta), Sep 16, 21, 29, and Oct 8, 10, 20, 28, 29, 1875.
24. Ibid, Sep 11, 1875.
25. Oct 6, 1875.

asserting that Adam A. Wilson's letter "is false in every particular." The newspaper wrote:

> She says she has written to Salt Lake City, as well as to several prominent gentlemen in Utah, making inquiries about Wilson, and can neither hear from nor about him. She is satisfied that there is no such man in Salt Lake City, or that if there is, nobody has heard of him."

The reporter added, "Mrs. Bonner has several letters which would seem to establish her identity" and that she had just arrived to "superintend a book, giving her war history, and shortly to be published by the Southern Publishing company." The *Constitution's* reporter seemed focused on establishing Velazquez's identity and probably did not think to substantiate Velazquez's claims or claims against her.

Velazquez brilliantly discredited Wilson's statement by implying that he did not exist in Salt Lake City, even though Wilson did not claim to be an established resident there. He claimed that he was in Austin, Nevada when Velazquez arrived there during the winter of 1867-1868 and she did not refute that. The odds are that she knew him in Austin, since the town was small enough. The 1870 U.S. Census for the Austin area reveals two men named "A. Wilson," both were miners. One was from Kentucky and 37 years old, and the other from Iowa and 31 years old. Surely the writer was one of these men, take your pick. He knew her and wrote about her, no doubt, for his own reasons.

If Adam A. Wilson was correct in his claim that Velazquez "applied" for a divorce, the divorce was not finalized- this conclusion reached by the absence of court records in Salt Lake City which would have been found if true. If Velazquez went with another man to San Francisco, she returned to Bonner and did not divorce Bonner. She claimed many times after the date of Wilson's letter to be married to Bonner and Mr. and Mrs. E. H. Bonner, together, briefly managed a hotel in Silver City and that was after their departure from Salt Lake City. Of course, when she left Bonner, she married Bobo in Texas.

Nine days later the *Constitution*[26] again reported on Velazquez in an article titled "The Woman in Battle" and the reporter was now satisfied as to Velazquez's identity:

> This is the title of a new book soon to be published, giving the history of Lieutenant Harry F. [*sic*] Buford, of Confederate fame, who is now in the city supervising the work. She has resumed her maiden name of Velasquez. We have seen her, and she has shown us numerous letters of identification. She is well known to citizens of Atlanta, among them our Col. Acton, and there can be no

---

26. Oct 15, 1875.

doubt of the fact that she is the veritable Lieutenant Buford. The book will soon be out and we trust it will have a good sale, for it will doubtless be most interesting.

Colonel Acton and his significance will be discussed further along.

In the meantime, the Augusta *Constitutionalist* wrote a flattering article about Velazquez. The newspaper's correspondent, Martha, who steadily supplied Atlanta news in a section titled "Letter from Atlanta," wrote:[27]

Belle Boyd and Harry Buford- Extraordinary Adventures of a Female Soldier- A Cuban Patriot in a Pullback- Cupid and Mars-

The names of Belle and Harry Buford occupy a conspicuous place in the history of the late unpleasantness, as Confederate spies and valuable aids to a glorious cause. Poor Belle, now in California, was unfortunate. She had all the opportunities to make a name that would go sounding down all ages; but her fame was only a sudden burst, passion-like, to finally die away. She had a pretty face and that was her trouble. Flattery spoilt her and she did more gallant service under Cupid than Mars. She has been, since the close of the war, an inmate of an insane asylum, in which her baby was born.

With Harry Buford the case was different. She went into the army with her husband, disguised as a soldier and won her way to a lieutenancy by sustaining an unblemished reputation, valiant service in battle, and discharge of important offices of trust. A Cuban by birth, she enlisted her sympathies in the cause for liberty of the South and right royally did she serve it. Her sex was discovered by reason of being wounded, at New Orleans, but was known only to a few, afterwards her sex was again discovered in Atlanta when it became generally known and of course compelled her to abandon the disguise. In September, 1863 she was again married (her former husband having been killed) at the Atlanta Hotel, on the site where the Kimball House now stands, to Captain T. C. De Caulp, in the presence of Dr. Jos. Thompson, A. F. Finney and Dr. Hammond and others. Those names are in Atlanta now, and testify to the identity of Harry and Mad. Loveta [sic] J. Velazquez who is now in the city.

Since the war closed, Harry has roamed nearly all over the world. Having a little son, about six years of age, to support and educate, she has devoted many years to the preparation of a book to be called "The Woman in Battle." In this remarkable book is recounted all of her daring exploits, by land and sea, while in the service of the Lost Cause. The proceeds of the sale of this work will be applied to the maintenance of herself and child. Knowing that Mad. Velazquez was in the city and desiring to see and talk to the famous Harry Buford, of whom I had read so much during the war, I called on her in behalf of the *Constitutionalist* and interviewed her.

She is a tall graceful woman, something over thirty I would judge, with a face somewhat masculinish [sic]. The cheek bones are rather prominent, and she has a delicate shade of down on her upper lip that reminds one of the average young America[n]'s first effort at raising a moustache. Her eyes, blue in color, have a way of brightening up and sparkling when she speaks of her native land, struggling Cuba. Although having passed through all the roughness of camp life, among

---

27. Oct 7, 1875, article dated Oct 6.

soldiers of every grade, who never suspected her true sex, she bears that modest demeanor that belongs to woman, and you can't for the life of you detect anything in her deportment or conversation that would be expected from a woman who has gone through her many trials and mingled with so many men.

In her apartments [*sic*] she has many photographs of distinguished men, Confederate and Cuban officials, and one of herself in uniform. She showed me letters from prominent men in the North and South commending her and her book. One from G. W. Alexander, formerly commander of the famous Libby Prison at Richmond, now editor and proprietor of the Washington, D.C., *Gazette*, addressed to her as "Dear Harry." He knew her under that pseudonym during the war. There were also several from W. J. Clarke, Jr., Philadelphia, Max Adeler's brother, who has rendered her great service in the preparation of her book.

She is an enthusiast on the subject of Cuba. She believes firmly that, provided the Island is recognized by England or America, that the Cubans will eventually win the fight. Since the successful landing of vessels containing guns and munitions, that the army has been strengthened and more victories won. Over five thousand Cuban refugees are in Key West, unable to return to Havana, and that these patriotic refugees send all their money for the support of the Cuban army. She is anxious that the Southern press should impress upon Southern Congressmen the importance of using their influence to have Cuba recognized as a nation by our Government. Then, she says, the ports of Savannah, Charleston, Mobile, New Orleans and Galveston will be opened to and receive from the Island large imports of sugar, coffee, rum, tobacco, cigars, fruits, etc., which will tend to enrich the South and make her that much more independent.

Madame Velazquez certainly loves the South. She has done a great deal for it, and is willing to do more. Yet, there are newspapers, the Atlanta *Constitution* for one, which have endeavored to have the public believe that she is an imposter. She has convincing proofs of her identity, and refers to such men as Dr. Thompson, Dr. Hammond and other well known men, right here in the city. These and other strong proofs that she is the identical daring Harry Buford, and withal a lady of unquestionable reputation, are to be shown to any one who may doubt her. The *Constitution* should, by all means, retract its erroneous statement. Mr. Salem Dutcher, Mr. Randall and Mr. Hewitt, of your city [Atlanta], will perhaps remember her. She refers to those gentlemen and certain they will identify her as being the veritable Harry Buford.

First, the reporter addressed the veracity of Velazquez's identity, not the veracity of Velazquez' claimed deeds. Today, there is no question that Velazquez was the same as alias Lieutenant Harry T. Buford. It's the claimed deeds which are in doubt and the important ones are provably false.

Second, the reporter briefly contrasted Belle's fate as "an inmate of an insane asylum," to Velazquez's, whose "case was different." In fact, Belle Boyd had been admitted briefly to the asylum in October 1869, received medical treatment, recovered and was released by 1870. While there, she had a son. After her release she had three more children. She pursued a full life, dying at the age of 56. The reporter noted Velazquez's considerable inner and outer strength which seemed to exclude her from Belle's fate, but the reporter, accurate to that date, could never (and didn't try) have imagined Velazquez's fate.

Third, it is not to be doubted that Velazquez married DeCaulp in September 1863, probably the first week. To date the marriage certificate is not found. It is surely true that Dr. Joseph Thompson was present at the wedding, since he was the proprietor of the Atlanta Hotel. Dr. Hammond also attended; he wrote, as will be seen, in the publisher's testimonial that he did. The identity of A. F. Finney is unclear.

Fourth, of the three named Augusta men who were stated to "perhaps remember her," at least two were prominent citizens of that city. Mr. Salem Dutcher, later in 1890, published a history of Augusta titled *Memorial History of Augusta*. And Mr. Randall must have been James Ryder Randall, editor, for many years, of the Augusta *Chronicle* to whom Velazquez might have told her story, but it can be certain that he was not a witness to any of her claims.[28] The identity of the third man, Mr. Hewitt, was likely John Hill Hewitt, who had lived in Augusta, but in 1875, was no longer living there, but was instead in Maryland.

John Hill Hewitt was well-known as an author, a poet, a musician, a composer, and a playwright. During the war he wrote plays which supported the Confederacy. (He tried to enlist at the age of sixty.) His first war-time play, *The Scouts; or, The Plains of Manassas*, produced in 1861, presented women as capable soldiers when they "dress[ed] as Zouaves[29] in order to capture a federal picket." Also, within the story is "a comic love plot provided by an Arkansas 'free-fighter' who falls in love with Jeanette, another of the female soldiers." The similarity of Velazquez's narrative- Arkansas soldier Captain DeCaulp falls in love with Loreta "Janeta," a female soldier- seems only a coincidence without any connection. Hewitt could not have modeled his Arkansas soldier on DeCaulp, since DeCaulp only entered the picture in 1863. However, did Velazquez take her middle name from Jeanette?

Hewitt's most successful play was titled *The Vivandiere* and was performed in February 1863 in Augusta. The lead character is Louise, a Southern heroine who joins the soldiers at Manassas and captures a Union soldier, who turns out to be her brother. "She carries a pistol and wears pantaloons."[30] If Velazquez's Mr. Hewitt is not one and the same as

---

28. Lucian Lamar Knight, *Georgia's Landmarks, Memorials, and Legends, Vol 1 Part 1* (Atlanta: Byrd Printing Co., 1913), 45.
29. Civil War soldiers who dressed in the fashion of the French army which served in North Africa beginning in 1831.
30. Charles S. Watson, *The History of Southern Drama* (Lexington, KY: Univ Press of Kentucky, 1997), 77-79.

playwright John Hill Hewitt, then the coincidence of their mutual interest is unexplainable.

Fifth, Velazquez named "W. J. Clarke Jr." of Philadelphia as a person who rendered great service with the preparation of her book. This was not the man who was ultimately claimed as the book's editor. That was one "C. J. Worthington" and much more will be said about him.

Besides her fuss with the Atlanta *Constitution*, Velazquez also struck back at the Louisville *Courier-Journal* when she wrote a letter to its editors on October 7, 1875. She used the Southern Publishing Company's very attractive letterhead stationery which contained in the upper left corner a printed note for "The Woman in Battle, The Greatest War Book Ever Published- Agents Wanted." Velazquez's letter[31] is presented verbatim:

> Editors of the Corier [*sic*] Journal
> Gentlemen
> I have before me an Article published in the Constitution purporting to be a letter. Published in the Columns of the Courier Journal. last winter. from Mark Twain. denying any knowledge of my history. the Constitution claims they clipped it from your paper. I therefore ask you to produce Said Letter. as I am in Possession of Several Letters. from Mark Twain denying the writing said Letters to your Paper. as to his writing my Book. he had nothing to do with it. now injustice I Either wish you to forward to my Publisher the Letter from Sam. Clemens or Mark Twain. Or correct the statement you have made. my marriage name is Mrs. E. H. Bonner and Velazquez is my fathers [*sic*] name. which I have chose [*sic*] for the Title of my Book. now in Press. the Woman in Battle. let me hear from you at your earliest
> Yours Respectfully
> Mrs L. J. Velazquez

Velazquez rather indignantly asserted that Twain had nothing to do with the writing of her book which was <u>not</u> what she had claimed prior, in September and November of 1874, when she said he would write her story. But most impressive is the fact that Velazquez boldly claimed she had in her possession a letter from Mark Twain in which he denied that he ever wrote a letter to the newspaper in which he denied any knowledge of her history, when the newspaper had in its possession the exact denunciation letter. She then audaciously asked that Twain's denunciation letter be sent to her publisher. Was Velazquez trying to get the letter in order to take it out of the newspaper's possession and thus the public realm?

In Velazquez's original handwritten letter to the newspaper, where she wrote that "Velazquez is my fathers [*sic*] name," she first wrote V-E-L-A-S, but then wrote over the S with a Z. For her entire life she was conflicted

---

31. Mrs. E. H. Bonner to Louisville *Courier-Journal*, 7 October 1875, Atlanta, GA., (UCLC 32217), Courtesy of the Mark Twain Project, The Bancroft Library, University of California, Berkeley.

how to spell the name of her revered father, the one of noble Castilian heritage. It also should be noted that the letter sounds like the writer was not a native writer of English, another sliver of evidence of Velazquez's origins.

When Henry Watterson of the *Courier-Journal* received this letter he wrote on the back, "Dear Clemens, What have you done to this woman" and forwarded it to Samuel Clemens. Clemens then wrote on Watterson's envelope, "Female fraud."

It can be imagined that these were difficult times for Velazquez and the fact that she next fell ill must have been the straw that almost broke the camel's back:

> Lieut. Harry T. Buford.- Madame Velasquez, otherwise known as "Lieut. Harry T. Buford" has been quite ill in this city for ten days past, and on yesterday was taken with convulsions, which lasted about 9 hours. She is some better now, and the Dr. is hopeful of her recovery.[32]

In the meantime Southern Publishing Company was having trouble with one of their contract sales agents for the city directory and William Ramsay warned, "CAUTION!," that one T. M. Haddock was no longer their agent and all contracts for the directory written by Haddock were returned by the court to the rightful owner, Ramsay. The contracts by Haddock would be honored, but future contracts written by him would not.[33] Velazquez, two weeks after Haddock's firing, presented herself in Marietta, Georgia "in the interest of a Directory of Atlanta, Marietta, and other towns."

The local newspaper said:

> Madame Loreta Jauneta [*sic*] Velazquez is also getting out a book of 600 pages, entitled "The Woman in Battle," reciting her romantic career as a disguised Confederate officer, spy, & c. She evidently will get out a work worth reading and patronizing.[34]

The Woman in Battle seemed to be on a positive course for publication. The *Sunny South* (Atlanta) of December 18, 1875 reported:

> The new sensational book... the experiences of Madame Velasquez as a spy, a soldier, and an officer of the Confederate army, is now ready for the press, the plates being all electrotyped. We have been favored with a sight of the very unique table of contents. The book is written by a distinguished Northern writer, and Mark Twain is reported to have said that it will be *the* book of the season.

It is astounding that Velazquez would not let go of the Mark Twain connection, especially after Twain had completely denounced her. She may

---

32. *Constitution* (Atlanta), Oct 31, 1875.
33. Ibid, Nov 3, 1875, noticed dated Oct 30, signed by Wm. A. Ramsay.
34. *Marietta Journal*, Nov 19, 1875.

have been trying to plant a different version of events in the mind of the public, hoping they would forget the true earlier version, that is, the thrashing she had received from Twain. She was trying to drum up interest in her book and she rightly figured that a word of praise from Twain would help sales. Of course, she falsely claimed his praise.

In December 1875 and January 1876, the Southern Publishing Company placed help wanted advertisements for book sales agents in South Carolina and Tennessee newspapers and maybe others. The advertisements ran from one to seven months and were substantially the same as the one that appeared four months prior in the Atlanta *Constitution*.[35]

The publisher was seeking agents and the book was "ready for the press," but there was one obstacle. The newspaper announced, "Marshall's Sale for January 1876... three presses and fixtures... levied on as the property of the Southern Publishing Company, for their city tax for the years 1874 and 1875."[36] Surely now Velazquez feared, if not completely understood, that Southern Publishing Company's financial problem was going to hurt her book.

Velazquez the Reporter

While Velazquez waited in Atlanta for progress on her book, she apparently occupied herself as a newspaper reporter. At least, that is what one Atlanta correspondent[37] thought Velazquez was doing and wrote of events at the State House:

... I will tell you instead of our fair reporters Mde. Velasquez, for instance, whom I met yesterday coming out of the State House- note book in hand. Her life has been a strange romance- married to a Confederate officer, she accompanied him throughout the whole war dressed as a soldier. She acted as a spy, and in any military capacity, she was wounded three times- in her foot, neck, and breast. She has, of late years, interested herself in the Cuban war. Dame Rumor says she is soon to be married to a Count, an officer in the Cuban army. She can write three kinds of short hand.

If it is assumed that the reporter got the facts exactly as stated by Velazquez when they met, there are plenty of assertions to question.

First, she never married any "Count, an officer in the Cuban army," her history shows. So, either Velazquez spoke too soon or fibbed.

Second, the wounds' locations on her body, the "foot, neck and breast," are different than reported in her memoir or in many other articles. One

---

35. The *Newberry Herald* (South Carolina) ads ran for seven months (Dec 1, 1875- Jun 14, 1876). The *Pickens Sentinel* (South Carolina) for three months (Jan 6- Jun 8, 1876). In Tennessee newspapers: *Morristown Gazette*, Jan 12 & 19, 1876, maybe other dates; *Fayetteville Observer*, Dec 9, 16, 23, 1875; and *Herald Tribune* (Jonesborough), Dec 2, 9, 16, 23, 1875.
36. *Constitution*, Dec 28, 1875.
37. *Georgia Weekly Telegraph and Georgia Journal & Messenger* (Macon), Feb 1, 1876.

year and five months earlier, on September 4, 1874, the Atlanta *Constitution* reported she was wounded on her right foot, right shoulder and hand. And ten days prior to that, the *Mobile Register* newspaper[38] stated she was wounded in the right shoulder. In *TWIB* (page 225) she stated that she was wounded in the "arm and shoulder." The great discrepancy of her claimed wounds is covered in more detail elsewhere.

Third, the article stated that she had only one Confederate army officer husband whom she was with the entire war. This contradicts her book and all prior and later newspaper statements. The reporter might have gotten this part wrong or Velazquez just too briefly told her story because she was in a hurry to go find some lunch.

Fourth, it is hardly believable that Velazquez wrote three kinds of short hand, when it is clear from her many known letters, she poorly managed English.

Whether Velazquez got paid for any reporting or for whom she might have worked, is not clear. Her interest could have been genuine, or she might have simply been seeking the prestige of the title of reporter. Or she might have been seeking contact with politicians. Her life's history shows that she relished contact with people of office, title and money, often seeking letters of recommendation and other acknowledgement from them.

To her credit, she was paying attention to legislation enacted by the Georgia State House. One piece of legislation outraged her, an amendment to the convict lease law. The original law had passed on March 3, 1874 and allowed penitentiaries to lease out prisoners for ten hours a day. The prisoner had to be serving a minimum of five years, but could be leased out for twenty years, if their sentence was that long. Now the amendment repealed the 10-hour maximum work day, virtually enslaving the prisoner. The Macon and North Georgia Railroad was supplied with "250 convicts free of charge."[39]

A Letter to President Ulysses S. Grant

Velazquez, in protest of prisoner treatment, wrote to the President of the United States, Ulysses S. Grant on February 24, 1876. The letter[40] is presented retaining original punctuation, spelling and syntax:

> Hon. U.S. Grant
> His Excellency.
> I beg your attention to a late bill passed by the Legislature of Georgia, to let out [*sic* lease] convicts to private individuals Such as RR [railroad] Companies who place Overseers over them who use them most brutally under the lash, and starvation.

---

38. Aug 25, 1874.
39. Matthew J. Mancini, *One Dies, Get Another: Convict Leasing in the American South, 1866-1928* (Columbia, SC: Univ of South Carolina Press, 1996), 87.
40. Ulysses S. Grant Papers.

those men pay nothing to the State, for there [*sic* their] Services, they pretend to clothe them and board them. this they do not do, and when one of them ask for food he is Striped [*sic* stripped] of his clothes and lashed till the blood trickles to his feet. now I beg of you to Send and have this thougerly [*sic*] investigated and in the name of humanity and Christianity for god sake put a stop to this Human Cruelty, and Murder. it is not been long Since one poor fellow was whipped until he fell exhausted. they then drenched his body with water, then had two Other prison convicts Rub his back with Salt and turpentine and next morning repeated the same treatment until he fell and died in the most agonizing groans. President. his family as well as hundreds of Others are paying taxes to keep up this penitentiary and have the poor wives and relatives of these unfortunate men to have this cruel acts performed under their Eyes. Oh god forbid when you remonstrate with them they will tell you are a Yankee using the most bitter Epithets and threaten to assassinate you if you write anything to the government against them. President. I have done this under the threat of making me leave the State. and now I wish to ask Your Excellency if there is not a law [to] sustain honorable law abiding citizens and to protect the unfortunate prisoner from Barberous treatment under the mask of Republicanism is this Rebellious Conduct to go on a disgrace to this honorable body of Politicians. I will close trusting you will hear this from only one who does not fear to Express the truth before her god and man. there are Others who would gladly do the same if they were properly protected. their families and properties is [*sic* are] at Stake. may god help all the Afflicted and bring the guilty to a speedy Justice is the prayer of the writer. With Honor, allow me to Escribe myself Your friend

Mrs. L. J. Wasson

Velazquez's heartfelt emotion is evident in her concern for the convicts and was surely sincere.

This letter was received at the Executive Mansion on March 4, 1876 and, by direction of President Grant, forwarded on March 6 to the U.S. Attorney General who sent it to Honorable Powell Clayton in the U.S. Senate. The complaint was then referred to the Committee on the Judiciary on March 14, 1876. The action card which was filed indicated that the letter was received from a "Mrs. John L. J. Wasson of Atlanta." Velazquez did not use Wasson's first name "John" in her signature, so it must have been taken from the envelope's return address.

Velazquez clearly meant for her identity to remain a secret, fearing threats as stated, or why would she have signed the letter with a long past married name when her name after Wasson had been Mrs. E. H. Bonner, starting in 1868, and then Mrs. Bobo? If secrecy was her intent, then she must have been rusty in her self-proclaimed clever spy skills because she used Southern Publishing Company letterhead stationery, complete with address, No. 3 Marietta Street, Atlanta, Ga. which certainly had an obvious connection to her. Or it might be supposed that she wished to cause trouble for William A. Ramsay and that was part of her motive for using his stationary. It was at this time that Ramsay's Southern Publishing Co. was failing to fulfill its contract with Velazquez.

More about the convicts will be addressed further along.

The Southern Publishing Company Fails Velazquez

Now a battle erupted between Velazquez and Ramsay, and Velazquez swore out a warrant for his arrest on charges of "cheating and swindling." "Madame Velasquez, better known as Lieut. Harry Buford of confederate fame" and Mr. Wm. Ramsay, appeared before Judge McConnell on Tuesday afternoon March 7 and "the prosecutrix alleged that Ramsay made certain statements to her relative to his means and capacities for publishing the book, which were untrue, and occasioned her loss." It was explained that "about a year ago" Ramsay had contracted to publish her book and several dates to do so had been postponed. Ramsay claimed "he had done the best he could" and "that he had been harassed and hindered by being sued by various parties, that the editor of the book lived in Philadelphia, and that he had been subjected to various other delays." The court ruled "no intent to deceive" was proven and the case was dismissed.[41]

In addition to the battle with Ramsay, Velazquez might now have worried about the Georgia newspapers which had become aware of Mrs. Wasson's letter to President Grant and the letter's subsequent forwarding to the U.S. Attorney General. The newspapers reprinted a version of the letter (with punctuation and spelling corrected for readability). Some readers called her accusations "lies" and stated:

> Who and what is this Mrs. Wasson? In the absence of any specific knowledge on these points I should judge she was a lineal descendent of that worthy couple Ananias and Saphira."[42]

The allusion was Mrs. Wasson was a liar related to the Biblical couple who lied to Saint Peter and to God, and fell dead.

The *Augusta Chronicle*[43] reported that the "Charge of Cruelty to the Penitentiary Convicts of Georgia" will be investigated by the Judiciary Committee. The next day the *Chronicle*[44] said it hoped the Georgia governor would "order a speedy and searching investigation." It questioned, "Who is Mrs. L. G. [*sic*] Wasson that writes to the Attorney General of the cruel 'scourging and straining' of penitentiary convicts in Georgia?" The newspaper concluded, "We fail to see what the Federal Government has to

---

41. *Atlanta Constitution*, Mar 9, 1876.
42. *Macon Weekly Telegraph*, Mar 28, 1876, the Washington correspondent filed the report on Mar 17, 1876.
43. Mar 21, 1876, "From Washington."
44. Mar 22, 1876.

do with the matter." Of course, Georgia, and all Southern states, resented Federal involvement in state issues.

The *Atlanta Constitution* finally got into the action by reprinting[45] the article which had run in the March 17 *Macon Weekly Telegraph*. Then again, the *Constitution*, this time taking from the Augusta newspaper, addressed the issue on March 25:

"Mrs. L. J. Wasson's" letter, the Augusta Chronicle says: We have heard nothing of the cruelties which the lady in the Southern Publishing company so graphically portrays. We have seen no evidence of the inhumanity she describes. The courts have no cognizance of the murders which she charges to have been committed. We repeat the hope expressed yesterday that Governor Smith will have the matter promptly and thoroughly investigated. The United States government has no jurisdiction in the premises.

The Augusta newspaper asked, who is this Wasson and shouldn't the president of the Southern Publishing Company "look into the matter a little?" Soon the newspapers figured out that Ramsay was the president of the Southern Publishing Company and sought him out for explanation. The *Macon Telegraph and Messenger*[46] wrote under the topic LETTER ON THE CONVICTS:

There is no little excitement in town over the letter on the convicts, copied in your editorial correspondence. Ramsay, the owner of the Southern Publishing House, knows nothing of it- so he assured me. He says his letter paper was taken out of the office by someone unknown. Still he suspects, and he is determined to ferret out the writer and has detectives on her track. Ramsay is unlucky with the women- he got into terrible trouble with Madame Velasquez about her "Woman in Battle"- and now this female is using up his paper, with printed address. It appears to me that this foul slander is but a revival of the old stories which so excited the country some years ago, but, which on examination, turned out to be all lies. Some wretched creature, of course, trying to curry favor with the paternal Government at Washington, has repeated them.

At this same time Ramsay had "A Card" printed in the *Constitution* in which he emphatically said his company had not sanctioned the letter and he could not account for the use of his letterhead except that "the author of the letter had evidently appropriated" some of his stationery.[47]

The turmoil caused by Mrs. L. J. Wasson's letter, at this date, still had not caused her any public trouble, as she remained unidentified. Ramsay surely by now realized she was the author of the letter. More troubles were in store for William Ramsay. After the warrant sworn out by Velazquez for Ramsay's arrest, she took final steps to terminate their association. Velazquez wrote

---

45. Mar 23. 1876.
46. Mar 26, 1876.
47. *Daily Constitution* (Atlanta), Mar 26, 1876.

"A Card to the Public" which was printed in the *Atlanta Constitution*[48] which announced:

> I hereby notify the public that W. A. Ramsay alias Southern Publishing Company, have no right, title or claim, to give or receive agencies or subscriptions to the Book entitled "Woman in Battle." All persons are Cautioned and Warned, from this date not to negotiate with him for this Book, as said W. A. Ramsay is in no way connected with the "Woman in Battle," either as Agent or Publisher. All papers that have advertised said Book will please copy this notice. All orders for Agencies or Books should be addressed to Madame L. J. Velasquez, S 1-2 Marietta street, Atlanta Georgia. Madame L. J. Velasquez

Ramsay responded immediately:[49]

> Caution. A card is going the rounds over the signature of "Madame L J Velazquez" "cautioning the public against Wm A Ramsey" and asserting that he is in no wise [*sic*] connected with the book entitled "Woman in Battle," either as agent or publisher, etc.
>
> CAUTION. I hereby caution the public against the said Madame L J Velazquez or any other person, or persons representing themselves as proprietor of said book, as I, Wm A Ramsey, am sole proprietor of the book entitled "Woman in Battle." I further state that negotiations are pending between Madame Velazquez and myself. She proposes to buy me out but as yet nothing has been done, she having failed to come to terms. I will give due notice to the public should I sell out. Respectfully, Wm. A. Ramsey Of the Southern Pub. Co., Atlanta, Ga.

It can be assumed that Velazquez had no money to buy out Ramsay and Ramsay did not have enough money to publish her book. After all, Ramsay had been in financial straits for some time and Velazquez stated plainly (*TWIB*, p5-6) that she was "anxious for the money." Abandoned husband, E. H. Bonner wasn't likely supporting Velazquez and his son, and abandoned husband Bobo certainly was not. Both Velazquez's and Ramsay's lack of money was a sure death sentence for any further business association.

A Woman in a Street Fight

Velazquez and Ramsay continued with their battle. The *Atlanta Constitution*[50] reported, "Madame Velasquez and W. A. Ramsey had a street rencon're on Marietta street yesterday without serious results." Of course, a rencon're is a hostile meeting.

Adding some specifics, the *Marietta Journal* wrote the dispute was "about publishing her book, The Woman in Battle. She plugged Ramsey under the

---

48. Apr 2, 1876, card dated Mar 24.
49. *Atlanta Constitution*, Apr 9, 1876.
50. Apr 11, 1876.

eye and pulled out her little knife and Ramsey fled. She ought now get out a book entitled 'A Woman in a Street Fight.'"[51]

The Atlanta *Times*[52] gave the details:

> A Woman in Battle. The corner of Marietta and Peachtree streets, near Castleberry's furniture store, was the scene of a very lively and interesting little action yesterday afternoon. The parties engaged were Madame Loreta Juaneta Velasquez [sic], known in the confederate army as "Lieut. Buford," and W. A. Ramsey [sic] of the Southern Publishing company. Madame Velasquez is a Spanish Cuban, and served in the late war between the states on the side of the confederates as a spy, etc. She has written a book, giving an account of her exploits, and named "Women [sic] in Battle." Ramsey contracted with her to publish the work. They have fallen out about it, and have published cards about each other. Sunday Ramsey published a card about it, and yesterday she met him at the corner designated and asked him: "Did you write that?" He said he did, when she plugged him under the chin with her fist, and he fell backward. She then drew a knife, when he ran up Marietta street, she pursuing with the knife in hand, making thrusts at his coat tail. A policeman was encountered, when he arrested Madame Velasquez and carried her to the station-house. Ramsey went off to consult a lawyer to ascertain what kind of case to bring against her. He finally told the policeman that he did not want to prosecute her if he could help it. Upon this Madame Velasquez was released.

Another newspaper[53] provided somewhat conflicting, though entertaining, additional details of the fight:

> Mme. Velasquez frightened Ramsay nearly to death... His last rencontre with Mme. Velasqueezher (as the people pronounce the name) was exceedingly ludicrous. It appears Mme. is not satisfied with the manner in which Ramsay has published her book, and they have been publishing each other in the daily papers. So when they met on the street Madam called Ramsay to account for his last card and after arguing and gesticulating excitedly for a few minutes she raised her hand some say with a knife in it. Be this so or not, the gesture floored Ramsay, who fell into the gutter, crying frantically "murder! police!" At last, scrambling up, he took to his heels. Madam, who was laughing heartily, pursuing; but when a policeman arrived she walked off with him apparently highly enjoying the fiasco, while Ramsay crept back, and with the assistance of the boys, found his hat. Poor fellow! he has apparently read Madam's adventures in "The Woman In Battle" to such good effect that he has imbibed a holy terror of her prowess.

Clearly, Velazquez was of bold character to stand-up for herself. In any case, it seems their dispute abated, or at least, it may be assumed they kept out of each other's way from then on and went about their respective businesses as nothing more has been found regarding their conflict.

---

51. Apr 14, 1876.
52. As reprinted by the *St. Louis Republican* of Apr 14, 1876.
53. *Georgia Weekly Telegraph and Georgia Journal & Messenger* (Macon), Apr 25, 1876.

About this time a newspaper reported that "Lt. Harry Buford" was burglarized, "Detective W. L. Jones yesterday arrested J. A. Scheiff and J. L. Cozart upon the charge of burglary in the daytime. They are supposed to have robbed Lt. Harry Buford."[54] Nothing more could be found in Atlanta court records, which implies that the charge was dismissed. Suspect John L. Cozart was recorded in the 1870 U.S. Census as working as the Barlow Hotel bar keeper and 21 years of age. At the time of the burglary, he would have been 27 years old, but nothing more is known of him. Nothing at all was found on Scheiff, and nothing was found connecting the two men to Ramsay, who probably wasn't foolish enough anyway to be involved with this act.

Uncle Remus Knows

It was shortly after the street fight that Madame Velazquez was finally identified as the "Mrs. L. J. Wasson" of the Georgia convict letter. The Macon newspaper[55] made the revelation in two sentences:

> Harris of the Savannah *News* intimates that Madame Velasquez and Mrs. L. J. Warson [*sic*] are one and the same. Goody gracious, hadn't he better hide out when the Lieutenant goes to Savannah!

Harris of the Savannah *News* was none other than Mr. Joel Chandler Harris and he had correctly identified "Mrs. L. J. Wasson." At this date, the 27-year-old journalist was reporting for the *Savannah Morning News*. Although he had not yet become famous for his later Uncle Remus books, or his 24-year tenure at the *Atlanta Constitution*, the gentleman was as wily as Br'er Rabitt and Br'er Fox, the characters he created. He loved his native state of Georgia and only left it once, when he took a job, for six months, with the New Orleans *Crescent Monthly*. At the first opportunity he returned to Georgia, never to leave again.

His stay in New Orleans coincided with the time when Mrs. Mary DeCaulp came to town on January 1, 1867, married John Wasson of Kentucky on January 17 and departed on January 31 with the Venezuela Company. Harris probably remembered her from when the group landed in criminal court on January 23 over their chartered boat. Also in January, Harris published in the *New Orleans Times* a poem titled "The Sea Wind." Coincidentally, one line, although not in any way referring to Velazquez, said, "Tell her I never forget." Nine years and four months after Harris had met Mrs. Wasson, he indeed had not forgotten her. He had correctly identified her.

---

54. *Constitution*, Apr 29, 1876.
55. *Georgia Weekly Telegraph and Georgia Journal & Messenger* (Macon), Apr 18, 1876.

Even though the mystery of Mrs. Wasson's identity had finally been made public, there appears to have been no repercussions. Her letter of complaint about the leased convicts was rather old news by then.

Velazquez had no more trouble with Ramsay. After his many financial troubles and his failure to publish Velazquez's book, it is doubtful that he had any assets remaining. He left Atlanta, moving to Philadelphia, surely anticipating a new start. Shortly after his arrival there, he contracted typhoid fever and died on April 27, 1877 at the age of 34 years. His death certificate[56] stated his occupation as "Publisher." But not of Velazquez's book.

Ostensibly, it had been a long time since Velazquez had any significant cash flow, and now, she thought to remedy that. She applied to the City Council for a permit "to give a gift concert." The Council replied at their May 1 meeting, with at least one councilman approving and at least another one disapproving- the request was denied.[57] It can only be thought that this concert was to be a charity fund raiser for herself. Remember her charity ball in Memphis in 1866? If the concert was for the benefit of a real charity, it can be guessed the council would have approved.

---

56. Return of a Death in the city of Philadelphia, Physician's Certificate.
57. *Daily Constitution* (Atlanta), May 2, 1876.

Chapter 11

The Woman in Battle is Born

After many delays, Velazquez's "life and adventures during the late war as an officer in the confederate service" was "issued from the press" in July 1876. The *Atlanta Constitution*[1] wrote favorably of the book:

> *The Woman in Battle*... is rather a readable book and but for a series of reverses would have been published several years ago. Its typographical work is excellent and reflects much credit upon the publishers. Madame Valasquez [*sic*] is now canvassing the city for subscribers, and we hope she will receive that patronage which her past service in the lost cause deserves.

On August 1, the *Constitution* added, "We are informed that five hundred copies of this work are now on the way to Atlanta to supply subscribers."

Now energized, Velazquez left Atlanta and traveled to Raleigh, North Carolina where she checked into the Yarborough House on August 23.[2] She apparently had an agreement with the publisher that North Carolina was her sales territory and she immediately placed an advertisement, to run two months, in the local paper to recruit sales agents. Besides selling the book, the agents were to sell "Steel Engravings of the author."[3] The ad stated her office was at the Grange Hotel, one block from the Yarborough House; the Grange Hotel might have been her new lodging considering the Yarborough House was premier lodging.

By September the book had been delivered to several Georgia newspapers which printed reviews. The *Columbus Daily Enquirer*[4] said it had "received from the publishers, Messr. Dustin, Gilman & Co., Richmond, Va., a copy of an elegantly bound" book with wood cut illustrations "well executed." It concluded:

> Much of the book is tame, but oftener quite interesting and exciting, and throughout possesses a peculiar interest. The narrative is simply told, the only objection being there is too much of detail. Female readers will be pleased with it.

The reviewer did not address the book's credibility or veracity and the review might be considered one of the first of many reviews to get the facts wrong. For example, it stated, "she participated as a Confederate officer" in numerous battles, which, of course, implied that she was a real commissioned officer with a real regiment with all the real duties and responsibilities of the position.

The *Newberry Herald* which had already carried seven months of advertising for the book, reviewed the book and in part wrote:[5]

---

1. Jul 19, 1876.
2. *Raleigh Sentinel*, Aug 24, 1877.
3. *Raleigh News*, Aug 31, 1877, indicating the ad was started on Aug 25.
4. Sep 7, 1876.
5. South Carolina, Sep 13, 1876.

It gives thrilling descriptions of the many battles in which she participated, of her perilous performances as a spy, a bearer of dispatches, as secret service agent and as a blockade runner; of her adventures behind the scenes at Washington, of her career as a bounty and substitute broker in New York, and in fact, is record of the most thrilling adventures and hair-breath escapes it has ever been the lot of woman to encounter.

The *Weekly Sumter Republican*[6] heralded at the head of its review, "A Woman in Male Attire: or, the Female Spy, THE MOST REMARKABLE BOOK OF THE AGE."[7] The article opened with, "We have before us a book to which we can give our most unqualified endorsement." The reviewer echoed:

a record of the most thrilling adventure and hair-breadth escapes it has ever been the lot of a woman to encounter... a career of adventure which has never been paralleled on this continent... [a] fascinating volume.

However, the reviewer might have harbored doubts:

For knightly daring and bold strategy, history has hardly a parallel, and the reader can with difficulty persuade himself that the story is real and not a wild creation of fancy.

In that sentence, the reviewer inadvertently hit the heart of the matter; can the story be believed? The reviewer then copied some of the content of the "publisher's circular" (which will be introduced shortly) which defended the integrity and character of the book's author:

Few persons in any part of the Southern States have not heard of the famous female officer, who distinguished herself in the late conflict between the South and North; for stories concerning her- absurdly exaggerated- have been told and retold thousands of times both during and since the war. Some have refused to believe that there was such a person; but these are comparatively few in number, for Lieut. Harry T. Buford, or Madame Loreta Juaneta Velasquez (which is her true name), is well known to thousands of officers and soldiers of the Confederate army; and there is the most abundant testimony of the kind that cannot be disputed, to the effect that she did participate in a number of battles, and that she rendered invaluable services to the Confederacy, both as a soldier and as a spy, and also as a secret service agent.

In fact, there was not then, and there is not now "the most abundant testimony of the kind that cannot be disputed." There has not been found any diary or firsthand account in which the writer exclaimed something such as, "You are not going to believe what happened today in battle! You see there was this dandy Lieutenant Harry T. Buford...." Even in the post-war

---

6. Americus, Georgia, Sep 15, 1876.
7. The same article ran in the September 21 edition of the Dallas (Texas) *Daily Herald*; there were probably other papers.

years, among the thousands of soldiers who wrote of their experiences, not one soldier-chronicler wrote something like, "I wish I knew what happened to that dandy, brave young man who assumed command of our company when all of our officers were killed?" (Velazquez claimed in her memoir she did this, more than once.) The same soldier-chronicler might have written (but did not), "Gee, he wasn't even officially in our company or regiment, but helped us anyway. Wow, what a leader! Too bad we didn't have more of that kind." Or maybe the comrade-chronicler wished to know what became of Lieutenant Harry T. Buford since the War, and desired to give thanks because Buford had "rendered invaluable services to the Confederacy."

The closest thing supporting this reporter's assertion about the abundance of testimony was the "publisher's circular" of testimonials about her good character. This circular accompanied her book and appears to be strong testimony. But it must be realized that the circular was a self-serving promotional tool, so by its very nature, is suspect and should be examined in great detail.

One last observation about the Americus *Weekly Sumter Republican* review- The reviewer surely had not read the book because he erred about what it said and instead made an assertion which he clearly copied from the "publisher's circular," which was, "She was wounded at the Battle of Ball's Bluff, and in a skirmish just after the battle of Shiloh." No, she wasn't, and in her memoir, she never made this claim! Even her "publisher's circular" failed to accurately repeat the contents of the memoir it was promoting! She did not claim she was wounded at Ball's Bluff; she only said that afterwards she was tired and that evening dropped "into a sound and dreamless sleep." Also, she did not claim in her memoir that she was in a "skirmish just after the battle of Shiloh," but that a stray shell sent shrapnel wounding her while she was burying some soldiers of the 10th Tennessee Regiment, when in truth the 10th Tennessee was nowhere near Shiloh! This falsehood is addressed elsewhere.

Now that Velazquez had made Raleigh, North Carolina her headquarters, she placed an advertisement on September 15, 1876, booking it for three months, in the *Tarborough Southerner* (Tarboro', North Carolina) seeking agents to help sell her book:[8]

WOMAN IN BATTLE!
AGENTS WANTED to canvass every town and county in the State for "Woman in Battle!" one of the most intensely interesting books ever published, being the Life and Exploits of Lieut. Harry T. Buford, (C. S. A.) or Madame L. J. Velasduez [*sic*]. No subscription book ever published has offered the chances this

---

8. The ad is evident on Oct 6 and 13. No other Oct editions are found. The ad does not appear in Nov or Dec as booked, possibly indicating a change of sales strategy after considering the limited potential customers to be found in the small population of the area.

one does for wide awake agents to make money rapidly, and as territory is being taken up very fast those who desire to canvass for it should make application without delay.

MADAME L. J. VELASQUEZ, Agent for North Carolina; office, Grange Hotel, corner Wilmington and Davie sts., one block from the Yarboro House, Raleigh, N. C. Any information required, can be had at this office, or from Dr. Blacknall.

Shortly after the beginning of the advertisements, the newspaper[9] presented a review and noted that the book was just from the press and "it had been promised to the public a long time and has come at last":

> It is handsomely gotten up. The style is clear, strong and graphic. The name is sufficient to attract the attention; a glance at its contents to interest; while the reader of a few pages will not willingly lay it down until he has gone thought the six hundred pages the book contains... The book is beautifully printed and profusely illustrated, while the most inferior of the three styles of binding is quite handsome. It is sold by subscription only, at $3.50, $4.00 and $4.50 according to the style of binding.

The three binding types were: In Extra Fine English Cloth, $3.50; In Leather, Library Style, $4.00; and In Half Turkey Morocco, $4.50.[10] Surviving examples of the cloth edition show the most common was green with gold and black trim and lettering, and there were brown cloth editions, as well.

The last paragraph of the review provides news of Velazquez which helps place her now living in Raleigh:

> Madame Velazquez intends making Raleigh her Home and is agent for the State of North Carolina and will no doubt give good Agents in every town and County a fine opportunity for making money. See advertisement elsewhere.

Velazquez placed advertisements in many North Carolina newspapers from September 1876 into February 1877, seeking "wide awake agents to make money rapidly."[11]

Advertisements were placed as far away as Opelousas, Louisiana by the book's publisher, Dustin, Gilman & Co.[12]

---

9. *Tarborough Southerner*, Sep 29, 1876.
10. "Publisher's circular" archived at David M. Rubenstein Rare Book & Manuscript Library at Duke University.
11. *Raleigh Christian Advocate*, Oct 11, 1876- Feb 21, 1877; *Biblical Recorder* (Raleigh, N. C.), Oct 18, 25 and Nov 1, 8, 15, 22, 1876; *Durham Tobacco Plant* (Durham, N. C.), Jan 10, 1877; *Randolph Regulator* (Asheboro, N. C.), Oct 25, 1876, Jan 10, 1877; *Alamance Gleaner* (Graham, N. C.), Jan 16, 1877; *Weekly Ansonian* (Polkton, Anson County, N. C.), Jan 24, 31 and Feb 14, 1877.
12. *Opelousas Journal*, Mar 3, 1877.

Southern Historical Society's Criticism

Probably in September the publisher's agent, Rev. Aaron Jones, sent a book to the Southern Historical Society, surely wishing for a favorable review. The Society published a periodical called *Southern Historical Society Papers* and it was the October 1876 edition which carried the book's review under, "Book Notices." By this date the Society was well regarded with about 1560 members receiving its periodical.

The Southern Historical Society had been founded in 1868 in New Orleans by Major General Dabney Herndon Maury. The Society's purpose was to counter what it believed was the North's one-sided history of the war and to preserve the memory of the just, but lost, cause. The organization shortly afterwards moved its headquarters to Virginia in an effort to boost membership. Maury was Chairman of the Executive Committee of the Society at the time of the book's submission. It is hugely ironic that Maury was the commander and friend of William Burnet, the same William Burnet whom Velazquez falsely claimed she married. It was General Maury who wrote a letter to William Burnet's father in April 1865 telling of William's death:

My Dear Sir: With deep regret and grief I announce the death of your son William E. Burnet, my Chief of Artillery and my most Christian friend. He was shot through the head and instantly killed, while on a reconnaissance in Spanish Fort....

The shot had come at about noon from about 150 yards away from the Union rifle pits occupied by the 7th Vermont, Captain R. B. Stearns' Company K. All morning the "musket fire by his men was exceedingly troublesome" to the Confederates in their fort. "[Burnet] had for a moment taken a rifle in his hand, and was in the act of aiming it from behind the breastworks through a wooden embrasure." The Yankee minié ball passed through the embrasure and hit Colonel Burnet in the head.[13]

Maury's letter to Burnet's father continued, "My wife, who esteemed him very highly, and other good ladies here, took into their charge the sad duties relating to his funeral." William's friends paid high tribute to his memory and General Maury praised William's good character:

He was a rare compound of excellent qualities. He was the best educated soldier I have ever seen. His information varied- he was accurate in his reflections and deductions. His courage was of the highest order. He was kind to all- had no antipathies nor prejudices against persons; and so modest and unobtrusive that only persons of rare discrimination, or who knew him intimately, appreciated him

---

13. Christopher Columbus Andrews, *History of the Campaign of Mobile* (New York: D. Van Nostrand, 1867), 84; OR, Ser I, Vol 49, Part II, p1179.

adequately. His death is a loss to his country and comes at a time when I feel it profoundly.

William's father, David G. Burnet, said that William's death was "the most costly sacrifice that could be expected of me in this life, the last member of a once dear family." The elderly Burnet was now alone, his wife had already died and so had all of his children; William was the last living of his children.[14]

William Estes Burnet, aged 30-years, was buried in the Twelves family burial plot in the Protestant Cemetery, now Magnolia Cemetery, on Ann Street, Mobile, Alabama. He had roomed with the Twelves family since his arrival in Mobile and had clearly gained the family's friendship. No marker is on Burnet's grave, which is in the southwest corner of the Lot 40.[15]

It is understandable that William Burnet's grave never received a monument. Mobile's citizenry was preoccupied with the Union army's tightening of the conquest noose, and besides, the citizens had exhausted their resources by this late date in the war. Burnet's 77-year-old father lived in distant Texas; he had no income for a marker, as he was living on the generosity of friends.[16]

Please see the photo of William Burnet's grave in Illustrations, Figure 19.

Contrast the tribute paid by William's true family and friends, to Velazquez's sparse memorial. Velazquez wrote (*TWIB*, p87) only that she was "terribly shocked and wild with grief" upon learning of William's death. She did not praise the man whom she claimed she had married when she was only fourteen years old and claimed fathered her first three children. Well, her treatment of William's memory is understandable, since it was a lie that she was ever married to him.

Surely, General Maury was not aware that Velazquez had claimed, in the September 4, 1874 Atlanta *Constitution* interview (prior to her book), that she married William E. Burnet "in 1857" and that he was killed in "the latter part of 1861." Had General Maury been aware of this interview, he would have surely denounced her. In her memoir, Velazquez did not provide claimed husband "William's" surname, but intimated it was William Burnet by saying that he resigned his commission when his state, Texas, left the Union and that his father, residing in Texas, urged him to resign. Even if General Maury had read her book, he would not have recognized that "William" was supposed to be one and the same as his dear friend and comrade-in-arms, William Burnet. However, if Maury had read both the earlier interview and then the book and connected the two items, one can

---

14. *Chronicles of Oklahoma*, Vol 39 (1961): 193.
15. Mobile Public Library, Local History and Genealogy Division- "*Departed this life on this day* March 31, 1865."
16. *Southwestern Historical Quarterly*, Vol 49 (Oct 1949).

only imagine what General Maury's reaction would have been. At the least, he would have refused to print a review, or maybe taken greater measures and publicly lambasted her.

But the review did get printed and the reviewer, at the onset, expressed his skepticism stating that the book "purports to give her adventures...." The reviewer admitted that the book would be "eagerly read by those who are fond of the marvelous" and that general readership would find it interesting. "As to the reality of the existence of such a personage, there can be no reasonable doubt," asserted the reviewer, and he acknowledged the "publisher's circular" (more on this later), repeated the names of the men giving testimonials and stated that they all testified that Madame Velazquez and Harry T. Buford were one and the same. "We have also met with several Confederate officers who were cognizant of the fact that such a personage *did* figure in the Confederacy, and who saw her upon several occasions." The reviewer wrote, "How far it can be received as history is altogether another question" and protested the same thing that Ex-Confederate General Jubal Early will later, in May 1878, protest, that Velazquez claimed to be in two very separate locations at the same time during the Battle of Bull Run (or Manassas).

General Jubal Early was President of the Southern Historical Society at the time of her book's submission, but was away on business, so he must not have been aware of its submission.[17] He became aware of the book at a later time and place, he explained.

The Society's reviewer further questioned how Buford could have been "at so many battles fought by the different armies in different sections of the country- or how he [Buford] managed to accomplish various other physical impossibilities." The review concluded on a gentle note, "We can only say that it is a very *readable* book, and would serve well to while away a winter's evening."

The book reviewer's name was not stated, but it was surely Reverend John William Jones, editor of the *Southern Historical Society Papers*. He was the Society's Secretary, serving in that capacity until 1886. Please see the Appendix, Item 5 for the review.

Velazquez considered Reverend Jones to be the reviewer, because that is to whom she addressed a letter of protest. Her letter, dated October 27, 1876 from "Roliegh [*sic*] NC," was typical of her hurriedly written letters (and maybe emotionally written). See the Appendix, Item 6 for a transcription of the letter.

She first thanked Reverend Jones for his "liberal and kind words" and for speaking in her "behalf." She wrote, "Yet suffer me to call your attention to a few points." She proceeded to explain something that Jones had not

---

17. The Society's meeting minutes on Nov 2, 1876 note that General Early was away.

contested, as if this was a point on which he was confused. She pointed out that Beauregard was in command of the entire army and referenced page 96 of her book. She then said that General Johnston came onto the battlefield later and referenced page 98 of her book. These two accurate points had nothing to do with the lie she told about her participation in the battle. Her protest did not address Reverend Jones' contested point of her flying overland a distance of fifty miles during the night while she lay down to sleep.

She wrote that her book was not "intended as a history," but that her "opinion of men and events" was "given as [she] was impressed at the time." She then stated something which she never claimed in her book or elsewhere, "You will call to mind my commission was a recruiting, that I only was 5 months in the Army regular, after that I belonged to the Independent Scouts...." She said that this gave her the freedom to move from army to army around the country and she further claimed she had "satisfactory evidence" to support the assertion. She concluded by thanking Jones for his "kindness" and "accepting all criticism...." She signed the letter Madame L. J. Velasquez, using an "s" in place of the first "z," contrary to the spelling of her name, Velazquez, as the author of her own book.

Her claims in the last paragraph of her letter conflict with the claims in her memoir.

First, in the letter she said that her commission was a "recruiting" by which she meant a recruitment officer. However, on pages 105-106 of *TWIB* she explained that General Jackson only "gave [her] a recommendation to General Bragg for a recruiting commission." She said, "This I did not care about, for I thought that I did not need his permission or his aid to do recruiting duty...." She rejected this assignment and went on to other adventures. A commission is not the same as a recommendation for recruiting duty. And if any real commission (whether it had been in recruiting or other) had been offered, she would have taken it, as that was the theme of her book and her major source of bragging rights. She wrote in her memoir that she rejected the recruiting duty, so even if she was confused, thinking a duty assignment constituted a commission, she rejected it. Therefore, she could not truthfully claim to have been a commissioned officer for recruiting.

Second, in her letter she stated that she was only in the regular army for 5 months. On page 182 of her memoir, she stated the one time that she was in the regular army was with the 21st Louisiana Regiment. She claimed she purposefully joined the men in order to slip out of New Orleans unobserved by the mayor, who had given her some trouble. She left the regiment in a "short time." Credulity is stretched to its limit here, since at this date during the war, anyone recruited was signed for the duration of the war. It was an impossibility that the 21st Louisiana Regiment would let her walk away from a soldier's duty, if it was believed she was a man. Only by revealing her true identity could she have gotten herself kicked out. She did not claim she did this or used any other trick, only that she left with regrets. Major John Newman of the 21st Regiment, whose testimonial is later analyzed and discredited, did not explain how she got out.

Third, in her letter she claimed to have been in the "Independent Scouts." The Independent Scouts was a particular organization and it also was called Independent Tennessee Cavalry or Independent Cavalry. She did not claim in her book to have been a member of this organization. However, between pages 60 and 61, on an unnumbered illustration page, is Velazquez disguised as Harry T. Buford and the illustration is labeled "1st Lt [Lieutenant] Indpt [Independent] Scouts C. S. A." Recall that she claimed in the March 7, 1866 St. Louis *Republican* newspaper that she was "elected 1st Lieutenant in Capt. Phillips' Company of Independent Tennessee Cavalry." In that article, she said she proceeded to Corinth, Mississippi with the company and reported to General A. S. Johnston and "at the battle of Shiloh, Capt. Phillips fell mortally wounded, and the command then devolved upon her." Of course, this was not true.

It is a fact that Capt. Phillips did not die at Shiloh (April 6-7, 1862), but surrendered at Fort Donelson on May 5, 1865. So, whether she rode and served in some capacity with this company is overshadowed by the big lie of Capt. Phillips' death. It should be noted that in her book she does not mention Captain Phillips' death, or of her taking command of Phillips' company or even of her serving in the company. In summary, she first made this false claim before the publication of her book and then she wisely did not make the claim in her book, only leaving in the labeled portrait. She then again made the claim after the publication of her book.

Velazquez was not through with her protest to the Reverend Jones. She wrote a second and equally grammatically mangled letter on November 12, 1876. Please see the Appendix, Item 7 for a transcription of the letter.

She was still in "Roliegh, NC," but had not yet learned how to spell the city's name, even though she had lived there 81 days, since August 23. From the letter's context, it would appear that Jones had not replied to her first letter; Velazquez was still trying to defend the same negative points of the book review. She, this time, claimed there were "many living who will cheerfully testify" that she was in "different sections of the country" and that she could provide "any required amount of testimony as to [her] acts [her emphasis] and identity." She again said that she only wrote down her own impressions and some people may have different opinions. She voiced her protest more strongly, "Your notice is unfair and unjust to me and would ask you to reconsider the matter, I only ask Simple Justice...." She told the

Reverend that if he still doubted her movements to let her know and that she would with "much Pleasure" give "a Satisfactory Solution of what appears to [him] as a Physical impossibility."

Velazquez assured Reverend Jones that she "went to Leesburg from Manassas via Richmond & Linchburg [*sic* Lynchburg, Virginia] to be in that Battle." She was referring to the Battle of Leesburg by its Confederate name, also called the Battle of Ball's Bluff, which occurred on October 21, 1861. She, at this point, very cleverly does not state that she was in the battle, but that she only "went to Leesburg... to be in that Battle." There is a difference. The real problem and important point is that it was impossible that she went to Leesburg with the intention of being "in that battle" since that battle was the result of an accidental encounter of enemies, therefore totally unpredictable. Velazquez narrated (*TWIB*, p115-125) her participation in the Battle of Ball's Bluff; her claim is false and is addressed elsewhere.

Velazquez closed her letter by stating that she enclosed a postage stamp for his reply. It is not known if he replied, but it is doubtful. She again signed the letter Madame L. J. Velasquez, not Velazquez, the name of authorship of her book.

The Publisher's Circular

The Southern Historical Society's book reviewer mentioned the "publisher's circular" and the five men who testified that Velazquez and Buford "were one and the same individual."

The circular was a four-page promotional pamphlet for enhancing the sales of the book.[18] The first page consists of an illustration of "Lieutenant Harry T. Buford, C. S. A." which occupies half of the page with the heading, "A True Heroine. The Woman in Battle: The Adventures, Exploits, and Travels of Madame Loreta Juaneta Velasquez...." It is perplexing that this official pamphlet failed to spell Velazquez's surname and middle name the same as her authorship name. On the lower half of the page is printed "Agents Wanted," indicating that interested individuals should contact "Madame L. J. Velasquez, Agent for North and South Carolina. Headquarters, Raleigh, N. C."

The second page begins a general narrative of her war activities and one (aforementioned) assertion stands out, "She was wounded at the battle of Ball's Bluff, and in a skirmish just after the battle of Shiloh." Amazingly, the pamphlet's assertion contradicts Velazquez's memoir, that she came away from the Ball's Bluff only tired- not wounded; and that the day after the Battle of Shiloh she was wounded by the shrapnel of a stray shell while burying some dead soldiers- not in a skirmish!

---

18. A copy at David M. Rubenstein Rare Book & Manuscript Library at Duke University, North Carolina.

The third page continues with the general narrative of her activities, but it contains two noteworthy points. The pamphlet claimed that her editor C. J. Worthington was "late an officer of the United States Navy, who participated in the war on the Federal side." The assertion is a provable lie and much more will be said about it. The second point of contention is that the book was "profusely illustrated with pictures of the most striking scenes, drawn by one of the best artists in America Mr. E. B. Bensell."[19] It is strange that only Bensell was credited as the book's illustrator, when Jeremiah Rea was clearly the main contributor with his sole signature on six drawings. Bensell's signature is evident on only one drawing. There are two drawings which are jointly signed; one signature is clearly Rea's and the second is simply a "B," ostensibly Bensell's. There are some nine illustrations signed by seven other artists and about ten illustrations with no signature evident.

The fourth and last page of the circular contains testimonials from five people and four Georgia newspapers. The first paragraph asserted that the testimonials were "unsought" and that the gentlemen were of "high character" and that they could identify "the person" and vouch for the "character of Madame Velasquez." An analysis of these gentlemen and the newspapers, and their connection to Velazquez is in order.

Of the four newspapers, the first three newspapers are Atlanta papers and the last is from Augusta, Georgia:

1) The *Kennesaw Gazette* rendered a short book review. It stated that the book is "popular and highly romantic," placing the author "side by side with the proudest heroines of ancient or modern history." The book has "engravings and is ably written," and "everyone should buy and read it." The review did not attempt to address the truthfulness of the memoir or character of the author.

2) The *Daily Commonwealth's* contribution also was a simple book review, calling the book "well gotten up and elegantly written." The review said that Velazquez's adventures equaled those of any heroine ever "recorded in history." Again, the newspaper made no attempt to address the truthfulness of the memoir or character of the author.

3) The *Daily Constitution* did vouch for Velazquez. It stated that her "fame is well known to the citizens of Atlanta; among them our Col. Acton. There are numerous certificates from good and reliable judges as to the excellencies and truthfulness of the literary features of the work." This testimonial paragraph seems to be pieced together from previous *Constitution* articles. The first sentence was taken from the October 15, 1875 article which was right after Velazquez rebutted Adam A. Wilson's denunciation. It was then

---

19. Philadelphia-born Bensell (June 11, 1842) attended the Pennsylvania Academy of the Fine Arts and together with others formed the Philadelphia Sketch Club. Bensell's illustrations appeared in the leading publications of the day.

that Colonel Acton's name was first brought up. No evidence, to date, connects the Colonel to Velazquez during the War. His testimonial in no way verifies her participation in a battle. Their first meeting was certainly after the War and he was impressed by her and her story.

At the date of the publication of Velazquez's book, Colonel Tom McCarroll Acton (1821-1895) was the traveling sales agent for the *Constitution*. He served in that capacity for eighteen years, 1868 to 1886. In his earlier years he was the owner of the *Jackson Republican* (Tennessee) newspaper and worked for several others. During the War he "served as general news agent in Johnston's department of the army of Tennessee."[20] In other words, Colonel Acton was not in the army as a soldier. He is not found in Broadfoot's *Roster of Confederate Soldiers, 1861-1865* or in the National Park Service's data base of Civil War soldiers or the www.Fold3.com data base. Colonel Acton was not a military colonel. His title seemingly was a courtesy title. Recall, that Colonel Acton did not say that he knew Velazquez during the War, only that her "fame [was] well known." If he had known her, he would have written something, after all, he was a newspaper man.

The source of the second sentence in the testimonial is not known. Without details about the "numerous certificates," it is difficult to give value to the phrase.

4) The *Augusta Constitutionalist* was the longest, most detailed testimonial. It was an extract of the article which had appeared on October 7, 1875, which was prior to the book's actual printing. This article (previously presented) was by the *Constitutionalist's* "Regular Correspondent" in Atlanta named "Martha" and she immediately made a huge error by stating that Velazquez "won her way to a Lieutenancy." Velazquez never, in her memoir, claimed that she earned a rank, but only that she gave herself the disguise of rank. Martha asserted that Velazquez won the rank because she sustained "an unblemished reputation, [was] valiant in battle, and discharged important offices of trust." This was more than Velazquez ever claimed or dared to claim in her memoir.

The reporter (and testimonial) said that they "interviewed her" and described Velazquez as "a tall, graceful woman, something over thirty. Her eyes, blue in color, have a way of brightening up and sparkling when she speaks of her native island...." This description conflicts with that of other reporters who also spoke with Velazquez. The *Indianapolis Journal* (Dec 1879) called her a "slight-built person, slender" and that she had "eyes that seem to change from gray to black as you look at them." A reporter from the *St. Louis Evening Post* (June 1878), who "conversed" with her, said she had "steely gray glittering eyes" and that she was 5 feet 5 ¾ inches in height,"

---

20. *Atlanta Constitution*, Jan 31, 1895, obituary.

calling her "a woman of medium height and of a slight-built form." The *Atlanta Constitution* (Sep 1874) stated that she was "slightly above the average height." A reporter from the *New York Times* (Dec 1884) stated she was "black-eyed." Many years later, the New Orleans *Times-Picayune* (Oct 1900) said she was "tall and fine looking." Her book's editor, in his preface, probably settled the question of height when he wrote (p12), "She is slender, something above medium height" and that "her frame is firmly knit."

The height discrepancy might be explained by varying high-heeled shoes which Velazquez would have worn underneath the long, full dresses of the time. On the question of eye color, the *Constitutionalist* reporter might have had difficulty distinguishing between blue and gray. Despite Martha's contradictory description, there was only one Madame Velazquez.

Martha wrote that, by Velazquez's "modest demeanor... her deportment or conversation," one would not suspect she had seen the "roughness of camp life" or suspect "her many trials and mingling with men." Martha concluded by saying, "She showed me letters from prominent men in the North, West, and South, commending her and her book." That would have been her not yet published book, so one wonders how these prominent men could have commended it.

In summary, the testimonial was in no way a firsthand account of Velazquez's actions during the War. There is no doubt that it was Velazquez who took the alias, Lieutenant Harry T. Buford, but the "letters from prominent" men are not evidence enough to substantiate that she did what she claimed. It is easily suspected that these letters, some or all, were forgeries as it has been shown that Velazquez was a forger.

Next an examination of the five "gentlemen of high character" in the "publisher's circular" testimonials is in order:

1) "M. D. Lorme McLeod, M. D., Late of Denver, Col, now of Atlanta, GA." wrote that Velazquez was of "unsullied character and acknowledged ability" and that her book was "ably written" and would place her among history's heroines. McLeod obviously believed his own words, was impressed and later married her.

Doctor Moses DeLorme McLeod did not know Velazquez during the War. He may have met her when she traveled through Denver in 1873 and followed her to Atlanta. Or maybe he happened to come to Atlanta in 1876 (or earlier), met her and subsequently married her in 1877. He had no way to know if her narration of her War years was true. Much more about McLeod is elucidated further along.

2) "G. W. Alexander, Proprietor *Washington Gazette*, Washington, D.C." wrote that she was "brave, noble, and generous in disposition." He also said that "she made many sacrifices" and "was particularly distinguished for her devotion to the cause."

George W. Alexander met Velazquez during the War when she became his prisoner in "Castle Thunder" Prison, which Alexander commanded as the Assistant Provost Marshal in Richmond.

Her incarceration was covered in the local newspaper in July 1863. She was reported to have been brought before General Winder on July 1 as a suspicious character. She was discovered to be a woman in a man's disguise and sent to Castle Thunder while the authorities considered what to do with her. No hostile intentions were charged against her, as she was a supporter of the Southern cause. The newspaper announced her release on July 11:

She quite took to the Castle before she left. She got acquainted with everybody, ordered everybody about, and by her bustling manner and busy ways threw the commandant [Alexander] quite in the shade.

Velazquez addressed (p278) her incarceration in her memoir:

It was the very best thing that could have happened to me... Major Alexander, and his lovely wife, both showed the greatest interest in me, and they treated me with such kindness and consideration that I was induced to tell them exactly who I was, what my purposes were in assuming male garb, what adventures I had passed through, and what my aspirations were for the future. They not only believed my story... but rendered assistance....

In summary, Alexander knew Velazquez for 10 days in July 1863 when she was his prisoner. Velazquez did not even get Alexander's rank correct; he was a captain, not a major. Alexander did not know her as a soldier on the battlefield, nor was he witness to any of her claimed acts on the battlefield. She told Alexander and his wife her story which Velazquez said "they believed." Velazquez might have visited them again in 1864, after her marriage in Atlanta, when she was again reported to be in Richmond. It is certain that Velazquez contacted him during her trip North in 1875 when she went seeking an editor. At that time, he was the editor of the *Washington Gazette* located at 931 D Street.[21] He most graciously gave her a character reference based on their happy acquaintance from her imprisonment days. It is noteworthy that he did not comment on her book and its veracity, since it was not completed and he had not seen it.

3) "Geo. Anderson, Late Brigadier General C. S. A., of Atlanta" wrote, "It affords me great pleasure to certify that Madame L. J. Velazquez is the person known during the late war ... as Lieut. Harry T. Buford, C. S. A."

It is not doubted that Madame Velazquez posed as Lieutenant Harry T. Buford; even a cursory investigation confirms this. Anderson did not claim he witnessed her presence on any battlefield and since he said very little about her, it is reasonable to think he knew very little. He may have seen her

---

21. *Congressional Directory* (Washington, DC: GPO, 1875, 1876).

in her costume, as many people did and as the newspapers reported. However, there has not been found any credible comrade-in-arms war connection between Anderson and Velazquez.

She wrote in her book (p534) that she saw "General G. T. [Tigh or Tiger] Anderson" in Atlanta after the War. She said that Anderson called her "Lieutenant" when he came into a hotel parlor where she happened to be speaking to a Federal officer. The Federal officer was completely astonished to hear her called "Lieutenant" and to learn of her wartime spying. Velazquez claimed the Federal officer, who had met her during the War, only then understood that he had been duped by spy Velazquez during the War.

However, there is a big conflict between her narration (p531-536) and the truth. She claimed at the time of this meeting with Anderson in Atlanta, she had departed New York and was on a cross-country trip on her way to New Orleans. She claimed stops in Baltimore, Washington, Richmond, Charlotte, N. C., Columbia, S. C., Charleston, Atlanta, finally arriving in New Orleans. Upon her arrival in New Orleans, she decided to join the Venezuela emigration group and with them left the country. The truth was far different.

She did not make a cross-country trip which took her through Atlanta and terminated in New Orleans, but she actually arrived there on January 1, 1867 aboard the steamship *Montgomery* which had departed on December 22 from New York. She could not have made the stop in Atlanta, the location of her related story about General Anderson and the Federal officer.

However, Velazquez indeed made a wide sweep of the country in 1866 looking for opportunities. The first part of the year, she claimed to the newspapers, she was trying to set up a dry goods store, but lost all possessions in the steamboat *Miami* explosion, escaping only with her life. She was in Memphis and St. Louis the first week in March, then went to New Orleans the last of March. In the middle of the year, she was trying to sell subscriptions to three books she claimed to be writing. She found her way to Atlanta, then Augusta and, then Savannah and Charleston in May. She now rather backtracked to Meridian, Mississippi and then Nashville in June. She headed north and was in Richmond, then in Washington in August where she sought "an interview with the President in relation to the building of an asylum for the disabled and destitute of the South."

Velazquez, in her book, did not write truthfully about her cross-country trip. She told an untrue variation of actual events. She could not have stopped in Atlanta on her way to New Orleans simply because she was instead on a boat bound for New Orleans. The untruthfulness of the storyline cast doubts on whether she met General Anderson as described in her book.

The bottom line is that General Anderson did not vouch for the truthfulness of her book, he wrote, "Her book cannot but be one of unusual interest." This statement indicates that he had not read the yet-to-be published book.

4) "John Newman, Major of the 21st Regiment of Louisiana Volunteers, New Orleans" wrote the most positive of all the testimonials, vouching for her "unblemished character." What he specifically stated is the heart of the matter:

> I have been personally acquainted with her for the past thirteen years. She served under me with distinction as a soldier for three months, and was afterwards promoted for her great efficiency and integrity to the position of 1st Lieutenant in the Confederate Service.

At first glance this one sentence would seem to be the firsthand account of Velazquez for which we have been searching! Newman stated that Velazquez served as a genuine soldier in the army and was promoted to a 1st lieutenancy. But problems abound.

Velazquez, on page 182 of *TWIB*, explained how she was connected to the 21st Regiment of which Newman was major, though she does not mention him in her book. Velazquez stated that she "enlisted in Captain B. Moses' company, of the twenty-first Louisiana regiment." It is true that Captain B. (Bernard) Moses was the captain of Company "D" of the 21st Louisiana Regiment.

Upon her alleged enlistment in Captain B. Moses' company, Velazquez narrated, "The next day we started for Fort Pillow, to join the balance of the regiment. In this manner I contrived to get clear of New Orleans...." She stated that this enlistment was the first time she officially joined the army and her enlistment was solely to enable her to slip out of New Orleans and away from the problems created for her by the mayor when he arrested her. She wrote that she "had no fancy for going on duty as a private soldier any longer than was absolutely necessary...." and that she only stayed with the regiment for a "short time," which is in general agreement with Newman's account that she served "three months."

Recall, the New Orleans *Daily True Delta* (April 24, 1862) stated that she was arrested on April 23. She claimed (*TWIB*, p181) she was in prison for 10 days and then released. It was after her release that she wished to leave the city undetected by the mayor. It can be concluded that her enlistment, if true, was on, or after, May 3, 1862. Velazquez, in her book, claimed she departed for Fort Pillow the "next day" after her enlistment. Fort Pillow, at this time, was under continuous mortar shelling by Federal gunboats. The shelling commenced on April 14 and ended June 4, when the Rebels evacuated the Fort. If she had arrived at the Fort in May, she would have been duly impressed and would have written of it, and very excitedly, no doubt. She does not mention the assault of the siege. By May 28 the regiment had evacuated Fort Pillow and had fought a skirmish near Corinth, Mississippi.[22] A careful reader of her book will note that she did not state that she actually arrived at Fort Pillow, only that she departed for Fort Pillow. It also might be noted that Newman did not specifically state that she served in combat; however, Newman did say she served.

Recall that in the March 7, 1866 edition of the *St. Louis Republican* she claimed she went from Island No. 10 (in the Mississippi River), and <u>not</u> from New Orleans, to Fort Pillow and that at Fort Pillow "she was elected First Lieutenant in Captain Phillips' Company of Independent Tennessee Cavalry." This clearly contradicts her book's version and it raises a question; how could she have been in the 21st Louisiana Regiment and the Independent Tennessee Cavalry at the same time?

Despite Newman's claim that she served as Harry T. Buford in his Louisiana Regiment and even became 1st Lieutenant, no record has been found of this alias in *Military Records of Louisiana Confederate Soldiers and Louisiana Confederate Commands* compiled by Andrew B. Booth, Commissioner Louisiana Military Records, 1920. Neither is her alias found in *The Roster of Confederate Soldiers, 1861-1865* by Janet B. Hewett, Broadfoot Publishing Co., nor in the National Park Service's "Search for Soldiers" online database. If Velazquez had successfully served as Harry T. Buford in the 21st Louisiana Regiment, as she claimed, a record would be found; Velazquez was clear (p182) about her enlistment, "This was the first time I had ever been regularly mustered into the service...." If on the other hand, her disguise and sex was discovered and she was run off, it is possible a military clerk might have just thrown out her papers thinking it served no purpose to retain them. However, Newman did not say Velazquez's sex was discovered or that she was run off. Neither did Velazquez say it.

Newman stated that she "served under" him for three months "and was <u>afterwards</u> <u>promoted</u>." If interpreted exactly as written, she left his command and only later, out of Newman's sphere, she was promoted. In that case, he would have not been a witness to the promotion.

If interpreted that she was promoted while still under Newman's command, the question arises, why did she leave this company and regiment after she finally won a 1st lieutenant's commission which she coveted? After all, the entire focus of her book was her seeking this honor and the various reasons for failing to obtain it! It is contradictory, at best and ridiculous at worst, that she would leave this company after finally attaining a promotion.

If she had indeed received a 1st lieutenancy from Newman, or the 21st Regiment, where is her prideful statement of this fact in her book or anywhere else? Velazquez stated in her book that she never succeeded in

---

22. Bergeron Jr., 125.

obtaining a commissioned rank from anyone, which would include Newman. Newman did not promote her to 1st lieutenant, and his testimonial of any "promotion" was not a firsthand account.

The flaw in Newman's testimonial is that he over-embellished what Velazquez had in mind as a character reference. Newman made a claim which even Velazquez did not make or try to make! Newman claimed she was promoted to a 1st lieutenancy based on merit, specifically citing, "great efficiency and integrity." If that had been the truth, Velazquez would have made it the centerpiece of her book and rightly deserving glorification. But even Velazquez, did not dare claim she was promoted to 1st lieutenant based on merit! Recall, that Velazquez titled Chapter Four of her book, "Disguised as a Confederate Officer," and not how she merited and obtained a commissioned rank of a Confederate officer! She asserted she only named herself a lieutenant.

What of the "three months" which Newman claimed Velazquez served under him? No military records found, to date, show her participation in the 21st Regiment. It is certainly possible that Velazquez tagged along with Newman's command at some time and maybe for three months. Newman may have met her then and developed a fondness for her which motivated him to write a testimonial thirteen years later.

Captain Newman probably wrote the character reference when Velazquez traveled through New Orleans in 1874 since Newman did not mention her book in his testimonial. The book did not yet exist. Even though Newman said that he had known Velazquez for thirteen years, it is possible that this 1874 meeting was their first. In a likely scenario, she might have told Newman that she was with the 21st Regiment and had met him then. Newman might have politely accepted her claim. Why should he doubt her seemingly sincere words? Velazquez, according to accounts, was a most fascinating and convincing person. Besides, how would Newman have known her, in her Harry T. Buford disguise, among a regiment of 1000 men? Newman might have simply accepted her story, not wanting to refuse a lady's request for a reference and finding no harm in it, wrote the reference.

One last possibility exists- Velazquez forged Newman's testimonial. To date, Newman's fate has not been discovered and it is unknown whether he was still living at the date of the "publisher's circular."

5) "J. F. Hammond, M. D., Asst. Surgeon Empire Hospital, Atlanta" was Joel F. Hammond, whose testimonial was strong and cross-checks with other facts:

> Dear Sir: It affords me great pleasure to state that no one knew Madame Laureta Juaneta Velasquez under her assumed *pseudonym* (Lieut. Harry T. Buford) better than I did. I knew much of her history, especially that part which relates to the field service. Lieut. Buford was admitted into Empire Hospital on July 26, 1863;

suffering at the time from a wound. Captain Decaulp was at that time a patient of mine. He afterwards became her husband; I witnessed their marriage at the Thompson Hotel. I certainly knew her private character, and I cheerfully state, and will make oath, if such a thing should become necessary, that it was good and above suspicion; her conduct was that of a brave soldier, whose life was at the disposal of home and country. Her work is founded on facts.

Dr. Hammond, I Presume, or Not

Confederate Service Records show that J. F. Hammond enlisted at the age of 24 as a private in company "E" in the 35th Georgia Infantry on August 12, 1861 at Campbellton, Georgia for "during the war or three years." About 4 months later, Hammond was detached from his company and detailed as a hospital nurse.[23]

By late 1862 he was assigned to the Empire Hospital (a converted hotel) in Atlanta. The Hospital's Muster Roll for January 1 to February 1, 1863 shows that he was "attached to hospital" on Oct 20, 1862 and employed as nurse. A later Muster Roll, for March & April 1864, stated he was attached to the hospital on Oct. 18, 1863 and was employed as a ward master. It appears that he left the Empire Hotel Hospital, but then returned. There were many busy hospitals in Atlanta and he might have been working at one of those. The records are incomplete and do not place him at Empire Hotel Hospital precisely on July 26, 1863, the date that Hammond stated he met Lieut. Harry T. Buford there. This record gap does not mean he wasn't there, of course.

Was "Lieut. Buford admitted into Empire Hospital on July 26, 1863, suffering at the time from a wound," as claimed "Dr. Hammond"? Exactly when could she have received the wound? Recall, that Velazquez had just been released from Castle Thunder in Richmond on July 15 and was "sent away... to Atlanta, Georgia."[24] Should it be concluded that Velazquez received the wound on the train ride from Richmond to Atlanta? Maybe she twisted her ankle on the platform, but it can be reasonably sure she did not receive a wound in battle during the noted eleven-day time frame. Maybe it was an old wound.

Was Hammond "Asst. Surgeon Empire Hospital, Atlanta"? Military records show he served as "nurse," then "ward master," then "hospital steward." <u>Hammond, at the date of his contact with Velazquez, July 26 to mid-September 1863, was a nurse.</u> His military record shows that it was only later that he was promoted to rank of ward master, on October 18, 1863, three months after Velazquez's admission and one month after her release and marriage.

---

23. Dec 28, 1861.
24. *Examiner* (Richmond), Jul 16, 1863.

The three positions in which he served were non-commissioned positions. Position of Assistant Surgeon was a commissioned officer's position, which carried the rank of a captain or 1st lieutenant.

There is no evidence that Hammond served, as he claimed, in the position of "Assistant Surgeon." Is it possible that as the war dragged on and conditions became desperate in the Confederacy, Hammond assumed the duties, even occasionally, of an "Assistant Surgeon" long after Velazquez left the scene? Not likely, since the gap in qualifications and rank was large. It was unlikely that a "hospital steward" was promoted to "Assistant Surgeon," but near impossible for an enlisted "private," who had been detached as a "nurse," to attain the rank that an "Assistant Surgeon" would hold. Plus, a hospital steward did not have time to serve as "Assistant Surgeon." The duty of a hospital steward was the management of the hospital in all aspects; the job was intense and critical to the operation of the hospital. These duties included the oversight of the dispensary, the kitchen, the toilettes, the ward and general hygiene of all departments. It was only under the surgeon's instructions that hospital stewards, ward masters and nurses were allowed to treat patients. They were not permitted, on their own, to make a diagnosis.[25]

J. F. Hammond has yet to be found in the roster for Confederate "Assistant Surgeon" in *The Medical and Surgical History of the War of the Rebellion (1861-1865)*[26] and Editor Jesse Alemán, in the notable 2003 reprinting of Velazquez's book, wrote in his preface:[27]

J. F. Hammond is not listed in William B. Atkinson, ed., *The Physicians and Surgeons of the United States* (Philadelphia: Charles Robson, 1878) or Joseph Jones, 'Roster of the Medical Officers of the Army of Tennessee,' *Southern Historical Society Papers* 22, No. 3 (Jan-Dec 1894): 165-280. The mobility of medical personnel during the war may explain the lack of documentation on Hammond.

As just made clear, "mobility" was not the reason for the failure to find Hammond listed as a doctor. And the Empire Hospital was firmly planted in Atlanta at the time of which Velazquez spoke.

Velazquez correctly named (*TWIB*, p314-316) Dr. Hay, Dr. Benton and Hammond, which leaves no doubt that Velazquez was familiar with the Hospital. Of the doctors, she wrote:

---

25. For ranks and duties of medical personnel see Alfred Jay Bollet, *Civil War Medicine* (Tucson, AZ: Galen Press, Ltd., 2002); Joseph Janvier Woodward, *The Hospital Steward's Manual: For the Instruction of Hospital Stewards, Ward-Masters and Attendants in Their Several Duties* (Philadelphia: J. B. Lippincott & Co., 1862); *Medical and Surgical History of the War of the Rebellion* (Washington, DC: GPO, 1870).
26. Washington, D.C. Printing Office, 1888.
27. Page xxxviii.

I was first admitted into Dr. Hammond's ward, and then subsequently into that of Dr. Hay. Dr Hay, who was a whole-souled little fellow, is dead, but Dr. Hammond is still living, and I am glad of such an opportunity as this of testifying to his noble qualities. During the entire period I was under his care in the hospital, he treated me, as he did all his patients, with the greatest kindness.

She went on to say that while she was a patient in Dr. Hay's ward, Thomas DeCaulp, her soon to be husband, was admitted into Dr. Benton's ward which adjoined Hay's ward. It must be remembered that Hammond said in his testimonial that DeCaulp was his patient; Hammond did not say DeCaulp was in Dr. Benton's ward. If Benton and Hammond ran their own wards, then Velazquez's and Hammond's statements concerning DeCaulp's care seem contradictory. In any case, it was probably true that the DeCaulp was attended by nurse Hammond at some point.

The "Dr. Hay" mentioned, was Acting Assistant Surgeon J. L. Hay and he served in that capacity at Empire.[28] Even though Velazquez expressed her like for Dr. Hay she must not have respected him because she told (p333) him a lie, "I was with [Captain DeCaulp] at the battle of Shiloh, and he behaved like a true hero." Or maybe she didn't tell Dr. Hay anything, but instead falsely told her readers she said it. In any case neither she nor DeCaulp fought at Shiloh.

Please note, the mentioned Dr. C. H. Benton was <u>appointed</u> Assistant Surgeon by the Secretary of War and was at Empire Hospital from Feb 11, 1863 to Oct 30, 1863,[29] when Velazquez was there.

No discovered documentation substantiates that Hammond was ever commissioned as an officer or appointed "Assistant Surgeon" by the Secretary of War or anyone else. At best, under the pressures of war, Hammond might have had to perform the duties of assistant surgeon, but it is too much to believe that he was commissioned as an officer and served as assistant surgeon.

In any case, at the time of Velazquez's hospital admission and marriage to DeCaulp, the records show that Hammond was a nurse and not an assistant surgeon, which his testimonial asserts.

When Velazquez was in Atlanta trying to get Southern Publishing Company to publish her book, Dr. Hammond resided there. It was at this time he wrote his testimonial. Hammond was a Georgia native. He and his family briefly resided in Alabama, but had returned to Atlanta by 1874. He is found in the city directory that year and each year until 1881. His address was different every year (1875, no address given) which may be an indication

---

28. Jack D. Welsh, *Two Confederate Hospitals and their Patients: Atlanta to Opelika* (Macon, GA: Mercer Univ Press, 2005), 158.
29. Joseph Jones, "Roster of the Medical Officers of the Army of Tennessee," *Southern Historical Society Papers*, Vol 22 (1894): 174.

of financial problems. The "Marshal's Sale for December, 1876" announced the sale of a city lot belonging to Dr. Hammond to pay "taxes due" to the city as a result of "mayor and council vs Dr. J. F. Hammond."[30] This was probably a residential piece of property, as his office address was at 26 Whitehall Street which was the Live Drug Store. His office address was more stable, remaining the same from 1877 to 1879 in the city directory.

It can only be thought that Hammond inflated his true title as nurse, held from July-September 1863, in the 1876 testimonial so as not to diminish the prestige and profitability of his ongoing Atlanta medical practice.

Hammond's Firsthand Account

Hammond stated, "I knew much of her history, especially that part which relates to her field service." There is great weakness in his claim since Hammond was on staff at the hospital and therefore not witness to anything regarding her "field service." He undoubtedly learned of her "history" from her. Hammond stated that he witnessed her marriage to DeCaulp and there is no reason to doubt him on this. He stated that he knew her "private character" to be "good and above suspicion." He wrote she was a "brave soldier" ready to sacrifice herself for "home and country."

It is satisfying to read of Hammond's praise of Velazquez and it is true they were mutually positive of their acquaintance and had kind words for each other some 13 years later. Velazquez was his patient in the hospital and grateful for the care given her. While there, she no doubt presented herself in the best light to Hammond. However, the fact remains that he was not witness to the "field service" which he praised.

Hammond concluded with, "Her work is founded on facts." If a loose interpretation of this sentence is taken, it means that her work was "based" on facts, but can be filled-in with non-factual information, as well. If his statement is strictly interpreted, then it would mean all information in her "work" was factual. Clearly, her "work" is not factual, but is instead full of falsehoods which cannot be attributed to forgetfulness or honest mistakes.

It is rather curious that Hammond said he would "make oath, if such a thing should become necessary" as to her "private character... that it was good and above suspicion...." Why not just swear right then and there in the testimonial, instead of waiting until "a thing should become necessary." After all, that is what a testimonial is for, isn't it?

Conclusion of Publisher's Testimonials

All of the publisher's testimonials fall short of turning Velazquez into one of the "heroines of history." None of the testimonials was/is a true firsthand account of her claimed deeds in battle. The editor of *The Woman in Battle*, one C. J. Worthington, stated in the book's Preface (*TWIB*, p10):

---

30. *Atlanta Constitution*, Nov 19 and Dec 5, 1876.

...there are thousands of officers and soldiers who fought in the Confederate armies who can bear testimony, not only to the valor she displayed in battle, and under many circumstances of difficulty and danger, but to her integrity, her energy, her ability, and her unblemished reputation... there are abundant witnesses whose testimony will not be disputed.

Where is the one person out of the "thousands" of soldiers and "abundant witnesses" who gave their firsthand testimony of her "valor displayed in battle?" These "thousands" should have been pushing to the head of the line just to have their name forever associated with that of Lieutenant Harry T. Buford. Yet, they appear nowhere. No testimonial presented to date supports the falsehoods told by Velazquez.

1876, Other Book Reviews

The Salt Lake City *Herald* printed a review noticing the book's publication.[31] It was more of an advertisement than a review, stating the book could be purchased by subscription by addressing the party in Raleigh, N. C. The paper explained, besides her adventures as a soldier and a spy, she "spent some time in Utah a few years ago." If the article wasn't a paid placement, then the newspaper must have been just pleased to have Salt Lake City evoked in a book. The newspaper did not recognize that the author was Mrs. E. H. Bonner. Of course, in her memoir Velazquez never revealed husband Bonner's name.

The *Rural Carolinian* reviewed *The Woman in Battle* favorably.[32] Even though the magazine's reviewer admitted that he had "only been able to glance hastily at the contents," he said he was "enticed" and found the book "captivatingly attractive." The long review was basically a repeat the book's narrative and concluded:

Say what we will of the life of the Madame, it has been romantic and wonderful, and though we would not have cared to have been her husband, or to have had her for our wife, we can but admire the courage of any one, even though it be a female, who would undertake such perilous adventures, and after all is over, have the boldness and candor to relate them even to particulars. We think this book well worthy of perusal by every Southerner who wishes to keep alive upon the tablets of his memory the bold and daring deeds of the Confederate spies and scouts.

The review was typical of the reviews of the time, in contrast to the aforementioned Southern Historical Society's review, which was the exception, because it questioned the book's truthfulness. But in the end, it too spoke kindly of the book, claiming it highly readable which it was and still is.

---

31. Oct 10, 1876.
32. Cokesbury, S. C., Dec 1876.

One impressed reader was in Franklinton, N. C. about 30 miles north of Raleigh. Recall at this time Velazquez was in Raleigh and the vicinity, recruiting sales agents for her book and she herself selling books. This customer-reader submitted a seemingly unsolicited, long, glowing review, the highlights are:[33]

Madame Velasquez can wield the pen as well as the sword... she acquitted herself as a recruiting officer and a gallant... her narrative will be highly appreciated by all Southern women... her finesse, singleness of purpose, heroism and patriotism can best be admired among all the intelligent people North and South... her many marvelous adventures during that period are intense, exciting and thrilling interest... It is no wishy-washy, sensational tale, but real matter-of-fact alone, told in an able and eloquent manner, in simple, pure, chaste and elegant language... In her rare elements of character are concentrated, quickness of perception, love of glory and country, true courage and chivalry, love of danger and the finesse necessary to self-preservation. Such are some of the characteristics of this truly remarkable woman...."

Surely Velazquez enjoyed this praise, and with the arrival of the New Year, the *Raleigh News* provided more of the same with a one paragraph review, calling the book "one of the most remarkable books of the age" and asserting "the work is highly romantic, and will amply repay perusal."[34] The Raleigh *Observer*, not to be outdone, wrote, "The Woman in Battle.- A well written book in glowing terms, rehearsing the trials, deeds of daring and patient sufferings of a brave, fearless and patriotic woman, Madame Valesquez [*sic*], who is the author, has been placed upon our table."[35] Velazquez seems to have hand-delivered the book, so for the moment she was still in Raleigh.

Another Letter to Alexander H. Stephens

On December 28, 1876, Velazquez wrote another letter to the Honorable Alexander H. Stephens, Ex-Vice-President of the Confederate States:[36]

Central Hotel Roliegh [*sic*] December 28 1876

"Hon" A. H. Stephens
Washington City, D.C.

Hon'rd Sir,

---

33. *Observer* (Raleigh), Dec 20, 1876, review by J. W. W., dated Nov 30, 1876.
34. Jan 7, 1877.
35. Jan 13, 1877.
36. Used by permission, the letter is in Alexander H. Stephens Papers, Correspondence 1823-1883, Box 5: Correspondence, 1876, Letter date is Dec 28, 1876, David M. Rubenstein Rare Book & Manuscript Library, Duke University, North Carolina.

Your letter of the 26th to hand and contents noted. it affords me great pleasure to have one so distinguished and esteemed numbered among my many correspondence, which extends to all portions of Europe & the <u>west Indies</u>. I send you a copy of my book. by to days mail. which you will I hope read. not as a mere Story or romance but as one of truth, though the writer may have transgressed upon conventionalities of Society. by donning male attire. You will have generosity enough to see what prompted this part of the actor. I hope you will excuse farther trespassing upon your most valuable time when I offer you the apoligy of my native Island, Cuba. any effort of mine or any write I can offer to induce the Statesmen of America to give attention to her claims for freedom and independence will afford Satisfaction to mind

[page 2]

that I have in my feeble way done all that a human could to effect her freedom and to arrest the inhumane butchery going on there, I see that President Grant has long favored the acquisition of San Domingo why Should this government go arround Cuba when it possesses every advantage Over San Domingo in climate, Soil population, and Commerce. I have presented an Appeal to the American People through the "Hon" George F. Hoar & General John T. Morgan. which you can See by calling upon them or I will forward Copy of the Same if you desire. which will Show to you that my heart is with the South and her interest. <u>God help her People</u>, Hoping I may kindle a Spark in your generous and Christian breast for my down trodden Countrymen

I have the honor to be

Yours most Respectfully

Madame. L. J. Velasquez

PS. please be kind enough not to loan the book where it will interfere with my agents and oblige yours LJV

The first (and petty) observation is that Velazquez had been in Raleigh at least four months and still did not spell the city's name correctly. She, earlier on December 6, 1876, had announced she was moving her office from the Grange Hotel to the Central Hotel, which is now noted in the letterhead.[37] She was likely living in the hotel.

The content of the referenced Stephens' letter of the 26th is unclear. This letter may yet be discovered in some repository and would be of interest. It could very well have a connection to the soon-to-be presented article from the August 11, 1878 Brooklyn *Eagle* which states, "Madame Velazquez bears with her certificates as to her high character and integrity, to which is attached the signatures of ex-Governor Throckmorton, A. H. Stephens and others." Of course, the question is, did A. H. Stephens actually endorse Velazquez's high character or did Velazquez take liberty with his signature attained through these letters, and attach it along with others to some certificate?

---

37. *Raleigh News*, Jan 4, 1877.

Velazquez continued to espouse the cause of Cuba, as she had already done in her June 27, 1875 letter to Ex-Confederate President Jefferson Davis, and now to the Ex-Confederate Vice-President. Velazquez wrote that she had "presented an Appeal to the American People" in support of Cuban independence to Honorable George F. Hoar and Honorable John T. Morgan.

This "Appeal" is surely the same document (a copy of which is located in the Library of Congress) as the "Address to the American Congress on Cuba," written by "Madame L. J. Velasquez" in which she asked the U.S. Legislature for its help in securing Cuba's independence from Spain. Her name is the only name of authorship on the five-and-a-half-page document and she did an adequate job of challenging America to support Cuban independence. The "Address" apparently was never delivered orally by her to Congress since it is not found in the Congressional record. Instead, the document was delivered to the named members of Congress, Hoar and Morgan, and through them the "Appeal" became preserved, although, to date, the "Appeal" has not been found referenced in either man's archived manuscripts.

It is a curiosity that she claimed she delivered her "Appeal" to the two named gentlemen who happened to be polar opposites during the American Civil War and afterwards, as well. John Tyler Morgan, during the War, rose to (Confederate) Brigadier General and later in 1876 was elected to the U.S. Senate from Alabama. He was one of the foremost racist ideologues of the time, serving as the second Grand Dragon of the Realm of Alabama of the Ku Klux Klan from 1871 to 1876.[38] He also was a proponent of Cuba's annexation to the United States. On the other hand, George Frisbie Hoar was staunchly anti-slavery before the War and during the War served as a Massachusetts State Senator. After the War, he served in the House of Representatives from 1869 to 1877 and then was elected to the U.S. Senate, serving from 1877 to 1904. He was one of the foremost proponents of freedmen rights and favored Cuba's independence.

There has been found no other association of the men with Velazquez and there probably was none.

1877, Married McLeod

In the final pages of *TWIB* (p597) Velazquez tells of her departure from the Salt Lake Valley and of "the first place of importance reached," which was Denver, Colorado, "a well built and thriving town, of about eight or ten thousand inhabitants." While staying over in Denver she may have met one Doctor Moses DeLorme McLeod, who was living and working there. Upon

---

38. Susan Lawrence Davis, *Authentic History Ku Klux Klan, 1865-1877* (NY: American Library Service, 1924).

departing Denver, Velazquez continued her travels and ultimately reached Atlanta by September 2, 1874 and it might be suspected that McLeod followed her there in 1875 or 1876. However, it might have been only a coincidence that he returned to Georgia, a state where he had once lived, and chanced to meet Velazquez. He left his wife and children in Denver. By 1876 and maybe earlier, Doctor Moses DeLorme McLeod was singing Velazquez's praises in the publisher's advertising circular previously discussed.

Recall as early as August 23, 1876 Velazquez had established herself in Raleigh, North Carolina. The "publisher's circular" and a local newspaper advertising campaign also establishes her presence here. Moses McLeod was probably with her at this time. From Raleigh, Velazquez traveled to Wilmington, North Carolina and now it will become clear that she had Moses McLeod in tow. No doubt, the reason Velazquez went to Wilmington is the fact that it had a large population, making it a good market for her book. Once there, she busied herself selling books.

On Thursday, January 25, 1877 the *Morning Star* reported:

> Madame L. J. Velasquez, otherwise known as Lieut. Harry T. Buford, C. S. A., is in the city canvassing her book, "The Woman in Battle." She is staying with Mrs. Bowden, corner of Chestnut and Second Streets.

Mrs. Bowden ran a reputable boarding house in Wilmington. Then three days later the newspaper[39] wrote:

> Madame Loreta Juanita Velasquez... informs us that she is making very good progress in the sale of her book. She also states that she is getting up commercial, financial and manufacturing statistics in this city for a forthcoming work devoted to these subjects in the Southern States. She visited Messrs. Wilder & Morton's turpentine distilleries, and found them an object of considerable curiosity, being the first she had ever seen, and she says that she will have a photograph taken of them to form the subject of one of the illustrations of her proposed work. Madame Velasquez expresses herself as delighted with Wilmington.

Wilmington, after twelve years of reconstructing its destroyed naval stores industry, was showing vigor again. During the War "most of the turpentine stills had been seized by the Confederate government, probably for the sake of the copper used in their construction."[40] Velazquez saw new equipment and energized businessmen making up for lost time and profit.

---

39. *Morning Star*, Jan 28, 1877.
40. W. McKee Evans, *Ballots and Fence Rails, Reconstruction on the Lower Cape Fear* (New York: W. W. Norton & Co. Inc., 1974), 36, first published by the Univ of North Carolina Press, ©1966, 1967.

Another Wilmington newspaper, the *Daily Journal* lavished praise on *The Woman in Battle* after Velazquez gifted it a book:[41]

Madame Loreta Janeta Valesquez [*sic*]. This lady, otherwise known as Lieut. Harry Buford, has furnished us with a copy of her book. The volume is of thrilling interest. Hair-breath escapes from dangers, flirtations with susceptible girls, real attachments, &c., &c., present a medley to the lover of sensational literature, that must necessarily entertain. The book is nicely bound, well printed and contains a number of illustrations. Madame Valesquez is now in the city.

While Velazquez was busy selling books, receiving praise and herself lavishing praise on the reviving naval stores industry, McLeod was busy setting up his medical practice. Dr. McLeod purchased a month's (February 10- March 4) worth of newspaper ads in which he gave his office location at "the Corner Second and Chestnut Streets," which should be noted to be Mrs. Bowden's boarding house where the couple was staying. The ad stated:

M. DeLorme McLeod, M. D. Surgeon. Cancer, Ulcers, Piles, Fistula, Tumors, Varicose Veins, Hare-Lip, Scrofula, Rheumatism, Asthma and Dropsy cured. Special attention given to diseases of Eye and Ear and Obstetric Surgery.

The busy pair took time on February 17, 1877 to purchase a $3.00 marriage license which stated:

Mr. M. D. McLeod having applied to me for a license for the marriage of Mr. M. D. McLeod of Wilmington, N. C. aged 44 years, color White, the son of M. B. and M. J. McLeod living at South Carolina and Mrs. L. J. Bonner of Wilmington aged 34 years, color White, the daughter of [blank] living at Mexico.[42]

The marriage took place on 25th of February "at the house of Mrs. John C. Bowden," which was Mrs. Bowden's boarding house. The fact that the couple's activity and circle of acquaintances was seemly limited to Mrs. Bowden's boarding house is an indication that the couple did not have relatives or maybe even any friends in Wilmington.[43]

The age Velazquez gave herself on the marriage certificate corroborates her birth date she claimed in her book. This is not surprising, as she did not have much choice, since any discrepancy was sure to be noticed. If the date given in her book was factual, then she would have been 34 years and 8 months old.

It is curious that she left blank spaces for the names of her parents, especially considering the praiseworthy heritage which she assigned to them in her book. It also is curious that she claimed her parents were "living" in

---

41. Jan 30, 1877; On this date publisher Dustin, Gilman & Co. advertised for book agents, under the ad headline of "The Female Spy, Thrilling Adventures of Madame Velasquez" in the *Yazoo Valley Democrat*, Yazoo City, Mississippi.
42. North Carolina State Archives, New Hanover County Marriage Licenses, 1867-1937.
43. Ibid, certificate.

Mexico or maybe this should be understood to mean the New Mexico Territory where she left her husband Bonner, then it is not so curious. It will be seen later, in a July 26, 1900 interview with the *Weekly Republican*, she claimed both her parents died prior to the War. This July 1900 claim and her many other interviews, mentioning her parents, contradict this marriage certificate and her book's claims.

Who was Doctor McLeod?

Doctor M. D. McLeod indeed had the professional expertise he advertised in Wilmington. Only a few years before, Dr. McLeod had a practice in Denver and he is found listed in the Denver city directory in 1873 and 1874, the time period when Velazquez traveled through.[44] It is possible that they met at this time and he later followed her to Georgia. When he did leave, McLeod left his wife, Mary Francis, and their children.

Jumping ahead to the 1880 Census, it is possible to see the family members he left in Colorado. His wife, Mary McLeod, then living in Boulder, aged 43, was listed as married, but no husband was listed in the house. The children were Carrie, aged 18, single; son Hollingsworth, aged 15, "working in gold mine"; Sallie, aged 13 and Della, aged 8.

Prior to moving to Colorado, in 1870 Dr. McLeod had lived with his Georgia-born wife Mary and their children in Americus, Georgia and he earned his living as a doctor. His stated age was 41 years.[45] Some thirteen and a half years prior, on December, 23, 1856, McLeod had married Mary Francis Hollingsworth in Marion, Georgia.

Already by the age of twenty-two Dr. McLeod was a physician, according to the 1850 U.S. Census. He was living at home in his native state of South Carolina, Sumter County, with three sisters and a brother, and his father, Moses B., a financially secure planter who owned 44 slaves.

Taking note of McLeod's age in the censuses, it can be understood that the stated age on the marriage license to Velazquez was a fudged age, making him about four years younger than his true age.

Doctor McLeod's medical training was called upon with the eruption of the Civil War, when he was employed as a Confederate "contract surgeon" at the rank of Captain and was posted in Tallahassee, Florida. The 1860 Slave Census shows him owning eight slaves. He remained in Florida, at least, from 1860 to 1867 as indicated by the births of five children there.

By 1870 the family had moved to Americus, Georgia, where his sixth child was born in 1872; however, the *Denver Rocky Mountain News* placed Dr. McLeod already in Denver that year, meaning that McLeod went ahead of his wife and kids to get established. Now in Denver McLeod purchased

---

44. *Directory of the City of Denver 1873*, Vol. 1, printed by the *Denver Tribune* Association.
45. U.S. Census 1870.

advertisements from January 5, 1872 to May 8, "Dr. M. D. McLeod, will do an office practice of Medicine & Surgery... Patronage respectfully solicited." By January of 1873 he had relocated his office, and then in February, he moved again.[46]

Outside of his medical practice McLeod was interested in minerals of the region. He bought into a partnership with Presbyterian Reverend Lewis Hamilton and formed the Hamilton & McLeod's Museum, which also sold "minerals, fossils and precious stones in great variety."[47] The partners renamed themselves the Denver Museum of Natural Science and sold "cabinets from $5.00 to $1000.00" of Rocky Mountain gems, mineral ores and fossils. In addition, they offered "mineral lands examined and reported upon."[48] By mutual consent McLeod and Hamilton dissolved their partnership in June 1872 and McLeod assumed "all liabilities of the firm."[49] McLeod then entered into a partnership with Rudolph Borchardt, a taxidermist and they announced the Denver Museum of Natural Science was to be moved to Borchardt's address "opposite the Post Office."[50]

Dr. McLeod was earnest about his mineral collection and entered some specimens in the (Denver) Colorado Fair in September 1872. While the judges were deliberating,

> Mr. P. P. Peck and Dr. McLeod, rivals for premiums, came together with doubled fists and uncontrolled rage, and settled their differences then and there. The doctor struck Peck in the "smeller" and drew blood, when Peck returned the blow and extracted a copious amount of claret from the doctor. They were finally parted by friends.[51]

It is not clear who hit first, but Dr. McLeod certainly was not one to shy away from a fight.

Possibly Velazquez visited the mineral museum and at that time met McLeod. Or maybe she sought Dr. McLeod's medical help for herself or child. Both scenarios of a meeting in Denver are possible. Or, as already mentioned, maybe McLeod only met Velazquez upon his return to Georgia and they had an interest in minerals in common.

---

46. *Denver Daily Times*, Jan 11, 1873; *Denver Daily Times*, Feb 14, 15, 19, 1873.
47. *Denver Rocky Mountain News*, Jan 7-Apr 12, 1872.
48. *Denver Daily Times*, May 18, 1873.
49. Ibid, Jun 8, 1872.
50. Ibid, May 28, 29, 1872.
51. *Rocky Mountain News* (Denver, CO), Sep 28, 1872.

Chapter 12

Going, Going, Gone from Wilmington

The delight expressed by Velazquez with Wilmington must have worn off because she soon left. Only 47 days after her wedding there, her presence in Baltimore, living at 77 North Pearl Street, is made clear by an advertisement she placed for three months in a local newspaper.[1] She heralded:

> Agents Wanted! To canvass every town and county in the State, for one of the most interesting books ever published, 'Woman in Battle,' being the adventures and exploits of 'Lieutenant Harry T. Buford, C. S. A., or Madame L. J. Velasquez.' No subscription book offers the chances this one does for agents to make money rapidly. Address- Madame L. J. Velasquez, 77 N. Pearl St., Baltimore, Md.

She placed this same advertisement in a distant Mississippi newspaper; interesting because of a suspected connection there.[2]

The *Baltimore Sun* of May 5 presented a lengthy, positive book review and stated she was in Baltimore "offering the work in person for sale."[3] Then on July 3 the *Easton Star* presented probably the longest book review to ever appear, with typical praise, in part, stated:[4]

> It is the most intensely interesting personal narrative we have ever read... Madame Velazquez is the most remarkable woman the New World has produced, and the Old World has given birth to very few, if any, who have surpassed her.

There is no doubt that the review was part of the advertising campaign which began on June 12 in the Easton newspaper and ran in every weekly issue until October 30. Silas Lane's Tobacco store was selling the book and Silas, together with Arthur Mitchell had acquired the "General Agency" for the book for Talbot and Caroline counties. The advertisement also stated that Velazquez was looking for agents in every Maryland county and to contact her at No. 77 N. Pearl Street, Baltimore.[5] It is unclear if Velazquez visited Easton, Maryland, on the opposite side of the Chesapeake Bay from Baltimore; if she did, it was a long steamboat or train trip, but no doubt easy for expert traveler Velazquez.

Apparently, Velazquez and McLeod had separated only days after the marriage. It seems Velazquez never mentioned McLeod by name or number in later newspaper interviews.

Dr. McLeod must have left Wilmington when Velazquez left, evinced by the fact that he is not found in the Wilmington city directory for 1877-1878.[6] He did not return to his family in Denver according to the 1880 U.S. Census.

---

1. *Aegis and Intelligencer* (Bel Air, MD), Apr 13, 1877.
2. *Columbus* (Mississippi) *Democrat* as late as October 19, 1877.
3. 1877.
4. 1877.
5. *Easton Star*, Jun 12- Oct 30, 1877.
6. *Sheriff's Wilmington, N. C. Directory, and General Advertiser for 1877-1878* compiled and published by Benjamin R. Sheriff.

Instead, "McLeod, Delorme" is found living in East Feliciana Parish, Louisiana (north of Baton Rouge) with Louisiana-born "wife" Josephene, age 32, and working as a physician. McLeod's age was stated at 50 years which was two years younger than his age should have been, based on his given age in the 1850 U.S. Census.[7] McLeod's fate after 1880 is not clear.[8]

Did McLeod divorce Mary Francis before marrying Velazquez? No record was uncovered indicating that he did. In fact, Mary Francis in 1899, living in Salt Lake City, called herself his widow.[9] By 1905, Mary F. was living in Anderson, South Carolina, still calling herself widow of Moses D.[10] If it is correct that McLeod died in Texas in 1903, (as a source claimed), a question arises as to why Mary F. prematurely claimed in 1899 to be Moses' widow. Maybe after not hearing from him in years she concluded he had died. Or did she wish to avoid the stigma of an abandoned woman or divorcee and chose the more respectable status of widow? Or did she know of his true death? In any case, she did not revile Moses McLeod enough for his abandonment not to use or mention his name. Mary F. returned to Salt Lake City, lived with an unmarried daughter and died there in 1908 while taking a mineral springs bath.

Did Velazquez divorce E. H. Bonner or A. J. Bobo before marrying McLeod? No record was uncovered indicating that she did. In 1874, Velazquez claimed that her husband, Bonner, was working in New Mexico and she presented herself as "Mrs. E. H. Bonner" routinely, up until the time of her marriage to McLeod in 1877.

In 1887 Velazquez got married again, to William Beard. At the time of the Beard marriage, she did not acknowledge her McLeod marriage or her Bobo marriage on the "Return of a Marriage" document because she called herself Mrs. Bonner. Much more will be said about future husband William Beard.

A Good Book Review

Velazquez's book was being promoted rather widely and in Fort Smith, Arkansas, it found a sales agent by the name of Mrs. S. M. Tillotson who was "canvassing the city and environs for subscribers to a work of thrilling

---

7. East Feliciana Parish marriage records do not show Josephene's and McLeod's marriage.
8. The 1890 U.S. Census record was destroyed by fire, so is of no help; he has not been found in the 1900 U.S. Census. Several online genealogical family tree entries state that Doctor Moses DeLorme McLeod died July 20, 1903 in Red River County, Texas, but an extensive search by a local genealogist found no evidence to confirm the claim and McLeod's death there is doubtful. Sources checked: Most every resource at the Red River Historical Society, plus most every online, paid and free, resource.
9. *1899 Salt Lake City Directory.*
10. *Walsh's Directory of the City and County of Anderson, S. C. for 1905-06.*

interest...." The local newspaper[11] admirably assisted Mrs. Tillotson in the promotion of the book:

> It is perhaps the most intensely war book ever published, being the true narrative of the romantic career of a remarkable woman who participated in the disguise of a rebel officer in some of the hardest fought battles of the late war and who played a very prominent part as a spy and secret service agent... Mrs. T will call upon all our prominent citizens.

In New Orleans, Velazquez's book found an agent, J. C. Brown[12] at #80 Camp Street, who, in a local newspaper[13] under "New Publications," provided a review which, in part, stated:

> Much of the romance of the great American civil war is found in memoirs of personal adventures of participants charged with delicate and dangerous duties which remove them from the conspicuous report of military bulletins and of the war correspondent. Among the most noted of these emissaries was Madame Velasquez, otherwise known as Lieut. Harry T. Buford, C. S. A.
>
> In this book, "The Woman in Battle," there is recorded the narrative of the romantic- we might say the most romantic- career of a most remarkable woman. In address, in adroitness and fertility of resource, in readiness, in cool self-possession, in courage and in intelligent and patriotic devotion to the cause which she espoused, M'me Velasquez was distinguished among her compeers in the dangerous service in which she was engaged. The story of her exploits and adventures is told with modesty, with vivacious candor and with the sprightliness and grace of a bright-witted woman. Full as the book is of romance, it is yet more valuable for the light thrown upon many transactions which were inexplicable at the time, and particularly respecting the organization and operation of that extensive system of secret service established by the Confederate Government within the Federal territory.

Mr. Brown repeated with accuracy the adventure contained in the book. It should be noted that as the book's agent, he was not trying to validate the book's claims, but was promoting its sale. His review might be characterized as a promotional effort which probably succeeded in not getting charged for advertising space.

1878, Promoting Her Book, Herself and Cuba's Freedom

A reporter's routine telegram to the Chicago *Daily Inter Ocean* (Dec. 5, 1877) told that Velazquez was in Washington, D.C. and was an agent of Cuban rebel sympathizers. At this time Cuban rebels were seeking independence from Spain and the reporter stated there was concern that steamer, *Estelle* at Bristol, Rhode Island, might be used by the rebels against

---

11. *Fort Smith New Era*, Apr 4, 1877.
12. *Soard's 1877 New Orleans* city directory, 702.
13. *Times-Picayune*, Apr 17, 1877.

the Spanish in Cuba. There was concern about those who might be involved. The article, in part, asserted:

> Cuban sympathizers in New York have an agent here in the person of a woman named Velasques [*sic*], who was a spy during the rebellion, and who was known as Lieutenant Harry Buford. She has written a sensational narrative of her adventures during the war. She pretends to be a newspaper correspondent here, and has a ticket to the reporters' gallery as a means of covering her operations.

It is difficult to imagine that Velazquez was a paid agent for the rebels since the rebels never had enough money for real needs. However, she clearly represented herself as an agent, no doubt because of her interest in the issue. The fact that Velazquez took the time and trouble to voice her support of Cuba's independence lends credence to her claim of her birth there.

Washington D.C. correspondent Kate King[14] wrote that Velazquez was in attendance at a Woman's Convention there. King gave a sparse rendition of Velazquez's history and expressed her skepticism, but went no further in seeking veracity in Velazquez's claims:

> Among the auditors [listeners] at the convention one noticed Madame Loreta Juaneta Velasquez a Cuban woman of the adventuress type, who served in the Confederate army under the pseudonym of Lieutenant Harry Buford. She claims to have participated in several battles and to have acted the part of spy to the very great advantage of the Confederacy. She was engaged in getting up an insurrection among the prisoners on Johnson's Island, and was the go-between of the projectors of a raid along the entire lake coast. She further claims to have been in collusion with Treasury officials who were supplying the counterfeiters with duplicate plates, by means of which the Government suffered to the extent of several millions. If everything set forth in her work is true, she has earned the plaudits of rascals the world over, and for herself a good, quiet nook in the Penitentiary. Her history seems to be well authenticated. She is of the dark, Spanish type, and seems to be one of the persons of note here this winter. Her life, written by herself, and edited by C. J. Worthington, is an acquisition to the startling and marvelous in literature.

To her credit, Kate King understood that Velazquez had claimed she had served "under the pseudonym of Lieutenant Harry Buford," meaning false rank and false name. It seems that King got a book from Velazquez and read it. However, King failed to probe into the correctness of Velazquez's claims relating to the Treasury department and the Johnson's Island prison plot, when clearly King was skeptical. King thought that Velazquez's book "is an acquisition to the startling and marvelous in literature," and in that King was correct.

---

14. *Cleveland Leader*, Jan 12, 1878, dateline Jan 9.

Velazquez was actively promoting her book in Washington, D.C. and she sought through the newspaper to increase her sales force: "WANTED- SIX LADIES and SIX GENTLEMEN, to solicit for a new publication. Call at Windsor House, 1327 F St., Madame L. J. Velasquez."[15]

The *Evening Star* also ran an announcement which did a fine job of promoting *The Woman in Battle* under the heading "New Books."[16] After giving the name of the book, its editor and publisher, the advertisement stated:

In this curious volume Madame Velazquez tells how, disguised as a man, she fought in the confederate service and afterwards acted as a spy, blockade runner, &c., and in various ways showed a woman's wit, coupled with man's courage, in her adventurous career during the civil war and later.

Another Washington special correspondent, this time from the *News and Courier* (Charleston, South Carolina), reported that he had met Velazquez:[17]

One of the most notable feminines now in Washington is Madame Velasquez, the author of the "Woman in Battle." It will be remembered that she was a lieutenant (Lieut. Buford) in the Confederate army. I met her the other day, and had quite a chat with her. She is slim, youthful looking, very bright eyed, weighs 128 pounds (while lieutenant weighed 148) and is loquacious as a mimic. She was born in Cuba, came to the United States at five years of age; when seventeen married an army officer, who resigned his commission in 1861 and joined the Confederacy, and was killed early in the war. She determined to avenge his death, through army influence secured a commission of lieutenant from Mr. Davis, was assigned to Gen. Bragg's army, took sick, was sent to the hospital at Atlanta, recovering was betrothed and subsequently married to an officer whom she nursed in Atlanta when she became convalescent; he was killed; she went to Richmond, was discovered, and by order of Mr. Davis put in Libby prison, released by the kindness and sympathy of Mrs. Davis, afterwards married Velasquez, who died, got killed or somehow and somehow else was put out of the way; and now she is here espousing the cause of Cuba, which she says is recognized by Peru and one or two other of the South American governments, and if it were only recognized by the United States would in a short time be the "sweetest little republic" afloat. She says the insurgents in Cuba have a minister here now knocking at the doors of the White House and Capitol. Perhaps he is at the backdoor, for I have not yet seen him.

Although the article was wonderful in its description of Velazquez, there are many troubling contradictions when compared to her book.

First, the article stated she married at age seventeen. In her book Velazquez said fourteen, and in another newspaper article she said thirteen. It is certain that the reporter recorded her age as he was told and was not

---

15. *Evening Star* (Washington, D.C.), Jan 24, 25, 1878.
16. Jan 26, 1878.
17. Feb 5, 1878 with a dateline of Washington, Jan 31.

mistaken; he would have known the difference between a fourteen-year-old bride and a seventeen-year-old bride. Even at that date, a marriage at the age of fourteen would raise eyebrows, whereas a marriage at the age of seventeen would have been in the realm of normal even though still underage and in need of parental consent if married in New Orleans.

Second, the article stated she was put in Libby prison, which is in error. The newspapers of the times noted her imprisonment in Castle Thunder prison and Velazquez, in her book, wrote of her time in Castle Thunder. The reporter's error may have stemmed from the fact that both prisons were in Richmond and two blocks apart.

Third, the article stated that she was released from prison through the kindness of Mrs. Davis. Velazquez, in her memoir, never made this claim.

Fourth, it was a lie that Velazquez "secured a commission of lieutenant from Mr. Davis" and furthermore she never claimed it in her book and it is a tribute to her audacity to claim it now. If it was true, Velazquez would have proudly referred to it on every other page of her book and included a reproduction of the commission document. And the document would probably have survived in the military records, just as the commission document of Sally L. Tompkins as captain has survived, and is archived at the Museum of the Confederacy in Richmond. Tompkins is unanimously acknowledged by historians as the only female to have been given a commission as an officer by the Confederate Government.

How did the reporter bungle the facts as told to him? Did the reporter make so many mistakes in a single paragraph because the story was collected 4 or 5 days before it was published? Or did Velazquez forget her own memoir and retold it incorrectly?

Velazquez and her book continued to receive the attention important to her financial success. The *Washington Post* of March 2, 1878, in its Literary Notes column, said her book was a "very interesting volume, profusely illustrated and well printed." Then on March 3, another Washington correspondent[18] met Velazquez "soliciting subscriptions for books" and he wrote:

> One woman who calls herself Velasquez, I believe, works for female suffrage, is agent for a book of which she professes to be the author, is pressing the claims of the downtrodden Cuba for recognition by the United States, and still has time to cultivate friendly relations with employees in the Capital.

At this time there was a strong women's lobby for the 19th Amendment, to give women the right to vote. Even though Velazquez was among the women suffragist, she was talking about her book and Cuba, and it will be seen at a later date, she claimed she was not one of the suffragist women.

---

18. *Brooklyn Eagle*, Mar 5, 1878.

Velazquez was seemingly more interested in the promotion of her book and the promotion of Cuban independence. She also was interested in meeting and charming politicians. The sitting Congress was the 45th and it was likely at this time that she buttonholed U.S. Representative Glover from Missouri and told the story of her involvement in an alleged U.S. Treasury fraud during the War. He believed it, for which he would be lambasted, as will be seen.

Mostly newspapers accepted Velazquez's story, never attempting to question its veracity and in this category was the *Cleveland Leader* of May 21, 1878. Under the title "All For Her" and subtitle "Notes About Women and Fashion" was a collection of short statements concerning women in the news. For example, "Vinnie Ream sings at parties a ballad written for her by Joaquin Miller," and a second example, "Kate Field says she 'is over thirty, but won't tell how much over." The sixth news item in the column stated, "Madame Velasquez fought in the Southern army three years, during the late war, rising to the rank of Lieutenant." Such a simple statement would have been accepted as fact by virtually all who read it. This single sentence is the perfect example of the lie which grew into fact.

Startlingly, the newspaper claimed facts about Velazquez which even she never claimed in her book! The sentence implied she enlisted in the Southern army for three years and achieved her rank through advancement because of ability and leadership. Velazquez only claimed in her book to have enlisted briefly in the regular ranks and that was with the 21st Louisiana Regiment when she "contrived to get clear of New Orleans." At the first opportunity, she left the regiment. In any case, all claims about the 21st Regiment were false. She explained that, except for this one time, she never joined the regular army so as not to restrict her movements, but instead wandered about seeking opportunities. Velazquez never wrote she was "in the Southern army for three years."

And Velazquez never "[rose] to the rank of Lieutenant." Velazquez readily stated in her book that her rank was never earned or commissioned, but instead was a rank she gave herself. On many occasions she ignored her own book's account and gave widely conflicting accounts to the newspapers of how and from whom she received a commission. Just seen in the February 5 article, Velazquez claimed she "secured a commission of lieutenant from Mr. Davis." And it will be seen in June 1878 that she asserted she obtained "her commission from the Governor of Arkansas, dated May 28, 1861."[19] She never claimed either version in her book and it is a tribute to her audacity to contradict her own book at these later dates. She obviously forgot or did not care what she had previously written in her book, maybe being only interested in impressing at the moment her interviewer.

---

19. *St. Louis Evening Post*, Jun 25, 1878.

1878, Defending Her Book from General Jubal Early

The Woman in Battle was selling and being read, and naturally some people emerged who did not believe that Velazquez's story was true. One un-named reader asked Ex-Confederate General Jubal Early his opinion of the book which Early readily gave. About the first week of May 1878, Jubal Early was staying at a hotel in Richmond and made the acquaintance of "a gentleman from Richmond" who told General Early that he had just traveled by train from Danville to Richmond and had met Velazquez, from whom he bought her book.

By chance, General Early had already encountered the book in the winter of 1877 when he was in New Orleans. He had given the book "a cursory examination" and was "satisfied that the writer of that book whether man or woman, had never had the adventures therein narrated." So, he told the Richmond gentleman that Velazquez "could not be what she pretended to be" and Jubal Early pointed out "several inconsistencies, absurdities and impossibilities in it which [he] thought proved beyond all question, the writer of it to be a mere pretender."

This Richmond gentleman or another person (since Early "expressed the same opinion to several persons") in Richmond passed on General Early's negative opinion to Velazquez. Velazquez responded to this criticism by writing to General Early on May 18, 1878 from Washington, D.C. Her letter was designated "House of Representatives, care of Hon W. H. Slemmons [*sic* W. F. Slemons]." She protested General Early's negative opinion of her book and asked that he, as a gentleman, not harm her book sales, as it was support for her "little son." She proclaimed her devotion to her child and said that "Hon. J. M. Glover, A. H. Stephens, Ex. governor John C. Brown & a host of others" could vouch for her dedication.

She specifically excused "inaccurate dates" because she said she had to trust her memory since she lost "many of [her] notes." She further excused herself explaining she could only know the facts from her area of the battlefield which may not be consistent with events from other areas of the battlefield. She admitted she might have been more explicit with facts and the names of those involved, but she had to keep the cost of the book down by employing brevity. As for her failure to name the criminal governmental officials described in her book, she explained she was protecting the crooks' families, particularly the "young ladies." She "did not wish to taint their innocent names with their parents' misdeeds."

She signed her letter to Jubal Early, "Madame L. J. Velasquez or H. T. Buford C.S.A., Correspondent *Le Buletin De Commercial*, Rio de Jaunario [*sic* Janeiro], Empire Brazil." A quick examination of her signature and accompanying title unearths a curiosity. 1) Can't she spell the city of her employer? 2) Is she working for a French newspaper in Portuguese speaking

Brazil? The name of the newspaper was not Portuguese, but French. She did claim (p365 & 522) to speak French. To date, no record has been found of this newspaper, and it can be doubted that it ever existed. Her signature raises a question, as well. Doesn't she know how to spell her own surname? Previously, on October 7, 1875 she signed a letter, spelling "Velazquez" with two "zees" and she used "Velazquez" as her author's name in 1876, as well. Then in letters she wrote in October and November of 1876 she spelled "Velasquez" with one "zee" and one "s" and now here too.

General Early was convinced that she had not written the book, at least, not without the book being "very much changed and improved in style by her editor." General Early could recognize no skill of an author in her letter. Indeed, her letter to him was poorly written. (However, her letter was wonderfully passionate.)

Velazquez, soon after mailing her letter to General Early, showed up at his Richmond hotel asking, through a servant, to see General Early. They met in the parlor. It should be noted that authors of a popular 2002 book[20] implied that Early sought out Velazquez and initiated the meeting, "Early then arranged 'a brief interview' with Velazquez herself...." However, of this meeting Early wrote, "I subsequently had a brief interview with Madame Velasquez, upon being informed by a servant that a lady wished to see me in the parlor of the hotel...."

This difference is important because Velazquez supporters routinely portray Jubal Early as an aggressor in his efforts to discredit Velazquez. More on this point will be addressed.

After the meeting, Early was sure "Velasquez [was] not of Spanish birth or origin, but [was] an American and probable from the North." The same aforementioned authors thought that Early might be correct on this point, but then hedged their conclusion with the fact that "[Velazquez] landed a job as a newspaper correspondent in South America" as "lend[ing] credence to her claim of Spanish heritage." In addition, the authors wrote: "At the time she wrote to him, in May 1878, she was living with her child in Rio de Janeiro, Brazil, and working as a newspaper correspondent." No, no, no.

First, it is pure assumption that Velazquez had her child with her, in Rio de Janeiro or anywhere else. The last news item relative to this child had placed this child in New Orleans under someone's care while Velazquez was in Atlanta pursuing the publication of her book. And there is no information discovered which subsequently reunited the mother and child.

Second, Velazquez was not in Rio de Janeiro at this date! Instead, the historical record firmly places Velazquez in Washington, D.C., with a trip to Richmond. Velazquez's letter to General Early was dated May 18, 1878, and

---

20. DeAnne Blanton and Lauren M. Cook, *They Fought Like Demons*, (Baton Rouge: Louisiana State University Press, 2002), 180.

he said on May 22 that he received the letter three days ago. In other words, Velazquez's letter did not travel from Brazil in one day! But the letter did travel from Washington in one day. And Early said by May 22nd, he had already met her in the hotel parlor.

Recall that she was identified shortly before, on March 5, in Washington, D.C., soliciting books. She would have not had enough time to travel to Brazil and return, and besides she was busy selling her books. And how could Velazquez have found out from a gentleman from Richmond that General Early was talking bad about her book if she was living in Rio de Janeiro? Velazquez was not implying that she was physically located in Brazil. Velazquez only sought the prestige of being able to call herself a correspondent, and by claiming to be one for a South American newspaper, she could not be easily proven false. Recall an earlier report from the *Daily Inter Ocean* of Chicago, dated December 5, 1877, stated, "She pretends to be a newspaper correspondent here [Washington, D.C.]," and "has a ticket to the reporters' gallery as a means of covering her operations."

General Jubal Early was now pulled into the current by her accusation, that he was "endeavoring to injure her book." He decided to address the issue by writing to the go-between which Velazquez had indicated to use, U.S. Congressman from Arkansas, William F. Slemons. But before Early sent the letter to Slemons, General Early was overcome with doubt about how to address the issue, not wanting to escalate any conflict or involve Slemons if not warranted. So General Early wrote a letter, dated May 24, to a trusted third party, Congressman John Randolph Tucker, asking his opinion and saying he would abide by his good judgment whether or not to give Velazquez any attention whatsoever. General Early enclosed an exact copy (including all errors) of Velazquez's letter received by him, and the letter which he thought to send to Slemons. (General Early indicated that these letters were enclosed on May 26, 1878.) It is clear that J. R. Tucker received the letters because they are preserved in the Tucker Family Papers. It is not clear if the letters were ever sent to Slemons, but probably not, since there seems to be no historical evidence of continued contact between Velazquez or Slemons and Early.[21]

Jubal Early explained in his letter (dated May 22, 1878) to Slemons that he received a letter from Velazquez three days ago and was responding using Slemons as the go-between indicated by Velazquez. General Early asked to be pardoned by Slemons and to please disregard the letter, if Velazquez had involved Slemons without Slemons' knowledge. However, if Velazquez did have Slemons' "sanction" then Early said, "You can show Madame Velasquez what I will write to you."

---

21. These three letters are in the Tucker Family Papers, #2605, Southern Historical Collection, The Wilson Library, University of North Carolina at Chapel Hill.

Jubal Early explained that he had "no disposition of injure the alleged author," and even less her child, but when "a book... is sought to be palmed on the public as true" then he "has the right to speak... whether the author be man or woman."

It should be pointed out that in a 2002 book about women in the Civil War, the authors opined:[22]

If the adventures put forth in her memoirs had been written by a man, such a controversy definitely would never have arisen. No one would have questioned a man's ability to perform military duty, raise a company, fight in battle, and act as a secret agent. And no one would have looked so askance at his personal morality for having numerous wives.

In rebuttal to that assertion- if a man had written the lies which Velazquez wrote, he would have been broadly and loudly branded a liar. Velazquez escaped being broadly and loudly branded a liar because of the fact that in those days a lady was simply not called a liar by a chivalrous society. The authors of the aforementioned book should have noted what General Early wrote- that when a book is "palmed on the public as true" then he will speak against its author, "whether the author be man or woman." Neither General Early, nor anyone else on record, said that a woman could not do things as well as a man. The General said that Velazquez lied: "the writer of the book is not telling the truth...."

The 2002 book called General Early "the most outspoken critic of Loreta Velazquez." General Early seems to be the only prominent critic whose opinion has been preserved in an archive, but he was by no means a persecutor of Velazquez. Early's letter of criticism was sent to a private party and it was never known to the public at that time. Had Early wished to damage her, he could have, as several of Early's post-war adversaries found out. General Early was a strongly opinionated (rightly or wrongly) person who fought on principle. For example, General Early faced down- retract or duel- a man who had criticized Early as a soldier. "In these encounters, Early generally displayed himself at his most contentious, self-serving, vindictive, and effective; he was not to be deflected, silenced or overcome."[23] If General Early, in truth, had persecuted Velazquez, it can be certain that her destruction would have been complete.

The authors of the 2002 book seemingly failed to consider that General Early was a product of the time and place of which Velazquez wrote; for that reason, he was a credible detractor. Instead, the authors dismissed the General as a simple brute "who was irate that a married woman used her

---

22. DeAnne Blanton and Lauren M. Cook, *They Fought Like Demons*, (Baton Rouge: Louisiana State University Press, 2002), 182.
23. Charles C. Osborne, *Jubal, the Life and Times of General Jubal A. Early, CSA, Defender of the Lost Cause* (Baton Rouge, LA: LSU Press, 1992), 454.

maiden name." This was simply not the case. The General protested that Velazquez refused to supply proper names for her various husbands by which her account of her life could be substantiated. He wrote:

> Then her failure to give the name of her first husband who she says, was an officer in the United States Army and resigned therefrom to go into that of the Confederacy States, is a suspicious circumstance. She has no hesitation about giving her own maiden name, with an account of her descent from a noted Spanish family whose name she still bears after four marriages; but then we have no means of ascertaining the correctness of her story in that respect, while if she had given the name of her first husband and he was an officer of the U.S. Army who joined that of the Confederacy, then the correctness or incorrectness of the story might be easily ascertained.

Jubal Early was correct in that all U.S. Army officers who resigned and joined the Confederacy were known, so her husband "William" could have been identified.[24] As it has been shown the General's suspicions were correct. General Early was interested in determining the truth of Velazquez's claims by examining her claim that this husband resigned from the Union army and joined the Confederacy. Jubal Early was not protesting that Velazquez was running around using her maiden name.

General Early had many other very specific objections and these he wrote in his letter to Slemons and explained that he had found the points of contention simply upon a "cursory examination" of Velazquez's book.

General Jubal Early's Objections

1) General Early explained to Slemons that he had made a copy Velazquez's letter "verbatim et literatim," that is, word for word and letter for letter, and had enclosed it. Early was shocked at the poor "orthography, punctuation, and grammatical structure." He stated that "her style must have deteriorated" since she had written her book. Early pointed out, that in spite of her book's claim that Velazquez had "received a thorough English education," the errors he saw were of an American not properly educated and not the errors of a foreigner.

It is clear from discovered Velazquez letters, some 24 in number, that her hurried letters were grammatical nightmares. She seldom capitalized the first word of a sentence, and many times failed to place a period at a sentence's conclusion. In contrast, her cursive handwriting can be described as generally pretty and when she took her time, very pretty. Because of her improper and bad writing habits, General Early doubted she was the author of the book, but he was wrong on this point. Early wrote the book must have been "very much changed and improved in style by her editor" and he

---

24. *Register of Officers and Agents, Civil, Military and Naval in the Service of the United States on the Thirtieth September, 1859* (Washington, DC: GPO, 1859).

was correct on this point. Velazquez, in her memoir, wrote: "I have been greatly aided by the gentleman who has consented to act as my editor" and she praised the editor's "remarkable skill."

2) General Early was critical that Velazquez, in her book, failed to name her first husband, who she claimed was a U.S. Army officer who had resigned his commission and joined the Confederacy, but freely named her dead second husband and her dead third husband. She also refused to name her fourth husband, or to "account for his disappearance." Velazquez knew (and Early understood, no doubt) that husband number four was still alive and could be contacted.

The resignation of a U.S. Army commissioned officer (husband number one) was hugely significant and noted in those turbulent days, although the significance today may not be so apparent. In 1861 there were not that many commissioned officers and all were known and mostly admired, and their treasonous resignation was shocking. Their names were documented in registers of officers who resigned. Verification of alleged first husband's resignation would have been simple and if it was true that he was killed, as Velazquez asserted, then there was no reason not to name him, except her claim could be proven false. General Early apparently never read the 1874 William Burnet husband claim, or the lie would have been even clearer to him.

3) General Early pointed out an impossibility which Velazquez had written in her book:

she states her husband (no. 1), on the 8th of April 1861, dressed in full Confederate uniform, [went] to Richmond, to meet General R. E. Lee and a number of others, when Virginia had not seceded at that time and was not expected to secede, and General Lee was still an officer in the U.S. Army; and when the Confederate uniform had not then been adopted.[25]

General Jubal Early was correct in full. He was himself in Richmond during this time as a delegate to the Southern Convention which was considering the secession question. The attack on Fort Sumter, commencing the war, was on April 12, 1861; Virginia voted for secession on April 17 (finalized by referendum on May 23); General Lee resigned by official letter dated April 20; the uniform was adopted by General Order No. 9 on June 6, 1861.[26]

4) General Early pointed out another impossibility, that Velazquez had

in four days in the month of April 1861 raised a battalion of volunteers comprised of 236 men... she equipped at her own expense appointing all the

---

25. See *TWIB*, p52 for Velazquez's claims.
26. *Delta* (New Orleans), May 23, 1861; *1861 Gardner's New Orleans Directory*, p88, 483- Mr. E. Cain, merchant tailor, designed the uniform.

officers… a sergeant and a corporal, and afterwards of a 1st and 2nd Lieutenant… all being appointed by herself.

Early identified the flaw:

This battalion had been raised without the instrumentality of the Governor of Arkansas, or of the President of the Confederacy, or without her saying to others as much as 'by your leave' and carried just alone she thought proper, all the expenses being paid out of her own pocket; though where the money came from is an unsolved mystery, as her father had cast her off on her marriage, and it does not appear her husband had anything but his pay as an officer in the army.

Early challenged Slemons, "If you were then a resident of Arkansas, especially if you entered the Confederate Army, you can form some opinion of the correctness of this story. If not, ask Colonel Cravens and Colonel Van Manning about it."

Slemons would have seen the pointed-out impossibility. He was practicing law in Arkansas at the outbreak of the war and joined as a lieutenant, then rose to brigadier-general. Both of the referenced men, Cravens and Van Manning also were lawyers in Arkansas and had joined the Confederacy and attained high rank as officers. By 1878, they were serving alongside Slemons as U.S. Congressmen from Arkansas. Even if Slemons would have agreed that comparing notes with these men was a good idea, the suggestion certainly never reached him since evidence indicates that Early never mailed the letter and Slemons never received it. Instead, as already explained, the letter stayed in the possession of Tucker to whom Early sent it, wishing Tucker to review it.

Indeed, it was an impossibility that Velazquez raised and equipped a battalion of 236 men in four days; if true, she set a record never bested by another battalion, Confederate or Yankee. All historical accounts of such activity make clear, it was not a four-day operation. Considering the rural area in which she claimed to have raised the troops, the absurdity is even more apparent. To gather such a group, across the rural distances, alone would have taken more than four days. Besides, there were probably not even 236 eligible farm boys in the surrounding area.

The total white population of Crittenden County, where she claimed she raised her "Arkansas Grays," in 1860 was 4920. Males in the age range 15 to 20 numbered 109, in the age range of 20 to 30 numbered 399 and in the age range of 30 to 40 numbered 287.[27] The three categories added together makes 795. The area of Crittenden County is about 637 square miles making the density of eligible men per square mile about 1.2 men. The County is an

---

27. *Population of the United States in 1860* (Washington, DC: GPO, 1864), 12, Subsecton titled- "Classified Population of the States and Territories, by Counties on the First Day of June 1860" State of Arkansas Table No. 1, Population by Age and Sex.

odd shape, narrow in the south and broad in the north, roughly 25 miles wide by 65 miles long. This is the great distance from which Lieutenant Harry T. Buford had to recruit. (Admittedly, some men could have come from the closest, but still distant, adjacent county). In reality, the numbers would have been less because the first volunteers were generally younger than the men conscripted later in the war. Taking only the first two age groups into consideration would make a total of 508 men for the 637 square miles or a density of 0.8 men per square mile.[28] Averaging the two density numbers gets one man per square mile. Very roughly stated, she would have had to pull in men from 236 square miles (in four days!) to make-up her "Arkansas Grays battalion." It did not happen!

The raising of companies of men at the start of the war was highly publicized and praised by the local newspapers which reported on the fanfare. There were speeches by leading citizens, company flags presentations, flags which were made by local talented seamstresses, and fundraising drives to provide personal items the soldiers needed. It was a very public event. No mention of the formation of her so-called "Arkansas Grays battalion" is found.

Velazquez narrated that after she raised her 236 men, she marched them to a landing on the Mississippi River. There she met her Memphis friend who gave her a letter from her husband which contained the news that "he had gone to Pensacola." Velazquez then loaded her men on the steamboat *Ohio Belle* which took them to New Orleans. To her credit she accurately named the steamboat which was providing this exact service at that time. She disembarked her men "a short distance above" New Orleans. There she purchased all the supplies the men would need, "perfected" her military attire disguise and bought a fine horse from "Dr. Elliot, on Union Street." Again, to her credit, she accurately named Dr. Elliot on Union Street who was likely capable of providing her a horse, as he was a veterinarian.[29] It is clear that Velazquez was knowledgeable about steamboat *Ohio Belle* and Dr. Elliot, but this in no way turns the lie, about raising a battalion, into the truth.

Any company's progress or travel was followed closely by the newspapers and any company that arrived, transited or departed New Orleans, as she claimed her company did, routinely received a flattering newspaper report, evident by the many articles of the times. "Another

---

28. The estimated average age for Union soldiers is generally given as 25.8 years and the average age for Confederate soldiers is characterized as indeterminable because of the shortage data. The military enlistment forms for many states, both Union and Confederate, did not ask for an age. Civil War historian and author Bell Irvin Wiley wrote that the average Civil War soldier was "between 18 and 29."

29. *New Orleans Bee*, Jul 31, 1862; *1861 Gardner's New Orleans Directory*, 157, listed Elliot, Joseph veterinary surgeon.

detachment of Zouaves leaves this evening for Pensacola."[30] In addition, the newspaper picked up reports of troops passing through other cities and headed to Pensacola, "Montgomery, April 9… The Mississippi brigade of eighteen hundred men arrived at Pensacola on the 7th. Three hundred and seventy Georgia troops, for Pensacola, passed through here within the last forty-eight hours."[31] Her "Arkansas Grays" were not mentioned by any New Orleans newspaper.

She proudly stated, "No finer body of men ever went out of New Orleans than the Arkansas Grays, as my battalion was called." Velazquez claimed the battalion, on its way to Pensacola, marched through Mobile, Alabama and it was "heartily cheered, the men waving their hats, and the women their handkerchiefs." Mobile newspapers of this time abound in stories of the many military companies' movements to Pensacola. It reported on the aforementioned Zouaves transiting Mobile. No Mobile newspaper mentions Velazquez's "Arkansas Grays."

The Pensacola newspapers continuously reported the arrival of Southern troops:

April 25… Another company, the Pensacola Guards, tendered their services to the Governor last night… Two companies of Louisiana troops arrived at noon today… I visited the camp of the Orleans Cadets; *April 26*… Soldiers still arrive by every train. Three companies from Louisiana arrived to-day, also a hundred water soldiers (marines) from New Orleans.[32]

The arrival of Georgia and Mississippi troops was announced.[33] Yet there is no mention found of Velazquez's "Arkansas Grays."

Not only do the newspapers not mention the "Arkansas Grays," but no Civil War record mentions the "Arkansas Grays."

But listen to this! At the commencement of hostilities, Alabamian James P. Stephens joined the Southern ranks and kept a war diary in which he wrote on its first page, "Notice, If I should fall in Battle I wish this book returned to my relatives at Centre, Cherokee County Alabama" and he signed it and dated it March 5, 1861. Stephens served in Company C of the 7th Alabama Infantry, CSA, which was sent to Pensacola and arrived at the Rebel-seized Federal Navy Yard on April 4.

Stephen's diary entry for Saturday April 20 stated, "I take the following from the Pensacola daily Observer" newspaper and he noted the news of the surrender of Fort Sumter and then noted:

---

30. *Times-Picayune*, Apr 12, 1861.
31. Ibid, Apr 10, 1861.
32. Ibid, Apr 30, 1861, repeating the Pensacola *Advertiser*.
33. Ibid, Apr 17, 1861, repeating Pensacola papers.

April 15th [1861] We understand that a company numbering one hundred and fifty men has arrived here from Arkansas to tender services to General Bragg they have organized and traveled here at their own expense, and are determined to participate in the assault on Fort Pickens whether received or not. All honor to these brave and gallant men.[34]

Stephens' diary ostensibly confirms that a company of men from Arkansas arrived in Pensacola. This may very well be the basis of Velazquez's claim. However, there are problems. The newspaper reported that the men came at "their own expense," not at the expense of any recruiter/commander named Lieutenant Buford, which she claimed. Worse is the fact that the date of the company's arrival, April 15, does not at all fit Velazquez's narrative. It is two months too early! Recall, she claimed that after she delivered her Arkansas men to her husband in Pensacola, who was a few days later killed, she immediately headed for Virginia and gave the date as June 16. And 150 men are not 236 men. These men could not have been Velazquez's men.

No Arkansas troop histories mention this company and no newspapers mention this Arkansas company, and there was an abundance of newspaper reports about all troop formations and transits. Because of the lack of other substantiation, it leads one to wonder if the Pensacola *Observer* erroneously reported that the company was from Arkansas.

A reader might be ready to believe that Velazquez provided a basic truth about the "Arkansas Grays," but abruptly the spell is broken by a contradiction found in the already presented August 25, 1874 *Mobile Register* article titled "An Adventurous Lady." This was an interview with "Mrs. E. H. Bonner" in which she told of her participation in the War- two years before the publication of her book. The article, in part, stated:

During the month of June 1861, she left New Orleans, in full uniform of a recruiting officer, and went direct to Arkansas, where she soon succeeded in raising a company of veterans. As First Lieutenant, under Capt. Weatherford, she left Arkansas with the company and went to Key West. Here she was reluctantly compelled to leave the command which she had organized....

First, she wisely understood she could not state to the Mobile, Alabama newspaper and its readership that she had marched through Mobile to deliver her battalion to Pensacola, Florida. The Mobile people would have remembered such a transit, if true. In addition, Pensacola is only 50 miles away and in very good communication with Mobile, and a false claim of activity in Pensacola would have been noticed.

---

34. James P. Stephens, *If I should fall in battle...: The Civil War Diary of James P. Stephens* (Huntington, WV: John Deaver Drinko Academy for American Political Institution and Civic Culture, Marshall University, 2003), 39 or page 8 of the diary.

Second, this Key West claim does not hold water. There was never any Confederate company which traveled to Key West! That island always remained in strong Union control and the Rebels never even approached it. Wisely she never again tried to make this ridiculous claim.

Third, there has not been found, to date, any Captain Weatherford associated with an Arkansas company. If he had existed, the record would exist.

Fourth, in her book, she claimed she was the sole organizer and financial source for the formation of a "battalion," not a company... there is a difference.

Fifth, she failed to mention her husband "William" anywhere in this version; she had not yet thought of it.

But wait! A week after the Mobile interview, she traveled to Atlanta, Georgia and "a representative of the *Constitution* had the pleasure of an introduction" to Mrs. Bonner; the reporter wrote:[35]

> It was arranged between her husband and herself that she should raise a company and join him in Pensacola, thus making him a battalion commander. She accordingly donned the full uniform of a second Lieutenant in the regular confederate army, and went to Arkansas, where she succeeded in raising a company of one hundred and thirty-six men... The lieutenant, with her company, joined her husband in New Orleans, to which place he had been ordered, and the two companies were merged in the 'Louisiana Greys.' In the later part of 1861 her husband was killed....

First, Velazquez did not tell the same version of the story in a period of only 10 days. Not only do the stories contradict each other, they contradict the claim found two years later in her book. In any case, all versions were simply lies.

Second, in her book she claimed she raised (implying as a <u>first</u> lieutenant) a "battalion" of 236 recruits, but in this article, she claimed she raised a "company" of 136 men all the while disguised as a <u>second</u> lieutenant. It is a fact that second lieutenants did not raise companies. And there is a difference between a "battalion" and a "company." The custom at that time was that a battalion consisted of 4 to 8 companies and a lieutenant colonel or major commanded a battalion, not a lieutenant, the rank she claimed she designated herself. Recall, she claimed (*TWIB*, p86) that in her lieutenant's disguise, she surprised her husband in Pensacola by delivering a battalion of 236 men to him.

Third, in her book she claimed her husband died in June 1861, not "the later part of 1861" as claimed in this article. In any case, she made various claims regarding this husband and of his death, and all were untrue.

---

35. *Constitution*, Sep 8, 1874.

But wait again!! Years earlier, in 1866, when Velazquez was traveling throughout the South trying to raise money by subscription for her forthcoming "books," she claimed in a March *St. Louis Republican* article that she raised "a company of cavalry and equipping them at her own expense, proceeded to Virginia and served for months on the Peninsula under the command of the celebrated Col. Dreux...." A Savannah, Georgia newspaper, in May, stated that she "in male disguise raised a company in Texas, which she commanded at Manassas."

But wait, wait again!!! Earlier still, in 1863, after Velazquez was released from a New Orleans jail, she traveled to Jackson, Mississippi where the *Mississippian* announced her presence and in an extensive article stated in part, "... she proceeded to Texas, where she raised and equipped an independent company and went to Virginia with it as 1st Lieutenant."

The Woman in Battle's account of this battalion is in painful contradiction with these many and varied accounts she told the newspapers.

In conclusion, General Jubal Early was right. Velazquez never raised a company or battalion, at her own expense or otherwise. She never raised a company in Arkansas or Texas. She never raised and commanded a Texas company at Manassas. She never "raised and equipped an independent" Texas company and went with it as first lieutenant to Virginia. She, as second lieutenant, never raised an Arkansas company which then merged into the "Louisiana Greys" in New Orleans. She never raised an Arkansas company and, as its "First Lieutenant, under Capt. Weatherford," went Key West. She never took an Arkansas company to New Orleans, Mobile or Pensacola. She never raised a cavalry and served with it on the Virginia Peninsula with Colonel Dreux. If any variant of a claim has been overlooked and not included, it too was a lie.

5) General Early objected to Velazquez's claim that she took the railroad from Greensboro, North Carolina to Richmond, Virginia around the middle of June 1861. He correctly pointed out that this portion of the railroad on that date had not yet been constructed. General Early rightly said, "the road was made later in the war."

As her life's history shows, Velazquez was an experienced railroad rider and probably the most traveled woman of her time. She even claimed in her book to have been a ticket checker on the railroad. She knew the railroad; therefore, it is hard to believe that she made an innocent mistake of placing a railroad where one did not exist. It is easier to believe that she fabricated railroad track to facilitate her narrative.

6) Jubal Early protested that Velazquez

> has Memphis at that time in a ferment about the approaching war, with a number of officers in uniform carousing around the drinking saloons and

threatening to demolish the Yankees immediately, though Tennessee had refused to secede- See pp 52 to 69.

Please see "In a Bar-Room in Memphis" drawing from *TWIB* in Illustrations, Figure 20.

General Early was correct again. The night of Velazquez's visit to the "bar-rooms" was stated as April 7, 1861, but Tennessee did not secede until June 8th. However, emotions for secession were high in Memphis in mid-April, but Tennessee as a whole was not in favor of secession. In addition, Velazquez specifically recalled that her husband was wearing "his elegant new gray uniform" on April 5, 1861, taking particular notice of the date since it was their wedding anniversary. Again, the Confederate gray uniform was adopted two months later, so it is not clear just exactly what "elegant new grey uniform" her husband or the "numbers of officers in uniform" were wearing.

7) Jubal Early objected to one of Velazquez's most profound lies, though he himself did not call it profound. He wrote:

Then she fought on the 18th of July 1861 at Blackburn's ford on Bull Run, she being at Mitchell's ford a mile off, and being put in command of a company whose captain was killed, though she had no commission. She then slept on the battle field all night until daybreak on the 19th when she put on her boots and took after the line of march through Ashby's Gap in the Blue Ridge & Piedmont on the Manassas Gap rail-road, from whence she went over the rail-road to Manassas. See pp 95 to 98.

General Early suggested to Slemons that he contact General Hunter and Colonel Cabill, if he did not understand the geography. General Early did understand the geography and stated the impossibility of Velazquez's movements without the help of "seven league boots of which we read in fairy tales." These boots, featured in European fairy tales, allowed the wearer to make a single stride of one league or roughly three miles. So, with seven strides, the wearer could complete the distance that a normal human could walk in a day assuming a seven-hour walking day, or seven leagues.

Jubal Early was correct once again. Her version of her participation in the First Battle of Bull Run (or Manassas) contains a major flaw and several minor ones. The major flaw was not an innocent mistake of bad memory or lost notes, but was a flaw of trying to keep her lie straight and failing.

Velazquez wrote of her days in Richmond just before she departed to the developing battlefront at Manassas Junction. She narrated she, "bought two horses and shipped them" to the front. In the next paragraph she said she took the train to Clifton, Virginia, then two paragraphs later, she said, "At Clifton I bought a couple of fine horses...." In the space of three paragraphs, she bought her two horses twice. She forgot she already bought her horses and her editor did not catch the error. This was a minor error, to be sure, and faulty memory could be attributed. Well, anyway, one can never have too many horses, yeehaw.

Velazquez wrote she approached the battlefront from the southeast, first arriving in "Clifton- a supply-station about a dozen miles from the headquarters of the army in the field." She proceeded to the front, where she sought out Brigadier General Bonham, who was holding Mitchell's Ford. She next claimed she fought at Blackburn's Ford, a mile away.

Lieutenant Harry T. Buford's notable day at the Blackburn's Ford skirmish was concluded with her helping to bury the dead. She "was tired out, and lying down on the bare ground, slept soundly until four o'clock the next morning." Then:

> At daybreak, on the 19th, I was in my boots, and ready to march. Passing through Ashby's Gap we reached the little town of Piedmont, on the Manassas Gap Railroad, where we halted.

What? Velazquez went to sleep at Blackburn's Ford and woke up on the other side of Ashley's Gap some 50 miles away to the northwest, and proceeded to march back to the battlefront, where she had just slept the night. This was the major flaw which General Early pointed out. The lie is so big that it casts doubt on even her presence at the First Battle of Manassas and it is certain that she did not do what she said she did.

When the *Lynchburg Republican* newspaper of September 26, 1861, reported her arrest on Wednesday the 25th, she made no claim (that is, which was reported) to have been in that recent Manassas battle, two months prior. If she had been there, she would have freely and proudly stated so; it would have been out of character for her not to claim credit. Instead of reporting her presence at the battle, all that the newspaper reported was, "She said her reason for dressing in soldier's clothes was that she determined to fight the battles of her country, and thought such disguise more likely to enable her to accomplish her object." The paper explained she was arrested for suspicion of being unfriendly to the Southern cause.

8) Jubal Early complained:

> Nearly all the Confederate officers she describes are drunken, gasconading brutes, whose mouths are constantly filled with obscene language, and the women, especially the young and pretty ones, are in ready to throw themselves into the arms of the dashing 'Lieutenant Harry T. Buford', and surrender without waiting to be asked, all that is dear to women of virtue.

In addition, Early said, that Southern men and women should not "patronize" the book "for it is libel in both." Jubal Early was quick to defend Southernism and its men and women, and he was mostly correct. Considering the looseness with which Velazquez handled the truth, it is likely that she invented the scenes in which she portrayed, in unflattering terms, Southern men and women. It was most certainly not true that Velazquez visited the Memphis bars, prior to the war, while in male disguise, so any observed behavior of the men she claimed she witnessed was a fib. It was most certainly not true that Velazquez recruited a "battalion" in "Hurlburt Station," Arkansas, so the description of Sadie's attraction (p75-76) to Lieutenant Buford was false. The love letter (p221-222) from Miss M of Memphis, which Velazquez claimed she received after the Battle of Shiloh, has been proven a plagiarism. Velazquez's nasty characterization (p312-313) of "General F… employing his time in getting drunk at Atlanta, instead of doing his duty at the front leading his men" and the sordid story of their conflict has been shown fake. Since these claimed incidents were untrue, it follows that the descriptions and actions of the people involved in the incidents also were untrue. One might suppose that Velazquez did not intend to disparage Southerners since the theme of her book was that she herself was a devoted Southern patriot, who stood by the Southern cause until the end. She rather seems to have lost herself in the embellishment of her story regardless of who got disparaged. In any case, at least one person, General Early, was offended.

Who Was General Jubal Early?

General Early, at the time of his contact with Velazquez, was an accomplished, educated and intelligent individual. He graduated in 1837 from the United States Military Academy at West Point, eighteenth out of a class of fifty. He was an officer in the Mexican War. He had a successful law practice. He had briefly served as a "judge of the General Court of Virginia" and had served in the Virginia Legislature, 1843-1847 and as State Attorney, 1848-1852.

Upon joining the Confederacy, he was placed in command of the Confederate army's Sixth Brigade which fought at Blackburn's Ford, at the First Battle of Manassas. The Washington Artillery, which Velazquez praised in her book, was under his command. He commanded troops on the exact ground on which Velazquez claimed to have fought and he saw the "impossibilities" of Velazquez's claims. General Early commanded troops in many other battles and was praised by General Robert E. Lee, "Stonewall" Jackson and others.[36]

General Early understood the foolishness of Velazquez's military claims. He declared her "a mere pretender." He wrote:

> There are many other statements which I could point out to show that the writer of the book is not telling the truth.

---

36. Douglas Southall Freeman, *Lee's Lieutenants* (New York: Scribner, 1949), Vol 2, 260.

In that, he was correct, but he did not persecute her. The discord between Velazquez and Early entailed no more than her letter to him and her brief visit to him.

Certainly, General Early understood that persecuting and calling a lady a liar was a no-win proposition; the lady would not be admonished by the public and only his gentlemanliness would be damaged for his efforts. General Early even doubted the wisdom of sending a private letter, in which he rejected Velazquez's claims, to Congressman Slemons; therefore, he sought his friend Tucker's advice whether he should; Early's letter was never sent to Slemons.

The quandary of calling a lady a liar was considered by Margaret Mitchell in her hugely successful 1936 novel *Gone with the Wind*. Mitchell, who was reputed to have thoroughly researched the attitudes and culture of the times,[37] wrote (p663):

> [Scarlett] knew she was perfectly safe in lying about them [other lumber dealers, all men]. Southern chivalry protected her. A Southern lady could lie about a gentleman but a Southern gentleman could not lie about a lady or, worse still, call a lady a liar.

Please consider that on this point Margaret Mitchell knew of which she wrote, or if unwilling to consider it now, then fiddle-dee-dee, at least think about it tomorrow.

After the War, General Early worked for many years "defending Southernism" and writing about the "Lost Cause." He was an officer in the Southern Historical Society, but he seemingly was not aware of the Society's review of Velazquez's book at the time. Jubal Early died in 1894, at the age of 77, and to the end he was an unrepentant Rebel.[38]

Departed Washington

Velazquez was still in Washington on March 12, 1878 when a correspondent for the Raleigh, North Carolina *Observer* wrote:

> [I] was the delighted recipient of a visit yesterday from Mme. Velasquez, the sprightly author of the 'Woman in Battle,' and who performed two years of gallant service in the Southern army. She is canvassing for her book and otherwise making herself useful. On her Southern tour she will give you a call. She is not as *petite* and chirrupy as Vinnie Ream, but is quite interesting. [signed H]

The reporter thought Velazquez was not as petite and chirrupy as Vinnie Ream, who was just five-feet tall, weighed slightly more than 90 pounds and had long dark flowing hair and dark eyes. Nevertheless, Velazquez should

---

37. Marianne Walker, *Margaret Mitchell & John Marsh, The Love Story Behind Gone With the Wind* (Atlanta: Peachtree, 1993), 174, 178, 179, 193, 220, 366-367.
38. Andrew F. Rolle, *The Lost Cause, the Confederate Exodus to Mexico* (Norman, OK: Univ of Oklahoma Press, 1965), 190.

have been flattered to be mentioned in the same paragraph as the brilliant sculptress, who in 1864 at the age of 17 sculpted a marble bust of Lincoln and later in 1866 was awarded a commission to create a full-sized statue of Lincoln which today stands in the U.S. Capitol rotunda. At this date Reams was world-renowned.

The "quite interesting" Velazquez departed Washington, D.C. sometime after March 12, 1878 and next made her presence known on May 30, 1878 in Cincinnati, "Madame L. J. Velazquez, of Washington, D.C., correspondent of *Le Bulletin Courrier*, is at the St. James Hotel." Forever the hotel dweller, Velazquez chose this one which was located on Fourth Street between Main and Sycamore.[39] No doubt she was selling her book, but she would have been looking for opportunities, as well. Her claim to be a correspondent for *Le Bulletin Courrier* should not be believed. No evidence of this periodical is found;[40] it seems a fabrication, similar to her claim to General Early that she was a "Correspondent [for] *Le Buletin De Commercial*, Rio de Jaunario [*sic* Janeiro], Empire Brazil." Or maybe it was an idea that went nowhere. It will be seen shortly she had an interest in foreign trade and journals rather related to that.

About a month later she appeared in St. Louis and a *St. Louis Evening Post* reporter said he "conversed yesterday" with her and that, "Mme. Velasquez is now in the city and intends making it her headquarters for some time."[41] The article, titled "A Woman's Romance," was wonderfully long, but there was little original inquiry by the reporter. After the main title, there were four subtitles written large:

Two Years a Lieutenant in the Confederate Army; Present at the Battles of Bull Run and Leesburg; Wounded by a Shell at the Battle of Shiloh; Becomes a Spy and Secret Service Agent and Engages in Financiering.

The four assertions came straight from Velazquez's book from which the reporter gleaned them.[42]

The most interesting part of the article was the description of Velazquez:

A woman of medium height and of a slight-built form, with a pleasant face, strongly tinctured with masculinity, especially in the firm, determined jaw, and the square chin, so indicative of inflexibility and persistency of purpose; a complexion which, without being course, has lost its feminine softness; a pair of steely gray glittering eyes that bespeak indomitable sternness of will that no danger could turn from its aim—such was the lady with whom an EVENING POST reporter

---

39. *Daily Star*, May 30, 1878; *Williams' Cincinnati City Directory* for Jun 1878.
40. *Pettengill's Newspaper Directory* for 1878; *Geo. P. Rowell & Co's American Newspaper Directory* for 1879.
41. Jun 25, 1878.
42. The same article was repeated in distant newspapers, for example, the *Lockport Daily Journal* (New York) of Jul 6, 1878.

conversed yesterday. Yet with all these traits, there was no obtrusive personality perceptible in her appearance, nothing to denote a career as strange and romantic as any ever portrayed by that ingenious prince of marvelous fiction Dumas *pere*. A quiet, undemonstrative ladylikeness of demeanor characterized all her actions. No one to gaze upon her would have imagined that she was a woman whose life had been passed entirely out of the old ruts of FEMININE EXISTENCE. One would scarce have dreamed that this was a modern Joan of Arc.

The reporter continued with hard numbers, "Mme. Velazquez is 5 feet 5 ¾ inches in height, and weighs 139 lbs. When she was a lieutenant in the Confederate army her weight was 159 lbs." Recall, less than five months prior Velazquez told a reporter for the *News and Courier* (February 5, 1878) that she weighed 148 pounds when she was a soldier. It might be facetiously noted she was the only Confederate soldier of record who weighed less after the War than during.

The article illustrated her seeming success seeking endorsements in Washington:

The following testimonial, signed by prominent southerners, is a proof of Mme. Velazquez' identity. Washington, D.C., March 1, 1878

Madame L. J. Velazquez (author of the "Woman in Battle") has undertaken to make a tour of the Middle, Southern and Western States in the interest of the popular work, and also to aid in the establishment of direct commercial trade between the United States and Brazil, via her native island—Cuba, starting from the City of New Orleans. She is correspondent of several foreign, as well as native journals, through which she can give much aid to the great enterprise in which she is engaged. Every branch of industry is interested in this grand project, and wherever Madame Velazquez goes we hope she will receive a courteous and hospitable reception. She is a lady of talents, energy and high personal character. Signed by Richard Coke, D. B. Culberson, D. A. Giddings, Jr.; John H Reagan, and Ex-Gov. J. W. Throckmorton, Congressmen from Texas; <u>A. H. Garland, Congressman from Arkansas</u> [emphasis by author]; Wm. Walsh and W. Kimmel, Congressmen from Maryland; J. B. Ellard, Congressman from Louisiana; Wm. A. Phillips, Ex-governor of Kansas; J. B. Gordon, Senator, and A. H. Stephens, Milton A. Candler, H. P. Beil, Julian Hartridge and Phil Cook, Congressmen from Georgia.

It is now clear what Velazquez had been doing in the U.S. Capital during March; she was selling books and collecting signatures. Whether any of the signatures were forged is impossible to say at this late date. Her history makes it clear that she was not above forgery. In this case, it probably wasn't necessary that she forge any Congressman's signature. She would have found that at her request, the gentlemen would have kindly complied and felt good about helping a lady; after all, they did not have in mind to judge her. Neither would they have bothered themselves with verifying her claims, even if they had read her book. The men would have found her pleasant, personable and would have had no reason not to say that she was a person of good character. If there was a disparaging gentleman who refused to sign her good character list, Velazquez would not have included him in her trophy documents, would she? None of the Congressmen gave a firsthand account supporting Velazquez's claims and the reporter, like reporters before, was content with verifying she was a real person, not the veracity of her story.

One sentence midway in the article reads, "By some means she procured her commission from the Governor of Arkansas, dated May 28, 1861." For Velazquez to make this claim in 1878 is startling because in her 1876 book she asserted she never received a commission and that her rank was self-designated. It is a fact that she never received a commission; however, <u>to her credit, she did try</u> to obtain a commission while she was in Mobile, Alabama, but failed. Military records document her effort.

A commission from Governor of Arkansas should have been clearly untrue to people then (and to people now). If the commission was factual, then it would have been documented in state records or military records. At least one of the signers of the previous testimonial, A. H. Garland, would have been unhappy to read this claim. Not only was he a Senator from Arkansas at the date of the testimonial, but he was a former Arkansas Governor serving from 1874 to 1877. He would have understood the significance of such a false claim. In any event, this newspaper article appeared after he signed the testimonial (or his signature forged) and he likely never saw the article.

Notice that the March 1, 1878 testimonial stated she was trying to establish commercial ties with Brazil and that "she is <u>correspondent of several foreign</u>, as well as native journals, through which she can give much aid to the great enterprise in which she is engaged." Recall Velazquez wrote in her May letter to General Early that she was "Correspondent *Le Buletin de Commercial*, Rio de Juanairo [*sic*] Empire Brazil" The testimonial is further evidence that Velazquez claimed she was a <u>foreign</u> correspondent and not that she was a correspondent located in Brazil as some researchers have asserted.

She was a Former Arkadelphian

Four days after the *St. Louis Evening Post*'s long article about Velazquez, the *Southern Standard* newspaper[43] from Arkadelphia, Arkansas (about 412 miles southwest of St. Louis and 68 miles southwest of Little Rock) noted that Madame Velazquez "was in St. Louis a couple of days ago" and the newspaper recognized the former resident:

---

43. Jun 29, 1878.

Many of our citizens will remember her, then Mrs. M. A. Arnold, as she was considered quite a dashing character in this place in ante-bellum times.

This revelation presents a problem!

Never in her memoir did Velazquez claim an antebellum (pre-war) residency in Arkadelphia or a marriage to anyone named Arnold. However, the *Southern Standard's* assertion has some corroboration. Recall her first arrest in New Orleans in April 1862, the newspaper said she went by the name "Mrs. M. M. Arnold, but has flourished under several aliases, such as Gibbons and Lieut. Buford." When she was arrested the second time in New Orleans, then sent to the hospital in November 1862 after a health complaint, the hospital admission book recorded that the "Last Place From" was Arkansas and that "Residence in N. Orleans" had been seven months.

She told a Memphis newspaper, on March 1, 1866, that she intended to open a dry goods business in Jefferson County, Arkansas and five months afterwards she told a Richmond newspaper (August 10, 1866) that "Her home is in Dallas County, Arkansas." It should be noted that Arkadelphia is in Clark County and 33 miles to the east is Dallas County and another 63 miles further to the east is Jefferson County. Clearly Velazquez knew the area and it was most surely from before the War, just as she was identified.

A search for a Mr. M. A. Arnold or a M. M. Arnold or his marriage was not successful and at this distant date it is difficult (but possible) to discover more. Recall when she was arrested in Virginia on September 1861, she said she was Mrs. Mary Ann Keith from Memphis, Tennessee, which is only across the River from Arkansas.

"She was considered quite a dashing character" in Arkadelphia before the War which oddly goes against her represented behavior. She wrote (*TWIB*, p49-50) that in those years she was busy as a wife and mother of three children in St. Louis and Fort Leavenworth.

Velazquez's Son Died in New Orleans

The last public reference to Velazquez's son was in the *Atlanta Constitution*, September 4, 1874; it stated that her son was in the care of someone in New Orleans. All the while she was in the Washington, D.C. area there are no discovered mentions of him, except in May 1878 when she begged General Jubal Early to be mindful not to hurt her son by damaging her book sales by speaking against her book. She proclaimed her dedication to her son, "I live for him and him alone."

In the interview with the St. Louis newspaper, Velazquez made no mention whether her "little son" accompanied her. It was unlikely she had her child with her. Her habit of continuously moving and her busy nature seems to indicate a solo operation, without childcare in the mix. It can be reasonably assumed that her son continued living under the care of someone in New Orleans. What became of her son?

A boy named Jeff Bonner, aged 9, died in New Orleans at #82 St. Peter Street on September 18, 1878 of yellow fever. Yellow fever was rampant in the city and for the week ended on September 22, the victim count was 408, "388 whites and 20 colored." If it was any consolation the number of deaths was down by 93 from the prior week.[44] One of the victims was most certainly Velazquez's son.

Remember that Velazquez identified her son by name, Jefferson, and by age, five, in her October 16, 1874 letter to Jefferson Davis. And shortly before that, she told the *Atlanta Constitution* (September 4, 1874) that her son was five years of age. Jeff Bonner, who died in New Orleans in 1878 and was identified as being nine years old, seems a perfect match. However, the death certificate stated that Jeff was a native of Baltimore, which at first glance would seem to rule out that Jeff could have been Velazquez's son since Velazquez wrote in her book that he was born in Salt Lake City. It is likely that the New Orleans people caring for him thought that he was from Baltimore because they had received letters and/or money from Velazquez who spent time in Baltimore during that period. A Maryland newspaper clearly placed her in Baltimore offering her work in person as early as April 13, 1877 and she was still there, living at 77 N. Pearl Street in October 1877. She was reported in nearby Washington, D.C. throughout January to May of 1878.

Jeff Bonner's death certificate was witnessed by three people; Mr. G. (Gadane) Casanave was the undertaker; Mr. P. H. Lanauze and Mr. H. Kohlhaase were probably officials at the Board of Health. Mr. Lanauze was listed as a clerk in the 1878 city directory and Mr. Kohlhaase was found listed as a "sanitary officer." Jeff Bonner's place of death, #82 St. Peter Street, was a boarding house. There were no obvious family ties found in New Orleans for young Jeff Bonner and it appears that Jeff was under the care of non-family.

It was not possible to confirm whether a child named Jeff Bonner was in fact born in Baltimore because record keeping there commenced in 1875, so no birth certificate exists for his birth year. The Bonner surname is found in Maryland in the 1870 and 1880 Censuses, but none could be linked to Jefferson Bonner. An extensive search for a birth record for Jefferson Bonner in Salt Lake City and vicinity found nothing.

After 1878, there are no more mentions of Velazquez's son found in any newspapers which addressed Velazquez and her activities. This lack weighs heavy as circumstantial evidence that Jeff Bonner, who died in New Orleans, was her son.

---

44. *New Orleans Times*, Sep 24, 1878; *Times-Picayune*, Sep 24, 1878.

An Opportunity in the Theatre

In contrast to the unpleasant news of the death of her son in New Orleans, an incident, no doubt considered pleasant, occurred shortly afterwards, in October, in St. Louis. Velazquez's life's story, based on her book, was considered for a dramatic stage presentation. The *St. Louis Post Dispatch* under the section titled "Local Green Room Gossip" stated:[45]

> Mme. Velasquez, who under the sobriquet of Lieutenant Harry Buford, raised and commanded a company of the Confederate army during the war, is to have her book, "Woman in Battle," dramatized, and may bring it out here.

Apparently, the rumor had been circulating since August that Velazquez "has written both a drama and a novel... The former will probably be produced in the fall."[46]

No evidence was uncovered that the stage production was made, even though it is a fact that at this time Saint Louis had an active theatre industry. It is likely the news story was the result of Velazquez doing a little self-promoting or speaking too soon and nothing more developed.

1878 and 1879, All Business in St. Louis

In June of 1878 Velazquez stated her intention was to remain in St. Louis and to establish commercial trade between the U.S. and Brazil which she expected to go through New Orleans, then via Cuba and to Brazil. Whether she truly tried is unknown, but she did not succeed in that endeavor. She remained in St. Louis with excursions to neighboring states.

The *Daily Arkansas Gazette* of November 28, 1878 noted her as the author of *The Woman in Battle* and said:

> [she] spent several days in Little Rock, and particularly at the Fair, where she exhibited and got the premium on the Star Cotton Planter, returned to St, Louis yesterday. She is evidently a lady of great force of character, modified by a lady-like bearing and polished education.

By November 1878 Velazquez had found work with the St. Louis firm of J. M. Stone & Co. at 215 Market Street. The company was an agent for agricultural machinery and Velazquez was selling cotton machinery, no doubt the Star Cotton Planter for which she won a ribbon. The company also was ostensibly the publisher of the *Cotton Plant* of which Velazquez was editor. It was probably her idea. The local newspaper[47] explained:

> The "Cotton Plant" is the title of a new journalistic aspirant for business favors. It is a twenty-seven-column folio, and the first number contains a large amount of interesting information. It is edited by Madame L. Velasquez, a lady of a great deal

---

45. Oct 19, 1878.
46. *Daily Shreveport Times*, Aug 14, 1877.
47. *St. Louis Post and Dispatch*, Feb 10, 1879.

of energy, and no doubt literary qualifications sufficient to make the "Cotton Plant" valuable. Mme. V. says she aims high, but desires to have as many readers as there are bales of cotton grown.

It is difficult to imagine that she was a very precise editor since she was not an accurate writer of the English language. She seemingly would have needed assistance editing the magazine and surely her partners helped.

J. M. Stone & Co. was listed as "cotton planter" in the 1879 St. Louis city directory and the three principals in the firm were listed as James M. Stone, Alphonso W. Gillett and "Velasquez." These men were found in various censuses with wives and large families. Gillett was listed as "stock dealer" and Stone as a "speculator." It does not seem that Velazquez was intimate with either, unless it was kept hidden. Suspicion of this is triggered when it is learned that in 1885-1886, she cohabited with a married business associate, Edward Goddard. More on that later. For now, the publication the *Cotton Plant* and the sale of machinery seem to have been her main interests.

Three months after her aforementioned visit to Little Rock, she was once again there on February 20, 1879 and the local newspaper[48] wrote:

> Mrs. L. J. Velasquez, editress and publisher of the "Cotton Plant," St. Louis, the lady who is deeply interested in southern manufacturers and southern development generally, is now in the city.

It is clear that Velazquez traveled for her job, also seen by a visit to a Vicksburg, Mississippi newspaper. On this occasion she had news worth telling; there was an exodus of blacks from the plantations. It is possible that she wished to stop the exodus which damaged the plantation owners who were her customer base. In any case, no doubt she was happy to be in touch with the newspapers, as she was accustomed, and might have even been paid for the report. (It is curious the newspaper did not say she was promoting her book, but maybe she was and the newspaper failed to mention it.) The Vicksburg newspaper[49] reported under the title "A Southern Paper on the Negro Migration":

> We had a call yesterday from Mme. L. J. Velasquez, of the St. Louis firm of J. M. Stone & Co., agents for agricultural machinery, and also publishers of the *Cotton Plant*. Mme. Velasquez came South on a business trip from St. Louis and has made several stoppages in Louisiana and Arkansas. She says that at nearly every landing negroes are flocking to the river, seeking transportation to St. Louis, and willing to trust to luck for their further passage to Kansas. She further states that a man has been traveling through Arkansas, claiming to be a dentist, but practicing exclusively

---

48. *Arkansas Democrat*, Feb 20, 1879; Velasquez might have been a regular visitor to Little Rock evinced by a letter noted remaining in the Post Office the week ending April 5, 1879.
49. *Vicksburg (Miss) Herald (Dem)*, Mar 12, 1879, article repeated by the *Chicago Daily Tribune*, Mar 19, 1879.

among the negroes. The practice is not so much teeth extracting as the circulation of illustrated handbills and embellished information as to the great advantages offered to colored emigrants by the State of Kansas.

One of the handbills, we are informed, represents a large sheaf of wheat, and another a very enticing picture of a potato roasting in a large fireplace, that is, one end of the potato roasting, and the other affording a happy colored citizen a spacious seat. Underneath is stated. 'This is the sort of potatoes that grow in Kansas, the colored man's heaven.' This is done, it is said, in the interest of the Kansas Pacific Railroad, which is put to this strait to secure the Government land-grants. If so, the Railroad Company must certainly take very little interest in their colored friends after they leave here. The impression is that the railroad takes the negroes from St. Louis to homes in Kansas free of charge, but this is doubtful. A letter from St. Louis tells of a well-to-do colored man who left one of the plantations in this immediate vicinity, paid transportation for himself and mule, and when he reached St. Louis had to sell his mule to obtain means to continue his journey to Kansas.

Mme. V. states that within two or three blocks of her office in St. Louis there are fully 200 negroes who have emigrated from the South, and have only succeeded in getting that far on their way to Kansas. They are perfectly destitute, and are only kept from actual starvation by the meager contributions of colored people in St. Louis, and who, for the most part, are little better off than the miserable emigrants. She further says she was present when some of them went aboard a Southern bound steamer at St. Louis and begged to be allowed to work their way back to the Southern cotton fields, but were refused, the Captain telling them that they were worthless, and that the South or any other section would be more benefited by their absence than by their presence.

We don't know how to prevent the negroes from being duped into so silly and ruinous a move, for they will seldom listen to reason, though we are told that a party of sixty were dissuaded and turned back from one of the landings—Providence, we believe it was—by a little good advice and the refusal of the Captain to take them on his boat for any price. That this wholesale migration of the negro is ruinous to the planting interest of this country is palpable, and not to be disputed, for they take away not only that labor, but in the aggregate a good deal of the wealth of the country in the shape of money, stock, and chattels. A little concert of action on the part of the planters might rid the country of the Kansas emissaries, and put a quietus upon this emigration.

There were many follow-up articles monitoring the migration. Story titles like "A Darkey Deluge, Still Coming From the South Dead Broke and Hungry" illustrated the problem.[50] The migrants had little money and it ran out before reaching their destination. The steamboat captains were not interested in transporting anyone for free, either to their destination or returning them to their starting point. The captains said that they could not very well let them starve, so they were obligated to exhaust the boat's food

---

50. *St. Louis Post,* Mar 19, 1879.

supplies. The newspapers asked who was responsible for the mess, but no real answer was found. Local citizens could not let the migrants die of starvation, so charitable groups stepped up to help. Some migrants returned from whence they started and others continued on their way with strangers' help. By April 8 the migration was reported to have slowed and those remaining in St. Louis were going to be carried by steamer *Durfee* to Kansas City.[51]

After Velazquez left Vicksburg, she went to New Orleans where a local newspaper[52] noted her visiting the city:

> Mme. Velasquez is now a member of the firm of J.M. Stone & Co., St. Louis, editors and proprietors of the St. Louis Cotton Plant, a journal that is well edited and rapidly growing in public favor.

The newspaper also noted that she had a "widespread reputation" during the War and had published a book of her participation in it as Lieutenant Harry Buford. No mention of her son's death there was made, but she possibly at this time visited his grave, if its location known.

Departed St. Louis

Velazquez soon quit the company and with expressed regrets gave up her *Cotton Plant* publication. She published "A Card" of her imminent departure:[53]

> St. Louis, July 1, 1879.- To the Subscribers and Patrons of the *Cotton Plant*.- In justice to myself and to you, it is proper I should announce the temporary suspension of the publication of the *Cotton Plant* on account of my ill health; my physician and friends advising me to visit my native clime of Cuba and the States of South America. To thank you for a generous patronage would be insufficient, and I desire to state that I have completed arrangements to resume the publication of my paper on the first of next September, under the name of *North and South American Trade Journal*, to be devoted to the growth and interest of commercial intercourse between the two continents. My patrons will be furnished with that paper in fulfillment of all obligations. In the meantime I shall thoroughly acquaint myself with the present conditions of the commercial affairs and the products of the countries referred to, and shall be able to furnish you with the best results of my labors and observations. I desire to add that I will take the cards and represent the interests of the merchants and manufacturers of St. Louis in that country. Communications may be addressed care *Globe Democrat Job Printing C.*, St. Louis. [signed] Madame L. J. Velasquez

To date, no edition of the *Cotton Plant* has been located, but it is certain that Vol.1, No.1 was published because a copy was sent to the Arkadelphia,

---

51. *St. Louis Post-Dispatch*, Apr 8, 1879.
52. *New-Orleans Price-Current, Commercial Intelligencer and Shipping List*, Mar 22, 1879.
53. *St. Louis Daily Globe-Democrat*, Jul 2, 1879.

Arkansas newspaper[54] which stated, "It is a 28 column and very ably edited paper, devoted principally to cotton interest, and subjects of peculiar interest to the South." The newspaper also noted, "Mme. Velasquez is a Spanish lady, and we had the pleasure of meeting her at the State Fair last Fall, where she had a Cotton Planter on exhibition. We wish her success." The Arkadelphia newspaper remembered her from the Fair, but one wonders why the newspaper made no connection to Mrs. M. A. Arnold, a former Arkadelphian and "quite a dashing character" in ante-bellum times, which the newspaper had noted on June 29, 1878 when she was selling her book.

It is doubtful that Velazquez traveled out of the country, as she implied she might, because she showed up too soon in New York City. She was reported there, clearly full of energy after her ill health in St. Louis, "preparing to publish her book- Woman in Battle- under a new name, 'The Adventures of L. J. Velazquez, the Great American Heroine,' and her paper, *The North and South American Journal*."[55] Her book never reappeared under this title, but she stuck with her news journal awhile, as will be seen.

---

54. *Southern Standard*, Mar 29, 1879.
55. *Raleigh News* (North Carolina), Dec 12, 1879.

Chapter 13

1879, the Ridiculous Story and Investigator Glover

A newspaper correspondent was told of her presence and he seized the opportunity to interview her. The *Indianapolis Journal* published the resulting article, but as an introduction, the *Journal*'s editor struck first with his opinion:[1]

Our New York correspondent this week gives some hitherto unpublished particulars concerning an adventuress calling herself Madame Velasquez. Among other things, the woman tells a preposterously absurd story about a plot for the stealing of greenback plates from the Treasury Department during the war, in which she implicates along with herself the late Chief-justice Chase, then Secretary of the Treasury, and several other officials of that department. Yet this story, preposterous and incredible as it is, was accepted as true by the gifted Glover, who conducted an investigation into the affairs of the Treasury Department a year or so ago, and occupied a prominent place in his suppressed report. We print the story just as it was furnished by the woman herself, in order that our readers may see what sort of stuff Democratic investigations are built upon.

This is the first found instance of a newspaperman boldly calling Velazquez a liar, without saying the word.

The *Journal's* correspondent's article, titled "Madame Harry Buford," followed:

I was calling the other evening on a friend at a well-known boarding house here, when he suddenly broke out with:

"By the way, there's a lady up-stairs whom you ought to see, a character, indeed."

"Who is she?" I asked.

"Madame Velasquez," he said, and went on, volubly, "Madame Velasquez, you know dressed in uniform during the war, so as to fight by the side of her husband, William Burnett, who was a Confederate officer. She fought her way to a commission, and was known for a whole year in the rebel army as Lieutenant Harry Buford. Her husband was killed by her side, and the commanding officer commended Lieutenant Harry Buford for gallantry."

"A strange story, surely." I said.

"But not the strangest, by any means," my friend went on. "The sex of Lieutenant Buford was discovered in hospital. She married again, and in five weeks was again a widow. Then she offered herself to the confederacy as a spy. She crossed the lines, and arrived in Washington in 1863 as 'Sue Battle.' In Washington she was employed by Colonel Baker as a government detective and learned a good many government secrets, and at last she organized a conspiracy, of which she says the chief members of the Republican party were members, which stole the currency plates from the Treasury Department, and had millions of dollars printed from them in this city."

---

1. Dec 20, 1879, interview Dec 11.

"See here!" I exclaimed, as new light suddenly broke on me, "isn't this Madame Velasquez the woman whose testimony Glover, the Missouri bilk, tried in vain to get printed last winter for the purpose of ruining the Republican party?"

"The very same," he said.

"Then I want to see her."

It was not difficult. I sent up my card to the lady. We met in the parlor. A slight-built person, slender, tired-looking, with a sensitive mouth and eyes that seem to change from grey to black as you look at them- evidently Spanish born.

"I am glad to see you," she said, offering her hand. "I am glad to see any journalist. Newspapers are afraid of me, and they won't print anything I say. Glover tried to print one report, but the House wouldn't allow it. Nobody dares to print the truth. I have printed it myself, here in my little book just out," and she handed me a volume of 900 pages, abundantly but not very artistically illustrated, containing her record as a soldier, politician and spy for both armies at the same time.

"So, you were a member of the famous bogus money syndicate?" I asked.

"Yes," she said, "and I want some paper to print the whole story. They're afraid to. And I can't get them to arrest me. If I could get Garfield to arrest me, I could prove the truth of what I say by producing papers." And she gave me the names of the men who, she said, were associated with her in robbing the nation.

"I should think they would arrest you," I said, "as a lunatic."

"I can produce papers to prove all I say," she went on. "They are in England, locked up in a bank."

"Nobody will believe what you say," I said, frankly. "Your story is quite incredible."

"Please reduce it to writing," said she, "and I will sign it and swear to it before a notary public."

Then I drew up her statement, as follows, from her dictation:

New York City, December 11. "To Hon. James A. Garfield: I hereby confess and allege that, with the assistance of officials in the Treasury Department, I, on or about September 5, 1864, procured the abstraction from that department two steel-plates, each capable of four United States hundred-dollar notes at each impression; that I transferred those plates to a combination of conspirators of which Salmon P. Chase, Schuyler Colfax, Jay Gould, James A. Garfield, Fred. W. Seward, Judge Burnett, Superintendent S. M. Clark and Solicitor Jordan were members; that about thirty-three million dollars in bills were printed from those plates in New York, and nearly as much in England, and that these bills were distributed between myself, the gentlemen above named and others not herein mentioned, and used by them; and I hereby make oath that I have in my possession a written contract signed by the persons whose names are above mentioned, and others, agreeing to a fair division of the so called money, and that I can and will produce this document whenever legally required to do so."

She said after I read it, "that's it to the crossing of a 't.' I'll sign it and attest it whenever you choose to go before a notary with me."

She gave me many other particulars of the great sixty-million dollar robbery, and I inquired, "May I ask what became of the several millions you received, Madame Velasquez?"

"Certainly!" she said; "I spent it all in buying war vessels for the Confederacy. I organized the only navy that Mallory ever had."

I have not yet been to a notary's with the lady. Her story is too preposterous for consideration. She is far from being an idiot, for she is very brisk and alert in conversation, and she does not talk like a lunatic- but lunatics seldom do, I believe. But remember that this utterly impossible yarn was swallowed by Glover, chairman of one of the chief committees of the Democratic party, and then no longer wonder at the fatuity which has followed that party like the shadow of doom.

Velazquez was supposed a lunatic; her lunacy will again be questioned at a later date. The correspondent understood her tale did not pass any test of logic and he might have been more aggressive with a few simple questions.

For example, why had Velazquez failed to include in her book her praiseworthy act of Southern patriotism, that of organizing "the only navy that Mallory ever had"? In her book, she never failed to tout her other Southern patriotic acts. If she spent her millions on navy vessels, wouldn't Stephen Mallory, Secretary of the Confederate navy, have gratefully named at least one vessel after her? Yet before his death in 1873, he never identified Velazquez as a benefactor.

The Confederacy's chief European secret agent in charge of clandestinely building Confederate navy ships, James Dunwoody Bulloch, had nothing to say about Velazquez's contribution. Bulloch, who called himself the "Naval Representative of the Confederate States in Europe during the Civil War," wrote an extensive two volume history of some 898 pages in which he explained how the financing (particularly its difficulty) of Confederate vessels was accomplished.[2] And of the many books written by officers and sailors in the Confederate navy, dissecting virtually every remembrance of the War, not one book mentions Velazquez as a benefactor or in any other capacity.

Another question should have been: how could such damning documents have been sitting for years, since the end of the War, in an English bank vault, when enemies of the Republican administration would have given a king's ransom to obtain them? If these same enemies thought there was any chance such documents existed and could be retrieved, they would have treated Velazquez to the most luxurious trans-Atlantic voyage, holding her hand and polishing her boots every morning and evening, just to get possession of the documents. Even after the *Journal* article refreshed the public's awareness of the "conspiracy," no one sought her out to take advantage of such valuable and damnable evidence she held against the Republican administration.

---

2. James D. Bulloch, *The Secret Service of the Confederate States in Europe or, How the Confederate Cruisers were Equipped* (London: Richard Bentley and Son, 1883).

Besides the enemies of the Administration, Velazquez herself could have used such damning "conspiracy" evidence to force the U.S. Congress to acquiesce to her demands for the recognition of the Cuban revolutionaries or any other pet project she wished. If the evidence existed, she would not have failed to use it to her advantage. Her personal history shows that she was always in the pursuit of money and/or high station in life, and empowered with such damning information in an English bank vault, she would have been set for life.

Worse still, the information she was peddling in 1879 does not corroborate the information in her 1876 book's relevant chapter, "An Electrotype Plate Bargained For." In her book she claimed (p483) a stolen "plate for one hundred dollars' compound interest notes" was delivered to her room at the Kirkwood House. This would have been a bond printing plate which offered interest. But now, she was talking about currency printing plates, "two steel-plates, each capable of four United States hundred-dollar notes at each impression." Clearly, she would have had no need to print bogus bonds, as she claimed in her book, and then go to the trouble of selling them, if she had currency printing plates to print all the cash she wished, as she now claimed!

In addition to the claim in her book to have received the stolen printing plate capable of turning out "one hundred dollars' compound interest notes," she also claimed she later "obtained another one for printing fractional currency." This claim of "fractional currency" should not be confused and thought to be the same claim as having stolen "two steel-plates, each capable of four United States hundred-dollar notes at each impression" of the newspaper interview. Fractional currency was small denomination paper money issued during the war in amounts of cents: 3, 5, 10, 15, 25 and 50, again cents! Of course, it is false that Velazquez obtained printing plates for fractional currency, but if she had, she and her American friends probably wouldn't have been able to find enough paper to print "thirty-three million dollars" worth of currency! Or found wagons enough to haul it away! Then there were her claimed British friends who would have had the same problem.

The *Chicago Daily Tribune* repeated the *Journal's* original report, but gave it a more dramatic and political headline, "Madame Velasquez: The Ridiculous Story Which Investigator Glover Swallowed."[3] The "Investigator" and "the Missouri bilk," as the newspaper called him, was John Montgomery Glover, U.S. Representative from Missouri, who served in the 43rd, 44th and 45th Congresses. During the 45th Congress he served as chairman of the Committee of Expenditures in the Department of the Treasury and tried to

---

3. Dec 23, 1879.

investigate departmental issues. His report, Velasquez claimed, was suppressed and it was.

The "Truth about the Glover Report" was detailed in the *Portland Daily Press* (Maine) on July 31, 1879:

"What is the truth about the Glover report about which we hear so much?" is a question which a great many people are asking nowadays. Mr. Glover of Missouri is one of those excellent gentlemen whose discretion is inferior to their valor. He never seemed to one very much of a Democrat, and in personal qualities he was, while in Congress, the equal, if not the superior, of most men on the Democratic side of the House. He was appointed chairman of the committee on the expenditures of the Treasury Department, and through two Congresses he carried on a secret investigation into the management of certain business of the Treasury Department.

Mr. Glover's investigation had two peculiarities. It was conducted chiefly by himself, without the aid or knowledge of the other members of the committee. It was aided by certain so-called experts, some of whom were notoriously crack-brained fools, whom no Congressman or any other person with any regard for his own reputation, would be likely to ask to assist him in any matter of business whatever. Add to this the fact that Glover did not know a liar or a blackmailer from an honest man on the witness stand, and you have the principal characteristic of this extraordinary investigation. Glover listened to the narrative of fools, liars, blackmailers and some honest men, and out of all their stories he got a vast mass of evidence, some of which was important, and most of which was untrue or ridiculous.

Like many other Democratic investigators, he did not get ready to make any report until too near the end of the session to get it before the House. He had also succeeded in stirring up certain mare's nests of evidence the publication of which would be derogatory to prominent Democrats, and when he came to ask to have his report printed there was a combined effort on both sides of the House to suppress it.

Mr. Glover is an honest man, but terribly weak-headed, and about as useless in Congress as it is possible for a man to be. He might have made a strong and telling report on abuses in the Department, but he utterly failed. Now he has become a sore-head, and is making a nuisance of himself by circulating his worthless testimony in obscure newspapers throughout the country.

Glover's term ended in March 1879 and after the House "snubbed him so unmercifully, Glover tried the *World*, the *Sun*, the Washington *Post*, the Cincinnati *Enquirer*, and other democratic papers, but could induce none of them to become his medium for reaching the public." Congressman Singleton of Mississippi, who "sat down upon" Glover, "in a personal explanation... stated his belief that Glover was crazy."[4]

---

4. *Oregonian* (Portland, Oregon), Jul 28, 1879.

Glover was not the first, nor was he the last to be persuaded, if not charmed, by Velazquez and worse off for his credulity. In her 1878 letter to Jubal Early, Velazquez said that J. M. Glover, among others, could vouch for her devotion to her son and to the "glorious Sunny South." It seems Glover was an easy target. The *St. Louis Post-Dispatch*, about six months prior to this Velazquez interview, suggests how she captured Mr. Glover's attention, "John M. Glover is a bachelor. It is said he is only in love with the law and has his eye on a race for the Senate in the far away future. Yet he finds time to be agreeable to the ladies."[5] Recall, Velazquez was in St. Louis from about July 8, 1878 to sometime after July 2, 1879, at which time she might have associated with Glover; she already knew him from her time in Washington.

One final refutation remains of Velazquez's claim, that on "about September 5, 1864" she "procured" printing plates for one-hundred-dollar bills. Recall on August 1, 1864 she was still under house arrest at the St. Cloud Hotel in Nashville. She was released and by August 4 she was in Louisville. By August 11 she was in St. Paul in confortable quarters with her husband, according to General Sibley. That leaves 25 days for her to go to Washington, D.C., to earn the trust of fellow criminals, and to commit history's greatest robbery. Velazquez, in her book, does not tell of her Nashville arrest, a lie of omission to be sure, which is troubling considering she said her book was truthful. If she willingly omitted a truth, wouldn't she willingly insert a lie? Velazquez should have understood how a reader would want to know the details of how she won her freedom from a Nashville jail and then rushed to Washington, D.C., arriving just in the nick of time to commit such a wonderful crime and patriotic service for the Confederacy. Such a fabulous affair warrants its own book, *The Woman Who Built a Navy*, or at the least, the incident should have been included in *The Woman in Battle*, yet it was not.

A Firsthand Account from One Who Believed

It was in 1879 that a Confederate officer, who claimed he had worked at Castle Thunder Prison in Richmond during the War, wrote an article titled "History of Lieutenant Harry Buford- A Woman Who Fought Bravely at Manassas by An Officer of Castle Thunder" for a Richmond newspaper[6] in which he claimed that he had met Velazquez and had firsthand information of interest to readers:

Sometime in the year 1864 two of our detectives came down to the Castle from Gen. Winder's office, having in their charge a person dressed in the uniform of a

---

5. Jul 3, 1879
6. *New Orleans Item* (Louisiana), Oct 6, 1879, repeating the *Southern Intelligencer* (Richmond) article.

cavalry lieutenant of the Confederate army, which looked as if it had seen service in the field. The person was below the ordinary height of a man, was well formed, and had the bearing of a soldier. He was a good looking man, and the wonder was, why he had been committed?- what offense was he charged with? Very soon our curiosity upon this point was gratified.

One of the officers handed us a note from Gen. Winder, which directed Capt. Alexander to take charge of "Lieutenant Harry Buford" and keep him in the Castle until further orders. It further informed him that the said lieutenant was a woman, who had been sent to Richmond with no military offense charged against her, but to wait until the Secretary of War, or President, should determine what were her rights in the army, and therefore, that she should be given good apartments and all proper courtesy and respect paid her.

This intelligence, as was natural, excited great surprise amongst us at the Castle, for no one could suspect from her appearance and dress that she was any other than a cavalry officer. We assigned her to proper apartments among the women prisoners, and all of them were astonished to see one whom they supposed to be a man put in among them, and it was a source of much merriment with them when they found out she was a woman in man's attire. Her presence amongst us in such unusual garb for a woman to wear at once created a curiosity among everybody to know her history. I shall now tell it to my readers as I heard it from Harry herself and from others who were conversant with it at that time.

At this pause, let it be noted that "Officer of Castle Thunder" asserted Velazquez's disguise was very convincing to him and all others. "Officer" made no mention of a mustache and goatee, about which he surely would have commented, just as he did about the women prisoners' reaction upon Harry Buford's entrance into their room. He continued:

At the outbreak of the war she was living in the State of Arkansas, in which State she was born. Before the war she married a Northern man named Williams, who settled in that State, and had acquired considerable wealth. When hostilities commenced Mr. Williams left his home and joined the Federal army and fought on that side until he was killed in battle.

His wife, after his departure, determined that she would join our forces, and getting together a sum of money, and donning man's apparel, she proceeded to Texas, where she assisted in raising and equipping a cavalry company, of which she was appointed first lieutenant, having declined the captaincy, which had been offered to her, because she preferred that someone who was more skilled in military affairs should take the responsibility of that position. When her company was fully equipped it was mustered into service, and ordered to Virginia along with many of the Southern troops who came here during the first year of the war.

Her regiment bivouacked for a time near Richmond, where it received all possible drilling the time afforded, when it was ordered to Manassas, and arrived in time to be engaged in the first battle of Manassas, in which Lieut. Harry fought with the skill and bravery of a veteran officer. She remained in Virginia for about a year, performing all the duties appertaining to her position as an officer, and nobody during that time ever suspected that she was a woman, but thought her to be what she looked to be- a brave, efficient officer.

Her regiment then was returned to the South, and was in action at the battle of Shiloh. There Lieut. Harry was badly wounded, and was left on the field in the hands of the enemy. There, for the first time, the surgeon who cared for her wounds ascertained her sex, and she was sent to New Orleans, where she remained under medical attention until her wounds were healed and her health recovered.

When she was fully restored to health, she left New Orleans and came up to the Confederate army, near Corinth, and requested to be reinstated in her cavalry company. The commanding general, who learned then that she was a woman, was uncertain what to do, and refused her request, and sent her under escort to Richmond, that authorities here might decide the matter. And, indeed, it seemed that they were as much puzzled what to do in the premises as was the general at Corinth, for they allowed some months to pass by before a conclusion was reached.

During that time she was under our charge at the Castle. She wore her uniform all the time, and, although she was good-natured and amiable, she chafed a good deal at her confinement, and was somewhat indignant that the President or Secretary of War did not send her back to her command. She had committed no offense, she was charged with no crime, and her only fault was that she was a woman who had the independence and the courage to step out of the sphere in which her sex, it was presumed, ought to fill, and had played the *role* of a soldier in man's attire. True, all said she acted the part she had assumed with fidelity, courage and efficiency, and she thought it hard that she should be cooped up in prison and not be permitted to play it out to the end.

While she remained at the Castle full liberty was given her to go about the prison as she pleased, and we gave her employment as clerk in the office whenever her services as pensman was needed. She was not allowed to go out on the streets without being in charge of an officer, because the ordinances of the city forbade a woman in man's clothing going at large about the city. I recollect a conversation I had with my much-esteemed and highly-respected friend, his honor, Joe Mayo, about Lieut. Harry, which I will relate, as it was very characteristic of him.

"Officer" then narrated in four paragraphs how he asked Joe Mayo, who was mayor of Richmond and an honorable Virginian, whether Velazquez could be permitted to walk about "without being under the charge of an officer" since she "was in prison for no crime." The mayor refused, because Velazquez was still wearing male attire, and doing so was against the city ordinance and his officers would just arrest her. "Officer" explained the mayor was adamant in doing his duty, giving no exceptions. He asserted:

Finally it was determined that Lieut. Harry should not be allowed to retain her commission as lieutenant and re-enter the army. When this was told her she was greatly distressed, but she requested that she should be sent down to Atlanta, Georgia, where she had friends. This was done, and her career as a soldier closed. Dressed in female attire, she left the Castle for Atlanta. Sometime afterwards I learned that she had married a Confederate officer named Col. De Caulp, who was soon killed in battle.

The article was surely interesting to 1879 readers, but it is even more so for readers today because of its now easily identifiable falsehoods.

It should be recalled that Velazquez was taken into custody in Mobile and taken to Richmond and committed to Castle Thunder Prison in 1863, not 1864 as "Officer" wrote. There is no doubt that "Officer" accurately described her arrival, the surprise of staff and prisoners, and Velazquez's activities while incarcerated, such as her working as a clerk. The clerkship also was reported in the newspapers.

The problem is "Officer" said he learned of Velazquez's history and war activity from her, for example, she helped raise a cavalry company in Texas and got appointed its first lieutenant and went with it to First Battle of Manassas. "Officer" should have been wise to the battle's historical facts which were available by this date. And he had available to him Velazquez's 1876 memoir, which he knew existed (as evinced momentarily), and which is in total contradiction to what she said to him.

Velazquez's claim to have been, at the outbreak of the war, living in Arkansas, "in which State she was born" is in violent contradiction to her memoir. And her claim to have been married to "a Northern man named Williams, who settled in that State, and had acquired considerable wealth" and "when hostilities commenced, Mr. Williams left his home and joined the Federal army" also is in total contradiction to her memoir. However, there is a dusting of truth in this claim, as this was likely Williams of the Federal 13th Connecticut to whom she claimed to the newspapers to be married and she had already used his surname in New Orleans, Jackson and Richmond.

The claim that she again met with her Texas "regiment" and fought with them at Shiloh is an impossibility because there was no Texas regiment which fought at both First Manassas and Shiloh. However, there were Texas regiments at Shiloh, but none was Velazquez's Texas regiment because she didn't have one. Besides, the Texas regiment version contradicts her book and all the newspaper interviews in which she claimed multiple versions, all of which also were false and contradictory to her book.

"Officer" then made a claim which he, of all people, should have been suspicious, he wrote, "Finally it was determined that Lieut. Harry should not be allowed to retain her commission as lieutenant and re-enter the army." One would think that "Officer" would have understood the nature of acquiring a commission and been mildly curious from whom Velazquez obtained a commission in the first place while so cleverly disguised. And if he had bothered to read her memoir, he would have seen a great contradiction because she wrote (*TWIB*, p37) she never was a commissioned officer, but only acted "under the *pseudonyme* of Lieutenant Harry T. Buford."

"Officer" correctly narrated that Velazquez was sent down to Atlanta, Georgia, where she married, but it was not to "Colonel DeCaulp," as he incorrectly wrote, but to Captain DeCaulp, as the historical record shows.

Perhaps the most interesting was in the last few sentences:

> In the fall of 1865 Mrs. De Caulp came to Richmond, and she told me she was on her way to New York, where she had obtained employment to write for the press. This was the last time I have seen her, but not long since I saw a large book written by her, containing a history of her life. Her later experiences were as chequered and romantic as those I have narrated. She married a third time to a Spaniard in Central America, and with him traveled all through that country and California. She gives thrilling accounts of the dangers and trials through which she passed in that rough country of miners, desperadoes and gamblers.

If "Officer" had read her "large book," which he "saw," he would not have mistakenly said that she married a Spaniard in Central America, etc. More importantly, he would have discovered his own obvious contradictions and would have written a very different article for the Richmond newspaper.

And finally, recall there is a large knowledge gap as to Velazquez's whereabouts during 1865. At least now, one location, Richmond in the fall of 1865, is identified as a possibility. It also was discovered in "Officer's" story that Velazquez expressed, as early as 1865, an interest in writing for the press.

1881, *North and South American* in New York

Recall that at the time Velazquez left St. Louis where she worked with J. M. Stone & Company and edited the *Cotton Plant*, she stated that she was going to visit her "native clime of Cuba and the states of South America." It is doubtful that she did because she showed up only a short time later in New York, giving a newspaper interview on December 11, 1879.

Prior to her St. Louis departure, Velazquez had promised to produce a new publication, *North and South American Trade Journal*, which was to replace the terminated *Cotton Plant*. Now a year later she had not forgotten her promise and was still of the same mind. Someone was following her progress! Remember J. W. W. who wrote the wonderful book review which was presented in the December 20, 1876 Raleigh *Observer*? Well now, on May 11, 1880 the same J. W. W. informed Raleigh *News* readers:

> Madam Loreta Juaneta Velasequez [*sic*], a native of the Isle of Cuba, of Confederate notoriety as Lieutenant Harry T. Buford, the relict of five husbands, has her book, "A True Heroine" out and is publishing "The North and South American Commercial and Trade Journal" in New York City, in the English and Spanish languages.

Velazquez had not given up selling agricultural machinery as a Vicksburg, Mississippi newspaper[7] explained:

> Messrs. L. J. Valesquez [sic] & Co., of New York, has appointed Mr. T. R. Foster full representative for this State [Mississippi] and Louisiana, to take charge of their machinery and agricultural implements, and also the representative and agent for their "North and South American and Commercial Trade Journal," published by them, at No. 150 Nassau Street, New York. Mr. Foster is a young man, energetic and wide awake, and will prosecute the interest of this firm with great perseverance and success.

It is unknown if Mr. Foster prospered in his new job, but he was a gentleman of above average luck. Four months earlier he had won "a beautiful, pyramidal bouquet" raffled at the festival at Bovina, for the benefit of the Episcopal Church.[8] And three months later, he luckily recovered from "a severe attack of swamp fever."[9] Mr. Foster was probably lucky enough to survive his employment with "Messrs. L. J. Valesquez & Co.," as well.

About this time Velazquez announced "The partnership heretofore existing between L. J. Velasquez and John R. Bedan, under firm name of L. J. Velasquez & Co., is this day dissolved."[10] The nature of the partnership must have been related to the publication of her new journal since John R. Bedan, age 46, by occupation was a printer.[11] Of course, it could have been Mr. Bedan who broke the partnership.

By the end of 1880, Velazquez was temporarily living in Washington, D.C. and had landed a job, described by the newspapers as a "female attaché" to the Nicaraguan minister in Washington and as "attaché of the Nicaraguan legation." She was at the meeting of the U.S. House Committee on Foreign Affairs, related to the canal across Nicaragua. Shipbuilder William H. Webb said he and Commodore Vanderbilt had obtained the canal concession in 1849, but the Nicaraguan government hadn't been cooperative afterwards. Minister Jerez, feeling insulted, objected, thereupon, the chairman of the Committee said such language by Webb was acceptable in these meetings. Mr. Jerez, in gentlemanly fashion, "bowed himself out of the committee," and with his secretary and the "ever faithful female attaché of the legation, Madame Velasquez" in tow, departed the Capitol.[12]

It can be guessed that Velazquez skedaddled back to New York City, shortly after March 19, 1881, the day she placed a fake "Special Notice" in

---

7. *Daily Commercial*, Aug 12, 1880.
8. Ibid, Apr 23, 1880.
9. Ibid, Jul 6, 1880.
10. *Truth* (New York), Aug 21, 1880.
11. U.S. Census 1880, John had a wife and six children.
12. *National Republican*, Jan 19, 1881; *Times* (Shreveport, Louisiana), Jan 7, 1881, J. M. Scanland's letter is dated Jan 1, 1881.

a Washington newspaper, "Notice has been served on Madame L. J. Velasquez to appear in Havana by the 12th of June to attend a suit pending for her property through her representative agent in New Orleans."[13] The ad must have been to reassure people to whom she owed money or people from whom she sought money, of her ability to repay upon receiving her "property." It can be certain she left Washington and her attaché job well before her required June 12 appearance in Havana. She would have lost her job anyway on August 11 had she stayed, as Mr. Jerez suddenly died that day.[14]

In 1881 Velazquez was connecting herself to the *North and South American* publication. The San Francisco *Evening Bulletin* of July 6 picked up a short news item, though from where is unclear, and wrote, "The editor of the *North and South American*, Madame L. J. Velasquez has just completed arrangements to establish an agricultural college in the Republic of Nicaragua, Central America."

No evidence of this agricultural school has been found. It appears to have been a venture stimulated by her association with Mr. Jerez that went nowhere. Maybe Velazquez was looking for investors who never materialized. Nicaragua had for many decades been the focus of investors; from Cornelius Vanderbilt, the tycoon who tried to own it, to William Walker, the filibusterer who tried to conquer it. Considering that former President U. S. Grant had in January expressed his belief in "an American canal built and owned by Americans," and that the construction of a Nicaraguan ship canal was a possibility, it would have made it a likely place to entice investors. In any case, nothing more has been found linking Velazquez to anything in Nicaragua.

To date, no surviving copy of the *North and South American* publication has been found and it might be suspected that it did not gain wide circulation, thus no easily found copies. A directory of publications for 1881 listed the *North and South American Commercial and Trade Journal*, but left unreported circulation numbers.[15] The directory shows the journal was established in 1880, was a monthly publication containing 4 pages, measuring 26 by 42 inches, and cost three dollars a month for ten lines of advertising.

Recall Velazquez arrived in New York City by the end of 1879; the city's 1881 directory shows "Velasquez, Loreta J. publisher, 150 Nassau h [home]

---

13. *National Republican*, Mar 19, 1881.
14. *Evening Star* (Washington, D.C.), Aug 12, 1881.
15. *N. W. Ayer & Son's Directory of Publications*. The *North and South American* is found in the *Directory's* section for Commercial, Financial and Trade Publications (p587) and in the section for New York-based (p64) publications.

78 Fourth Av."[16] The fact that she identified herself as a "publisher" no doubt was related to the *North and South American* journal. Her "publisher" title also could have facilitated her selling copies of her memoir. These two are the only known publications of her creation, but the *Cotton Plant* was likely her idea too. Recall she claimed a connection with *Le Buletin de Commercial* and *Le Bulletin Courier* (both of which seem never to have existed), but as a correspondent.

Velazquez's *North & South American Commercial and Trade Journal* was listed as a monthly in an American newspaper catalog, under the Commercial, Financial and Trade Publications section for years 1882, 1883, and 1884.[17] No circulation for 1882 is provided, but for 1883 and 1884 circulation was recorded as 5,000 per month, a highly suspicious number. That would mean 120,000 copies placed in the public for those two years, yet, no surviving copy has been discovered. Compare another New York publication, the monthly *Railroad Age* for 1884 with a circulation number of 2,000. Copies of this are easily found in archives. In any case, by 1885 her *Journal* was no longer in existence.[18]

1884, the Cigar Makers and President Grover Cleveland

By 1884 Velazquez had left behind cotton agricultural machinery and the Nicaraguan school, but international trade was still her interest. Related to that, she now focused on a favorite and reoccurring theme of hers- Cuba. The *New York Times* reported that she was in town supporting the cigar makers, ostensibly many of whom were Cuban. The newspaper stated that she was "of Washington," but she, in fact, resided in New York. Whether she lied to the reporter or the reporter just made a wrong assumption is not clear. She may have been trying to hide the fact that she was living in New York with Edward A. Goddard, without the benefit of marriage, pretending to be Mrs. Goddard. Mister Goddard, in an April 30, 1886 explanation, stated they were living together in New York during this period, "the first day of our acquaintance [was] two years ago last November [1883]." Their relationship will be addressed.

Velazquez had started an import/export company, and using the company's very attractive letterhead stationery, she wrote to President-elect

---

16. *Trow's New York City Directory*, Vol XCIV, for the year ending May 1, 1881. She is listed twice in the *Directory* on page 1584; two lines down from the first is found "Velasquez L. J. & Co. publishers, 150 Nassau."
17. *Edwin Alden & Bro.'s American Newspaper Catalogue*.
18. Neither the 1884 nor the 1885 edition of the *N. W. Ayer & Son's American Newspaper Annual* shows the journal; The *Edwin Alden Co.'s American Newspaper Catalogue* for 1886 also fails to show the journal. A copy of the 1885 *Catalogue* was not located, thus not checked for the *North and South American's* inclusion.

Grover Cleveland on November 29, 1884 expressing her joy at his election.[19] She wrote she was opposed to a trade treaty drafted by John W. Foster, a representative appointed by U.S. President Chester A. Arthur, to go to Spain to talk treaty. She thought the treaty contained "trickery," would negatively impact trade with Cuba, and she preferred annexation of Cuba.

Her letter is reproduced to aid in determining her ability as an author and the truth of her claimed Cuban birth:

New York
His Excellency
Grover Cleveland
Albany, NY
November 29, 1884

Hon Sir,
It would be useful to express our joy upon your success to the highest Gift. of this great Nation. It is Enough to say we done all we could to help the Democratic cause by Electing one of New York's favorite sons. to preside over our future dealing which is hailed with welcome throughout the South. Especially in our Sister Republic. in which our special correspondent at the Palace in the City of Mexico is a letter just received he says language is in adequate to Express the Joyful surprise of Cleveland Election. for much of our future prosperity depends upon this satisfactory change of Administration. of both U. S. and Mexico for Diaz. will make a radical change. Politically and commercially which cannot
[page 2]
fail to unite us commercially. which is the stepping stone to a political union of three governments. US. Mexico and Central America. for this reason we want continental free trade. to the ismuth [sic isthmus] of Panama. which means protection of American interest. we want no more French invasions on our soil. protection to American citizens life and property private and public. will be safe in your hands is my reply to all our correspondents want is Treaty with Spain. The Foster Teaty means. trickery- to which End Cuba my native Iland [sic island] will go to pay Germany endebtedness [sic]. Anexation [sic] is our hope to our parrent [sic parent] Country. US of America,- could say volumns [sic volumes] upon this subject. will leave it to our able statesman to. settle. Wishing your 4 years 8 or during life, knowing the country is safe I now commit the whole to the care of our heavenly father – beleive [sic] me Ever to be your Friend. Loreteta J. Velasquez

Noticeably, Velazquez signed with a new variant of her name, "Loreteta."

In contrast to the letter's awkward content is her company's splendid letterhead. It occupies a third of the page, with "Continental Exporting & Importing Co." at the top center and much description of services offered. On the left is a picture of a clipper ship under full sail and on the right is a locomotive engine chugging along leaving an overhead smoke trail. Centrally

---

19. Grover Cleveland Papers, Microfilm Ser 2, Reel 2.

placed is a large illustration of two hands shaking with the word "Reciprocity" in quotations. This was a catchword at the time which basically meant international fair trade. At issue were government-imposed tariff trade barriers, favored by some politicians while others desired tariff free trade. It was a topic about which Velazquez was clearly conscious because of her designated business; fewer or no tariffs potentially encouraged more transactions. The Democrats of that date generally favored fewer tariffs, thus Velazquez's expressed support for the newly elected Cleveland, the first Democrat since before the Civil War.

December 8, 1884 found Velazquez in New York speaking on behalf of the cigar makers' opposition to the Spanish Treaty which they deemed injurious to their livelihood. The proposed treaty would remove the import duties on tobacco products. This would make imported Cuban cigars cheaper and cause the U.S. cigar makers to work for less money in order to stay competitive or outright lose their jobs. The *New York Times* stated:[20]

A black-eyed and black-haired woman came into the meeting room, and after giving her name to the Chairman, was introduced as Mrs. Velasquez, of Washington. She spoke English fluently and said that she was a Cuban and had come to help the cigar makers. She was an old worker in Congress, although she wanted it to be understood that she was not a woman's rights agitator. She had been requested by several Senators to come on to New York and confer with the cigar makers and sugar manufacturers. One hundred and forty members of Congress and 41 Senators were decidedly opposed to the treaty. The speaker said she was very well acquainted with Messrs. Edmunds, Blair, Sherman, Randall, and numerous other Senators and Congressmen. Mr. Foster's object in drafting the treaty was to further his own individual interests and the interests of his friends, and they would do all that lay in their power to push it through the Senate.

Mrs. Velasquez was not only opposed to the treaty, but she wanted to see Cuba annexed, and there were many in Washington who wanted that, too. Mr. Hill, of Ohio, was in her office on Saturday, and she had a letter from Senator Blair asking her to see the different societies in this city. She urged the cigar makers to send representatives to Washington, where committees would arrive from New Orleans, [&] California.

At least one out-of-town newspaper reported similarly:[21]

The cigar makers of this vicinity held their usual Sunday meeting to protest against the adoption of the Spanish treaty. A Mrs. Velasquez said Senator Hill told her he would speak against the treaty. One result of the negotiation over the treaty has been the shutting down of the largest cigar manufactory in the United States, that of Straston & Strom, in this city, and the consequent throwing out of employment of 2,300 workmen. The shutdown was announced to the men

---

20. Dec 8, 1884.
21. *Wheeling Register* (West Virginia), Dec 9, 1884.

Saturday night. The firm says they stopped work in order to see what the effect of the treaty will be upon the importation of raw materials.

Whether Velazquez was a paid agent of the cigar makers or anyone else is not clear and it is doubtful that she was instrumental in the treaty's ultimate failure of ratification by the Senate. She probably figured the treaty would hurt her business, or rather the drumming up of business; there was no real business claimed her common-law husband Goddard, as will be seen. Curiously, her letter to the President-elect and her support of the lifting of tariffs was in conflict with her support of the cigar makers who were opposed to the lifting of the tariffs, but her overriding interest seems to have been annexation of Cuba. There is no more discovered evidence of her association with the cigar makers.

1885, the People's Party and Another Letter to Cleveland

It might be supposed that her association with the cigar laborers led to a brief contact with the People's Party. She does not seem to have become a member of the political party, or at least, a notable one. Velazquez appeared at a People's Party meeting held in Clarendon Hall on January 13, 1885. "There was fire in the air at the meeting [and] the people's party was there in force [giving] sweeping sentiments on matters of various public interest." This boisterous group called for the resignation of the state's two Senators who had recently voted against a bill which the party favored, then "moved a resolution recommending the abolishment of the United States Senate as a useless appendage."[22]

It was in this atmosphere, "Mr. John G. Huhn said Mme. Velasquez was in the audience, and would like to take the platform for five or six minutes, but the chairman ruled Mr. Huhn and Mme. Velasquez out of order." What Velazquez wanted to say is unknown, but it might be supposed she was there to promote workers' rights somehow related to the cigar makers.

Whether she embraced the political philosophy of the People's Party is not certain, but the party's objective was:

> To provide by law that laboring men may combine and organize for their own protection, and that all devices, either by contract or terrorism, or otherwise, to obstruct and set aside this right in laboring men, are oppressive and in derogation of the rights of an American freeman and should be made penal by law.[23]

If indeed she embraced the People's Party's platform, an interesting irony presents itself. The creation of the party had been the work of her old Civil War foe, Union General Benjamin Butler. In the just held presidential election of November 1884, the Anti-Monopoly party and the National

---

22. *New York Herald*, Jan 14, 1885.
23. *Brooklyn Eagle*, Oct 31, 1884.

Greenback-Labor party had nominated General Butler for their candidate. In the last weeks of July, General Butler "consolidated the minor parties into a third party called the 'People's Party.'" Butler was "one of the hardiest campaigners in history" and he ably railed against both the Republican or Democrat parties, standing on ideals which he thought favored a stronger nation. He spoke against railroads which would "not allow grain and consumers to be brought together so as to live," he supported an import tariff to protect American labor and goods, he supported greenback currency rather than a precious metal standard, so that money would be more readily available to the populace and he spoke against monopolies.

Butler did not delude himself that he would win, considering he did not have a solid national organization or sufficient finances, and he was correct. However, he seemed satisfied to present to the American people his "certain principles" attained in the course of his life's "long experience and judgment" as his "memorial and legacy."[24]

March 3, 1885 found Velazquez in Philadelphia from where she wrote another letter,[25] on American Hotel letterheaded stationery, to newly seated President Cleveland:

American Hotel
Opposite Independence Hall
Philadelphia
Jas, D. McClellan, Prop'r
March 3, 1885

Mr. Grover Cleveland.
President USA.
Washington DC.

Honored Sir.

The course you have adopted is one which will reclaim the vital interest of your government from a downward grade to commercial and financial ruin. Economy. is the success of all classes of business. You will win a spot in every true Americans heart. And win for yourself, a name that will do credit to the Father of your country in front of whose. Statue. I write this. All Nations of the Earth. will proclaim you a hero. I have no voice. in the politics of this
[page 2]
gigantic country. owing to my sex. how do I desire to have. I am a merchant interested in the commercial and financial welfare of the whole continent. to the Ismuth [*sic* isthmus] of Panama. which. Should be one commercially. with. the three Local governments. U. S. A. Mexico, and Central America_ with our. R. R.

---

24. Richard S. West, *Lincoln's Scapegoat General, A Life of Benjamin F. Butler, 1818-1893* (Boston: Houghton Mifflin, 1965), 377-407.
25. Grover Cleveland Papers, Microfilm Ser 2 Reel 6.

communications and intercourse the Latin Americans will adapt themselves to modern uses and customs as far as climate. will admit of I trust. and pray. that if it is consistent with the policy of the US to bring about a Federal union of those five little Republics of Central America. making them self sustaining. my three years observation and knowledge of the condition has proven. their inability to. remain. longer. in there [sic] impoverished condition, with the untold hiden [sic] wealth. now waiting development. and know [sic no] one

[page 3]

more thougerly [sic thoroughly] understands. and deplores these facts than myself. Señor Romero will give you a better idea of my last five years work in the interest of the two countries. the Aglo. [sic Anglo] and Latin Races. as a merchant. I should like to. See for Post master of New York. Dorohiemer, Roswell. P. Flower, John Kelly, &. member B J. Willis. since it is not consistent with your policy to permit Mr. Pearson to remain, if the majority of the business classes. in the State of New York were Satisfied. I should be glad to see him remain. while he is not my choice, but I believe he. is thougerly [sic] able and competent. to. manage. this branch trust you will pardon me for daring to pressure to offer

[page 4]

an opinion in the matter which is agitating the minds of our citizens daily. You have my prayers for your future that god will continue your health to carry out your great work. I am

Very Truly Yours
Lorateta. J. Velasquez
102 Chambers Street
New York

Accompanying the letter was her attractive business card:

Continental Importing & Exporting Co. Exporters of American Manufacturers for Introduction to Central America, Mexico and West Indies, for which we can Offer Special Inducements, and Importers of Productions from above Countries. 102 Chambers Street New York City, U. S. A

Curiously, she flipped the name of her company since her first letter to him. Handwritten at the top of the card on the front was "my house, 16 months old." This was her business house address and she was indicating it had been in existence for 16 months. At the bottom was written "(over)" and on the card's reverse was handwritten:

Madame Lorateta. J. Velasquez
I forgot to state I am now arranging with a large publishing house to have my manuscript. of my travels. through Central America & Mexico. my interviews with the leading men. commercial and trade relations showing the true condition of affairs- LJV

It is an impossibility that she was going to write anything about which she said she was, simply because it was false that she had traveled in Central America and probably Mexico too. She knew nothing firsthand about those places and most likely the leading men she interviewed were not that leading. Anyway, no book resulted.

Velazquez's boldness is illustrated by her willingness to express political opinions and even lamenting, "I have no voice in the politics of this gigantic country, owing to my sex, how do I desire to have." She was clearly avant-garde.

Instead of signing "Loreteta" of her first letter to Cleveland three months prior, Velazquez now varied the variant, signing "Lorateta." She had come a long way since March 23, 1867, when she wrote to President Andrew Johnson and signed "Lauretta."

Note Velazquez said she started her business 16 months ago which would mean November 1883 which matches the date Mr. Goddard claimed he first met her.

1886, Cohabited with Edward Goddard in New York

By the spring of 1886 Velazquez had relented in her efforts to aid the cigar makers, to address the People's Party and to annex Cuba. She now claimed to be an importer of products from Mexico. She established an import business which was totally entwined with her personal life and when her personal life took a turn for the worse, the business failed. More precisely, the business never had an income, thus the failure. The *New York World* of April 27, 1886 told of the business' failure and of a saucy chapter in Velazquez's life under the title "Mrs. Goddard Explains, Justifying Her Conduct to a Big Crowd at the Bowling Green":

Mr. E. A. Goddard and his wife have fallen out. They formerly imported merchandise from Mexico to this port and had an office at N. 102 Chambers street. They have lived unhappily for several months, when, on the 7th inst., their infant child was laid in its tiny grave, the last link that bound them together apparently was broken. Since then their domestic relations have been growing more and more unpleasant, and yesterday the difficulty came to a climax.

Mr. Goddard went into the Stevens House barbershop yesterday and had his whiskers trimmed. He had just left when a very trim little woman in black called.

"I'm Mrs. Goddard," she said in a very businesslike way that almost made the hair on the shears stand up. "Has my husband been here? Don't say no, for I saw him go in that door not fifteen minutes ago."

"I believe he's upstairs, ma'am." said the barber meekly.

Mrs. Goddard went up with a determined tread. Her husband saw her at the door and turned red and pale in rapid succession. He seemed about to make a break for the door, but the little woman in black was down on him before he knew it, and what a tongue-lashing she did give him! The husband backed his way out to the door and his wife followed him, growing more animated and excited at every step. On the sidewalk she backed him up against a railing, shook a bundle of legal documents in his face, and promised to have justice if it cost her the last cent she possessed. The little kid-gloved fist came closer with every shake. At just the last moment Mr. Goddard gathered himself together and fled. He bowled nimbly around the green at the foot of Broadway and disappeared down Whitehall street. The little woman in black watched him out of sight and then turned to the crowd which had gathered before her. She told various stories concerning her husband, and was going to say something more, but interrupted herself to catch a [street] car which was passing uptown. She boarded it neatly while it was still in motion, and was seen no more.

A call at the old office in Chambers street elicited the fact that it had been vacated.

Mr. E. A. Goddard was now compelled to reply to Mrs. Goddard's public tirade against him with an explanation and confession. The *Brooklyn Eagle* gave his version of his domesticity with Velazquez under the title "Mr. Goddard Explains, His Extraordinary Experience at the Hands of a Woman Who Claims to be His Wife, but Whom He Stigmatizes as an Adventuress":[26]

To the Editor of the *Brooklyn Eagle*:
On Tuesday last the *World* published a scandalous article concerning myself. My attention was called to it by a friend late Wednesday evening. I immediately wrote a reply and carried it to the *World* office myself, but for some reason they have not seen fit to print it. What can be thought of a paper which will print scurrilous articles against private citizens and refuse to print anything they may wish to say in their own defense? Knowing your love of justice and fair play, I do not hesitate to ask you to print the statement inclosed [*sic*]. Yours truly, E. A. Goddard, New York, May 1, 1886

New York, April 30, 1886.
My attention has just been called to an article in the *World* of last Tuesday entitled "Mrs. Goddard Explains." There is not a word of truth in the article except the fact that a woman who has the effrontery to call herself Mrs. Goddard did publicly disgrace herself by reciting the story of her wrongs, as she terms them, to those who chanced to listen in the parlor of the Stevens House. The rest of the article "that she backed him up against the railing and shook a bunch of legal documents in his face," etc., is but the fanciful work of some reporter's lively imagination. In justice to myself, to my friends and especially to my wife, who has been insulted by this shameless pretender to my name, I ask you to publish the following statement:

First- This woman is known as Madame L. J. Velasquez, and there never was any pretense of marriage between us.

Second- She knew that I was a married man from the first day of our acquaintance two years ago last November, and many will testify to this fact when called upon to do so.

Third- It is true that we had business relations together. She represented that she had property in Mexico and had established agencies in various places

---

26. May 1, 1886.

throughout Mexico and Central America. She had many schemes for making money, and urged them with a plausibility which unfortunately completely bamboozled me, and through me, many of my friend and acquaintances. It is sufficient to say that not one of her schemes have [*sic*] ever been realized, nor a single representation as to her property has been verified. She did not have a dollar during my connection with her, except what she borrowed from her friends or through myself.

Fourth- So long as I was willing to live with her, she had no criticism to make either of my business or personal relations with her, but from the very first of our intimacy she gave me to understand that if I ever left her to go back to my wife, she would ruin me. I soon found that I had to deal with an unscrupulous adventuress, as vindictive and cruel as she was cunning and deceitful, and I was moral coward enough to live under the shadow of this threat for more than a year, dreading the scandal and disgrace of an exposure, and hoping that some of her many representations might prove true as to her property and thus save the financial part of the connection by paying those of my friends who had parted with their money on her representations and mine.

Fifth- Within forty-eight hours after I left her, she went to many public places of business, carrying a babe supposed to be hers, proclaiming me to be a villain of the deepest dye and parading her own shame in a manner which the lowest outcast would have shrunk from doing. She also wrote to my wife a cruel and ingenious letter, which almost broke her heart, and followed it up with others of a like tenor to every friend and acquaintance whose name she chanced to know.

Sixth- This woman claims to have been married five or six times prior to my meeting her, and if these men are all dead it is not to be wondered at, judging from my own experience. I have reason to believe, however, that at least one of these supposed husbands is living, and his story no doubt would prove interesting. In conclusion, I would say that I deserve all the punishment visited upon me by this disgraceful connection, and bow my head in shame when I think of the disgrace I have brought upon my friends, my family and myself by consenting to a life which made my every act a lie. It is with reluctance that I make this statement, but I know of no better way than to boldly face the truth, and assure my friends that in the years to come I hope to redeem myself in their estimation. But what safety is there for any man against the slanderous tongue of an abandoned woman, who cares nothing for her own reputation and who will descend to anything for the sake of revenge? No doubt this woman will attempt to repeat the disgraceful scene of Monday whenever and wherever we may meet, but in due time her power to injure others as she has injured me will be ended. E. A. Goddard.

The *National Police Gazette: New York* picked up the "Mrs. Goddard Explains" story and added an illustration of Velazquez with Mr. Goddard in her clutches.[27] It might be reasoned that the illustrator only guessed how Velazquez looked and he positively had no idea of how Mr. Goddard looked, evinced by the lack in the illustration of the whiskers described. The

---

27. May 15, 1886.

odds are nil that the illustrator happened to witness the domestic dispute and captured the scene. The *Gazette* simply picked up the original story from the news. Whether the feuding co-inhabitants reacted to having their story published in the seedy *Gazette* has not been found.

Please see the *Gazette's* drawing of Velazquez in Illustrations, Figure 21.

Who was Mr. E. A. Goddard? Who was the real wife, about whom Mr. Goddard claimed that Velazquez had "almost broke her heart"? Edward A. was a native of Massachusetts and Goddard's real wife, Jennie H., was from Connecticut. Both were 47 years of age in 1886. Six years prior to the Velazquez episode, in 1880, Edward and Jennie were living together as boarders in South Elliot Place, New York. At that time Jennie was listed as having "no occupation" and Edward was listed as working in "paint manufacture."[28]

By late 1884 or early 1885, Edward had started living with Velazquez. But somehow Edward must have kept his estranged wife's feelings in mind, probably not having completely broken his relationship with his wife. At the time of the Velazquez domestic eruption, Velazquez and Goddard were indeed living together and working together. This fact is shown by the 1886 New York City directory which lists Edward A. Goddard as a "merchant" with an office at 102 Chambers Street and a residence at 217 E. 118th; these same addresses are given for "Velasquez, Lorateta J.," who was listed as an importer. Velazquez had another partner, David McCormick. "Velasquez L. J. & McCormick" are listed as importers at 102 Chambers. Curiously, McCormick's residence address also was 217 E. 118th. All three must have boarded there. Nothing of McCormick's association with Velazquez is known.

After the domestic blow-up, it can be certain that Mr. E. A. Goddard kept clear of Velazquez and had no more relationship with her.

Oh, and Edward Goddard was a liar because there was a "word of truth in the article." Sure enough, their infant did die on "7th inst," that is, April 7, 1886 and was buried on April 8 at Green-Wood Cemetery, lot # 8839, in Brooklyn.

The child's name was Joaquin V. Goddard and he was three months and twenty-six days old when he died of bronchitis on April 7 at 4 p.m. Doctor I. H. Reiley of 167 W. 23rd Street had attended to the sick child from March 31 until his death.[29]

Joaquin's death certificate listed the father as Edward A. Goddard, born in Lowell, Mass, and the mother as Loretta J. R. Goddard, born in Havana, Cuba. The certificate showed them living as a single family on the 3rd floor

---

28. U.S. Census 1880.
29. The Certificate of Death spelled the child's name Joquin; Green-Wood Cemetery spelled his name Joaquin.

of 131 W. 23rd Street.[30] They ostensibly had relocated from the address which was noted in the 1886 New York City directory.

A search for Joaquin's birth certificate failed, though the death certificate clearly stated that he was born in Fordham, New York and this is where the search was directed. It would seem that Joaquin was born at home and no certificate was issued.

Recall, Edward asserted that Velazquez was "carrying a babe supposed to be hers"? This will be addressed further along.

1887, Married William Beard

Although Velazquez's phony marriage to Goddard failed in a most public way, she did not swear off men or marriage. She remained in New York and sixteen months later she married a bona fide husband, William Beard. Details about the marriage can be gleaned from both the "Certificate of Marriage" and the "Return of a Marriage" documents.

Please see the documents and image of Beard in Illustrations, Figure 22.

The marriage took place on August 20, 1887 and Velazquez gave her name as "Loratita Juanita Bonner." Please recall her authorship name of "Loreta Janeta." Here it seems that she was trying to make the diminutive of Loreta which should have been Loretita. And with middle name, Juanita, it seems she finally got a correct Spanish name instead of the invented Janeta.

The documents asked for "Maiden Name, if a Widow," and she wrote, "Velasquez." Well yeah, she was a widow in the distant past, but not of her three most recent husbands! Recall that her most recent married name was McLeod. She also ignored stagecoach driver A. J. Bobo, and miner Bonner, the husbands before McLeod. Moses DeLorme McLeod, at this date, was likely alive (though possibly dead, but how would she know), and E. H. Bonner and A. J. Bobo were positively alive.

When she filled-in the space stating "Number of Bride's Marriage," she wrote, "three." Just which two prior marriages did she wish to credit? Recall that Mr. E. A. Goddard said that she claimed to have been "married five or six times." Let's see what husbands Velazquez claimed in her book; in order, she married a "William" (no surname given), Captain Thomas C. DeCaulp, Major Wasson, and an unnamed miner (Bonner). That's four. Marriage documents have been found for Wasson, followed by Bonner. Although no marriage record has been found to date for DeCaulp, letters between DeCaulp and Velazquez show they called each other "husband" and "wife."

One wonders whether husband Beard ever read her book and caught the discrepancy in the numbers. Beard would have seen that he was husband

---

30. New York City Department of Records, Municipal Archives- "If a Dwelling, by how many families, living separately, occupied, *one*, Floor # *3*."

number five, at a minimum, based on Velazquez's own and prior claim, and not number three. But of course, there also were husbands A. J. Bobo and Dr. McLeod, which would have then made William Beard number seven. Not yet included in this count is her 1862 claim to be married to "Williams" of the 13th Connecticut and the newspapers' claim that she had married a Bachman from Arkansas and that she also had gone by the name of Mrs. Arnold. Oh, and recall that in 1861, when Velazquez was arrested using the name Mrs. Mary Ann Keith, she claimed to the newspaper that "she had been married twice, the first husband having been a member of Sherman's famous Battery; her second was in the Southern army." The reader may wish to add four husbands to the count which would then make husband William Beard number eleven. (The alleged husband in "Sherman's famous Battery," and surely a lie, has been left out of the count since a name was not provided and she may have already referred to him. Also left out of the count is the name "Gibbons," since the New Orleans newspaper did not say that she was a Mrs. Gibbons. And there was her 1886 false claim to be married to E. A. Goddard. Should he be counted?)

She would later, in December 1900, claim to reporters that William Beard was her second husband.

Velazquez gave her place of birth as "Havana de Cuba, W. I. [West Indies]" and her "Age next Birthday" as 44 years which was younger than her age should have been if the date of birth, June 26, 1842, given in her book was true. She would have been 46 at her next birthday and was 45 years and almost 2 months at the marriage. She gave her father's name as "Juanquin R. Velasquez" and her mother's name as "Marie Antoneta DeChaump."

William Beard stated that he was born in Cornwall, England and gave "Age next Birthday" as 52 years. The document stated that this was his first marriage and he was a mining engineer. His father's name was John and his mother's name Elizabeth Bunney.

English census records for 1841 and 1851 confirm that William Beard was born in St. Austell, Cornwall, England to parents, John and Elizabeth (Betsy) and his stated age on the "Return of Marriage" document is confirmed. William Beard, as well as his brothers and a sister, are shown attending school in 1851. William's assertion that this was his first marriage is suspect- A record from July 17, 1854 shows William Beard marrying Elizabeth Stephens at the St. Allen Parish Church in Cornwall County.[31] This seems to be our William, who would have been about 21 years old, but there is a small chance it was another.

The marriage documents show Velazquez and Beard living at the same address, 116 Lexington Ave. The witnesses who signed the "Return of

---

31. England, Cornwall Parish Registers, 1538-2010, www.familysearch.com.

Marriage" document were Walter R. Lord and Thomas J. Purdy, both New York City attorneys. Mr. Purdy also was found as a witness on the "Certificate of Marriage" along with Anna R. Eddy, probably the spouse of the marriage ceremony minister, Clayton Eddy.

Although William Beard and Velazquez gave their residence address as 116 Lexington Avenue, it is unclear how long they stayed there. A letter written in 1890 by William's brother, Thomas, gave a different address. Thomas, two years younger than William, had immigrated in 1862 and was living in Ironton, Massachusetts. It was on January 26, 1890 that Thomas[32] wrote to his nephew (son of the brother Joshua, who was 4 years younger than William) with general family news and gave William Beard's address as No. 57 Broadway, New York.[33]

Who was William Beard?

William Beard departed Liverpool and arrived at the Port of New York on October 5, 1863 aboard steamship *Glasgow*, listed as passenger Wm. Beard, a 30-year-old miner.[34] It will be seen in 1898 Velazquez claimed to a newspaper[35] that he was "a member of the Geodetic Survey Commission which went over the country in 1859 and 1860." And similarly, another newspaper[36] reported that he went to Alaska "in 1857-1858 in company with his brother and a small party." No evidence of these events has been uncovered and besides his brother did not come to the U.S. until 1862 and William in 1863.

Prior to his marriage, William Beard spent the 1880's in Arizona mining districts and generally traveled the West. The Globe hometown newspaper, *Arizona Silver Belt*, mentioned him and his travels frequently. It is clear that he was in demand as a mining specialist. Velazquez and Beard may have met during these earlier years, but if not, then at least their common experiences and interest in mining certainly helped the attraction.

Beard's early activity in the West is known somewhat. He is noted employed as the Mining Superintendent for the Alice Mine in the Globe District in Gila County in 1881.[37] William apparently later became at least part owner of the Alice and sold it and other mines and "amassed a fortune of $150,000 in cash. This was lost in other unfortunate enterprises...."[38]

---

32. U.S. Census 1900; *Iron County Register*, Jul 21, 1898, Thomas was still living in Ironton in 1898 at the time of William's death.
33. Family papers of Andrene Messer, Falkirk, England. The address was that of William's attorney.
34. New York Passenger Lists, 1820-1891, www.familysearch.com.
35. *Philadelphia Enquirer*.
36. *Springfield Republican*, Jul 22, 1898 quoting the *Philadelphia Ledger*.
37. *Arizona Business Directory and Gazetteer* (San Francisco: W.C. Disturnell, 1881), 71.
38. *Arizona Daily Star* (Tucson, Arizona), Aug 21, 1894.

In August 1882 William Beard went to Denver to show ore specimens at an exposition. Four months later, he and Con Burns went East, with ore samples "from Globe District mines which will please the eye and convince the judgment of non-residents, that Globe District abounds in precious metals."[39] Two years later Beard exhibited this same mineral collection at the New Orleans World's Industrial Exposition, which opened December 1, 1884. Beard was stated to be "Commissioner for Gila County to the New Orleans World's Industrial Exposition."[40]

Besides expositions, Beard attended his normal work. He and Con Burns went to "the San Carlos coal fields [about 21 miles away] with a view of satisfying themselves in regard to supplying copper furnaces with coke."[41] Beard's partnership with Con Burns helps to positively identify William Beard since Con Burns shows up later as a co-plaintiff with Beard against one Major Safely.

One trip had a social element. He and fellow Masons went to San Francisco for a Masonic convention, "The procession with its gorgeous banners and plumed knights, was a grand affair."[42] Beard was a member of the White Mountain Lodge 3F and A.M. at Globe and of Arizona Commandery K. T. No.1 in Tucson.[43] Organization records show that he became a Master Mason in 1882, but was subsequently suspended in 1887,[44] surely for the simple reason he had departed the area, and had gone to New York, where he married in August 1887.

William Beard became the Superintendent of the Harris M. and M. Company's ore stamping mill in Harrisburg, Arizona which was to commence operation on December 1, 1886 under Beard's "skillful direction." The news was said "encouraging,"[45] but Beard did not stay there a full year; he probably figured it was not going to be a king maker and left. The mine played out in short order.

Other places were named where Beard supposedly lived: Mexico, New Mexico and California. At the time of his death, it was reported that he had recently returned from South Africa,[46] but his claim came from Velazquez and is provably false. No doubt it is true Beard traveled to the other mentioned locations.

Beard's constant moving was not conducive to marriage and it is a credit to Velazquez that she attracted 52-year-old Beard. He certainly had good

---

39. *Arizona Silver Belt* (Globe, Arizona), Aug 12, Dec 23, 1882.
40. Ibid, Sep 13, 1884.
41. *Tucson Daily Citizen*, Nov 1, 1882.
42. *Arizona Silver Belt*, Aug 25, 1883.
43. *Arizona Daily Citizen* (Tucson), Aug 16, 1898.
44. White Mountain Lodge No. 3 archives.
45. *Arizona Weekly Journal Miner*, Nov 10, 1886.
46. *Seattle Post-Intelligencer* Jul 14, 1898.

looks enough which must have caught many women's attention. William's picture, presented in the *Philadelphia Inquirer* article announcing his death, showed he was a handsome man, appearing very fit. Please see Illustrations, Figure 22. In addition, Beard was industrious, educated and apparently intelligent. No doubt, these were attributes to which Velazquez was attracted. She might have been aware that Beard was owed $25,000 by one Mr. Safely, if only Beard could collect.

William Beard is Swindled

In August 1882, Beard together with Con Burns, George H. Sisson and John J. Safely agreed to procure "certain contracts or bonds for the purchase" of land and water rights, and some copper mines, the Lone Pines Group near Clifton, Arizona Territory. The men, using a contract agreement with the owners, put down a little option money for its future purchase. This was a speculative maneuver which enabled them to have a few months' time to find a real buyer with real money before their option to purchase expired. The men avoided locking-up their own money in the full purchase price while they attempted to do a quick resale. Once sold, the men were to split the profits.

The property they purchased on paper for $85,000, they resold for $185,000 in cash in February 1883. Major John Safely collected the money in New York and Mr. Sisson received his $25,000 share. At the time of the sale, Beard was absent from Arizona and did not receive his portion. John J. Safely kept Beard's $25,000 and Beard claimed it was "wrongfully and fraudulently converted to [Safely's] own use...."

When Beard saw Major Safely in Arizona in the "early part of 1884," Safely said that the land had been sold, but no money had been collected pending an "examination by the purchaser's expert." Four- or five-months later Beard was informed by someone in Tucson that the sale had concluded.

Beard sought out Major Safely and finally located him in July 1887, at the Fifth Avenue Hotel in New York. When confronted for the money, Safely said that he could not get it at the moment as he was obliged to leave the city, but would return in a few weeks. Beard waited several weeks for Safely's return and when he didn't, Beard wrote him several letters asking for the money, but Safely never answered. It was about this time, on August 20, 1887, Beard married Velazquez.

Beard caught John Safely in New York "about the 29th of November 1888" and demanded to be paid. Safely told him "to meet him the next day… between ten and eleven o'clock in the forenoon, and he would fix the matter up with [him]." The following day Beard waited, but Safely "did not come."

Beard requested an arrest warrant on December 18, stating that Safely "intends leaving within a few days." Judge Truax of the Superior Court issued a warrant the next day and set the bail at $25,000.[47]

Two deputies arrested Safely on the 19th, just after he left the Fifth Avenue Hotel dining room and entered the parlor. William Beard and his attorney accompanied the officers. Safely was "so surprised and annoyed that he used strong language." He protested that "it was particularly inconvenient to be disturbed just then, as he had tickets for the theatre and had also invited two ladies to accompany him. Moreover, he said, the proceeding was an outrage." The officers were accommodating and took Safely to visit his lawyer at his home, but then took Safely to Ludlow Street Jail, where he spent the next two nights. On Friday the 21st, Safely got bail posted and was released.[48]

John Safely left right away for his home in Indiana to spend Christmas. A reporter contacted Safely's attorney, who on behalf of Safely, "denied every charge in Beard's complaint" and in a detailed explanation denied facts surrounding the Bentz Group Mine, which the complaint did not even mention. Instead, the complaint had stated the money owed was related to the sale of the Lone Pines Group Mine. The attorney's answer might be construed as evasive, but an honest answer probably would have been incriminating.

Beard had pursued Major Safely with the conviction and determination of someone with the facts on his side. Beard caught Safely two months shy of the statute of limitations. The disposition of the complaint has not been found, but it can be guessed that Beard started the New Year, 1889, paid in full. The fact that no court record exists indicates that Safely paid-up before the case made it to trial.

Velazquez seems to have kept a low profile at this time. She is thought to have become pregnant shortly after her marriage and was surely busy tending to her child. Later (1898) newspapers stories state her son's age, indicating this was probably the case.

1888, Ex-Confederate General Longstreet's Letter

By 1888 public interest in Velazquez had seemingly faded, but had not died. A probable reader of her book, named Emmy W. Park, took it upon herself to write a letter (dated June 15, 1888) to Ex-Confederate General James Longstreet asking for some explanation of the famous woman-soldier, Harry Buford. Her exact questions to Longstreet can only be guessed, since her letter has not been found and has probably not survived.

---

47. Both Con Burns and William Beard filed suit against George H. Sisson and John J. Safely, according to the January 18, 1884 *New York Times*. Con Burns must have gotten paid soon after because Burns was a not a party in later actions.
48. *World* (New York) Dec 25, 1888.

Fire burned down Longstreet's Gainesville, Georgia home in April 1889, and all of his Civil War memorabilia and library were lost. The Longstreets moved into a cottage also on the farm, but 3 years later it too burned down.[49] One of the fires surely consumed Emmy Park's letter. The content of Longstreet's reply (dated June 18, 1888) makes it clear that Emmy Park was asking for confirmation of the existence of Velazquez and the veracity of her story.

Longstreet replied,[50] "There was a woman in the ranks with us who became Lieutenant and called her name Buford though I did not know her until some years after the war." On the second page of his short letter he similarly wrote, "I had not known of her in the ranks nor as Lieutenant and could only attest of points she gave for identification." Please see Longstreet's letter in the Appendix, Item 4.

"There was a woman in the ranks with us" is clearly negated by "I had not known of her in the ranks" and "though I did not know her until some years after the war." The question which arises is: Who told him that Velazquez was in the ranks? He further explained, "She... passed through New Orleans when I was there and then I met her, the only time of my life." That meeting took place in 1874. Longstreet was living there until the summer of 1875 when he moved to Georgia.[51] Recall Velazquez passed through New Orleans in August 1874.

General Longstreet's reply letter was clear and simple enough, but one archivist/author unwittingly read more into it than exists. In May 1997, they wrote, "None other than General Longstreet vouched for the service of Loreta Velasquez. His letter, is at Duke [University]; all those historians who dismiss her as a fraud must think he is a liar. But I digress."[52]

Longstreet did not vouch for Velazquez's service! He wrote in his letter that he did not know Velazquez in the service; he, in effect, said it three times. He said that he "could only attest of points she gave for identification." In other words, he could declare true that she was a real person who identified herself by telling her story to him. Historians don't think that General Longstreet vouched for Velazquez's service or that Longstreet was a liar. What some historians know and others ought to know is that Velazquez was a liar and she most certainly lied to General Longstreet.

Longstreet said he met her only after the War. It is easily surmised that Velazquez herself told Longstreet, at the time of their meeting, that she was in the ranks. He would have given her the benefit of the doubt, not knowing the nature of his new acquaintance. Even if he doubted her, he would have

---

49. Jeffry D. Wert, *General James Longstreet* (New York: Simon & Schuster, 1994), 421.
50. Letter in Rare Book, Manuscript, and Special Collections at Duke University Library.
51. Wert, 417.
52. H-Net Discussion Networks, May 19, 1997.

not been so crass as to call her a liar. He could not have known and probably did not try to judge the truthfulness of her claimed service record. And there is no discovered evidence that he was even motivated to seek out the truthfulness of her story.

Longstreet might have been charmed by Velazquez, at least a little, because he recalled and bothered to retell a tale Velazquez personally related to him- the tale is not found in any newspaper account or her book. Longstreet wrote:

Her enterprise after the war was a trip to the Rocky Mountains, with a party of men in her disguise as Lieutenant Buford. The party had much trouble with the Indians, lost their horses and had to travel afoot a great distance. When she gave out and her comrades had to assist her, in that way she became known.

Clearly, this tale contradicts her book's narrative and no doubt the tale was untrue. In any case, Longstreet was impressed enough to remember the tale, and he may have believed it, though he would not have had any way to verify it.

Recall that Longstreet wrote that there was "a woman in the ranks with us who became Lieutenant." However, Velazquez never wrote that she "became Lieutenant." She claimed only that she called herself (*TWIB*, p37) by that rank. It is clear that Longstreet was completely uninformed about her service and was completely in the dark about what she wrote.

It is obvious that General Longstreet had not read Velazquez's book and did not know the extent of her claims, or surely, he would have denounced her- he had a temper. One claim which Velazquez made would have been of interest to the General and that was of her fighting at the First Battle of Bull Run. Even of greater interest would have been her claimed activity three days prior, at Mitchell's Ford and at Blackburn's Ford on Bull Run.

The defense of Blackburn's Ford was General Longstreet's assignment and he was everywhere in the skirmish line that day, flawlessly directing his troops to victory. Velazquez claimed she fought at Blackburn's Ford and that when the Union forces "broke and ran, [she] fired a last shot at them with a dead man's musket." She said that after this skirmish she was "placed temporarily in command of a company, the senior officer of which had been killed...." This would have been under Longstreet's command! Yet Longstreet said he did not know her. Remember, military records show no Confederate company lost its senior officer at Blackburn's Ford. Velazquez's claim would have outraged General Longstreet had he known of it.

Velazquez's most loathsome statement concerning Bull Run is found in the 1874 interview with the *Atlanta Journal*. Recall, she said she was "in the first battle of Manassas (Bull Run) with Col. Charley Drew's [*sic* Dreux] Battalion, and was near Drew when he was killed." But Colonel Charles

Didier Dreux had been killed before then and 150 miles away at Young's Mill, Virginia. Dreux had received information about Union soldiers who routinely patrolled a nearby sector and he was determined to ambush the patrol. The surprise was prematurely revealed and the Union patrol succeeded in defending itself and it inflicted two deaths among the Confederates, Colonel Dreux being one of them.

Colonel Dreux's body was returned to his native Louisiana and the ensuing funeral procession was the largest ever beheld by New Orleans; it took an hour and twenty minutes to pass the Cathedral. Three to four thousand soldiers and some eight to ten thousand civilian mourners marched with the hearse. It was estimated another thirty thousand lined the sidewalks and balconies as observers. Colonel Dreux, a most beloved native son and practicing attorney who left the bar to join the cause, was the first Confederate officer killed in the war, an unfortunate distinction. Southern sensibilities were greatly insulted, Northern tyranny was blamed and the death was widely covered in the newspapers.[53] Louisianans by 1874 had not forgotten the details of his death. It was fortunate for Velazquez that she did not try to make her claim of Dreux's death to the 1874 New Orleans newspaper instead of the Atlanta newspaper or she would have been run out of town on a rail!

General Longstreet surely was not aware of Velazquez's claim about Colonel Dreux. There is only a slight chance that Longstreet ever met Dreux, even though Longstreet had traveled through New Orleans in May of 1861. When Longstreet moved to New Orleans in September 1865,[54] he, no doubt, learned of the high regard for Dreux's memory.

Even though Longstreet claimed he never met Lieutenant Harry T. Buford during the War, but only after, Velazquez wrote that she met Longstreet during the War. Under the subtitle of "An Interview with Longstreet," Velazquez wrote (p290) that she, as Lieutenant Buford, and some fellow officers were trying to catch the train to Atlanta. The train was filled to capacity with Longstreet's men and would not take Lieutenant Buford and her companions. She proposed that they should speak to Longstreet to ask permission, but no one took the initiative:

> I therefore went up, and making a salute, stated to General Longstreet that a number of officers who were ordered to join their regiments immediately were unable to proceed for lack of transportation, and asked if we might not go on with him; for, if we did not, great inconvenience would be caused to ourselves and to the army. The general hesitated somewhat, but after asking me several questions

---

53. *Charleston Courier*, Jul 19, 1861 reprinting the *Richmond Whig*.
54. Wert, 408.

about who we were, and how many there were of us, where we were going, &c., he acceded to my request.

Note that Velazquez claimed she identified herself, "who we were," to General Longstreet in a rather unique situation, no less, yet Longstreet said he never knew her in the army.

In summary, it is certain that Longstreet never read Velazquez's memoir and never validated its truthfulness and never tried to. Longstreet was not witness to any of Velazquez's claimed military service. He never saw her, in or out of disguise, in the service and he only confirmed that she existed as a person after the War. So, no, no, no, it is not true that "None other than General Longstreet vouched for the service of Loreta Velasquez." It might be recalled that General Samuel P. Heintzelman also met Velazquez, as a civilian, and "feared she is a scamp."

Another Respected Man Who Just Didn't Know

Later in 1888, another respected man, Dr. Simon Peter Richardson, a Methodist Reverend, had something to say about Velazquez. Under the story title of "War Reminiscences," an Athens, Georgia newspaper[55] wrote that Dr. Richardson "is one of the best-informed men on all subjects there is in our county. He never forgets anything and to listen at him for an hour is most interesting." The article continued:

Dr. Richardson recollects Lieutenant Harry Buford, the woman that served as a Lieutenant in the Western army. He says that Lieutenant Buford <u>informed him</u> that she once had a chance while in the army to kill General Grant; that she with a party of soldier men hid in a rocky cliff in the mountains and that General Grant passed very close to where she was concealed and she had her finger on the trigger of her pistol and a dead sight on the General when something prevented her from firing.

Recall, in her book (p213), Velazquez weaved a different tale.

The mountains of the Reverend's story do not equal a riverbank. The rocky cliff does not equal bushes. A party of soldier men does not equal being alone. Grant passing very close-by on a road does not equal floating-by in a boat. The great discrepancy between the two versions makes at least one of the stories a lie, but the truth is, both were lies.

Had Reverend "never forgets anything" Richardson read Velazquez's book, he would have caught the lie the moment when she "informed him." Did he ask her why one of the other "party of soldier men" hidden in the rocky cliff with her did not take the shot? Her explanation would have been most interesting, no doubt.

---

55. *Weekly Banner-Watchman* (Athens, Georgia), Sept 4, 1888.

In *The Woman in Battle*, Velazquez narrated that two generals, one being Grant, rowed a small boat out to one of the gunboats in the river and boarded it. However, Grant wrote in his autobiography[56] that he stayed on shore that evening, under a tree in a miserable rain. And both Velazquez and Grant make clear that they were writing of the same night! It must be noted that no navy or army man mentioned a visit by Grant that evening aboard a gunboat; memoirs abound by seemly every literate soldier or officer who participated in the War and such a meeting would not have been left unrecorded.

The article about the Reverend concluded:

Lieutenant Harry Buford was probably the only soldier who was known to be a woman and served in the Confederate army. She wore a beautiful Lieutenant's uniform and was said to be as brave a soldier as ever went into the field. She married in Atlanta a Major of the Confederate army and laid aside her sword and uniform. Her husband dying, she went to Cuba and again married and the last heard of her she went by the name of Madame Velasquez and was selling a history of her life during the war.

Confirming that the Reverend had not read her book, or at least not with care, he erred that she married a major and that after the major died, she went to Cuba and there remarried. No, Velazquez did not write this. She wrote she married a captain and she did not write that she remarried in Cuba.

Reverend Richardson, like General James Longstreet, met Velazquez after the War and listened to her persuasively tell of her adventures, even though those adventures varied from her memoir's version. Neither gentleman gave a firsthand account of Velazquez's participation in the War, nor was in a position to know whether her story, or any other version of it, was true. And they had not read her book.

1889, William Beard's Interest in Railroads

A year and a half after his marriage to Velazquez, Beard returned to Arizona. The Globe, Arizona newspaper[57] wrote:

William Beard, a former resident of Globe, but for several years living in the East, arrived from New York on Wednesday on mining business. Mr. Beard is personally interested in organizing the proposed railroad from San Diego to Salt Lake.

The newspaper explained that $180,000 had been spent grading and laying ties at the San Diego end for forty miles and 300 miles had been surveyed. It remained to be seen if the railroad would pass through Yuma

---

56. *Personal Memoirs of U.S. Grant*, Vol 1 (NY: C. L. Webster & Co., 1885), 349.
57. *Arizona Silver Belt*, Feb 23, 1889.

and Yavapai counties in Arizona. The article concluded, "Mr. Beard expresses confidence in its early construction."

William Beard informed the newspaper that he had read news before departing New York that a "London banking house" was marketing bonds for the Tucson and Globe railroad. This railroad had already been chartered in 1882 and it seems the financing was for improvement and replacing the narrow gauge with standard gauge.

The decade of the 80's had witnessed energetic railroad construction in the Arizona Territory and no doubt Beard was a proponent along with many others. His great interest in railroads will be seen later to have rubbed off on Velazquez.

It appears that William Beard spent a significant amount of time over the next five or six years in the West. His name shows up in several news reports and it seems he is one and the same. Surely, he took occasional trips back East to check on his wife and kid, but no record of his coming and going has been found.

1891, Still in New York, as Businesslike as a Man

In 1891 Velazquez reappeared and the *New York Herald* noticed. Her absence was probably due to time demands of motherhood. She had a son in 1888, that is, according to 1898 newspaper articles which reference her ten-year-old son.

The February 1 article titled "As Businesslike as a Man, Mrs. L. J. Beard and Her Various Enterprises on the American Continent" heralded:

A woman of business, a woman who can run things like a man, is rare in the world. Once in a while such a woman comes to the front and she is regarded as a curiosity.

I had a talk yesterday with one of these fascinating curiosities. Her name is Mrs. Loretta J. Beard and her office is at No. 401 Broadway. In a word, she is at the head of a variety of schemes. She is a promoter and apparently an indefatigable one.

At first Mrs. Beard was disinclined to say anything about herself personally, fearing that she would be "written up" in the style of some gushing journals. When she got started in her plans, however, I saw that she could talk for a year and a day on them.

She was born in Cuba, forty-six years ago. The name of her father, who was a Spaniard, was Joaquin Velasquez. Her mother was a French woman. Mrs. Beard is a typical, go-ahead Western woman, not only in manner but in dress. She has two accents, one the normal Western, the other, when excited, the Spanish. She has a firm mouth, pale face and remarkably keen eyes.

She has been over the greater part of the world; has wondered over a considerable portion of South America with whose resources she says she is particularly well acquainted, and has done some literary work for various periodicals, home and foreign.

Her husband, "Colonel W. Beard, is an Englishman, many years in this country, so she told me, who has seen some service on the Indian frontier, but was never a soldier. He is now in the West. The name of her first husband Mrs. Beard would not give me. She told me that that marriage cut her off from her family.

According to the letters she showed me yesterday Mrs. Beard has had an extensive acquaintance with public men, to whom she was known as Mrs. J. Velasquez. Some of these letters were from Senator Blackburn of Kentucky; W. P. Hill, of Ohio; the late Senator and ex-Judge L. Q. Lamar, Senator Gordon, Senator Blair and several Congressmen and foreign officials. They all appeared to be in answer to some request, and some were commendatory of her business ability.

She told me she had given $125,000 for mines in South America, and that she was the possessor of silver mines in Arizona. Mrs. Beard has a large number of "concessions" from Mexico and Honduras. One is for a canal, another for a railway, another for a steamship company and so on.

One of her special enterprises is a mining investment and trading company incorporated in West Virginia in August last. The incorporators are L. J. Velasquez, George G. Bowen, W. G. Beard, W. Fearing Gill, all said to be of New York, and L. K. McKinney of Elizabeth, N. J. The officers are B. W. Nichols, of Fall River, Mass., president; G. P. Streeter, of New York, treasurer; E. R. L. Tighe, secretary, and Mrs. Beard, correspondent and general manager.

Mrs. Beard said that she had two bills in Congress in furtherance of some of her projects. She was acquainted with the late Secretary Windom, whom she first met in 1857 in Minnesota.

There is no doubt Velazquez showed to the reporter the document which had established on July 22, 1890 a new company named The New York and Montezuma Investment Company. The organizers applied for incorporation in West Virginia and it was certified on August 1, 1891 by the Secretary of State, who asserted he had received from the applicants an agreement (with proper affidavits) which stated:[58]

The undersigned agree to become a corporation by the name of the New York and Montezuma Investment Company, for the purpose of transacting and carrying on a general brokerage and commission business, and the promoting of enterprises, companies and corporations of any and every kind and dealing in railways, steamships, navigation property and properties, concessions and subsidies of all kinds, railway and steamship securities, and all corporate securities, and securities of every kind whatsoever; contracts, leases, notes, bonds, stocks of any and every kind, and mines, quarries, telegraph companies, water works, gas works, irrigation and every kind of property, or properties real or personal, in any manner not prohibited by law, and to do all things that may be necessary and requisite for the successful carrying out the purposes of the company.

---

58. *Acts of the Legislature of West Virginia, at its Twentieth Regular Session Commencing January 14, 1891* (Charleston: Moses W. Donnally, 1891), 1316-1317.

In short, the company was a sales company which would sell anything for anyone for a commission. The Company's principal office was to be located in New York City and the incorporation papers were valid until July 1, 1940.

"The said corporation… subscribed the sum of two hundred thousand dollars to the capital thereof, and have paid in on said subscriptions the sum of two hundred thousand dollars" and "the capital so subscribed is divided into shares of twenty (20) dollars each." Shares were placed as follows: L. J. Velasquez Beard, New York City, 5050 shares; Ramon Velez, NYC, 500 shares; George S. Bowen, NYC, 500 shares; W. Fearing Gill, NYC, 500 shares; L. K. McKinnry, Elizabeth, N. J., 500 shares; Wm. G. Beard, New York, 2950 shares. In addition, the corporation maintained "the privilege of increasing the said capital, by the sale of additional shares from time to time."

Considering that the company did not claim to own any assets, it is inexplicable that such a large sum of money was raised. It is doubtful that the investors, including the Beards, put up the stated full amount. For "L. J. Velasquez Beard" and "Wm. G. Beard" the total dollar amount would have been $160,000 (8,000 shares at $20 per share) and a huge amount in 1891, equal to roughly 5.8 million dollars in 2023, and an amount which the Beards never seemed to possess. ("Wm. G. Beard" could only have been husband William Beard and it is the only time a middle initial was found connected to William Beard.) Each of the other four investors would have had to put up $10,000 (500 shares at $20 per share), also a large amount (about $370,000 in 2023 dollars) considering there were no collateralized assets.

No evidence for the claimed schemes was found and logic dictates that a man or woman of wealth with successful businesses for a canal, a railway and a steamship company would be easily and prominently found in recorded history. Instead, what Velazquez possessed was a sales company (which then incorporated) to sell businesses, and the identified businesses seem never to have gotten past the promoting stages.

Velazquez may have hoped to drum up additional investors with subsequent stock offerings as per the incorporation papers, but no further investors have been discovered. Maybe she had access to the $40,000 put up by the four aforementioned investors to run the office where the reporter found her. The investors were of means and not inconsequential. Ramon Velez was editor of *Revista Popular*, a Spanish newspaper in New York with agents in Mexico and Nicaragua.[59] George S. Bowen seems to have been the wealthy merchant, manufacturer and capitalist with many investments and a great interest in Mexico, evident by his 1878 trade mission there. However, Bowen was stated in the incorporation papers to be living in New York City,

---

59. *New York Herald*, Sep 24, Dec 7, 1891; *Evening Star* (Washington, D.C.), Sep 5, 1891.

when in fact he was living in Chicago, although a native of New York.⁶⁰ William Fearing Gill was the biographer of Edgar Allan Poe (pub. 1880), editor of several books of poems, stories and essays, and married the younger sister of Mrs. Cornelius Vanderbilt.⁶¹ L. K. McKinnry of Elizabeth, New Jersey has not yet been identified. The fact that Velazquez enlisted these four investors is surely a credit to her charming persuasiveness. Even if Velazquez did not have the four investors' money, she likely had the money collected in William's 1888 lawsuit with which to maintain the office from which to promote her schemes.

Back down to earth, there is evidence that she and William were dealing in real estate. The 1891 New York City directory listed both "Beard L. J. lands, 64W 55ᵗʰ" and "Beard Wm, lands, 64W 55ᵗʰ." It is unclear if the 64W 55th address was occupied before or after the 401 Broadway address mentioned in the article. To date, no more is known about her real estate business in New York.

There are several curiosities in the newspaper article. The claimed age of 46 made her three years younger than her book's claim. And Velazquez implied that Beard was her second husband.

Velazquez claimed she gave $125,000 for South American mines. It is simply false that she possessed $125,000 (2.6 million in 2023 dollars) to invest. Did she buy the mines when in Venezuela? Remember in Venezuela she begged the Guayana governor for work because she was broke, the U.S. Navy passed the hat to collect money for her, and she wrote in her memoir she was "destitute." If she had that kind of wealth, then what was she doing dabbling in New York real estate and what was her husband doing working in the West?

How is it possible that Beard was a colonel "who has seen some service on the Indian frontier, but was never a soldier"? Doesn't one become a colonel by becoming a soldier? Well, if William Beard never was a soldier, but was a colonel, then maybe he was the original fried chicken colonel!⁶² Later in 1901, it will be seen that instead of claiming her husband "was never a soldier," she claimed her husband was "a Mexican army officer."⁶³

She claimed, "She was acquainted with the late Secretary Windom, whom she first met in 1857 in Minnesota." The question arises as to how she could have met the man in Minnesota in 1857 when she claimed (p49) in her book that at that time she was in St. Louis with a new born child. She claimed that

---

60. George S. Bowen Papers, 1856-1928, Chicago History Museum.
61. *New York Times*, Jun 29, 1888.
62. "Kentucky colonel" is a title and honor given to people of accomplishment, such as Colonel Sanders of fried chicken fame, by the governor of Kentucky.
63. *Evening Telegram* (New York), Aug 28, 1901.

her husband was away on the Mormon expedition and when he returned, they went to New Orleans, then to Fort Leavenworth, Kansas.

Hold on, maybe it was false that she was living in St. Louis with her baby. Recall that in 1862 when she robbed the Chesters in New Orleans, the newspaper wrote,[64] "[She] then went to the house of another lady [Mrs. Chester] whom she had known at St. Paul, Minnesota, and when the lady was out one morning she absconded, taking with her a watch and other articles." Velazquez's acquaintance with the Chesters in Minnesota possibly verifies as true that she was there before the War. This New Orleans report was some 14 years before Velazquez weaved her memoir.

Velazquez neglected to mention her autobiography, but only said she had "done some literary work for various periodicals, home and foreign." Why wouldn't Velazquez have proudly presented a copy to show the reporter? Had criticism she received about the book discouraged her? Maybe she no longer sold enough books to make it worth mentioning. Or maybe she had sold away royalty rights for cash, so wasn't motivated to promote it.

She named her father, "Joaquin Velasquez," and almost used the same spelling, "Juanquin R. Velasquez," as found on the 1887 "Return of Marriage" to William Beard. Of course, the variation might not have been by Velazquez, but by the reporter.

The reporter noted that Velazquez had "two accents, one the normal Western, the other, when excited, the Spanish." Thirteen years earlier, General Jubal Early also made note of her accent and in his 1878 letter wrote, "Her appearance and voice are those of an American woman, and has no resemblance to those of a cultivated Spanish lady." In addition, the General wrote that he believed "that Madame Velasquez is not of Spanish birth or origin, but is an American and probable from the North." There seems to be no explanation for the divergence of opinions.

---

64. *Daily Delta* (New Orleans), Oct 31, 1862; *Picayune* (New Orleans), Nov 2, 1862.

Chapter 14

1891, Saving George Washington's Mother

It is clear that Velazquez reemerged in 1891 with tremendous energy. Following the February 1 *New York Herald* article praising her business acumen, she again was the recipient of flattery because of a new project which was reported in the *New York World* of May 17, 1891 under the title "Washington's Mother, A New Monument to be Erected Over Her Grave, Patriot Women at Work, They Will Raise Money for the Purpose by Selling the Portrait of the Hero's Mother":

> Mrs. L. J. Beard, a New York business woman and a most patriotic American, has been empowered by Mrs. John T. Goolrick, President of the Mary Washington Monument Association, of Fredericksburg, Va., to take steps towards the raising of a fund to aid in the erection of a new monument to be placed over the grave of Mary Washington, the mother of George Washington, at Fredericksburg. The present monument was erected many years ago, and has not only never been finished, but has fallen into partial decay. The patriotic feelings of the ladies of Virginia became aroused over this fact some time ago, and the present Association was formed for the purpose of erecting a new monument.
>
> Mrs. Beard's plan is to have a large number of steel engravings made of Mary Washington, taken from an oil painting now in the possession of descendants of George Washington living at Fredericksburg. This is the only likeness of Mrs. Washington in existence and was painted in England. While being brought to this country the face of the picture was slightly damaged. Fifty-five years ago an effort was made in Philadelphia to remedy the injury, but with slight success.
>
> The proposed engravings will be made by a New York firm of acknowledged ability and will be quite large in size. It is estimated that four months will be required to complete the work. The engravings will be placed on sale in all parts of the country at a moderate price. Special arrangements will be made for its sale at the World's Fair. The receipts will be placed in the hands of the Executive Committee, among them being several citizens of New York whose high standing will be a guarantee that the money will be properly applied. A caveat to secure the copyright of the engraving has been filed by Mrs. Beard at Washington. She intends to offer a prize for the best poem embodying the virtues of Mrs. Washington and making reference to the erection of the new monument. The poem will be inscribed on a slab of onyx to be inserted in the base of the monument. The material composing the present monument will be used in the construction of the one to be erected. Any portion of the fund remaining after the new monument has been completed will be devoted to purchasing all relics formerly belonging to the Washington family which may be for sale. These will be preserved in some public institution hereafter to be selected.

A detractor might note that Velazquez would like such a job, if her motive was to skim the proceeds. Recall in July 1864 she obtained permission to solicit donations for "disabled soldiers' children" from the Union garrison at Fort Columbus, New York Harbor. It's easily suspected she skimmed because at that time, by her own admission (in letters), she had no money. Ten years later she claimed that she collected $780 "from the

United States soldiers of Commodore Brissol's fleet, then at Bridgeport, Barbados, and sent to Southern hospitals, although the money was supposed to have been given for the benefit of Federal soldiers."[1] In this case the assertion was a lie, so in truth, she did not misappropriate the money, but it hints at an attitude. Well, maybe the suspicion is unfounded.

At this date there was great interest in placing a new monument over the grave of Mary Washington. The country became outraged when it heard news that a commercial real estate company was going to auction, on March 5, 1889, the land which contained the grave and its very old unfinished and damaged monument. Two groups, headed by women, organized to raise contributions to purchase the land and erect a fitting marker for the mother of the "father of our country." The two organizations were the (Fredericksburg) Mary Washington Monument Association and the National Mary Washington Memorial Association.

The (Fredericksburg) Mary Washington Monument Association was chartered on November 8, 1889 and Mrs. John T. Goolrick was its first Vice-President. This was the organization and the woman who Velazquez claimed sanctioned her fund-raising efforts.

One hundred and two years earlier, in August 1789, Mary died of cancer in Fredericksburg. George, who understood the severity of her illness, had said his good-bye prior and was attending to his duties as the first President of the United States. Upon being informed by letter of his mother's death, George wrote to his sister, "When I was last in Fredericksburg I took a final leave of my mother, never expecting to see her more."[2]

The U.S. Congress, wearing "mourning crepe for thirty days" and with great respect for the President and his mother, passed a resolution to supply a monument for her grave. History shows a small stone marker resulted.

In 1826 an appeal was made for a new marker and by 1830 the residents of Fredericksburg had raised two thousand dollars. Silas E. Burrows, a New Yorker of wealth was inspired to join the effort and took charge, spending his own money. The corner stone was laid on May 7, 1833 and President Andrew Jackson attended the great ceremony. The work proceeded for four years with all the necessary money already paid in full by Burrows. Burrows subsequently went to China where he died. The contracted stone mason, "working in the hot sun, was stricken with brain fever and died" and his family failed to complete the work. Also given as reason for the work stoppage was that the bank which held the funds failed and the money was lost.[3] The monument languished with un-mounted stones lying on the

---

1. *Mobile Daily Register*, Aug 25, 1874.
2. Susan Rivière Hetzel, *The Building of a Monument: A History of the Mary Washington Associations and Their Work* (Lancaster, PA: Wickersham Co., 1903), 3.
3. Ibid, 20.

ground and the site in general poor maintenance, until the two organizations sprang into action to save the historically significant sight.

As the two organizations grew, the National Association emerged as the stronger organization, but the Fredericksburg Association had obtained and held the deed to the land. The two organizations met in January 1891 and agreed that the Fredericksburg organization would convey the deed to the National organization[4] and with their differences smoothed-out, they co-operated in the final push to get the monument completed. The National organization set up a network of vice-presidents in many of the States to co-ordinate fundraising by various means, among them, holding balls, theatrical plays, concerts and lectures. Steadily the organization's coffers filled and the goal amount reached.[5]

The new monument was ready after five years of commitment and work, and was dedicated on "the 10th of May 1894, an ideal spring day with a cloudless sky, a bright sun tempered by a refreshing breeze."[6] All the citizens in gaily decorated Fredericksburg celebrated. The Marine Band of Washington marched and played. Many organizations also marched, such as the Masons, the Odd Fellows, plus militia companies and a cavalry company. In attendance was United States President Grover Cleveland who delivered "an impressive address… in a strong, mellow, penetrating voice." The "orator of the day" was Senator John W. Daniel of Virginia. Also present were U.S. Vice-President Stevenson, the U.S. Chief Justice of the Supreme Court, members of the U.S. Executive Cabinet, Virginia Governor O'Ferrall, Fredericksburg Mayor Rowe, other dignitaries too many to name and a crowd of thousands. All the dignitaries were accompanied by their wives. It was, after all, the women who were the true force behind the successful project, as was duly noted on the monument itself, "Erected by her Country-Women."

Two points of interest are found in the *New York World* article and one question needs answering.

First, Velazquez's grandiose plan hinged on whether she could "secure the copyright" of the portrait of Mary. Without the copyright, the outlined scheme was empty words and maybe a ready excuse for failure of the plan. In any case, the newspapers made no further mention of the plan and there is no evidence discovered that this plan was implemented.

Second, Velazquez claimed that she would hold a contest for the best poem and the winner would have their poem "inscribed on a slab of onyx to be inserted in the base of the monument." It is easily understood that

---

4. Ibid, 73.
5. Ibid, 106.
6. Ibid, 137.

Velazquez thought of creating a poetry contest since previously, in 1866, Velazquez claimed that she was writing a book of poems, clearly an interest.

The question is: Was Mrs. L. J. Beard connected to the Mary Washington Monument Association?

Please recall that Velazquez claimed that "Mrs. John T. Goolrick, President of the Mary Washington Monument Association" had "empowered [her]...." Mrs. John T. Goolrick was Francis Bernard (White) Goolrick, and along with some other women created the Mary Washington Monument Association. Francis was elected the Association's first Vice-President.[7] Today, Francis Goolrick's papers concerning the rebuilding of the Mary Washington Monument are archived with the Virginia Historical Society. A search was conducted of this collection for Mrs. L. J. Beard or her activity. <u>None</u> was found.[8]

Author Susan Rivière Hetzel tells in detail in her 1903 book, *The Building of a Monument: A History of the Mary Washington Association and Their Work*, of the organization's fund-raising activity. Hetzel was intimately familiar with the organization's activities and supporters since she became the second Secretary of the organization, after her mother first held the position. She carefully identified individuals by name and the activity in which they participated. In addition, her book contains a list of "Hereditary Life Members." These were patrons who donated $25 or more and were awarded a "badge" or medallion in the shape of a five-pointed star with a likeness of Mary Washington in the center and the letters NMWMA on the star points (one letter per point). Six hundred patrons were identified. Mrs. L. J. Beard is <u>not</u> found in the list.[9]

Think back to 1867 when Mrs. Mary De Caulp [*sic*] claimed she was "the agent for the Southern states for a Venezuelan Emigration Company, the President of which is a Mr. John Walker of St. Louis, Mo."[10] In reaction, John A. Doll, Director and Treasurer of the emigration company, wrote, "My opinion is, that Mrs. De Caulp [*sic*] is a self-constituted agent, and does not know even the title of our company...." Mr. Doll pointed out that the true President was Dr. H. M. Price (and the true New Orleans agent was Benjamin P. Vancourt).[11] The ready conclusion is that Velazquez falsely claimed that she was an agent and misnamed the emigration company's President, who she implied had given her the agency.

---

7. The first President was Mrs. James P. Smith. Source is S. J. Quinn, *The History of the City of Fredericksburg Virginia* (Richmond: Hermitage Press, 1908), 158.
8. Virginia Historical Society, Mss G6434 a 337-514.
9. Ibid, 90-95.
10. *Daily Picayune* (New Orleans), Jan 5, 1867.
11. *Times-Picayune* (New Orleans), Feb 9, 1867.

Mrs. L. J. Beard's claim that she was "empowered by Mrs. John T. Goolrick, President of the Mary Washington Monument Association" was false because Mrs. John T. Goolrick was never President of that association, just like Mr. John Walker was never President of the Venezuelan Emigration Company! Mrs. Goolrick performed many valuable and admirable functions for the organization, only she was never its President. She served as Vice-President of the Mary Washington Monument Association and Vice-President for the State of Virginia for the National Association.

Archivist L. Eileen Parris, at the Virginia Historical Society, wrote,[12] "No, Francis Goolrick was NEVER (Parris' emphasis) president of the National Mary Washington Monument Association. Neither was she president of the Fredericksburg Mary Washington Monument Association."[13]

There is no discovered corroborating evidence of Velazquez's participation in the Mary Washington project. Considering that well-regarded people from all across the nation became involved in the project and were mentioned time and again in the newspapers, it is curious that other than the single article about Mrs. L. J. Beard's participation, she was never again discovered tied to the monument. Neither was her plan.

In conclusion, Velazquez's claimed connection to the Mary Washington Monument Association seems to have been self-promotion, presumably with a hope of success for her scheme. Recall, only three and a half months prior, she told the newspaper she was "at the head of a variety of schemes." She was the owner of a South American mine and silver mines in Arizona. She had "concessions" from Mexico and Honduras. One was "for a canal, another for a railway, another for a steamship company and so on." Velazquez claimed she was one of the incorporators, as well as the correspondent and general manager, of "a mining investment and trading company incorporated in West Virginia in August last." Well, this last one was true. The incorporation was factual though her claimed description was not exactly honest. And it might have been true that she or her husband retained some ownership in an Arizona silver mine, but common sense prohibits the belief that the rest of the claims were true. Mostly Velazquez flourished in an environment of contrived important schemes and the Mary Washington Monument Association claim was just the latest.

Maybe Velazquez thought her idea would be recognized as good and adopted, and she would reap praise. Clearly it did not happen, but her idea was good.

---

12. Oct 2013 correspondence.
13. Mrs. James P. Smith was the first President. Mrs. Vivian M. Fleming was the second. Source- H. R. Ball, "The National Mary Washington Memorial Association," *The Colonial Magazine*, Vol 1, No. 1 (November 1895): 136; *Clinch Valley News* (Jeffersonville, Virginia), Feb 21, 1890; *Times* (Richmond), Nov 4 and 13, 1892.

1890 to 1893, Awarded $4,000

Velazquez took a lease on houses No. 62 and 64 West 55th Street in New York City with the view of running a boarding house. The lease was a reasonable sort, requiring no large investment. The lease was for three years at $7,600 per year, payable monthly, starting May 1, 1890. All Velazquez seemly needed to do was keep the boarding house full to realize a net income, but on July 28, 1890 she found herself in a legal battle.

The owner of the house, Elizabeth Vandenburg, apparently failed to pay her lender and the property went into receivership of John Hayes, who then commenced to act as "receiver of the rents, issues and profits" for the premise. Hayes filed a lawsuit against "Mrs. William Beard" to recover $750 "for alleged willful and malicious injury and destruction of real and personal property."

Hayes had Velazquez arrested and thrown in jail. It took her three days before she found the $1000 bail; Mr. Beard must have been out of town and unable to help. When she did emerge from the "loathsome jail" where she had been "obligated to remain," she was determined to settle the score with Hayes.

She countersued claiming that Hayes had her arrested on charges he knew "to be false" and that he "willfully and maliciously" omitted facts in the warrant by which she had been arrested. Hayes had claimed she "maliciously" cut and defaced walls, had taken down stone pillars and had removed three stone tubs, a furnace heater, a refrigerator,[14] a cooking range, etc., charges which she refuted. She stated that his claim was "wickedly, willfully and maliciously done." She maintained that she had first obtained "consent and permission" from both Vandenburg and Hayes to make changes to the houses for the convenience and comfort of the boarders.

Velazquez succeeded in having her "order of arrest vacated and set aside by [the] court" on the 12th of August. But Hayes continued to "persecute and annoy" Velazquez by serving another complaint on Velazquez's attorney on August 21, 1890. Velazquez countersued on June 18, 1891.[15] Hayes defended himself by claiming that he had earlier appealed the vacating of the arrest warrant which had been served on Velazquez. The judge found no evidence that he had, and did not believe that he had made this appeal, so the judge rejected his defense.

Velazquez claimed, in conclusion, that she had been "greatly injured in her person and in her business." She complained that she suffered "severe nervous prostration" and that her business outside of her boarding house

---

14. Yes, court records say a refrigerator.
15. In the Summons, the name of the parties was handwritten as, "Loratita J. V. Beard against John Hayes." In later documents Velazquez's name became confused and written as "Loratitia J. P. Beard."

"was greatly injured and impaired, in consequence of many persons hearing of the said arrest and supposing her to be a person of bad and malicious character." She sought damages of twenty thousand dollars, plus court cost.

When Velazquez got her day in court on February 10, 1893, the court ruled in her favor. She was awarded $4,000 plus cost of $345.29 (total of $162,400 in 2023); it took two years, but the woman in battle won.[16]

It is clear that Velazquez was still living in New York in February 1893, but by May she took up residence in Washington, D.C., that based on letters written by her. Remaining from her New York residency is a listing for "Velasquez Beard (L. J.)" found in the Spanish language Cuban *Boletín del Archivo Nacional* with her address as 35 Broadway on the date June 24, 1895. Of course, by that date she was no longer there.[17] Velazquez likely became listed in this bulletin because of her "Address to Congress" in support of Cuba's liberation from Spain. The 35 Broadway address was surely an office and not a residence. Prior, in 1891, she had another office address of 401 Broadway.

1893, the Southern Immigration Scheme

With her troubling lawsuit concluded and money in her pocket, Velazquez now considered an immigration venture which was reminiscent of the Venezuela emigration scheme. Velazquez knew that the Venezuelan scheme never made its organizers rich and she probably should have taken that as a warning of her scheme's likely success.

Velazquez wrote on May 10 from Washington, D.C., where she now had moved, a letter to the Secretary of the Treasury in which she promoted a plan of attracting European settlers to abandoned Southern land which had fallen out of cultivation as a result of the War. The letter was forwarded to the Department of Immigration which, at the time, was under the Treasury Department. A register of received letters noted Madame L. J. V. Beard "Asks aid to locate 'Southern Immigration' at Savannah, Ga. or Baltimore, for landing immigrants adapted to Southern climate." Clearly, Velazquez did not have sufficient capital to initiate her plan and she sought money from the Federal Government.[18]

---

16. Loratitia J. P. [*sic* Loratita J. V.] Beard v John Hayes, County Clerk, New York County; W. S. Gibbons, ed., *The New York State Reporter*, Vol XXXVII (Albany, NY: W. C. Little & Co., 1891), 536; *New York Times*, Feb 10, 1893; *New York Herald*, Feb 10, 1893.
17. This publication was authored by Archivo Nacional de Cuba, Vol 25, 1928.
18. NARA, Her letter was received on May 11 and it was given a reference number of 4721 in Records of Correspondence (Register of Letters Received 1891-1903), RG85, Records of the Immigration and Naturalization Service, Book Vol 3 (of 27), entry 3, Aug 9, 1892-Jun 23, 1893. The file box which contains the numbered received letters has many gaps and her letter is one of the missing. RG85, Records of the Immigration and Naturalization Service, Numbered documents, Letters received, 1882-1906, 3035-4980 with gaps, Box 19, A1, entry 7.

Velazquez's letter is lost, but its content is substantially known because of newspaper reports:[19]

MRS. VELASQUEZ BEARD'S PLAN, She Writes Secretary Carlisle about Southern Immigration-

Washington, May 13- Madame L. J. Velasquez Beard, in a letter to Secretary Carlisle, sets forth at great length the objective of the Southern immigration society in which she is deeply interested. She desires to locate, at either Savannah, Ga., or Baltimore, Md., a bureau for landing emigrants, adapted to the various pursuits of the Southern climate. There are more than 700 emigrants, she states, with money ready to move to the South, where already many parcels of lands have been put into a syndicate to form a colony. A prospectus will be issued soon, giving the details of her plan, which, from her letter, is not clear. She is emphatic, however, in stating that "we desire to be entirely separate from the branch in New York city [sic], and that New York of today is not the great New York of the past." She does not want our "beautiful country overrun by the Russian Jews and criminals of Siberia." Superintendent Hermin Stamp [sic Herman Stump was Superintendent of Immigration, under the Treasury Department.], to whom Secretary Carlisle referred Madame Beard's letter, replied that the bureau of immigration was in entire sympathy with the object of her plan, as far as understood, and would await her promised prospectus.

The *Charleston News and Courier* printed the same story, but it was not kind to Velazquez in the headline: "A FEMALE CRANK, The Alleged Emigration Plan of Mme. L. J. Velasquez Beard."[20] The plan had detractors.

The Superintendent of Immigration replied immediately, May 12, 1893:[21]

Madam L. J. V. Beard
Washington, D.C.
Madam:

Your letter of the 10th instant, addressed to the Hon. John G. Carlisle, Secretary of the Treasury, has been referred to me for reply.

This Bureau is in entire sympathy with your project, and will await the prospectus of your plans in order to further discover your objects and purposes, which you have provided at an early date. Each port of the United States is entirely separate and distinct from the other, and therefore any landing of immigrants at the ports of Savannah or Baltimore or any other port you may select, has no connection whatever with the port of New York. All are responsible to this Bureau and all orders and regulations regarding immigrants emanate from this Department, copy of which I enclose herewith. It also relates to the Contract-Labor Laws to date, and we desire that you particularly examine the same so far as they relate to your project. I would particularly call your attention to the proviso contained in

---

19. *Alexandria Gazette*, May 13, 1893; *Columbus Daily Enquirer* (South Carolina), May 14, 1893; *Baltimore Sun*, May 14, 1893.
20. (South Carolina) May 14, 1893.
21. NARA, RG85, Records of the Immigration and Naturalization Service, Letters Sent, 1882-1912, Book Vol 8 (of 355), entry 8, p376.

section 3 of the act approved March 3, 1891, which states, "This action shall not apply to States and immigration bureau of States advertising the inducements they offer for immigration to such States," and in this connection would suggest that your operations be conducted under the Bureaus of the several States that you desire to benefit by your project.

I regret exceedingly that your desire to see me without coming in contact with Dr. Senner, Commissioner of Immigration at the port of New York, prevented my giving you an audience, as Dr. Senner had another engagement of very great importance on the day you called. Enclosures-2).

Respectfully yours,
Herman Stump
Superintendent

The *News and Courier* again took notice of Velazquez on November 22, 1893 when it printed a letter written by Velazquez to Mr. W. B. Whaley asking that "people of Charleston" supply ships to transport the settlers:

IMMIGRATION. A Company Organized to Bring Scandinavian Settlers to the South. The following letter, which was received here yesterday, will explain itself:
WASHINGTON, D.C., November 18, 1893.
Mr. W. B. Whaley- Dear Sir: You remember meeting me at the Capitol, some weeks ago passing through to New York. I was speaking to you about settling the States of the South with the better class of Scandinavians and Swiss. We are about organizing a company for this purpose, with our head office in Washington, with branches in each of the Southern States, and with another main office in Paris. We publish a journal devoted to the interests of Southern resources. We reproduce this in French, in Scandinavian, German and Swiss. Col. Donan edits our paper. William T. Riggs has the matter in hand. I would be glad to hear from you as to procuring lands, and what inducement will the people of Charleston give to put on one or two lines of first-class ocean steamers. We shall only bring good thrifty settlers; no Polish Jews or serfs will be allowed under our charters. I shall be glad to hear from you at your earliest convenience, and await your reply.
Yours truly, Madame L. J. V. Beard

Surely it wasn't true Velazquez had "branches in each of the Southern States." Furthermore, the proposed "main office in Paris" would not have been at all convenient for "a better class of Scandinavians," but maybe the Swiss might have found convenience in a Paris office, if it had ever been opened. And what languages are "Scandinavian" and "Swiss"?

Velazquez astutely selected the right man of whom to ask favors. Mr. W. B. Whaley was Charleston's resident entrepreneur and capitalist. He was one of the directors of the Royal Fertilizer Company and one of the incorporators of the Courtenay Manufacturing Company as well as the Indianola Manufacturing and Power Co., which proposed to develop cotton mills with power harnessed by damming the Catawba River to operate

200,000 cotton spindles and 5,000 looms.[22] The ambitious Mr. Whaley married one of the three daughters of "The Wealthiest Resident of the City of Charleston," Mr. Williams Burroughs Smith, who at the time of his death in June 1892, left an estate of two and a half million dollars, that is, 93.5 million in 2023 dollars.[23]

The local newspaper[24] reported:

Mr. Whaley will submit the letter to the Cotton Exchange and endeavor to secure the necessary co-operation of the different commercial bodies of Charleston and the State authorities to ensure the success of the movement.

However, it seems Mr. Whaley did not pursue it or make an investment of his own.

The newspaper[25] pointed out how and why the scheme might succeed:

The State owns some very valuable "forfeited lands," which might be offered to settlers upon favorable terms, and there are hundreds of thousands of acres in the State which could be purchased far below its actual value. And as for ocean steamers, they would not be hard to find, the passengers and cargoes being provided.

In spite of this positive notice, the emigration scheme seems not to have taken hold in the Charleston area. Still Velazquez pursued her scheme.

The *Roanoke Times* (Virginia) of December 14, 1893 gave credit to Velazquez for originating the newly created immigration organization and made its name known:

The National Immigration and Colonization Association has been organized in Washington and incorporated under the laws of Virginia with a capital stock of $500,000 with the authority to increase it, as the demands of the company may require, to $3,000,000. The announced object of the company, says the *Washington Post*, is to turn immigration and capital to the Southern States, to select and provide lands and homes for immigrants and to secure for them every possible advantage and protection in the new regions to which they go.

The idea of such an organized movement originated with a woman, Mme. Velazquez-Beard, and the preliminary work has been actively going on for many months. Pledges of earnest co-operation have come from hundreds of leading Southern men in all the States and Territories from Maryland and Virginia to Texas, New Mexico and Arizona. Tens of thousands of acres of land have been tendered, accompanied by assurances of personal assistance to intending settlers, in a number of instances including offers to build suitable houses on the lands selected. The

---

22. *Charleston News and Courier* (South Carolina), Feb 17, 1893 and Jun 15, 1893.
23. *State* (Columbia, S. C.), Jun 24, 1892.
24. *Charleston News and Courier* (South Carolina), Nov 22, 1893.
25. Ibid.

governors, immigration agents and other officials of numerous States have sent written guarantees of interest and aid, and....

Although the organization's President, Vice-president and Secretary were mentioned by name in later newspaper reports, there is no more record of Velazquez in this venture.[26]

It appears that Velazquez had the opportunity to tell of her plan directly to the *Roanoke Times*, evident by the second paragraph:

Pledges of earnest co-operation have come from hundreds of leading Southern men.... The governors, immigration agents and other officials of numerous States have sent written guarantees of interest and aid....

This information seemingly came directly from Velazquez; where else could the newspaper have developed this information? It will be seen that Velazquez used the same "all on board" sales technique later in 1900 when she promoted a railroad scheme.

Velazquez now traveled to Norfolk to consider the project, "Madame L. J. Velasquez Beard of Washington, D.C., who is interested in immigration matters, is at the Atlantic [Hotel]."[27]

Questions must be raised about Velazquez's role in the immigration scheme. Long before Velazquez's May 13 newspaper mention, the governor of Virginia had already sent out invitations on March 17 to the Southern governors for an April 12 meeting "to consider questions relating to immigration."[28] And as early as March 7, it was reported that Governor Brown of Maryland was in favor of immigration to help develop the state's resources.[29] He thought that the efforts and money of capitalists was what was needed to succeed in an immigration scheme, but suggested that the state back the capitalists with $10,000 of state money. It seems that Velazquez grabbed an idea already proposed; this is reminiscent of when Velazquez promoted the Venezuela Company as its agent, and also the Mary Washington Monument scheme.

Velazquez's letter of November 18 made clear that she knew Colonel Donan was one of the organization's officers and it may be believed true that Velazquez tried to associate with the organization. However, after December 1893 there is no more mention in the press of Velazquez in connection to the organization. In January 1894, Colonel Donan was reported to have made Washington, D.C. his home and had been chosen as Vice-president of the National Immigration and Colonization Company.[30]

---

26. *Gazette* (Raleigh, North Carolina), Dec 16, 1893.
27. *Virginia-Pilot* (Norfolk), Feb 21, 1894.
28. *Dallas Morning News*, Mar 19, 1893.
29. *Baltimore Sun*, Mar 7, 1894
30. *Bismarck Tribune* (North Dakota), Jan 2, 1894; *St. Paul Daily Globe* (Minn.), Jan 1, 1894.

480

When Colonel Pat Donan was interviewed at the Southern Convention in June 1894 he said, "We are succeeding slowly but surely."[31] The company failed to attract support enough for the scheme to thrive and it is last found in the 1896 Kansas City Directory, where it was listed as "Land Companies, National Immigration and Colonization Co."

1894, Second Try, New Company

Velazquez wasn't finished with immigration schemes and started another which she called the International Colonization Company, incorporated in Norfolk, Virginia in November.

This time Velazquez cleverly attached herself to Captain Emil Lindburg, a very prominent name in the immigration business. Already in 1870, he had associated himself with the Swedish Emigrant Association, Chicago.[32] He had been "General Agent of the Land Department of the Atlantic and Pacific Railroad Company"[33] and in August 1874 he was in St. Louis working as a clerk[34] and was then recognized by the President as the Vice-consul of Sweden and Norway. By 1881 he was operating out of New York City as general manager of the General European Colonization Agency and Bureau of Southern Immigration vigorously encouraging Southern states to make lands available for purchase.[35] Lindburg traveled to Memphis and delivered a presentation explaining that the steamship and railroad companies had given him reduced prices for his immigrants and he asked the locals to "sell them land at fair prices… we don't ask alms; we merely want encouragement and fair play."

In August 1888 Mr. Lindburg, living in Brooklyn, was arrested for perjury. He protested he "was an honest and respectable man, and he could bring witnesses to prove it," but in December a jury found him guilty. Mr. Lindburg appealed to the judge "for mercy, declaring that he was an innocent and greatly abused man." The Judge sent Lindburg to Sing Sing State Prison for two years. Lindburg had served as bondsman, for one Frank Harrison who had been accused of grand larceny and when doing so, Mr. Lindburg had asserted to the Bond Clerk that he owned four houses worth $27,500, which in truth he no longer owned.[36] The false affidavit resulted in the conviction of perjury.

---

31. *New York Times*, Jun 24, 1894.
32. Letter Apr 2, 1870, to James Sykes, Rufus Ward Collection, Acc. No. 73, Ser I, Mississippi State Univ. Library.
33. *Madison Daily Democrat* (Wis.), Apr 23, 1872; *Daily City Item* (New Orleans), May 9, 1881.
34. *Chicago Tribune*, Apr 8, 10, 1891.
35. *Comet* (Jackson, Mississippi), Jun 18, 1881; *Southern Standard* (McMinnville, Tenn.), Sep 3, 1881; *Patron of Husbandry* (Columbus, Miss.), Sep 17, 1881.
36. *Sun* (New York), Aug 18, 1888, Dec 20, 1888; *World* (N.Y), Dec 21, 1888; *New-York Tribune*, Dec 20, 22, 1888; Sing Sing Prison Admissions Record, New York State Archives.

In any case, he emerged from his trouble and resumed his immigration efforts. In July 1892, Lindburg was living in Brooklyn and was "Manager of the Scandinavian Homestead Society." He endeavored to place immigrants in the South and assured Southerners that "all" the immigrants "have money with which to buy farms and get a start in business."

Now Mrs. L. J. Velasquez-Beard was energized, she departed Norfolk, Virginia and headed for New Bern, North Carolina, with a brief stop in Elizabeth City, N. C., where she told the newspaper that she represented the International Colonization Company of Norfolk.[37] She arrived in New Bern by steamer *Neuse* on Friday November 23, 1894 and checked into Hotel Chattawka. Wasting no time, she contacted the local newspaper to explain the purpose of her visit:

> to bring over not less than 1,250 families of a desirable class of immigrants... from Finland, Norway, Denmark, Sweden and north of Scotland, men who have means to pay for lands and then in some instances have capital left besides, who are skilled laborers, and who will erect factories, and develop localities....

She noted that a "grand reliance" of the success of her plan was Mr. Emil Lindburg. The newspaper hoped for good results.[38]

Velazquez received the attention she needed, and a tour of the area. At the Honorable H. R. Bryan's plantation, she noted yucca plants, and asserted and demonstrated that the leaves make good fiber, better than sisal. With proper cultivation and a factory, a fine income could be realized from rope production. She told her listeners that she had seen this in Cuba and Mexico.[39] She also told the newspaper she had enough subscribers, some residents, others not, to build a cotton factory and it would be on Judge Bryan's land opposite the city. This effort was an aside, not connected to the International Colonization Company. The newspaper supported the plan and thought all citizens would favor it.[40]

In response to the many inquiries about immigration to the South, Mr. Lindburg asked the editors of the New Bern newspaper to publish his letter of response. He stated the positive which would result, that the immigrants "come to buy and work their own lands... and are a value to the community." He asked persons having land for sale to contact at the International Colonization Company, Major D. J. Turner, President, Columbia Building Norfolk, Virginia. The writer signed Emil Lindburg, 243 Broadway, New York.[41]

---

37. *Economist-Falcon* (Elizabeth City, North Carolina), Nov 23, 1894.
38. *New Berne Daily Journal*, Nov 24, 1894.
39. Ibid, Nov 29, 1894.
40. Ibid, Dec 1, 1894.
41. Ibid, Dec 1, 1894.

Velazquez then departed to Morehead and Beaufort, North Carolina to see if she could engage the citizens there and returned on December 4, again checking into Hotel Chattawka and "expressing herself well satisfied with the progress."[42] She said Morehead had been decided upon as the arrival port for the immigrants. She did not stay long, but departed for Raleigh on business. The newspaper publicly asked if Mr. Lindburg could not be "induced to pay our city a visit himself."[43]

In Raleigh, Velazquez visited the local newspaper and stated she felt confident of the success of the International Colonization Company. The newspaper said that she was "a writer of note and has acted as American correspondent for a number of journals" in Europe.[44] She once again returned to New Berne's Hotel Chattawka on December 10 and on the 13th a citizens' meeting was called for at City Hall "to discuss matters pertaining to immigration, which subject is rife here now."[45] The newspaper said it is informed the International Colonization Company has immigrants only awaiting the word to come. Mrs. Beard said they would not be all located as a whole, but in their own separated locale in groups of origin. Also, to be discussed was the cotton factory, estimated cost $110,000, and the capitalists said ready to build it.[46]

About fifty people attended and Mayor Ellis introduced Mrs. Beard who briefly stated the Company's purpose and its progress. She claimed there were 3,000 families waiting to come and "it remained for the people here to say if they wanted them." A motion was made that the Mayor should invite Mr. Lindburg and Mr. D. J. Turner, President of the Company, to New Bern to see what New Bern had to offer. The newspaper said the "meeting passed off very pleasantly" and it awaited "the next move."[47]

Mr. Turner answered the invitation offer, stating he would "arrange for an early visit to New Berne in company with [his] general agent, Capt. Emil Lindburg."[48] Emil Lindburg also answered. He could not come, but would try at a future date to come with President D. J. Turner. The newspaper said it wished he would have come right away as the proposed cotton factory needed discussing.[49]

On December 18 Velazquez visited Wilmington, N. C., but stayed only a day. This visit produced a big article by the *Wilmington Messenger* of December 20:

---

42. Ibid, Dec 1 and 5, 1894.
43. Ibid, Dec 6, 1894.
44. *News and Observer* (Raleigh, N. C.), Dec 7, 1894.
45. *New Berne Daily Journal*, Dec 11, 1894.
46. Ibid, Dec 13, 1894.
47. Ibid, Dec 14, 1894.
48. Ibid, Dec 19, 1894, published the letter dated Dec 17, 1894, at Norfolk, Va.
49. Ibid, published the letter dated Dec 15, 1894, at 243 Broadway, New York.

COLONIZATION SCHEME. Fifty Thousand Acres of Land Wanted for 3,000 Families of Settlers- A Chance to Get Them for North Carolina.

The MESSENGER is pleased to acknowledge a visit from Mrs. L. J. Velasquez-Beard, whose husband Col. Wm. Beard, is vice president of the International Colonization company (incorporated) which was organized a little over six weeks ago in Norfolk with headquarters in that city.

Mrs. Beard, who has been spending some time at Newbern, as the guest of that city, came over to Wilmington on Tuesday and returned to Newbern yesterday afternoon. She is the duly authorized agent of the International Colonization company and will probably revisit our city at an early day and go hence to Raleigh and Greensboro.

We learn that the object of the company she represents, is to colonize 3,000 families in some section of the South, and they want to move as soon as suitable lands can be secured for them. For their use 5,000 acres of land in one tract is wanted, and it is desired that the ground shall be high and fertile. A cotton factory is one of the enterprises proposed by the colony as soon as it locates. Alabama and Virginia are making bids for these settlers, but we have no doubt that North Carolina can secure them by proper efforts.

With reference to Mrs. Beard's visit to Newbern the *Journal* says:

Her object in this first visit is to get the people informed upon and interested in the work which it is proposed to accomplish, and also to have someone to look after lands and take stock in the company.

The company proposes to carry on its operations in all the country lying south of a line running through Washington city westward to the Pacific; the principal object is to attract good settlers and capital to the South; to develop the resources of special localities, and to encourage the establishment of profitable industries that will give impetus to every branch of business and trade where such industries are established. It is proposed to bring over not less than 1250 families of a desirable class of immigrants to this country every year and to give bond guaranteeing the bringing of this number of desirable families.

The class of immigrants which it is proposed to bring are the sturdy and thrifty peasantry of Finland, Norway, Denmark, Sweden and north of Scotland, men who have the means to pay for lands and then in some instances have capital left besides, who are skilled laborers, and who will erect factories, and develop the localities in which they settle or colonize.

A grand reliance of the company for the successful culmination of its plans is the man who is its general agent at New York. This is Mr. Emil Lindburg who has held the position of consul general to Sweden, who from the circumstance and from experience in immigration work [is] in a commanding position relative to such changes of settlement. Not only does he wield wide influence among those spoken of but he is also in receipt of thousands of letters from settlers in the Northwest who have their eyes turned longingly southward. Many letters from those still in the "old countries" cite Eastern North Carolina as the place which they wish to make their new home.

Mrs. Beard is a native of the West Indies, a Louisianian [*sic*] by adoption (the family removed there when she was but a child), is thoroughly Southern in attachment and for twenty-seven years she has been engaged in efforts looking to the development of the Southern States. She is a writer, and not only contributes to publications in this country but now contributes also to forty-two papers in Sweden and Scotland, the countries among the citizens of which the International colonization company is directing its chief efforts.

Mrs. Beard has letters of strong endorsement from some of the most prominent men of the South, of recent date and running back for a number of years.

Two observations are in order. Her husband was not a colonel and her claim that her family removed to Louisiana "when she was but a child" is in painful contradiction to her memoir, published 18 years prior, in which she claimed her family stayed in Cuba and sent her to live with her aunt in New Orleans.

In addition, the article contains plenty of unbelievable foolishness such as Velazquez contributed to forty-two newspapers in Sweden and Scotland and that she had for twenty-seven years made efforts to develop the South. Does moving to Venezuela in 1867, then living in the West from 1868 to 1874, then living in New York qualify as efforts to develop the South? Those distant residencies were in the last 27 years.

The article was rather positive, but it identified the need in the headline, "Fifty-thousand Acres of Land Wanted," which was called 5,000 acres in the article. The immigrants would move "as soon as suitable land can be secured for them." Velazquez returned to her New Bern Hotel Chattawka on December 19.[50]

The newspaper claimed Mrs. Beard received a letter from President D. J. Turner and that Mr. Bryan received one from Mr. Lindburg, both men repeating their acceptance of the invitation, but no date was set.[51]

"A correction of some wrong ideas in reference to the colonization work" was offered by Velazquez to the newspaper. She said the immigrants are not coming as one body to be settled on one tract of land, but will come in intervals and spread out. She also explained that the proposed cotton factory "is not the work of the Colonization Company, but of others, as is also the planned iron bridge across Trent River." She said a company proposed to build a toll bridge which would open the other side of the river to manufacturing enterprises.[52]

Mrs. Beard "went down the Wilmington, Newbern & Norfolk Railroad in the interest of the colonization scheme."[53] While she was in adjacent Jones County on Saturday the 22nd she addressed some citizens as to the Company's progress, but mostly she seems to have been trying to acquire

---

50. Ibid, Dec 20, 1894.
51. Ibid.
52. Ibid, Dec 22, 1894.
53. Ibid.

land. She returned to New Bern by Monday December 24, but did not go to Hotel Chattawka, where she had been staying free as a guest of the city. It might be speculated that at this point she had lost her support. In any case, she instead checked into Hotel Albert.

The newspaper[54] asserted:

> She has opened an office there which she designs to be permanent, her husband and family having decided to make New Berne their home. Mrs. Beard will remain here until after the visits of Messrs. Lindburg and Turner, the General Agent and the President of the Company to this city and will then be away for a short time preparatory to moving to the city.

Mr. Lindburg and Mr. Turner never came. Nor did Mrs. Beard and her family move to New Bern. When she left, she left for good. All news of Mrs. Beard and her Colonization Company and the gentlemen vanished from the newspapers. It is unbelievable that the newspapers just stopped coverage of Mrs. Beard and her Company, after so much attention, but that is the fact. The newspaper and/or Judge Bryan might have been embarrassed and they simply couldn't take any more talk of it.

The hard fact is that Mrs. Beard never acquired any free land, the only land she could afford, so her scheme went nowhere! Even Mr. Lindburg's reputation as an immigration specialist and his alleged general agency (if truthful) to Mrs. Beard Colonization Company could not produce success without land. And the cotton factory went nowhere, a sure indication that it was not true that Mrs. Beard had subscribers as she had claimed! To her credit though, she had expended tremendous energy in her effort.

Velazquez probably had no operating cash remaining and the city was no longer hosting her. There was nothing left for Velazquez to do, but to abandon the immigration scheme. By 1895-1896, she was living in Norfolk, Virginia, working as a stock broker of sorts.

Captain Emil Lindburg continued with immigration schemes and in 1904 obtained some large tracts of land in South Carolina.[55]

1893, Ménie Muriel Dowie's *Women Adventurers*

In 1893 Ménie Muriel Dowie edited and published a 288-page book, *Women Adventurers*, which elevated the myth of Velazquez to such a level that its everlasting life was assured. The book contained the biographies of four women and the first chapter (51 pages) was allotted to Velazquez with reproduced images of her in and out of uniform, as well as the original title page of Velazquez's memoir. The chapter was a condensed, edited version of the memoir with a brief retelling of events to the point where Dowie lets

---

54. Ibid.
55. *Reports and Resolutions of the General Assembly of the State of South Carolina*, Vol 1(Columbia, S. C.: Gonzales and Bryan, 1906) 913.

Velazquez's memoir pick up the narration. Dowie did not contribute new information and it should be noted that Dowie was never in a position to learn anything other than what Velazquez wrote about herself. Dowie never met Velazquez and did not even travel to the United States until 1941, when she immigrated.

Ménie Muriel Dowie was born (1867) in England, educated there and in Germany and France. She was the author of several books which raised feminist issues. Her first novel was published in 1891 and it was about a heroine who dressed as a man. *Women Adventurers* was her second book and she wrote others. Dowie was later known by her married name, Mrs. Henry Norman (1891), and was sometimes associated by that name with her *Women Adventurers* book.[56]

All sorts of newspapers and book reviews gave attention to Ménie Muriel Dowie and her new book. The reviewers treated the Velazquez chapter of the book as if it was factual, for example, the *New York Times* (June 19, 1893) wrote:

> The narrative of Mme. Loreta Janeta Velasquez, who appeared as Lieut. Harry T. Buford of the Confederacy, has to be treated with more respect. There is reason to believe that there is some foundation of truth in it. She was a spy, and at the beginning of the troubles may have been present at some of the engagements. Mme. Velasquez was clever, energetic, and certainly ran many risks.

It is ironic that the *New York Times* and the U.S. publisher of *Women Adventurers* were located in New York, where Velazquez was living at that time. Velazquez obviously did not feel it necessary to reveal herself to them; at least no record was uncovered that she did. Maybe Velazquez felt no need to because she no longer made money on her book. By then she may have sold away the rights.

As some people had before, Dowie gave credence to Velazquez's story and perpetuated it. Later researchers and authors borrowed from Dowie.

H. W. Hageman and Richard Worthington

Probably trying to ride the coattails of Ménie Muriel Dowie book's success, in 1894 the H. W. Hageman Publishing Co. in New York reissued Velazquez's book. The reissue was not under the original title of *The Woman in Battle*, but instead, *Story of the Civil War or The Exploits, Adventures and Travels of Mrs. L. J. Velasquez (Lieut. H. T. Buford, C. S. A)*. It was not Hageman who made this title change, since it had already been executed in November 1890 by the Worthington Co. of 747 Broadway, NYC. The name change was apparently a fresh marketing effort to describe the contents of the book. Notable is that the author's name had been adjusted to "Mrs. L. J.

---

56. Dowie divorced in 1903 and married a Fitzgerald and separated from him in 1928. She died in Tucson (Arizona) in 1945.

Velasquez," with an "s" and no "Madame." The Worthington 1890 reissue, which sold for $1.50, seems to have had little or no success and no discovered newspapers mention Velazquez promoting her book under the new title, which would seem to indicate that she no longer had royalty rights and no chance of financial reward.

The Woman in Battle was first published by Dustin, Gilman & Company, Richmond, Virginia in 1876. How Velazquez came to an agreement with this publisher is unknown. Velazquez's book fit the genre of a woman's autobiography which interested this publisher, evident by its recently published (1875) autobiography by Ann Eliza Young, *Wife No. 19, or The Story of A Life in Bondage, being a Complete Exposé of Mormons, and Revealing the Sorrows, Sacrifices and Sufferings of Women in Polygamy*.[57] Ann Eliza and Mormon Church President Brigham Young married in 1868, she was 24 and he was 66. In 1873 Ann Eliza initiated divorce proceedings claiming neglect, cruelty and desertion against Brigham. Her book about her experience was a bestseller, and on the lecture circuit, she was a national sensation.

Dustin, Gilman & Company was owned by Charles E. Dustin and Julius S. Gilman. These two men had formed the company after their partnership with the Alfred D. Worthington was dissolved in about July 1873.[58] The A. D. Worthington Company continued for years as a publisher and was widely known, but it was not associated with *The Woman in Battle*.

However, a different Worthington, one Richard Worthington was associated with *The Woman in Battle*. It is unclear how the (Richard) Worthington Company of 747 Broadway, NYC obtained rights to publish the book, which it did in November 1890. It was this company which first reissued the book with the title *Story of the Civil War*.

Richard Worthington came to New York in 1885 and formed his publishing company that year. In January 1893 the Worthington Company failed and went into the receivership of John J. Little publishing company.[59] It appears that Velazquez's book was not among the assets taken over by the Little Company and it is probable that the publishing rights had already gone to Hageman Publishing Co.

Mr. H. W. Hageman, in his younger years worked for Scribner, Armstrong & Company. When Richard Worthington bought out D. Appleton & Company, Mr. Hageman saw opportunities with an expanding company and "cast his lot with Mr. Worthington." When the Richard Worthington business was closed, Hageman started his own business in the

---

57. Ann Eliza, chronologically, was 52nd of Brigham's fifty-five wives, but "according to the laws of the Mormon Church" she was his 19th.
58. Michael B. Frank and Harriet Elinor Smith, ed., *Mark Twain's letters, Vol. 6*; *Vol. 9* (Los Angeles: Univ California Press, 2002), 91 of Vol 6.
59. *New York Times*, Oct 9, 1894, Obituary.

Mohawk Building at 160 Fifth Avenue. It would have been at this time that Hageman acquired rights to publish Velazquez's book.[60]

Was C. J. Worthington the Editor of *The Woman in Battle?*

At this point it is necessary to sort out who's who among the Worthington name. Mr. Alfred. D. Worthington was a well-known publisher in 1876, but he had nothing to do with Velazquez's book and was not related to the book's alleged editor, C. J. Worthington. Another Worthington, Mr. Richard Worthington (married, no children),[61] did get the rights to the book, but that was many years later, in 1890, and in any case, he was not related to Alfred. D. Worthington or to the nebulous C. J. Worthington.

Evidence leads one to conclude that the name of C. J. Worthington was a fabricated name, selected to imply a respectable connection with the well-known publishing name of Alfred D. Worthington. If C. J. Worthington was not the editor's real name, then who was the real editor of *The Woman in Battle?* The answer is Charles A. Dunham. The evidence and argument follow:

1) The editor, C. J. Worthington, in the memoir's "Prefatory Notice," stated (p9) that he "was in the United States naval service from near the beginning to the end of the civil war." However, *Naval Enlistment Weekly Returns, 1855-1891* archived at NARA fails to reveal a C. J. Worthington; neither does the National Park Service's database of Civil War sailors.

Some recent writers have credited C. J. Worthington to have been a naval officer, though he never claimed it. It was only the "publisher's circular" which stated that Worthington was "an officer of the United States Navy" and this is the source for these writers' assertions. If C. J. Worthington was an officer, he would be more easily found.

A search of *List of Officers of the Navy of the United States and of the Marine Corps from 1775 to 1900* shows no officer named C. J. Worthington.[62] Neither does *The Records of Living Officers of the U.S. Navy and Marine Corps* by Lewis R. Hamersley, published in 1870.

Velazquez wrote (Prefatory Notice, p6) only that he "was on the other side."

2) Recall when Velazquez sued William Ramsay (in 1876) for "cheating and swindling"? Ramsay, in his own defense stated that one of the delays he encountered was "that the editor of the book lived in Philadelphia"[63] and

---

60. *Publishers' Weekly*, Apr 1, 1899. Hageman died suddenly on March 18, 1899. He had been born in Pomerania (now divided between Poland and Germany) fifty years prior and had come to the U.S. as a young man.
61. *New York Times*, Oct 9, 1894.
62. Ed. Edward W. Callahan (NY: L. R. Hamersly & Co, 1901), Compiled from the Official Records of the Navy Department.
63. *Atlanta Constitution*, Mar 9, 1876.

earlier, on September 11, 1875, Ramsay's Southern Publishing Company identified C. J. Worthington as the editor.

The book's illustrator, Mr. Jeremiah Rea, also lived in Philadelphia.[64] He drew the portraits of Velazquez in male disguise and as herself. In addition, there was another illustrator, Edmund Birchhead Bensell, also from Philadelphia who contributed to the book; he was stated in the "publishers circular" to be the illustrator of *TWIB*.

In 1875 Velazquez stated that one "W. J. Clarke Jr." of Philadelphia "rendered her great service in the preparation of her book."[65] William J. Clark Jr. was a prominent Philadelphian and editor.[66] He was President of the Philadelphia Sketch Club,[67] Vice-president of the Press Club of Philadelphia[68] and wrote "Critical Notices" which first appeared in the Philadelphia *Evening Telegraph* in December 1874, where he was a staff editor.[69] Clark was the author of *Great American Sculptures* published in Philadelphia in 1878.

If Clark helped at all, it was minimal because at that time Clark was busy working on his own books and performing his regular newspaper editorial duties, and besides, Velazquez's book was not in Clark's area of interest. Velazquez demonstrated her correct knowledge when she mentioned that Clark was the brother to "Max Adeler." Max was a humorist, author, and editorialist who wrote for Philadelphia newspapers and enjoyed great popularity. Velazquez was name dropping them both, as she did to Mark Twain. The point is, the brothers lived in Philadelphia where Velazquez sought and found an editor and also found illustrator Rea. But William J. Clark Jr. was not the editor of Velazquez's book.

3) No C. J. Worthington has been found in Philadelphia public records. He did not exist.

4) Charles A. Dunham was working in Philadelphia when Velazquez went North looking for an editor. Dunham is placed in Philadelphia as the editor and publisher of the *Philadelphia Market Journal*; the first issue under his name was July 11, 1874.[70] It must be suspected that his ownership was brief because the 1874 *American Newspaper Directory*[71] listed W. H. Kilpatrick

---

64. *Philadelphia Inquirer*, Mar 18, 1900.
65. *Constitutionalist* (Augusta, Georgia), Oct 6, 1875.
66. James Gospill, *Gospill's Philadelphia City Directory for 1875* (Philadelphia: James Gospill, 1875), 315.
67. *Philadelphia Inquirer*, Jan 9, 1875; Jan 5, 1878; Jan 5, 1880.
68. Ibid, Dec 27, 1873.
69. William J. Clarke, Jr., *Exhibition of Prints (Claghorn Collection)* (Philadelphia: Rue & Jones, 1875).
70. Carman Cumming, *The Devil's Game, The Civil War Intrigues of Charles A. Dunham* (Urbana and Chicago, IL: Univ. of Illinois Press, 2004), 258, 289.
71. Ed. George P. Rowell.

as the editor and publisher of the *Journal* and the 1875 *American Newspaper Directory* listed B. Salinger as the editor and publisher of the *Journal*. Since Dunham's ownership occurred after the middle of 1874, his name would not have been in the 1874 *Directory* and he must have sold out by the time the listings were compiled for the 1875 *Directory*. The *Philadelphia Market Journal* apparently wasn't desirable because in 1876 it again changed ownership.

After Dunham sold his Philadelphia newspaper in 1874, it is likely that he went to New York, later in the year. His enduring presence in New York is established by the birth of seven of his children there, from 1858 to 1875. Velazquez's presence there is reported by a New York newspaper on September 9, 1874. She remained in New York for some eight months, after which she was documented in Key West, in June 1875. Five years later Dunham was still in the New York area, just across the Hudson River in New Jersey.[72] So Velazquez could have dealt with Dunham in both Philadelphia and New York. And C. J. Worthington circumstantially placed her in both cities during this time when he wrote (*TWIB*, p13), "In New York [and] Philadelphia… she has a large number of very warm friends…."

5) Velazquez already knew Dunham from Castle Thunder in Richmond. Dunham was imprisoned there from the end of April (or beginning of May) to the end of July 1863 and Velazquez was there in July 1863.[73] Dunham was released from prison and sent North across the military lines. It was then that Dunham, under his alias of "Harvey Birch," wrote to the *New York Herald*, that he had met "in July last the celebrated she-Lieutenant Buford" and that she was released from prison and was probably now in the North spying and "serving the rebels with such information as she can acquire." He wrote, "The day before the fair lieutenant left, she said in a jocular way to me that she hoped I would soon be released, and that she should see me in Baltimore."

6) Charles A. Dunham was a brilliant wordsmith, but he would not have dared associate his real name with the book, unless he wished it to fail. No doubt Velazquez concurred. Dunham had the right combination of writer's ability and a deficiency of scruples which made him highly qualified to edit her book and then apply an alias to his work. Dunham had used many aliases for evil during and immediately after the Civil War and adding C. J. Worthington to his list of aliases was probably the least harmful name he ever used.

Dunham's greatest contribution to history, and the reason Dunham dared not use his own name as Velazquez's editor, was that he, using the alias Sanford Conover, fabricated a huge fraud on the 1865 United States

---

72. U.S. Census 1880.
73. *Staunton Spectator*, Jul 7, 1863, repeating the *Richmond Enquire*, Jul 2, 1863.

Government's investigation of President Lincoln's assassination.[74] Judge Advocate General Joseph Holt had been appointed by President Lincoln and was subsequently tasked to investigate his own boss's assassination. Confederate President Davis was suspected in a conspiracy and Judge Holt sought evidence. One shady character decided to give Holt evidence, even if it had to be fabricated. Alias Sanford Conover promised Judge Holt through a letter that he could "procure witnesses and documentary evidence sufficient to convict Jeff Davis."

Judge Holt arranged a meeting with Conover who convinced the Judge to hire him. Conover departed for New York on his witness search. He located one witness and delivered him to Washington, where he testified before the Bureau of Military Justice to the satisfaction of Holt. Holt was now convinced of Conover's ability to produce witnesses and Conover, on the payroll, left for Richmond and southward in further search. Holt was kept on a baited hook by Conover's crafty letters and telegrams detailing Conover's progress. Conover routinely requested money, he said transportation and food were expense, because of a lack of it, and Southern hotels charged "rates far exceeding that of the Washington hotels." Judge Holt paid regularly.

Conover, on October 10, 1865, crafted a letter which was a totally believable narrative of his activities in securing witnesses, and it illustrated Dunham's knowledge of Velazquez:

> The witnesses mentioned by me include all that I have so far obtained, but investigations have led to the discovery of another plot, approved by Davis, for the murder of the late President quite as diabolical as the one which resulted in his death. The witnesses to establish this charge-- one of whom is a Miss Alice Williams, who was commissioned in the rebel army as a lieutenant under the name of Buford, the would-be Charlotte Corday, except that she proposed to employ poison instead of a dagger -- being mostly females I thought better not to produce them without a conference on the subject with you.

French woman Charlotte Corday met with Jean Paul Marat, a prominent French Revolution leader, under the pretense of promising to betray some political enemies. Unbeknownst to Marat, Charlotte was a royalist sympathizer and considered him an enemy of France. He was soaking in a bathtub, treating a skin disease, as he was known to meet visitors. Needless to say, the Monsieur was unarmed and Mademoiselle Corday pulled a concealed dagger from her clothing and plunged it into his chest; he died almost instantly.

Miss Alice Williams was indeed no Charlotte Corday and Conover never again mentioned Williams or the female poison plot simply because Conover

---

74. OR, *The War of the Rebellion*, Ser 2 Vol 8, 932-945.

knew nothing more of Williams other than what he had learned of her years earlier at Castle Thunder.

Recall, that Velazquez narrated in her book how she refused to assassinate General Grant because "it was too much like murder," but yet, she was ready to poison President Lincoln? Both were lies, one from Velazquez and one from Dunham.

Before long Judge Holt was convinced to send money to Conover's witnesses who promised to collect more witnesses. Conover arrived in Washington with some witnesses and their depositions were taken at the Bureau of Military Justice. Two of the witnesses were female; one was "Mrs. Douglass" who turned-out to be Dunham's real wife, Ophelia.

Subsequently, the House of Representatives formed an investigative committee which summoned Judge Holt, who gave his findings and produced the depositions he had collected. Several of the witnesses were rounded up and asked to address the committee; they recanted their testimonies. Conover's "School of Perjury" was exposed. The witnesses had fabricated their testimonies per Conover's instructions. Judge Holt was compelled to tell the committee that "Conover has been guilty of a most atrocious crime" and to "discard the testimony produced by [Conover]." Judge Holt asked the committee to "understand under what constant encouragements and apparently trustworthy assurances" he had been caused to be duped.

Judge Holt said that Conover's crime was "committed under what promptings" he was "wholly unable to determine." Judge Holt could not believe that Conover was motivated by hopes of financial gain. Conover had only been promised expenses and "fair compensation… in view of their importance and of the extreme danger to which it was supposed they might expose him… but nothing beyond this."

But financial gain was always part of Conover's motives. What Judge Holt did not realize was that, what he considered small money was real money to Conover. Conover needed a job, and trickery, forgery, deceit and fraud for money was what he knew how to do. In addition, Conover was no doubt getting a good share of the money Holt sent to Conover's witnesses. The money was clearly needed by Conover, evident by Conover's letter of September 4, 1865 in which he wrote, "I took the liberty of sending $50 of the amount received from you [Holt] to my family, knowing that they would need some during my absence." When one newspaper printed the story of one witness's recantation, it reported the witness said Conover "got up the testimony to obtain the reward."[75]

---

75. *Daily News and Herald* (Savannah, Georgia), Jun 15, 1866; *OR, The War of the Rebellion*, Ser 2 Vol 8, 932-945.

The greater motive for Conover's criminality was that he was a pathological liar; certainly, a noxious talent by which to earn a living, but it gave him great job satisfaction. "He took malicious pleasure in duping fools."[76] A newspaper, in 1865, wrote that Dunham "among his acquaintances bears the reputation of one of the most audacious liars imaginable."[77] Judge Holt could have scarcely known Conover's history or recognized his proclivities, thereby avoiding involvement with him.

Dunham, caught in his conspiracy of lies, and with the investigators greatly embarrassed, was prosecuted and sentenced to prison. He served just over 2 years and was pardoned in February 1869. The reason for his pardon may have been because he had served as a Union spy. The record shows an association with Colonel L. C. Baker of the U.S. Secret Service.[78] However, it also can be speculated that Dunham spied for both sides. Even at this date it is unclear if he was loyal to his Northern roots. He was mostly loyal to himself and his own wallet.[79]

Dunham's career during the Civil War might be described as that of forger, liar, opportunist and spy. He was a man of many aliases. Eleven of his aliases are known, not counting Charles A. Dunham and C. Augustus Dunham. It is suspected that he used at least nine other aliases. "Sanford Conover" and "Harvey Birch" are the names he used in connection with Velazquez. Dunham traveled both North and South crossing military lines, at which time it can be thought he was spying, and possibly for both sides. He wrote brilliant letters to the newspapers in which he subtly, and not so subtly, disparaged both sides of the conflict. Under one alias, he would write a letter to a newspaper which published it, and then write a second letter using another alias criticizing the first letter and the stupidity of the newspaper for having believed and published it. At times, the aliases "would accuse each other of notorious crimes and misdemeanors."[80]

Dunham's creative mind invented an alias used during the War, Colonel George W. Margrave, who wrote letters to the newspapers and invented a report which was printed in the newspapers.[81] Dunham crafted other aliases who submitted stories about Margrave to the newspapers to solidify Margrave's existence.[82] "His use of the name Margrave may have been an

---

76. Cumming, 13.
77. Ibid, 25.
78. NARA, Turner Files, #1561, letter from C. A. Dunham to Col. L. C. Baker; ed. George Gardner Smith, *Spencer Kellogg Brown: His Life in Kansas and His Death as a Spy, 1842-1863* (New York: D. Appleton & Co., 1903), 350. Dunham helped Union spy Brown communicate with Baker.
79. Cumming.
80. Cumming, 7.
81. Ibid, 10.
82. Ibid, 72-74.

inside joke: a villain named Margrave ('master of demoniac arts, and the instigator of secret murders') showed up in a popular melodrama of the day, Edward Bulwer Lytton's *A Strange Story*."[83] When a son was born to Dunham in about 1865, he named him Margrave.[84]

Charles Dunham had no compunction about creating aliases, committing fraud or forgeries and lying before, during or after the War. Dunham's inborn affinity to commit deception was his strongest character trait. Dunham directed his own wife, alias of Mrs. Douglass, to falsely testify to the Bureau of Military Justice. By comparison the task of editing a book under an alias which contained lies, and probably adding his own to them, seemingly would not have been very disconcerting for him.

Dunham possessed the talent for quality creative writing. Carman Cumming, the author of *Devil's Game* and a professor of journalism, points out that Dunham worked "brilliantly in his journalism to craft and deploy" the frauds. Dunham on two occasions "spoke of his '*coethes scribendi*,' a deep urge to write." When Dunham was in the Albany prison, after his perjury conviction, "he admitted for a longing for pencil and paper."[85] Dunham's exploits are extensively told in *Devil's Game* and it should be read to more fully understand the talents of Dunham.

7) Author Carman Cumming was the first (to my knowledge) who was suspicious that Dunham might have been the editor of Velazquez's book, though he said that there was "no proof Dunham wrote or helped to write" it.[86] Cumming noted that Velazquez's book "touched on a remarkable number of other places in Dunham's career path, moving from New York and Baltimore to Washington and Richmond and even to Martinsburg, then on to Canada where Velazquez was assigned (as Dunham claimed he had been) to scout Johnson's Island before an attempt to free the prisoners there."[87]

Cumming's observations are keen. It can be easily believed that Dunham substituted into Velazquez's narrative his own activity, even his falsely claimed activity. During the War Dunham placed himself, truthfully or not, at these places by writing and submitting, under aliases, stories to the newspapers. Velazquez has been caught many times in lies about where she was and what she was doing; for example, she lied about the duration of her imprisonment in New Orleans, claiming several days instead of the true six months, and she omitted her arrest in Nashville. There can be no doubt that

---

83. Ibid, 13.
84. Ibid, 262.
85. Ibid, 12.
86. Ibid, 260.
87. Ibid.

Velazquez would have been appreciative of Dunham's help with the timeline and places to account for time periods which Velazquez wished to omit.

Cumming pointed out that in Velazquez's story she managed to dupe "at least three men" who were on "Dunham's hate list: Generals Winder, Butler and Colonel Baker." It has been shown that Velazquez lied about her interactions with each of the three generals. It is certainly possible that Dunham took revenge by belittling the men. Or maybe Velazquez was simply trying to excite her readership and Dunham helped.

Cumming said that Velazquez's "writing... seemed to echo Dunham's lawyerly style." This observation is accurate. Velazquez's book is free of idioms that one might expect because of her origins and education; this was due to good editing by Dunham. Dunham's letters show the same lack of idioms or idiosyncrasies. In contrast, all of Velazquez's known letters reveal astoundingly poor grammar, poor spelling, odd sentence construction and odd word usage or idioms. She credited her editor for his great contribution to the book, and rightly so. In addition, the embellishment of detail, so abundant in Velazquez's book, also is evident in Dunham's known writings.

Since there is a lack of idioms with which to compare Dunham's writings to Velazquez's book, a second-best comparison method must be used, that of regular word usage and it is not a perfect test. For this test, we are looking for similarities found in Dunham's many letters to Judge Holt, found in *Official Records (OR) of The War of the Rebellion*, Ser 2 Vol 8, pages 932-945, and *The Woman in Battle (TWIB)*.

OR, page 935, Sep 4 letter by Dunham, "The [witness]... is <u>exceedingly anxious</u> to give his testimony...." Similarly found in *TWIB*, page 61, "... for I was <u>exceedingly anxious</u> to carry out a magnificent idea I had in mind...." Also found five more times, on pages 203, 286, 305, 377 and 406.

OR, page 936, Oct 10 letter by Dunham, "... my efforts to find certain persons as witnesses for the Government have been <u>crowned with</u> complete <u>success</u>." Similarly found in *TWIB*, page 435, "...an effort that, if <u>crowned with success</u>, would bring me more credit and renown...." Also found in *TWIB*, page 452, "... I felt that if all the rest had done their duty as efficiently as I had done mine, <u>success</u> would have <u>crowned</u> our efforts" and on page 341, "final victory... would <u>crown</u> our efforts."

OR, page 940, Dec 20 letter by Dunham, "Mrs. Douglass said to him that she was opposed to her husband engaging in such a project; that it looked <u>too much like murder</u>." Similarly found in *TWIB*, page 214, "It was <u>too much like murder,</u> however, and I could not bring myself to do the deed...."

OR, page 941, Dec 20 letter by Dunham, "To recount all, or even a <u>tithe</u>, of what was said on these various occasions would occupy more time and space that I have at my disposal." Similarly found in *TWIB*, page 466, "I knew only too well how guilty they were, and I knew that Baker had ample evidence against them, although he was not informed of a tithe of the villainies they had committed."

8) In summary- The person named C. J. Worthington, editor, did not exist. He did not exist in the Union navy, sailor or officer. He did not exist as a resident of Philadelphia. He did not exist as an editor of other works prior to or after *TWIB*.

Charles A. Dunham did exist. Dunham and Velazquez were acquainted. Dunham bothered to mention her in his writings in 1863 and again in 1865.

The memoir's editor was identified as living in Philadelphia by William Ramsay of Atlanta. Dunham lived in Philadelphia, evident by the fact that he was editor and publisher of the *Philadelphia Market Journal*. The illustrator of *TWIB*, Jeremiah Rea, lived in Philadelphia. A second illustrator, E. B. Bensell also lived in Philadelphia. Velazquez left Atlanta and traveled North looking for someone to work on her book. She found Rea and Bensell in Philadelphia and ostensibly found Dunham in Philadelphia, as well. "W. J. Clarke, Jr." of Philadelphia was mentioned by Velazquez as lending assistance, but he was not her editor.

Dunham had the ability to edit her book. He knew the history of the War, intimately. Dunham's writing style is very similar to the style of *TWIB*. Dunham would not have had any compunction creating an alias editor and falsely claiming himself a navy veteran. The clever selection of the name C. J. Worthington, implying an association with well-known publisher A. D. Worthington, is nothing less than what would be expected from Dunham's creative mind, the same mind which created Margrave after which Dunham named his son.

Both Dunham and Velazquez were born pathological liars who thrived on creating falsehoods. This commonality, no doubt, was important to the successful completion of the book. An editor with scruples would have refused the project or quit it. With no scruples to hinder him, Dunham would have willingly edited the memoir.

1895, 1896, 1897 Norfolk, Philadelphia and Wilmington

William Beard seems not at Velazquez's side during her immigration schemes. William, from February 1889 to the first half of 1894, was mostly in Arizona involved in railroads and mining, and "lived for some time at Casa Grande on a ranch."[88]

Recall that when Velazquez was promoting her immigration scheme to New Bern, a newspaper said (December 1894) that she had organized her immigration company "a little over six weeks ago in Norfolk with headquarters in that city" which indicates her presence there by November. An even earlier August Arizona newspaper reported that William Beard "is

---

88. *Arizona Daily Star*, Aug 21, 1894.

now the general manager of the Norfolk, Va., Mining Exchange and is also engaged in the stock and brokerage business, and that of promoting industrial enterprises."[89]

In any case, by the end of 1894, the Beards had established themselves in Norfolk, Virginia, according to the 1895-1896 city directory. They set up a company called "Beard & Co. (William and L. J. V. Beard)" and were listed as "brokers" with office rooms 407 and 408 Columbia Building at 26 Granby Street. The business section listed "Beard & Co." under "Brokers-Stock." Their home was at 40 Highland Avenue.[90]

Besides the Arizona newspaper article, which sounds like it was submitted to the paper by Velazquez herself- "His wife, a distinguished and much accomplished lady"- no articles or advertisements which mention the couple was found in local newspapers. Nothing about their stockbroker business has been discovered, and it apparently did not flourish. The Beards may have departed Norfolk as early as September 1896 because at that time another business was occupying room 407 at the Columbia Building.[91] By 1897 the company and the couple had disappeared from the Norfolk directory.

Velazquez next is found claiming, in September 1897, residency in Philadelphia.[92] However, the Beards were not firmly established in Philadelphia because William had taken work as a wheelwright in Wilmington, Delaware (as 1901 information reveals) and Velazquez went there too. On September 17, 1897, she presented herself to the Wilmington *Evening Journal* explaining she was the "wife of Professor Beard, who has been all through the Klondike region" and she advised "Eastern people" not to put their money in placer gold mines because they soon wear out, instead put their money in gold-quartz mines.[93]

A "special telegram" from Wilmington to the *Philadelphia Times* said Mrs. William Beard of 1602 Mount Vernon Street, Philadelphia had visited the Wilmington newspapers and said she was an agent for the Columbia Mining, Trading and Transportation Company of Alaska and "employed by H. P. Bush, a mining engineer, who is now in Alaska."[94] It can easily be thought that the "special telegram," which targeted Mrs. Beard's presently claimed hometown newspaper, was sent by Mrs. Beard. She made a mess of the name of the company for which she claimed she was an agent; it was the Alaska & Klondike Gold Mining and Prospecting Company which had in

---

89. Ibid.
90. J. H. Chataigne, ed., *Chataigne Directory of Norfolk 1895-96* (Chataigne Directory Company, 1895), 101, 532, 763.
91. *Norfolk Virginian*, Sep 6, 1896.
92. *Times* (Philadelphia), Sep 19, 1897.
93. Sep 18, 1897.
94. *Times* (Philadelphia), Sep 19, 1897.

August been incorporated in New Jersey, with H. P. Bush from Bellefonte, Pennsylvania as one of the listed stockholders.[95]

Mrs. Beard may have been in earnest selling that company's stock; after all, she had just spent the last years in Norfolk claiming she was a stockbroker and Bush's company would not have been particular who was selling its stock. The company had recently, on September 5, advertised a stock offering in a Philadelphia newspaper. That advertisement offered additional information- that "our President, Mr. Bush has returned from the Yukon district, after locating four very rich claims. He will start back as soon as possible with a fully equipped party."

Recall on September 19 Mrs. Beard claimed that Bush "was now in Alaska" Well, it wasn't true. On December 9, 1897 Bush was still in the Pennsylvania, visiting his Uncle John S. Tomb, prominent millionaire lumberman, in Jersey Shore, Lycoming County.[96] It is likely that Bush found all the financing he needed for his expedition from his factually proverbial rich uncle. The newspaper explained that Bush had returned from Dawson City some months ago (another newspaper placed him in the Klondike about August 1897) and that he would return to Alaska the first part of March, departing Seattle then. He and a Philadelphian friend intended "to devote their time to relocating claims in the Canadian territory." The assertion in his stock offering, that he had staked four claims, seems supported as true.[97]

Bush did go to Alaska. He left Bellefonte by January 21, 1898, with three others accompanying him, one was ostensibly his 32-year-old cousin, George C. Tomb. Another was identified as "W. S. Hughes, a mining engineer from Philadelphia," who was noted in the stock offering as the company's treasurer. The newspaper said the party expected to arrive at their destination in April and be gone for two years.[98] By June 9, 1900 Bush was back in his hometown of Bellefonte, Pennsylvania, according to the U.S. Census and called himself a prospector.

Nothing seems to have become of Bush's Alaska company, though he was a very experienced miner.[99] Years earlier (1891 to 1897), he had worked in Columbia, South America.[100] It was after Columbia that he first went to Alaska; by September 1897 he was in Philadelphia starting his company. At this time the Alaska gold discovery was thrilling the nation and ambitious men were forming Alaskan mining companies and selling public stock.

---

95. *Trenton Evening Times*, Aug 24, 1897.
96. *Philadelphia Inquirer*, Nov 15, 1898; *Wilkes-Barre Record*, Dec 17, 1898.
97. *Columbian* (Bloomsburg, PA), Dec 9, 1897; *Philadelphia Inquirer*, Jan 22, 1898.
98. *Philadelphia Inquirer*, Jan 22, 1898.
99. U.S. Consular Registration Certificates, 190-1918.- Ancestry.com. Bush later went to Chile's mining regions, arriving there in May 1901.
100. U.S. Passport Applications, 1795-1925, 1923 passport application.- Ancestry.com

One such company was the Caribou Mining Company, formed by gas magnate J. Edwards Addicks. Velazquez claimed her own company was "hostile" to it and her company was "doing all it can to defeat the plans of the gas king." The conflict, if it in fact was real, might have been competition for purchasers of company stock or it may have been simply Velazquez seeking recognition for herself, and her misnamed company by inciting controversy with the very well-known Addicks.[101] Addicks purchased elaborate advertisements in local newspapers for several months offering company stock for sale, but by December 3, 1897, he closed the company and offered full refunds to stock purchasers. He explained, "It started in good faith, but soon a whole raft of fake companies blossomed forth and killed the business."[102]

Two days after the Wilmington *Evening Journal's* first notice of Mrs. Beard, it titled an article "She Is A Whole Mine" and wrote "Mrs. Sallie Beard" had recently stopped at the *Journal's* office.[103] Where the name Sallie came from is anyone's guess! One guess is pathological. The newspaper said she had been to the Alaska gold fields and that she "is a whole book full of knowledge about the Yukon, and relates some interesting stories of the great country and its people." It added, "She was born of French-Spanish parents, in Cuba, and has traveled extensively in India and all of the European countries." Of course, it was untrue that Velazquez had been in Alaska, much less all the countries of Europe and even less true India. She said her husband's "report of the exploration of the silver, gold and copper mines of Alaska is expected to be published." There was no gold report in the making. And that "they are traveling in this section of the country in the interest of traders" is questionable since Mr. Beard was (noted by another source) working then as a wheelwright. It seems that she alone was doing the promoting; at least she was the one seeking publicity in the newspapers.

About this time someone floated a bogus story. They claimed that "Mrs. John A. Logan would head a syndicate to build a great hotel at Dawson City." Mrs. Logan wrote a denial from her Washington, D.C. residence to the newspaper:

> Mr. William Beard: I have nothing whatever to do with any enterprise contemplating investment in Alaska or a trip to that country, and no one has authority to use my name in connection with any company or expedition of this kind.[104]

She further denied that

---

101. *Times* (Philadelphia), Sep 19, 1897.
102. *Kansas City Journal*, Dec 3, 1897.
103. *Evening Journal*, Sep 20, 1897.
104. *Daily Inter Ocean* (Chicago, Illinois), Oct 2, 1897.

she is heading an expedition of women to the Klondike region and in a most emphatic manner denounces those who have without her permission connected her name with it. She says she is constantly being made use of in this way and is tired of it.[105]

At this date Mrs. Logan was the widow of the esteemed Union army Major General John Logan who also had served as a U.S. Representative, a U.S. Senator, and a U.S. Vice-presidential candidate (failed). She was said to be the "best-known woman in the country" because anywhere there was a reunion of the Grand Army, she was honored. "Mrs. Logan has long enjoyed a great amount of distinction, both here [Philadelphia- where Velazquez might have taken note of her] and Washington and elsewhere, on account of her undeniable individuality and charm, together with her unvarying cordiality of manner."[106] The rumor generator, who smelled of Velazquez, could not have picked a more recognizable name to evoke, but Mrs. Logan's denial quickly got rid of the stink. The purpose of the bogus story is undiscovered.

1896, Myth Building

On March 29, 1896, the *Atlanta Constitution* perpetuated Velazquez's story in an article titled "From Maid to Martyr." Most notable is that the article attributed things to Velazquez which she never claimed. The article stated that she "entered the service as one of the regular volunteers" which Velazquez specifically said she avoided and did not do, except on one brief occasion when she claimed to enlist in Captain Moses' company, 21st Louisiana Regiment in order to escape New Orleans undetected. In any case, the roster of the 21st Louisiana Regiment does not support her claim. The article continued:

This is by no means a fictitious romance. The lady belonged to one of the best families of the south and after the war she published quite a handsome volume, giving a detailed account of her adventures.

If one's family lives in Cuba, does that qualify them as "one of the best families of the south"? The reporter did not explain who this "best" family was, although he implied, he knew. Clearly, the reporter did not try to validate any of Velazquez's claims.

Other newspapers continued with the business of myth creation. The *Age-Herald* (Birmingham, Alabama) on April 12, 1896, echoed the *Atlanta Constitution* with its own article under the section "Our Social World":

---

105. *Valentine Democrat* (Valentine, Nebraska), Sep 30, 1897.
106. *Philadelphia Inquirer*, Sep 26, 1897.

This courageous woman arrayed herself in masculine attire and entered the service as one of the regular volunteers. She subsequently achieved distinction for bravery and pluck....

To repeat, Velazquez plainly stated she avoided service as a regular volunteer. And in order to achieve "distinction for bravery" is it enough to claim one's own bravery?

The April 1896 edition of the *Confederate Veteran* magazine (Nashville, Tennessee) published a remembrance by B. L. Ridley, ex-military man, from Murfreesboro, Tennessee which was titled "Heroines of the South" and he gave a seemingly firsthand account (one paragraph) of Velazquez's presence during the War, "I recollect another heroine, a Lieut. Buford of an Arkansas regiment... She has written a book." Bromfield L. Ridley, who served on staff of Lieutenant-General A. P. Stewart, wrote his own book *Battle and Sketches of the Army of Tennessee* and it was published in 1906. Ridley, in his book, repeated the Velazquez paragraph, failing to add any new information. His account has the ring of credibility, but will be shown problematic when his book is again mentioned.

It is notable that in no other editions of the long-published *Confederate Veteran* magazine is there any mention of the military feats of Lieutenant Harry T. Buford or Velazquez. Hundreds of veterans sent in their war stories, covering all matters great or small. The classified ads helped veterans find one another. Yet no other person spoke of or asked about Lieutenant Harry T. Buford. Consider this. If Lieutenant Harry T. Buford had indeed assumed command of a company at Blackburn's Ford (prior to the First Battle of Bull Run) after its captain had been killed, as she claimed, it would have been a highly notable feat, especially since she claimed to have arrived on location only the day before. No doubt the men would have been amazed and wondered for years afterwards who the young stranger was who came to the aid of this unfortunate company. The grateful men would have sought-out the fill-in commander to offer thanks and praise, through this highly circulated publication.

The only other mention of Velazquez in *Confederate Veteran* was 47 years after the publication of her book. A reader, Judge Henry D. Wood of Dallas, Texas, asked fellow readers in a 1923 edition of the magazine where he could get a copy of Velazquez's book. No documentation was found to connect Judge Wood to Velazquez. He appears only to have been a curious reader.

Chapter 15

1898, the Death of William Beard

When the steamship *Portland* arrived in Seattle, Washington in mid-July 1897 with news of large Alaska gold discoveries, and a ton of shiny gold as proof, the country was electrified. The Alaska gold rush was on! One hundred thousand people from all walks of life let their exuberant optimism overwhelm their good senses and they set out for the Klondike mining area. Only about 30,000 actually arrived and mined.

Newspapers nationwide echoed with stories of the goldfields and the newspapers of Philadelphia were no different. One advertisement[1] announced that the Philadelphia and Alaska Gold Mining Syndicate had already held a "large stock sale," and the books would still be "open for a few days for those that did not get in." The ad tempted with, "This may help you get rich, and be the chance of a life time."

The gold rush news played precisely into the strengths of William Beard. By this date, Velazquez and her son were living in Philadelphia and William Beard was away working as a wheelwright in Wilmington, Delaware, though she too went there and stayed part of the time.[2] In Wilmington, Mrs. Beard had already promoted herself as an agent of a gold mining company and now Velazquez approached the newly formed Philadelphia-based North Star Mining and Developing Company of Alaska to promote her husband as the best candidate-prospector they could hire to send to Alaska.

The company's headquarters was at "513 and 514 Fidelity Mutual Building, Broad above Arch Street" and the company filed incorporation papers with the Department of State on September 14 in Camden, New Jersey. One hundred thousand shares at one dollar each were authorized and it commenced with a thousand-dollar reserve. North Star Mining advertised, "A chance to own a part of the Klondike riches, this will pay you to investigate, as only enough shares will be sold to enable the Company to transact a safe investment."[3]

It seems that Beard did not invest his own money in company stock, as he probably had no money, indicated by his employment as a wheelwright. It will later be revealed that Dr. Hancock of the North Star Company provided the money for the prospecting expedition. It can be assumed that Beard was promised shares in exchanged for his expertise. The Company wasted no time in sending their mining expert, William Beard, to Alaska; he departed Philadelphia on December 17, 1897.[4]

William Beard came from a family of miners. His father was listed as an "Iron Mine Agent" in the 1851 Cornwall, England census and his brother, Thomas, called himself a "Mining Expert and Real Estate Agent" in a letter

---

1. *Philadelphia Inquirer*, Jul 30, 1897.
2. *Times* (Phila., Penn.), Nov 21, 1901; *Morning News* (Wilmington, Del.), Oct 17, 1898.
3. *Philadelphia Inquirer*, Sep 26, 1897.
4. *Philadelphia Ledger*, Jul 16, 1898.

written in Ironton, Massachusetts on January 26, 1890. William referred to himself as a "mining engineer." The newspapers called him "a mining expert," "Professor" and even "Doctor," but no found evidence confirms a formal education backing those titles. In any case, he had a lifetime of experience and was no doubt very capable.

Beard left Seattle, bound for Port Valdez, Copper River, Alaska, aboard the steamer *Alliance* on January 3, 1898, along with sixty-nine fellow passengers. He was among the first-class passengers which numbered thirty-five. The *Seattle Post-Intelligencer* stated, "William Beard represents an Eastern syndicate and claims that 200 men are coming in the spring."[5] Surely that was a true statement providing Beard found a profitable mining claim.

Steamer *Alliance* landed its passengers six miles from their intended destination of Valdez because frozen sea ice blocked the vessel; the remaining distance had to be traversed on foot. Beard formed a working relationship with another first-class passenger, H. C. Watkins. It was imperative to work together in order to sleigh supplies across the wide ice pack of the frozen bay. No sooner had the men started the difficult task when a snow storm hit. The wind howled the entire day and at 2 pm, with the snow "like small pieces of ice," the men were plunged into total darkness. The blowing snow obliterated their trail; they groped and crawled along for two hours exhausting themselves, "shouting at intervals to attract attention of those in camp." Their cries were finally heard by the men in camp, but were unable to discern the direction of the cries and a search was fruitless. Beard and Watkins had laid down in the snow, ready to surrender to the beautiful sensation of exhausted sleep, knowing they would freeze to death when two rescuers wearing snowshoes and carrying lanterns found them.

Although saved, the storm lasted ten days and the men had other difficulties to overcome. They had to dig down ten feet into the snow in order to protect the tent from being ripped up by the wind. The excavation of the tent area left the men suffering "all kinds of aches."

Beard and Watkins sent a letter detailing their near demise to the *Seattle Post-Intelligencer* which published parts of the letter on March 26, 1898. The headline read: "Rescued from a Blizzard, Narrow Escape of Watkins and Beard at Valdez, They had lain down to die." Watkins was identified as a New York newspaper man and as a broker by the newspapers, but he was neither and had a dark past which will be revealed. Now Beard and Watkins reassured their readers that having survived their test, they are "pretty well hardened, feeling well and can eat almost anything, even porcupine." They were optimistic that once they got "across the glacier [they] expect[ed] to have plenty of game." They were now crossing an inland glacier.

---

5. Jan 4, 1898.

Optimism for a successful expedition was soon dashed with the first public notice of Beard's death. The July 14, 1898 headlines of the *Seattle Post-Intelligencer* heralded: "Smothered in Snow, Tragic Fate of Dr. William Beard of Philadelphia, Buried in a Deadly Slide."

Mr. H. C. Watkins had written the news to a Seattle friend, but had asked that the news be "kept quiet." This request was probably to allow time for a similar letter bearing the news to reach addressed parties in Philadelphia.

Velazquez must have learned (before the newspaper story) of Beard's death from the President of the North Star mining venture, Dr. Hancock, who said he received a letter in "early June" from one of Beard's companions who had dated the letter May 10 from Valdez.

On June 19, 1898 Velazquez wrote a letter to United States President McKinley asking him to ascertain the cause of Mr. Beard's death. The White House tasked the Department of Interior to look into Velazquez's appeal which then, in a letter,[6] requested Alaska Governor John Brady to investigate. Governor Brady answered[7] that he would investigate to the best of his ability, but was a little hampered because he had "no independent means of transportation." The results of Governor Brady's investigation will be presented momentarily.

Upon receipt of news in Philadelphia of Mr. Beard's death, Mrs. Beard "believed that [Beard] had been murdered, as he had a large amount of money in his possession" and she immediately wrote to Mr. DeLorme Harbaugh of the Rainer-Grand Hotel in Seattle seeking information and expressed her suspicions. Mrs. Beard knew that William Beard and H. C. Watkins had stayed at the Grand while in Seattle. The newspaper explained, "When Mrs. Beard's suspicions of murder were given out, however, Watkins' friend decided to make public the letter."

Watkins' letter contained the details of Beard's death which the *Seattle Post-Intelligencer* now published. The next day, July 15, 1898, the *Philadelphia Inquirer* also published the details of Beard's death. The newspaper said that Velazquez was "completely prostrated by the news" and that "she is a member of the well-known Spanish American family of Velasquez, who possessed large estates in Louisiana before the war." Notably, in the middle of the crisis, Velazquez was still telling falsehoods to newspapers. In her book, Velazquez claimed her father's estate was in Texas, and later had another one in Cuba, which, in any case, also were false. In prior newspaper interviews she did claim her family settled in St. James Parish, Louisiana, (which, of course, contradicts her book), but she never claimed her family possessed "large estates in Louisiana," and now at this late date, how can this new claim be true or believed?

---

6. Jun 25.
7. Jul 16.

No wealthy Velazquez family existed in Louisiana at that date, "before the war." The 1860 Census shows one family named "Velasquez" in the entire state of Louisiana and that was in New Orleans. The family was headed by a woman with three young daughters, but none of these too young females could have been Velazquez. There was no "Velazquez," at all, in the 1860 Census. Suppose for a moment that her family did have "large estates in Louisiana before the war," which, of course, indicates a family of great wealth and surely known to the history and records of the State and is not, then why would Velazquez have been at Nelly Bremer's New Orleans whorehouse when money could not have been her motivator for being there?

The details of the several accounts of Beard's death did not corroborate one another. This disturbing discrepancy triggered Mrs. Beard's suspicion of murder. The President of North Star Mining, Dr. Hancock, said, "there are things in connection with the Professor's death that need clearing up."

The *Seattle Post-Intelligencer* (July 14, 1898) gave an account:

The two men, according to the letter, had a terrible time crossing the Valdes glacier. Dr. Beard was greatly troubled with rheumatism, and was compelled to lie in his tent for days at a time. This pulled him down greatly in health. The first of May found the two men on a mountain 5,000 feet high, with their outfit scattered along the trail. One of the terrible snow blizzards common to that season of the year swopped down on them, having no timber for a fire, the two men started back to the timber line. It seemed their only chance for life, according to Watkins.

A small snow slide came down the mountain and caught Beard in its smothering grasp. It passed on and Watkins escaped uninjured. For ten days he struggled around through the drifts day and night. The nights were bitter cold and it snowed continually. He had to keep moving for fear he would freeze to death. During this time he subsisted on raw bacon, uncooked rice and rolled oats, minced with snow. At last he struck the trail leading back to Valdes, and landed there without a cent. He wrote to friends here for money on which to come back to Seattle.

A suspiciously different account was given by the *Philadelphia Inquirer* (July 15, 1898):

The writer stated that on the morning of April 27, Mr. Beard started out from camp ahead of the rest of the party in order to mark the trail which they were to follow. Shortly after he left camp a heavy snowstorm came on during which they lost sight of him. When the storm abated somewhat they proceeded in the direction in which he had disappeared but could find no trace of him. Their path led them directly onto the glacier which was full of wide crevasses covered with drifted snow. Their belief is that the Professor fell into one of these and was lost, a belief which was strengthened by the circumstances attending another of the party, who almost met the same fate, and would probably have perished had it not been for the assistance rendered him by his companions.

In addition, the *Philadelphia Inquirer* further explained that Dr. Hancock had received a letter from Beard in which he had written that he had three companions. But in contradiction, the *Seattle Post-Intelligencer's* version of Beard's death stated that Watkins was Beard's only companion. The simple explanation is that Dr. Beard had expanded his party and later information makes this clear. The circumstance of Beard's death was not clear to Dr. Hancock which prompted him to pose a question upon the occasion of him speaking to the *Philadelphia Inquirer:*

There is one thing about the story which puzzles me. Mr. Beard was lost on April 27. According to one of the letters the party remained eight days on the ground in the hope that some trace of him could be found. They then started back for Valdes about May 5. Another letter I received is dated May 10. How is it possible that the men could traverse in five days the trail which it had taken them all of six weeks prior to cover with the assistance of an expert in ice traveling, such as Mr. Beard was? According to our calculation the Professor must have had about $500 in his pocket at the time he met his death. He left Philadelphia with $1500 in his possession.

Dr. Hancock's question might be answered thus: The outbound men were moving tons of supplies uphill along the trail by stages, an arduous and slow task. The retreating men carried only sufficient supplies to make it back to Valdez, either abandoning the rest of their equipment, or more certainly, selling it to one of the groups of men on the same trail bound for the Copper River. In any case, Dr. Hancock was diligent in his search for the facts, which must have been frustrating because of conflicting information, such as the letter he received on July 18 from J. A. Ward, an engineer from Seattle, which stated that "Beard was seen alive north of Valdes Glacier in the latter part of May, a month after his reported death."[8]

It seems that all of the opinions of those close to the expedition or Copper City (now Valdez) thought the death was an accident. Captain Abercrombie, who was in command of the U.S. Army Regulars at Valdez, declared that "the explorer came to his death accidentally."[9] Dr. Hancock stated that Postmaster Allen of Valdez, through a letter, had informed him "that he had a talk with the men, and that their story was the same" as to the fate of Beard.[10] The people who Watkins and Beard befriended in Seattle during their stopover there were "positive that the unfortunate expert was not murdered."

But Velazquez was positive it was murder. The *San Francisco Chronicle* of July 14, 1898 said, "she is alone in this belief." The *Philadelphia Ledger* of July 16 stated that she "entertains a strong belief that her husband was

---

8. *Philadelphia Record,* Jul 19, 1898, titled "THINK BEARD IS ALIVE."
9. *Phildelphia Inquirer,* Jul 31, 1898.
10. Ibid, Jul 15, 1898.

murdered" and that "he had $685" remaining in his possession of the initial $1500 travel money. The newspaper added, "Her suspicions are confirmed, she says, by contradictory accounts regarding the manner of his death."

When Mr. Watkins arrived in Seattle on July 22 from Alaska, aboard the steamer *Al-Ki*, he gave an explanation of William's death to the newspaper which reported:[11]

> A party of four men, including Professor Beard and myself, were traveling on the other side of the river divide on April 29 last. Professor Beard started ahead of the party to investigate and make a trail. We saw him go up the valley for almost a mile to a point where the valley turned. We followed with our sleds as fast as we could, and found that he had turned into another valley. It had begun snowing, and we decided to make camp at the turn. I followed up the other valley for a short distance, but Beard's trail had been obliterated by the snow.
>
> All that night we waited for Beard, expecting him to come back at any time. He did not return, so we started out after him as soon as it was light. We went to the head of the valley, which was about two miles long, and there found a small glacier. It extended across the valley, and one might come on it in a snowstorm without noticing. F. L. Hildreth,[12] who was one of our party, slipped and all but went into a big crevasse. He saved himself by catching his foot in a small hole. This showed us how Professor Beard probably came to his death.

Mrs. Beard departed Philadelphia to the West Coast sometime after July 22. Her presence in Seattle, Washington on August 6 is made clear by the *Seattle Post-Intelligencer*:[13]

> Mrs. William Beard of Philadelphia, is numbered among the guests of the Rainier-Grand hotel. The object of her visit to Seattle is to learn, if possible, additional information regarding the death of her husband, which is known to have occurred in the Copper river country. Mrs. Beard firmly believes that her husband was murdered for his money, and emphatically declares that the one object of her life will be run down the assassins. She has asked for and has been given the assistance of the government, and President McKinley and Secretary Bliss, of the interior department. The heartbroken widow stated to a Post-Intelligencer reporter yesterday that government officials at Washington had promised to send special emissaries to the Copper river country to investigate her husband's death, and it was possible that she would go to Alaska while making the exhaustive investigation undertaken.
>
> To the reporter Mrs. Beard said; "According to the information I have received I cannot believe that my husband died a natural death. It has been reported to me that he either perished in a snowstorm or was lost in a glacier, but these reports sound absurd. When my husband left Seattle for the Copper river country he was

---

11. *Philadelphia Record*, Jul 31, 1898 repeating the *Seattle Post Intelligencer*, Jul 23.
12. Hildreth traveled to Valdez by steamer *Alliance*, as did W. Beard. Source- *Seattle Post Intelligencer*, Jan 4, 1898.
13. Aug 7, 1898.

known to have over $2,800 in his possession. I believe he was made the victim of a conspiracy, and that he was murdered for the money he had when he left here."

"It is not my desire to do a single person injury, and I will refrain from making statements which would reflect on any person. I now have information which will greatly assist me in prosecuting my investigation, and I actually believe that I shall be able to fasten the crime on the guilty people before I leave this part of the country. While in Seattle I shall also look after the effects which my husband left here, and shall also make a formal demand for that part of his belongings which were taken from Port Valdes, where it is said he was buried. I have been told that the body was buried in some gravel, and I have also been informed that the body was never recovered. Since coming to Seattle I have retained the services of a prominent attorney, and shall spare no expense or energy in having my interests properly cared for. I was accompanied to Seattle by my young son, and it is our intention to remain here until such time as the murderers of a dutiful father and a loving husband are avenged."

"Mr. Beard was in Alaska in the early fifties, was familiar with the country, and was under instructions to make a survey for a railroad to be built from Prince William Sound to the Yukon country. He was also interested in the North Star Mining and Development Company, of Philadelphia."

While telling her story Mrs. Beard broke into tears on several occasions. The lines of pain, grief and suffering in Mrs. Beard's face plainly indicate that she is laboring under great strain, and has endured much since receiving the sad message from Copper river.

Also reporting from Seattle was the *San Francisco Chronicle* (August 10, 1898) which added, Mrs. Beard "claims to have received a letter from Valdes that he was killed with the butt of a revolver." It further asserted that Velazquez claimed "to have financial help of President McKinley" and that she was "assisted by the Masonic order, of which her husband was a member." It is unlikely McKinley provided financial help, but it seems possible the Masonic order helped her out. She must have had some money in reserve upon which to live while her husband was away on the expedition and, as will be seen, "Mrs. Beard was furnished money to go to Alaska and investigate," said Dr. Hancock in November 1901.

On July 28, a half-dozen North Star Mining officers met at Dr. Hancock's house to consider the facts known of Beard's death and to discuss how to proceed with their mining venture. Although most of the men did not doubt that Beard had died, two members thought he might still be alive. The men conceded that it would do no good to send out another man to investigate the matter and "felt disposed to accept the story of the accident as first received." The men agreed to continue the company until November to wait to see if further information emerged. The members agreed that the various land officers in Alaska should be contacted to determine if Beard had staked any claims, and if so, then Dr. Hancock's brother-in-law, William Wilkins would be sent to Alaska.[14]

Accomplishing little in Seattle, Velazquez left and went to San Francisco arriving no later than September 14 to continue her investigation, that Beard "was murdered by his associates for the money that he carried." She booked a room at the Brooklyn Hotel.[15]

In the meantime, Alaska Governor Brady submitted the results of his investigation to the Assistant Secretary Thomas R. Ryan at the Department of Interior by a letter dated August 4. Brady explained he had spoken to Dr. Allen, the same aforementioned Postmaster, and Brady was "convinced that there was no foul play." Furthermore, Brady wrote, "Dr. Allen is thoroughly acquainted with the case and he has also investigated it; and he states that the man was lost in a very severe snow storm, and his body could not be recovered." Governor Brady noted, "The personal effects of Mr. Beard are in the charge of Capt. Abercrombie."

Following the Governor's conclusion, the Secretary Cornelius Bliss of the Department of Interior replied in an August 23 letter to Mrs. Beard, at 2428 North 20th Street in Philadelphia:

> In further reply to your letter of the 19th of June... requesting the aid of the United States authorities in determining the cause of death of your late husband, Professor William Beard, whom you believe to have been murdered near Valdes... I transmit herewith for your information a copy of a letter from the Governor of Alaska in which he states that Professor Beard was lost in a severe snow storm and his body could not be recovered.

Of course, Velazquez was not in Philadelphia to receive the letter, but it was probably forwarded to her if she made her address known to Dr. Hancock.

While Velazquez was staying at the Brooklyn Hotel in San Francisco, she wrote another letter to President McKinley.[16] The President's private secretary Mr. John Addison Porter, on September 26, responded to Mrs. William Beard, writing, "Dear Madam... your letter of the 18th instant" was received and "its contents have been noted." Her letter to date has not been found, so the exact nature of this letter is unknown.[17]

There were conflicting reports as to whether William Beard's body was recovered. The *Seattle Post-Intelligencer* of July 14, 1898 stated, "From another source it is learned that Beard's body was recovered and taken to Valdes on a sled, where it was buried." But Velazquez wrote a letter (dated August 10, Seattle) telling of Beard's death to Mr. Samuel Hughes, a merchant in

---

14. *Philadelphia Inquirer*, Jul 31, 1898.
15. Ibid, Sep 15, 1898 (dateline San Francisco, Sep 14); *San Francisco Chronicle*, Sep 18, 1898.
16. Sept 18. The letter's return address was the Brooklyn Hotel in San Francisco.
17. Wm McKinley Papers, MS Div., LOC, Off. Ltr. Book, Sep 16, 1898 to Oct 1, 1898.

Tucson and a mining investor, and apparently an old friend of Beard's, in which she stated that "no attempt has yet been made to recover the body."[18]

Velazquez's presence is next noted in Los Angeles by the *Los Angeles Herald* of October 6, 1898 in the "Personal" column: "Mrs. Wm Beard and son arrived yesterday from Sitka, Alaska, where Mrs. Beard's husband was recently murdered."

It was only the week before, on September 30, when the *San Diego Union* published an American Press Association article titled, "Women as Soldiers," in which, Velazquez was given a paragraph and her image (dressed as a woman) from her book was reproduced. The appearance of the article in a California newspaper seems to be merely a coincidence with the fact that she was then in California, since the article was too broad in its scope and did not singularly highlight Velazquez.

Velazquez was interviewed shortly after her arrival in Los Angeles which resulted in a long October 14 *Herald* article in which she asserted that Beard's body was finally found. The wordy headline seems a veiled reference to her book:

BEARD IS FOUND/ Wife Of The Scientist Says He Was Murdered/ BRAVE WOMAN'S BATTLE/ Searching For Proof To Convict The Slayer/ HER SEARCH FOR HIS REMAINS/ A Snow Blind Companion Now in the County was Left in the Tent When Beard Started.

There arrived in this city yesterday, after months of fruitless search amid the snow and ice of Prince William's Sound country, in Alaska, Mrs. Valasquez-Beard [*sic*], the wife of Prof. William Beard, the eminent geologists, scientist and mining expert, who went to the gold fields with a party from New York in 1897, and who was reported to have been buried beneath a snow slide on the Valdes glacier.

From her own research Mrs. Beard believes her husband was foully murdered and she claims to have proof which substantiates her claim. Her coming to this coast at this time is to arrange for the settlement of her husband's mining interests and to arrange for the bringing out of the frozen vastness of Alaska his body.

Mrs. Beard says that the place where her husband's body was found, which was discovered, after she had left Alaska, completely disproves the story of his death as told by the only man with him when he perished, which man returned in safety to camp.

The following from the *Philadelphia Herald*, where Prof. Beard lived with his wife and boy before starting to Alaska, tells the story of his venture and the news first received of his death. That paper says:

"Prof. Beard left this city in December last to explore Northwest Alaska and penetrate to the Yukon river in the interests of the North Star Mining company of this city, of which Dr. Joseph Hancock is president. It was the intention of Prof.

---

18. *Arizona Daily Citizen* (Tucson), Aug 16, 1898. A search of the "Samuel Hughes Papers, 1861-1951" archived at the Arizona Historical Society Library and Archives failed to find a letter from Mrs. Beard.

Beard to explore the southern part of Alaska before going further north into the Yukon river district, where he was to examine the gold and copper mines controlled by the Philadelphia syndicate.

Arriving at Seattle, Washington, in April, Prof. Beard was joined by three companions, among them H. C. Watkins, a former New York broker, and the party shortly afterward made the start north. When they had traveled into the midst of the Valdes glacier, an eight days' snow storm prevented their progress. After the storm ceased, Prof. Beard, according to a letter received from Watkins, went ahead to explore the route, and was found underneath a snow slide. The rest of the party, subsisting on scant food supplies, waited his return for over a week, and finally reached Valdes half-starved.

Another version of Prof. Beard's death, telegraphed from the police authorities at Seattle, states that Watkins and his party returned without Beard, and they have been detained to await developments. Prof. Beard's body, it is reported by the dispatches, has been recovered.

Prof. Beard was born in Wales in 1836, and was from a family of iron operators and mine owners. He was a great traveler and after leaving college explored Africa and Oriental countries. From 1857 to 1861 Prof. Beard traveled through Alaska and Oregon and afterward controlled a large silver mine in Oregon. Prof. Beard organized the North Star Mining company in this city last year."[19]

"It was with the sole intention of recovering my husband's body," said Prof. Beard's widow yesterday, "that I went to Alaska. Dr. Hancock, president of the company, and I were both suspicious of the story of his death, but you know how things get garbled from a far-away country like that and I made up my mind to learn the truth."

"As the clipping given you says, H. C. Watkins, a New York broker and one, not two others were with my husband in camp the day he met his death. The other man besides Watkins is in this county now and was left snow blind, in the tent, when Watkins and my husband went out that fatal day."

"On my arrival in Alaska I found my work almost impossible for a woman to accomplish. Fortunately I am well known in Washington and not only President McKinley but others high in official circles, aided me. This is what I learned:"

"My husband and Watkins left the tent together to mark out the trail after, not during the storm, and left their snow-blind companion in the tent. How far the men went only God and Watkins know and what happened only the Great Father and the man who returned alone to the tent know. This I know:"

"When my husband left the tent he had on his person $2300 in money and gold dust. He was an old and experienced traveler in Alaska and knew its dangers.

The other man was a penniless greenhorn, so far as Alaska was concerned, and yet he returned to the tent, well and hearty and later on wore my husband's clothes and shoes into an Alaskan hotel when he reached semi-civilization."

"When my husband's body was found there was not a penny on it and it lay six miles away from any glacier and six miles away from any possible snowslide. It was buried where found and when the snows melt we will bring it home. Whether or

---

19. This rendition also was found in the *Philadelphia Record*, Jul 15, 1898.

not the poor body of one of the bravest and best men that ever lived will aid Dr. Hancock and myself in having justice done I do not know but I believe that the God of the widow and the orphans will aid me to bring the truth to light."

Mrs. Beard was Miss Velasquez [*sic*] of New Orleans, well and favorably known throughout the South during the rebellion for the work she did for the starving Confederate soldiers. As a young woman she became an heiress to great sugar plantations in Cuba- where by the way, she was born- and in Louisiana and Mississippi. The war stripped her of her fortunes and she went to Washington where she met and married Prof. Beard.

It is probable Mrs. Beard, who is at the Baltimore [Hotel], will remain in this city until the date of her return to Alaska, as she has large mining interests left herself and son in this state, Mexico and Arizona.

Velazquez was correct to suspect H. C. Watkins of foul play. Newspapers earlier had identified Harry C. Watkins, an alias, by his true name, Harry C. Wiltshaw. He was English-born and this may have endeared him to Beard, thus their partnership. Wiltshaw had worked in New York at the United States National Bank for eight years, almost from the bank's inception, starting at clerk, working his way to bookkeeper. In 1888 he started embezzling and on November 14, 1891, he "left the bank hurriedly in his thin alpaca office coat" and disappeared. (Another report states he left in August.) A subsequent investigation revealed he had taken $32,072.94.[20] He hid in rather plain sight, using his alias, until March 3, 1894 when he was arrested in Buffalo, New York by a U.S. Marshal. Watkins at first denied his identity, until his trunk was searched and his identity proven. The man was five feet five inches, 120 pounds, a 28-year-old blond, though looked younger, with a slight mustache. He was sent back to New York City and held on $20,000 bail.[21] On March 14 he pleaded guilty and was sent to Erie County Penitentiary for five years.[22] It appears he received a reduced sentence, was released, then put a lot of miles between the penitentiary and himself, showing up in Alaska in January 1898.

Watkins was a convicted thief, but it cannot be proven at this distant date that he was a murderer, as Mrs. Beard then was insinuating. It can be believed, Watkins would have emptied the pockets of an already dead Mr. Beard, if the opportunity arose.

A quick visit of the falsehoods contained in the article is in order before raising a significant question and answering it.

First, it is curious that the reporter did not mention Velazquez's book which detailed her war adventures, but only referenced Velazquez's "work

---

20. *Sun* (New York), Apr 24, 1892; *New-York Tribune*, Mar 6, 1894; *Utica Weekly Herald* (New York), Apr 19, 1892.
21. *New-York Tribune*, Mar 6, 1894; *World* (New York), Mar 9, 1894.
22. *New-York Tribune*, Mar 15, 1894; *Sun* (New York), Mar 31, 1894.

she did for the starving Confederate soldiers" which Velazquez never claimed to do in her book.

Second, Velazquez stated that "As a young woman she became an heiress to great sugar plantations in Cuba- where by the way, she was born- and in Louisiana and Mississippi. The war stripped her of her fortunes...." In her book she did not claim plantations in Louisiana and Mississippi. She did say that her father inherited a "valuable estate" in Cuba, but she did not claim that she in turn inherited it. In fact, recall she claimed her father disowned her for eloping with "William." And if she had inherited the plantation, the war would not have "stripped her of her fortunes," as commerce was booming in Cuba during the War so she would have profited even further. Indeed, if she had owned plantations in Louisiana and Mississippi, she would have lost them, but she didn't. It was simply untrue that she inherited anything.

Third, she did not go to "Washington where she met and married Prof. Beard." She married him in New York.

Fourth, it was stated that Mrs. Beard had "large mining interests left herself and son in [California], Mexico and Arizona." Surely, she had no such mining interests and if she did, the mines failed to provide her an income, evident by her lack of money at this time and afterwards. Recall, Velazquez just said she got "financial help of President McKinley" and from "the Masonic order" to enable her to search for her husband. Also Dr. Hancock said (in 1901) he had to give her travel money. It is absurd that Velazquez had "large mining interests," yet had no money!

Fifth, Velazquez stated, "When my husband left the tent he had on his person $2300 in money and gold dust." In contradiction, Dr. Hancock stated, "According to our calculation the Professor must have had about $500 in his pocket at the time he met his death. He left Philadelphia with $1500 in his possession." Even Velazquez stated earlier that Beard left Philadelphia with $1500, so how is it possible that he now had $2300 remaining after having paid substantial travel costs? And how is it possible that Beard had gold dust when he had yet to arrive at the mining district to extract any? Arguably he could have purchased the gold dust while on the trail and written Velazquez about it.

The article stated, "Mrs. Beard says that the place where her husband's body was found, which was discovered, after she had left Alaska completely disproves the story of his death...." How could she have learned this news if she had been on board a boat in transit to Los Angeles from Alaska?

The significant question is: Did she really go to Alaska at all? The quick answer is, no. Please follow the evidence. She was identified as having arrived in Seattle, from the east, on August 9. The newspaper, at that time, did not report she was heading to Alaska. She then was identified on

September 14 in San Francisco as "having come from Seattle." Note that the article did not state that she had been in Alaska. Her September 18 letter to the President McKinley still places her in San Francisco.

On October 6 she was reported just arrived in Los Angeles, having come from Alaska "after months of fruitless search amid the snow and ice of Prince William's Sound country." If it is accepted that she did not go to Alaska from Seattle, then she must have gone from San Francisco. In that case, the only time frame in which she could have gone was from September 18 to October 6, a window of 19 days, which certainly isn't "months." This would have necessitated departing from San Francisco and backtracking to Seattle from which she had just come, since all the passengers from San Francisco to Alaska changed steamers in either Seattle or Portland. It took four days by steamer from San Francisco to Seattle, some 920 statute miles.[23] The distance from Seattle to Sitka, where she claimed she had just departed, is about 1500 statute miles which would have taken the boat about six and a half days. So, a round-trip from San Francisco to Sitka took about twenty-one days. But Valdez is farther away still by some 551 statute miles (479 nautical miles) from Sitka, which would add another four days round trip. Clearly, with a time window of only 19 days she could not have done something which would have taken her a minimum of 25 days. It was positively a lie that she spent "months" in Alaska in a fruitless search.[24]

In a little confusion the *San Francisco Chronicle* of October 15, 1898 reported (with a dateline of Los Angeles, October 14), "She is preparing to start for a trip into Alaska." Some papers repeated the same erroneous detail, but others stated that she had just returned, as was made clear by the aforementioned *Los Angeles Herald* article.

Two years and two months later, in an interview with the *Atlanta Constitution* of December 27, 1900, Velazquez still maintained that Beard was murdered, but did not mention if his body had been recovered and properly buried.

It can be assumed that she never saw her husband's body and that he was buried in Alaska, though no discovered burial record reveals this. The expense and difficulty of returning his body to Philadelphia was prohibitive and besides there was no news of his return and funeral.

Velazquez stated that one of the men who had been with her husband was "in this county" and that was the reason she visited Los Angeles, to question him about the death and to see what happened to the money. If the money had been taken by him, it most likely was spent, but recall

---

23. F. W. Allen, ed., *Traveler's Official Railway Guide*, 31st Year No. 3 (New York: National Railway Publication Co., Aug 1898), 542. This book contains steamship information, in addition to railway information.
24. *Distance Between United States Ports*, 12th Ed. (Wash., DC: Dept. of Comm., NOAA, 2012).

Governor Brady wrote, "The personal effects of Mr. Beard are in the charge of Capt. Abercrombie." It is unknown if she recovered the money, but it can be certain that Velazquez persevered (and rightfully so) until she got it.

The North Star Mining and Developing Company of Alaska met its end as well. The company was listed in state records as "Charter no longer in force" by 1902, but it was probably defunct by the end of 1899.

The tragedy of Beard's death brought forth in the press[25] the name of their son, who may have gone otherwise unnoted, "Professor Beard… leaves a wife and a 10 year-old boy, Waldemar, both of whom reside at 1939 North Twentieth Street."[26] It is clear that when Velazquez left Philadelphia in search of her husband, she took along her son. The *San Francisco Chronicle* [27] stated that she was in the city "stopping at the Brooklyn Hotel, having come from Seattle with her son, Waldemar" and again the *Los Angeles Herald* [28] noted her son with her. She will have her son in tow for the next two and a half years.

1899, Fans of the Legend

Upon Velazquez's October 1898 arrival in Los Angeles, she seemingly found it to her liking and/or was in need of an income and established a business. She was listed under "Brokers- Mining" (among some 50 mining brokers) in the *Directory of the City of Los Angeles* for 1899 as "Beard, L. J. V. Mrs., 600 Frost Bldg." In addition, she was listed under "Real Estate Agents and Dealers" with the same name and address. The double listing is understandable since the sale of a mine would likely include the sale of the land. She, no doubt, sold land without mines, as well.[29]

One Miss Emma Brophy, on December 11, 1898, found employment as a stenographer and typist in the same office room with Velazquez, who purportedly handled the mining business portion for real estate man, S. P. Creasinger, who occupied a distinct room.

When the troubled Miss Emma was not paid on payday, Velazquez reassured her that Creasinger would pay, since he was her employer, and that Velazquez would have a word with him. After two months and eight days of work and receiving no pay, only excuses, Miss Emma questioned Creasinger and he explained he had not hired her.

---

25. *Philadelphia Inquirer*, Jul 15, 1898.
26. This Philadelphia address was a room-for-rent and not a permanent residence. Only the month prior, on June 19, 1898, when Velazquez wrote to President McKinley, her return address was 2428 N. 20th Street which was a boarding house. Source- *Philadelphia City Directory*.
27. Sep 18, 1898.
28. Oct 6, 1898.
29. *1899 Classified Business Directory of the City of Los Angeles* (Los Angeles Directory Co., 1899), 1018, 1120.

Miss Emma took Velazquez and Creasinger to court to recover her $85.50 pay due. Justice James found fault only with Velazquez who was ordered to pay Miss Emma.[30]

Mrs. Beard must have made herself and her history known to someone in town. The Eclectic Book Store (corner of Main and Second streets) placed a request in the "Books Wanted" section of the *Publisher's Weekly*,[31] along with its other requested books, for "Woman in Battle, by L. J. V. Beard." The requester apparently had some knowledge of Mrs. Beard and her connection to the book, but had not learned under which name the book had been published many years before.

Book stores, newspapers and the public rarely made the connection between the woman and the legend. Journalists emerged from time to time repeating the legend. One writer, Robert Adamson, gushed, "This story here, a lost epic of the south, I rescued the other day from a ponderous old scrapbook in Columbia College." His huge article was printed in the *Atlanta Constitution*, January 22, 1899, under the title, "The Joan of Arc of the Confederacy, Thrilling Story of a Young Woman's Active, Daredevil Service as Spy and Soldier for the South, as Told in Journals Many Years Ago."

Adamson wrote:

To forestall the impression sure to form in the minds of those who read it to the end, let it be said here that it is not fiction. I took it from the files of newspapers, serious-minded, laconic dailies published at a time when newspapers were not sensational...

and adding that the news of that time was sensational enough without trying to make it startling. Although "conservative editors of her time" had attributed to her, beauty, Adamson supposed that the "heroine" was even "more beautiful":

Clear of eye, sure and clean of limb, superb in height and shapeliness, with the rich coloring of a perfectly healthy woman who is much out of doors, she enraptured the vision, as the eye of the artist is enraptured by a glorious sunset or a majestic landscape. ... How grand a picture she must have made in her saddle, cheeks aflush, eyes asparkle, her whole face aglow with youth, innocence, enthusiasm and beauty.

The "ponderous old scrapbook" obviously did not follow Velazquez through to the publication of her book, so Adamson did not know of her book. Had he read her book and then compared the newspaper clippings he had before him, he might have tempered his adoration and added a touch of skepticism upon seeing the obvious contradictions. The several newspaper clippings from which he worked were from her tour through

---

30. *The Los Angeles Times*, Mar 18, 1899.
31. Mar 25, 1899.

Atlanta, Augusta and Savannah in May and June of 1866, when she was trying to sell subscriptions to the three books she claimed to be writing: "The Cruise of the Shenandoah," "A Personal History of the War" and "Poems of Buford."

Adamson lamented, "Where are the books and where is the author?" He searched Columbia College literary volumes "for some further trace of her. Not a line. Who was she? Whence did she come?" And of the books which Adamson thought Velazquez succeeded in writing, he said he would especially like to read the "Buford's poems." He concluded:

> I suppose they are lost to literature just as their writer's story seems lost to history. Perished, perhaps, those books, and gone the author these many years from the sight of editors and men.

Two years later, "Mrs. L. J. Velasquez Beard of Arizona" trod the same ground as Adamson, when she was interviewed by the *Atlanta Constitution* (presented shortly). It can be certain that Robert Adamson failed to recognize the connection between the real woman, "Mrs. L. J. Velasquez Beard of Arizona," and the legend he found in the newspapers.

Adamson triggered another journalist[32] to help fill-in the gaps which Adamson had left. Helen Gray explained that she had more information on this heroine because she had found a copy of Velazquez's autobiography "last summer upon the dusty shelf of a second-hand book store... which enables me to tell more minutely the thrilling story of this beautiful woman."

Gray's article was titled "Sensational Story of Confederacy's Joan of Arc, as Told by Herself in her Thrilling, Well-Written Life." Gray, possibly trying to more accurately define Velazquez's beauty upon which Adamson had lavished praised, stated, "The editor of Mistress Loreta's book... informs us... that 'she has more than the average of good looks....'" Other than this, Gray did nothing to point out the contradictions that should have been apparent to her when she compared Adamson's article to Velazquez's book which Gray implied she read. Unfortunately, Helen Gray succeeded only in providing a synopsis of the book, emphasizing its adventure and romance, and even then, Gray doesn't repeat some details correctly as Velazquez wrote them.

Gray concluded by asking, "Where is she? Is she among the living or the dead?" and acknowledged that "someone else must answer" these questions. She wondered if Velazquez had returned to Cuba to join the freedom fighters to end Spain's colonial rule, and "were her sons and daughters among the volunteers for Cuban freedom...." Gray asked if they "gathered around their mother's knee to listen to the story of her warrior life, did their young hearts thrill as did hers for military glory?"

---

32. *Atlanta Constitution*, Feb 11, 1899.

Ultimately, Helen Gray's article simply perpetuated the legend, as had Adamson's article. In all likelihood Helen Gray, like Robert Adamson, failed to recognize that Mrs. L. J. Velazquez Beard was the missing Southern heroine, when Velazquez visited Atlanta two years later promoting her railroad.

More typical in size and character, rather than the large articles like those by Adamson or Gray, was one titled "New Century Woman in Trousers" found in the *Grand Rapids Herald* of November 19, 1899. It stated, "We in America have had our amazons... but none has eclipsed the fame of Lieutenant Harry Buford...." In typical fashion, the article claimed more than Velazquez herself claimed, "She even succeeded in raising a regiment of volunteers for [her husband] and accompanied him in uniform as his lieutenant." The first obvious error is that a regiment consists of one thousand men, and Velazquez never claimed to have raised one thousand men, but instead 236 men. The second error is that she never claimed to have served as her husband's lieutenant.

1900, Railroad Promoter

By May 1899 Velazquez had seemingly ceased the search for William Beard's body. She was still working in Los Angeles, but it is wondered if she found much success as a mining broker because she now focused her attention on the expanding enterprise of railroads.

She once again wrote a letter to President McKinley (received May 12), this time in reference to the "Mexican [railroad] concessions granted to A. C. [*sic* B.] Smith." Her letter was passed to the Department of State for a response, but what her letter specifically addressed and the answer it elicited is unknown since the letter, to date, have not been found.[33] Velazquez was just starting her Mexican railroad phase with more to come.

In the meantime, she tried her hand at starting a local railroad in San Bernardino, California.

> Mrs. L. Velasquez of Los Angeles and her son are guests of the Stewart [Hotel]. Mrs. Beard is here in the interest of the electric road to Waterman canyon and Arrowhead Springs. Those who wish to see the plans of the proposed work should call on her.[34]

A follow-up story three days later (June 16) provided details and was complimentary to Velazquez:

> The success of the San Bernardino, Waterman and Arrowhead electric road may not be assured beyond all controversy, but as Colonel Sellers would say, "the scheme looks well." If energy can make a success of the road that element will not be wanting.

---

33. William McKinley Papers, Ser 6, Reel 89, p27.
34. *San Bernardino County Sun*, Jun 13, 1899.

The actual head of the company, the general who lays all the plans and conducts the battles, is a woman, but a remarkably smart business woman. Her name is Mrs. L. J. Velasquez Beard of Los Angeles, a woman who numbers among her business correspondents, and to whom she can at any time refer as to her capability and responsibility, such men as Hon. Thomas Reed, ex-President Cleveland and a score or more Senators and Congressmen.

She is the widow of Prof. Beard, the geologist who was lost in the crevasse of an Alaskan glacier two years ago, while exploring that country. It is supposed that he was thrown down the crevasse by his men while occupied in laying out the Yukon railroad, as he added to his other scientific qualities that of civil and mining engineer.

Upon his death Mrs. Beard opened an office at Los Angeles to deal in mines, mining stock, railroads, real estate and other branches of business and is considered an authority upon all such deals, her sharp business acumen and indomitable energy being peculiar traits of her character.

She has planned out the electric road that is to connect this city with the foothills and is working to make it a success. She was in the city yesterday morning, stopping at the Stewart, and had with her the complete draught of the road and the plans of the hotel and grounds at Waterman canyon, which look very feasible. She is a walking encyclopedia on the subject and has evidently her whole soul bound up in the success of the scheme. She is a good talker, and yet talks to a purpose and not at random, putting her words where they will all tend to one object, the success of the road and the Waterman improvements. The Arrowhead Springs are to come next, but the grounds around them are not large enough for her plans without the aid of the Waterman ranch as a foundation.

She does not claim to be after the money of the rich, but is seeking those of more moderate means to interest in the scheme and enable them to reap the harvest that is sure to follow.

Mrs. Beard had just come from Redlands, where she had two objects in view, placing the stock of the new company, which is capitalized at $500,000, and to look after the motive power with which to operate the road. In both she met with great encouragement and hopes to see the "dirt fly" on her new road within a few weeks.

To add to the interest attaching to the electric road just at present is the fact that F. M. Coulter, son of one of the owners of Arrowhead springs property, arrived last night from Los Angeles to look after the prospect of including this valuable location for a tourist hotel in the deal with the Waterman ranch. The only trouble hitherto has been the owners, knowing its immense value, have held it at a figure that was almost prohibitory to those who have thought of buying. In connection with the electric railroad scheme, however, this price put upon it would not be exorbitant.

Velazquez's energy and business acumen were similarly described many years before, in 1876, by her book's editor (p12), "She is a shrewd, enterprising, and energetic business woman" and "is quick and energetic in her movements."

Whether the proposed electric railroad from San Bernardino up the foothills to Arrowhead Springs originated with Velazquez is unclear, but if so, it was a commendable and logical project in light of the fact that nearby Redlands, California had just, in 1899, converted its mule drawn street cars to a new electrified rail system and San Bernardino was working towards a similar line.

Arrowhead Springs for many years had been promoted to tourist who sought health benefits of the hot springs. By this date two previous hotels at that location had burned and soon a fine third hotel was built in 1905. Velazquez was too early to benefit from the impetus the new third hotel could have provided. The first segment of the San Bernardino railroad was built, but without Velazquez, and opened for service in 1902 and the Arrowhead line to the Hotel was built 1906-1907.[35]

The luxury resort became the playground of famous movie stars of the day which included Loretta Young, Mary Pickford, Spencer Tracey and Humphrey Bogart. Then this hotel was lost in a November 1938 forest fire. It was rebuilt bigger and better and opened in December 1939. The stars came back, "Judy Garland, Al Jolson and Rudy Vallee were among those featured at the all-star grand opening." World War II interrupted the fun and the hotel was converted to a naval hospital. At the conclusion of the War, attempts were again made to attract the celebrities, but with less success. In 1950, screen star Elizabeth Taylor spent her honeymoon with first husband Conrad "Nicky" Hilton at the hotel. It ceased operating in 1962 though the historic, beautiful building and grounds are maintained. The huge and naturally occurring arrowhead shape in the soil of the slope of the mountain, from which the springs derived its name, can still be seen from miles away as it has for centuries.[36]

In the newspaper article, Velazquez, in typical fashion, name-dropped Congressmen and Senators, even ex-President Cleveland, who could vouch for her "capability and responsibility." It is debatable that they were "business correspondents" because, as seen, these communications were usually her asking for something and not getting it.

In an effort to impress her audience with her knowledge of railroads obtained by association with her dead husband, she let fly a lie, "It is supposed that he was thrown down the crevasse by his men while occupied in laying out the Yukon railroad, as he added to his other scientific qualities that of civil and mining engineer." Actually, she let fly three lies in one sentence. Her husband did not work on the Yukon railroad. He was not thrown into a crevasse by anyone. He was not a civil engineer. Velazquez's ability to custom-fit falsehoods to any occasion was indeed impressive.

---

35. Electric Railway Historical Association of Southern California, www.erha.org.
36. City of San Bernardino's website, www.sbcity.org.

Velazquez had no money of her own, failed to raise the $500,000, in spite of the fact that she was "a good talker," and besides she did not have the owners of Arrowhead Springs on board. Though the railroad to the Springs was a failure for Velazquez, it was a good warm-up for her, when eleven months later she will get back to the aforementioned Mexican railroad.

Velazquez left California, traveled to Arizona and set up shop in Tucson. She bought advertising in the *Arizona Daily Star* from the middle of September 1899 to the end of July 1900:

> L. J. V. Beard, 35 East Congress St., Tucson, Arizona. Mines Dealt in, Copper and Gold, Lands and Colonization a Specialty. Correspondence solicited.

Maybe she had occasional success in the mining/land business therefore continued in the same manner as she had operated in California. However, she had only seen failure in the colonization business, but one supposes it could correctly be called a specialty.

She next made splashy news in the *Weekly Republican* (Phoenix) of May 24, 1900 which reported that "while the delegates from Florence [Arizona] to the democratic territorial convention were waiting at Casa Grande, they were entertained at great length by a woman named Mrs. William Beard." The reporter added that she "was a woman of hardly middle age, attractive personality, and a strong flow of language." There can be no doubt that Velazquez could capture an audience. It might be recalled her editor wrote (*TWIB*, p12) that she "in society is a most brilliant and most entertaining conversationalist, abounding in a fund of anecdotes, and endowed with a mimetic power that enables her to relate her anecdotes in the most telling manner" and "is very vivacious in conversation."

The newspaper said Mrs. Beard was determined to "tap [Phoenix] with a railroad." She claimed to have obtained concessions from the Mexican government to run the railroad from the U.S.-Mexico border to "a bay south of Topolobampo" (this near Los Mochis in the state of Sinaloa). The concession granted "10,000 acres of land and a subsidy of $10,000 a mile."

Velazquez tried to create a competitive environment to spur and entice her Arizonan audience by asserting that she had been offered $50,000 to send the railroad across the New Mexico-Mexico border connecting at Deming, New Mexico, "but she had declined." She further claimed that her deceased husband had "told her that central and northern Arizona was the richest and most promising mineral region in the world," which he certainly might have.[37]

---

37. A railroad from Arizona to the Gulf of California was not a new idea. In 1874, Mr. James C. Truman of New York, agent for some capitalists, and Mr. D. B. Blair of San Francisco scouted the topography for a railroad to Guaymas in the state of Sonora. Velazquez's proposed railroad terminus was some 220 miles further south, in the state of

It is unclear why Velazquez did not stick with her initial sales pitch, but she may have let her braggadocio personality get the best of her. She further dismissed New Mexico's alleged offer of $50,000, stating that the amount was "a bagatelle hardly worth considering since she was backed by capitalists of the Hague [Netherlands] to the extent of $44,000,000." Still, this gross exaggeration did not satisfy Velazquez. She then added that she had other capitalists who wanted to invest $80,000,000, but she saw no reason for their money, as $44,000,000 "was enough." It might be questioned why she even sought the likes of small-fry Phoenix investors, when she had 44 plus 80 million dollars at her command. It is laughable that she so graciously and sportingly would not let $50,000 change her mind as to the routing of the railroad, when the truth was, that for $50,000 she would have built a railroad over her own mother's grave and used her mother's bones for cross-ties. As will be seen, when Velazquez finally departed Phoenix, she did so "aided by money furnished by sympathetic citizens." She was broke.

Velazquez claimed that she had made a "preliminary survey" of the railroad route by "riding over the entire route on horseback or in a buckboard." There were variations of this alleged survey reported in other newspapers, such as, "She recently completed a trip lasting twenty-eight months and covering 3000 miles on donkeys...."[38] This 28-month travel claim was simply not true. Recall her presence was established in California in June 1899 and her presence in Arizona clear by the middle of September 1899. That makes only three months unaccounted for and therefore available for her claimed 28 months of travel. However, it is conceivable that she made a brief trip to Mexico. She could have taken an ocean vessel from Los Angeles to the Pacific Coast of Mexico and then worked her way north to Arizona. But remember that she had an eleven-year-old (approximately) boy in tow and she was probably short of cash, particulars which would have made such a trip difficult and unlikely. It will be seen that in November 1901 Velazquez's son claimed "he knew nothing of Mexico, and declared he had never been astride a mule." In other words, this preliminary survey trip never happened.

She further claimed in the *Weekly Republican* that the "settlement" of Topolobampo was "turned over to her by the Mexican government, the original concessionaire Owens [*sic* Owen] having failed in his contract [to build a railroad] with the government."[39] This "settlement" was the co-operative colony land grant which took socialist Albert Owen years to obtain from the Mexican government.

Sinaloa. Sources- *Arizona Miner* (Prescott, AZ), Sep 11, 1874; *Daily New Mexican*, Sep 23, 1874.
38. *San Francisco Chronicle*, Jun 7, 1900.
39. May 24, 1900.

About Albert Owen

Albert Owen was part of an 1872 railway survey party which sought out a pretty bay described and recommended to them by a Mazatlan doctor. Owen set eyes upon it in September and later wrote, "Everything which we examined combined to impress us the importance of these straits and bays for a safe, deep and extensive anchorage."[40] He was enamored by the location and as early as 1874, Owen went before the U.S. Congress asking support for a railway to reach the projected harbor, but received none.[41]

Albert Owen was a believer in the socialist philosophy and communal living, and was determined that this Mexican location would be right for a socialist colony. Owen, in 1879, wrote to Mexican President Porfirio Díaz espousing his plan as "simple and easily of accomplishment," and that President Díaz "would have the proud satisfaction of having largely stimulated the industries of the Mexican People...." Through Owen's "winning personality and exceptional executive ability," he successfully cultivated the "friendship and assistance" of the President, who offered "favourable conditions."[42]

Owen was granted the concession in June 1881 and the first Topolobampo colonists arrived in 1886. However, Owen failed to meet the concession requirements, most important among them was the building of a railway. The Mexican government offered a second chance to the colony and in June 1890 extended the concession. But the colony failed their second chance and the concession was canceled by January 1891, and Mr. Owen lost "$30,000 in bonds... he had deposited as a guarantee."[43]

Albert Kimsey Owen was an Englishman and a surveyor and civil engineer by education. He had "studied Socialism for many years," having met and befriended all the "leading Socialists of the world." He had studied other "communal undertakings" and felt he had identified their failures. He lectured and wrote prolifically on the topic of socialism and on his version of "integral co-operation" at Topolobampo, believing he would have success.

However, angry ex-members, who left the commune, wrote, "we were often hungry... the water we had to drink was totally unfit for use" and we had "little medicine... [and] musty flour." One ex-member pointed out that

---

40. Albert Kimsey Owen, *Integral Co-Operation at Work* (New York: John W. Lovell Co., 1890), 213.
41. Owen was not the discoverer of the bay, since in 1869 the bay had already been surveyed by the U.S. Navy and described in glowing terms the potential harbor. Source- Alexander D. Anderson, *The Topolobampo Pacific Railway* (Washington, DC: Gibson Brothers, 1881), 55.
42. W. L. Courtney, ed., "Correspondence," *The Fortnightly Review* (Jan to Jun, 1908): 762-764; J. Leon Williams, *An Experiment in Socialism, and What Came of It* (London: Chapman & Hall, 1908).
43. *Railroad World*, Jan 3, 1891.

Owen had "figured prominently in the labor agitations of 'Frisco about 1886" and further complained that Owen "manifested great sympathy for labor by avoiding and living off it." This critic asserted that Owen "had been engaged in the pleasing task of depicting through various publications the idyllic joys of life on the co-operative plan in Mexico… meanwhile [Owen] has remained in the United States trying to eke out an existence under the old order of things."

In fact, Owen stayed in New York City, occupying the headquarters office at 32 Nassau Street. He and his colony received newspaper coverage, favorable and unfavorable, on a regular basis. Velazquez might have heard about Owen, his colony and his railroad during her residency in New York.

Mrs. Beard's claim of the Owen concession was false. She would not have been able to offer $30,000 bond money (as Owen had to) or other money to secure anything. She had not cultivated the necessary political connections in Mexico. The bureaucracy which took Owen two years to navigate, Velazquez could not have steered in a matter of months. A concession document, similar to the 30-page Mexican/Owen concession document does not exist for Mrs. Beard. Mrs. Beard never again mentioned that she had been given this valuable Topolobampo concession. If it had been true, it would have been claimed time and again and she would have continued her efforts to develop it, but instead, it will be seen that she completely dropped it.

1900, the Promotion of the Railroad Continued

Velazquez's railroad promotional efforts continued to receive newspaper coverage and on May 25, 1900 the *Tucson Daily Citizen* identified Lyman Bridges as "the chief engineer of the company being promoted by Mrs. William Beard." The article titled "A Railroad to The Coal Fields," stated that J. A. Reavis and Lyman Bridges went to San Carlos to "investigate the fields with the view of building a railroad from Tucson to that rich mining country."[44] There was work already on-going in the coal field and the workers anticipated the arrival of a diamond drill bit. The article implied that the coal mined there could serve the railroad from Phoenix (through Tucson) to Mexico which was being promoted by Mrs. Beard.

On June 7, 1900, the Arizona *Weekly Republican* revealed the railroad's name, the American, Mexican & Pacific, and stated that "Mrs. L. J. Velasquez Beard" has "for several days" been in Phoenix promoting it and "outlined the plan to the reporter." The route of the railroad was now said to be to "Banderas Bay." This newly claimed terminus was south of

---

44. According to the 1900 U.S. Census, the men were civil engineers. Mr. J. A. Reavis' correct name was Mr. J. Peralta Reavis.

Topolobampo by some 425 miles. So much for the Owen concession at Topolobampo!

The newspaper reported, in variance to the previous reports, about the financial backing, "Mrs. Beard says that $84,000,000 in German and Holland capital is back of the Mexican end...." Mrs. Beard asserted that "concessions from the Mexican government have been secured for virtually all of the line." It is curious that with such huge financial backing, Velazquez was still looking for local investors. The article continued, "Incorporation papers have been filed for the Arizona part of the road... with capital stock of $9,000,000...." Listed in the article were twenty-two incorporators by name; the first eleven were listed as temporary directors, L. J. Beard and Lyman Bridges among them. Among the incorporators were Alexander K. Coney, San Francisco and A. B. Smith, Los Angeles, the two men who probably played a role, directly or indirectly, in exciting Velazquez's interest in the railroad. More on Coney and Smith momentarily.

A short time later, on June 16, a special correspondent for the *Los Angeles Herald* reported similarly, but added a little more detail as to who Velazquez was targeting as investors, "She will have the support of several hundred business men of Maricopa county [Phoenix area], beside the large number she has already secured in Pima county [Tucson area]...." In a complimentary fashion the reporter wrote, "Mme. Beard is losing no time in her work, and while at first her plan was regarded as extravagant, she is rapidly converting prominent people to the belief that her scheme is practicable and that her assertions are not altogether without foundation."[45]

About Alexander K. Coney and Mr. Alphonso B. Smith

Besides being listed as one of the incorporators by the newspaper, Alexander K. Coney, according to Mrs. Beard, was a key figure supporting her involvement in the railroad scheme. "She was aided in getting the concession by high Mexican officials, among them A. K. Coney, Consul-General of Mexico at San Francisco, who is very close to President Díaz."[46] Coney was Consul General of Mexico at San Francisco at the time Velazquez was there in September 1898 looking for the facts of her husband's death.

Coney and President Porfirio Díaz indeed had become lifelong friends, after Coney saved his life. During a revolutionary episode, Díaz fled Mexico and traveling under an alias, he hid onboard a Ward Line ship. At the port of Tampico, a regiment of Mexican soldiers boarded for passage to Vera Cruz. The colonel, for unknown reasons, became suspicious that Díaz was hidden away. He offered Coney, the purser of the vessel, "$50,000 dollars

---

45. *Los Angeles Herald*, Jun 19, 1900.
46. *San Francisco Chronicle*, Jun 7, 1900.

for information of the insurgent." Coney replied, "I know nothing of Díaz." When Díaz later triumphed as President, he appointed Coney, who had married a Mexican, to several consular posts, and lastly, he was appointed Consul General at San Francisco. Later when Coney retired and "fell on hard times" Díaz loaned him money. Coney was a Mason, which stood him in good stead; "many (perhaps most) of Díaz's early *yanqui* supporters were Mason," and Díaz rewarded them with "appointments as Mexican consuls."[47]

Coincidentally, William Beard had been a Mason, and Mrs. Beard, while in Seattle in August 1898, claimed that she was "being assisted by the Masonic order" in the search for her deceased husband. The following month, September, when she was in San Francisco, it is possible she made an appeal to some Masons there. This may have resulted in her introduction to Coney who would have known about the concession which had already been taken away from Albert Owen.

Recall that when Mrs. Beard left San Francisco, she traveled to Los Angeles where she was noted on October 14, 1898.[48] It was probably then, somewhere in southern California, that she met Mr. Alphonso B. Smith who was said to be "well known in San Diego, where he has lived for years."[49] As seen, Smith was listed as one of Beard's railroad scheme incorporators.[50] Earlier, on January 13, 1899, the *Railway Age* reported that Smith had been granted a Mexican railroad concession. It is unclear the nature of the railroad concession, but it is known that he also had been granted and obtained a Mexican coastal steamship concession.

Smith was reported in March 1900 to have created the Mexican Coast Steamship company which ran between San Francisco, San Diego and ports in Mexico. This business was based on a Mexican concession which was secured "several years ago" and it gave "subsidies for carrying the mail" plus "certain rights to fisheries and to the guano on certain islands."[51]

It was explained that A. B. Smith "was always in close touch with the Mexican authorities" and that Smith was a distant relative to the Mormon Prophet Joseph Smith. A. B.'s father or grandfather went to Mexico to settle and "suffered from the depredations of the Indians to such an extent that he had a claim against the Mexican government, which was recognized as more or less valid." A. B. Smith pressed the claim and the government awarded the steamship line concession and the other rights.

---

47. William Schell Jr., *Integral Outsiders: the American Colony in Mexico City, 1876-1911* (Wilmington, Delaware: SR Books, 2001); Fanny Chambers Gooch Iglehart, *Face to Face with the Mexicans* (New York: Fords, Howard & Hulbert, 1887).
48. California *Evening News*.
49. *San Diego Union*, Mar 20, 1900.
50. *Weekly Republican* (Arizona), Jun 7, 1900.
51. *San Diego Union*, Mar 20, Aug 9, 1900.

By August Smith had sold out his interest in the steamship line.[52]

Another San Diego newspaper[53] credited Smith "with the intention of building a railway system" and said that "there is no doubt as to his having the concessions from the Mexican government, as he has documents to show… and that he has had the concessions for some time…." The report noted the railroad was to run from "Yuma to San Diego and from Yuma down the Mexican coast, with a branch to Phoenix."

The truth of the history of the concession and Smith's ownership is unclear. However, Velazquez must have believed true Smith's claim, evident by the aforementioned May 1899 letter she wrote to President William McKinley in reference to the "Mexican [railroad] concessions granted to A. C. [sic B.] Smith." It seems that this was the concession which Mrs. Beard initially promoted, but then later promoted a variation of it as her own scheme.

Regardless of the origins or truthfulness behind Beard's claims of a concession, her projected American, Mexican & Pacific railroad failed before it got started. She had put in two months work at Phoenix and now she said that because of "a disagreement with chief engineer, Lyman Bridges, the project was abandoned."[54] This alleged disagreement seems a false defense of the true reason- she was forced out. After the company's board of directors met on June 25, they published a resolution:

> That public notice is hereby given that Mrs. L. J. V. Beard is not authorized to make appointments for, nor to contract any indebtedness against the American-Mexican Pacific Railway [signed] J. L. Powell, Secretary of American-Mexican Pacific Railway.[55]

Velazquez had said that the railroad had "a capitalization of $5,000,000, most of the stockholders residing in Tucson." But the money was never raised, it was only a goal; she never raised a dime. This will become clear momentarily.

After she was forced out of the company, the newspaper said she had been "busy organizing a new company and declares that there is now no obstacle to the completion of the line." She named six local capitalist men in the Arizona Territory who were behind the project and named "Roosevelt and Sullivan, a New York engineering firm" in charge of the survey.

Another Try with a New Railroad Company

Beard told the newspaper that the new organization was called the "American-Mexican Commercial Railway company and was to have a total

---

52. Ibid, Mar 20, 1900.
53. *Evening Tribune*, Mar 23, 1900, taking from the Los Angeles *Herald*.
54. *Weekly Republican*, Jul 26, 1900.
55. *Arizona Daily Star* (Tucson), Jun 29-Jul 31, 1900.

capitalization of $55,000,000." She had failed to raise five million dollars in her previous stock offering, so how she expected to raise ten times that amount is unimaginable. Besides she had lost the prior 22 incorporators. She now said that the local Mexican consul, Señor Navarro, was assisting her in her work.

The *Weekly Republican* (July 26, 1900) interviewed her and she revealed some of her life's history which greatly conflicts with her memoir:

> She was born in Havana, Cuba, in 1845 and is of French-Spanish extraction. Her father served in the diplomatic corps there and later removed to Mexico, and during the war with the United States was wounded at Chepultepec [*sic* Chapultepec]. After her parents died she was put in charge of an aunt at New Orleans, and when thirteen years of age was married to William E. Burnett. "It was a runaway match," says Mrs. Beard, "and I either had to do that or marry young Rafael Francisco Rodriguez, whom I hated. When the civil war broke out my husband enlisted and was killed. Later I married Professor William Beard, a noted scientist, geologist and mining expert, and it was he who planned part of my railway scheme. The Spanish-American war temporarily hindered the work and we went to Alaska, where my husband died. Several months ago I returned to this country and am now trying to complete his life work, a railway which will be the key to the vast resources of old Mexico."

At this date of maturity, her penchant for lying still chugged away.

First, Velazquez shaved three years off her age, stating her birth year at 1845. In her book, the year was 1842 and in other newspaper interviews she gave varying dates of birth, the earliest was 1838. Shaving three years might have been due to vanity and is forgivable. The rest of the inconsistencies are not forgivable.

Second, in her book she <u>never</u> claimed that her father was at the Battle of Chapultepec (though she <u>did</u> claim that her father was an officer in the Mexican army during the Mexican-American War). This battle is hugely historical and reverberates with Mexican national pride to this day. If her father's presence as an officer at that battle was true, it would have merited him a statue! And it is inconceivable that she failed to write before now that he was a participant, especially considering her memoir's predominant theme of military duty, honor and bravery. For her to claim, at this late date, that her father was at Chapultepec and to think she would have it believed is a credit to her audacity. One supposes her other claimed fathers, "Major J. B. Roche of Mississippi," "Rear Admiral Rosche of the English Navy," "Commodore J. B. Roach of the British Navy," and "Samuel S. Clapp" of Texas, were also at Chapultepec!

Third, she claimed that she was sent to New Orleans <u>after</u> the death of her parents. In contradiction, she explained in her book that she was sent away by her parents from Cuba in 1849 to her aunt's house in New Orleans to further her education. In her book her parents are alive after her 1856 marriage. She also has her mother alive after 1857, the year she claimed she herself became a mother. In an interview with the *Atlanta Constitution* in 1874, she stated her mother died in 1860. *The Woman in Battle* (p69 and 290) has her father alive in April 1861 and still alive in the summer of 1863, when she received two letters from him.

Fourth, Velazquez, amazingly and falsely, still claimed her first marriage was to "William E. Burnett" and the claim had never been exposed by the newspapers. (The gentleman's surname was spelled "Burnet" and Velazquez probably did not know it or at least she never spelled it for the reporters so they could get it right.) In her book she said she was 14 years old when she married, not 13 as she stated here. She did not identify Burnet by his surname in her book, only by his first name, but used Burnet's name in newspaper articles before and after the publication of her book. In her book, she deftly omitted using his full name, knowing someone could check the facts. The article said that after the death of her first husband, she "later" married Beard. The claim is substantially true, however, the newspaper failed to enumerate her husbands in between Burnet and Beard, of which there were several. She had cohabited and claimed to be the wife of Williams of the 13th Connecticut in New Orleans, she married DeCaulp, she married Wasson, she married Bonner, she married Bobo, she married McLeod and she cohabited with Goddard, had his child and posed as his wife. During her earliest known years, the various newspapers identified her as Mrs. Mary Ann Keith, Mrs. Arnold and claimed she married a man from Arkansas named Bachman.

Fifth, the Spanish-American War, which commenced on February 15, 1898 and ended in December, had no effect on William Beard's departure for Alaska in December 1897 and his death there in April 1898. The war played no part in any of his or her prior visits to the western territories or Old Mexico.

Sixth, Mrs. Beard did <u>not</u> go to Alaska <u>with</u> her husband, as she now claimed.

Seventh, it is noteworthy that here is the one and only time found mentioned the full name of the suitor of her young years in New Orleans, "Rafael Francisco Rodriguez." Her book only gave the young Spaniard's name as "Raphael R," which should be noted as inconsistent with the correct Spanish spelling of the name, a habit of which Velazquez was all too fond. But there was more than a young Spanish suitor lurking at the door; there was a lie lurking. Velazquez claimed "Raphael" was selected by her parents as her betrothed and the time frame identified by Velazquez would have made her betrothed at the tender age of nine. It is just not believable that her alleged worldly parents, a Spanish father, educated in Madrid and Paris, and a French-American mother, would have forced her into this arrangement! Either the parents were a lie or the betrothal was a lie, but it can be guessed both were lies. Unfortunately, the name Rafael Francisco Rodriguez, as a potential clue to her early years, leads to nothing of use.

Eight, Velazquez stated that it was her husband "who planned part of [her] railway scheme." It might be recalled that it was while her husband was still alive, the *New York Herald* of February 1, 1891 reported, "Mrs. Beard has a large number of 'concessions' from Mexico and Honduras. One is for a canal, another for a railway, another for a steamship company and so on." It is clear that as early as 1891 Velazquez had railroads on her mind, but then, so did the entire nation. Prior, in February 1889, it was seen that William Beard went to Globe on mining business and at that time expressed his great interest in two railroad lines. Her husband probably was her inspiration for the railroad business.

Ninth, striking is the fact that Velazquez avoided any mention of her participation in the Civil War or of her book.

1900, Mrs. Velazquez Beard Departed Phoenix

Mrs. Beard departed Phoenix on Saturday night, July 28, 1900. Before leaving she announced her intention to go to El Paso to secure "Texas influence and coin to build her railroad."[56] In seeming contradiction, the *San Francisco Call* of July 29, 1900 stated she was going to Chicago "in an effort to secure backing" for the railroad. She did both. She traveled to El Paso, then north to Albuquerque, and then Denver before turning east towards Chicago.[57]

The *Arizona Republican* (July 30, 1900) wrote that she had tried for the past two months to interest "Arizona capital in her project" and that her husband had conceived of the railroad idea three years ago and that she had gone to Alaska with him where he died. The reporter, exceeding today's standards of sexism, wrote, "Mrs. Beard's case is a pathetic instance of a woman's efforts to fulfill a man's mission, and the consequent failure." Mrs. Beard gave the reason for failure was the "treachery on the part of men whom she had associated in her enterprise," and now she "sought new aid." None was "forthcoming, her cash was exhausted and she was unable to meet current expenses." She "gave up hope and aided by money furnished by sympathetic citizens, left Phoenix."

By now, Velazquez knew that the millions she sought would never be realized. In any case, the money for her immediate needs was also probably an objective and that money did materialize, and with it, she moved on.

Before leaving Arizona, she mailed still another letter to U.S. President William McKinley. It was received by the White House on August 1, 1900.

---

56. *Arizona Republican* Jul 30, 1900; *Weekly Republican-Herald* (Arizona), Aug 2, 1900.
57. *El Paso Daily Herald*, Oct 2, 1900, recalled her passing through "last summer."

The President's letter book stated the nature of the letter, "Wants money for International Railway Scheme." The request was referred to the Department of State; its response is undiscovered, but it is clear by subsequent history that she was not given money.[58] It can never be said that Velazquez was not bold when representing herself or her grandiose plans. One might as well go to the top.

It is certain that Velazquez had no concession from the Mexican government for a railroad, yet she solicited support from the U.S. Government for the project. It can only be supposed that her intention was that if she could obtain the Federal Government's promise of support of the railroad, she then would approach the Mexicans with this fact and entice it into supporting the project, as well. If this supposition is accepted, then one might believe her efforts honest in a manner. In any case, she exhibited a remarkable boldness in seeking out support for the railroad.

The progress of Velazquez's eastward travel and arrival in Albuquerque was noted at the Highland Hotel by the *Albuquerque Citizen* of Aug. 2, 1900, under "Hotel Arrivals." She was listed as "Madame L. J. V. Beard and son." It is clear that Waldemar was still traveling with her.

Velazquez then showed up in Denver where the newspaper reported, "Senora Dona L. J. Velasques Beard... desires to enlist some $40,000,000 capital in building of a railroad through the Mexican states of Jalisco, Tepic, Sinaloa, Sonora and Chihuahua, some 1050 miles." The report stated she had concessions and grants from President Diaz for the railroad. Velazquez tried to make a personal connection with the Coloradans by stating she "desires to take the stump in Colorado for Bryan and incidentally dispose of bonds to build the railroad." This was William J. Bryan, Democrat candidate for the U.S. Presidency, who in the coming November lost to incumbent President William McKinley. And as always, Velazquez evoked the names of prominent people, and, no doubt, was ready to exhibit forged letters:

> She carries letters of introduction from President Diaz, Chauncey Depew, J. Pierpont Morgan, Henry Clews, Li Hung Chang and several United States senators and governors of various states.[59]

Velazquez next appeared in Chicago. Her arrival date there is unclear, but her presence might have been the impetus for the August 31, 1900 *Chicago Tribune* article titled "Woman in the Civil War." The article presented short biographies of several women with accompanying images, and Velazquez's image, with mustache and goatee, in male military uniform was clearly taken from her book. Velazquez's biographical sketch contained errors or falsehoods which will be addressed later.

---

58. William McKinley Papers, Ser 6, Reel 90, p38.
59. *Denver Post*, Aug 23, 1900.

By September 21, 1900, Velazquez was solidly placed in Chicago.[60] The newspaper introduced her:

Mme. L. J. Valasquez Beard of Washington, D.C., was in the city Friday. She is on her way to Mexico, where she is building a railway. This lady is a native of Cuba, and the widow of Professor Beard of Washington, the mining expert, with whom she at one time spent two years in Kimberley, South Africa.

It was untrue that Velazquez was on her way to Mexico, but had instead just traveled away from the Southwest. It was a great stretch for her to claim that she was from Washington; the claim must have been selected to impress the reporter. And it was an outright lie that she "spent two years in Kimberley, South Africa" with her husband "Professor Beard." First of all, Beard was not a professor. Furthermore, from the time the couple married on August 20, 1887 to the time that William Beard departed Philadelphia, on December 17, 1897, for his Alaska death trip, Velazquez never left the country. Her presence in the United States is documented for every year of that ten-year time frame.

Velazquez persisted in her claim that she had "obtained the concession for her railway from President Diaz...." This claim, as will be seen, will derail.

The article continued:

Mme. Beard says she has already placed $40,000,000 in bonds for her railway. Senator Wolcott of Colorado is interested, as are German capitalists. [And] Senator Wolcott desires the connection of the Denver & Rio Grande, and the German capitalists have schemes of their own.

Of course, it was untrue that she had sold 40 million dollars of bonds and if she had the 40 million, she wouldn't have had any concern about what German capitalists thought and the named-dropped Senator Wolcott of Colorado would have asked that the line be connected in his own backyard.

Velazquez fabricated a fresh Mexican terminus of the railroad, "on a harbor at Cape Corrientes, on the Pacific, due west from the City of Guadalajara." She further described the harbor as "indenting the land deeply and having sufficient water for any boat that floats on the Pacific." It just was not and is not true! There is no natural harbor at Cape Corrientes. This is the Cape just south of the Bay of Banderas. If she meant instead, the rather nearby Bay of Banderas, it too is not a natural harbor for big shipping. Neither location indents the land at all.

The reporter gave an interesting description of Velazquez:

---

60. The *Seattle Daily Times* of Sep 26, 1900 ran the article in a column titled "In the Windy City." It is unclear from which Chicago newspaper it was taken.

She is 50 years old, tall and vigorous. She speaks English with a Spanish accent, but is entirely American in her sentiments and her energy.

Her stated age of 50 would have made her born in 1850 which conflicts with her memoirs claim to have been born in 1842. Vanity age fudging is surely the explanation for the discrepancy.

It is unclear if Velazquez diligently sought investors in Chicago, but it is easy to suppose that she did not entice the city's financial community. She may have even had difficulty duping the citizens out of their pocket money to enable her to move on.

"Mrs. Beard Bobs Up" next in Springfield, Illinois:[61]

Mrs. J. Velasques Beard, the eccentric lady who spent several months of the summer in Phoenix, laboring on a plan to build a railroad from here to Banderos bay, on the southwestern coast of Mexico, has turned up in Springfield, Ill. A paper from there, speaking of Mrs. Beard says: "During the civil war she was actively connected with the confederate army, following it through with her husband, Colonel Burnett. Her husband was killed in the war and she afterwards married William Beard, a geologist and scientist, who was killed in Alaska a few months ago. Mrs. Beard is now on her return from Alaska where she went for her husband's body and to secure some evidence that he was foully dealt with. She left this city this afternoon for New Orleans, going via St. Louis. From there she goes to Washington to arouse interest in her plans for a new railroad route to the Pacific coast through Mexico, stopping at Banderos Bay, Mexico. This gives a straight western route to the Pacific. Mrs. Beard claims that her scheme has the support of the brother-in-law of President Diaz of Mexico. She also has the support of many political leaders in this country and has letters from President McKinley, Candidate Bryan and probably half the senators in the United States and nearly all the cabinet officers."

It appears that Velazquez did not try to raise any money in Springfield, probably understanding if there was none in Chicago, there was none there. It was certainly not true that she had letters of endorsement from all the politicians she claimed; but if so, some were sure to have been forgeries. Velazquez's claim to have had the support of the brother-in-law of President Díaz must have elicited a grin from readers then and it should now. Yessiree Bob, there is nothing better than an influential "hold my cerveza and watch this" brother-in-law.

As the article stated, Velazquez was headed south to New Orleans via St. Louis and she is found en route registered at the Gleason Hotel in Little Rock, Arkansas on October 5, 1900 as "I. [sic] J. Velasquez and son, Phoenix."[62]

---

61. *Arizona Republican*, Sep 27, 1900.
62. *Arkansas Democrat*, Oct 5, 1900.

1900, Traveled to New Orleans, Then to Atlanta

The New Orleans *Times-Picayune*,[63] in "Woman Building a Railroad," repeated much of the same information previously published, no doubt picked up off the telegraph wire. It stated that she "is now in Mexico building a railway," which was not correct and it will be seen nine days hence she made an appearance in New Orleans. Again, the same description of Velazquez was presented, "Mme. Beard is about 50 years of age, tall and fine looking. She speaks English with a Spanish accent."

Recall that she claimed in her book to have been born in 1842, so her age would have been 58. Whether she told the reporter her age or whether he guessed, she would have been satisfied by the eight-year reduction. Whether she had a permanent Spanish accent, and not one which could be put-on, is questionable. How did this accent go unnoticed by General Jubal Early and by the many other reporters to whom she spoke?

By October 25 Velazquez's presence was positively noted in New Orleans by the *Times-Picayune* in an article titled, "A Woman's Glorious Dream." Like a good salesman, she endeavored to connect with "the business people" by telling them she was "formerly of this city" and "that being a native of this state she has refused to have the [rail]road diverted to any other point, and ask the co-operation of the people here to consummate what she believes would be a splendid thing for the city."

The article continued, "She desires to get up a company with $150,000 capital here" and the whole cost of the project would not be over $35,000,000. She reminded the public that her deceased husband, Professor Beard, had been in New Orleans when he had a mineral exhibit at the Exposition. That was the truth, but it was long before he was her husband. The Exposition had opened on December 1, 1884.

The *Times-Picayune*, in a November 1 follow-up article, "The Only Woman Railroad Builder," wrote:

> Mme. L. J. Velasquez Beard is probably the only woman in the world who is engaged in building a railroad. Mme. Beard herself is a Cuban by birth, but her railroad is in Mexico. She is now on her way to Mexico, and says that she has placed $40,000,000 in bonds for her enterprise. Mme. Beard is 50 years old, tall and handsome. She speaks English with a Spanish accent, but is thoroughly American in spirit and energy. She herself secured the concession for the railroad from President Díaz. She has done much traveling, and has familiarized herself with many lands....

Well, Velazquez was once again born in Cuba and in a mere seven days she placed forty-million dollars in bonds. Of course, Velazquez was not on

---

63. Oct 16, 1900.

her way to Mexico. Take note that she claimed she had "secured the concession for the railroad from President Díaz."

She had no success in New Orleans, so next traveled to Atlanta where she, "endeavoring to form a company," promoted a steamship line connecting Savannah, Georgia, to Mexico and then a railroad across Mexico. She readily admitted that "she did not receive the proper encouragement" in New Orleans. She claimed that she had "a number of Savannahians" interested and they "will meet with the Atlanta people Monday." Like a good salesman, applying some competitive pressure, she made it understood that if the Atlantans did not embrace the project that she would take it to New Yorkers who had already "signified their willingness to place money in the enterprise."[64]

From experience, Velazquez had learned that seeking huge amounts of money was not well received so now sought "to organize in Atlanta a development company, with a capital not to exceed $50,000 and not less than $30,000." The company was "to aid in the construction of this continental railroad and to own all of the concessions along the line." Velazquez said "the capitalization of the enterprise is suggested as $15,000,000, and not less than $10,000,000."

She further stated, "The rights of the road have been applied for in Mexico, and all of the preliminary surveys have been made." It should be noted that it was an impossibility the preliminary surveys had been made because she constantly changed the route of the tracks! And it is curious that previously she claimed that the rights had been secured, but now they were only "applied for." If the rights were only applied for, it can be certain that any wily investor would have balked and she obviously failed to get any investors. However, it is possible that she collected some travel money to get her to her next stop.

To the *Atlanta Constitution* reporter Velazquez related some of her personal history. Once again, she stated she was born in Havana, Cuba, by Spanish parents, dropping her French-American mother. She stated, "Her second husband was William Beard...." and she still maintained he was murdered. Of course, the "second husband" statement was designed for polite company, who would have been flabbergasted at Beard's actual place in the husbands' numbers count. She said that her husband had "vast mining interest in Arizona... She took charge of the mines, with a partner...." Even if this mining interest was true, she did not collect money enough to keep her in pocket change for her travels. The article concluded, "She is accompanied by her little son." This places her son, Waldemar, still on the road with her, now for over two years and four months, at least since August 10, 1898 when they arrived in Seattle. And Velazquez herself must have told

---

64. *Atlanta Constitution*, Dec 27, 1900.

the reporter that her son was "little," because no reporter would have called a 12-year-old "little."

Only 20 days after the first Atlanta newspaper report, again the *Atlanta Constitution*[65] reported that she was still cultivating support for the "gigantic railroad system," this time meeting with government officials in the capitol. "She called on the governor and all the other officials to show them plans...." She tried to make a salesman's connection with her customers by claiming that "she was in Atlanta during the siege" and that she was a Confederate veteran.

Velazquez's presence during the siege was just not true! At that time, she was under Union army arrest in Nashville and upon release she went to Minnesota. Even if she had tried to go to Atlanta, it would have been impossible to cross the Union lines encircling the city. The Union army targeted Atlanta with continual artillery bombardment, some 5000 shells landing during one day alone and most of the residents had abandoned the city. If she truly crossed the lines, it would have been a deed worth bragging about and until now she had never said a word. For her to claim it now was brazened and not to be believed.

The article concluded:

She exhibited her plans to all the statehouse officials and asked them if she might refer to them in seeking to interest capital in her enterprise. "You may tell them you showed me your plans," was the reply one of them gave her. She thanked him and went away, seemingly perfectly satisfied.

1901, Tampa Could Not be Persuaded

She did go away and reappeared in Tampa, Florida. The *Morning Tribune* of February 24, 1901 reported that Mrs. Beard's had arrived three weeks ago, which placed her there the first week of February. The newspaper said she registered at the Palmetto Hotel and that it was clear "from the mysterious air with which she interrogated the clerk that she was a woman with a purpose." In a facetious tone, the reporter told the story of Mrs. Beard, under the headlines, "Big Scheme of One Woman, She Desired to Build a Railway and Start Shiplines, But the Lawyers Laughed," which, in part, follows:

...The purpose was not long showing itself. The day after her arrival, Mrs. L. J. Velasquez Beard, loaded down with a heavy bundle of credentials, went about seeking whom she might devour. She had no difficulty in obtaining audiences with several prominent citizens, to whom she unfolded the great, glaring, glittering scheme outlined above. She had millions at her immediate disposal; the government of Mexico and the richest syndicate of Holland were behind her; so promising was her project that J. Pierpont Morgan had offered her $50,000 cash to

---

65. Jan 16, 1901.

allow him to work it for her; she had been sent as the chosen emissary to select the American port at which the steamer line was to have its terminus. She had been thinking, and, after several good, strong thinks, she decided that Tampa was the place; and all that she wanted Tampa to do was to give her dockage for her ships.

Not water enough in the Hillsborough River? Why that was a small consideration, she said. Wire Mr. Sparkman to be at ease; bid the republican watchdogs of the treasury begone; her Holland syndicate would at once dig out a channel to the docks of Tampa, not twenty, not thirty, but fifty-five feet deep.

Mrs. L. J. Velasquez Beard... finally got together a company of capitalists... one afternoon last week. Those present were C. C. Whitaker, E. P. Hopkins, G. L. Larimore, Paul Worth Smith, George P. Raney, all well-known magnates....

Before this august assemblage... she orated, eloquently, on the future greatness and glory that she brought to Tampa and its people. All went well in the meeting until Judge Raney asked, in his usual earnest and dignified manner, if Mrs. L. J. Velasquez Beard wouldn't be so kind as to deposit $10,000 in cash with him as a guarantee of good faith. At this Colonel Whitaker laughed a quiet little goo-goo laugh, and the other capitalists did likewise.

This ended the meeting. Mrs. L. J. Velasquez Beard stalked from the room, angered to desperation, informing them as she went, that she would carry her line to some other port.

And this woman, with millions at her command, sometime before breakfast yesterday morning, departed from the Palmetto Hotel, leaving a small satchel containing a few business cards in settlement of three weeks board and shook the dust of Tampa from her feet.

To repeat the obvious, Velazquez had no money. However, Velazquez did have vision; today the Tampa Bay ship channel is dredged to a depth of some 42 feet.

Curiously, many years later, the *Tampa Tribune* of February 23, 1916 referred to this episode in a terribly misleading news brief. The article, in total, stated:

Tampa News in Other Years, Fifteen Years Ago Today, Feb. 23, 1901, "Mrs. L. J. Velasquez Beard" a mysterious woman, who had been talking to citizens about financing a steamship line to Mexico, disappeared from her hotel.

Yes, but she reappeared in Philadelphia.

1901, Last Chance in Philadelphia

Obviously, Mrs. L. J. Velazquez Beard did not have "millions at her command," but she knew of one more place to look for it. She headed north to Philadelphia (arriving in March, as it will be seen) where she knew existed investors who had paid to get into the gold mining business, and just maybe, they would be interested in a railroad.

A "Special Dispatch" from a Philadelphia correspondent dated August 27 told of her success in finding investors. The article was titled "A Railroad Across Mexico" and in part stated:[66]

Through the untiring efforts of a woman nearly three-score years of age a company has been organized and chartered under the corporation laws of Delaware to build a railroad across Mexico, which, with the proposed connections in this country, will make it possible to journey from Philadelphia to the Pacific Coast in eighty hours and will bring the Philippine Islands 1,700 miles nearer than by any other route at present used.

Senora L. J. Valasquez [sic] Beard of Tepic, State of Tepic, Mexico, the widow of a Mexican army officer, is the woman, and the company is the Mexican Continental & Steamship Company, and is composed partly of Philadelphians.

The Mexican Continental & Steamship Company was indeed created and her old Philadelphia friend Dr. Joseph Hancock, from the North Star gold mine venture, became the company's secretary and treasurer. The other officers were: president, Henry Heil of Philadelphia; vice-president, J. L. Ober of Mexico; and attorney, Thomas A. Gurney of Philadelphia. The newspaper stated that General Longstreet of Washington, D.C., and Señor Alcase of Mexico also were interested.[67]

The company's capitalization was stated at $150,000 with the amount increasing "after the concessions are in the hands of the company," that is, transferred from Velazquez to the company. The reporter explained how Velazquez had gained the concessions, no doubt repeating what Velazquez told him:

Senor Beard was a prominent officer in the Mexican army, a very rich man, and a close friend of President Diaz. He was wounded once while fighting by the side of Diaz. He went to the Klondike at the beginning of the gold fever and died there soon afterwards. It was rumored that he was murdered for his money. His widow has a large fortune, part of which consists of rich mineral lands in Arizona and Mexico.

While Senor Beard was alive President Diaz had promised to Senora Beard the right of way across Mexico for a railroad. The concession was not granted outright, but the assurance was given that any regular corporation of which Senora Beard was a member would receive the concession. Senora Beard came to Philadelphia in hope of interesting capital.

At this point the article narrated how Mrs. Beard arrived four months ago and vigorously searched out investors. Also explained in detail was the

---

66. *Cleveland Leader* (Cleveland, OH); The *Evening Telegram* (NY) of Aug 28, 1901 carried a slightly varied article.
67. The *Philadelphia Inquirer*, Sep 28, 1901, reported the formation of the company, "Philadelphia and Mexican Capitalists Plan Scheme for Transcontinental Lines," citing the *Manufacturers' Record*.

route the railroad was to take, naming several Mexican towns and stating "the road will be practically without competition." And the concessions, well:

> The concessions are expected every day. When they are received several corps of surveyors will start at once to survey the line, and it is believed the work of construction will be started in less than a year.

At this point, the concessions which Velazquez was claiming to have been promised her were still believed true by investors.

The last paragraph of the article addressed Velazquez's appearance and history:

> She is a little woman, not much more than five feet high, and of slight build. She is always dressed in somber black. She was born of Louisiana parents in Cuba and raised in Louisiana. She is said to be a very good business woman and a firm believer in the rights of secession.

First, it was not true Mrs. Beard was left a large fortune. William Beard died before he reached the gold fields, so he could not have filed a claim, thus no gold (as implied) or large fortune. When Mrs. Beard traveled to the West Coast to investigate her husband's death, she was furnished the money by Dr. Hancock of the North Star mining company (this fact is established later). Also, in her hunt for her husband, Velazquez claimed "to have financial help of President McKinley" and from "the Masonic order." Why would a widow with "a large fortune" need financial assistance? There certainly was no indication that Velazquez possessed a large fortune judging from her eagerness to seek out Beard's Alaska partner who supposedly recovered from Beard's body any remaining grubstake. And if Velazquez had been left a large fortune, why did sympathetic people have to give her money to facilitate her departure from Phoenix and why did she have to cheat the Tampa hotel out of her room and board?

Second, it was false that Mr. Beard had been an officer in the Mexican army, but still more, it was a contradiction. Mrs. Beard specifically stated in February 1891 that Mr. Beard was "never a soldier." And Velazquez's audacity to claim that her husband was "wounded once while fighting by the side of [President] Diaz" is a true marvel.

Third, it was untrue Mrs. Beard was "of Tepic, Mexico." She never made any prior claim to this. It is possible that she could have visited Tepic if one supposes that she traveled through Mexico in 1899, between her last known presence in Los Angeles and her arrival in Arizona three months later. Tepic is near the Bay of Banderas which she designated as the termination of the projected railroad. However, later evidence will negate any likelihood that she ever went to Tepic; her son said (later) he knew nothing of Mexico.

Fourth, Velazquez claimed "she was born of Louisiana parents in Cuba and was raised in Louisiana" which of course is a contradiction to her memoir's assertions and is a novel claim contradicting all prior newspaper claims.

Fifth, her age was stated at "nearly three-score," or 60 years, which fits tightly with the birth year given in her memoir. The description of her as "a little woman, not much more than five feet high and of slight build" is less height than newspapers previously reported. At the advanced age of about sixty, her skeletal structure might have lost some of its height.

Despite all the falsehoods told to the newspapers, Velazquez was making positive progress towards the formation of the company. The upstart Mexican Continental Railroad and Steamship Company paid the Delaware state tax due, $22.50, for incorporation for the year 1901.[68] The creation of the corporation clearly indicated that the principals thought there was a chance of financial gain through floating stocks.[69]

The proposed route which the railroad was to take had changed greatly from the earliest versions. Now the idea was that the railroad would cross Mexico from Tampico, on the Gulf of Mexico, to the Bay of Banderas on the Pacific coast. Steamships would depart from various U.S. ports, from Philadelphia to Baltimore, even Pensacola, all destined for the port of Tampico.

It is surprising that the development of this company got as far as it did. Any smart money should have understood that such a railroad would be bankrupted by the completion of the Panama Canal which had been begun by the French, but at the moment was suffering terribly in its progress. By June 1902, the U.S. Senate supported buying out the French and in 1904 the Americans bought the remaining French equipment and the Panama Canal was completed in 1914.

---

68. *Annual Report of the State Auditor of the State of Delaware 1901* (Dover, DE: Sentinel, 1902).
69. *Minneapolis Journal*, Aug 30, 1901; *Railway Age*, Sep 6, 1901; *Philadelphia Inquirer*, Sep 28, 1901; *St. Louis Republican*, Sep 29, 1901; *International Railway Journal*, Nov 1, 1901.

Chapter 16

Mrs. Velazquez Beard's Train Wreck

The headlines came crashing head-on:

Mexican Railway Stock Called In – Officers of Company Recently Organized Decide to Investigate Franchises – Senora Beard the Promoter –Philadelphia Business Men Who Invested in Project to Build the Road Across Mexico Say They Were Deceived.

The *Times* of Philadelphia[1] explained:

All stock of the Mexican Continental Railway and Steamship Company, with its central offices in this city, has been called in for purposes of investigation.

A few months ago the company was incorporated under the laws of Delaware. The project was the building of a transcontinental railway between Tampico, Mexico, on the gulf coast, to the Bay of Banderas, on the Pacific coast, making a route from New York and Philadelphia to San Francisco and the Orient, several hundred miles shorter than that by way of Panama. The establishment of a steamship line between Tampico, Mexico, and Pensacola, Florida, the institution of telegraph and telephone lines and the development of valuable mining land were also planned.

Government concessions, franchises and right of way for these projects were in possession of Senora Velasquez Beard, a woman said to be of Cuban nativity, married to an Englishman name Beard, who, after an adventurous life, is supposed to have been murdered while prospecting in Alaska for gold in the employ of a Philadelphia company. Senora Beard was the promoter of the great project, and her late associates give her credit for much shrewdness. The immediate and urgent reason in calling the stock is, as President Henry Hill, Attorney Gummey and others interested asserted, their conviction that Senora Velasquez Beard does not legally possess the concessions, rights and franchises upon the basis of which she induced the organization of the company.

The persons most directly interested are Thomas A. Gummey, an attorney, with offices in the Stephen Girard building; Dr. Joseph Hancock, a physician with offices and residence at Seventeenth street and Columbia avenue; J. F. Horton, Drexel building, promoter and investor; Henry Hill [*sic*], president of Quaker City Mining Company and president of the company under discussion; F. L. De La Barra, a Mexican official; Charles E. Foster, formerly agent in the Betz building of Douglas, Lacey & Co., brokers, whose main office is at 66 Broadway, New York, and many other business men connected in a lesser way.

MRS. BEARD'S FIRST APPEARANCE. Senora Velasquez Beard, according to the story of Mr. Gummey, the attorney, first came to be known to Philadelphians ten years ago, when she wrote to Mr. Gummey from New York, saying that important papers connected with business matters of a client of his were in her possession. The papers were wanted and Mr. Gummey found the statement to be true. He negotiated with Mrs. Beard and secured the papers, the woman explaining that she had come upon them in an office where she had desk room. Mr. Gummey next met Mrs. Beard five years later when he one day walked into the offices of

---

1. Nov 21, 1901.

Leland & Power, investors and promoters, in the Drexel Building. Leland & Power were organizing the North Star Improvement Company, for Alaskan prospecting, and Mrs. Beard was urging the employment of her husband as agent and prospector.

For the third time Senora Beard came upon the horizons of Mr. Gummey, when she walked into his office last March with a mass of documents under her arm, containing the sweeping Mexican franchises, upon the basis of which the Mexican Continental Railway and Steamship Company was organized. Every detail seemed not only plausible, but legal as well, and Mr. Gummey agreed to act as attorney and lend influence and material assistance to the project.

Previous to this time, however, Dr. Hancock, through interests in the North Star Improvement Company, had invested in the Beards. Out of his own pocket, as he yesterday told a reporter for THE PHILADELPHIA TIMES, he gave Mr. Beard, in 1897, $1500 for the Alaskan tour. Casting about for a reliable prospector several persons were considered. Senora Beard stepped in and secured the place for her husband, then working as a wheelwright in Delaware, but according to Mrs. Beard, an experienced prospector and mining expert and an ex-employee of the Government Coast and Geodetic Survey. Beard went to the Copper River country. Several encouraging letters were received from him. Then came a silence only broken by letters from one of his companions saying he had been lost in a blizzard while attempting to conquer the journey over a thirty-mile glacier. Mrs. Beard was furnished money to go to Alaska and investigate. At Seattle, as he says, Mrs. Beard was convinced she saw one of her husband's Alaskan companions sporting her husband's clothes.

COMES TO PHILADELPHIA DESTITUTE. When she returned to Philadelphia last March with her son Wallie, aged 15, she was, as she admitted, quite destitute. Dr. Hancock, on account of his former association with her and her husband, told her he would board her and her son if she would find lodgings in the neighborhood. She did so at the home of William F. Binder, carpenter and builder, 1545 Bouvier street. There she remained taking her meals at Dr. Hancock's until a short time ago, when the stockholders of the Mexican company decided to investigate the company's prospects. Dr. Hancock, for that reason and also because, as he asserts, Mrs. Beard was a great source of annoyance on account of her imperative and exacting temperament, closed his doors to the feminine promoter. Since that time the Binders have been giving the Beards a portion of their meals.

"I have no fear about my six months' room rent, however." said Mrs. Binder last evening.

"I believe in Senora Beard. Why, she has letters from Diaz, of Mexico, and from every member of his cabinet, all with big red official seals attached, and President Diaz says that all concerned place implicit trust in Senora Beard. Besides, only three weeks ago, a gentleman interested in the Senora's project guaranteed the lodging bill, of which I have not yet received one dollar."

Mr. Gummey, the company's attorney, said yester [*sic*] to a PHILADELPHIA TIMES reporter:

"When Mrs. Beard first came to me I asked for the most explicit proof that she possessed the concessions and franchises she claimed. She refused to exhibit all her documents, as, she said, other schemes were involved. Finally, after repeated consultation with Mr. Hile [*sic*] and others whom she had interested, we decided that the legal proofs were sufficient, and J. F. Horton, a most cautious man in his line, organized the company. Mrs. Beard was to be paid $10,000 and to receive an allotment of stock. The first revelation came when we were informed that Charles E. Foster, in charge of the branch office here of Dorsey & Lacey, New York brokers, had purchased all of Mrs. Beard's alleged grants for a cash consideration. This led to a correspondence between me and F. L. De La Barra, whom Mrs. Beard claimed to be her counsel at the City of Mexico. Senor De La Barra disclaimed all knowledge of Mrs. Beard, except that she had written to him for government maps and documents which he had sent to her."

"Here is a letter from De La Barra which asserts that no record existed of any grant made to Mrs. Beard, and that she was unknown personally to any Mexican official. I was then convinced that she had used her information of a prospecting tour once made by her husband to invent the project of the railway. She claimed to have made a journey upon muleback over the route within the last year or two, accompanied by her boy. The boy, I found later, knew nothing of Mexico, and declared he had never been astride of a mule."

"I accused Mrs. Beard of gross deception. She became abusive, and I ordered her from my office. Again she returned, and I threatened her with arrest if she did not at once leave and never again show herself."

FOSTER NOT TO BE FOUND. Inquiry was made at the branch office, in the Betz Building, of Douglas & Lacey in regard to Charles E. Foster, who is said to have purchased all of Mrs. Beard's alleged Mexican grants prior to her negotiation with the organized company. It was found that Mr. Foster had been succeeded as agent of the New York firm by D. B. Carroll and J. D. Allen.

"Douglas & Lacy would like to know where Foster is," said Mr. Allen to the reporter for THE PHILADELPHIA TIMES. "We have a warrant out for him, and officers with two other warrants are seeking him. He was arrested upon charges of misuse of money entrusted to him. He secured bail and has disappeared. He told friends that he did not care for this picayune office as he would soon be president of a Mexican railway company, at a salary of $25,000 a year."

Another person associated with the Mexican project was an elderly man, who for several years had been an attendant at the department store. In that capacity Mr[s]. Beard made his acquaintance, and, as both Mr. Gummey and Dr. Hancock state, induced him to invest in the project. She made him an award of stock, and promised him an official position at $10,000 a year. He went security with his employers for purchases by Mr[s]. Beard to the extent of several hundred dollars, and resigned his position, despite the advice of his friends and employers, that he might become a railway magnate.

J. F. Horton, the organizer of the company, went to Washington yesterday to lay the matter before authorities at the Mexican Legation. Mr. Binder, Mrs. Beard's landlord, said last evening that "the Senora" had just gone to New York accompanied by her son, and that she had promised to return Friday evening.

And it can be certain that she never returned.

The truth had finally caught up with Velazquez. She did not have a Mexican concession for anything. And she had no promises of concessions. And the Mexican government had not given her Albert Owen's Topolobampo concession, either. Remember that one? She had flogged the Mexican concession lie for an amazing 18 months, a credit to her tenacity or maybe her insanity, but certainly not her honesty. It seems that she never before this time was asked to prove possession of the concession. It is now clear what her con was. She claimed with full confidence that she was granted the concession because she correctly calculated that no gentleman would demand proof of a lady thereby insinuating that she was a liar. And as seen in the August *Cleveland Leader* article, Velazquez said she had been "promised" the concession, which might have left her a good excuse for her investors, that the Mexican government reneged. However, she never got to use the excuse since the attorney Gummy discovered she did not have even a promise of concessions.

Until Philadelphia, Velazquez seemingly had never induced investors to the point that they might ask for proof. Even if her ruse became too hot to handle over the course of the 18 months she had promoted her scheme, she could always move on, just as she did. By the time she reached Philadelphia she had perfected her storyline and false documents enough to finally get investors to believe her and incorporate a company.

Velazquez, in writing (*TWIB*, p363) about attributes of a good spy, which she considered herself, possibly revealed a thinking which she carried to the railroad con:

> The fact is, that human nature is greatly given to confidence; so much so, that the most unconfiding [*sic*] and suspicious people are usually the easiest to extract any desired information from....

She continued, that women could "more easily deceive other people, and are less easily imposed upon." No doubt Velazquez was right, but in this case, Mr. Gummey was bent to impose upon her.

It is most interesting the way Velazquez connected the name of "F. L. De La Barra, a Mexican official" to the project, implying he had a direct interest in the project, when in truth, in a reply letter to Mr. Gummey, De La Barra "disclaimed all knowledge of Mrs. Beard, except that she had written to him for government maps and documents which he had sent to her." Here is a clear example of how Velazquez used people's names to endorse her or her claimed deeds! Do you suppose Mr. Gummy double-checked with "the brother-in-law of President Díaz" just to make sure it wasn't Mr. De La Barra who was the liar here?

Also interesting is the article's revelation as to how the Beards made their acquaintance with Philadelphia and its citizens, and how William Beard was furnished with the $1,500 dollars for the Alaska misadventure and how Dr. Hancock gave Velazquez her travel money to search for her husband.

Validated (as though it was needed) is the fact that Velazquez never made a survey trip through Mexico. Son Waldemar, who was always with her throughout this period, said he never went to Mexico or was astride a mule.

It is disturbing that her son was identified as a 15-year-old because that would have made him born in 1886 and therefore not the son of William Beard, as has been thought the case. Previously, Waldemar was identified by the *Philadelphia Inquirer* of July 15, 1898 as the Beards' 10-year-old son residing "with his parents in Philadelphia." That would have made Waldemar born in 1888 and the Beards were married August 20, 1887, which is a good fit. However, an August 21, 1894 Arizona newspaper stated that "their" son was 7 years-old.[2] This would have made the child born on the day of the wedding, at best, or sometime before.

Recall, in 1886 Velazquez was living with Edward Goddard and she confronted Goddard in public with a baby in her arms and proclaimed to her listeners that the child was Goddard's. Goddard more insinuated than asserted, that it was not his. He said, "she… carrying a babe supposed to be hers, proclaiming me to be a villain of the deepest dye…." Was the baby in her arms Waldemar? Clearly, Goddard did not give a firm denial that he was "a villain," or rather, the daddy; Goddard implied that the child wasn't even hers. Goddard also said it was untrue that he was the father of the deceased infant, but he was.

Later, in a 1912 document, Velazquez's son will be identified as 28 years old which would have made him born in 1884. It would appear that there is a two out of three chance that Waldemar was not William Beard's son. To date, conclusive evidence of Waldemar's birth and fate (though he makes another brief appearance) has not been found and is waiting for discovery by some future researcher.

Disquieting is Velazquez not only targeted investors who probably could survive a financial cheating, but she took advantage of her simple landlords, the Binders. On the other hand, the cheating of Charles E. Foster, the agent of dubious character, evokes little sympathy. But what of the elderly department store attendant who "went security" for her purchases? In other words, if Mrs. Beard failed to pay for her department store purchases, the elderly gentleman would be forced to pay the bill. And it is difficult to believe that Velazquez ever paid her bill, since she abruptly departed Philadelphia.

It will be seen that Velazquez was not yet finished with railroads.

Also not yet finished was the American-Mexican Railroad Company which had found "new signs of life" under "several reputable citizens of Tucson." They sought "a continuation [a variation] of the scheme pushed…

---

2. *Arizona Daily Star*, Aug 21, 1894.

last year by a weird female, Mrs. J. Velasquez Beard, who claimed to have concessions galore... exhibited her reticule of documents... tried to organize a corporation... and then disappeared."³

1901, Author Marian West was Skeptical

During Velazquez's railroad years, no newspapers seemingly made the connection between promoter, Madame Velazquez Beard and Madame Loreta Janeta Velazquez, author of *The Woman in Battle*. The stories about the Civil War "heroine" still appeared in the press and, as always, were presented as true. The stories were usually synopses of the memoir and at times the writers failed in their accuracy, although they had presumably read *The Woman in Battle*.

A case in point was a nicely written and illustrated article by Marian West in *Munsey's Magazine* (New York) of May 1901 titled "Women Who Have Passed as Men." Marian West wrote:

[Velazquez's] editor remarks that in the course of her varied career as soldier and spy, she found time to be married three times and to give birth to four children, which is manifestly an impossibility, unless we include the three children who were born and died in Cuba before the war.

Poor Marion West must have gotten very confused.

First, Velazquez's editor never wrote (*TWIB*, p7-13) a word on the topic of Velazquez's marriages or children.

Second, Velazquez, in her book, claimed four marriages, of which only one was during the War when she was reputed to be a soldier. Of the other three, one was before the War began and two were after the War ended.

Third, Velazquez claimed (*TWIB*, p50) her three children by her first husband died in the fall of 1860, in St. Louis, before the war commenced. She did not state where the three children were born, but named three cities in which she resided during that time frame: St. Louis, New Orleans and Fort Leavenworth. The fourth child mentioned in *TWIB* was born to her and husband E. H. Bonner, while in Utah, long after the War. No children were born to Velazquez in Cuba and Velazquez never claimed such a thing. Velazquez claimed she herself was a child during her years in Cuba. Because of her erroneous reading of *TWIB*, Marian West concluded that these marriages and births were "manifestly an impossibility." Unfortunately, Marion West searched no deeper for answers to the riddle which confounded her. Had she searched, she might have located Velazquez once again residing (about 1902) in New York City where West's story was published.

Marian West was perfectly capable of investigative reporting as evinced by her later *Munsey's Magazine* article of January 1902 titled:

---

3. *Los Angeles Times*, Mar 11, 1902, by special correspondent, Tucson (Arizona) Mar 9.

The Truth About Barbara Frietchie,- The Heroine of the [John Greenleaf] Whittier Poem and the Historical Reason for Believing that she did not Perform the Brave Deed Ascribed to Her.

This well-received patriotic poem is mostly forgotten today.

Barbara, who was reputed to have been almost 96 years old, "hung out the Stars and Stripes when [Confederate] Stonewall Jackson marched through the town of Frederick [Maryland] on his way to Harper's Ferry and had bidden him shoot her if he must, but spare [the] country's flag."

Marian West concluded the poem was just a poem, and not historically accurate. Colonel Douglas of General Jackson's staff concurred, "I was with him every minute while he was in the town, and nothing like the patriotic incident so graphically described by Mr. Whittier in his poem ever occurred."[4] Had West pursued the historical accuracy of Velazquez's story as she did for Barbara Frietchie, Marian West would have had much to write about.

Nine months prior to Marian West's Velazquez article, the *Chicago Tribune* ran a story about a military reunion in Chicago.[5] One Michigan veteran praised female nurses in general, but particularly Annie Etheridge who was "with the Second Michigan as regimental nurse." The veteran then spoke of several other women, among them, Velazquez:

Certainly the most sensational part played by a woman in the Civil War was that of Mme. Velasquez, a pretty young Southern woman of Spanish descent, who disguised herself as a man and for many years served as a Lieutenant in the Confederate army under the name of Lieutenant Harry Buford. In this capacity she took part in several battles, leading her men with great fearlessness and skill and winning the compliments of her superior officers for gallantry on the field of battle. In the later part of the war she was made an agent of the Confederate secret service, and in various disguises spent months in the North, traveling repeatedly from New York to Chicago, Philadelphia, and other cities. At one time she even succeeded in getting employment under the head of the United States secret service in New York City, and in that position was able to secure information of great value to the Confederacy.

At the Battle of Ball's Bluff she was in command of a regiment, and the men under her charge captured more than a hundred Federal prisoners. It was the scene of bloodshed of which she was forced to witness here that finally led her to give up active service in the army and go into the secret service, which, while quite as dangerous, did not lead her constantly into the presence of wounded and dying. During the whole of her service she was never wounded, though it is said that she often took greater chances than were necessary.

---

4. Henry Kyd Douglas, *I Rode with Stonewall* (Chapel Hill, NC: Univ of North Carolina Press, 1940, 1968), 151-152.
5. Aug 31, 1900.

The veteran clearly knew nothing first-hand about Velazquez and he positively never read her memoir if his accuracy is used as evidence. In her memoir, Velazquez did <u>not</u> claim she "for many years served as a Lieutenant," or that she commanded a <u>regiment</u> at Ball's Bluff, or that "during the whole of her service she was never wounded." It is impossible to understand where the veteran got his erroneous information.

The *Richmond Planet* and the *New Orleans Item* repeated the article in part, leaving out the other women, who were Northern and presumably of no interest to their Southern audience. These newspapers presented just the section about Velazquez under the title "A Brave Southern Woman."[6]

1903, Some Heroic Women

In 1903 the State Committee Daughters of the Confederacy edited and published a 413-page book titled *South Carolina Women in the Confederacy*.[7] The editors wandered outside the title of the book and included stories of women who were not from South Carolina and one of these was Velazquez.

The chapter titled "Some Heroic Women" gave a routine summary of *The Woman in Battle* and about Velazquez said:

Of all who have gained a reputation for reckless daring and deeds of valor during the Civil War, there are none who outranked the brave Cuban girl, Loretta Valesque [*sic*].

Author Mrs. White then proceeded with claims about Velazquez which Velazquez herself never made, such as, Velazquez's husband "helped to drill her [Velazquez's] soldiers" and that Velazquez "succeeded in having her company transferred to Virginia, and marched into line at the Battle of Bull Run." In her memoir, Velazquez never claimed her husband helped her drill her men or that she took these men to Virginia. Mrs. White's concluded, "The last that was heard of this wonderful woman, she had gone to California as a miner." Velazquez never claimed she was a miner herself, but did say truthfully that her husband was. Clearly Mrs. White had not glimpsed the cover of, much less read, *The Woman in Battle* or she might have correctly spelled Velazquez's name.

South Carolina Women in the Confederacy must have excited interest in South Carolina about Velazquez and her book, judging by a request from the Gonzales Book Co., in Columbia, S. C. for "Woman in Battle by Lt. Buford" in the Books Wanted classified section in the *Publishers' Weekly* for the July 2, 1904 edition. Obviously, the requester did not know or remember the

---

6. Feb 9, 1901 and Apr 26, 1901, respectively.
7. State Committee Daughters of the Confederacy, ed., *South Carolina Women in the Confederacy* (Columbia, SC: State Co., 1903). The "records [were] collected" by Mrs. A. T. Smythe, Miss M. B. Poppenheim and Mrs. Thomas Taylor. Chapter "Some Heroic Women" by Mrs. James H. White.

book's author and Velazquez seemly was not making any public displays of her association with her book during the 1900's.

1905, Returned to New York

After her train wreck in Philadelphia, Velazquez hastened to New York, likely arriving in November 1901. About three and a half years later she is found listed in the 1905 New York City Census taken on June 1st: "*Name*- Beard, L. J. V.; *Relation of each person to the head of the household*- lodger; *Color or race*- w; *Sex*- m; *Age at last birthday*- 60; *Nativity*- US; *Citizenship, Number of years in the United States*- blank; *Alien or citizen*- cit; *Occupation*- promoter."

The census information abounds in contradictions and raises questions. Her age, as recorded, would make her born in 1845, not 1842, as claimed in her book. Her country of birth was recorded as the United States, not Cuba, as claimed in her book and in so many newspapers which interviewed her. But the most curious was that her sex was recorded as "m" for male. Did a careless census-taker mark an inaccurate, but perfectly clear "m"? Did Velazquez present herself as a man to the census taker when he came knocking? Was she once more donning the attire of a man? All the lodgers at the boarding house were listed as male. Did she dress as a man for the purpose of securing lodging? Did she dress as a man so that she could live with one of the male lodgers and thereby avoid the criticism of neighbors? The next listed person at that dwelling was a male lodger, sixty-two years of age, born in Cuba, living in the U.S. for fifteen years and a lawyer. Was she living with him? It is not clear if any of these possibilities is fact. It is curious that the boarding house operator, Andres Muro, was also born in Cuba.

L. J. V. Beard did not claim her occupation was author, but instead "promoter." Indeed, she was still promoting a railroad, as will be seen momentarily. And she had years of experience promoting railroad and colonization schemes. It is possible she had sold away her book rights or if she still held them, she was not touting her authorship or her book.

This New York City Census makes clear her son Waldemar was not at the boarding house with her (or anywhere else in the census). He was likely off on his own because he was at least 17 years old at this time. And he could have been older, this possibility raised by one newspaper account and by a forthcoming document.

The debacle in Philadelphia did not stop Velazquez's tenacious promotion of railroad schemes. A new incorporation was announced in Maine:[8]

Augusta, Me., May 24, 1905. The Mexican American Construction Company, with capitalization of $10,000,000 today filed a certificate of incorporation at the office of the secretary of state. It was organized at Portland to build and operate

---

8. *Boston Herald*, May 25, 1905, special dispatch to the *Boston Herald*.

railroads and to develop real estate. Nothing of the capital stock is paid in and the par value of a share is $100.

The fee for the organization is $1695 [rather unclear number], and as the certificate of incorporation was filed before June 1, the company will be obliged to pay a state franchise tax of $275. The incorporators are J. B. Woolworth, Gregor Landes, John J. Whittemore and L. J. V. Beard of New York city, Julian Kleisler of South Hampton, N. Y., and M. T. Osgood and George F. Gould of Portland.

One incorporator, John J. Whittemore, was a boarder where Velazquez was living. The census indicates he was a 60-year-old US-born lawyer. Clearly, Velazquez was still persuasive and Whittemore was clueless of her history. This group adopted the old name which Albert K. Owen used in his failed effort to build the railroad to the socialist Topolobampo colony.

The corporation was still on the books of the Maine Bureau of Taxation for the year ending November 1, 1907 with $10,000,000 in "Capital Stock" and a tax of $525.[9] The fate of the company is unknown, but if it ended in scandal, or thrived, it would seem that its history would have been found. An off-the-cuff guess is that it faded away for lack of money and interest. This was the last railroad company found associated with Velazquez. In spite of her many energetic promotions, she never succeeded in building a railroad.

1905 to 1908, the Myth Revived

Velazquez, the author and person, seemingly disappeared, but her story had not. Only days after the June 1, 1905 New York City Census, which showed her living in obscurity, or maybe more correctly, disguise, the *Sunny South* (Georgia newspaper)[10] revived her past glory, reprinting the old 1863 "A Female Lieutenant" article:

The following interesting item appeared in *The Richmond Examiner* in 1863. Lieutenant Buford, the female lieutenant from the south, arrested in this city, and sent to Castle Thunder....

This was the article which explained she had been arrested for wearing military attire, but was released by General Winder and that her "real name is Mrs. S. T. Williams... her father is Major J. B. Roche, of Mississippi, but she was born in the West Indies." Her family was wealthy, "her annual income before the war was $20,000 most of which she spent in getting medicines for the confederate government"... she nursed the wounded and fought "in several battles."

Of course, if any patron of the *Sunny South* read the article and by chance during the passing years had read *The Woman in Battle*, they would have been

---

9. *Seventeenth Annual Report of the Board of State Assessors of the State of Maine 1907* (Augusta, ME: Kennebec, 1907), 295.
10. Jun 17, 1905.

left wondering how her father, "Major J. B. Roche" from Mississippi, had undergone a name change to "the noble name of Velasquez," and was instead born in Spain. They might also have wondered at the contradiction that she spent all her money helping the wounded, when she made no such claim in her book and claimed instead, she spent her money raising a "battalion."

Then on April 8, 1906 the *New-York Tribune* published an article titled "Women as Warriors" by Edward G. Holden who presented a historical record of women participating in wars of all eras around the world. The long article included one paragraph about Lieutenant Buford:

> A picturesque figure of the Civil War was Loreta Velasquez, a Cuban maid, who left her native land and joined the Southern forces. She began her career by marrying a Northern officer, who she persuaded to go over to the Confederate side. "Lieutenant Harry Buford," as she was known, fought with energy and valor in the first battle of Bull Run. Afterward she became a spy, and by the wearing of male or female costume whenever it suited her purpose, gave valuable aid to the Confederacy. She finally went to California as a miner.

It is curious that a New York newspaper article should appear coinciding with Velazquez's presence there. It brings to mind the earlier and similar article in Chicago at a time when Velazquez traveled there.[11] Is it possible that she sold, or in some manner put forth the topic to the New York paper? Years earlier, in 1878, Velazquez wrote to General Jubal Early that "correspondence with the Press" was one way she earned her money and she claimed this several times later.

The *New-York Tribune* writer, Edward G. Holden, was more than a staff writer; he published articles under his own name, rather uncommon for the times. It is paradoxical that Lieutenant Harry Buford was living in the same city as the sixty-six-year-old Holden,[12] yet Holden ostensibly did not know of her presence there and failed to secure an interview.

It was in 1906 that Ex-Confederate Lieutenant-General Bromfield Ridley, of General A. P. Stewart's staff, published his book, *Battles and Sketches of the Army of Tennessee*, in which he repeated the passage which he had earlier written in the *Confederate Veteran Magazine* of April 1896 identifying "Lieutenant Buford" in a seemly firsthand account. This passage is the best-known account of Velazquez in a military environment:

> I recollect another heroine, a Lieutenant Buford of an Arkansas regiment. She stepped and walked the personification of a soldier boy; had won her spurs on the battlefield at Bull Run, Fort Donelson, and Shiloh, and was promoted for gallantry. One evening she came to General Stewart's headquarters, at Tyner's Station, with

---

11. *Chicago Tribune*, Aug 31, 1900.
12. New York City Census 1905.

an order from Major Kinloch Falconer to report to duty as a scout, but upon his finding the 'he' was a woman, she was sent back and the order revoked. She has written a book.

It is clear that in the first sentence Ridley was parroting Velazquez's published story. Ridley was not at Bull Run, or Fort Donelson or Shiloh, so he had no firsthand knowledge if she was there. Ridley implied that he understood that Velazquez was with "an Arkansas regiment" at Bull Run, Fort Donelson and Shiloh. However, in her book, Velazquez wrote that at Bull Run she was with troops other than "an Arkansas regiment." In addition, she claimed that at Fort Donelson she operated independently, but finally kept company with some Virginians. And lastly, Velazquez explained that at Shiloh she had the good fortune of reuniting with her old Arkansas company and commanding the company was her friend (and soon to be husband) Captain Thomas DeCaulp. The problem with the claim is that DeCaulp's Arkansas company was part of the 3rd Arkansas Cavalry and it was not present at the Battle of Shiloh. In 1862 when she was arrested in New Orleans for stealing, she made a contradictory claim to the newspaper, that she was at Shiloh with the 11th Louisiana Regiment.

The second sentence might indicate Ridley's firsthand knowledge of her, that is, her appearance at Tyner's Station, (first station stop east of Chattanooga) where he said she sought scouting duties. To date, this is the closest thing to a firsthand account verifying any portion of her claims to military activity. However, Ridley's testimony is rather weak. He does not say that he saw her- what she looked like or what she was wearing. He may have been away from headquarters at the time of her appearance and was only told about the incident afterwards. In fact, Ridley implied that A. P. Stewart made the discovery of her disguised sex and not himself.

Velazquez did not write of this episode. She did not write she sought a job as a scout from General Stewart by order of Major Falconer. She did not even mention General Stewart or Major Falconer. She only wrote (*TWIB*, p293) that she passed through Tyner's Station on the way to find Captain DeCaulp who she learned was near Spring Hill with Van Dorn:

> Getting off at Tyner's Station, I obtained a horse, and started off in the direction of Chickamauga. At this point I fell in with General Pegram's cavalry, and had the great pleasure of seeing the handsome General Frank Armstrong, an officer for whom I entertained an intense admiration.

Velazquez placed this event in the summer of 1863 and a contradiction becomes apparent when it becomes known that Van Dorn was already killed on May 7, 1863. Furthermore, Velazquez wrote (p291) the reason for her trip was she was most anxious to again see Captain DeCaulp:

I had not seen the captain since the battle of Shiloh, where I fought by his side, or at least under his eye, during nearly the whole of the conflict, succeeding in winning his commendation for my courage, without exciting any suspicion in his mind that I was the woman upon whom his affections were bestowed.

It is simply untrue that Captain DeCaulp was at Shiloh, so Velazquez could not have fought with courage beside him. Did she even go looking for Captain DeCaulp who she thought "was near at hand"?

It's a pity that Velazquez wrote nothing to corroborate Ridley's assertion, but instead only injected falsehoods which bolster doubt.

Ridley's third sentence, "She has written a book," in conjunction with his first sentence, implies that Ridley may have read the book, and if in fact he did, it may have tainted his testimony in the sense that he was charmed by her story rather than relied on the accuracy of his own memory.

It is curious that Ridley alleged Major Kinloch Falconer sent her seeking the job. Falconer was from Holly Springs, Mississippi where he was a newspaper editor and at the beginning of the War joined the old Company B, 9th Mississippi Infantry as a private. This is the second person from Holly Springs with whom Velazquez seeming had an association. Recall, that Velazquez wrote that before the Battle of Ball's Bluff that she encountered Colonel Featherston who she claimed she knew when she was only a child. Colonel Featherston also was a resident of Holly Springs. These associations and Velazquez's Mississippi connections are covered elsewhere.

In conclusion, Ridley's one paragraph does not validate the many claims of her participation in battles or of her wounds or of her heroism contained in *The Woman in Battle* or newspapers. The paragraph, at most, tells of her presence among troops during the War, which is not in doubt and never was. And recall Confederate soldier Robert Hodges Jr. saw a female lieutenant at the train station, which matches the place of Ridley's narration and soldier Van Buren Oldham reported her, by name, in Chattanooga.

Typical newspapers of this time simply repeated Velazquez's memoir. The *Weekly Banner*[13] (Athens, Georgia) of September 13, 1907 was such a case; it published an amazingly long article of approximately 2200 words titled "The Thrilling Deeds of a Woman Soldier." The author, R. M. Rawls, did nothing to enlighten the public as to the true person behind the legend, but was satisfied to repeat the romantic and interesting points of the memoir.

Some newspapers of this time failed, as others had failed, to retell accurately what Velazquez wrote; a case in point was the *Washington Post* of March 8, 1908[14] which ran an article titled "Famous Women in Male Attire, Some Remarkable Cases of Female Soldiers Who Have Won Fame." The

---

13. Copying the *Birmingham Age-Herald*.
14. Copying the *Kansas City Star*.

article applied only one paragraph to Velazquez and it stated that she served in the army for the "pure love of adventure… obtained a Lieutenant's commission… distinguished herself at the battle of Bull Run… [and] had an adventurous and thrilling career as a soldier and spy." Well, Velazquez never claimed in her book to have "obtained a Lieutenant's commission," but only that she gave herself the rank of lieutenant.

Not everyone thought to honor Velazquez. In 1906 a new and substantial book of 313 pages was published titled *The Women of the Confederacy* by Reverend John Levi Underwood, Master of Arts, Mercer University, Captain and Chaplain in the Confederate army. He failed to mention Velazquez. The author was an ex-Confederate and contemporary of hers, yet he seemingly did not know her or of her or maybe he knew of a reason not to include her.

1908, a Heroine in Need of Rescuing

Unlike romantic storybook characters, frozen in time and youthful health, real people age and get sick. And that was how Velazquez next appeared in a public notice. The *New York Times* announced, "Mrs. Beard Ill and in Want- Once Wealthy War Nurse and Friend of ex-President Cleveland." The article[15] explained:

Mrs. L. J. V. Beard, once wealthy and numbering among her friends ex-president Cleveland and other prominent men, and who was a nurse in an army hospital in Richmond, Va., during the civil war, lies in New York Hospital, critically ill and reduced to want.

Doctors say she will die unless she can have the quiet of a room to herself and special treatment. These she is too poor to obtain. She is now 68 years old.

For twenty-five years Mrs. Beard has been a familiar figure in New York, and only recently has become helpless. She is widely known in Washington and the South. While the civil war was in progress she went to Canada and obtained thousands of dollars for the Southern cause, in addition to nursing wounded soldiers.

Her first husband was a member of the personal staff of Gen. Joseph E. Johnston. She is now a widow, with one son too young to be of much help to her in her present extremity.

First, Velazquez was elusive, as always, about her age, stating it at 68. This would have made her born in 1840, which contradicts the 1842 date she gave in her book. Now instead of claiming a younger age, as she previously did, she claimed an older age, seemingly seeking sympathy and help which might be directed to an elderly person.

Second, in her book, she never claimed to have nursed soldiers in Richmond. It appears she might have been playing to her audience, seeking reciprocating medical attention for herself. Of course, it is possible that she

---

15. Mar 21, 1908.

tried a nursing job during the War, did not like it, and so didn't bother to mention it in her book. She did claim in a newspaper article[16] to have nursed Confederate prisoners held at Camp Chase, Ohio, but never in Richmond. A Mobile newspaper in 1874 credited her with the same; "The starved, inhumanely treated prisoners of camp Chase, have every reason to remember her who nursed them, fed them, and furnished them every cent she could spare, day after day." There has been no record found to date of her activity at Camp Chase. She, in her book, never claimed to have nursed prisoners at Camp Chase, only to have gone there to get her brother released, and this brother's very existence was likely untrue and his life's story certainly is a lie. However, she did claim she nursed Captain Thomas C. DeCaulp, her husband-to-be, in Atlanta and that should be believed. After all, if you don't keep him alive, you can't marry him.

It is believable that Velazquez went (at least once) to Camp Chase, because of her accurate description of one of its officers. Velazquez wrote (p381):

> On reaching Todd [*sic* Tod] Barracks, where the prisoners were confined, I found a one-armed major in command. He was very polite indeed, and entered into quite a conversation with me, during which he told me that he lost his arm in the Mexican war. When my brother came, the major gave us his own private room, so that we might talk together without fear of interruption.

It is not believable that at Camp Chase she visited a brother of the specific history which she gave about him. Velazquez may have had a brother, just not the one she described.

The one-armed major was Uniontown, Pennsylvania-born Major John W. Skiles, who, at that time, was a major in the 88th Ohio Volunteer Infantry, Commanding Tod Barracks. He was indeed a Mexican War veteran, but had not lost his arm in that war.

> Mr. Skiles was a member of Colonel Roberts' regiment in the war with Mexico, and again entered the service of his country in the 23rd Ohio regiment, and was wounded September 14, 1862, near Frederick, Maryland, and had his arm amputated.[17]

In spite of her accurate mention of the one-armed major, the nature of her claimed interaction with him was likely false. It is right to be suspicious when one recalls her claim that British Consul George Coppell got her released from jail, which was a lie, and her claim to have met "General Wessells, the Commissary General of Prisoners," when at that date, he was far from holding that job, thus another lie. Velazquez had a knack for pulling prominent people into her storyline and Major Skiles was prominent. In

---

16. *St. Louis Republican*, Mar 7, 1866.
17. James Hadden, *A History of Uniontown* (Place and publisher not identified, 1913), 113.

addition to his position commanding Tod Barracks, he was Provost Marshal for the city of Columbus, Ohio. Every stranger's presence in town was his business and he likely looked into Velazquez's presence there and in that way, she met him.

Later, on April 28, 1865, in anticipation of Lincoln's funeral procession's arrival in Columbus and visitation of Lincoln's body in the state's capitol rotunda, Major Skiles was "appointed Chief Marshal of the ceremonies in honor of the remains of the late President Lincoln, in the city of Columbus." Major Skiles was in "entire control" of the "procession attending the transfer of the remains from and to the depot."[18]

Major Skiles was certainly a prominent individual worthy of name-dropping, but it cannot be correctly stated that Velazquez evoked Major Skiles name because, clearly, she did not give his name. She rather acted like the Major was an obscure person and she hadn't gotten his name. At this point an attentive reader should be puzzled; throughout her book she recalled the names of almost everyone, from the hotel keeper, Mr. Jones, in Meridian, Mississippi, to Lieutenant B who told her of her brother's captivity, to Lieutenant Shorter who gave her a mission, to Major Bacon and Lieutenant Chamberlain who talked her out of fighting with General F, to Mr. B who told her where she could find friendly Southern sympathizers (p379), to "Captain Marriotta, the provost marshal" of Okolona (p352) who granted her a travel pass to go see General Ferguson. It would seem asking for a travel pass from "Captain Marriotta" must have involved only the briefest association, yet Velazquez still remembered him. Let it be noted that to date no evidence of "Captain Marriotta" has surfaced in any military records and he surely was an invention. There were many, many other people she recalled, even though her meeting them was most fleeting. For example, she named an Orinoco River pilot, Antonio Silva, who briefly came aboard the vessel of the emigrants upon their arrival in Venezuela! So why is it she forgot the name of a most unique, important official who treated her with great courtesy, gave her access to her prisoner brother and loaned his private quarters so that she could speak with her brother in private, hmm?

Third, the most bold and contradictory statement, and a lie, was that her first husband was on the "personal staff of Gen. Joseph E. Johnston." In her book she stated that her first husband, "William," left Memphis, joined the Confederacy, went to Pensacola and died there prior to June 16, 1861 He, therefore, would never have had a chance to be on the "personal staff of Gen. Joseph E. Johnston."

---

18. John Carroll Power, *Abraham Lincoln: His Life, Public Services, Death and Great Funeral Cortege* (Chicago and Springfield, IL: H. W. Rokker, 1889), 173.

When Velazquez told the *Atlanta Constitution* (September 4, 1874) that her first husband, "William," was William E. Burnet from Texas, it becomes even more obvious that she was prevaricating. Burnet did not die in Pensacola in 1861, but died in Spanish Fort, Alabama, across the river delta from Mobile, in 1865. It was a lie that Burnet was her husband, and besides, Burnet did not serve on the staff of General Joseph E. Johnston.

Fourth, her "one son too young to be of much help" would have been Waldemar and 20 years of age. (He was identified in 1898 newspaper articles as a 10-year-old.) He also could have been 22 or 24 years old according to other sources. He may have been no help to her, but he was hardly too young.

The nature of her illness and the "special treatment" sought can only be guessed since the hospital's records no longer exist. Although some records for New York Hospital for this date do exist,[19] the file for Mrs. Beard is not one of the surviving records. The fact that the "quiet of a room to herself and special treatment" was needed indicates a nervous disorder or flight of fancy which needed calming.

How or whether she succeeded in getting the requested financial help to enable a full recovery is not clear, but she left the hospital and seems to have rallied. On October 22, 1908 in Albany, New York, the "World Finance Company" was incorporated by directors: L. J. V. Beard at 200 Broadway; C. L. Thorne at 213 E 24th St and the aforementioned J. G. B. Woolworth at 260 Sixth Avenue.[20] James G. B. Woolworth was a Lewis County, NY native and a driven, successful man who in 1891 had purchased the famous Grand Union Hotel in Saratoga Springs, New York; he met with U.S. President Harrison to plan the President's August 1891 visit there.[21] It is unclear who C. L. Thorne was. In any case, the World Finance Company seems to have gone nowhere.

Relocated to Washington, D.C.

Velazquez relocated to Washington, D.C. sometime between late 1908 and 1911; her presence is noted in the 1911 *Washington DC City Directory*, as "Beard, L. J. Velasquez, real est. 1329 G nw." The listing indicated she was a real estate agent of some sort, but it can be reasonably doubted that she had any great financial success, as events will show.

In the meanwhile, the newspapers continued with the flattering stories about Velazquez's legend in particular, and/or female soldiers in general. It was the *Salt Lake Herald's* turn this time.[22] Over the next dozen Sundays, the newspaper ran a series, "Twenty Women Soldiers of the World," which

---

19. Medical Center Archives, New York-Presbyterian/Weill Cornell Medical Center.
20. *New York Times*, Oct 23. 1908.
21. *Frank Leslie's Illustrated Newspaper*, Apr 4, 1891.
22. Mar 7, 1909.

profiled one or two women each week. The week of May 2, 1909 was Velazquez's turn and it was the standard repeat of her published story.[23]

In Velazquez's own backyard, the *Washington Herald* of July 11, 1909 published an article titled "Amazons of the Civil War" in which Pauline Cushman and Belle Boyd were given their due, but in a rare departure from other newspapers, Velazquez was discredited:

> There was... a Spanish girl, Loreta Velasquez; a Confederate sympathizer, and many others, all famous in their time, and responsible for reams and volumes of writing- autobiographical, biographical, apocryphal, and frankly fictitious.

More typical were flattering articles such as the *Chicago Daily Tribune's* titled "Some Joans of Arc" which stated, "The public will remember, says the *Richmond Examiner*, Sept. 13, 1863, the numerous paragraphs published concerning one 'Lieut. Harry Buford....'"[24] The article proceeded with the exact article from that date, presented as factual. Or the *Oregonian* article of July 31, 1910 titled "Women in Trousers Lead Lives as Men" which presented the two illustrations of Velazquez from her book, one in and the other out of disguise. The article repeated, as fact, the same claims found in Velazquez's book, but added more than even Velazquez claimed. It stated, "in later life she joined a miner's camp as a man," which she did not do and did not say she did.

Interest in her book persisted even if some of the people looking for copies did not know the book's title. The *Publishers Weekly* of May 13, 1911 contained in the "Books Wanted" section a request from Geo. D. Smith of 48 Wall St. N. Y. who asked for "Life of Janeta Loreta Velasquez (wife of a Confederate Officer)." At an earlier date, Geo. D. Smith of New York might have shared the New York sidewalk with Velazquez or she might have even been able to hand-deliver a copy of her book, but at this date she was residing in Washington, D.C.

It was in 1911 that Velazquez's story made its first known appearance in a children's book, *The All Sorts of Stories Book* by Mrs. (Leonora Blanche) Lang. This London and New York published book was part of "The Fairy Book Series" edited by Andrew Lang. A book guide characterized Mrs. Lang's book as "historical stories" of "persons whose adventures were exciting in the extreme."[25] The twelve-page chapter, "Loreta Velazquez, the Military Spy," recounted portions of Velazquez's memoir. Mrs. Lang explained that she had searched with the help of one Professor Brander Matthews for an edition of Velazquez's book, but failed to locate one. Lang

---

23. The May 9 edition, in error, was titled "No. 10- Madam Loreta Janetta Velasquez," but it does not mention of her. May 2 addresses Velazquez.
24. Feb 7, 1909.
25. *A. L. A. Booklist, a Guide to the Best Books* (Chicago: American Library Ass., 1911), 416.

said that she was "forced to rely on the portions reprinted in *Women Adventurers*." Recall, this was Ménie Muriel Dowie's 1893 book which had reprinted portions of Velazquez's memoir.

Since Mrs. Lang did not know the full scope of Velazquez's story, she supplied a very loose retelling of Velazquez's memoir. Lang did not understand Dowie's too brief of an introduction and misunderstood Dowie's explanation of Velazquez's meeting of her first husband. So, in error, Lang asserted that Velazquez at the age of fourteen was still living in Cuba with her parents who "expected her to marry some rich planter in the island, and gave but a cold welcome to the young American officer who frequently rode over from the house where he was staying to lounge about under the shady trees with Loreta." Of course, by now readers know Velazquez made no such claim and can easily see Lang's error. Author Lang concluded:

Is she alive now? It is quite possible, for she would only be sixty-nine. But her life by her own choice was a hard one, and may have worn her out before her time.

Of course, Velazquez was alive, but she had faded from public view as the author of *The Woman in Battle* and apparently willingly. Thus, it is surprising that she sought a re-emergence which was reported by the *Washington Times:*

Woman Writer Here to Collect Data with the purpose of rewriting her book, "The Woman in Battle," which described her experiences in the civil war. Mrs. L. J. V. Beard is again making a visit to Washington, gathering data. She is also contemplating the writing of a volume on relations existing between the United States and Mexico. She has recently made a protracted study of political and social conditions in the latter republic.[26]

It would seem that Velazquez was maintaining a facade as a visitor because she can plainly be identified living in Washington in 1911 by her listing in that year's *City Directory*. It also is curious that she sought attention for her book after many years of not doing so. It has been speculated that she no longer had the rights to her book and that was why she had not been noticeably promoting it. In any case, it will be seen that she did not rewrite her book and she never wrote anything about Mexico, either.

The Woman in Battle was getting attention without Velazquez's promotion and was included through the years in various catalogs, encyclopedias, compilations and indices of literary works or of authors or of library holdings. They all inadvertently promoted the story as true just by giving a synopsis of the work and even made claims about Velazquez which she herself never made. For example, the *Library of Southern Literature (Volume*

---

26. Jun 4, 1912.

XV) Biographical Dictionary of Authors,[27] in its short biographical paragraph on "Velasquez, Loretta Janeta, Madame," included these facts, "Heroine" and "Her girlhood days were spent in Texas" which Velazquez never claimed in her book.

That assertion was echoed in 1913 by *Writers and Writings of Texas* with the simple sentence, "Girlhood days in Texas."[28]

Jumping ahead to the next century finds authors DeAnne Blanton and Lauren M. Cook in 2002 claiming, "Ten years after the close of the war, Velazquez resided in Texas, where she penned her memoirs."[29] And writer Maggie Van Ostrand in a 2009 *Texas Escapes* magazine article, "A Confederate Soldier in Texas: Full Metal Corset," borrowed from them and wrote, "Lt. Harry T. Buford may not have been born a Texan but, after serving in the Confederate army during the Civil War, when it came time to pen memoirs, Texas was the place chosen to do it."[30]

Let's examine the "Girlhood days in Texas" and Texas writer issue.

Velazquez stated (*TWIB*, p40) that her father "fell heir to a large estate in Texas, which was then a part of the republic Mexico" thus resigned as a Spanish government official working in Cuba and so "in 1844 removed with his family to San Luis Potosi, in Central Mexico" to manage this "very large tract of land and immense herds of cattle...." Velazquez related that the family was settled in San Luis Potosí, barely a "twelvemonth," when the Mexican-American War broke out, so the family fled to the West Indies and the estate was abandoned. (The war started April 25, 1846, not in 1845 as Velazquez wrote.)

Velazquez did not claim that she spent 12 months in Texas, but instead in San Luis Potosí, 400 miles south, where her father had moved the family. Only the alleged estate was in Texas not the family. She never claimed to set foot on the estate; would a stroll there (She said part of Mexico.) make her "girlhood days in Texas"? (Prior to 1836 Texas was part of Mexico; Texas was then an independent republic from March 2, 1836 to February 19, 1846 and annexed to the U.S. on February 19, 1846. The disputed ownership of the land lying between the Rio Grande and the Nueces River gave rise to the Mexican-American War of 1846-1848.) Does any child who lived for 12 months in San Luis Potosí, Mexico (which Velazquez did not do anyway) and whose father had an estate 400 miles to the north in Texas (which he never had anyway) qualify them as having a childhood in Texas?

---

27. Compiled by Lucian Lamar Knight, copyright 1907 & 1910.
28. Davis Foute Eagleton, compiler and editor, (NY: Broadway Publishing Co., 1913), 388.
29. DeAnne Blanton and Lauren M. Cook, *They Fought Like Demons*, (Baton Rouge: Louisiana State University Press, 2002), 177.
30. *Texas Escapes* magazine, Jun 18, 2009.

Did her father, who she characterized at that time as "a careful and accurate business man," manage this "very large tract of land and immense herds of cattle" located in Texas from more than 400 miles away, the distance to San Luis Potosí in Central Mexico? Why not live on the estate or in a nearby town? Surely nearby San Antonio would have been the place chosen to live by "a careful and accurate business man" rather than the very distant San Luis Potosí.

When the United States won the Mexican-American War, Mexico ceded (and sold) Texas. Velazquez wrote (p41) that her father abandoned his "estates [which] were included in this territory, refused to live under a government which he disliked so intensely...." But recall, Velazquez said that her father and the family were living 400 miles away in San Luis Potosí, which was not ceded to the United States, so he would not have been <u>living</u> under the United States government.

Velazquez then said her father returned to Cuba where he became heir to "another estate... engaged actively in the sugar, tobacco and coffee trade... speedily acquired great wealth, and was able to surround his family with every luxury." But behold, on page 69 of *TWIB*, Velazquez told that she wrote a letter, in April 1861, to her husband in which she "stated that [she] was going to Texas, for the purpose of accompanying [her] father to Cuba." What was her father doing in Texas? She said that he left a long time ago, in 1848. Surely, he was not living "under a government which he disliked so intensely." But wait, Texas was no longer controlled by the "government which he disliked so intensely" since it had left the Union on February 1, 1861. Why then was he leaving when he might have had a chance to petition the new Confederate Government to recover his land taken by the despised United States?

Velazquez did not adopt the Texas estate story or her proud Velazquez patriarchal heritage, until 1876, with the publication of her book. Prior to this, in July 1863, she told the newspapers, "Her father is Major J. B. Roche, of Mississippi." In August 1864, Velazquez wrote in a forged letter to Gen. Sibley that her father was "Rear Admiral Rosche of the Eng Navy." In December 1864 she forged another letter, under the name of "Don Augustus V. Steinhosse, of Havana," reporting the death of her father, "Commodore J. B. Roach, of the British Navy." Then in April 1866, the newspapers wrote that her "maiden name was Roach, was born in the West Indies in 1838... [and that] at an early period her parents moved to the United States and settled in the Parish of St. James, Louisiana." In 1874 she told the *Atlanta Constitution* her father was "Samuel S. Clapp." Then two years later, in 1876, her father became Velazquez.

Perhaps the most outrageous of the accounts of her parentage and childhood comes from the September 1874 *Atlanta Constitution* newspaper.

The reporter interviewed her and wrote, "Her childhood days were spent in Mississippi, but after she grew up to girlhood her family moved to Texas." How can that be?! In her memoir she asserted her childhood was in Cuba, then at the age of nine she was sent to New Orleans to live with her aunt. The explanation is simply that Velazquez altered the Texas storyline in order to facilitate another falsehood claimed in this interview. She claimed "while the family were [sic] residing in Texas, [she] made the acquaintance of Mr. William E. Burnett [sic Burnet]... and they were married in 1857." If she had failed to alter her story, then her meeting of Mr. William E. Burnet, who she claimed to have married as her first husband, would have been out of whack. She would have met him when she was a child, when her father inherited the Texas cattle ranch, instead of when she was a young woman. She then said that they were married quietly in Texas, the marriage known to only their families. This contradicts her book in which she claimed they were married in New Orleans and the marriage was kept a secret from their families. Any and all versions of this marriage were lies; she never married William E. Burnet!

In the 1874 *Atlanta Constitution* interview, Velazquez fabricated an entirely different parentage, not previously told. She told the newspaper that her maiden name was "Loretta Jeanett Clapp" and that her father was "Samuel S. Clapp," and one of her uncles was "Mr. Theodore Clapp, [who] flourished for many years in New Orleans as a Universalist minister." In addition, she said, "Her father, Samuel S. Clapp, died a confederate prisoner in Fort Hamilton, N. Y., in 1863." Actually, Velazquez had already tried on for size the Clapp surname on November 10, 1868 when she supplied the San Francisco newspaper with a fake obituary for a fake brother named Colonel R. D. Clapp who was to be buried in San Luis Potosí, a place where the family had a fake connection.

The lies in the *Constitution* interview are more plentiful than the prickly pear cacti of Texas. These Clapps never lived in Texas. And "Samuel S Clapp" was not her father. Samuel S. Clapp's correct name was Theodore S. Clapp and he was the son of Reverend Theodore Clapp, who was a renowned New Orleans minister. Reverend Theodore Clapp, a native of Massachusetts, was married on May 31, 1822 to Adeline Hawes and soon after moved to New Orleans. The 1850 U.S. Census lists their son T. S., as a Louisiana born, twenty-two-year-old. Theodore S. (Samuel) Clapp became a doctor of medicine.

Early during the Civil War, the Confederacy employed Samuel Clapp as a contract surgeon. His command was captured and he was taken prisoner, but released as medical officers at that date were not held as prisoners of war. It appears that Dr. Theodore S. Clapp then joined the Union army. In any case, Dr. Theodore S. Clapp did not die as "a confederate prisoner in

Fort Hamilton, New York in 1863" as asserted by Velazquez in the Atlanta interview. Fort Hamilton was never used as a confederate prison and Clapp did not die during the War, but lived long after. He practiced medicine in New Orleans' Charity Hospital and later worked in Kentucky where he died in 1905 at age 77.

Clearly, the Atlanta newspaper version of Velazquez's father as "Samuel S. Clapp," contradicts her book in which she claimed her father was a wealthy Spaniard, "Velazquez," of prominent and noble heritage. It elicits a chuckle of disbelief to realize that these two versions were told in Atlanta only two years apart, yet no one there seemed to have caught on.

Author Maggie Van Ostrand, in her 2009 magazine article, "A Confederate Soldier in Texas: Full Metal Corset," concluded, "What daddy would have hated most was that [Velazquez] would write it in Texas." In other words, Velazquez's father would have been upset if he had known that Velazquez had chosen Texas in which to write her book, considering that the American war with Mexico caused him to abandon his estate in Texas and how he hated America for that.

Velazquez ended her memoir (last two pages of her book) with her traveling through Texas by stagecoach as an adult; the last section was subtitled "The Stage Route Across Texas." Traveling through Texas does not qualify her as a Texas writer. And it is not true that "Velazquez resided in Texas, where she penned her memoirs" as her subsequent history proves. In other words, Velazquez was not a Texas writer!

1914, Swan Song

A June 1914 article in *Pearson's Magazine*,[31] which appeared shortly after Velazquez disappeared from public view, might be considered her swan song. The article, "Secret Service of Miss 'Harry Buford'" by William Gilmore Beymer, was a solid eight pages of the retelling *The Woman in Battle*. It was subtitled "THE WONDERFUL STORY OF A CIVIL WAR WOMAN SPY- A STORY OF ADVENTURE MORE THRILLING THAN ANY FICTION." Beymer's opening paragraph is illustrative of how he, as well as readers, researchers and historians have been captivated:

BELIEVE, if you will, that every statement here recorded is a fact. I think I do. You will not as you read this narrative. I did not when I read the autobiography from which this is taken. But when I had put the book away and had thought it over,- that was different. And so it will be with you. Doubt all you please while you read, for when you have finished, and have matched, as I did, this woman's character with her deeds you will see how convincingly they dovetail together.

Beymer continued with an admirable and accurate enough job of repeating Velazquez's autobiography and concluded:

---

31. Vol. 31, No. 6, 749.

How does it all end? God knows. This story of a strange life comes to an abrupt termination, leaving the autobiographer midway on a journey across the plains en route to the Northwest. Doubtless, it is all that we shall ever know.

Perhaps she is living to-day, a dear old granddame of seventy-odd. Perhaps she may chance upon this story, and as she reads there will again come the old battle-light into 'Lieutenant Harry Buford's' age-dimmed eyes.

One obvious, but minor error is that Velazquez did not conclude her story with her traveling to the "Northwest." Of course, to a weary traveler who is off his intended course, the error isn't so minor, but upsetting. Velazquez wrote she traveled through Texas, "eastward again." Beymer must have meant the Northeast which would have been closer to correct.

Beymer's question of "How does it all end?" has been asked many times, by many people through the years. Though Velazquez's final years are not as heroic as a romantic might wish, they have been discovered and can be told.

1912, Petition, a Matter of Insanity

Velazquez's wanderlust was brought to a sudden stop by the Commissioners and the Supreme Court of the District of Columbia. On the 15th of August 1912 the Commissioners petitioned the Court to adjudicate "Lorette J. Beard" insane and commit her to the asylum. (Court documents spelled her name Lorette with one exception when they spelled her name, Loretta.)

The Commissioners petitioned the Court to hold "an equity court in the matter of the insanity of Lorette J. Beard" and the document stated, in part, that:

...one Lorette J. Beard, who is believed to be insane or of unsound mind, has been apprehended and is now at the Government Hospital for the Insane in this District pending a judicial inquiry into her mental condition; that said Lorette J. Beard is represented to your petitioners and is by them believed to be, an indigent insane person or person of unsound mind, so that she has not sufficient capacity for the government of herself. Your petitioners further believe if said Lorette J. Beard be not an indigent insane person that she is an insane person of homicidal or otherwise dangerous tendencies, so that she has not sufficient capacity for the government of herself and her property; that said Lorette J. Beard has been insane or of unsound mind since, to-wit, the 5th day of August, 1912, that the cause of her insanity or unsoundness of mind, if in fact, it exists, is unknown to your petitioners; but if the representations made to your petitioners be true, the said Lorette J. Beard is unfit to be at large, and is a fit subject for detention and treatment on account of her mental condition; and your petitioners believe that if she be permitted to remain at large within the District the rights of person and property therein will be greatly endangered, the preservation of public peace imperiled, and the commission of crime rendered probable.

The Commissioners concluded their petition with a request for a "writ *de lunatico inquirendo* [lunatic inquiry]." The Supreme Court of the District of Columbia assigned the case: "No. 4734, Lunacy Docket, In regard [to the] alleged lunacy of Lorette J. Beard, Insane Asylum."

On August 22, 1912, the Court, in the name of "the President of the United States" summoned six witnesses "to testify the truth touching the above matter… you are hereby commanded to be and appear before the Justice of this Court assigned to the hearing of lunacy cases." The hearing was set for court room No. 1 on the 29th day of August at 10:30 a.m.

Of the six witnesses, "Wallie J. Beard" is of the greatest interest. He was noted to be her "son" and living at "1219 10th St. N. W." This clearly was her son Waldemar. However, court documents show that Wallie J. Beard was "not to be found." The other witnesses were: one Dr. B. R. Logie, 1792 Columbia Road; three doctors from Washington Asylum Hospital; and W. E. Owens, M. P. [Metropolitan Police], No. 1 Police Station. The document stated that these five witnesses provided testimony.[32]

On August 29, 1912 the "jury of good and lawful men," twelve in number found:

Lorette J. Beard to be of unsound mind, suffering from Paranoid state accompanied with homicidal tendencies; she has not sufficient capacity for the government of herself, and her property; that she has been so insane since July 26, 1912, that said lunatic has not alienated any lands or tenements, that no real estate remains to her; and that she has 1 child, Wally J. Beard, age 28 years.

Wally's (or Wallie) stated age of 28 would have made him born in 1884, and if true, then he could not have been William Beard's son. This point has been addressed earlier.

It can be speculated that on or about July 26 some event, illustrative of Velazquez's mental instability, triggered some neighbor or son Wally to summon Policeman W. E. Owens, who detained Velazquez. At this date 45-year-old Officer William E. Owens had been on the police force for twenty years and would serve another 18 years before retiring.[33] Doctor Logie may have been summoned at this point and recommended further observation, thereby landing Velazquez in the insane asylum by August 5. Her subsequent insanity hearing and the court's ruling sealed her fate as an inmate of St. Elizabeth's Hospital for the remainder of her life.[34]

Please see the photographs of William Owens, of St. Elizabeth's Hospital and the Order of the Court related to Velazquez's lunacy hearing in Illustrations, Figures 23 and 24.

---

32. No testimony documents were located.
33. NARA, RG 351, Records of the Government of the District of Columbia, Metropolitan Police, Personnel case files, entry 119.
34. A search of the newspapers failed to locate a report of her arrest or confinement.

1913 to 1922, Out of Sight, but Not Out of Mind

Although confined to the Government Hospital for the Insane (St. Elizabeth's Hospital) and her person lost to the public, her story was not. Francis Henry Gribble wrote a 342-page book titled, *Women in War* which ambitiously addressed the history of women in wars worldwide.[35] With so many scores of women to cover the author didn't linger long on Velazquez (pages 5 & 6), but Velazquez was there just the same, among the most famous. Gribble's short synopsis was the usual repetition, but it made one claim which Velazquez herself never made, that her husband, "taught her how to drill her men." Velazquez might have taken issue with this misstatement. Velazquez stated (*TWIB*, p71) that she read her manual of tactics on the train ride to "Hurlburt Station" so that she would know how to "get recruits into something like military training immediately." She added that since she was a military wife and "had seen soldiers drilled hundreds of times" she was able to take full credit for the training of her men. She never claimed her husband had a hand in it.

With World War One in progress and on everyone's mind, the newspapers addressed it and also addressed the topic of women in war. The *Wyoming State Tribune* (Cheyenne) of July 1, 1918 published "Women Who Have Played Their Part on Battlefields," subtitled "Sketches of the Most Prominent Women Who Have Fought with Men in the Ranks for Their Country's Cause."[36] The writer must have gleaned information about Velazquez from Gribble's book because it contained "the husband taught her how to drill the men." No doubt the routine repetition of the memoir was accepted as fact by the reading public.

While Velazquez was a patient at St. Elizabeth's Hospital, the national census of 1920 was conducted. The hospital is found in Enumeration District 361, pages 1A through 41A. The census taker recorded the employees and the patients at the hospital, but inexplicably no patient named Beard was discovered recorded and no other patient (or employee) listed seems to be Velazquez. This failure is a loss of information which might have revealed some facts about Velazquez, that is, if the information was provided truthfully.

Velazquez, even as a confined patient, somehow successfully avoided getting counted. During her entire adult life, she successfully avoided the national census time and again. She, to date, has not been found in any national census from 1850 to 1920 under any of the appropriate married names of the date of their use or otherwise.

If she arrived in America in the 1840's, as she claimed in her book, then the first national census in which she might have been counted would have

---

35. Francis Henry Gribble, *Women in War* (NY: E. P. Dutton & Co., 1917).
36. Other newspapers ran the syndicated article.

been the 1850 Census. However, without knowing her true maiden name, the task of finding her in 1850 is insurmountable.

The next likely census in which to search is 1860. However, at this time, as revealed by the newspapers, she might have been going by one of four possible surnames: Keith, Arnold, Gibbons or Bachman. A search on those names revealed nothing of recognized value. It also is possible she simply avoided the census taker in 1860.

During the 1870 U.S. Census she was married to miner E. H. Bonner and likely living in Utah. Neither of them was found in that census, in Utah or anywhere. During the 1880 U.S. Census she was living in New York City and using the name "L. J. Velazquez." She does not appear in that census. The 1890 U.S. Census record was mostly destroyed by fire and offers no help. The 1892 New York State Census has lost its Manhattan and Bronx listings, where she was likely living, so she is not found.

During the 1900 U.S. Census she was in Arizona promoting her railroad and using the name, "Madame L. Velasquez [sic] Beard." A careful search for Arizona does not reveal her name or that of her son, Waldemar, also called Wally, who was with her then. They were not found in any other state, either.

During the 1910 Census, she was probably either in New York City or Washington, D.C. and using the name "L. J. Velasquez Beard." She had recently moved to Washington, but the exact date is unclear, therefore she could have been in either city. Still, no record shows her in either or anywhere else.

The last census conducted during her lifetime was that of 1920, which failed to list her among the many patients of St. Elizabeth's Hospital. Velazquez's determined avoidance of all the national censuses might be credited to an underlying paranoia, at worst, or at best, her determination and consistency.

The only census that recorded her was the New York State Census of 1905 and it revealed no secrets, but only raised more questions. (It has been covered.)

1923, a Death Hardly Noticed

A simple notice of her death appeared on January 8, 1923, "Loretto J. Beard, 79 years, St. Elizabeth's hospital." The *Washington Post* published her name among dozens of names under "Deaths Reported." Neither this newspaper nor any other recognized this was "Madame Loreta Janeta Velazquez," author of *The Woman in Battle*. But she had already been lost to the public even before her death.

She died on January 6, 1923 at 6 a.m. from "Organic Heart Disease" which had been diagnosed one year prior, with a "contributory" factor of "General Arteriosclerosis" which was noted to have been more than five years of duration. She had no operation preceding death and no autopsy was performed.

On the "Certificate of Death," an attending physician certified that she had been at St. Elizabeth's Hospital from August 5, 1912 to January 5, 1923, when "last seen alive." Velazquez most likely died in her sleep.

The death document contains spaces for "Personal and Statistical Particulars" which does little to identify the origins of Velazquez. Across the spaces for "Name of Father, Birthplace of Father, Name of Mother, Birthplace of Mother" was scribbled "unknown."

The "Birthplace" for Velazquez was given as "United States." Her age was given as 79 years. This age would yield a calculated birth year of 1844, in contradiction to the 1842 birth year she claimed in her book. Other "particulars" were "Sex- Female; Color or Race- White; and Single, Married, Widowed or Divorced (write the word)- Widowed (?)" with a question mark.

Please see Velazquez's certificate of death in Illustrations, Figure 25.

The entry in the document for "Occupation of Deceased" is recorded "Writer." How this fact entered the hospital record and survived the years, 10 years and 5 months, is not clear. It seems that it was entered in the record upon her admission; recall she had recently said she intended to rewrite her memoirs. It might be supposed Velazquez, during her residence, told the staff of her autobiography and of her many adventures. Could the staff believe anything told to them by an inmate of an insane asylum? Even if she had related only the true portions of her life's story, the staff would have found them unbelievable. Surely Velazquez told her story anyway, just as she had so often done, regaling the people around her. It is possible some of her narratives were recorded in her medical files in doctors' efforts to understand her mental instability.

Velazquez is found in an index, *Register of Cases*, for the Government Hospital for the Insane (St. Elizabeth's Hospital) and it assigned to "Beard, Lorette J." a file number of 20081. The *Register* contained the same information found already mentioned on the death certificate and added only a little more about her and her medical case. It stated the "Form of Disease on Admission" as "art. scl. dementia" and the "Supposed Cause" as "age & arteriosclerosis." The register stated that she was 69 years old on "8. 5. [19]12" when admitted and discharged on "1. 6. [19]23" because she died. Her place of "Nativity" was left blank; her marital status was marked with a question mark; her "Religion" was "Episcopal"; her "Residence at the Time of Admission" was "D.C."; her "Occupation" was "Writer"; and her "Station in Life" was recorded as "Indigent."

A quick bit of math shows that the stated age at admission does not exactly match her claimed birth date of June 26, 1842 in her book. On

August 5, 1912 she would have been 70 years, 1 month, and 10 days- rather close to the 69 years mentioned.

All of the St. Elizabeth's Hospital records of that era were transferred to the National Archives in Washington, D.C. and are stored there today. Understanding the potential value of such a medical file to the unraveling of Velazquez's life, an exhaustive search was launched to locate the file. The St. Elizabeth's Hospital record collection was and is huge and, in an effort, to fit the collection in the physical space available some of the records were destroyed... and the "Lorette J. Beard" file #20081 was one of the many destroyed. Unfortunately, any life story which might have been contained in her medical files will never be known. Oddly, only admissions from years which are multiples of five were kept and archived, plus those of notable persons.

The "Certificate of Death" provides one last piece of the Velazquez puzzle. Her "Place of Burial, Cremation or Removal" is stated to be Cedar Hill, Maryland, on January 8, 1923. The Cedar Hill Cemetery is located at 4111 Pennsylvania Avenue, Suitland, Maryland, only three and a half miles from the hospital.

The haste at which the burial was performed suggests that it was a burial not by family or attended by family members, since gathering-up family usually takes several days. In any case, there was no family, except her son Waldemar and there is no reason to believe that he was present for the burial since he was not present at her lunacy hearing many years earlier. Further evidence that Waldemar was not present and/or had no interest is indicated by the lack of a grave marker in remembrance. It has not been discovered, to date, whether Waldemar was still alive then. No more information has been uncovered about Waldemar, his life, occupation, marriages or children. Surely, this path of research has not yielded all that remains to be found.

Madame Loreta Janeta Velazquez's final resting place is Site 59, South D row, in Section 10 of Cedar Hill Cemetery. Her boundless energy, bold adventurous spirit, wanderlust, and restless heart were never contained in life, but her mortal remains are contained where the plots are "about 3 feet in width."[37]

Please see the location of Velazquez's grave in Illustrations, Figure 26.

Was Velazquez Cuban?

Velazquez claimed she was born in Havana, Cuba; she had "every reason to be proud" of her name and the blood which flowed in her veins was "that of Castilian nobles." She pointed out two examples of the Velazquez name which were "well known and highly honored: Don Diego Velazquez, the

---

37. Notation on Cedar Hill Cemetery section map.

conqueror and first Governor of Cuba... and Don Diego Rodriguez Velazquez, the greatest artist that Spain ever produced...."

She gave her father's native city as "Carthagena," clearly misspelling Cartagena, (Spain) and explained that her father had "received a very thorough education at the universities of Madrid and Paris." He then went to Paris as an *attaché* of the Spanish embassy. While in Paris he married the "daughter of a French naval officer, by an American lady, the daughter of a wealthy merchant." The couple soon moved to Madrid, "where three sons and two daughters were born."

Velazquez wrote:

In 1840 my father was appointed to an official position in Cuba, and two years later I, his sixth and last child, came into the world in a house on the Calle Velaggas [*sic*], near the walls in the city of Havana, on the 26th of June, 1842. I was christened Loreta Janeta.

In typical Velazquez fashion of erroneously spelling almost every Spanish name in which she came in contact, she misspelled the street name where she was born as "Calle Velaggas." The error is clear if one understands that double "g" does not exist in Spanish. One may deduce that she meant Calle Villegas which is indeed a street in Old Havana. Even though she claimed she was educated in Cuba until the age of seven, she did not know what any first grader knows- there is no double "g" in Spanish. In addition, she also used double "p" and double "c," which is not done in Spanish. These errors are evident in her misspelling of place names in Venezuela: "Coraeppa," instead of Curiapo, and "Caraccas" instead of Caracas. Also, a problem is "Baranco," instead of Barrancas and "Los Tablos," instead of Las Tablas.

Velazquez provided solid information about her birth by which verification should be possible. She gave an exact date, location, and the fact that she was christened or baptized, implying in the Catholic Church since two paragraphs prior she had explained that her father "was a very strict Catholic." With sufficient information to conduct a search, a retired Catholic Church employee in Havana was tasked to examine Church records, which by the way, he noted to be excellent.[38]

The baptismal records of Havana churches near Calle Villegas were searched. Since Velazquez claimed she was baptized "Loreta Janeta," this was the primary name searched, but any similar name was considered. It should be noted that "Janeta" is not a Spanish name and seems to be an attempt at the name Juanita, which is a Spanish name meaning "Little Jane." The error is reminiscent of her spelling her brother's name, "Josea," which seems to be an attempt at the name José. The search included several years

---

38. Señor Eduardo Erigoyen García, who lives at 207 Calle Villegas between Calles Obispo and Obrapía, in La Habana Vieja (Old Havana).

before and after her claimed birth date, just in case the given birth date was not true. Searched were six Churches: El Espíritu Santo (Cuba y Acosta), El Cristo del Buen Viaje (Plazoleta del Cristo), Santo Ángel Custodio (Compostela y Tejadillo), Iglesia Nuestra Señora de Regla, Jesús del Monte and the Catedral de Habana.

No record of Loreta Janeta Velazquez was found. Simply put, Velazquez's narration of her birth into the noble, wealthy and "Calle Velaggas"-residing Velazquez family can only be concluded to be untrue.

However, she still might have been born in Cuba, but not of the Velazquez family, and left Cuba as a small child, moving to Louisiana or Mississippi. Or she may have been born in America to a Cuban family which had moved. Her habitual and long-term involvement in Cuban issues demonstrated an emotional connection to that country and suggests Cuban roots. Velazquez wrote (p248), "… for I was, despite my Spanish ancestry, an American, heart and soul.…"

A Father by Any Other Name

It is necessary to compare the many newspaper stories about Velazquez, and more specifically her father's identity, to her memoir in order to see how Velazquez selected her father's name, thus her own history. The first mention of her father was in the *Richmond Examiner* of July 11, 1863 when she was reported arrested and sent to Castle Thunder. She said her father was "Major J. B. Roche, of Mississippi, but she was born in the West Indies."

Military records show two Confederate "Roche" officers, one a clerk who was enlisted in Tennessee and the other a lieutenant and adjutant from Virginia. Neither fit her story. Searching alternate spelling, "Rosche," shows no one. Another alternate, "Roach," shows eight soldiers' names, but none are a match for a "Major J. B. Roche."

It is interesting that she stated she was born in the West Indies. Recall, upon her admission to Charity Hospital in New Orleans in November 1862 (eight months prior to her Richmond arrest), she told the admitting clerk that she was born in "Nassau, N. [New] Providence, West Indies." She also gave her name as "Lauretta Williams born Clark." This was the only discovered time in which she claimed Clark as a family name and this was prior to that of Roche. However, since she sought admission into the hospital probably with escaping in mind, she might have evasively invented the name Clark. Research into the surname Clark failed to discover anything useful.

In September 1863, in Atlanta, Velazquez married Confederate Captain Thomas C. DeCaulp. Within two weeks of the marriage, DeCaulp deserted the Confederate army and then later joined the Union army. Velazquez, in an effort to get favorable treatment for her husband, forged a letter dated August 4, 1864, in which she called her father "Rear Admiral Rosche Eng

Navy," of course, meaning the English Navy. Velazquez next raised her father's name in a fake inheritance letter which was published in the *Daily Constitutionalist* of December 31, 1864, only this time it was to announce the death of her father "Commodore J. B. Roach of the British Navy." It is unclear why Velazquez demoted her esteemed father from a "Rear Admiral" to a "Commodore," but that was not the only change. Velazquez changed the spelling of her father's name from Rosche to Roach and it is clear that she was the speller of both variations because she was the forger of both documents. It is unclear if the first variation of "Roche" was her own spelling or that of the reporting newspaper.

Skip forward two years to after the War, when she traveled throughout the South trying to sell subscriptions to books she said she was writing. It was on March 7, 1866 that the St. Louis *Republican* wrote Velazquez claimed her "maiden name was Roach" and that she "was born in the West Indies in 1838." It was a familiar claim, with the 1864 spelling variant, but maybe more interesting is that she contradicted her memoir's given date of her birth, June 26, 1842.

In January of 1867, Velazquez went to Venezuela with the ex-Confederates and just prior to their departure she married John Wasson. On May 24, 1867 the St. Louis *Daily Missouri Republican* wrote that it had been shown a letter dated in March from Ciudad Bolívar which gave the news of the Venezuelan colonists, some of which hailed from Missouri. The news included the names of six of the men who had recently married and their wives. The newspaper quoted the letter, "Mr. John Wasson has been united in wedlock with Madame Lauretta J. De Caulp, a widow lady, young, gay and fascinating, who is the daughter of an English Admiral...." It has been previously pointed out that Velazquez was probably the author of the letter, since it would seem that she alone was impressed with who her father was. If another colonist wrote the letter, then it is plain that they simply repeated what was told to them by Velazquez.

Velazquez soon left Venezuela, arrived by ship in New York and went by train and stagecoach to Austin, Nevada where she married miner E. H. Bonner. It was after this marriage that the San Francisco *Daily Alta California* on January 9, 1869 published a curious announcement which stated that the brother of "Mrs. Lauretta J. Bonner of Austin," one "Colonel R. D. Clapp," had died in Peru. There can be no doubt that the information was submitted to the newspapers by "Mrs. Lauretta J. Bonner" herself. Of course, this would also make her father's surname Clapp. This deceased and fake brother has previously been dissected.

By 1874 she ostensibly left husband Bonner in New Mexico and husband Bobo in Texas, and went to Atlanta where in a September 4 interview she claimed "her maiden name was Loretta Jeanett Clapp." Her father was

"Samuel S. Clapp" and one of her uncles was the renowned New Orleans minister "Theodore Clapp." This father and uncle claim has been shown an unholy lie.

One year and thirty-three days later Velazquez obtained a new father. The first discovered record in which Velazquez claimed, "Velazquez is my father's name" is found in a letter dated October 7, 1875 to the Louisville *Courier Journal* when she refuted Mark Twain's letter to the *Courier Journal* in which he had denied any association with her. It should be noted that in her handwritten letter she clearly overwrote the letter "s" in V-e-l-a-s-q-u-e-z with a "z." A facetious person might note that it is often difficult for some people to decide how to spell their father's name especially when it is a famous and noble name. Finally, with the publication of her book in July 1876, she cast in the bronze of history for all to admire, "Velazquez," her father's noble name, spelled with two zees. Well, that is, almost permanently cast... afterwards she regularly used an "s" in the place of the first "z."

In a final insult to her dear father's name, she entered on her August 20, 1887 marriage certificate to William Beard that her father's name was "Juanquin R. Velasquez" using an "s" in place of the first "z." But worse still was her use of "Juanquin" which was clearly an erroneous attempt at the correct Spanish name of Joaquín. Maybe a case could be made that she was not the one who wrote the name on the certificate, but in any case, she, the self-professed fearless fighter, should have fought the clerk to get the noble name of her father correct, that is if Velazquez knew what correct was.

In the entirety of her memoir, Velazquez never told her readers when, where or how her father died. It seems that a father as accomplished and of noble heritage as Velazquez claimed, would have merited from her a heartfelt tribute. Oh, and her mother's given pedigree was admirable as well, yet after the pedigree introduction, Velazquez only mentioned her once more, when her mother visited Velazquez in St. Louis. Why no eulogy to her noble Spanish father or her exotic French-American mother?

Making the Case that She was a Cuban

Clearly, Velazquez was not, in truth, the Velazquez of her claims, however, she may have indeed been born in Cuba and left when a child. That part could easily be true. Or she may have been born in America to Cuban parents whose interest in Cuba rubbed off on her. Her documented continued interest in Cuba surely reflects a connection there.

Her first found claim to have come from the West Indies was when she was admitted to Charity Hospital in New Orleans in 1862. She told the admitting clerk that she was born in "Nassau, N.[New] Providence, West Indies." Of course, this is the Bahamas and not Cuba. A similar claim popped-up later in March 1866 when the St. Louis *Republican* wrote that

Velazquez claimed that she "was born in the West Indies in 1838." Velazquez claimed in her book that she was born on June 26, 1842, which makes year 1838 suspect which in turn makes the West Indies suspect.

Recall the letter Velazquez wrote from Venezuela to U.S. President Andrew Johnson on March 23, 1867 in which she stated that the United States was her "Land of adoption for 17 years"? Unfortunately, she did not state her native land. Curiously, it was at this time that Velazquez was claiming to fellow Venezuelan colonists that she was the "daughter of an English Admiral."

The earliest date found in which she claimed she was born in Cuba was in a June 27, 1875 letter, from the St. James Hotel in Key West, Florida, to Jefferson Davis in which she wrote, "Noble Cuba where I was borned." She also said Cuba was her "native Land" and that America was her adopted home. She asked Jefferson Davis to help support her "poor Country [Cuba]."

In about 1877, "Madame L. J. Velasquez" (with an "s") wrote a six page "Address to the American Congress on Cuba" encouraging America to support the Cubans in their fight to end Spain's colonial rule of Cuba. The document is reasonably done, though rather rambling. It clearly had some editing; it does not contain the overwhelming errors typical of her letters. However, the "Address" is rather awkward, as if written by someone whose first language was not English. The document showed much effort on her part and indicated a passion for and connection to the cause of Cuba, which one would assume was real, since faking this passion would seem illogical and of questionable value to her.

Seven years later, in December 1884, Velazquez was found in New York supporting the U.S. cigar makers' opposition to a Spanish Treaty. The cigar makers (surely some of Cuban heritage) believed that the pending treaty was going to be injurious to their livelihood as it would remove the import duties on tobacco products. Cheaper imported Cuban cigars would cause the U.S. cigar makers to lose their jobs or, at least, to work for less money. She spoke on their behalf and her involvement shows her interest in Cuban issues.

The 1905 New York City Census taker found Velazquez on June 1 living in a boarding house owned by a Cuban-born man. For the entry designated "Nativity" Velazquez did not claim she was Cuban-born, but instead "US." The entry for "Citizenship, Number of years in the United States" was left blank, meaning her entire life, and the entry for "Alien or citizen" was designated as citizen. Considering that Velazquez frequently touted that she was born in Cuba, she certainly did not take this opportunity to tell it to the census taker and one wonders why. Curiously, one of the other boarders was Cuban born and four others Spanish born.

Possible evidence regarding Velazquez's Cuban background is found on page 320 of her book where she retold the Spanish love story of Estela and Don Carlos:

> I recollected, as I reviewed the circumstances of my own case, an old Spanish *novela*, which I had read when a girl, and which had long since passed out of mind with other childish memories, but the incidents of which now came back to me with singular vividness, on account of a certain resemblance they had to points in my own career. The author's name I forgot, but I distinctly remembered the story, which was one of a collection in an old book I was fond of perusing when at home under my father's roof at the Puerto de Palmas plantation in Cuba.

The *novela* of Estela and Don Carlos is the tale of lovers separated through treachery. Estela was kidnapped and sent to a foreign land by the evil machinations of a woman vying for Don Carlos' affection. After suffering terribly, Estela was helped to freedom at which time she disguised herself as a man and joined the Spanish army. She won recognition and served as an officer. By chance she found Don Carlos serving under her command. He had been charged with murder at the time of Estela's disappearance and sent to prison from which he escaped and had joined the army. Of course, Don Carlos did not know Estela in her male disguise. Estela succeeded in inducing Carlos to tell his sad life's story of how Estela had mysteriously disappeared and now seemed lost forever, yet he still loved her.

Since Estela had served in the king's army with honor, she was given the governorship of her home province. She took with her to her newly appointed office her now trusted assistant, Don Carlos. At Don Carlos' reappearance in the province, the police authorities and Estela's family renewed his prosecution since he had escaped justice and he was put on trial again. Estela, now as governor of the province, must serve as the judge at his trial. Don Carlos, again claimed his innocence, that he would never have harmed Estela, and declared his love for Estela. Judge Estela stated that if she must reach a verdict using the available evidence then she must conclude that he is guilty and only the reappearance of Estela could establish his innocence. Estela then revealed herself to Don Carlos and all present, to their amazement. The people of the province, but especially the king, were amazed upon learning the news. Estela accepted Don Carlos' love and the two married and lived happily.

At this point, Velazquez explained in great detail that while wearing her Lieutenant Harry T. Buford disguise, she found the object of her love, Captain Thomas C. DeCaulp, in an Atlanta hospital. Lieutenant Harry T. Buford induced DeCaulp to talk about the lady of whom he was so fond, which of course was Velazquez. (It should be pointed out that Velazquez had explained that DeCaulp knew her as Lieutenant Harry T. Buford, as well as the widow of "William," his dead comrade-in-arms, but did not know Buford and Velazquez were one and the same.) Velazquez wrote how the story of Estele inspired her:

> This is but a feeble and incomplete recital of a very pretty story, and is only entitled to a place in this narrative of my own adventures, because it was so much in my thoughts at the particular period of which I am now writing, and because it inspired me to imitate Estela's example so far as to seek to obtain a confession of love from Captain De Caulp, before I should reveal myself to him. I was filled with an eager desire to hear what he would say of me to his friend, the supposed Lieutenant Buford, and having arranged in my mind what I should say to him when we met, I waited, with ill-disguised impatience, for the time to come when I could put my plan in execution, trying to imagine, all the while, what would be the effect upon him when the whole truth was made known.

With much more flowery prose Velazquez explained how she then revealed her disguise to Captain DeCaulp, who then married her.

The story of Estela comes from a Spanish book of short love stories, *Novelas Amorosas y Ejemplares*,[39] published in 1637 by author Doña María de Zayas y Sotomayor, a native of Madrid. The book consisted of ten short stories and the story concerning Estela, was called "El Juez de Su Causa" which can be translated as "Judge of One's Cause" or "Judge Thyself."

The reason that the story of Estela is good evidence of Velazquez's possible Cuban connection is that the story had not yet been published in English at the time of Velazquez's memoir. Only one of the ten short stories found in the book had been translated into English and it was not the one recited by Velazquez.[40] Velazquez could not have read the Estela story in English. Her knowledge of the story would have seemingly had to come from the original Spanish source.

Is it possible that Velazquez, "when a girl," was so proficient a Spanish reader that she read this adult story? She claimed she read it. If so, then her Spanish knowledge diminished drastically into adulthood, evident by her gross errors in writing Spanish place names and people names. However, the story could have been read to her or told to her in Spanish. It also might have been told to her in English after someone read it themselves in Spanish or French. Also possible is that Velazquez read it in French; she claimed (*TWIB*, p522) she spoke French. There was a 1656 French translation of six

---

39. Given the English title *The Enchantments of Love*.
40. A 1922 book implied, in effect, that the *novela* about Estela had not been translated into English: "In English, there seems to be only a single translation of the *Novelas*, and that is *The Miser Chastised* to be found in the *Spanish Novelists*, vol. ii, by T. Roscoe, 1832." Source- Lena Evelyn Vincent Sylvania, *Doña Maria de Zayas y Sotomayor, A Contribution to the Study of her Works* (New York: Columbia Univ Press, 1922), 22.

of the short stories which included the "La Juez de Su Causa."[41] At the time of Velazquez's childhood, on the Gulf Coast of the United States there was a large population of both Spanish and French, and her family might have been part of this population.

It should be accepted that Velazquez told the Estele story from memory as she claimed. She would have been more accurate with her details if she had the story in front of her from which to copy and she probably wouldn't have claimed to have forgotten the author's name.

Similarly, Velazquez identified (*TWIB*, p34) "Catalina de Eranso [*sic* Erauso], the *Monja Alferez* or the nun-lieutenant" as one of her Spanish heroines. Velazquez did not relate in detail Catalina's autobiography, but it can be suspected that Velazquez took inspiration from Catalina's amazing and surely exaggerated story.

Catalina, at the age of four, was committed to a Catholic convent only to run away as a fifteen-year-old teenager. She cut her hair and assumed the attire of a young man and lived life as a man. For the next year she found various supporters and was then employed as a page for two years and was "well treated and well dressed." "On a whim [she] left that comfortable position" visited her hometown where she sat near her mother at a church service who "looked right at [her] without knowing [her]." She left San Sebastián and went to Sanlúcar where she signed on as a cabin boy aboard a galleon bound for the New World. In the New World, as the ship was preparing for the return voyage, loading a cargo of silver in Panama, Catalina jumped ship.

She worked her way to Peru and obtained a respectable job as a manager of a mercantile store in Saña (Zaña). All was pleasant until she had a conflict at a theatre with a Señor Reyes, who was blocking her view. The conflict reignited the following morning when Reyes showed himself twice in the store's doorway. A fight resulted in which she slashed his face with her knife. When a friend rushed to Reyes' aid, he was run through by Catalina's sword. She was thrown in jail, but her employer managed to get her released. Two months later another friend of Reyes accosted her and she stabbed him.

She became a soldier for three years, was then promoted to lieutenant and served another five years; the soldiers had many conflicts with the Indians and killed many. She was an inveterate gambler, got into a fight with a fellow soldier and killed him with her sword. She fled the army.

No matter where she went, she found fights. Catalina claimed that during her sojourn in Peru she stabbed some twelve men, at least five died. She was many times arrested. On one occasion when she was jailed, a sympathetic church bishop sought to help "him." It was then, after so many years, that she revealed her secret, to the bishop's disbelief. The bishop was now even

---

41. Sylvania, 21.

more motivated to help and he extracted her from her troubles. Upon her release she returned to Europe where she was admired for her exploits. "Erauso became a legend in her own time with at least two editions of her story published [in Spanish] shortly after her return from America to Spain in 1624 as well as a popular play."[42] Catalina once again departed Spain in 1645 for New Spain (Mexico) where she died in 1650.

By the time of Velazquez's 1876 memoir, Catalina de Erauso's story had already been published in English so Velazquez could have read it in either English or Spanish.[43] The point is- Velazquez was an admirer of the story of Spanish Catalina when most Americans of non-Spanish descent probably would not have even heard of Catalina.

Making the Case that She was a Mississippian

There are references in her book which show that Velazquez had a strong connection to Mississippi.

She (*TWIB*, p117) explained that at Leesburg, Virginia, at Hunton's headquarters, she "had the pleasure of meeting Colonel Featherstone [*sic*]" who she "had known when [she] was quite a small child." Of course, the Colonel did not recognize her dressed as Lieutenant Harry T. Buford. It has been previously shown that before the War, Winfield S. Featherston was elected to the U.S. Congress representing northern Mississippi. If her statement about Featherston was true, then it can only be surmised that she, as a child, was living in northern Mississippi and not in Cuba as she claimed in her book. Recall, that she wrote that she spent her youth, until the age of seven, in Cuba and it was only then that she moved to New Orleans, when she would no longer have been exactly "quite a small child." It can be sure that the contradiction is indicative of a lie somewhere. She finished the narration of her youth by explaining that she lived with her aunt in New Orleans until the age of about 14 years and 2 months when she revealed to her aunt that she had secretly married "William" about six months prior. Is it possible that Winfield Featherston came to New Orleans and she met him when she was a rather old "small child"? Not likely.

Another reference was on page 228 where Velazquez explained that she was on her way from the Battle of Shiloh to New Orleans when her poor health and spirits caused her to make a halt in Osyka, Mississippi where "resided one of the best friends [she] ever had." She stayed with him, and apparently his family, and they "treated her with the greatest kindness."

---

42. Joaquín María de Ferrer, *Historia de la Monja Alférez (Doña Catalina de Erauso)*, edited and annotated by Daniel Harvey Pedrick, Early Americas Digital Archive (EADA), Maryland Institute for Technology in the Humanities (MITH), University of Maryland.
43. Madame Laure Junot, *Memoirs of Celebrated Women of All Countries* (London: Edward Churton, 1834), 34; Leopold March, *A Walk Across the French Frontier into Northern Spain* (London: Richard Bentley, 1852), 217.

Osyka is a small town along the main road which runs the entire length of Mississippi from New Orleans to Memphis. It is curious that she claimed such a friendship in Mississippi, but never claimed similar friendships in New Orleans where she spent half her youth and where logic dictates that she should have claimed friendships, that is, with the exception of her schoolmate friendship with Nellie V, which did not last.

Similarly, she claimed another friendship just over the northern state line of Mississippi. She narrated (p227) that after the Battle of Shiloh when she was wounded and not well, she went to Grand Junction, Tennessee, which is just 4 miles from the Mississippi state line, where she stayed at the hotel of which the proprietor was "an old and true friend of [hers]." This town is some 26 miles from Holly Springs, Mississippi and some 93 miles from Houston, Mississippi; both are towns where Featherston lived. It so happens Grand Junction is about 63 miles from Memphis where Velazquez claimed she started her military masquerade. From Memphis it is 5 miles to "Hulburt [*sic* Hulbert] Station," where she claimed she recruited a battalion. Hulbert is today part of West Memphis, Arkansas.

Other references to Mississippi come from the newspapers, which would have taken its information from Velazquez's own statements. The *Richmond Examiner* wrote that her father was "Major J. B. Rosche of Mississippi, but she was born in the West Indies."[44] The *Daily Richmond Examiner* stated, "The heroine of this sketch is a native of Mississippi, and a devoted Southern Woman."[45] Recall that after the explosion of steamboat *Miami* Velazquez went to New Orleans and the *Daily Picayune* reported that she registered at the Saint James Hotel as Mrs. L. J. De Camp from Mississippi.[46]

In 1868 she married E. H. Bonner, who was a native of Mississippi. This might have been a commonality which caused them to notice one another. They married in Nevada and went to live, briefly, in California. At this time in San Francisco convened the Independent Order of Odd Fellows at which the Mississippi delegation submitted a "grateful acknowledgement" for some unspecified kindness to "the ladies of San Francisco, who presented to them, through Mrs. E. H. Bonner, a native Mississippian...."[47]

In February 1874 Velazquez registered at the Cosmopolitan Hotel in Galveston claiming she was from Jackson, Mississippi and then in September 1874 Velazquez told the Atlanta newspaper:

Her maiden name was Loretta Jeanett Clapp; she was born in Havana... The family moved from Havana to the United States while Mrs. Bonner was quite

---

44. Jul 11, 1863.
45. Sep 16, 1863.
46. Mar 29, 1866.
47. Independent Order of Odd Fellows, *The Journal of Proceeding*, Vol 6 (Baltimore: James L. Ridgely, 1874), 4690, submitted on the sixth and last day of session, Sep 27, 1869.

young. Her childhood days were spent in Mississippi, but after she grew up to girlhood her family removed to Texas.

Again, Velazquez referenced her childhood in Mississippi and in the process completely contradicted her book.

Although the Mississippi references are plentiful and surely Velazquez had connections there, it cannot be proven (at this date) that she was born in the state.

Other Claimed Places of Residence

Velazquez made several, though brief, claims to the newspapers to have resided as a child in St. James Parish, Louisiana. The first found claim appeared in the *Daily Constitution* (Augusta, Georgia) of December 31, 1864 when that newspaper printed the phony notice of the death of her father, "We clip the subjoined Personal from the *Richmond Enquirer:* Madame Laure De Caulp, formerly of St. James' Parish, La...."

The second occasion was about a year and two months later when she told the *St. Louis Republican* of March 7, 1866, "At an early period her parents moved to the United States and settled in the parish of St. James, Louisiana."

The problem with the St. James Parish claim is that it contradicts what she wrote in her book, which was that she moved to New Orleans and lived with her aunt until Velazquez married and then moved away. She wrote her parents remained in Cuba at that time. In her book, she never claimed she or they ever lived in St. James Parish. No discovered documents, to date, corroborate the St. James Parish claim.

Arkansas is another state which received much attention. After the War, an Arkadelphia (Clark County), Arkansas newspaper in June 1878 wrote it remembered her there before the War as "a dashing character." And "Officer of Castle Thunder" in 1879 wrote he knew her while she was imprisoned in Richmond and Velazquez claimed to have been, at the outbreak of the war, living in Arkansas, "in which State she was born."

Velazquez claimed to the *Memphis Daily Avalanche* of March 1, 1866 that she was on her way to St. Louis in order to purchase dry goods to start a store in Mulberry Grove, Jefferson County, Arkansas, implying that she was living there. Jefferson County might have had some attraction for her since nearby Pine Bluff was the County's principal city and is on the Arkansas River which empties into the Mississippi River, a commercial connection maybe obvious to Velazquez. Mulberry Grove is thought to have been swallowed by today's Pine Bluff.

However, five months and ten days afterwards she stated to the *Richmond Whig* of August 10, 1866, that her home was in Dallas County, Arkansas. The distance from Jefferson's County seat to Dallas' County seat is some 42 miles to the southwest and more remote from the Arkansas River. It is difficult to guess what connection she might have had to Dallas County since that county was very rural, except that she clearly knew this county since it is neighboring Arkadelphia's Clark County in which she positively lived. Before the War, Dallas County had a population of some 8200 (1860 U.S. Census) and after the War, by 1870, it had experienced a 31% decrease (1870 U.S. Census). Maybe Velazquez named the more remote Dallas County believing that nobody would check if it was true that she resided there. It was during this time in 1866 that newspapers reported her traveling through the South selling book subscriptions and it is clear that she did not go back to Arkansas during this five-month period to relocate to a new domicile.

In her 1876 memoir she did not claim to have taken-up residence in Arkansas, but she did claim it to the Jackson *Mississippian* newspaper of June 6, 1863, which wrote, "At the breaking out of the war Mrs. Laura J. Williams was a resident of Arkansas." And when the New Orleans *Daily True Delta* of April 24, 1862 reported her arrest, it wrote, "She gave the name of respectable houses here in the city who knew her in her proper sphere, when she resided in Arkansas, where she says she owns a plantation." The New Orleans newspapers further wrote that an Arkansas man named Bachman took her home and married her. When she registered as a patient at Charity Hospital on November 16, 1862, she wrote that seven months prior to her arrival in New Orleans her "Last Place From" was Arkansas.

One last possibility remains as the reason for her claim to be living in Jefferson or Dallas County, Arkansas. Recall, her husband Captain Thomas C. DeCaulp enlisted in the 3rd Arkansas Cavalry Regiment, Company C, in Pocahontas, Randolph County, Arkansas. His Confederate military record fails to show the distance traveled to the location of enlistment, which would have indicated where he was living; the notation of distance traveled was a common entry in military records. Since the call for volunteers could have extended to nearby counties, it is difficult to pinpoint from where DeCaulp came. Recall, DeCaulp deserted the Confederacy, joined the Union army, became sick, was given a medical discharge and it seems died in Philadelphia in December 1865. After DeCaulp's death and with the War ended, Velazquez possibly went briefly to Arkansas as DeCaulp's widow to visit friends from the Arkansas regiment (and maybe of whom to ask favors). Whether DeCaulp had a connection to Mulberry Grove, (Jefferson County) or Dallas County is unclear, however, it is likely that of the many soldiers in DeCaulp's Arkansas regiment, someone may have been from these places and it is possible Velazquez felt a connection.

And finally, recall the *Lynchburg* (Virginia) *Republican* of September 26, 1861 reported the earliest known arrest of "Mrs. Mary Ann Keith, of Memphis, Tennessee, but [she] registered at the Piedmont House as Lieut. Buford." It is notable that Memphis is only across the Mississippi River from

Arkansas and also about 50 miles distance from Holly Springs, Mississippi. It is logical that a person would name this large city as home if their home was in some lesser-known town in Arkansas or Mississippi near Memphis.

It is clear that the landscape is just too vast, with Cuba, the Bahamas, Louisiana, Mississippi, Arkansas and Tennessee as choices, from which to pluck the real Velazquez. Surely, some future researcher, with additional relevant information, will discover her true connections to these places and more importantly her birthplace and parents.

Chapter 17

Parade of Books, Newspapers, Magazines and Films

Velazquez, in her elderly years, was mostly unknown and unrecognized as the "heroine" of *The Woman in Battle*. When she died in 1923 the newspapers had forgotten her completely. However, her story has remained alive because books, newspapers and magazines sustained the story- even until today with a reissue of her memoir and with three films. Many of these works, since her death, are now presented to give an understanding how the myth of Velazquez evolved and persists; in particular, entry **2013** film *Rebel* excels in this area. Some of these works are brutally beaten down and bloodied, but hopefully, the pressure of the tourniquet of fact and logic will stanch the flow of myth. Please don't flinch at this sight of blood, but soldier on until the satisfying and victorious end! (Warning: entry **1999**, *Disarming the Nation* by Elizabeth Young contains graphic language which may offend readers.)

1923, *Times-Picayune* (New Orleans, LA) April 29 article titled "Adventures of Madame Loreta Janeta Velazquez, 21st Louisiana Regiment" by Harriet Geithmann. The author presented Velazquez's story, with a great portion quoting Velazquez's memoir and accepting and giving credit to Velazquez for her claimed enlistment as Harry Buford in the 21st Regiment. Of course, the records do not show that a Harry Buford enlisted and the claim should be considered false, unless documentation is ever found to prove otherwise. In addition, Geithmann wrote, "She fought with Stonewall Jackson at Bull Run, with Polk in Tennessee, dug mud in trenches, ran blockades, was wounded with shrapnel and filled out her life by marrying three times." Evidently Harriet Geithmann failed to read accurately the memoir's husband count which Velazquez claimed was four.

1930, *Women-at-Arms: Their Exploits Throughout the Ages* by Reginald Hargreaves. This London published book addressed Velazquez in Chapter VIII which is titled "Loreta Janeta Velasquez. (1842?-97)." Author Hargreaves indicates that her birth year was uncertain, but Velazquez claimed in her book the date was June 26, 1842; it is the death year about which Hargreaves should have been uncertain.

Hargreaves retold the memoir in the course of 21 pages, but with poor accuracy. He noted that Velazquez failed to give William's surname: "the multiplicity of her matrimonial adventures presumably accounts for a quite understandable little laxity of memory on Loreta's part in the matter of her husband's respective surnames." Hargreaves was only half correct. Velazquez, in her book, provided the surnames of two of her four claimed husbands, DeCaulp and Wasson. Miner-husband Bonner was not named at all.

Hargreaves wrote, "Of her own parents, it has been established that her father was a native of Cartagena, educated in Madrid and Paris, and a member of the Diplomatic Service." The fault, of course, is that Hargreaves implied that this fact was "established" by a source outside of Velazquez's own claim, which is not the case. It has been shown that Velazquez's many (newspaper) accounts of her father contradict one another.

The author asserted that Velazquez delivered her recruits to her husband in New Orleans and that she was with her husband in Pensacola when he was killed. That is not what Velazquez wrote. She said she delivered her men to her husband in Pensacola and that it was when she went alone to New Orleans that she received word of his death.

Hargreaves wrote that Velazquez received a "sincerely regretful farewell from her comrades" of the 21st Louisiana Regiment. Velazquez did not write any such thing, but wrote (*TWIB*, p182) only that she "had many regrets parting with the officers and the men" of the Regiment. There is a big difference and it is indicative of the inaccuracy of Hargreaves' retelling. Instead of seeking accuracy, Hargreaves was only going for literary effect, at least if his use of the words "quondam," effulgence," and "aureoled" on a single page can be used as evidence.

One final error is worth noting. Hargreaves repeated Velazquez's claim to have been present at the siege or Battle of Fort Donelson, he wrote:

On the 13th of February the assault was opened by the Federal troops. Their attack was accompanied by a driving hail of sleet and snow, and Loreta, who had consented to take over a comrade's tour of duty in the outworks, found herself committed to as deadly a struggle as any in the whole course of the war. And truth compels the admission that fight right valiantly she did, playing her part manfully in beating off the incessant waves of attack, which came on almost without intermission for the ensuing forty-eight hours.

Velazquez did not write that she fought at Fort Donelson. In fact, she explained in detail the activities in which she participated, which might easily convince a reader that she was there, but she never claimed she fought. She said that she stood guard duty during the freezing night and was compelled to listen to the cries of the wounded from out in the darkness. When her relief came, she then "[sought] shelter and the repose [she] sorely needed." She described the surge of the enemies against one another, but never once mentioned she fought. She wrote (*TWIB*, p172) the casualties were heavy and that she endeavored "to make the wounded men as comfortable as possible."

Reginald Hargreaves seemingly accepted as true all narrated by Velazquez, yet he was critical of the "type" of woman he determined her to have been. He thought her "vehement, imperious, headstrong" and an egoist, not capable of introspection, which "spared the brutality of an accurate mental audit" of her own total performance. Hargreaves wrote that she had dreamed of great things, but left them unaccomplished and that she was a "mountain of such infinite labour that produced so small a mouse of actual performance" and "hers was a nature capable of persuading itself it was swimming in the depths when it was doing little more than paddle in the shallows." However, on the positive side, he thought she possessed the "spirit which animate[d]" her actions and her "self-dramatization."

1936, *Women of the Confederacy* by Francis B. Simkins and James W. Patton. This substantial book of 306 pages dedicated one paragraph of 159 words to Velazquez, a very succinct summation to be sure. However, it is the relevant footnote which refines the authors' sentiments into one sentence:

These adventures, many of which are doubtless apocryphal, are described at great length in ... *The Woman in Battle*....

The definition of apocryphal is "of doubtful authenticity, although widely circulated as being true."

Francis Butler Simkins (1897-1966) was a Ph.D. history professor and author of eight history books. James Welch Patton (1900-1973) also was a Ph.D. history professor and author of history books. Both were career research historians and it is not insignificant that they found Velazquez memoir apocryphal.

1939, *Richmond Times-Dispatch* May 21 article titled "A Lady in Gray Fighting for the Confederacy, Madame Velasquez, Cuban, Had Remarkable Career as Soldier" by Perrin F. Shaw Jr.

This attractive article of some 1500 words included two illustrations of Velazquez, in and out of disguise, taken from her book. The author recited Velazquez's memoir with good enough accuracy and it is clear that he had read the book. Author Perrin both praised and criticized Velazquez and her deeds:

The war record of this remarkable woman is not impressive. If she had been content to employ altogether her talents as a spy rather than a soldier in an army that had no place for a woman, she probably would have been very useful to the Confederacy. As it was, she enjoyed fighting, but was unwilling to do her share of less exciting and harder work.

First of all, she was a woman, who loved and was loved, and had borne children. Even at the height of her military career, she married a Captain De Caulp, resuming her adventures after his death.

As a woman, she sought to justify her actions to other women.

"My career," she said, "has differed materially from that of most women, and some things I have done have shocked persons for whom I have every respect, however much my ideas of propriety may differ from theirs."

On the other hand, regardless of her individualism which might have been admired had it not been so misdirected, she cannot be considered in the same as Joan of Arc and Appolonia Jagiello… although she egotistically compared herself to them. As she frankly admitted, her ambition was solely to win personal distinction.

[Skip four paragraphs.]

Her egotism was staggering.

[Skip one paragraph.]

Such frank egotism needs no apology, and gives a ring of truth to her adventures as she related them. On the other hand, much of what she told is for the same reasons to be taken with a grain of salt.

[Skip two paragraphs.]

There were still more [women in the Civil War] but of them all, Loreta Velasquez was the most ambitious and had the most colorful career and personality.

Author Perrin said that it cannot be "reasonably doubted" that Velazquez disguised herself and was in the army. He named two other women who had done likewise which he thought added credence to Velazquez's story.

1941, *New York Times* February 2 article titled "Women as Warriors." With the outbreak of war in Europe, the reporter told of how "Greek peasant women [were] toiling beside men to defend their country against Italian invaders." He wrote:

They have labored to keep their armies' roads in repair and free of snow; they have clambered up mountainsides with supplies and ammunition; they have even rolled boulders down on Italian soldiers in narrow passes. In so doing they have added to a long tradition of women active in war.

The reporter then cited histories of women who had fought in conflicts. He named Countess Matilda of Tuscany and Joan of Arc. In America he named Molly Pitcher and Margaret Corbin in the War of Independence and in the Civil War he named Velazquez. He said:

Women fought on both sides in the War Between the States, some of them disguised as men. Loreta J. Velasques [*sic*], a New Orleans girl of Cuban descent, entered the Confederate Army under the name Harry T. Buford and rose to be a lieutenant.

At this point, is it truly necessary to state that Velazquez did not rise to any rank much less to that of lieutenant, but asserted she designated herself that rank, applying it to her alias?

1941, *Springfield Sunday Union and Republican* (Massachusetts) August 10 newspaper article by Andreas Dorpalen titled "When Women Go to War." Dorpalen reflected,

Today's conflict [WWII] finds modern Amazons fighting in armies of the world, their shouldering guns beside their men. And history provides heroic examples for them to follow.

Mr. Dorpalen surely took a cue from the *New York Times* article from six months earlier and wrote:

During the Civil war, a number of women distinguished themselves as spies. Few women, however, participated in the actual fighting. Those who did, followed personal motives- love of their husbands or love of adventure- rather than patriotic reasons. Best known among these women soldiers was Loretta J. Velasquez, a New Orleans girl, who disguised as a man, enlisted under the name of Harry T. Buford. Except for her rather boastful memoirs, however, little is known of her military career.

1943, *The Life of Johnny Reb: the Common Soldier of the Confederacy* by Bell Irvin Wiley. In 2008, an updated edition was issued with a new foreword which established Wiley's (deceased 1980) credentials as a scholar and Civil War historian. He was an unsurpassed University professor with "more than 50 years of classroom experience," and "indefatigable researcher" and writer about the Civil War with a hand in 24 books, either as author, co-author or editor.[1] Wiley stated his suspicion:

A story so remarkable as to create a doubt of its authenticity is that of one Madame Loreta Velasquez as told by herself… If Madame Velasquez's account be true, her career was indeed a phenomenal one; if it be false, she deserves high rating as a fictionist.

1950, the June 18 *American Weekly*'s 1,500-word article by Stewart Kelsey titled "The Girl in Gray" grabs the reader's attention because of its attractive two-page illustration which consists of three focal points. On the left is a row of five cannon with sentries. On the right is Velazquez in an officer's uniform, carrying a flapping Stars and Bars Confederate flag, mounted erectly on a fiery white horse rigged in ornate saddle tack, a kind never used in the War. In the background are troops marching with shouldered rifles, bayonets fixed. In the middle of the illustration is a large detailed highly romanticized portrait of Velazquez which does not in the least resemble Velazquez's portrait in her memoir. A man's handsome mustached face is located above her, somewhat mixed in with the sky's clouds, looking down admiringly at her.

The article is an exciting and mostly inaccurate recital of Velazquez's book. It begins with a dialog between Velazquez and her first husband, which was contrived and does not exist in Velazquez's book. Author Kelsey then wrote, "At 14, her family sent her to a convent to stay there until she

---

1. Center for Civil War Research, University of Mississippi.

was old enough to marry the man they had picked out for her." Velazquez never wrote she was sent to a convent at the age of 14! She claimed (*TWIB*, p41) that in 1849, making her seven years old, she was sent to live in New Orleans with her aunt under whom she studied "for two years." She then attended the school run by the "Sisters of Charity, to learn the ornamental branches," (p41) all the while living with her aunt (p47). Velazquez said (p48) she eloped on 5th of April, 1856 which would have made her 82 days shy of her fourteenth birthday.

Author Kelsey made up other stuff as well, for example: 1) Kelsey wrote that at the Battle of Bull Run that Velazquez "met[ed] out death with a saber and pistol," but Velazquez did not claim she used a saber and pistol at Bull Run. She wrote only that three days prior to Bull Run, at the Battle of Blackburn's Ford, she picked up a dead man's musket and took a shot at a fleeing Yankee. 2) Kelsey wrote that after husband Wasson died in Venezuela, "Loreta did not marry again, nor did she seek out more wars. She wandered restlessly through the West Indies, and spent some time in the Western states. Finally, she returned to Texas, where she wrote two volumes of memoirs. The last appeared in 1894."

It is necessary to set the record straight. 1) Velazquez did not claim that she did not remarry after Wasson's death in Venezuela; instead, she wrote (p587) she remarried in Austin, Nevada, to a miner. Her time with this miner is a significant portion of her book, covering 12 pages, and she got a baby out of the deal, as well. 2) Velazquez did not claim "finally she returned to Texas." The first time she did mention Texas was when her father inherited a ranch there, the second time was when she was going to meet her father there and the third time was when she was traveling through by stagecoach. Velazquez never claimed or implied she went to Texas to write her memoirs; instead, she wrote (p597), "...I started on a long journey through Colorado, New Mexico, and Texas...." The last subtitled section (p604) of her book is titled, "The Stage Route Across Texas." The memoir clearly ends with her traveling through Texas and history shows that she did not stay. 3) Velazquez did not write two memoirs; the second volume to which Kelsey referred was an 1894 reprint of the 1876 original under the new title, *The Story of the Civil War*. Understandably, Kelsey could not have found anything inside the 1894 edition citing that it was previously published in 1876, under its first title, since it did not contain that information. But he could have opened the second book and seen the same pages as contained in the first book!

1955, *Heroines of Dixie (Confederate Women Tell Their Story of the Civil War)* by Katherine M. Jones. This book was reprinted in 1973. Author Jones reproduced the writings of some 100 Southern women who recorded and opined on the progress of the War. Some of the ladies were prominent and others obscure and several have more than one entry in the book. Among the prominent ladies were Varina Howell Davis, wife of President Jefferson Davis of the Confederacy and LaSalle Corbell Pickett, wife of George E. Pickett, renowned for Pickett's Charge at the Battle of Gettysburg. Readers also would recognize the infamous spies Belle Boyd and Rose O'Neal Greenhow. Author Jones carefully introduced each woman, their entries pertaining to the time frame of the War which author Jones was addressing.

"Loreta Janeta Velazquez- Special Agent" was a reprint of Velazquez's narrative found on pages 408-419 of *TWIB*. A portion of the information for Velazquez's introduction was clearly taken from the *St. Louis Republican* article of March 7, 1866 or one of the many newspapers in which it was repeated. Jones wrote:

> Loreta was born in the West Indies in 1838, married a New Orleans planter named Roach and was living in St. James Parish, Louisiana, in 1861. After her husband's enlistment and early death in the Confederate cause, she raised a company of cavalry in Arkansas and equipped it at her own expense. Disguised as a man, she proceeded to Virginia where she took part in First Manassas and served for many months under Colonel Dreaux [*sic* Dreux] before her sex was discovered....

Clearly, Jones never read Velazquez's book.

First, Velazquez did not write that she was married to a planter named Roach; she claimed her first marriage was to a Federal officer whose first name was William.

Second, Velazquez claimed she raised a "battalion" of infantry, not a "company" of cavalry, and it was before her husband died, in fact, she delivered her men to him.

Third, author Jones unwittingly repeated the Colonel Dreux lie which has already been exposed.

Jones wrote, "Her contemporaries described her as 'the beautiful Confederate spy whose black eyes bewitched passes from Union generals.'"

In correction, it was not "her contemporaries" who made that statement, but it was author James D. Horan, who in his 1954 book, *Confederate Agent: A Discovery in History*, wrote that spy Felix Stidger in the summer of 1863 went to St. Louis "where he met the beautiful Madam Valesque [*sic*], the Confederate spy whose black eyes bewitched passes from Union Generals." Horan put words in Stidger's mouth! Felix Stidger, in his 1903 autobiography[2], never claimed to have met Velazquez. He did not write he went to St. Louis, but instead Louisville. Velazquez never went to St. Louis

---

2. Felix Grundy Stidger, *Treason History of the Order of Sons of Liberty* (Chicago: Felix G. Stidger, 1903).

summer of 1863 and never claimed it. She did write (p449) she went on a spy trip there when she was in Indianapolis, but this would have been between May and June 1864, according to her documented locations. The narration of the trip has been shown likely fabricated and is addressed in "The Yankee Spy within Her" section.

1958, a single paragraph space filler, printed in many newspapers, stated as fact:

Loreta J. Velazquez, posing as Lt. Harry T. Buford, was a noted woman spy on the confederate side in the War Between the States. She had to wear a special brace to make her appear masculine.[3]

It can only be surmised that newspaper editors sometimes do not review the paper's content for clarity. Did the woman posing as a man named Harry, work as a woman spy while wearing a special brace to make her appear masculine?

1959, *The Civil War Dictionary* by Mark Mayo Boatner III. This 974-page volume contains a 135-word paragraph entry for Velazquez, starting with "VELAQUES, Loreta Janeta. Confederate officer and spy. 1840-?" No and no, Velazquez said she was born in 1842 and that she only disguised as an officer. The rest of the entry is equally inaccurate. "They [she and her husband] were stationed at Fort Leavenworth when the war began...." No, she said she was in Memphis and he on the road to Richmond. Boatner wrote, "her husband said that she might go to war as his A.D.C. [aid-de-camp]" No, she never wrote her husband told her this. And Boatner further wrote, she "serv[ed] first as a temporary company commander under [General] Bee at 1st Bull Run." No, it was at the skirmish at Blackburn's Ford three days prior to Bull Run that she claimed she took command of a company and that by her own initiative, not by orders as the dictionary implies. General Bee was not there. She said she only hoped to continue in command of the company when the expected battle (Bull Run) began. At Bull Run she claimed she fought under General Bee.

This dictionary was revised in 1988; the entry for Velazquez was unchanged.

1964, the April 23 *News-Gazette* (Halifax County, VA) reported on the Virginia Woman's Club meeting at which the evening's speaker, Mrs. A. P. Bohannan, gave "a paper on women of the Civil War... She told of the

---

3. *Niagara Falls Gazette* (NY), Aug 14, 1958; *Union-Sun & Journal* (Lockport, NY), Aug 14, 1958; *Times-Picayune* (New Orleans, LA), Sep 8, 1958; *Trenton Evening News* (NJ), Nov 13, 1958; *Greensboro Record* (NC), Dec 5, 1958.

achievements of Capt. Sallie Thompson, Belle Boyd of Virginia, Sarah Cumming of Alabama, and Loretta Janeta Velasquez, who raised a troop of cavalrymen and disguised as a man fought in some battles." Of course, Velazquez, in her memoir, never claimed to have raised "a troop of cavalrymen."

1965, the March *South Atlantic Bulletin* published an address given at the South Atlantic Modern Language Association luncheon on November 13, 1964. The scholarly speech informed about the composition of the armies during the Civil War, noting that one in five soldiers in the Union army was a "foreign born, foreign-language-speaking soldier." The Confederate army too was noted to have had many foreign language military companies. The presenter stated:

There were also some foreign language women soldiers in both the north and the south. The one who, in my opinion, led the most exciting life, was the foreign-born, foreign-language-speaking Loreta Janeta Veláquez [*sic*]. She became a foreign-language soldier in the Confederate Army and was known as Lt. Harry T. Buford. In her autobiography she tells us that she was born in Havana of Spanish parents.

No, Velazquez wrote her mother was French and American, not Spanish. In addition, the presenter stated that Velazquez "actually succeeded in recruiting and equipping a whole regiment." Velazquez, in her memoir, never claimed this! Recall, that a whole regiment consists of 1000 men.

The speaker concluded:

Eventually [Velazquez] settled down and became a clever business woman and a leader in southern social circles, admired by some but held in contempt by others because she had once fought in men's clothes.

Extensive research has failed to reveal one incident in which Velazquez was held in contempt because she "had once fought in men's clothes." If she was held in contempt for some reason, it would likely have been by a person who read her book and understood Velazquez was a prevaricator. Or possibly they met her and caught one of her falsehoods and felt contempt because of it.

1966, *Bonnet Brigades* by Mary Elizabeth Massy who stated that she included Velazquez in her book about women in the Civil War because, "as Mrs. Livermore[4] noted," there was "an element of fact" in Velazquez's account.

There indeed is an element of fact, but any claim which was important, was all or mostly false. However, Massey was skeptical:

---

4. This was likely Mrs. Arthur L. (Henrietta Wells) Livermore, the suffragist, who was active in New York.

The most famous Confederate woman soldier was Mme. Loreta Janeta Velasquez, but it should be noted that her fame rests entirely on her fantastic account published more than a decade after the war. Nor has it been definitely established that the author might conceivably have had any of the experiences described. It seems impossible that any one woman could have done all she claimed....

Massey noted the newspaper articles about Mrs. Laura J. Williams and Lieutenant Henry Benford and thought they seemed connected to Velazquez. Massey considered it possible Velazquez took these news items or rumors of the day and made a composite picture, "enlivened by [her] vivid imagination," and presented it as her own story. Today, it is clear that these various accounts in the newspapers were all Velazquez.

Massey recounted mostly accurate Velazquez's narrative, but with some errors. For example, Massey said that Velazquez's fourth husband died "in the seventies [1870's]." Massey must have assumed his death had occurred then because that was when Velazquez dropped him from her narrative. Recall that Velazquez never named miner husband Edward H. Bonner in her book for the simple reason that he was alive and well and she did not wish to invite scrutiny. Bonner did not die until 1906.

Massey briefly tackled the controversy between General Early and Velazquez and in the process did not quite get the facts correct. Author Massey said that General Early sent his letter through "an intermediary who promised to forward it" to Velazquez. This was not true. General Early sent a letter to a friend and included in the envelope were two other letters, one letter that General Early had not yet sent to Congress Slemons and a copy of Velazquez's letter to Early. The General, harboring doubts if he should send this letter to Slemons, asked this friend his opinion whether Early should send it. In the letter to Slemons, General Early explained that it appeared that Velazquez, by notation in her letter, had chosen Slemons as an intermediary thus the reason why Early was making his reply through Slemons. General Early asked forgiveness of Slemons for bothering him if Slemons had not sanctioned Velazquez; Early asked that the letter be disposed. If Slemons had indeed sanctioned Velazquez, then Early said Slemons could show to her the letter which General Early wrote to Slemons. This was the letter which contained the General's criticism of Velazquez's book. As noted previously, none of these letters ever left the hands of the friend to whom General Early sent them, judging from their known history. In other words, the letter was never sent to "an intermediary who promised to forward it" to Velazquez.

Although Mary Massey got close to picking-up the scent of the trail, the trail was rather old and she failed to nip at the evidence enough to flush out the game. Massey must be praised for her skepticism.

1967, *Women in Battle* by John Laffin who dedicated ten pages to Velazquez; Chapter 13 was titled "Loreta Velasquez 1842- ?, Irrepressible and Irresponsible." Laffin's rendition of Velazquez's memoir was romanticized and a little inaccurate:

> The authorities took her at her own evaluation and she emerged from the recruiting office as Lieutenant Harry T. Buford of the Independent Scouts.

This, of course, is not what Velazquez claimed at all. Laffin also put words in Velazquez's mouth when he wrote that during the Battle of Fort Donelson, Velazquez "did more than her share in leading and actual fighting." No, Velazquez wrote (p164-173) about her time at Fort Donelson and she never stated she participated in the fighting or led men in the battle. She wrote only that she stood guard duty and she implied she worked in the presence of Dr. Moore when she tried "to make the wounded men as comfortable as possible." (There, indeed, was a Dr. Moore at Fort Donelson which is a credit to Velazquez's correctness and maybe to her presence there.)

Laffin wrapped up his presentation of Velazquez:

> Several writers over the years have tried to trace her life from this point [the conclusion of her book], but none has unearthed a clue. To know her last married name would help, but any records that were kept in Nevada in the 1870's have long since vanished. Her own family were [*sic*] still well established and descendents exist today, but they always denied that they had ever again heard from Loreta. They were not proud of her, though I think they should have been. Loreta Velasquez was unconventional, but she did not disgrace her family or race, and though she acted the man neither did she disgrace her sex. If ever there was a human being who combined the best qualities of a man and of a woman it was Loreta Velasquez-Lieutenant Buford.

Laffin must not have tried to find records "in Nevada in the 1870's" because they do exist and have **not** "long since vanished." As for Velazquez's family, Laffin must have dreamed about the existence of descendents who "denied that they had ever again heard from Loreta." He certainly did not state who these descendents were or support his claim with fact. No descendents have been discovered, to date.

1972, *Women Who Spied for the Blue and the Gray* by Oscar A. Kinchen who retold some of Velazquez's memoir, but not accurately:

> After her husband's early death in the Confederate army, she dressed herself in the uniform of a Confederate soldier and raised a company of cavalry in Arkansas, equipping it at her own expense.

No. Velazquez wrote she raised "a battalion" of infantry, not a company of cavalry, and delivered it to her very alive husband. Kinchen continued, "She was married at an early age to a man named Rouch [*sic*] and was living in St. James parish in Louisiana at the outbreak of war between the North and South." Velazquez never claimed this in her memoir and Kinchen did not state his source for this bit of information, though it surely came from the March 7, 1866 St. Louis *Republican* which stated in part, "... whose maiden name was Roach... At an early period, her parents moved to the United States and settled in the parish of St. James, Louisiana."

Kinchen claimed that "Rouch" was her husband's surname when it is clear that the newspaper said "Roach" was her maiden name. The microfilmed newspaper used by Kinchen must have made the "a" appear as "u." The variant "Rouch" will be seen to show up again in year 2010.

1978, *Sunday Advocate* (Baton Rouge, LA), January 8. Fred Brooks' article was titled, "Antebellum Amazons: Soldiers in Disguise" and it was accompanied by a nice illustration of two female soldiers facing off with bayonets fixed on their rifles seemingly ready to jab at each other. The occasion of the article was the chance discovery in a flower garden of nine skeletons in a common grave. The skeletons were forensically identified as soldiers by their decayed uniforms and surprising to the investigators, one skeleton was that of a female. The skeletons were reburied "in the Shiloh National Cemetery and marked 'unknown.'" Author Brooks ably gave of the history of some of the world's female soldiers and then addressed women in the Civil War. He somewhat cautiously considered Velazquez's history:

> If the book... be true, then she too fell at Shiloh. Lieutenant "Buford" was found to be a woman in disguise when she was wounded while helping to retrieve Rebel casualties from the battlefield. She was again unmasked when discovered by military authorities in New Orleans but continued to serve the Confederacy as a spy and in other capacities....

Velazquez never claimed she "retrieved Rebel casualties," only that she buried some dead. But the dead she claimed she buried, she also claimed were soldiers from the "tenth Tennessee regiment" and it is false that this regiment was at the Battle of Shiloh. Everything Velazquez wrote or said about Shiloh was likely a lie and has been covered elsewhere.

1978, June *Civil War Times Illustrated*. The article by Sylvia D. Hoffert was titled "Heroine or Hoaxer?" and it was reprinted in the August 1999 *Civil War Times*.

Hoffert recounts accurately enough the general events of Velazquez's memoir. However, in error, Hoffert wrote that after Velazquez returned to America from Venezuela she went "West, stopping long enough in Salt Lake

City to have a baby and meet Brigham Young. In Nevada she claimed to have married again for the fourth time to an unnamed gentleman." No, Velazquez clearly wrote she first married her fourth husband in Nevada, then had their baby in Salt Lake City.

The real strength of Hoffert's article was her attempt to weigh the available evidence which might verify Velazquez's story. In only little detail, Hoffert told of the nature and content of General Jubal Early's letter of criticism and how he did not believe Velazquez's book. Hoffert failed to mention that General Early was visited by Velazquez, or that Early was an ex-Confederate general who had trod the same ground as Velazquez and knew the nature of the army and its soldiers in great detail; in other words, he was a highly qualified contemporary whose opinion should have carried great weight.

Hoffert countered Early's criticism with:

> Two other contemporaries believed her story. Her editor, C. J. Worthington, understandably wrote that he had complete confidence in her veracity.

Hoffert then questioned the "value of his testimony" because the editor also wrote that Velazquez was a "typical Southern woman of the war period" and Hoffert said that anyone who read Velazquez's book could plainly see Velazquez was not typical. Hoffert, like most people, did not and could not have even considered the editor's credibility. Hoffert did not know a single thing about C. J. Worthington; the only thing she could have known about him was what he himself claimed, that he had been in the Union navy. As a witness and contemporary, C. J. Worthington falls very short of General Jubal Early. "C. J. Worthington's" true identity has been analyzed in the book in hand.

The other Velazquez contemporary who Hoffert noted was the reporter (*Daily Picayune*, January 5, 1867) who wrote about Velazquez's return to New Orleans when Velazquez, as "Mrs. Mary De Caulp," claimed to be an agent of the Venezuela Emigration Company. The article gave a rendition of Velazquez's war time escapades and the reporter recalled that during the War, she was arrested in New Orleans and "brought before Mayor Monroe." The reporter remembered seeing "her at the time, dressed in a rough gray jacket and pants, the suit rather worse for wear, with her hair cut short, and supporting a bandaged foot with a crutch of the most primitive pattern." And now "Mrs. De Caulp" was "a very different looking person" from the 'bould soger boy' who came to New Orleans during the war" because she was now "an elegantly attired lady." Hoffert nearly stumbled onto the key to the lock of truth when she wrote:

> The article described her adventurous life in some detail, most of it inaccurate if one accepts the story she published nine years later as true. For example, the

article asserted that she was a first lieutenant in a Texas cavalry company and mentions nothing about her espionage activities.

Distracted by the supposed reporter's inaccuracy because he failed to mention Velazquez's spying activity, Hoffert herself failed to notice a huge contradiction between the article and what Velazquez later wrote in her book. The reporter wrote that Velazquez "was a first lieutenant in a Texas cavalry company" when Velazquez should have told him that she was the first lieutenant of an Arkansas infantry "battalion" she raised at "Hurlburt Station," Arkansas, by her own effort and expense, because that was exactly what she later claimed in her book! Hoffert should have understood, and been very troubled, that the reporter could not have possibly gotten his facts "inaccurate" to this degree. Hoffert failed to understand that the reporter simply wrote the falsehoods told to him by Velazquez. Interestingly, the reporter must have harbored some doubt as to what he was hearing and hedged his report, stating "Mrs. De Caulp's life, according to her account...."

Hoffert pointed out that Velazquez, in her memoir, "made no attempt to hide her ability to tell a convincing lie and even defended it by saying that 'lying was as necessary as fighting in warfare.'" Hoffert stated in conclusion, that she couldn't judge if Velazquez was "a brave soldier and spy or merely a literary opportunist- or both" and noted that there just wasn't "enough evidence available to substantiate it." Hoffert concluded:

And since in every lie there is usually a seed of truth, we may assume that Madame Velazquez has expanded on that seed."

Recall that Velazquez wrote (p5) that she related her story "with simplicity and truth" and her editor, C. J. Worthington, wrote (p12-13) "it is a true story in every particular." Their vociferous claims of truthfulness leave no room for seed expansion.

1980, Castle Thunder: The Confederate Provost Marshall's Prison, 1862-1865 by Alan Lawrence Golden. This 155-page Master of Art thesis in History briefly touched (p122) on women who were jailed in Castle Thunder and gave Velazquez as the best known. Golden wrote:

In her memoirs published after the war, she tells of disguising herself as a man for the first years of the war so that she could obtain valuable information for the Confederacy.

No. She wrote she dressed as a male soldier and fought, not collected information. Golden further asserted that upon her release from Castle Thunder, she "continued her career in male attire." No again. She said she retired her male soldier impersonation upon her release, and as a female, spied for the benefit of the Confederacy. Even though Velazquez's memoir was given as the sole Velazquez source, it seems Golden never read it.

1984, the Winter *Southern Studies* periodical published an article by Janet E. Kaufman titled "'Under the Petticoat Flag': Women Soldiers in the Confederate Army." Although Kaufman recited the stories of several female soldiers, she dedicated much of her article to retelling Velazquez's narrative. Kaufman addressed social aspects of women in society of that time and how Velazquez sought to prove herself "equal or superior to men both on the battle field and in the courting parlor, even if only in print." Kaufman wrote, "The memoir is profoundly revealing as the author's struggle for personal and sexual identity," and that "Velazquez's story is so incredible as to raise doubts about its authenticity."

Kaufman relied almost entirely on Velazquez's memoir and reported only a little outside of it. Kaufman used Mary Massey's 1966 book, *Bonnet Brigades* as a source citing, "[Velazquez's] narrative is flawed by factual errors and internal inconsistencies." The one time Kaufman located an article which might have been used to the search for the truth, it simply confused her. Kaufman noted the story about "Mrs. Laura J. Williams" who adopted the name "Henry Benford" which Kaufman found in Felix Gregory DeFontaine's 1864 *Marginalia; or, Gleanings from an Army Note-Book*. DeFontaine had reproduced the original Jackson *Mississippian* newspaper article which appeared on June 6, 1863. In the end, Kaufman was unsure if Mrs. Williams was a woman other than Velazquez, or if there were two women with a similar story, or if Velazquez "grafted her own autobiography on to the other woman's life," or if this was Velazquez.

1985, *Boston Herald* November 3 article titled "The Pentagon: More than 5 sides- Surprise treasures tell the horror story of war" by Anita Zelman. Reporter Zelman wrote of her tour of the Pentagon and of the "display cases filled with items… used in the Civil War." She noted, "The Military Women's Corridor was dedicated in 1983, honoring the women who have served our country since the days of the American Revolution." She saw displays honoring the memory of women, such as Molly Pitcher, Margaret Corbin, Deborah Sampson and … Loreta Velazquez. Zelman wrote:

It was discovered that during the Civil War, Lt. Harry T. Buford of the Confederate States Army was really Loreta Janeta Velazquez and this fact is noted in her display case.

If Velazquez is still represented in the Military Women's Corridor among noteworthy women who have served the country, please Pentagon officials, read Velazquez's autobiography. You will find Velazquez said she gave herself the rank of lieutenant and falsely represented to those she met that she was a lieutenant. If all a person needs to do is falsely represent themselves in order to get honored in the display cases, please anticipate adding a sixth side to the building to accommodate the influx of new honorees which can be expected. And is it truly necessary to point out that Velazquez was not serving "our country" since she adamantly claimed she was fighting against it?!

1986, *Historical Times Illustrated Encyclopedia of the Civil War* edited by Patricia L. Faust. This 849-page volume presents Velazquez on page 779 in her alphabetical slot. Included in the two-paragraph synopsis is an erroneous claim which Velazquez never made, that she "raised a company of cavalry in Arkansas, became lieutenant of the unit, temporarily commanded it under Brig. Gen. Barnard E. Bee at First Bull Run...." However, to the editor's credit, Faust also wrote the memoir is "an unbelievable series of adventures with more characteristics of fiction than fact" and her book "is the least credible of the Civil War spy literature."

1988, *Who Was Who in the Confederacy: A Comprehensive, Illustrated Biographical Reference to More Than 1,000 of the Principal Confederacy Participants in the Civil War* by Stewart Sifakis. Author Sifakis incorrectly identified Velazquez's life span as "(1838-?)." Recall, Velazquez wrote she was born on June 26, 1842. Otherwise, Sifakis adroitly wrote, "If there has ever been a case of exaggeration with a hidden element of truth, it is likely to be in the claims put forward by Loreta J. Velazquez in her book...." A flash synopsis identifying some of her claims was presented, which was then followed with:

> Little in her work can be even circumstantially supported. Yet there may be an element of truth. She may have done some of the things she claimed, but this will never be definitely known due to her penchant for exaggeration.

Sifakis noted that Velazquez "may have written the work solely to provide an income for herself and her infant <u>daughter</u>." Yes and No. Yes, Velazquez said she hoped to earn money. No, she said a <u>son</u>. Sifakis also noted that General Early was "one of her harshest critics."

1990, *The United Daughters of the Confederacy* magazine, August, Vol LIII, Number 8. Historian General Francis W. McGill presented a three-paragraph summary of Velazquez's memoir ostensibly taken from the reference which McGill gave, *Our Incredible Civil War* by Davis Burke, published in 1960. This book was later renamed *The Civil War, Strange and Fascinating Facts*. Astonishingly, almost every point presented by McGill was an inaccurate retelling of Velazquez's claims. For example, after Velazquez turned over her men to her husband's command and then her husband was killed, "Loleta [*sic*] assumed command once more and led the regiment through a series of battles as an independent force." And, "She survived the war to enjoy three marriages and raise four children." McGill probably never came within ten feet of Velazquez's memoir and hadn't a clue about the claims it contained.

However, Francis McGill showed skepticism of the memoir which she seemingly never read, "The story of Loleta Velasquez [*sic*] must be classed as folklore even though the one concerned insisted that it was real life drama." Velazquez's book is not folklore; it is a memoir of some truths and many lies.

1993, *Patriots in Disguise (Women Warriors of the Civil War)*. Author Richard Hall, in detail and in forty-six pages contained in three chapters, accurately retold Velazquez's memoir.

In the last three paragraphs of the admirable recitation, Mr. Hall opined about Velazquez, "Having squandered her fortunes, she wrote the memoirs (rather hastily, judging by internal evidence) to support herself and her young son." Hall's belief in this single sentence got him off on the wrong foot. Logic dictates that Velazquez, in truth, did not have or inherit or earn a fortune to squander; her own storyline supports this. She claimed she was sent to the Sisters of Charity school (which records show was for the "care and training of needy girls") and her father disinherited her when she eloped. In addition, and outside of her storyline, recall, Velazquez lived at Nelly Bremer's house of prostitution, not exactly the lodging for a person of wealth. None of her war time activity earned her a fortune and she abandoned post-war husband Bonner and his earnings.

Hall's second misstep was that he claimed the memoir had been hastily written. Hall failed to note the 1866 articles, which abound in the record, in which Velazquez claimed she was already in the process of writing her book. The time period from 1866 to 1876 can hardly be characterized as "hastily." In fact, as early as April 24, 1862 a newspaper said:[5]

Her reason for the course she has adopted is, that she is collecting material for a history of the war, and that she adopted male attire as the plan best calculated to enable her to carry out her design.

In his "Chapter Notes," Mr. Hall tried to make some sense of the shortcomings of Velazquez's narrative. Hall figured that since Velazquez included her disappointments, failures, confusion and indecisiveness over what to do during the course of the war, etc., she was not simply trying to put-on a "good story." He wrote:

---

5. *Daily True Delta* (New Orleans).

On balance, this tends to support the interpretation that she was trying to give an honest account of her experiences, rather than consciously trying to deceive anyone for some ulterior motive.

Mr. Hall listed some points of Velazquez's narrative which made no sense to him and then said, "The Velazquez narrative leaves many puzzles unexplained." He noted that Velazquez, in her memoir, stated she spent 10 days in jail, yet "A contemporary news story reports that she was imprisoned for three months." Hall confused her two arrests in New Orleans. On the first arrest she was held briefly, the second she was incarcerated for six months. When Velazquez was released after the second arrest, she lied to the newspapers that she had been jailed by General Butler for three months for her Southern loyalty. This is the three months referenced by Hall. The truth is that she was convicted of stealing some jewelry from the Chesters, who were ostensibly trying to give her a place to stay and she was sent to prison for six months. Velazquez certainly couldn't tell the newspapers or her book's readership that she was jailed for stealing. In fact, Velazquez lied to her readership, saying that she was released immediately through the efforts of British Consul Coppell. All of this has been covered.

Hall addressed the encounter between Jubal Early and Velazquez, stating, "General Jubal Early denounced her as a fraud, even refusing to believe that she was a southern woman." More precisely, what General Early wrote was that after he had met her, he expressed to someone "the belief that Madame Velasquez is not of Spanish birth or origin, but is an American and probable from the North."

Richard Hall wrote about General Early's objections, but failed to mention them in their entirety and/or whether the objections had merit. That is, with the exception that Hall admitted that the General was correct that Velazquez could not have ridden on a particular railroad, as she claimed, because at that time it had not been completed. Hall wrote (p211), "On the other hand, this could be a simple failure of memory [of Velazquez's]."

At this date, Hall was mostly an apologist for Velazquez (p192), "Her apparently carelessly written memoirs are Velazquez's worst handicap when it comes to credibility." In addition, he wrote (p207):

In preparing this book, I made a substantial effort to check the factual accuracy and credibility of her story, and found that a *lot* in her work could be "circumstantially supported."

Hall continued:

The issue, as I see it, is to evaluate whether the errors the book contains can be explained convincingly as resulting from careless mistakes or faulty memory, or whether the evidence points more toward outright fabrication.

Toward that effort, Hall contacted Calvin L. Collier the author of *The War Child's Children*, a book which relates the story of the 3rd Arkansas Cavalry. This was the regiment to which Velazquez's husband, Captain Thomas DeCaulp, belonged. Collier stated, "DeCaulp could not have been either at Pensacola or the battle of Shiloh." In this Collier is correct; the facts of DeCaulp's military service are perfectly clear. Velazquez, in her book, lied that DeCaulp was at Pensacola and Shiloh. She lied about the time and place his death. She lied that he was a loyal Southerner. Not only did she lie about DeCaulp's fate in her memoir, she lied about him and his fate to the newspapers. Hall wrote, "I have thought of a few theories to explain the discrepancy between her story of his death at Chattanooga and all of the records showing that he did not die...."

Hall then presented a couple of possible explanations, but none of which was totally satisfactory to him and he stated the need for more investigation. Hall thought, at least in this part of her memoirs about Thomas DeCaulp, that "Velazquez mixed fiction with fact in some unknown but significant proportions." In his search for an explanation, what Richard Hall failed to consider and therefore understand, was that Velazquez was a purposeful and compulsive liar. He, like many others, suffered from gentlemanliness and it was not in his nature to believe that Velazquez was simply a liar.

Richard Hall made one interesting discovery which was worth examining. He noted that John W. Headley's 1906 book *Confederate Operations in Canada and New York* contains a photograph of a "young woman [that] bears a *strong* resemblance to the engraving of Velazquez that appears in her memoirs." He said he made an effort to positively identify that woman, but had not been successful. This photograph has been addressed earlier in detail and will be mentioned again in 2006 when Hall becomes convinced the photo was Velazquez.

Hall was understandably taken by Velazquez's story which he noted was "rich in descriptive detail of people, places and events, including many verifiable names and unit designations." He said he checked out as many clues as possible, but there remained much more to investigate, "In fact, I intend to continue this research." True to his word, Richard H. Hall will publish a follow-up book in 2006.

1994, *The Story the Soldiers Wouldn't Tell (Sex in the Civil War)* by Thomas P. Lowery, M. D., who in a page and a half, presented Velazquez. Even in brevity, Lowery asserted in error (echoed by future authors), "A decade later, she was in Brazil, at which point she fades from history." Lowery concluded:

Is her story true? Are her memoirs, *The Woman in Battle*, to be believed? Researchers who have devoted years to this question say yes- but. Some of her adventures seem to be true and can be verified, while others, of more doubtful validity, stand as wonderful examples of imagination.

1995, *The War the Women Lived (Female Voices from the Confederate South)* edited by Walter Sullivan. The author used various women's narratives to fill the timeline of the Civil War. Sullivan endeavored to cover the "Fall of 1863" of the War by repeating pages 351-372 of *The Woman in Battle*. This he did in some sixteen-and-a-half pages, taking the whole of his Chapter 15, but contributed nothing new. Curiously, Sullivan spelled Velazquez's name in a novel fashion. Sullivan wrote, "Loréta Janéta Velazquez," with accented "é" in Loreta and Janeta. Shouldn't it be trusted that a person knows how to spell their own name?

1995, *Swindler, Spy, Rebel (The Confidence Woman in Nineteenth-Century America)* by Kathleen De Grave. In her coverage of several women, author De Grave used Richard Hall's *Patriots in Disguise* for her information about Velazquez, as well as Velazquez's own book. De Grave accepted Richard Hall's warning that the truthfulness of Velazquez's memoir is not "clear-cut" and De Grave said that "with all these caveats in mind" she proceeded to retell what Velazquez herself wrote and characterized Velazquez's claimed deeds within the structure of the theme of *Swindler, Spy, Rebel*.

1996, *Women War Heroines* by George and Anne Forty, published in London by Arms and Armour Press and distributed in the USA by Sterling Publishing Company. This 190-page book addressed Velazquez in Chapter 5 in a six-page subsection, "Loreta Velázquez," and "Following the Loved One." Reproduced is Velazquez's "Making a Charge" from her book. See Illustrations, Figure 5.

The Fortys retold Velazquez's memoir, but omitted many points which would have, no doubt, caused disbelief in their readership. The authors added their own flavor and an impressive number of inaccuracies for such a short synopsis. For instance, "She enrolled 236 men in four days and one can image her husband's surprise when Loreta triumphantly burst into his room at the barracks in Pensacola and told him of her success!" No, that is not what Velazquez wrote. She wrote (p86) that her husband met her and her troops at the train station "in response to a telegraphic despatch [she] had sent to him, signed by [her] *nom de guerre*." Her husband did not know it was her until she "took him aside where [she] could speak to him privately, and disclosed her identity."

A greater transgression was the authors' retelling of Velazquez's activity at Fort Donelson:

Loreta arrived at Fort Donelson just in time to see its surrender, playing her part in the battle, being on duty on the outworks when the Federals first attacked. She fought valiantly, helping to beat off wave after wave of attackers, in sleet, snow and high winds of a bitter February in 1862; the battle went on without pause for forty-eight hours.

No, no, no. Velazquez never claimed she fought at Fort Donelson. She never claimed she was standing guard when the first attack came. She never claimed she fought off wave after wave of attackers. Velazquez wrote (p166-167) only that she stood guard during the painfully cold night, listening to the agonizing cries of wounded men pleading for water. She also wrote that she helped with the wounded.

Another wrong example is, "Poor Loreta, her happiness was again short-lived, for de Caulp was killed in action shortly after their marriage." No, that is not what Velazquez wrote. She wrote (p337), "Before reaching his command, Captain De Caulp was taken sick again... died in a Federal hospital in Chattanooga."

Suffice it to say there are still more inaccuracies which could be cited.

Authors Forty included some 42 women from different times and wars. Interestingly, the authors titled the second-to-last chapter, "Fact or Fiction?" and in it noted that the majority of the stories related could be "verified by factual evidence," but some "must be classified as unsubstantiated." They chose three women upon whom to cast doubt, one being Lucy Brewer of the United States, who was alleged to have fought disguised as a man in the War of 1812 aboard frigate USS *Constitution* as a marine sharpshooter.[6]

The Fortys contacted the U.S. Marine Corps for background information on Lucy and the authors said that the "[Corps] were careful to point out that as far as they were concerned, she was just a myth." Just the same, one of the streets at U.S. Marine Corps Base Camp Lejeune in North Carolina is today named Lucy Brewer Avenue. According to the Fortys, in 1947 the veracity of Lucy's story was questioned which had arisen from the naming of the Avenue. One of the historians involved in the issue, John L. Zimmerman, stated, "I think it would have been wise if someone had looked into the matter of Lucy before nailing up the street markers." The Fortys pointed out that not everyone was of the same sentiment and "well-known military historians, such as John Laffin," author of the 1967 book *Women in*

---

6. Lucy's story of serving three years while dressed as a man, and never being found out, was first published with success as a pamphlet titled *An Affecting Narrative of Louisa Baker* in 1814. A successful sequel was published in 1815 titled *The Adventures of Lucy Brewer (alias) Louisa Baker*. Then a third successful pamphlet was produced titled, *An Awful Beacon to the Rising Generation of Both Sexes* by Mrs. Lucy West (having married one Charles West). The three stories were gathered under one title in 1816, *The Female Marine, or the Adventures of Miss Lucy Brewer* and that work was greatly successful as well.

Battle, believed Lucy's story. Laffin's book has already been presented in this chronology and his treatment of Velazquez analyzed. Laffin was likely the Fortys' source of information, or at least one of their sources, about Velazquez which they used in their own book.

Velazquez was not included in the "Fact or Fiction?" chapter of the Fortys' book.

1996, *Passing and the Fictions of Identity* edited by Elaine K. Ginsberg and published by Duke University Press. The chapter addressing Velazquez (p181-217) was written by Elizabeth Young and is titled "Confederate Counterfeit: The Case of the Cross-Dressed Civil War Soldier." The back-cover notes explain the title of the book: "Passing refers to the process whereby a person of one race, gender, nationality, or sexual orientation adopts the disguise of another."

The chapter opens with recent history, the recounting of North Carolinian Lauren Cook Burgess' lawsuit against the United States Department of Interior. Lauren and her husband Fred were Civil War reenactors who participated at Civil War battlefields, many of which are under the auspices of the National Park Service. Fred wore a man's uniform and Lauren did likewise, impersonating a male soldier. She had been successful in her disguise on prior occasions, but at an August 1989 reenactment at Antietam Battlefield the Park Service discovered her and "ordered her to remove her uniform or to leave the park." Lauren refused and sued for sexual discrimination. The defendant, the Park Service, asserted that her disguise lacked authenticity, but the seemingly more dominant issue was that her gender lacked authenticity. Lauren effectively made her case that she portrayed a male soldier with ability "not only sufficient but superior" to most of the men out there pretending to be Civil War soldiers. The Battlefield Park's superintendent asserted that no women dressed as men soldiers were present at Antietam and Lauren countered with "extensive research on Civil War cross-dressers present at Antietam." Lauren won her suit in March 1993.

Prior to this date, Lauren had devoted some years researching women's participation as soldiers in the Civil War with published articles in leading magazines. Then in 1994, she published her first book which was titled *An Uncommon Soldier: The Civil War Letters of Sarah Rosetta Wakeman, alias Pvt. Lyons Wakeman, 153rd Regiment, New York State Volunteers, 1862-1864*. And it will be seen in 2002 of the chronology that Lauren Cook co-authored, along with DeAnne Blanton, *They Fought Like Demons (Women Soldiers in the American Civil War)*.

Author Elizabeth Young argued that disguised female Civil War soldiers' narratives, and most strongly that of Velazquez's, "take up precisely the same issues of gender and authenticity that frame the story of Lauren Cook Burgess...." It seems unfair to equate Lauren's authenticity to that of Velazquez's, considering that Velazquez has been shown to have been a lifelong liar. In any case, the comparison steered the essay into the historical realm.

Young explained (p184) that in her essay (or chapter) she was less concerned with "the documentary recovery of the lives of the women per se than their significance in the cultural imagination of Civil War America." In other words, Young was not looking for the truth in Velazquez's memoir. Young wrote (p185):

When we treat this work as a picaresque nineteenth-century novel rather than as an evidentiary account of the Civil War, however, *The Woman in Battle* becomes a productive site for an extended inquiry into the meanings of cross-dressing, as constructed by the intersecting axes of gender, sexuality, race, region, and nation. The importance of cross-dressing in *The Woman in Battle*, I will argue, inheres in its figurative as well as literal meanings and particularly in its ability to forge fictional links between disparate ideas and images. Military masquerade functions in this text as a metaphorical point of exchange for intersections between individual bodies and the body politic in Civil War and Reconstruction America. From the phantasmatic possibilities of a "lesbian confederacy" to the cultural myths of the postwar South, *The Woman in Battle* offers insights into the meaning of cross-dressing for identity- both individual and national- in the nineteenth-century America.

Hmm...huh...wait a moment. Elizabeth Young, a literature professor, continued her analysis (p188-189):

Velazquez's text responds metaphorically to the enlarged spectrum of possibility for Southern white women during wartime; [and] If the Civil War functions as a psychic space of release even in its most literal register- as the historical setting for *The Woman in Battle*- then its thematic of internal conflict is even more inseparable from the fictional biography of Loreta Velazquez herself; and, Velazquez's first marriage symbolically maps national boundaries onto individual identities....

Please do not feel alone or despair or consider self-harm if you haven't a clue what you just read; please stay with the group and let's ease onward, all holding hands.

In some 35 pages of analysis the reader is battered with contorted metaphors and symbolisms about sexual identity, racial identity, and national identity, but worse still is that Young unwittingly (or otherwise) accepts Velazquez's false claims and extracts meanings and applies metaphors to those false claims.

For example, Young points out that Velazquez fought at the First Battle of Bull Run and at the Battle of Ball's Bluff. Rather than considering whether

Velazquez's specific (and provably false) claimed deeds at those battles were true, Young searched for a profound metaphor and found one: "On the suggestively named battlegrounds of 'Bull Run' and 'Ball's Bluff,' both Velazquez and the Confederacy prove their 'manhood.'" Oh, I think I get it, do you mean, suggestively named, like Testicle's Bluff? Is it really necessary to explain that these locations of the battles were not "suggestively named" by forefather settlers with the "manhood" of Velazquez or the Confederacy in mind?

Bull Run, a small tributary creek of the Occoquan River, originates in the Bull Run Mountains (in the Blue Ridge Mountains) some miles away in Loudoun County, Virginia; and Ball's Bluff was named for Colonel Burgess Ball, who was a friend and relative (cousin) to President Washington. George Washington's mother was Mary Ball.[7]

Interestingly, the Battle of Bull Run is also known as the Battle of Manassas and the Battle of Ball's Bluff is known by two other names, the Battle of Harrison's Island and the Battle of Leesburg, yet Young failed to point out how those names might be "suggestively" construed.

To her credit author Elizabeth Young gets one of the most important facts correct, Young wrote, "the book narrates Velazquez's adventures while disguised as an officer of her own invention, Lieutenant Harry T. Buford." Velazquez wrote exactly this (p61 and 341) and it is clear to all who wish to read it, but it is invariably ignored by many of Velazquez's admirers who wrongly claim she was commissioned an officer. Even her seemingly most reliable supporter, Major John Newman of the 21st Louisiana Regiment, claimed (in the publisher's testimonial circular) Velazquez earned the rank, which contradicts what Velazquez herself wrote.

There remains much more which could be probed about Young's essay, but suffice it to say that Elizabeth Young was just getting warmed-up for the publication of her own book, *Disarming the Nation (Women's Writing and the American Civil War)*, three years later in 1999, which will be addressed momentarily.

1997, *Valor and Lace: The Roles of Confederate Women 1861-1865* edited by Mauriel Phillips Joslyn. (Previously published in 1996) The 186-page book was the product of nine contributing writers, each with a chapter topic, and author Norma Jean Perkins covered Velazquez in Chapter 4, titled "The Soldier," on pages 58-69.

Author Perkins retold Velazquez's memoir rather accurate, but made claims on Velazquez's behalf which Velazquez never made.

---

7. *History of Union County Kentucky* (Evansville, IN: Courier Co., 1886), 241; "Notes and Queries," *Publications of the Southern History Association* (Oct 1898, Vol II, No. 4): 375.

First, "Velazquez's unit has also been referred to as Arkansas Independents in her book." No, Velazquez wrote they were the "Arkansas Grays." Nowhere in her memoir does Velazquez call them the "Arkansas Independents." A unit, by either name, never existed.

Second, "DeCaulp was wounded and even though they married, he died of his wounds not long after." No, Velazquez never wrote DeCaulp was wounded or he died of wounds. She wrote he was ill and died of illness. Anyway, DeCaulp did not die in the manner Velazquez claimed or how Perkins misstated.

Third, "Supporting the child, (the husband had died), was the reason given for writing the memoirs." No, Velazquez never wrote that this husband, the miner from Austin, Nevada, had died. She said nothing about his fate. History shows he lived long after their separation.

Fourth, "[General Early] stated that she got some of the dates of the battles wrong." No, General Early never said that, but he said many other things worth mentioning which Perkins didn't.

Author Perkins used as sources some of the previously mentioned sources, so it is understandable that she carried forth erroneous statements. Perkins did express some skepticism, "Was she really a dedicated soldier in it for the excitement and challenge? Or was she really a woman of questionable character?"

1997, *Civil War Heroines* by Jill Canon, illustrations by Alan Archambault, Bellerophon Books. This 56-page soft-cover "coloring book" for juveniles presents short biographies of fifty-nine women, some rather unknown and others very well-known, such as Sojourner Truth, Harriet Tubman, Harriet Beecher Stowe, Belle Boyd, Rose O'Neal Greenhow and Sarah Emma Edmonds (who in male disguise joined the Union army).

On page 28 is Loreta Janeta Velazquez's three-paragraph biography and an illustration of her in an officer's uniform with a sword shouldered at full attention. The brief biography mentions some of the by now familiar claims, but in addition makes an original claim, "In a book she wrote after the war, Loreta claimed to have duped several officials, including President Lincoln." No, Velazquez described (*TWIB*, p141) her (as a woman) alleged introduction to Lincoln and in no way claimed or implied that she duped Lincoln or even tried; in fact, she said she "did not have an opportunity to exchange a great many words with Mr. Lincoln."

1998, *Washington Post* staff writer Tara Mack, in a May 2 article titled "Personal Histories Get a Rare Display: 26 Lives Offer Glimpse of Battle," reported that the Manassas Museum (Virginia) opened yesterday a new exhibit titled "Shared Destiny: Encounters Along Bull Run, 1861." The purpose of the display was to "offer tiny glimpses into the lives of 26 people whose paths crossed during one of the defining battles of the Civil War."

They were from Cuba, Georgia and Illinois. They were West Point graduates and former slaves. They went on to become governors, generals and high school principles. But on a grisly day in 1861, they had one thing in common: they all played a role in the First Battle of Manassas.

Included in one short paragraph was "Loreta Velazquez, a native of Cuba who moved to New Orleans as a child with her family... she organized a cavalry unit and joined the fighting." Of course, Velazquez wrote nothing of the kind in her memoir. She wrote her family remained in Cuba when they sent her to live with an aunt in New Orleans. And Velazquez never wrote she raised a cavalry which she took to Manassas. Instead, she wrote she raised an infantry battalion which she took to Pensacola. When she claimed she went to Manassas, she claimed she went there alone.

The display existed until January, so for seven months the public was treated to fabricated and erroneous claims which Velazquez never made in her memoir.

1998, *Those Courageous Women of the Civil War* by Karen Zeinert, Millbrook Press, Inc. The *School Library Journal* characterized the book as written for Grades 6-10 and stated it was "well-written, well-researched... a solid work."

Chapter Two, titled "On the Battlefield," presented Velazquez, including the portrait of her in male military disguise. Author Zeinert asserted:

Velazquez left her home in New Orleans and purchased a commission (officer's title), which was a common practice in the 1800's. From then on, she was known as Lieutenant Harry T. Buford. She eventually attached herself to a regiment from Alabama, where she served with General Barnard Bee.

No, no, no. Velazquez did not claim New Orleans was home at the time she donned her male military disguise. She said she was in Memphis when she put it on. Velazquez did not claim she purchased an officer's commission; she said (p96) she tried and failed to do so, but that was long after she had already named herself an officer. And Velazquez did not claim she attached herself to a regiment from Alabama. What Velazquez claimed (p101) was that she, during the First Battle of Manassas "remained with [General Bee's] command during the entire day." However, she was vague as to which regiment she attached herself and General Bee commanded the 4th Alabama, the 2nd Mississippi, the 11th Mississippi (Companies A and F), the 6th North Carolina and the Staunton Artillery. Curiously, Velazquez claimed (p106) that after the battle she "remained for some time with [her] acquaintances of the fifth and eight Louisiana regiment, hoping that another battle would come off at an early day." The problem is that the 5th Louisiana was not at the First Battle of Manassas and the 8th Louisiana was under General Bonham. (Velazquez correctly made no claim that the 8th Louisiana was under command of General Bee.)

Zeinert ignored the overwhelming theme of Velazquez's memoir when Zeinert wrote in the caption below the illustration of Velazquez, "Loreta Velasquez served under her husband in the Confederate Army, disguised as a man known as Harry T. Buford." Velazquez did not do it and did not claim it either. She claimed that in the opening days of the war, she, in disguise, recruited 236 men, delivered them to her husband in Pensacola to prove herself to him. Within only days of this delivery, he was killed and she left for Virginia. That hardly qualifies her as having served under her husband in the Confederate army, which implies, she served long-term with him. In any case, every word of Velazquez's claim about this husband was a lie.

1998, *Battle Cries and Lullabies (Women in War from Prehistory to the Present)* by Linda Grant De Pauw. This substantial book covers the history of women in war through the ages and around the world. Velazquez was represented briefly with two paragraphs. Author De Pauw noted that Velazquez's "many extraordinary stories" seemed "impossible for a single individual to have experienced." De Pauw continued:

> Gen. Jubal Early called her a fraud and doubted that she was even the Southern woman she claimed to be. But Gen. James Longstreet believed her, and her story definitely has a core of truth.

General Early did not call Velazquez a fraud, however, he did not believe that Velazquez's story was truthful. It also is correct that Velazquez's story contained some truth, however, to say there was a "core of truth" might not be the best phrase to use. One might as easily have stated that it contained a "core of lies." However, it is a misrepresentation of the facts to say that General James Longstreet "believed her." The evidence which De Pauw cited for this assertion was James Longstreet's 1888 letter to Emmy. However, Longstreet wrote no such thing. He said that he did not know Velazquez during the War and only met her afterwards, which should be understood to have been a mere acknowledgement that Velazquez was a real person. Longstreet's letter has been explained in detail already.

1999, *All the Daring of the Soldier (Women of the Civil War Armies)* by Elizabeth D. Leonard who retold Velazquez's story in the course of about eleven pages and included images of Velazquez, in and out of disguise. Leonard addressed the controversy over the authenticity of the memoir citing General Jubal Early as one of the critics. Then Leonard reproduced several of the well-known newspaper articles "to support the theory that at least the broad outlines and even more precise details of the Velazquez story, as presented in *The Woman in Battle*, have their basis in fact."

When Leonard wrote (p253) about Velazquez's claim to have raised her own battalion, Leonard did not express even the mildest disbelief, but instead accepted the claim:

> Velazquez's initial plan is to raise a battalion at her own expense and then present the men to her husband and offer him their command. Gather troops she does: 236 men in four days- not enough for a battalion but certainly enough for the core of a regiment.

However, 236 men were enough for a battalion. A battalion consisted of 2 to 8 companies and a full company consisted of 100 men. A full regiment was 1000 men or ten full companies. Clearly, the 236 men would constitute a battalion or at least "a core" of a battalion <u>before</u> they would constitute "a core" of a regiment.

More important, Leonard positions herself as an apologist for Velazquez's lack of credibility by excusing her or explaining away any problem. Leonard asserted that Velazquez and her editor took artistic license to make Velazquez's memoir more readable at the expense of making it a "pure memoir." Leonard wrote:

> Both Velazquez and Worthington, therefore, confessed up front that *The Woman in Battle* was not a pure memoir per se- if such a thing exists- but rather a product of their combined efforts, a product of memory as well as research which also benefited from the stylistic skill and judgment of an editor sensitive to the demands of a popular readership.

This assertion is simply not true because neither Velazquez nor Worthington made the claim.

Velazquez wrote (p5) that she related her "story with simplicity and truth" and that (p37) her memoir was "unpretending, but truthful." Velazquez asserted (p38):

> Some of the most distinguished officers of the Confederate army and many equally distinguished civilians, can and will testify to the truthfulness of the story I am about to relate, and to the unblemished character I bore while in the Confederate service.

No upfront confession here that the memoir was not a pure memoir! Worthington, Velazquez's alleged editor, wrote:

> While Madame Velazquez does not pretend to any literary accomplishments, her style has a certain flavor which is far from unpleasant; and the editor has been careful, in making such changes and alterations as have seemed necessary, to retain the author's own words wherever practicable.

He also said her story was "a true story in every particular" and that it was "the only authentic account of the career of a Confederate heroine that has issued from the press," and that she had an "unblemished reputation." What up front confession?

Neither Velazquez nor Worthington "confessed up front" that they were presenting anything other than "a pure memoir." Worthington wrote that he was "careful" to make only "alterations as have seemed necessary" and that he retained "the author's own words wherever practicable." Worthington did not claim he provided "stylistic skill" and it was not the "stylistic skill and judgment of an editor sensitive to the demands of a popular readership" that caused an untruthful memoir. It was not a memory failure which caused an untruthful memoir. It was untruths which caused an untruthful memoir.

Leonard further asserted:

> Ten years, even a hundred and ten years after Appomattox [the end of the war], commenters expressed disgust at the idea that a woman would do what Velazquez claimed to have done, serving not only for the glorious cause but also for money as a Civil War soldier and spy, and then writing a memoir about her military adventures for profit.

It is a mystery as to who Leonard's "commenters" were; in the course of research for the book in hand, no discovered source "expressed disgust at the idea that a woman would do what Velazquez claimed to have done," and no discovered source criticized Velazquez for her profit motive of writing the book. Velazquez was, however, criticized by General Early for "palm[ing]" off on the public a book which was in "want of authenticity."

It will be seen that in the 2013 film *Rebel*, Elizabeth D. Leonard is one of the contributing scholars and is still making excuses for Velazquez's book:

> The absolute truth of one thing or another in the book is not the most important contribution that the book makes. It's the presence of the book, the fury that it provoked, the claims that it makes, the reality it tries to portray.

1999, *Disarming the Nation (Women's Writing and the American Civil War)* by Elizabeth Young. Author Young was previously presented in year 1996 as the author of a chapter, which seemingly was a warm-up for this book.

Associate Professor of English Young's presentation of Velazquez is reminiscent of the "compare and contrast" essay assignments which sends English Literature students into convulsions. Noting criticism leveled at *The Woman in Battle* and General Early's criticism, in particular, Young wrote:

> In these condemnations, moreover, what emerges in the absence of authenticity is the presence of the literary. [Skip the rest of the paragraph.] This opposition between truth and fiction is a stagnant one if it focuses on the issue of the book's

empirical truth-value, but what happens if we embrace rather than repudiate the label of fiction for this text? Velazquez herself invokes fictional frames of reference for her story. [Skip the rest of the paragraph.] Reading *The Woman in Battle* as a picaresque novel, we can interpret its presentation of cross-dressing as a literary fantasy prompted by the real-life transformations of Southern white women during wartime.

It is clear that Young had no intention of weighing the truthfulness of Velazquez's memoir, but was only interested in interpreting the narrative metaphorically and giving symbolism to every aspect of the memoir, even to the most obviously false claims of Velazquez. Young leaves no interpretation and symbolism unstated. Young covers: coming of age, race, gender, gender indeterminacy, sexism, same-sex eroticism, cross-dressing, heterosexuality, femininity, masculinity, national and individual identity, and too many more to mention without the continued infliction of pain.

For example, "When Velazquez becomes a Confederate spy, her geographic movements between regions provide a metaphorical gloss on her oscillation between genders (p166)." And, "*The Woman in Battle* offers similar instances of sexual ambiguity, with military masquerade providing a symbolic frame for the representation of male homoeroticism (p169)." And one last example, which will make the reader grateful not to still be sitting in an English Literature class headed by a metaphorical maniac of a teacher, "Expanding the narration of Confederate nationalism to include protolesbian plots, Velazquez's text also offers an early corrective to a model of lesbianism that might translate nineteenth-century desire between women into a domesticated version of domestic feminism (p173)." Well, but of course.

If on the other hand, the reader is aroused by Young's academic propensity for developing a metaphor for everything, even the length of the drive-up window lane at a fast-food restaurant (Just joking- see anyone can play the metaphor game.), here's one more of the many:

So too does *The Woman in Battle* hint at the specifically sexual dimensions of Confederate loss. When the Confederate army, aided by Buford, is triumphant, its representation is that of victorious rapist. Describing the optimistic beginning of the battle of Shiloh, Velazquez announces proudly, "We took possession of their camp... almost without resistance" (203). Conversely, when the South loses the war, its sexual relation to the North is that of potential rape victim, as when the strength of the Union army "compelled the Confederates... to think about the means of resisting invasion" (108). The relation of Velazquez to her Northern editor reinforces the heterosexual dynamics of Confederate defeat. As Northerners secured political control over the South, Worthington has editorial control over Velazquez's text: "It has been necessary ... while expanding in some places, to make large excisions in others... The excisions, therefore, have been carefully made" (11). Yet the gender valences of such military "invasions" and textual "incisions" are not entirely clear. For if the South symbolically emerges from the war as a woman, it also assumes the posture of defeat as a feminized man; the North takes on yet more masculinity through its victory in the war. Hence the South risks being "raped" by the remasculinized North both heterosexually and homosexually. In a process of cultural feminization that addresses two sides of the male body, what the Confederacy faces in remembering its defeat is, symbolically speaking, both losing its phallic potency and being raped from behind.

Velazquez's text does not, to be sure, speak explicitly about the South as a victim of male rape. But the text nonetheless raises this figurative possibility in displaced form, through a strand of imagery that constructs Southern military aggression as anal penetration. In a chapter entitled in part "Preparations for an Attack on the Federal Rear," Velazquez discusses a plan for the Confederate army to liberate a prisoners' camp by entering the Federal lines through Canada; the idea is "to make such a diversion in the Federal rear as would compel the withdrawal of a large force from the front" (441). (*Disarming the Nation*, p182)

Anal penetration?! Diversion in the Federal rear?! An apology for this last example is probably wanted, so consider it given. And probably the apology should have been upfront of the example rather in the rear of the example so as not to allow another insufferable metaphor to be made.

If an author claims to have written a "truthful" memoir, and it is revealed that the memoir is not truthful, does that make its author a metaphorical liar or just a liar? It would seem that the primary symbolism found in a lie should be that the author is a liar. Author Elizabeth Young clearly rises to a higher level of explanation as to how a lie contains symbolism and how one might interpret it. The reader is remiss not to admit that they could have produced similar metaphorical results had they paid better attention in Literature class.

2000, *Encyclopedia of the American Civil War; A Political, Social, and Military History*, editors David S. Heidler and Jeanne T. Heidler, published by ABC-CLIO. The entry for Velazquez, on pages 2018-2019, was provided by Elizabeth D. Leonard, who also is the author of the 1999 book, *All the Daring of the Soldier (Women of the Civil War Armies)*.

Leonard began by explaining that "few if any of women's Civil War service as soldiers or as spies are as difficult to sort out and verify" as found in *The Woman in Battle*. In the retelling of Velazquez's memoir, Leonard immediately faltered when she wrote, "According to *The Woman in Battle*, Loreta Velazquez was born in Cuba (her year of birth is not known) to a Spanish father and a Franco-American mother." No, Velazquez plainly wrote (p40) in her memoir that she was born on "26th of June, 1842." Velazquez made a big fuss over her birth and christening in Havana and the subtitle of that section of Chapter I is "My Birth," all of which is impossible to miss.

Leonard further misrepresented Velazquez:

When her father inherited a large estate in Texas, the family immigrated to the United States, and Velazquez herself spent time in Texas and then in New Orleans, where her family sent her to complete her education.

No, no, no. Velazquez did not write that; she wrote (p40-41) that her father inherited "a large estate in Texas, which was then a part of the republic Mexico," so the immigration was to Mexico, not the United States! Actually, Velazquez stated (p40) that the move was in 1844 and at that date Texas was an independent Republic, so was not part of Mexico. Furthermore, Velazquez claimed she lived in San Luis Potosi, Mexico which was a great distance from the Texas estate and San Luis Potosi never became part of the United States. Velazquez never claimed to have even visited the Texas estate, much less claimed to have lived in Texas! And she never claimed her "family immigrated to the United States."

Then Leonard wrote that Velazquez "assumed the pseudonym Harry T. Buford, and began to gather troops to form her own regiment, the 'Arkansas Grays,' for Confederate service." No, Velazquez never claimed she formed a regiment; she wrote (p84) she raised a battalion. There is a difference! No, Velazquez did not write her pseudonym was Harry T. Buford, but instead wrote (p37) that she acted, specifically, when she raised a battalion, "under the *pseudonyme* of Lieutenant Harry T. Buford." There is a difference! In addition, Chapter IV (p61) of the memoir contains the subtitle, "Disguised as a Confederate Officer" and Velazquez called (p62) "Lieutenant H. T. Buford, C.S.A." her "military *pseudonyme*." And much later on page 341, Velazquez again plainly stated she "disguised as an officer." In other words, the rank was made up along with the name.

Leonard concluded with, "clearly *The Woman in Battle* is hardly a work of pure nonfiction…" but thought Velazquez and her memoir significant "for the study of women's involvement in Civil War military life." And if Velazquez's memoir "is not entirely an accurate representation of its author's own wartime experiences… that much, if not all, of it could have been," that is, based on what is known of other "women's wartime activities as soldiers and spies." Well, those other women soldiers and spies might have taken offense by the characterization of their activities as being represented by the false representations of Velazquez.

Criticism of Leonard's biography of Velazquez should in no way be taken as criticism of the *Encyclopedia's* entire and extensive work. The *Encyclopedia* was reissued by W. W. Norton & Company on September 16, 2002.

2000, *Loyal and Lethal Ladies of Espionage* by Tom Moon who provided a six-page summary of Velazquez's memoir, concentrating more on the espionage parts rather than the battle parts. Moon concluded:

She disappeared from the records somewhere in Texas in about 1880. Because of the incredible tales many have suspected outright fabrication or at least considerable embellishments of her stories.

In *Who Was Who in the Confederacy* Stewart Safakis [sic Sifakis] states after painstaking research much of her story can be confirmed. Many names, dates, and places fit in with her story. Others such as conflicting dates or places could be explained as loss of memory. Many other details cannot be verified one way or the other. But overall he feels the basic stories do fit historical records.

Stewart Sifakis' book, *Who Was Who in the Confederacy*, has been presented in year 1988 of the chronology.

2000, *Civil War* by John E. Stanchak, published by DK (Dorling Kindersley) Eyewitness Books series, second edition. The entry for Velazquez is titled "A Dubious Soldier" and stated:

Loreta Velazquez was a Southerner of Cuban-American descent. She claimed she had donned a disguise and served in the Confederate army as Lieutenant Harry Buford so that she would be near her soldier-husband. She also claimed to have been widowed twice during the war and to have served as a spy. Most veterans found Madame Velazquez's claims outrageous. Yet the memoirs she wrote after the war, titled *The Woman in Battle*, sold well.

The two portraits of Velazquez, in and out of disguise, were presented.

The biographical summary is innocuously brief and fails to interject any controversy which might cause a reader doubt, despite the title "A Dubious Soldier." The assertion that "most veterans found [her] claims outrageous" is arguable since to date the only veteran that has been found who criticized her memoir was General Jubal Early and he more exactly said her claims were not truthful.

2002, *They Fought Like Demons (Women Soldiers in the American Civil War)* by DeAnne Blanton and Lauren M. Cook who wrote (p2) in the Introduction:

Readers may be surprised by our inclusion of Confederate officer Loreta Janeta Velazquez, labeled a fraud by a number of historians. Our research shows that they have been too quick to dismiss her.

And include Velazquez the authors did, to the tune of many pages. Their book succeeds in becoming a major contributor to the misrepresentations, whether accidental or not, of the real Velazquez, and a perpetuator of the Velazquez myth.

2002, *Foreigners in the Confederacy* by Ella Lonn who retold Velazquez's memoir in brief, but not very accurately. She opened with (p380), "Among the extraordinary and dramatic characters... none was stranger than Mrs. Velazquez...." No, Velazquez never married a Velazquez; therefore, she was never a <u>Mrs.</u> Velazquez. Another misstatement was, "She did ultimately attain the rank of lieutenant, being known as Lieutenant Harry T. Buford." No, from the very beginning she self-designated the rank. Lonn concluded with, "[she] married three times." No, Velazquez wrote four times.

2002, *Cubans in the Confederacy* edited by Philip Thomas Tucker. Richard Hall contributed Chapter 3, titled "Loreta Janeta Velazquez: Civil War Soldier and Spy." Recall Hall wrote *Patriots in Disguise* (1993). His contribution to *Cubans in the Confederacy* is the continuation of his research which will be seen to result in another book in 2006. In *Cubans in the Confederacy*, Hall's chapter is divided into sections.

In the first section, Hall retold Velazquez's memoir enough to enable the reader to grasp the scope of her book.

In section "Assessing Her Claims," Hall considered the memoir's veracity in what he called a "preliminary report." Hall pointed out some of the problems and noted:

> What errors she does make probably are attributable to faulty memory and careless mistakes made in haste rather than deliberate fabrication. Overall, the internal evidence suggests that she was not consciously fabricating.

At this date Hall was an apologist for Velazquez's memoirs. Hall conceded that Velazquez's tale of husband DeCaulp suffered from "incomplete and inadequate explanation." He wrote, "There is little doubt that, for whatever reasons, she engaged in false and misleading reporting about her alleged relationship with DeCaulp."

In section "Confirmations of Her Memoirs," Hall gives "a number of subtle points of her memoirs" which have "proved to be accurate upon thorough investigation." Yes, Hall was correct; there are points in Velazquez's memoir which are accurate. She was a real person who widely traveled, was interviewed and reported on often. Hall availed himself to newspapers and government documents (most of which have been presented in the book in hand) which confirm Velazquez's presence, so it is puzzling why Hall failed to understand that the severe contradictions found in the many Velazquez newspaper interviews were the results of lies told by Velazquez. Hall did not grasp that Velazquez lied habitually and purposefully to newspaper interviewers.

In section "New Eyewitness Report," Hall reported on the discovery that Bromfield L. Ridley mentioned Velazquez in his own memoirs, which has been discussed in the course the book in hand.

Hall ended with "Summary and Preliminary Conclusions" in which he acknowledged that it was "problematical" to accept as factual all of Velazquez's adventures and again blamed the haste in which Velazquez wrote her book.

2002, *Fields of Fury (The American Civil War)* published by Atheneum Books for Young Readers, written by James M. McPherson (Pulitzer Prize Winning author of *Battle Cry of Freedom*). McPherson wrote (p58):

The most sensational thing some women did was disguise themselves as men and fight on the front lines. One woman who did this was Loretta Janeta Velazquez, who fought for the Confederacy as a soldier. Disguised as Lieutenant Harry T. Buford, she fought at the First Battle of Manassas, at Fort Donelson, and the Battle of Corinth, in Mississippi, where she was wounded. She would continue her fight both on the battlefield as a soldier and behind the Union lines as a spy. After the war, she published a memoir of her incredible exploits.

Velazquez's claimed participation in these battles has been addressed ad nauseam and the proverbial dead horse will be spared further beating here. However, the historian will not be spared the beating; it is unimaginable that McPherson actually read Velazquez's memoir and then derived his summary with a belief of the memoir's truthfulness. Had he read the memoir, and with his life-long gained knowledge as a remarkable historian of the Civil War, he would have immediately seen many lies. At the least, McPherson could have noted that some historians are much troubled by the memoir's claims, even if he wasn't.

Oh, please permit just one more beating. McPherson claimed Velazquez was at the Battle of Corinth. Velazquez never claimed it and she wasn't. This includes both the First Battle and the Second Battle of Corinth. In addition, McPherson claimed she was wounded at the Battle of Corinth. Velazquez did not claim this; she claimed she was wounded <u>before</u> the First Battle of Corinth. During the time frames of First Battle (April 29-June 10, 1862) and the Second Battle (October 3-4, 1862) Velazquez claimed she was in New Orleans, with a blockade run to Havana and a secret mission trip to Robertson's Plantation. (The newspapers reported her presence in New Orleans on April 24, 1862, and again on October 31, 1862.)

Criticism of McPherson's handling of Velazquez should in no way be construed as criticism of his good and impressive body of historical works.

2002, *Historical Dictionary of the Civil War* (Vol 2, M-Z) by Terry L. Jones and published by Scarecrow Press. History Professor Jones, University of Louisiana at Monroe, summarized Velazquez's memoir in one large paragraph in Volume 2 of this 1701-page dictionary. (Vol 1 was 1784 pages.) To his credit he stated, "little of it can be proved," called her life's story "improbable," and he even threw in the disclaimer word, "supposedly." The real problem with his summary is that he made claims on Velazquez's behalf which she never made:

This Confederate spy claimed to have led a fascinating life, but little of it can be proved. A native of Cuba, she moved to New Orleans, Louisiana, with her family and married a U.S. Army officer in 1856. Velazquez claimed she raised a volunteer company under the assumed disguise of Harry Buford when her husband joined the Confederate army and that she eventually accompanied her husband to war as an aide and lieutenant. He subsequently was killed in an accidental shooting. Velazquez supposedly fought at First Manassas, Ball's Bluff, Fort Donelson, and Shiloh (being wounded in the latter two battles) before her true identity was discovered in 1863....

Velazquez did <u>not</u> claim her family moved to New Orleans, instead she wrote (*TWIB*, p41) that they stayed in Cuba. Velazquez did <u>not</u> claim she raised a company, she said (p84) it was a battalion. Velazquez did <u>not</u> claim she raised her volunteers under the disguise of Harry Buford, but instead under the disguise of Lieutenant Harry Buford- there is difference. Velazquez did <u>not</u> claim she "accompanied her husband to war as an aide and lieutenant," instead she wrote (p86) she, in disguise, led her battalion to his location (Pensacola). He did not recognize her until she, in a whisper, revealed herself. She claimed she then immediately left Pensacola for New Orleans by herself (never having had time to act as "an aide and lieutenant") and while away her husband was killed in the accidental explosion of a carbine, <u>not</u> by "an accidental shooting." There is a difference. Velazquez did <u>not</u> claim she was wounded at Fort Donelson, but instead she wrote (p174) she left there "utterly used up from fatigue, exposure, anxiety, and bitter disappointment." And by now, the reader is aware that Velazquez, while disguised as Lieutenant Harry T. Buford, was discovered as early as September 1861 and identified herself as "Mrs. Mary Ann Keith," even if Professor Jones (understandably) was not aware of this arrest and discovery.

Please note that the disparagement of this one-half-page paragraph should in no way reflect badly on the 3485 pages of this substantial two-volume dictionary set.

2002, *Civil War, A to Z: The Complete Handbook of America's Bloodiest Conflict* edited by Clifford L. Linedecker. Velazquez's one paragraph entry is found alphabetically on page 312, exactly between "Van Lew, Elizabeth 'Crazy Betty'" and "Venereal Disease." The editor noted that Velazquez's "exciting life reads more like fiction." Ok, so far. Then in error, the handbook stated Velazquez left her home in Louisiana to join the Confederacy. No, Velazquez said she had already left Louisiana some five years prior and was in Memphis at the time she assumed her military disguise. And that she was "cited for gallantry before she was exposed as a woman...." No, Velazquez never wrote she was cited for gallantry.

2003, *Women in World History: A Biographical Encyclopedia*, Vol 15 Sul-Vica, editor Anne Commire. This gargantuan encyclopedia covers more than 10,000 women in the course of 17 volumes, each volume running about 900 pages. Velazquez's entry is on page 864 and is provided by Lisa S. Weitzman, freelance writer, Cleveland, Ohio. The three-paragraph biographical sketch starts in error and ends in error. Author Weitzman titles the sketch "Velásquez, Loreta (1842-1897)." No, Velazquez never used an accent in her name and moreover Velazquez used two zees in her authorship name. Weitzman asserted, "After [Velazquez] married a Confederate Army officer... [and] Under the assumed name of Harry T. Buford or Burford, she enlisted with a group of independent volunteer scouts." No, Velazquez wrote she married a U.S. Army officer who five years later resigned his commission and joined the Confederacy. No, Velazquez never wrote she used Burford as an alias and Velazquez never wrote she "enlisted" in a group of independent volunteer scouts.

Weitzman said Velazquez "earned praise for her efforts from General Stonewall Jackson, who never discovered her true identity." No, Velazquez never wrote such a thing and General Jackson never wrote such a thing.

Weitzman wrote, "At this point, she joined the 21st Louisiana Regiment, engaging in guerilla warfare before she was wounded." Velazquez claimed (p181) she joined the 21st Louisiana Regiment, but Velazquez never wrote she engaged in guerilla warfare with this regiment. Weitzman also claimed Velazquez later "dabbled in gold mining and traveled on the women's lecture circuit." No, Velazquez wrote only that her husband was a miner and there is no discovered history that Velazquez went on the lecture circuit though it certainly is possible and reasonable that she might have.

Weitzman concluded by informing her readers that Velazquez "ultimately published her story in 1876 as *The Woman in Battle: A Narrative of the Exploits, Adventures, and Travels of Madame Loreta Velásquez*. She died in 1897." Understandably Weitzman could not have correctly known Velazquez's date of death, but the erroneous spelling of Velazquez's authorship name makes it clear that Weitzman never saw Velazquez's memoir. Most troubling is that Weitzman did not claim to have used Loreta's memoir as source material. Instead, Weitzman cited three inaccurate and inadequate sources: *Famous Americans You Never Knew Existed* by Bruce Felton and Mark Fowler, 1979; *The Book of Women's Achievements* by Jack Macksey, 1976; and *American Women's History* by Doris Weatherford, 1994. This last book provided three paragraphs on Velazquez, Doris Weatherford wrote, "Ungrateful Confederate officers responded to her enthusiasm by fining her ten dollars and sentencing her to ten days in jail." The assertion is not true; Velazquez wrote (p180) that it was the mayor of New Orleans who fined her and put her in jail, not ungrateful Confederate officers. The reason for the arrest was because, at that time, it was unlawful for a woman to dress like a man.

The Book of Women's Achievements by Macksey provided a single paragraph which begins with "Loreta Velasquez (Spanish, 1842?-97)." No, Velazquez used as her authorship name, Velazquez with two "zees" and Velazquez never claimed she was Spanish, but Cuban; in fact, in 1875 she wrote in a letter she wished to "drive the detestable Spanish from the Island." Velazquez harbored no doubt about her 1842 birth; she said it was June 26, 1842. By now readers understand the death date of "97" is wrong. The rest of the paragraph is misleading with assertions, such as, Velazquez "became engaged in guerrilla warfare before she was wounded...." Velazquez never wrote she fought as a guerrilla.

Famous Americans You Never Knew Existed by Felton and Fowler provided a single paragraph, as well, which also is painfully inaccurate, indicating the authors did not read Velazquez's memoir and didn't have a clue about which they wrote: Velazquez "left her husband and joined the Confederate Army as 'Harry T. Burford' [*sic*]... and "She served with distinction in many important battles, including Bull Run, and was praised by Stonewall Jackson, who never found out she was a woman." Now it is clear from where the error of Burford originated. First, no, Velazquez claimed she joined the Confederacy so she could be with her husband. Second, no, in order to serve with distinction, it is necessary to receive the recognition from others. One cannot recognize themself for distinction, which is what Velazquez did throughout her memoir. Third, no, Stonewall Jackson never praised Velazquez and she never wrote that he did, instead she wrote, General Jackson gave her a "recommendation to General Bragg for a recruiting commission." Velazquez continued, "This I did not care about, for I thought that I did not need his permission or his aid to do recruiting duty, and determined to wait and see if something better would not offer." Is a recommendation, praise?

In summary, contributing author Lisa S. Weitzman for *Women in World History: A Biographical Encyclopedia* semmingly never read Velazquez's memoir and neither did the authors of her cited three inaccurate sources.

2003, *Women in the Civil War*. Author Larry G. Eggleston devoted Chapter 5 to "Loreta Janeta Velazquez: Woman Soldier and Spy" in which he wrote (p33), "During the battle of Fort Donelson, on February 13-16, 1862, Lt. Harry Buford was wounded in the foot and required medical attention." In clear contradiction Velazquez wrote (*TWIB*, p174-175) that she left Fort Donelson only fatigued. She claimed she then went to Nashville where she was in some skirmish and was "wounded in the foot."

Then Eggleston wrote (p34), "During the Battle of Shiloh, Lt. Harry Buford was assigned temporary command of her original unit, the Arkansas Grays, after the lieutenant in command was killed." However, that is not quite what Velazquez wrote, "We had not been long engaged before the second lieutenant of the company fell. I immediately stepped into his place, and assumed the command of his men." It is clear that Velazquez did not write that she was "<u>assigned</u> temporary command," but instead she claimed to have simply stepped in and assumed command. Recall, her "original unit" was a battalion of 236 men. She did not claim she was assigned command of them, but only took command of a second lieutenant's men.

The problem (but one not in the purview of author Eggleton's efforts) is that second lieutenants did not command companies, unless something had happened to the captain and first lieutenant, and Velazquez makes clear that Captain DeCaulp was alive after the battle. A greater problem is that Velazquez wrote that these men were her original battalion of "Arkansas Grays" now under the command of Captain DeCaulp. Military records show that DeCaulp was a captain of a company in the 3rd Arkansas Cavalry and the 3rd Arkansas Cavalry was not at Shiloh, so neither was DeCaulp. In other words, her Arkansas Grays (which never existed) were not at Shiloh, so it follows that Velazquez did not assume the command of a company that wasn't there!

Eggleston continued, "Captain DeCaulp did not know that he had fought alongside her at First Manassas/Bull Run, Balls Bluff and Shiloh." No, Velazquez never claimed this. Velazquez only claimed (falsely) that DeCaulp was at the Battle of Shiloh; she never claimed that he was at the First Manassas or at the Battle of Ball's Bluff.

There are other less important inaccuracies. Eggleston wrote that Velazquez went to Nevada, married, had a son and moved to California correct enough, but then in error, he stated, it was in California "where she wrote a book about her four years of service to the Confederacy." Velazquez did not claim that she wrote her book in California. Eggleston did not address the remainder of the book's events which occurred after she left California. Then Eggleston incorrectly stated that Velazquez "died in 1897 at the age of 55," but he could not have possibly known the facts and did not.

Eggleston concluded the chapter, "She went far beyond the call of duty, and is worthy to be remembered for her courageous spirit."

2003, *Commercial Appeal* (Memphis, TN) May 1 article in the "Neighbors" section by Perre Magness titled "Loreta Stars in Thrilling War Story." In this 1297-word article, Memphis freelance writer Magness repeated, as factual, Velazquez's story. Ms. Magness claimed three sources for her information:

the 1972 Arno Press' reprint of Velazquez's 1876 *The Woman in Battle*; Richard Hall's 1993 *Patriots in Disguise*; and Walter Sullivan's 1995 *The War the Women Lived*. In her final paragraph Magness noted, in somewhat of a disclaimer, what author Walter Sullivan had written:

> Some scholars have considered Velazquez's memoir to be, at least in part, spurious. However, her accounts of her undercover work for the Confederacy ring true, and are typical of those of many Southern women who served their country as spies and couriers.

In riposte to Magness' assertion- There may be a ring of truth in Velazquez's memoir of her stealing bond printing plates (or currency plates, as Velazquez claimed to the *Indianapolis Journal* reporter), but it was a rich lie. And there may be a ring of truth in Velazquez's account of her trip to St. Thomas about at which time she claimed she saw commerce raider *Florida* under command of Captain Maffitt escape the Union navy, but this too is a huge and provable lie. Of course, there are other claims which "ring true" that have been shown to be falsehoods, if one wishes to recall them.

2003, *The Woman in Battle (The Civil War Narrative of Loreta Velazquez, Cuban Woman & Confederate Soldier)* is a reprint of Velazquez's 1876 book with editing and an introduction titled "Authenticity, Autobiography, and Identity; *The Woman in Battle* as a Civil War Narrative" by Associate Professor of English Jesse Alemán of the University of New Mexico.

In Alemán's Preface, he explained:

> I have not attempted to verify the narrative with historical documentation, since Velazquez's history and the history of the text are so embattled in a debate over their authenticity. Instead, *The Woman in Battle* stands as readers confronted it in 1876- a sensationalist, secessionist, and suspicious autobiographical account of a Cuban woman who participated in the Civil War as a cross-dressed Confederate (page v).

But contrary to his word, Alemán did not let the book stand "as readers confronted it in 1876" because he added his own parenthetical title. Nowhere in the very long original title did Velazquez write she was Cuban, but Alemán changed the title by inserting and asserting that Velazquez was a "Cuban Woman." It was only in the narrative that Velazquez asserted to have been Cuban born. It is a little troubling that based on Velazquez's assertion alone, apparently with no corroborating documentation, Alemán accepted her Cuban birth as the truth and changed the title of the original book.

The Preface's questionable start gained careless speed when Alemán misrepresented the facts surrounding General Jubal Early's criticism of Velazquez's book:

When Confederate General Jubal Early came across Loreta Janeta Velazquez's *The Woman in Battle* (1876), he was so outraged by it that he wrote to Tennessee Congressman William H. Slemons to protest the book's authenticity.

No! It is not true that General Early was an "outraged" aggressor who sought out Slemons to whom to complain. The facts are these. General Early came across the book in New Orleans shortly after its publication, gave it a cursory read and was "satisfied that the writer of that book whether man or woman, had never had the adventures therein narrated." Much later, General Early met, in a Lynchburg (Virginia) hotel where Early was boarding, a man from Richmond who had met Velazquez on the train from Danville to Lynchburg and the man had bought her book. Upon Early being told of the book and its heroine, Early replied that he recognized her name; Early wrote, "He produced the book, and I pointed out to him several inconsistencies, absurdities, and impossibilities in it which I thought proved beyond all question, the writer of it to be a mere pretender."

Word got around to Velazquez that Early had spoken ill of her book. Velazquez wrote a letter to Early asking him not to disparage her book as it would hurt its sales on which she was depending for income for her and her child. Before he had a chance to reply she showed-up in the parlor of his hotel and sent a request to his room for a visit. They met in the parlor and he was not impressed that she was Spanish and thought she might be a Northerner and also thought her "no true type of Southern woman...." Jubal Early was not convinced that she was the author of the book because he had read her poorly written letter and thought her incapable of the task. However, it was her book, though greatly improved by her editor, exactly as Jubal Early said it must have been.

After Velazquez's letter and this meeting, General Jubal Early felt compelled to explain his voiced criticism of the book and wrote to Congressman Slemons. Jubal Early explained to Slemons the reason he addressed the letter to him. He said that Velazquez had indicated that Slemons was to be used as a go-between. General Early said that if he was mistaken in this fact, and Slemons had not sanctioned Velazquez, then please disregard what he wrote and destroy the letter. The General then said that if indeed Slemons had sanctioned Velazquez, then he was free to show to Velazquez the contents of the letter.

But before General Early sent the letter, he had second thoughts about getting further involved, so he sent the letter intended for Slemons to friend Congressman J. R. Tucker and asked his opinion as to whether Early should sent it at all. In this letter to his friend, Jubal Early gave his reasons and concerns about addressing Velazquez and her book, and in part he wrote that he did not want Velazquez to "say she has written to me and silenced me." The letter intended for Slemons was ostensibly <u>never</u> sent to Slemons, but remained with the friend and today is archived in the Tucker Family Papers, #2605, Southern Historical Collection, Wilson Library, University of North Carolina at Chapel Hill.

Alemán further misrepresented General Early's criticism by stating that General Early objected to Velazquez's narrative "mainly because the book challenged the supposed gentility of Southern gender codes." No, General Early mainly objected because the book was being "palmed on the public as true." Alemán added:

Indeed, Early found it downright offensive that a narrative about a woman masquerading as a Confederate soldier would be in circulation, which is why he centered his attack on the authenticity of the book and its supposed author.

No, that was not the reason for Early's criticism; he said the book was not "a true narrative." In addition, his "attack" was not a public "attack," but a criticism which was written in a private letter which was never even sent to its intended recipient.

Alemán, apparently used his literary analytical skills to read General Early's mind and wrote:

Rather, Early implies that only a Yankee hack would have the nerve to imagine a Cuban woman who dressed in men's clothes, took up arms for the South, seduced unsuspecting women, and then wrote about it for money.

No, General Early did not imply anything of the kind and he had no need to imply anything. Well, first of all, General Early wrote he believed "that Madame Velasquez is not of Spanish birth or origin," so how did Early imply she was "a Cuban woman"? Second, the General was sharp tongued and would have said it if he meant it. In the letter, General Early wrote plenty of objections that were not implied, but were real, and Alemán could have spent his time proving or disproving them, instead of gazing for implications in a literary cloud. It is one thing for Alemán to state that he would not spend time trying to authenticate anything, but it is beyond the pale that Alemán then searched the nebulousness for implications with which to deprecate General Jubal Early. Please read Jubal Early's letter in the Appendix, Item 3 to understand the facts of what Early wrote.

Alemán repeated the often-asserted claim that editor C. J. Worthington was a "former Yankee naval officer," thus elevating Worthington as a character witness. Worthington never claimed in his preface that he was an officer, but claimed only to have been in the Union navy. (It was the "publisher's circular" which (falsely) claimed Worthington was an officer.) If Alemán had sought to "verify the narrative," which he said he would not try to do, he would have discovered that there was no C. J. Worthington in the navy, officer or enlisted, which in turn should have raised a suspicion as to his identity. But then again Alemán wasn't trying to question anything which might have cast doubts on Velazquez's memoir, which Worthington wrote was "a true story in every particular."

Alemán supplied some high points of many of the newspaper articles about Velazquez found by author Richard Hall. These are the articles presented in the book in hand, and by now, the reader understands the articles are full of contradictions, or more accurately, lies. Alemán wrote, "Notice how these pieces of documentary evidence blend into each other, cross-dressing, if you will, from one account to the other...." It is curious that Alemán thought the evidence was blending rather than contradictory. And it is even more curious that he metaphorically associated the perceived blending to cross-dressing, which brings us to the second section.

This section is subtitled "Gender and the Genuine Thing" and it opens with:

> The act of cross-dressing, which is so central to *The Woman in Battle*, may in fact trouble the notion of authenticity altogether in autobiography, authorship, and even identity.

Who knows what that means, but if the sentence means that it is doubtful that Velazquez had success staying undiscovered for any length of time, and therefore it is doubtful that she did most of the things she claimed while in disguise, then that is the truth. The records of the times indicate Velazquez was regularly found out.

Alemán discussed Velazquez's changing of clothing, transvestism, etc., but then in a flourish of something or another stated that Velazquez was a "double agent in drag." No, Velazquez claimed she always performed her double agent spying activity dressed as a woman. She was a woman dressed as a woman, thus no "drag." Still later in 2004 Alemán would not turn loose of this drag idea when he titled an essay contribution, "Crossing the Mason-Dixon Line in Drag: The Narrative of Loreta Janeta Velazquez, Cuban Woman and Confederate Soldier."[8] No, Velazquez never claimed that she crossed the Mason-Dixon Line dressed as a man; she always claimed she went North clothed as a woman, thus, once again, no drag.

Mercifully, Alemán concluded this section with a representative and final sentence:

> In this sense, Velazquez's identity is not so much genuine as it narrated through cultural signs that describe gender, historical documents that frame identity, and even the supposed autobiography that recounts her life- all of which can only represent Velazquez, rather than embody her, through the medium of language and are thus subject to all of the impossibilities of fiction.

---

8. Jon Smith and Deborah Cohn, ed., *Look Away! The U.S. South in New World Studies* (Durham, NC: Duke University Press, 2004).

Please dear reader, do not brutalize yourself if you failed to comprehend Alemán's astute point; there will be other opportunities to demonstrate your comprehension.

In the next subsection, titled "Genre and the Civil War's Gender Crises," Alemán explained (correctly) that during the war with the men away as soldiers, women many times had to take on the men's duties at home. He continued; they became "an empowered class exactly at a moment when the war feminized Southern men." Really?! Did the fighting of the Civil War and the Confederate army's slow and final defeat actually feminize Southern men? Surely you knew that to be the case and did not think otherwise! It seems someone should take offense here, maybe females or males or soldiers or female soldiers or maybe just Southern men. Someone's been disparaged!

Alemán asserted, "This type of gender trouble manifests itself in *The Woman in Battle* as a cultural truth that legitimates the text's transvestism as an authentic symptom of the Civil War." And "Velazquez's inverted hoopskirt, then, symbolically indicates the South's collapsing gender roles and class categories. It also mirrors the South's fluctuating power, as Elizabeth Young points out." Please recall Associate Professor of English Elizabeth Young, who believes the symbolism of the memoir is more important than the falsehoods it contains.[9]

Alemán wrote:

> Ironically, in a heterosexual moment, when Velazquez and DeCaulp confirm their wedding plans in fact, Velazquez's cross-dressing registers a fissure in the construction of Southern masculinity and femininity, with Velazquez wearing Buford's pants and Captain DeCaulp helplessly feminized in a hospital bed.

What?! Is a male in a hospital bed "helplessly feminized"? If the reader has always supposed that a male in a hospital bed was sick, then apparently the reader has been mistaken. Again, offense should be taken by someone, only it is not clear if it should be a sick male who was called feminized, or a feminine someone who has been called a sick male. Or should any person who is feminine be considered helpless, and thus offended? Someone has been savaged!

Why Alemán called the occasion when Velazquez and DeCaulp confirmed their wedding plans a "heterosexual moment" is a mystery. Is Alemán implying that all the other events covered in Velazquez's memoir are all homosexual? If so, then he clearly missed the fact that the overwhelming part of the memoir portrays Velazquez as a woman. Even when she is a soldier, she still does not represent herself as a homosexual, only a woman disguised as a male soldier. When "Lieutenant Buford" flirts

---

9. *Disarming the Nation (Women's Writing and the American Civil War)*, 1999.

with women, she is pleased with herself because she claims her male comrades-in-arms think she is a good ladies' man, thus reinforcing to her readers what a clever male soldier disguise she is capable of maintaining. Never once did Velazquez claim that while out of uniform, she disguised as a civilian man and flirted with the girls... maybe in a homosexual moment. When dressed as a woman, Velazquez never claimed or implied she had a homosexual moment, either.

"Cuba, the Confederacy, and their Cross-Dressed Civil Wars," is the final subsection. Alemán connected the American Civil War to the on-again, off-again Cuban revolution for independence from Spain and throws cross-dressing in the mix. Alemán wrote:

> In this sense, Velazquez's performance as Buford must be read as reactionary rather than revolutionary. That is, her cross-dressing symbolizes a culturally true connection between Cuba and the Confederacy during the Civil War, but it also enacts an ideologically authentic postwar Confederate reaction to radical Reconstruction that imagines an independent Cuba disguised as an independent South to create a new Southern slavocracy that provides an alternative yet equivalent slave system to sustain the white privilege Velazquez enjoyed under Cuba's Spanish colonial rule.

Whether the reader understood the last paragraph probably makes no difference; the main point to keep in mind is that this subsection is entirely based on Alemán's acceptance of Velazquez's claim to have been Cuban born and at this date it is still an unproven claim. There is no doubt that everything Velazquez claimed about her family's history in Cuba is a lie, but that does not necessarily mean that she was not born in Cuba, just not under the circumstances she asserted. Until historical documentation of Velazquez's Cuban birth is discovered, is an analysis of Velazquez in the context of "Cuba, the Confederacy, and their Cross-Dressed Civil Wars" even worth the effort?

Alemán wrapped it up:

> In the end, then, perhaps the most important cultural truth *The Woman in Battle* and its ostensible author offer is that gender, race, and nation are simple matters of clothing that, when cross-dressed, challenge the ideologies of authenticity that determine the battle lines between masculinity and femininity, black and white, North and South, autobiography and fiction, and ultimately, self and Other.

This summation should have helped clear-up any lingering misunderstanding of Alemán's opinion.

In all fairness to author Jesse Alemán, please read his entire Preface, Acknowledgment and Introduction plus Notes; it is only some thirty-five pages. That way it can be sure that you have not relied on an unintentional misrepresentation of his work. On the other hand, Alemán was not sensitive to his own seemingly intentional misrepresentation of what General Early wrote so he probably doesn't mind how his own work is represented. Just the same, please read it.

2003, *Women in the American Civil War: An Annotated Bibliography* by Theresa McDevitt. This volume contains literary works which address Velazquez, all of which are included in this chronology.

2003, *Notable Caribbeans and Caribbean Americans: A Biographical Dictionary* by Serafín Méndez-Méndez and Gail A. Cueto, published by Greenwood Press. This large volume presents Velazquez on pages 412-413 under the title, "Loreta Janeta Velázquez (Lieutenant Harry Buford) (1842-1897) Cuban Military Officer and Writer." Just the title harbors three points of contention: First, Velazquez never in her book, in any letter or document placed an accent above the "a" in her surname. One would think that she wished to spell it that way and did not wish correction by anyone. Second, Velazquez was not a "Cuban Military Officer." She claimed she was a Cuban-born Confederate Officer. Third, she did not die in 1897, an error which is understandable.

The dictionary's entry recounts Velazquez's memoir in general terms, avoiding Velazquez's particularly unbelievable claims which might raise an eyebrow from a reader. There are the predictable errors such as, "She presented [first husband "William"] with the recruits for his command, but while training them in the use of arms he was accidentally shot and killed." No, Velazquez claimed (p87), "while drilling his men, my husband undertook to explain the use of the carbine to one of his sergeants, and the weapon exploded in his hands, killing him almost instantly." Clearly her husband (who was a lie anyway) was not "shot and killed."

And that Velazquez arrived in Salt Lake City, had a baby, "and shortly thereafter married an unnamed gentleman...." No, Velazquez wrote she married a miner in Austin, Nevada and they subsequently moved to Salt Lake City where she then had a baby.

The authors correctly stated that there are contradictions in Velazquez's memoir, but that there is "enough evidence [for historians] to assert that she did exist and that there is some truth to her account." Yes, she did exist and yes there is some truth in her memoir- and many lies, especially on any point of importance. It seems that Méndez-Méndez and Cueto never read the memoir.

2004, "The Lady in Gray" was written by New Orleans freelancer writer Bill Sasser and was published in New Orleans' *Gambit* newspaper, September 14. This 3,251-word article was inspired by the presence of a film crew in New Orleans, under the direction of María Agui Carter, filming a documentary about Velazquez to be titled *Rebel*. The film's director hoped that the film would be ready and shown on Public Broadcasting Service (PBS) in 2005.

Author Sasser repeated Velazquez's story accurate enough, but was seemingly unaware that Velazquez's claims are easily shown untrue. Sasser wrote, "In her memoir, Velazquez describes fighting for the last time at Shiloh, temporarily taking command of her Arkansas volunteers when their commander was killed." If Mr. Sasser had undertaken the mildest of research pertaining to the Order of Battle at Shiloh, he would have understood that "her Arkansas volunteers" were not at Shiloh. Velazquez claimed that Captain DeCaulp (her future husband) was with this company at Shiloh, but it is a fact that DeCaulp was not there and neither was his company. Velazquez could not have and did not assume command of a company that wasn't there.

Also in error, Mr. Sasser wrote that Velazquez "was living in Texas raising a young son when her memoir was first published. Then she vanished from history." This living-in-Texas error has been covered elsewhere and can be reviewed if necessary.

Sasser noted there exists controversy and reviewed some points raised by Sylvia Hoffert in her 1978 "Heroine or Hoaxer" article. He interviewed Tulane University History Professor Lawrence Powell and the New Orleans Confederate Museum Director Pat Ricci and neither was familiar with Velazquez's story. Sasser wrote, "Her life story runs counter to the history of the Civil War as we know it- which is why she remained in the margins until being rediscovered recently by a new generation of historians." This assertion simply is not accurate. As can be seen by this chronology, Velazquez has not "remained in the margins," instead she has been continually rediscovered with each and every new generation of writers. And the reason for her alleged obscurity is not because "her life story runs counter to the history of the Civil War as we know it." If the implication is historians have entered into some secret agreement to suppress her story, it certainly is not the case.

Mr. Sasser misrepresented what two of Velazquez's contemporaries, Reverend William Jones and General Jubal Early, wrote about her book. Recall, Reverend William Jones was editor of the *Southern Historical Society Papers*, Secretary of the Society and apparently the person who reviewed *The Woman in Battle* in the *Society's* journal. Sasser wrote:

> An editor for the Southern Historical Association (SHA) reviewed the book favorably. While he wrote that parts seemed to be embellished, he also noted that he contacted several of the men quoted in the broadside who confirmed that they had in fact known Velazquez during the war.

Sasser's statement requires refuting on two points, but first, a probing reader should read the review, presented in the Appendix, Item 5.

The first point of contention is that the Reverend William Jones "reviewed the book favorably." Editor Jones wrote only that the book would be "eagerly read by those who are fond of the marvelous" and it will be of "interest for the general reader." The editor rejected the book as the truth, "How far it can be received as *history*, is altogether another question." The editor, in criticism, gave the example of how Velazquez placed herself in two very separate locations at the same time at the Battle of Bull Run. Jones concluded, "We can only say that it is a very *readable* book...." He gave the book a favorable review based only on its enjoyment potential and not on its truthfulness.

The second point of contention is the assertion that Reverend William Jones "contacted several of the men quoted in the broadside who confirmed that they had in fact known Velazquez during the war." This is not what Jones wrote! Editor Jones named the men of the broadside and briefly repeated their testimony, then wrote, "We have also met with several Confederate officers who were cognizant of the fact that such a personage *did* figure in the Confederacy, and who saw her upon several occasions." The editor made clear that these "several Confederate officers" were not the same people as those of the publisher's broadside testimonies. Furthermore, it must be assumed that these "several Confederate officers" knew of her because they had seen her, as well as many other people, for example, every time she got arrested in Richmond and was in the public's awareness. These officers indeed confirmed she was a real personage, but they in no way credited or confirmed the battlefield deeds she claimed!

Sasser also misrepresented General Jubal Early's criticism of Velazquez. Sasser wrote, "[Early] began a letter campaign denouncing the book as a hoax, calling Velazquez a fraud and a 'camp follower'- a euphemism for a prostitute." First, let's be clear exactly what General Early wrote about the memoir. He wrote it was "entirely inconsistent with the character of a truthful chronicle," and he also said that he has the right to speak out when a book which has "want of authenticity" is "palmed on the public as true." General Early never called the book a hoax, but condensing his several words, he said it contained lies. General Early wrote, "Madame Velasquez may have been a follower of one or the other army in some capacity, but the book that is given to the public in her name cannot be a truthful narrative of the adventures of any person." Early did not call Velazquez a prostitute, but an 1862 New Orleans newspaper article stated as much, "She is known also to have been an inmate of Nelly Bremer's" which was a New Orleans "house of ill fame."[10] Further along this equating a camp follower to a prostitute will be addressed.

Sasser wrongly asserted that General Early began "a letter campaign denouncing the book." General Early, in fact, wrote in his private letter to Slemons that he had "no disposition to injure the alleged author of that book, and still less to deprive her of the means to training and educating her child," but "whether the author be man or woman," he was compelled not to let the lies go unaddressed. This letter was written only after Velazquez had written a letter to the General and then paid him a visit to protest that she had heard he had spoken ill of her book. Early explained in his letter, that when someone had asked for his opinion of the book, he replied he believed the book was full of lies. This was how Velazquez heard that the General had disparaged her book. The General's private letter to Slemons does not constitute "a letter campaign denouncing the book." The letter never was sent to the intended recipient, since it was first sent to General Early's friend, Tucker, for review and Tucker ostensibly never forwarded it to Slemons and the letter remains in the Tucker family papers to this day.

The fact is, if General Early had so desired, he could have decimated Velazquez. General Early was the President of the Southern Historical Society at the time of Velazquez's book submission and from this position of power, through its monthly journal, he could have fatally damaged her book. But he did not, history clearly shows. Sasser reported that María Agui Carter stated, "It's doubtful [Early] gave Loreta Velazquez a fair consideration." However, that is exactly what General Early did give Velazquez.

The greatest voice, given by Sasser, was to María Agui Carter, the film's writer/director. Sasser wrote, "For the project, [Carter] spent five years researching Velazquez." If so, then Carter's research should have revealed that Velazquez did not "vanish" from history after the publication of her book, as Sasser asserted, but instead Velazquez is easily found promoting her railroad in the 1900's.

Author Sasser wrote that "[Carter] searches for the truth about Velazquez, comparing the memoir with the historical record." Carter claimed that during her research, she located the military records of Velazquez's "second husband," meaning Thomas DeCaulp. How is it possible that Carter compared the facts of DeCaulp's record to the lies Velazquez wrote about DeCaulp's service and death and failed to understand Velazquez lied profusely and completely about this husband?! Perhaps most distressing is the fact that Carter claimed to be a documentarian, yet when she uncovered this fact, she failed, at best, to

---

10. *Daily True Delta*, Nov 2, 1862; Nov 1, 1861.

understand it or, at worst, she purposely ignored it and refused to make it part of her documentary film, as will be seen.

2004, *Women During the Civil War: an Encyclopedia* by Judith E. Harper. On pages 394-395 the author summarized Velazquez's memoir and took some outside information to round it out:

> In 1867, she settled in New Orleans to assist in efforts to establish a community of Confederate exiles in Venezuela [and] she and her son from her fourth marriage relocated to Rio de Janiero, Brazil, with the proceeds from her 1876 memoir. There she found work as a journalist. Nothing is known of her later life and death.

By now the reader easily understands these assertions are erroneous.

2005, *Civil War Women: Their Roles and Legacies* by Trish Chambers supplies one paragraph about Velazquez (plus the typical two portraits) which retells Velazquez's story inaccurately. Author Chambers wrote that Velazquez raised "approximately 236 men." No, Velazquez said (p85) she raised "two hundred and thirty-six in all." Chambers also wrote, "[Velazquez] became the unit's lieutenant and commanded the unit in the first battle of Bull Run (First Manassas)." No, Velazquez wrote she first disguised herself as a lieutenant and then she raised the troops while wearing the lieutenant disguise. And Velazquez positively never claimed (p95) that she fought at Bull Run with "the unit" she raised! Author Trish Chambers will later appear in the 2007 film *Full Metal Corset, Secret Soldiers of the Civil War*, as a contributing authority on Velazquez.

2005, *Latina Legacies (Identity, Biography, and Community)* edited by Vicki L. Ruiz and Virginia Sánchez Korrol. Chapter 3, titled "The Adventures of Loreta Janeta Velázquez, Civil War Spy and Storyteller," was written by Amy Dockser Marcus who "has written extensively about women soldiers during the Civil War and is preparing a book on the subject."

The thirteen-page recitation emphasizes Velazquez's Latina roots and her defiance of feminine cultural norms of accepted behavior. The chapter is replete with errors harvested from aforementioned published sources. For example, "Her memoir ended in Texas, where she said she planned to settle and to write her book." And that editor C. J. Worthington was an ex-Union naval officer which Worthington never claimed, but only said he was in the Navy. (It was the "publisher's circular" which stated Worthington was an officer, but it was a lie anyway.)

Marcus asserted that Velazquez was in Brazil when she wrote her letter to General Early, which she was not, and that Early persecuted Velazquez, which he did not. Almost to Marcus' credit, she wrote, "Jubal Early made several prescient points, and it is true that her book has its share of factual problems." Yet the Marcus dismissed the "factual problems" by minimizing them and not seeing easily recognized falsehoods.

2005, *The History of Southern Women's Literature*, editors Carolyn Perry and Mary Louise Weaks. One long paragraph addresses Velazquez's book, but oddly the editors made no comment on its quality as literature (it's good), which they did for the other books of female Civil War writers. The editors only commented about Velazquez:

> Most scholars discount Velazquez's account of her activities on behalf of the Confederacy, and it seems extremely doubtful that she could have dressed as a man, as she claims, and participated in battle disguised as a Confederate officer. Her stories of being a courier for Confederate spies in Memphis and New Orleans cannot be substantiated, but they are in close accord with the same sort of activities in which many Confederate women were engaged and are therefore valuable. Velazquez is a shadowy figure. There is no reason to doubt her claim that she was born in Havana in 1842, but when and where she died remain a mystery.

2006, *Women of the Civil War Battlefront* by Richard H. Hall. This is Mr. Hall's second book in which Velazquez is considered; recall the first, *Patriot in Disguise*, gave a good rendition of Velazquez's claimed deeds. In this second book, in Chapter 5, titled "The Secret Service: Spies, Scouts, and Saboteurs," Hall retold Velazquez's story, but only briefly and referred readers to his first book for a more complete retelling.

A minor error is immediately apparent when Hall stated that Velazquez's miner husband, with whom she had a son, was her third husband. Velazquez wrote this miner husband was her fourth. The error does not mean that Mr. Hall had not read Velazquez's book. He positively did read it, evident by his detailed retelling of her story in his *Patriots in Disguise*. He just lost count.

In the years between his books, Hall had no luck tracking Velazquez during her years <u>after</u> the publication of *The Woman in Battle*. He wrote:

> Except for one or two brief mentions of her after 1876, what became of her and her son remains a mystery. She apparently died in obscurity, but no date or place of death is known.

Hall did discover much written about Velazquez <u>prior</u> to the publication of her book. He wrote, "Historical evidence has been found that supports some of the key elements of her story, though in certain portions fact and fiction appear to be inextricably entwined" and he presented his findings in Chapter 9 which was titled "Case Studies" and also in Appendix B.

Hall wrote, "Much more has been learned about Velazquez after ten additional years of research...." Indeed, Mr. Hall found many newspaper references to Velazquez by her many names and he listed the sources chronologically and summarized each, stating pertinent information. (All of these have been presented.)

Hall noted in the *Official Records* the existence of a letter from Major H. Winslow which "reported placing a female secret service agent in the field who had been operating in the West and North."[11] Hall thought this was Velazquez, he wrote, "Velazquez reports this assignment and the circumstances in her memoirs." Hall's suspicion has been previously examined in detail and the facts do not allow the conclusion that this was Velazquez.

Another misstep by Hall was when he reported that the July 15, 1863 *Richmond Examiner* told of the arrest of "Mrs. S. T. Williams, whose husband was reported to be a lieutenant in the 13th Connecticut Infantry," Hall was flummoxed because "the 13th Connecticut roster contains no officer named Williams at all." Wouldn't Velazquez happily lie about her husband being a lieutenant when she happily lied about herself being a lieutenant? Yes, there were no lieutenants by that name, but other "Williams" soldiers are likely husband candidates and has been addressed.

In the intervening ten years, Hall was still confident that the photograph he had found in John W. Headley's 1906 book, *Confederate Operations in Canada and New York*, and Hall had reported in his first book, was that of Velazquez. Hall wrote that the photograph was "an apparent photograph of her during a trip to Canada in which she was helping Confederate soldiers who were prisoners there." This impossibility has been covered.

By now Richard Hall was beginning to catch on:

Evidently she also engaged in considerable deception, and possibly some embellishment, severely complicating the effort to pin down the whole truth about her. The problem centers around the difficulty of filtering out the myths, the garbled and distorted information in newspaper stories, and her own deceptions, and then isolating and more clearly establishing the facts.

Mr. Hall's problem was of his own creation. He refused to understand that the newspapers wrote what Velazquez herself said. The newspapers did not make-up information which (unfortunately) conflicted with the "truth" in Velazquez's later written memoir. Hall wrote that one newspaper reported on her in "a highly distorted news story about her career" when she passed through St. Louis in April 1866. It should have been clear to Mr. Hall that when Velazquez visited the St. Louis, she went to the newspaper and gave her life's story. How else would any newspaper have known such details? The Atlanta *Constitution* of January 15, 1875 said this exactly was the case:

Some months ago [referring to the September 4, 1874 extensive article] a woman, who gave her name as Mrs. E. H. Bonner, appeared in our city, claiming

---

11. OR, *The War of the Rebellion*.

to be Harry Buford, the female lieutenant of the confederate army. <u>Upon the authority of Mrs. Bonner</u>, an article was written in the *Constitution*, giving briefly <u>her history just as she detailed it</u>.

Any contradictory-appearing details were told to the newspaper by Velazquez. She was not worried that at some later date, someone, a researcher maybe, would be troubled when they detected the contradictions. By the time she published her book some ten years later, even she, most likely, did not remember her previous lies.

Mr. Hall wrote, "In time and with continued intensive research, more reliable details may also come to light about her military and spying activities." Richard H. Hall apparently never accepted the fact that Velazquez was a compulsive liar; he died on July 17, 2009.

2006, *She Went to the Field: Women Soldiers of the Civil War* by Bonnie Tsui. In thirteen pages Tsui presented Velazquez's memoir. Tsui explained:

> In 1878 Confederate general [*sic*] Jubal Early, outraged at the depiction of Loreta's immoral behavior in *The Woman in Battle*, wrote an angry diatribe to Congressman W. F. Slemons of Arkansas, stating that she was "no type of Southern woman."

General Early's letter was far from an "angry diatribe" and it was not initiated by him out of the blue. He was responding to the letter from Velazquez and a personal meeting with Velazquez, both of which she initiated. The letter to Congressman Slemons was not addressed to him for no reason; Slemons was the intermediary who Velazquez indicated to Early she wished to use. And Early was not "outraged" by "Loreta's immoral behavior." Early wrote, "the manner in which she claims to have supplanted in love her bosom friend, and married her first husband, is not calculated to produce a favorable impression of her character." He never said she was of "immoral behavior." He did denounce Velazquez's depiction of Southern officers as "drunken, gasconading brutes" and Southern women as "ready to throw themselves into the arms of the dashing 'Lieutenant Harry T. Buford,' and surrender without waiting to be asked, all that is dear to women of virtue." General Early continued, "Velazquez herself is no true type of Southern woman, and the women she describes are not fair specimens of the pure and devoted women who followed with their prayers the armies of the Confederate States through all their struggles and trials."

Instead of paying attention to or answering General Early's very important points of contention (which have been detailed previously) Bonnie Tsui misrepresented the true nature of General Early's letter and was quick to condemn the General.

Tsui then wrote, "When it comes to her specific exploits and actual participation in battle, many Civil War scholars believe that Loreta Janeta

Velazquez's story was significantly exaggerated for her audience's reading pleasure." For some unknown reason, Tsui failed to understand that General Early was Velazquez's reading audience and he, in fact, provided facts relevant to Velazquez's claimed "specific exploits and actual participation in battle." General Early was Velazquez's contemporary, was at Bull Run, had tremendous military experience and he knew of which he spoke. Is a Civil War scholar, some 150 years after the War more knowledgeable than was General Early? And why was "Velazquez's story significantly exaggerated for her audience's reading pleasure" when Velazquez stated multiple times that her story was the plain truth! Even Velazquez's editor said that Velazquez wrote only the truth!

Bonnie Tsui mentioned briefly what Elizabeth Leonard opined in her 1999 "pivotal work *All the Daring of the Soldier*," that Velazquez's book was "a kind of fictionalized memoir on which editor and publisher C. J. Worthington worked substantially 'refining Velazquez's prose for a popular audience and having corrected certain errors of detail....'"

The one point which Tsui made and is of some value is that "the very writing of her memoirs is a daring exploit and extraordinarily revealing of contemporary attitudes and thoughts on the conflict between the North and South." It is a stretch to believe that Velazquez was representative of the "attitudes and thoughts of the conflict" considering Velazquez's eccentricity and mythomania. However, the writing and publication of Velazquez's book was a "daring exploit" in that it took great energy and dedication to see it to completion.

2006, *Her Best Shot: Women and Guns in America* by Laura Browder. This 304-page book examines gun-toting women from historical to contemporary and their fit in American society. Author Browder notes that the "first armed women to become the subjects of popular ballads and fiction were female soldiers...."

The book's first chapter is titled "Military Heroines, Narratives of Female Soldiers and Spies in the Civil War" and in it, Browder correctly repeated two of Velazquez's claims; that Velazquez took up arms for the thrill of it and that Velazquez claimed to outsoldier the men- as well as other claims. Reproduced in the chapter is the illustration from the memoir, showing Lieutenant Harry T. Buford "Making a Charge," thrusting her rifle with bayonet fixed, stabbing at a Yankee who fends off the bayonet with his sword. See Illustrations, Figure 5.

Author Browder noted that General Early had criticisms of Velazquez and that General Early "angrily dismissed [Velazquez] was as 'a mere pretender.'" It is arguable whether General Early "angrily" dismissed Velazquez; his surviving letters do not show anger. Yes, he dismissed

Velazquez as a mere pretender; however, it is clear that Early presented his civil tongued (not angry) criticism to Congressman Slemons factually and methodically, in a manner which was designed not to offend Slemons, since General Early believed Slemons was one of Velazquez's adherents.

Browder, in addition, wrote that General Early "could not contain his vitriol about someone he considered 'no true type of a Southern woman.'" If vitriol is defined as "cruel and bitter criticism" then a defense of General Early is warranted. General Early's criticism shows that he was trying to be accurate with logical conclusions using the information Velazquez provided and was not cruel or bitter. Again, it must be stated that General Early throughout his letter maintained a civil tongue so as not to offend the Congressman.

Please read General Early's letters in the Appendix, Items 2 & 3 and determine whether the General wrote in anger and with vitriol.

Never was Velazquez identified as a gun-toter by any newspaper reporter who interviewed her or described her. Only she herself claimed in her book to have carried a gun. For example, on the occasion of her recruiting trip into Arkansas when she stayed at the home of the Giles family, she wrote (p81) she placed her revolver beneath her pillow. On this trip she claimed she recruited a battalion of 236 men, a provable lie. Does that make her pistol claim a falsehood as well?

At the Battle of Ball's Bluff, Velazquez narrated (p122) she looked into a ravine, saw a Yankee sergeant reach for his musket with the intention of shooting her, but she "leveled a pistol at him" and captured him. Then sometime later she "fired [her] revolver at another officer- a major who was in the act of jumping into the river" and implied killed him (p125). This occurred just after she had commanded a company, "which had lost all its officers." It is provable lie that a Confederate company "lost all it officers" in that battle, so does that make it a lie that she leveled a pistol at the Yankee sergeant or shot and killed a major, especially when military records show no Union major was killed at Ball's Bluff?

However, on one occasion Velazquez is positively identified in possession of two pistols. Please recall her July 27, 1864 letter written to Captain Stockdale, while she was detained at the St. Cloud Hotel in Nashville, in which she explained her possession of two pistols, "I received my passes & permit from his provost marhial [*sic* marshal] for to carry two pistols & A Rebbel belt I captured from A Rebbel." On that occasion it must be understood that she had two guns, but it is also clear that she lied about capturing them from a Rebel since she claimed (in her book) she herself was a Confederate Rebel. Worse still, she never in her memoir or to any newspaper claimed she fought <u>against</u> the Rebels. In fact, she always espoused her perfect Southern loyalty. How did she capture "two pistols and A Rebbel belt" from "A Rebbel" who she never fought against?

A cynic might suppose that she captured, rather, stole the guns from a Rebel in the South, upon her departure for the North, that is, if she in truth had acquired the guns from a Rebel at all. One would suppose the guns could have been sold for travel money. A defender of Velazquez may wish to object by saying Velazquez was in the North as a Confederate spy so she would have had to lie about where and why she had two pistols. The problem with this defense is that Velazquez lied to the readers of her memoir, as well as the newspapers, that she went to the North as a loyal Confederate spy and to help her brother, when the truth is, she followed her deserter husband there. She even had the gumption to kill off her husband in her memoir before she went North. The reality seems to be that Velazquez was a spy of negligible accomplishment (for either side, take your pick), with this conclusion derived from the documents discovered to date. And furthermore, she might be considered to have been an inept spy, if the discovery of two pistols in her possession would cause her to be unveiled as a spy.

Browder cited both author Richard Hall, saying that Hall "confirmed many details of her story" and Jesse Alemán, editor of Velazquez's reissued memoir, who wrote that Velazquez's memoir "rests somewhere in between history and story."

2006, *Boston Globe*. The August 22 article, titled "Stealth Fighter," written by staff member Johnny Diaz, included the two images of Velazquez, one in male military uniform disguise and the other in female attire. The occasion of the article was an interview with María Agui Carter, filmmaker and the owner of her own production company, Iguana Films, which was making *Rebel*, which Carter hoped would be presented on PBS in the spring.

Diaz wrote the basics of Velazquez's participation "at the battles of Bull Run and Ball's Bluff, and at the siege of Fort Donelson," then produced quotes by the film team in which they expressed their wonderment. "'Loreta's story was an unbelievable story, because it's not what proper women did at that time,' says Sabrina Aviles of Roslindale, co-producer of *Rebel*. 'She was also a Latina, a Cubana who spoke Spanish!'" Diaz quoted María Agui Carter, "This is an incredible woman we have never heard of… I want people to say 'Why haven't we heard of this woman, and why hasn't history included her?'" And "This is a detective story. Who was she?" It will be apparent that when Carter completed the film in 2013, she failed to produce a detective story.

To his credit, author Diaz noted that a debate about the validity of the memoir continues today, however, he did not state the nature of the problems.

2007, *Transgender History & Geography, Crossdressing in Context, vol. 3* by Dr. G. G. Bolich who is author of numerous books, holds doctorates in both Psychology and Religious Studies and "teaches graduate students in counseling at Webster University- Greenville." He writes about Gender, Transgender, Psychology and Religion.[12]

Under the subtitle "Who are some famous crossdressing women?" and still another subtitle "Who is Loretta [*sic*] Janeta Velazquez?" author Bolich wrote (p162-165):

The Woman in Battle... is generally regarded today as untrustworthy as an historical document, but in her own life it serves to secure Velazquez a measure of fame. Whatever the accuracy of the details, her narrative offers a richly detailed story of a crossdressing woman and its various elements may truly reflect experiences some women had during the Civil War.

Dr. Bolich rather capably presented a synopsis of the memoir, making points about Velazquez's attire.

However, some familiar errors are obvious. Velazquez raised "a regiment of volunteers." No, a regiment is 1000 men; Velazquez claimed she raised a "battalion" of 236 men. Velazquez's husband William was "killed by an accidental discharge of a carbine." No, Velazquez claimed the carbine exploded- there is a difference. In any case, this husband and his death were lies. Velazquez married "a fourth time, to an older widower, whom she meets as she travels through the American West." No, Velazquez did not claim this husband was a widower. It was a different man, a sixty-year-old miner she met prior to her husband who was the widower and who, after knowing her for "a couple of days," asked to marry her and offered half his mining interest in the deal- she refused.

Dr. Bolich tells about Velazquez's claimed spy trip to Washington when Velazquez acquired some female attire from a slave woman, "Persuading a slave woman to procure clothes for her- and thus becoming a woman pretending to be a man pretending to be woman- she enters the North." What? No, Velazquez simply removed her disguise and put on her normal female attire. Besides, this claimed trip to Washington has been shown to be a lie. So maybe a better observation is that Velazquez was a liar pretending to tell the truth.

---

12. G. G. Bolich, *Transgender Realities* (Raleigh, NC: Psyche's Press, 2008), About the Author.

2007, article titled "On the move again, Tracking the 'Exploits, Adventures, and Travels of Madame Loreta Janeta Velazquez'" by Coleman Hutchison, Assistant Professor of English from the University of Texas at Austin. This article appeared in *Comparative American Studies, An International Journal*, Vol 5(4): 423-440. In 18 pages, including sources, author Hutchison presented Velazquez's memoir from a point of view of internationalism. Hutchison summarized:

> This essay considers an under-studied aspect of both the Velazquez narrative and its historical context. I argue that *The Woman in Battle* elegantly 'embodies and enacts' the international dimensions of the American Civil War. *The Woman in Battle* is a restless text, one that moves dexterously and recurrently across lines of nation and region. As Velazquez travels from state to state, nation to nation, and continent to continent, her narrative effectively remaps the American Civil War within a global system of immigration, foreign intervention, transnational capital, transatlantic slavery, and competing nationalisms. In *The Woman in Battle* the Civil War is played out not only on the battlefields of Shiloh and Manassas but also in a series of unexpected contexts: Europe, South America, and the Caribbean. Perhaps because of her cosmopolitan background, Velazquez as narrator has a particularly keen eye for the international aspects and implications of the war. Indeed, her narrative recapitulates and her rhetoric underscores such internationalism, forcing readers to acknowledge the ways that this bloody and harrowing conflict exceeded the provincial limits and logics of 'North versus South.' In all, Velazquez's awareness of a world outside of the United and Confederate States helps to disrupt the insularity of Civil War narrative convention and to tell the belated story of a Confederacy in and of the world.

Velazquez would have been flattered that academia found a use for her, though she most likely would not have understood, or worse, felt a little nauseous in the effort.

Before scholar Hutchison credited her extensive travels it might have behooved him to verify the truthfulness of these travel claims. For example, it has been proven that Velazquez lied that she saw Confederate commerce raider *Florida* escape from St. Thomas. Did she also lie about her presence in St. Thomas?

It has been shown that Velazquez most certainly lied about her trip to Havana, departing from New Orleans, with a dispatch for commerce raider *Alabama*.

Velazquez lied about her trip to Richmond when she met Jefferson Davis. She was still in jail in New Orleans. (Velazquez did travel to Richmond on other occasions as documented by the newspapers.)

She claimed she took a trip to Europe with her brother, but Velazquez told so many lies about her brother that his very existence is not believable. If the brother with whom she claimed she traveled to Europe never existed, maybe her trip to Europe never happened. As has been pointed out, her visit to Europe certainly did not help her learn how to spell "Parris" and it is a provable lie that she met the Minister to France, William Lewis Dayton, who was already dead at the date when she claimed she met him.

It is true that Velazquez traveled to Venezuela, however, she lied to the newspaper that she was an agent of the emigration company, she lied to her readers about her role in the trip and she lied to her fellow colonists that she was the "daughter of an English Admiral."

Does an academic analysis and its conclusions have any value when many of the collected data points are false? Hutchison stated that he understood that "the narrative... rests somewhere in between history and story," yet, he proceeded with the analysis.

2007, *Full Metal Corset, Secret Soldiers of the Civil War* is a film made by Indigo Films for the History Channel, A&E Television Network. This film is ostensibly the first film in which the story of Velazquez was told. (It was presented before the completion of *Rebel* which still was in the making.) *Full Metal Corset* presented the memoir-based stories of alias "Frank Thompson" Sarah Emma Edmonds and alias "Harry Buford" Loreta Janeta Velazquez.

The film supposedly retold Velazquez's story, but it failed to stay accurate and truthful to the memoir.

First, the film's narrator stated that Velazquez, at the age of 16, eloped with "William," which was an incompetent misrepresentation of what Velazquez wrote; she wrote she was 14. Recall she was born on "26th of June, 1842" and eloped on the "5th of April, 1856." At the time of her elopement, she would have been 13 years, 9 months and 10 days of age. Did the film's writer avoid this fact because they were afraid the audience would refuse to believe it? It is curious that the narrator (thus writer too) just moments before, <u>correctly</u> recalled 1849 as the date which Velazquez claimed she moved to New Orleans from Havana.

Second, the film depicted Velazquez as an officer, waving a sword and firing a pistol as she commanded troops at the skirmish at Blackburn's Ford. Recall, Velazquez claimed (p97) that at Blackburn's Ford she had "been placed temporarily in command of a company- the senior officer of which had been killed...." If the filmmakers had conducted the simplest search of military records, they would have found that no Confederate company at Blackburn's Ford lost its senior officer.

Third, Velazquez was depicted at the Battle of Bull Run, again waving a sword, firing a pistol and commanding a company. Velazquez never claimed she commanded anyone at the Battle of Bull Run. In fact, she wrote (p99) that she was not "attached to a regular command" and that "being an independent enabled [her], to a great extent, to choose [her] own position in the battle...."

Fourth, Velazquez was shown at the Battle of Fort Donelson, again with her sword and pistol, and commanding a company. Velazquez never claimed she commanded a company at the Battle of Fort Donelson or even fought or fired a shot there.

The film maker's depiction of Velazquez commanding a company at these battles is a blatant misrepresentation of what Velazquez wrote.

It should be noted that the film depicted her first claimed husband, "William," (about whom all claims have been shown to have been lies) while it failed to mention her second claimed and a real husband, "DeCaulp," about whose life and death Velazquez freely lied and provably so. It might be suspected the film wished to avoid bringing attention to the messy facts.

Throughout the film, scholars provided a running commentary, describing the times and more particular retelling Velazquez's story. They were: Elizabeth D. Leonard, author of *All the Daring of a Soldier* (1999); Trish Chambers, author of *Civil War Women: Their Roles and Legacies* (2005); Judith Bellafaire, Ph.D., Chief Historian, Women's Memorial; DeAnne Blanton, author of *They Fought Like Demons* (2002); Jesse Alemán, Associate Professor, University of New Mexico. It should be recalled, Jesse Alemán wrote the introduction to the 2003 reprint of Velazquez's book and added his own parenthetical title, *The Woman in Battle (The Civil War Narrative of Loreta Velazquez, Cuban Woman & Confederate Soldier)*.

All of the contributors were/are Velazquez's advocates and no opinion was presented contrary to theirs and no refutation of the truthfulness of Velazquez's memoir was presented. The narrator gingerly handled the criticism which *The Woman in Battle* has incurred and said that Velazquez "receive[ed] heavy criticism for her candid and highly dramatized story." No, Velazquez did not receive "heavy criticism for a candid and highly dramatized story," she received criticism for producing an untruthful story which was sold as the truth.

In the last three minutes of the film, criticism of Velazquez reached a whispered crescendo when DeAnne Blanton stated:

> In many ways her memoirs are over-the-top. She presents herself as larger than life and because of that some have said that she just couldn't be real, that women just didn't act that way, most women didn't, she did.

Yes, she was real. Yes, most women and men did not act this way, that is, impudently lie to the public! Does "over-the-top" mean, lying?

The narrator picked up the point, "Recently uncovered documents confirm not just her existence, but also many of the claims she makes in her book." Yes, Velazquez was a real person. Yes, the newspapers identified her when she was in town, when she was arrested or otherwise; however, the newspapers did not and do not "confirm… the many claims she makes in her book." Instead, the newspapers regularly and hugely contradict her book, since Velazquez always made-up lies during the course of the War and only settled on the version she would tell in her book ten years after the War's end.

The one newspaper article which was chosen to be flashed on the screen was from the July 2, 1863 *Richmond Examiner* and it was one of the least revealing of many known articles which so clearly contain the contractions and lies Velazquez told the press. It simply announced her arrival in Richmond and imprisonment at Castle Thunder after having been sent from Mobile upon her arrest there. Blanton continued, "There are wartime newspaper articles about Lieutenant Harry Buford. These are accounts of a cross-dressing Confederate woman soldier." Yes, and yes, those are true statements, but it does not make truthful Velazquez's memoirs. Yes, there are articles and the articles contain enough contradictions to Velazquez's memoir to trigger anyone's inborn intuition that they are being lied to.

2007, *Leading Ladies, American Trailblazers* by Kay Bailey Hutchison. Author and statesman Hutchison explained in the Preface, that she wrote the book because of comments by readers of her previous book, *American Heroines*, who suggested "women and professions that should have been included. Among the most common: Why not the military?"

In *Leading Ladies'* first chapter, vignettes of some 14 women with military histories are presented with Velazquez at number six, covered on pages 17-18. In the remaining chapters, some 50 women from many eras and accomplishments are presented; among them are first ladies, women suffragist and civil rights pioneers.

About Velazquez, Hutchison wrote, "Despite the extravagant claims the author makes, many authorities have concluded that there is at least a kernel of truth in Loreta's memoir, though most people agree with the assessment of Confederate Jubal Early...." Hutchison mentioned some of the more significant of Velazquez's claims and noted:

> Most scholars believe that Loreta combined other accounts of Civil War experiences- such as those of Laura Williams, who fought under the nom de guerre Lieutenant Henry Benford- with her own exploits and those of literary works to fabricate an epic tale of warfare, intrigue and romance.

Of course, it has been shown that this was not the case and Benford was Buford and Laura Williams was Velazquez. This same erroneous conjecture, that Laura Williams was a separate individual from whom Velazquez borrowed, was previously proffered by author Janet E. Kaufman in 1984.

January 2008, article titled "Unmasking the Gentleman Soldier in the Memoirs of the Two Cross-dressing Female US Civil War Soldiers" by Matthew Teorey, "teacher of literature, composition, and business writing at Peninsula College in Port Angeles, Washington." Teorey's 19-page article appeared in *War, Literature & the Arts: An International Journal of the Humanities*, Vol 20, Number 1-2, and featured "Frank" and "Harry," that is, respectively Sarah Emma Edmonds and Loreta Janeta Velazquez, by retelling their memoirs.

Teorey identified no problems with Velazquez's memoir and his most severe criticism was: "Velazquez did add a little embellishment and sentimentalization." Teorey then recounted Velazquez's good opinion of Abraham Lincoln upon her meeting him and her decision not to assassinate General Grant when the opportunity presented itself; Teorey wrote, "Regardless of whether these experiences actually happened or not, her message was the importance of recognizing and respecting good people." What?! One would imagine that the "importance" would be the historical truth of whether one chose not to assassinate General Grant, rather than an obvious truism of "respecting good people." It might be pointed out that one method of "respecting good people," for example her readership, is by not lying to them!

Teorey used as sources some of the previously cited books as well as adding his own misstatements.

1) "[She] raised her own regiment for the Confederate army." Teorey, a "son and grandson of air force officers," (as noted in his credits) did not grasp the distinction between a "regiment" and "battalion," what Velazquez actually claimed she raised.

2) "After she and her husband move to New Orleans, curiosity about male freedom and independence caused her to dress in her husband's suits, copy his mannerisms, and carefully observe those around her as she walked through town and visited men's clubs." Velazquez claimed this event was in Memphis, <u>not</u> in New Orleans, and they visited "a bar-room," not "men's clubs," there is a difference.

3) "Velazquez's own commanders jailed and fined her several times when they discovered her dressed as a male soldier." No, Velazquez never claimed this and the newspapers of the times never reported this. To clarify, a mayor was never her commander and neither was a provost marshal and these were the only officials who had a hand in her arrests.

4) Addressing the death of second husband DeCaulp, Teorey wrote, "… the second [husband] dying of an illness brought on by a wound purportedly less severe than either of Velazquez's battle wounds." No! Velazquez never claimed in her book that DeCaulp's illness was a result of a wound. And she never compared his illness to her wounds. She plainly wrote (p326-327) that DeCaulp had "a spell of sickness" in an Atlanta hospital and once sufficiently recovered returned to duty. Velazquez wrote, "Before reaching his command, Captain De Caulp was taken sick again… he died in a Federal

hospital in Chattanooga." In any case, the story of DeCaulp's death is a murderous lie. He factually survived the war; this has been addressed.

In support of Velazquez's battlefield claims, Teorey wrote, "Velazquez also distinguished herself in battle." Teorey, in pointing out Velazquez's disgust with big talkers who proved "not always the best fighters," wrote, "This gap between the soldiers' posturing among civilians and their cowardly performance on the battlefield annoyed Velazquez even further because her performance was exactly the opposite- courageous on the battlefield and understated at home." And, "Velazquez took command of a company when its commanding officer slunk away, and she considered her soldiering and leadership abilities equal, if not superior, to his." Author Teorey must not have considered, while awake, the plausibility of Velazquez's battlefield claims in order to reach these conclusions.

Teorey had something to say about General Early's criticism of Velazquez, "Some men and women, at the time of the war considered these women's unsexing as a condemnation of femininity. For example, Confederate General Early considered Velazquez as sex-less, refusing to accept her as either a true man or a 'true type of a Southern woman.'" Matthew Teorey's assertion is totally false! General Early never wrote that he "considered Velazquez as sex-less," and he never wrote that he did not accept her as a true man.

General Early wrote in his letter, "I was satisfied that the writer of that book whether man or woman, had never had the adventures therein narrated."

In summary, General Early was not worried about Velazquez's sexuality, rather, he simply objected to a liar getting away with lies. Please read General Jubal Early's complete letter in the Appendix, Item 3.

2008, *I'll Pass for Your Comrade (Women Soldiers in the Civil War)* by Anita Silvey. This 115-page book, written for "juvenile" readers (with nice illustrations) addresses some of the known Civil War women soldiers, with Velazquez figuring prominently. Silvey wrote, "Although many of the facts that Loreta Janeta Velazquez reported in her memoir, *The Woman in Battle*, cannot be verified, some of the details appear to be accurate." Some interesting parts of Velazquez's narrative are quoted and the familiar illustrations of Velazquez in and out of disguise are presented.

In conclusion, Silvey wrote:

Extremely controversial, the book was denounced by some Confederate officers, who believed the story a fabrication; but others, including General James Longstreet, vouched for her service.

No, General Longstreet did **not** vouch for Velazquez's service; this has already been covered. And no denouncements by Confederate officers other than Jubal Early have been discovered. It is a pity that the "extremely controversial" statement was not placed at the beginning of Silvey's narration, instead of the end, so that the young reader might be attentive to assertions.

2008, *Women in the American Civil War*, Vol II, editor Lisa Tendrich Frank. The entry on "Velazquez, Loreta Janeta [Harry T. Buford] (1842-1897)" was written by María Agui Carter who is the writer/director of the film *Rebel*, still in the making at this date.

The sources Carter used, all found in this chronology, contain inaccuracies; therefore, Carter's entry suffers from inaccuracies.

Carter wrote, "[Velazquez] fought as a self-appointed officer and served the Confederacy as a secret agent." Here are two unproven assertions and one truth. It is unproven, or unconfirmed by any source other than Velazquez's claim, that she fought in battle. It also is unproven, or unconfirmed by any source other than Velazquez's claim, that she was a secret agent for the Confederacy, though she could have been. Velazquez did work as a "special agent" for the Union. The one truth Carter correctly represented is that Velazquez was "a self-appointed officer."

María Agui Carter misrepresented the facts when she wrote:

Prominent General Jubal Early began a public campaign to discredit Velazquez as a liar and prostitute. Based almost exclusively on his testimony, her work and wartime experiences were considered a hoax for over a century.

No! General Early waged no such campaign, as has been explained ad nauseam!

The writing of his private letter does not constitute "a public campaign" and it is unlikely that the public was even aware of "his testimony" until found by researchers years later. General Early, in part, wrote:

I gave this opinion [that she was not the author, judging from the horridly written letter he had received from her] also to the gentleman from Richmond referred to, at the same time expressing the belief that Madame Velasquez is not of Spanish birth or origin, but is an American and probably from the North.- This is the extent to which I have sought to deprecate Madame Velasquez or her book so far as Richmond is concerned, and I have expressed the same opinions to several persons in this city [meaning Lynchburg, Virginia].

How General Early's expressed opinion can be construed by Carter as a "public campaign to discredit Velazquez as a liar and prostitute" is incomprehensible. Furthermore, Early's comments most certainly cannot be determined the cause of her book being "considered a hoax for over a century" since the comments were in a private letter and not known to the public. This prostitute assertion will be put to bed later.

Please see General Early's letter in the Appendix, Item 3.

May 2010, "The Civil War: A Soldier's Life" was created for the Traveling Trunk Program which provides "a hands-on approach to learning about a soldier's life during the Civil War" and is sponsored by Special Collections Library/Center for the Book, Albuquerque Public Schools-Teaching American History Grant.

The display material consists of replicas and authentic items and is offered to teachers for programs for their students. To accompany the Trunk Program, is an eight-grade level three-week Civil War lesson, in which the class is introduced to "Lieutenant Harry T. Buford aka Loreta Janeta Velazquez who fought at the battle of Bull Run on the side of the confederacy." The program states, "[Velazquez] was also the only Latina woman to disguise herself as a man to fight in the Civil War." One wonders how the program knows there weren't other Latina women- after all, they would have been in disguise, right?

2010, *Stealing Secrets: How a Few Daring Women Deceived Generals, Impacted Battles, and Altered the Course of the Civil War* by H. Donald Winkler. In 28 pages of Chapter 17 titled "Hired to Find Herself" Winkler recounted Velazquez's story, especially the story Velazquez wove about how U.S. Secret Service Chief Lafayette C. Baker hired her to find herself. Winkler consumed about 7 pages, quoting from Velazquez's book.

Author Winkler apparently tried to pull-in outside information to aid in the narrative. About Velazquez's alleged first husband, Winkler wrote, "He was a U.S. Army officer named William Rouch." No, Velazquez never stated in her book William's surname and author Winkler obtained William's surname from some unnamed and unknown source, but it was probably Kinchen's 1972 book. The name has previously been seen in various sources as "Roach," "Roche," and "Rosche." Velazquez told the newspapers that first husband was William Burnet.

Winkler noted:

> The accuracy of Loreta's memoir continues to be an issue with scholars. Some claim it is all fiction, but in doing so they ignore a newspaper report about the arrest of a Lieutenant Bensford (undoubtedly Buford) when it was discovered that he was actually a woman. The article gives her name as Alice Williams, one of the aliases Loreta used. Other scholars have noted that the details in Loreta's memoir show a familiarity with the times that would be difficult to completely simulate.

Yes, the newspaper reports were all real, but the lies they contained and the lies contained in her memoir also are real and easily proven as such, thus the "issue with scholars."

2010, "The Multiple Metaphoric Civil Wars of Loreta Janeta Velazquez's *The Woman in Battle*," published in *Southern Quarterly*, Fall 2010, by Robin C. Sager who received a PhD in History and a certification in Women, Gender, and Sexuality Studies from Rice University. She is Assistant Professor in History at University of Evansville, Indiana. The 19-page article is an unnecessary academic presentation about something or another, but luckily author Sager explained:

…The multiple metaphoric civil wars that appear within Velazquez's *The Woman in Battle* speak to the ways that individuals contested the traditional constructions of race, ethnicity, class, gender and sexuality during the U.S. Civil War and Reconstruction periods. Despite being written more than 130 years ago, Velazquez's text anticipates the current direction of U.S. Civil War historiography through its depiction of the intersectionality of identity markers. Using the definition of civil wars as rebellions in which people challenge normal binaries, I will briefly summarize the plot of *The Woman in Battle*, place this article in dialogue with the work of other Velazquez scholars, and provide an analysis of the embattled ideas of race, ethnicity, class, gender, and sexuality that appear within the text and hint at future research possibilities focusing on the U.S. Civil War period.

Dr. Sager wrote she was inspired by authors Jesse Alemán's (2003, "Authenticity, Autobiography, and Identity: *The Woman in Battle* as a Civil War Narrative") and Elizabeth Young's (1999, *Disarming the Nation: Women's Writing and the American Civil War*) "explorations of gender and sexuality," which goes a long way to explaining why historical facts were excluded, erroneous or ignored by Dr. Sager, who said "the efforts of literary scholars" Alemán and Young "stand out" and that Jesse Alemán was "the foremost Velazquez scholar." Remember Alemán is the editor of the reprint who wrote, "… I have not attempted to verify the narrative with historical documentation, since Velazquez's history and the history of the text are so embattled in a debate over their authenticity." A scholar who refuses to "verify the narrative with historical documentation" or investigate the authenticity of their subject would seem to be the wrong scholar upon which to hook one's wagon, doncha think? And remember Elizabeth Young, the other scholar? She evoked the symbolism of "anal penetration." It is curious that Dr. Sager, whose doctorate is in history depended on English or literature professors as sources.

First, Sager opined that Velazquez's travels ended with "her eventual settlement in post-war Texas." For the umpteenth time, Velazquez did not settle in Texas!

Second, Sager wrote, "After raising her first regiment, according to the text, Velazquez dressed as Buford fights in the major Civil War battles of Bull Run, Balls Bluff, Fort Donelson, and Shiloh." No, Velazquez did not write that she raised a regiment. Velazquez claimed she raised a "battalion."

Sager called the regiment Velazquez's "first," implying she raised others after the "first." Velazquez never claimed to raise more than one "battalion" and she lied about that one; she raised nothing.

Third, Sager asserted Confederate General Jubal A. Early "claimed that [Velazquez] presented an overly dramatic, brutalized image of southern men and women." General Early did indeed protest Velazquez's representation of southern men and women, but it was not the "take-away" of his letter which was instead, Velazquez was not truthful. It is a misrepresentation of Jubal Early's letter to imply the take-away was anything else. See General Early's letter in the Appendix, Item 3.

Sager goes to the trouble of analyzing social "class," Velazquez's rearing, and behavior as it pertained to her upper-class family history, "Her parents also sent her to school in New Orleans, another marker of wealth." Of course, by now the reader should understand that the Sisters of Charity school, which Velazquez claimed she attended, was not a marker of the wealth of the parents who sent their kids there. Nor did wealthy parents let their child live in a New Orleans whorehouse. If the reader does not understand the whorehouse reference, please re-read the newspaper articles from Velazquez's 1863 arrest in New Orleans.

Sager examined Velazquez's sexuality and concluded, "Over all, Velazquez's sexuality remains in question throughout the work and is not resolved even with the birth of her first living child." Robin Sager, upon reading Velazquez's book, must have missed Velazquez's claimed engagement to Raphael and Velazquez's four claimed marriages. The first marriage, Velazquez claimed, produced three children who all died from fever, before the war began, and her last marriage produced a son born in Salt Lake City. Just how many marriages or children does it take to determine a female's sexuality? And still there were other marriages not claimed in Velazquez's book, but reported by the newspapers of the times. The 1863 New Orleans newspapers said she had been known as Mrs. Arnold, and had been married to a Bachman from Arkansas, and at that moment was married to Williams of the 13th Connecticut Infantry. Earlier, an 1861 newspaper called Velazquez, Mrs. Mary Ann Keith. After the publication of Velazquez's book, there were at least three more marriages and at least one co-habitation (a year in duration) and two more children, all covered in the course of the book held in hand. Does Velazquez's sexuality remain in question?

Velazquez was clear on her own sexuality even if Robin Sager is not. Velazquez explained her flirtatious manner with ladies was to keep her disguise well-hidden, she wrote (p75), "if I was to figure successfully in the role of a dashing young Confederate officer, it would be necessary for me to learn how to make myself immensely agreeable to the ladies." On one occasion, just after the death of her first husband (which was a lie), by chance some woman was attracted to Lieutenant Harry T. Buford, but Velazquez, who was in no mood to deal with the advances the woman, explained (p88), "The necessity of playing the character I had assumed, however, in a successful manner, pressed on me," so Velazquez, in spite of her bereavement, continued with her role. Of her "love adventures" while in male disguise, the previous mentioned included, Velazquez said (p88) she had "a comical interest for [the woman]." On another occasion, Velazquez claimed (p196) she was in Memphis shortly before the Battle of Shiloh, when she became the object of Miss M's affection which Velazquez wrote was "all very absurd" and she "could not help being amused" and that she "wished [herself] out of the scrape." In conclusion, Velazquez never wrote of a desire for a sexual liaison with any woman, much less had one, whether Velazquez was Lieutenant Harry T. Buford or herself.

One point remains to be made about Velazquez's sexuality as it relates to other women. The "love letter" which Velazquez, rather Lieutenant Harry T. Buford, claimed (p221-223) she received from a female admirer has been determined fake. This lie cast doubt on whether Velazquez was truthful about <u>ever</u> attracting the admiration of any females at all while wearing her attire as Lieutenant Harry Buford.

Sager analyzed Velazquez's ethnicity or race and how as a Cuban, thus a foreigner, she fit in. Sager asserted that since Velazquez was Cuban, she was sensitive that people might not regard her as white. Sager tried to further support her assertion when she speculated on Velazquez's motive for buying a slave, "Velazquez tries to demonstrate her whiteness by buying a slave, Bob, to assist her during her time in the military." The problem is that Velazquez herself rejected Dr. Sager's assertion before Dr. Sager ever made it. Velazquez wrote (p68) that she hid her whiteness to give herself "a more manly air" by applying "a solution… to stain [her] face, in order to make it look tanned." And Dr. Sager's analysis of Bob the slave is all very interesting and extensive, but it took its cue from what is most certainly a lie; Velazquez had no slave named Bob or by any other name. Bob will be further analyzed momentarily.

Sager's analysis of Velazquez's ethnicity, though interesting, might be considered premature since Velazquez's claim to have been born in Cuba is still, at this date, not proven. And it is certain that the specifics Velazquez told of her birth in Cuba are a lie. She lied about her birth into the wealthy Velazquez family on "Calle Velaggas" and about her christening shortly afterwards. Her father may have or may not have been a "native of the city of Carthagena," Spain, but it is certainly untrue that he received "a very thorough education at the universities of Madrid and Paris" and then moved to Cuba and achieved wealth and prominence. She most certainly lied that her mother was "the daughter of a French naval officer, by an American lady, the daughter of a wealthy merchant." It must be conceded that her parents may have been of the stated ethnic backgrounds, but it is a lie that her parents came from the claimed backgrounds of education, wealth, prominence and her father from the "noble" Velazquez lineage. Is there really any purpose of a detailed analysis of Velazquez's race, ethnicity, or whiteness, when the analysis takes it cue from probable lies?

2011, "Vindicating the Confederacy: Confederate Female Spies and their Memoirs, 1863-1876" by Melissa Renee Matthews. This 90-page Master of Art thesis in History analyzed the memoirs of Belle Boyd, Rose O'Neal Greenhow and Loreta Velazquez.

Matthews claimed all three of the women's memoirs were "pieces of Confederate propaganda because they supported Confederate nationalism and vindicated Confederate men." Well, Velazquez's book was published ten years after the war, so to call it "Confederate propaganda" is inaccurate if not harsh. The Confederate States of America had long been defeated and since propaganda is intended to influence opinion, the question arises as to who Velazquez was trying to influence- Southerners to another rebellion?

And to say that Velazquez's book "vindicated Confederate men" would be also inaccurate since Velazquez often and freely spoke against them. She denounced a Confederate General's brutish behavior (p312); she called a Confederate first lieutenant a coward (p121); she got into a quarrel with a drunken first lieutenant and slapped his face (p199). In fact, the disparaging of Confederate officers was one of Jubal Early's points of contention against Velazquez's book. In addition, Velazquez said (p107) the Rebels thought too highly of themselves, believing one Rebel could whip five Yankees and she asserted (p121) that her "colored boy Bob was a better soldier than some of the white men who thought themselves immensely his superiors."

Matthews explained the path to be taken in her thesis:

> It is not in the interest of this work to discuss the authenticity of these women's writing. The main focus of this study is to look at these memoirs as contributions to Confederate nationalism, and how these women used their stories as Confederate propaganda. While it seems evident that Greenhow and Boyd both wrote their own accounts, Velazquez's memoir is still debatable. Still, it does not matter in this context whether or not these women's stories were completely true. It does matter that each of these women wanted to express their sentiments about the Confederacy. They saw a unique opportunity to tell unusual stories to draw an audience in to supporting the Confederacy or in Velazquez's case vindicating what has already passed."

It should be noted that the author downgraded Velazquez's memoir from "Confederate propaganda" to a case of "vindicating what has already passed." But more important is the issue of authenticity. If authenticity of the memoir is not the bedrock, then any claimed deed or "sentiments about the Confederacy" is surely questionable and any conclusion about them is on a slippery slope.

Matthews inaccurately asserted (p5), "Loreta Velazquez supposedly wrote *The Woman in Battle* as a way to earn money after divorcing her fourth husband." Yes, Velazquez said she wrote it to earn money. No, Velazquez never wrote she <u>divorced</u> her fourth husband. Then in short order, Matthews contradicted herself (p21), "While it seems rather unorthodox to remarry so many times, in each case, Velazquez stated she was <u>widowed</u> and <u>not divorced</u>." No! Velazquez did not say she was widowed by the fourth husband, either. But then Matthews changed her mind again and wrote (p39), "She needed the money to support her infant son after her fourth husband <u>disappeared</u>." In fact, Velazquez neither wrote she was divorced nor widowed from the fourth husband and she never claimed he disappeared; she said nothing about his fate. His fate has been covered in the course of the book in hand.

Matthews was seriously not worried about facts when she wrote, "Velazquez took on the name Harry T. Buford and joined an Arkansas regiment." This is not what Velazquez wrote! She did not <u>join</u> a "regiment," she wrote she <u>raised</u> a "battalion." By now we all know that Velazquez designated herself Lieutenant Harry T. Buford, traveled to the Arkansas countryside, raised (enlisted) 236 men and supplied them with all their military equipment at her own expense, trained them and delivered them to Pensacola. There is a huge difference and it can only be concluded that Matthews carelessly (or willfully) misrepresented Velazquez's memoir.

In summary, Matthews extensively repeated Velazquez's memoir (and not always accurately), simply accepted it as true (as she said she was going to do) and then applied meaning, in great detail and over-analysis, to everything Velazquez claimed.

How was a master's thesis in History, which bluntly stated it will ignore the authenticity of the memoir, even accepted?

2011, *Women in Combat* by Rosemarie Skaine. The author, said nothing about Velazquez, but simply listed her among six selected "women who served as men," only the author mistook Velazquez's name as "Loreta James Velazquez." The mistake might have been due to a word processor's auto-correction which preferred the popular and award-winning American singer Etta James.

2011, *Women in the United States Military: An Annotated Bibliography* by Judith Bellafaire. Entry 116 is Velazquez and the 2003 reprint of Velazquez's book.

Velazquez claimed she was a soldier in the Confederate States of America Army which was at war with the United States of America? Ok, the wayward path of our Southern brethren will be ignored since their reconciliatory return back into the family of the United States is fact. What will not be ignored is the museum's statement that "Velazquez was the wife of an officer who decided to disguise herself as a man, raise a cavalry company, and join her husband in battle." No, a simple reading of Velazquez's memoir reveals she did not claim she raised a cavalry company! She wrote she raised a battalion which was on foot. And, of course, the museum didn't understand that Velazquez lied about joining her husband in battle.

To the museum's credit, it did not include anything about Velazquez in its 2015 physical display for the Civil War years, but presented short biographies and images of nine remarkable women of the times.

2013, *Washington Times* May 20. On the occasion of the forthcoming showing (May 24) on PBS of the film *Rebel*, writer Martha M. Boltz gave a synopsis and astutely opined:

[Velazquez] is the woman who wrote her 600-page memoir, 'A Woman in Battle' in 1876, and for the last 147 years others have been trying to convince readers to believe her story.

Boltz then rather inaccurately retold Velazquez's story, seemingly not having read the memoir, and maybe only taking her information from the film. It might have been a good thing that Boltz had not read the memoir because she would have been extremely distressed when she learned that the film's makers did not even try to accurately retell the memoir.

Writer Boltz correctly pointed out that "[Velazquez's] highly embellished narrative simply falls apart as she fights at Ball's Bluff" because Velazquez claimed that a Confederate unit lost all of its officers and military records show this is not true. Boltz noted that "most scholars have embraced the rationale that if one story is so lacking in authenticity, how can comparable exploits at other battle sites be accepted as factual?"

Boltz summed up the problem with *Rebel* when she wrote, "While the PBS program comes backed by some fairly well-known authorities, it fails to provide any substantive material to refute the longstanding criticism about her book's content." Boltz thought the film was worth watching, "but the questions go on."

2013, the internet magazine *Cuban Art News*, addressing "Cuban art and culture worldwide," published Part One of a May 22 article titled "Rebel: A Cuban-American Woman in the U.S. Civil War." The author was Nadine Covert, "a specialist in visual arts media with a focus on documentaries."

Again, the occasion of the article was the anticipated showing of the film *Rebel*.

Covert's summation of Velazquez's story could have come only from the film as the summation is in no way an accurate retelling of the actual memoir; surely Covert did not read the memoir. For example, Covert asserted that Velazquez's three children fathered by "William" died in the "fever that ravaged New Orleans in that era." No, Velazquez's wrote those children died in St. Louis. Covert wrote Velazquez disguised herself <u>after</u> the death of husband William. No, Velazquez wrote that she donned her disguise, enlisted 236 men at her own expense and delivered the men to her alive husband. And Covert wrote, "During this time she acquired a slave, Bob, who presumably helped to keep her secret." It's a good thing that Covert only presumed that was the case, because Velazquez made clear that Bob was not told her secret.

Reaching a climax Covert asserted:

> The book was denounced by critics of the time, and especially by former Confederate General Jubal Early, as a hoax. She was accused of being a camp follower and a prostitute, and was virtually erased from history.

No, no and no. General Early did not say the book was a hoax, he said it was not truthful. No one claimed Velazquez was a prostitute. Author DeAnne Blanton asserted that General Early said Velazquez was a prostitute, which he did not. He did say she was a camp follower, which will be explained momentarily. And Velazquez was <u>not</u> "virtually erased from history." Is Covert implying a conspiracy to keep Velazquez's memoir hidden from the public? And by whom?

Stay turned for part two of the article appearing on May 28, 2013.

2013, the 55-minute film *Rebel* was presented on PBS television. Writer/director María Agui Carter, who claims to be a documentarian, inaccurately retold Velazquez's memoir. For example, Carter narrated that Velazquez's husband, William, left home to join the Confederacy and Velazquez remained at home. When William was killed in a gun accident at Pensacola, she received (at her home) a dispatch announcing his death. Velazquez <u>then</u> decided to disguise herself as a soldier. That is <u>not</u> what Velazquez wrote!!!

Velazquez wrote that after William left for the war, she cut her hair, put on the uniform of a Confederate lieutenant and even glued on a mustache. She then took a train ride west of Memphis to a rural Arkansas community where she raised a "battalion" of 236 men in four days. She said she financed all the battalion's military equipment and provisions out of her own pocket. She marched her troops to the Mississippi River, loaded them on a river boat to New Orleans. From there she proceeded to Pensacola, Florida, marching her men through Mobile, Alabama to the cheering of the crowd. When she arrived in Pensacola, she presented her men to her husband who did not recognize his wife in her disguise. She, in a whisper, let him know it was her and he was astonished at her accomplishment. She then returned to New Orleans for provisions for her troops and it was then that she learned through a message of her husband's death.

The most basic tenet or the heart and soul of Velazquez's book was her claim to have raised her own troops while in a soldier's disguise; Velazquez wrote (p340), "I had attired myself in the uniform of an officer, had enlisted a large body of men by my own unaided exertions, had marched them from Arkansas to Pensacola…."

The film's director omitted even a mention of this actual claim and instead gave a dishonest and an invented version of Velazquez's story probably because Carter feared the audiences' rejection of Velazquez's actual claim. If one wishes to argue that Carter justly simplified and romanticized the story for film adaptation, then the film ceases to be a documentary of Velazquez's own story and the film should not have been represented as a documentary! And the invention could not have been a simple mistake because Carter is a documentarian and surely Carter read Velazquez's memoir.

Writer/director Carter presented images of the pages of Velazquez's book and provided a "Velazquez" voice-over narrative which implied the words were taken from Velazquez's book, which they were not. In some cases, the Velazquez voice-over stated points which were contradictory to what Velazquez wrote. An illustration follows, along with another point of contention.

María Agui Carter paraded out supporting narrators in the form of "scholars," i.e., historians, writers and archivists, who have previously addressed Velazquez in their own works, almost all of which have been presented in the book in hand. These contributors unwittingly, or otherwise, supported the inaccurate retelling of Velazquez' story, but worse still, many of them made their own inaccurate or false statements which could have been rectified had they simply read Velazquez's memoir for themselves. Or maybe they did read it, yet still made the statements.

One of these contributors was Jesse Alemán, "American and Latino Literatures Scholar" who, recall, is the literature professor who wrote a 35-page introduction titled, "Authenticity, Autobiography and Identity," to the 2003 reprint of Velazquez's book. His opinion and those of other scholars from a segment of the film about Bob the slave follows: Alemán stated, "Loreta also buys a slave named Bob and Bob always struck me as a very important character in this narrative. Bob becomes part of the way Loreta Janeta Velazquez, Cuban woman, passes as Harry T. Buford, Confederate soldier." Then Vicki L. Ruiz, "Scholar of U.S. History and Latino Studies," interjected, "Here she is trying to have her own, expand her own boundaries of possible while enslaving another human being." The Velazquez voice-over, in an accurate enough quote, stated, "My colored boy Bob is a better soldier than some of the white men, who think themselves immensely his superiors." Renee Sentilles, "Gender Studies Scholar," then stated, "When Loreta makes him a comrade in arms and really to the level of a warrior as the white soldiers and herself, it's really fascinating what she is doing. She is essentially humanizing the slaves." The Velazquez voice-over, in another accurate enough quote, stated, "He fights as well, as well as he knows how, like the rest of us. I confess that I am proud." Rene Sentilles, in somewhat of a tangent, continued:

> You only allow citizens who have the full rights of citizenship to fight. And women and African Americans don't really own this country. They're not- they're not citizens in the same way. They don't have full rights of citizenship. And once you allow someone to fight and put their life on the line, can you deny them those rights anymore?

Then Alemán stated, "For someone like Loreta Velazquez you have an immigrant trying to find a sense of identity within this country, and the way she does it is by fighting for it." Jesse Alemán continued, "There is a question about the relationship between Buford and Bob. They fight alongside side each other. They ride together. So, if anyone is in the know about Buford's secret, it would be Bob." The Velazquez voice-over, then stated, "My life depends on his keeping my secret."

Here are the problems with the passage.

First, Velazquez, in her book, made clear that Bob never knew her secret, so it is false for the Velazquez voice-over to represent Bob as willfully keeping her secret.

Second, if these scholars are trying to represent Bob and Buford's relationship as something special, maybe with some commonality in their goal for individual freedom and citizenship, it might be instructive to read what Velazquez wrote (p96):

> I... went to look after my boy Bob. The darkey was just beginning to have some appreciation of what fighting was really like, and was badly scared. I told him that if he ran off and left me, I would kill him if I ever caught him again.

Upon reading this, one might conclude that it would be a misrepresentation to state that Velazquez was "essentially humanizing the slaves." However, Velazquez did express her admiration at Bob's capacity to dig trenches and how he soon became accustomed to battle and was a good fighter. When Bob was lost to her (he ran away), she did not write she lost her comrade or some such thing, instead she stated (p218) she was deprived "of his valuable services."

Third, Velazquez never had a slave named Bob or any other. No newspaper reporter of the times ever said they saw an accompanying Bob. The Richmond *Examiner* of July 11, 1862 wrote that she claimed she followed the Confederate army with "medicines, bandages and servant," spending most of $20,000 doing it. This is the only newspaper discovered that mentions a servant. The servant was a lie, the nursing was a lie and the $20,000 was a lie.

Velazquez had little or no money (Remember the theft of the Chester's gold watch and chain?) with which to purchase an expensive eighteen-year-old male slave, the age and sex of which commanded the highest of premium, about $1,800 in 1860 money (or $66,300 in 2023).[13] To put the price in perspective, at this date a laborer made about 90 cents a day. Did Velazquez have the money for such a purchase? No. It has been shown beyond a doubt that Velazquez lied about her father and his source of wealth, thus her source of wealth was a lie.

Besides, she claimed (p49) that her father cut off her money upon his disapproval of her marriage. Recall the less than fourteen-year-old bride's marriage in 1856? But then amazingly Velazquez claimed (p68) she possessed $88,000 dollars with which to equip the battalion she raised in Arkansas in 1861. So, did fourteen-year-old Loreta have a bank account with $88,000 dollars (3.3 million dollars in 2023 money!) at the time her father disinherited her? She certainly had no time to earn any money, much less that kind of money, after her marriage because she was busy birthing her alleged three children. She claimed (p50) these children all died in 1860 and it was afterwards she commenced her military exploits.

Fourth, her inclusion of Bob in narrated events in which claimed her own, but provably false, participation would make his participation false as well, wouldn't it?

The fifth point of contention about the previous passage deals only with Velazquez and not Bob. Velazquez at no time stated her purpose for fighting was that as "an immigrant [she was] trying to find a sense of identity within this country." It is not clear on what basis scholar Jesse Alemán made this assertion since Velazquez's sole stated reason for fighting was that she had martial ambitions.

Moving on- the most reprehensible and seemingly purposeful misrepresentation of a fact is when the film addressed Ex-Confederate General Jubal Early involvement with Velazquez. By now, readers should

---

13. Robert Evans, Jr., *Aspects of Labor Economics* (NY: Aron Press, 1975, 1962),199. The relevant chapter is titled "The Economics of American Negro Labor."

be aware that General Early wrote a letter which contained criticism of Velazquez and her book, and if not, do some rereading.

The film quoted from General Early's letter:

> I came across Madame Velasquez's book, entitled "Woman in Battle," and gave it a cursory examination, from which I am satisfied that the writer of that book whether man or woman, had never had the adventures therein narrated. And I have expressed the same opinion to several presses in the city.

In other words, the film represented General Early as making complaints to the newspapers in order to damage Velazquez. This is simply untrue. There is no record that Jubal Early ever went to the newspapers with his criticism and the sole known criticism is a letter which was ostensibly never delivered to whom General Early thought to send it. The letter seems to have stopped with the man from who General Early sought advice on how to address Velazquez's appeals to him.

It is clear that the filmmaker and its historians, at best, misunderstood General Early's letter, or, at worse, purposefully misquoted General Early. Between the two sentences of the film's quote are an additional 295 words and these words need reading! To more accurately represent the truth of the quote, a larger swath is taken encompassing some of the avoided words:

> I gave this opinion also to the gentleman from Richmond referred to, at the same time expressing the belief that Madame Velasquez is not of Spanish birth or origin, but is an American and possible from the North.- This is the extent to which I have sought to depreciate Madame Velasquez or her book so far as Richmond is concerned; and I have expressed the same opinions to several persons in this city [Lynchburg, Virginia].

General Early did not write the word "presses," as asserted by the filmmaker, but instead wrote the word "persons." The content of the sentence makes clear that the word he wrote was "persons." General Early spoke to the gentleman from Richmond and then to spoke to several persons in Lynchburg. Is that clear, now? Did Lynchburg even have several presses?

At this point in the film, "Civil War Scholar" Gary Gallagher explained how General Jubal Early had "acquired a great deal of power." Gallagher continued, "If he disagreed with something that someone wrote and they didn't make the changes that he wanted he could be very effective in attacking them or having others attack them in various print forms." Of course, filmmaker Carter used Gallagher's statement to support her misrepresentation that General Early persecuted Velazquez. If Gallagher is correct that General Early was so effective in persecuting those with whom he had a disagreement and if General Early persecuted Velazquez, then where "are the various print forms" denouncing Velazquez. There is no known record of a public denunciation of Velazquez by General Early!

The film, moments later, showed an image of the book review which was published by the Southern Historical Society in its journal *Southern Historical Society Papers* which expressed mild criticism of the memoir. If the filmmaker's intent was to imply that Jubal Early, as an officer in the Society, had a hand in the review, it is not substantiated by fact or logic. The fact part is: Jubal Early wrote on May 22, 1878 that he first saw Velazquez's book "last winter" which was after the book review was published. In any case, Reverend Jones, Secretary of the Society and editor of the journal, most certainly wrote the review and that is who Velazquez understood wrote the review. The logic part is: if Jubal Early was so opposed to Velazquez and her book, why would he write such a mildly critical review when his alleged nature was to attack effectively all those he opposed? If Jubal Early had wished, he could have decimated Velazquez in the Society's book review (which he did not write anyway) or elsewhere. But he didn't, did he?

The film then depicted Jubal Early flipping Velazquez's book on a veranda table in disgust and Vicki L. Ruiz, "Scholar of U.S. History and Latino Studies," narrated, "How could this woman have infiltrated his ranks? Not only how could this woman have infiltrated his ranks, but how dare she write about his troops in that manner?" Ruiz's first question must have originated within Ruiz herself because Jubal Early never posed the question as to how Velazquez could have infiltrated his ranks. As for the second question, Jubal Early made clear his objection; he wrote that the book should not "be patronized by Southern men or women, for it is libel in both."

Ruiz implied General Early was only defensive of "his troops," but he, in fact, also was defensive of civilian women who Early thought Velazquez slandered. Please read Early's letter in the Appendix, Item 3.

Jesse Alemán explained about General Early, "He himself is at the start of an entire print culture that is remembering the Confederate cause through an ideological lens we now know of as the Lost Cause." Following up was "Rene Sentilles, Gender and Women's Studies Scholar," who stated, "Loreta is incredibly dangerous to the creation of a Confederate nationalism." How Sentilles arrived at this assertion is a mystery since the facts demonstrate that Velazquez and her book never received enough attention or sales to have been deemed "a danger to the creation of a Confederate nationalism." And besides the memoir would not have been a danger, but instead a boost to Confederate nationalism, as the entire theme of the memoir is Southern loyalty. Sentilles must have meant that Loreta was an aid in the creation of a Confederate nationalism which is dangerous thing.

Then the firm voice of a male narrator quoted from page 8 of General Early's letter, "Madame Velazquez may have been a follower of one or the other army in some capacity, but the book cannot be the truthful narrative of an army person [The underlining is mine, to be addressed momentarily]." There are several problems with this quote.

The first problem is that the quote is incomplete. Curiously, the camera is focused on the page of the letter as it is being read and it zooms-in just in time so that a viewer following the quote doesn't see the part of the quote which was omitted.

The second, and a greater problem, is that the quote is in error. The full and correct quote is, "Madame Velazquez may have been a follower of one or the other army in some capacity, but the book that is given to the public in her name cannot be a truthful narrative of the adventures of any person." It is impossible that a documentarian or historian with the habit of modest attention to his work could mistake the two words, "any person," for three words, "an army person." The error clearly changes the meaning of the sentence and certainly lowers the confidence level in the ability of the "scholar."

General Early's quote is further misused when DeAnne Blanton, "Senior Military Archivist, National Archives," explained to the viewer that the "sub context" of the term "camp follower" was Jubal Early's "way of saying [Velazquez] was a prostitute." Blanton's assertion is unfounded. Read the quote! General Early did not say that and Blanton is assuming he meant that. General Early said that Velazquez was a "follower" of the army "in some capacity."

To review: the "follower" quote was taken from Early's letter addressed to U.S. Congressman Slemons, whom Velazquez indicated she wished to use as a go-between. In this letter also is found an important sentence which settles whether or not General Early, in a sub contextual manner, called Velazquez a "prostitute." General Early wrote:

If the Hon. [Congressman] J. M. Glover, the Hon. [Congressman] A. H. Stephens, and Ex-Governor Brown, to whom Madame Velasquez refers me, can state that they are personally cognizant of her antecedent, or have any authentic knowledge or information of the part she had in the late war, and from such knowledge or information can vouch for her claims to consideration as a lady of character, then I will be willing to make every possible atonement for the wrong I may have done her, in thought as well in speech; but must not be expected under any circumstances, to accept the "Woman in Battle" as a true narrative.

In addition, to his friend Congressman Tucker, General Early wrote, "You must take into consideration the fact that she has the apparent endorsement of some forty-five Southern members of Congress."

Does Blanton believe that General Early was so stupid and vile that he would call a lady, whom he had just briefly met and was not even sure was the real author of the book to which he objected, a "prostitute" within the hearing (or reading) of powerful men, mostly Congressmen, whom Velazquez had identified, and General Early believed, to be her adherents and friends?!!!

If the reader chooses not to accept this defense of General Early, then consider this. The 1862 New Orleans newspapers identified Velazquez as an "inmate" of Nelly Bremer's "house of ill-fame." Clearly this was no accusation hidden in a "sub textual context," but a deliberate assertion. What, no criticism of that newspaper?!

Ok, everyone take a deep breath. General Early did not call Velazquez a prostitute. However, the newspapers did suggest that Velazquez was a prostitute. Velazquez rid herself of any association with that endeavor and she certainly had every opportunity to pursue the business in the mining camps of the American West if she so desired. She did not.

Just what was a "camp follower"? Author of *Battle Cries and Lullabies*, Linda Grant De Pauw ably wrote (p20):

> Female camp followers were usually wives, widows, or daughters of soldiers. Although most historical sources call them prostitutes, that usually meant that the women slept with their men after the day's work was done. Men without wives might pay for such service when they could not successfully court a sweetheart. Sweethearts as well as wives were valued for more than satisfying a pressing sexual urge. Caring for the soldier's physical needs- preparing his food, keeping him warm, dry, and clean, nursing him in illness- was the usual work of his woman.

So, does this description fit Velazquez? Recall, the New Orleans newspaper, when announcing her arrest in November 1862, wrote, "The police at once got on her track, and officer Conner finally succeeded in arresting her at Camp Lewis, where she was living as the wife of a soldier named Williams." By De Pauw's definition, does the reader dare conclude that Velazquez was a "camp follower"?

Historians Simkins and Patton in their 1936 book *The Women of the Confederacy* wrote (p75):

> The women who lived in camps usually did so in order that they might be near a soldier-son or soldier-husband. Among their many activities, conventional and unconventional to women, were rescuing the wounded, nursing the sick, praying for the dying, cooking delicacies, and mending worn clothes.

These historians then named several women who became renowned as camp followers:

> Another outstanding camp follower was Betty Sullivan, also an Irish woman attached to a Louisiana regiment. With canteens and bandages suspended from her

shoulders, she stood near the soldiers during battles in order to stanch their wounds and moisten their lips. Often she slept on the frozen ground, a blanket her sole covering, and a knapsack her only pillow. She was so beloved by the men of her regiment that they affectionately named her "Mother Sullivan," and it was said that there was not a man among them who would not have shed his blood for her.

Clearly the men of the regiment would have objected that their camp follower, Mother Sullivan, was considered a prostitute by the "sub context" of the term "camp follower" as DeAnne Blanton asserted.

The filmmaker then presented the scene when Velazquez called on General Jubal Early in the parlor of the hotel to protest that General Early had said to a mutual acquaintance that he believed her memoirs untruthful. The "General Early" character then raised his voice in hostility towards "Velazquez" and claimed, "You are no true type of Southern woman. I have the right to speak my opinion. I will speak it whether the author be a man or woman." Offended, the victimized Velazquez hurried away in near tears. The basis for this scene was solely the imagination of the director. Recall, this is the same courageous Velazquez who stood in many battles, exchanging musket shots with the enemy and survived years in the company of brutish soldiers, yet she went away, reduced to near tears by an elderly defeated ex-Confederate general, the likes of whom she claimed she routinely duped during the War.

Only Jubal Early left a record of the meeting and he in no way indicated that it was volatile. And it was most certainly not. Jubal Early represented himself as a gentleman; it is scarcely believable that he would have treated in such a rude manner a lady who called on him. Recall that General Early objected to how Velazquez had portrayed Confederate officers as "brutes." If he disliked that anyone thought Confederate officers were brutes, why would he conduct himself as a brute? Throughout the War, General Early associated with the Confederate officers whom he considered to be gentlemen. For the record, there were indeed some Confederate officers who were not gentleman and Jubal Early most likely would never have intended to include them in his defense of Confederate officers.

Catherine Clinton, "Women and Civil War Scholar," continued with the character assassination:

Jubal Early was an old soldier, glorious and here was this woman coming along making-up stories and he felt it was very easy, she was Hispanic, she was marginal. She was someone who he could easily attack and discredit and he did, so effectively that I think this label of hoax stuck with her book for almost a century.

Clinton's Freudian slip was showing when she said that Velazquez came "along making-up stories," because that was exactly the reason for Jubal Early's objections!

The true problem is that Clinton did not let the facts get in the way of her assertions. The facts are: First, General Early wrote that he did not believe Velazquez was Hispanic, so how could he have attacked Velazquez on that basis? Second, the public did not know of General Early's criticism, as that information was contained in a private letter, so to claim that General Early criticism caused the book to be viewed by the public as a hoax is simply unsubstantiated. In any case, the public did not need General Early to tell them the book was a hoax since the public too had suffered through the War and could recognize the innumerable exaggerations and lies in a book which represented itself as scrupulously true. The public, without Jubal Early's help, could make its own determination whether the memoir was truthful.

DeAnne Blanton, towards the film's end, referred to a portion of General Early's letter and said, "When General Early was criticizing Velazquez and her book and proclaiming loudly to anyone who would listen that she was a fraud, one of the things he specifically critiqued was her time she spent as a double agent in Washington, D.C. But what General Early couldn't have known is that in the files of the Provost Marshal, there was this document." Blanton then read (somewhat paraphrased) from the document while tracking the words with her finger as the camera took a close-up view:

This certifies that the bearer Mrs. Alice Williams on this day [Blanton pointing to the date], has been appointed as a U.S. Special Agent in Middle Department until further orders. This Alice Williams is indeed Loreta Velazquez.

In order to proceed with an analysis of Blanton's representation, it is informative to read exactly what General Early wrote on page 8 of his letter when he criticized Velazquez's double agent claim:

[Velazquez's] statements about flitting from one army in the Confederacy to another- of her being employed as a secret agent and going on business for the government to Washington, New York, Havana, Canada etc., and always having abundant means provided for her, and of her being in the secret service of the United States, at the same time she was in that of the Confederacy are simply incredible.

General Early found Velazquez's claims "simply incredible" and it is acceptable to restate that General Early "specifically critiqued" Velazquez's claim to have been a double agent. It is true that Velazquez went by the name Mrs. Alice Williams, as has been shown in the course of the book in hand. It is true that this document, Schenck's orders, shows a Mrs. Alice Williams was a "U.S. Special Agent." It has been shown previously why it is not believable that this "Mrs. Alice Williams" was Velazquez. However, a second document, Captain Ewald Over's (6th West Virginia Infantry) travel order "No. 330," makes it clear that "Lauretta DeCaulp" was "in secret service" of the United States. The Ewald document makes General Early wrong about the Union half of the double spy claim; so Early was at least half-wrong on that point. Just because Velazquez was employed as a Union agent does not make true her claimed marvelous deeds. And it was the claimed marvelous deeds which caused General Early to think them "simply incredible."

There is no Confederate record discovered to date which proves that Velazquez served in the Confederate secret service. It has been shown that her claimed mission (the trick General Winder played on her) as a Confederate agent delivering a message to the General Van Dorn was a lie because Van Dorn was already dead. It has been shown that her claim to have stolen Federal government bond printing plates which in turn helped finance the Confederate government was a lie. And it has been shown that her claimed spy trip to Richmond to carry back instructions to the plotters of the Johnson's Island prison break was a lie. It was these sorts of marvelous claims which General Early labeled "simply incredible." He did not call the claims lies, but as has been shown, he should have, because they were, so a reader might wish to conclude that the General understood what he was talking about.

Velazquez's explained (p399) her employment as a Southern agent, "Shortly after this my brother went South on a cartel of exchange, and in due time I received information that my message had been delivered, and that I was recognized as a Confederate secret service agent." But there are problems with the assertion.

First, notice that Velazquez did not name the head of the Confederate secret service and claim it was he who hired her (or anyone else by name); she probably didn't even know his name. And Confederate General Winder does not count as her employer. She wrote (p345) Winder gave her "a letter of recommendation to the commanding officer of the forces in the South and West." This letter was supposedly given to her when she was in Richmond, but it was a lie she was in Richmond then. She was in jail in New Orleans. A few pages afterwards she embellished (p349) the letter, "I was travelling under credentials from General Winder, and was in a manner an attaché of the Secret Service Department." No, she was given a letter of recommendation, and even that was a lie. So, she refused to name her Confederate employer, but she willingly told readers that Colonel Baker hired her for the Federal secret service.

Second, her brother carried her message South? Nothing Velazquez wrote about this brother was true. Velazquez did not go North to help him out of prison; she went to be with her deserter husband. Velazquez invented the brother in order to avoid any admission that her husband went North. Her brother, at least this brother, did not exist. After this mention of her brother, her next mention of him places him in New York and the war is in progress. How is it he went South to recommit to the Southern Cause and yet Velazquez has him surprisingly still (or once again) in the North just when it is convenient for her to include him in her European trip storyline? "Simply incredible."

DeAnne Blanton was either blissfully ignorant or purposefully deceitful about the contents of the document she presented. Didn't Blanton read in totality the document in her hand? Didn't Blanton compare the contents of the document to what Velazquez wrote in *The Woman in Battle*, which Blanton ostensibly had read?

What Blanton did not tell the audience and what the camera angle prohibited the viewer from seeing was that the order's signatory was Maj. Gen Robert C. Schenck. The camera angle also makes it difficult to read the order's contents: "She will report only to me...." It might be supposed that the signatory's name and the content of the order were omitted purposefully by the film's director in order to avoid the messy task of an explanation.

The explanation is this. Velazquez, in her book, did not claim she was hired by Maj. Gen Robert C. Schenck, but instead she claimed she was hired by Colonel Baker of the U.S. Secret Service. Velazquez claimed she reported to Baker, which is in contradiction to this document which instructed her to report only to Schenck. One of Velazquez's most dubious claims (p516) was that Baker hired her to find herself. No document discovered shows that Velazquez worked for Baker. A discerning reader, upon reading Velazquez's "simply incredible" claims of association with Baker, will conclude Velazquez lied. Please see elsewhere in the book in hand other facts which contribute substantially to doubts about her ridiculous claim to have been hired by Baker "to find herself."

Much earlier in the film, Carman Cumming, "Journalist and Civil War Scholar," made a keen observation relevant to Velazquez's spying:

> Then she disappears from the South and according to her story, she crossed the line to come north to spy. It appears that she works at the Baltimore Provost Marshal Office keeping watch on spies and smugglers and so forth. And the records there seem to indicate that her job there was to turn in disloyal people or to search female suspects. The big question is, was she spying on the north or was she defecting. The records in the North have to do with the Baltimore hiring of Alice Williams. They seem to suggest that instead of spying on the North, she was defecting.

Cumming's question of Velazquez's possible defection is reasonable and better than maybe he realized. The reason that Velazquez went North was to reunite with her husband, Confederate Captain Thomas DeCaulp, who had deserted, gone North and even joined the Yankee army. However, to say that Velazquez defected might be too harsh, as her allegiance to the

South is questionable in the first place. Recall, prior to her marriage to DeCaulp, she was married to Williams, a Yankee soldier of the 13th Connecticut Regiment which was then occupying New Orleans. Recall as well, when she was arrested in New Orleans in 1862 at the time of her alleged marriage to Williams, the newspaper wrote of her statement to the court, "She declared that she was now strongly for the Union, and was raising her children up to revere the old flag."

At this point in the film, 1860's newspaper articles about Velazquez are floated passed the camera with sentences or paragraphs highlighted. These are the same articles scattered throughout the book in hand and have been analyzed in detail. This display was seemingly used to imply the veracity of Velazquez's claimed deeds as told in her memoirs. At best, the articles confirm the existence of Velazquez, which was never in question anyway. If the filmmaker and scholar contributors had examined the articles with curiosity, the huge contradictions contained in the articles would have made Velazquez's lies clear. Velazquez told multiple versions of her forever changing story to the newspapers and they printed what she said. The newspapers did not and could not have known what to print without her telling them. Her claimed deeds were not and are not validated in any manner by the floating past of these newspaper articles.

Curiously, neither the filmmaker nor the film's "scholars," mentioned that these articles were hugely contradictory to Velazquez's book. A case in point is the flashed article which was originally from an 1862 New Orleans newspaper when "Anne Williams" was arrested for stealing jewelry. She told the newspaper (or court) that she had been "wounded in the engagement [Battle of Shiloh] as a member of the 11th Louisiana." How is it possible that the filmmaker and the "scholars" did not see this statement as a lie, since Velazquez wrote (p205) in her book, "I was delighted beyond measure in an opportunity to take part in a great battle [of Shiloh] with my own company that I had raised over in the Arkansas swamp…." Then she wrote, "Glancing over the field [of Shiloh], I saw the eleventh Louisiana regiment, with a friend of mine, and a brave officer, Colonel Sam. Marks, at its head…." And when she wrote of her wounding, she claimed it was <u>after</u> the Battle of Shiloh when she was burying some dead soldiers. At least, one of the two versions should have been an apparent lie to the "scholars."

This, and a hundred other contradictions and lies, could have been investigated by the filmmaker and its "scholars" if they had wished to make a true documentary. Instead, they made a film which was a misrepresentation of the authentic Velazquez, and worse, it was a misrepresentation of what Velazquez wrote about herself and her deeds.

The reason for this failure might be explained by one of the "scholars" in her concluding monolog. Elizabeth D. Leonard, "Civil War Scholar," stated:

> The absolute truth of one thing or another in the book is not the most important contribution that the book makes. It's the presence of the book, the fury that it provoked, the claims that it makes, the reality it tries to portray.

Let's rephrase these two sentences into four sentences to see if it is possible to understand them better. 1) The truth is not important for a "truthful" memoir. 2) The memoir is important because of "the fury that it provoked" in the people who were sold a "truthful" book, but found it to be an untruthful. 3) The memoir is important because of "the claims it makes," even if the claims were untrue. 4) The memoir is important because of "the reality it tries to portray," even if the reality or its portrayal was untrue. This rephrasing is possibly too complicated.

For a true simplification it might be instructive to look seven minutes earlier in the film when DeAnne Blanton stated, "The way I view Loreta's book is that she took her life story and she made it a little better." Blanton included a hand gesture indicating abundance and radiated an impish smile. If embellishments make Velazquez's memoir "a little better," then may it be concluded that lies could make the memoir greatly better? Curiously, Blanton was either oblivious to the lies or purposefully avoided their mention. Of course, any acknowledgement of Velazquez's lies would have thrown the film off of its storyline.

It would be time consuming and painful for the reader to view a list of every misrepresentation and/or omission worthy of commentary. If the reader harbors any doubts that the film is a failure as a documentary, read Velazquez's memoirs, then view the film and form one's own conclusion. To echo, but alter somewhat, Jubal Early's admonition: This film "ought not be patronized by [any] men or women, for it is libel," that is, to the definition of the word, "documentary."

This film put words in Velazquez's mouth and misrepresented Velazquez's memoir. Worse still, the filmmaker did not even try to address the contradictions found in the historical record or the obvious lies in her memoir. Recall that Velazquez claimed her memoir was "relate[d] with simplicity and truth." Sadly, the film is a "documentary" which lacks truth about an autobiography which lacks truth!

Most abhorrent is the fact that the film was a hit piece on General Jubal Early. This contemporary of Velazquez's wrote, in his now infamous letter, very precise objections which identified falsehoods. He identified failures in the memoir which caused him to believe Velazquez was not truthful. With the exception of General Early's doubt about Velazquez's double agent roll, which was a minor part of the General's objections, the filmmaker did not address General Early's more important objections to see if they had any merit. Instead, Director Carter and her contributing "scholars" assassinated Jubal Early's character and portrayed him as a wild-eye misogynist, instead of presenting historical or factual evidence to prove his assertions wrong.

To conclude on a positive note, the film is attractive with good cinematography, enjoyable music, and interesting settings and period costumes.

It will be seen that the film gets further attention in 2014 in this chronology.

2013, Part Two of the *Cuban Art News* (May 28) article "Rebel: A Cuban-American Woman in the U.S. Civil War" by Nadine Covert. In this second part the author interviewed María Agui Carter, director/maker of the film *Rebel*. The interview was likely before the PBS showing *Rebel*, but the article was published after.

Carter revealed that she came across Velazquez's memoir "in the Harvard Widener Library" and then "began to question why [Velazquez] was not part of our national history." In 2000 Carter started her research and finished cutting the film in 2013, and explained:

Part of the theme of this film is an examination of the politics of memory. History is always crafted; there is never just one objective version of a story, because each story is filtered through personal and cultural and political experience and viewpoint.

Velazquez crafted lies into her history? The "politics of memory" caused Velazquez to write two different versions about her approaching First Manassas, each from a different direction, and then forgetting to remove one of the lies? And when a "story is filtered through personal and cultural and political experience and viewpoint" does that filter remove the lies or just ignore them?

Carter concluded, "Loreta's personal journey starting out as a Confederate soldier and ending as a double agent spying for the Union, and ultimately speaking out against slavery later in life, echoes a very fascinating personal growth of an immigrant who comes to embrace the American ideals of democracy." It is not clear where Carter's assertion that Velazquez spoke out against slavery later in life derives- none was found during research of the book in hand. And if cheating investors out of money to build a fake railroad; cheating Miss Brody, the Los Angeles typist, out of pay; cheating the Binders out of six months room rent and cheating the old gentleman attendant at the Philadelphia department store with his co-signing her purchases constitute coming to embrace American ideals of democracy, then what more can anyone say?

2013, *Civil War Times*, October, Vol 52, Issue 5, pages 26-27. Sarah Richardson interviewed *Rebel* documentary filmmaker María Agui Carter, who explained she "became so intrigued with the historical evidence surrounding Velazquez's account that she spent 10 years researching Velazquez's story."

The occasion of the interview was mostly an opportunity to promote the film, but the interviewer did ask two good questions which Carter managed with soft answers. One question was, "Have people challenged the film's accuracy?" Of course, Carter did not name any historian who might have criticized the film, but instead answered, "The point of the film is to make people think critically about historical storytelling and to say historical storytelling is interpretation, and you need to understand who is telling that story and what their interpretation is." And Carter went on for three more sentences. What happened to documentarian Carter's "detective story"?

The next question was, "Has Velazquez's combat experience been verified?" Carter answered that Velazquez wrote about Fort Donelson, about being wounded at Shiloh, about being at the First Battle of Bull Run and at the Battle of Ball's Bluff, but said "you won't find her in regimental histories," which is correct. Carter then explained that Velazquez and other women soldiers were discovered in other ways, for example, "doctors discovered the dead bodies in the battleground," women soldiers were mentioned in letters home by men soldiers and the newspaper reported women being discovered and arrested. Carter concluded with, "I can't verify Loreta's service from regimental histories, but I can verify from arrest reports that she's wandering around in uniform and injured." Yes, it is well documented that Velazquez was arrested wearing a male military uniform. It also is documented that Velazquez told the newspapers many conflicting versions of her battlefield wounds, which obviously means that some claims, if not all, are false. The newspapers in no way verified her claimed injuries as battle related or her claimed deeds on the battlefield and neither could Carter.

Just to clarify a point which Carter didn't; Velazquez claimed while in soldier's disguise she operated as an independent, never enlisting in any regiment or company, so naturally there would be no record. But Velazquez claimed (p181) one exception, when she successfully enlisted "in Captain B. Moses' company, of the twenty-first Louisiana regiment" in order for her to slip out of New Orleans undetected by the mayor. A soldier's record for "Harry T. Buford," Velazquez's alias, should exist in the records for this company and regiment, yet it does not. Wonder why?[14]

---

14. NARA, CMSR, Washington, D.C.

2013, *The Routledge Encyclopedia of Civil War Era Biographies* by John D. Wright. In this 752-page volume author Wright presented the biographies of a vast number of Civil War era people and Velazquez was included alphabetically. In three extensive paragraphs Wright retells Velazquez's memoir with some accuracy, but also with inaccuracies.

Wright wrote that Velazquez "was educated at a convent school in New Orleans." No, Velazquez did not write the school was a convent school, she wrote only that it was run by the Sisters of Charity. Wright also wrote, "Velazquez joined her original Arkansas regiment at Shiloh where she was wounded in the side, and camp doctors discovered her sex." No, Velazquez did not write that! She wrote (p225-226) she was wounded "in the arm and shoulder" and the wounding occurred on the day after the two-day Battle of Shiloh and she did not claim at the time of the wounding that she was with her "Arkansas regiment." Velazquez did not write she was discovered by "camp doctors," but instead wrote that she went to Corinth, Mississippi where she sought treatment from "a young surgeon whom [she] knew intimately." When the doctor examined her arm, she saw the puzzled look on the doctor's face and she then decided "concealment would be useless" and told the doctor who she really was, of course to his total astonishment.

Wright noted Velazquez's life span was "1840- c.1897," which conflicts with the birth date, June 26, 1842, Velazquez claimed in her memoir. Of course, author Wright had no way to know her death date.

Wright concluded her memoir "is the only information about her, and some have distrusted Velazquez's claims...."

Criticism of Wright's handling of Velazquez is in no way intended to reflect negatively on the hundreds of other biographies of the robust *Encyclopedia*.

2014, a brochure by the National Park Service, U.S. Department of the Interior, titled "Shiloh" and subtitled "The Contributions of Women in the Civil War" and sub-subtitled of "With Bayonet and Sword They Served." The first paragraph of the article begins, "In one way or another all women were involved in the Civil War," which is true. The second paragraph begins with, "Not all who wore the uniform were men," which is true. The third, fourth and fifth paragraphs address Velazquez:

Loretta [*sic*] Velazquez donned the Confederate uniform, enlisted as Lieutenant Harry T. Buford and recruited a company of volunteers from Arkansas. In the spring of 1862, after fleeing from authorities who had discovered her sex, she enlisted with the 21st Louisiana Infantry. According to Loretta, her participation in the Battle of Shiloh was her greatest military triumph. On the battlefield, her regiment became engaged alongside the men she had recruited in Arkansas:

We had not long been engaged before the second lieutenant of the company fell. I immediately stepped into his place, and assumed the command. This action was greeted by a hearty cheer from the entire company... This cheer from the men was an immense inspiration to me...(it) encouraged me to dare everything, and to shrink from nothing to render myself deserving of their praises.

After the battle Velazquez was wounded by a shell while burying the dead. An army doctor once again discovered that she was a woman. Believing that too many people knew her true identity, she finally gave up the uniform.

The National Park Service has unwittingly accepted falsehoods, and worse still, misread what Velazquez wrote.

First, Velazquez never claimed that she "enlisted" as a "Lieutenant." She just called herself one. Velazquez explained (*TWIB*, p37) that she assumed "the *pseudonyme* of Lieutenant Harry T. Buford." Velazquez never claimed to have "recruited a company," but instead claimed she recruited 236 man "battalion." The Park Service should understand that lieutenants did not recruit companies or battalions. Captains recruited companies. Generally, after companies were formed, an election was held by the men to select their lieutenants.

Second, the Park Service historian must have gotten very confused. Velazquez in her book did not claim that she was with "her regiment" (the 21st Louisiana Infantry Regiment?) which fought beside the men she had recruited in Arkansas; the Park Service seems to be saying this, maybe not intentionally. Velazquez claimed somewhat the opposite! She wrote (p205) she was with her Arkansas men and Captain DeCaulp, and looked over to see her friends in the 11th Louisiana Infantry Regiment. In her memoir, Velazquez did claim she enlisted in the 21st Louisiana Infantry, but that was before the Battle of Shiloh and she said she had left that regiment well before that battle. In any case, the 21st Louisiana Infantry did not fight at Shiloh because the 21st was not there! For the record, the 11th Regiment was there.

Third, her alleged "company of volunteers from Arkansas" did not participate in the Battle of Shiloh simply because they too were nowhere near that field. Velazquez unwittingly trapped herself in her own lie when she told her readers that Captain Thomas DeCaulp and her Arkansas boys were there. Military records are clear that Captain DeCaulp was with the 3rd Arkansas Cavalry and the 3rd was not at the Battle of Shiloh! It logically follows that if her Arkansas boys were not there, then she could not have assumed command of them, as she claimed she did in her memoir or she could not have looked over at them during the battle, like the National Park Service asserted she did.

The Park Service brochure gave suggestions for further reading on the topic of contributions of women in the Civil War and *The Woman in Battle* was not among the five books listed. The original date of the brochure's creation is not clear, but it is placed in year 2014 of the chronology because it was noted then; it may or may not still be in print.

There is another National Park Service publication (in print in 2015) titled "Vicksburg" with the subtitle, "A Culture Transformed- Women in the Civil War." On page three of the four-page brochure is found Loreta Velazquez, under the subtitle "They Fought as Men." Velazquez's picture in uniform is presented along with those of other women who served during the Civil War: Pauline Cushman, Frances Clayton, Sarah Edmonds, Jennie Hodgers alias Albert Casher, and Almeda Summer Butler Hart alias James Strong. Only the last two women's stories were given in summary; nothing of Velazquez was written.

2014, the National Museum of Civil War Medicine in Frederick, MD, placard exhibit:

Loreta Janeta Velazquez
Loreta Janeta Velazquez was born in Havana, Cuba, in January 1842. At age seven she was sent to New Orleans, Louisiana, to live with an aunt. She left school at age fourteen, against her family's wishes, to marry an officer of the United States Army. In 1861, her husband resigned to join the Confederate Army, and Velasquez [sic] disguised herself as an army officer named Lieutenant Harry T. Buford in order to join her husband in Florida, where he was assigned. Her husband died from a carbine explosion a few days after her arrival.

Velasquez [sic] then headed to the front, still dressed as Buford. She fought at Blackburn's Ford and First Manassas, and at Ball's Bluff in October of 1861 she was given temporary command of a company whose officers were killed. Velazquez then went west to join her dead husband's regiment and was at the Battle of Fort Donelson in February of 1862. While working as a scout she received a wound to the foot and sought medical attention, did not stay in the hospital because she feared discovery. She was wounded in the arm at Shiloh in April of 1862 while on a burial detail.

Her next adventures entailed carrying dispatches and working to catch spies in Richmond, and later as a double-agent in Washington, DC. In 1864 Velasquez [sic] became a Confederate operative in Canada and Great Britain, selling counterfeit United States bonds in an attempt to bankrupt the Union. Following the war she went to Europe with her family, then returned to New Orleans, remarried, and moved to Venezuela. She was last heard of in 1878, living in Rio de Janeiro, Brazil.

Velazquez never claimed she was born in January 1842, but instead said (p40) her birth was on June 26, 1842, all explained in subchapter "My Birth."

It is not totally correct to assert that Velazquez "left school at age fourteen, against her family's wishes, to marry an officer of the United States Army." Precisely, Velazquez wrote (p48) she married "William" on April 5, 1856 which would have made her 13 years, 9 months and 10 days of age. Furthermore, Velazquez did not state her family's sentiment about her leaving school; she only said that her family harshly rejected William's request to marry her.

Velazquez did not claim she "went west to join her dead husband's regiment," instead she said (p204) she went west where she by chance happened upon the company she raised in Arkansas.

Velazquez did not assert she went to Europe to sell "counterfeit United States bonds in an attempt to bankrupt the Union," instead she wrote (p505) she went to dump Confederate bonds at any price she could get before the bottom fell out.

These points are simply the ones the historian could have learned had they read Velazquez's memoir; instead, the historian invented claims on Velazquez's behalf. Of course, the outright (and more important) errors contained in the exhibit have already been covered and will not be repeated here.

Velazquez's exhibited biography was presented in a manner that a casual reader would be willing to accept as true, in other words, devoid of any of Velazquez's unbelievable claims which might cause a reader to doubt the truthfulness of Velazquez's story. If Velazquez's story is wonderful and worthy of belief, why didn't the historian present the best of Velazquez's claims up front? Remember the claims? Velazquez, while disguised as a Confederate lieutenant, raised a "battalion" of 236 men at her own expense! And, Velazquez took command of two different companies in two different battles whose officers had all been killed! And, Velazquez refused to assassinate General Grant at Shiloh when she had the opportunity because it felt too much like murder! Did the historian fear that if they presented what Velazquez actually wrote, the audience would reject it? Was the historian promoting a memoir they knew contained lies? Or was their complicity unintentional because the historian was simply uninformed? Either way, the exhibit sustains the myth of Velazquez, not to mention twisting the truth.

The condemnation of this one exhibit should in no way be taken as criticism of the totality of the National Museum of Civil War Medicine.

2014, *Unsung Heroes: The Story of America's Female Patriots*. This two-hour film was presented on Public Broadcasting Service (PBS) in May and the production's stated goals were "to educate the American public about the heroic service of America's Female Patriots" and "to facilitate discussion and strategic thinking at the high school and college levels about the service and contributions of American service women throughout history." The film is well-done, admirable in its goals and successful.[15]

However, the film stepped out of its stated goals and injected Velazquez's name among the American Female Patriots. Recall, Velazquez fought

---

15. unsungheroeseducation.com.

against America. (Must we accept Robert E. Lee was an American Male Patriot?) The production included in its photo gallery the sketches of Velazquez both as herself and as disguised soldier Lieutenant Harry T. Buford.

Commentor Francoise Bonnell, Ph.D., evoked Velazquez (for the Confederacy) and Sara Edmond (for the Union) as examples of women who disguised themselves as men and fought in the Civil War. Bonnell said that Velazquez disguised herself as a man, "joined the Confederate Army" and that both Edmonds and Velazquez fought and "survived the battle of Bull Run and would go on to fight in other conflicts as well." The production noted that "Dr. Bonnell is the director of the U.S. Army Women's Museum at Fort Lee, Virginia and a recognized authority in women's military history" and that she is a retired U.S. Army lieutenant colonel.

There is more to the project than just the film; there is an accompanying "Education Package, Advanced Classroom Version, U.S. Army Educational Edition Teacher's Guide" written by Krewasky A. Salter, Ph. D:

> While there are varying accounts of women's participation during the Seminole Wars and Mexican American War, the best-documented depictions of women warriors and participants emerged during the Civil War. [Skip three sentences.] Loreta Janeta Velazquez, a somewhat controversial historical figure because some have strongly disputed her claims of service, was believed to have disguised herself as Confederate Lt. Harry T. Buford and served in various locations and roles throughout the war.

Almost to author Salter's credit, he noted that Velazquez was "a somewhat controversial historical figure," but his sentence is rather curious. Is Salter saying that Velazquez unjustly became a controversial historical figure because there are those who have disputed her claims of service which others believe present no problem, and therefore, she should never have become a controversial figure?

In addition, it is a huge stretch to call Velazquez's memoir a "best-documented depiction" of a woman warrior when even the meekest of readers can see it is clearly embellished and now the informed reader understands it is full of lies. Shouldn't a claim of extraordinary feats be verified by just a modicum of documentation?

But Krewasky A. Salter did not speak for all involved in the project, evident by the accompanying disclaimer to the Guide which stated:

> The views within this curriculum represent the opinions of the author and should not be taken to represent the views of the Department of the Army, the Department of Defense, the United States Government, or the Office of the Assistant Secretary of the Army, Manpower and Reserve Affairs or its members.

hair, wore a false mustache and beard, and called herself Harry Buford. She became an officer, even led men into battle. She claimed, "Fear was a word I did not know the meaning of."

No, Velazquez did not <u>become</u> an officer, she simply called herself an officer and the other assertions supporting Velazquez's claims can, by now, be readily determined erroneous by the reader.

Excepting the Velazquez representation, all the museums of the quartet, and particularly the Civil War Museum of the Western Theater, are impressive.

2016, *Inventing Loreta Velasquez, Confederate Soldier Impersonator, Media Celebrity, and Con Artist* by William C. Davis. In 358 pages including notes, author Davis astutely explains many falsehoods of Velazquez's creation.

2019, *Behind the Rifle, Women Soldiers in Civil War Mississippi* by Shelby Harriel. Author Harriel was mostly warned off of Velazquez by William Davis' inventing Velazquez book, so presented only some likely sightings of Velazquez. Harriel noted the *Charlotte Times* newspaper of September 30, 1864 had reported "a woman soldier from Mississippi passed through the city on a train bound for Richmond... may well have been... Velazquez." (pages 166-67) But it was not, since at that date Velazquez was with her deserter husband Decaulp at Fort Snelling, Minnesota, as noted by General Sibley in his August 11, 1864 letter (previously addressed).

Author Harriel correctly noted (page 98) two soldiers who in their diaries wrote of Velazquez when she was in Chattanooga. Soldier Hodges saw Velazquez, and soldier Oldham wrote she was in town. These events have been addressed.

Sustained Myth Concluded

In her author's preface, Velazquez questioned how the public would receive her memoir and gave somewhat of an explanation what actions or activity the reader was going to find therein. Here at the end of the book in hand, it is good to review what she said her readership might read about and compare it to discovered, and now known, facts:

> I do not know what the good people who will read this book will think of me. My career has differed materially from that of most women; and some things that I have done have shocked persons for whom I have every respect, however much my ideas of propriety may differ from theirs. I can only say, however, that in my opinion there was nothing essentially improper in my putting on the uniform of a Confederate officer for the purpose of taking an active part in the war; and, as when on the field of battle, in camp, and during long and toilsome marches, I endeavored, not without success, to display a courage and fortitude not inferior to the most courageous of the men around me, and as I never did aught to disgrace the uniform

I wore, but, on the contrary, won the hearty commendation of my comrades, I feel that I have nothing to be ashamed of. Had I believed that my book needed any apologies on this score, it would never have been written; and, having written it, I am willing to submit my conduct to the judgment of the public, with a confidence that I will at least receive due credit for the motives by which I was animated.

1) It is unclear what "good people" think of her memoir, but fact driven researchers think the memoir contains an unacceptable mass of lies, that is, for a memoir which Velazquez claimed was written with "simplicity and truth."

2) No "shocked persons" were discovered during research, maybe with the exception of General Early, who was not shocked, but thought Velazquez had slandered the reputation of Southerners, and expressed that opinion in a private letter.

3) Velazquez told her readers how they might read about her "active part in the war," for example, "on the field of battle, in camp, and during long and toilsome marches." However, her every account of a field of battle has huge flaws (and lies) which simply render her accounts unbelievable. Even though Velazquez presented a section titled "Camp Life" in Chapter III, she never gave enough detail of her activity in any camp to convince the reader she lived in one. She claimed she was on "long and toilsome marches," yet never once did she write of a single one. She always conveniently had plenty of horses for transportation and always claimed she was a solo act, never with others on "long and toilsome marches." She might have inadvertently told the truth when she wrote (p340), "I had seen enough of fighting, enough of marching, enough of camp life...." Yes, "seen," not participated in them.

4) Velazquez claimed she "displayed courage and fortitude not inferior to the most courageous men around [her]" and that she "won the hearty commendation of [her] comrades," but as has been seen, no research has yet revealed a battlefield comrade who vouched for her. However, recall there were people who stated they knew of her during the War, saw her in her disguise, under arrest, or at a train station, etc. Velazquez existed.

5) Velazquez wrote she wished to "at least receive due credit for the motives by which [she] was animated." Simply restated, Velazquez wished, invented or imagined much animation and for that she wished to get credit. Remember her professed meeting with Jefferson Davis which has been shown a lie? Credit anyone, anyone?

One wonders if Velazquez inadvertently truthfully stated the facts when, early in her memoir, she wrote (p37) that she would narrate the "many adventures that befell [her] while playing the part of a warrior." If taken at her word, was she "playing" warrior? She might have more easily written that she was a warrior, if it was the truth.

One also wonders if Velazquez didn't cryptically address her readers when she wrote (p131):

The way to keep a secret, as I had long since found out, is not to tell it to anybody; and acting upon this very excellent principle, I have generally succeeded in keeping my secrets- and I have, in my time, had some important ones- until the proper moment for revealing them came.

Velazquez has been successful in keeping probably most of her secrets.

Writers, scholars and historians, particularly those who never bothered to read the memoir, and who have asserted, or unwittingly supported, Velazquez's memoir to be truthful, now know. Velazquez was not truthful, was not what she professed to be and did not do what she claimed she did on any matter of importance. Enough about her life and memoir has been discovered to reach this conclusion. Some of her narrated travels and activities were truthful, even though twisted in the telling.

Curious readers, who simply wished to untangle the lies from the truths in Velazquez's memoir, now know. Velazquez was seldom content to give an honest account of her activities, but instead she was pathologically driven to lie.

Proponents of women in the military, who have held up Velazquez as a success story, now know. They should seek safer ground by selecting as their Civil War model a praiseworthy woman of the estimated 400-1000 women who served during the War.

And proponents, who have found metaphorical meaning in Velazquez's memoir which led/lead them to elucidate on cross-dressing, transsexuality, lesbianism or any sexuality at all, now know. Velazquez's lies were simply lies and not a mechanism to connect the American Civil War to sexual symbolism.

Everyone now knows General Jubal Early was/is a victim of misrepresentation and has been unjustly lambasted. Everyone now knows Velazquez was not a Texas writer. Everyone now knows the difference between a company, a battalion and a regiment. You say you are still not clear about these points? Oh, please do let me explain…

A Parable

Maybe a variation of a rather unknown joke about Mr. Boudreaux and his duck-retrieving dog, Buddy, illustrates the point.

Boudreaux was a Louisiana bayou-roaming duck hunter who was renowned for bagging his limit in record time, every trip out to the swamp. Other hunters begged him to take them along so that they might learn the secret of his success. One day Boudreaux relented and allowed Pierre to accompany him and his bird dog, Buddy.

The hunters had barely gotten settled in the hunting blind when some ducks flew overhead and they opened fired. Pierre was rather off balance so fell from his seat and hit his head on a rib of the skiff and lost consciousness. At that same moment Buddy went over the side of the boat with a splash and swam about retrieving all the ducks, a boat load at that. Boudreaux had his hands full trying to revive Pierre and getting Buddy back in the boat. Boudreaux made Pierre comfortable and waited for him to regain consciousness. In the meantime, he dried off Buddy and brushed out his shiny coat and then the dog sat very pleased in the warm sunshine and fresh breeze.

After a long time, Pierre awoke with man and dog staring at him and was rather embarrassed at his rather wimpy nap. The self-professed superior huntsman Pierre did not wish to admit how long he had been out, so he woozily marveled that the boat was full of ducks, but Buddy was dry- so Buddy must have walked on the water to retrieve the ducks. Boudreaux grinned at this narcotic notion and mischievously asserted that it was indeed true and confessed that was the reason he had never let anyone come along before, to witness this wonder.

Later in town, when Pierre was asked about their very successful hunt and was pressed on details, he told how Buddy walked across the water to retrieve the ducks. Pierre wasn't about to admit he slept away the day in the bottom of a skiff. His listeners raised their eyebrows, but Pierre insisted it was true- he was there. In short order, Pierre died when a crawfish he was eating got crosswise in his throat. Pierre had so convincingly told and retold his story that now the town folk marveled and hounded Boudreaux to take them on a hunt.

Boudreaux was so pestered that he pulled-up stakes and went to the Florida Everglades to bag ducks. There, hunters asked him about his home and he told them that he had to leave because everyone wanted to see his dog walk on water. One Florida hunter was sure that his leg was being pulled so wrote a letter to the Louisiana town folk and they replied, yes, it is true Louisiana water dogs are superior in every way to Florida retrievers, especially the one that walks on the water.

One day a Florida hunter took a shot which peppered nearby Buddy. Boudreaux thought the shot a purposeful, jealous one. After the hunter apologized, Boudreaux understood the shot was accidental and it had not injured Buddy anyway. Then the following day an alligator charged a nearby hunter's skiff causing great damage and injury to that hunting party. Boudreaux and Buddy soon wearied of these sorts of things, so departed and next traveled to the Chesapeake Bay.

Boudreaux was astounded to see wall to wall ducks floating in the Bay. Unfortunately, he was driving on the Bay Bridge and was in no position to hunt ducks. Anyway, he had no money to buy shotgun shells. He tried to console himself.

It was time for a break from hunting, so Boudreaux, a dog lover to his core, headed to New York to see the Westminster Kennel Club competition. Boudreaux, of course, made no attempt to enter Buddy in the competition, the old scarred working dog that he was, but Buddy sat contented in the stands with Boudreaux and likewise enjoyed the competition.

Since the hunting duo was in New York, the Mecca of book publishing, Boudreaux figured to write a book about his amazing hunting adventures with Buddy. Boudreaux asserted, "I will 'relate my story with simplicity and truth,' but also due to the fact that some of my notes got soggy in the bottom of the skiff, I was 'compelled to rely entirely upon my memory.'" The book's editor asserted, "There are thousands of hunters who can bear testimony [and] there are abundant witnesses whose testimony will not be disputed."

Boudreaux wrote:

Buddy is a special dog- many can "bear testimony" that he can walk on water, for example, the "thousands" of the Louisiana hometown folk....

Once in Florida in the pursuit of ducks, Buddy was shot by a stray shell. Actually, he was wounded one, or two, or three, or four times on day one, or day two, or day three of the hunt. The wound was in his "right shoulder," or "hand," or "foot," or "neck," or "wrist," or "breast," or "his shoulder was found to be out of place and his arm cut and his little finger lacerated"....

Later we experienced a brutal alligator attack on our skiff. We count ourselves lucky to be the sole male survivor and the sole dog survivor of the catastrophe.

This in no way dampened our courage; we sought bigger water and more challenges and thus went to the Chesapeake Bay. There we saw so many ducks we felt it would have been "too much like murder" to hunt them, and "we could not bring ourselves to do the deed," so we continued on our way to New York where I got Buddy into the Westminster Kennel Club show. Well, Buddy didn't win, but some dog flesh experts who knew of his "unblemished reputation" back home protested that he should have won because of "his integrity, his energy and his ability."

Over the years, Boudreaux's book has had its detractors because of the seeming falsehoods; readers do believe true Boudreaux's and Buddy's existence, only not their adventures- and this in spite of the fact that the book's editor claimed Boudreaux's "narrative is exact in every particular, with regard to the facts" and is an "authentic account."

The book has been successful to some degree and is still in print and should be read by those "fond of the marvelous," it is titled: *Lying Like a Dog: the Adventures of Buddy and Boudreaux*.

Acknowledgements

Sandy Heaxt, Administrative Officer at the West Florida Public Library Genealogy Branch, stands out for her tireless work locating historical microfilms throughout the country. Señor Eduardo Erigoyen García in La Habana Vieja (Old Havana) conducted a search for Velazquez's claimed birth and baptism. Journalist Albor Rodríguez in Ciudad Bolívar, Venezuela found two Velazquez letters. Irene Wainwright, Archivist, Greg Osborn and other staff at the New Orleans Public Library, Special Collections located microfilm of Velazquez's marriage to Wasson, Charity Hospital admission records and newspaper articles about the Venezuelan emigration scheme.

Thank you to the staff at the A. S. Williams III Americana Collection, Amelia Gayle Gorgas Library, University of Alabama, Tuscaloosa for access to the *Battle House Guest Register 1863* which contains the registration of "Lieut. H. Buford" and thanks to A. Steve Williams for donating this and his entire collection to the University.

Sue Nelson, Senior Deputy Recorder at the Lander County (Nevada) Recorder Office, located the marriage certificate of E. H. Bonner and Velazquez. A thank you to Lander County Recorder, Idonna M. Trevino, and staff, Barbara Brooks and Donna Kelley, for access to the records room which contains mining records for Reese River Mining District, Austin, Nevada which revealed business transactions of E. H. Bonner. Nancy Gordon, Director of the Austin Museum, opened the museum which led to the discovery of three ore assays for E. H. Bonner. Gail Morehead, owner of the International Cafe and Bar in Austin since 2007, served up some good meals and provided some information about the International. Cindy Garcia, owner of the Cozy Mountain Motel, showed Austin's hospitality, lent me a book about historic Austin and directed me to some residents with whom to speak. Gail Utter at the Austin Court House provided access of 1860's and 70's *Reese River Reveille* newspaper. In Salt Lake City at This is the Place Heritage Park, Jim Davis, provided a personal tour of the Andrus House and a thank you to the friendly and helpful staff and volunteers at the Family History Library.

The North Carolina State Archives located the marriage documents of McLeod and Velazquez. The New York City Archive located marriage records for Beard and Velazquez. Andrene Messer of Falkirk, England, supplied valuable information on William Beard, who was her great-great uncle. New York County Clerk of the Court provided the lawsuit records of Beard vs Hayes. The Clerk also provided the legal documents of William Beard's lawsuit against John J. Safely.

Andrew Goldstein, Curator of the Valdez (Alaska) Museum, provided gold rush information and a contact for Andrene Messer of Falkirk,

England. John M. Coski, Historian and Director of Library and Research at The Museum of the Confederacy provided Velazquez's letters to J. William Jones. The Library of Congress and the New York Public Library provided copies of Velazquez's "Address to the American Congress on Cuba." The Vital Records Division, District of Columbia, Department of Health located the death certificate for Velazquez.

The Cedar Hill Cemetery in Suitland, Maryland provided the location of Velazquez's grave and Mr. Martin E. Evans, Family Service Counselor, at Cedar Hill Cemetery assisted me in locating the gravesite.

Kelly Wooten, Librarian at Research Services and Collection Development, David M. Rubenstein Rare Books & Manuscript Library at Duke University Library provided a copy of General Longstreet's letter to Miss. E. W. Parks. Thanks to Wakefield Harper and Matthew Turi at the Southern Historical Collection, University Archives, Southern Folklife Collection, Louis Round Wilson Special Collections Library at The University of North Carolina at Chapel Hill for providing the Velazquez letter to Jubal Early and Jubal Early's letters to J. R. Tucker and Congressman Slemons.

The Mobile (Alabama) Public Library, Local History and Genealogy Services, and Mr. H. F. "Tige" Marston, Cemetery Specialists and City Sexton for Magnolia Cemetery, aided in locating the grave of William Burnet. Archivist L. Eileen Parris, at the Virginia Historical Society, provided information on the Mary Washington Monument Association. The Louisiana Secretary of State, Division of Archives, Records Management, and History provided the death certificate for Jeff Bonner.

Dr. Anita J. Morgan, History Professor at University of Indiana-Purdue University Indianapolis provided the location at the Indiana State Archives of the payroll records for Indiana Arsenal which contains Lauretta DeCaulp's payroll record and Michael Vetman, Archivist at the Indiana State Archives, sent them to me. Dr. Morgan provided a copy of Mrs. Lauretta J. DeCaulp's letter to Indiana Governor Morton and the location of the letter in the archive.

Tom Hester, volunteer at the Silver City Museum, located references to E. H. Bonner's mining years in Silver City, New Mexico and researcher Doc Campbell located the Bonners' advertisement for the Keystone Hotel in Silver City and information about Bonner's activity as Justice of the Peace and Bonner's correct date of death. Steve Meadow from www.waroftherebellion.com (Civil War Photographs, Albumen's, CDV's, Ephemera, Memorabilia & Other Interesting Historical Items for the discriminating Collector) provided the photo of General Milo S. Hascall. The University of West Florida and the West Florida Regional Library provided microfilm and an abundance of books about the Civil War, necessary background reading. The U.S. National Archives and Records Administration (NARA) in Washington, D.C. and Atlanta provided Civil War military records and documents on Velazquez's insanity hearing and confinement at St. Elizabeth's Hospital.

James A. Morgan III, preeminent Ball's Bluff historian and the author of *A Little Short of Boats: The Civil War Battles of Ball's Bluff and Edwards Ferry* (2004 & 2011), gave me a first-class tour of the battlefield of Ball's Bluff and his book provided information necessary to know in order to consider the truth of Velazquez's claimed participation in the battle.

Thank you to Dr. Richard A. Weaver, retired Captain Medical Corps US Navy, for reading and commenting on an early manuscript. Alan Manning, author and attorney, read the manuscript and wrote the backcover praise for which I am grateful. John Nevin Shaffer Jr., retired Navy Commander, patent attorney and author, read and offered suggestions on the manuscript. Retired Marine Brig. General Larry Garrett read the proof and gave much appreciated guidance.

A special thanks to John Leo Post, my brother, and Jeanne Demory Post, his wife, for valuable suggestions and encouragement.

I am indebted to the authors who have earlier endeavored to address Velazquez's memoir, *The Woman in Battle*. It is because of their efforts my work was less strenuous in some regards, but more difficult in others.

A thank you is given to all who contributed and my apology for any omission of organizations and people who helped.

Appendix

The letters presented are transcribed by the author of the book in hand and any errors are mine. Original punctuation and spelling are retained. The handwritten letters were on narrower stationery so the sentences were shorter per line and here have been allowed to fill the page space available. An occasional word is unclear/unknown and is indicated by [?]

Item 1

Madame L. J. Velasquez's [*sic*] letter to General Jubal Early of which he made a copy, verbatim et literatim, and sent the copy to friend J. R. Tucker. Today this letter is archived in the Tucker Family Papers, #02605, Southern Historical Collection, The Wilson Library, University of North Carolina at Chapel Hill; by permission.

Velazquez's letter is read with some difficulty because of her lack of correct usage of capitalization, commas and periods.

A Copy-   Enc. [5-26-78]
House of Representatives
Washington D.C. May 18, 1878

General Jubal Early,
My diar [*sic*] Sir

I am prompted by a high sense of honor to write you the following. while I have been advised by gentlemen who know me and my position Socially and Publickly [*sic*] information has reached me from a Richmond that you was Endeavoring to injure me and my <u>Book</u>. owing to Some incorrect dates. which I will call your attention to my Editors <u>Preface</u> I had to trust to memory having lost many of my <u>notes</u>. You know that a Subordinate had not the Same opportunities of knowing the order of their Superior Officers. I had to gather my information from my own personal Observation of the movements of our army and the officers under who I had the honor to serve with. We can not See such a gigantic Struggle from the same Stand Point for no writer ever seen or wrote alike. I do not pretend to know Even one tenth

[page 2]

that transpired upon any one Battlefield I served upon. I only Endeavor to give the most important facts. that came under my immediate observation. I might have been more Explicit in some points in my work, and ought have given names connected with the facts. but let me say to you my reasons for this is first I had to condense my manuscript on account of Pecuniary [?- embarrassments]. Second I felt for many of those men's families who was concerned in defrauding the Government, for some of the members of their families who was young ladies. whom I did not wish to taint their innocent names with their Parents misdeeds. they may read the statement while their names were not exposed to the public. it would not offend the innocent. for none of us want our parents faults heralded to the <u>world</u>. Now General, if you have any suggestions to make please let me hear from you. for my Book and Correspondence with the Press is my entire support of myself and little Son. (My health is failing,) and my whole souls devotion is the education of him who is to live after I have passed away. This know [*sic* no] one

[page 3]

knows than the "Hon" J.M. Glover, A.H. Stephens, Ex Governor John C. Brown & a host of others who know my labors and devotion this writer has been to him and the prosperity of our glorious Sunny South- No one man or a section of men can deter me from my duty to her (may god Bless her and her people.) for I have had trials Enough to have driven almost any proud spirited woman to madness, or to commit suicide. but I have struggled and born my lot with the hope of prosperity before me. casting the buffeting of my inferiors. beneath my feet and with Gods Protection I have lived above it all. and all I now ask from you is justice to my <u>child</u>. I live for him and him alone. with the most profound regard for you as a gentleman of culture and a patriot I have the honor to remain

Yours Most Respectfully
Madame L. J. Velasquez or H. T. Buford C.S.A.
Correspondent Le Buletin de Commercial
Rio de Juanairo
Empire Brazil
House Representatives care of "Hon" W.H. Slemmons. Washington DC.

[General Early added an explanatory "Note."] Note- The within letter is copied literally with capital letters, punctuation and all just as they are in the original. There are one or two instances in which a and is wanting, and in such cases the deficit was probably from mistake or oversight. Certain words are underscored as in the original. J.A.E.

Item 2

Jubal Early's letter to Congressman John Randolph Tucker, in the Tucker Family Papers, #02605, Southern Historical Collection, The Wilson Library, University of North Carolina at Chapel Hill; by permission.

Lynchburg May 24, 1878

Dear Sir:

Since I wrote you I have received a letter from Madame Velasquez. I'm sending in an envelope to the Hon. W. F. Slemons of Arkansas, an exact copy of the Madame's letter and a letter to him in reply to it. I desire you to read these, and they will explain themselves.

After writing the letter I have had some hesitation about sending it. My question is whether I should take any notice of Madame Velasquez's letter to me. I have some doubts on the subject, though I don't want her to be able to say that she has written to me

[page 2]

and silenced me. I have no idea of having a direct correspondence with her and under the circumstances it has occurred to me that if I notice the letter at all it would be proper to do so by a letter to the gentleman to whose care she requests me to direct my answer.

I submit this matter to your judgement and decision, and I wish you to read the letter to me & same to the Hon. Mr. Slemons, and then say whether the letter shall be delivered. I do not desire to involve a gentleman against his will in any complications with Madame Velasquez.

It has struck me that

[page 3]

if Mr. Slemons is not cognizant of the liberty Madame Velasquez has taken with his name, then he should not be then [?] of any communication with him directly or indirectly. But if he was informed of her purpose, and authorized the use of his name, then it occurs to me that there would be no impropriety in my writing to him directly.

I submit the whole matter to your judgment and will be content to abide by it.

If you prefer you can consult Colonel Crittens in the subject- You may not, I wish Mr. Slemons to understand that [?] [?] indignity in discounting to him is intended. I will leave for New Orleans

[page 4]

in the morning and if it becomes necessary for me to have seen you, you can within the next three weeks direct a letter to me at New Orleans, care of Box No. 692.-

Excuse me for troubling you with this matter, but as you are on the ground, you can better understand whether Madame Velasquez's status is such as to require any notice of her. [Above the last three words of the sentence there is a three-word insertion which looks like "Then I can."]

You must take into consideration the fact that she has the apparent endorsement of some forty-fifty Southern members of Congress.

                            Yours most truly

Hon. J. Ran Tucker   JA Early

Item 3
Jubal Early's letter to Congressman Slemons, in the Tucker Family Papers, #2605, Southern Historical Collection, The Wilson Library, University of North Carolina at Chapel Hill; by permission.

[Enclosure 5-26-78]
Lynchburg, Virginia, May 22nd 1878

Dear Sir:

I must first explain why I address this communication to you. Three days ago I received from "Madame L. J. Velasquez or H. T. Buford CSA" as she calls herself, a letter of which I send enclosed a copy made <u>verbatim et literatim</u>, with the orthography, punctuation, and grammatical structure just as they are in the original. Being indisposed to have a correspondence with Madame Velasquez personally in reference to the subject mentioned in her letter, I address this communication to you directly, because I understand, from the memorandum at the bottom of her letter, that she desires any reply I may make to that letter to be addressed to your care. If this memorandum of hers is without warrant from you, then you must pardon the liberty I take, and make such disposition of this communication as you may think proper; but if it has your sanction, then you can show to Madame Velasquez what I will now write to you.

In reference to the statement she makes that she has received information from Richmond that I have been endeavoring to injure her and her book, I have

[page 2]

this to state: When I was in New Orleans last winter I came across Madame Velasquez's book, entitled "Woman in Battle," and gave it a cursory examination, from which I was satisfied that the writer of that book whether man or woman, had never had the adventures therein narrated. I saw no one who could give me any information about any such character as the heroine of the story, and the whole subject had passed out of my mind until two weeks ago._ At that time I met at the hotel here at which I am boarding, a gentleman from Richmond, who informed me that he had traveled, on the [railroad] cars from Danville to this place, with a lady who had served in the Confederate Army as an officer, and since published a book containing a history of her adventures, which he had bought. On his giving me the name of the lady and her <u>nom de guerre</u>, I recognized them as that of the person whose adventures was narrated in the book I had seen and I at once said to him that she could not be what she pretended to be. He produced the book, and I pointed out to him several inconsistencies, absurdities, and impossibilities in it which I thought proved beyond all question, the writer of it to be a mere pretender. I subsequently had a brief interview with Madame Velasquez, upon being informed

[page 3]

by a servant that a lady wished to see me in the parlor of the hotel, and I thus became satisfied that she had not written the book of which she professed to be the author, or that it had been very much changed and improved in style by her editor. I gave this opinion also to the gentleman from Richmond referred to, at the same time expressing the belief that Madame Velasquez is not of Spanish birth or origin, but is an American and probable from the North. This is the extent to which I have sought to depreciate Madame Velasquez or her book so far as Richmond is concerned; and I have expressed the same opinions to several persons in this city [Lynchburg]. My reasons for entertaining them are as follows:

In the first place, the manner in which she claims to have supplanted in love her bosom friend, and married her first husband, is not calculated to produce a favorable impression of her character. See her book pp 45 to 49. Then her failure to give the name of her first husband, who she says, was an officer of the United States Army and resigned therefrom to go into that of the Confederate States, is a suspicious circumstance. She has no hesitation about giving her own maiden name, with an account of

[page 4]

her descent from a noted Spanish family whose name she still bears after four marriages; but then we have no means of ascertaining the correctness of her story in that respect, while if she had given the name of her first husband and he was an officer of the US Army who joined that of the Confederacy, then correctness or incorrectness of the story might be easily ascertained. She has no hesitation about giving the names of her 2nd and 3rd husbands, but their histories cannot be traced, and she fails to give that of the fourth, or, so far as I have been able to discover, to account for his disappearance. In the next place, she starts her husband (no 1), on the 8th of April 1861, dressed in full Confederate uniform, to Richmond, to meet General R. E. Lee and a number of others, when Virginia had not seceded at that time and was not expected to secede, and General Lee was still an officer in the US Army; and when the Confederate uniform had not then been adopted._ Moreover, she has Memphis at that time in a ferment about the approaching war, with a number of officers in uniform carousing around the drinking saloons and threatening to demolish the Yankees immediately, though Tennessee had refused to secede- See pp 52 to 69.-

[page 5]

Then directly after her husband left for Richmond she assumed male attire, putting on the Confederate uniform, and ran over to Arkansas where at a way station suggested to her by the rail-road conductor, she got out and in four days in the month of April 1861 raised a battalion of volunteers comprised of 236 men enlisted for three months. These she equipped at her own expense appointing all the officers for the battalion, who consisted at first of a sergeant and a corporal, and afterwards of a 1st and 2nd Lieutenant in addition all being appointed by her sole authority. She marched the battalion to Memphis, and then carried it down the river to New Orleans, and from there through Mobile to Pensacola, where she turned it over to her astonished husband, who was killed in a very few days by the explosion of a carbine while he was drilling the battalion and showing a sergeant how to handle the weapon. This battalion had been raised without the instrumentality of the Governor of Arkansas, or of the President of the Confederacy, or without her saying to others as much as "by your leave" and carried just as how she thought proper, all the expenses being paid out of her own pocket; though where the money came from is an unsolved mystery, as her father had cast her off on her

[page 6]

marriage, and it does not appear her husband had anything but his pay as an officer in the army. See pp 70 to 87. If you were then a resident of Arkansas, especially if you entered the Confederate Army, you can form some opinion of the correctness of this story. If not, ask Colonel Cravens and Colonel Van Manning about it. After the death of her husband, Madame Velasquez, still in male attire, left Pensacola on the 16th of June 1861 for Richmond, Va, via Montgomery, Ala & Columbia, S. C. At the latter place she stopped for several days, and then took "the train bound North" for Richmond, and passed through Lynchburg in her route where she stayed over night thus filling up the gap in the rail-road from Greensboro N. C. to Lynchburg Va though (except from Greensboro to Danville where the road was made during the war,) the road here not really been made until since 1870. See pp 88 to 90.

Then she fought on the 18th of July 1861 at Blackburn's ford on Bull Run, she being at Mitchell's ford a mile off, and being put in command of a company whose captain was killed, though she had no commission. She then slept on the battle field all night until daybreak on the 19th when she put on her <u>boots</u> and took after the line of march through Ashby's Gap in the Blue Ridge

[page 7]

& Piedmont on the Manassas Gap rail-road, from whence she went over the rail-road to Manassas_ See pp 95 to 98. If you don't understand the geography of that part of the country ask my friends General Hunter and Colonel Cabill, whose names I observe in Madame Velasquez's credentials, about the matter. To perform that feat her boots must have been made out of the same matter with the seven league boots of which we read in fairy tales.

Another remarkable exploit of hers was in the fall of 1863, when she joined Longstreet at Charlotte N. C., then on his way to join Bragg at Chickamauga, and went with him to Atlanta, where she received information that Van Dorn's head-quarters were at Spring Hill, and that her then betrothed (husband no 2) was with him. She endeavored to get to them, but failed it is presumed because Van Dorn was killed in the May previous. See pp 288 to 293.

These are some of the points of her narrative which struck me while merely skimming over her book, as being entirely inconsistent with the character of a truthful chronicle. There are many other statements which I could point out to show that the writer of the book is not telling the truth and they can not seem statements of facts about which men engaged in battle might differ because they

[page 8]

viewed these from different stand-points. Her statements about flitting from one army in the Confederacy to another_ of her being employed as a secret agent and going on business for the government to Washington, New York, Havana, Canada, etc, and always having abundant means provided for her, and of her being in the secret service of the United States, at the same time she was in that of the Confederacy, are simply incredible.

Madame Velasquez may have been a follower of one or the other army in some capacity, but the book that is given to the public in her name cannot be a truthful narrative of the adventures of any person. If intended as a work of fiction, then it is one which ought not to be patronized by Southern men or women, for it is a libel in both. Nearly all the Confederate officers she describes are drunken, gasconading brutes, whose mouths are constantly filled with obscene language, and the women, especially the young and pretty ones, are in ready to throw themselves into the arms of the dashing "Lieutenant Harry T. Buford", and surrender without waiting to be asked, all that is dear to women of virtue.

Madame Velasquez herself is no true type of a Southern woman, and the women she describes are not

[page 9]

fair specimens of the pure and devoted women who followed with their prayers the armies of the Confederate States through all their struggles and trials.

This is the impression made on me by reading the "Women in Battle" even very cursorily, and the more I see of it the deeper my convictions become._ I have no disposition to injure the alleged author of that book, and still less to deprive her of the means of training and educating her child;

but I cherish most devotedly the character and fame of the Confederate armies, and of the people of the South, especially of the women of the South, and when a book affecting all these is sought to be palmed on the public as true, and has on its face the evidence of its want of authenticity, then I have the right to speak my opinion and will speak it whether the author be man or woman._

I should be sorry to believe that either of the Southern members of Congress, who have signed Madame Velasquez's credentials, would, after having read her book carefully, be willing to place it in the hands of his wife or daughter, with a commendation of its morality.

If the Hon. J. M. Glover, the Hon. A. H. Stephens, and Ex-governor Brown, to whom Madame Velasquez

[page 10]

refers me, can state that they are personally cognizant of her antecedent, or have any authentic knowledge or information of the part she had in the late war, and from such knowledge or information can vouch for her claims to consideration as a lady of character, then I will be willing to make every possible atonement for the wrong I may have done her, in thought as well as in speech; but must not be expected under any circumstances, to accept the "Woman in Battle" as a true narrative.

If the author of that book is the same with the author of the letter to me, then her style must have deteriorated very much since the former was written. It will be seen, according to the story in the book, that Madame Velasquez received a thorough English education, and the solecisms in grammar contained in her letter do not result from the broken English of a foreigner, but are the blunders of an American whose education is imperfect._ Her appearance and voice are those of an American woman, and has no resemblance to those of a cultivated Spanish lady._ If she is really Spanish in origin, then her association with Camp life have thoroughly Americanized her.-

[page 11]

Pardon me, sir, for thus troubling you with my reasons for doubting Madame Velasquez's story and identity with the character she has assumed.

Having been taken to task for questioning the claims if [?-you] [?-ask] has, to some extent the endorsement of a number of members of Congress from the South, I deem it necessary and proper to give the reasons which impelled me to do so, and I do not know how I could better do it than by addressing them to you to whom she refers me.-

Very Respectfully
Your Obt Sert
JA Early
Hon W. F. Slemons M. C. [Member Congress]

Item 4

General James Longstreet's letter to Miss Emmy W. Park, in the David M. Rubenstein Rare Book & Manuscript Library at Duke University, Durham, North Carolina; by permission.

Gainesville Ga [Georgia]
18 June 1888

Miss Emmy W Park
Dorchester Mass
Dear Lady
Your favor of this 15th instant is received and noted.

There was a woman in the ranks with us who became Lieutenant and called her name Buford though I did not know her until some years after the war. Her enterprise after the war was a trip to the Rocky Mountains, with a party of men in her disguise as Lieutenant

[page 2]

Buford. The party had much trouble with the Indians, lost their horses and had to travel afoot a great distance. When she gave out and her comrades had to assist her, in that way she became known. Afterwards she had success in gold speculations, and became a belle of course in Nevada. She referred her suitors to me, but I had not known of her in the ranks, nor as Lieutenant, and could only attest of points she gave for identification. She was married out west and passed through New Orleans when I was there and then I met her, the only time of my life. I cannot now recall her maiden name, nor her name after marriage. Her adventures as she gave them and as they were given by his [*sic*] western suitors were remarkable.

Most respectfully yours
James Longstreet

Item 5

The Southern Historical Society published a review of *The Woman in Battle* in its journal, *Southern Historical Society Papers*, October 1876 edition, Vol. II, No. 4.

Book Notices

The Woman in Battle- Madame L. J. Velasquez [*sic*], otherwise known as Lieutenant Harry T. Buford, Confederate States Army. Richmond, Virginia: Dustin, Gilman & Co. 1876.

We have received this book from the publishers through their agent, Rev. Aaron Jones. It purports to give the adventures of a woman who disguised herself as a man, fought gallantly in a number of battles, rendered most important services as a Confederate spy, and had various hair-breath escapes, and most romantic and thrilling adventures. As to the reality of the existence of such a personage, there can be no reasonable doubt. The publishers' circular contains certificates from Drs. J. F. Hammond and M. D. L. McCleod of Atlanta, Georgia; Major G. W. Alexander, of Washington, Georgia [sic D.C.]; Major John Newman, of New Orleans, and General George Anderson, of Atlanta, all testifying that Madame Velasquez [sic] and Lieutenant Harry T. Buford, Confederate States Army, were one and the same individual. Major Alexander says that she was well known to him, and that "she was particularly distinguished for her devotion to the cause, for which she made many sacrifices. She was also brave, noble, and generous in disposition, ready at all times to do anything in her power for the Confederacy." We have met with several Confederate officers who were cognizant of the fact that such a personage did figure in the Confederacy, and who saw her upon several occasions.

The book is one which will be eagerly read by those who are fond of the marvelous, and is undoubtedly one which possesses much interest for the general reader. How far it can be received as history, is altogether another question. E. g., we may read with interest this narrative of personal adventure without being forced to explain how this dashing Lieutenant could have fought with Beauregard at Blackburn's ford on the 18th of July, 1861, and yet have been with Johnston, who marched from Winchester to Beauregard's relief on the same day- how he happened to be at so many battles fought by different armies in different sections of the country- or how he managed to accomplish various other physical impossibilities. Nor could we endorse many of the opinions of men and things so confidently expressed.

We can only say that it is a very readable book, and would serve well to while away a winter's evening.

Item 6

Velazquez wrote a letter which acknowledged and protested the review; this letter is archived in the Eleanor S. Brockenbrough Library, The Museum of the Confederacy, Richmond, Virginia; by permission.

All original syntax, spelling, capitalization and punctuation are retained. Velazquez seldom used commas, but periods instead, so many of the periods must be read as commas. The original handwritten letter consisted of shorter sentences on narrower stationery, but here the sentences have been allowed to fill the page. The use of [sic] is omitted.

Roliegh. NC. October 27 1876

Rev W. Jones
Respective Sir,

I have received a copy of your Southern Historical Society Papers for Oct Vol II. No 4 in which you have given my work (Woman in Battle) a Short notice, accep my thanks for the liberal and kind words you Speak in my behalf, Yet Suffer me to call your attention to a few Points- 1st the work was not intended as a history of the late war between the States, 2nd I was with Beauregard on the 18th at least he was in Command of the Entire Command of the Army he Ranked General Johnston. only as a Senior Officer. for both were Major Generals. if you will take the trouble to reread my work on Page 96 You will find I state this fact, and on page 98. I state that General Johnston. came on the Field at noon on the 20th from Winchester. Where he was holding the enemy in Check. Commanded by Gen Patterson on the 18th. You will call to mind my commission was a recruiting. that I only was 5 months in the Army regular. After that

[page 2]

I belonged to the Independent Scouts. and my movements was comparatively free. If it were necessary I could give Satisfactory evidence of all my movements from Army to Army- in different Sections of the country. My opinion of men and events are given as I was impressed at the time and of Course are only my Own Opinions made up from the stand point I occupied-

Thanking you again for your kindness and accepting all criticism with proper appreciation I am

Very Respectfully
Madame L. J. Velasquez

Item 7

Velazquez followed her first letter with a second which indicates that Reverend William Jones did not answer the first. This second letter is archived in the Eleanor S. Brockenbrough Library, The Museum of the Confederacy, Richmond, Virginia; by permission. The letter is presented verbatim; the use of [*sic*] is omitted.

Roliegh NC Nov 12 1876

J. William Jones D.D
Richmond, Va
Dear Sir

I wrote you a letter some time ago calling Your attention to your own Error of date in the notice You were pleased to give my Book. I was with the Army in different Sections of the country which many living will cheerfully testify. I do not expect Every One to endorse my Opinions of men and things as they are my Own and Expressed as I was impressed by them. I think your notice is unfair and unjust to me and would ask you to reconsider the matter, I Only ask Simple Justice and can give you any required amount of testimony as to my <u>acts</u> and identity. I went to Leesburg from Manas. [Manassas] via Richmond & Linchburg. to be in that Battle. Troops are moving. during war. all the time. Will you

[page 2]

please to mention to me by letter the Other physical impossibilities I accomplished. it will afford me much Pleasure to give you a Satisfactory Solution of what appears to you as a "Physical impossibility" Enclosed please find stamps for you reply.

  Very Respectfully Yours
  Madame L. J. Velasquez

Abbreviations

Ass- Association
Chap- Chapter
CMSR- Compiled Military Service Records
Comm- Commerce
CSS- Confederate States Ship, designation for Confederate Navy
Dept- Department
Ed- Edition
GPO- Government Publishing Office
LOC- Library of Congress
Ltr- Letter
M- Microfilm
MS- Manuscript
NARA- National Archives and Records Administration
NOAA- National Oceanic and Atmospheric Administration
Off- Official
OR- *The War of the Rebellion: a Compilation of the Official Records of the Union and Confederate Armies*
RG- Record Group
Sec- Section
Ser- Series
TWIB- The Woman in Battle
USS- United States Ship, designation for United States Navy
Vol- Volume
Wash- Washington

About the Author

William L. Post Jr. is a keen enthusiast of U.S. Civil War history and of early U.S. history. He enjoys traveling and exploring sites of Civil War action. In particular, he relished his trip to the "Old West" researching this book. Over the years, he has travelled to many overseas destinations, some of which, by chance, were also claimed destinations of Madame Velazquez.

William is a 1975 Auburn University, Bachelor of Science graduate.

Index

A

Abercrombie, Captain William R. 507, 510, 516
Acton, Tom McCarroll 377
Adams, George Rollie 232
Adamson, Robert........................ 517–19
Addicks, J. Edwards...............................499
age
    1874 interview, about 35 years.....326
    1891 interview, 46 years 464
    1900 interview, 50 years 534
    1900 newspaper, "nearly three score" 539
    1905 New York City Census, 60 years..551
    at death, 79 years 570
    at Tyner's Station, "about 17 years" 189
    betrothed, 9 years 530
    married
        Beard, "Age next Birthday," 44 years..454
        Bobo, 31 years 274
        Burnet
            (implied), interview, 17 years 401
            13 years... 46
            intieview, 13 years 529
            interview, "under fourteen" 307
        McLeod, 34 years 394
        onboard *Elba*, 28 years 227
Alaska, Velazquez did not go to. 514–15
Albuquerque, New Mexico, visit, August 2, 1900 532
Alemán, Jesse...... 386, 624–30, 640, 644, 650, 659–63
Alexander, Captain G. W.....94–96, 353, 437
    in Harvey Birch's letter...................106
    publisher's circular...........379–80, 702
alias
    Arnold.. 19
    Mrs... 35
    Mrs. M. A. 423
    Mrs. M. M. 26
Bachman... 36

Beard
    Madame L. J. V. 477
    Mrs. Loretta J................................ 464
    Mrs. Sallie 499
    Mrs. William................................... 508
Benford, Henry.................. 51, 92, 345
Benford, Lieutenant..................... 83
Bensford, Lieutenant 90, 92
Bonner
    Loratita Juanita........................... 453
    Mrs. E. H.. 301
    Mrs. Lauretta J............................. 256
Buford
    H. T..404
    Lieutenant H. T...........................78, 97
    Lieutenant Harry T..................301
    Lieutenant, first newspaper use 17
Burnett, Mrs. William E. 307
Clapp, Loretta Jeanett.................... 307
DeCamp, Mrs. Loretta 153
DeCaulp
    Mrs. Jeruth 101
    Mrs. Lauretta J............................ 109
    Mrs. Lorreta J. 166
    Mrs. Major L. J. 131
    Mrs. Mary 185
Gibbons 26
Goddard, Loretta J. R................... 452
Keith
    Mrs. Martha 17
    Mrs. Mary Ann 13, 17
McLeod, Mrs. M. D. 394
Roach
    Lieutenant 153
    maiden name............................. 153
    Rouch, in error................ 596, 649
Velasquez
    Lorateta J.................................... 448
    Loreteta J.................................... 444
    Madame L. J............391, 404, 428
Velazquez
    Loreta Janeta................................ 2
Wasson
    Laura 227
    Lauretta 198
    Lauretta J.................................... 251

Loretta J. 274
Williams
    Anne 35
    Lauretta, born Clark...................47
    Mrs. Alice..................................90
    Mrs. Laura J..............................51
    Mrs. Lauretta J. 97
    Mrs. Lauretta Tennett................78
    Mrs. S. T. 92, 93
Alliance, steamer...................................504
Alta City, Utah 260–64
Anderson, General George T. 380–82
Andrus Halfway House.......................266
Andrus, Bishop Milo...........................265
apocryphal, asserted
    Francis B. Simkins and James W.
        Patton...587
    Washington Herald..............................560
Arkansas
    Arkadelphia, living in 422–23
    Hulbert Station4, 5, 22, 418, 568, 598
    resident 48, 51, 423
Arnold, Philip............................... 329–37
    death..337
    Great Diamond Hoax of 1872 .. 335–37
    visit to jailed Arnold................ 329–30
arrested
    Lynchburg, taken to Richmond 12
    Mobile, taken to Richmond 83–96
    Nashville................................... 129–37
    New Orleans, first...................... 19–21
    New Orleans, second................ 35–37
    New Orleans, second, escaped and
        recaptured....................................47
    New York City 474–75
    Richmond...17
Arrowhead Springs, California.... 519–22
As Businesslike as a Man article..........464
asylum for the disabled.................183, 207
Atlanta Hotel.....104, 171, 309, 352, 354,
    See Thompson Hotel
Atlanta, Georgia
    visit
        December 27, 1900....................536
        defended husband's honor, May
            9, 1866.....................................167
        September 4, 1874....................307
Augusta, Georgia
    visit
        May 12, 1866 168

        under Forrest and Stuart claim,
            May 22, 1866 175
Austin, Nevada 243–58
    cost of living...................................244
    International Hotel........................246
    Reese River Mining District..........245
Ayers, Captain Romeyn B. *See* Sherman's
    Battery

B

Bailey, Captain Theodorus....................27
Baker, Lafayette C.
    analysis of Velazquez hiring. 146, 669
    Dunham, association with.... 493, 495
    hired Velazquez....111, 124, 127, 343,
        431
    hired Velazquez to find herself 146
    Velazquez, alleged resignation.....130,
        132
Baltimore, Maryland, living in............397
Banderas Bay 525, 533, 540, 541, 543
Barnouw, Erik, Honorable Mention
    Award...679
Battle House Hotel 76–78
    Buford, Lieut. H., C.S.A., registered
       77
    companions 77
    guest register....................................81
Battle of
    Ball's Bluff............................... 58–64
        Baker, Colonel Edward D., death
            of..61
        Confederate artillery in battle....61
        Devens, Colonel Charles, escape
            62–63
        expected battle.............................59
        Featherston, Colonel Winfield63–
            64
        Harrison's Island 61
        Morgan III, James A. [author,
            historian]................................61
        shot and killed a Union major...61
        Testicle's Bluff 608
        took charge of a company 60
    Belmont..20
    Bull Run (Manassas)........93, 173, 501
        7th Louisiana Regiment, a
            member.............................. 42–44
        already occured 18
        claim by

film 643, 678
newspaper 19, 35–37, 180, 420, 553, 556, 585, 609, 640
Traveling Trunk Program .. 649
writer .. 550, 553, 590, 592, 600, 608, 610, 619, 622, 623, 634, 650, 673
Colonel Charley Dreux *See* Dreux, Colonel Charley
contradiction 179
first claim at 19
Full Metal Corset, depiction in 643
General Bonham gave permission 11
General James Longstreet 460
General Jubal Early
   objection 416–17, 698
   presence 638
memoir 18
mention, lack of 16
Mitchell's Ford 316
Reverend W. J. Jones, mentioned in letter to 376
Texas company .... *See* Texas, company claim
two separate locations 373, 632
Chapultepec 529
Harrison's Island ... *See* Battle of Ball's Bluff
Leesburg .... *See* Battle of Ball's Bluff
Manassas .... *See* Battle of Bull Run
Rowlett's Station .... *See* Battle of Woodsonville
Shiloh
   10th Tennessee Regiment, not at 70, 369
   11th Louisiana Regiment .. 36, 44–45
   Hastings, Lieutenant Philip 70–72
      analysis of 72
   motivation 21
   participation 21–24
   wounded 69–70
   Woodsonville 6, 155
Battle, Sue 431
Beard, William 453–58
   death of 503–16
      murder asserted 505–13, 515, 536, 539, 543
   Freemason 456, 527
   Globe, Arizona, in .. 455–56, 463, 531

Mexican army officer, was a 539
railroads, interest in 463
soldier, was never a 465
son 509, 513, 516, 547
swindled 457–58
wheelwright 503, 544
who was 455–57, 503
Wm. G. Beard 466
Bee, General Barnard E. 592, 600, 610
Bellafaire, Judith 644, 654
Benford, Henry 51, 73, 83, 92, 599
Benford, Lieutenant Harry 345
Benford, Lieutenant Henry 594, 645
Bensford, Lieutenant 90–92, 345, 649
Beymer, William Gilmore 565–66
Birch, Harvey ....*See* Dunham, Charles A.
   alias 105, 490, 493
   letter to the *New York Herald* 105
birth
   baptismal record search 573
   date 2
   Nassau 48
black eyes bewitched passes from Union Generals 591
Blackburn's Ford 590, 592
   analysis of participation ... 43–44, 316, 417, 460
   depiction
      Full Metal Corset, film 643
      National Museum of Civil War Medicine 676
   General James Longstreet, command at 43, 316, 460
   General Jubal Early, command at 418
   General Patterson 703
   objection
      General Jubal Early 416, 698
      Southern Historical Society 702
   participation 4
Blanton, DeAnne
   as authority for
      film Full Metal Corset 644
      film *Rebel* 658, 664–69, 671, 679
   co-author of *They Fought Like Demons* 606, 617
   Texas claim 562
Bliss, Secretary Cornelius 508–10
Blunt, Orvis P. ... *See* National Union Life & Limb Ins. Co.
boarding house, as operator 474–75
Boatner III, Mark Mayo 592

Bob 18, 59, 81–82, 652–53
   analysis 658–61
Bobo, Andrew Jackson 273–75
Bohannan, Mrs. A. P. 592
Bolich, Dr. G. G. 641
Boltz, Martha M. 657
Bonner, Edward Hardy 251–56, 259, 264–65, 267–72
   Austin, Nevada mining 252
   death 271
   Department Recorder 253
   Justice of the Peace 269
   origins 252, 272
   Silver City, New Mexico mining .. 270
   son .... *See* Bonner, Jefferson
   Utah mining 259
Bonner, Jefferson 266, 343, 423–24
Boyd, Belle. 338, 560, 591, 593, 609, 653
   compared to 185, 352–54
Brady, Governor John 505, 510
Brewer, Lucy 605
Brissol, Commodore 302–4
Brooks, Fred 596
brother 107
   aided by
      General Wessells 66–67
      Lieutenant B. of Arkansas 89
   Camp Chase 556–58
   Clapp, Colonel R. D., obituary 256
   College de France 107, 145, 218
   Cuba 224, 227
   European trip 145, 669
   Harry, Acting British Consul at Haiti 142
   Josea 107, 146, 218, 257, 572
   New Orleans 254
   no brothers living, 1874 307
   St. Lucia 217
   went South 668
Browder, Laura 638–40
Bulloch, James D. 433
Burgess, Lauren Cook .... 606, *See also* Cook, Lauren M.
Burnet, William E. 307–15
   claimed attended West Point 307
   attended Kentucky Military Academy 313
   claimed death in Pensacola 1861 ..... 4, 315
   death in Spanish Fort, Alabama 1865 .... 315, 371

   claimed married in 1857 307
      General Early unaware of 409
      General Maury unaware of 372
   claimed married in New Orleans ... 46
   claimed married in Texas 307
Burrows, Silas E. 470
Bush, H. P. 497
Butler, General Benjamin
   commanding New Orleans 29–32
   contest of wits 53–58
   education and legal prowess 54
   People's Party 446
   the Beast 54

C

Camp
   Chase
      Andrew Jackson Bobo 273
      feed and nursed prisoners 302, 557
      Lieutenant B informs brother is prisoner 89
      Major John W. Skiles 557–58
      prisoner brother 107, 258
      Tod Barracks 557
      watched over Confederate prisoners 154, 157, 167
   Lewis 35–39, 41, 665
camp follower 632, 658, 664–66
Canon, Jill 609
Carberry, Thomas A. 246–50
Carter, María Agui. 630–34, 640, 648–49
   Rebel 658–72
      interview 673
      preview 655–56
      screening 679–80
Casa Grande, Arizona, visit, May 24, 1900 522
Castle Thunder
   Birch, Harvey 105–6
   incarceration 91–95
      Alexander, Commander G.W. ... 94
      behavior 94, 438–39
Cedar Hill Cemetery 571
Chambers, Trish 634, 644
Charity Hospital Record 47
Charleston, South Carolina
   visit, horseback ride, June 2, 1866 171
Cheyenne, Wyoming 241–42
Chicago, Illinois

visit, September 21, 1900 533
childhood
  Mississippi
    asserted in interview 307
    implied in memoir................ 63–64
  Texas
    asserted girlhood there by others
    561–64
    asserted girlhood there in
      interview................................ 307
children
  DeCaulp infant
    my present condition................ 117
    support my infant...................... 121
  Jefferson Bonner
    at Galveston hotel..................... 275
    death............................. 423–24
    in her arms................................ 267
    mother of newborn 266
    Mrs. Bonner has one child 309
    my little son is named Jefferson
    343–45
  Joaquin V. Goddard................ 451–53
  lost three by 1860 3
  lost two by 1874.............................. 309
  mother of three................................ 423
  raising her children to revere the old
    flag... 37
  Waldemar Beard
    mother's burial........................... 571
    mother's lunacy inquiry............. 567
    not found in censuses....... 551, 569
    question of father............ 547, 567
    ten-year-old boy 516
    too young to help............ 556, 559
    traveling with 532, 536
Cincinnati, Ohio, visit, May 30, 1878420
Civil War Times 10, 596, 673
Clapp, Samuel S......... 257, 307, 310, 529,
  563–65, 575, *See* Clapp, Theodore S.
Clapp, Theodore S. 310, 564–65
  Reverend Theodore Clapp, father
    .... 307, 310, 564
Clark Jr., William J. 353–55, 489, 496
clerk, as
  Castle Thunder................... 93, 438–39
  War office 178–79
Cleveland, President Grover
  at Mary Washington Monument
    dedication 471

first letter to, asking for Cuba's
  annexation...........................443–45
friend of 556
praise for Velazquez.............. 520, 521
second letter to, supporting trade
 447–49
College de France................ 107, 145, 218
Collier, Calvin L. 603
Columbia Mining, Trading and
  Transportation Company
  as agent.. 497
Commire, Anne................................. 621
commission
  applied for.................................. 78–83
    record book................................. 78
  by
    Adjutant General, rank of 1st
      lieutenant 153
    Confederate Government, rank
      of captain 101
    General Pillow, rank of 1st
      lieutenant 308
    General Villepique, rank of 1st
      lieutenant 301
    Governor of Arkansas, May 28,
      1861 422
    Jefferson Davis, rank of
      lieutenant 401–2
      in-person request................... 80
    Secretary of War, rank of 1st
      lieutenant 208
  pseudonyme of lieutenant..............4, 616
  self-designated 2nd Lieutenant 308
  tried to buy for $500 .... 315, 610
  variance of 315
Coney, Alexander K.......................... 526
Confederate Veteran............................... 501
contempt, held in, asserted................ 593
Continental Exporting & Importing
  Company.. *See* Continental Importing
  & Exporting Company
Continental Importing & Exporting
  Company, as owner........ 444, 448, 450
Cook, Lauren M............. 562, 606–7, 617
Cooper, Adjutant General Colonel
  Samuel
  letter to.. 97
Coppell, George C. [British Consul] 56–58
Corbin, Margaret......................... 588, 599
Corcoran, Michael 112, 113

Corday, Charlotte 491
cotton machinery salesman, as a 425–29, 441
Cotton Plant, as publisher of 425–29, 440, 443
Courier-Journal
   article
      An Interesting Visitor................326
      What Mrs. Bonner Knows About It..329–30
   gave prominence to Velazquez.....340
   Henry Watterson.............. 340–42, 356
   Velazquez letter to 355
court orders Velazquez to pay Emma Brophy 517
Covert, Nadine..............................657, 672
Crawford, Governor Samuel J. 233–34
CSS
   Florida...219–24
      escape 624, 642
      in Indies with dispatches for ..302, 304
   Shenandoah
      in Canada mailed packages to .129
      in Indies with dispatches for ...302
      not believable.........................304
      prepared book about 177
      preparing book about...............169
         impossibility..........................170
Cuba, interest in
   Address to the American Congress on Cuba...................... 392, 576, 656
   asked for influence
      A. H. Stephens...........................391
      Grover Cleveland.......................444
      Jefferson Davis..........................348
   enthusiast...353
   exiled Cuban community................348
   supported Cuban cigar makers......445
   sympathizer's agent................399–403
   tried to join insurgents 345
   war...357
Cueto, Gail A. 630
Cumming, Carman..........494–95, 669–70

D

Davis, Jefferson
   condemnation of General Butler....30
   elected 11
   implicated by Dunham...................105
   letter to
      first..342
      second 347–49, 656
   meeting 78, **79**, 642, 682
Davis, William C....................................681
Dayton, William Lewis 147–48, 643
De Grave, Kathleen...............................604
De Pauw, Linda Grant 611
death and burial 569–71
DeCaulp, Thomas C.
   alias
      Benjamine F. Carter.. 117–18, 324
      Captain Byron DeCamp...........318
      Thomas R. DeCalp 118
      William Irwin 138, 322
   Arkansas 583
   Battle of Shiloh........5, 21–24, 44, 319, 554, 603, 623, 631, 675
   bigamist..118
   Colonel, not 438–40
   death
      "shortly after her alliance with him"...167
      Corinth, Mississippi 309
      Federal hospital in Chattanooga 104, 319, 325
      Federal prison 178–79
      in Confederate service.80, 175–77
      New York........................... 153, 167
      true, probable.............................325
   education, alleged...........................119
   Empire Hospital, patient in
      "helplessly feminized" 628
      Dr. Benton..................................387
      Dr. Hammond 385
   Indianapolis, offered to recruit Rebel prisoners for Yankees...............109
   letter
      from Velazquez 117–18
      to wife Nettie (Velazquez) 118–23
   Major, not...... 131, 134, 157, 178, 180
   marriage proposal 6–8, 103–4, 577
   married Velazquez....8, 100, 104, 453
   military record 320–25
      "incomplete and inadequate explanation"............................618
      30th Wisconsin Regiment........114, 322–24
      Camp Reno, Wisconsin.. 114, 121, 322
      capture and exchange 321

deserted the Confederacy 106, 167, 322
discharge from Union Army ... 323
documentarian fails 633
enlistment
    Confederacy 320
    Union 322
    Fort Snelling, Minnesota. 119, 323
    William Irwin, alias 138, 322
nursed by Velazquez 120, 165, 557
origin, alleged 320, 324
Pennsylvania
    born in 109, 320
    Philadelphia
        lives in 322
        to be address at 324
Pensacola 157, 328, 603
surname, origin 324
defended her book 404–8
DeFontaine, Felix Gregory 599
Denver, Colorado, visit, August 23, 1900 532
description
    apparently quite intelligent 112
    attractive personality, strong flow of language 522
    average height, thoroughly educated and very fluent 307
    below ordinary man height, bearing of a soldier 437
    black-eyed, black-haired, spoke English fluently 445
    brave, but eccentric 93
    can talk gibly 35
    dressed *a la militare* 171
    dressed in black 112
    great force of character, lady-like bearing, polished education 425
    height 421, 535, 541
    intelligence and gentle breeding 19
    intelligent-looking, refined appearance 302
    middle sized tolerably full 112
    not particularly handsome, countenance rather attractive .. 326
    not quite as pretty as 90
    rather graceful and elegantly attired 186
    sharp business acumen, indomitable energy, good talker 520
    slight lisp, missing some front teeth 100
    slight-built, pleasant face strongly tinctured with masculinity 420
    slim, youthful looking, very bright eyed, loquacious as a mimic 401
    still quite a handsome woman 37
    tall and fine looking 535
    variance in 378
    weight 401, 421
    well dressed 189
    well made, but not pretty, soldier attire 74
    young, good-looking and lady-like 102
Devens, Charles
    meeting General Devens in Charleston 173–75
    seeing Colonel Devens at Battle of Ball's Bluff 62
diaspora of ex-Confederates 192–93
Diaz, Johnny 640
Díaz, President Porfirio .. 524, 526, 532–34, 539, 544–46
disguise
    creation of 4, 411
    discovered 90, 94
    facial hair, effectiveness 13–16, 437
    friend helped 182
    secret, did not try to keep a 79, 97
    Yankee, as a 114–16
Dixon, Billy 229, 235
Doll, John A **192**, 472
Dorn, General Earl Van
    dead already 554
        General Jubal Early concurs ... 699
    dead general burst into a laugh 96
Dorpalen, Andreas 588
Dowie, Ménie Muriel 485
Dreux, Colonel Charley 72, 153–55, 301, 308, **316**, 415, 591
Dunham, Charles A 488–96
Dustin, Gilman and Company, publisher 487

E

Early, General Jubal
    criticism of 602, 624–26, 647–49, 661–68
        angrily dismissed, accused of .. 638

angry diatribe..............................637
double agent........................667–70
intermediary, asserted...............594
vitriol..639
encounter with Velazquez........404–8
objections to *The Woman in Battle*
....408–18
    camp follower...632, 658, 664–66, 699
    Confederate uniform.......409, 416, 697
    no commission...................410, 698
    railroad line not constructed..415, 698
    raised a battalion...............410, 698
    Robert E. Lee still in U.S. Army
....409, 697
    seven league boots 416, 699
    Virginia had not yet seceded..409, 697
    who was..418–19
education.............3, *See* Sisters of Charity
Eggleston, Larry G...................622
El Juez de Su Causa.*See* Estela and Carlos
Elba, bark, passenger Laura Wasson..227
Eleventh Louisiana Regiment.36, 42–44
Emma mine............................260–62, 331
Empire Hospital..............................384–89
Erauso, Catalina de 1, 579–80
Estela and Carlos, love story...204, 577–79
Exchange Hotel, Montgomery..............11

F

Falconer, Major Kinloch...............553–55
fans of the legend..........................517–19
father
    Commodore J. B. Roach of British Navy..............................142
    English Admiral...............................200
    Joaquin Velasquez...........................464
    Juanquin R. Velasquez 454
    Major J. B. Roche of Mississippi....92
    question of name 356, 573–75
    Rear Admiral Rosche of English Navy..............................138
    Samuel S. Clapp.................................307
    Velazquez 355
Faust, Patricia L. 600
Featherston, Colonel Winfield.....63–64, 86, 99, 555, 580
Felton, Bruce..621
fictionist, asserted Bell Irvin Wiley....589
film..*See* Full Metal Corset, *See* Rebel, *See Unsung Heroes*
Fitzgerald, Captain Ross of Hussars, meeting...................................102
forgery
    "genuine documents".....................302
    congressmen in question...............421
    Hascall letter to General Sibley . 137–41
    letter
        announcing father's death........142
        from General Casey 340
    letters of introduction....................532
        to prominent gentlemen, in question..................................302
    Newman's testimonial, in question
....384
    obituary for brother........................256
    Samuel Clemens, "forged my handwriting"..........................340
Forrest, Nathan Bedford
    3rd Arkansas Cavalry 138
    claim rode with.................175–76, 306
    dispatch for..84
    Henry Watterson rode with..........342
    raid...87–89
Fort
    Arbuckle..3
    Columbus...............126, 133, 304, 469
    Donelson..6, 619, 620, 640, 650, 673, 676
        fought at
            claimed by others.......553, 586, 595, 604
            Velazquez never claimed...**586**, 595, 644
        Full Metal Corset, depiction....644
        helped wounded 165
        wounded
            during Battle of.....................622
            shortly after Battle of............70
    Leavenworth.............................315, 592
        first husband assigned to 3
        lived at........................230, 468, 548
        Sherman's Battery at....................16
        Velazquez was a mother at......423
    Massachusetts....................................56

Monroe 125, 129
Morgan 223
Pickens .... xiii, xiv
Pillow 153–56, 308, 315, 382–83
Snelling 16, 116, 124, 127, 136, 681
   reference to husband at.... 137–38, 141
   Thomas DeCaulp
      letter written at 119
      presence at 323–24
Forty, George and Anne 604
Fowler, Mark 621
Frank, Lisa Tendrich 648
frankly fictitious, asserted the *Washington Herald* 560
Freemasons 255, 456, 509, 514, 527, 540
Fremantle, Lieutenant Colonel Arthur L.
   saw a female soldier 74–76
   analysis 75
Frietchie, Barbara 549
From Maid to Martyr article 500
Full Metal Corset, Secret Soldiers of the Civil War 634, 643–45, 655, 656

G

Garidel, Henri
   meeting 100–101
      Velazquez missing some front teeth 100
Geithmann, Harriet 585
General F fiasco 98–100
Georgetown, Guyana, visit 215
Gill, William Fearing 467
Ginsberg, Elaine K. 606
Globe, Arizona 455–56, 463, 531
Glover, John M. 431–36
Goddard, Edward A.
   child with 452
   cohabited with 449–53
Government Hospital for the Insane
   568–69
Grant, Ulysses S.
   Battle of Belmont 20
   canal, interest in 442
   envelope addressed to 141
   General Casey's letter to 340
   insurance business with 125
   Santo Domingo 391
   Velazquez letter to 358

Velazquez refused to assassinate 5, 20, 23, 492, 646, 677
   Dr. Simon P. Richardson's variation 462
   relative to blowing up the arsenal 122
grave 571
Gray, Helen 518
Great Diamond Hoax of 1872 335–37
Greenhow, Rose O'Neal ... 591, 609, 653

H

H. W. Hageman Publishing Company
   .... *See Story of the Civil War*
Hall, Richard H. 624, 627, 640
   Cubans in the Confederacy, contributed to 618
   female spy put across lines, on 152
   Patriots in Disguise 601–4
   St. Alban's messenger, on 149
   Women of the Civil War Battlefront. 635–37
Hammond, Doctor J. F. 384–88
Hancock, Doctor Joseph ... 503–14, 539–40, 543–47
Hargreaves, Reginald 585
Harney, General William S. 228–36
   athleticism 235
   attraction 234
   Indian Commission 229
   loyalty to Union 229, 231
Harpending, Ashbury 329–36
Harper, Judith E. 634
Harriel, Shelby 681
Harris, Joel Chandler 364–65
Harrison's Island 61, 608
Hascall, Colonel M. D. .. *See* Hascall, Milo Smith
Hascall, Milo Smith 137–41
Hastings, Lieutenant Philip 70–72
Havana, Cuba, visit 224
Headley, John W. 149–51, 603, 636
health
   convulsions, 1875 356
   critically ill, 1908 556
   insane, 1912 567
   organic heart disease, 1923 death 569
   prolapsus of womb, 1862 48
   teeth, 1863 100
Heidler, David S. and Jeanne T. 615

Heintzelman, Samuel P. 112, 462
Hell on Wheels.. *See* Julesburg, Colorado
Hetzel, Susan Rivière 472
Hewitt, John Hill 354
Hoar, George Frisbie 392
Hodges Jr., Robert 189, 555
Hoffert, Sylvia D. 10, 596, 631
Holden, Edward G. 553
Holladay, Benjamin 242
Holt, Judge Advocate General Joseph
.... 490–92
Horan, James D. 591
horseback
    bought horses twice 417
    dashing about in New Orleans 186, 188
    horse race in Charleston 171–73
husband, alleged or real
    Andrew Jackson Bobo 274
    Arnold 38
    Bachman 36, 38
    Dr. Moses DeLorme McLeod 394
    Edward Hardy Bonner 251
    Gibbons 38
    John Wasson 198
    Keith 13
    Thomas C. DeCaulp 104
    William Beard 453
    William E. Burnet 307
    Williams of the 13th Connecticutt Infantry 36, 38–42
Hutchison, Coleman 642
Hutchison, Kay Bailey 645

I

Iguana Films .... *See Rebel*
Indian Commission 229–30
Indianapolis 89, 109–12, 120–23, 210, 322
    arsenal 120–23
        reason for not blowing up 122
Indigo Films .... See Full Metal Corset
insanity inquiry 566–67
Irish Tom .... *See* Carberry, Thomas A.
Irwin, William .... 322–25, *See* DeCaulp, Thomas C.
    letter
        General Sibley 141
        M. D. Hascall 138
Island No. 10 .... 153–55, 383

J

Jackson, Mississippi
    visit, June 6, 1863 51–52
    visit, rare bird, June 24, 1863 73
Jackson, President Andrew 470
Jackson, Thomas "Stonewall" 11, 374, 418, 549, 585, 621, 622
Jagiello, Apolonia 1
Johnson, Captain Frederick A. 186, 195–98, 201, 204–13, 309
    denunciation by Velazquez 211–12
Johnson, President Andrew
    build an asylum requested by Velazquez 183
    impeachment and Benjamin Butler 54
    letter to 206–7
    remind him of her 209
    signed "Lauretta" 449
    wants to expose him 343
Johnson's Island 9, 127, 129, 219–20, 400, 494, 668
joined, claims of
    11th Louisiana Regiment at Shiloh
.... 36, 44
    12th Mississippi Regiment 308
    13th Mississippi Regiment, implied
.... 60
    21st Louisiana Regiment 301, 382–84
    3rd Arkansas Cavalry 22–24
    5th Texas Volunteers, to Virginia with 51
    7th Louisiana Regiment at Manassas
.... 36, 42–44
    8th Louisiana Regiment 301
    Colonel Charley Dreux at Manassas
.... 301, 308, 460
    General Patterson at Blackburn's Ford 703
    Independent Scouts 375, 703
Jones, John B. [secretary and diarist] .11, 18
Jones, Katherine M. 590
Jones, Reverend J. William 373, 631, 702–4
Jones, Terry L. 619
Joslyn, Mauriel Phillips 608
Julesburg, Colorado 236–39

K

Kaufman, Janet E. 599, 645

Kelly, Marta C. 656
Kelsey, Stewart 589
Kidder, Lieutenant Lyman 239
Kinchen, Oscar A. 595
kinship
    Diego Rodriguez Velazquez [painter]
    2
    Don Diego Velazquez [first Cuban governor] 2
Kinsman, Judge Lieut. Col. J. B. 36
Korrol, Virginia Sánchez 634

L

La Barra, F. L. de 545–46
Laffin, John 595
Lang, Leonora Blanche 560–61
Laporte, Colorado 241–43
lawsuit, won 474–75
Lee, Robert E.
    age 232
    American Male Patriot by equivalency? 678
    namesake, A. J. Bobo's son 275
    still in U.S. Army 409, 697
    surrender 41, 146
Lent, William 333–37
Leonard, Elizabeth611–13, 615–16, 638, 644, 671
letter to
    Adjutant General Colonel Samuel Cooper 97
    Brigadier General Webster 136
    Captain Stockdale
        letter 1 135
        letter 2 135
        letter 3 135
        letter 4 137
    card to *St. Louis Daily Globe-Democrat* 428
    Colonel Donaldson 134
    Daily Alta California 256
    Ex-Confederate President Jefferson Davis
        letter 1 342
        letter 2 348
    Ex-Confederate Vice-President A. H. Stephens
        letter 1 345
        letter 2 390
    General Henry H. Sibley 138

    General Jubal Early 404, 693
    Governor of Guayana "John Dala Costa" 208
    husband Thomas DeCaulp 117
    Indiana Governor Oliver P. Morton 109
    Louisville *Courier-Journal* 355
    Mr. W. B. Whaley 477
    Reverend J. William Jones
        letter 1 .... 373, 702
        letter 2 .... 375, 703
    Samuel Clemens (Mark Twain) 339
    U.S. President Andrew Johnson .. 206
    U.S. President Grover Cleveland. 447
    U.S. President Ulysses S. Grant ... 358
    U.S. President-elect Grover Cleveland 444
Libby Prison 353, 401, 402
Lincoln, Abraham
    assassination investigation ... 105, 491
    burned in effigy xiii
    duped 609
    Edward Baker, friend of 61
    good opinion of 646
    Hurrah for Lincoln 29
    marble bust sculpture 420
    meeting 66
    monument 680
    Ohio funeral procession 145, 147, 558
    poison 492
    re-election 150
    Velazquez mentioned
        1867 letter 209
        1874 letter 343
Linedecker, Clifford L. 620
Little Cottonwood Canyon, Utah 262
Logan, Mrs. John A. 499
Longstreet, General James 458–62
    "believed her" assertion 611
    "vouched for her service" assertion 647
    Blackburn's Ford, at 43, 316, 460
    Emmy Park's letter to 458, 701
    Mexican Continental & Steamship Co., interest in 539
    referenced by General Early 699
    three Texans on staff 169
Lonn, Ella 617
Loomis, Gustavus 126–27, 304
Los Angeles, California, living in 516

Louisiana Greys ...308, 311–13, 414, 415
Louisville, Kentucky
    visit, September 6, 1874..................326
love letter, plagiarized......................24–26
Lowery, M. D., Thomas P. 603
Lucy Brewer Avenue ... *See* Brewer, Lucy

M

Mack, Tara..609
Macksey, Jack...621
Maffitt, Captain John Newland... 219–24
    praise..221, 223
    yellow fever......................................222
Magness, Perre.......................................623
Mallory, Stephen R......................223, 433
Manzano y Manzano, Joaquín del.. 224–27
Marcus, Amy Dockser.........................634
married
    Andrew Jackson Bobo....................274
    Doctor Moses DeLorme McLeod
   394
    Edward A. Goddard (common law)
   452
    Edward Hardy Bonner....................251
    John Wasson.....................................198
    Thomas C. DeCaulp........................100
    William Beard..................................453
Mary Washington Monument Association
    as an agent................................469–73
Massy, Mary Elizabeth.........................593
Matthews, Melissa Renee 653–54
McDevitt, Theresa.................................630
McGill, General Francis W...................600
McKinley, President William
    aided by............................509, 512, 514
    has letter from.................................534
    letter to
        first, asking for investigation of Beard's death....................505
        fourth, requested money for railroad....................................532
        second..510
        third, referenced Mexican railroad
        ....519, 528
McLeod, Doctor Moses DeLorme. 392–98
McPherson, James M............................619
Medicine Lodge Creek..........................229

Memphis
    visit
        Grand Ball, June 27, 1866........181
        March 1, 1866............................152
        March 21, 1866..........................163
Méndez-Méndez, Serafín....................630
Meridian, Mississippi
    visit, three books now prepared, June 2, 1866.................................177
meted out death with a saber and pistol
....590
Metropolitan Life ......*See* National Union Life & Limb Ins. Co.
Mexican-American War 2, 16, 529, 562–63
Miami, explosion of steamboat ... 158–63
    Ashley Band.....................................161
    Levy, Captain E. A. 159
    one of two lady passengers saved 154
    only lady passenger saved.............163
Military Women's Corridor*See* Pentagon
Mobile, Alabama
    visit
        August 25, 1874........................301
        defended her honor, May 1866
       166
Monja Alferez........ *See* Erauso, Catalina de
Monroe, Mayor John T. 27
Moon, Tom...616
morality..2, 407, 700
Morgan, John Tyler...............................392
Mormon Rebellion. *See* Utah Expedition
Morton, Governor Oliver P...............109
Moses, Captain Bernard......................382
mother.58, 100, 146, 570, 575, 593, 615, 653
    birthplace...217
    brother and sister................................2
    death...307, 530
    French...464
    French-American.............................530
    Marie Antoneta DeChaump..........454
    Spanish...536
    surname in Spanish culture...........107
Mumford, William Bruce 28–32
    hanging..30
    meeting..29
    widow and children..........................32

N

Nashville, Tennessee
  visit
    June 16, 1866 178
    photographs for sale, June 20,
      1866 180
National Museum of Civil War
  Medicine 676–77
National Park Service 674–76
National Police Gazette, New York 451
National Union Life & Limb Ins. Co.
  .... 125, 130–33, 136
  poster 131
New Orleans, Louisiana
  departed as a Registered Enemy .. 48–50
  Mint flag affair 27–32
  surrender demanded of 27
  visit
    March 29, 1866 163
    Mrs. Mary DeCaulp, Jan. 5, 1867
    185
    October 25, 1900 535
New York City
  1905 Census 551
  living in 441–55, 464–75, 551–59
  visit, September 1866 183
New York Hospital, in 556–59
Newman, Major John 382–84
Nicaragua
  agricultural school, as founder 442
  attaché of legation 441
Nielson, Roger B. 38
Norfolk, Virginia, living in 497
North and South American Trade Journal
  as publisher of 428, 440–43
North Star Mining and Development
  Company 503–16
Northup, Solomon 85
nurse, as 92, 164–65, 552
  Camp Chase 302
  Richmond 556–57
  Thomas DeCaulp 120

O

Oath of Allegiance 110, 322
Officer of Castle Thunder, article by
  436–40
Oldham, Van Buren 190, 555
Oreto .... *See* CSS *Florida*

origins
  Cuba
    was Velazquez Cuban? 571–73
      making the case 575–80
    Mississippi, making the case ... 580–82
    other places 582–84
Ostrand, Maggie Van 565
Over, Captain Ewald
  "in secret service" 112, 668
  travel pass 112
Owen, Albert 523–25, 552
Owens, Officer William E. 567

P

Park, Emmy W. 458, 701
Parton, James [biographer of Gen.
  Butler] 27–31
Patton, James W. 587
Pelouze, Louis H. 112, 113, 323
Pensacola
  delivered battalion 413, 604, 610, 611,
    620, 654
    contradiction 154, 169, 311, 327
    memoir 4, 157
  departure 11
  husband
    death of 7, 586, 658
      exploding carbine 327–28
  prelude to war .... xiii–xv
  railroad 541–43
  referenced by General Jubal Early
    698
  Robert H. Purdom 165
  Thomas DeCaulp 5, 103–4, 157, 321,
    603
  troops arrived 411–15
  William E. Burnet 314–15, 559
    ordered to 308
Pentagon 599
People's Party 446
Perry, Carolyn 635
Perry, Governor Madison S. xiii
Philadelphia, Pennsylvania
  living in
    March 1901 538
    September 1897 497
Phillips, Captain Bruce L. 72, 153–56,
  375, 383
Phillips, Mrs. Eugenia Levy 28, 55–56
photographs of Velazquez for sale

Charleston 173
Nashville 180
Pierce, George F. [Pensacola historian]
 xv
Pinkerton, Reverend Samuel J. 104
Pinkington, Reverend .... *See* Pinkerton, Reverend
Pitcher, Molly 51, 588, 599
Polk, General Leonidas 155
polygamy, opinion of 265
Powell, Lawrence 631
Price, Dr. Henry M. ....183, 191–96, 203, 206–15, 302, 309, 472, *See also* Venezuela Emigration Company
 death of miners mentioned in letter
 210
 denunciation by Velazquez 211–12
prostitution
 Nelly Bremer's House of
  Prostitution 36, 45–47
 prostitute 632, 648, 658, 664–66
publisher's circular... 368, 369, 373, **376–89**, 488, 608, 626, 634, 702
Pulaski, Tennessee
 visit, June 22, 1866 180
Purdom, Robert H., knew her 164

Q

Quantrill, William Clarke 301, 305–7

R

railroad, entrepreneur
 Arrowhead Springs, California .. 519–22
 Mexico, to 522–48
  last chance in Philadelphia 538
   deceit discovered 543–48
    renewed effort 551
  Tampa could not be persuaded
   537–38
raised company or battalion
 analysis of the claim 410–11
 Arkansas
  Arkansas Grays 311
  company of veterans 301
  company, 136 men 414
  infantry battalion, 236 men,
   memoir claim 4
  conclusion about the claim 415
 General Early's protest of the claim
  410
 location unknown
  company of cavalry 153
 Texas .... *See* Texas, company claim
 company commanded at
  Manassas 169
 company of 136 men 208
 independent company 51
Raleigh, North Carolina, living in 367
Ralston, William C. 333–36
Ramsay, William A. 338, 349–50, 356, 359–64, 365, 488, 496
 street fight with 362–64
realtor, as a 467, 516, 520, 552, 559
Ream, Vinnie 419
Reavis, Logan 232
Rebel 613, 631, 640, 643, 648, 655–73, 679–80
reporter, as **357–58**, 404, 420–22, 440, 443, 694
reputation, claim by
 editor .... xv, 389, 613
 Edward A. Goddard 451
 newspaper ..35, 45, 181, 302, 352–53, 378, 428
 Velazquez .... xv, 2
 writer 550
Ricci, Pat 631
Richardson, Sarah 673
Richmond
 visit, August 10, 1866 182
Ricketts, James B. 112, 113
Ridley, Lieutenant General Bromfield
 .... 501, 553–55, 618
Roberts, George D. 329–36
Robertson Plantation 33–34
Rodriguez, Rafael Francisco 530, 651
Rosecrans, General William S. 109–10, 138
 deceived 42
 released Thomas C. DeCaulp 322
Ruiz, Vicki L. 634, 660, 663

S

Sager, Robin C. 650–53
Salt Lake City, Utah
 Adam A. Wilson letter 346, 351
 Brigham Young 265
 Herald book review 389

hotel arrivals 260
Mary Francis McLeod....................398
not divorced at........................ 271, 351
rested at 244
son born in 9, **267**, 424, 597, 630, 651
stagecoach travel........................ 242–44
This is The Place Heritage Park...266
Salter, Krewasky A.................................678
Sandy Station, Utah 265
Sasser, Bill.................................... 630–34
Savannah, Georgia
visit, May 14, 1866 168
Schenck, Major General Robert C...115, 124, 132, 146, 667, 669
appointed Mrs. Alice Williams agent 111
Emma Silver Mining Co................261
Seventh Louisiana Regiment.......... 42–44
Shaw Jr., Perrin F. 587
she wolves ....106, *See* Birch, Harvey
Sherman, Captain Thomas W............. *See* Sherman's Battery
Sherman, General William T.... 136, 145, 229
Sherman's Battery 16, 454
Ship Island 39, 40, 55–58
Sibley, General Henry Hastings 138, 140
siblings................................ 2, 142, 217–18
Sifakis, Stewart............................ 600, 617
Silver City, New Mexico 268–72
Keystone House 269
living in..269
Tremont House 272
Silvey, Anita...647
Simkins, Francis B.................................587
Sisters of Charity 3, 46, 64, 601, 651, 674
convent, asserted 590
Skaine, Rosemarie 654
skeleton of a female..............................596
Skiles, Major John W................... 557–58
Slemmer, Lieutenant Adam J..............xiii
Slemons, William F. 404–7, 408–11, 416, 419, 594, 625, 633–34, 637–39, 664, 694–700
Smith, Alphonso B. 519, 526–28
smuggling
Havana 32
Robertson Plantation 33
San Diego and Havana, buying coffee and sugar 302

South Atlantic Modern Language Association 593
South Carolina Women in the Confederacy 550
Southern Historical Society
book review................................701–2
letter 1 from Velazquez.............702–3
letter 2 from Velazquez.............703–4
review and criticism 371–76
Southern immigration, as agent...475–85
A Female Crank headline.............. 476
letter from Herman Stump........... 476
letter to Mr. W. B. Whaley............ 477
Southern Publishing Company, fails .. 360–64, *See also* Ramsay, William A.
Spanish
proficiency in.............................202–4
accent 225
brother's name.................. 107, 146
Caracas..213
Señor 210
Spanish-American War 529–30
Springfield, Illinois
visit, September 27, 1900 534
spying
Canada, trip to 128
Johnson's Island prison break..... 127, 219
Memphis, trip to 83–89
fooled General C. C. Washburn 87
helped General N. B. Forrest ... 87
New Orleans 27
Richmond 127
St. Louis and Hannibal............123–25
Washington, D.C........ 64–68, 667–69, 676
obtaining female attire 65, 641
reason to resume 65
St. Alban's Raiders 148–52
photograph of a woman................ 149
St. Cloud Hotel, Nashville..135–37, 180, 436, 639
St. Elizabeth's Hospital *See* Government Hospital for the Insane
St. James Parish 142, 153, 505, 563, 582, 591, 596
St. Louis
living in..............................420, 425–29
departure announcement......... 428
visit, March 7, 1866 153
St. Lucia, visit...................................217–18

St. Thomas, Virgin Islands, visit........218
stagecoach
    discomfort and danger....................239
    driver, Andrew Jackson Bobo 273–75
    Echo Canyon accident....................243
    Julesburg to Cheyenne............240–42
        drunken woman........................240
    Laporte to Salt Lake City...............243
    Laporte, Colorado.................... 241–42
    Omaha to Julesburg.......................236
    Salt Lake City to Austin, Nevada
       243–44
Stanchak, John E. 617
Stephens, Alexander H........ 96, 404, 421, 664
    letters received from Velazquez..345, 390–91
    referenced in Jubal Early's letter to W. F. Slemons.............................700
    referenced in Velazquez's letter to Jubal Early....................................694
Stidger, Felix......................................591
Stockdale, Captain S. A. 135–37
Story of the Civil War or The Exploits, Adventures and Travels of Mrs. L. J. Velasquez (Lieut. H. T. Buford, C. S. A)...486
Stuart, "Jeb" James Ewell Brown ... 175–76, 306
Sullivan, Walter.................................604
swan song....................................565–66

T

Talcott, William M. 244
Tampa, Florida
    visit, February 1901 537
Teorey, Matthew............................ 645–47
Terrill, Captain William R. 24
Texas
    company claim 74, 168–69, 177, 185–87, 415, 437–39, 598
        5th Texas Volunteers....................51
        in letter to Governor Della Costa
       208
    girlhood in....................... 307, 561–64
    memoir written in, asserted by others
        ....562, 590, 631, 634
The Woman in Battle
    binding types................................370
    editor, C. J. Worthington........ 488–96
    illustrators...................... 377, 489, 496
    issued..367–70
    publisher, Dustin, Gilman and Company...................................487
    stage production...........................425
    treatment relative to
        Cuban..............618, 624, 629, 652
        ethnicity.................................652–53
        foreigner.................... 593, 617, 630
        gun-toting............................. 638–40
        internationalism.................. 641–43
        Latina..................................634, 649
        Pentagon, honoree at...............599
        propaganda/vindicating the past
       653–54
        pure memoir. xv, 602, **612–13**, 671
        sexuality...606–8, 613–15, 627–30, 641, 650–52
        slavery................629, 652, 659–61
        social class...................................651
Thompson Hotel 8, 104, 385, *See* Atlanta Hotel
Thompson, Doctor Joseph........352, 353, 354, *See* Atlanta Hotel and Thompson Hotel
three books forthcoming............. 168–70
Tiffany, Charles Lewis..........................336
Topolobampo, Mexico 522–26, 546, 552
Transcontinental Union Pacific Railroad
   239–41
Tsui, Bonnie......................................637
Tucker, John Randolph.... 406, 410, 419, 625, 633, 664, 693–95
Tucker, Philip Thomas........................618
Twain, Mark.................................. 337–42
    letter from Owen S. McKinney....340
    letter to Watterson of the *Courier-Journal*...341
    Velazquez asserted memoir to be written by............................309, 346
        Adam A. Wilson's letter denouncing.............................347
        Twain's refutation 341, 346
    Velazquez asserted praise from....356
    Velazquez letter to *Courier-Journal* about Twain................................355
Twenty-first Louisiana Regiment
    enlistment asserted by
        analysis of 374, 382–84
        National Park Service 674
        newspaper....................................301

Velazquez 403, 500
farewell to 586
guerilla warfare 621
Major John Newman 608
two pistols captured from a Rebel ... 135, 639–40
Tyler, Brigadier General Erastus B., travel pass 125, 127, 129
Tyner's Station, presence at 186, 189–90, 553–55

U

U.S. Army Women's Museum .. 656, 678
Union Navy
  capture of New Orleans 26–32
Unsung Heroes, The Story of America's Female Patriots 677–79
USS
  Constitution 221, 605
  Penobscot 216
  Pensacola 27
  Wachusett 219
Utah Expedition
  Harney, General William S. 230
  she was not with 37, 230
  she was with, claim to newspaper .. 37

V

Vanderbilt, Cornelius 441, 442
  sister of Mrs. Vanderbilt 467
Venezuela
  Caracas 205, 213–15
  crocodile ate Dixie 205
  Emigration Company 185–215
    claim agent for 186
    claim rebut 192
    creation of 190–97
    dissatisfied colonists 213
    Dr. Henry M. Price .. *See* Price, Dr. Henry M.
    Elizabeth, schooner
      arrived Ciudad Bolívar 204
      departed New Orleans 201
      emigrants taken to court 197
      Orinoco River pilot 201–3
    F. A. Derbyshire's account . 201–3
    first interest in 183
    Frederick A. Johnson *See* Johnson, Captain Frederick A.
    John Wasson ..... *See* Wasson, John

land grant size 193
letter to President Andrew Johnson 206–7
La Guaira 213
Volunteers Institute (NY) 126

W

Walker, Leroy P., meeting 11–12
Washington, D.C.
  living in 441, 559
  Old Capitol Prison 147
  visit, wants to build an asylum, August 13, 1866 182
Washington, Mary 469–73, 608
Wasson, John
  asserted a Major 198
  not a Major 199
  death, alleged and probable 205, 210–11
  no grave in Caracas 215
  married Velazquez 197–200
  went to Venezuelan gold mines .. 205, 210
  who was 200–201
    asserted "John W. Wasson of Kentucky" 309
Watkins, H. C. 504–7, 513
Watterson, Henry 340–42, 356
Weaks, Mary Louise 635
wealth
  annual income before the war 552
  Arizona, possessor of silver mines in 465
  Arkansas, owns a plantation in 583
  battalion, financed a 4, 93, 128, 661
  California, large mining interest in 513–14
  Cuba
    father became heir to another estate 563
    father's plantation in Puerto de Palmas 577
    heiress to great sugar plantations in 513–14
  destitute 544, 567
  Indianapolis, no money from Thomas DeCaulp 121
  Julesburg 238
  Milwaukee, aided by Minister's wife 117

New York Hospital 556
Philadelphia 544
Phoenix 76
Tampa 538
USS *Penobscot* 216
every luxury 46, 108, 171, 563
family 2, 92, 216, 552, 651
   mother, daughter of a wealthy merchant 572, 653
indigent 566, 570
inheritance 142
   disinherited 3, 410, 661, 698
Louisiana
   heiress to great sugar plantation in 513
   large estates in before the War 505
Mexico
   father fell heir to large estate in 562, 616
Mexico and Arizona
   large fortune, rich mineral lands in 539
   large mining interest in 513–14
Mexico and Honduras, concessions in 465
Mississippi
   heiress to great sugar plantations in 513–14
nurse
   once a wealthy war nurse 556
   spent fortune on medicines for Confederacy 552
school 64
   Sisters of Charity 46, 651
slave, purchased 661
South America, mines in 465
squandered 601
whorehouse, lived in 506, 651
Weatherford, Doris 621
Webster, Brigadier General Joseph D. 136
Weitzman, Lisa S. 621
Wessells, General Henry W. ...67, 89, 557
   meeting, discussed prisoner brother 66
West, Marian, *Munsey's Magazine* article 548–50
Whittier, John Greenleaf .... *See* Frietchie, Barbara
Wiley, Bell Irvin 589
William, first husband

eloped 3, 643
   did not 308
marriage
   altered story 564
   caused Velazquez's father to disown her 171, 514, 698
married
   New Orleans, in 3
   no underage marriage 311
   Texas, in 307
   Velazquez's age
      13 years, 9 months, 10 days ..3, 46, **311**, 676
      seventeen, claimed by an 1878 newspaper 401
      sixteen, claimed by film Full Metal Corset 643
Nellie's boyfriend stolen by Velazquez 46
Velazquez tribute to 372
Williams, Alice
   Columbia, South Carolina 96
   detective commission, surrrendered 132
   first use of name 90–93
   meeting
      Harvey Birch 105–6
      Henri Garidel 100
   mentioned by
      Carman Cumming 669
      H. Donald Winkler 649
   poison plot 105, 491
   U.S. Special Agent, appointed 111
   analysis of 115, 124, 132, 146, 667
Williams, Lauretta 47–48, 573
Williams, Mrs. Laura J. 91, 583
   at Battle House (Hotel)? 81
   at Jackson, Mississippi 51, 72
   confusion
      Hutchison's 645
      Kaufman's 599
      Massey's 594
Wilmington, Delaware, visit, September 17, 1897 497
Wilmington, North Carolina, visit, January 28, 1877 393
Wilson, Adam A. 257, 267, 271, 351, 377
   letter denouncing Velazquez 346
Wiltshaw, Harry C. ..... *See* Watkins, H. C.
Windom, Secretary William 465, 467
Winkler, H. Donald 649

Winslow, H.
    placed female spy across lines 152
Women of the Civil War Museum 680
Worthington, C. J. 346, 350, 355, 400
    as a witness 597
    editor 488
    naval officer question 377, 626, 634
    praise for Velazquez 388, 598
    style or control question 612, 614, 638
    who was .... *See* Dunham, Charles A.
Worthington, Richard *See Story of the Civil War*
wounded 69–70
Wright, John D. 674
wrong initial usage 110, 138, 155, 339, 404, 528

Y

yellow fever
    Jeff Bonner 424
    John Newland Maffitt 220
    John Wasson 205
Young, Brigham 265, 487
Young, Colonel William H. .... *See* Volunteers Institute (NY)
Young, Elizabeth 606–8, 613–15, 628, 650
Young, Lieutenant Bennett H. 148–51

Z

Zayas y Sotomayor, Doña María de ... *See* Estela and Carlos
Zeinert, Karen 610
Zelman, Anita 599
Zouave, eaten by shark 327

www.ingramcontent.com/pod-product-compliance
Lightning Source LLC
Chambersburg PA
CBHW020655060526
44119CB00068B/25